Yearbook on International Communist Affairs 1988

Yearbook on International Communist Affairs 1988

Parties and Revolutionary Movements

EDITOR: Richard F. Staar
ASSISTANT EDITOR: Margit N. Grigory

AREA EDITORS

Thomas H. Henriksen • Africa
William Ratliff • The Americas
Ramon H. Myers • Asia and the Pacific
Richard F. Staar • Eastern Europe and the
Robert Conquest Soviet Union
James H. Noyes • The Middle East
Dennis L. Bark • Western Europe

HOOVER INSTITUTION PRESS
Stanford University, Stanford, California

The text of this work is set in Times Roman;
display headings are in Melior. Typeset by
Harrison Typesetting, Inc., Portland, Oregon.
Printed and bound by Braun-Brumfield, Inc.,
Ann Arbor, Michigan.

The Hoover Institution on War, Revolution and Peace, founded at Stanford University in 1919 by the late President Herbert Hoover, is an interdisciplinary research center for advanced study on domestic and international affairs in the twentieth century. The views expressed in its publications are entirely those of the authors and do not necessarily reflect the views of the staff, officers, or Board of Overseers of the Hoover Institution.

Hoover Press Publication 380

First printing, 1988
Manufactured in the United States of America
91 90 89 88 9 8 7 6 5 4 3 2 1

International Standard Book Number 0-8179-8801-7
International Standard Serial Number 0084-4101
Library of Congress Catalog Number 67-31024

Contents

ASIA AND THE PACIFIC

EASTERN EUROPE AND THE SOVIET UNION

THE MIDDLE EAST

WESTERN EUROPE

Preface

This edition of the *Yearbook*, the twenty-second consecutive one, includes profiles by 80 contributors, covering 122 parties and revolutionary movements as well as twelve international communist fronts and two regional organizations (the Council for Mutual Economic Assistance and the Warsaw Pact). In addition, eleven biographic sketches of prominent communist leaders follow individual profiles. The names and affiliations of contributors are given at the end of each essay.

This *Yearbook* offers data on the organization, policies, activities, and international contacts during all of calendar 1987 of communist parties and Marxist-Leninist movements throughout the world. Information has been derived primarily from published sources, including official newspapers and journals, as well as from radio transmissions monitored by the U.S. Foreign Broadcast Information Service. Dates cited in the text without indicating a year are for 1987.

Whether to include a party or a group that espouses a quasi-Marxist-Leninist ideology, yet may not be recognized by Moscow as "communist," always poses a problem. It applies specifically to certain of the so-called national liberation movements and, more significantly, to some ruling parties. In making our decisions, the following criteria have been considered: rhetoric, the organizational model, participation in international communist meetings and fronts, and adherence to the USSR's foreign policy line. It seems realistic to consider the regime of Nicaragua, for example, in the same category as that of Cuba. The ruling parties in the so-called "vanguard revolutionary democracies" appear to be clearly affiliated with the world communist movement. They also are discussed in the Introduction.

Our thanks go to the librarians and staff at the Hoover Institution for checking information and contributing to the bibliography. The latter was compiled by the *Yearbook* assistant editor, Mrs. Margit N. Grigory, who also provided liaison with contributors.

Richard F. Staar
Hoover Institution

The following abbreviations are used for frequently cited publications and news agencies:

CSM	*Christian Science Monitor*
FBIS	*Foreign Broadcast Information Service*
FEER	*Far Eastern Economic Review*
IB	*Information Bulletin* (of the *WMR*)
JPRS	*Joint Publications Research Service*
LAT	*Los Angeles Times*
NYT	*New York Times*
WMR	*World Marxist Review*
WP	*Washington Post*
WSJ	*Wall Street Journal*
YICA	*Yearbook on International Communist Affairs*
ACAN	Agencia Central Americano Noticias
ADN	Allgemeiner Deutscher Nachrichtendienst
AFP	Agence France-Presse
ANSA	Agenzia Nazionale Stampa Associata
AP	Associated Press
BBC	British Broadcasting Corporation
BTA	Bulgarska Telegrafna Agentsiya
CANA	Caribbean News Agency
ČETEKA	Československá Tisková Kancelář
DPA	Deutsche Presse Agentur
EFE	Agencia EFE, Spanish News Agency
KPL	Khaosan Pathet Lao
MENA	Middle East News Agency
MTI	Magyar Tavirati Iroda
NCNA	New China News Agency
PAP	Polska Agencja Prasowa
RFE	Radio Free Europe
RL	Radio Liberty
TASS	Telegrafnoe Agentstvo Sovetskogo Soiuza
UPI	United Press International
VNA	Vietnam News Agency

Party Congresses

Country	*Congress or National Conference*	*Date (1987)*
Lesotho	7th	early 1987
Philippines (CPP)	9th	January
Lebanon	5th	3–5 February
Switzerland	13th	27 February–1 March
Sri Lanka	13th	22–26 March
Mexico (PSUM)	Merger	23 March
Austria	26th	25–28 March
Bangladesh	4th	7–11 April
Denmark	28th	16–19 April
Norway (NKP)	19th	23–26 April
Greece (E.AR)	1st, Founding	24–26 April
Spain (PCPE)	2d	25–27 April
Greece (KKE)	12th	12–16 May
West Berlin (SEW)	8th	15–17 May
Sweden (VPK)	28th	23–27 May
Peru	9th	27 May–2 June
Finland (SKP-Y)	1st	5–7 June
Australia (CPA)	29th	6–8 June
France	National conference	12–13 June
Tunisia	9th	12–14 June
Finland (SKP)	21st	12–15 June
South Yemen	4th	20–21 June
Morocco	4th	17–19 July
Brazil	8th	17–20 July
United States	24th	13–16 August
Costa Rica (PPC)	15th	23–24 August
Afghanistan	National conference	18–21 October
China	13th	25 October–1 November
Iceland	Biennial	7–10 November
Great Britain (CPGB)	40th	14–18 November
Mexico (PMS)	1st	25–30 November
Japan	18th	26–28 November
France	26th	2–6 December
Martinique	9th	12–13 December
Romania	National conference	14–16 December

Register of Communist Parties

Status: * ruling, + legal, # unrecognized, 0 proscribed

Country: Party(ies)/Date Founded	*Mid-1987 Population (est.) (World Factbook)*	*Communist Party Membership (claim or est.)*	*Party Leader (sec'y general)*	*Status*	*Last Congress*	*Last Election (percentage of vote; seats in legislature)*
AFRICA (12)						
Angola	7,950,244					
Popular Movement for the Liberation of Angola (MPLA), 1956 (MPLA-PT, 1977)		35,000 cl.	José Eduardo dos Santos	*	Second 9–11 Dec. 1985	(1980); all 203 MPLA approved
Benin	4,339,096					
People's Revolutionary Party of Benin (PRPB), 1975		fewer than 2,000 est.	Mathieu Kérékou (chairman, CC)	*	Second 18–24 Nov. 1985	(1984); all 196 PRPB approved
Congo	2,082,154					
Congolese Party of Labor (PCT), 1969		9,000 est.	Denis Sassou-Ngouesso (chairman)	*	Third 23–30 July 1984	95.0 (1984); all 153 PCT approved
Ethiopia	46,706,229					
Workers' Party of Ethiopia (WPE), 1984		50,000 est.	Mengistu Haile Mariam	*	First (Const.) 6–10 Sept. 1984	85.0 (1987); 835 all WPE members
Lesotho	1,621,932					
Communist Party of Lesotho (CPL), 1962		no data	Jacob M. Kena	0 (tolerated)	Seventh "early 1987"	(1985)
Mozambique	14,535,805					
Front for the Liberation of Mozambique (FRELIMO), 1962		130,000 cl. (*WMR*, Apr. 1987, p. 53)	Joaquim Albert Chissano	*	Fourth 26–29 Apr. 1983	(1986); incomplete

Nigeria	97,383,000					
Socialist Working People's Party (SWPP), 1978 (Socialist Workers and Farmers Party, 1963)	*(Political Handbook of the World, 1987)*	no data (probably defunct)	Dapo Fatogun	0	First Nov. 1978	(1983)
Réunion	549,697					
Réunion Communist Party (PCR), 1959		2,000 est.	Paul Vergès	+	Fifth 12–14 July 1980	29.2 (1986); 13 of 45 left coal.: 7 for PCR (local assembly); 2 in Paris
Senegal	7,064,025					
Independence and Labor Party (PIT), 1957		no data	Amath Dansoko	+	Second 28 Sept.–2 Oct. 1984	0.5 (1983); none
South Africa	34,313,356					
South African Communist Party (SACP), 1921		no data	Joe Slovo Dan Tloome (chairman)	0	Sixth Dec. 1984 or early 1985, in London	n/a
Sudan	23,524,622					
Sudanese Communist Party (SCP), 1946		9,000 est.	Muhammad Ibrahim Nugud Mansur	+	Fourth (legal) 31 Oct. 1967	1.67 (1986), 5 of 301; 2 in territ., 3 in grad. constituencies
Zimbabwe	9,372,000					
Zimbabwe African National Union–Patriotic Front (ZANU-PF), 1963		no data	Robert G. Mugabe	*	Second 8–12 Aug. 1984	75.0 (1987); 77 of 100 (in by-election for 30 formerly white Parl. seats)
TOTAL	249,442,160	237,000				

Country: Party(ies)/Date Founded	*Mid-1987 Population (est.) (World Factbook)*	*Communist Party Membership (claim or est.)*	*Party Leader (sec'y general)*	*Status*	*Last Congress*	*Last Election (percentage of vote; seats in legislature)*
THE AMERICAS (29)						
Argentina	31,144,775					
Communist Party of Argentina (PCA), 1918		80,000 est.	Athos Fava	+	Sixteenth 4–7 Nov. 1986	5.3 (1987); none Broad Front coal. parliamentary and provincial by-elections 6 Sept. 1987; none
Bolivia	6,309,642					
Communist Party of Bolivia (PCB), 1950 (split, 1985)		500 cl.	Simón Reyes Rivera to July Humberto Ramírez from July (majority faction) Carlos Soria Galvarro (minority faction)	+	Fifth 9–13 Feb. 1985 Extraordinary 26–29 April 1986	2.21 (1985); 4 of 130 FPU coal.
Brazil	147,094,739					
Brazilian Communist Party (PCB), 1922		15,000 est. (*Jornal do Brasil*, 16 July 1987)	Salomão Malina	+	Eighth (called National Meeting of Communists) 17–20 July 1987	(1986); 3 of 487
Canada	25,857,943					
Communist Party of Canada (CPC), 1921		2,500 est.	William Kashtan	+	Twenty-sixth 5–8 Apr. 1985	.05 (1984); none
Chile	12,448,008					
Communist Party of Chile (CPC), 1922		20,000 est.	Luís Corvalán Lepe	0	Sixteenth June 1984 (clandestine)	n/a

Colombia	30,660,504					
Communist Party of Colombia (PCC), 1930		18,000 est. (incl. youth org.)	Gilberto Vieira	+	Fourteenth 7–11 Nov. 1984	1.4 (1986); 9 of 199 Patriotic Union
Costa Rica	2,811,652					
Popular Vanguard Party (PVP), 1931		3,500 est. (prior to split)	Humberto Vargas Carbonell	+	Fifteenth 15–16 Sept. 1984	0.8 (1986); 1 of 57 Popular Alliance
Costa Rican People's Party (PPC), split from PVP, 1984		no data	Manuel Mora Valverde	+	Fifteenth 23–24 Aug. 1987	(1986); 1 of 57 United People's Coalition
Cuba	10,259,047					
Cuban Communist Party (PCC), 1965		523,639 cl. 500,000 est.	Fidel Castro Ruz	*	Third 4–7 Feb. and 30 Nov.–2 Dec. 1986	(1986); all 499 PCC approved
Dominican Republic	6,960,743					
Dominican Communist Party (PCD), 1944		750 est.	Narciso Isa Conde	+	Third 15–17 Mar. 1984	0.3 (1986); none
Ecuador	9,954,609					
Communist Party of Ecuador (PCE), 1928		500 est.	René Mauge Mosquera (member of parliament)	+	Tenth 27–29 Nov. 1981	3.6 (1986); 3 of 71 Broad Leftist Front, FADI 4.0 (1984) in pres. elec.
El Salvador	5,260,478					
Communist Party of El Salvador (PCES), 1930 (One of five in FMLN)		1,000 est.	Jorge Shafik Handal	0	Seventh Apr. 1979	(1985)
Grenada	84,748					
Maurice Bishop Patriotic Movement (MBPM), 1984		no data	Kenrick Radix (chairman)	+	First Oct. 1985	5.0 (1984); none
Guadeloupe	336,354					
Communist Party of Guadeloupe (PCG), 1958		3,000 est.	Guy Daninthe	+	Eighth 27–29 Apr. 1984	no data (1986); 22 of 41 left coal. (PCG: 10 of 22), local assembly; also 1 of 3 in Paris

Country: Party(ies)/Date Founded	Mid-1987 Population (est.) (World Factbook)	Communist Party Membership (claim or est.)	Party Leader (sec'y general)	Status	Last Congress	Last Election (percentage of vote; seats in legislature)
Guatemala	9,622,387					
Guatemalan Party of Labor (PGT), 1952		500 est.	Carlos González ("Camarilla" faction) Daniel Rios (National Leadership Nucleus Faction)	0	Fourth Dec. 1969	(1985)
Guyana	765,844					
People's Progressive Party (PPP), 1950		200 est.	Cheddi Jagan	+	Twenty-second 3–5 Aug. 1985	16.8 (1985); 8 of 53 elected members
Haiti	6,187,115					
Unified Party of Haitian Communists (PUCH), 1968		350 est.	René Théodore	+	First 1979	(1987) incomplete
Honduras	4,823,818					
Communist Party of Honduras (PCH), 1954 (one of six in the Honduran Revolutionary Movement, MHR, 1982)		200 est.	Rigoberto Padilla Rush (in exile) Mario Sosa Navarro (leader in Honduras)	0	Fourth Jan. 1986 (clandestine)	n/a (1985)
Jamaica	2,455,536					
Workers' Party of Jamaica (WPJ), 1978		75 est.	Trevor Munroe	+	Third 14–21 Dec. 1984	(1983) (WPJ boycotted)
Jamaican Communist Party (JCP), 1975		no data	Christopher Lawrence	+	no data	
Martinique	344,922					
Martinique Communist Party (PCM), 1957		1,000 est.	Armand Nicolas	+	Ninth 12–13 Dec. 1987	no data (1986); 3 of 41 (local assembly); none in Paris

Mexico	81,860,566					
Unified Socialist Party of Mexico (PSUM), 1981		90,000 cl.			(Merger Congress, 23 March 1987)	3.24 (1985); 12 of 400
Mexican Socialist Party (PMS), 1987		no data	Gilberto Rincón Gallardo	+	First 25–29 Nov. 1987	
Nicaragua	3,319,059					
Nicaraguan Socialist Party (PSN), 1937		no data	Gustavo Tablada	+	Tenth Oct. 1973	1.3 (1984); 2 of 96
Sandinista Front of National Liberation (FSLN), 1961		1,400 est.	Daniel Ortega (Coord. of Executive Commission)	*		63.0 (1984); 61 of 96
Panama	2,274,833					
People's Party (PDP), 1943		13,089 est.	Rubén Darío Sousa	+	Eighth 24–26 Jan. 1986	(1984); none
Paraguay	4,251,924					
Paraguayan Communist Party (PCP), 1928		4,000 est.	Julio Rojas (acting) Antonio Maidana (arrested in 1980)	0	Third 10 Apr. 1971	n/a
Peru	20,739,218					
Peruvian Communist Party (PCP), 1930		2,000 est.	Jorge del Prado Chavez	+	Ninth 27–30 May 1987	26.0 (1984); 48 of 180 United Left Coalition; 6 PCP repr. of 48
Puerto Rico	3,320,520					
Puerto Rican Communist Party (PCP), 1934		125 est.	Frank Irrizarry	+	unknown	0.3 (1984); none
Suriname	388,636					
National Democratic Party (NDP), 1987		2,000 est.	Desire Bouterse	+	First 7 June 1987	10.4 (1987)
25 Feb. Unity Movement (25 FM), 1983		no data	Harvey Naarendorp		First 12 May 1984	
United States of America	243,084,000					
Communist Party USA (CPUSA), 1919		17,500 cl.	Gus Hall	+	Twenty-fourth 13–16 Aug. 1987	0.01 (1984); none

Country: Party(ies)/Date Founded	Mid-1987 Population (est.) (World Factbook)	Communist Party Membership (claim or est.)	Party Leader (sec'y general)	Status	Last Congress	Last Election (percentage of vote; seats in legislature)
Uruguay	2,964,052					
Communist Party of Uruguay (PCU), 1920		11,000 cl. (*Pravda*, 14, 22 Dec.)	Rodney Arismendi	+	Twentieth Dec. 1970	6.0 (1984); none Frente Amplio coal.
Venezuela	18,291,134					
Communist Party of Venezuela (PCV), 1931		4,000 est.	Alonso Ojeda Olaechea	+	Seventh 24–27 Oct. 1985	2.0 (1983); 3 of 195
TOTAL	692,876,806	792,089				

ASIA AND THE PACIFIC (20)

Country: Party(ies)/Date Founded	Mid-1987 Population (est.) (World Factbook)	Communist Party Membership (claim or est.)	Party Leader (sec'y general)	Status	Last Congress	Last Election (percentage of vote; seats in legislature)
Australia	16,072,986					
Communist Party of Australia (CPA), 1920		1,000 est.	Judy Mundey	+	Twenty-ninth 6–8 June 1987	0.3 (1987); none
Socialist Party of Australia (SPA), 1971		500 est.	Peter Dudley Symon	+	Fifth 28 Sept.–1 Oct. 1984	negl. (1987); none
Bangladesh	107,087,586					
Communist Party of Bangladesh (CPB), 1948		5,000 cl.	Muhammed Farhad (died, Oct. 1987) Saifuddin Ahmed Manik	+ (banned in Nov.)	Fourth 7–11 Apr. 1987	(1986); 6 of 330
Burma	38,822,484					
Burmese Communist Party (BCP), 1939		3,000 cl.	Thakin Ba Thein Tin (chairman)	0	Third 9 Sept.–2 Oct. 1985	n/a

Cambodia	6,536,079					
Khmer People's Revolutionary Party (KPRP), 1951		7,500 est.	Heng Samrin	*	Fifth 13–16 Oct. 1985	99.0 (1981); all 117
Party of Democratic Kampuchea (PDK), or Kampuchean Communist Party (KCP), 1951		no data	Pol Pot	0	Third 14 Dec. 1975	n/a
China	1,064,147,038					
Chinese Communist Party (CCP), 1921	(1,072,330,000 Peking Central Office of Statistics)	46,011,951 cl. (*Beijing Review*, 2–8 Nov. 1987)	Hu Yaobang until 16 Jan. Zhao Ziyang	*	Thirteenth 25 Oct.–1 Nov. 1987	(1987); all 3,202 CCP approved
India	800,325,817					
Communist Party of India (CPI), 1928		479,000 cl.	C. Rajeswara Rao	+	Thirteenth 12–17 Mar. 1986	2.71 (1984); 6 of 544
Communist Party of India-Marxist (CPM), 1964		361,500 cl.	E. M. S. Namboodiripad	+	Twelfth 25–30 Dec. 1985	5.96 (1984); 22 of 544
Indonesia	180,425,534					
Indonesian Communist Party (PKI), 1920 (split)		1,400 est. ca. 200 exiles	Jusuf Adjitorop (pro-Beijing faction) Satiadjaya Sudiman (pro-Moscow faction)	0	Seventh Extraord. Apr. 1962	n/a
Japan	122,124,293					
Japan Communist Party (JCP), 1922		470,000 est.	Tetsuzo Fuwa (Presidium chairman to Nov.) Hiromu Murakami Kenji Miyamoto (CC chairman)	+	Eighteenth 26–28 Nov. 1987	9.47 (1986); 27 of 512
Korea (North)	21,447,977					
Korean Workers' Party (KWP), 1946 (as united party, 1949)		2,500,000 est.	Kim Il-song	*	Sixth 10–15 Oct. 1980	100 (1986); all 706 KWP approved

Country: Party(ies)/Date Founded	Mid-1987 Population (est.) (World Factbook)	Communist Party Membership (claim or est.)	Party Leader (sec'y general)	Status	Last Congress	Last Election (percentage of vote; seats in legislature)
Laos	3,765,887					
Lao People's Revolutionary Party (LPRP), 1955		40,000 cl. (*WMR*, June)	Kaysone Phomvihane	*	Fourth 13–15 Nov. 1986	(Dec. 1975); Supreme People's Assembly (all 46 appointed by LPRP)
Malaysia	16,068,516					
Communist Party of Malaya (CPM), 1930		1,000 est.	Chin Peng	0	1965 (last known)	(1984)
Communist Party of Malaysia (MCP), 1983		800 est.	Ah Leng	0	unknown	(1984)
Mongolia	2,011,066					
Mongolian People's Revolutionary Party (MPRP), 1921		88,150 cl.	Jambyn Batmonh (Dzambiin Batmunkh)	*	Nineteenth 28–31 May 1986	93.5 (1986); 346 of 370, MPRP approved
Nepal	17,814,294					
Nepal Communist Party (NCP), 1949 (factions)		10,000 est. (75% pro-Beijing and neutral)	Man Mohan Adhikary	0	Third 1961 (before split; right wing held its own third in 1968)	n/a
New Zealand	3,291,600 (N.Z. Dept. of Stat.)					
Communist Party of New Zealand (CPNZ), 1921		50 est.	Richard C. Wolfe (died, 19 July) Harold Crook (since July)	+	Twenty-third 22 Apr. 1984	(1987); none
Socialist Unity Party (SUP), 1966		300 est.	George H. Jackson	+	Seventh 26–27 Oct. 1985	(1987); none
Pakistan	104,600,799					
Communist Party of Pakistan (CPP), 1948		under 200 est.	Ali Nazish	0 (since 1954)	First 1976 (clandestine)	n/a

Philippines	58,100,000 (*Asia Yearbook, 1987*)					
Philippine Communist Party (PKP), 1930		200 est.	Felicismo Macapagal	+	Eighth 1980	(1987)
Communist Party of the Philippines (CPP), 1968		15,000 est.	Rafael Baylosis	0	Ninth Jan. 1987 (First legal since 1946)	(1987); participated indirectly via Partido ng Bayan
Singapore	2,616,236					
Communist Party of Malaya, Branch (CPM), 1930		350 est.	Chin Peng	0	unknown	(1984)
Sri Lanka	16,406,576					
Communist Party of Sri Lanka (CPSL), 1943		5,000 est.	Kattorge P. Silva	+	Thirteenth 22–26 March 1987	2.0 (1977); 1 of 168
Thailand	53,645,823					
Communist Party of Thailand (CPT), 1942		250 est.	Thong Jaensri (unconfirmed; pseudonym?)	0	Fourth Mar.–Apr. 1984 (clandestine)	n/a
Vietnam	63,593,000					
Vietnamese Communist Party (VCP), 1930		1,900,000 est.	Nguyen Van Linh	*	Sixth 15–18 Dec. 1986	98.8 (1987); 496 of 614; all VCP endorsed
TOTAL	2,698,903,591	51,901,851				

EASTERN EUROPE AND USSR (9)

Albania	3,085,985					
Albanian Party of Labor (APL), 1941		147,000 cl.	Ramiz Alia	*	Ninth 3–8 Nov. 1986	100.0 (1987); all 250 Democratic Front
Bulgaria	8,960,749					
Bulgarian Communist Party (BCP), 1903		932,055 cl.	Todor Zhivkov	*	Thirteenth 2–5 Apr. 1986	99.9 (1986); all 400 Fatherland Front

Country: Party(ies)/Date Founded	Mid-1987 Population (est.) (World Factbook)	Communist Party Membership (claim or est.)	Party Leader (sec'y general)	Status	Last Congress	Last Election (percentage of vote; seats in legislature)
Czechoslovakia	15,581,993					
Communist Party of Czechoslovakia (KSC), 1921		1,705,490 cl. (*Rudé právo*, 3 Sep. 1987)	Miloš Jakeš	*	Seventeenth 24–28 Mar. 1986	99.94 (1986); all 350 National Front
Germany: German Democratic Republic	16,610,265					
Socialist Unity Party (SED), 1946		2,324,386 cl. (*Neues Deutschland*, 18 April 1987)	Erich Honecker	*	Eleventh 17–21 Apr. 1986	99.94 (1986); all 500 National Front
Hungary	10,613,000					
Hungarian Socialist Worker's Party (HSWP), 1956		870,992 cl.	János Kádár	*	Thirteenth 25–28 Mar. 1985	98.9 (1985); all 352 Patriotic People's Front
Poland	37,726,699					
Polish United Workers' Party (PZPR), 1948		2,130,000 cl. (*FBIS-EE*, 28 May 1987; *Süddeutsche Zeitung*, 25 May 1987)	Wojciech Jaruzelski	*	Tenth 29 June–3 July 1986	78.8 (1985); all 460 Fatherland Front
Romania	22,936,503					
Romanian Communist Party (RPC), 1921		3,640,000 cl.	Nicolae Ceauşescu	*	Thirteenth 19–22 Nov. 1984	97.8 (1985); all 369 Socialist Democracy and Unity Front
USSR	284,008,160					
Communist Party of the Soviet Union (CPSU), 1898		19,037,946 cl. (*WMR*, Apr. 1987, p. 53)	Mikhail S. Gorbachev	*	Twenty-seventh 25 Feb.–6 Mar. 1986	99.9 (1984); all 1,500 CPSU approved (71.4% are CPSU members)

Yugoslavia	23,430,830					
League of Communists of Yugoslavia (LCY), 1920		2,168,000 cl. (2,150,000 est.)	Milanko Renovica Boško Krunić (president of Presidium)	*	Thirteenth 25–28 June 1986	(1986); all 308; all LCY approved Socialist Alliance
TOTAL	422,954,184	32,955,869				

MIDDLE EAST (15)

Afghanistan	14,183,671 est.					
People's Democratic Party of Afghanistan (PDPA), 1965		40,000 est. (185,000 cl. incl. cand. members)	Mohammed Najibullah	*	Second nat'l. conference 18–19 Oct. 1987	(1985) (local council)
Algeria	23,460,614					
Socialist Vanguard Party (PAGS), 1920		450 est.	Sadiq Hadjeres (first secretary)	0	Sixth Feb. 1952	(1982)
Bahrain	464,102					
Bahrain National Liberation Front (NLF/B), 1955		negligible	Yusuf al-Hassan al-Ajajai (chairman) Saif ben Ali (sec. gen.)	0	unknown	n/a
Egypt	51,929,962					
Egyptian Communist Party (ECP), 1921		500 est.	Farid Mujahid (apparently)	0	Second 1984 or early 1985	(1984)
Iran	50,407,723					
Communist Party of Iran (Tudeh Party), 1941 (dissolved May 1983)		1,500 est.	Ali Khavari (first sec. of CC; party leader in exile)	0	National Conference 1986	(1980)
Iraq	16,970,000					
Iraqi Communist Party (ICP), 1934		no data	Aziz Muhammad (first secretary)	0	Fourth 10–15 Nov. 1985	(1984)

Country: Party(ies)/Date Founded	*Mid-1987 Population (est.) (World Factbook)*	*Communist Party Membership (claim or est.)*	*Party Leader (sec'y general)*	*Status*	*Last Congress*	*Last Election (percentage of vote; seats in legislature)*
Israel	4,222,118 (excl. E. Jerusalem and the West Bank)					
Communist Party of Israel (CPI, "RAKAH"), 1948 (Palestine Communist Party, 1922)		2,000 est.	Meir Vilner	+	Twentieth 4–7 Dec. 1985	3.4 (1984); 4 of 120
Jordan	2,794,000					
Communist Party of Jordan (CPJ), 1951		no data	Ya'qub Zayadin	0	Second Dec. 1983	n/a
Lebanon	3,320,522					
Lebanese Communist Party (LCP), 1924		3,000 est. (14,000–16,000 cl.)	George Hawi	+	Fifth 3–5 Feb. 1987	(1972)
Organization of Communist Action in Lebanon (OCAL), 1970		1,500 est.	Muhsin Ibrahim	+	First 1971	
Morocco	23,361,495					
Party of Progress and Socialism (PPS), 1974 (Moroccan Communist Party, 1943)		3,000–5,000 est. (30,000 cl.)	'Ali Yata	+	Fourth 17–19 July 1987	2.3 (1984); 2 of 306
Palestine Communist Party (PCP), 1982	4,500,000 Palestinians (incl. E. Jerusalem, Gaza, Jordan and the West Bank)	200 est.	Bashir al-Barghuti (presumably)	0	First 1984	n/a
Saudi Arabia	14,904,794					
Communist Party of Saudi Arabia (CPSA), 1975		negligible	Mahdi Habib	0	Second Aug. 1984	n/a
Syria	11,147,763					
Syrian Communist Party (SCP), 1924 (as separate party, 1944)		5,000 est.	Khalid Bakhdash	+	Sixth July 1986	(1986); 8 of 195

Tunisia	7,561,641					
Tunisian Communist Party (PCT), 1934		2,000 est. (4,000 cl.)	Muhammad Harmel (first secretary)	+	Ninth 12–14 June 1987	(1986); none (PCT boycotted elections)
Yemen (PDRY)	2,351,131					
Yemen Socialist Party (YSP), 1978		31,000 cl. (incl. cand. mbrs.)	'Ali Salim al-Bayd	*	Fourth 20–21 June 1987	(1986); all 111 YSP approved
Total	231,579,536	91,150				

WESTERN EUROPE (23)

Austria	7,569,283					
Communist Party of Austria (KPO), 1918		15,000 est.	Franz Muhri (chairman)	+	Twenty-sixth 25–28 Mar. 1987	0.72 (1986); none
Belgium	9,873,066					
Belgian Communist Party (PCB/KPB), 1921		5,000 est.	Louis van Geyt (president)	+	Twenty-fifth 18–20 Apr. 1986	negligible (1987); none
Cyprus	683,651					
Progressive Party of the Working People (AKEL), 1941 (Communist Party of Cyprus, 1922)		12,000 cl.	Ezekias Papaioannou	+	Sixteenth 26–30 Nov. 1986 Extraordinary Congress 20 Dec. 1987 (*Pravda*, 21 Dec. 1987)	27.4 (1985); 15 of 56
Denmark	5,130,260					
Communist Party of Denmark (DKP), 1919		10,000 est.	Poul Emanuel (party sec.) Jørgen Jensen to Apr., Ole Sohn since Apr. (chairman)	+	Twenty-eighth 16–19 Apr. 1987	0.9 (1987); none

Country: Party(ies)/Date Founded	*Mid-1987 Population (est.) (World Factbook)*	*Communist Party Membership (claim or est.)*	*Party Leader (sec'y general)*	*Status*	*Last Congress*	*Last Election (percentage of vote; seats in legislature)*
Finland	4,939,880					
Finnish Communist Party (SKP), 1918		20,000 cl.	Esko Vainionpää (sec. gen.) Arvo Aalto (chairman)	+	Twenty-first 12–15 June 1987	9.4 (1987); 16 of 200 SKDL Front (11 of 16 for SKP)
Finnish Communist Party-Unity (SKP-Y), 1986		16,663 cl.	Jouko Kajanoja (gen. sec.) Taisto Sinisalo (chairman)	+	First 5–7 June, 1987	4.3 (1987); 4 of 200 DEVA Front
France	55,596,030					
French Communist Party (PCF), 1920		604,282 cl. (*L'Humanité*, 3 Dec.)	Georges Marchais	+	Twenty-sixth 2–6 Dec. 1987	9.8 (1986); 35 of 577
Germany: Federal Republic of Germany	59,131,000 (FRG Consulate, San Francisco)					
German Communist Party (DKP), 1968		40,000 est. (64,000 incl. student & youth org.)	Herbert Mies (chairman)	+	Eighth 2–4 May 1986	0.5 (1987); none for Peace List in which DKP participated
Great Britain	56,845,195					
Communist Party of Great Britain (CPGB), 1920		9,700 est.	Gordon McLennan	+	Fortieth 14–18 Nov. 1987	0.01 (1987); none
Greece	9,987,787					
Communist Party of Greece (KKE), 1921		42,000 est.	Kharilaos Florakis	+	Twelfth 12–16 May 1987	9.9 (1985); 13 of 300
Communist Party of Greece–Interior (KKE-I), 1968:		(split into two factions)		+	Fourth May 1986	1.8 (1985); none

(KKE-I Renovating Left), 1987; and		no data	Giannis Banias	+		
Greek Left (E.AR), 1987		no data	Leonidas Kyrkos	+	24–26 April	
Iceland	244,676					
People's Alliance (AB), 1968		3,000 est.	Olafur Ragnar Grimsson (chairman)	+	Biennial Congr. 7–10 Nov. 1987	13.2 (1987); 8 of 63
Ireland	3,534,553					
Communist Party of Ireland (CPI), 1933		500 est.	James Stewart	+	Nineteenth 31 Jan.–2 Feb. 1986	(1987); none
Italy	57,350,850					
Italian Communist Party (PCI), 1921		1,505,000 cl.	Alessandro Natta	+	Seventeenth 9–13 April 1986	26.6 (1987); 177 of 630
Luxembourg	366,127					
Communist Party of Luxembourg (CPL), 1921		600 est.	René Urbany (chairman)	+	Twenty-fourth 4–5 Feb. 1984	4.9 (1984); 2 of 64
Malta	344,479 (Malta Office of Statistics)					
Communist Party of Malta (CPM), 1969		300 est.	Anthony Vassallo	+	Extraordinary 18–25 May 1984	0.08 (1987); none
Netherlands	14,641,554					
Communist Party of the Netherlands (CPN), 1909		12,000 est. (27,000 cl.)	Elli Izeboud	+	Thirtieth 29 Nov.–2 Dec. 1986	0.6 (1986); none
Norway	4,178,545					
Norwegian Communist Party (NKP), 1923		5,500 est.	Kaare Andre Nilsen (chairman)	+	Nineteenth 23–26 Apr. 1987	0.2 (1985); none
Workers' Communist Party (AKP), 1973		10,000 est.	Kjersti Ericsson (chairman)	+	Third (or Fourth?) Dec. 1984	(1985); none
Portugal	10,314,727					
Portuguese Communist Party (PCP), 1921		over 200,000 cl.	Álvaro Cunhal	+	Eleventh Extraord. 2–6 Feb. 1986	11 (1987); 30 of 250 United People's Alliance Coalition (25 of 30 for PCP)

Country: Party(ies)/Date Founded	*Mid-1987 Population (est.) (World Factbook)*	*Communist Party Membership (claim or est.)*	*Party Leader (sec'y general)*	*Status*	*Last Congress*	*Last Election (percentage of vote; seats in legislature)*
San Marino	22,791					
Communist Party of San Marino (PCS), 1921		1,200 cl.	Gilberto Ghiotti	+	Eleventh 27 Jan. 1986	24.3 (1983); 15 of 60
Spain	39,000,804					
Spanish Communist Party (PCE), 1920		60,000 est.	Gerardo Iglesias	+	Eleventh 14–18 Dec. 1983	4.6 (1986); 7 of 350 United Left Coalition
Communist Party of the Peoples of Spain (PCPE), 1984		25,500 est.	Juan Ramos (sec. gen.) Ignacio Gallegos (chairman)	+	Second 25–27 Apr. 1987	included above
Spanish Workers' Party-Communist Unity (PTE-UC), 1987		14,000 est.	Adolfo Pinedo (sec. gen.) Santiago Carrillo (chairman)	+	First 8 Feb. 1987	1.12 (1986); none
Sweden	8,383,026					
Left Party Communists (VPK), 1921		17,800 cl.	Lars Werner (chairman)	+	Twenty-eighth 23–27 May 1987	5.4 (1985); 19 of 349
Communist Workers' Party (APK), 1977		5,000 cl.	Rolf Hagel (chairman)	+	Twenty-eighth 7 Nov. 1986	(1985); none (withdrew)
Switzerland	6,572,739					
Swiss Labor Party (PdAS), 1921 (re-established, 1944)		4,500 est.	Armand Magnin (until March) Jean Spielman	+	Thirteenth 27 Feb.–1 Mar. 1987	(1987); no data
Turkey	52,987,778					
Communist Party of Turkey (TCP), 1920		negligible	Haydar Kutlu	0	Fifth Oct. or Nov. 1983	(1987)

West Berlin						
Socialist Unity Party of West Berlin (SEW), 1949	1,869,000 (FRG Consulate, San Francisco)	7,000 cl.	Horst Schmitt (chairman)	+	Eighth 15–27 May 1987	0.6 (1985); none
TOTAL	409,567,801	2,646,545				
GRAND TOTAL	4,705,324,078	88,624,504				

MAJOR INTERNATIONAL FRONT ORGANIZATIONS*

Organization (12)	*Year Founded*	*Headquarters*	*Claimed Membership*	*Affiliates*	*Countries*
Afro-Asian Peoples' Solidarity Organization (AAPSO)	1957	Cairo	unknown	87	–
Christian Peace Conference (CPC)	1958	Prague	unknown	–	ca. 80
International Association of Democratic Lawyers (IADL)	1946	Brussels	25,000	–	ca. 80
International Federation of Resistance Movements (FIR)	1951	Vienna	5,000,000	68	29
International Organization of Journalists (IOJ)	1946	Prague	ca. 250,000[1]	–	120 plus
International Union of Students (IUS)	1946	Prague	10,000,000	122	112
Women's International Democratic Federation (WIDF)	1945	East Berlin	200,000,000	142[2]	124[2]
World Federation of Democratic Youth (WFDY)	1945	Budapest	150,000,000	ca. 270	123
World Federation of Scientific Workers (WFSW)	1946	London	740,000	ca. 46	70 plus
World Federation of Teachers' Unions (FISE)	1946	E. Berlin	26,000,000	137	79[3]
World Federation of Trade Unions (WFTU)	1945	Prague	ca. 214,000,000	92	81
World Peace Council (WPC)	1950	Helsinki	unknown	–	143

*All known or presumed participants in meetings of "closely coordinating" international nongovernmental organizations during 1981–1987.

1. Prague, ČTK, 29 January.

2. *Women of the Whole World*, No. 3, p. 14.

3. *Flashes from the Trade Union*, 27 Nov.

Introduction: The Communist World, 1987

The world communist movement has been affected by the "new thinking" that reportedly permeates the Kremlin. It is apparently based on a more realistic assessment of the limitations that constrain Soviet power and influence. Moscow's policies are aimed at achieving a reduction of external pressures on the USSR so that economic and social problems can be solved at home. Communist parties, both inside and outside the Soviet empire, are expected to support these objectives. These guidelines are being disseminated through the CPSU Central Committee's department of liaison with ruling communist parties under Vadim A. Medvedev and the International Department for all other such movements, headed by Anatolii F. Dobrynin.

A rebuilt and economically more powerful Soviet Union would again project an image of a model sociopolitical system for the rest of the world and, thus, ultimately benefit all national communist parties. To achieve such a revival, a period of global détente is the main prerequisite. Interdependence and cooperation, thus, should replace East-West confrontation during this interim of *peredyshka*.

The nonruling communist parties are being told by Moscow to subordinate the class stuggle, albeit temporarily, to the worldwide peace campaign. They will do so by joining other left-wing movements in the struggle against the arms race. However, these foreign communists should not aspire to a leading role in the anti-imperialist effort, and they should not lecture their domestic allies "but seek to learn from them."[1]

The message to the Third World's revolutionary democratic parties is that they should use extreme caution in deciding whether or not to invoke armed struggle. Various manifestations of leftist extremism should be renounced because "any local conflict has a tendency to grow into a regional or even a world conflict."[2] The implication appears to be that revolutionary forces cannot count on automatic Soviet military intervention.

This less dogmatic approach could be seen at the 70th anniversary of the Bolshevik Revolution 4–5 November (in advance of the actual date), which attracted 178 delegations from 119 countries.[3] These included not only recognized communist parties but also social democratic parties and Marxist-Leninist movements from the Third World.

Mikhail S. Gorbachev, CPSU general secretary, had given the main 70th anniversary address two days earlier in which he stated that "the days of the Comintern, of the Informburo, and even of binding international conferences, have passed."[4] He also reportedly listed six generally recognized principles that should apply to relations between the CPSU and other ruling communist parties:

1. Unconditional and total equality
2. Responsibility of the ruling party for affairs in its own country
3. Concern for the general cause of communism
4. Respect for achievements in other bloc countries
5. Voluntary cooperation
6. Strict observance of peaceful coexistence.[5]

The assembled delegates heard Gorbachev say in his opening comments two days later that "the communist movement needs renewal and qualitative changes." He rejected the "arrogance of belief in one's omniscience" and extended an invitation "not only to fraternal parties, communists, but also socialists and social democrats, and representatives of other trends in political thought and action . . . to cooperation and search jointly."[6] Absent from this gathering were the Albanians and Chinese.

Over the past one-and-a-half decades, it is claimed that the world communist movement has expanded from 88 parties and about 50 million members in the early 1970s to almost 100 parties and more than 82 million members in the mid-1980s.[7] Of this 82 million, more than 77 million live in the sixteen communist-ruled states and fewer than 4.7 million in other countries (see Table 1).

Parties in the communist-ruled states—part of the Soviet "commonwealth of nations"—now total twelve with the addition of the former revolutionary democracy in Cambodia,[8] which has only observer status with the Council for Mutual Economic Assistance (CMEA). The four ruling movements out-

Table 1: Growth of Communist Parties (CPs) in Non-CP-Ruled States

Region	1970 Number of CPs	1970 CP members (millions)	1986 Number of CPs	1986 CP members (millions)
Asia, Australia, and Oceania	19	0.60	22	1.40
The Americas	25	0.38	25	0.40
Africa	9	0.02	11	0.08
Western Europe	21	2.27	22	2.80
Total	74	3.27	80	4.68

SOURCE: N. F. Shumikhin (chief ed.), *Sotsializm i sovremennyi mir* (Kiev, Vyshcha shkola, 1987), p. 20.

side the so-called commonwealth are those in Albania, China, North Korea, and Yugoslavia (associate CMEA member). It is expected that other "revolutionary democratic" parties will advance to membership in the commonwealth. One Soviet source claims that approximately 40 such movements exist in the Third World,[9] although he does not list them.

The Register of Communist Parties in this volume includes 108 countries or geographic entities with communist parties recognized by Moscow as well as the more radical revolutionary democratic and national liberation movements. The CPSU acknowledges the existence of more than one party in Australia, Costa Rica, Finland, India, New Zealand, Spain, and Sweden. It also recognizes parties in such nonsovereign territories as Guadeloupe, Martinique, Palestine, Puerto Rico, Réunion, and West Berlin. The so-called vanguard revolutionary democratic parties[10] in the Register operate in Afghanistan, Bahrain, Benin, Cambodia, Congo, Ethiopia, Grenada, Mozambique, Nicaragua, South Yemen, and Zimbabwe. All are in power except the movements in Bahrein and Grenada. A few communist parties not recognized by Moscow (some are pro-Chinese) are also listed in the Register.

The acronyms for those movements not designated as "Communist Party of..." appear in the Register, with the full name provided in the Basic Facts section of the text. Population data are estimates[11] as of July. Also given are names of party general secretaries (with other titles in parentheses), dates of most recent congresses or national conferences, status of the movement, percentage of the vote, and seats in parliament where applicable.

Most of the sixteen ruling communist parties had insignificant changes in membership with the exception of increases claimed by China (two million), Romania (80,000), the Soviet Union (500,000), and Vietnam (an estimated 200,000). Among the nonruling movements, it is suggested that Brazil lost one-fourth of its members. The communists in Uruguay claimed an increase of almost 50 percent. The estimates for Bangladesh and Singapore grew by two-fifths, but those for Indonesia dropped about that much. Malaysia, the Philippines, and Thailand dropped even more. Considerable disparities exist between some communist claims and our estimates: Afghanistan—185,000 claimed; our estimate, 40,000; Morocco—30,000 and 2,500; Tunisia—4,000 and 2,000; West Berlin—7,000 and 4,500.

New leaders emerged in nine communist parties: five due to resignations (Bolivia, Japan, Jordan, Iceland, and Switzerland), three because of deaths (Brazil, Bangladesh, and New Zealand), and one based on an unconfirmed report (Thailand). The Table of Party Congresses in this volume lists the 35 party congresses and national conferences that took place during 1987.

Parliamentary voting was held in nineteen countries around the world during 1987. The communist or revolutionary democratic regimes in Albania, Vietnam, Ethiopia, and Zimbabwe achieved overwhelming victories in uncontested elections. Among the other states where the people voted, only Turkey maintains a ban on the communist party. Argentina, New Zealand, and the Philippines registered no seats in their respective parliaments for the local communist parties. In Western Europe, the same results applied to Belgium, Denmark, and Malta. However, communist parties did obtain parliamentary seats in Switzerland (1), Iceland (8, down from 10), Finland (16, down from 27), Portugal (30, down from 38), and Italy (177, down from 198). Major developments in various regions of the world are discussed below.

Sub-Saharan Africa. The most newsworthy event affecting a Marxist-Leninist party took place in Ethiopia, where a new constitution was approved by 81 percent of those voting on a referendum in February. When the constitution went into effect during September, the country became officially known as the People's Democratic Republic of Ethiopia. Additionally the *dergue*—the provisional military administrative committee—transferred its power to the newly established national *shengo*, or parliament. These adjustments represent Ethiopia's continuing effort to become a ruling communist party state instead of one dominated by strongman Mengistu Haile Mariam and his military clique. Mengistu retains his positions as commander in chief of the armed forces and as general secretary of the Workers' Party of Ethiopia.[12] The national *shengo* elected him president of the country in September. Ethiopia also pushed ahead on its resettlement and ruralization programs, despite dislocation of agriculture and attacks by Eritrean rebels.

Leadership reshuffling characterized the main activity of the South African Communist Party (SACP). The Central Committee, which operates in exile from Europe and elsewhere in Africa, elected Dan Tloome as chairman, replacing Joe Slovo, and shifted Slovo to the general secretaryship, a post vacant since Moses Mabhida died in March 1986. These leadership moves recall the earlier party organization whereby the chairman concentrated on diplomatic and public aspects while the general secretary focused on political and administrative functions of the SACP. The party was heartened by the continuing turmoil inside the Republic of South Africa, viewing rent strikes, white defections from the "ruling class," and widespread disturbances as making "even more effective the conduct of the revolutionary struggle on all fronts."[13]

Zimbabwe witnessed a strengthening of the leadership in the ruling Zimbabwe African National Union–Patriotic Front (ZANU-PF). On 31 December 1987 Robert Mugabe was installed as the country's first executive president. As a consequence, he is now party, government, and state leader. As in previous years, Mugabe continued gravitating toward a single-party state, but 1987 marked significant movement toward this goal. The 30 parliamentary seats reserved for whites, who make up less than 2 percent of the population, were abolished and then filled during an election by ZANU-PF candidates, including fifteen whites. Mugabe co-opted Joshua Nkomo, the leader of the opposition party—the Zimbabwe African People's Union (ZAPU)—and incorporated part of ZAPU into his ZANU-PF.[14] Other elements of ZAPU—which represents the Ndebele people, the second largest ethnic community—resisted the merger with the Shona-dominated ZANU. Antigovernment violence continued from the ZAPU dissidents. Mugabe also moved against opponents to merger within his own party and replaced Marxist ideologues and ethnic chauvinists with moderates, paving the way for an official one-party state.

In neighboring Mozambique, leadership changes took place when President Joaquim Chissano reshuffled his council of ministers and the military high command in hopes of containing the guerrilla warfare successes of the opposition movement, the Mozambique National Resistance (RENAMO). The military position of the ruling Front for the Liberation of Mozambique (FRELIMO) remained difficult but was stabilized by the presence of some 30,000 foreign troops, mainly from Zimbabwe and Tanzania, as well as about 3,000 advisers from the Soviet bloc.[15] In an effort to reverse its economic slide, FRELIMO enacted an economic rehabilitation program that formalized, in part, recent moves toward a market-type economy and away from a hard-line Marxist economic structure. FRELIMO also maintained its previous pragmatic policy toward the West and international financial institutions in order to gain assistance and investment.

To the south, the Communist Party of Lesotho (CPL) continued to be in an ambiguous position in the country. The CPL is illegal, but its general secretary, Jacob M. Kena, operates openly. The purported Seventh Congress was held "in utmost secrecy in early 1987."[16] The main task of the CPL is to develop organizationally throughout the country.

The Sudanese Communist Party (SCP) has functioned above ground since 1985 when the Ja'far Numayri government was overthrown. Winning 5 of 264 contested seats the following year, the SCP is presently a visible part of the parliamentary opposition. During 1987 the SCP initially opposed the government's handling of the war in the south between the predominantly Arabic-speaking Muslim northerners and the non-Muslim southerners. Toward the end of the year, however, it moved to support some governmental military measures. But the SCP, which advocates a secular state, opposed other government policies, including the decision not to abrogate the 1983 Islamization laws.

Across the continent in Senegal, the country's several communist and leftist parties remained divided and without meaningful impact on national politics. The Party of Independence and Labor, which now enjoys official recognition by Moscow as a communist movement,[17] was represented at a number of Soviet bloc–sponsored meetings. Domestically the Marxist parties tried to form fronts, without much success, and criticized the government's austerity policies required by the International Monetary Fund (IMF) and the World Bank in return for financial assistance.

In Nigeria, the Marxists operate from less organized platforms than those in Senegal. Nigerian Marxists joined the national debate on the structure of a new political system with the release of a manifesto by the Nigerian Labour Congress, which called for socialism in Nigeria. The appeal of socialism is centered mainly among the intelligentsia, not in functioning parties.

The three ruling Marxist-Leninist parties in Benin, Congo, and Angola had a difficult year. The People's Revolutionary Party of Benin (PRPB) made efforts to improve the economy, provoking opposition from public servants and students, who staged demonstrations. The PRPB has moved to revitalize the private sector, increase the performance of state corporations, and improve relations with Western countries. Public employees protested the lack of salary raises, and students demonstrated for payment of their scholarships. But the poor economy remained the most unsettling challenge for the regime in Benin.[18]

More serious and dramatic events rocked the People's Republic of the Congo, which also experienced opposition to its policies dealing with economic problems brought on, in part, by the decline in oil prices. Government reports of the failure of an attempted plot to kill the chairman of the Congolese Workers' Party (PCT), Denis Sassou-Ngouesso, led to a purge that removed Camille Bongou, the regime's number-two man and the party's ideologue. Bongou was linked to the June plot, which was led by a rival of Chairman Sassou-Ngouesso, retired Captain Pierre Anga. In an operation to capture Anga and his followers, the government used French military assistance rather than Soviet bloc equipment, which was based in the country. The French-aided expedition seemed to emphasize the growing cooperation between Paris and the ruling PCT.

In the People's Republic of Angola, the ruling Popular Movement for the Liberation of Angola–Labor Party (MPLA-PT) confronted, as in years past, the twin problems of a badly faltering economy and an escalating insurgency. Since 1975 the MPLA has been waging a struggle in the south against the National Union for the Total Independence of Angola (UNITA). For survival as well as ideological reasons, the MPLA has relied on substantial support from the Soviet bloc. During 1987 the USSR provided more than $1 billion in military equipment, and Cuba increased its troop strength to 40,000 in an unsuccessful effort to eliminate UNITA.[19]

The deteriorating economy served as a reason to replace a number of high government officials. President José Eduardo dos Santos dismissed Foreign Trade Minister Ismael Gaspar Martins and Internal Trade Minister Adriano Pereira dos Santos, Jr., in May, citing food and medicine shortages. Maria Mambo Cafe, in charge of social and economic affairs, was fired in December. She had been an opponent of expanded economic ties with the West, including an application to IMF for membership.[20]

The Americas. In August the five Central American presidents signed an agreement in Guatemala that pledged to take the region's peace process into their own hands. The strength of the plan, drawn up by Costa Rican president Oscar Arias, was the series of deadlines set for its implementation.[21] Compliance with major provisions was set for 5 November, postponed to 5 January 1988, and then postponed to 15 January. After a meeting of the Central American presidents on the last date, the deadlines were extended for another month. The plan called for simultaneous and equal implementation of a number of provisions to end the conflict and outside support for indigenous belligerents, to institutionalize democracy in the region so as to prevent future conflicts, and to verify—but not enforce—compliance.

From the beginning of 1987, Arias stressed that the main obstacle to peace in the region was the government in Managua, remarking that "with or without *contras* and with or without military aid, I continue to think that there will be violence in Nicaragua if the Nicaraguan people cannot elect their leaders freely."[22] On 15 January 1988 Arias (who won the 1987 Nobel Peace Prize for his efforts) and two other presidents—Napoleón Duarte of El Salvador and José Azcona of Honduras—

pointed their criticism mainly at Nicaragua for failing to comply with the plan's provisions. This particularly applied to Managua's refusal to negotiate a cease-fire directly with the resistance movement; its halfhearted democratization at home; its continuing to receive aid from abroad; and its assisting other guerrilla movements in the region. As one analyst has noted, the other Central American countries, while sometimes falling short, all complied more fully and more honestly.[23]

In the face of this pressure and under the threat that the U.S. Congress would vote more aid for the resistance, the Nicaraguan government made additional concessions, including an agreement to negotiate directly with the resistance. These negotiations began on 28 January 1988.[24] The Reagan administration renewed its call for more aid to the resistance as the only way to obtain serious concessions and (possibly) compliance from the Sandinistas, though of the requested $36 million package only $3.6 million was for military aid and that was to be placed temporarily in escrow.[25]

In Nicaragua, the economy continued to deteriorate, with inflation increasing to more than 1000 percent and rationed food often unavailable. The armed resistance, approximately 16,000 men, operated in half of Nicaragua's territory—though not on the populous Pacific coast. According to press reports, it seemed to have made considerable headway in building support for the movement among Nicaraguan people. In October, two months after the Guatemala peace accord had been signed, the opposition paper *La Prensa*, which had been outlawed for more than a year, was allowed to reopen and resume criticism of the government.

At the end of January 1988, the Sandinista government braced itself for even wider criticism as concessions made after the session that month came into effect. Speculation on divisions within the Sandinista leadership continued to surface. According to Major Roger Miranda, who, until his defection in October 1987, had served as a top aide to defense minister Humberto Ortega, the Sandinistas intend to double the size of their army and militia to about 600,000 by the mid-1990s and have agreed to train Salvadoran guerrillas in the use of surface-to-air missiles.[26]

Both the Salvadoran and the Guatemalan governments held direct talks with guerrillas operating in their countries after initially refusing to do so; there is no significant guerrilla movement in Honduras. President Duarte met with representatives of the Farabundo Martí National Liberation Front (FMLN) in San Salvador, and rebel leaders had wide access to the general news media, though no cease-fire was reached. The FMLN fought a defensive war in the countryside but stepped up its movement into the capital of San Salvador. FMLN political front leaders Rubén Zamora and Guillermo Ungo visited El Salvador after the Guatemala accords.

The National Revolutionary Unity of Guatemala (URNG) forces have declined from about 10,000 in 1981–1982 to fewer than 2,000 in 1987. During the year URNG concentrated more on propaganda and reorganization than on military encounters; it set up a radio station, La Voz Popular, clearly modeled on the Salvadoran FMLN's Radio Venceremos. The government met with guerrilla leaders in Madrid without resolving their differences.[27] The communist Guatemalan Party of Labor continued to call the URNG "pseudo-leftist."[28]

In Colombia the truce between government and some guerrillla groups continued to fall apart even as evidence mounted concerning cooperation between the guerrillas and the country's powerful drug rings. In October, the leaders of six major guerrilla organizations formed the Simón Bolívar National Guerrilla Coordinating Board. Defectors tied to the Communist Party of Colombia claimed that the guerrillas have Cuban instructors and an air base with modern Soviet-made weapons. The so-called America Battalion claims to incorporate guerrillas from Colombia, from the Alfaro Lives! movement in Ecuador, and from the Tupac Amaru II group in Peru. An international seminar on democratization in Latin America was held for Colombians and representatives from five other countries in Bogota during mid-June, sponsored in part by the *World Marxist Review*, with speakers from the Soviet Union and the German Democratic Republic.[29]

A variety of Marxist-Leninist movements in Peru operated at high intensity. The United Left (IU) remained the second-largest political force in that Andean country, making Peru one of only two countries—the other being Guyana—whose major opposition is Marxist-Leninist. The IU—a coalition of organizations ranging from moderate to extreme left—is becoming the only alternative to the American Popular Revolutionary Alliance (APRA) government of Alan García, which is finding intractable political and economic problems on all sides. The Peruvian Communist Party, which held its Ninth Congress in 1987, is a major actor in the coalition. The Soviet bloc remains the major outside influence on the Peruvian military; in May, Peru purchased five Antonov-32 military transport planes to replace An-26 planes bought a decade earlier. It is reported Cuba wanted to buy some of the An-26s.[30]

Widespread terrorism continued during 1987 with the main group, the Maoist Sendero Luminoso (Shining Path), forcing the García government to maintain seventeen provinces under a state of emergency. In a tactical shift, the Maoists turned to political activities in some instances in an effort to compete more successfully with other leftist political forces. Sendero Luminoso has announced that it will hold its first national party congress during 1988.[31]

In Chile, the communist party joined other leftist groups during June to form the United Left Coalition (IU), the most widely based leftist opposition group since the Popular Unity Coalition of the early 1970s. Tensions continued within the party and the IU, however, because of continuing communist support for terrorism through the Manuel Rodriguez Patriotic Front. Not until October did the communist party begin encouraging registration for voting in the 1988 presidential candidate plebiscite.

Communist parties participated in many of the region's countries through legislatures; they had substantial representation and influence in Peru, Guyana, Martinique, and Guadeloupe but minimal representation in Brazil (where the party had its Eighth Congress, the first held legally in the country), Venezuela, Colombia, Ecuador, and Bolivia. In some countries—including Panama—communists applied pressure indirectly through fronts, other parties, and student and labor groups. In Bolivia a prominent communist was elected head of the large Bolivian Labor Central (COB). For the first time in history, the United Party of Haitian Communists ran a candidate for president. The movements in Argentina and Uruguay were highly critical of their governments for amnesty bills with deadlines for filing charges against military personnel accused of breaking the law during antiguerrilla campaigns in the 1970s.

The Cuban economy remained in a state of decay during 1987, but Fidel Castro opposed the trend in the socialist world toward decentralization and material incentives. Instead, the Cuban leader reverted to an emphasis on volunteer work and moral incentives characteristic of the 1960s, though these policies wrecked the economy then. Unlike current general secretaries in other major communist countries, particularly the Soviet Union and China, Castro can not blame earlier leaders for his country's problems; they are of his own making. To adopt Chinese and Soviet-style reforms would be to admit Cuba has been on the wrong track since 1959. Several high-level officials from Cuba and Nicaragua defected during the year and revealed domestic and international secrets and plans: for example, both countries are infested with substantial corruption and favoritism.[32]

Despite Castro's refusal to follow the Soviet model in economic reform, the Cuban leader played a prominent role at the celebrations of the 70th anniversary of the Bolshevik Revolution in November and returned home, saying his ties to Moscow have never been better. Trade with the Soviet Union was expected to reach a turnover of $9 billion in 1987, some $200 million more than in 1986. Part of the massive Soviet support for Castro, about $5 billion annually in economic and military aid, continued to come in the form of Soviet purchase of half the Cuban sugar crop at three times the world market price.[33] Meanwhile, though U.S.-Cuban relations deteriorated in the first part of 1987, they improved somewhat in the final months of the year as several agreements were signed, including an immigration pact. Castro stated his support for the Arias peace plan and met several times with Sandinista leaders to discuss it.

The Soviet Union made advances in the hemisphere, both before and after Foreign Minister Eduard Shevardnadze's trip through a number of Latin American countries during October and November. These advances included expansion of the already extensive trade with Argentina, securing resupply facilities for the Soviet fishing fleet in Uruguay, military sales to Peru, permission for Aeroflot to land, and a service contract to provide dry-dock and other shore facilities to the Soviet fishing fleet in Panama.[34]

The Communist Party USA claims continuing growth, which is denied by some analysts. However, it has decided not to run a candidate of its own in the 1988 presidential election. Instead it will continue to expand its positions in the national "peace movement," among blacks, and within the Democratic party, where its favorite candidate is Jesse Jackson.[35] The membership decline in the Socialist Workers' Party, the second largest Marxist-Leninist group in the United States, continued during 1987. The communist movement in Canada remained at a very low level.

Asia and the Pacific. Except for the regime in North Korea, the other continental communist-ruled states were involved in nurturing reforms to make their systems work more effectively. The Communist Party of China (CPC) successfully put down large-scale student demonstrations in early January 1987 and responded with an antibourgeois liberalism campaign drive to rid the CPC of overzealous critics. By spring the writer Wang Ruowang, the astrophysicist Fang Lizhi, and the journalist Liu Binyan had been expelled from the party. By summer nearly 400,000 college graduates and postgraduate students were being sent to rural areas for two years instead of being assigned to government agencies,[36] and another one million were to spend the summer recess working in factories, offices, and rural villages as part of a program to "remold their views." Security organs continued to search out and arrest counterrevolutionaries everywhere. Between late January and early June, authorities reportedly discovered 15,000 anticommunist posters in eleven counties of Sichuan province alone.[37]

The CPC held its Thirteenth Congress during early November. Delegates approved a new slate of leaders for the Politburo and elected fewer and younger persons to the Central Committee, cutting that body from 210 to 175 members and an average age of 55 instead of 59. For the first time since a communist regime was established on the mainland, fewer people with military experience were in the Politburo and a new generation of leaders had replaced the "long march" survivors. Deng Xiaoping, Chen Yun, and Peng Zhen are gone, but they still serve as elder statesmen.

The Thirteenth CPC Congress upheld the party line set forth in late 1978 that had as its primary goal modernization and the reforms to achieve it. The new general secretary, Zhao Ziyang, strongly emphasized that although the CPC was pursuing reforms, it would firmly apply the "four cardinal principles": follow the socialist road, support the dictatorship of the proletariat, uphold the dictatorship of the communist party, and adhere to Marxism-Leninism and Mao Zedong thought. Zhao admitted that China still remained in the "primary stage of socialism" and that the road to modern socialism would be long and arduous, but the party would persevere in leading the Chinese people.

However, the Chinese agricultural reforms, which permitted more privatization and free market determination of prices, suffered serious setbacks. China had to import 14 million tons of grain in 1987 at a cost of $1 billion (U.S.), the largest annual grain import in this decade.[38] Pork, vegetable oil, and sugar became scarce enough in the cities that the state had to reimpose rationing in December. These developments took place because farmers transferred their land and labor to high-price crops and products like *chuanxiong*, a leafy medicinal plant grown in Sichuan province whose price had risen from $40 per ton to $8,000 per ton.

On 10 January 1988 the Chinese weekly *Liaowang* published an interview with Mikhail S. Gorbachev in which he proposed a summit meeting with Beijing's leaders to speed up re-establishment of normal relations between the two largest communist-ruled states.[39] China refused the invitation several days later on the grounds that Moscow had not fulfilled the three demands made by Beijing as initial conditions for normalization: withdrawal of all Soviet troops from Afghanistan, an end to support for the Vietnamese occupation of Cambodia, and sharp reductions in USSR troops and missiles deployed along China's northern border.

In communist-ruled Vietnam the new "circle of five" leaders who replaced Truong Chinh, Pham Van Dong, and Le Duc Tho are now headed by 72-year-old Nguyen Van Linh. They concentrated on reshuffling personnel, ridding the party of inept and corrupt members, and building networks of supporters throughout the country. Although they discussed reform, few positive steps were initiated.[40] By year's end Linh was in charge, with his colleagues' position greatly strengthened. The new leadership now stresses *cong khai* (openness) in conducting party business and learning from previous mistakes.

On 21 January 1988 Linh announced to a group of foreign journalists that Vietnam could learn lessons from the capitalist world. He revealed that under "centralized bureaucratic subsidization, it was the people in this Ho Chi Minh City [formerly Saigon] who were striving to break all the restrictions that were checking their production."[41] Linh expressed hopes that ties with China could be improved and that it was time for the United States and Vietnam to put their war behind them. Admitting that farmers could not buy fertilizers, that factories worked at 30 to 70 percent of capacity, that inflation was rampant, and that the family-planning system is in disarray, Linh said that Vietnam could not solve all its problems over night.

The Mongolian People's Revolutionary Party, with some 88,000 members, responded to Moscow's call for reform by holding meetings to discuss how to bolster the sagging pastoral economy. The

United States established diplomatic ties with Mongolia; the Soviets removed some troops from the country; and the People's Republic of China slightly improved its ties with Ulan Bator.

The Korean Workers' Party continued to mobilize support for Kim Chong-il to succeed his father, Kim Il-song, as the heir apparent. North Korea will boycott the September 1988 Olympic Games in Seoul and probably caused the crash of a Republic of Korea (ROK) airplane over Burma in November 1987, which killed all 115 aboard. The United States added Pyongyang to its list of terrorist regimes.[42] North Korea refrained from any serious negotiations with the ROK during its year of political turbulence.

In Indonesia, where the communist party is illegal, little evidence surfaced about its activities. During the spring, 653 members of the Marxist-Leninist faction of the Malaysian Communist Party surrendered to the government, leaving an undisclosed but greatly reduced force of guerrillas in that country's border area.[43] In Thailand, defections from the communist party continued, and police in Bangkok arrested a handful of leaders who were holding a top-level meeting to plan the Fifth Party Congress for October. The Burmese Communist Party (BCP) leaders are aging yet remain committed to expanding their base areas in the north, which are protected by their People's Army. According to a Western journalist who visited these base areas in early 1987, serious splits in the BCP leadership exist and the party has failed in recent years to re-establish a foothold in central Burma.[44]

The communist party and its military arm, the New People's Army (NPA), escalated their activities to destabilize the Republic of the Philippines. Rebel leaders broke off their cease-fire negotiations with Corazon Aquino's government and resumed armed struggle. The NPA escalated killings of government officials and their key supporters. Rebel forces increased contacts with international support groups outside the Philippines. The government, late in the year, reversed its policy of reconciliation with the communists and ordered military and paramilitary activities against the NPA. Finally, the United States gave more aid to the Philippines. But widespread poverty, a lackluster economy, and social anarchy have made it impossible for government forces to suppress the NPA, and the conflict has become a standoff.

The total population of the independent island states in the South Pacific, including Papua New Guinea, is about 5.5 million. Although there is no communist party in this region, several formal Marxist groupings exist in the French territory of New Caledonia. Over the last few years, various student and youth associations in New Guinea, Fiji, West Samoa, Nauru,[45] Tuvalu, Belau, and Tonga have sent their representatives to youth and women's organizations in Eastern Europe, the USSR, and Australia to participate in the activities of certain labor unions that are pro-Soviet. When USSR foreign minister Shevardnadze visited Canberra, Australia, in March, he surprised his hosts by adding Tuvalu, Papua New Guinea, and Tonga to the list of island nations that have shown an interest in developing agreements with the Soviet Union. For example, Crown Prince Tupouto, the conservative Tongan minister for defense and foreign affairs, traveled to Moscow in February reportedly to discuss another fishing agreement, although he had previously assured Australia that his country had no fish to sell to the Soviets.

In countries where the communist party is free to operate like other political movements, there were minor successes. The Bangladesh Communist Party held it Fourth Congress in April at Dacca and endorsed the objective to promote a "national democratic revolution," which calls for working with all "progressive liberal democratic forces" to topple the current regime. In New Zealand, communist-led front organizations organized support for Nicaragua and tried to oppose the new economic policies of the government to privatize social welfare and reduce budget deficits. Although unsuccessful in the latter effort, some of their members did win seats on the 1987 Council of Trade Unions.

During early July, the Mongolian People's Revolutionary Party hosted a congress for the purpose of initiating a campaign to transform Asia and the Pacific Basin into a peace zone. Twenty communist parties of the region, not including China (not invited), Japan, and North Korea, participated. Gorbachev sent greetings to the congress.[46] The delegates discussed means by which the region's communist parties and front organizations could promote nuclear-free zones and prevent the United States, Japan, and South Korea from strengthening their security ties.

In November and December, Soviet diplomats met in Tokyo with Japanese foreign minister Sosuke Uno and stated that Moscow would like to improve relations with Japan.[47]

The Middle East. The political as well as the military fortunes of the ruling People's Democratic

Party of Afghanistan (PDPA) continued to deteriorate, despite efforts to co-opt opposition leaders and a modest increase in Soviet military strength, back to the approximate level of 120,000 existing before the previous year's force cutback.[48] With its rule effective only in a few principal towns during daylight, the PDPA made an effort to broaden its appeal by altering the name of the state from the Democratic Republic of Afghanistan to the Republic of Afghanistan[49] and the name of its general secretary from Najib to the more religiously significant Najibullah.[50] As discussions about the withdrawal of Soviet occupying forces intensified, PDPA reform efforts became marked by an air of desperation. Internal party reorganization and purges occurred, together with major state reforms, all designed to create a national coalition PDPA superficially purified of Soviet and communist identity. This effort appeared no more successful than were attempts to stem mass military defections and draft dodging by doubling military salaries in June.[51]

The only other ruling Marxist-Leninist movement in the region, the Yemeni Socialist Party (YSP) in the People's Democratic Republic of (South) Yemen (PDRY), also struggles for internal and international legitimacy yet controls its territory without Soviet occupation forces. Since the bloody civil war of January 1986, most of the veteran Marxist ideologues who gave the regime its legitimacy either have been killed or are exiled in North Yemen. This complicates the PDRY-Soviet relationship, although Moscow supports large advisory programs to YSP organizations apparently in the hope of strengthening the regime's roots. Gorbachev's "personal representative," Karen N. Brutents, held two days of high-level talks in Aden toward the end of the year.[52]

For members of the two illegal tiny communist movements on the Arab side of the Persian Gulf—the Communist Party of Saudi Arabia (CPSA) and the Bahrain National Liberation Front (NLF/B)—the new high-profile regional Soviet diplomatic visibility must have presented anomalies. CPSA general secretary Mahdi Habib, for instance, called for "an end to the absolutist administration,"[53] whereas Moscow was redoubling its efforts to achieve establishment status in the Gulf and for the first time officially received a Saudi oil minister, newly appointed Hisham Nazir.[54] Similarly, although the thrust of the NLF/B's propaganda focused on the late 1986 arrests of some eighteen of its members, Soviet deputy foreign minister Vladimir Petrovsky toured Iraq, Kuwait, the United Arab Emirates, and Oman suggesting security guarantees for shipping in the region and agreeing to lease three USSR tankers for the transport of Kuwaiti oil.[55] This dual-track policy of support for local communist parties that in turn are working to overthrow states courted by Moscow, while hardly new, is just now appearing on the Arab side of the Persian Gulf.

Iran's deteriorating economic and social conditions gave some credence to Communist Party of Iran (Tudeh) claims on its 46th anniversary that "the number of party cells has increased throughout the country."[56] Although all opposition groups in Iran, legal or illegal, have new opportunities as the country's economy worsens, there is no sign that the Ayatollah Khomeini regime faces a threat to its physical control of the country.

Like the Tudeh, the Iraqi Communist Party (ICP) blames the war on its own country's central government. Although the conflict remains unpopular in both Iran and Iraq, neither state has generated a major antiwar movement to which either party could graft itself. The ICP retains its goal of a national front uniting all parties opposed to the ruling Baathist regime, but in fact the ICP remains buried in a front with the Democratic National Party of Kurdistan/Iraq and some smaller organizations dominated by the Kurds.[57]

The Syrian Communist Party (SCP) plays the role of a restive lap dog, used and tolerated by the Baathist regime of Hafiz al-Assad and restricted to occasional oratorical objections to Syrian policy. Veteran SCP leader Khalid Bakhdash in a Moscow speech mentioned "Syria's great economic difficulties," contrasting the condition of "the workers, peasants, and working masses" with that of the parasitic bourgeoisie and the bureaucratic apparatus.[58] Assad's own relations with the USSR have been affected during the year by apparent Soviet cutbacks in arms shipments (an effort to join the peace process). These problems manifested themselves last April during Assad's visit to Moscow when Gorbachev said, in a toast, that the lack of relations with Israel was abnormal and that military expansion was not the way to achieve peace in the area.[59]

Communist parties from the Middle East convened twice in Athens and once at Beirut. On each occasion, they attacked the United States and other NATO countries for their presence in the Persian Gulf.[60]

Eastern Europe and the USSR. Ever since

the CPSU announced that it would convene its Nineteenth National Conference next summer, five ruling parties in the East European bloc countries have indicated that they too will hold special conferences[61] between the end of 1987 and June 1988. The first took place in Bucharest during 14–16 December on the "new stage of building socialism" and the "advance toward communism." The remaining ones have been scheduled to open 28 January (Bulgaria), during the first half of the year (Hungary), in March (Yugoslavia), and the middle of 1988 (Poland). Neither the East German nor the Czechoslovak communists have mentioned a special conference as of this writing.

The Albanian Party of Labor (APL) continued to experiment with domestic reform, albeit in a more limited fashion than in the bloc countries. Centralization of the economy was slightly reduced and local managerial authority somewhat increased.[62] Otherwise, cultural stagnation continued despite some effort to relax the general atmosphere. Elections on 1 February registered 100 percent participation, a world record.

However, ruling-party leader Ramiz Alia did expand his contacts with other countries. The foreign minister of Greece lifted the state of war with Albania and signed eight agreements at Tirana in August; West Germany established diplomatic relations in October and sent its Bavarian premier with a loan; and the Albanian regime accepted an invitation to attend a Balkan conference during February 1988. Only relations with Yugoslavia continued to involve polemics, and relations did not exist with either the USSR[63] or the United States.

Bulgaria has imitated, at least on the surface, the Soviet examples of openness and reconstruction more closely than any other East European client state. Campaigns against alcoholism and corruption were followed by a reorganization of the government. No relaxation occurred, however, in regime treatment of ethnic Turks who refused to become Bulgarized and change their names.[64]

Leading communists, including 75-year-old General Secretary Todor Zhivkov, visited Moscow frequently. They all emphasized full support for USSR foreign policies. Zhivkov also made a week-long trip during May to China that seemed to be part of the continuing East European rapprochement with that country. One Soviet objective, a nuclear and chemical-free zone in the Balkans, received endorsement by the Greek prime minister, who traveled to Sofia in July.[65]

Czechoslovakia was visited by Gorbachev in April, and he apparently moved its cautious leadership toward economic reform. By July the regime had begun issuing draft laws on changes in industry, agriculture, and cooperatives. Toward the end of the year, Gustáv Husák (almost 75) retired, and Miloš Jakeš replaced him as general secretary.[66] Jakeš, a top collaborator during the August 1968 invasion of his country by the USSR, subsequently directed a purge that expelled half a million communists from the party. This does not augur well for the future, although Jakeš (66) may be only a transitional figure.

The German Democratic Republic continues under the aging Erich Honecker (75) with no designated heir apparent. He presides over the most successful economy in the bloc, although a chronic energy shortage may affect this status in the future. Much of the success is due to financial support coming from the Federal Republic of Germany (FRG).

Honecker made a five-day visit during September to the FRG, including his birthplace in the Saarland. Although he adhered to the "two-state theory" in official statements, the number of East Germans under 65 allowed to visit the FRG in the first eight months of the year totaled more than 866,000 compared with 66,000 for all of 1985. The final communiqué after Honecker's visit mentioned establishment of an economic commission for closer contact between small- and medium-sized enterprises in the two Germanys.[67]

Hungary, under János Kádár (75), had proceeded farther than any other Soviet client state in market-oriented economic reforms, which date back to 1968 and have almost run out of steam. However, at the end of June a new prime minister, Károly Grósz (57), introduced an effort to begin stabilizing the faltering economy. An inflation rate of 15 percent has been caused by rising prices for consumer goods and the highest per capita foreign debt in the bloc.[68] A reduction in imports from the West and in the standard of living may improve the situation. The budget for 1988 includes drastic cuts in government subsidies.

Despite these difficulties, the Hungarian economic model has been praised in both Moscow and Beijing. Credits, however, came from Bonn, which offered one billion FRG marks in October 1987. Kádár visited Brussels and attempted to obtain a trade agreement with the European Economic Community. All of this is part of the three- to six-year stabilization period, to be followed by a ten- to fifteen-year full development stage.[69]

Poland is also engaged in a "second stage" economic reform, which began with a reorganization of the central government in October. The following month, only two-thirds of all registered voters took part in a referendum. Of these, some 44 percent supported the new economic policies and 46 percent the official plans for liberalization, which meant that neither proposition had been approved by the required simple majority. Ignoring public opinion, the regime announced that prices would increase from 40 to 200 percent in 1988, in part offset by a 20 percent pay raise.[70]

General Wojciech Jaruzelski (63), party and state leader, scored a victory when the United States lifted all economic sanctions early in 1987. Poland's $37 billion foreign debt is the largest of any East European country. Vice President George Bush paid a visit during September, and a U.S. ambassador was appointed to Warsaw. Back in Moscow, Jaruzelski stood on top of the Lenin monument with the CPSU Politburo for the Bolshevik Revolution's anniversary parade salute in November,[71] together with Zhivkov, Honecker, and Nicolae Ceauşescu.

Romania's party and state leader Ceauşescu celebrated his 69th birthday in January amid a cult of personality unknown anywhere except perhaps in North Korea. The family seems to run the country, with Ceauşescu's wife, Elena, in charge of appointing key personnel; his son Nicu, the party first secretary for Sibiu County; his brother Nicolae A., the head of cadres for the interior (police) ministry; and his brother Ion, first deputy chairman of the State Planning Committee. When CPSU general secretary Gorbachev visited Bucharest, he criticized the Brezhnev era's "nepotism" in the Soviet Union,[72] perhaps drawing an implied parallel with Romania.

County first secretaries and government officials continued to be rotated and, thus, frustrated from building any power base. However, that measure did not stop several thousand workers from ransacking the city hall in Brasov as a protest against harsh living conditions. Arrests broke up the demonstrations. Before the end of the year, half the profit-sharing fund was paid out in advance to workers.[73] The U.S. Congress removed most-favored-nation status from Romania because of its human rights violations and its repressive policies toward the Hungarian minority.

Yugoslavia's economic outlook is also bad. Nearly 1,500 strikes by a quarter of a million workers took place during the first 50 weeks of 1987. Inflation reached 164 percent by December. A revised bankruptcy law went into effect at midyear, and the unemployment rate of 20 percent will increase after some 200 firms are permanently shut down.[74]

Meanwhile, the ruling League of Communists of Yugoslavia continued to lose workers and young members because of disharmony and corruption. Party purges and resignations could not reverse the deterioration. Payments on a $20 billion foreign currency debt are being postponed through extensions. According to a former finance minister under Marshal Tito, the country is in a "civil war," that is, law and order have broken down.[75]

Western Europe. What had been a bright picture for the region's communist parties at the beginning of this decade has steadily deteriorated. Cohesion has been replaced with interparty strife. Whatever appeal Marxism-Leninism offered earlier had declined markedly, and the earlier communist challenge to the West had been transformed into a challenge to the parties as to what kind of role they could play in the future.

West European communist parties saw "the idea of socialism" fade as well. It seemed clear that a return to the marketplace, incentives, and free enterprise had a vastly greater appeal than the ephemeral promises of socialism.[76] Only 12 of Western Europe's 23 communist parties were represented in their respective parliaments—Cyprus, Finland, France, Greece, Iceland, Italy, Luxembourg, Portugal, San Marino, Spain, Sweden, and Switzerland. With the exception of San Marino, party members held no cabinet posts for the fourth consecutive year.

The Italian Communist Party (PCI) lost strength, dropping from slightly less than 30 percent of the parliamentary mandates to 26.6 percent. Of the others with legislative representation, the communists on Cyprus held the highest (27.4 percent), followed by San Marino (24.3 percent), Iceland (13.2 percent), Portugal (11.0 percent), Greece (9.9 percent), France (9.8 percent), Finland (9.4 percent), Sweden (5.4 percent), Luxembourg (4.9 percent), and for the 1987 Swiss election there is no accurate data. The eleven parties without seats received between 0.03 percent (Great Britain) and negligible (Belgium) support from their respective electorates.

By the end of 1987, the region's communist parties found themselves in a dilemma. If they do not "change their ideology and their slogans," they have no appeal to the so-called working classes they claim to represent. If they do change, they lose their credibility, as the French Communist Party (PCF) proved in the latest elections. Thus, they must "either reassert their traditional philosophy, at the risk of losing more support, or move toward the social democratic center, at the risk of losing their identity."[77]

Communists in Italy, Belgium, Denmark, West Germany, Great Britain, and Sweden have advocated creation of the "Euroleft." Gianni Cervetti, a member of the Italian PCI leadership, defined it as follows:

> We see the Euroleft as a composite entity comprising, first and foremost, the traditional parties of the working class and democratic movement with all their differences and in all their diversity, as well as other major movements—trade union, cooperative, peace, environmentalist and women's—together with the youth associations and cultural organisations.[78]

In an effort to restore unity to the PCF, Chairman Georges Marchais announced that he would not run in the May 1988 presidential elections. Nevertheless rancor intensified during the year as party leaders struggled with the grim prospect of a strife-torn PCF. Disaffected functionaries—including at least one former minister and several Central Committee members—finally resigned from the party or from their offices, and many of them rallied to the alternative candidacy of Pierre Juquin. Marchais and Poltiburo "conservatives" forced Juquin's expulsion from the PCF at almost the same time that the Twenty-sixth Congress, convened in December 1987, met to ratify Central Committee secretary André Lajoinie, who is Marchais's hand-picked presidential candidate.

The PCF leadership persistently deflected demands for open debate from self-styled "renovateurs" by emphasizing party unity. Roland Leroy, *L'Humanité* director and Politburo member, attacked dissidents for failing to dissent within the rules of democratic centralism.[79] As the year progressed, the party became increasingly concerned with the possible consequences of two presidential candidates when communist voter support remained at or below 10 percent. The Twenty-sixth PCF Congress, however, re-elected Marchais to a seventh term as general secretary and returned all members of the Politburo.

The Spanish Communist Party (PCE), under the leadership of Gerardo Iglesias, also has attempted to heal internal party friction. Despite these efforts, this communist movement, fragmented into three main parties, is one of the most divided in Europe. Pro-Soviet dissidents are led by Ignacio Gallego, who heads the Communist Party of the Peoples of Spain (PCPE). The third group, initially called the Board for Communist Unity but which changed its name to Workers' Party—Communist Unity (PTE-UC) in 1987, is led by Santiago Carrillo.

Iglesias sought during the year to eliminate differences among the three parties by emphasizing a new climate of unanimous goodwill toward the CPSU. In September he proclaimed that the party crisis was over.[80] However, it was also announced that the major discussion at the PCE's Twelfth Congress, scheduled for February 1988, would be reunification of all communist groups in Spain.

Alvaro Cunhal has served as general secretary of the Portuguese Communist Party (PCP) for almost 27 years. The PCP is controlled by an aging leadership and remains one of the most Stalinist, pro-Soviet movements in Western Europe. The year was highlighted by domestic developments that should affect the debate on the future direction of the PCP when it convenes its Twelfth Congress in March 1988.

Parliamentary elections in July gave the PCP (in coalition with "many independent democrats") only 10 percent of the vote, a drop from more than 15 percent two years earlier. Cunhal justified the party's relative isolation from other political parties by explaining that the communists "resolutely defend the interests of workers . . . against capitalist exploitation."[81] Portugal's voters apparently did not agree.

The San Marino movement is an extension of the Italian Communist Party, just as the other political parties are extensions of their Italian counterparts. It holds one-fourth of the seats in parliament. The Communist Party of Malta (CPM) participated in its first general election during May. Out of 236,169 ballots cast, the movement received only 119 and the leader Anthony Vassallo, just 13 votes. Pro-Soviet in orientation, the CPM plays a marginal role in political life but maintains extensive contacts with other communist parties throughout Europe and with the CPSU.

The Communist Party of Cyprus (AKEL) is supported primarily by the Greek Cypriot majority, which comprises approximately 80 percent of the island's population, and is proscribed by the Turkish Republic of Northern Cyprus. In municipal elections held during May, the AKEL received 32.5 percent of the vote and took over the offices of mayor in nine of the eighteen cities on the southern part of the island; it thus enjoys an opportunity to influence local politics. Party leadership remains in the hands of Ezekias Papaioannou (79), who has served as general secretary for almost 40 years; the average age of all leaders is over 65. To what extent this may dampen AKEL's appeal to younger voters during the presidential elections in February 1988 is unclear. AKEL announced at midyear that it intends to support the independent candidacy of Yeoryios Vasiliou.

In Greece the party remains divided between pro-Soviet and Eurocommunist factions: the Communist Party of Greece (KKE) and the KKE-Interior. The latter underwent a major reorganization at its most recent congress but emerged split into two major groups. One, which adopted the name "Greek Left," is led by Leonidas Kirkos and seems to enjoy relatively greater support. The other, under Giannis Banias, retained the designation KKE-Interior and added the subtitle "Renovating Left."

The KKE is headed by Kharilaos Florakis, and its policy views have often paralleled those of Andreas Papandreou's governing Panhellenic Socialist Movement (PASOK). Relations between both party leaders remain cooperative, although KKE is vehemently anti-American and opposes the presence of U.S. military bases in Greece. In addition, it rejects austerity measures designed to strengthen the economy. KKE is plagued by a generational gap between the leadership and younger members. Its Twelfth Congress in May called for compromise and cooperation among "democratic and progressive forces" of the left.

The Communist Party of Great Britain (CPGB) continued to decline, membership having dropped by 50 percent since 1980. Its influence is exercised primarily through the trade union movement, but this too is diminishing. Party leader Gordon McLennan argues that "Marx's classical working class... is a declining minority. If Britain's communist party is to survive... it must adapt and seek support among a broader range of interest groups."[82]

The communist parties of Belgium, Denmark, the Netherlands, and Luxembourg played marginal roles in the political affairs of their respective countries. In Luxembourg, the movement remains under control of the Urbany family, which founded it. René Urbany (60) continues to follow a strongly pro-Soviet line.

The Communist Party of Denmark (DKP) has not been represented in parliament since 1979, when its vote fell below the 2 percent minimum required for proportional representation. The year under review, however, saw more change than usual. The party chairman, Jørgen Jensen, died on the eve of the Twenty-eighth DKP Congress in April. His successor is 32-year-old Ole Sohn. In the September parliamentary elections, the movement received less than 1 percent of the vote.

The Belgian Communist Party (PCB) did poorly, with a negligible percentage of the vote in national elections three months later. In an effort to be responsive to changing conditions, the movement's leader declared throughout the year that regional economic differences would require varying approaches in Flanders, Brussels, and Wallonia but within the framework of a federalized party structure. These efforts did not produce measurable results, however, and the PCB's poor performance at the polls foreshadowed continued stagnation for 1988.

Communist activity in the Nordic countries, while extensive, exerted only minimal impact. The People's Alliance (PA) in Iceland has participated in coalition governments on a regular basis. Its setback during national elections in April was the second in a row and occurred despite a strong showing in the previous year's local balloting. The PA lost 4 percent of the vote and two of its seats in an expanded parliament. The party chairman resigned and was replaced by Olafur Ragnar Grimsson, a political scientist at the University of Iceland.

The Communist Party of Norway (NKP) competes for popular support with several other leftist groups, especially the Socialist Left Party (SV). Without representation in parliament, the NKP remains a staunchly pro-Soviet and Stalinist movement. Its chairman endorses the SV idea of a united front for all left-wing parties in the country as well as joint election lists. Yet the NKP remains one of the weakest communist organizations in Western Europe and shows no indication of increasing its political support. At its Nineteenth Congress in April, the NKP adopted a new program that reaffirmed adherence to Marxism-Leninism and "proletarian internationalism" at a time when many of its West European counterparts were seeking to de-emphasize ideology and broaden their electoral base by endorsing the vague concept of the "Euroleft."

The internal affairs of the Finnish Communist Party (SKP) have been dominated by factional strife. This rift, according to chairman Arvo Aalto, has alienated 150,000 supporters and 20,000 party members. Public opinion polls indicated that both factions were suffering a loss of popular support, and national election results in March confirmed this prognosis. The SKP lost 4.6 percent of the vote and eleven of its seats, whereas the Stalinist Finnish Communist Party-Unity (SKP-Y) received almost that percentage. Neither of the two party leaders was elected to parliament.

At the SKP-Y's first congress in June, differences developed over who should be supported in the 1988 presidential election and whether the party should drop the fiction of being the legitimate SKP. Taisto Sinisalo was re-elected chairman and proposed Jouko Kajanoja, general secretary, as a presidential candidate. The Twenty-first SKP Congress was held the following week, and Aalto was re-elected chairman. Twenty of the 50 Central Committee members were newcomers, the average age was 43, and 22 members were women. The new program is regarded as Eurocommunist or Euroleft both in its description of Finnish socialism and in its disassociation from the CPSU.[83] Despite efforts by both factions to improve their popular image, they remain outside the mainstream of political life.

The communist parties of Austria (KPÖ) and Switzerland (PdAS) occupy roles of negligible importance. The KPÖ is not represented in the Austrian parliament, remains pro-Soviet, and adapts its domestic and foreign policy positions to those of the CPSU. Thus, throughout 1987, party chairman Franz Muhri extolled the virtues of *glasnost'* and condemned Austria's coalition government as procapitalist. The Swiss Labor Party received less than 1 percent of the vote in 1987 national elections. Also a pro-Soviet movement, it has long suffered a lack of significant support among younger voters. At its Thirteenth Congress, PdAS sought to rejuvenate the leadership by electing Jean Spielmann (43) as general secretary. In the new Central Committee, almost two-fifths of the members are under 40 and another fourth are between 40 and 50 years of age.

The Socialist Unity Party of West Berlin (SEW) has never had any representation in the city's parliament. It is dependent financially on the communists in East Germany and mirrors their positions. In a city divided by the Berlin Wall and surrounded by mine fields, the SEW does not appeal to inhabitants in the western sectors. Indeed, the party slogan for its Eighth Congress—"With the SEW for Peace, Work, Democracy, and Social Progress"—had a hollow ring.

The West German Communist Party (DKP) also has never been represented in parliament and received only 0.5 percent of the vote in the January national elections. Loyalty to the East German SED and the CPSU reduces its electoral appeal. Both DKP leader Herbert Mies and SED chief Erich Honecker received the Lenin Peace Prize for 1987 in Moscow. The policies of Gorbachev, however, are causing problems.

On the one hand, the CPSU leader's call for *glasnost'* has been embraced by the DKP rank and file, long restless over the "lack of possibilities for intraparty influence and participation," according to party author Erasmus Schöfer.[84] On the other hand, both the DKP and the SED are seeking to control, if not dampen, the enthusiasm caused by the "strong impulses" coming from Moscow. Mies cautioned that in a capitalist country like West Germany, "there can be no imitation of the Soviet approach" and that one must not "reduce the splendid history of the Soviet Union . . . to economic and moral problems."[85]

Richard F. Staar
Hoover Institution

NOTES

1. Vitalii Korionov, "Soznavaia otvetstvennost'," *Pravda*, 9 May.
2. E. G. Plimak, "Marksizm-Leninizm i revoliutsionnost' kontsa XX veka," *Pravda*, 14 November 1986.
3. Editorial, "Socialism's Decisive Contribution," *Za rubezhom*, no. 46, 13–19 November.
4. M. S. Gorbachev over Moscow television, 2 November; *FBIS-Soviet Union*-87-212, 3 November.
5. Cited by Vladimir Kusin, "Gorbachev, Eastern Europe, and the Communist Movement," *RAD Background Report*, no. 220; RFE, Munich, 13 November.
6. M. S. Gorbachev over Moscow television, 4 November; *FBIS-Soviet Union*-87-213, 4 November.
7. N. F. Shumikhin (chief ed.), *Sotsializm i sovremennyi mir* (Kiev, Vyshcha shkola, 1987), p. 20.
8. Cambodian representatives attended meetings during 1987 with bloc newspaper editors, heads of official press agencies, and deputy directors from Central Committee international departments, all in Moscow. *Pravda*, 7 May, 19 June, and 16 December. In addition, Cambodia is featured as one of the sixteen "socialist" countries in a supplement to *New Times*, Moscow, 8 November.
9. K. N. Brutents, "Osvobodivshiesia strany: antiimperialisticheskaia borba," *Pravda*, 10 January 1986.
10. For a listing of 24 of these revolutionary democratic movements, see Table 1.3 in Richard F. Staar, *USSR Foreign Policies After Détente*, rev. ed. (Stanford, Calif.: Hoover Institution Press, 1987), p. 14.
11. U.S. Central Intelligence Agency, *The World Factbook: 1987*, CPAS WF 87-001 (Washington, D.C.: U.S. Government Printing Office, 1987).

12. See the Russian-language proceedings of its founding congress in *Uchreditel'nyi s"ezd rabochei partii Efiopii: Addis-Abeba, 6–10 sentiabria 1984 goda* (Moscow: Politizdat, 1987), pp. 256.

13. *African Communist* (London), no. 109, 2d quarter.

14. "Ob'edinenie partii," *Pravda*, 24 December.

15. *NYT*, 25 January 1988, pp. 1 and 4; Richard Grenier, "Weaning Mozambique," *National Review*, 5 February 1988, pp. 41–44.

16. *WMR*, November.

17. Shumikhin, *Sotsializm*, p. 21 (see note 7).

18. "Life in Benin Without Embellishments," Moscow radio, 3 December; *FBIS-Soviet Union*-87-248, 28 December.

19. *CSM*, 1 April; *Prensa Latina*, Havana, 7 January 1988.

20. Luanda Domestic Service, 22 August; *FBIS*, 26 August.

21. Susan Kaufman Purcell, *Evaluation of the Central American Peace Plan* (Washington, D.C.: Central American Peace and Democracy Watch, January 1988), p. 1.

22. XEW Television, Mexico City, 6 February; *FBIS-Latin America*, 10 February.

23. Purcell, *Evaluation*, pp. 1–10.

24. *NYT*, 29 January 1988.

25. *NYT*, 27 January 1988.

26. *NYT*, 24, 28 January 1988; Miranda interview at U.S. Department of State on 8 December in undated State Department release headed "Robert Miranda Bengoechea"; and Humberto Ortega comments, saying the troop level sought is 600,000, on Managua Domestic Service, 12 December; *FBIS-Latin America*, 14 December.

27. *WP*, 7 June; *FBIS-Latin America*, 3 September.

28. *IB*, Toronto, February.

29. *El Siglo*, Bogota, 4 August; *WMR*, September; AFP, Paris, 2 October.

30. AFP, Paris, 26 May; *FBIS-Latin America*, 27 May.

31. Lima Panamericana Television, 20 November; *FBIS-Latin America*, 23 November; *Quehacer*, Lima, no. 50.

32. *NYT*, 11 October; *WSJ*, 27 November.

33. *Granma*, Havana, 19 January.

34. *Critica*, Panama City, 27 November; *FBIS-Latin America*, 2 December; *WP*, 16 December.

35. *People's Daily World*, New York, 24 September; *NYT*, 20 November; *Washington Times*, 21 January 1988.

36. *Wen Wei Po*, Hong Kong, 1 July.

37. *FBIS-China*, 7 July.

38. *WSJ*, 19 January 1988.

39. *NYT*, 11 January 1988.

40. "Communist Party of Vietnam Central Committee Plenum," *Pravda*, 21 December.

41. *NYT*, 22 January 1988.

42. *NYT*, 21 January 1988.

43. *FBIS-East Asia*, 8 June.

44. Bertel Lintner, "The Rise and Fall of the Communists," *Far Eastern Economic Review*, Hong Kong, 4 June.

45. Note the announcement of diplomatic relations with Nauru in *Pravda*, 30 December.

46. *FBIS-East Asia*, 10 and 13 July.

47. *CSM*, 18 November; *Pravda*, 2 December.

48. *Afghanistan: Eight Years of Occupation* (U.S. Department of State, Washington, D.C.: December 1987), Special Report no. 173.

49. *Kabul New Times*, 29 November.

50. TASS, 4 October; *FBIS*, 5 October.

51. Radio Kabul, 28 June; *FBIS*, 2 July.

52. *Middle East International*, London, 24 October; *Pravda*, 24, 28 December.

53. *WMR*, March.

54. TASS, 22 January; *FBIS-USSR*.

55. TASS, 19 April; *FBIS-USSR*, 23 April. For a visit by K. N. Brutents to Kuwait, see *Pravda*, 8 January 1988.

56. *Tudeh News*, London, 14 October.

57. *Le Monde Diplomatique*, Paris, October 1986.

58. *Sovetskaia Rossiia*, Moscow, 4 November.

59. *WP*, 12 October; *NYT*, 11 September.

60. *Pravda*, 31 August, 8 September; Moscow radio, 22 October, in *FBIS-Soviet Union*, 87-205, 23 October.

61. Vladimir V. Kusin, "Communist Parties to Hold Special Conferences," *RAD Background Report*, no. 237; RFE, Munich, 11 December.

62. Louis Zanga, "Albania," *RAD Background Report*, no. 250, 30 December.

63. *Rruga ë partisë*, Tirana, no. 10, October; *FBIS-Eastern Europe*, 9 November.

64. *Bulgaria: Continuing Human Rights Abuses Against Ethnic Turks* (Amnesty International, London: July 1987).

65. BBC, Current Affairs Research and Information Section, no. 86/87, 15 July.

66. Peter Matuska, "Czechoslovakia," *RAD Background Report*, no. 250, 30 December. A biography of Jakeš appeared in *Pravda*, 18 December.

67. *Neues Deutschland*, East Berlin, 9 September.

68. Alfred Reisch, "Hungary," *RAD Background Report*, no. 250, 30 December.

69. *Magyar hirlap*, Budapest, 20 August; *FBIS-Eastern Europe*, 27 August.

70. Jan B. de Weydenthal, "Poland," *RAD Background Report*, no. 250, 30 December on the referendum; *NYT*, 31 January 1988 for prices.

71. Photograph in *The Boston Globe*, 8 November.

72. *Scînteia*, Bucharest, 27 May.

73. *NYT*, 22 November; *Scînteia*, 12 December.

74. Milan Andrejevic, "Yugoslavia," *RAD Background Report*, no. 250, 30 December.

75. Ibid.

76. Joseph C. Harsch, "Fading Socialism," *CSM*, 18 June.

77. William Echikson, "West Europe's Communists Running Out of Steam," *CSM*, 2 October.

78. Quoted in *WMR*, October.

79. *L'Humanité*, Paris, 28 January.

80. *WMR*, September.

81. *L'Avante*, Lisbon, 20 August; *FBIS*, 24 August.

82. BBC Central Talks and Features, "British Communists: a Dying Species?" 6 January.

83. *Uusi Suomi*, Helsinki, 12 February, discussed the draft program.

84. *Der Spiegel*, Hamburg, 7 September.

85. *Unsere Zeit*, East Berlin, 20 May.

AFRICA

Introduction

This year saw Ethiopia formally become a Marxist state. A new constitution, which resembles the Soviet document, was approved by 81 percent of those voting in a referendum in February. The new constitution became legally effective in September, and the country became officially known as The People's Democratic Republic of Ethiopia. The dergue, or Provisional Military Administrative Committee, transferred its power to the newly established National Shengo, or parliament. From a state dominated by strongman Mengistu Haile Mariam and his military clique, Ethiopia has moved toward a communist state since the overthrow of Emperor Haile Selassie in 1974. Mengistu remains commander in chief of the armed forces and retains the position of general secretary of the Workers' Party of Ethiopia, founded in 1984. The National Shengo elected Mengistu president of the country in September.

Ethiopia's earlier problems carried into 1987. Eritrean rebels continued their guerrilla war of separation. The Marxist regime remained committed to relocating peasants in government-controlled villages. It was this villagization program and the displacement of potential adversaries that pushed Ethiopia into world headlines in 1985, when some 100,000 people perished. Resettlement caused starvation and death. As in the Ukraine, Cambodia, and Tibet, where communist resettlement programs were also violently implemented, famine became one of the by-products.

In South Africa, the government released from prison Govan Mbeki, who had been sentenced in 1964 for sabotage and conspiracy to overthrow the white minority regime. Upon his release, Mbeki maintained that he was still a member of the African National Congress and the South African Communist Party (SACP). Furthermore, he said, "I still embrace Marxist views." (Johannesburg SAPA, in English, 5 November; *FBIS*, 6 November.) The SACP itself witnessed leadership changes. The Central Committee, which operates in exile from Europe and elsewhere in Africa, elected Dan Tloome as chairman, replacing Joe Slovo. Slovo was shifted to the general secretaryship—a post vacant since Moses Mabhida died in March 1986. The reshuffling harkens back to an earlier party organization where the chairman concentrates on the diplomatic and public aspects and the general secretary focuses on political and administrative functions. The SACP noted its encouragement of the continuing turmoil inside the Republic of South Africa; it viewed rent strikes, white defections from the "ruling class," and widespread disturbances as making "even more effective the conduct of the revolutionary struggle on all fronts" (*African Communist*, no. 109).

Across the border in Zimbabwe on 31 December, Robert Mugabe was installed as the country's first executive president. As a consequence, he now holds the positions of head of the government, state, and ruling Zimbabwe African National Union–Patriotic Front (ZANU-PF) party. Mugabe continued moving Zimbabwe toward a single-party state, and this year marked significant movement toward his objective. He abolished the 30 parliamentary seats reserved for whites, who constitute less than 2 percent of the population, and filled them during an election with candidates nominated by ZANU-PF, including fifteen whites.

His other actions paved the way for a nonparty state. He co-opted Joshua Nkomo and part of his opposition party, the Zimbabwe African People's Union (ZAPU), into ZANU. Some members of ZAPU—which represents the Ndebele people, the second-largest ethnic community—resisted the merger with the Shona-dominated ZANU. ZAPU dissidents persisted in their violence against the government. Mugabe removed opponents to the ZANU-ZAPU merger within his own party and replaced Marxist ideologues and ethnic chauvinists with moderates.

Leadership changes took place in neighboring Mozambique, where President Joaquim Chissano reshuffled his cabinet, or Council of Ministers; Chissano also shook up the military high command in hopes of containing the military successes of the opposition movement, the Mozambique National

Resistance (RENAMO). He replaced Sebastião Mabote with General Antonio Hama Thai as chief of staff. The Front for the Liberation of Mozambique (FRELIMO) military position has remained a problem but was stabilized somewhat, due largely to the presence of some 30,000 foreign troops, predominantly from Zimbabwe and Tanzania, as well as advisers from the Soviet bloc. The domestic economy also remained precarious. FRELIMO enacted an Economic Rehabilitation Program, which formalized, in part, moves since 1984 toward a market-type economy and away from a hard-line Marxist economic plan. The FRELIMO government continued to pursue its previous pragmatic policy toward the West and international financial institutions in order to gain assistance and attract investment. These maneuvers met with great success as some $600 million government and commercial loans were rescheduled. Mozambique also secured substantial new loans from Western countries.

Southward in Lesotho, the Communist Party of Lesotho (CPL) holds to its ambiguous status in the country. The CPL is illegal, but its general secretary, Jacob M. Kena, operates openly. The purported Seventh Congress was held "in utmost secrecy in early 1987" (*WMR*, November); the congress set two main objectives for the party. First, the CPL must strengthen its organization by developing three- to five-member cells throughout Lesotho and must revitalize its trade union activities. Second, the congress also resolved to strengthen its contacts with South African trade unions.

The Sudanese Communist Party (SCP) operates legally in the Sudan. The SCP has enjoyed this status since 1985, when the Jafar Numayri government was toppled. Since winning 5 of 264 contested seats in 1986, the SCP has been a visible part of parliamentary opposition. In June 1987, the SCP opposed the government's handling of the war in the south. This regional conflict is between the predominantly Arabic-speaking and Muslim northerners and the non-Arabic-speaking and African southerners. The SCP has been more or less consistent in its sympathetic expression for the separatist movement, the Sudan People's Liberation Movement. Toward the end of the year, however, the SCP moved to support the government's position. But the SCP, which advocates a secular state, strongly criticized other government policies. For example, the SCP opposed the government's decision not to abrogate the 1983 Islamization laws imposed by Numayri.

In Senegal, several communist and leftist parties have remained divided and without meaningful impact in national politics since becoming legal in 1981. The Party of Independence and Labor, which enjoys official recognition from Moscow, was represented at a number of Soviet bloc–sponsored meetings. But it had a less visible presence domestically. Of the Marxist parties, the Democratic League/Movement for the Party of Labor projected the most significant presence in left-wing Senegalese politics and joined with other groups pressing for electoral reform. The Marxist parties joined in criticizing the government's market reforms and austerity policies required by the International Monetary Fund (IMF) and the World Bank in return for financial assistance.

In Nigeria, political party activities have been banned since 1983, and this ban has restricted Marxists and non-Marxist organizations. The Socialist Working People's Party appears defunct as an organization. The appeal of socialism resides mainly among some of the Nigerian intelligentsia and not in functioning parties. Nigerian Marxists joined the national debate on the structure of a new political system with the release of the Nigerian Labour Congress's manifesto, calling for socialism in Nigeria.

The three ruling Marxist parties in the People's Republic of Benin, Congo, and Angola faced a difficult year. In Benin, the Revolutionary Party of the People of Benin's (PRPB) efforts to improve the economy provoked opposition from public servants and students, who staged demonstrations. The People's Republic of Benin sought to revitalize the private sector and increase the performance of state corporations, while improving relations with Western countries. Public employees protested the lack of salary raises, and students demonstrated for payment of their fellowships. Benin's poor economy remained the most unsettling challege for the PRPB regime.

The People's Republic of Congo experienced more serious opposition to the government's policies to restore the failing economy brought on, in part, by the decline in oil prices. The government reported the aborted plot to assassinate the chairman of the Congolese Party of Labor (PCT), Denis Sassaou-Ngouesso. This led to the ouster of Camille Bongou, the regime's number-two man and the party's ideologue. Bongou was linked to the June plot led by a rival of Chairman Sassaou-Ngouesso, retired Captain Pierre Anga. The PCT government called on French military assistance to quell a threatened ethnic clash between followers of Anga and those of Sassaou-Ngouesso, rather than using Soviet bloc equipment, which was based in the country. The French-aided expedition highlighted the growing cooperation between Paris and the ruling PCT.

The ruling Popular Movement for the Liberation of Angola–Labor party (MPLA-PT) in Angola confronted, as in previous years, the two problems of a badly collapsing economy and a spreading insurgency. The MPLA has been waging a struggle against the National Union for the Total Independence of Angola (UNITA) in the south since 1975. The MPLA has relied upon substantial support from the Soviet bloc. In 1987 the Soviet Union provided more than $1 billion in military equipment (*CSM*, 7 April), and Cuba increased its troop level to 40,000 (*Prensa Latina*, 7 January 1988) in an unsuccessful effort to eliminate UNITA.

The MPLA government used the deteriorating economy as its rationale for purging several top officials. In May, President José Eduardo dos Santos fired Foreign Trade Minister Ismael Gaspar Martins and Internal Trade Minister Adriano Pereira dos Santos, Jr. citing shortages in food and medicine as his reasons. In December, he dismissed Maria Mambo Cafe, minister for social and economic affairs. She had been an opponent of expanded economic ties with the West, including Angola's application to the IMF for membership (Luanda Domestic Service, 22 August; *FBIS*, 26 August).

On the island of Réunion, the Réunion Communist Party (PCR) requested economic assistance from the Paris government, which administers the Indian Ocean island as a French overseas department. But French officials' plans for complete integration of the island with France occasioned concerns by the PCR for the preservation of Réunion culture and the Creole language. The party supported several strikes by the communist-affiliated trade union, the General Confederation of Réunion Labor, during 1987.

Thomas H. Henriksen
Hoover Institution

Angola

Population. 7,950,244
Party. Popular Movement for the Liberation of Angola–Labor Party (Movimento Popular de Libertação de Angola–Partido do Trabalho; MPLA-PT)
Founded. 1956 (renamed 1977)
Membership. 35,000 (*African Communist*, no. 105 [2d Quarter, 1986])
General Secretary. José Eduardo dos Santos
Politburo. 11 members
Central Committee. 90 members
Status. Ruling party
Last Congress. Second, 9–11 December 1985
Last Election. 1980; all 203 candidates MPLA-PT approved
Auxiliary Organizations. MPLA Youth (JMPLA); Organization of Angolan Women (OMA); Angolan Teachers' Association; National Union of Angolan Workers (UNTA)
Publications. No data

The MPLA-PT, the ruling Marxist-Leninist political party of Angola, was founded as the MPLA in 1956. The party, a secret movement to resist Portuguese rule in Angola, was led for the most part by urban-based mestizos and intellectuals with roots in the Portuguese Communist Party. (Its subsequent history is outlined in prior editions of the *YICA*.) In 1974–1975, the MPLA was catapulted into power in Luanda by virtue of covert support from influential members of the revolutionary military leadership in Lisbon as well as massive external support from Cuba and the Soviet Union that resulted in a military showdown with the two other major factions in Angolan politics, Holden Roberto's National Front for the Liberation of Angola (Frente Nacional de Libertação de Angola; FNLA) and Jonas Savimbi's National Union for the Total Independence of Angola (Uniao Nacional para a Independência Total de Angola; UNITA).

The MPLA was renamed the MPLA-PT in December 1977 at the first major postindependence party congress. The move was considered necessary to enhance the role of labor in the governing party, toward which end labor was allocated 20 percent of the party congress seats by statute.

Leadership and Party Organization. The MPLA-PT and its Central Committee monopolize political power in the half of the country under the control of the central government. Day-to-day control is exercised by the eleven-member Politburo, headed by José Eduardo dos Santos, the current president of Angola and chairman of the MPLA-PT. Dos Santos was educated in the Soviet Union and is married to a Russian. In recent years, his principal rivals having suffered setbacks, dos Santos increasingly has centralized Politburo decisions in his hands, but this power is not absolute. Since 1980 a vast political infrastructure has been created on paper consisting of a People's Assembly, provincial assemblies, and a number of electoral colleges meant to represent the various constituencies appropriate to a Marxist-Leninist state. The People's Assembly met in August but wound up its business in just three days (Luanda Domestic Service, 14 August; *FBIS*, 18 August).

More germane to the running of the country, the Central Committee met in late June to focus on the economic situation (Luanda Domestic Service, 24 June; *FBIS*, 25 June). Indeed, the deteriorating economy became the issue that served to replace a number of top-level officials in the government. As the new policies were put in place, they were sufficiently focused for dos Santos to announce an economic reorganization in August (Luanda Domestic Service, 17 August; *FBIS*, 19 August). The destruction of the economy is discussed below, but the traumatic effect on the leadership was clear. In May, seeking to place blame for the sad state of the economy, dos Santos sacked two cabinet ministers: Foreign Trade Minister Ismael Gaspar Martins and Internal Trade Minister Adriano Pereira dos Santos, Jr. (AFP, 8 May; *FBIS*, 12 May). The severe shortages of food and medicines were the immediate causes for the move against the two ministers. By July, the firings were escalating. Evaristo Domingos Kimba, minister of agriculture, lost his job on 3 July, along with his deputy, Joaquim Antonio Russo. Four provincial commissars (in Bie, Zaire, Huambo, and Namibe) also lost their jobs (Luanda Domestic Service, 3 July; *FBIS*, 6 July). The final shoe dropped in December with the firing of Maria Mambo Cafe as the senior leader of social and economic affairs. As a candidate member of the Politburo, she had been the principal resister to expanded economic ties with the West, and her dismissal was a clear signal that the Angolan economy, internally and externally, was on a new track (Luanda Domestic Service, 14 December; *FBIS*, 15 December).

Domestic Party Affairs and Mass Organizations. With the tensions of the leadership over economic issues and with the ongoing war with UNITA showing no progress, the MPLA showed few signs of strengthening domestically. A variety of mobilization efforts continued, along with realignments of personnel, to attempt to deal with the political malaise in the Luanda regime. A national conference of ideological workers was held in early 1987 to increase motivation (*WMR*, April 1987). The media were a particularly nettlesome sector in 1987, and thus the editors of ANGOP, the national news service, and the *Jornal de Angola* were replaced on 7 April by the Central Committee Secretariat (Luanda Domestic Service, 24 April; *FBIS*, 27 April).

The party showed great concern during the year as policies became increasingly pragmatic. The more ideological members of the Politburo attempted to maintain "revolutionary vigilance" as the country focused on conventional issues. Methodology seminars were held for political cadres stationed with the army, which was under serious siege from UNITA (Luanda Domestic Service, 28 April; *FBIS*, 1 May). The bureaucracy showed every sign of simply getting along, with ideological rigor rapidly ebbing (*WSJ*, 19 February). The usual calls for purging the local party organs and reinforcement of discipline did not evoke any evident action on the part of the cadres (Luanda Domestic Service, 23 July; *FBIS*, 28 July).

The greatest domestic difficulty faced by the party was the weakness of the economy. As reported by the *Washington Post* (30 August), the economy was run on a currency consisting of beer cans rather than the nominal currency of kwanzas, with even some salaries paid by cases of beer. Water shortages in the spring provoked demonstrations in Luanda and Lobito when the water company began selling water for the first time (Clandestine KUP, in French, 19 February; *FBIS*, 19 February). President dos Santos laid out the dimensions of the Angolan economic decline in August: 600,000 people displaced by the war, capital investment in 1986 only 20 percent of the 1985 figure, and imports of consumer goods off by 50 percent. Given the state of Angolan production, that could mean almost a 50 percent drop in the standard of living. The drop in the price of oil, along with continuing war expenses and imports, meant that foreign debt had climbed to $4 billion. The party was thus being forced, according to dos Santos, to "find ways to economic relations with Western countries advantageous to the People's Republic of Angola (Luanda Domestic Service, 17 August; *FBIS*, 19 August), which included a formal application to the International Monetary Fund for membership. The party got behind that effort at the grass roots (Luanda Domestic Service, 22 August; *FBIS*, 26 August), but the cost was the sacrificing of some senior leaders, as noted above.

International Activities and Views. As in past years, Angolan relationships with the Soviet Union and Cuba were central to the country's international situation. The Mikhail Gorbachev era in Moscow created uncertainty in Luanda, especially as it became clear that Soviet allies were increasingly expected to pay their own way. That meant stronger economic ties with the West, which President dos Santos embraced more quickly than did some of his advisers. (The resistance of the Cubans to such advice created tensions that required the entire year to work out.)

Other areas of concern to Luanda were the evolving relationship with the United States, U.S. support for UNITA, and South Africa's continuing incursions into the southern part of the country in support of UNITA's military defense. Talks with the United States occurred off and on throughout the year, clearly enriched by the desire of President dos Santos to reap greater economic benefits from the West.

Tensions were reported as early as February, when Cuban sources began whispering about their unhappiness with dos Santos and about their evident search for an ideologically more faithful person as president (*Cape Times*, 16 February; *FBIS*, 18 February). The tripartite Soviet-Cuban-Angolan consultations that took place 10–11 March were apparently crucial in planning the approach to be taken against UNITA in the 1987 dry season military offensive (Luanda Domestic Service, 14 March; *FBIS*, 16 March). With the offensive expected in late April or early May, the inflow of Soviet arms reached record levels in prior months, more than $1 billion in one year, a clear sign that it was time for a "final push" (*CSM*, 7 April). Cuban troop levels began climbing and were later acknowledged by Cuban leaders to reach 40,000 (*Prensa Latina*, 7 January 1988; *FBIS*, 7 January 1988).

In the meantime, talks with the United States went forward, with meetings between Foreign Minister Alfonso Van Dunem and U.S. assistant secretary of state Chester Crocker (Luanda Domestic Service, 15 April; *FBIS*, 16 April). Terms of Cuban withdrawal were evidently discussed, primarily in terms of first ending outside support of UNITA and then Cuban troops out. One new element in the talks focused on the possible neutralization and reopening of the Benguela railroad, which UNITA leader Savimbi indicated his willingness to guarantee (*The Johannesburg Star*, 25 April; *FBIS*, 28 April). The proposal, however, came to nought. Talks with the United States were also pursued by Politburo member Pedro de Castro Van Dunem and the deputy foreign minister in early June (Luanda Domestic Service, 14 June; *FBIS*, 15 June). Crocker visited Luanda in September as well, with no results.

President dos Santos traveled widely in 1987. A trip in April to India and North Korea yielded little except rumors that he asked the North Koreans for troops to replace the Cubans, later publicly denied despite some plausibility (AFP, 14 April; *FBIS*, 14 April). He then visited Cuba in July and August in an apparently friendly sharing of views. In October, dos Santos traveled to Portugal, where he was much more cordially received than in the past, and addressed the Portuguese assembly and audiences of Portuguese businessmen. He went on to France, Belgium, and Italy. Finally, he went to Moscow for the 70th anniversary celebrations of the Soviet Revolution.

Little of importance was seen in the visiting socialist delegations in Luanda in 1987. The greatest attention was given to a Supreme Soviet Presidium delegation, led by Pavel Gilashvili, that arrived for several days in March (Luanda Domestic Service, 16 March; *FBIS*, 17 March). More tangible issues were addressed by a Council for Mutual Economic Assistance delegation in May, which reportedly agreed on twenty major projects for support (RL 187/87, 14 May). Several delegations from East Germany revealed that foreign aid to Angola would reach about 8 million marks in 1987 (Luanda Domestic Service, 9 October; *FBIS*, 9 October).

Richard Bissell
Washington, D.C.

Benin

Population. 4,339,096
Party. Revolutionary Party of the People of Benin (Parti Révolutionnaire du Peuple du Bénin; PRPB)
Founded. 1975
Membership. Less than 2,000
Chairman. Mathieu Kérékou (also president of the republic)
Politburo. 11 members, elected November 1985: Mathieu Kérékou, Martin Dohou Azonhiho, Joseph Deguela, Gado Giriguissou, Roger Imorou Garba, Justin Guidehou, Sanni Mama Gomina, Romain Vilon Guezo, Vincent Guezodje, Idi Abdoulaye Mallam, Simon Ifede Ogouma.
Central Committee. 45 members
Status. Sole and ruling party
Last Congress. Second (ordinary), November 1985
Last Election. 1984, all 196 National Assembly members on PRPB list, all elected.
Auxiliary Organizations. Organization of the Revolutionary Youth of Benin (OJRB); Organization of the Revolutionary Women of Benin (OFRB); National Federation of Workers' Unions of Benin (UNSTB); Committees for the Defense of the Revolution (CDR)
Publications. *Handoria* (PRPB publication); *Ehuzu* (government-controlled daily); *Bénin Magazine* (monthly), published by the National Press publishing and printing office (government enterprise).

Party and Domestic Affairs. The year was dominated by continuing economic difficulties and austerity policies, resulting in growing dissatisfaction on the part of the privileged groups, especially students and bureaucrats. Increasingly it appears that President Kérékou's attempts to revitalize the private sector, privatize or improve the management of the parasitic state corporations, and improve relations with France and the United States have led to growing opposition from the dogmatic yet influential Marxist-Leninists.

The public servants and students are most affected by the austerity measures imposed by the newly influential technocrats led by Idi Abdoulaye Mallam and having the ear of Kérékou. Both groups, long overabundant in Benin, are politically active and influential as well as in the forefront of radicalism. The bureaucratic grievances are mostly economic and directly related to the regime's decision not to increase the salaries of state employees since 1982 and to impose new taxes (takué), including a 2,500 Communauté Financière Africaine franc (CFAFR) tax at the international airport of Cotonou-Cadjehoun (*Jeune Afrique*, 27 May). Furthermore, a hiring freeze in the public sector and some firings by state enterprises have also served to alienate the bureaucracy. This alienation was made clear when the public employees staged a series of demonstrations during the spring specifically directed at irregular payment of wages and a 10 percent compulsory deduction. (Ibid.)

The Beninese students, especially those at the national university campus at Abomey-Calavi, have a long tradition of radicalism and political activism. In March they staged massive demonstrations protesting the government's failure to pay their fellowships. Beninese students abroad have complained about the same problem—those in Dakar, unpaid for seven months, occupied Benin's consulate in that city—as well as the policy of allowing a trip back home every three years instead of the traditional two.

The government's reaction to the students was, rhetorically at least, extremely harsh. The Politburo declared that, while the party and state are "constantly preoccupied with the problems of our pupils and students, stern instructions have been given to the comrade minister of defense, the minister delegate . . . in charge of interior, public security . . . the minister of secondary and higher education, and to . . . all prefects of provinces" (*FBIS-Africa*, 19 March). Kérékou himself promised "no pity" for the "infiltrators" of "reactionary international groups" and that "we will deal with resolute force" (ibid.). In contrast, the regime tried to legitimize its rule by emphasizing the "political stability and social peace" it has brought to the country since 1972 (*FBIS-Africa*, 20 March), still a convincing argument for the older generations.

More generally, patronage continued to characterize the political system: obscure ministers or simple advisers assumed major policy decision-making powers because of their relationship to Kérékou. Thus, Idi Abdoulaye Mallam, a "simple" adviser, is now in charge of the portfolios of the sacked finance minister, Hospice Antonio, and planning and statistics minister, Zul Kifl Salami (*Jeune Afrique*, 27 May). Similarly, Gado Giriguissou, formerly public works minister and since February minister of commerce, crafts, and tourism; Baba Moussa, director of the Lomé-based West African Bank for Development; and Soule Dankoro, ex-minister of commerce and now minister of equipment and transportation (*Africa Confidential*, 29 April; *FBIS-Africa*, 10 February) are, in fact, the main policy makers of Benin's economic and even foreign policy.

The economic crisis, admitted throughout the year by dignitaries of the regime including President Kérékou, deepened in 1987. On 14 August the National Revolutionary Assembly formally approved a budget estimating a deficit of 6 billion CFAFRs (revenues 50 billion CFAFRs, expenditures 56 billion CFAFRs), the first time since the 1972 coup that brought Kérékou to power that a deficit was officially admitted (*FBIS-Africa*, 18 August). Meanwhile, the national debt of $800 million has resulted in Benin's losing its capacity to borrow from abroad, while economic aid from Libya, the Soviet bloc, and China has declined from small to negligible amounts.

Foreign Affairs. In such circumstances, it became clear that the only recourse available to the regime was a drastic reassessment of its economic and, by implication, foreign policies. Ideological, cultural, and diplomatic ties to the Soviet bloc and China generally remained unchanged. Meanwhile, economic and political relations with the West expanded rapidly, while those with Libya declined.

Benin's relations with the Soviet bloc in general have continued at the same pace since 1980, characterized by numerous exchanges of low-level Soviet bloc delegations with less frequent but higher-level Beninese officials traveling to the USSR or other Soviet bloc capitals. In February Valentin Pavlov, the Soviet ambassador to Benin, reviewed bilateral ties and pointed out two major aspects of cooperation: the ties between Komsomol and the OJRB and the Soviets' building the Lenin Square in Cotonou (*FBIS-Africa*, 13 February). As if to strengthen the ambassador's point, a Komsomol delegation, led by Yevgeny Samotesol, visited Benin in February; in March a Lithuanian Soviet Socialist Republic minor official, Ringaudas-Bronislovas Songayla, briefly stopped over in Cotonou and was received by Roger Garba, the deputy chairman of the Revolutionary National Assembly's Permanent Committee. In April a Soviet trade union delegation, led by Peter Guitchenkov, visited Benin for a week; at the end of the visit a joint communiqué restated the close relations between the two countries' unions, as well as condemnation of South Africa's treatment of trade unions. (Ibid., 21 April.) A relatively high Soviet military delegation, led by Major General Novochesky, visited Benin in April and was received by the top military officers of Benin: Colonel Charles Bebada, chief of staff of the People's Armed Forces; Colonel Leopold Ahoueya, chief of staff of the Public Security Forces; and Gaston Coovi, chief of staff of the National Defense Forces (*FBIS-Africa*, 16 April). On the political level, the Soviet military team was received by Romain Vilon Guezo, acting chief of state and chairman of the Standing Committee of the National Assembly (ibid., 23 April). Another Komsomol delegation, led by the Armenian Komsomol boss, visited Benin in June, and signed a cooperation agreement between the Komsomol and the OJRB. In August a CPSU delegation—led by the Central Committee member and first secretary of the Kalinin *obkom*, Nikolay Fedorovich Tatarchuk—arrived in Benin for party-to-party talks (*Pravda*, 13 August) and on 24 August was formally received by Kérékou. On the other hand, Benin's Ousmane Batoko, the minister of education, spent two weeks in the Soviet Union in February (*Pravda*, 3 March). In April Nicaragua's foreign minister D'Escoto spent three days in Benin, most of the time delivering rabidly anti-U.S. speeches. Interestingly and significantly, Kérékou's reactions to D'Escoto's statements were discreetly avoided by the official Beninese media to avoid upsetting the country's Western aid donors. Ties with China continued on the same low but public level as before, as did relations with North Korea.

Relations with the West were drastically improved. An agreement with the International Monetary Fund (IMF) was negotiated and is soon to be approved. Once again, Benin refused to support the Soviet invasion of Afghanistan and abstained on the issue at the U.N. Not only did Benin's official rhetoric against French "imperialism" disappear, but bilateral ties reached unexpected dimensions. The most spectacular of those was the decision to establish a military training center in Porto Novo, worth 6 billion CFA francs, suggested by General Saulnier, the French army's chief of staff, during his November 1986 visit to Benin. Loudly attacked by Beninese radicals, particularly students, as a "return of Dodds" (the French conqueror of precolonial

Abomey) (*Jeune Afrique*, 27 May), the project, involving mostly French-speaking West Africans, went ahead. Idi Abdoulaye Mallam, asking for French support at the IMF, defined Paris as "the defender of African countries, the doctor who knows how to sweeten the potion of the IMF to make it palatable to the sick" (ibid.). As for the United States, Kérékou's meeting with President Ronald Reagan in June served to improve bilateral relations, long strained by Cotonou's rhetoric and close ties to Libya.

Michael Radu
Foreign Policy Research Institute, Philadelphia

Congo

Population. 2,082,154
Party. Congolese Party of Labor (Parti Congolaise du Travail: PCT)
Founded. 1969
Membership. 9,000 (estimated)
Chairman. Denis Sassou-Ngouesso
Politburo. 10 members
Central Committee. 60 members
Status. Ruling and sole official party
Last Congress. Third, July 1984, in Brazzaville
Last Election. 1984, 95 percent, all 153 members PCT approved
Auxiliary Organizations. Congolese Trade Union Confederation (CSC); Revolutionary Union of Congolese Women (URFC); Union of Congolese Socialist Youth (UJSC)
Publications. *Mweti* (government-controlled daily); *Etumba* (weekly organ of the PCT Central Committee); *Elikia* (party quarterly)

Domestic Affairs. Economic difficulties caused by both government policies and the sharp decline in oil prices are beginning to threaten the stability of President Sassou-Ngouesso's rule. The president's frequent absences from the country between June 1986 and June 1987, when he served as chairman of the Organization of African Unity (OAU), further encouraged his domestic opponents, both within and without the ruling PCT.

In June Lieutenant Gilbert Iloki led a coup plot involving a number of active military officers and retired senior officers and a former chief of staff of the army. According to the government, the plotters intended to shoot down the presidential plane on Sassou-Ngouesso's departure to the OAU annual summit in Addis Ababa. (*Jeune Afrique*, 21 October.) The secret police, led by the director general of state security, Colonel Gouelo-Ndele, promptly arrested the plot leaders. More than twenty officers were arrested, including a number of majors, captains, lieutenants, and four colonels, one of whom, Jean-Michel Ebaka, was a former director of national security. All of them came from the Kouyou ethnic group. (*FBIS-Africa*, 26 July.)

Following a well-established pattern dating from the creation of the People's Republic of Congo in 1969, the plot served as an auspicious justification for another spectacular purge. The target of that purge was surprisingly important: the number two man of the regime and the party ideologue, Camille Bongou. Bongou, a devoted and orthodox Marxist-Leninist, had long been known for his radicalism and was the leader of the shadowy faction M-22 (Mouvement 22 du Février). The movement sprang originally from an attempt by Lieutenant Ange Diawara in 1972 to overthrow then-president Marien Ngouabi. The army killed Diawara a year later, but his followers made a spectacular comeback in 1979 when Sassou-Ngouesso needed their help against the "revisionist" Yhombi-Opango.

As a Politburo member, Bongou chose the members for the forthcoming PCT Congress of 1989, and they will decide its outcome, including the election of the Central Committee and Politburo. As the Central Committee secretary in charge of both organization and coordination, he held sway over the PCT "mass organizations," including youth and women as well as unions and journalists. In July Bongou was purged from his most important position, organization secretary of the PCT (ibid.), and replaced by Andre Obami Itou, previous chairman of the PCT Control and Verification Commission. More important, the government discreetly linked him to the June plot and to Pierre Anga.

There are very good reasons to believe that Anga's alleged plot was nothing more than a government decision gone awry. Indeed, Pierre Anga, retired captain of the ANP and a former member of the junta that succeeded the assassinated Ngouabi in 1977, lost his bid for the defense ministry to Sassou-Ngouesso, whom he has hated ever since. Placed under house arrest until 1984, as was

Yhombi-Opango, he was then sent to his native Owando. Trying to find a scapegoat, the regime accused Bongou of ties with the exiled captain. At any rate, by the end of August Anga and Yhombi-Opango were called to Brazzaville for interrogation; Anga refused and declared that he would never again allow himself to be arrested. Supported by his relatives among the Kouyou ethnic group, Anga began distributing a tape cassette, which accused President Sassou-Ngouesso of involvement in the 1977 assassination of Marien Ngouabi, and apparently received some arms and ammunition from his Brazzaville supporters in the army. Meanwhile, the regime continued to use the incident to discredit the president's rivals. Camille Bongou and former Prime Minister Louis-Sylvain Goma were dispatched to Owando to try and convince Anga to surrender, but both failed.

By the beginning of September the entire affair became extremely serious or at least was perceived as such in Brazzaville. By the end of the first week in September, events turned for the worse for the government. Anga's friends killed between 4 (government sources, in *FBIS-Africa*, 9 September) and 50 (*Jeune Afrique*, 16 September) soldiers and civilians. Anga escaped and took refuge in the Manga swamps of his native area. On 9 September former President Yhombi-Opango was arrested under vague charges.

The most interesting aspect of the affair, however, was the fact that Brazzaville requested and received French military aid to put down what threatened to become an ethnic clash between the two dominant northern peoples—Anga's Kouyous and Sassou-Ngouesso's Mbochis. Congolese commandos landed at Owando on a French military plane based in neighboring Gabon on 6 September. This use of French military support has heavy political implications, for it demonstrates that the army's Soviet transport planes were unreliable or, probably, that the air force itself was unreliable. As for the numerous Cuban and other Soviet bloc military personnel in the Congo, the fact that they were not requested to aid the Owando expedition may prove that the recent pro-Western changes in Congolese policy may be deeper than previously thought.

Foreign Affairs. The level of political, ideological, and cultural exchanges between Congo and the Soviet bloc continued at the same pace as in previous years, but those with the West became more important. In April a CPSU delegation, led by the first secretary of the Kerson *obkom*, A. N. Girenko, visited Brazzaville and discussed a number of issues with Congolese officials, particularly matters pertaining to agricultural development and collectivization (*FBIS-USSR*, 10 August); the delegation's main interlocutor was Planning Minister Pierre Moussa, also a Central Committee secretary. In June, an East German delegation from the Socialist Unity Party of Germany's Control Commission, met in Brazzaville with Jean-Pierre Obembe, the PCT Central Committee secretary in charge of propaganda and information (*FBIS-Africa*, 11 June). The same month, a personal message from CPSU leader Mikhail Gorbachev, underscoring the "proximity of positions" between Brazzaville and Moscow on southern Africa, the OAU, and disarmament and development, was delivered in Brazzaville by a special emissary. In July, a Supreme Soviet delegation, led by a Moldavian Soviet Socialist Republic official, A. A. Mokanu, visited Congo and was received by Sassou-Ngouesso (*FBIS-USSR*, 22 July).

Relations with the West in general, and France in particular, continued to improve. Congo participated in the francophone summit in Canada, attended the French-African summit in France, and renewed military ties with Paris, as demonstrated by the Owando episode. Furthermore, Congolese cooperation with the IMF, the reduction of rhetoric against the United States, and an increasingly nonpartisan approach to such African issues as Chad indicate a steady movement on the part of Sassou-Ngouesso toward nonalignment and pragmatism.

Michael Radu
Foreign Policy Research Institue, Philadelphia

Ethiopia

Population. 46,706,229
Party. Workers' Party of Ethiopia (WPE)
Founded. September 1984
Membership. 50,000
General Secretary. Mengistu Haile Mariam (46, career soldier)
Politburo. 11 full members: Mengistu Haile Mariam, Fikre-Selassie Wogderess, Fisseha Desta,

Tesfaye Gebre Kidan, Berhanu Bayih, Legesse Asfaw, Addis Tedlay, Hailu Yimenu, Amanuel Amde Michael, Alenu Abebe, Shimelis Mazengia; 6 alternate members.

Secretariat. 8 members: Fisshea Desta, Legesse Asfaw, Shimelis Mazengia, Fasika Sidelil, Shewandagn Belete, Wubeset Desie, Ashagre Yigletu, Emibel Ayele

Central Committee. 136 full members, 64 alternate members

Status. Ruling party

Last Congress. First, 6–10 September 1984, in Addis Ababa

Last Election. Parliament (National Shengo), June 1987; 85 percent (13.4 million) elected 835 deputies; all are WPE members.

Auxiliary Organizations. All-Ethiopian Peasants' Association; Kebelles; All-Ethiopia Trade Union; Revolutionary Ethiopia's Women's Association; Revolutionary Ethiopia's Youth Association

Publications. *Serto Ader*, *Meskerem*, *Yekatit*, *Addis Zemen*, *Ethiopian Herald*, *Negarit Gazeta*

Of primary importance in 1987 were Ethiopia's conversion to a People's Democratic Republic, the adoption of a new constitution, elections for a new parliament, and, once again, the spread of famine and starvation. Resettlement and villagization policies continued, while the secessionist wars in Eritrea and Tigre heated up again.

Leadership and Party Organization. On 12 September—the 13th anniversary of the Ethiopian revolution—the third constitution of Ethiopia became legally effective (see *YICA*, 1987, for the constitution's provisions). Only two days earlier the dergue, or Provisional Military Administrative Committee (PMAC), transferred its powers to the newly established parliament, the National Shengo. These events were set in motion on 22 February when a new constitution was approved by 81 percent of those voting in a referendum; 96 percent of Ethiopia's 14 million voters participated (*Pravda*, 18 April). As the constitution went into effect, the country became officially known as the People's Democratic Republic of Ethiopia.

Elections to the National Shengo were held 14 June. Some 13.4 million people participated in the vote, which resulted in the election of 835 deputies, all of whom were selected as candidates by the ruling WPE (*Pravda*, 5 July). Among those elected were Mengistu Haile Mariam, who was chosen to be president of the country by the National Shengo in September; Fisseha Desta, vice president; and Fikre-Selassie Wogderess, prime minister.

The interconnections between party, military, and government are apparent in that the hierarchy of the WPE and the now-defunct PMAC are the leaders of the newly installed government. Mengistu is general secretary of the WPE, commander in chief of the armed forces, and president of Ethiopia. L. N. Zaykov, secretary of the CPSU Central Committee and a member of the Soviet Politburo who led his country's delegation to the anniversary celebrations in Ethiopia, reinforced Soviet support for Ethiopia's political changes: "We regard the Workers' Party of Ethiopia as an associate in the common struggle . . . The proclamation of the People's Democratic Republic marks the start of a new stage in the development of the Ethiopian revolution" (*Pravda*, 11 September).

International and Political Activities. Two to five million people are "at risk" from starvation, and Ethiopia announced it will need 950,000 metric tons of grain in 1988 to cope with the disaster. The United States will provide 115,000 metric tons of grain, and the European community will ship 85,000 metric tons (*WP*, 22 September). The USSR agreed to aid in the development of livestock and irrigation programs (Addis Ababa Domestic Service [AADS], 9 October; *FBIS*, 12 October) and to set up a caustic soda plant to help produce "industrial raw materials locally" (AADS, 6 October; *FBIS*, 7 October). In April Foreign Minister Berhanu Bayih traveled to East Germany in an attempt to acquire additional economic and political support (ADN, 30 April). Mengistu in 1987 visited the Soviet Union, where he met with General Secretary Mikhail Gorbachev, the Democratic People's Republic of Korea, and the Yemen Arab Republic. Among the leaders that visited Ethiopia during the September anniversary celebrations were Prime Minister Robert Mugabe of Zimbabwe, President Hassan Gouled Aptidon of Djibouti, President Yoweri Museveni of Uganda, and Yassir Arafat, chairman of the PLO (Palestine Liberation Organization).

It was reported in 1987 that over the past eighteen months two more officials had defected: Abebe Kebede, ambassador to Japan, and Mesfin Makonnen, first secretary in the embassy in Czechoslovakia. In April 1987 Tesfaye Lemma, theater manager for the folk group People to People Ethiopia, defected in Washington, D.C.

Ethiopia moved ahead with its resettlement and

villagization programs, moving some 300,000 people from the drought-stricken areas of the north to the southwest. To date 800,000 people have been relocated with a total resettlement of 1.2 million planned. Seven million peasants were moved from rural to centralized villages by the end of the year, and plans call for the eventual relocation of 30 million people.

In November an Ethiopian relief column of 32 vehicles was attacked by Eritrean rebels. All the vehicles and food supplies were destroyed. Although Ethiopia has gained the upper hand in the secessionist wars in the north, the government has been unable to defeat the rebels. Directly after the attack, Ireland announced it would send $375,000 in emergency food aid and Sweden granted $630,000 for famine victims. The People's Republic of China announced a loan of $5.3 million for additional relief.

Peter Schwab
State University of New York at Purchase

Lesotho

Population. 1,621,932
Party. Communist Party of Lesotho (CPL)
Founded. 1962
Membership. No data
Chairman. R. Mataji
Secretariat. Jacob M. Kena (general secretary), John Motloheloa, Khotso Molekane
Status. Illegal (but tolerated)
Last Congress. Seventh, early 1987
Last Election. September 1985
Auxiliary Organization. Mine Workers' Union
Publication. *Mozhammokho* (Communist)

The CPL claims to have held its Seventh Congress "in utmost secrecy in early 1987" (*WMR*, November), thus continuing to ignore the Seventh Congress purported to have been held in November 1984 (*YICA*, 1987). According to the recently published documents of the 1987 congress, the main task of the party is organizational: to develop three-to-five-man cells countrywide and to revitalize its trade union activities (*WMR*, November). The congress also vowed to strengthen ties with the South African trade unions, especially the National Union of Mineworkers (in which some 200,000 Lesotho immigrants are alleged to be involved) (ibid.). This is a logical policy for the CPL in that party leader Kena continues to operate legally in his capacity as secretary general of the (Lesotho) mineworkers union (see *YICA*, 1987).

The congress account noted that a split had earlier developed in the CPL, with some of the "splitters" taking sides with the new regime (ibid.). This probably refers, among others, to Planning Minister Michael M. Sefali and Law Minister Halaki Sello, who were described early this year as former CPL members (*Africa Confidential*, 21 January; see *YICA*, 1987, to see them characterized as pro-Soviet and pro-African National Congress [ANC]). The article describing them predicts that they will have a hard time staying in the government (*Africa Confidential*, 21 January), but they have survived, apparently because of the support they receive from King Moshoeshoe II (*YICA*, 1987).

The CPL in fact pictures the king as a relatively progressive figure within the Lesotho power structure who "keeps his distance from the Pretoria authorities and leans toward nonalignment" (*WMR*, November). The aforenoted article that discussed the status of Sefali and Sello agreed that the king wants to cultivate a liberal image and implied that he is chiefly opposed by the two dominant personalities on the Military Council, the "overtly pro-South African" Thaabe and Sekhobe Letsie (*Africa Confidential*, 21 January). (The article regards Military Council chief Justin Metsina Lekhanya as a figurehead.)

That the king has been able to steer the country along a nonaligned path is seen in the good relations Lesotho maintains with the Soviet Union and China as well as with South Africa; the domestic parallel is that while the CPL is not legal, its members are not persecuted (as the CPL itself has said, "there are no witch hunts for the Communists") (*WMR*, November). But at least on one occasion during the year, the regime appeared to have leaned leftward: three of the four Lesotho delegates to the June Moscow World Congress of Women—one of the two major communist front conferences of 1987—were government officials (apparently including Minister of State for Women and Youth Affairs Matelima Hlalele) (The World Congress of Women's *Preliminary List of Participants* on page 12 names government minister Anna Hlalele, an apparent reference to Matelima). Thus, it would seem that the characterization of Lesotho as a "Bantustan" by the quarterly of the Soviet-line Christian Peace Conference is not warranted, even though the evidence cited—the in-country presence of a South African "hit team" targeted against ANC members and sympathizers and the Military Council's prohibition of church involvement in political activities—appears to be true (*Christian Peace Conference*, vols. 1–2, nos. 89–90).

The CPL's publicized activity abroad was minimal during 1987, and what there was appeared to have been centered around the *World Marxist Review* (*Problems of Peace and Socialism*), the Prague-based international communist theoretical monthly. The July issue listed the CPL as sending a delegation to its May Prague symposium entitled "The October Revolution and the Main Problems of Our Age" (*WMR*, July). The September issue had the magazine's CPL representative, Sam Moeto, as a participant in its meeting devoted to the "U.S. Policy of Neoglobalism, the Military-Industrial Complex, Contemporary Militarism, and the Working Class" (time and place unstated) (ibid., September). Finally, the November issue carried the aforenoted account of the party's Seventh Congress, reported by party member Jeremia Mosotho (*WMR*, November).

Wallace H. Spaulding
McLean, Virginia

Mozambique

Population. 14,535,805
Party. Front for the Liberation of Mozambique (Frente de Libertação de Moçambique; FRELIMO)
Founded. 1962
Membership. 130,000 (*WMR*, April)
President. Joaquim Alberto Chissano
Politburo. 10 members: Joaquim Alberto Chissano, Marcelino dos Santos, Alberto Chipande, Armando Emilio Guebuza, Jorge Rebelo, Mariano de Araújo Matsinhe, Sebastião Marcos Mabote, Jacinto Soares Veloso, Mário de Graça Machungo, José Óscar Monteiro
Secretariat. Julio Zamith Carrilho, Pascoal Mocumbi, Aduardo Aaro, José Luís Cabaço
Central Committee. Approximately 130 members
Status. Ruling party
Last Congress. Fourth, 26–29 April 1983, in Maputo (600 delegates)
Last Election. 1986
Auxiliary Organizations. Organization of Mozambican Women (Organização da Mulher Moçambicana; OMM); Mozambique Youth Organization (OJM); Mozambique Workers' Organization (OTM)
Publications. *Notícias* (daily); *O Tempo* (weekly); *Diário de Moçambique* (daily); *Domingo* (Sunday paper); *Voz de Revolução* (Central Committee organ); *Economia* (Chamber of Commerce magazine)

The FRELIMO party celebrated its 25th anniversary amid continuing problems. The People's Republic of Mozambique remains a deeply troubled country with a virtual civil war, atrocities and massacres, widespread starvation, and a dislocated economy. The Population Crisis Committee announced that its human suffering index showed Mozambique to be the most miserable country in the world during 1987. The severity of Mozambique's plight has prompted the ruling communist party to adopt a degree of pragmatism in running the country over the past few years. The FRELIMO leadership turned toward the West for aid and investment and lessened state controls on some small-scale enterprises to encourage development. Western countries have responded in hopes of moving Mozambique away from its staunch alignment with the Soviet Union. Despite the war and hunger in this southeast African country, official figures report an increase in a few agricultural products, limited improvement in port facilities at Beira, and a greater degree of transport safety across the Beira corridor to and from landlocked Zimbabwe.

Yet the opposition force, the Mozambique National Resistance (Resistência Nacional Moçambicana; RENAMO, formerly MNR), continues to be an active player in much of the countryside. The state of Mozambique's economy also remains precarious. War in the rural areas and recognition of RENAMO's challenge also grew in the year under review. The guerrilla struggle persisted as the dominant political feature, which reflects the divisions of

Mozambique's recent history (for background, see *YICA*, 1982, 1987).

Organization and Leadership. Notwithstanding FRELIMO's greater pragmatism in domestic policies and foreign relations, the party's leadership and organizational structure remain wedded to the standard operating procedures of communist movements. Three small factions merged to form FRELIMO in 1962. Both in appearance and in organization FRELIMO resembled a national front organization in the early years of its existence. FRELIMO's radicalization process became delineated in both the organizational structure and its Marxian phraseology after its Second Congress in 1968. FRELIMO moved to implement democratic centralism and a cell structure as left-wing elements consolidated control over the national front; this leftward movement was accompanied by bitter internal struggles that resulted in several murders. The first president, Eduardo Mondlane, was assassinated by a book bomb in 1969. A troika ran FRELIMO for six months until Samora Moisés Machel, head of the military arm, took over the presidency as well as the army. Machel presided over the transformation of FRELIMO from a nationalist front to a communist party organization. He died in an airplane crash in October 1986, and Chissano was chosen by the Central Committee to be the president (for additional information on Chissano, see *YICA*, 1987). As expected, the new president carried on his predecessors' policies of domestic pragmatism and dealings with Western countries and financial institutions without altering FRELIMO's basic policies and principles.

In 1977 the Third Congress approved the Central Committee's recommendation to transform FRELIMO into a "Marxist-Leninist vanguard party." Even before this announced change, FRELIMO had already structured its organization along typical communist party lines. The Central Committee (now 130 members), for example, is approved by the congress and is to carry out its policies. As in most communist structures, the Politburo shapes policy for FRELIMO. Many of its members also have ministerial portfolios and as such have seats on the Council of Ministers—the government's cabinet. According to Mozambique's constitution, the People's Assembly (250 members) is the country's highest legislative organ, with delegates chosen by an elaborate election process held every five years. But because of the countrywide warfare, an election was postponed until late 1986, and even then the war forced the abandonment of polling in dangerous areas. The first session of the second legislature was held in January, and dos Santos was elected chairman unanimously (Maputo Domestic Service, 13 January; *FBIS*, 14 January). FRELIMO also introduced local, district (112), and provincial assemblies (10). Constitutional provisions empower the president (who is also head of the party) to appoint provincial governors and members of the Council of Ministers, among others. Additionally, the president has the power to annul decisions made by the provincial assemblies. The Third Congress abolished the office of vice president, and FRELIMO officials have been relieved of ministerial duties and dispatched to posts as provincial or district leaders. They also serve as first secretaries of the party in their areas. The practice of strong, appointed district administrators follows the Portuguese tradition.

Ministerial reassignments and cabinet shuffles have been of a prevailing character. Before his death, Machel constituted the post of prime minister and appointed da Graça Machungo to fill it; he still holds the position. Early in the year under review, the president reshuffled the Council of Ministers and appointed Armando Nuno Guebuza minister of transport and communications, Matsinhe security minister, Mocumbi minister of foreign affairs, Feliciano Salomão Gundana minister in the presidency, Fernando Vaz health minister, Luís Bernardo Honwana minister of culture, Aguiar Real Mazula minister of labor, José Maria Igrejas Campos deputy health minister, Danial Simeão Mutemba Tete Province governor, Julião Massunchola Niassa Province governor, and António Fernando Materrula Zambezia Province governor. The president announced that this reshuffle was necessary after the Mbuzini (site of President Machel's plane crash) tragedy to implement the decisions adopted by the FRELIMO party Central Committee after its recent sixth session (Maputo Domestic Service, 12 January; *FBIS*, 12 January).

Mass Organizations. Like other ruling communist parties, FRELIMO set up mass organizations for different sectors of the population. During the guerrilla war for independence, the insurgent leadership focused on two key elements of the population—women and youth—that were important to winning the rural insurgency. The mass organizations of women and youth owed their initiation to wartime demands but grew and developed in the early independence period. The objectives of the

OMM focused on freeing women from their traditional roles and bettering them economically and politically. Specifically, OMM has sought to end child marriages, polygamy, and the bride price and to promote the role of women in the professions and the party. Like other mass organizations, the OMM also seeks to publicize and implement the party line in the country as a whole. Formed in 1973, it is the oldest and most active of the mass organizations.

FRELIMO founded the OJM after the Third Party Congress to mobilize young men between the ages of 18 and 35. Originally, OJM concentrated on urban youths to combat "bourgeois habits," but with the spread of the RENAMO insurgency, it has striven to solidify support for the regime and its military efforts.

FRELIMO set up Production Councils in 1976 to mobilize the workers' participation "in an active, collective and conscious way in the discussion and resolution of their problems, especially in relation to production and productivity" (*Notícias*, 12 November 1976). The war has slowed the countrywide establishment of councils at all mills, foundries, and factories. FRELIMO plans to establish national organizations for artists; journalists and others remain in rudimentary stages because of the demands of the war and the faltering economy. Reportage of representatives of the mass organizations attending meetings and rallies occurred several times during the year.

The People's Forces for the Liberation of Mozambique (FPLM). The FPLM remains a weak reed for the government to lean on. Demoralized and often beaten by RENAMO, the FRELIMO army depends on about 12,000 Zimbabwean troops who mostly patrol the Beira corridor. In Harare banking sources reportedly stated that the war costs Zimbabwe half a million dollars a day (*CSM*, 24 September). The Soviet Union is estimated to have as many as 1,000 advisers present, Cuba, some 2,000, and East Germany, 500. Soviet military assistance since independence was estimated by one source at $1 billion (*Insight*, vol. 2, no. 45, October 1986).

Soviet bloc specialists, particularly the East Germans, have played an important role in training the National Service for the People's Security (*Serviço Nacional de Segurança Popular*; SNASP), FRELIMO's secret police, which operates the prisons and re-education camps along with its security functions. On 11 October President Chissano addressed a Vigilance Day rally in Maputo to mark the 12th anniversary of the founding of the security organization. He proclaimed, "This is a working apparatus of the people, and its aim is to ensure that our people, state, and party take the right steps in their long march" (Maputo Domestic Service, 11 October; *FBIS*, 14 October).

The government issued stern warnings to the FPLM. Punitive measures would follow against "tardiness, drunkenness, black marketeering, and lack of control and responsibility over war materiel." (Maputo Domestic Service, 7 June; *FBIS*, 9 June.) Identifying such abuses called attention to the continuing problems plaguing FRELIMO's armed services whose ranks are filled by conscripted soldiers. Another census for the draft is scheduled for spring 1988.

Widespread recognition of the FPLM's inefficiency and poor performance was behind the government's far-reaching reshuffle of top military positions in June. President Chissano promoted General Antonio Hama Thai to chief of staff of the armed forces with the status of a deputy defense minister as he had done for Hama Thai's predecessor, Mabote. Formerly head of the Mozambican Air Force, General Hama Thai also served as governor of Tete Province, military commander of Inhambane Province, and chairman of the Maputo City Council. Hama Thai received credit for military success in the central province of Zambezi this year. Chissano announced no new post for General Mabote, who had held the post of chief of staff since Mozambican independence. The president also announced new commanders for the army, air force, and navy. He additionally named three new general directors to the Ministry of Defense along with other senior staff changes including appointing new military commanders in nine of the country's ten provinces. (Maputo in English to southern Africa, 20 June; *FBIS*, 23 June.) Despite the poor showing of the FPLM, Mozambique's defense consumes close to 50 percent of the state budget. FRELIMO hopes to reduce military expenditures to about 20 percent over the next three years in connection with its plan for international financial help (*Financial Times*, 13 July).

Heavily supported by foreign troops, FRELIMO achieved some military successes in the central region of the country. To the south, however, the FPLM proved unable to stop a series of RENAMO attacks, designed to isolate the capital, on buses, trucks, and railroad cars. A series of assaults occurred both north and south of Maputo toward the end of the year (*CSM*, 4 November). FRELIMO alleged that the rebels committed several massacres in the course of the year, the most internationally publicized of which reportedly took place at Homoine in Inhambane Province. RENAMO denied the charges and pointed to the lack of independent observers. Such charges and denials are a familiar pattern of guerrilla wars and have become a prominent feature of the war in Mozambique in 1987.

The heavy toll exacted by the ten-year war prompted Mozambique's Roman Catholic bishops to appeal, in a May pastoral letter, to both sides to negotiate. A month later, the FRELIMO government staged a rally in Maputo to criticize "a strange minority." One newspaper covering the rally stated that "some apostles of treason seek to present themselves piously as representatives of the people" (*Notícias*, 27 June).

Domestic Affairs. President Chissano continued the domestic program begun by his predecessor. Like Machel, the current president emphasized the central role of Marxism-Leninism in the country's economy but sought foreign assistance. Speaking in February before the secretariat members of some 400 party cells and representatives from mass organizations, Chissano explained that socialism is "the path to development." He made it clear that even though negotiations had transpired with the International Monetary Fund and "other financial organizations, this does not mean that it is relinquishing its principles." (Maputo Domestic Service, 3 February; *FBIS*, 6 February.)

A month earlier, the People's Assembly gave its approval to the Economic Rehabilitation Program (ERP), one important dimension of which called for adequate defense against RENAMO attacks. Another aspect is encouraging farmers to grow more agricultural produce by liberalizing the previously fixed prices. Without adequate compensation for food, farmers preferred to barter their produce for salt or clothes rather than sell to the urban centers. From green belts around Maputo, Beira, and Tete, farmers with new higher price incentives began to supply the town markets. Since July 1986 homegrown fruits and vegetables have been available to urban dwellers, albeit at high prices. The government announced large price increases in February for foodstuffs. In small towns, where the cost of living is lower than in large cities, the increases were greater than in Maputo and Beira. As part of the economic recovery program, some wages were also increased and the currency, the metrical, was devalued (Maputo in English to southern Africa, 26 February; *FBIS*, 27 February).

The ERP also called for the channeling of resources to agriculture, especially family farms. The new plan calls for 1981 production levels by 1990 and also entails a drop in the urban population as its living standard drops due to dismissals of thousands of state employees and workers in nonprofitable enterprises. The government intends to encourage these people to return to the countryside and take up farming (*Country Report: Tanzania, Mozambique*, no. 2, 1987).

Much of the economic activity of the year focused on Beira, the country's second-largest city and port terminus for the land corridor stretching across Mozambique from Zimbabwe. Repeated attacks on the rail and road traffic in the Beira corridor made Beira a virtual ghost town. Stepped-up security during the past eighteen months increased usage of the port by landlocked Zambia and Zimbabwe. According to Mozambican figures, traffic along the Beira corridor increased 87 percent between January and May over an equivalent period in 1986 (*African Business*, South Africa, September). Mozambican trade minister Aranda de Silva reported in late August that industrial growth increased 34 percent in the first six months. He added that exports expanded by 32 percent and that agriculture went up 17 percent in comparison with last year (Maputo Domestic Service, 29 August; *FBIS*, 1 September).

Food production increases were noted around the capital. The figures were usual compared with those of 1981, the last year of improved output in foodstuffs for specific areas. The Gaza market, for example, announced that it had achieved 86 percent of its rice quota (Maputo Domestic Service, 6 November; *FBIS*, 10 November). The fall harvest figures were widely reported in government newspapers and magazines (see, for example, *Tempo*, 25 October).

Such increases should be taken into account as only comparisons with previous years. Mozambique remains a desolate and impoverished land. Progress is marked by pockets of development rather than a broad, even expansion of production across the country or within one industry. Outside these areas of increased production life continues to be precarious. Prices fixed by the government, disastrous planning by FRELIMO's rigid and ill-suited central bureaucracies, and RENAMO sabotage exacted heavy tolls in agricultural and industrial output. Since 1980 exports have declined by two-thirds. Mozambique's gross national product has fallen by 50 percent from 1981, and its foreign debt stands in excess of $3.2 billion, requiring $90 million in annual interest payments. Exports reach only about $80 million a year (*WSJ*, 20 April). Mozambique managed a rescheduling of $400 million in repayments in June in government loans at the Paris Club and $200 million in commercial loans with the London Club. It also secured $700 million for 1987 from donor states at the July meeting of the World Bank (*Financial Times*, London, 13 July).

International Affairs. The insurgency remains as pivotal a factor in the conduct of FRELIMO's foreign affairs as the handling of domestic policies. In this regard, President Chissano's first year in office as head of state witnessed no significant departures from his predecessor in Mozambique's international policies. Chissano continued pragmatic relations with Western states and international financial institutions, signaled by Mozambique's signing of the 1984 Nkomati Accords with South Africa. This nonaggression pact forbade either signatory from offering support to insurgent groups opposed to the respective governments. Hence, it required that FRELIMO deny aid to the African National Congress and the South African Communist Party; South Africa is prohibited from supporting RENAMO. This year as last year, both sides charged the other with violations of the accords. FRELIMO has found it difficult to provide demonstrable proof to independent observers of Pretoria's aid (*NYT*, 30 August).

FRELIMO's successful overtures to Western states and financial institutions are detailed above. These loans were directed toward rebuilding the domestic economy. Mozambique also received much foreign food assistance. The European Economic Community, for example, announced that the Southeast African country was to receive the latest amount of its new aid—55 tons of cereals. The United States provided $10 million in economic aid and $75 million in food aid in 1987 in an effort to wean Mozambique from the Soviet orbit. As one proof of American success, U.S. State Department officials pointed to Mozambique's vote at the U.N. on the Afghanistan issue. In the years immediately following the Soviet invasion of Afghanistan, FRELIMO voted against U.N. resolutions calling on Moscow to withdraw. More recently, Mozambique has not voted against the measure. In November, the FRELIMO government's vote was recorded in the "absent or not voting" category (*NYT*, 11 November). Nor did Mozambique abstain. Therefore, it did not vote with 123 nations calling for a Soviet withdrawal of military forces.

America's friendlier relations with Mozambique generated opposition by conservatives in the United States. In the Senate, the opposition, led by Senator Jesse Helms, held up the confirmation of Melissa Foelsch Wells, the Reagan administration's nominee as ambassador to Mozambique, for almost a record-breaking ten months because, in part, of her labeling RENAMO as "bandits"–the FRELIMO characterization of its opponents. She was confirmed by the Senate in September (*LAT*, 10 September). The opposition also raised questions about the thrust of U.S. policy toward Mozambique as devised by the assistant secretary of state for Africa, Chester Crocker (*WP*, 6 May). Opposition to warmer relations between Washington and Maputo may have been responsible for a halt in plans to provide additional aid to Mozambique toward the end of 1987. Chissano met with President Ronald Reagan in November but was unsuccessful in securing more assistance. FRELIMO opponents staged demonstrations and met with high administration officials in Washington, D.C. (*WP*, 10 November).

Italy canceled Mozambique's $100 million debt and transformed a loan for a Maputo glass factory into a grant. FRELIMO also sought to establish diplomatic relations with the Vatican; Chissano raised the issue again during his audience with Pope John Paul II this year. But the Holy See wants the removal of restrictions on the movements of priests, the return of confiscated church property, and the reopening of closed Catholic missions in the country (*Inform Africa*, vol. 1, June).

Mozambique also received substantial military assistance to restore its combat capability. This year witnessed the dispatch of Malawian troops to Mozambique to protect the railway to the northern port of Nacala (*STAR*, South Africa, 5 March). Previously, Malawi had been viewed as a client of South Africa and a supporter of RENAMO. The British government expanded its military aid, and its army training base at Nyanga, Zimbabwe, doubled the intake of Mozambican officers from 60 to 120. By year's end, some 480 Mozambican officers were to be trained by British officers. The Commonwealth nations meeting in Vancouver during October decided to make "appropriate contribution to the security needs of Mozambique and other front-line states requiring such help (*NYT*, 8 November). They specified that their aid was to protect the rebuilding of the transportation routes across Mozambique.

Although FRELIMO's pragmatic foreign policy dictated responsiveness to the overtures from the West and international financial institutions in return for economic aid, it maintained friendly relations with the Soviet bloc. The minister of information, Teodato Hunguana, while in London stated that, "Mozambique is not shifting from one side to another, from West to East. We are staying at the same point, defending our independence." He added, "The Soviet Union has been an historic ally" (*Times*, London, 7 March). In November FRELIMO "saluted the 70th anniversary of the Great October Socialist Revolution" (Maputo Domestic Service, 5 November; *FBIS*, 6 November). In return, Moscow dispatched "anniversary greetings" on the occasion of FRELIMO's celebration of 25 years since its founding. The *Pravda* article also noted "the friendship and cooperation between our countries is cemented by the treaty whose 10th anniversary was widely marked in the spring of this year." The CPSU Central Committee wished, "dear comrades, the FRELIMO party, and the entire Mozambican people, success in your just struggle" (*Pravda*, 25 June; *FBIS-USSR International Affairs*, 1 July).

The Soviet Union also furnished nonmilitary aid to Mozambique, announcing in March that it would provide $15 million in fuel, food, and consumer goods for 1987 (Maputo Domestic Service, 27 March; *FBIS*, 30 March). In May the USSR issued a grant of a three-year commercial credit for $48 million along with $8 million in supplementary aid (Maputo Domestic Service, 8 May; *FBIS-USSR International Affairs*, 21 May). The Soviet Union also announced an accord to rehabilitate the Mozambican National Petroleum Enterprise, modernize a foundry, and restore the Beira-Moatize railroad (Maputo Domestic Service, 11 March; *FBIS*, 12 March). At a dinner held in the Kremlin to honor him, President Chissano stated that "we are guided by the same wish to foster the bonds between our two nations." Later in the same address, he held that Mozambique was equal to its problems "by the will of our parties, the realism of their leadership, the inexhaustible potential of socialism, and the friendship and solidarity of our peoples" (*IB*, October). The Soviet Union demonstrated its continuing support of FRELIMO, despite the party's pragmatic relations with the West, in another way. In November, Moscow dispatched several warships from the Soviet Navy to Maputo. Rear Admiral Vitaly Dornopik, commander of the fleet, stated that the ships "are ready to repel any enemy attack" (Maputo Domestic Service, 9 November; *FBIS*, 10 November).

Relations with South Africa remained strained this year. The two countries charged each other with harboring and aiding their enemies who strike across their common border. The African National Congress, the South African opposition movement, did hold its 75th anniversary celebration at the Mozambique Trade Fair grounds in Maputo (Maputo Domestic Service, 8 January; *FBIS*, 9 January). Relations fell still further when FRELIMO held South Africa responsible for the airplane death of Machel, the then-president, on October 19, 1986. A South African commission of inquiry, on which a number of prominent international aviation experts sat including former U.S. astronaut Frank Borman, pointed to errors by the crew on Machel's plane. Midyear, however, Mozambique and South Africa agreed to set up a joint commission to investigate the Homoine massacre. Maputo had accused South Africa of complicity in the massacre in which 400 villagers were reputedly killed by RENAMO guerrillas. The establishment of such a joint commission was viewed at the time as a positive step in smoothing relations between the two (*WP*, 7 August). Mozambique also entered into meetings with South Africa and Portugal on tripartite means to restore power lines from the giant Cahora Bassa dam on the Zambesi River. The Mozambicans and South Africans have set up an ad hoc military commission to protect the 800 kilometers of lines from the dam to South Africa. In addition to providing military support, Pretoria is also assisting in the financing to repair some 522 sabotaged power pylons. South Africa also appeared to be pressuring RENAMO not to repeat its attacks on the power lines (*Inform Africa*, vol. 1, December). These South African overtures indicated a possible alteration in Pretoria's policies and actions toward Mozambique at year's end.

Publications. FRELIMO controls the media. The party uses a number of print publications as well as broadcasts to put forth information and messages, using, for example, the daily paper *Notícias*; the *Diário de Moçambique* in Beira; a Sunday paper, *Domingo*; and a national magazine, *O Tempo* (for additional background, see *YICA*, 1982), *Voz da Revolução* deals with Marxist theory and FRELIMO policies. This year the party initiated *Economia*, a new publication under the direction of the Chamber of Commerce, in line with FRELIMO'S pragmatism in stimulating limited commercial enterprise.

Thomas H. Henriksen
Hoover Institution

Nigeria

Population. 97,383,000 (*Political Handbook of the World, 1987*)
Party. Socialist Working People's Party (SWPP)
Founded. 1963 (SWPP, 1978)
Membership. No data
General Secretary. Dapo Fatogun
Politburo. 4 members: Chaika Anozie (chairman), Wahab Goodluck (deputy chairman), Hassan Sunmonu, Lasisi A. Osunde
Central Committee. No data
Status. Proscribed
Last Congress. First, November 1978
Last Election. August–September 1983, SWPP ineligible
Auxiliary Organizations. No data
Publications. *New Horizon*

The ongoing ban on political party activity, dating from the December 31, 1983, coup, continued to restrict the possibilities for Marxist (as well as non-Marxist) political organization and mobilization in Nigeria during 1987. However, Marxist and socialist sentiment was again evident in intellectual and political life, and the adoption of a plan for transition to a new civilian, democratic political system appeared to open renewed opportunities for popular political mobilization by the socialist and Marxist left in coming years.

Although explicitly communist parties have never been a significant presence in Nigeria and although the defunct (Marxist) SWPP never established a base of support during the late Second Republic (1979–1983), the general secretary of the SWPP, Dapo Fatogun, has recently become visible again through his publication of the journal *New Horizon*.

In the latter part of 1986, the Marxist left joined the national debate over the structure of a new political system for Nigeria with the release of a manifesto by the Nigerian Labor Congress (NLC). Present at its launching, along with Fatogun, were some of Nigeria's leading socialist and Marxist trade unionists, including Michael Imoudu, Wahab O. Goodluck, and Hassan Sunmuno (recent past president of the NLC and now secretary general of the Organization of African Trade Union Unity). The introduction to the manifesto, by current NLC president Alhaji Ali Chiroma, seeks to rebut the argument that socialism is alien to Nigerian tradition and culture. Characterizing Nigeria as a capitalist, neocolonial country incapable of independent development, the manifesto asserts "that only a socialist option can ensure a viable and stable political and economic arrangement in Nigeria." It goes on to call for "socialization of the means of production, distribution and exchange" and a working class political party, along with extensive state efforts to improve mass welfare and to ensure "equal participation of all ethnic groups in politics." In addition to being published in full by *New Horizon* (September 1986), the manifesto was given prominent attention in *The African Communist* (no. 109, 2d Quarter).

The appeal of socialism to a significant segment of the Nigerian intelligentsia was indicated in the report of the Political Bureau, a seventeen-member committee—composed largely of university professors—appointed at the beginning of 1986 to propose a new political system for the country. In addition to extensive political proposals for a presidential system of two (and only two) parties, the Political Bureau (or "Politburo," as it became popularly known) also recommended a socialist economic system for Nigeria. State ownership should be extended, it said, throughout the "commanding heights" of the economy. The private sector would not be abolished but would be limited to agriculture and small-to-medium-scale enterprises. Each party would have to subscribe to a national philosophy of socialism.

Although the military regime rejected the Political Bureau's recommendations of a socialist system and a constitutionally mandated national philosophy of socialism, it largely accepted the political recommendations, while extending the timetable for the transition from 1990 to 1992. The program got off the ground (albeit rather shakily) at the end of 1987 with nationwide voter registration and elections on 12 December, on a nonpartisan basis, for local government councils. These steps are to be followed by the lifting of the ban on party politics in the second quarter of 1989; the recognition of two political parties (third quarter, 1989); partisan local government elections (fourth quarter, 1989); election of state legislatures and governors in the first half of 1990; election of a National Assembly in the first half of 1992; and election and inauguration of a president in the second half of that year.

Although party formation and organization remain proscribed until 1989, behind-the-scenes maneuvering and public gesturing have already begun in earnest. Among the groupings that figure to be significant in the competition for party recognition is the former People's Redemption Party (PRP), which controlled the two most powerful northern states, Kano and Kaduna, during the Second Republic. Based largely in the Muslim north, the PRP established a considerable following among peasants and the urban poor of that area, along with intellectuals and university students around the country. Its platform was a combination of Marxist rhetoric and ideology and democratic socialist programs.

The PRP's most popular political leader, Alhaji Abdulkadir Balarabe Musa—who was impeached and removed as governor of Kaduna State in a power struggle with conservative interests in 1981—is one of the few prominent politicians of the Second Republic to have been cleared of any wrongdoing during the military tribunals of the past four years. Although he, like all other former government and party officeholders from the two civilian regimes, will be banned from taking part in electoral politics until after 1992, he has begun to reassert his political presence through public lectures and interviews and the formation in 1986 of *The Analyst*, a new monthly features magazine. Balarabe Musa, the publisher, wrote in its first edition that the magazine was born at a time when Nigeria was searching for a new social, economic, and political order. A leading Marxist intellectual said the magazine would serve as a rallying point for Nigerian radicals (*Newswatch*, Lagos, 6 April).

Radical left (socialist and Marxist) elements will no doubt play a significant role in the emerging new political system, but, ironically, they may be disadvantaged by the political recommendations of the left-leaning Political Bureau because the mandatory limitation of the new political sytem to two political parties makes it unlikely that the radicals will be able to have a party of their own. Rather they will probably have to settle for inclusion in a broad progressive party in which they may have a strategic but nevertheless minority status. Furthermore, the popular base of the radical left in the Muslim north is in danger of erosion from competing populist mobilization by Islamic fundamentalists. Relations between leftists and Islamic fundamentalist student groups in the north have been tense, and many radicals believe that northern conservatives have helped finance and foster radical Islamic mobilization—which exploded into violent confrontation with Christians in the north during 1987—as a way of diverting popular support from the radical left.

In foreign affairs, Nigeria continued to balance its generally Western orientation with limited but cordial Eastern bloc ties. In mid-December, Nigeria signed a new bilateral trade agreement with the Soviet Union. The Nigerian minister of trade noted, at the signing ceremony in Abuja, the cordial relationship the two countries enjoy in cultural and economic affairs, as reflected in the development of the Ajaokuta steel complex being built with Soviet assistance. The Soviet ambassador extraordinary, Yuriy Kuplyakov, said his country was determined to expand other frontiers of agreement with Nigeria in cultural, scientific, and technological fields (*FBIS*, 11 December). In August, Nigeria signed a trade agreement with Czechoslovakia that will provide $120 millon in credit facilities to finance public sector projects and small- and medium-sized industrial ventures in Nigeria (ibid., 18 August). Reiterating its commitment to liberation in South Africa, the Nigerian government offered in November to provide military training facilities to cadres of the African National Congress.

Larry Diamond
Hoover Institution

Réunion

Population. 549,697
Party. Réunion Communist Party (Parti communiste réunionnais; PCR)
Founded. 1959
Membership. 7,000 claimed; 2,000 estimated
General Secretary. Paul Vergès

Politburo. 12 members: Julien Ramin; remaining members unknown
Secretariat. 6 Members: Paul Vergès, Elie Hoarau, Jean-Baptiste Ponama, Lucet Langenier; remaining members unknown
Central Committee. 32 members: Bruny Payet, Roger Hoarau, Daniel Lallemand, Hippolite Piot, Ary Yee Chong Tchi-Kan, Laurent Vergès; remaining members unknown
Status. Legal
Last Congress. Fifth, 12–14 July 1980, in Le Port
Last Election. Legislative election, 16 March 1986, 29.2 percent; regional election, 16 March 1986, 28 percent; 13 of 45 in local assembly; 2 in Paris
Auxiliary Organizations. Anticolonialist Front for Réunion Autonomy; Réunion Front of Autonomous Youth; Réunion Peace Committee; Réunion General Confederation of Workers (CGTR); Committee for the Rally of Réunionese Unemplyed (CORC); Committee for the Rally of Réunionese Youth (CORJ); Réunion Union of Women (UFR); Réunion General Union of Workers in France (UGTRF); Réunion General Confederation of Planters and Cattlemen (CGPER)
Publications. *Témoignages* (daily), Elie Hoarau, chief editor; *Travailleur Réunionnais* (semimonthly), published by CGTR; *Combat Réunionnais*, published by UGTRF

Unlike communist parties in two other French overseas departments, Martinique and Guadeloupe, the PCR made no claims for autonomy and eventual independence of its island. On the contrary, the party leaders consistently called for greater integration with metropolitan France. "Equality" with the people of metropolitan France must be achieved, and anything short of it is racism and colonial oppression, in their view.

Differing from communist parties in France and overseas departments, the PCR is dominated by two families, the Vergès and the Hoaraus. Raymond Vergès was one of the founders of the PCR, and the 30th anniversary of his death was marked on 2 July with considerable solemnity. His portrait hangs in party headquarters with a portrait of his son Paul superimposed on it. Paul Vergès, the current secretary general of the party, served as one of Réunion's deputies in the French National Assembly until he resigned on 14 October to protest the alleged inequality of French citizens in Réunion compared with French citizens in the metropolis. He was succeeded by Laurent Vergès who early in the year led a general assembly of party members at Saint-André. Paul's twin brother, Jacques, is also a well-known personality in Réunion; most recently he served as the defense attorney for Arab terrorists in a Paris court as well as the attorney for former Gestapo chief Klaus Barbie.

The other communist deputy, Elie Hoarau, resigned as a representative to the French National Assembly when Paul Vergès resigned and was succeeded by Claude Hoarau. Roger Hoarau served as vice president of the Regional Council.

Vergès' and Hoarau's resignations stemmed from their assertion that social benefits, particularly with respect to family allowances, are higher in metropolitan France than in Réunion, which is supposed to be an integral part of France. They also were protesting the judicial system in the island, which they claimed discriminated against communists. They said that the results of the many cases of electoral fraud and related infractions of the law showed communists receiving greater penalties than noncommunists.

Electoral fraud led to three elections for seats on the General Council and one for a seat on a municipal council. The candidates of the PCR won two seats on the General Council; the results of the third election were disputed by the party. The party claimed its candidate had won, but a court ruled otherwise. In the course of the year a scandal concerning the issuance of false identity cards to permit citizens from the neighboring island of Mauritius to vote in Réunion was revealed. The PCR claimed that its opponents had organized the Mauritian vote to weaken the left.

Throughout the year the party called on Paris to help Réunion's economy. Exports pay for only 12 percent of imports; unemployment has reached 80,000, and the party expects it to climb to 110,000 in 1992. Agriculture, the traditional mainstay of the majority of people, has steadily declined, and French prime minister Jacques Chirac's government proposes a program of outside investments and tourism to solve the island's problems. (From the party's point of view, outside investments and tourism will only weaken the local economy.) Hurricane Clotilda damaged thousands of fields and houses in January 1987, and the French government sent aid. The party complained that Réunion has become a center for drug trafficking.

In an effort to deal with some of Réunion's problems and to build electoral support, Prime Minister Chirac visited Réunion and promised more assistance. The minister for overseas departments and territories, Bernard, also stopped in Réunion and promised eventual and complete equality with metropolitan France. Complete integration with France and equality with other French citizens would be compatible, in PCR eyes, with a particular Réunion cultural identity. Thus, the PCR supported the extended use of the Creole language, and its daily newspaper, *Témoignages*, devoted several issues to a discussion of this language. PCR journalists complained that efforts to promote Creole by writing letters to the local administration in Creole were rebuffed by officials, who requested the exclusive use of French. The party newspaper praised the publication of a new Creole-French dictionary as well as the publication of a novel, *Faims d'Enfance* by Axel Gauvin, that evoked the distinctiveness of Réunion's culture. The party noted with approval the publication of another book by the socialist Albert Ramasamy and was also pleased with the author of *La Réunion: Décolonisation et intégration*, who called for the island's complete absorption politically and economically by France.

Integration into the European Economic Community, projected for 1992, raised concerns for the economy of Réunion. The disappearance of barriers to the free flow of goods, services, and people would devastate the local economy, in the PCR view. Local products and labor would be unable to compete effectively, and an influx of workers from outside the island would weaken Réunion's special character, in their view. Paul Vergès delivered a report on these issues to the European parliament. By year's end the matter had not been resolved, although the European community expressed the desire to help France's overseas departments adjust.

The communist-affiliated trade union, General Confederation of Réunion Labor, conducted several party-supported strikes during the year. They also held their Sixth Congress 6–8 November, during which they discussed the economic problems facing Réunion. *Témoignages* newspaper carried the party banner throughout the island, and party members celebrated the annual fete for the newspaper 2–11 October.

Brian Weinstein
Howard University

Senegal

Population. 7,064,025
Party. Independence and Labor Party (Parti de l'indépendance du travail; PIT)
Founded. 1957
Membership. No data
General Secretary. Amath Dansoko
Politburo. 14 members: Amath Dansoko, Samba Dioulde Thiam, Maguette Thiam, Mady Danfaka, Sadio Camara, Seydou Ndongo, Semou Pathe Gueye, Makhtar Mbaye, Bouma Gaye, Mohamed Laye (names of other 4 not known)
Secretariat. 7 members: Amath Dansoko, Semou Pathe Gueye, Maguette Thiam, Samba Dioulde Thiam, Mady Danfaka, Makhtar Mbaye (replacement of Seydou Cissoko not yet named)
Central Committee. 55 members (secretary: Semou Pathe Gueye)
Status. Legal
Last Congress. Second, 28 September–2 October 1984, in Dakar
Last Election. 1983, 0.5 percent, no seats
Auxiliary Organization. Women's Democratic Union
Publications. *Daan Doole*, *Gestu*

There were no major developments or inroads for Senegal's several Marxist and leftist parties in 1987. In the six years since the full legalization of opposition parties in 1981, Senegalese communists, Marxists, and assorted leftists and Trotskyites remained badly splintered among several parties and completely overshadowed by the ruling Socialist Party (PS), which controls 111 of the 120 seats in the National Assembly. Even among the fifteen opposition parties, the liberal ("bourgeois") Senegalese Democratic Party (PDS) remained, despite a serious internal split, the most dominant and active force. (For a brief guide to Senegal's Marxist and other parties, see *YICA*, 1986.)

Of the half-dozen or more Marxist parties, the PIT continued to enjoy the official recognition of Moscow but remained more active on the international than the national stage. The two best-known figures of the PIT—Dansoko, 50, general secretary since 1984, and Gueye, a Politburo member and

Central Committee secretary—continued to appear frequently in *WMR* and at Soviet-sponsored international conferences. Gueye was among two dozen international communist leaders attending an international seminar in Prague on "The Developments of the Peace Movement in the 1980s and the Communists," where he delivered the usual appeals for international peace and disarmament and praise for Mikhail Gorbachev's peace initiatives (*WMR*, July). In a previous *WMR* contribution (November 1986) on the 1986 congress of the Socialist International in Lima, Peru, Gueye echoed the Soviet line at great length on such issues as preventing the militarization of outer space, declaring a moratorium on nuclear tests, and condemning the policies of the United States. He also reiterated his party's interest in a combined front of communists, socialists and Social Democrats taking part in the struggle for a new international economic order and other common goals, such as the ending of apartheid in South Africa.

In his own article (*WMR*, January), Dansoko condemned capitalist development strategies in Africa—and their recent resurgence under the direction of the World Bank and the International Monetary Fund (IMF)—while conceding that at some stages of the transition to socialism, "capitalism still has definite potential and possibilities in the Third World." But if its pernicious influence is to be controlled, "*the concentration of power in the hands of genuine spokesman of the people is essential*" (ibid., emphasis in the original).

Although contemptuous of democratic institutions and processes, the PIT is happy to operate in the relative freedom of Senegal's semidemocratic system. But at the level of real domestic politics, the PIT has yet to demonstrate significant popular support. Among Marxist parties, a more substantial presence on the Senegalese political scene in 1987 was the Democratic League/Movement for the Party of Labor (LD/MPT), and in particular its general secretary, Dr. Abdoulaye Bathily. (The LD is another pro-Soviet communist party, though not officially recognized by the USSR.) Bathily, a leading member of the loose and volatile alliance of opposition parties, early in the year joined with PDS leader Dr. Abdoulaye Wade (with whom he was arrested in a 1985 demonstration) in calling for sweeping reforms of the electoral law (now blatantly rigged to favor the ruling party) and a broad opposition alliance against the PS. But President Abdou Diouf again rejected firmly all appeals for electoral reform, and repeated efforts at unification of the opposition met with renewed frustration. Significantly, the two problems are linked because the electoral law forbids party alliances from sponsoring candidates for election.

The most persistent opposition grouping has been the five-party Democratic Alliance of Senegal, formed in 1985 by Wade (PDS), Bathily (LD/MPT) and three more-obscure Marxist parties (the Socialist Workers' Organization, the And Jef, and the New Democratic Union). But most opposition attempts at unity have been fragile and fleeting. In February eleven of the fifteen opposition parties, led by the PDS, joined in a statement denouncing government policies, including their violent suppression of a student strike at Dakar University and of separatist agitation in the Casamance region. But the hoped-for broad front failed to congeal.

Shortly thereafter, three smaller Marxist parties inaugurated a front of their own. Its organizing committee included the three party leaders—Majhmout Diop of the African Independence Party (the first legal communist party in Senegal, which follows a Marxist-Leninist line); Doudou Sarr of the Workers' Communist League (Trotskyist); and Abdoulaye Thiaw of the People's Democratic Movement (self-managed socialist)—along with some independent professionals (*FBIS*, 10 March). Also prominent in sponsoring the new group was Mamadou Dia, leader of the Democratic People's Movement and a powerful leader in the postindependence government, whose militant socialist views led him into a losing power struggle with President Senghor followed by a long prison sentence in 1962.

In a September interview with the influential London-based journal *West Africa* (28 September), Bathily said the LD/MPT and other major opposition parties had decided to adopt Wade as their candidate for the 1988 presidential elections. Bathily also condemned the economic liberalization and austerity policies being "imposed" on Senegal by the IMF and the World Bank, under pressure as well from the United States, and further denounced the growing political and military cooperation between Washington and Dakar.

In fact, the grim economic situation left the regime vulnerable to opposition protest and mobilization, especially from the left. The familiar package of IMF austerity measures—cutbacks in state employment and intervention, abolition of state subsidies for staple foodstuffs and petrol, and so on—has taken a harsh toll on the standard of living since 1983 without generating economic growth at a rate much beyond that for the rapidly burgeoning population. External debt ($2.6 billion in 1987) consumes about 20 percent of export earnings in service payments and 45 percent of real budgetary earnings (*FBIS*, 27 July). Although Diouf's liberalization measures have won high praise from American and international officials, they have not brought any increase in economic assistance (*CSM*, 8 September), and a low world price for groundnuts has required heavy state price subsidies to farmers. These circumstances give credence to the claims of leftist leaders, such as Bathily, that capitalist economic reforms cannot work, and escalate the public disaffection that might be mobilized either by the left or by the Islamic fundamentalists.

The continuing economic malaise was compounded by other problems for the ruling party. The February strike of university students was followed in April by a shattering, nationwide police strike in reaction to the jailing of seven policemen for torturing a criminal. Both developments grew in part out of the diffuse social and economic malaise, and the police strike resulted in the dismissal of the entire police force, only part of which was reinstated. Continuing separatist agitation in the culturally distinct Casamance region adds to the insecurity.

On the foreign front, Senegal continued to maintain warm relations with the Soviet Union, despite its increasing economic, diplomatic, and military ties with the United States. Senegalese foreign minister Ibrahima Fall gave a warm reception for Soviet ambassador Yuriy Belskiy on 4 July, the occasion of the latter's departure from his six-year mission in Dakar. Fall praised "the signing of over fifteen agreements, notably in the fields of culture, economy, water resources, and shipbuilding," and thanked the Soviet Union for its aid to the cause of liberation in southern Africa. In May PIT leader Dansoko, in Bulgaria for a five-day visit, was hosted by the Bulgarian Communist Party, which reiterated its "solidarity with the African peoples' struggle against imperialism and apartheid," and joined with Dansoko in hailing the historic initiatives of the USSR on nuclear disarmament and world peace (*JPRS*, 4 June). The Romanian Communist Party, in contrast, sent a message of greetings and "close militant solidarity" to a rival communist party, the PAI, on the occasion of its Fourth Congress on 1 February (*JPRS*, 12 March).

Larry Diamond
Hoover Institution

South Africa

Population. 34,313,356
Party. South African Communist Party (SACP)
Founded. 1921
Membership. No data
Chairman. Dan Tloome (68, teacher)
General Secretary. Joe Slovo (61, barrister)
Leading Organs. Composition unknown
Status. Proscribed
Last Congress. Sixth, late 1984 or early 1985
Last Election. N/a
Auxiliary Organizations. None
Publications. *African Communist* (quarterly, published abroad); *Umsebenzi* (published clandestinely in South Africa)

Africa's oldest Marxist-Leninist party, the South African Communist Party (SACP), continues to operate illegally both within the country of its birth and in exile in close alliance with the also banned and clandestine African National Congress (ANC), South Africa's major black nationalist organization, presently headquartered in Lusaka, Zambia. Founded in 1921 in Cape Town as the Communist Party of South Africa, the party operated as a fully legal but often harassed multiracial political party until it dissolved itself in June 1950 in the face of an impending ban under the Suppression of Communism Act. Reconstituting itself underground in 1953 as the SACP, the party was active internally but only revealed its existence in the post-Sharpeville state of emergency in 1960 when the ANC was also proscribed and forced underground.

In the new clandestine conditions, which were contrary to the ANC tradition of open and legal existence that had prevailed since its establishment in 1912, the ANC and SACP drew together. Leaders of both organizations (including the now imprisoned Nelson Mandela of the ANC and Slovo, the present general secretary of the SACP) joined together secretly within South Africa in 1961 to establish Umkhonto we Sizwe, the military wing of the ANC that was organized to conduct sabotage and train cadres for eventual armed struggle. Forced into exile in the early 1960s by the successful campaign of the South African government to smash the infant internal underground organizations of Umkhonto, the ANC, and the SACP, those leaders who escaped imprisonment crafted an ever closer relationship built on their shared commitment to oust the Nationalist government and to end apartheid. Strengthened by the resurgence of black opposition within South Africa in 1970s and by an infusion of younger recruits fleeing South Africa in the wake of the Soweto uprising of 1976, the ANC, Umkhonto, and the SACP have successfully reestablished an underground presence within the country, highlighted by often widely publicized successful sabotage and armed attacks by Umkhonto cadres on government forces and installations.

In the guardedly optimistic view of the Central Committee of the SACP, "the situation in our country is characterized by a sharpening confrontation between the revolutionary forces on one hand and the fascist regime on the other . . . it is clear that the heightened political and military offensive [under the liberation alliance headed by the ANC] served further to shift the balance of forces in favor of the democratic revolution. This has forced the apartheid regime to resort to extreme reaction, confirming the tendency we have observed before, that this regime can no longer rule in the old way." (*African Communist*, no. 109.) "The prestige of our liberation alliance, headed by the ANC, has grown to unprecendented levels both inside the country and internationally. The ANC stands in an uncontested position as the leader of the democratic forces that represent the future just social order which both our people and the rest of the world wish to see established in South Africa . . . the broad democratic movement and the masses of our people have continued decisively to rebuff the enemy's efforts to turn them into an appendage of the reactionary anticommunist forces. On the contrary, thanks to their selfless contribution in the political and military struggle for the destruction of the apartheid system, the communists of our country have won for themselves and their party, the SACP, the respect of the masses of our people. This has put our party in an even better position to make its own contribution to the victory of the people's cause." (ibid.)

Organization and Leadership. Operating in exile in Africa and in Europe, the top leadership of the SACP was reshuffled by the Central Committee early in the year. Tloome, longtime member of the Central Committee, was elected chairman, replacing Slovo, who was named general secretary, thus filling a post that has been vacant since the death of Moses Mabhida in March 1986. The shifting of the chief party officers suggests a return to traditional party practice in which "the Chairman has been the premier diplomatic and public presence, while the General Secretary has been the principal political and administrative figure" (*African Communist*, no. 106).

Both Tloome and Slovo are representative of the older generation who joined the then-legal party in the 1940s but who subsequently were active in reestablishing the clandestine SACP in the 1950s before following party orders in 1963 to leave the country to work with the exiled leadership of the ANC. In his more than two decades in exile, Tloome has served in a variety of representational posts, whereas Slovo has been at the center of strategic planning within Umkhonto and prominent as an articulator of policy for the SACP and its allies.

Tloome, the new chairman of the SACP, is a 68-year-old African who originally trained as a teacher. From the early years of the World War II until he was banned from open political activity in 1953, Tloome participated widely in the trade union movement and the ANC in the Johannesburg area. After a decade of behind-the-scenes activity within South Africa, in exile he returned to more visible positions, serving on the executive committees of the ANC, the South African Congress of Trade Unions, and the Central Committee of the SACP, representing "one or other of these organizations at many international conferences" (*African Communist*, no. 109).

Slovo, now in the position of general secretary, is a 61-year-old Lithuanian-born barrister who has been active in the party since the late 1940s. Prominent in the 1950s and early 1960s as a defender of members of the ANC and its allied organizations charged by the government, Slovo, since going into exile, has been intimately involved with organizing armed struggle for the ANC. In 1964 he became a member of the Revolutionary Council of the ANC and subsequently, chief of staff of Umkhonto, receiving recognition as the first white elected to the National Executive Committee of the ANC in 1985 when non-Africans became eligible for membership on the ANC's directing body. In the assessment of a party writer, Slovo "has, in recent years, become acknowledged as the party leader who makes many of the important keynote speeches of the organization . . . he has certainly become the movement's foremost writer on themes of military-political strategy and the draftsman of many crucial theses which have shaped the present strategy and tactics of the whole South African revolution" (ibid., no. 106).

Slovo's installation as general secretary apparently reflected a Central Committee assessment that his demonstrated administrative and leadership talents would ensure that the SACP maximized opportunities for strengthening and growth. In this vein Chairman Tloome successfully requested that the ANC leadership relieve Slovo of his functions of chief of staff of Umkhonto, arguing that "the tasks and duties which now rest on his shoulders have multiplied immensely. As the leading public officer of our party and its chief spokesman, he is called upon increasingly to devote himself to elaborating and projecting its policies and perspectives and to participate in numerous exchanges with both internal and international groups. In addition he must play an important part in ensuring that our leading collective vigorously pursues its task of ensuring that our party carries out its duties as part of our great liberation alliance and as a force representing the historic aspirations of our working class." (*African Communist*, no. 110.)

The nature of the relationship between the SACP and the ANC in the "liberation alliance" continues to be a central issue for leaders of both organizations, particularly amidst continuing charges in the European and American press that the SACP dominates the ANC and in the wake of the January publication of the Department of State brochure "Communist Influence in South Africa," in which the ANC was characterized as deeply obligated to the Soviet Union and to the SACP for military assistance to wage armed struggle and in which it was claimed that "roughly half" of the ANC National Executive Committee were known or suspected party members. Both organizations readily and explicitly recognize their intimate cooperation, but each organization is clear about its separate and independent status.

Reacting to the suggestion of the State Department brochure that the Soviet Union and the SACP would exploit their association with the ANC to seek domination of any future ANC government, Oliver Tambo, president of the ANC, asserted, "because we are getting arms from them for free does not mean we are mortgaging ourselves. And I dominate the ANC. Yes, I dominate, I am not dominated and controlled." (*NYT*, 24 January.)

An ANC commentator offered a broader assessment of the linkage between the ANC and the SACP in the offical ANC publication: "If there is any kind of influence that the communist party has had on the ANC, in our own experience, it has been to make us stauncher nationalists and democrats. Communists have demonstrated by personal example what is meant by dedication and heroism in the struggle against national oppression. When some groups and individuals have criticized the ANC for being 'backward' or even 'bourgeois' by not including a socialist clause in its program, it has been members of the communist party who have been the first to defend the ANC's national democratic program, and the need for the ANC not to 'narrow' its objectives." (*Sechaba*, July, 1987.)

Brian Bunting, editor of the *African Communist*, offers a complementary long-term assessment from the SACP perspective: "A process of cross-pollination occurred between the communist party and the national movement. On the one hand the communist party achieved and incorporated in its program a truer understanding of the nature and importance of the national movement than it ever had before. On the other hand the national movement was moved toward an appreciation of the class forces which underlie the national conflict in South Africa and to perceive the relationship between the national struggle of the oppressed people of South Africa and the international movement against imperialism and war. The nationalism of the ANC . . . developed an international dimension; the communist party was indigenized." (*Communist Viewpoint*, March.)

From the perspective of Slovo, general secretary of the SACP, "the alliance between the ANC and our party has very deep roots in our South African condition. There are no secret clauses and no hidden agenda in this alliance. The stability and closeness of the relationship and the participation of individual communists in the leading echelons of the national, trade union, and other mass movements has its roots in our party's historically evolved style of work in relation to the mass movements. We have always respected and defended the independence, integrity, and the inner democratic processes of the mass organizations. To act otherwise is to suffocate them as creative organs and to confuse manipulation with leadership." (*WMR*, June.) Speaking of the ANC he stated that "we consider it to be a sort of parliament, which at present represents the interests not only of the workers' class, but of all components of the national liberation movement. We think it is correct that the ANC is at the head of our struggle for freedom." (*FBIS*, 4 February.)

In keeping with the SACP program of 1962, which postulates that South Africa must first undergo a national democratic revolution before the possibilities of achieving socialism can be entertained, the SACP has a very specific view of the role of the party beyond its responsibilities as an integral component of the "liberation alliance." As Slovo put it on the occasion of the party's 65th anniversary celebrations in 1986, "unlike the ANC, which does not and should not commit itself exclusively to the aspirations of a single class, the SACP owes allegiance solely to the working people. And it is our prime function both as an independent party and as part of the alliance to assert and jealously safeguard the dominant role of the class whose aspirations we represent. In our book this does not imply that the party itself must seek to occupy the dominant position in the liberation alliance. On the contrary, if correct leadership of the democratic revolution requires the strengthening of the national movement as the major and leading mass organization force, then this is precisely the way in which a party exercises its vanguard role in the real and not the vulgar sense of the term." (*African Communist*, no. 107.) Party writers have indicated, however, that conditions may well be such that with the achievement of the national democratic revolution "the working class will already have one foot on the ladder to socialism, to put it metaphorically. Under these conditions, there exists an objective possibility in South Africa for the national democratic revolution proceeding at once, without any interruption, without procrastination, without waiting for the advent of another 'October'... Whether this transition will be effected only by the communist party or it will be joined by a developed ANC (developed in the manner in which the MPLA [Popular Movement for the Liberation of Angola] and FRELIMO [Front for the Liberation of Mozambique] respectively reconstituted themselves as workers' parties), is a pure speculative question, to which we shall not address ourselves at this instance." (*African Communist*, no. 110.)

At present the exiled SACP and ANC members work together throughout Europe and Africa, primarily in the major centers of activity in Zambia, Tanzania, and Angola, as well as in the more dangerous underground in South Africa, almost certainly concentrated in the larger urban areas where support for both organizations is greatest. The party faces a special challenge establishing party structures within the country and linking them to the exiled leadership. In the candid estimation of Tloome, chairman of the SACP, the party has suffered substantially from government efforts to thwart its activities. "Over the past decade [the government] has managed to destroy a large section of our party apparatus and to seize and torture to death a number of our activists and leaders. But harassment has not prevented our party from organizing closer contact between its units and reinforcing the collective efforts of their activities." (*WMR* September.)

Domestic Activities and Attitudes. Party spokesmen have been heartened by developments in South Africa since the declaration of the first state of emergency in mid-1984. In the estimation of Gerneral Secretary Slovo, two crucial psychological barriers have been breached: "the people are now convinced that however long it may take, race rule can be destroyed and they are prepared to sacrifice life to bring this about" and conversely, "in the face of years of uninterrupted upsurge and resistance, confidence in the permanent survival of race rule has been very badly eroded" among "our ruling class and its support constituency in the white community, triggering off fragmentation, defections, in-fighting, and other symptoms of the beginnings of political disintegration of the previously relatively monolithic racist power bloc." (*WMR* June.)

On the one hand white workers are supporting the right-wing opposition Conservative Party and the extraparliamentary *Afrikaner Weerstandsbeweging*, while growing numbers of the white middle class, including Afrikaner students, are selectively identifying with important positions of the ANC and its allies. Elements within the "ruling class" are also expressing opposition to elements of government policy, finding that their "class interests are no longer served by old-style apartheid... this sector senses the inevitability of change and is beginning to seek a change involving the extension of varying forms of political democracy within the framework of capitalism and the retention by them of the ownership of all or most of the means of production. Despite these limitations, the reform-oriented bourgeoisie cannot be regarded as part of the main enemy camp. A serious revolutionary movement must work to broaden the base of opposition to the *main* enemy, implying everwidening varieties of opposition, some of which may not be motivated by revolutionary intentions. The same reasoning applies to the churches, disaffected sectors of the white middle strata, the growing liberal wing among white academics and students, and so on." (Ibid.)

Even more promising are the advances made by the black opposition—direct and open political challenges through rent strikes, opposition to government policies and institutions in both urban and rural areas, and periodic general strikes coordinated by the United Democratic Front and its more than 700 affiliated organizations, as well as by the still rapidly growing Congress of South African Trade Unions. "Their success demonstrated that we have the organizational capacity to respond to the increased resolve of the people to act, in fact to draw them into united national and local action as well as further to expand the organized strength of the democratic movement. In this connection one of the most significant developments is the establishment and multiplication of organs of people's power arising directly out of the stuggle to make the country ungovernable and apartheid unworkable. The emergence of street and area committees, people's courts, self-defense units, and workers' councils represents the birth of new organizational forms which root the revolutionary movement among the people and create additional elements which make ever more effective the conduct of the revolutionary struggle on all fronts." (*African Communist*, no. 109.)

According to General Secretary Slovo, "in the coming period we will continue to face many serious challenges not only in the theoretical field but, more importantly, in the field of revolutionary practice. The internal underground leadership, both of the party and of the national liberation movement, has to be strengthened. New ways have to be found to enable the mass legal organizations to adjust to the conditions of siege in which the country has been placed by the emergency. It is clear that room for open mass maneuver has been narrowed. High-profile street actions are no longer the answer and other ways have to be elaborated to sustain the offensive... But the narrowing of opportunities for mass legal and semilegal opposition makes even greater demands on the armed wing of our liberation movement. One of the key tasks is to find effective ways of providing links, leadership, and logistical support to the combat units that are emerging among the youth and among the workers. In general we are also called upon to streamline the organizational framework for broadening the base of the liberation front, to help bring even greater unity to the Trade Union Movement, and to continue to develop appropriate tactical responses to the enemy's counteroffensive in a situation which remains filled with promise for revolutionary advance." (*WMR*, June.)

The possibility of eventual negotiations with the South African government is recognized unambiguously: "*the bottom line for engaging in serious negotiations must be an acceptance of the principle of majority rule* (one person, one vote) *in one united democratic South Africa*. Once this is accepted as a starting point, many other questions can be tossed about including legislative provision to secure the rights of the individual, the safeguarding of the diverse cultural and linguistic heritage of the ethnic entities which make up our nation, and the precise shape of the democratic institutions which will replace the apartheid tyranny." (Ibid.)

"Another vital question relates to the postliberation economic structure. In approaching this question two imperatives must be reconciled: the need to begin bringing about changes in the relations of production in the direction of economic equalitarianism, and the need to meet the people's economic requirements and expectations. In the long term there is harmony between these two imperatives; indeed, the one is the necessary condition for the other. But enough experiences have been accumulated of disastrous great leaps forward to teach us to be wary of clumsy and overhasty pole vaults into socialism. In our South African context there will clearly be a place in the postliberation stage for many levels of nonmonopoly private enterprise." (*WMB*, June.)

International Views and Activities. Under the heading, "Soviet Union: A True Friend," a party commentator observed that "from our experience we know that the Soviet Union and the countries of the socialist community are our most consistent allies" (*African Communist*, no. 109). Other party commentators have spoken warmly of *glasnost'* and *perestroika* as well as of General Secretary Gorbachev's pronouncements on the national question in the Soviet Union (*African Communist*, no. 110), reflecting the continued favorable attitude of the SACP toward the Soviet Union. For the most part, however, party publications and spokesmen have had little comment upon matters concerning "the socialist community."

The general stance of the SACP on its international role was stated baldly by Chairman Tloome: "our party regards itself as an integral part of the world communist movement. No matter how difficult our struggle is, no matter how difficult our situation is, and no matter what the obstacles are for us, we see our duty as a communist party to strengthen the international communist movement, which we regard as the main instrument for the revolutionary renewal of the world. We attended the 1960 and 1969 international meetings of communist and workers' parties and were active in convening a meeting of communist and workers' parties of Tropical and Southern Africa [in 1978]. We believe that contacts between fraternal parties should continue to be developed so that exponents of Marxism-Leninism on our continent are able to get together regularly, exchange opinions, and openly discuss many questions with a view to making an even greater contribution to the struggle against imperialism and neocolonialism." (*WMR*, September.)

Publications. The most visible of the SACP publications is the party quarterly, *African Communist*, printed in East Germany and distributed from London; a special illegal edition is distributed inside South Africa. The journal, since its inception in 1959 "published quarterly in the interest of African solidarity and as a forum for Marxist-Leninist thought throughout our Continent," is devoted primarily to articles about South Africa but contains a regular section, "Africa Notes and Comments," in which developments elsewhere on the continent, particularly those pertaining to Marxist parties, are reported. Extracts from Soviet, East European, and Cuban publications also occasionally appear. Since 1985 the SACP has been producing a clandestine newspaper within the country six times a year entitled *Umsebenzi*, the Zulu/Xhosa word for worker and the name of the legal party newspaper from 1930 to 1936. Within the country the party is also "distributing works of the classics of Marxism-Leninism published in separate small booklets. Each has a different color and the format is such as to make it very difficult for the racist police and security to detect them." (*WMR*, September.) The party also disseminates propaganda flyers and leaflets, including specially targeted ones such as "White Worker—Your Future Lies With Democracy" (*African Communist*, no. 108). The party is also working on a Zulu translation of the *Communist Manifesto*.

SACP publications are paralleled by those of the ANC, also published in exile and clandestinely within South Africa; this year marked the 20th year of publication of *Sechaba*, the ANC monthly published with the support of the Afro-Asian Solidarity Committee of the German Democratic Republic. The ANC also broadcasts regularly to South Africa, using the shortwave facilities of the state radio services of Angola, Ethiopia, Madagascar, Tanzania, and Zambia.

Sheridan Johns
Duke University

Sudan

Population. 23,524,622
Party. Sudanese Communist Party (al-Hizb al-Shuyu'i al-Sudani; SCP)
Founded. 1946
Membership. 9,000 (estimated)
General Secretary. Muhammad Ibrahim Nugud Mansur
Secretariat. Muhammad Ibrahim Nugud Mansur, Ali al-Tijani al-Tayyib Babikar, Izz al-Din Ali Amir, Abu al-Qasim (Gassim) Muhammad, Sulayman Hamid, al-Gazuli Said Uthman, Muhammad Ahmad Sulayman (Suleiman)
Central Committee. Sudi Darag, Khidr Nasir, Abd al-Majid Shakak, Hasan Gassim al-Sid, Fatima Ahmad Ibrahim, Ibrahim Zakariya, and the members of the Secretariat
Status. Legal
Last Congress. Fourth, 31 October 1967, in Khartoum
Last Election. 1986; 1.67 percent of the total vote in territorial constituencies; 5 seats out of the contested 264 (2 in territorial constituencies and 3 in special ones for "graduates") (Sudan News Agency [SUNA], 25 May 1985)
Auxiliary Organizations. Democratic Federation of Sudanese Students; Sudanese Youth Union; Sudan Workers' Trade Union Federation; Sudanese Defenders of Peace and Democracy; Union of Sudanese Women
Publications. *Al-Maydan* (official party newspaper); *al-Shuyu'i*

Organized communist activity in the Sudan began in the 1920s, but it was not until 1946 that Sudanese intellectuals and students created a formal party organization. The SCP has been both publicly and clandestinely active in Sudanese politics since then.

It was active through the Anti-Imperialist Front in the first era of parliamentary politics (1953–1958) and then was part of the opposition to the first military regime (1958–1964). SCP members played a leading role in the 1964 revolution, which overthrew military rule, and participated in the transitional government. However, despite winning eleven seats in the 1965 parliamentary elections, opposition to the SCP by the new prime minister, Sadiq al-Mahdi, led to the party's exclusion from parliament (see *YICA*, 1968). When the second era of civilian politics was brought to an end by a military coup in 1969, the SCP gave strong support to the coup's leader, Ja'far Numayri.

Communists were very influential in the first two years of the Numayri regime, but tensions led to an abortive, communist-supported coup in the summer of 1971 and to the subsequent vigorous suppression of the SCP and the execution of many of its leaders. The SCP joined other civilian parties in opposition to Numayri and again in 1985 played a leading role in popular demonstrations that led to the overthrow of military rule. The SCP became an active participant in the restored partisan civilian political arena and won five of the 264 contested seats in the 1986 elections. Because of its experienced leadership and ties with other social and political groupings, the SCP is now a visible part of the parliamentary opposition.

Leadership. General Secretary Nugud and others in the party Secretariat have long been active in civilian politics in the Sudan. Nugud was already on the SCP executive committee in the 1960s, and he and others have participated in important events like the favorably viewed revolutions of 1964 and 1985. As a result, even though the party is small compared with the traditional parties, its leaders have visibility and are respected by most Sudanese. In addition, SCP members are important in a variety of economic and social associations within the Sudan (for instance, in the unions) and internationally.

Domestic Issues. In 1987 the SCP leadership believed that the situation in southern Sudan represented "the most serious and complex obstacle in the way of a better political, national, and constitutional life" (*al-Maydan*, 18 January; *JPRS*, 17 March). The SCP has a long history of working for a resolution of the conflict, which is based in part on differences between the predominantly Arabic-speaking and Muslim northern Sudan and the southerners, many of whom are neither Muslim nor Arabic speaking (see *YICA*, 1985). During 1987, the SCP suggested a major initiative to end the war (SUNA, 16 June; *FBIS*, 17 June). The government, however, ignored it, and the leader of the Sudan People's Liberation Movement (SPLM) rejected it as presenting nothing new (Radio of the Sudanese People's Liberation Army, 9 November; *FBIS*, 18 November). Although the SCP had been relatively consistent in expressing sympathy for the SPLM and opposition to the more hard-line position of the government, the SPC moved closer to the position of Prime Minister al-Mahdi by the end of 1987. In late November, for example, SCP general secretary Nugud supported a government policy of mobilization to recapture a town recently taken by the SPLM (SUNA, 29 November; *FBIS*, 2 December).

On other issues the SCP remained sharply critical of government policy but within the limits of participatory opposition. Nugud stated the approach of the SCP clearly in June: "We will confine ourselves to a strict policy of constructive criticism... The present 'limited democracy' in the Sudan is greatly preferable to a military dictatorship oriented toward the left or embellished with progressive watchwords." (*Le Monde*, 10 June; *FBIS*, 15 June.)

This position did not hinder the SCP from strongly opposing a variety of government policies, including the Islamization laws imposed by Numayri in 1983, or from criticizing al-Mahdi for not formally abrogating them. The SCP's position is in favor of a fully secular state; during 1987 it rejected proposals by al-Mahdi that changed specific aspects of the legal situation but did not totally secularize the legal system and state.

International Positions. The SCP is a relatively orthodox, Soviet-oriented communist party. Its leaders exchange visits with Soviet bloc party officials on a regular basis. General Secretary Nugud took a major trip to eastern bloc countries during the year, visiting East Germany, Bulgaria, and the Soviet Union during May and June. On the occasion of the 70th anniversary of the Russian October Revolution, the SCP had a series of meetings and entertained a special communist party delegation from the Soviet Union.

These contacts did not isolate the SCP from the government because al-Mahdi and his coalition government had similar contacts. The foreign minister (from the Democratic Unionist Party in the coalition government) visited Bulgaria in April, a trade protocol with the Soviet Union was signed in February, and the head of the Supreme Council of State supported good relations with the USSR and visited Romania in October. In this situation it was possible for the SCP to continue its initial favorable view of the government's foreign policy in "its course towards expanding relations with many, including socialist, nations" (*WMR*, November 1986).

In regional affairs, the SCP supported the idea of a negotiated settlement of the Arab-Israeli conflict through an international conference. In this it sided with the Soviet Union and many of the more moderate Arab states. It continued to affirm its strong support for the Palestinian cause and also associated itself with opposition to apartheid in South Africa. The party also opposed the influence of the International Monetary Fund in the development of Sudanese economic policy.

In general, the SCP remained a party of students, intellectuals, and organized working groups. It continued to face the challenge of the newer Islamic ideological groups, especially the Muslim Brotherhood, in competing for support. During 1987 the SCP does not appear to have made significant progress in expanding its base of support. The new activisim is found in the Islamic organizations, with the SCP being a more traditional-style participant in Sudanese politics.

John O. Voll
University of New Hampshire

Zimbabwe

Population. 9,372,000
Party. Zimbabwe African National Union–Patriotic Front (ZANU-PF)
Founded. 1963
Membership. No data
First Secretary and President. Robert G. Mugabe
Politburo. 15 seats: Robert Mugabe, Simon Muzenda (holds two seats), Meyor Urimbo, Tapumaneyi Mujuru, Maurice Nyagumbo, Enos Nkala, Emmerson Munangagwa, Nathan Shamuyarira, Didymus Mutasa, Dzingai Mutumbuka, Teurai Nhongo, Sydney Sekeremayi, Josiah Tongamirai, Ernest Kadungura
Central Committee. 90 members
Status. Ruling party
Last Congress. Second, August 1984
Last Election. October 1987 (for 30 new parliamentary seats)
Auxiliary Organizations. People's Militia, Youth Wing.
Publications. *Zimbabwe News*. Nearly all news organs are government owned in whole or part. The major exception is the privately owned weekly, *The Financial Gazette*, which operates independently of party and government.

Party Organization and Domestic Political Conditions. The real power in Zimbabwe lies with the ZANU Politburo, although ultimate authority rests with Mugabe, who serves as party head. Mugabe's position in both government and party continues to grow as a result of the new party structure established at the Second Congress in 1984 and through the constitutional amendment of 1987, which created a more powerful presidency. On 31 December Mugabe was installed as the country's first executive president (*NYT*, 1 January 1988). Consequently, he simultaneously holds the positions of head of party, government, and state. Although Mugabe has committed himself to the ultimate establishment of a Marxist state, his increasingly pragmatic economic policies and purges of radical ideologues from party leadership have won the collaboration of key white leaders in the capitalist sectors and contributed to the viability of those areas of private enterprise that are considered essential to economic growth.

Throughout 1987, Mugabe and his supporters in ZANU-PF increased their pressure for the creation of a one-party state under a powerful and centralized executive presidency. In that endeavor they were remarkably successful but at the cost of greater domestic turmoil. Mugabe vigorously pressed his strategy of seeking a party merger with the opposition Zimbabwe African People's Union (ZAPU) under its aging leader, Joshua Nkomo. In an effort to win over moderates within ZAPU, in early 1987 Mugabe released Dumiso Dabwengwa, ZAPU's second-ranking leader, from detention (*Economist Intelligence Unit* [*EIU*], no. 1). Some elements in South Africa capitalized on ZAPU opposition to the merger by resupplying antigovernment Ndebele rebels based in rural Matabeleland (African Consulting Associates, Special Country Reports for Corporate Clients, October). As ZAPU-ZANU unity talks reopened, violent dissident activity in Matabeleland resumed after a lull of nearly eighteen months. Between April and June, guerrilla sabotage destroyed several white farms and government facilities and killed a dozen people, including white commercial farmers and West German tourists (*NYT*, 12 October). The government used this resurgence of violence to ruthlessly clamp down on anti-ZANU elements. In June it banned ZAPU from holding rallies, meetings, and demonstrations. In September, all ZAPU district councils in Matabeleland North were dissolved, and in a raid on party offices, twelve ZAPU-PF officials were arrested and accused of collaborating with the dissidents (*FBIS*, 30 September).

Mugabe also dealt forcefully with opponents to merger in his own party, purging several key party leaders, including the influential firebrand Edgar Tekere, ZANU-PF chairman of Manicaland province (Frost & Sullivan, Zimbabwe Country Report, annual [F.&S.], October). Indeed, Mugabe's quest for a one-party state on his own terms became a pretext for removing from party leadership the Marxist ideologues and those who harbored strong clan or ethnic prejudices. Inevitably, as Mugabe moved moderates, including white businessmen, into positions of influence, he drew strident criticism from Marxist hard-liners, who accused him of betraying the revolution.

A major step towards Mugabe's consolidation of power was made in September when President Canaan Banana signed a law that abolished the 30 parliamentary seats that had been reserved for whites, who make up less than 2 percent of the population. In internal parliamentary elections held a month later, the vacated seats were filled by candidates nominated by ZANU-PF, including fifteen whites. Thus, ZANU was able to gain control over 77 of the 100 parliamentary seats. To the distress of the Ndebele, who comprise about 17 percent of the population, not a single additional seat was secured by a member of ZAPU (*NYT*, 24 October). Interestingly, the new seats in the Senate and House of Assembly were filled by people representing certain occupations and economic sectors, including agriculture and commerce. Nevertheless, 1987 was marked by an increasing number of defections from white parties as well as from ZAPU, including its national chairman (*CSM*, 2 October).

These constitutional measures, as well as the new momentum toward the incorporation of ZAPU into the ruling ZANU-PF structure, led to a further escalation in antigovernment violence, spearheaded by a small band of former officers in ZAPU's preindependence guerrilla army. Their aim was to sabotage the unity talks and drive a wedge between ZANU-PF and the white community, which was gradually moving toward closer cooperation with the Mugabe regime. The dissidents gained fresh support from uprooted and unemployed peasants in rural areas waiting impatiently to be resettled by the government on lands belonging to whites. In late November, sixteen white missionaries were massacred just south of Bulawayo. It was alleged that they died at the hands of dissidents with cooperation from the area's landless peasants (*Africa Economic Digest* [*AED*], 4 December). Clearly, white farmers, regardless of their political orientation, had become symbols of the government's failure to achieve land reform, and the rebels were capitalizing on squatter frustrations over the slow pace of resettlement (*CSM*, 30 November).

Despite the turmoil, unity talks resumed late in 1987 and led to a merger agreement in December. ZAPU would be incorporated into ZANU-PF. Nkomo would become one of two vice presidents and a second secretary of the enlarged and reconstituted ZANU-PF, and a number of former ZAPU officers would gain seats on the Politburo. The agreement, which still had to be ratified, paved the way for the establishment of an official one-party state in Zimbabwe.

Domestic Economic Conditions. By mid-1987, the economy found itself slipping back into a recession, its worst since independence. The decline stemmed from a crushing combination of drought, rising debt-service burdens, and a reduction in aid and other capital inflows (*Economic Review*: Zimbabwe Banking Corporation, April). The weakening economy and soft world prices for agricultural commodities contributed to a deepening foreign exchange shortage. This led to drastic reductions in imports, which starved the manufacturing sector of desperately needed spare parts and industrial inputs. The currency was allowed to depreciate to new lows in order to render exports more competitive in world markets. But the move also made vital imports more expensive and contributed to greater inflation (*African Business* [*AB*], September).

Zimbabwe's severe liquidity crisis forced the government to resort to more barter or countertrade arrangements, which meant more trade with the communist bloc countries. It also resulted in a slight deterioration in the terms of trade for Zimbabwe

(*Economic Bulletin*: Standard Chartered Bank, no. 31).

The deteriorating economic situation placed strains on the decisionmaking process. Criticism within the party over the slow pace of socialist growth made it politically impossible to significantly reduce government spending. Subsidies to parastatals remained high, and overall public spending was projected to increase by at least 14 percent in the current fiscal year (*Financial Times* [*FT*], 30 July). The 1987–1988 budget was the largest in history and called for an eleven percent increase in expenditures over the previous year. Debt interest and repayments were already absorbing nearly 25 percent of budget expenditures (*FT*, 31 July). Bowing to pressures from within the Politburo, the government refused to seek a rescheduling of its debts to western creditors or to negotiate new loan facilities with the International Monetary Fund. Consequently, by midyear the debt-service ratio rose to nearly 40 percent, and the budget deficit exceeded 12 percent of the gross domestic product (*EIU*, no. 2).

The economic policies contributed to escalating labor turmoil and criticism from the private sector, especially from the Zimbabwe Chamber of Commerce and the powerful Confederation of Zimbabwe Industries. The latter complained of the 50 percent cut in allowable corporate dividend remittances (*AB*, August). In August organized labor, in the face of an unemployment rate approaching 18 percent (*FT*, 5 June), responded to the government freeze on wages by launching a series of wildcat strikes.

The government drew mixed responses to its crackdown on corruption and inefficiency among management echelons in the parastatals. A number of executives were fired, including several with powerful connections to the inner circles of ZANU-PF. However, unlike most African countries in 1987, the government continued to acquire greater equity in key private enterprises, which ran against the continentwide trend toward privatization of the public sector.

In the final quarter of 1987, the economy showed signs of a slight recovery. The new export promotion schemes began to show results, and the government relaxed regulations to encourage reinvestment by multinational corporations (*AB*, December). Zimbabwe was able to improve its current account and trade balance by selling off a portion of the reserve bank's gold stock. The mining sector, particularly gold, increased its exports at a time of firmer world prices for gold, asbestos, copper, and other metals (*AED*, 4 December). Continuing low prices for petroleum imports gave the economy additional relief as did the unusually good rains in early December (*AED*, 17 December). Moreover, labor tension was eased somewhat after the government promised to review wage policies in early 1988.

International Relations. Zimbabwe in 1987 strengthened its trade, cultural, and diplomatic relations with Marxist countries not out of a new ideological fervor for communism but in keeping with Mugabe's position as chairman of the Nonaligned Movement and in response to the country's need to lessen its dependence on South Africa. Zimbabwe made an aggressive approach to the Soviet Union for defensive weapons against South Africa and the Mozambique National Resistance (RENAMO), which was attempting to disrupt the vital Beira corridor to the sea, and to the Netherlands and the Nordic countries for economic support and for funds to rehabilitate the corridor's infrastructure.

In March, Air Marshal Josiah Tungamirai and Maurice Nyagumbo, a high-ranking member of the Politburo, paid a visit to Moscow (TASS, 17 March). The Russians expressed satisfaction over Zimbabwe's establishment of diplomatic relations with Afghanistan, but they turned a deaf ear to requests for military hardware and substantial economic assistance. Indeed, in April and May, the foreign ministers of Angola, Tanzania, and Zimbabwe held extensive though desultory talks in Moscow with Mikhail Gorbachev and Foreign Minister Eduard Shevardnadze over the question of stronger Soviet backing to enable the front-line states to strengthen their sanctions against South Africa (*Pravda*, 26 May). In late June Mugabe returned from a visit to the Kremlin without an agreement for the purchase of Soviet MiG-29s (Moscow TV Service, 25 June). Consequently, in July, after a bitter internal struggle between moderates and radicals and after intensive lobbying from the private sector, the government announced it would postpone its decision to apply comprehensive air and trade sanctions against the apartheid regime (BBC World Service, 30 July). It was an embarrassing volte-face that caused hard feelings among members of the cabinet and the Politburo. In the final analysis, Mugabe had to face the reality that 21 percent of his country's imports came from South Africa and that 10 percent of its exports went there

(*FT*, 1 August). Moreover, the Beira corridor and harbor were not yet sufficiently rehabilitated to handle Zimbabwe's trade in the event of a cessation of trade with South Africa (F.&S., October).

Zimbabwe's relations with the People's Republic of China remained extremely cordial. New economic and technical cooperation agreements have been signed with China, and Beijing has extended several large interest-free loans (F.&S., October). In January Mugabe visited Beijing en route to a Nonaligned conference in India (*EIU*, no. 2), and in May, the Chinese foreign minister, Wu Xueqian, stopped in Harare on a seven-nation African visit to inspect the newly completed Chinese-built National Stadium (Harare Domestic Service [HDS], 26 May).

Zimbabwe's relations with several communist bloc countries deepened in 1987. There were substantially more cultural exchanges and countertrade with East Germany, Czechoslovakia, and Romania. An agreement was signed with the USSR on a new plan for cultural and technical exchanges (TASS, 10 August). Earlier, in February, an accord on tourism was concluded with the Bulgarians, and in March a delegation went to Yugoslavia to discuss a joint production of automobiles for the Zimbabwe market (*AED*, 11 March). Political and economic relations with Yugoslavia warmed considerably in 1987. Yugoslavia's Energoprojekt will soon begin to rehabilitate and upgrade eight district hospitals. Zimbabwe has also taken a keener interest in Hungary. In September, the Harare-based Merchant Bank of Central Africa signed a $6 million countertrade agreement with the Hungarian foreign trade bank Magyar Külkereskedelmi (*FT*, 29 September). Zimbabwe also reached an agreement with the Hungarians for an exchange of tobacco for pharmaceuticals and textile machinery, and its growing trade with the bloc countries was revealed by the participation of East Germany, Cuba, Czechoslovakia, and the Soviet Union in the annual Zimbabwe International Trade Fair. Nevertheless, Zimbabwe has been relatively unsuccessful in obtaining substantial capital inflows from communist bloc countries, including loans on favorable terms.

Zimbabwe's relationships with the African National Congress (ANC) and the South African Communist Party (SACP) have slowly improved. Bowing to pressure from South Africa, Mugabe has steadfastly refused to permit either organization to establish headquarters or any kind of guerrilla operations within Zimbabwe. However, Zimbabwe did allow a huge antiapartheid conference to convene in Harare in September (*AR*, November). It was the largest gathering ever of top ANC leaders and included Joe Slovo, who is also a leader in the SACP. The presidents of the ANC and the SACP were also invited to the inaugural celebrations for President Mugabe in late December and given a prominent place on the podium.

A degree of tension persisted between Zimbabwe and the Western powers, largely over the Zimbabwean government's strident criticism of the powers' continuing involvement in South Africa and also because of Zimbabwe's conciliatory gestures toward the Eastern bloc countries. In 1987, Zimbabwe angered the United States by signing a ten-year protocol with the Sandinista government in Nicaragua (*FBIS*, 21 October). In May Mugabe condemned the U.S. Senate for voting to ban aid to any southern African country that refuses to halt crossborder attacks against South Africa (HDS, 22 May). Such statements and votes have strained relations and generated conflicting perceptions of Zimbabwe's business and political environments. They have also had a stultifying effect on bilateral aid, trade, and investment.

The country's relations with fellow members of the Southern African Development Coordination Conference remain productive, and trade within the region is gradually increasing. However, in late 1987 Zimbabwe angrily accused neighboring Botswana of providing sanctuary for antigovernment dissidents.

In regard to Mozambique, the Politburo remains divided over the amount and nature of military support to the Front for the Liberation of Mozambique (FRELIMO) government forces. At great cost, the Zimbabwe National Army (ZNA) trains FRELIMO soldiers in counterinsurgency and guards Mozambique installations vital to landlocked Zimbabwe's access to the sea. RENAMO, which seeks to overthrow Joaquim Chissano's regime, expanded its operations into the Mozambique countryside in 1987 and staged raids across the 600-mile border with Zimbabwe (SAPA, 4 November). The incursions alarmed the Politburo and pressure began to build for a major offensive against the allegedly South African–backed guerrilla movement. At least 7,000 members of the ZNA were already stationed inside Mozambique, many of them guarding the 183-mile Beira corridor, at a cost now exceeding $500,000 a month. Military spending is rapidly rising and consumes $460 million of Zimbabwe's $3.1 billion budget (*CSM*, 24 September).

In conclusion, ZANU-PF, under the astute leadership of Mugabe, emerged from 1987 politically stronger though more racially and ethnically heterogeneous. However, in the process of incorporating a wider spectrum of members and neutralizing the hard-liners, it gave the appearance of being less ideologically committed, domestically, to a program of Marxist-Leninist economic development.

Richard W. Hull
New York University

THE AMERICAS

Introduction

In August 1987 the five Central American presidents signed an agreement in Guatemala—the Esquipulas II accord—pledging to take the region's peace process into their own hands. Although often presented as an outgrowth of the Contadora peace process, which primarily involved Mexico, Panama, Colombia, and Venezuela, the new plan was in fact a recognition that Contadora could never succeed. The strength of the new plan, drawn up by Costa Rican President Oscar Arias, was that it put the peacemaking process in the hands of Central Americans themselves, focused on the need for democratic reform (above all in Nicaragua), and incorporated a series of deadlines for implementation of the provisions. The deadlines were repeatedly postponed, however: compliance with major provisions—dialogue, cease-fire negotiations, a general amnesty, and democratization—was set for 5 November, then put off until 5 January 1988, and then set at 15 January. After a meeting of the Central American presidents on the latter date, the deadlines were effectively extended again for an unspecified period of time. The plan, which won the Nobel Peace Prize for its author, also called for the simultaneous and equal implementation of the provisions, outside support for indigenous belligerents, lifting of the states of emergency, freedom of association and information, and verification—but not enforcement—of compliance.

From the beginning of 1987 Arias had stressed that the main obstacle to peace in the region was the government in Managua; he remarked on Mexico City television on 6 February that "with or without *contras* and with or without military aid, I continue to think that there will be violence in Nicaragua if the Nicaraguan people cannot elect their leaders freely." At the 15 January 1988 session and in January interviews Arias and presidents José Napoleón Duarte of El Salvador and José Azcona of Honduras pointed criticism mainly at Nicaragua for failing to comply with the plan's provisions. Above all the Sandinistas had: (1) failed to negotiate a cease-fire directly with the armed resistance movement; (2) only played at democratization at home, with President Daniel Ortega pledging as recently as December 1987 that the Sandinistas would never "give up power"; (3) planned to greatly expand their military, active and reserves (which in 1987 numbered 175,000 with an active army of 80,000) to 600,000 by 1995; and (4), according to Major Roger Miranda, who had served as a top aide to Defense Minister Humberto Ortega until defecting in October, continued assisting other guerrilla movements seeking to overthrow governments in the region—for example, in October, fifteen Salvadoran guerrillas were trained in the use of surface-to-air missiles. President Ortega admitted Nicaraguan support for Salvadoran guerrillas in a debate with President Arias on Costa Rican television on 14 January 1988.

The Sandinistas continued to claim that the contras were nothing but puppets of the United States, and condemned Honduras for failing to throw all the resistance forces off its territory, but analysts noted that the other Central American countries, while sometimes falling short of full compliance, all made a more wholehearted and sincere effort to comply than the Sandinistas. In addition, the Soviet bloc gave Nicaragua more than $1 billion in military aid during 1986–1987.

Within Nicaragua, economic conditions deteriorated further: inflation rocketed to over 1,000 percent, and food, water, and electricity were rationed all or part of the time and were often unavailable. In October, two months after the Guatemala peace accord was signed, the opposition paper *La Prensa*, which had been outlawed for more than a year, was allowed to reopen and was highly critical of the government.

During the year the U.S.-armed resistance movement, which numbered approximately 15,000 and was by far the largest guerrilla force in Latin America, began operating in half of Nicaragua's territory, though not yet on the populous Pacific coast. According to numerous press reports, the resistance seemed to have made considerable headway building support among the Nicaraguan people.

Both the Salvadoran and Guatemalan governments held direct talks with guerrillas operating in their countries, after initially refusing to do so; there is no significant guerrilla movement in Honduras. President Duarte met with representatives of the Farabundo Martí National Liberation Front (FMLN) in San Salvador, although, to no one's surprise, no cease-fire was concluded. The FMLN normally fought a defensive war in the countryside but stepped up its military and political activities in the Salvadoran capital, and FMLN political front leaders Rubén Zamora and Guillermo Ungo visited El Salvador after the Guatemala accords and had wide access to the general news media.

The National Revolutionary Unity of Guatemala (URNG) forces declined from about 10,000 in 1981–1982 to less than 2,000 in 1987, and during the year it concentrated more on reorganization and propaganda than on military encounters. It set up a radio station, La Voz Popular, which was clearly modeled on the Salvadoran FMLN's Radio Venceremos. The government met with guerrilla leaders in Madrid but did not resolve their differences. The communist party in Guatemala, the Guatemalan Party of Labor, continued to call the URNG "pseudo-leftist."

In Colombia the truce between the government and some guerrilla groups continued to fall apart even as evidence mounted that there is some cooperation between the guerrillas and the country's powerful drug rings. In October the leaders of Colombia's six major guerrilla organizations formed the Simón Bolívar National Guerrilla Coordinating Board. Defectors from the Revolutionary Armed Forces of Colombia (FARC), a group tied to the Communist Party of Colombia, claimed that the guerrillas have Cuban instructors and an airbase with modern Soviet-made weapons. The so-called America Battalion claims to incorporate guerrillas of the M-19 in Colombia, the Alfaro Lives! movement in Ecuador, and the Tupac Amaru II movement in Peru. An international seminar on "Democratization in Latin America" was held for Colombians and representatives from five other countries in Bogotá in mid-June, sponsored in part by the *World Marxist Review*, with speakers from the Soviet Union and East Germany.

A variety of Marxist-Leninist movements operated at high levels in Peru. The United Left (IU) remained the second largest political force in that Andean nation, making Peru one of only two countries—the other is Guyana—whose major opposition is Marxist-Leninist. Increasingly the IU is the main alternative to the government of Alan García, which is finding seemingly intractable political and economic problems on all sides, though the IU is a coalition of organizations ranging from the moderate to the extreme left who rarely agree on any significant issue. The Peruvian Communist Party, which held its Ninth Congress in 1987, is a major actor in the coalition.

In 1973 Peru became the first and only country in South America to receive Soviet arms; the value of these arms in 1987 exceeded $1.5 billion. In May Peru purchased five Antonov-32 military transport planes to replace An-26 planes bought a decade earlier; it is reported that Cuba wants to buy some of the An-26s. There were about 115 Soviet military advisers in Peru during the year; at least 500 other Soviets worked there in other capacities. Some 3,000 Peruvian military personnel had been trained in the Soviet Union through 1985, and such training continued in 1987.

Widespread terrorism continued in Peru, mostly by the Maoist Sendero Luminoso (Shining Path), which had grown to an estimated 10,000 members. Sendero launched attacks in 22 of 24 departments and by the end of the year forced the García government to maintain seventeen provinces in a state of emergency. Announcing that "anything that has to do with terrorism must be fully investigated," García sent 4,000 police and military units onto four university campuses in February looking for evidence of subversive centers. In a partial tactical shift, the Maoists turned at times to political-type activities in an effort to compete more successfully with other leftist political forces. Sendero held its first plenary session in September and announced that it will hold its first national party congress in 1988.

In June the Communist Party of Chile (PCC) joined other leftist groups in forming the United Left Coalition. This coalition also included the Clodomiro Almeyda branch of the Socialist Party and the Movement of the Revolutionary Left (MIR), among others, and has been the most widely based leftist opposition group in Chile since the Popular Unity Coalition of President Salvador Allende in the early 1970s. Tensions continued within the PCC and United Left, however, because of ongoing communist support for some terrorism through the Manuel Rodríguez Patriotic Front. Not until October did the PCC begin encouraging registration for voting in the 1988 presidential candidate plebiscite.

Communist parties participated in legislatures in many of the region's countries: they had substantial representation and influence in Peru, Guyana, Martinique, and Guadeloupe; their representation was minimal in Brazil (where the party had its Eighth Congress, the first ever held legally in the country), Venezuela, Colombia, Ecuador, and Bolivia. In some countries communists applied pressures indirectly on fronts, other parties, and student or labor groups; indirect influence was applied in Panama, for example, on the Democratic Revolutionary Party, the political front of the Panama Defense Forces. In Bolivia a prominent communist was elected head of the large Bolivian Labor Central (COB); the Soviet Union remained a major importer of Bolivian tin. For the first time in history, the Unified Party of Haitian Communists ran a candidate for president.

Communists in Argentina and Uruguay were highly critical of their governments because of differing amnesty bills that put a deadline on filing charges against military personnel for their activities during antiguerrilla campaigns in the 1970s.

The Cuban economy remained in a state of decay during 1987 but Fidel Castro bucked the trend in the socialist world toward decentralization and material incentives. Instead, the Cuban leader reverted increasingly to an emphasis on volunteer work and moral incentives characteristic of Cuba in the 1960s, though these policies wrecked the economy then and promise to make it worse now. Castro's problem is that, unlike current leaders in other major communist countries, particularly the Soviet Union and China, he cannot blame earlier leaders for his country's problems; they are of his own making, and to adopt Chinese and Soviet-style reforms would be to admit he has been on the wrong track most of the time since 1959. What is more, Castro probably actually thinks that such reforms mean caving in to capitalist methods. Several high-level officials from Cuba defected during the year and revealed domestic and international secrets and plans: Cuban intelligence has long controlled most CIA activity in Cuba, for example, and Cuba is infested with corruption and favoritism.

Despite Castro's refusal to follow the Soviet lead in economic reform, the Cuban leader played a prominent role at the celebrations of the 70th anniversary of the October Revolution in November, and he returned home saying his ties to Moscow have never been better. Trade with the Soviet Union was expected to reach $9 billion in 1987, some $200 million more than in 1986, and part of the massive Soviet support for Castro—about $4–5 billion annually in economic and military aid—continued to come in the form of Soviet purchases of half of Cuba's sugar crop at three times the world market price. Cuba's hard currency earnings have fallen dramatically in recent years, and Havana has responded by trading still more with the Soviet bloc. Meanwhile, although U.S.-Cuban relations deteriorated for the first part of 1987, they improved somewhat in the final months of the year as several agreements were signed, including an immigration pact. Castro stated his support for the Arias peace plan and met several times with Sandinista leaders to discuss it and advise them.

The Soviet Union made advances in the hemisphere before and after Foreign Minister Eduard Shevardnadze's visits to Argentina, Brazil, Uruguay, and Cuba in October and November. The overall expansion of ties included increasing the already extensive trade with Argentina, securing resupply rights for the Soviet fishing fleet in Uruguay, selling military supplies to Peru, and getting the Noriega government in Panama to allow Aeroflot to land in Panama and to sign a service contract to provide drydock and other shore facilities for the Soviet fishing fleet.

The Communist Party USA claims continued growth, which is denied by some analysts, but has decided not to run a candidate of its own in the 1988 presidential election. Instead it will continue to push its positions in the so-called national peace movement, among blacks and within the Democratic Party, where its favorite candidate is Jesse Jackson. The membership decline in the Socialist Workers' Party, the second largest Marxist-Leninist group in the United States, continued during 1987. The communist movement in Canada continued at a very low level.

William Ratliff
Hoover Institution

Argentina

Population. 31,144,775
Party. Communist Party of Argentina (Partido Comunista de la Argentina; PCA)
Founded. 1918
Membership. 80,000 (claimed; 25,000 militants)
General Secretary. Athos Fava
Politburo. 12 members: Athos Fava, Jorge Pereyra, Patricio Echegaray, Luis Heller, Ernesto Salgado, Fanny Edelman, Guillermo Varone, Miguel Ballato, Eduardo Sigal, Rodolfo Casals, Enrique Dratman, Francisco Alvarez
Central Committee. 100 members, 15 alternates
Status. Legal
Last Congress. Sixteenth, 4–7 November 1986
Last Election. 1987 (parliamentary and provincial midterm elections), no representation
Auxiliary Organizations. Communist Youth Federation, Union Argentine Women, Committee in Solidarity with Nicaragua, local branch of the World Peace Council; the party effectively controls the Argentine Permanent Assembly on Human Rights.
Publications. *¿Que Pasa?* (weekly); *Aquí y ahora* (monthly). The popular political gossip magazine *El Periodista* (weekly) is generally regarded as controlled by party members.

The democratically elected government of Raúl Alfonsín weathered another difficult year, surviving a small-scale barracks revolt, growing economic problems, and a setback in congressional elections in which the rival Justicialist (Peronist) Party took control of both Senate and Chamber of Deputies. Of particular significance for left-wing politics was a "full-stop" law passed by Congress just before Christmas 1986. It set a period of 60 days (ending 22 February 1987) for the courts to receive any further charges against alleged human rights violations during the previous period of military rule (1976–1983) and for the accused in turn to be cited to appear before the courts for investigatory hearings. After that date, any of the accused not cited would be free from further judicial action.

By the deadline about 150 summonses had been issued by the courts, including about 30 for active duty army and navy officers. Eleven human rights organizations claimed to have submitted a list of about 650 military and police officers to the courts, including 20 percent of the serving high command.

Domestic Party Affairs. At their Sixteenth Party Congress in November 1986, the communists abandoned their conditional support for the Alfonsín government and, perhaps more important, began to attack the Peronists frontally; they particularly attacked Antonio Cafiero, who as governor-elect of the province of Buenos Aires was generally assumed to be his party's presidential candidate in 1989. The congress set the stage for the creation of a new, exclusively leftist coalition, the so-called Broad Front, comprising the PCA, the Intransigents, the Movement Toward Socialism (MAS), nearly a dozen small Marxist and semi-Marxist parties, and a tiny offshoot of the Justicialist Party that styled itself "Revolutionary Peronism."

As Organizational Secretary Pereyra explained, recent developments had forced the party to re-evaluate the Alfonsín administration, which he now called "a bourgeois government that represents the interests of the monopolistic high bourgeoisie and that is not in a position to carry out the 1983 campaign platform . . . There is a basic contradiction between the top echelon of the Radical Party, which is in control of the administration, and great masses of Radicals who have other interests" (*El Periodista*, 14–20 November 1986; *JPRS*, 8 January).

In the 6 September elections, the Broad Front polled 1,100,099 votes (out of 19,419,963 cast). Under the complicated procedure by which individual parties can elect deputies while belonging to electoral coalitions, the Intransigents maintained their five seats in the lower house of Congress and the communists and others (such as MAS) obtained no representation.

Leadership and Party Organization. The congress also signaled a purge of party leadership, although General Secretary Fava remained at the helm. More than half the Politburo was replaced; eighteen major party activists were expelled, including veterans like Rubens Iscaro—who had been the party's presidential candidate in 1983—and Angel Bustelo. Iscaro had accused his victorious adversaries of being interested in armed revolution and of harboring exaggerated prospects of going it alone (that is, without an alliance with one of the two major parties). As he explained to a journalist after his expulsion, "Those who contend that the bourgeoisie is worn out are making a serious historical mistake . . . spurning potential allies and friends, handing over to the enemy a force that is also seeking a way out." Iscaro had also opposed the party's alliance with MAS on the grounds that "if groups say they are left wing but in the final accounting work to divide the left, we must combat them." (*El Periodista*, 14–20 November 1986; *JPRS*, 8 January.)

International Views, Positions and Activities. General Secretary Fava had a busy traveling year. In May he visited North Korea as the guest of Kim Il-song; in June he was in Cuba. In September he went to Bulgaria, and in November he was in both Vietnam and the Soviet Union for the 70th anniversary of the October Revolution, where he and two other members of the PCA Central Committee were received by CPSU General Secretary Mikhail Gorbachev.

Relations with the Soviet Union and Other Bloc Members. The cordial relationship with the Soviet Union and other members of the bloc that apparently exists under all regimes in Argentina—civil and military, democratic and dictatorial—continued in 1987. However, the radical asymmetry of the relationship—whereby the Argentines bought practically nothing from the Soviets, who nonetheless took 60 percent of Argentine cereal exports and paid in hard currency—finally came to an end. During his 1986 visit to Moscow, President Alfonsín agreed to clear at least a portion of commercial accounts through barter arrangements and the purchase of Soviet technology. Thus, it was revealed in the course of 1987 that Soviet enterprises would participate in the construction of four hydroelectric turbines for the Piedra de Aguila dam in Neuquén province and in the construction of generators and electric transformers at the same site. Further, it was announced in September that Soviet and Argentine engineers will work jointly to reconstruct and electrify the Retiro-Pilar-Mercedes railway in the province of Buenos Aires; locomotives made in the USSR will also replace worn-out diesel models on the San Martín line. Finally, the Soviets are currently supplying 20 percent of the enriched uranium used by Argentine nuclear reactors.

The importance of these new arrangements was underscored by the visit to Argentina of Soviet foreign minister Eduard Schevardnadze 30 September–5 October, the first ever by anyone in his position. During the course of the visit the two countries agreed to a program of cooperation to increase bilateral trade beyond the traditional rubrics; a series of supplementary protocols were signed at the tenth meeting of the Joint Argentine-Soviet Commission for Economic, Scientific, and Technical Cooperation a few days later. In the final communiqué, the two governments emphasized their coinciding views on such matters as the Malvinas (Falklands) Islands, the Antarctic, Central America, and the Strategic Defense Initiative (which both oppose). In the Argentine official perspective, these points of agreement did not signify support for Soviet interests as such, but rather were an effective expression of nonalignment.

Argentine governments have always looked to the Eastern bloc countries as new markets for exports to counterbalance serious losses within the European Community. In 1987 Argentina bid to provide services in the construction of nuclear plants in Czechoslovakia, competing for the first time with more traditional suppliers such as West Germany and Canada. A reciprocal credit agreement with Bulgaria facilitating the barter exchange of goods went into effect in May. In August the deputy foreign minister of East Germany, Bernhard Neugebauer, visited Argentina. He was followed in November by President Károly Németh of Hungary. The People's Republic of China sent a trade mission to Argentina in September.

In the United Nations in March, Argentina voted against a proposal advanced by the United States to investigate the state of human rights in Cuba. Foreign Minister Dante Caputo denied that he was opposed to the substance of the resolution but said that in view of a motion simultaneously introduced by Cuba condemning the United States, it was better to support an Indian compromise proposal "to act on both"—that is, to vote down both. Responding to criticism from conservatives in Congress and the press, Caputo said, "If some [in Argentina] are worried because the Argentine policy follows a zigzag course, it is because our policy sometimes does not side with either Moscow or with Washington, but with Buenos Aires." (*Noticias Argentinas*, 17 March; *FBIS*, 19 March.)

Other Leftist Groups. Since Argentina's return to democracy, leftist groups have proliferated; there are now nearly a dozen within the framework of the party-dominated Broad Front and several outside of that framework. Most are extremely small, sometimes containing no more than a few hundred (or even a few dozen) members. Some groups—such as the Mothers of the Plaza de Mayo or its offshoot, the Grandmothers of the Plaza de Mayo—claim to be human rights organizations but in fact are pursuing an agenda far beyond their advertised purpose. During 1987 all of these groups focused on protesting the "full-stop" law, both by gathering signatures on a petition demanding a referendum and by filing legal briefs impugning the law's constitutionality. Nonetheless, on 23 June the Supreme Court upheld the new legislation.

The largest single party of the left outside of the PCA is the Intransigent Party led by Oscar Alende, a former Radical and one-time governor of the province of Buenos Aires (1958–1962). At one time the Intransigent Party seemed likely to emerge as a major third force between Peronism and radicalism, but it has now been overtaken by the rightist Union of the Democratic Center (UCD) party, which leapt from three to seven deputies in the September elections.

MAS is often referred to in communist publications as Trotskyist but might be more accurately described as independent Marxist. MAS general secretary Luis Zamora criticized Shevardnadze during his visit for his evident support for Alfonsín "although," Zamora said, "the people massively reject Alfonsín's economic policies" (*TELAM*, 6 October; *FBIS*, 8 October). Both MAS and the Intransigents were sharply divided over PCA front policies, though both avoided formal schisms.

As in 1986 there were frequent allegations by far-right personalities that Argentina was on the verge of another round of leftist terrorism. Facundo Suárez, the civilian head of the Secretariat for State Intelligence (SIDE), found it necessary in June to pointedly deny a rumor that there had been a recent high-level meeting of Latin American terrorist organizations in northern Argentina. At a dinner in July for retired army officers, which included two former military presidents, General Julio Alsogaray (retired) claimed that "government organizations" and radio and television were plagued with "subversive infiltrators" (*Diarios y Noticias*, 7 July; *FBIS*, 8 July). Despite these fears, however, in May one of the intellectual authors of the guerrilla war of the 1970s, former Montoneros chief Mario Firmenich, was sentenced to life imprisonment for kidnapping, extortion, and murder.

Biography. *Ernesto Salgado.* Born in 1945, Salgado joined the Communist Youth Federation in 1964 after activity (during high school years) in the Peronist movement and passage through the youth movement of the since-dissolved Argentine Socialist Party. In the Buenos Aires Communist Youth he was in charge of mass movements and organization, and he eventually became provincial general secretary. In August 1983 he became a full party member, taking over the propaganda secretariat in the first southern region and, later, the Quilmes (Buenos Aires province) committee secretariat. In March 1986 he became, consecutively, secretary of organization and general secretary of the southern region. Re-elected by acclamation at the regional conference preceding the Sixteenth Congress, he was named two weeks later to the Politburo. He is currently also a member of the National Secretariat for Ideological Propaganda.

Mark Falcoff
American Enterprise Institute

Bolivia

Population. 6,309,642
Party. Communist Party of Bolivia (Partido Comunista de Bolivia; PCB)
Founded. 1950 (latest split, 1985)
Membership. 500 (claimed)
General Secretary. Simón Reyes Rivera (majority faction until mid-year, then Humberto Ramírez); Carlos Soria Galvarro (minority)
Status. Legal
Last Congress. Fifth, 9–13 February 1985; Extraordinary, 26–29 April 1986
Last Election. July 1985; the United People's Front (FPU), the electoral coalition supported by the PCB, won 4 of 130 seats in the Chamber of Deputies; 1987 Patriotic Alliance formed electoral front with other parties.
Auxiliary Organization. Communist Youth of Bolivia
Publication. *Unidad* (majority and minority editions)

The most important events in Bolivia during 1987 were the continuance of—and reactions to—the new economic policy of the government of President Victor Paz Estenssoro, the government's campaign to eliminate the cocaine export problem, and changes in the leadership of the Central Obrera Boliviana (COB), the country's central labor organization. The communists played a role in all of these events.

The PCB was founded in 1950 by a group of young people who broke away from the country's first pro-Stalinist party, the Left Revolutionary Party (Partido de Izquierda Revolucionaria; PIR), which had collaborated with conservative governments of the 1946–1952 period. After the Bolivian National Revolution, led by the Nationalist Revolutionary Movement (Movimiento Nacionalista Revolucionario; MNR), the PCB remained a minor force in national politics and the labor movement. However, after the overthrow of the MNR regime in 1964, the communists became the largest single group in the organized labor movement and particularly among the tinworkers of the Miners' Federation (FSTMB).

During the elections of 1978, 1979, and 1980, the PCB formed part of the Popular Democratic Union (UDP), a coalition that backed the candidacy of former president Hernán Siles Suazo of the Left MNR (MNRI). After Siles was finally inaugurated as president in October 1982, the PCB was represented in his cabinet by two ministers, those of Mines and Labor, who left the government in January 1985.

After the Fifth Congress of the PCB in February 1985, the party suffered a split. The faction headed by General Secretary Reyes soon emerged as the much larger faction, and it clearly enjoyed the Moscow franchise. The dissident group, which used the same name and was headed by Carlos Soria Galvarro, generated virtually no news in 1987.

A public opinion survey in March showed that the PCB was the sixth most popular party in the country. However, only 1.6 percent of those polled said that it had "the most attraction" for them. (*El Diario*, 29 March.)

Programs of the Government. After coming to power in August 1985, President Paz Estenssoro launched what he called the New Economic Program to curb inflation (reportedly running at 24,000 percent), reduce the deficits of government-owned sectors of the economy (particularly the mining industry), and curb smuggling by practically reducing tariffs. That program continued during 1987, although in the middle of the year Paz Estenssoro announced measures to "reactivate" the economy.

By mid-1987 inflation had been cut to an annual rate of 10–12 percent. Yet unemployment had grown substantially, particularly among the tin miners, of whom some 20,000 had been dismissed. Although those let go were given dismissal payments equivalent to about $2,000, many miners had exhausted these grants by mid-1987 and many had gotten involved in the illegal cocaine trade, particularly in the Chaparé area of Cochabamba (*CSM*, 4 August). In April an agreement between the government and the COB was announced under which no more miners would be fired, and those found to be in surplus in some mines would be transferred to new mines being developed (*La Red Panamericana*, 7 April).

Another agreement, in November, provided that the government would seek jobs in the private sector for the unemployed miners, and it set up a committee to study further plans for closing mines (ibid., 4 December).

Communist Attitudes and Campaigns. Throughout 1987 the communists strongly opposed the programs of the Paz Estenssoro government. They called for the formation of a united front of all opposition groups to try to defeat those programs.

Typical of these efforts was an appeal by the PCB Central Committee in January. It proclaimed that "While the rightists are closing their ranks to make their oligarchic, imperialist plans for authoritarian rule a reality, the people and their political organizations are still in suicidal disarray." The appeal urged, "What we should do now, without closing our eyes to all the differences or abandoning our own concepts—or seeking to force them on all the others—is to deal with the pressing problems, in search of more unity and on the basis of both specific and common demands by all classes and social groups victimized by the 'new economic policy.' This requires coordination of efforts to fight common enemies—imperialism and oligarchy. There is now a pressing need for minimal agreement among public and political organizations to foster unity of action against the regime's economic policy." (*Unidad*, 15–22 January.)

The PCB used, at least to a limited degree, the December municipal elections—the first to be held in 40 years—to mobilize opposition to the Paz Estenssoro government and its policies. It was reported that in La Paz, the Patriotic Alliance, which the communists had formed with the left-wing Patriotic Convergence Axis, came in third (EFE, 7 December).

The PCB and the COB. From the point of view of the PCB, the most important event of the year was the election of its general secretary, Simón Reyes, as head of the COB at that organization's Seventh Congress in July. Three years earlier, at the Sixth Congress, Reyes had first run against Juan Lechín, the founder and head of the COB since its establishment in 1952, but Reyes had been defeated by a coalition of personal supporters of Lechín, Trotskyists, and other political groups opposed to the PCB.

In 1986, when Lechín had resigned as head of the FSTMB, Reyes had temporarily succeeded him but had been forced to resign when his policies were repudiated by an extraordinary congress of the federation. He was succeeded by Víctor López Arias, a compromise candidate.

It was López who presided over the COB's Seventh Congress. There were two major factions in the meeting: "the Axis," comprising supporters of Juan Lechín; and "the 17," the core of which comprised delegates who were members of the PCB. There were also a number of delegates who were not associated with either faction.

The different positions of the factions surfaced during the congress's political debate. According to journalist Jorge Lazarte, "the Axis felt that from the popular point of view the way out of the present situation could only be through 'revolution' and that labor's demands must therefore be combined with a 'general offensive' against the government, to the point of destabilizing and overthrowing it by means of more effective forms of struggle (implicitly armed struggle, as several Axis advocates in the Policy Committee debate declared)." In contrast, "for 'the 17' the ways of conducting the struggle could not be freely chosen since they were determined by the situation at any given moment and, under the present circumstances and given the balance of power in the country, closing off the channel of negotiation to embark on the path of revolution could only unfailingly lead to defeat and, therefore, the Axis approach was adventurous and suicidal." This cautious approach undoubtedly reflected the position of the PCB.

Lechín participated in the debate on the political resolution and was strongly hissed, which is rare in COB history. Subsequently, Lechín announced his decision to run again as head of the COB but insisted that, in re-electing him, the congress must completely support his political position. The majority of the delegates were unwilling to do this, and so the PCB, which had been hesitant to assume the leadership of the COB, ended up putting forth and supporting Reyes, who was elected. The PCB also won the largest—although not majority—representation on the new National Executive Committee of the COB (*Presencia*, 26 July).

As a result of his election as head of the COB, Reyes resigned as general secretary of the PCB. Humberto Ramírez was chosen in his place. (Prague, *Rudé právo*, 29 July.)

International Relations of the PCB. The Reyes and Ramírez PCB maintained close relations during the year with the pro–Soviet Communist Party (CPSU) bloc. It was represented at discussions organized in Prague by the *World Marxist Review* on "Christian/Marxist Dialogue in Latin America" and "Can the Military-Industrial Complex Be Bridled." The party was also represented at the Second Conference of South American Communist Parties in Lima in December 1986.

At the time of the choice of Ramírez to succeed Reyes as general secretary of the party, Gustáv Husák, Czechoslovakian general secretary, sent his congratulations. Earlier, in April, a delegation from the CPSU Central Committee headed by Leonid Sharin had visited La Paz on the invitation of the PCB, apparently to demonstrate Soviet support for Reyes. While meeting with the delegation, Reyes "declared himself to be in favor of the further strengthening of inter-party links with the CPSU on the principles of proletarian internationalism..." (TASS International Service, 2 April). The Soviet delegation also met with Vice President Julio Garrett (*Pravda*, 3 April).

Other Radical Groups. Although the Reyes/Ramírez PCB remained the largest single Marxist-Leninist element in Bolivian politics, it competed in the labor movement and elsewhere with various other groups. These included at least two factions of the Movement of the Revolutionary Left (Movimiento de Izquierda Revolucionaria; MIR), a Maoist party, and several Trotskyist groups. Some guerrilla-oriented factions also apparently continued to exist.

The faction of the MIR headed by Antonio Aranibar Quiroga had allied itself with the PCB in the 1985 elections. In the Seventh Congress of the COB in July 1987, that group, too, allied itself with the communist forces (*Presencia*, 26 July).

The Marxist-Leninist Communist Party (PCB-ML), headed by Senator Oscar Zamora Medinacelli, was formed as a Maoist party in 1964. It did not play any major role in national politics during the year.

Bolivian Trotskyism, once the largest element in the far left, remained splintered, with at least four groups proclaiming loyalty to Trotskyism. The most significant faction was the Revolutionary Labor Party (POR), led by Guillermo Lora, which was influential in the student federation of San Andres University in La Paz and still had some influence among the miners. It was not affiliated with any faction of International Trotskyism.

Another group, the so-called United POR (POR-U), was affiliated with the United Secretariat of the Fourth International. It had been formed by a merger of two other groups in 1983.

The Bolivian affiliate of the "Morenoite" faction of International Trotskyism is the Socialist Workers' Party (PST), originally established as a faction of the Socialist Party of Marcelo Quiroga in the late 1970s. It had some influence in the teachers unions and the factory workers of La Paz. Finally, the tiny Trotskyist-Posadist POR (POR-TP), headed by Felix Aranda Vargas, continued to exist as the Bolivian affiliate of the faction of International Trotskyism founded by the late J. Posadas.

Most of those arrested in Bolivia for attempted guerrilla activities during the year were reported to have some relationship with the Sendero Luminoso and the Patria Roja extremist factions in Peru (*La Red Panamericana*, 24 February, 3 April).

Robert J. Alexander
Rutgers University

Brazil

Population. 147,094,739
Parties. Brazilian Communist Party (Partido Comunista Brasileiro; PCB), pro-Soviet; Communist Party of Brazil (Partido Comunista do Brasil; PCdoB), pro-Albanian; Workers' Party (Partido dos Trabalhadores; PT), strong Marxist-Leninist-Trotskyist influence
Founded. PCB: 1922; PCdoB: 1961 split from PCB; PT: 1981
Membership. PCB: 15,000 (*Jornal do Brasil*, 16 July); PCdoB: 50,000 claimed, 20,000 estimated (*Folha de São Paulo*, 28 June)
Top Official. PCB: General Secretary Salomão Malina (65); PCdoB: President João Amazonas (75); PT: President Luis Inacio "Lula" da Silva (45)
Executive Committee. PCB: 15 members, including Salomão Malina, Roberto Freire, Ivan Pinheiro, Hercules Correa, Givaldo Siqueira, Almir Neves, José Paulo Neto, Regis Frati, Paulo Elisario, Sergio Morães, Amaro do Nascimento; PCdoB: José Duarte, Dyneas Fernández Aguiar, José Renato Rabelo, Roberto D'Olne Lustosa, Ronaldo Cavalcanti Freitas, Elza de Lima Monnerat, João Batista de Rocha Lemos, Pericles Santos de Souza, Alanir Cardoso, Maria do Socorro Morães Vieira; PT: 19 members, including Luis Inacio da Silva, General Secretary Olivio Dutra, José Genoino, Eduardo Jorge, Eduardo Suplicy, Helio Bicudo, José Dirceu
Central Committee. PCB: 63 active members, 23 alternates
Status. All legal
Last Congress. PCB: Eighth, 17–20 July
Last Election. November 1986, for governors, state legislatures, and 487-seat National Congress, which became Constituent Assembly in 1987. Deputies elected: PCB: 3; PCdoB: 3; PT: 16.
Auxiliary Organizations. PCB: dominant in Agricultural Workers' Confederation (Confederação Nacional dos Trabalhadores na Agricultura; CONTAG), some leadership in General Workers' Central (Central General dos Trabalhadores; CGT); PCdoB: dominant in National Student Union (União Nacional dos Estudantes; UNE), minor position in CGT; PT: dominant in Single Workers' Central (Central Unica dos Trabalhadores; CUT), influence in Basic Christian Communities (Comunidades Eclesiais de Base; CEBs) and Landless Movement (Movimento dos Sem Terra)
Publications. PCB: *Voz da Unidade*, João Aveline, director; PCdoB: *Tribuna da Luta Operária*, Pedro de Oliveira, director

Popular esteem for mainstream political groups dropped precipitously in 1987 as the circus-like Constituent Assembly seemed to bring day-to-day government to a standstill. The economic crisis and deteriorating trade relations with the United States took a back seat to splits within both the governing coalition and the majority party. The coalition had comprised the majority Party of the Brazilian Democratic Movement (Partido do Movimento Democrático Brasileiro; PMDB) and the centrist Liberal Front Party (Partido do Frente Liberal; PFL); the PFL left the coalition and three tendencies appeared in the PMDB. After ten months of often chaotic debate, the assembly decided on a parliamentary system to be adopted in March 1988, with presidential elections in November 1988 (shortening President José Sarney's term by one year). As the assembly prepared to recess for Christmas, however, a new question on rules left both issues up in the air once again. The leftist parties failed to capitalize on these conditions and only added to the confusion with some demonstrations for immediate elections, an unsuccessful general strike, and land invasions.

PCB. With the exception of the general strike, the PCB generally eschewed street activity and concentrated on its Eighth Congress, the first ever to take place legally. A speech written by President Sarney was read by a spokesman at the congress, and PCB leaders and their foreign guests were received by Sarney. The extraordinary congress was called primarily to name the successor of General Secretary Giocondo Dias, who had already resigned because of illness (he died in September). The newly elected Central Committee chose Salomão Malina to replace him and named Roberto Freire deputy secretary. In conformity with Brazilian political party regulations, they are called president and vice president (see biographies below).

Freire reportedly had strong support for the top post but eventually withdrew his candidacy. Distribution of tasks remains the same, with Malina as party organizer and Freire as political spokesman in the assembly. The PCB did not grow as it had hoped after its 1985 legalization; it has only three deputies, little presence in student organizations, and a secondary position in labor. Malina says the party is "redoing its house," that is, strengthening the ideological profile without radicalism (*Jornal do Brasil*, 20 July).

Documents approved at the congress reveal the intention of maintaining the current political line of peaceful party co-existence, distinguishing adversaries from enemies, and promoting broad alliances in defense of democracy (ibid.). The PCB supports Sarney's transition government but, according to Malina, "has already opted for a four-year presidential term and a parliamentary system" (*O Estado de São Paulo*, 21 July). The congress also approved a moratorium on foreign debt with renegotiation after a minimum of five years nonpayment. It defended the right to job stability after 90 days on the job, the 40-hour work week, and the right to strike for all categories; it called for repeal of the National Security Law. Another congress will be convened in two years to define post-Constitution strategy.

An October plenum of the Central Committee resolved that Sarney's government must be supported as the only guarantee of a democratic transition; to that end he should broaden his political base, incorporating more parties, and make greater efforts to solve pressing economic problems (*Neues Deutschland*, 20 October).

Auxiliary and Front Organizations. The PCB's José Francisco da Silva heads the agricultural confederation CONTAG and is also vice president of the CGT, a confederation comprising federations and unions dominated by the PMDB, PCB, and PCdoB. In August the CGT joined the PT-dominated CUT in a singularly unsuccessful general strike. This second joint effort of the rival confederations (see *YICA*, 1987) was called to protest erosion of wages by the government's austerity economic program, but many firms negotiated last-minute increases to avert the strike. The two confederations also sponsored a Latin American–Caribbean trade union conference on foreign debt at Campinas State University in May. Travel expenses for most of the 160 foreign delegates were paid by the Prague-based World Federation of Trade Unions.

International Views, Positions, and Activities. The Eighth Congress adhered to the concept of *glasnost'* and inaugurated its own version. As elsewhere, differences exist between those who consider the recent developments in the USSR a logical evolution of socialism and others who see a clear and highly positive process of renovation. The resolution on the topic follows the conservative line, describing the Soviet reforms and acceleration of economic development as "a notable deepening of political, social, and economic democracy" (*Jornal do Brasil*, 26 July).

Foreign delegates from 23 countries, including the People's Republic of China, spoke at the PCB congress in favor of peace, demilitarization, denuclearization, and an end to hostilities in Central America. Among others, the USSR delegation, led by CPSU Central Committee member G. P. Bogomyakov, praised both the Brazilian initiative to turn the South Atlantic into a zone of peace and cooperation and the country's participation in the Contadora process (*O Estado de São Paulo*, 19 July; *Jornal do Brasil*, 16, 18 July).

PCdoB. A rift of some proportions is developing between supporters of a policy of conciliation with the transition government and those who favor radical opposition. Since the press is barred from most committee meetings, information tends to be sporadic and frequently contradictory. A document released by the Executive Committee in June spoke of the "cynical corruption and sellout" of the "reactionary government" and the PMDB; noting that the PCdoB "started to oppose the government in March 1986," it adds that "opposition does not mean the seeking of unrealistic goals" (*Folha de São Paulo*, 28 June; *FBIS*, 9 July).

Shortly after this statement appeared, a number of militants were expelled. One, Amelinha Teles, later spoke to *O Estado de São Paulo* and denounced the remaining leadership as corrupt—interested only in maintaining access to sources of power and wealth. Teles said that expulsions applied to those dissenting from the official line of conciliation with Sarney's government. Yet Antonio Neto Barbosa, former head of the regional directorate, was expelled presumably for the party's poor performance in the 1986 elections, even though he had acted as liaison with the office of São Paulo governor Orestes Quercia (*O Estado de São Paulo*, 20 December).

The PCdoB has likewise created uncertainties as to its position in the CGT. It participated in the defeated CUT slate in the São Paulo metalworkers' election (an independent liberal won in that key federation) and supported the CUT tickets for the commercial workers in Brasília. At CGT meetings its delegates are told to "go join the CUT" (*Jornal do Brasil*, 21 July).

Like the PT, the PCdoB has openly promoted land invasions and squatters' movements, particularly in eastern São Paulo and Pará. National Security Council reports on radical activities in the Catholic Church said that PCdoB militants are active in the church's Federation of Social and Educational Welfare Groups (Federação de Orgãos para Asistencia Social e Educacional; FASE). FASE works with the approximately 150,000 CEBs (*O Estado de São Paulo*, 11 November).

The São Paulo directorate denied having incited supermarket lootings in July but called them a legitimate defense of starving people. Although PCdoB and PT activists were among those arrested during a demonstration protesting Sarney's visit to the city of Belém in November, security forces said the principal organizer was João Carlos Batista of the small Brazilian Socialist Party.

PT. The PT has announced the candidacy of party president and founder, Luis Inácio "Lula" da Silva, to succeed President Sarney. The campaign has not officially opened, since elections in 1988 are not yet a certainty, but two large rallies were held in São Paulo and Rio de Janeiro to press for the early election. In both, Lula shared the stand with Leonel Brizola, presidential candidate of the Democratic Workers' Party (Partido Democrático dos Trabalhadores; PDT). Of almost equal importance, four pre-candidates are being considered for the São Paulo mayoral contest. Deputy José Cicote, who heads the regional São Paulo office, is trying to return the party to its origins in the labor movement, and this may favor the candidacy of Luiza Erundina, who has a long labor history. (Ibid., 5, 6, 13, 19 December.)

Clandestine parties within the PT are again a subject of discussion. Olivio Dutra of the "PT puro" would like the groups to organize legally and leave the PT. Fortaleza mayor María Luiza Fontenelle, who has ties to the clandestine Revolutionary Workers' Party (Partido Revolucionario Operário; PRO), does not see how the PT can "launch national candidacies if it does not know where to shelter its own tendencies." (The PRO is a splinter of PT leader José Genoino's Revolutionary Communist Party, which is in turn a PCdoB splinter.) The PT reportedly now harbors some twelve clandestine groups. Eduardo Suplicy sees no problem so long as the groups adhere to PT directives—that is, no flaunting discipline and then "loudly proclaiming PT membership when they get in trouble." (Ibid., 6 December.)

CUT president Jair Meneguelli is proposing yet another general strike in early 1988 to protest attempts to undo popular constitutional amendments such as job stability, the 40-hour week, and 120-day maternity leave. The unions hope to broaden the movement to include the Bar and Press Associations and other civic groups. This may further fuel already intense political activity in the so-called ABCD cities of São Paulo's industrial outskirts, where the CUT and the PT originated. The CGT expects to make some inroads among the CUT metalworkers, with an eye to strengthening PMDB candidates in the 1988 municipal elections. The

CUT is working hard to win the General Motors unions of São Caetano do Sul as well as the rapidly growing ABCD tradesmen. As counterweights to the leftists, a new Liberal Party is organizing in the region, and some right-wing groups, such as National Action and the anticommunist Unification Church, have been established. The greatest threat may eventually come from the conservative evangelical churches, including the Assembly of God, Brazil for Christ, and God Is Love (ibid., 20 December). Nationwide, this movement has almost doubled the number of its communicants to about twelve million since 1980, and as many more regularly attend services (*NYT*, 25 October).

The PT and CUT, in cooperation with the Landless Movement and Catholic Church groups, particularly the Pastoral Land Commission (Comissão Pastoral da Terra; CPT), continued to promote and support urban and rural land invasions and squatter movements. Under the agrarian reform law, of the 460,000 families who should have been settled in 1986–87, only 17,000 have received plots and their conditions are precarious (ibid., 10 September). Effective campaigning by the Democratic Rural Union, a landowners' group, has slowed the process considerably, chiefly by blocking disposition of expropriated land in law suits. In these and other cases the leftists move their squatters into the disputed properties, sometimes with violence and always with indoctrination. At the Annoni Ranch in Rio Grande do Sul, expropriated two years ago and illegally occupied since then by 1,500 families, the squatters recently fired the directors of the camp, accusing them of diverting foreign donations to PT political campaigns. In the same area, where construction of 25 dams is planned, the PT, CUT, and a church group called the Regional Commission for Those Affected by Dams (CRAB) reportedly offer courses with heavy Marxist-Leninist content and have sent directors to Cuba and Nicaragua for training. (*O Estado de São Paulo*, 21, 22, 24 November.)

Similar conflicts are taking place in many states; violence has been greatest in the northeastern and Amazon regions. In the Amazon, the church is protesting mining grants on Indian territory and the army's Calha Norte project, which would establish military bases in the region as a barrier against the entrance of narcotics and guerrillas from neighboring countries.

International Views and Activities. A delegation of Brazilian theologians and sociologists, including Franciscan Leonardo Boff and Dominican Fra Betto, visited the USSR for fifteen days at the invitation of the Russian Orthodox Church. Boff returned full of praise, saying that he encountered much knowledge of and respect for liberation theology: "They consider the synthesis we make between Christian faith and Marxist ideology as something promising, to be encouraged." Betto noted that the publication of his book, *Fidel and Religion*, "opened the possibility of a similar work" that would intensify the Catholic-Socialist dialogue in Eastern Europe. *Folha de São Paulo* reported that the Vatican Secretariat of State reportedly supports the efforts of the Brazilians to improve relations between the Catholic Church and the Socialist bloc, but the support is apparently not shared by other sectors of the Curia Romana. (*Folha de São Paulo*, 25 June, 10 July; *JPRS*, 8 September.)

Guerrilla Activity. The release in São Paulo of Chilean army colonel Carlos Carreño, who was kidnapped by the Chilean Manuel Rodríguez Patriotic Front (Frente Patriótico Manuel Rodríguez; FPMR), has focused attention on Brazil as a possible haven and supply center for Latin American guerrillas. Peruvian and Surinamese guerrillas are known to have received arms from Brazil, and the Colombian M-19 attempted to buy rifles from the Brazilian jungle infantry battalion at the border. *O Estado de São Paulo* quotes a report from Peruvian military intelligence on a 1985 meeting near Tacna of guerrilla leaders from Argentina, Bolivia, Chile, Ecuador, Peru, and Venezuela and representatives from Paraguay, El Salvador, Guatemala, and Nicaragua; the elusive Abimael Guzmán of Sendero Luminoso was present as well as two Brazilians identified as militants of the Brazilian Revolutionary Communist Party (Partido Comunista Brasileiro Revolucionario; PCBR; see *YICA*, 1986, 1987). *O Estado* also cites U.S. intelligence to the effect that some Brazilian guerrillas have received training in Nicaragua and at least eight Brazilians serve in the Nicaraguan International Brigade (*O Estado de São Paulo*, 10 December). As Brazilian police investigate the FPMR's support network, Chilean exiles there are desperately seeking asylum elsewhere. They fear that the Chilean secret police will join the search, unleashing a general repression against all the Chilean refugees (ibid., 9 December).

Biographies. *Salomão Malina.* Malina was born in Rio de Janeiro in 1922. He has been a PCB member since 1942. As a volunteer in the Brazilian Expeditionary Force in Italy, he received Brazil's highest honor, the Combat Cross first class, and was one of two Brazilians decorated for bravery by the U.S. Army. When Malina's political rights were canceled by the military government in 1974 ("cassacao"), he also lost the Brazilian decoration. Of his 45 years in the PCB, 2 were spent in prison, 35 clandestinely, and 4 in exile. He is not an orator but is considered the party's most capable organizer.

Roberto Freire. Freire is a 45-year-old lawyer from the state of Pernambuco. He joined the PCB in 1962 and was elected state deputy on the MDB (legal opposition party) slate in 1978 and federal deputy four years later. In 1985 he ran unsuccessfully for mayor of Recife on the PCB ticket and was returned to Congress in 1986. An effective speaker, Freire is considered to be one of the more competent legislators but has little experience with party machinery.

Carole Merten
San Francisco, California

Canada

Population. 25,857,943
Parties. Communist Party of Canada (CPC); Communist Party of Canada (Marxist-Leninist) (CPC-ML); Revolutionary Workers' League (RWL); Trotskyist League (TL); International Socialists (IS)
Founded. CPC: 1921; CPC-ML: 1970; RWL: 1977; TL: 1975
Membership. CPC: 2,500; CPC-ML: 500; RWL: 200 (all estimated)
General Secretary. CPC: William Kashtan; CPC-ML: Hardial Bains; RWL: John Riddell
Central Committee. CPC: 77 members
Status. All legal
Last Congress. CPC: Twenty-sixth, 5–8 April 1985, in Toronto; CPC-ML: Fourth, 3 April 1982, in Montreal; RWL: Sixth, 28 July–3 August 1986, in Montreal
Last Federal Election. 4 September 1984; CPC: 52 candidates, average vote 162; RWL: 5 candidates, average vote 127; no representatives
Auxiliary Organizations. CPC: Parti communiste du Quebec, Canadian Peace Congress, Conseil québecois de la paix, Association of United Ukrainian Canadians, Congress of Canadian Women, Young Communist League, Workers' Benevolent Association of Canada; CPC-ML: People's Front Against Racist and Fascist Violence, Revolutionary Trade Union Opposition, Democratic Women's Union of Canada, Communist Youth Union of Canada (Marxist-Leninist), Canada-Albania Friendship Association; RWL: Young Socialist Organizing Committee, Comité de la jeunesse révolutionnaire (CJR)
Publications. CPC: *Canadian Tribune* (Tom Morris, editor), *Pacific Tribune*, *Combat*, *Communist Viewpoint*, *Le Communiste*, *Rebel Youth*, *Jeunesse militante*; CPC-ML: *Marxist-Leninist*, *Le Marxiste-Leniniste*, *Voice of the Youth*, *Voice of the People*, *Democratic Women*, *Peoples' Front Bulletin*, *Canadian Student*, *BC Worker*; RWL: *Socialist Voice* (Michel Prairie, editor), *Lutte ouvrière*; TL: *Sparticist Canada*; IS: *Socialist Worker*

A number of Marxist-Leninist organizations exist legally in Canada. The oldest, largest, and best organized is the CPC. Founded in 1921, it has adhered faithfully to a pro-Moscow line. The CPC-ML began in 1970 as an ardent follower of the Chinese brand of communism but since then has eschewed Beijing for the Albanian model. In addition, there are several Trotskyist groups functioning, the most active of which is the RWL.

Since Brian Mulroney's resounding victory in the 1984 federal election, the political fortunes of the Conservative government have taken a decided turn for the worse. The Conservatives have seen their popular support steadily erode, reaching a low point in July (23 percent), while that of the Liberals and New Democratic Party (NDP) climbs.

There is an ongoing controversy in Canadian-American military cooperation. Canada's future involvement in the Strategic Defense Initiative (SDI), continued testing of the cruise missile on Canadian territory, and the proposed overhaul of the Distant Early Warning (DEW) line have mobilized a plethora of peace groups into forming a loosely knit lobby organization: the Canadian Peace Alliance (CPA). Composed of some 40 affiliates, including Operation Dismantle, Physicians for Social Responsibility, and the Canadian Labour Congress

(CLC), the CPA has launched vigorous campaigns for an "independent Canadian foreign policy of peace," which among other items calls for an abrogation of Canada's North American Air Defense Command (NORAD) agreement and the establishment of Canada as a nuclear-weapons-free zone. The Soviet-U.S. treaty to eliminate intermediate range nuclear forces (INF) from their respective arsenals, signed by those two countries at the December summit in Washington, D.C., has provided added incentive for the CPA to continue its activities.

CPC. The CPC operates from its national office in Toronto on a meager budget of about $300,000 (Canadian) a year. In the 1984 federal election the party fielded 52 candidates, electing none and garnering just over 8,000 votes. It ran nine candidates in the 1987 Ontario provincial election; all were defeated, receiving a negligible vote (approximately one-tenth of 1 percent of all votes cast).

There has been no general meeting of the CPC since its Twenty-sixth Congress in 1985. However, the Central Committee did convene in May 1987 and again in September to discuss a draft update of the CPC program, *The Road to Socialism*, and to make preparations for the next party congress scheduled for May 1988 (*Canadian Tribune*, 1 June, 14 September).

During the year, CPC general secretary Kashtan, the party's Quebec president Sam Walsh, and educational director Maggie Bizzell attended celebrations in Moscow marking the 70th anniversary of the October Socialist Revolution in Russia (ibid., 16 November). In July, Kashtan went to Moscow and met with Alexander Yakovlev, a member of the Politburo of the CPSU Central Committee (ibid., 27 July; *Pravda*, 18 July). Chris Fraser and Line Chabot, representing the Canadian Young Communist League (YCL), participated in the Twentieth Komsomol Congress, which brought some 5,000 Soviet delegates and foreign guests together in Moscow (*Canadian Tribune*, 27 April); Nan McDonald, CPC women's director, and 80 other Canadian delegates partook in the World Congress of Women held in Moscow, 23–27 June (ibid., 11 May, 13 July). In addition, a CPC delegation headed by Kashtan made an official trip to the People's Republic of China (14–30 April) as guests of the Central Committee of the Chinese Communist Party (CCP). The discussions that took place there (the first in 24 years) were aimed at normalizing relations between the two parties (ibid., 20 April, 15 June). According to Kashtan, much progress was made in renewing bilateral ties; however, significant differences remain. The CPC could not agree with the CCP's assertion that the USSR and the United States share equal responsibility for the arms race, nor could the Canadian party endorse the Chinese position in relation to other socialist countries and regional questions such as Afghanistan, Cambodia, and Vietnam (ibid., 11 May).

Two prominent party figures died in 1987. Emil Rosenthal (77) joined the party in the early 1920s; he played a strong leadership role for half a century in the Toronto Typographical Union as well as being a valued member of the party's Central Print Bureau (ibid., 13, 27 April). Rose Kashtan, the sister-in-law of the general secretary, had also been active in the CPC for over 50 years (ibid., 1 June).

The problem of new recruitment has continued to be a high priority as has increased circulation of the *Canadian Tribune*. The party has set a goal of 5 percent overall increase in membership and a yearly target of 15 percent growth in the newspaper's subscription. In both cases it is difficult to ascertain if these objectives have been achieved, since the party does not publish precise figures. The *Tribune* was relatively successful in a $100,000 sustaining drive (the money needed to operate the newspaper), collecting $91,400 (ibid., 19 October). However, its $30,000 "modernization" campaign, necessary to purchase new equipment and upgrade the editorial facilities, raised only $8,000 (ibid., 12 October). Given this state of affairs, it appears that the *Tribune*'s aim of eventually producing a daily rather than a weekly is still a long way off.

The CPC rejoices in the downward slide of the Conservatives in public polls—which, according to the party, reflects doubts by Canadians about the prime minister's ability to cope with the basic economic and social problems confronting the nation—and decries what it believes is the unabashed "sellout" of Canada, primarily to U.S. interests (*Communist Viewpoint*, June; *Canadian Tribune*, 21 September). The party maintains that since the demise of the National Energy Program and the Foreign Investment Review Act, the policy of "Canadianization" has been replaced by a policy of "Continentalism" (*Canadian Tribune*, 2 November). The CPC cites a plethora of recent foreign takeovers—for example, Mitel Corporation, Canada Trust, Kootenay Light and Power, B.C. Forest Products, Bank of British Columbia, Continental Bank of Canada, Husky Oil, and Versatile Farm

Equipment—as well as Amoco's proposed purchase of Dome Petroleum.

Of particular concern to the CPC has been Mulroney's free-trade initiative. Editorials in the *Canadian Tribune* have consistently argued that free trade with the United States is a bad deal that in the long term would result in the loss of Canada's economic as well as political independence (ibid.; *Canadian Tribune*, 12 October). Now that a free-trade agreement has been reached, the party urges Canadians to organize an "all-out collective struggle" against it (*Canadian Tribune*, 30 November). It also demands that Mulroney call an election over the issue (ibid., 21 September). There are, the CPC insists, better alternatives than "throwing all of Canada's eggs into the U.S. basket," such as developing a policy of multilateral trade with all countries, including socialist states (*Communist Viewpoint*, June).

Another area of chagrin for the CPC has been the so-called Meech Lake Accord signed on 3 June. This constitutional amendment ostensibly ends Quebec's constitutional isolation from the rest of Canada. Yet the CPC believes that the document is seriously flawed because it denies the right to self-determination for French-Canadians while subverting the legitimate interests of the aboriginal peoples and other minority groups (ibid.). Moreover, it "seriously undermines the ability of the federal government to determine its own policies by giving greater power to the provinces" (ibid.; *Canadian Tribune*, 21 September).

Ottawa's policies in the agricultural sector have also received a harsh review. Noting that Canadian wheat prices are the lowest in eight years (due to the U.S. Farm Bill, which boosted subsidies to U.S. farmers while driving down the world price of wheat), the party has lambasted the government for doing little to protect the Canadian farmer (ibid.). Its own program includes guaranteeing farmers parity prices while providing interest-free loans to low-income family farmers, free crop insurance, a moratorium on farm debts, and an end to foreclosures. To achieve these aims, the party calls for "worker-farmer unity against the government, banks, and other monopolies" (*Canadian Tribune*, 14 April 1986).

On the domestic scene generally, the CPC has been highly critical of the Tories; it accuses the Mulroney administration of a "neoconservative drive to dismantle the public sector, ravage social services, and shift an ever larger share of the social wealth into the hands of the monopolies and multinationals" (*Canadian Tribune*, 29 June). It labels Finance Minister Michael Wilson's White Paper on tax reforms—the core of which is a Business Transfer Tax (BTT)—as a scheme "to make the rich richer and the poor poorer" (ibid., 27 April). If implemented, the party avers, the BTT would result in increased prices and additional burdens on the populace, particularly those in the low-income bracket (ibid.). The CPC's tax reform platform advocates the elimination of income taxes for those earning less than $25,000 a year and an increased corporate tax based on the "recognition that corporations and banks do not carry a fair share of the tax burden" (ibid.).

To combat these and other "disastrous" policies of the Mulroney government, the CPC urges the formation of a "people's majority outside of Parliament." In this regard, the party favors a broad coalition of communists with the NDP, left Liberals, and the trade union movement (ibid., 27 April, 7 September). While guarding against the Liberal Party becoming the main beneficiary of discontent with Tory policies, the CPC endeavors to press the NDP to advance a "more coherent program against state monopoly capitalism," to oppose deregulation and privatization, and to do battle for Canadian independence. The NDP sweep of all three seats in the 20 July federal by-elections was thus welcomed by the party (ibid., 27 July). Nevertheless, although it supports a "minimum program of unity," the CPC is wary of the top leadership of the NDP, which may not be trusted to represent the "true interests" of the working class (ibid., 7 September).

The CPC follows a similar strategy in its approach to trade unions, particularly to the CLC. The party recognizes that, as the largest organized section of the working class, the CLC "offers the potential to lead the nation into a fundamentally new path for peace, independence, and social progress" (ibid., May 1986). In a show of solidarity with organized labor, the *Canadian Tribune* (28 September, 19 October) has given wide coverage to a number of strikes and lockouts, especially the protracted labor disputes between Canada Post and its militant postal workers' unions.

The CPC has whole-heartedly endorsed the Soviet Union's fifteen-year peace proposals (announced in 1986) and gives full credit to Mikhail Gorbachev for his peace initiatives, which resulted in the INF treaty (ibid., 2, 9 November). The treaty is seen as a "hopeful start" that "must serve as the basis for increasing the struggle for a nuclear-free and violence-free world" (ibid., 30 November, 7 December).

The main threat to the achievement of peaceful co-existence and a globe free of nuclear arms, according to the CPC, is still U.S. imperialism (*Communist Viewpoint*, June). The Reagan administration, it argues, continues to pursue a confrontationist policy, provoking new situations and areas of tension. The CPC cites "American gunship diplomacy" in the Persian Gulf as proof, suggesting that such actions "increase the danger of an all-out war" (*Canadian Tribune*, 10 August, 28 September). The party maintains that the U.S. objective is to achieve military superiority in space (via the SDI) while wearing down economically the Soviet Union and the socialist countries in order to exact concessions from them.

The CPC accuses the Mulroney government of complicity in these U.S. strategic aims. It points to Ottawa's White Paper on defense (which in part advocates the building of ten to twelve nuclear submarines for use in Arctic waters) as evidence, suggesting that the document is a blueprint to promote Canada's military integration with the United States by further militarizing the North and tying it more directly to the NORAD command structure and SDI planning (*Communist Viewpoint*, June; *Canadian Tribune*, 15 June). Numerous editorials in the *Canadian Tribune* reiterate CPC demands that Canada halt the testing of cruise missiles on Canadian territory; that the government reject all plans to upgrade NORAD and the DEW system; that it publish all secret U.S.-Canada military agreements; and that, ultimately, Canada pull out of both NORAD and the NATO alliance (17, 31 August). The above actions are necessary, the party contends, if Canada is to develop an independent foreign policy rather than be reduced to "a U.S. satellite" (ibid., 31 August).

In international affairs generally, the CPC follows a two-tiered line of stoutly supporting the Soviet position while condemning that of the United States. Editorials in the *Canadian Tribune* have particularly chastised Reagan for his rejection of Oscar Arias's plan for peace, which was accepted by all Central American nations, and for his ongoing support of the *contras* in their war against Daniel Ortega's regime in Nicaragua (ibid., 24 August, 23 November).

The CPC also accuses the Canadian government of becoming an accomplice to "American adventurism" by surreptitiously condoning U.S. actions around the globe (ibid., 15 June, 31 August). Canadian Secretary of State for External Affairs Joe Clark's recent visit to Central America, for example, was labeled a sham for his failure to denounce U.S. policy in the region (ibid., 14 December). Canada's ambassador to the United Nations, Stephen Lewis, is described as the "enfant terrible" for his continued criticism of the Soviet occupation of Afghanistan (ibid., 9 February).

CPC-ML. The CPC-ML operates from its national headquarters in Montreal. Although there has been no party congress since 1982, First Secretary Bains has been active writing polemical pamphlets and giving lectures to various Marxist-Leninist study groups. In relative terms, however, 1987 has not been a good year for the party. It continues to produce *Marxist-Leninist*, but that publication appears on an irregular basis and is not widely distributed or easily obtained. Moreover, the party's "progressive" bookshop in Kitchener, Ontario, has been closed indefinitely, and a number of the leading CPC-ML members find themselves charged with numerous offenses under the criminal code.

The CPC-ML remains a doctrinaire organization which believes that the transformation of society from capitalism to socialism can only be ensured through "revolutionary violence." Although the party concludes that the class struggle has deepened in Canada, it acknowledges that there is some confusion among the workers who have been diverted from the true Marxist-Leninist course by "class-collaborationists" and "labour aristocrats" (*Marxist-Leninist*, 4 May 1986). For this state of affairs the party blames the NDP, which "desires that the proletariat should make their peace with the bourgeoisie," and the CLC for its collaboration with the bourgeoisie and betrayal of the working class (ibid.).

On domestic issues, the CPC-ML accuses the Mulroney government of condoning increased U.S. economic and military domination of Canada. It condemns the free-trade agreement as a "national betrayal" and sees closer military cooperation with the United States as a direct threat to Canada's sovereignty. It urgest Ottawa to withdraw from NATO and NORAD, to refuse further testing of the cruise missile on Canadian soil, to oppose the overhaul of the DEW system, to prohibit any U.S. military bases in Canada's north, and to reject completely the SDI program (ibid., 16 March, 13 April). To make its views known, the CPC-ML organized a number of "militant pickets" and demonstrations in Toronto, Montreal, Quebec City, Winnipeg, and

Vancouver as part of its "mass actions on May Day" (ibid., 11 May).

On the international level, the CPC-ML sees U.S. imperialism, together with Soviet "social-imperialism," as "the greatest enemy of the struggles of the peoples for national and social emancipation" (ibid., 4 May 1986).

Seventeen years after its founding, the party remains very much on the political fringe with a tiny (albeit hard core) following.

RWL. The RWL is the Canadian section of the Trotskyist Fourth International. The league's aim is "to build the mass revolutionary party needed to lead the entire working class and its allies in the fight to take political power away from the ruling rich and establish a workers' and farmers' government in Ottawa" (*Youth and the Socialist Revolution* [RWL publication], March). In the past several years, however, the RWL has been preoccupied with internal restructuring due to a decrease in membership and financial difficulties (see *YICA*, 1986, 1987). Its Montreal and Toronto offices are run on shoestring budgets.

In accordance with a decision reached at the RWL's 1986 convention, the Young Socialists and the CJR—youth committees of the league in Toronto and Montreal, respectively—held a joint congress in Montreal (16–18 May) to launch a new pan-Canadian revolutionary youth organization. A funding drive begun immediately after the founding congress raised almost $18,000, surpassing the rather modest target of $16,500 (*Socialist Voice*, 27 July). In the course of the funding campaign (May to July), four new members joined the Young Socialists (ibid.).

On domestic issues, the RWL berates the Conservative government at every turn—from its "repressive" immigration bill (C-55) to the Canadian Security Intelligence Service's "covert spying and disruption activity against individuals and organizations which oppose federal government policies" (ibid., 27 July, 31 August). At the same time, it gives favorable press coverage to militant unions involved in national labour disputes, the most notable of which was the three-week rotating strike of the Letter Carriers' Union that witnessed some picket-line violence (ibid., 27 July). The league notes with evident satisfaction that support for the NDP in both English Canada and Quebec is on the rise. Although quite critical of the New Democrats in the past, it believes that the NDP can be reformed to assume a truly "pan-Canadian character" (*Youth and the Socialist Revolution*). The Quebecois, the league maintains, are an oppressed nationality with second-class status as a result of institutionalized discrimination based on language (ibid.). The return of the Liberals to power in Quebec (after nine years of separatist Parti Quebecois rule) and the recent signing of the Meech Lake Accord are seen as victories for the profederalist forces over the goal of Quebec self-determination (*Socialist Voice*, 31 August). To rectify this situation, the league proposes the creation of a new, trade-union-based party in the province (*Youth and the Socialist Revolution*).

In foreign affairs, the RWL is pro-Soviet and anti-American, focusing primarily on U.S. activities in Central America, particularly the Reagan administration's war against Nicaragua (ibid.). In general, the RWL sees U.S. imperialism as the main obstacle to world peace and criticizes the Canadian government for kowtowing to U.S. interests (ibid.). Like the CPC-ML, the RWL is very much on the political periphery, with no more than about 200 members throughout the country.

Other Groups. The TL and IS are two other Marxist-Leninist groups that appear to operate, at least nominally, in Canada. The TL believes in "permanent revolution," denounces all other Trotskyist organizations and advocates a reforged Fourth International while the IS is more populist in nature calling for the building of socialism from below by the establishment of well organized branches in major cities. The best-organized IS branch seems to be in Ottawa, where a number of "socialist forums" were held (*Socialist Worker*, July–August). On the whole, however, whether through lack of funds and/or personnel the activities of the TL and IS during the year have been minimal.

J. Petryshyn
Grande Prairie Regional College,
Grande Prairie, Alberta, Canada

Chile

Population. 12,448,008
Party. Communist Party of Chile (Partido Comunista de Chile; PCC)
Founded. 1922
Membership. 20,000 (estimated)
General Secretary. Luís Corvalán Lepe

Politburo. 20 members (clandestine and in exile)
Secretariat. 5 members (clandestine and in exile)
Central Committee. Over 100 members (clandestine and in exile)
Status. Illegal, but functions underground and through front groups.
Last Congress. Sixteenth, June 1984, held clandestinely in Chile and simultaneously outside the country; clandestine Central Committee plenum held in Santiago in October 1987.
Last Election. March 1973, 16 percent, 23 of 150 seats in lower house
Auxiliary Organizations. Communist Youth (illegal); Popular Democratic Movement (MDP), replaced by United Left Coalition in June (see below); Manuel Rodriguez Patriotic Front (FPMR; terrorist group with independent lines to Havana and Moscow)
Publications. *El Siglo* (clandestine newspaper); *Principios* (clandestine theoretical journal)

During the last part of 1986, two events had fundamentally altered the position of the left in Chile. The first was the discovery in August of a cache of weapons designed for use in a large-scale guerrilla war and the subsequent identification of Cuba as their source.

The second was the failed attempt to assassinate President Augusto Pinochet, on 7 September, by members of the FPMR. These events, combined with the opening of registration lists in 1986 and the promulgation of a Political Parties Law in early 1987, posed the issue of violence versus nonviolence more dramatically than had been posed earlier, and they created significant tensions not only within the PCC and other extreme leftist groups but also between them and the rest of the forces opposed to Pinochet.

In December 1986 eleven leftist parties—including the Radicals and the Nuñez faction of the Socialists that were allied with centrist groups opposing Pinochet—had met in a Conclave of the Left to work out areas of common agreement. It soon became evident, however, that the Nuñez Socialists were not enthusiastic about working with the communists, and the Radicals were internally divided on the issue—a division that finally led to a split in that party in May 1987.

The PCC did not help matters when in February its Politburo issued a statement that the "struggle of the masses" against "the Fascist regime" would inevitably involve "the use of violence, which will only end when the will of the people is allowed to be expressed." So long as "the imperialists and internal reactionaries show their determination to impose, here and everywhere, their law through armed violence, we feel obliged to support those who resort to armed action to enable the people to defend themselves." (*FBIS*, 12 March.) In a clandestine news conference several weeks later, two leaders of the PCC stated that the party favored free elections but that such elections were impossible so long as Pinochet was in power. They added, "We made a historical error in the past when we overlooked military force as a means of defending the popular and democratic government" (*FBIS*, 27 March).

In early April Pope John Paul II visited Chile, and leftist groups threw rocks and lit fires at a papal mass in O'Higgins Park that was attended by almost a million people. The FPMR denied involvement since it said it was observing a truce during the pope's visit, and the PCC also claimed that it had asked its militants to avoid any violence during the visit. Once the visit was over, however, the FPMR returned to its previous tactics of blowing up electrical transmission towers, planting bombs, and seizing radio stations in order to broadcast their communiqués.

In June the National Intelligence Center trapped and killed twelve FPMR leaders under mysterious circumstances. Nevertheless, on 1 September the FPMR kidnapped the deputy commander of the army ordinance section, Colonel Carlos Carreño. The PCC was critical of the kidnapping, and Carreño was released on 3 December in São Paulo, Brazil.

In September, *El Mercurio* reported a division within the PCC between a more moderate "historical" sector comprising labor leaders and former politicians and a more radical line favored by intellectuals and youth. The latter group was close to the FPMR and even provided some of its membership until the PCC took measures against double affiliation. (*FBIS*, 24 September.)

Confirming the *El Mercurio* report, former PCC deputy Maria Maluenda spoke out against the party's position opposing electoral registration by its members. She was reprimanded by the party, but in October when the Central Committee met, the party reversed itself and began to encourage registration. The turnabout was explained as a response to pressures from other parties on the left, but it seems also to have resulted from the feelings of PCC members themselves about grass-roots participation.

Like the other parties on the left, the PCC as an

institution did not take steps to register under the new Political Parties Law, since Article 8 of the Constitution outlawing totalitarian parties was clearly aimed at the communists and had already been invoked against its MDP front group. Article 8 was also invoked against Allende's former foreign minister, Clodomiro Almeyda, after his clandestine return to Chile. As in the cases of two communist leaders—Mireyra Baltra and Julieta Campusano—who had also returned illegally, the transitional constitutional provision allowing the government to send opponents into internal exile ("relegation") for a period of 90 days was applied to Almeyda after his return. A number of other socialist leaders, including Aniceto Rodríguez, Erich Schnake, and Raúl Ampuero of the Popular Socialists, were permitted to return legally as part of the government program to reduce the number of those in exile.

One 26 June a significant broadening of the left took place when the United Left Coalition was formed. Besides the PCC, Almeyda Socialists, and Movement of the Revolutionary Left (MIR), which had been the principal members of the MDP, the new group also included the Christian Left (its leader, Luis Maira, had already signed a joint communiqué with the PCC and Almeyda Socialists at the end of 1986), the United Popular Action Movement (MAPU), which had split from the Christian Democratic Party in 1969, and a minority faction of the Radical Party headed by Luis Fernando Luengo. The coalition elected Almeyda as its president, but Luengo took the post of acting president due to Almeyda's problems with the government (*FBIS*, 30 June). The group's program called for free elections, repeal of the 1980 Constitution, and dissolution of repressive organizations.

The election registration issue became increasingly important since, according to the 1980 Constitution, a plebiscite on a presidential candidate for the 1989–1997 presidential term must be held by late 1988 or early 1989. The left had its own Command for the Struggle for Free Democratic Elections, which was parallel to the Committee for Free Elections headed by Sergio Molina, a former Christian Democratic cabinet member. Both groups hoped to change the presidential plebiscite into a competitive election. The Nuñez Socialists were also instrumental in the establishment of a Party for Democracy to group all those supporting competitive civilian elections; its first head was Ricardo Lagos, a Socialist academic. The new party immediately refused to follow the cumbersome registration procedures established in the Political Parties Law.

In February *El Mercurio* reported that the MIR was divided on the issue of the appropriateness of violence and that a MIR-Renewal group had called for a new approach after the failure of the assassination attempt (*FBIS*, 6 March). In April that newspaper also reported that, during the Fourth Congress of the MIR beginning on 15 April, the division between the "militarized" faction and the renewal group had led to a schism whereby each group was claiming to represent the authentic organization (ibid., 30 April).

As the political system in Chile opens up in preparation for the plebiscite and for the congressional elections scheduled for 1990, the PCC is still playing a double game: calling for alliances with the rest of the opposition, but at the same time accepting and even endorsing the selective use of violence that the other parties reject. However, the violence/nonviolence issue has become more difficult for the communists—as well as for the MIR and the FPMR—as the opportunity to use the plebiscite against Pinochet approaches. The issue is exploited by the government to keep the opposition divided, and the communist position continues to provide some justification for government repression against far-left groups.

At the end of 1987 there appears to be little or no likelihood of a successful national uprising against Pinochet similar to the one led by the Sandinistas against Somoza in Nicaragua, but the PCC continues to insist on "all forms of struggle." However, now that it is no longer urging a boycott of the plebiscite, the estimated 8–15 percent of the electorate that is sympathetic to the communists could provide a decisive element in using the vote to defeat Pinochet. For that reason 1988 will be a decisive year.

Paul E. Sigmund
Princeton University

Colombia

Population. 30,660,504
Party. Communist Party of Colombia (Partido Comunista de Colombia; PCC)
Founded. 1930.
Membership. 18,000 (estimated, including youth organization)

General Secretary. Gilberto Vieira (76)
Executive Committee. 14 members
Central Committee. 80 members
Status. Legal
Last Congress. Fourteenth, 7–11 November 1984
Last Election. 1986: presidential, 4.5 percent; municipal and state assembly, 1.4 percent; congressional, 1.4 percent, 5 of 114 senators, 9 of 199 representatives
Auxiliary Organizations. United Workers Confederation (CUT); Federation of Agrarian Syndicates; Communist Youth of Colombia (JUCO), claims 2,000 members
Publications. *Voz* (weekly), 40,000 circulation; *Margen Izquierda*, political journal; Colombian edition of *World Marxist Review*, 2,000 circulation

The political situation in Colombia in 1987 was dominated by a resurgence of guerrilla and other politically motivated violence. According to a report by Colombian security agencies, a total of 1,679 people died as a direct result of political violence during the first ten months of the year. There were 408 terrorist actions, 27 attacks on small villages, particularly in remote areas, and 229 skirmishes between the armed forces and police and guerrilla units. In addition, 186 citizens were kidnapped (*El Siglo*, 7 November).

The three-year-old truce between the Colombian government and the Revolutionary Armed Forces of Colombia (FARC)—the country's largest guerrilla movement—experienced its worst moments during the year, with frequent violations occurring on both sides. It is clear that the Liberal administration of President Virgilio Barco is less tolerant of cease-fire abuses than the previous government and inclined to coordinate its policy more closely with the military. Approximately four hundred soldiers and seven hundred guerrillas were killed in clashes believed to be more intense now than at any time since the late 1970s. The government's fragile agreement with the FARC has been further eroded by mounting evidence of cooperation between the guerrillas and Colombia's powerful drug rings.

The threat to peace in Colombia is exacerbated by persistent charges that middle-level army officers may be involved in the paramilitary groups and right-wing death squads that were responsible for the murder of almost two hundred leftist political leaders and activists in 1987, including Senator Jaime Pardo Leal, head and former presidential candidate of Colombia's major opposition party, the Patriotic Union (Unión Patriótica; UP). Although the PCC and UP still remain committed to the peace process, there is growing concern among their leadership that if political violence continues to escalate, it may prove impossible to hold local elections in emergency zones in March 1988. The UP has practically been annihilated by political violence in regions like Meta and Caquetá departments, where the majority of UP candidates or precandidates for mayor have been assassinated. Colombia is in no immediate danger of being taken over by leftist extremists or by a security-conscious military, but uncontrolled violence is seriously undermining the country's democratic institutions.

PCC. The communist movement in Colombia has undergone various transformations in both name and organization since the party's initial formation in December 1926. The PCC was publicly proclaimed on 17 July 1930. In July 1965 a schism within the PCC between pro-Soviet and pro-Chinese factions resulted in the latter's becoming the Communist Party of Colombia, Marxist-Leninist (PCC-ML). Only the PCC has legal status. It has been allowed to participate in elections under its own banner since 1972. In 1986 the PCC participated in municipal council, state assembly, congressional, and presidential elections as the leading member of the leftist coalition UP. The UP was formed in 1985 on the initiative of the FARC as a broad front to achieve political, economic, and social reforms (*Voz*, 12 February). From the day the movement was founded, the PCC has been active in its leadership and work. The UP won or shared five senate and nine house seats in the March elections (compared to one senate and three house seats for the Democratic Front coalition in 1982). It also elected a total of nineteen deputies in twelve departmental assemblies (compared to eight in 1982), and 323 councilmembers (compared to 108 in 1982). The UP's presidential candidate received 4.5 percent of the popular vote in the May 1986 presidential election, which represents the highest level of support for the left in Colombian history in terms of number of votes (328,641).

According to U.S. intelligence sources, the PCC has 18,000 members, including communist youth. Although the party contends that its ranks have increased "by more than 5,000" in recent years, the party's growth has been less rapid than its leaders had hoped, especially outside the Federal District of Bogotá. Most of the party's success in establishing new primary party organizations has occurred in

Arauca, Urabá, César, Caquetá, Meta, Bolívar, and Santander (*WMR*, July). The PCC exercises only marginal influence in national affairs.

The highest party authority is the congress, convened at four-year intervals. A major source of the party's influence is its control of the CUT, reportedly Colombia's largest trade union confederation with 800,000 members. Although the party officially disclaims any control over the CUT, it insists on the right to "occupy and exercise any leadership positions that may be assigned to it" (*Voz*, 30 April). The CUT's vice president, Gustavo Osorio, and its general secretary, Angelino Garzón, are members of the PCC's Central Committee.

The PCC's youth organization, the JUCO, plays an active role in promoting party policy among university and secondary school students. The JUCO's Central Committee held a plenum in Bogotá on 24–25 January to review its recent accomplishments and to plan activities for 1987. According to JUCO's organizational secretary, its ranks have grown stronger in Antioquia, Meta, Santander, Arauca, Caquetá, Córdoba, and North Santander. The Central Committee called on JUCO to "forge greater student unity and organization" (*Voz*, 22 January). During the year JUCO figured prominently in the National Student Encounter, held in Bogotá on 15–17 May; the Fifth National Human Rights Forum, held on 24–26 April; and the Third National Youth Festival, which took place in Cali on 10–12 October. The JUCO's political role in support of the PCCs electoral and organizational objectives is carried out through the Union of Patriotic Youth. The JUCO's general secretary is José Anteguera.

Guerrilla Warfare. Although not a serious threat to the government, guerrilla warfare has been a feature of Colombian life since the late 1940s; the current wave began in 1964. The four main guerrilla organizations are FARC, long controlled by the PCC; the M-19, which began as the armed hand of the National Popular Alliance (ANAPO); the pro-Chinese People's Liberation Army (EPL), which is the guerrilla arm of the PCC-ML; and the Castroite National Liberation Army (ELN). Other, smaller guerrilla movements that have emerged in recent years include the Trotskyist-oriented Workers' Self-Defense Movement (ADO); the Revolutionary Workers' Party (PRT); the Free Fatherland (Patria Libre), which some observers believe to be a spinoff of the EPL; and the Quintín Lamé, a pro-Indian group that operates primarily in the Valle del Cauca and Cauca departments. In late 1985, leaders from the various guerrilla organizations that no longer observe the 1984 cease-fire agreements or, in the case of the ELN, that did not agree to them in the first instance, formed the National Guerrilla Coordinating board (CNG). The principal leadership within the CNG is provided by the M-19. Among the guerrilla columns functioning under the umbrella of the CNG's coordinated command is the so-called America Battalion, said by its leader to consist of leftist rebels from Colombia, members of the Alfaro Lives movement of Ecuador, and guerrillas from the Tupac Amaru II movement of Peru. Colombia's defense minister reported on 16 December that there are 7,000 guerrillas operating in the country (EFE, 16 December; *FBIS*, 17 December).

In October the leaders of Colombia's six major guerrilla groups, including the FARC, met in La Uribe and announced their merger as the Simón Bolívar National Guerrilla Coordinating Board (Simón Bolívar CNG). In a three-page declaration, the new rebel command explained that as a result of "the unprecedented critical situation" that the country is experiencing, it is working on the formation of a single guerrilla army "as a guarantor and defender of life and the national and people's sovereignty" (AFP, 2 October).

The FARC. According to Colombia's defense minister, the FARC has a total of 4,500 men (other estimates range as high as 12,000) operating on 39 fronts (EFE, 16 December; *FBIS*, 17 December). According to the movement's principal leader, Manuel Marulanda Vélez, the FARC has expanded its areas of influence in recent years to include portions of the departments of Huila, Caquetá, Tolima, Cauca, Boyacá, Santander, Antioquia, Valle, Meta, Cundinamarca, and the intendance of Arauca. The FARC's general headquarters is located in La Uribe. Jacobo Arenas is Marulanda's second-in-command; other members of the FARC's central staff are Alfonso Cano, Raúl Reyes, and Timoleón Jiménez. Although Marulanda has never confirmed officially that the FARC is the armed wing of the PCC, it is widely believed that the leadership mechanisms and general policy of the FARC are determined by the PCC's bylaws, and political resolutions emitted at party congresses and plenums are presumably transmitted to the fronts through Marulanda's directives.

In February FARC commanders accused the Barco government of not wanting to revive the peace commission nor being able to halt "the surge of militarism" (*Voz*, 5 February). Colombia's defense minister, in turn, claimed to have "clear evidence" of the FARC's continued involvement in guerrilla attacks in some of the country's regions (*El Tiempo*, 21 February). Following a tour of so-called red zones, military commanders verified the deterioration of public order in Arauca, Santander, North Santander, Huila, Antioquia, Córdoba, Meta, and Caquetá (ibid., 31 March).

In April the FARC and the EPL issued a joint communiqué expressing their willingness to "continue seeking the unity of the guerrilla movement" and to work for a political solution to the current crisis in the nation (ibid., 16 April). Marulanda explained that the FARC would continue to seek rapprochement with other guerrilla groups "in order to work out agreements that will allow us to carry out joint political activities and to find ways to normalize the situation" (EFE, 22 April; *FBIS*, 23 April). On 7 May, the FARC's leadership sent an open letter to President Barco reaffirming their commitment to the peace process and requesting an audience to discuss means of combatting the escalation in political violence (*Voz*, 14 May).

In what a military spokesman called "the worst guerrilla attack on the army in 15 years," two FARC fronts ambushed a truck convoy near Puerto Rico, Caquetá, on 16 June, leaving 27 dead and 42 wounded (*El Tiempo*, 17 June). In an address to the nation, President Barco declared that the government "will assume the cease-fire is over anywhere in the nation where the police are attacked," thus giving authority to the armed forces to determine where the truce is in effect (ibid., 24 June).

Clashes between army troops and various FARC fronts continued during July and August. According to FARC deserters, the FARC has Cuban instructors attached to each of its fronts and maintains a sophisticated airbase with modern Soviet-made weapons in the southeastern region of the country, where drug trafficking and gun running are common (*El Siglo*, 4 August). The commander of FARC's second front and eleven other guerrillas were killed on 21 September in a clash near the border between Huila and Tolima departments (*El Espectador*, 22 September).

Colombia's government minister announced in September that the La Uribe agreements "no longer had any value for the country" and that the government would take no steps to revive them unless the FARC agreed to demobilize and lay down its weapons (*El Tiempo*, 22 September).

In an interview published in October, Marulanda complained that "not 10 percent of what was agreed upon in the La Uribe agreements has been complied with." Apart from the popular election of mayors, scheduled for 11 March 1988, other FARC demands such as agrarian and urban reform and the lifting of the state of siege remain unfulfilled. Marulanda admitted that the government's military operations have been "very costly" for the FARC. Nevertheless, he announced that the FARC would continue to support "a great national electoral campaign to defeat militarism and allow the people to undertake the changes through some means other than war" (Montevideo, *La Hora*, 11 October). Following a meeting on 30 October with the presidential adviser for rehabilitation, reconciliation, and normalization, Jacobo Arenas announced that the FARC would resume a dialogue with the government (*El Espectador*, 31 October).

The commander of the FARC's thirteenth front was killed in December in a skirmish with government troops in the region of Belén de los Andaquies municipality (*El Tiempo*, 2 December). Approximately eighty members of the FARC's fourth and fourteenth fronts occupied Canta Gallo, San Pablo municipality, on 27 December, but they failed in their attempt to seize a local military outpost (*El Espectador*, 28 December).

Domestic Attitudes and Activities. The PCC recognizes the experience of the Communist Party of the Soviet Union (CPSU) as an ideological source, but it also takes "maximum account of the national characteristics and revolutionary and democratic traditions of the Colombian people." This has enabled the party to devise its own tactics, which combine diverse forms of struggle ranging from electoral campaigns to guerrilla warfare. The documents and declarations approved by the PCC's Fourteenth Congress indicate that the strategy and tactics of the PCC will continue to be a combination of all forms of struggle. According to Vieira, "We are partisans of all forms of mass struggle and we strive to combine them to meet adequately each political situation. We have always stated and will repeat whenever necessary that the Colombian Communist Party justifies armed mass struggle against tyrannical oppression and military aggression" (*Voz*, 31 July 1986).

Much of the PCC's political activity in 1987 directly concerned its participation in the leadership and activities of the UP. The UP's political growth has been substantial in remote areas like Urabá, Middle Magdalena, Arauca, and Meta. The UP insists that it is a legal movement, unlike the FARC, and can therefore demand guarantees for its followers' lives and its political activities. Most of the recent political crimes in Colombia have been committed against UP members. According to *Voz* (8 January) 342 UP leaders and activists were killed in 1986, most of them by right-wing groups.

The PCC held a plenary session in Bogotá on 9–11 January to consider the political situation in the country and internal party matters. Vieira cited the consolidation of the UP and the establishment of the CUT as the most important results achieved in recent class struggles. In the face of continued persecution of party activists and UP members, he called on the Colombian people to form a united front in defense of democracy (*Voz*, 15 January). According to Manuel Cepeda, "The army's aim is to get the Patriotic Union out of the game before next year's municipal elections." He called on the party to intensify its propaganda effort and expose "reactionary plans" aimed at undermining the democratization process (*NYT*, 27 January).

At the UP's fifth national plenum, held on 20–22 February in Bogotá, party leaders sought to dispel the belief that the movement is the FARC's political arm. UP president Jaime Pardo Leal insisted that the UP's decisions are made solely by its National Coordinating Committee, consisting of 24 members. The plenum approved a proposal calling for a special session of Congress to consider agrarian, urban, and political reforms and to demand a moratorium on interest payments on Colombia's foreign debt. It also condemned the government's "militaristic policy, inspired by the Pentagon" and called for the creation of broad alliances to take part in the popular election of democratic mayors and municipal bodies in 1988 (*Voz*, 26 February).

A PCC delegation headed by Cepeda, Hernado Hurtado, and Gustavo Osorio met with the communications minister in February to complain about the suspension of one of the party's radio outlets and its inability to obtain airtime on any of the major radio networks. The delegation also protested the late evening hour assigned to the PCC by the National Electoral Commission for television broadcasts (ibid.).

The party's Central Committee met on 14 March to discuss preparations for the "union of democratic forces" to compete in the 1988 local elections. Carlos Romero emphasized the need to step up the PCC's propaganda and canvassing work and to strengthen ties with other leftist political organizations (*Voz*, 19 March; *WMR*, June).

According to Secretariat member Alvaro Vásquez, an essential element in raising the people's consciousness is the struggle against militarism. This means the party's continued opposition to the state of siege, paramilitary actions, disappearance of popular leaders, persecution of the UP, discrimination against the labor movement, and militarization of the universities and popular barrios. The PCC has repeatedly denounced the military's Condor Plan and charges that military intelligence carries out some of its actions under cover of dissident guerrilla groups, which it claims are acting in the name of the FARC. According to Vieira, militarism in Colombia is "above all at the service of North American imperialist interests." The only way to defeat it, in the party's view, is through the broadest patriotic coalition possible, and "that is what we [the PCC] are promoting in Colombia through the work of the UP." (*Voz*, 31 July 1986.)

The assassination of UP leaders continued in various regions of the country during the early months of the year. Following the assassination of seven UP leaders during the first week of March, the PCC and UP issued a joint declaration demanding that the Barco government provide effective political guarantees for the 1988 elections (ibid., 12 March). On 18 March, UP leaders in Meta took over the governor's office to demand guarantees for their lives, claiming that 44 of their members had been murdered in Meta since the movement started (ibid., 26 March). In a meeting with President Barco, UP leaders asked the government for better guarantees to carry out political activities and more security for party members. In addition, the UP called on the president to establish a verification committee, dismantle paramilitary groups, investigate the activities of a group of military officers denounced by the UP, establish a general plan of demilitarization, and remove the state of siege (ibid, 2 April).

In April a CPSU delegation visited Colombia at the invitation of the PCC leadership. Vieira reported that the decisive problem in Colombia "continues to be the struggle for peace and a democratic opening." He spoke about the PCC's work to strengthen the unity of democratic forces and to increase the party's influence in student organizations, labor unions, and women's groups as well as among antimilitarist liberals and conservatives (*Pravda*, 26 April).

A powerful bomb exploded at the main headquarters of the PCC in Bogotá on 20 June, allegedly in response to the FARC attack of 17 June in which 27 soldiers were killed (*El Espectador*, 21 June).

On 11 October, Jaime Pardo Leal was assassinated near La Meza by unidentified gunmen. The UP organized a nationwide protest on 13 October in the form of work stoppages, marches, barricades, and street demonstrations to express repudiation of the assassination (AFP, 12 October). At Pardo's funeral, Vieira demanded the dismissal of Defense Minister General Rafael Samudio, saying that "only a civilian respected by all political sectors" could restore the country's confidence in the government. Vieira also welcomed the creation of the Simón Bolívar CNG, which he called "an important step in the search for a political solution to the internal armed conflicts of Colombia" (EFE, 13 October; *FBIS*, 14 October).

A UP plenum in Bogotá on 16 October confirmed Bernardo Jaramillo Ossa (33) as the new president of UP and announced that the party would "continue legal political activities with renewed strength" (*Voz*, 22 October). Jaramillo is a member of the PCC's Central Committee. In one of his first interviews, he proposed that the government begin talks with the guerrillas' coordinating board. He denied that the UP has any direct relations with insurgent movements and reaffirmed that the UP's immediate political objective was to participate in the 1988 popular election of mayors (*El Tiempo*, 18 October).

By November an estimated 187 political leaders had been murdered since the beginning of the year, most of them belonging to the UP (*El Siglo*, 7 November). Talks between the government and the UP have ended in stalemate for lack of government guarantees for the political group, according to Jaramillo. He described a meeting with President Barco on 9 November as "negative" and said that "the government's position continues to be inflexible on the possibility of talks with the Simón Bolívar CNG." He added that the UP would continue its political activities, but "as long as the violent incidents continue, we cannot participate in the mayoral elections in March 1988" (*El Tiempo*, 10 November).

International Views and Positions. The PCC faithfully follows the Soviet line in its international positions. According to Vieira, the party is engaged primarily in the struggle for the emancipation of the Colombian people. However, the PCC insists that it is impossible to remain neutral in the "great international struggle" between socialism and capitalism. The party therefore "enthusiastically" supports the socialist countries and particularly the Soviet Union "because it defends genuine socialism, despite its imperfections" (*YICA*, 1987). At the same time, the party claims that it is not dependent on Moscow, Havana, or "any foreign place" nor does it serve as the agent for the international policy of any foreign country. The PCC wants a Colombian international policy that is "independent and autonomous." The PCC believes that its experience in employing all forms of popular action is proving useful in other Latin American countries.

The PCC is consistently internationalist and invariably displays solidarity with the struggles of fraternal parties and peoples. The party proclaims its unconditional support for the Cuban revolution and solidarity with the Nicaraguan Sandinistas. At the Central Committee plenum on 14 March, the party expressed solidarity with the peoples of Chile, El Salvador, Haiti, and Paraguay. It also passed resolutions in support of the World Labor Federation; the "continental struggle" against payment of foreign debt; the New International Economic Order; and Latin American integration (*Voz*, 19 March). The party supports the Soviet Union's position on arms control and the elimination of intermediate range missiles. According to Vieira, the U.S. "industrial and military complex" gravely threatens world peace whereas the world Socialist system, headed by the Soviet Union, works to defend it.

Vieira headed the PCC's delegation at the celebration of the 70th anniversary of the October Revolution. He praised Mikhail Gorbachev's report for its "innovative approach to the fundamental problems of the present day" (*Pravda*, 15 November).

The Maoists. The PCC-ML is firmly pro-Chinese, although in recent years the party has looked more toward Albania for political guidance. Its present leadership hierarchy is not clearly known. The PCC-ML has an estimated membership of one thousand. Unlike the PCC, it has not attempted to obtain legal status, and its impact in terms of national life is insignificant. Its official news organ is *Revolución*. The Marxist-Leninist League of Colombia publishes the monthly *Nueva Democracia.* PCC-ML statements are sometimes found in Chinese publications and those of pro-Chinese parties in Europe and Latin America.

The PCC-ML's guerrilla arm, the EPL, was the first to attempt a "people's war" in Latin America. The EPL has conducted only limited operations since 1975, although according to Colombian intelligence it still has an estimated 750 guerrillas organized over fifteen fronts (EFE, 16 December; *FBIS*, 17 December). The EPL operates mainly in the departments of Antioquia, Córdoba, and Risaralda, with urban support networks in several of the country's larger cities.

The EPL was among the guerrilla movements to conclude a peace agreement with the government in August 1984. However, the murder of several prominent EPL leaders in late 1985 led the movement to disavow the truce.

In February, newspapers in Bogotá reported that the EPL had decided to resume peace talks with the national government (*El Siglo*, 12 February). Only days later it was officially reported that Ernesto Rojas, one of the EPL's two principal commanders, was killed in a clash with police in Bogotá. Rojas, whose real name was Jairo de Jesús Calvo, allegedly served as secretary for international affairs of the PCC-ML (*El Espectador*, 19 February).

According to a report provided by state security agencies, a total of 102 EPL guerrillas were killed during the year in clashes with counterinsurgency units (*El Siglo*, 7 November). In October EPL supporters briefly occupied a radio station in Bogotá and transmitted slogans against the government and in favor of the Simón Bolívar CNG (AFP, 27 October; *FBIS*, 27 October).

The Independent Revolutionary Workers' Movement (MOIR) has aspired since 1971 to become the first mass-based Maoist party in Latin America. Its leadership and organization are independent of those of the PCC-ML. The MOIR has no military branch and has been unable to strengthen its political position in recent years. The MOIR's general secretary is Francisco Mosquera.

The M-19. The M-19, which first appeared in January 1974 as the self-proclaimed armed branch of ANAPO, takes its name from the contested presidential election of 19 April 1970. Since 1976 the M-19 has been actively involved in Colombia's guerrilla movement, pursuing "a popular revolution of national liberation toward socialism." The Colombian Defense Ministry's official estimate of the M-19's strength is 450 members operating on two fronts (EFE, 16 December; *FBIS*, 17 December). Other estimates on the movement's size range up to several thousand.

The M-19 held out for what it considered a "broader peace agreement" from that reached by the government with the FARC. For most M-19 leaders, the peace accord signed with the government on 24 August 1984 constituted an agreement to end hostilities in order to open the way to a "national dialogue." Unlike the FARC, the M-19 has lacked a consistent policy regarding the cease-fire, the national dialogue, or its political future. In addition, the movement's loss of leadership in recent years has created internal dissension. Since resuming guerrilla activities in June 1985, the M-19 has been engaged in continuous warfare with the armed forces. The M-19 supplies most of the manpower and leadership for the guerrilla columns operating through the self-styled CNG, including the America Battalion. The M-19's principal commander is Carlos Pizarro Leongómez. Other surviving members of the M-19's high command are Antonio Navarro, Germán Rojas Patiño, Vera Grave, Pedro Pacheco, Rosemberg Pabón, and Libardo Parra.

In April, Policio Ricardo Coral, commander of the Antonio Nariño Front, and three other M-19 members were arrested. According to military sources, the Antonio Nariño Front is in charge of logistical support for the America Battalion that operates in the Santo Domingo mountain range along the Colombian-Ecuadoran border (*El Espectador*, 3 April).

In a message addressed to FARC leaders in early July, the M-19 proposed a meeting between their respective general staff members to agree on common strategies to continue the armed struggle (AFP, 3 July). According to clandestine documents, the M-19 believes that armed struggle is "the only current option for Colombians to find peace and democracy." Advancement toward a single revolutionary army represents "a first step in unified development." Toward this end, it is essential to find a rapprochement between the CNG and the FARC (*El Siglo*, 14 July).

In a message signed by Antonio Navarro Wolff and sent to national news media in September, the M-19 called for a "national pact for a government of peace" and stated "it would respect such a commitment" (AFP, 30 September). At least one faction of the M-19 now appears to be insisting on a dialogue for peace. However, the Barco government has said repeatedly that it will only consider a dialogue with the M-19 when the movement demobilizes and disarms itself.

The ELN. The ELN was formed in Santander in 1964 under the inspiration of the Cuban revolution. It undertook its first military action in January 1965. Once recognized as the largest and most militant of the guerrilla forces operating in Colombia, the ELN has never recovered from the toll exacted on its leadership and urban network by an army offensive in 1973. According to Colombian intelligence, the ELN has approximately 950 members distributed over fifteen fronts. It operates in a vast region of northeastern Colombia, North and South Santander, Bolívar, Cauca, and Antioquia, and the intendance of Arauca. Because of its revenue from kidnappings, extortion, and bank robberies, the movement is believed to be financially self-supporting. It reportedly purchases black-market weapons without direct Cuban assistance (*WSJ*, 23 January).

The ELN was the only major guerrilla movement that did not sign a cease-fire agreement with the government in 1984. The Simón Bolívar and Antonio Nariño fronts accepted a peace agreement with the National Peace Commission in December 1985. Members of the Gerardo Valencia Caño front, which operates in Cauca, Nariño, and a large sector of the Atlantic coast, signed a similar agreement in April 1986.

Most of the ELN's operations during the first half of the year were directed against foreign oil companies working in the eastern Llanos. ELN units carried out numerous attacks on Colombia's main petroleum export outlet, the Caño Limón–Covenas oil pipeline linking the eastern plains and the Caribbean coast. In a communiqué sent to news media in January, the ELN said that it would continue attacks against pipelines and oil installations throughout the country as an expression of its opposition to "agreements and contracts that harm national sovereignty" (*El Tiempo*, 19 January). The ELN announced in June that it would suspend its sabotage actions against oil installations if the government agreed to change its energy policy. Specifically, the ELN demanded that the government lower the price of fuel, impose an $800 million fine on the Occidental Oil Company, and establish a $1 "social tax" on every barrel of crude oil extracted by multinational enterprises. The government's position is that it will not negotiate a change in energy policy with "an armed minority who attempts to destroy national property" (ibid., 3 June). On 28 December the ELN sent a communiqué to radio stations in Ocana announcing it will resume attacks on the country's oil pipelines (ibid., 29 December).

In a clandestine communiqué issued by the ELN's National Directorate in Bucaramanga, the ELN said that it would no longer "sign agreements" or "have relations" with the FARC, which it termed a "counterrevolutionary organization." ELN leaders charged the FARC with acting militarily in the name of the ELN and disavowed responsibility for the 24 January ambush in Middle Magdalena in which seven soldiers were killed (*El Espectador*, 3 February). The ELN subsequently accused the FARC of "opportunism" and stated it would launch a strong military offensive against "the FARC and its political arm, the Patriotic Union" (*El Tiempo*, 20 February). In April the ELN publicly admitted that it was engaged in a "guerrilla war" against the FARC, which it accused of "causing more ELN casualties than the regular army" (ibid., 23 April). The ELN claimed responsibility for the murders of two UP members in Meta and César departments in May (Radio Sutatenza, 19 May; *FBIS*, 20 May).

In a clandestine note sent to newspaper offices in Bucaramanga, the ELN revealed the formation of a new guerrilla front in North Santander (*El Tiempo*, 4 May). The Domingo Laín Sáenz front claimed responsibility for the September attack on a Venezuelan National Guard post in the border town of Ureña. The ELN stated that the attack was a reprisal for "the injustices perpetrated by the Venezuelan National Guard against Colombian smugglers" (AFP, 28 September). Ten policemen were killed on 30 October when their van was blown up by an ELN guerrilla column operating in Arauca (*El Espectador*, 31 October).

Daniel L. Premo
Washington College

Costa Rica

Population. 2,811,682

Party. Popular Vanguard Party (Partido Vanguardia Popular; PVP). A splinter faction is the Costa Rican People's Party (Partido del Pueblo Costarricense; PPC), led by PVP founder and former general secretary Manuel Mora Valverde and his brother Eduardo. Other secondary leftist parties are the Movement of the New Republic (Movimiento de la Nueva República; MNR)—formerly the Revolutionary People's Movement, led by Sergio Erick Ardon, and the Costa Rican Socialist Party (Partido Socialista Costarricense; PSC).

Founded. PVP: 1931; PPC: 1984; MNR: 1970 (as MRP); PSC, 1972

Membership. PVP: estimated at 3,500 to 10,000 before 1984 split of PPC. Other left parties have only minuscule memberships.

General Secretary. PVP: Humberto Vargas Carbonell; PPC: Manuel Mora Valverde;—Lenín Chacón Vargas, subsecretary general

General Undersecretary. PVP: Oscar Madrigal; PPC: Eduardo Mora Valverde

Central Committee. PVP and PPC each have 35 members, 15 alternates

Status. Legal in all cases

Last Congress. PVP: Fifteenth, 15–16 September 1984, in San José; PPC: Fifteenth, 23–24 August 1987

Last Election. 1986: Popular Alliance (Alianza Popular; AP), including PVP, less than 1 percent of the presidential vote, 1 legislator elected; United People (Pueblo Unido; PU), including PPC, less than 1 percent of the presidential vote, 1 legislator elected

Auxiliary Organizations. Unitary Workers' Central (Central Unitaria de Trabajadores; CUT); General Workers' Confederation (Confederación General de Trabajadores; CGT); National Peasants' Federation (Federación Campesina Nacional; FCN); Costa Rican Peace and Solidarity Council (umbrella group of approximately 50 union and solidarity committees)

Publications. PVP: *Libertad Revolucionaria* became *Adelante* (weekly), Francisco Gamboa Guzman, director; PPC: *Libertad* (weekly), Eduardo Mora Valverde, director

The year of 1987 will go down in Costa Rican history as the year of the Nobel peace prize. Many Costa Ricans will claim a part of the credit for that award, including the political parties of the left that had been clamoring for a negotiated settlement of the crisis in Central America. Neither President Oscar Arias' regional peace initiative nor his government's domestic policies met the political demands of the parties of the left that had contributed to his electoral success in 1986 (see *YICA*, 1987). However, opposition to the government from the left in Costa Rica is based on rhetoric rather than on actions.

It is the direct participation in the political system that sets the politics of the left in Costa Rica apart from many of its Latin American neighbors. The parties of the left suffered a political setback in 1986 (see *YICA* 1987), when they elected only 2 legislators—Humberto Vargas of the Popular Alliance coalition (the Broad Democratic Front and the PVP minus the Mora faction) and Javier Solis of the United People coalition (the Mora faction of the PVP, the PSC, and the MNR)—out of 57. This decline in electoral representation will be even more significant in the 1990 election, when the parties of the left will not qualify for public campaign advance financing due to the low vote totals in the 1986 election.

Future directions of the political left were a topic of concern at the Fifteenth Congress of the PPC in September 1987. Although Manuel Mora was reaffirmed as general secretary of the party, by year's end there were rumors that he was considering stepping down in favor of someone younger and more energetic who would be able to confront the problems of the domestic economy and the regional political and military crisis. A resolution adopted by the Central Committee of the PPC in October recommended that the party "explore the possibilities and present a proposal for creating a unitarian electoral block that should represent the most consistent and democratic sectors . . . and present an alternative in the 1990 elections besides the PLN [National Liberation Party] and the PUSC [Social Christian Unity Party]" (*Libertad*, 9–15 October). Following this recommendation, the Political Commission of the PPC began a series of talks with the parties in both the PU and the AP (*FBIS*, 21 October).

The PVP similarly pursued strategies to invigorate the party and to recruit more supporters. To this end its publication *Libertad Revolucionaria* was revised and released in late October under the masthead *Adelante*, which may be translated as "onward." Thus despite differences that produced the splintering of the PVP and the emergence of two leftist coalitions in the 1986 election, a rethinking of strategy may occur if those parties hope to regain ground in the next election.

All groups from the left, as is traditional in Costa Rica, remained politically active within the system during 1987. Parties of the left in Costa Rica play by the loyal opposition game, as opposed to taking up arms against the government. Opposition to the government is manifested through rhetoric and acts of civil disobedience rather than through armed struggle. The voices of opposition from the left continued to be heard throughout 1987 with respect to both domestic and foreign policies that frequently were intertwined.

Domestic Activities. In the absence of electoral concerns, the economy was the primary focus of attention in 1987. Costa Rica continues to suffer economic effects of the regional political instability that has forced the government to renegotiate aid, trade, and debt-financing agreements. Both coalitions of the left object strenuously to the omnipresent role of the International Monetary Fund (IMF) and the U.S. government in these economic agreements and negotiations.

The Costa Rican government spent much of 1987 trying to pass fiscal legislation that would provide budgetary relief and tax reforms that would guarantee compliance with IMF conditions for international loans and assistance (*Latin America Regional Reports* (*LARR*) 15 January; *Inforpress Centroamericana*, 5 February; *Tico Times*, 26 June; *LARR*, 24 September; *La Nación*, 11 November). Economic difficulties prompted a halt in servicing the country's foreign debt of $3.5 billion in 1987, and the Costa Rican government faced delays in the disbursement of funds from the U.S. Agency for International Development (AID), the World Bank, and the IMF. By the end of 1987 Costa Rica faced a major currency devaluation that would favor export sales to comply with IMF recommendations. Charges were lodged by the PPC against IMF austerity measures as being programs "that bring only hunger and deprivation" (*Libertad*, 9–15 October). In 1987 the Arias government proposed three different tax reform packages to reduce the fiscal deficit in accordance with IMF conditions (San José, *Rumbo Centroamericano*, 3 November). Finally, after ten months of negotiations, the Legislative Assembly approved the government's tax reform proposals on 9 November (*La Nación*, 10 November).

Editorials from *Libertad* and *Libertad Revolucionaria* vociferously criticized not only intervention by the IMF but also intervention by U.S. AID in Costa Rica's domestic economy. Specific opposition to AID activities focused on infrastructure and community development programs based primarily in the northern part of Costa Rica close to the Nicaraguan border. To receive AID assistance from the PL480 program, Costa Rica had to agree to complete highway and community development projects in the northern zone with the proceeds from those funds (*Tico Times*, February 20). Charging the U.S. government with having military motives, *Libertad Revolucionaria (13–19 February)* editorialized that "AID agents in our territory are ruling here in Costa Rica. It is a shame that in exchange for a few dollars a foreign organization meddles so shamelessly in our country and orders us around".

The U.S. "interference" in Costa Rica's domestic affairs, according to critics from the left, also included road improvement and bridge-building exercises by the U.S. Army Corps of Engineers. Approximately 247 U.S. troops set up Camp Gallo Pinto outside Quepos on the Pacific coast of Costa Rica. Their task was to build "Bailey" bridges along the Pacific coast highway (*La Nación*, 26 January; *Tico Times*, 13 February). As with the AID projects in northern Costa Rica, the bridge-building exercises have been challenged by the left as being motivated by military concerns within the region. Humberto Vargas, general secretary of the PVP and member of the Legislative Assembly, declared that these operations are intended to acclimate Costa Ricans to the presence of U.S. military troops and to prepare an infrastructure for the transfer of troops from Panama to Nicaragua. Speaking for the PVP he called for the withdrawal of U.S. troops that intend "to build up an extensive infrastructure that would make it possible to use Costa Rica's national territory and its public forces in the event of direct aggression against Nicaragua" (*IB*, May). Throughout 1987 voices from the left suggested that Costa Rica was the victim of the U.S. promotion of "low-intensity conflict" by accepting U.S. projects that "appear to address both security concerns and political and social needs, offering military access if needed while satisfying local demands for long-needed improvements" (*NYT*, 14 July).

One economic issue addressed by parties of the left that involved neither the IMF nor U.S. AID was the relocation of displaced gold miners. In March 1986 a group of approximately 800 gold miners and their families were forcibly removed by the Rural Guard from the Corcovado National Park on the Osa Peninsula when the government decided to expand the territory to be preserved under national park status (*La Nación*, 14 March 1986). Under pressure from the miners the Legislative Assembly passed Law 7056 in December 1986 that allocated 250,000 colones per miner. However, the assembly budgeted only 30 million colones, which was insufficient. In April hundreds of miners and their families pitched tents in front of the Legislative Assembly in San José in protest. Popular Alliance legislator Humberto Vargas participated in the negotiations for compensation for the miners (*Libertad Revolucionaria*, 27 March–2 April). Legislators and the minister of energy and mines, Alvaro Umana, worked throughout the year to attempt to resolve the issue. Another group of gold miners occupied the Metropolitan Cathedral in San José in August (*La Nación*, 26 August), and in October miners returned to San José and set up another tent city in Central Park (*Tico Times*, 9 October). By the end of 1987 the assembly had authorized compensation to the dislocated miners but did not have sufficent funds to appropriate payments.

International Views and Positions. Although the parties of the left sharply criticized the Arias government's relations with the U.S. military, AID, and international lending agencies, the government's active role in peace negotiations in the region brought support from both major coalitions. Both the AP and the PU had continuously attacked the undeclared U.S. war on Nicaragua and Costa Rica's "neutrality" that allowed Nicaraguan *contras* to operate from within Costa Rica during the Monge administration. The revelation in September 1986 of a "secret *contra* airstrip" was the beginning of the revelations that culminated in the Iran-*contra* scandal.

President Arias responded to the revelations and the implications of the scandal by calling a meeting in February of the presidents of Guatemala, Honduras, and El Salvador after which the Arias Plan was proposed. This plan was a scaled-down and refocused version of earlier proposals by the Contadora nations that called for a negotiated settlement of the various conflicts in Central America—not just Nicaragua. President Arias also called for a meeting of the five Central American presidents in Guatemala in June to sign the peace agreement. Although built on the earlier work of the Contadora negotiations, Arias' proposal that the five Central American presidents sign an accord to determine their own future peace negotiations was historic.

The June meeting was delayed, but on 7 August the historic signing of the peace initiative by the five presidents took place in Guatemala. No insurgent groups or outside powers were included in the meeting. The plan called for democratization, political freedom, and an end to states of emergency; dialogue between governments and unarmed oppositions including guerrillas who accept amnesties; a prohibition of the use of national territory by groups to attack another country; cessation of outside aid to insurgent groups; cease-fires and accompanying amnesties; renewed regional arms negotiations; economic and refugee assistance; and the election of a Central American Parliament. The initial steps toward the peace pledge were to be in place by 7 November and verified by an international verification commission.

That the peace initiative was signed by all five Central American presidents was heralded in Costa Rica by all political groups (*La Nación*, 8, 9 August). For many years the parties of the left in Costa Rica had objected to the operations of the *contras* against the Sandinista government of Nicaragua. Despite training by Special Forces of the U.S. military from 1985 to 1986, the Costa Rican Civil Guard was never sufficiently prepared to secure its northern border from *contra* activities or Sandinista incursions that happened throughout 1987 (*FBIS*, 7 May; *La República*, 22 May; *FBIS*, 15 July). Thus, although *contra* military activity violated Costa Rican law, the capability to enforce that law was lacking. Much to the satisfaction of the various factions on the left, the peace initiative clearly called for a cessation of support for the *contras* by the United States. Editorials in both *Libertad* (14, 20 August) and *Libertad Revolucionaria* (14–20 August) demanded that the United States cease support for the *contras* and that the Arias government ensure compliance with the prohibition of use of territory for attack against another nation.

Following an initial honeymoon period of euphoric support for the peace initiative, both *Libertad* and the PVP publication *Adelante* began to criticize President Arias about the *contra* presence within Costa Rica (*Libertad*, 25 September–1 October; *Adelante*, 30 October–5 November). Significantly, the principal complaints of the left were the continued *contra* presence and the U.S. support for the *contras* rather than "Costa Rican issues." National reconciliation, one of the tenets of the peace accord, was not a major concern for Costa Rica. However, to comply with the accord (and to ensure that Honduras would do so), the Costa Rican government did name a National Reconciliation Commission to verify that "a process is under way for the improvement of the conditions for social and political coexistence among Costa Ricans" (*La Nación*, 4 November). Alvaro Montero Mejía, PU candidate for president in the 1986 election, was selected as an alternate to the commission.

President Arias and Costa Rica's peacemaking initiative received international acclaim in October when the Nobel peace prize committee announced its recipient for 1987: Oscar Arias Sánchez. Arias's efforts did not cease, however. In November he met with Salvadoran guerrilla leaders (*La Nación*, 19 November), and in December he served as an intermediary in negotiations between the *contra* forces and the Sandinista government of Nicaragua that set the stage for face-to-face talks in San José between the warring factions. President Arias also notified the *contra* directorate leaders who were living in Costa Rica that they would have to relinquish their directorate positions or leave Costa Rica in order for Costa Rica to comply with the peace accord. Two of the three leaders—Pedro Joaquín Chamorro and Alfredo César—announced they would leave Costa Rica. Alfonso Robelo left the directorate so he could remain in Costa Rica with his family.

With respect to the issues of primary concern to the parties of the left in Costa Rica, 1987 was a year of varying success. All factions celebrated the historic Central American peace initiative spearheaded by President Arias; by year's end peace was not at hand, but serious negotiation efforts were on the table. Less successful were efforts to push the government to reject IMF and U.S. AID involvement in the Costa Rican economy. In organizational matters, the various factions of the left began to reconsider their split, that had led to the electoral disaster in 1986. The resolution approved by the People's Party in October to propose unity talks with members of the parties of the PU and the AP alliances was significant. Reconciliation of the splintered factions may be necessary for the left to survive in Costa Rica.

Jennie K. Lincoln
Mershon Center, Ohio State University

Cuba

Population. 10,259,047
Party. Communist Party of Cuba (Partido Comunista de Cuba; PCC)
Founded. 1965
Membership. 500,000; 75,000 candidates (both estimated)
General Secretary. Fidel Castro Ruz
Politburo. 14 members: Fidel Castro Ruz, Raúl Castro Ruz (second secretary), Juan Almeida Bosque; Julio Camacho Aguilera, Osmany Cienfuegos Gorrían, Abelardo Colomé Ibarra, Vilma Espín Guillois, Armando Hart Dávalos, Esteban Lazo Hernández, José R. Machado Ventura, Pedro Miret Prieto, Jorge Risquet Valdés-Saldaña, Carlos Rafael Rodríguez, Roberto Viega Menéndez; 10 alternate members
Secretariat. 9 members: Fidel Castro Ruz, Raúl Castro Ruz, José R. Machado Ventura, Jorge Risquet Valdés-Saldaña, Julián Rizo Alvarez, José Ramón Balaguer Cabrera, Sixto Batista Santana, Jaime Crombet Hernández-Baquero, Lionel Soto Prieto
Central Committee. 144 members, 77 alternates
Status. Ruling party
Last Congress. Third, two sessions: 4–7 February, 30 November–2 December 1986
Last Election. 1986, all 499 members of the National Assembly of People's Power PCC approved. Fidel Castro and Raúl Castro reelected as president and first vice president of the Council of State for 1987–1992. The council has five vice presidents, a secretary, and 23 members (ministers).
Auxiliary Organizations. Union of Young Communists (Unión de Jovenes Comunistas; UJC), Union of Cuban Pioneers (Unión de Pioneros de Cuba; UPC), Federation of Cuban Women (Federación de Mujeres Cubanas; FMC), Committees for the Defense of the Revolution (Comités de Defensa de la Revolución; CDR), Confederation of Cuban Workers (Confederación de Trabajadores de Cuba; CTC), National Association of Small Farmers (Asociación Nacional de Agricultores Pequeños; ANAP)
Publications. *Granma* (six days a week), official organ of the Central Committee; *Juventud Rebelde* (daily), organ of the UJC

Returning to old and failed remedies, the Castro government tried in 1987 to arrest a continuing economic and social decline of Cuba—a country that, on 1 January 1989, it will have ruled for 30 years. Although in all Soviet bloc countries new ways were being explored to change the stagnating and inefficient Marxist polity, there was no such effort in Cuba. Officially the Castro regime spoke of a "spirit of rectification," but it did not even pretend that the rectifying process had any new element in it. On the contrary, Havana went back to the 1960s, reviving the idea first advocated by Ernesto Ché Guevara that voluntarism and moral incentives were the solution of all problems in communist society.

Despite being plagued by profound social and serious economic problems and despite frequent admissions of these difficulties, which in 1987 followed President Fidel Castro's major speech at the December 1986 Third Congress of the PCC, Marxist orthodoxy was reaffirmed in the economic management. Revisionist trends in the Soviet bloc were rejected by Castro as inappropriate for socialist Cuba. Cuba, he said, would continue to adhere to the highly centralized style of governance. He left no doubt that he himself was, and would continue to be, making all major decisions in domestic and foreign affairs.

Mikhail Gorbachev's *glasnost'* (openness) and *perestroika* (reorganization) programs were rejected by Castro's Cuba. The reason was quite simple. Whereas Gorbachev has been rectifying policies and procedures put into effect by his predecessors and for which he is only marginally responsible, Castro, by accepting the Soviet leader's programs, would have to repudiate everything that he himself implanted, rationalized, fought for, and hotly defended in the public forum. Collective leadership, to a large extent a reality in most other communist countries, continued to be a myth in Cuba. In the Politburo and the party Secretariat there might be one or two able executors of policies, but certainly these bodies lack original thinkers with stature for anything more than following orders. The Soviet government, critical though it has been on occasions of Castro's economic mismanagement, continued to fully subsidize the Cuban economy, as though resigned that it could not dissolve or obtain a separation from its bad marriage with Havana.

In contrast, on the foreign front and especially in Latin America Castro could count a number of successes. His relations with the United States went from bad to tolerable in the course of 1987, and he gained acceptance of sorts from the leaders of the largest countries of the non-English speaking western hemisphere.

Leadership and Party Organization. There were no major changes in the Cuban communist and government leadership. Two members were removed from the Central Committee: Luis Orlando Domínguez, who was arrested and later convicted on charges of embezzling public funds; and Humberto Pérez González, who until 1985 headed the state economic planning board. No new names appeared on the Cuban political scene to indicate that younger communist cadres were making their way to the top.

Although criticism of internal problems intensified, the top leadership was exempt from it. Indeed, as Castro said in a 29 November speech addressing a meeting of the City of Havana provincial PCC, "criticism and self-criticism are open only to revolutionaries acting from revolutionary positions." This process, in which "liberal ideas" would be barred, will lead to a "new way of working in the Party." He did not explain what this "new way" really meant, except that a new task would be to urge "voluntary work" on the population. Voluntary work, a concept popular in the mid-1960s and abandoned a decade later as an inefficient use of human and material resources, was revived as a solution to Cuba's economic difficulties. So were the so-called minibrigades—groups of volunteers from different sectors, used mainly in the construction sector. Twenty years earlier these groups were called microbrigades, and their failure was recognized by Castro. For about ten years there were perennial and, for all practical purposes, compulsory mobilizations of Cubans for work after regular hours and on Sundays and holidays. The minibrigade movement is now to be instituted on a large scale, Castro indicated, saying that by 1990 those brigades would contribute approximately $1 billion to the country's "gross social product." (*Granma*, 13 December.)

In general, the "criticism and self-criticism" campaign was carefully orchestrated. It did not mean—as has been the case in the Soviet Union—that the official media would begin exposing examples of endemic problems in the country. *Granma* continued to be the most self-congratulatory and least interesting party newspaper in the communist world, according to knowledgeable analysts. In 1987 Jorge Enrique Mendoza, its executive editor for 20 years, was dismissed without explanation and replaced by Enrique Ramón Hernández. But no appreciable change in the newspaper's content took place. On the other hand, the quality of Cuban radio programming improved, and some observers attributed this to the competition of more lively, U.S.-supported Radio Martí broadcasts, which are being heard in many areas of Cuba despite jamming.

On occasion, however, *glasnost'* made small inroads into the Cuban media. In September *Somos Jovenes*, a monthly aimed at youth, published a fourteen-page article about prostitutes on the streets of Havana. It said that many prostitutes earn as much as 6,000 pesos each month, many times the salary of the highest paid government officials. The story, written in May, appeared apparently after young editors pressed higher party officials for its publication. In October, according to European diplomats in Cuba cited by the *Miami Herald*, some 50 University of Havana students and professors and government editors met at the Central Committee headquarters with Carlos Alfana, chief of the PCC's "revolutionary orientation" department. While they were "grilling" him about press freedom within socialist perimeters, Fidel Castro walked in. According to those sources, students continued to question the president why *glasnost'* had not been adopted in Cuba. His reply, if any, was not reported, but it appears that he continued to adhere to the premise that only he was permitted to practice *glasnost'*. (*Miami Herald*, 8 December.)

Nevertheless, the popularity of the Soviet-styled openness was evident in Cuba in 1987. Cubans, especially the young ones, who for decades had shown antipathy to Soviet cultural manifestations, have "recently developed fascination with" Soviet films and publications. Every issue of *Moscow News*, a *glasnost'*-influenced weekly, was sold out immediately in Havana. In November police dispersed angry, shouting moviegoers outside a theater in the capital after cultural authorities canceled a showing of a candid Soviet film portraying the underground youth culture in Lithuania, including pictures of punks and vandals. After an outcry, the state television broadcast the film, but it was preceded by a stern critique by a government movie critic who denounced its "bourgeois emotionalism." (Ibid.)

Castro's insistence on retaining Marxist orthodoxy as his regime's basic ideological and economic policy was evidenced in many areas. In early October, commemorating the twentieth anniversary of Ché Guevara's death, he stressed, without mentioning the Soviet Union, that Ché Guevara rightly believed in making socialism work through revolutionary spirit rather than through material incentives. "I ask modestly," Castro said, "that Ché's economic ideas be recognized. I'm not saying that they be adopted [by everyone] . . . I'm asking that Ché's economic thoughts be recognized" (*Miami Herald*, 10 October). The speech was significant in that it was made a day after Soviet foreign minister Eduard Shevardnadze left Cuba following a 28-hour visit.

Earlier in the year an interesting exchange of views on the Cuban economy was vented in the Spanish-language version of the Soviet weekly *New Times* (*Nuevos Tiempos*). In one of the publication's August issues, Vladimir Chirikov, a Soviet commentator, replied to a letter from a Colombian who wondered why Cuba had failed to raise its development level to that of the Council for Mutual Economic Assistance (CMEA) despite its fifteen years of membership in that group; in that reply, Chirikov noted Cuba's economic shortcomings and its misuse of CMEA aid. A few weeks later, *Nuevos Tiempos* printed a response by a deeply offended Cuban Politburo member and the country's delegate to CMEA, Carlos Rafael Rodríguez. The Cuban accused Chirikov of writing with "only secondhand information about Cuba" and succumbing to the "temptations to repeat generalities uttered by American Cubanologists."

The exchange stimulated great interest in Soviet publications in Cuba. In a November issue *Nuevos Tiempos* printed several letters from Cuban readers, one of whom praised "the democratic breezes" blowing from the Soviet Union. The weekly's circulation, which had been 150,000 copies an issue earlier in the year, was increased by 20–30,000.

Against the background of increasing interest by Cubans in *glasnost'* and *perestroika* and of Castro's resistence to it, Castro traveled to Moscow for the celebration of the 70th anniversary of the Russian Revolution. He met with Gorbachev as well as with other leaders, and the two appeared to have agreed to disagree on the issue of economic and political liberalization. Castro appeared quite satisfied with the visit. "This was my happiest trip to the Soviet Union," he said after arriving home on 8 November. "The results of my meeting with Gorbachev were excellent, really excellent." He ridiculed speculations in the Western press about Cuban-Soviet differences and said that one of the topics of discussion had been "economic reorganization being implemented in the Soviet Union." (*Granma*, 15 November.) Meanwhile, little was said about a plan, also announced in 1987, to send 10,000 Cuban forestry workers to cut trees in Siberia (ibid., 26 April).

The Economy. It was another bad year for the Cuban economy. On 27 July Castro, while contending that the country was advancing slowly, said it was trying to overcome its "enormous economic crisis." Cuba's output of sugar, which accounts for 70 percent of the country's total exports and is the principal provider of foreign exchange, was estimated by Western sources at 6.9 million tons, about 500,000 tons less than in 1986. (Havana did not announce sugar production figures.) Adverse weather—severe drought followed by heavy rains and devastating floods—seriously affected tobacco, livestock, and citrus fruit sectors. The country could not find buyers for most of its nickel production.

In addition to low agricultural production and admitted governmental mismanagement, which were in large measure responsible for the country's poor economic performance, weak world prices of sugar—about six cents a pound, or half of the production cost—and of petroleum had a strongly adverse effect on the Cuban financial situation. In 1986 Cuba had reportedly earned $150 million in foreign currency from re-exporting Soviet oil. In 1987 Moscow shipped to Cuba only enough petroleum to cover the country's internal needs. Trade between the two countries was supposed to reach $9 billion in 1987, $200 million more than in 1986 (*Granma*, 19 January), but Soviet trade is believed to have increased only slightly and was estimated at about $3.5 billion, or $10 million a day. The Soviet Union receives about half of the Cuban sugar production, paying twenty cents a pound, three times more than the world market price.

The shortage of foreign exchange caused Cuba to again stop servicing its medium-term loans to Western banks. Its debt with the West rose to $4.5 billion, about $300 million more than in 1986. For the second consecutive year, Cuban imports from the West were reduced, from $1.6 billion to $600 million, as Havana continued to discuss rescheduling its payment to the Paris Club, a cartel of West European creditors.

As it has done repeatedly in the past, the Castro government undertook what it called "detailed analysis of the process of rectifying mistakes on a countrywide scale . . . to improve production organization, increase labor discipline, and save raw materials and resources, as well as to involve Party organizations and all Communists actively in the struggle to rectify the errors that have occurred" (*Pravda*, 27 September). But rather than trying to reduce the bureaucratic procedure in the oversight and analysis process, Cuba created a "Central Group" composed of Politburo and PCC Secretariat members and other top officials who—in effect—were to be checking and reporting on themselves.

So far no conclusions of the Central Group's study have been announced by Havana, although it met several times during the year. Having abolished a free market for farmers in 1986, Castro—as though placing the blame for many economic problems on persons rather than on the system—denounced alleged greed of individual entrepreneurs both in the cities and in the countryside. He said that Cuba needed large collective farms to produce for the state, not small farms and plots growing for free-market sales.

In the regime of austerity that was tightened in 1987 even the previously sacrosanct military institution was not spared from criticism. Cuban defense minister Raúl Castro, in a rare admission, acknowledged concern over whether the nation's military buildup could be justified at times of economic crisis. Without specifying examples of "mistakes and deficiencies," he said they ranged from incompetence to waste in supplies.

Raúl Castro admitted that the size and strength of the Cuban military did not match Cuba's economic development but said that Cuba was "forced" to build "undoubtedly the most powerful armed forces of the Latin American continent" to discourage the "tangible possibility of an imperialist aggression." He noted that Cuba had not borne the cost of the military buildup alone and that most of it resulted from the "fundamental pillar of Soviet solidarity and generosity . . . In armament alone we have received totally free [from the Soviet Union] about 10 billion rubles . . . since the beginning of this collaboration." Castro said that the Cuban government also contributes to the military budget with millions of pesos. But sometimes, he noted, equipment lies idle for lack of spare parts or through incompetence. He said that at least 100 armored vehicles were out of commission at the time of his speech for lack of spare parts. (*Miami Herald*, 12 September.)

Domestic Affairs. The economy was not the only problem of the Castro government in 1987. In May, Brigadier General Rafael del Pino Díaz, one of Cuba's several deputy defense ministers, defected to the United States by flying with his family to Key West aboard a small twin-engine plane. In 1961, as a young pilot, del Pino had fought against the Bay of Pigs invasion and reportedly shot down two of four planes supporting the exile invading force; later he had served in Angola. In broadcasts and news statements in the United States, the 49-year-old del Pino said Cuban military commanders maintain a lifestyle much more comfortable than even that of civilian leaders. He said that cynicism pervades the Cuban military, with officers vying for senior positions to "steal more" than lower-ranking commanders. He also said that corruption was pervasive among government and communist officials and that there was discontent among Cuban troops serving in Angola. (*San Francisco Chronicle*, 26 October.)

Fidel Castro, whose rule was described as "whimsical and capricious" by del Pino, strongly attacked the defector calling him a "corrupt individual and a traitor." Urging his supporters to stay faithful to the revolution, the Cuban president said "there will always be rats who abandon the ship when there's a little turbulence."

Two months after del Pino's defection, Castro personally ordered the arrest of Luis Orlando Domínguez, head of the Civil Aeronautics Institute, a ministerial-level position. Domínguez was a member of the Central Committee and had previously been secretary of the UJC; he had been presented by the Cuban media as a prototype of the selfless "New Man" of the revolution. Among his former duties, for which this ex-protégé of Castro was eulogized, was the supervision of construction of the nuclear plant and oil refinery in Cienfuegos and the nickel plant in Moa, three of the largest industrial complexes in Cuba. The 44-year-old Domínguez was charged with embezzling hundreds of thousands of pesos in public funds. He was said to have built a mansion on a beach outside Havana and given large sums of money to his family members and friends. He was also accused of wasting large sums of foreign exchange, to which he had access, to purchase electronic equipment and electrical appliances abroad. More than $200,000 in Cuban currency was found in two of his homes. "It makes one ponder when one sees a new cadre like Luis Orlando, who supposedly represents the promise of the future, turning corrupt," Castro said. "It is difficult to imagine . . . You think we do not belong to a gang. This is a party, a movement, a revolution." (*Miami Herald*, 7 August.) Although Castro indicated that Domínguez was one of many cases of corrupted officials, no purge was reported by Cuba. Domínguez was tried and given a twenty-year prison sentence. No arrests of other officials were announced by Havana.

Cuba embarked in 1987 on one of the most aggressive programs of any country to control the spread of acquired immunodeficiency syndrome (AIDS). According to Hector Terry, a Cuban deputy minister of health, 1,446,541 Cubans had been tested in 1987 with 172 carriers detected, of whom 5 died. Terry said that AIDS initially detected only among homosexuals has spread to heterosexuals. Every Cuban was tested for AIDS between 1975 and 1986, including soldiers returning from Angola, but according to Terry "we detected a low number of infected people." Some scientists and others have speculated that Cuba probably has a higher infection-rate than is being reported, because since 1975 tens of thousands of soldiers and civilians have served in Africa, where the human immunodeficiency virus, the agent that causes AIDS, is widespread. (*Miami Herald*, 17 September.)

The Cuban government continued to maintain friendly relations with the Roman Catholic Church in the country as part of its effort to persuade Pope John Paul II to visit the island. In 1987 Havana gave permission to Monsignor Eduardo Boza Masvidal, a Cuban prelate expelled in 1961, to travel to the island, where he was given special treatment. Plans were underway in Havana to receive Cardinal O'Connor, the archbishop of New York, who announced he would visit Cuba in early 1988 to participate in the festivities on the occasion of the 200th anniversary of the birth of Father Félix Varela, a Cuban priest, educator, and philosopher. The Cuban Culture Ministry was collaborating with the Cuban Episcopal Conference and Monsignor Giulio Einaudi, the acting apostolic nuncio, in preparing the festivities.

Cuban-U.S. Relations. From open hostility at the beginning of 1987, Cuban-U.S. relations moved to near normalcy—within the confines of deep ideological differences—at the year's end. In March the United States tried unsuccessfully to obtain a United Nations censure of Cuba as a violator of human rights. Soon afterward, the senior U.S. diplomat in Havana, head of the U.S. Interest Section Curtis W. Kamman, was reassigned to Washington, leaving the mission without a principal officer for the first time since the re-establishment of limited diplomatic ties in 1977. In July relations reached the lowest point in years when the Cuban government, in an extensive television and newspaper campaign, charged that many U.S. diplomats in Cuba had been spying and plotting to assassinate President Castro. The United States, in a note to Cuba, "energetically" rejected the spying allegations and specifically denied any plans to harm Castro.

But as the Cuban newspapers were denouncing Americans as spies, a U.S. baseball team played a series of five games in Havana to packed stadium crowds, and Cuba was preparing to send a 450-athlete delegation to the Pan American Games in Indianapolis. The Cuban campaign, which quickly abated, appeared to be Havana's attempt to counteract the embarrassment of the May defection of

General del Pino, whose criticism of the Castro regime, broadcast by Radio Martí, was heard by many Cubans. Under the icy surface, relations between the United States and Cuba began to warm, with both countries softening their positions and indicating a willingness to reinstate a key immigration agreement that Cuba had suspended in May 1985 when the United States started Radio Martí, a branch of the Voice of America. In May, Kenneth N. Skoug, Jr., director of the State Department Office of Cuban Affairs, met with senior Cuban officials in Havana. A few weeks later both sides agreed on certain uses of chartered flights between the United States and Cuba (though this agreement was not announced at the time). In August and September Cuba released 30 political prisoners and permitted them to come to the United States. And late in September, John T. Taylor, a career diplomat, arrived in Havana to fill the vacant post of chief of the U.S. Interests Section there.

The most substantive sign of change was the renewal of the immigration pact, which was announced by the two governments on 20 November. The agreement to restore the December 1984 pact was reached in Mexico City apparently after Castro, shortly after his return from Moscow a month earlier, began to send signals that he wished to improve relations with Washington. On 13 November Cuban and U.S. diplomats met secretly in Montreal, and this led to the signing of the accord in Mexico City after a secret 19–20 November meeting there. The accord provided that Cuba would accept the return of 2,500 exiles with criminal records and mental problems from the 1980 Mariel boatlift, when 125,000 Cubans fled the island, in exchange for the annual emigration of 20,000 Cubans eligible as immigrants under U.S. laws and, on a one-time basis, 3,000 former political prisoners with their families.

One new part of the Mexico City accord was that the United States agreed to help Cuba find a medium-wave radio frequency so that it could begin broadcasting a program of its own to the United States. Discussions on this issue were scheduled for early 1988. (*NYT*, 21 November; *Granma*, 6 December.) The United States also agreed to increase considerably its Interests Section personnel in Havana to process thousands of Cubans, relatives of Cuban-Americans, and former political prisoners for departure to this country.

Shortly after Washington announced that it would begin to repatriate Mariel criminals to Cuba, Cuban inmates in the Oakdale, Louisiana, and the Atlanta prisons rioted, seized over one hundred hostages, and did severe fire damage to the two penitentiaries. The riots ended on 4 December with a promise by the U.S. Department of Justice that, before anyone was sent back to Cuba, each prisoner would have his case reviewed by a special panel.

Cuban Policy Toward Latin America and Africa. The presidents of eight principal Latin American countries met in Acapulco, Mexico, in late November for their first Summit Conference held without the participation of the United States. They agreed that Cuba should rejoin regional organizations from which it was excluded more than twenty years ago. The consensus of the presidents of Argentina, Brazil, Colombia, Panama, Peru, Uruguay, and Venezuela appeared to be the result of a resolute effort by Havana to improve its relations with Latin America. With the exception of Guatemala, Honduras, El Salvador, and Paraguay, Cuba has diplomatic or cultural and economic ties with all remaining countries of Latin America. The United States has consistently opposed Cuban participation in regional groupings, arguing that the Caribbean island should be considered a member of the Soviet bloc and should not be readmitted until it agrees not to interfere in the affairs of its neighbors and installs a democratic form of government.

The eight presidents disagreed with the U.S. position. Several weeks later, President Oscar Arias of Costa Rica expressed willingness to talk about peace in his region with Fidel Castro. For his part, Castro wrote a letter to the eight presidents emphasizing his willingness to cooperate with them on solving common problems. "This is not a time to look into differences but to confirm common stands," he wrote on 7 December. "It is not possible for us to overlook public statements" of the eight presidents that Cuba should rejoin the regional organizations. "Such manifestations alone point to the changes that have occurred on the continent since the unfortunate day when Cuba was removed from the Organization of American States. We think it convenient to emphasize here that Cuba has shown its unwavering faithfulness to the principles of Latin American and Caribbean unity and integration, which the Cuban Revolution, inspired by Jose Martí, has upheld as its permanent motto." (*Granma*, 22 December.)

Two days after Castro sent his letter, in New York Arias said he was ready to speak with Castro to "consolidate peace in Central America" because the Cuban president was "the leader" who could convince Salvadoran guerrillas to accept a cease-fire and governmental amnesty. Arias's statement indicated that he considered Castro an important factor in the process of settling the Central American conflict pursuant to the Esquipulas II plan fathered by the Costa Rican president. In August, immediately after the Esquipulas—or Arias—plan was signed by the presidents of Guatemala, El Salvador, Honduras, Costa Rica, and Nicaragua, President Daniel Ortega of Nicaragua flew to Havana apparently to obtain Castro's open endorsement of the accord, which at that time was reportedly opposed by hardliners in his regime. That opposition seems to have vanished after Castro, in a public statement, praised the Arias initiative and the Costa Rican president personally. Ortega flew again to Havana in mid-November after a visit to Washington, where he addressed the Seventeenth General Assembly of the Organization of American States. Many U.S. observers believe that Castro, either pressed by Moscow or on his own, favors peace in Central America on terms that would leave the Sandinista government in power even though it is forced to guarantee respect for political pluralism. Although the Reagan administration still speaks occasionally of Cuban expansionism as being the main danger to Latin America's stability, that view is apparently rejected by most governments of the region. Instead, they consider economic issues and their huge foreign debts to be the main problems destabilizing their societies.

Cuban involvement in the Angolan civil war continued at a high level in 1987; estimates of Cuban troop strength remained at about 37,000. For the third year in a row a massive dry-season offensive by the ruling, Cuban-backed Popular Movement for the Liberation of Angola (MPLA) was defeated by the National Union for the Total Indepencence of Angola (UNITA) under Jonas Savimbi. According to reports from the capital, Luanda, government losses were so heavy that Cuban troops were sent to the front line. UNITA continued to control about a third of the country, though its guerrilla activities have stretched to the very outskirts of Luanda. Several rounds of peace negotiations—which involved U.S. assistant secretary of state for African affairs Chester Crocker, Cuban Politburo member Jorge Risquet, and Angolan government officials—failed to make headway in 1987.

Cuban officials visiting the frontline states of Zambia and Zimbabwe reaffirmed Havana's support for movements fighting against apartheid in South Africa. Reports circulated of Cuban involvement in conflicts in Uganda and Sudan.

George Volsky
University of Miami

Dominican Republic

Population. 6,960,743
Party. Dominican Communist Party (Partido Comunista Dominicano; PCD)
Founded. 1944
Membership. 500–1,000
General Secretary. Narciso Isa Conde
Central Committee. 27 members
Status. Legal
Last Congress. Third, 15–17 March 1984
Last Election. 1986, 0.28 percent, no representation
Auxiliary Organizations. No data
Publications. *Hablan los Comunistas* (weekly), *Impacto Socialista* (theoretical journal, appears every two months)

The Dominican extreme left continued to be divided in 1987 and was unable to overcome the adverse political consequences of the telling defeat suffered by the PCD in the 1986 presidential election. In 1986 the PCD's presidential candidate, General Secretary Isa Conde, received only 0.23 percent of the vote, or five thousand out of over two million votes cast. In the 1982 election the united left—which had nominated a non-Marxist candidate—received 7.1 percent of the vote.

The Marxist left comprises some twenty organizations, several of which have just a dozen members. It was no nearer to achieving a semblance of unity than before. The 1983–1985 effort to form the Democratic Leftist Front all but collapsed. The leftist parties were competing for support with the non-Marxist Dominican Liberation Party (PLD), headed by former president Juan Bosch, and with the Dominican Revolutionary Party (PRD), whose president, José Francisco Peña Gómez, also presides over the Latin American committee of the Socialist International. It did not help Isa Conde that both leaders of the non-Marxist left were received with honors in the communist capitals: Peña Gómez in March in Havana and Bosch in September in Moscow.

"We have a heavy burden of many weaknesses, shortcomings in our style of work, stagnation and sectarianism, reformist deviations, impermissible radicalism, and a lowering of the standards in the struggle for our cause," wrote Isa Conde six months after his electoral defeat. "The party has failed to involve all its members in an active work. The Communists are devoting all their energy to building up, as soon as possible, an alliance of the forces of the Left, and an organized popular movement capable of the challenge of the day. The new times require a new approach and new actions." (*WMR*, November 1986.)

There were no indications, however, that in 1987 the PCD developed a new approach, let alone new action, in its effort to coalesce the scattered leftist forces even though precarious economic conditions in the Dominican Republic created social unrest. Owing $4 billion to the World Bank and $185 million to the European Market, the Dominican Republic under President Salvador Jorge Blanco (who did not run for re-election in 1986) had instituted a program of domestic austerity under an agreement with the International Monetary Fund. But the falling prices for agricultural products, principally sugar, have seriously affected the Dominican economy heavily dependent on foreign imports. The Dominican peso, once on par with the U.S. dollar, has fallen to a 5-to-1 ratio of exchange. Inflation reached 50 percent in 1987.

In April police arrested more than 500 farm laborers who occupied state and privately owned lands in the northwestern coastal region, and there were strikes in more than 100 rural communities demanding more public works and thus employment. In July a brief general strike took place, preceded by demonstrations in major cities for social improvements. Several persons were killed, among them the leader of a youth organization affiliated with the PCD. The strike, organized by the nonsocialist labor federation, was supported by the PCD, the Anti-Imperialist Patriotic Union, the Communist Labor Party, the Dominican Workers' Party, and the Movement of the United Left, all Marxist groups.

That the social unrest did not lead to a more serious upheaval was due to the popularity of President Joaquín Balaguer. The 80-year-old president, the only blind chief executive in the world, is regarded as an honest person in a country where graft among politicians has been common. He has repeatedly attributed the cause of the economic problems in the Caribbean to social injustice and has been seen by the Dominicans as attempting to remedy this inequity.

Another worry of the Dominican Republic was the political upheaval in neighboring Haiti. In April the two countries agreed to reopen their borders, but these were closed again before the 30 November elections in Haiti. The cancellation of those elections after an outbreak of military-led terror produced shock and concern in the Dominican Republic. Several hundred thousand Haitians live in the Dominican Republic, and officials fear that this number could grow if the situation in Haiti deteriorates further.

George Volsky
University of Miami

Ecuador

Population. 9,954,609

Party. Communist Party of Ecuador (Partido Comunista Ecuatoriano; PCE), pro-Moscow, participates in elections as part of the Frente Amplio de Izquierda coalition (FADI); Marxist-Leninist Communist Party of Ecuador (PCE-ML), participates in elections as the Movimiento Popular Democrático (MPD); Socialist Party (Partido Socialista Ecuatoriano; PSE)

Founded. PCE: 1928; PCE-ML: 1972; PSE: 1926

Membership. PCE: 500; PCE-ML: 100 (both estimated)

General Secretary. PCE: René Mauge Mosquera; MPD: Jaime Hurtado (National Director)

Central Committee. PCE: Milton Jijón Saavedra, José Solís Castro, Efraín Alvarez Fiallo, Bolívar Bolanos Sánchez, Ghandi Burbano Burbano, Xavier Garaycoa Ortíz, Alfredo Castillo, Freddy Almeidau, Luis Emilio Veintimilla, Edgar Ponce

Status. Legal

Last Congress. PCE: Tenth, 27–29 November 1981, in Guayaquil; FADI: Second, December 1985, in Guayaquil

Last Election. 1 June 1986 (for provincial deputies to Congress); FADI: 2 of 59 seats; MPD: 3 of 59 seats; PSE: 6 of 59 seats. Total representation in Congress: FADI: 3 of 71 seats; MPD: 4 of 71 seats; PSE: 6 of 71 seats

Auxiliary Organizations. PCE: Ecuadorean Workers' Confederation (Confederación de Trabajadores del Ecuador; CTE), comprises about 20 percent of organized workers; Ecuadorean University Students' Federation (Federación de Estudiantes Universitarios del Ecuador; FEUE); Ecuadorean Indian Federation (Federación Ecuatoriana de Indios; FEI)

Publications. PCE: *El Pueblo*; MPD: *Patria Nueva*

The temporary kidnapping of President León Febres-Cordero, a continuing economic crisis including suspension of payments on the foreign debt, and preparations for the January 1988 general election were the principal domestic events for the year in Ecuador. The most important issue was the presence in the country of several thousand U.S. army reservists, to which the opposition, including the communists, strongly objected.

On 16 January the president was kidnapped by air force enlisted men at the country's largest airbase, near Guayaquil. He was released twelve hours later, after he agreed to free air force general Frank Vargas Pazos, who had been jailed the year before after attempting a revolt (*LAT*, 17 January). Febres-Cordero had refused to conform to an amnesty law passed by Congress that had included Vargas among those to be freed (*NYT*, 21 January). Subsequently, Congress passed a resolution by a vote of 38 to 29 demanding the resignation of Febres-Cordero but did not go forward with formal impeachment proceedings (*LAT*, 23 January).

Early in March a serious earthquake disrupted the country's principal oil pipeline, temporarily ending export of petroleum, which is the principal source of foreign exchange. A week later Febres-Cordero announced suspension of any payments on the country's foreign debt for the rest of the year (*NYT*, 14 March).

In July oppositionists inside and outside of Congress launched a campaign for the withdrawal of thousands of U.S. reservists who were engaged in helping reconstruction in that part of the country ravaged by the earthquake. This campaign was led by the principal opposition candidate for president, Rodrigo Borja, head of the Izquierda Democrática, who had been defeated by Febres-Cordero in the 1984 election. (*CSM*, 23 July.)

The PCE. The PCE was established in 1926 as the Socialist Party of Ecuador, and in 1928 it became a "fraternal" member of the Communist International. In 1931 the party changed its name to "Communist," and those who opposed this move withdrew to reform under the original name.

The youth organization of the PCE is the Juventud Comunista Ecuatoriana (JCE). It has considerable influence in the country's principal student organizations, although it is being faced there by competition from other leftist groups. In December the JCE gained publicity when some of its members occupied the Colombian Embassy in Quito to protest "murders of more than 1,000 Colombian patriots" in the Colombian government's campaign against guerrillas and drug smugglers (EFE, 2 December).

The PCE had played a major part in organizing the CTE in 1944 and soon came to control it. Now one of the three major labor groups, the CTE is still under communist control—a PCE Central Committee member is its chairman—and is affiliated with the World Federation of Trade Unions. Its periodical, *CTE*, gives frequent publicity to the PCE.

The PCE has an Executive Council and a Central Committee as well as provincial, zonal, and cell divisions. During 1987 the party mounted a recruitment drive that was often discussed in the party periodical, *El Pueblo*.

For electoral purposes, the PCE operates as part of the FADI, to which the Partido Socialista Popular and the Partido de la Unidad Nacional also belong. René Mauge Mosquera, one of the two communist members of the National Congress, is both PCE general secretary and president of the FADI. The latter group elected three members of Congress in 1984.

A conflict developed within the PCE during the year between the national party leadership and that of the party organization in Pichincha. The 29 May–4 June issue of *El Pueblo* announced that on 31 May the Executive Council of the PCE had decided to reorganize the PCE Provincial Committee of Pichincha "for violations of the political line and statutes of the party" and had designated a new Provincial Committee to be headed by Efraín Alvarez Fiallo, secretary of the Central Committee and FADI member of Congress. In addition, a plenum of the Central Committee on 20 July "ratified the decision taken by the Executive . . . on reorganization" of the Pichincha party organization. It also expelled two candidate members of the Central Committee "for acts of treason" and called a provincial conference of the party in Pichincha (*El Pueblo*, 24–30 July). The reasons of policy or principle underlying this decision were not disclosed.

Domestic Views and Activities. The PCE carried on an intensive campaign throughout the year against the Febres-Cordero government. Typical of the campaign was a manifesto issued in March. It demanded the resignation of the president and opposed various aspects of the government's austerity program. Specifically, it demanded retraction of a decree raising gas and transport prices, the end of payments on the foreign debt, seizure of all foreign exchange "to cover the economic needs of the state," and "reduction of public expenditures without affecting popular sectors or expenditures on social areas." Finally, the manifesto called for "annulment of the agreement with the Pentagon with which North American military presence in Ecuador is permitted." (*El Pueblo*, 20–26 March.)

Much of the party's attention during 1987 centered on the campaign against the presence of U.S. reservists in the country. For example, an article on "National Sovereignty and the 'Reservists'" alleged that the troops were the result of "sinister plans against the sovereignty of the peoples" (*El Pueblo*, 29 May–4 June).

Throughout the year, the PCE carried on a campaign for unity of the left in the January 1988 election. In April it particiated in a "Programmatic Accord of the Left," in which twelve organizations participated. These included the PCE and its electoral front, the FADI; the Maoist PCE-ML and its electoral group, the MPD; and the PSE, the Partido Socialista Revolucionario, and various other groups (ibid., 24–30 April). However, that agreement did not end the conflicts within the left front.

One issue that divided the PCE from some other elements on the left was the PCE's advocacy of a presidential candidacy that would draw support from more than just the far-left parties. Thus, when the Maoists and MPD suggested Jaime Hurtado as the presidential candidate for the left, Alvarez Fiallo strongly opposed this. He argued that "the current situation does not justify any Marxist candidate, because the alternative of power for the Ecuadoran left is not present in the elections of 1988." Rather, Alvarez Fiallo suggested General Vargas Pazos, who had his own party, Acción Popular Revolucionaria Ecuatoriana (AFRE). He labeled Vargas Pazos "a democratic soldier, dignified and valiant, who confronted an authoritarian government." Alvarez Fiallo suggested Rodrigo Borja, of Izquierda Democrática, as the vice presidential nominee. When asked whether Borja would accept, he replied, "Of course, Borja is intelligent." (*El Pueblo*, 22–28 May.) However, General Vargas himself was not willing to be the candidate of the far left. Late in July he refused to be part of a coalition including the FADI and MPD. The PCE Central Committee then issued a reply to Vargas, deploring his position. (*El Pueblo*, 31 July–6 August.) Finally, agreement was reached on Mauge Mosquera as the head of the United Left ticket for the Congress, and Alvarez Fiallo was chosen as vice presidential candidate (*Pravda*, 18 August).

International Views and Activities. The PCE remained a loyal member of the pro-Moscow bloc during the year. It participated in the Second Conference of South American Communist Parties in Lima in December 1986 (*IB*, April). PCE Central Committee member Luis Emilio Veintimilla participated in a symposium of the *World Marxist Review* in Prague on "Christian/Marxist Dialogue in Latin America" (*WMR*, February). Later, Edgar Ponce, another Central Committee member, attended a meeting of the *WMR*'s Commission for Latin America and the Caribbean, where he talked about the situation in Ecuador (*WMR*, June).

On several occasions the PCE periodicals expressed support for the program of restructuring and openness being carried out in the Soviet Union by Mikhail Gorbachev. One article in *El Pueblo* posed the question, "Are There Conflictive Situations in the USSR?," answered it in the negative, and proclaimed that "We say that renovation (*perestroika*) initiated in the USSR is an authentically revolutionary process" (*El Pueblo*, 29 May–4 June). Another dealt with the "Road to Restructuring: New Step in the Development of Socialism in the USSR," written by Milton Jijón, member of the PCE Executive Council (ibid., 31 July–6 August).

The PCE-ML. The PCE-ML was founded in 1963 as the result of the breakaway from the PCE of a pro-Maoist faction. Although it subsequently suffered several splits, it survived. For electoral purposes it works within the MPD, which won 4 of the

71 seats in Congress in the 1984 election. The PCE-ML paper is *En Marcha*.

During the year there were polemics between the PCE-ML and the PCE. For instance, the PCE denounced the insistence of its rivals that the far left should name its own candidate in the January 1988 election rather than seeking an alliance with people and groups to their right. The PCE accused *En Marcha* of launching "gross calumnies and diatribes" against the PCE and its leader, Mauge Mosquera.

Guerrilla-Terrorist Groups. At the extreme left are the Alfaro Lives! movement and an element that broke away from it, Montoneras Patria Libre. In 1986 most of the leaders of Alfaro Lives! were killed, and in December 1986 it issued an appeal to politicians and church groups to join in a "dialogue for peace" (Reuters, 1 December 1986). However, in January it endorsed the kidnapping of Febres-Cordero as a "legitimate act of rebellion because of his continuous violations of the Constitution" (Panama, ACAN, 22 January). In February six members of the group seized a radio station in Guayaquil.

In April Alfaro Lives! announced that it had reorganized and was resuming its activities. The reorganization had taken place in Quito at a "meeting of commanders" to struggle for the dismissal of Febres-Cordero. It claimed credit for a bomb that exploded in a police station in Quito on 7 April. (EFE, 13 April.)

There were reported contacts of the Alfaro Lives! group with guerrillas in Colombia and with the Nicaraguan regime (EFE, 23 June).

In June the director of a radio newscast in Quito was captured and held prisoner by the Montoneras Patria Libre until a proclamation issued by that guerrilla organization had been published.

Robert J. Alexander
Rutgers University

El Salvador

Population. 5,260,478

Major Marxist-Leninist Groups

• Communist Party of El Salvador (Partido Comunista de El Salvador; PCES)

Founded. March 1930; destroyed two years later; reorganized during the late 1940s.

Membership. Less than 1,000

General Secretary. Jorge Shafik Handal

Governing Body. Central Committee

Last Congress. Seventh, April 1979

Status. Illegal

Fronts and Auxiliary Organizations. Nationalist Democratic Union (UDN) was the legal political front since 1965, now illegal; the Armed Forces of Liberation (Fuerzas Armadas de Liberación; FAL) is the party's military branch.

Publications. *Voz Popular* (irregular); *Fundamentos y Perspectivas* (theoretical, irregular)

• Farabundo Martí Popular Liberation Forces (Fuerzas Populares de Liberación Farabundo Martí; FPL)

Founded. April 1970, by dissidents from the PCES

Membership. Fewer than 1,000 cadres and fighters; about 20,000 civilian dependents and supporters

Leadership. Leonel González, first secretary of the Central Committee since August 1983, commander of the Popular Liberation Army (EPL; see below); Dimas Rodríguez, second in command of the EPL and the FPL; Ricardo Gutiérrez, chief of staff of the EPL; Salvador Guerra

Governing body. Central Committee (membership unknown, except for above)

Status. Illegal since inception

Last Congress. Seventh Revolutionary Council, August 1983

Front and Auxiliary Organizations. People's Revolutionary Bloc (BPR), established July 1975 as an FPL-controlled umbrella including unions and professional groups. The "subregional governments of people's power" in the department of Chalatenango were sporadically operative in certain areas until 1985, when the FPL lost permanent control over them; their leader was Evaristo López.

Publications. *El Rebelde* (irregular), *Farabundo Martí Weekly Informative* (external propaganda); the FPL also controls the second most active FMLN radio station, Radio Farabundo Martí. The BPR publishes irregularly the *Weekly Popular Combat* (abroad) and the *Juan Angel Chacón Bulletin*, since 1981.

• People's Revolutionary Army (Ejército Revolucionario del Pueblo; ERP)

Founded. 1971, as The Group (El Grupo), acquired present name following bloody internal purges in May 1975.

Membership. About 1,500 cadres and fighters; as many as 20,000 civilian supporters and dependents

Leadership. Main leaders Joaquín Villalobos (alias of René Cruz)

Political Commission. Villalobos, Ana Guadalupe Martínez; Ana Sonia Medina Arriola ("Mariana"); Mercedes del Carmén Letona ("Luisa"); Claudio Rabindranath Armijo ("Francisco"); Juan Ramón Medrano ("Balta"); Jorge Meléndez ("Jonas")

Status. Illegal since inception

Last Congress. July 1981

Front and Auxiliary Organizations. Party of the Salvadoran Revolution (PRS), Popular Leagues–28 February (LP-28); both were established in 1977 as generally fictitious expansions of the militaristic ERP and are now largely defunct or unoperative.

Publications. Controls (as ensured by "Luisa") the FMLN station Radio Venceremos.

• Armed Forces of National Resistance (Fuerzas Armadas de la Resistencia Nacional; FARN)

Founded. May 1975, as a result of the ERP purges, by dissident youths from the PCES, FPL, and Christian Democratic Party.

Membership. Fewer than 1,000 cadres and guerrillas; some 10,000 civilian supporters and dependents

Leadership. Fermán Cienfuegos (alias of Eduardo Sancho Castañeda), and "Luis Cabral" as second in command

Governing Body. Seven-member National Leadership (equivalent of a Politburo) that selects an "extended leadership" (i.e., Central Committee).

Status. Illegal since inception

Fronts and Auxiliary Organizations. United People's Action Front (FAPU), established by Marxist Jesuit priests in early 1970s and transferred to the FARN, largely nonexistent since 1981; Party of National Resistance (PRN), established in 1975, remains ineffectual.

Publications. *Pueblo Internacional* (irregular); *Parte de Guerra* (war bulletin)

• Revolutionary Party of Central American Workers (Partido Revolucionario de los Trabajadores Centro Americanos; PRTC)

Founded. January 1976, in Costa Rica as regional Trotskyist party with expected branches in Costa Rica and Guatemala, which were never formed, and in El Salvador and Honduras, which were formed and became independent in October 1980.

Membership. Fewer than 200 members, mostly urban; some 1,000 sympathizers and dependents

Leadership. Roberto Roca, supreme leader; Jaime Miranda, representative to Mexico; important Central Committee members include Mario González ("Mario"), Ismael Dimas Aguilar ("Ulysses"), Maria Concepción de Valladares ("Nidia Diaz")

Governing Body. Central Committee (complete membership unknown)

Front and Auxiliary Organizations. Popular Liberation Movement (MLP), established in 1979, largely disappeared in 1981.

• Revolutionary Democratic Front (Frente Democrático Revolucionario; FDR), an umbrella alliance including the guerrilla organizations of the FMLN, their parties and fronts, and a few minor civilian parties, including the allegedly social-democratic National Revolutionary Movement (MNR), led by Guillermo Ungo, a vice president of the Socialist International, and a smaller splinter of the Christian Democratic Party, the Social Christian Popular Movement (MPSC), led by Rubén Zamora.

Founded. 1980

Membership. A few hundred intellectuals and internationally connected professionals.

Leadership. Guillermo Ungo, Rubén Zamora.

Politico-Diplomatic Commission. Members include Ungo (MNR), Zamora (MPSC), Mario Aguinada Carranza (UDN), José Rodríguez Ruíz (FAPU), Ana Guadalupe Martínez (LP-28), and Salvador Samayoa (BPR).

Status. Illegal but tolerated

For El Salvador, as for most of Central America, 1987 was a year of protracted struggle, great hopes pinned on the Arias Plan, and no significant improvement. From a military viewpoint, the civil war remains a stalemate unlikely to be broken soon by either party; economically the country slid further into stagnation and poverty; and politically the ineptitude of both the government and its opposition remained undiminished.

Although relations between Farabundo Martí National Liberation Front (Frente Farabundo Martí de Liberación Nacional; FMLN) guerrillas and some of the FDR political figures remained less than cordial, there was unanimity on the leftist opposition side on at least one major point: that the Napoleón Duarte government simply cannot effectively run the country, that there is a de facto power vacuum. In a January interview, FDR leader Guillermo Ungo claimed that "Duarte is gradually losing the capacity to govern" (*JPRS-LAM*, 5 March). The previous month, FPL-BPR representative in the FDR, Salvador Samayoa, had claimed that "this president is rejected and opposed by all the country's political and economic sectors, as far as economic and political measures are concerned" (ibid., 23 January); on the guerrilla's side, high-ranking PRTC leader Nidia Diaz stated that Duarte is deserted by everyone except the United States (ibid.). As for President Duarte, he seems to have enjoyed alienating conservative opposition in Congress and among the private sector as well as leftist allies of the FMLN-FDR by claiming that "If we give in to the rightists . . . we would only jeopardize the social process . . . If we were to reach to an agreement with the sectors that advocate a violent revolution . . . we would end up like all those who fought in Nicaragua" (ibid., 5 March).

President Duarte's attacks against the conservative opposition (ARENA) often took a personal tone, as when he accused the president of El Salvador's Chamber of Commerce and Industry, Víctor Steiner, and his deputy José Antonio Rodrígues Porth, of murders before 1981 (ibid., 19 May). Furthermore, Roberto D'Aubuisson, the former main opposition leader and Duarte's rival in the presidential race, was formally accused of ordering the assassination of Archbishop Oscar Romero, a step widely perceived as politically motivated in light of the shaky evidence thus far available. For its part, ARENA stated that President Duarte suffers from "acute emotional disturbance" (ibid., 19 May).

In concrete economic terms, the Duarte government's policies of economic austerity—which are the result in part of the damages inflicted by the FMLN as well as by the 1986 earthquake and the incompetence of the government itself (*WSJ*, 14 September)—have resulted in a serious decline in the standard of living of the poor. In addition, productivity in the private sector, which is wary of government intervention, higher taxes, and rising inflation, has fallen.

As for the polarization within the legal political arena, the decision of Colonel Sigifredo Ochoa Pérez to resign from the military and engage in politics on ARENA's side signifies a new and revitalized threat to the Christian Democratic regime. Intelligent, independent, and nationalistic, Ochoa is a counterinsurgency expert as well as a national hero. In politics he will become the center of the anticommunist opposition if, as expected, he is elected to congress in 1988 and if he provides conservatives with a credible, charismatic, and—unlike D'Aubuisson before him—a clean presidential candidate after 1990. The conservative, war-winning temptation is also clear in Christian Democratic ranks, where ex-foreign minister Fidel Chavez-Mena is the front-runner for the presidential nomination against the Duarte-like, vacillating Rey Prendes, who is a symbol of the unpopular status quo.

Guerrilla Activities. From a strictly military viewpoint, the war continued at the same general level as the year before. It appears that both the insurgents and the army have significantly improved their professionalism, although the relative strengths of the two sides have favored the military. According to Defense Minister Carlos Eugenio Vides Casanova, the army's strength as of the end of June was 52,000, whereas the estimated number of guerrillas was 6,000 (*LAT*, 2 July). At the end of the year, Chief of Staff Adolfo Blandon estimated the number of insurgents at 4,000 (*FBIS-LAM*, 24 December), slightly less than the estimate of independent and U.S. government observers. Blandon also provided figures for the casualties suffered by both sides during 1987: some 450 soldiers killed and 1,082 wounded, most of them slightly, and over 1,000 guerrillas killed, over 600 wounded and 400 captured (ibid.). If these figures are correct, and they probably are, at least insofar as army casualties are concerned, the FMLN forces lost almost one third of their estimated January strength. Yet the intensity of the war has clearly slowed down, if one compares the level of casualties in 1987 with that of

June 1986–June 1987. According to Vides Casanova, from June 1986 to June 1987 the army suffered 2,706 casualties (killed and wounded) and the guerrillas suffered 4,434 dead, wounded, and captured (*LAT*, 24 July). Although such figures should be taken with caution, particularly on the guerrilla side, the relative magnitude of the mid-year figures and those of December indicate a reduction in the number and size of operations.

Some of the reasons for this reduction were admitted by Guillermo Ungo in a surprisingly candid interview with the *San Francisco Sunday Examiner & Chronicle* on 10 May. Ungo admitted that the FMLN received weapons and other forms of support from Nicaragua, that the activities of the *contras* "have impeded to some extent materiel support from that country, and we have felt the effects of their presence," and that the government's reconstruction campaign "has been successful to some extent."

Faced with a situation in which Nicaraguan support diminishes, its ranks become depleted, and the military pursues the war more consistently and successfully, the FMLN has adopted new tactics. One was to stage spectacular, albeit sporadic, large-scale attacks to improve its media image; the other was a return to the cities, particularly San Salvador, taking maximum advantage of the opening of the political process and the vacillations of the Duarte government. The first tactic was dramatically demonstrated in the 31 March attack against the major military base of El Paraiso, in the province of Chalatenango, which had long been an FPL stronghold. During the attack, made possible by infiltrators, 69 Salvadoran soldiers and one U.S. adviser were killed, at the probable cost of only ten guerrillas (*WP*, 1 April). In another spectacular attack, FMLN forces (largely ERP this time) attacked the even larger army base at San Francisco Gotera in the province of Morazán on 2 May, killing ten soldiers (*NYT*, 3 May). Despite Western media claims that such attacks "ruined the myth that the Army is winning" (*CSM*, 2 April), however, the basic trends and nature of the war remained unchanged; it is a conflict of attrition in which numbers and resources clearly favor the government.

From a political standpoint, the FMLN was far more successful in its attempts to reinfiltrate the cities and revitalize its legal fronts, particularly among unions and self-proclaimed human rights organizations in addition to its older strongholds at the University of Central America (UCA). Quite obviously the Duarte government has not succeeded in devising a strategy to cope with guerrilla-controlled legal organizations such as the National Union of Salvadoran Workers (UNTS), which is heavily penetrated by the PCES; the Committee of Mothers and Relatives of Political Prisoners, Disappeared, and Assassinated (COMADRES), a fully owned FARN organization (*Washington Times*, 15 July); the National University; and the UCA. Furthermore, there are important testimonies to the effect that the FARN has succeeded in establishing a network among Salvadoran illegal aliens in California.

The return of the FMLN to San Salvador was demonstrated by increasingly brazen demonstrations of support for the guerrillas on the university campuses, from both student activists and faculty, activities that culminated in physical attacks on President Duarte on the National University campus, political strikes staged by the UNTS, and a clear recrudescence of urban terrorism. The major danger of such activities and of government inability to put an end to them is the reappearance of vigilantism, the dreaded "death squads" of the early 1980s. There are sporadic signs that anticommunist vigilantism is reappearing in San Salvador, in direct proportion to the perceived military and political impotence on the part of the authorities, and that it is encouraged on both sides by the economic crisis facing the country (*WP*, 5 June; *San Francisco Examiner*, 10 May).

In the countryside the war has become a defensive one on the part of the FMLN despite the spectacular actions mentioned previously, a fact demonstrated by the guerrillas' extensive use of land mines, most of which maimed and killed civilians, particularly children. Even the large pro-FMLN Americas Watch, though stating that "the great majority of civilian casualties" is due to mines, admitted that "the main, civilian casualties result from mines placed by FMLN guerrillas" (*WP*, 20 April). On the other side of the coin, the FMLN's protracted war strategy and ability to survive have resulted in the creation of a "war generation" of people, often as young as thirteen (*LAT*, 7 April), for whom warfare is a way of life that is unlikely to change unless they are physically eliminated. Furthermore, the countryside remains the main operational area for the FMLN campaign of economic sabotage; nine bridges were destroyed in July and August alone (*CSM*, 13 August).

There were some important signs that the FMLN is in serious financial and political trouble in the rural areas. On the one hand, they once again engaged in kidnappings for ransom, including that of businessman Silvano Orellana in January; the captive's son, trying to deliver the 300,000 colones ransom, was killed in the cross fire (*JPRS-LAM*, 5 March). On the other hand, as the government's intelligence network expanded, the guerrillas resorted to killing civilians, prompting *The New York Times* (2 February) to define such abuses as "among the most severe human rights violations by the guerrillas in the war."

All these developments produced a significant change in the Salvadoran political body and within the military. Ochoa best defined it by accusing the United States of preventing the army from winning the war, of imposing "socialist" policies in El Salvador, and, most significantly, of providing the Salvadoran army with aid "with a dropper"—enough to survive but not to win (*WSJ*, 17 July). Whether Ochoa's views are correct or not, they clearly represent a new articulation of Salvadoran nationalism, which is the growing trend and increasingly subscribed to by anticommunists in the country. It is significant that both conservatives like Ochoa and the Marxist-Leninists of the FMLN were equally dismayed by President Duarte's kissing of the U.S. flag during his visit to Washington.

It is in this context that the impact of the Arias Plan, which was accepted by the five Central American presidents in Guatemala in August, should be seen. Both sides in El Salvador tried to take political advantage of negotiations in a country whose population is exhausted by the war and tends to want peace at almost any cost.

The government of El Salvador appointed a National Reconciliation Commission, led by ex-president Alvaro Magana, Bishop Marco René Revelo of Santa Ana, ARENA leader Alfredo Christiani, and Vice President Rodolfo Castillo Claramount. Talks were started in San Salvador on 4 October. Following the government's warning that it would not talk to front men of the FDR but only with actual guerrilla leaders (*FBIS-LAM*, 30 September), the FMLN-FDR delegation included PCES leader Jorge Shafik Handal, FPL commander Leonel González, ERP second in command Jorge Meléndez, and fellow travelers Ungo, Zamora, Héctor Oqueli, and Facundo Guardado (ibid., 5 October).

The government offered a cease-fire as a goodwill gesture and requested FMLN reciprocity, but the guerrillas claimed that no cease-fire is possible outside of an "overall political solution" that would include them in the government. Then, on 26 October, Herbert Anaya, the self-appointed head of the Human Rights Commission of El Salvador, was shot and killed, and the FMLN used his death as a pretext for ending peace talks with the government, alleging death-squad activity behind the assassination. The fact that the ERP and in particular its leader, Joaquín Villalobos, were never seriously interested in peace negotiations is well known (*NYT*, 9 September); a new development is that the PCES is more combative and has moved closer to the ERP's position. Communist party ideologues even quote Villalobos approvingly and claim that "Only a revolution can realize the people's aspirations" (*WMR*, May). Shafik Handal reacted to the Arias Plan summit requirement that peace negotiations should be started between governments and insurgent forces in the region by claiming that such demands amount to surrender, and that "We are not about to lay down our arms and we never will" (*WP*, 9 September). On the contrary, the PCES leader promised an intensification of the war (ibid.).

Although the FMLN-government talks were unsuccessful, the Duarte regime's vacillations and weakness resulted in allowing at least two FDR fellow travelers, Zamora and Ungo, to return to El Salvador to engage in legal political activities in support of the FMLN. Neither of the two accepted amnesty or any other restraint on his activities, and both imposed a heavy burden on the security forces to protect them against vigilantes (a far heavier burden than that required for protecting conservative politicians and businessmen). Once again, the Duarte government was perceived as weak, vacillating, and prepared to compromise with the FMLN, and thus as antipatriotic, soft on communism, and ineffective. The result is further polarization of the political body and clear chances for the conservative ARENA opposition to win the 1988 congressional elections. In addition, peace is as remote as ever, and so is economic prosperity, growth and, ultimately, democracy.

Michael Radu
Foreign Policy Research Institute, Philadelphia

Grenada

Population. 84,748
Party. Maurice Bishop Patriotic Movement (MBPM)
Founded. 27 May 1984
Membership. No data
Chairman. Kenrick Radix
Status. Legal
Last Congress. First, October 1985
Last Election. 3 December 1984; 5 percent, no seats
Auxiliary Organizations. The Maurice Bishop and Martyrs of October 19, 1983, Memorial Foundation; The Grenada Foundation, Inc.; The Maurice Bishop Youth Organization (MBYO)
Publications. *The Indies Times* (weekly), *The Democrat* (biweekly)

Grenada's political left maintained a low profile in 1987. This was due to general apathy toward the MBPM, and islandwide antipathy toward Bernard Coard (ex-deputy prime minister of the People's Revolutionary Government [PRG]), Hudson Austin (former People's Revolutionary Army [PRA] commander and chairman of the Revolutionary Military Council), and other members of the PRG now awaiting appeals following their 1986 convictions for the murder of PRG prime minister Maurice Bishop and members of his cabinet.

Although less visible than in previous years, members of the MBPM continued their ties with Cuba, the Soviet bloc, and international leftist support groups. In a statement issued from the MBPM's Havana office in November 1986, former PRG press secretary Don Rojas accused Coard of giving "to imperialism the popular Grenada Revolution on a silver platter" and "opening the door to the U.S. invasion" (St. John's, *The Worker's Voice*, 3 December 1986). In Grenada, MBPM chairman Kenrick Radix's occasional rallies failed to attract more than a handful of hardcore party members, most of whom were former junior and mid-level officials of the PRG. The noticeable lack of Grenadian popular support for the MBPM—regardless of lingering nostalgia for Bishop's dynamism and charisma—may be due to Radix's refusal to rule out violent revolution. The people of Grenada seem tired of political strife and disenchanted with revolutionary socialism. (*NYT*, 25 October.)

Regardless of the MBPM's limited popular support, the government of Prime Minister Herbert Blaize has not grown complacent about a possible security threat from MBPM members and ex-soldiers of the PRA. In June the Grenada Parliament passed an emergency powers bill giving the police sweeping powers of arrest in the event of a declaration of national emergency. The controversial legislation may also have been inspired by former prime minister Sir Eric Gairy's meetings with ex-PRA officers and men, most of whom had received training in Cuba. The former soldiers were reported to be providing security for Sir Eric and were quoted as having stated that although they loved Maurice Bishop, now that Bishop was dead "the only leader they recognize and love now is Uncle Gairy" (*Grenada Guardian*, 26 June).

The MBPM maintained close ties with the Communist Party of Cuba, which reportedly continued to provide funding for travel and other party activities. However, travel of MBPM party members to Soviet bloc countries showed a marked decrease from previous years, probably due to travel restrictions and increased vigilance by Grenada government authorities. MBPM support for radical groups and causes remains undiminished, and party members are committed to the goal of returning to power in Grenada.

Timothy Ashby
Washington, D.C.

Guadeloupe

Population. 336,354
Party. Communist Party of Guadeloupe (Parti Communiste Guadeloupéen; PCG)
Founded. 1944 as section of the French Communist Party (PCF), 1958 as independent
Membership. 3,000 (estimated)
General Secretary. Guy Daninthe
Politburo. 12 members: Henri Bangou, other members unknown

Central Committee. Christian Céleste (secretary)
Status. Legal
Last Congress. Eighth, 27–29 April 1984
Last Election. 16 March 1986, French National Assembly; 28 September 1986, Regional Council, 10 of 41 seats
Auxiliary Organizations. Union of Guadeloupan Communist Youth (Union de la Jeunesse Communiste Guadeloupéenne; UJCG; Fred Sablon, general secretary), Union of Guadeloupan Women (Union des Femmes Guadeloupéennes; UFG), General Confederation of Guadeloupan Labor (CGTG)
Publications. *L'Etincelle* (PCG weekly), *Madras* (UFG monthly)

In 1987 PCG reacted to events rather than taking the initiative, and it focused its attention on economic questions. There were no significant changes in internal party affairs, although Bernard Alexis, one of the party's founders in 1958, died. The same group continued to direct the PCG: Guy Daninthe completed another year as general secretary, and Christian Céleste, secretary of the Central Committee, led a public meeting at which general problems in Guadeloupe were discussed. Because an election had been nullified, a by-election in Pointe-à-Pitre was held on 10 May; the PCG candidate, Lucien Parize, won a seat on the General Council. Dr. Henri Bangou—member of the Politburo, mayor of Pointe-à-Pitre, and a senator—spoke widely. The party organized a course at the José Martí Cultural Center on materialism and a seminar on the functioning of party cells and democratic centralism.

Party leaders met in Fort-de-France, Martinique, with their counterparts from Martinique and Réunion to discuss the economic problems of the three French overseas departments. The slogan of the celebration marking the 43d anniversary of the party newspaper, *L'Etincelle*, was "Support Local Production, Struggle for the National and Social Liberation of the Country."

The Ninth Party Congress will be held in 1988 and will focus on relations with the European Economic Community (EEC). Economic questions—particularly in relation to France and the EEC—will be the most important matters on the agenda for two reasons: the government of Prime Minister Jacques Chirac has launched a new development program for the overseas departments, and by 1993 those departments will be more completely integrated into the EEC. The Paris program includes improvements in the infrastructure of Guadeloupe and training programs for Guadeloupan youth in France. Party leaders claim that the training programs are a form of camouflaged emigration and that the changes in infrastructure will encourage an influx of non-Guadeloupan capital. The Guadeloupan population in France may have reached 200,000 as compared with 330,000 on the islands themselves. In addition, plans to build a French military base at St. François have raised the level of verbal protest.

The PCG reasserted its goal of democratic and popular autonomy as a step toward independence with a socialist content. It continued to oppose forces and parties demanding immediate independence from France but expressed sympathy with the independence movement in New Caledonia. The party thus condemned bomb attacks by independence forces in Guadeloupe at the end of 1986 and the beginning of 1987. During the trial of German Gestapo chief Klaus Barbie, the only comment by writers in *L'Etincelle* was to reproduce testimony of a Soviet citizen who had been tortured by him during World War II. The French who suffered were not mentioned.

Party concern about the proposed end of customs regulations among members of the EEC stemmed from the fear that, without protection, Guadeloupan agriculture would collapse. Free movement of the population would also mean an influx of non-Caribbean peoples, thus changing the cultural character of the islands. The PCG called for special status or special protection for Guadeloupe after 1992.

The PCG showed its concern for Haiti and the reemergent communist party there, the Unified Party of Haitian Communists (PUCH). Party officials called on members to send books, pens, and medical supplies to the PUCH. The PCG asserted that the PUCH and the Roman Catholic Church were the only institutions trying to bring about significant change in that country. *L'Etincelle* reproduced an interview with Haitian communist leader René Théodore that had been originally published in the French communist newspaper, *L'Humanité*.

Daninthe called for closer ties with Haiti and with Senegal's Independence and Labor Party. He used Radio GATC, the PCG station, to broadcast his ideas. Allied organizations such as the UJCG and the UFG held joint affairs with the PCG. They all celebrated the International Day of Women. The UFG newspaper, *Madras*, has been published since 1958.

Brian Weinstein
Howard University

Guatemala

Population. 8,622,387
Major Marxist-Leninist Organizations
• Guatemalan Party of Labor (Partido Guatemalteco de Trabajo; PGT), in three factions
Founded. 1952 (under present name). A Guatemalan Communist Party was first created by the Comintern in 1922 and was destroyed in 1932. In September 1949 an illegal new party was formed, which became legal three years later.
Membership. Believed to be under 500 for all factions
Leadership. "Camarilla" faction: Carlos Gonzáles (general secretary and head of the Political Commission); National Leadership Nucleus faction: Daniel Rios (leader), Mario Sánchez ("in charge of general political matters"); Military Commission faction: unknown
Status. Illegal
Last Congress. Fourth, December 1969
Last Election. N/a
Auxiliary Organizations. Autonomous Federation of the Guatemalan Trade Unions (FASGUA); Patriotic Youth of Labor (JPT)
Publications. *Verdad* (irregular, published abroad)

• Rebel Armed Forces (Fuerzas Armadas Rebeldes; FAR)
Founded. 1962, though largely inactive 1968–1978
Membership. 1,000 (estimated)
Leadership. Jorge Ismael Soto García (alias Pablo Monsanto)
Status. Illegal
Auxiliary Organizations. National Committee of Trade Union Unity (CNUS), now practically defunct
Publications. *Guerrillero* (irregular, published abroad)

• Armed People's Revolutionary Organization (Organización Revolucionaria del Pueblo en Armas; ORPA)
Founded. 1971
Membership. 1,000 (estimated)
Leadership. Rodrigo Asturias Amado (alias Gaspar Ilom)
Status. Illegal
Auxiliary Organizations. Infiltrated the FAR's CNUS and the EGP's CUC
Publications. *Erupción* (irregular)

• Guerrilla Army of the Poor (Ejército Guerrillero de los Pobres; EGP)
Founded. January 1972, in Mexico
Membership. 1,000 (estimated)
Leadership. Rolando Morán (alias of Ricardo Ramírez de León)
Auxiliary Organizations. Peasant Unity Committee (CUC), January 31st Popular Front (FP-31), Revolutionary Christians Vicente Menchu and Robin García Revolutionary Student Front (FERG)
Publications. *Compañero* (irregular, published abroad; sometimes translated into English), *Informador Guerrillero* (irregular)

• National Revolutionary Unity of Guatemala (Unidad Nacional Revolucionaria de Guatemala; URNG), an umbrella organization including the FAR, ORPA, EGP, and National Leadership Nucleus faction of the PGT, their respective fronts, and other sympathetic groups, but it has never successfully unified all its members, which continue to operate autonomously.
Founded. February 1982
Bases. Operates largely out of Mexico, Nicaragua, and Cuba
Publications. *Noticias de Guatemala* (in Mexico); also press agency CESGUA, which serves as a political and diplomatic front for the insurgents

The first half of 1987 was characterized by a continuation of the increasingly desultory fighting between the national army and URNG elements; the second half witnessed significant political changes related to the Arias Plan for Central American peace and a renewal of military operations.

The first and perhaps best indications of the steady weakening of the insurgent forces throughout 1986 and the first months of 1987 were the decline in the number of "disappearances" and the increase of returned refugees from Mexico. The unofficial and rather indiscriminately antigovernment Human Rights Commission, which is based in Mexico and heavily influenced by URNG propagandists in that country, claimed 126 disappearances and 463 "political" murders in 1986, whereas the U.S. embassy mentioned 79 kidnappings and 131 possible political deaths for the same period (*CSM*, 23 March 1987). None of these figures can be taken as precise, although the embassy estimate is probably closer to reality. As for refugees, more than 300 returned from Mexico in January alone, as compared to 250 for all of 1986 (*LAT*, 15 March).

In the field, the strength of the total URNG forces seems to have dwindled from some 10,000 fighters in 1981–1982 to less than 2,000 in 1987 (*NYT*, 3 March), despite continuous shortages of helicopters and thus of rapid deployment capabilities on the part of the military. In fact, in May the Guatemalan government requested and received U.S. assistance in ferrying troops to the Playa Grande "development pole" when it came under EGP attack (*CSM*, 9 May), despite the official policy of "active neutrality" pursued by President Vinicio Cerezo Arévalo.

Although the guerrillas' activities in the field declined, leftist groups in the guise of "human rights organizations," particularly the Mutual Support Group, continued to press the Cerezo regime for reprisals against the military for alleged abuses against leftists during the pre-1986 military regimes, so far without significant success. It is also unclear to what extent the political opening offered by Cerezo's election in 1985 will present legal opportunities for the left to operate legal fronts. A congressional leftist group composed of Social Democrats, dissidents from the centrist PDCN, and a Revolutionary Party member was established in January (*JPRS-LAM*; Guatemala City, *La Prensa Libre*, 22 January). Reverend Andrés Girón, a gadfly from the Catholic left, continued to push for land reform, including confiscation of property, despite opposition from the Church and danger that the URNG would manipulate him (*WP*, 22 June).

Despite media claims that the PGT is a member of the URNG, the communist party continued to remain outside that umbrella organization and even to criticize it. In a statement on its 37th anniversary, the PGT labeled the Mexico-based URNG political fronts "a small emigré group," or pseudo-leftists, and it accused them of pursuing "policies of compromise and careerism" (*Information Bulletin*, February). Yet the PGT's analysis of the Guatemalan situation remained strikingly similar to that of the URNG groups, particularly in describing President Cerezo as a puppet of the military and "oligarchy." The most significant development on the left, however, was the apparent reconciliation between the "camarilla" faction and the National Leadership Nucleus; indeed, both Carlos González and Mario Sánchez signed the anniversary statement (ibid.). The implications of the reconciliation remain unclear, since although PGT statements were made public by CESGUA, the party itself did not publicly take credit for any violent action during the year.

Guerrilla Activities. There seems to be a consensus among Western media, independent analysts, and the Guatemalan military that the number of URNG fighters in 1987 was around 2,000, with some 6,000 civilians under their control (*NYT*, 3 March; *WP*, 7 June; *FBIS-LAM*, 9 April). Such figures should be compared with the peak strength of the guerrillas, which could have been as high as 12,000 fighters and over 300,000 civilians under their control in 1981 (*WP*, 7 June). With ever fewer civilians to recruit from, guerrilla casualties are harder to replace, and the resulting diminishing strength makes it difficult to maintain control over the civilian population. As a result of these developments, the military appeared increasingly confident that the situation is under control. Thus, Colonel Roberto Letona claimed that the "entire country is under control" (*FBIS-LAM*, 9 April); army chief of staff general César Caceres reiterated that "In general, terrorist crime in Guatemala is under control. Unfortunately we cannot speak of eliminating this evil, because in most of the countries where it exists it has become a way of life" (*La Prensa Libre*, 8 April). Such perceptions at the highest levels of the military explain the consistent scepticism it manifested vis-à-vis negotiations with the URNG, which the officers see as legitimizing a defeated force. Thus, Defense Minister General Héctor Gramajo publicly expressed doubts that the provisions for national reconciliation, cease-fire talks, amnesty, and dialogue contained in the Arias Plan applied to Guatemala, since the rebels are barely "a nuisance, not a military threat" (*FBIS-LAM*, 19 August).

Such assessments of the guerrillas' strength may be accurate inasmuch as they indicate the URNG's loss of both tactical and strategic initiative, but they should not be interpreted as proof that the insurgency in Guatemala is over. In fact, throughout the year armed clashes continued in a number of departments. The largest operation was the army's large-scale attack on ORPA strongholds in Suchitepéquez, Chimaltenango, and particularly

Sololá departments in April and May. The target was the ORPA's Javier Tambriz Front, centered around Santiago Atitlán. According to human rights groups generally sympathetic to the rebels, the army engaged in large-scale bombings of the area; according to the military, ORPA forces were "cornered" and "resorted to the criminal practice of laying mines" that inflicted civilian casualties (*FBIS-LAM*, 4 June). The ORPA has been under military pressure since 1986 (see *YICA*, 1987), and many of its redoubts in Sololá seem indeed to have been eliminated.

By June it appeared that the URNG's attempts to stage a comeback by expanding its operations in a number of departments had been largely checked. The FAR became more active in Petén, with unconfirmed rumors indicating that it was receiving supplies from Nicaragua via Belize (*El Gráfico*, 2 June). The EGP intensified its activities in Quiché and Huehuetenango and even attacked the garrison of Playa Grande; the ORPA was active in Quezaltenango and San Marcos as well as the departments mentioned above. Guatemalan media reports suggested that the EGP was forcing peasants to join its ranks, whereas the ORPA concentrated its efforts on propaganda among members of the civil patrols (ibid.). The number of casualties on both sides cannot be reliably assessed; the military claimed that the Javier Tambriz Front only had 40 fighters, which is probably an underestimate (*El Gráfico*, 26 May), and the ORPA wildly claimed to have "annihilated" a paratroop battalion (*La Prensa Libre*, 17 May). In fact it appears that the military felt confident enough to provide credible casualty counts, whereas the guerrillas desperately searched for a political impact with figures bearing little relation to reality. The ORPA's one major success took place on 29 August, when it successfully ambushed an army patrol in San Marcos, killing a major and wounding four soldiers at no cost to the insurgents (*FBIS-LAM*, 3 September). On the other hand, the clash between the army and the EGP in Quiché in late June resulted in nine guerrillas and two soldiers being killed (ibid., 30 June).

Militarily weaker than ever since 1979, the guerrillas concentrated most of their efforts on propaganda and internal reorganization. In December 1986 the URNG announced that it had started publishing an information bulletin to be printed in Mexico. More important, on 23 May the first guerrilla radio station, La Voz Popular, started broadcasting (ibid., 27 May). By the end of the year it was still unclear whether the station was based in Petén or on the Mexican side of the border. The establishment of the radio station, clearly intended as a replica of the Salvadoran FMLN's Radio Venceremos, aims at presenting a united position to the country and avoiding the former image of the URNG as a shaky coalition of historical enemies.

Throughout the first half of 1987 the URNG continued to claim that it wanted a dialogue with the government, but at the same time it made unrealistic and unobtainable demands. Those included trials of the officers involved in counterinsurgency operations of the past decade, the dismantling of such successful pacification efforts as "development poles" and civil patrols, and the guerrillas' "right" to maintain their military strength. More significantly, the insurgents have consistently declared that they will not lay down their weapons so long as "the sociopolitical conditions that led to the struggle still prevail" (*FBIS-LAM*, 27 July). In other words, according to the URNG nothing has changed in Guatemala since the late 1970s, which clearly contradicts their own expressed willingness to hold discussions with the Cerezo government. The government, for its part, has consistently declared that it refuses to treat the insurgents in any manner different from that of other opposition groups, whether in the Congress or in the private sector and unions.

During the Central American summit in Guatemala the URNG General Command announced a six-day truce on 3–9 August. On 11 August Pablo Monsanto, Gaspar Ilom, and Rolando Morán again offered to discuss "democratization" with the government but sharply criticized the army leadership for its "hard-line" (ibid., 18 August).

After a significant delay, and against almost public objections from the army, President Cerezo appointed a Reconciliation Commission to meet the rebels; the commission included Vice President Robert Carpio-Nicolle, co-owner of *La Prensa Libre* Teresa Bolanos de Zarco, Bishop Rodolfo Quezada Toruno, opposition politician Jorge Serrano Elias, and former 1982 military junta member Colonel Francisco Luis Gordillo. On 7–9 October in Madrid, members of the commission and military officers attached to it as "observers" met with a URNG delegation led by Gaspar Ilom, the ORPA's main leader. The military leadership, claiming that the URNG forces were reduced to only 900 by July, conditioned support for the talks on their representing "a political validation of the military victories" (*Latin America Regional Report*, 29 October).

There was clearly no meeting of minds in

Madrid, since the insurgent delegation repeated its previous demands, including trials for counterinsurgency commanders, political rights for the insurgent fronts in the absence of their renouncing violence, and a vague call for "humanization of the war," presumably including the army's unilateral renunciation of air attacks (ibid.). Although both sides stated that the Madrid meeting was useful and contacts would continue, there is little chance of any progress being made in the foreseeable future. The Guatemalan army considers the anti-insurgency war won on the battlefield and has no intention of losing it at the negotiating table; the URNG thinks it is only there it could recover its declining fortunes; and the Cerezo government has neither the strength nor the inclination to make significant concessions to the Marxist-Leninists and risk alienating the armed forces.

Michael Radu
Foreign Policy Research Institute, Philadelphia

Guyana

Population. 765,844
Party. People's Progressive Party (PPP); Working People's Alliance (WPA)
Founded. PPP: 1950; WPA: organized in 1973, became formal party in 1979.
Membership. PPP: 100 leaders and several hundred militants above non-Marxist rank and file; WPA: 30 leaders (both estimated)
General Secretary. PPP: Cheddi Jagan
Politburo. PPP, 12 members: Cheddi Jagan, Janet Jagan, Ram Karran, Feroze Mohamed, Pariag Sukhai, Clinton Collymore, Narbada Persaud, Isahak Basir, Rohit Persaud, Cyril Belgrave, Reepu Daman Persaud, Harry Persaud Nokta; WPA: collective leadership includes Eusi Kwayana, Clive Thomas, Walter Omawale, Moses Bhagwan, Rupert Roopnarine, Takuma Ogunsaye
Status. Legal but occasionally harassed
Last Congress. PPP: Twenty-second, 3–5 August 1985
Last Election. 9 December 1985. PPP: 45,926 votes, 16.84 percent, 8 of 53 seats in National Assembly; WPA: 4,176 votes, 1 seat in National Assembly
Auxiliary Organizations. PPP: Progressive Youth Organization (PYO), Women's Progressive Organization (WPO), Guyana Agricultural Workers' Union (GAWU)
Publications. PPP: *Mirror* (weekly), *Thunder* (quarterly); WPA: *Dayclean* and *Open Word* (weeklies)

Under the leadership of President Hugh Desmond Hoyte, the ruling People's National Congress (PNC) maintained in 1987 the two-track policy approach initiated the previous year in both domestic and foreign affairs. In doing so, Hoyte parlayed domestic and foreign policy adjustments, chiefly in the economic sphere, into improved relations with the private sector, neighboring countries, and the United States while preserving ties with the Eastern bloc and Third World radical states established during the tenure of the late Forbes Burnham.

Incremental economic liberalization, however, was not matched by political opening, despite Hoyte's suggestive address to the August PNC party congress. While allowing a controlled relaxation of media restrictions for the benefit of the private sector, the PNC maintained its authoritarian grip on the government and all repressive sectors of the state. But because Moscow, Washington, and their respective allies were generally sanguine about Hoyte's effort to revive a destitute economy through renewed Western contact, and because the West seemed willing to overlook the lack of domestic democratization, the Moscow-line PPP and the socialist WPA remained sidelined and with little leverage as the reign of the minority-backed PNC entered its 24th year.

President Hoyte declared 1987 "the year of purposeful economic adjustment" and opened in January with a 56 percent devaluation of the Guyanese dollar (*Latin American Weekly Report* [LAWR], 29 January). Subsequent implementation of wage restraints, limited privatization, increased foreign investment opportunities, and an increase in debt repayments lent credence to repeated news reports, denied by the PNC, that Guyana was secretly negotiating with the International Monetary Fund (IMF) for renewed funding eligibility (*Latin American Regional Reports: Caribbean*, 10 December). At the October Commonwealth conference in Vancouver, Canada, though he continued to deny that negotiations were taking place, Hoyte stated that his government had no objection to an "arrangement" with the IMF, which he said appeared to have undergone some "rethinking" (*Caribbean Insight*, November). If an agreement is announced in 1988, paving the way for creditors to consider refinancing Guyana's $1.6 billion debt, Hoyte is positioned to deflect criticism from the PPP and WPA, and from hardliners in his own party, by asserting that the IMF, not the PNC, had softened its position.

On the international front, Guyana's enhanced engagement with the West was most evident in the reciprocal state visits of President Hoyte and President Jaime Lusinchi of neighboring Venezuela. Venezuela's longstanding claim to the Essequibo region of western Guyana had led to an all-time low in bilateral relations during the last years of the Burnham era. Lusinchi seemed eager, however, to nurture apparent policy shifts under Hoyte. By the end of 1987 the two countries had formed a mixed commission for economic, cultural, and technical cooperation; extended an agreement whereby Guyana receives oil in exchange for bauxite; and agreed to leave the Essequibo question to United Nations Secretary General Javier Perez de Cuellar.

Further pursuit of Western ties was manifest in Guyana's renewed embrace of the Caribbean Community (CARICOM), whose summit conference in 1987 was chaired by Hoyte; Hoyte's presentation of one of the four keynote addresses at the annual Miami Conference on the Caribbean and his suggestion that Guyana would apply to be a designated beneficiary of the U.S.-developed Caribbean Basin Initiative (CBI); and a series of joint public and private ventures with international corporations and capitalist nations including Japan, South Korea, and Jamaica. Washington quietly expressed its approval of such initiatives by increasing the level of food aid renewed in 1986. Resumption of the entire U.S. aid program cut off in 1982 was not discussed, however, as Washington appeared to be awaiting a formal CBI application and the outcome of Guyana's unofficial talks with the IMF.

On the other side of the ledger, Guyana maintained—and in some cases strengthened—relations with the Eastern bloc and with revolutionary states and movements in the Third World. At the twelfth meeting of the Guyana-Cuba Joint Commission held in Georgetown in March, agreements were made to double trade between the two countries and increase Cuban medical, educational, and technical personnel in Guyana. Also in March, Guyana cooperated closely with Cuba, Nicaragua, and other radical states during the Nonaligned Movement Coordinating Bureau meeting hosted by Guyana. At that gathering, Cuban foreign minister Isidoro Malmierca delivered personal greetings from Fidel Castro to President Hoyte (Havana Television Service, 10 March; *FBIS*, 11 March).

In May, Guyana and Cuba agreed to a cooperative effort in Guyanese gold-mining, the first joint-venture economic project between the two countries. In June, Cuban Vice President Carlos Rafael Rodríguez paid an official four-day visit to Georgetown where he received Guyana's second highest award from President Hoyte and pronounced relations between the two countries as "excellent" (Havana Radio Progresso; *FBIS*, 22 June). At the end of the year, the Cuban ambassador in Georgetown held a press conference to state that, despite improved relations between Guyana and the United States, there had been no change in the Cuban-Guyanese relations forged during the Burnham era (Bonaire Trans World Radio; *FBIS*, 10 December).

Following an April visit to Moscow by Prime Minister Hamilton Green, the second-ranking government official, a Soviet technical mission traveled to Guyana to survey prospects for a joint venture in bauxite mining. In August, Soviet deputy foreign minister V. G. Komplektov received Noel Sinclair, permanent secretary of the Guyanese Ministry of Foreign Affairs, for a discussion of regional and international issues. TASS reported that "consultations passed in a businesslike, friendly atmosphere" (*Izvestiia*, 31 August; *FBIS*, 18 September).

From Moscow, Green led the Guyanese delegation to Pyongyang for the 75th birthday celebration of North Korean leader Kim Il-song and the Fourth Meeting of the Guyana-DPRK Joint Economic Commission (*New Nation*, 3 May; *JPRS*, 29 June).

In May a working protocol for the continuing of trade relations between Guyana and East Germany was signed in preparation for the Guyana-GDR Joint Commission meeting scheduled for the end of the year. In October, Haslyn Parris, Guyanese deputy prime minister in charge of planning and development, was received in East Berlin by Gerhard Schuerer, candidate member of the SED Central Committee Politburo and chairman of the State Planning Commission (*Neues Deutschland*, 21 October; *FBIS*, 23 October).

The Soviet Union, East Germany, Cuba, Poland, Bulgaria, Yugoslavia, North Korea, Iraq, the Palestine Liberation Organization (PLO), and the African National Congress (ANC) sent official delegations in August to the seventh biennial congress of the PNC held in Georgetown (*LAWR*, 3 September). The Soviet delegation was led by N. S. Perun, a member of the CPSU Central Committee Party Control Committee, and D. D. Muravyev, a senior member of the Central Committee International Department (*Pravda*, 8 August; *FBIS*, 17 August).

At the congress, Hoyte was unanimously reelected by acclamation as PNC party chief. In his at times contradictory address, he described PNC policy in terms suggestive of a Third World-style *glasnost'/perestroika* project. He dismissed speculation that under his leadership there had been a shift in the PNC's ideological position, stressing that "our party is a socialist party, as stated in the very first article of the party's constitution" (Caribbean News Agency [CANA], 11 August; *FBIS*, 18 August). He called for a "modification of method" not an "abandonment of basic goals," stating that the party must become a "finely tuned, efficient machine," ready to respond to the need for "urgent structural adjustment" (*LAWR*, 3 September). Then, seeming to disaffirm the concept of party "paramountcy" that is also embodied in the party constitution, Hoyte declared that "the party is not the government and we must make the distinction clear" (ibid.).

By the end of the year, however, there had been no practical changes in the relationship between the PNC and the government it continued to dominate. The promotion of a number of technocrats within the party secretariat seemed more an effort to facilitate the ongoing economic liberalization and reduce rampant corruption. The secretariat is the mechanism through which the PNC ensures that its policies are being implemented by all levels of the government ministries—the concrete manifestation of party "paramountcy" in government. It is significant that Hoyte also reappointed Ranji Chandisingh, a Soviet-trained ideologue and former PPP deputy, as PNC secretary general and deputy party chief. Chandisingh, who gave the second major address at the August congress, is also one of four vice presidents in the government as well as deputy prime minister in charge of national mobilization.

Given the extent to which Soviet structures provided a model for Guyana during the Burnham years, Mikhail Gorbachev's initiatives in the Soviet Union provide an interesting parallel to the balancing act evident in the PNC platform and government policies under Hoyte. Entering his third year at the helm following the death of Burnham, Hoyte for the time being appeared able to involve the private sector in the economy and lure Western capital without incurring the wrath of recalcitrant PNC hard-liners or jeopardizing his control of the government. Helping to appease the party ideologues was the substantial and positive reporting by Soviet news agency TASS on Hoyte's address to the PNC congress and the highlighting of Chandisingh's reappointment (*Pravda*, 8, 13, 18 August). For his part, East German leader Erich Honecker sent a personal message offering "Socialist greetings" to "Most valued Comrade Hoyte" and expressing "heartiest congratulations on the occasion of your re-election" (*Neues Deutschland*, 20 August).

For the main opposition PPP and WPA, however, the suggestion of political opening in Hoyte's August address faded in the fall. When they sought to take advantage of a major fuel shortage symptomatic of the still-destitute economy, the government responded with repressive police tactics reminiscent of the Burnham years. In addition, when the parties backed a Court of Appeal ruling on the unconstitutionality of a series of PNC-written labor laws, the PNC blocked publication of the ruling and overrode parliamentary procedure with a unilateral initiative to amend the Constitution. In a year-end report, the Guyana Human Rights Association—an internationally respected organization headed by independent church, labor, and university leaders—characterized the maneuver as "a clear illustration that the doctrine of paramountcy remains a central motivating factor of the ruling PNC" (*CANA, Carib News*, 5 January 1988).

PPP Domestic Views and Activities. The PPP Central Committee held a plenary meeting in January. In a subsequent *World Marxist Review* article entitled "Upholding the National and International Interests of Working People," rising PPP ideologue and Central Committee member Donald Ramotar outlined the party's positions. "In the face of the increasingly anti-democratic policy of the ruling PNC and its submission to imperialism and the International Monetary Fund," he stated, "we are using all legal methods of struggle and hope to expand them as far as possible . . . In parliament and in other elective forums the Communists expose the severe shortcomings of the regime, its corruption and incompetence, its sell-out to the IMF, and make concrete proposals on various issues" (*WMR*, June).

Ramotar further asserted that because "the expressed goal of 'socialism' announced by the PNC is at odds with the actual policy of the authorities," the PPP strives "to develop unity in the working masses, firstly in the working class, and in the mass organizations among youth and women." However, he continued, "this process is not proceeding as smoothly as we would have liked . . . Our struggle is developing in difficult conditions." After identifying the PNC's abuse of national armed forces and the courts as major domestic obstacles, however, Ramotar hinted that a lack of "proletarian internationalism" on behalf of the PPP was also a concern. In what could be interpreted as an indirect entreaty to Eastern bloc allies, he stated: "Back in 1917 Lenin wrote that to be a real internationalist means 'working whole-heartedly for the development of the revolutionary movement and the revolutionary struggle in *one's own country*, and supporting (by propaganda, sympathy, and material aid) *this struggle*, this *and only this* line in *every* country without exception.' This idea remains topical and has been repeatedly borne out by history." (Ibid.)

In this regard, it is significant that at the Second Conference of South American Communist Parties attended by the PPP in Lima, Brazil, in December 1986, one month before the PPP plenary session, there was no mention of Guyana in the final resolution (*IB*, April).

Following the plenary meeting, and throughout the year, the PPP attempted to balance, without success, two political initiatives. The first was the proposal, incorporated into the PPP platform at the 1985 party congress, calling for a "national patriotic front government" composed of the PPP, PNC, and WPA (*WMR*, December 1985). The second was the ongoing campaign for electoral reform by the Patriotic Coalition for Democracy (PCD), formed after the fraudulent 1985 elections by the PPP, WPA, and three tiny centrist parties—the Democratic Labor Party (DLP), the National Democratic Front (NDF), and the People's Democratic Movement (PDM).

Both initiatives, rejected by the PNC in 1986, were shrewdly disrupted by Hoyte in 1987 when he delegated Chandisingh to meet with PPP leader Cheddi Jagan, not on the PPP's national front proposal but on the issue of electoral reform. The move created tension within the PCD, since the other members, especially the centrist parties, were distressed at having the Marxist-Leninist Jagan negotiating democratic guarantees with his former deputy. As it turned out, Jagan pressed on the national front issue and came away with nothing, stating that prospects for PPP-PNC cooperation were even less than under Burnham (*Caribbean Insight*, September).

Jagan then secretly sought to ally with the WPA in an antigovernment left alliance, an approach exposed by the PNC-controlled media and reluctantly acknowledged by the WPA. The WPA, which in recent years had been steering a more social democratic course, appeared embarrassed to be seen considering association with the Marxist-Leninist PPP and claimed that this was only one of the proposals they had received from other parties (*Latin American Regional Reports: Caribbean*, 27 August). The net result was mounting distrust across the board.

The PCD, which had displayed unexpected unity in organizing a significant march and demonstration in March, appeared to be unraveling. But the PNC's heavy-handed repression during the fall fuel crisis, followed by its arbitrary manipulation of the Constitution on the wage issue, had drawn the coalition back together by the end of the year. At a November PCD meeting, initial discussions on political strategy led to frustration and finally spontaneous exhortations to violence as the only way to alter the PNC government (CANA, *Carib News*, 24 November). For the PPP, this fit the historical pattern of threatening violence after being outfoxed politically by the PNC. By December, however, the coalition and the PPP had retreated to planning demonstrations against the constitutional amendment and soliciting support from regional governments, the program with which they had begun the year.

PPP International Views and Activities. After the January plenary session, the PPP issued a statement on the international situation entitled "The Caribbean Must Become a Peace Zone." It combined standard condemnations of the "interventionist and reactionary actions by the Reagan administration" in the region, with "full support for the large-scale peace initiatives taken by the Soviet Union in favor of a non-nuclear world and a world without wars" (*IB*, May).

In the spring, following Brazil's suspension of interest payments on its foreign debt, Jagan reiterated condemnations of the IMF and called in the National Assembly for Guyana to join all Third World countries in a moratorium on debt payments. President Hoyte referred to Jagan's motion as "absolute folly, stupidity and nonsense" (*Caribbean Insight*, June).

In July the PPP called on the thirteen-member CARICOM to support the Costa Rican–sponsored peace plan for Central America. Jagan declared it was the "best hope" for ending the "low intensity war" waged by the United States against "a poor country and a courageous people who made such tremendous sacrifices to get rid of the fascist butcher Somoza" (CANA, *Carib News*, 4 August).

In September, Jagan paid a "two-week friendship visit" to Vietnam (Hanoi VNA, 24 September; *FBIS*, 25 September). He held talks with Nguyen Van Linh, general secretary of the Communist Party of Vietnam, as well as with other Politburo members. On his tour of the country Jagan "paid floral tribute" to President Ho Chi Minh at his mausoleum and visited the late president's home and office (ibid.).

From Vietnam Jagan traveled to Cambodia, where he was received by Prime Minister Hun Sen, member of the Politburo of the Kampuchean People's Revolutionary Party (KPRP) and chairman of the KPRP Foreign Relations Commission. Following an exchange of views, Jagan "reaffirmed the support of the PPP for the KPRP and the people of Cambodia in their national defense and reconstruction efforts" (Phnom Penh SPK, 22 September; *FBIS*, 22 September).

In November Jagan attended the 70th anniversary of the October Revolution in Moscow.

WPA Domestic Views and Activities. At the conclusion of a party conference in November, the WPA declared that it had changed "from an activist to a mass party, a revolutionary democratic and humanist party" (CANA, 4 November; *FBIS*, 12 November). To this purpose, the party had launched a membership drive and was prepared to embrace as members "all whose private beliefs allow them to take the side of the working people in class conflicts and to commit themselves to the genuine, multiracial, and democratic power of the working people" (ibid.).

The WPA further stated that conditions did not yet exist in Guyana "to build socialism in an authentic way," that what was needed first is "a broad-based government of national unity which would be able to embark on a program of economic reconstruction" (ibid.). WPA co-leader Rupert Roopnarine added that "Without a new set of electoral arrangements and some form of democratic government, this country is going to fall off the map" (*Caribbean Insight*, December).

Regarding internal party matters, it was announced that the leadership of the party would remain collective and not be concentrated in the hands of a single individual, although Eusi Kwayana would continue to occupy the WPA's sole seat in the National Assembly.

During the course of the year, as in 1986, Kwayana utilized the seat to pepper the PNC with legislative proposals on government accountability, electoral reform, labor rights, and the national budget. All his initiatives were overridden by the PNC majority in the assembly. Kwayana also sought to engage the PNC in the courts. An attempt to bring about an investigation into the assets of the late President Burnham failed. However, a year-long effort to secure an inquest into the 1980 bombing death of WPA founder Walter Rodney finally broke ground when the director of public prosecutions ordered a hearing at the end of the year.

In March the WPA was instrumental in organizing and carrying out the PCD demonstration for electoral reform. After the PCD lost its cohesion in the wake of the PNC-Jagan talks, however, the WPA unilaterally called for an emergency session of the National Assembly in response to the fuel crisis. Following the PNC's rejection of the proposal, Kwayana began in November a regionally publicized ten-day fast in support of the demand. During a religious ceremony in front of the National Assembly building to mark the end of the fast, WPA supporters—including Barbadian author George Lamming—were set upon by baton-wielding police and temporarily detained. (*Caribbean Insight*, December.)

Following the incident, Kwayana called on citizens to burn down petrol stations and "work for a political upheaval" unless the government agreed to multiparty negotiations (ibid.). His remarks caused a stir because in recent years the WPA had steered away from Walter Rodney's radical advocacy of removing the PNC by any means. Kwayana later seemed to soften his position, stating that he was using the language of biblical parable, which nonetheless did not alter the fact of the repressive nature of PNC rule (CANA, *Carib News*, 8 December).

WPA International Views and Activities. In March Kwayana traveled to the United States on behalf of the PCD and WPA. In Washington he briefed delegates to the Organization of American States (OAS) on the PCD's electoral reform campaign. Guyana remained excluded from the OAS because of the long-standing border dispute with Venezuela, but prospects for resolution had brightened with the recent turnaround in bilateral relations. Kwayana also visited the National Democratic Institute, the American Friends Service

Committee, TransAfrica, and members of the U.S. Congress. (*Open Word*, 16 March; *JPRS*, 11 May.)

In December Kwayana represented the WPA at a meeting in Caracas, Venezuela, of the Latin American Committee of the Socialist International. The WPA had become a "consultive member" of the Socialist International in 1986. As the result of Kwayana's persuasive presentation, the committee's published resolution contained an appeal to the Guyanese government to consider the democratic opposition's request for multiparty discussions of electoral reform (*CANA*, 17 December; *FBIS*, 18 December).

Douglas W. Payne
Freedom House, New York

Haiti

Population. 6,187,115
Party. Unified Party of Haitian Communists (Parti Unifié des Communistes Haïtiens; PUCH)
Founded. 1934 (PUCH, 1968)
Membership. 350 (estimated)
General Secretary. René Théodore
Politburo. René Théodore, Emmanuel Frédérick, Max Bourjolly
Status. Legal since 1985; in the open in Haiti with the return of Théodore in March 1986
Last Congress. First, 1979
Last Election. 29 November (incomplete)
Auxiliary Organizations. No data
Publications. Publications in Créole forthcoming

Haiti's provisional government, the National Government Council (CNG), used the growing violence against candidates, voters, and the Provisional Electoral Council to cancel the presidential and National Assembly elections on the day of the balloting, 29 November. According to observers, the violence was begun and almost exclusively maintained by the military and bands of former Tonton Macoutes, particularly after the independent electoral council excluded former dictator Jean-Claude Duvalier's allies from candidacy. One of those potential candidates had warned of violence, even though the new Constitution was the basis of the council's decision. The CNG also took advantage of the confusion to abolish the electoral council that the Constitution created, and it set a new date in January 1988 for elections. The U.S. government reacted by banning further nonhumanitarian aid to Haiti.

During the months leading up to these decisions, criticism of U.S. support for what was called Duvalierism-without-Duvalier grew louder. Duvalier supporters' and others' use of anticommunist slogans and claims of an imminent communist takeover probably increased the prestige of the PUCH and its leader, René Théodore, the first communist candidate for president in Haiti's long history.

In March the constitutional referendum convincingly showed Haitian enthusiasm for the ballot box when fairly used, but criticism of the ruling, military-dominated CNG reflected growing fear that someone would undermine the new Constitution. Jean-Bertrand Aristide, a popular parish priest in Port-au-Prince, called for the removal of the CNG and for radical change along the lines of socialism, but he was quickly labeled a communist and was physically attacked. A protestant church leader and presidential candidate, Sylvio Claude, claimed the communists wished to seize power; he also criticized the United States, which would be to blame, he said, if Haiti became a communist state. An army spokesman claimed Cuba was training Haitians for a communist takeover.

In June the CNG tried to suppress the reborn trade union, the Autonomous Confederation of Haitian Workers (CATH), but a general strike forced the council to retreat. It also failed in its attempt to wrest control of the electoral process from the Provisional Electoral Council. In September, two months prior to the presidential elections, political leader Eugene Athis was hacked to death, and others, also labeled communist, were threatened with a similar fate. In reaction, 57 organizations and parties founded the National Committee of Democratic Movements to apply pressure on the ruling council to abstain from interfering in the elections. PUCH leaders openly supported the committee and criticized the violence that dramatically increased after an October ruling by the electoral council that close associates of the Duvalier family were ineligible as presidential candidates. Yves Volel, an anti-Duvalier presidential candidate, was shot by the police, according to all witnesses, and armed gangs began openly to terrorize civilians. U.S. congressman Walter Fauntroy and Senator Bob Graham visited Haiti, expressed their support for the electoral council, and warned the CNG of a cut-off in funds if it prevented free elections. Yet the day of the election was marked by a new height in violence against voters, and it was then that the ruling CNG took control of the process in defiance of the Constitution.

During the escalating crisis, the communists may have gained unexpected prestige because the CNG and others blamed the PUCH for it. General Secretary Théodore consistently criticized the CNG and its policies, including the closure of state-owned companies that employed several hundred workers. He blamed the closure on U.S. pressure and advice. He supported the new Constitution and the Provisional Electoral Council, and more than anyone else he warned of the possibility of a military coup d'état—which by year's end did seem to be taking place. Théodore's comments about the powerful Roman Catholic Church were nuanced: he praised parish priests such as Aristide and Monsignor Romélus of Jérémie, but he generally criticized the church hierarchy.

In a hostile environment the PUCH tried to organize, recruit new members, and find ways to publicize its existence. It announced that it had held a congress in January, when representatives of what it called "popular committees" met. Théodore also held a news conference, during which he articulated a widely held fear that Duvalierism-without-Duvalier was alive and well. He announced the PUCH would soon have its own radio station, called Radio Vérité, but before most radio stations were closed by the military, the party only had a radio program called "Dialogue" on Saturdays. The program was recorded on cassettes that members then played and distributed outside Port-au-Prince. On 10 July, PUCH members marched in Port-au-Prince with others opposing the CNG. It was the first time that a communist flag flew over a popular march.

In addition to the CNG, the target of PUCH speeches was the United States. Théodore and his colleagues warned of alleged plans to invade Haiti. They blamed the Americans for putting and maintaining the unpopular General Namphy, head of the CNG, in power. Théodore called for solidarity of communists around the world, but he also stated that Haiti's culture was different from that of other countries. In other words, its uniqueness meant there would be unique political solutions to its problems. By the end of the year, it seemed that the communists of Haiti had gained in strength.

Brian Weinstein
Howard University

Honduras

Population. 4,823,818

Major Marxist-Leninist Organizations

• Communist Party of Honduras (Partido Comunista de Honduras; PCH)

Founded. 1927, dismantled by 1932, re-established 1954
Membership. Probably less than 200
General Secretary. Rigoberto Padilla Rush
Status. Illegal
Last Congress. Fourth, January 1986
Publications. *Vanguardia Revolutionaria*; *Voz Popular* (both irregular, published abroad)

• Revolutionary Party of the Central American Workers (Partido Revolucionario de los Trabajadores de Centro America; PRTC)

Founded. 1976 in Costa Rica, as Honduran branch of regional party, became independent in 1979
Membership. Probably less than 100
Leadership. Wilfredo Gallardo Museli
Status. Illegal
Last Congress. No data
Publications. No data

• Morazanist Front for the Liberation of Honduras (Frente Morazanista para la Liberación de Honduras; FMLH)

Founded. 1969 claimed, but was inactive until 1980
Membership. Claims a few hundred
Leadership. Octavio Pérez, Fernando López (both aliases)
Status. Illegal
Last Congress. No data
Publications. No data

• Lorenzo Zelaya Popular Revolutionary Forces (Fuerzas Populares Revolucionarias Lorenzo Zelaya; FPR-LZ)

Founded. 1980
Membership. 100 (estimated)
Leadership. No data
Status. Illegal
Last Congress. No data
Publications. *Lorenzo Zelaya* (irregular, published in Mexico)

• "Cinchoneros" Popular Liberation Movement (Movimiento Popular de Liberación Cinchoneros; MPL-Cinchoneros)

Founded. 1981, as successor to the People's Revolutionary Union, established in 1980 as Honduran front for the Salvadoran Popular Liberation Forces
Membership. Less than 200
Leadership. No data
Status. Illegal
Last Congress. No data
Publications. No data

Umbrella Organization

• Unified Directorate of the Honduran Revolutionary Movement (Dirección Nacional Unificada del Movimiento Revolucionario Hondureño; DNU-MRH)

Founded. 1982, though largely ineffective
Membership. All the above parties, as well as the Socialist Action Party (Partido de Acción Socialista de Honduras; PASOH), led by Virgilio Carias, headquartered in Nicaragua

The stagnation within the Honduran Marxist-Leninist organizations has continued throughout the year, without significant changes. The shadowy DNU-MRH continued to exist mostly on paper, and few references to it appeared in either leftist propaganda and statements or government declarations. Of the revolutionary groups the most active were the PCH, the FPR-LZ and, apparently, the Cinchoneros. At the same time, the PCH maintained a semi-legal existence and enjoyed the tolerance of the authorities. Previous statements advocating violence were muted in 1987; instead, PCH general secretary Rigoberto Padilla Rush professed that "The Communists have consistently advocated respect for the letter and spirit of the Constitution of our Republic" (*WMR*, April). The strategy espoused by the party is, on the one hand, to "unite all democrats, patriots and revolutionaries in the country" (ibid.)—a veiled admission that the DNU-MRH is still an ideal rather than a reality—and, on the other, to use patriotism rather than class struggle as the banner making such unity possible. As a result, the public goals of the party are the withdrawal of the U.S. "occupation troops" and the expulsion of the "Somoza bands" from Honduran soil (*FBIS-LAM*, 13 April).

Despite accusing the Azcona government of having surrendered Honduras' sovereignty to Washington, the PCH operated in a semi-legal manner, publishing a statement in Tegucigalpa on the occasion of the party's 33d anniversary on 8 April and even trying to raise funds openly on the Atlantic Coast. Indeed, at the end of April there were reports that the PCH was selling party bonds worth $2 and $50, with the inscription "Second National Financial Campaign–PCH" and the image of the Honduran flag together with the red banner and the hammer and sickle. (Ibid., 1 May.) The campaign was supported by party front organizations operating legally and included some unions and student and professional groups in La Ceiba and San Pedro Sula. Despite such open activities, the party was cautioned by the army commander, General Humberto Regalado Hernandez, not to "make the mistake and try to break the country's laws" (ibid., 20 May).

The government's tolerance for the PCH seems to have been related to the rather surprising move toward establishing trade relations with the Soviet Union. It is possible that the PCH played an intermediary role, along the lines previously established by the communist parties of Guatemala and Costa Rica during the 1970s. In January the economy minister stated that trade relations would be established with the communist states, intended to promote Honduran exports (Tegucigalpa, *La Tribuna*, 29 January). The idea received public support from the private sector and influential politicians from both major parties. In May a Soviet delegation led by Yuriy Vislousov, chief of the Costa Rica–based Soviet mission to Central America and the Caribbean, met Honduran officials in Tegucigalpa and discussed Soviet imports of coffee, lumber, and bananas (ibid., 11 May). The same month a Czech delegation arrived in Honduras for talks regarding imports of coffee. The significance of the Vislousov visit was underscored by the fact that, prior to it, Honduran economic ties to communist states had been limited to Yugoslavia and Czechoslovakia.

According to Honduran sources, the bilateral trade with the USSR will be conducted both in U.S.

dollars and on a barter basis; Honduras is interested in importing fertilizers and machinery, and the Soviet Union wants to buy coffee (Tegucigalpa, *El Heraldo*, 20 May). In August a draft treaty taken to Moscow by a Honduran delegation included a statement to the effect that the two countries share "the desire to strengthen friendly relations and increase trade and economic relations, based on the principles of independence and national sovereignty, noninterference in each other's internal affairs, equal rights, and mutual benefits" (*FBIS-LAM*, 24 August). The initial amount of two-way trade was estimated at $20 million (ibid.). During the same trip Honduras also signed an accord with Czechoslovakia that provided for joint ventures in Honduras and an increase in the volume of Czech imports of coffee from the current $23 million (*Latin America Regional Reports: Mexico and Central America*, 24 September).

Although the PCH continued its policy of nonviolence, the same restraint was not manifested by the revolutionary organizations on its left. Sporadic bombings occurred throughout the year, particularly in Tegucigalpa, La Ceiba, and San Pedro Sula. A bomb was deactivated at the Israeli Embassy on 6 January, and several were detonated near the residence of the Icaza family in Tegucigalpa on 6 March. The Icazas are connected with the main Nicaraguan insurgent (*contra*) organization, the FDN, and the bombs at their house were claimed by the "Froyl n Turcios Front" (*FBIS-LAM*, 9 March). The organization has previously been involved in bombings and appears to be a unit of the Cinchoneros.

The most important terrorist incident of the year occurred in San Pedro Sula on 13 March, when a safe house of the FPR-LZ was discovered by the security forces; two militants, Jorge Alberto Madrid and Amalia Bautista Rodríguez, were killed by the police. According to the authorities, carbines and assault rifles were captured as well as numerous documents (ibid., 18 March). Among those documents were accounting books of the organization, indicating a propaganda and student recruiting budget of 27,800 lempiras for 1987 and indicating that the main beneficiaries of such funds were high school students in Tegucigalpa and San Pedro Sula. Most of the funds originated from bank robberies during the past two years (ibid.). During the same raid, two revolutionaries, Freddy Nolasco and Hilda Rosa Rato, apparently committed suicide.

On 10 April a previously unknown "Bayardo Paguada" group claimed credit for a grenade attack in Tegucigalpa and promised more of the same "until Honduras has been liberated from U.S. imperialism" (ibid., 15 April). The group could have been a Cinchoneros unit, in line with that organization's habit of using ad hoc names for specific actions; it is also possible that such attacks are part of Sandinista intelligence attempts to intimidate the Honduran government into withdrawing support for the *contras*.

In June the leader of a PCH front organization, Rosa Dilia Rivera of the People's Organizations' Coordinating Committee (CCOP), was arrested in possession of party literature (*La Tribuna*, 4 June).

The most spectacular terrorist attack of the year took place in Comayagua on 9 August, when six U.S. soldiers and four Honduran civilians were wounded in an explosion in a restaurant. By 26 August four persons were arrested in conjunction with the blast and, according to the authorities, confessed to having participated in yet another bombing, at the National Autonomous University of Honduras, on 18 August. (Ibid., 31 August.) All four appear to have been students, possibly related to the PRTC.

Despite such incidents, it is clear that the Honduran revolutionary left is still in disarray, lacks any solid base of support outside some student groups, and is well under control by the security forces. In fact, so irrelevant is it perceived to be that the Arias peace plan signed in Guatemala does not even specifically require the Honduran government to open negotiations with the left, which is in contrast to the situation in Guatemala and El Salvador. Nevertheless, a perfunctory National Reconciliation Commission was set up, with little to do.

Michael Radu
Foreign Policy Research Institute, Philadelphia

Jamaica

Population. 2,455,536
Party. Workers' Party of Jamaica (WPJ)
Founded. 1978
Membership. 75 (estimated)
General Secretary. Trevor Munroe
Status. Legal

Last Congress. Third, December 1984
Last Election. 1983, legislative, WPJ boycotted; 1986, municipal, no representation
Auxiliary Organizations. No data
Publications. *Struggle*

The economic crisis that began in Jamaica in the early 1970s was at best mildly attenuated during 1987. In presenting his Budget Message to Parliament in April, Prime Minister Edward Seaga claimed that the economy had grown between 3 and 4 percent during the previous year, and he presented what he labeled a "growth budget" to expand social services (Bridgetown, CANA, 24 April). However, Seaga's claims were not accepted by the opposition.

The economic crisis continued to have political repercussions. In 1972 it had resulted in the victory of the democratic socialist People's National Party (PNP), headed by Michael Manley, which remained in power until 1980, when the opposition Jamaica Labor Party (JLP) won a landslide victory and Seaga became prime minister. The tenure of Seaga and the JLP in power was confirmed in a quick election in 1983—two years early—that the PNP boycotted because of Seaga's refusal to prepare a new electoral roll, which gave the JLP all seats in the Lower House.

Polls taken during 1987 indicated the likelihood of a clear victory for the PNP if elections were held then. For instance, in early June Carl Stone's poll, the most prestigious one in the country, showed that the PNP would get 49 percent as compared to 34 percent for the JLP (CANA, 20 July).

Leadership and Organization. The WPJ has had the Moscow franchise in Jamaica. The rival Jamaica Communist Party was organized in 1975 by Chris Lawrence, but it received no attention during the year. The WPJ emerged from study circles at the University of the West Indies in the early 1970s. In 1974 various groups were brought together in the League for Liberation of the Workers, which strongly supported the PNP in the 1976 election. Its principal leader was Dr. Trevor Munroe, a professor at the University of the West Indies.

The league became the WPJ in a congress in December 1978. It Third Congress was held in Kingston in December 1984, and 32.4 percent of the delegates were workers, as compared to 23.1 percent in the Second Congress in 1981. The principal labor organization in which the WPJ has influence is the Union of Workers at the University of the West Indies.

Domestic Attitudes and Activities. The WPJ suffered something of an internal crisis during 1987. This arose from the poor showing of the party in the July 1986 municipal elections. As Munroe wrote, the party's objective had been "to gain a maximum of 15 percent of the vote in some of the divisions we contested, less in others, and to win one or two seats to municipalities, in the most favorable areas. As is shown, this objective of the party was not met." Munroe admitted that the only union in the country the WPJ controlled was the 2,500-member University and Allied Workers' Union, which was one of the unions in the 10–15 percent of the labor movement not controlled by the country's two major parties. However, he claimed some recent success among nonworking-class elements, particularly those in the peace movement. He claimed that "We have developed our work in diverse social sectors and this has yielded important gains, particularly among the national religious leadership. In recent months, primarily because of the WPJ's work, important personalities and prestigious individuals have declared their support for the concrete, practical, and constructive steps being taken by the Soviet Union to safeguard world peace." (*WMR*, February.)

A resolution of the Fifth Plenary of the WPJ, although held in October 1986, summed up the problems of the WPJ during 1987. It said that "The poor performance in the elections was due to (a) the national character of the elections swamping the WPJ's local appeal; (b) anticommunism among the people; (c) unattainable targets set by the party based on wishful thinking." This resolution went on to note that "wishful thinking and trying to do more than the situation allows politically can now kill the party . . . Drastic change must now be made to match what party members and the Jamaican working people can manage in a time when they have to be taken up with survival and are placing some hope in reform." However, the resolution also noted that "A second less likely danger is the abandonment of our working-class principles. This must be resisted . . ." (*IB*, April.)

In September the party issued another document, this time on the problem of women's rights in Jamaica. It criticized the "machismo" characteristic of Jamaican society, which was also evident in the party itself. It was particularly critical of the emphasis the party had put on the rise of the cost of living as a "women's issue," instead of emphasizing the specific problems of women as wives, mothers, and workers. (*IB*, September.)

Throughout the year much attention was centered on the likelihood of a new election. An official Election Inquiry was established to propose modifications in the country's election laws. The WPJ presented its position to this body through John Haughton. He urged establishment of proportional representation, recall of elected members of Parliament and local elective bodies, and government subsidy of candidates' election expenses. (*Daily Gleaner*, 21 February.)

Over the years the attitude of the WPJ toward the PNP has varied considerably. The WPJ and its predecessor supported PNP candidates in 1976 and 1980 and joined the PNP in boycotting the parliamentary election of 1983. However, in 1986 it ran a number of candidates against those of the PNP in municipal elections.

In 1987 Munroe criticized the PNP's movement "to the Right" in preparation for forthcoming elections. He claimed that "The economic program of the PNP has become more 'moderate' than it was in the 1970s . . . It has made much more general and vague its policy regarding the expansion of the state sector . . . In relation to the working class itself, the PNP's original program of strengthening that class at the point of production by facilitating worker participation even in opposition to the bourgeoisie appears to be modified toward the center and the right." (*WMR*, February.)

International Views, Positions, and Activities. The WPJ maintained fairly close relations with other pro-Soviet parties in 1987. Elean Thomas, a member of the Politburo of the party, represented it at a round table of the *World Marxist Review* in Prague, Czechoslovakia, on "Christian/Marxist Dialogue in Latin America." She emphasized the party's success in involving various Christian individuals and groups in the WPJ's "peace" campaign. (*WMR*, February.) Thomas also participated in a *World Marxist Review* international symposium later in the year, also in Prague, on "Can the Military Industrial Complex Be Bridled?" (*WMR*, September).

Revolutionary Marxist League. The third and smallest Marxist-Leninist organization in Jamaica is the Revolutionary Marxist League (RML). It was organized in the late 1970s and identifies itself as Trotskyist. It is, however, aligned with the Revolutionary Socialist League in the United States, which repudiates the traditional Trotskyist position that the Soviet Union and other Soviet-bloc states remain "workers' states."

Robert J. Alexander
Rutgers University

Martinique

Population. 344,922
Party. Martinique Communist Party (Parti Communiste Martiniquais; PCM)
Founded. 1921 (PCM, 1957)
Membership. Less than 1,000
General Secretary. Armand Nicolas (62; French citizen)
Politburo. 3 members
Secretariat. 4 members
Central Committee. 33 members
Status. Legal
Last Congress. Ninth, 12–13 December
Last Election. 16 March 1986; in Regional Council, 3 of 41 seats
Auxiliary Organizations. General Confederation of Martiniquan Labor (CGTM); Martiniquan Union of Education Personnel (SMPE-CGTM); Union of Women of Martinique (Union des Femmes de la Martinique); Martiniquan Committee of Solidarity with the Peoples of the Caribbean and of Central America
Publications. *Justice* (weekly newspaper)

In September the very small PCM celebrated the 30th anniversary of its separation from the French Communist Party. During numerous banquets and fetes, members congratulated themselves on three decades of autonomy. The Ninth Party Congress took place on 12–13 December. Discussions focused on themes such as the crisis of capitalism and the reform or restructuring (*perestroika*) in the USSR, which, it was stated, will open a new and hopeful period for socialism. CPSU General Secretary Mikhail Gorbachev received special praise from the PCM.

More specifically, participants in the Ninth Congress called on Third World countries to repudiate their debts or refuse to repay them for the time being. They claimed that since the right is in power in France, vigilance and struggle must be increased. The PCM must struggle for decentralization or decisionmaking at the departmental level. Martinique nationhood is developing, they claimed, and French measures to develop the overseas departments are merely a continuation of imperialism. Participants denounced plans to integrate the departments further into the European Economic Community by 1993. The PCM, like the communists in Guadeloupe, lost some members to the local independence movement, but congress participants said they had reorganized themselves and were just as strong as ever.

During the year the party focused on economic questions. The French "law-program" passed on 31 December 1986 proposed a free zone for Martinique and other economic development measures that seemed to the PCM to encourage emigration. The PCM called for job creation for Martiniquans within Martinique; it called for greater decentralization by increasing the power of local institutions such as the Regional Council.

In two by-elections to the General Council, one communist won a seat and another member of the United Left won a seat. The PCM also joined with socialists and other members of the United Left to conduct study groups. Although the PCM denounced advocates of immediate independence for Martinique, it objected strongly to the police putting up pictures of seven independence advocates who are wanted by the police. The party criticizes the nationalists but does not consider them to be common criminals. A section of the affiliated trade union, CGTM, went on strike with party support. The PCM also praised the Union of Women of Martinique, headed by Solange Fitte-Duval. Both groups celebrated the International Day of Women on 22 May during a meeting at the town of François; that day was chosen as a holiday because of a slave revolt in 1848.

The PCM maintained close ties with communist parties in Guadeloupe and Réunion. Representatives of the three parties met in Fort-de-France, Martinique, to discuss the end of customs barriers in the European Economic Community in 1993. PCM General Secretary Armand Nicolas joined French National Assembly deputy Ernest Moutoussamy from Guadeloupe to travel to Brussels with Bernard Pons, minister for overseas departments. Discussions about the effects of integration in the Common Market in 1993 did nothing to assuage communist worries, they said. In April Nicolas and others visited the People's Republic of China, the first visit of Martinique communists since 1961. They met members of the Chinese Communist Party Central Committee and expressed hope for expanded relations in the future. In August a Chinese delegation visited Martinique.

Brian Weinstein
Howard University

Mexico

Population. 81,860,566
Party. Mexican Socialist Party (Partido Mexicano Socialista; PMS)
Founded. 1919 (PMS, November 1987)
Membership. 90,000 (claimed)
General Secretary. Gilberto Rincón Gallardo
Political Commission. Gilberto Rincón Gallardo, Jorge Alocer Villanueva, Raymundo Cárdenas Hernández, Heberto Castillo Martinez, Eduardo Valle Espinosa, José Luis Hernández, Jesús Ortega Martínez, Graco Ramírez Garrido-Abreu, Miguel Alonso Raya, Carmelo Enrique Rosario, Rodolfo Armenta, Camilo Valenzuela Fierra, José Domínguez, Manuel Terrazas Guerrero (*La Jornada*, 15 November)
Executive Committee. 36 members
National Committee. 159 members
Status. Legal
Last Congress. First, 25–29 November
Last Election. N/a
Auxiliary Organizations. Independent Center of Agricultural Workers and Peasants (CIOAC), Sole National Union of University Workers (SUNTU)
Publications. *Asi Es* (weekly, Mexico City; status not clear since November)

After only six years since its inception as the result of the unification of the Mexican Communist Party and other leftist groups, the United Socialist Party of Mexico (PSUM) was superseded by the PMS. This merger of groups to the left of the long-dominant Institutional Revolutionary Party (PRI) had been under consideration since August 1985; it was announced on 29 March 1987 and consummated in late November at the PMS First National Congress in Mexico City. The PSUM was initially joined in the new, communist-dominated organization by the small but influential Mexican Workers' Party (PMT) and by three little-known and politically marginal groups: the Patriotic Revolutionary Party, the People's Revolutionary Movement, and the Union of the Communist Left.

The five entities first revealed the extent and nature of their intended cooperation in a joint proclamation issued on 29 March during the Third National Congress of the PSUM. They declared that "Mexico once again is at a crossroads" and revealed their intention to struggle to "maintain national independence, establish a genuinely democratic national political system, and strive for the emancipation of workers." In addition, they announced their "decision to unite in a single revolutionary, patriotic, and socialist party." They denounced "U.S. intervention in Central America," called for international peace and disarmament, and endorsed a nonaligned foreign policy. Consistent with the traditional Eurocommunist attitudes of the Mexican communist movement, the five also declared that they would not "be subordinate to any center of international political direction." (*Asi Es*, 15 April.)

The creation of the PMS was motivated in large part by the desire of both the PSUM and PMT leaders to expand their parties' membership and showing at the polls during a period of intensifying political activity leading up to the national elections in July 1988. Although both parties were legal and had organizations and support in many areas of the country, neither had been able to attract large constituencies or to challenge effectively the PRI's monopoly of political power. Thus, although long-time PMT leader and nationally recognized socialist intellectual Heberto Castillo Martínez had refused to merge his party with the communist party in 1981, he was able to win important concessions from the PSUM in 1987. Most important, it was agreed that Castillo would run as the PMS presidential candidate and thus be the most conspicuous and quoted party leader during the nearly one year campaign period before the elections.

As a result, the PMS emerged as a hybrid party, dominated by militants of Mexico's frequently reorganized communist movement but with a social democratic and moderate orientation. For example, although the party adopted the "International" as its official hymn, Castillo and his PMT supporters prevailed in their long-time refusal to join in a party that used the hammer and sickle as its official emblem. Thus, that standard badge of Marxist-Leninist parties and ideology, which had been used prominently by the PSUM, has been dropped by the PMS.

Not surprisingly, then, the new party's relations with the Soviet and Cuban communist parties as well as with other pro-Moscow parties in Latin America remain cool. In fact, in mid-May, when it was still in a transitional stage of development, the PMS hosted a regional conference of fourteen Latin American socialist parties in Mexico City. Writing about that conclave in *Punto*, José Woldenberg, a ranking PSUM official at the time, indicated that "support for the parties varies widely in their countries, but what they have in common is their concern about combining socialism and democracy, their efforts to undo the huge prevailing social inequalities and to dampen the dynamics of blocs, as well as the fact that they are totally independent of any center of power." (*JPRS LAM-87-055*.)

The Third Congress of the PSUM. The PSUM's last congress was held explicitly to review and ratify the proposed merger with the PMT and the creation of the PMS. The three top PSUM leaders—General Secretary Pablo Gómez, International Department chief Gilberto Rincón Gallardo, and parliamentary group leader Arnoldo Martínez Verdugo—delivered opening addresses advocating the merger. Although, according to *Asi Es*, a good deal had been said and written against the plan, the nearly 1,500 delegates voted in favor; there were just seventeen abstentions.

The congress also installed a new 86-member Central Committee. During its first plenary session on 28 March, the Central Committee reinstated Pablo Gómez as PSUM general secretary, chose a 25-person Political Commission, a seven-member Secretariat, and a seven-member PMS Coordinating Commission. (*Asi Es*, 8 May.) These bodies and presumably the remainder of the PSUM organization and hierarchy remained intact until late November, when the PMS held its First Congress and named its own leadership.

The USSR was represented at the PSUM congress by Soviet Central Committee member and *Kommunist* chief editor I. T. Frolov (*FBIS*, 27 March). In his brief speech there, Frolov dwelled mainly on international issues where Soviet and Mexican government policies tend to converge. For example, he highlighted Mexico's "fruitful participation in the activity of the 'Delhi Six,' which makes a large contribution to the cause of nuclear disarmament." (Ibid., 31 March.) *Pravda* carried the text of Frolov's remarks and, in separate coverage, noted that the congress had approved "a proposal put forward by the PSUM leadership and four other left-wing political organizations to merge into a single party with a view to stepping up the people's struggle for democracy, socialism, and the defense of national sovereignty." *Pravda* did not, however, announce the name of the new party, and it noted cautiously that "a great deal of work will have to be done to insure that the future left wing party... really does unite the country's best forces and becomes the vanguard."

During the interim period between the PSUM's last congress and the PMS's first, the fledgling party made some important advances. In late June it won Mexican government recognition and thus the right to participate in national elections. And, in August a faction of the Socialist Workers' Party (PST) joined the five other parties and groups that were already members of the coalition. PST congressional deputy Graco Ramírez Garrido-Abreu announced that members of his party had agreed unanimously to join the PMS.

The First PMS Congress. Three thousand delegates participated in the new party's First Congress in Mexico City from 25 to 29 November—one delegate for every 30 militants the party claims as members (*Proceso*, 30 November). The congress described the party as "radical socialist" and, in keeping with such an orientation, called for the suspension of both interest and principal payments on Mexico's foreign debt in order to devote those resources to internal economic development. It urged, furthermore, that Mexico take a leadership role among other developing nation debtor states in forming an international front to push for the annulment of the Third World debt and to demand that governments of advanced capitalist countries renegotiate their economic relations with developing nations. In addition, the congress called for the reorganization of Mexico's internal financial system.

Long-time communist Gilberto Rincón Gallardo was elected PMS general secretary. Born in 1939, he began in politics as a member of the conservative National Action Party in the late 1950s but joined the Mexican Communist Party in 1963. During the late 1960s Rincón lived clandestinely and, according to his own account, was arrested eight times and imprisoned from July 1968 until December 1971, a period of acute political stress and radical and youthful militance against the PRI-dominated political system. (*Proceso*, 30 November.)

In public interviews and statements Rincón projects a moderate image intended to attract a broad following to the new party. During the PMS congress, for instance, he asserted in an interview that the people need to identify socialism with the PMS, "not with China, or Cuba, or with the USSR" (ibid.). On another occasion, referring to the diverse roots of Mexican socialism, he said that his country has to "resolve its socialist future realizing that it has a long border with the United States and that (this reality) influences its decisions." He went on to argue that Mexico must struggle for greater economic, cultural, and technological independence from the United States, "but at the same time it cannot detach itself economically from either North or South America." (Ibid., 23 November.)

Brian Latell
National Intelligence Council
and Georgetown University

Nicaragua

Population. 3,319,059

Major Marxist-Leninist Parties.

• Sandinista Front of National Liberation (Frente Sandinista de Liberación Nacional; FSLN)

Founded. 1961

Membership. 1,400 (estimated)

National Directorate. 9 members: Daniel Ortega Saavedra, Humberto Ortega Saavedra, Victor Tirado López, Tomás Borge Martínez, Bayardo Arce Castaño, Henry Ruiz Hernández, Jaime Wheelock Román, Luis Carrión Cruz, Carlos Nuñez Téllez.

Executive Commission. 5 members: Daniel Ortega Saavedra (coordinator), Bayardo Arce Castaño (deputy coordinator), Humberto Ortega Saavedra, Tomás Borge Martínez, Jaime Wheelock Román

Main Party Organs. Sandinista Assembly (105 members), supposed to convene yearly; routine party operations are under the control of seven auxiliary departments: general affairs (René Nuñez); organization (Lea Guido); agitation and propaganda (Carlos Fernando Chamorro); political education (Vanessa Castro Cardenal); international affairs (Julio López); finances (Plutarco Cornejo); studies of Sandinismo (Flor de Maria Monterrey).

Status. Ruling party
Last Congress. August 1985, FSLN Assembly
Last Elections. 4 November 1984; presidential race, 63 percent; Constituent Assembly, 61 out of 96 seats
Fronts and Auxiliary Organizations. Sandinista Defense Committees (Comités de Defense Sandinista; CDS), estimated membership 150,000, led by Leticia Herrera; Sandinista Youth–19 of July (Juventud Sandinista 19 de Julio; JS-19), led by Carlos Carrión; "Luisa Amanda Espinosa" Association of Nicaraguan Women (Asociación de Mujeres Nicaraguenses Luisa Amanda Espinosa; AMNLAE), led by Glenda Monterrey; Sandinista Workers' Central (Central Sandinista de Trabajadores; CST); Farmworkers' Association (Asociación de Trabajadores del Campo; ATC)
Publications. *Barricada* (party daily, circulation 110,000), *El Nuevo Diario* (government daily, circulation 60,000), *Nicarahuac* (ideological journal), *Segovia* (army journal), *Bocay* (Interior Ministry monthly); all television stations and the two major radio stations, Radio Sandino and La Voz de Nicaragua are party-controlled and owned.

• Socialist Party of Nicaragua (Partido Socialista de Nicaragua; PSN), oldest pro-Soviet communist party in the country
Founded. 1937 (first official congress, 1944)
Membership. Unknown
General Secretary. Gustavo Tablada
Political Commission. Gustavo Tablada, Domingo Sánchez Salgado, Luis Sánchez Sancho, Adolfo Evertz, José Luis Medina, Juan Gaitán
Status. Legal
Last Congress. Eighth Plenum, July 1985
Last Election. November 1984; less than 2 percent, two seats in Constituent Assembly
Auxiliary Organizations. General Confederation of Workers–Independent (CGI)
Publication. *El Popular* (weekly)

• Communist Party of Nicaragua (Partido Comunista de Nicaragua; PCN)
Founded. 1970, as splinter of PSN
Membership. Unknown
General Secretary. Eli Altamirano Pérez
Politburo. 7 members: Eli Altamirano Pérez, Ariel Bravo Lorio, Allan Zambrana Zalmeron, Angel Hernández Zerda, René Blandon Noguera, Manuel Pérez Estrada, Alejandro Gutiérrez Mayorga
Status. Legal
Last Congress. Second, June 1986
Last Election. November 1984; less than 2 percent, two seats in Constituent Assembly
Auxiliary Organization. Central for Trade Union Action and Unity (CAUS)
Publication. *Avance* (weekly, circulation about 20,000)

• Nicaraguan Marxist-Leninist Party (Partido Marxista Leninista de Nicaragua; PMLN), until 1986 called Popular Action Movement–Marxist-Leninist (Movimiento de Acción Popular–Marxista-Leninista; MAP-ML)
Founded. 1970, as splinter of FSLN
Membership. Unknown
General Secretary. Isidro Téllez
Other Party Leaders. Fernando Malespín, Alejandro Gutiérrez, Carlos Cuadra, Carlos Lucas
Status. Legal
Last Congress. National Conference, September 1985
Last Election. November 1984; less than 2 percent, two seats in Constituent Assembly
Auxiliary Organization. Workers' Front (Frente Obrero; FO)
Publication. *Prensa Proletaria* (bi-monthly)

In June one of the two full-time party organizers among the nine members of the FSLN National Directorate, Deputy-Coordinator Bayardo Arce, gave an interesting and revealing interview to a highly sympathetic Mexican newspaper; he described some of the internal and ideological characteristics of the FSLN, which was the first time information regarding membership, social background, and internal decisionmaking were made public in a detailed manner.

According to Arce, a decision was made after the revolution that the FSLN would not "open up the membership to all those people who regarded themselves as Sandinistas," but instead would "adhere to the concept of a party of cadres" (*Excelsior*, 25

June). Among those cadres the domination of the National Directorate is total: it appoints leaders of front or "mass" organizations as well as lower level party cadres, and Arce stated that "we have not made much progress in forms of party democracy" (ibid.). There are no plans for a congress in the foreseeable future.

The FSLN membership ranks have evolved as a result of a National Directorate decision made after the July 1979 political takeover. At that time it was discovered that there were less than 150 cadres with more than 5 years of membership; less than 500 had joined before 1977; and some 1,400 fulfilled the final criterion for membership, by having joined the FSLN by the time of the fall 1978 urban insurrections (ibid.). Most of those cadres had no political experience, and this, Arce admitted, raised some problems in filling even the top positions in the country, including 40 ministries, 18 "mass and social organizations," 70 "strategic enterprises," nine politico-administrative regions, and 61 National Assembly deputies. The result of the decision to retain the elite nature of the party while expanding its control over the national life was based on the notion that "a good collaborator is better than a poor militant." (Ibid.)

Regarding FSLN ideology, Arce consistently took refuge in negative definitions: "I can state categorically that I do not want Nicaragua to become like the USSR; I do not want it to become like the United States, or like France... The Cuban experience is not for us; we are not an island" (ibid.). As for the substance of the Sandinista ideology, Arce repeated older claims that it is a "synthesis" of Marxism-Leninism, Christianity, and nationalism, in that order; in a clearly tactical reversal of his own previous statements, he claimed that democracy "is not a tactical decision, but rather a strategic one" (ibid.). Arce also repeated the discredited notion that there is a "mixed economy" in Nicaragua, whereas in fact the FSLN controls prices, wages, credit, employment levels, and currency; it outrightly owns almost half of the industrial enterprises; and it has a complete monopoly on external trade and currency transactions.

The general orientation of the FSLN in the ideological field continued to be toward increasingly orthodox Marxism-Leninism and militarism. Culture Minister Ernesto Cardenal defined culture as "anti-imperialist" and said that all revolutionary activities, including defense, are cultural as well (*Barricada*, 21 July). Such definitions of culture are closely related to other FSLN policies aiming at controlling all forms of expression. Even the pro-government *El Nuevo Diario* admitted that there are only two types of journalistic criticism today in Nicaragua: "criticism of U.S. policy and of the system it represents (capitalism) and criticism of the domestic political parties or organizations that support the interests of their social classes and of the White House" (*El Nuevo Diario*, 19 November 1986).

To insure the revolutionary nature of even technical training, this year 423 youths, some as young as twelve, were sent to Cuba for six-year courses (*Insight*, 14 September), in addition to the thousands already there.

The FSLN accuses all other parties of either "penetration" by "imperialist forces" or of de facto betrayal (*FBIS-LAM*, 15 May). Thus, Daniel Ortega stated that the "ideological and political struggle, as well as the propaganda campaign must be carried out... against the rightist forces... and against the ultraleftist groups who, with their demagogic speeches and their false revolutionary language, are becoming accomplices of foreign aggression" (*Barricada*, 14 June).

In addition to the fact that political dialogue and acceptance of the legal and legitimate right of other parties to oppose FSLN policies are daily denied by top Sandinista leaders, the legal system itself is now under party control. The courts' decisions are openly rejected and dismissed by the CDS when those decisions do not allow CDS members to take over houses belonging to the "bourgeoisie" (ibid., 6 December 1986). More important, the existence and activities of the Anti-Somozista People's Tribunals, with their 97 percent rate of convictions, can only be justified by the regime's propaganda line claiming that all opposition, and particularly the armed one, is "Somozista." The abuses of the Sandinista penal system have been documented by a number of international human rights organizations, ranging from Amnesty International to Americas Watch, as well as by the independent Nicaraguan Human Rights Committee (CDHN); the number of political prisoners by the end of 1987 ranged between 9,000 claimed by CDHN and contradictory figures provided by government sources. For example, Tomás Borge claimed in June that there were 2,095 *contras* and 2,110 "Somozist guards" in the jails controlled by his ministry (Bogota, *Semana*, 9 June). In September, however, Borge said that the number of prisoners (political or otherwise, a distinction not always easy to make) was 8,000, of whom 3,000 were Somozist guards and over 1,000 *contras* (*FBIS-LAM*, 8 September).

The balance of forces within the FSLN core has further changed during the year toward increasing domination by the Ortega brothers. Despite Daniel Ortega's claim that "we are promoting collective leadership here . . . This eliminates any personality cult" (*JPRS-LAM*, 11 August), his power is increasingly unchallenged. The decisionmaking patterns of previous years are clearly undergoing a change, with power concentrated in Daniel Ortega's hands. Even Borge, the only surviving founder of the FSLN, has seen his power as interior minister circumscribed, and decisions normally pertaining to him are being announced—and probably made—by the president. One such decision was that allowing the opposition newspaper *La Prensa* and Radio Católica to operate again on 1 October (*NYT*, 4 October). The only other senior leader retaining his autonomy is defense minister and FSLN strategist Humberto Ortega, Daniel's brother.

The process of concentration of power in the president's hands was already formalized in December 1986, when attempts to limit the presidential mandate to one term were defeated in the National Assembly. In 1987 Arce lost his position as main party organizer, Henry Ruiz lost his position as minister of planning to a close associate of the Ortegas, Dionisio Marenco, and there are clear signs that the power of CDS leader Leticia Herrera, a long-time Ortega loyalist and friend, was enhanced. In addition, Omar Cabezas, a Borge loyalist and former secret police boss, was demoted to a position in the Economic Planning Ministry. Despite the growing domination of the National Directorate by the Ortega brothers, that body is now more united than at any previous time, with no signs of any significant disputes among its members. That there are no "doves" and "hawks" in the FSLN leadership was confirmed by Major Roger Miranda Bengoechea, Humberto Ortega's main collaborator, who defected to the United States in October.

The Economy. The process of formation of a Sandinista nomenklatura progressed rapidly during the year, and the economic crisis made the disparities between that group and the population increasingly glaring. Top FSLN and Sandinista People's Army (EPS) officials have exclusive access to special stores providing staples and luxury goods at heavily subsidized prices. They also have the right to exchange cordobas for dollars at the official rate (*NYT*, 29 December), which was 70 to 1 in January, as compared to 3,000 to 1 on the black market (*Foreign Report*, 29 January). By September the black market rate had reached 13,000 to 1 (*LAT*, 20 September). The most prominent cases of personal enrichment, according to Miranda, are the Ortega brothers themselves, who have over one million dollars in a Swiss bank account (ibid.). The economy remains the most dangerous problem facing the FSLN, and it is becoming more critical every month. The inflation rate is over 1,000 percent, food is rationed and often impossible to find. The monthly ration of rice, a staple of the Nicaraguan diet, is two pounds, at 40 cordobas per pound; in the nomenklatura stores the price per pound is 400 cordobas, and on the thriving black market it is 800 cordobas (*LAT*, 18 March). The cordoba, kept at a stable 10 to 1 exchange rate, is virtually worthless; a 1,000 cordoba note, which used to be worth $100 in prerevolutionary times, is now worth 3 cents and costs 2.7 cents to print. The gross national product is at the early 1950s level, and the monthly income of the average citizen is now between one-fifth and one-tenth of what it was in 1980. The public transportation system has collapsed for lack of fuel, vehicles, and parts; traditional Nicaraguan products such as coffee, sugar, meat, and cotton are impossible to find on the official markets.

The government blames the United States for the economic crisis but makes no allowances for the needs of the population. In February Daniel Ortega defined the "general guidelines" of the regime's economic policies: "First, top priority will continue to be [to] guarantee the military defense of the revolution . . . Second, the goal is to concentrate [on] export goods that will generate foreign exchange . . . goods that prop up or support the country's military defense . . . [and]the basic goods for the population" (*JPRS-LAM*, 9 February). With such a mentality, it is no surprise that the government has decided to label private market operations, mostly conducted by peasant women, as "speculation" and to crack down on them. With basic supplies absent, declining standards of living, and more workers forced to take a second job, the result was that, in 59 enterprises in the first half of 1986, absenteeism amounted to 403,715 man days, according to the government (*Barricada*, 9 February). Despite the regime's attempts to blame the economic collapse on the alleged U.S. aggression, the Soviet newspaper *Izvestiia* (24 June) also claimed that difficulties "are being intensified by parasitism, speculation and swindling." Even the many Cuban or Soviet bloc–trained experts have a hard time finding jobs in Nicaragua, and they complain bitterly (*El Nuevo Diario*, 4 August).

Opposition to the FSLN. The centralizing and polarizing trends in FSLN policies and attitudes, as well as the collapse of the economy, all combined to move the Nicaraguan opposition, whether legal, semi-legal, or illegal (military), toward unification. That process is far from complete, but there are clear signs that a trend toward coordination of action against the FSLN is progressing at both the legal and illegal levels. The relationship between the regime and the Roman Catholic Church developed to unexpected dimensions during 1987.

The opposition to the FSLN is largely structured at the following levels:

1. Most of the legal parties in the National Assembly, particularly the Independent Liberals, the Popular Social Christian Party (PPSC), and the PCN. The case of the PCN is perhaps the most ironic; in effect the communists accuse the FSLN of giving Marxism-Leninism a bad name (*Avance, Informe Politico*, 18 February).
2. The organizations (unions, business chambers, parties) included in the Democratic Coordinator umbrella, which are not in the National Assembly but have considerable mass support and external ties. These include the Conservative, Social Christian, and Social Democratic parties, the Council of Private Enterprise (COSEP), and the center-left union federation CUS.
3. The overwhelming majority of the Catholic clergy, led by Cardinal Obando y Bravo.
4. The armed opposition, now united under the label of the Nicaraguan Resistance and including political parties in exile, the military structure, and rebellious ethnic minorities on the Atlantic Coast.

The most important, perhaps decisive, change in the attitudes and effectiveness of the opposition in 1987 was the increasing trend toward cooperation and coordination among its various levels. On 5 February seven political parties from both the National Assembly and the Democratic Coordinator sent a letter to President Ortega demanding the formation of a National Peace Commission, a general amnesty, and a national pact between the FSLN and the opposition (*Avance*, 11 March). The letter was signed by the leaders of the PPSC, PCN, Social Democrats, Social Christians, Conservatives, and Constitutionalist Liberals—thus ranging across the entire political spectrum, from conservatives to Marxist-Leninists.

Some prominent Catholic priests, including the former bishop of Juigalpa, Pablo Antonio Vega, and the ex-spokesman of the Managua archdiocese, Bismarck Carballo, have made statements that could easily be construed as sympathetic to the *contras*; after being expelled from the country in 1986, they were allowed to return in late 1987.

The contras. The military situation changed quite dramatically during 1987, as did the political capabilities of the major armed opposition organization, the Nicaraguan Resistance (RN). At the political level, after a bad start at the beginning of the year when Arturo Cruz, a senior political leader, resigned from the *contra* leadership in March, a massive restructuring of the organization took place in May. The United Nicaraguan Opposition (UNO) was replaced by the RN and was consolidated into a single organization comprising practically all non-Indian external opposition groups, armed or not. A congress held in Miami in the first half of May elected a 54-member assembly, which in turn elected eleven members of the new directorate. Some of the top eleven were old military *contra* leaders like Adolfo Calero, Enrique Bermudez, and Aristides Sánchez; others were politicians, like Alfonso Robelo and Alfredo César, or representatives of parties in exile, like Azucena Ferrey of the Social Christian Party. (*LAT*, 8 May.)

On the military level, 1987 was unquestionably the best year for the anti-FSLN insurgents. Not only did they make great inroads in consolidating peasant support in the northern and central departments, particularly Jinotega, Matagalpa, Nueva Segovia, Boaco, and Chontales, but the insurgents have also succeeded in establishing permanent bases inside Nicaragua and greatly, if not totally, lessening their dependence on safe havens in Honduras. Furthermore, in addition to infiltrating as many as 14,000 fighters into Nicaragua and increasing the number of contacts with the EPS to almost ten a day, the insurgents have repeatedly demonstrated an ability to operate in large units against towns while retaining the element of surprise. Attacks such as those against San José de Bocay in July and against the Siuna and La Rosita gold mining installations in December involved hundreds of insurgents, yet they took the army by surprise. This tends to indicate that insurgent intelligence is better than that of the Sandinistas, which in turn reflects the sentiments of the local population.

The insurgent capabilities were greatly enhanced by the increasingly extensive use of sophisticated antiaircraft weapons (although they did not receive Stinger missiles), particularly British and Soviet-made. According to the insurgents, they had destroyed or damaged thirteen helicopters, or a quarter of the EPS's fleet, by June (*WP*, 26 June; similar though somewhat smaller figures in *CSM*, 23 July).

Perhaps even more significant is the fact that the insurgents have succeeded in somewhat increasing their numbers in 1987, despite casualties and the intensification of the war. The combination of small unit operations over most of the country, including for the first time areas close to or within the Pacific Coast strip where the country's population is concentrated, has forced the government to call in reserves, to spread its forces over a larger territory, and to accept at least temporarily the loss of certain areas.

At the strategic level the most important development took place in July and August, when the bulk of the insurgent forces in Honduras managed to infiltrate into Nicaragua around the Sandinista army's border defenses.

The government's reaction to the insurgent successes has been to intensify its internal relocation of the rural population in southern Zelaya, particularly Nueva Guinea, Boaco, and Chontales in the center of the country and Matagalpa and Nueva Segovia in the north. Although such standard anti-insurgency tactics may be relatively successful in the short term, in Nicaragua they tend to exacerbate the problems in the long term; indeed, the insurgents may lose valuable recruiting ground and intelligence support, but discontented peasants relocated to unfamiliar areas and living under severe economic conditions may in fact "infect" their new neighbors.

The signing of the Central American peace treaty in Guatemala in August led to a significant intensification of the war. Both sides tried to place themselves in a position of strength prior to the forthcoming negotiations, with an eye on the U.S. Congress's mood regarding renewed *contra* aid in the wake of the Iran-*contra* investigation and the Arias Plan. Significantly, the largest operation of the war—the *contra* attacks on Siuna and La Rosita in December involving some 4,000 insurgents—occurred at precisely the same time as indirect negotiations with the government took place in Santo Domingo, Dominican Republic, under the auspices of Cardinal Obando y Bravo (*Time*, 4 January 1988).

Indian resistance. In contrast to the main insurgent groups, 1987 was a very bad year for the ethnically based Indian resistance on the Atlantic Coast: not only did the Indians not reach the same level of political unity their *contra* counterparts did, but their military and political strategies were also clearly unsatisfactory.

In January Jimmy Emery Hodgson, a former leader of the Miskito Indian organization Misurasata, accepted an amnesty and, in fact, defected to the government's side (*El Nuevo Diario*, 23 January). Attempts by the Unity of the Nicaraguan Atlantic Coast Peoples (KISAN) to establish a southern front failed, and the group complained of receiving less U.S. money than it thought it deserved (San José, Costa Rica, *Tico Times*, 23 January). Misurasata leader Brooklyn Rivera complained about Sandinista attacks on civilians, "inhuman tortures, psychological intimidation, and constant persecution" (*FBIS*, 13 February). Finally, a number of KISAN leaders were arrested, threatened, and made ineffective by the Honduran authorities.

The Sandinista policy toward the Indians was quite predictable; a militia to "repel the *contras*" was formed in March under the nominal leadership of a former minor KISAN member, Forne Rabonia (*FBIS*, 20 March), and an indoctrination campaign was launched in the region (*El Nuevo Diario*, 30 June). Indeed, after blaming pirates, the British, and U.S. imperialism for the Indians' problems, Borge claimed that "we do not use the term 'nationality' [in regard to the Atlantic Coast] . . . We believe that the past hostilities on the Atlantic Coast were not ethnic strife but a patriotic battle against external aggression" (*WMR*, August).

The main problem facing the ethnic minorities, and particularly the Misurasata, is largely one of personality clashes among the top leaders. The most important of those are Wycliffe Diego of KISAN; Steadman Fagoth, former leader of the other major Indian opposition group, Misura, who still retains a significant following; and Rivera of Misurasata, who is the most ineffective and conciliatory Indian leader (*LAT*, 9 June). In addition, neither the blacks nor the Creoles are prepared to accept Miskito or "Spaniard" RN leadership for long. For the regime, such divisions present not only opportunities but also problems, inasmuch as the most conciliatory Indian leaders are also the weakest in terms of following. Practically all Indian fighters (600–1,000) are KISAN's, and Rivera has little to offer in the way of peace in Zelaya. Nevertheless, on 4 October one major local KISAN leader, Uriel Vanegas, signed an agreement with the government and met Borge in Puerto Cabezas; however, he only delivered a few dozen of the KISAN guerrillas in exchange for Sandinista support for vaguely defined "Indian rights" (*NYT*, 6 October). Whether people like Rivera and Vanegas can deliver peace to the Atlantic Coast is highly doubtful, and we must await the outcome of talks between the RN—which includes KISAN's main leaders—and the government before a prediction can be made.

Peace negotiations. Until August the government of Nicaragua was openly and consistently opposed to any form of negotiation with what it called the U.S. mercenaries or Somocistas. Arce and Borge were in the forefront of such opposition, and signs are that they may still harbor strong feelings against such policies. Nevertheless, the decision to slowly, conditionally, and temporarily make concessions to internal and particularly external pressure for negotiations was taken by the Ortegas and carried a majority of the FSLN membership.

The public policy of Managua in regard to the reconciliation and negotiations with the armed opposition went through a number of successive stages between the August summit in Guatemala and the January 1988 summit in San José, Costa Rica. The first stage was to claim that, although the FSLN intends to fully comply with the Guatemala agreements, the party "reasserts before our people the need to firmly continue intensifying the armed struggle against the mercenary aggression until peace is completely achieved" (*FBIS*, 18 August). If there were to be any negotiations, they should only involve Managua and Washington, not the RN.

The only implicit exception was in regard to the Indians, and in that respect the Sandinistas were quite successful in producing new divisions in the already fragmented Miskito leadership. In September Rivera once again created a splinter organization, Yatama, which accepted the "autonomy" proposed by Managua as a "starting point" for negotiations (*FBIS*, 17 September). In October negotiations between Yatama and the FSLN started in Nicaragua, but as of the end of 1987 there were no palpable signs of successful completion.

On 25 August Daniel Ortega appointed the National Reconciliation Commission headed by Cardinal Obando y Bravo and including Sergio Ramírez as vice president. In what he described as "another goodwill gesture," Ortega also declared that exiled prelates Pablo Antonio Vega and Bismarck Carballo could return to Nicaragua at any time (ibid., 26 August). However, Managua continued to insist that, unlike El Salvador, whose Marxist-Leninist insurgents are "supported by their own people," the *contras* are simply mercenaries of the United States and thus not included in the Guatemala requirement for government negotiations with armed opposition groups. This position was stated by both Daniel Ortega and Luis Carrión Cruz, who repeated that "The government has always maintained its position that it will hold no dialogue with the *contras*" (*FBIS*, 31 August, 10 September). Nevertheless, in an attempt to divide the field commanders of the insurgents from the political leadership, the FSLN offered and even unilaterally declared a cease-fire in a few areas. No important rebel commander accepted those conditions, and the RN leaders rejected them out of hand as "tantamount to surrender" (*WP*, 24 September).

Regarding the release of political prisoners, another key requirement of the Arias Plan, Ramírez stated that ex-Somoza National Guard members will not be released (*FBIS*, 24 September).

On 5 November, the date compliance with the Arias Plan was to be assessed, the Managua regime suddenly made a number of other concessions: it allowed the reopening of *La Prensa* without censorship and of Radio Católica on the condition that it does not broadcast news; more important yet, the government stated its willingness to talk indirectly to the armed opposition. Cardinal Obando y Bravo was appointed as a mediator between the FSLN and the RN, and in November he held talks with the rebel leadership in the Dominican Republic. Although those talks produced no concrete results and each side blamed the other for this, they took place in an atmosphere of growing militancy by the Nicaraguan legal opposition, with massive demonstrations against the Sandinistas taking place in Masaya and Managua.

There were also signs that there was a certain amount of dissatisfaction within FSLN ranks over the peace proposals and the decision to allow the opposition to become active once again. Such differences led Daniel Ortega to specifically deny divisions within the FSLN and to state that "there are no grounds for saying that some Sandinists agree and others disagree with the Esquipulas [i.e., Arias Plan] agreements" (ibid., 16 October).

International Views and Contacts. Foreign affairs, and particularly relations with the Soviet bloc and the United States, remained one of the top priorities of the government throughout the year. The highest ranking Soviet delegation to visit Nicaragua in 1987 was led by then Moscow party leader and Politburo alternate member Boris Yeltsin in March. On that occasion Daniel Ortega stated that "We are proud of our relations with the Soviet Union. We are never going to jeopardize those relations" (*FBIS*, 4 March). While in Nicaragua, Yeltsin claimed that his government "does not want the Nicaraguan revolution to be part of the Soviet bloc or the U.S. bloc," and he invited all parties represented in the National Assembly to meet with him; significantly, however, the only parties that rejected the offer were the PCN and the PMLN, although the pro-Moscow communists of the PSN did attend (*Barricada*, 5 March).

Although political and ideological relations between the Soviet bloc and the FSLN continued to be close, as witnessed by Daniel Ortega's visit to Havana immediately after the signing of the Esquipulas agreements and by the Soviets' awarding ex-priest and current foreign minister Miguel D'Escoto the Lenin Prize, economic relations were under a certain cloud. There were clear signs that the Soviets were unhappy with the Sandinistas' economic policies, and *Izvestiia* openly criticized them (*Izvestiia*, 24 June; *LAT*, 5 August). In more concrete terms, the Soviets made the decision to cut their costs in subsidizing Nicaragua. As a result, despite the fact that oil imports cost Managua $225 million while the country's total exports only reached $250 million (*El Nuevo Diario*, 29 May), Moscow did drastically cut its oil supplies to the Sandinistas. In fact, the Soviets cut their supplies of oil in half and shifted the cost to their East European and Cuban satellites. As a result, though the USSR was to deliver only 300,000 tons of oil, Cuba promised 60,000, Bulgaria 40,000 Czechoslovakia and East Germany 90,000 each, and Hungary "a large quantity" (ibid.). Nevertheless, according to Foreign Cooperation Minister Henry Ruiz, the "socialist countries . . . currently provide 75 percent of the foreign aid" (ibid., 8 April). According to the Czechoslovakian ambassador to Nicaragua, the economic aid provided by the Soviet bloc in 1987 amounted to $425 million (Douglas Payne, *A Chronicle of the Central American Peace Process* [New York: Freedom House, 1987], p. 17). Furthermore, almost all the enormous amount of materiel received by Nicaragua during the year was provided by the Soviet bloc. The total amount in 1987 included over 20,000 tons of armaments and a promise to arm an army of 600,000 by the mid-1990s.

Managua's diplomacy was fully engaged in trying to harness traditional Latin American anti-Americanism to the FSLN's advantage. It had some significant successes, such as when Peru sent 34,000 tons of oil and Mexico promised to deliver some of the 55,000 tons of oil still needed by Managua (*Latin America Regional Report*, 29 October). Furthermore, the so-called Verification Commission for the Esquipulas agreements—including Contadora countries (Colombia, Venezuela, Panama, and Mexico) and "support group" countries (Peru, Brazil, Argentina, and Uruguay)—was widely and accurately seen as favorable to the Sandinistas.

Nicaragua's policy of establishing fronts in Western countries through sympathetic organizations continued during 1987. One Sandinista sympathizer of U.S. origin, Benjamin Linder, was killed in an armed confrontation in April, and despite FSLN propaganda his death provoked congressional attempts to limit the activities of American left-wing activists in Nicaragua. Members of such pro-FSLN groups as Witness for Peace provoked their own "abductions" in Nicaragua as a means of discrediting the armed opposition, and organizations like Hands off the Americas, the Canadian Farmers for Peace, and West European, particularly West German, Dutch, and Scandinavian left-of-center parties, including some prominent leaders, have consistently provided moral, economic, political, and financial support to the FSLN.

Other Marxist-Leninist Parties. The far-left Workers' Revolutionary Party (Partido Revolucionario de Trabajadores; PRT) and its close ally, the Central American Unification Party (Partido de Unificación Centro Americana; PUCA), are spinoffs of the Revolutionary Party of Central American Workers. Both of these minuscule parties operate on the margins of legality; neither was allowed to participate in the 1984 elections, but they are still tolerated. Bonifacio Miranda is the leader of the PRT, and Alejandro Pérez Arévalo heads the PUCA. The PRT publishes a bi-weekly newspaper,

El Socialista, which is largely preoccupied with ideological attacks on the PCN.

Michael Radu
Foreign Policy Research Institute, Philadelphia

Panama

Population. 2,274,833
Party. People's Party (Partido del Pueblo; PDP)
Founded. 1930 (PDP, 1943)
Membership. 13,089 (500–1,000 militants); according to the government election office, 13,089 people had registered as members of the PDP by 21 June.
General Secretary. Rubén Darío Sousa (or Souza)
Politburo. Includes César Agusto De León Espinosa, Miguel Antonio Porcella Peña, Anastacio E. Rodríguez, Clito Manuel Souza Batista, Luther Thomas (international secretary), Felix Dixon, Darío González Pittí, Carlos Francisco Changmarín
Central Committee. 26 members
Status. Pending. Under current electoral law, 26 June was the deadline for party registration. Law requires that a party have at least 19,252 members before it can be legally recognized. Parties in formation with more than 10 percent of that figure can continue adding to their membership through 1988; those with less must start over again.
Last Congress. Eighth, 24–26 January 1986
Last Election. 1984, less than 3 percent, no representatives
Auxiliary Organizations. Panama Peace Committee, Committee for the Defense of Sovereignty and Peace, People's Party Youth, National Center of Workers of Panama (Central Nacional de Trabajadores de Panamá; CNTP), Union of Journalists of Panama, Federation of Panamanian Students (Federación Estudiantil de Panamá; FEP), National Union of Democratic Women
Publication. *Unidad* (weekly), Carlos Francisco Changmarín, director

The tension between the military-controlled government and the center-right opposition that had steadily increased since the fraudulent 1984 elections exploded in June following the forced retirement of Defense Forces chief of staff, Colonel Roberto Díaz Herrera. In a series of extraordinary interviews with the opposition press, Díaz confirmed popular beliefs that General Manuel Antonio Noriega, head of the Defense Forces since 1983, had rigged the 1984 presidential elections, removed two civilian presidents, and ordered the murder of prominent opposition leader Hugo Spadafora. Díaz's allegations triggered a wave of popular protest unprecedented under the military government established by the late General Omar Torrijos in 1968.

The series of strikes and demonstrations demanding the removal of Noriega and the establishment of authentic democracy lasted through the summer and into the fall. The protests were led by the National Civic Crusade, which is composed of more than 100 civic organizations backed by the business community. The crusade was further supported by a political opposition coalition that included the Christian Democratic Party (PDC) and the Authentic Panameñista Party (PPA) and represented at least half the electorate. Noriega responded by imposing a state of emergency, closing the opposition media, unleashing riot police against demonstrators, jailing hundreds of political prisoners, and sending thousands of troops into the street.

By mid-fall Noriega was seriously discredited, but the revolt had failed to dislodge him. Both sides appeared to be hardening their positions and preparing for a long struggle. Noriega's hold on the country had been undermined by the unexpected popular outburst, but he maintained the backing of the Defense Forces officers by portraying the protests as a direct attack on their institution that was orchestrated by the United States in an effort to renege on the 1977 Canal Treaties. By veering toward a left-populist position on domestic and economic policy, he restored key—if tenuous—support from the labor sector, which had been highly critical of the government in recent years.

Noriega also held onto the services of Eric Arturo Delvalle, the entrepreneur he installed as president in 1985. After expressing concern during the summer about the military's repressive tactics and lifting opposition hopes that he would resign, Delvalle, at the behest of Noriega, worked during the fall for a rapprochement with the business community. Private business and the banking sector were financing the National Civic Crusade, but the protests lost steam in the wake of the rapid economic decline caused by the crisis and Noriega's massive show of force. By the end of the year, much of the leadership of the anti-Noriega drive appeared to be passing back to the political party opposition.

U.S.-Panamanian relations, which had slowly worsened after Noriega took command of the Defense Forces, degenerated into direct confrontation during the crisis. At the outset, both the Reagan administration and the U.S. Senate called for the removal of the military from politics. Noriega retaliated by orchestrating an attack by government employees on the U.S. Embassy in Panama City. Washington countered by suspending the $26 million in U.S. aid to Panama and moving ahead with a Justice Department investigation of the general's involvement in the drug trade. In December the U.S. Congress moved to cut off all but humanitarian aid to Panama and prohibit the import of Panamanian sugar, prompting Noriega to personally order the U.S. Agency for International Development to close its operation in Panama.

In Latin America Noriega played the nationalist card to good effect; the permanent council of the Organization of American States (OAS) overwhelmingly passed a resolution criticizing U.S. interference in Panamanian affairs (*Latin American Regional Reports: Mexico and Central America*, 16 July), and in response to U.S. sanctions he accelerated the effort of recent years to strengthen political ties and obtain financial support from the Eastern bloc and Third World radical states. The primary agent of the stepped-up initiative was the Democratic Revolutionary Party (Partido Revolucionario Democrático; PRD), the political front and ruling instrument of the Defense Forces in the National Assembly. The PRD, whose leftward turn in 1986 had created tension between itself and Noriega, fully supported the general's domestic and foreign policy shifts in 1987.

By the end of the year Noriega's maneuvers appeared to have partially re-established the international and domestic balancing act through which he has kept himself in power. Having survived a heavy blow during the previous seven months, it nonetheless remained unclear whether he would continue to successfully navigate amid increasing U.S. pressure and the further economic deterioration and domestic flare-ups expected in 1988.

For the PDP, however, which has traditionally been on the margins of Panamanian political life, the sudden crisis, the general's response, and the subsequent alterations in the domestic political landscape opened the possibility for expanding the party's limited influence.

Party Organization. The PDP platform, adopted at the Eighth Party Congress in January 1986, called for a determined drive to recruit new members. In the 1984 elections the party had failed to garner the 3 percent of the vote required for representation in the National Assembly. According to current Panamanian electoral law, a party must have at least 19,252 members to receive legal recognition and run candidates in the scheduled 1989 elections. As of 21 June, according to the government elections office, 13,089 people had registered as PDP members (*Central America Report*, 7 August). That is approximately six times the highest membership estimate by outside observers in 1986, and it seemed to reflect successful recruiting efforts by PDP militants in the last year. By surpassing 10 percent of the required figure in 1987, the PDP was allowed to continue adding to its membership through 1988.

Domestic Views and Activities. On 1 January the PDP issued a statement on the joint exercises scheduled for later that month in Panama by the Defense Forces and the U.S. military. In keeping with the tacit approval of the Panamanian military displayed by the party in 1986, the statement sympathetically cautioned rather than criticized the Defense Forces. After an extended condemnation of U.S. "aggressive, militaristic policy," the PDP warned that by participating in the exercises, the Defense Forces "find themselves closely embraced by the aggressive Yankee interventionist policy, not unlike a David [embraced] by a giant Goliath" (*IB*, May). The statement concluded with a demand for an end to the maneuvers, which nonetheless took place as scheduled.

During the first five months of the year, the PDP was increasingly at odds with the government over economic policy. In order to implement an International Monetary Fund (IMF) stabilization program to alleviate one of the highest per capita debt burdens in Latin America, the government in 1986 had revised the labor code, reducing wages and job security. The result was a series of strikes lasting into 1987 by the National Council of Workers' Organizations (Consejo Nacional de Trabajadores Organizados; CONATO), the largest Panamanian union federation. Although the PDP-controlled CNTP participated in the demonstrations, the party criticized only President Delvalle, not the Defense

Forces, despite the fact that Delvalle could not make policy without clearance from Noriega.

In an April *World Marxist Review* article, PDP Politburo member and director of the weekly *Unidad*, Carlos Francisco Changmarín, labeled Delvalle as one of the "Trojan horses" infiltrated into the government by Washington and the IMF for the purpose of "removing Torrijos supporters from the leadership of the Panamanian armed forces and imposing upon us a puppet government." The infiltrators, he continued, "have now formed their own coalition, and it has been from this administration, in which the Revolutionary Democratic Party [PRD] has little say, that the IMF has in recent years wrested the most significant concessions."

Implicit throughout the article is criticism of Noriega for bowing, through Delvalle, to Washington and the IMF instead of adopting the populist measures and debt moratorium line advocated by the PRD, the party created by Torrijos. Changmarín also reiterated the PDP's goal, established at the 1986 congress, of creating a "broad, anti-imperialist, democratic front" formed by patriotic military officers loyal to Torrijism and the PRD, on the one hand, and by the PDP and the rest of the leftist parties and popular organizations, on the other. Although Noriega was not acknowledged as one of the officers loyal to Torrijism, he was defended as "the main target of U.S. criticism" and praised as "a fighter for the nation's sovereignty." (Ibid.)

The PDP's ambivalent backing of Noriega, however, evolved into clearer support following Noriega's policy shifts in response to the crisis. After the June protests began, Noriega rejected further economic stabilization measures, shelved planned social security reforms, began lowering food prices, and promised imminent worker bonuses. In response, the labor sector and the PDP stayed out of the tumult in the streets. At the end of June the PDP issued a statement "warning followers of the Torrijos line" that the protests were the result of U.S. interference and calling on the government to alter its "course of conciliation with imperialism, if it is not itself to fall victim to this imperialist conspiracy" (*IB*, October).

In July the PRD and the labor sector, with PDP support, created the Popular Organization Coordinator (Coordinadora de Organizaciones Populares; COPP). The group organized counterdemonstrations against the National Civic Crusade but demanded a debt-payment moratorium and wide-ranging nationalizations from the government in exchange for its position (*Latin American Weekly Report* [*LAWR*], 23 July). Noriega permitted COPP marches and personally received COPP leaders to discuss their demands. At a military ceremony in mid-August, he promised that the Defense Forces would be leading changes in government policy and asked President Delvalle to include the COPP at the government's "negotiating table" (*LAWR*, 27 August).

The subsequent PDP statement issued 24 September revealed not only clearer support for Noriega but sympathy for the civilian administration headed by Delvalle. The statement condemned the United States for "actions designed to topple the government and to throw out the Torrijists from the Defense Forces, primarily by ousting General M. A. Noriega" (*Matutino*, 30 September; *FBIS*, 2 October). This was the first time the PDP associated Noriega with "Torrijist" officers, signifying that he now qualified for inclusion in the broad, anti-imperialist front advocated by the party.

In an October *World Marxist Review* article, PDP general secretary Rubén Darío Sousa reaffirmed the party's newly unqualified support for Noriega. Sousa stated that "The Torrijist officers have a most important place within the context of renewing the political panorama" and that "General Noriega has come from the midst of patriotic officers as the man prepared to carry on the Torrijos legacy." Then, in a virtual endorsement of Noriega as the head of the broad front envisioned by the PDP, Sousa stated that "The General is being personally vilified in an effort to deprive the democratic and anti-imperialist movement of its leader."

By the end of the year, however, the labor sector was becoming recalcitrant again, demanding that the government carry through on promises Noriega had made at the height of the crisis. Striking government workers were temporarily mollified by a new commitment to increase wages, but the plummeting economy made it unlikely that Noriega would be able to continue populist economic policies for long. Those policies also ran counter to Noriega's efforts, through Delvalle, to restore the confidence of the business community and stem the massive capital flight that began in the summer. The question was whether the general's flagrant opportunism would begin to cool the PDP's enthusiastic endorsement of the newly designated "anti-imperialist" leader.

International Views and Activities. The PDP attended and approved the resolutions of the Second Conference of South American Communist Parties held in Lima, Peru, in December 1986 (the first such conference had been held in Buenos Aires in 1984). The conference fully supported Soviet peace and disarmament proposals and expressed solidarity with Nicaragua and "the widening patriotic and liberation struggle in all the countries of the [Central American] region" (*IB*, April). The participants also called for the strict observance of the 1977 Canal Treaties and the withdrawal of all U.S. troops from Panama.

In February the *World Marxist Review* reported that PDP Central Committee member Felix Dixon participated in an international roundtable in Prague on "The Dialogue of Communists and Christians Amid the Current Crisis in the Region," sponsored by the *WMR* Commission on Latin America and the Caribbean. The participants concurred that joint action between communists and "left-oriented" Christians "is by no means a short-lived policy of convenience rooted in tactical considerations, but a long-term *strategy* of the struggle for peace, social progress, democracy and national independence" (*WMR*, February).

In May Changmarín participated in a meeting of communist editors in Moscow to mark the 75th anniversary of *Pravda* (*Pravda*, 4 May; *FBIS*, 12 May).

Eastern bloc contacts. The trend toward closer relations between the Eastern bloc and Panama that began in 1985 and 1986 accelerated in 1987. The PRD continued to be the primary point of contact for the Soviet Union and Cuba in the Panamanian government. As the largest party in the Democratic National Union (UNADE)—the five-party government coalition—the PRD controls the National Assembly. In 1987 the tiny Panameñista party, another member of UNADE, also began to play an active role in relations with the Eastern bloc.

In January National Assembly president and PRD member Ovidio Díaz led an assembly delegation on a four-day visit to Havana where they were received by Flavio Bravo, Cuban National Assembly president and member of the Communist Party of Cuba Central Committee (Havana Television Service; *FBIS*, 27 January). In June, following the outbreak of the crisis in Panama, an opposition newspaper reported that PRD general secretary Carlos Ozores and deputy secretary general Ramiro Vásquez Chambonnet were received by Fidel Castro in Havana (*Extra*, 1 July; *FBIS*, 9 July).

In response to an invitation by the Supreme Soviet of the Soviet Union, Ovidio Díaz led an assembly delegation on a four-day visit to Moscow in February. The delegation met with leaders of the Supreme Soviet and Soviet deputy foreign minister V. G. Komplektov (*Izvestiia*, 27 February; *FBIS*, 2 March). Subjects discussed were the implementation of an agreement signed the previous year for an Aeroflot link between Moscow and Panama City; port access for Soviet fishing vessels in Panama; and increased economic and political ties between the two countries (*Critica*, 2 March; *FBIS*, 3 March).

In March Panama and Poland signed an agreement for educational, scientific, and cultural cooperation for 1987, 1988, and 1989 (*Matutino*, 18 March; *FBIS*, 20 March).

In November Vásquez Chambonnet led a PRD delegation to Moscow for the celebration of the 70th anniversary of the October Revolution. On his return he stated that "During the conversations I held with both the Soviet party as well as the parties from the other socialist countries, I found there was a very definite and clear show of solidarity as well as an affirmation of total willingness to offer any type of assistance—economic, political, and diplomatic—should the United States increase its pressures and aggressions against our Panamanian government and people" (Panama Televisora Nacional, 24 November; *FBIS*, 1 December).

On 26 November Aeroflot began twice-weekly flights to Panama according to the terms of a three-year agreement. The flights were to be used for transporting crew members of Soviet fishing vessels. (*Critica*, 27 November; *FBIS*, 2 December.) It was also reported that the two countries had signed a service contract to provide dry-dock and other shore facilities for the Soviet fishing fleet, another concession sought by Moscow (*WP*, 16 December).

In December, with Panama facing broader economic sanctions from Washington, including the elimination of its sugar quota for export to the United States, it was reported that the Soviet Union had offered to absorb all the sugar covered by the U.S. import quota at two cents per pound more than American importers were paying (South-North News Service, *New York City Tribune*, 10 December).

Throughout the year there was speculation in Panama that diplomatic relations long sought by Moscow would be established between the two countries. The Panamanian Foreign Ministry denied the reports, but in December a PRD official hinted that Panama would open a consulate in the

Soviet Union in 1988 (*Central America Report*, 18 December).

Radical Third World contacts. On 24 June, three weeks after the outbreak of the protests, Nicaraguan president Daniel Ortega and foreign minister Miguel D'Escoto were warmly received by both President Delvalle and General Noriega in Panama City. Ortega hailed the Panamanian authorities for being "brave and decisive" in handling the disturbances, stating, "The Panama Defense Forces are defending the sovereignty of the Panamanian people... There is a full-scale conspiracy to crush them and throw out the Torrijos-Carter treaties at the same time" (*Times of the Americas*, 1 July).

One month before, Captain Ricardo Wheelock, head of Sandinista military intelligence, attended at Nicaragua's request a Panamanian national intelligence seminar held by General Noriega in Panama City. Briefings on the situations in their respective countries were shared, and Noriega and Wheelock "toasted the friendship of the two countries" at the conclusion of the gathering (Panama City Domestic Service, 24 May; *FBIS*, 27 May).

According to Roger Miranda Bengoechea, a former top aide to Nicaraguan defense minister Humberto Ortega who defected to the United States in the fall, Wheelock had related to Noriega the details of a purported U.S. plot to kill the general. Miranda averred that it was a ploy to "sensitize Noriega and bring him closer to us" (*NYT*, 14 December). Miranda further alleged that Noriega was providing intelligence on U.S. movements in Panama to the Sandinistas and that in August Noriega had told Wheelock he was prepared to supply arms to the FMLN guerrillas in El Salvador after meeting with FMLN leaders in Panama (ibid.).

In October a progovernment newspaper reported that "Secret talks aimed at establishing diplomatic relations with Iran are well-advanced. This is another alternative for new markets and new frontiers for Panama" (*Critica*, 20 October; *FBIS*, 21 October).

At the end of November Noriega dispatched to Libya a delegation headed by Panameñista Party leader Luis Gaspar Suarez. The delegation was received by Libyan leader Moammar Khadafy (*JANA*, 23 November; *FBIS*, 24 November). According to a Panamanian exile source, Noriega was seeking $200 million in emergency economic aid plus a $100 million deposit by Libya in Panamanian banks to alleviate the capital flight problem (*WP*, 16 December). Panamanian foreign minister Jorge Abadia stated that Panama was "only implementing agreements on mutual assistance signed in 1977" (*Matutino*, 16 December; *FBIS*, 17 December). Suarez stated that the agreements were on cultural, economic, and overall mutual cooperation and that "Circumstances have caused these relations to become once again very important for both countries" (*Critica*, 11 December; *FBIS*, 14 December). The press officer at the Libyan People's Bureau in Panama said a Libyan delegation was expected in Panama by the end of the year "to resolve details about the agreements" (*La Estrella de Panama*, 15 December; *FBIS*, 16 December).

Douglas W. Payne
Freedom House, New York

Paraguay

Population. 4,251,924
Party. Paraguayan Communist Party (Partido Comunista del Paraguay; PCP)
Founded. 1928
Membership. 4,000 (estimated)
General Secretary. Júlio Rojas (acting); Antonio Maidana (official) is under arrest.
Status. Illegal
Last Congress. Third, 10 April 1971
Last Election. N/a
Auxiliary Organizations. No data
Publications. *Adelante* (underground weekly)

Paraguay's politics revolve around the slow but certain decay of General Alfredo Stroessner's 33-year-old dictatorship. Stroessner, now 74, long enjoyed the backing of the army, the United States, Paraguay's business leaders, and the peasant-based Colorado Party, but now those foundations are crumbling. Dramatic evidence of this came at the Colorado convention in early August, when the party split between two factions that were jockeying for position in the power struggle that must certainly come upon Stroessner's departure from the scene. The so-called militants (*militantes*), led by Interior Minister Sabino Montanaro and Stroessner's private secretary, Mario Abdo Benítez, got the upper hand over the traditionalists (*tradicionalistas*), headed by longtime party president Juan Ramón Cháves. Although Stroessner claimed to be neutral, he clearly preferred the militants, who are his inner circle of advisers, to the traditionalists, whose loyalty to the party comes first.

The traditionalists announced their intention after the convention of going into opposition by joining two other dissident Colorado factions: the Popular Colorado Movement (MOPOCO) and the so-called moralists (*éticos*). The MOPOCO also helps constitute another opposition front, the National Accord, along with the Authentic Radical Liberal Party, the social democratic Febrerista Party, and the Christian Democrats. Early in the year the Stroessner government seemed to be relaxing its pressure on the opposition. However, the screws were tightened again in late July.

Support for the National Accord became increasingly respectable: even such businessmen's associations as FEPRINCO (merchants) and the Unión Industrial (industrialists) were tacitly behind the opposition.

In this panorama, the PCP continued to play only a peripheral role because no other parties would invite it to join an alliance. Acting General Secretary Júlio Rojas spoke out in February, on the 59th anniversary of the PCP's founding, to call for the formation of a "national antidictatorial front" for the purpose of staging a popular uprising against the regime. Nevertheless, his speech, which designated the building of a "politically conscious fighting vanguard" as the "overriding goal," suggests that the PCP's organization is still weak. In addition, Rojas's constant lauding of the Soviet Union's "Great October Socialist Revolution" and its "genius theoretician and leader," V. I. Lenin, serves to keep it politically isolated. (*IB*, August.)

Paul Lewis
Tulane University

Peru

Population. 20,739,218
Party. Peruvian Communist Party (Partido Comunista Peruana; PCP)
Founded. 1930
Membership. 2,000
General Secretary. Jorge del Prado Chavez (b. 1910; member of Senate)
Central Committee. 47 members
Status. Legal
Last Congress. Ninth, 27–30 May; Sixteenth Plenary, 29–30 November 1986
Last Election. 1985 presidential and parliamentary. The PCP has six delegates and is part of a coalition of the United Left that has 26 percent of the delegates in the Chamber of Deputies. The PCP has two senators in the coalition that has 25 percent of the representation in the Senate.
Auxiliary Organizations. General Confederation of Peruvian Workers (Confederación General de Trabajadores Peruanos; CGTP), Peruvian Peasant Confederation
Publications. *Unidad* (newspaper of the PCP; Carlos Esteves, editor); other leftist newspapers: *La Voz*, *El Nuevo Diario*, *Cambio* (magazine)

The PCP celebrated its 59th anniversary and held its Ninth Party Congress in 1987. The venerable Jorge del Prado Chavez was re-elected general secretary of the party, a post he has held since 1966. In addressing the congress, del Prado exclaimed, "Never before have the left-wing forces, the revolutionaries and those who are fighting imperialism, and for socialism, had such a close possibility of winning power" (*WMR*, September). Indeed, as one of the major components of the electoral front, the United Left (Izquierda Unida; IU), the PCP is part of the second-largest political force in the nation. This makes Peru one of only two countries in South America—the other is Guyana—whose major opposition is Marxist.

Since the early 1980s the Peruvian population has voted overwhelmingly for reformist and revolutionary political parties. After President Alan García's three years in office, the ruling social democratic party, the American Popular Revolutionary

Alliance (APRA), faces increasing dissatisfaction, leaving the IU coalition as the popular alternative. The former Lima mayor and ex-president of the IU, Dr. Alfonso Barrantes Lingán, says he expects the left to be in power by the end of the century. But the cohesiveness necessary for a successful national campaign and the acquiescence of the Peruvian military to the assumption of power by a Marxist coalition are important obstacles to be overcome. (*Latin American Weekly Report* [*LAWR*], 14 May.)

Leadership and Party Organization. The PCP approached its Ninth Congress with renewed strength. The electoral success of the IU has been matched by the expanded influence of the leading labor organization in the nation, the CGTP. There were over 400 delegates to the congress, and invited guests included the leaders of all the component parties of the IU. There were also 36 foreign visitors from the communist parties in the Soviet Union, Bulgaria, Poland, Hungary, East Germany, Czechoslovakia, Yugoslavia, Romania, Cuba, thirteen other Latin American nations, and Japan. The theme of the congress was "For a Revolutionary Alternative to Power" (*Unidad*, 3 June).

The new Central Committee reflects the PCP's goal of "continuity and renovation." Among the 47 members are many veteran national leaders, but also included are a group of young newcomers who, although lacking national recognition, have substantial experience at the local or regional levels (ibid., 15 June).

Del Prado's address affirmed the PCP's support for the foreign policy of the Soviet Union and "all progressive peoples in their solidarity with Latin American nations facing U.S. imperialist aggression." He then turned to an analysis of the domestic situation. He asserted that the main political confrontation in Peru "is no longer between two traditionally right-wing parties or between those parties and [the] APRA, but between all of them put together and the Izquierda Unida, between a reformist alternative of half-conciliatory anti-imperialism and a revolutionary, emphatically anti-imperialist alternative of socialist orientation" (*IB*, October).

The two themes of del Prado's speech were the character of the APRA and the role of the IU in the immediate future. A major issue in the IU's development is its definition of the APRA's political orientation and, therefore, its relationship vis-à-vis the government. Given the APRA's social democratic principles and its eccentric, popular, left-of-center president, this has not been easy, leading to divisions within the left. Del Prado's address charged that the García administration's policies had fallen short of major systemic changes, that economic changes had been "tentative" and limited to foreign debt, and that no changes had been made in the ownership of production systems or the nationalization of state resources. (Ibid., October.)

Del Prado argued that the APRA's chief objective is "to stimulate capitalist development by using the classical principles of the bourgeois development theory . . . favoring big monopoly capital and conciliatory to imperialism" (ibid.). This pro-capitalist position leads to an "anti-worker orientation and the use of 'pentagon-like' repressive methods in counterinsurgency" (ibid.). Thus, the PCP leader characterized the APRA as "bourgeois, developmentalist, tied to national and transnational business, corporativist . . . [and] allied with militarism" (*Resumen Semanal*, 29 May–4 June).

Del Prado's evaluation of the APRA recognized that the party has adopted some measures suggested by the PCP, such as challenging the International Monetary Fund (IMF), but he believes that García has no intention of altering the system of private capitalist economy, thus underscoring "the duality and dichotomy between the government's internal and external policies." That is, the APRA can maintain foreign policy positions that are "patriotic" and coincide with the PCP and IU's desires while following a more reactionary internal policy. (*WMR*, September.)

The PCP leader stated that the IU "represents a true advance in the process of unification under the principles of a single front . . . for the revolutionary transformation of the country." But del Prado emphasized that the IU's success depends on the ability of the National Directive Committee (CDN) to define its political position in such a way as to bring all the organizations to work together in the name of direct democracy and self-defense (*Unidad*, 3 June). Thus, he urged the party congress to support (1) centralizing the leadership with democratic elections at all levels, (2) creating structures and norms to harmonize democratic principles with equal participation, and (3) broadening ranks to draw in all parties and organizations on the left, including the Social Christians. Del Prado claimed socialism, not Marxism, to be the unifying criteria. (*IB*, October; *El Nacional*, 25 February; *JPRS*, 15 April.)

For seven years the IU has served as the representative front for the political left, has provided consistent democratic opposition to the ruling parties, has accepted local and district governing responsibilities, and has grown electorally. As its opportunity for capturing national power increases, however, the IU structure is facing its gravest crisis, and its capacity to take advantage of the perceived opportunities is questionable.

Organically the IU retains its original composition as a coalition of parties with a large group of "independents" who support the front. Yet each entity wants to conserve its identity, and the member groups do not agree on what the IU's position should be in relation to the APRA, the appropriate path to power for the IU, or the front's response to political violence. The ideological spectrum within the IU is wide-ranging, which makes unity difficult and makes pronouncements in its name vulnerable to misinterpretation. The radical groups want firm opposition to the García administration. They stress the radicalization of the popular sectors rather than building electoral strength, and their calls for the development of "true revolutionary capacity" can be translated as qualified support for the guerrilla group, the Revolutionary Movement of Tupac Amaru (MRTA). They do, however, denounce the terrorism of the largest armed revolutionary movement, Sendero Luminoso. The groups in this category are the pro-Maoist coalition Union of the Revolutionary Left (UNIR), the two-year-old coalition Unified Mariateguista Party (PUM), which is now the largest of the six IU parties with major support from Andean peasants who swell the population of the Lima shantytowns, and the small Trotskyist Worker, Peasant, Student, and Popular Front (FOCEP).

Factionalism and realignment seem to be endemic to the more doctrinaire parties, and during 1987 two splinters—the Pueblo en Marcha and the Bolshevik factions of the Peruvian Communist Party–Patria Roja (a component of UNIR)—joined to form the UNIR-Combatiente. Its major influence is within two student unions in San Marcos University (*Resumen Semanal*, 3–9 April). Called "infantile dogmatists" by the rest of the IU, the UNIR-Combatiente characterizes the APRA as "fascist" (*LAWR*, 14 May). Del Prado feels that those who are so impatient as to call the APRA "fascist" represent theoretical deviations that do not serve the party's goals (*Unidad*, 16 June).

The less radical groups in the IU are the pro-Moscow PCP, the social democratic Revolutionary Socialist Party (PSR), and the Revolutionary Communist Party (PCR). These groups are willing to work with García because they define imperialism as the primary enemy, not the APRA. They want the rules of the democratic game observed since they feel they can play successfully. They clearly differentiate their methods of bringing about popular revolutionary change from those of antipopular guerrilla violence. As del Prado said at an IU rally, "We reject elitist forms of armed struggle and terror" (*LAWR*, 25 June).

What unity has existed in the front was forged by the personality of Dr. Alfonso Barrantes Lingán. Thus, a critical juncture in the front's development took place in May when he resigned from leadership. Barrantes's position of moderation and pragmatism opened him to charges of reformism, conciliation, and collaboration with the APRA. So long as García's popularity was high and social democratic policies were forthcoming, Barrantes's position was grudgingly accepted. But as the young president's fortunes declined, Barrantes found himself more and more on the defensive within the IU. His familiarity with García may have been tolerated, but the PCP was incensed when he welcomed the U.S. ambassador into his home. Moreover, his absence from the country during the May general strike and his persistent absence from the CDN meetings of the IU while he was mayor irritated his colleagues. (*Resumen Semanal*, 13–19 March; *Latin America Regional Reports* [*LARR*], 28 June.)

In his resignation speech, Barrantes regretted that he, rather than the orientation of the IU, had become the center of debate. He said, "The front has not forged a true spirit of confidence and fraternity . . . each constituent has a different position publicly" (*Resumen Semanal*, 29 May–4 June). Although he reiterated that he felt it was prudent to support the APRA's initiatives when they coincided with IU goals, he firmly underscored his fundamental differences with the ruling party's social and economic class orientation. Most important, he warned, his greatest concern with the APRA was its direct attack on the leftist popular organizations by undermining their programs and promoting parallel APRA-sponsored agencies. (Ibid.; Lima America Television, 1 June; *FBIS*, 2 June.) In fact, later in June IU congressmen charged Lima's APRA mayor, Jorge del Castillo, with deliberately poorly managing the milk program, which had been initiated by Barrantes, when Castillo allowed donated milk and oats from Holland to decompose rather than be distributed (*Resumen Semanal*, 12–18 June).

Barrantes condemned the terrorism of Sendero Luminoso and the constitutional violations of the government's repressive response. But his argument that stopping Sendero should be a primary goal, and that this would be more likely to bring about the end of militarism, is not a majority view in the IU. (Ibid., 29 May–4 June; Lima America Television, 1 June; *FBIS*, 2 June.)

To combat Sendero Luminoso, Barrantes called for the establishment of regional governments in which all popular organizations, the Catholic Church, professionals, and universities would launch massive protests against Sendero's methods. Although he acknowledged the "need for revolutionary violence in specific historic circumstances," Barrantes claimed that "revolutionary violence does not exist when small groups substitute themselves for the will of the people" (*LAWR*, 14 May).

After Barrantes's resignation, the IU did not designate another single leader; instead the leadership devolved to the CDN and its "coordinator in turn." Del Prado, as coordinator, was chosen as the only speaker at a major rally on 3 June to emphasize the front's unity. He criticized the CDN for not functioning regularly, for lacking initiative, and for failing as a vanguard. He then announced the objectives of the CDN to be (1) strengthening the organizational structure with a stable, permanent secretariat and work commissions, (2) creating membership norms with cards to define the organization's boundaries, and (3) creating intermediary and base organizations (*Unidad*, 15 June).

Toward this end, the Fifth Expanded CDN meeting was held 24–25 October at Huampani. The 225 delegates broke into two working commissions, one on policy and one on organization. The questions addressed were basic: What is the fundamental unit of the IU—the district committee or base community? Should the district committee be elected by party quota or universal suffrage? Should the regional comittees reflect the balance of forces in the CDN or begin to reflect base organizations? Though all admitted the need for change, the crucial question became: Should the principle of legitimacy be internal democracy from the grass roots up or emanate from the founding members of the CDN on down? (Lima, *Quehacer*, vol. 50, p. 29.)

The instinct for party survival still proved too strong for making much headway at Huampani. Answers to questions posed were not forthcoming, and the only policy statement made was to reiterate the accords adopted two years before. Steps were taken, however, to designate an organizing committee of eleven members, four independents, and seven party representatives to plan the First National Congress of the IU in September 1988. If the IU is to be a major contender in the 1990 elections, this congress will have to produce some concrete results in terms of party organization, strategy, and platform. (Ibid., p. 30.)

The potential strength of the left was highlighted by a four-day National Popular Assembly held 19–22 November in Villa El Salvador, a massive settlement on the outskirts of Lima that has been well-organized politically since the Velasco era in the late 1960s and early 1970s. The 2,364 delegates represented every major popular organization in the nation. The largest groups were: labor representatives, 43.8 percent; campesino organizations, 19.9 percent; neighborhood organizations, 12.9 percent; and local defense fronts, 10 percent. The twenty points that were derived from the work commissions were somewhat more radical than most IU positions, but the experience emphasized the benefits, as well as the difficulties, if these forces were to coordinate activity. (Ibid., pp. 9–15.)

Domestic Affairs. After two years of unprecedented popularity based on stirring rhetoric and an economic rebound, President García began his third year facing the fact that Peru's substantial problems cannot be talked away. His popularity declined as economic growth stalled, inflation almost doubled, and foreign reserves fell drastically. Increases in the cost of living and an inconsistent labor policy exacerbated tensions and precipitated the first general strike against the government on 19 May. From a 70 percent approval rating, García had fallen to just 34 percent by June. His bold move to regain popularity and seek an economic fix by nationalizing the financial system cost him far more political capital with the business community and the right wing of his party than it gained him. In fact, his relations with the IU opposition did not improve with this initiative. Finally, García's efforts to turn the tide in the struggle against terrorism by reorganizing the intelligence services, revitalizing the police, and coordinating the military under a single Ministry of Defense were hampered by a rebellion in the air force and a police strike. Little headway was made against the persistent armed revolutionary groups in a year that saw more terrorist activities and more government deaths than ever before.

Prior to May, labor tensions had been rising among government workers as "moralization" campaigns (ostensibly efforts to get rid of corruption and fraud) led to high dismissal rates in the Office of Public Registry, among prison workers, and in the transportation sector. The CGTP called a general strike against the government on 19 May, citing its preferred treatment of the private sector, lack of concern for the rights of workers, and continued violation of labor stability. The CGTP platform demanded, among other things, a regard for democratic rights and popular liberties, with an end to the states of emergency and the curfew; an affirmation of national sovereignty by breaking with the IMF; and no privatization of public companies, more nationalization, and fifteen different changes in the labor policy to help alleviate the high cost of living. (*Resumen Semanal*, 8–14 May.)

The government called the strike "unjustifiable" and retaliated by cutting the power off to the CGTP headquarters and violently suppressing demonstrations outside. Evaluations of success varied; the minister of labor said only 35 percent of the workers in Lima participated, but the leftist and centrist newspapers said that close to 50 percent of the city was paralyzed because transportation was down. (Ibid., 15–21 May; EFE, 19 May; *FBIS*, 20 May.)

Late in the year, labor tensions again resulted in multiple, lengthy strikes by thousands of workers. On 9 October the military industry workers walked out; on the 14th, the Intersectoral Committee of State Workers (CITE) took to the streets, 6,000 CENTROMIN miners left the job, and prison workers and Ministry of Health employees called a 48-hour stoppage. The teachers of the Unitary Peruvian Educators' Union (SUTEP) struck on the 21st. During this month strikers resorted to major attention-getting tactics. The communication and transportation workers, who had been out for 40 days, took over the Alliance Française just before President Mitterrand arrived for an official visit. After a 37-day strike, the government agricultural workers occupied the Costa Rican Embassy as President Arias won the Nobel Peace Prize (*Resumen Semanal*, 9–15 October). Ministry of Education employees held a sit-in at the Archbishop's Palace for fifteen minutes, and the prison employees went to the representative of the Vatican asking for mediation (ibid., 30 October–5 November).

García's response was to decree wage increases of 30 percent for state teachers, 28 percent for state doctors, and 25 percent for civil servants. The minimum wage was raised from 1,710 intis a month to 2,187 ($38). Despite the increases, inflation and the rise in the prices of controlled commodities meant that the "basic food basket" for a family was still six times the minimum wage. (*LAWR*, 5 November.)

The predominant feeling was a lack of responsiveness on the part of the government to any collective bargaining. In fact, the APRA's preference not to deal with the existing popular organizations was highlighted by the 1–2 December strike called by the Unitary National Agrarian Council (CUNA). It demanded that the minister of agriculture, Remigio Morales Bermúdez, resign for not fulfilling the agreements of the national agricultural accord. A few days before the strike the government convened a National Council for Agricultural Agreement. None of the major agrarian organizations—the Peruvian Peasant Confederation, the National Agrarian Confederation, or the CUNA—participated, arguing that the government was trying to by-pass existing organizations and create new ones of its own. The strike was ultimately successful in eleven of the nation's departments. (*Resumen Semanal*, 27 November–3 December.)

Two major initiatives of García's in 1987—nationalization of the financial system and the creation of a Defense Ministry—served to divide the IU even though they were moves that coincided with the front's platform. García surprised everyone on 28 July by announcing plans to nationalize the banks and credit institutions. Nationalization of the 30 percent of the banking system not owned by the state had long been an integral part of the PCP and IU "plans of government." The CGTP marched in favor, and Barrantes made a supportive TV speech saying, "It is unjust and antidemocratic that wealth is concentrated in a few hands and that credit is offered with egotistical motives" (ibid., 14–20 August).

García's motives in nationalizing the banks were both economic and political. First, he was frustrated that, despite efforts to stimulate an economic recovery with low inflation and the highest growth of any Latin American nation in 1986 (8.5 percent), new investment had not materialized. In fact, in the preceding two years capital flight had amounted to $1.5 billion. Thus, he said he needed to "break the stranglehold on the economy" by a small group of financiers who speculated with their money rather than investing in Peru's future. He argued that state control over the access to credit would direct investment to priority sectors and benefit the majority. Politically, García believed such a move would regain his initiative and strengthen his position in the center-left. (*LARR*, 3 September; *WSJ*, 9 October.)

The path to nationalization was long, chaotic, and marked by political polarization and the use of government force. During the three months it took to pass the legislation, legal maneuvering by the bank owners created a situation that could tie up the assets for years. The national debate produced the sharpest political strife since the early 1970s. The far right and the far left converged, calling the APRA move "fascist." The right wing of the Peruvian political spectrum consolidated around writer Mario Vargas Llosa, who spoke and wrote extensively on the totalitarian dangers exhibited by the nationalization and its attendant constitutional violations. (*LAWR*, 2, 6 August.)

Despite the support of Barrantes and the moderate line of the IU, including the PCP, there were many in the IU who denounced the move. Yehude Simons, editor of *Cambio*, warned that "no one can believe García is moving left. There must be no illusions because the nationalization of the banks is a mechanism needed by the bourgeois to impede the collapse of the system." The leftist newspaper *El Nuevo Diario* called the move a step toward absolute control, "an authoritarian grab for power" (*Resumen Semanal*, 31 July–6 August).

The IU position on the nationalization legislation became tied to APRA compliance with the demand for political amnesty for 150 members of the IU who were imprisoned for incidents during labor disputes. Negotiations with the president and the Interior Ministry had been carried on throughout 1987 as the list of persons to be released was debated. In August five congressmen from the UNIR and PUM went on a hunger strike to protest the delay. They warned they would vote against the nationalization bill if amnesty was not approved. (Ibid., 14–20 August.) But whatever chance the amnesty had was dashed by the assassination of Rodrigo Franco Montes, president of the State Food Marketing Enterprises (ENCI). García responded, in line with his party's hard-liners, that he could "be generous only when the guerrillas are defeated" (ibid., 28 August–3 September).

Another of García's major initiatives that had the critical support of the moderate IU faction was the creation of a Ministry of Defense. The president argued that consolidation of the armed forces would strengthen national security and eliminate duplicate efforts. It was also an attempt to exert more civilian control over the military by reducing its representation in the cabinet.

A single ministry had been part of the IU government plan drawn up under Barrantes's guidance in 1985. The problem was the means through which the APRA sought to establish the ministry. Most IU congressmen supported the creation of a bicameral commission to prepare the legislation. The APRA did not concur; instead a draft law was sent to congress that gave the executive the power to create the ministry. The vote on the draft saw the IU split, with the PUM and UNIR voting against and all others voting in favor. The Barrantes faction was accused of "shameless compromise"; the PUM and UNIR argued that a single ministry "would protect bourgeois interests . . . deal with rising popular protest, and be used for partisan ends." (*El Nuevo Diario*, 21 March; *JPRS*, 20 May.) The moderates, however, were more concerned with strengthening civilian power in relation to military power than with the possible abuse civilians could make of that power.

Two challenges to civilian authority from the forces of order were successfully squashed by García, but they took a toll in public confidence in the regime. The day the law creating the Ministry of Defense was promulgated, dissident air force general Luís Abram Carallerino ordered jets to overfly the presidential palace, and he held out at Las Palmas air base for 36 hours before accepting defeat and dismissal (EFE, 6 April; *FBIS*, 7 April; *NYT*, 12 April; *LAWR*, 16 April).

Perhaps more troublesome was a police strike that started on the eve of the seventh anniversary of Sendero Luminoso's emergence and two days before the 19 May general strike. It was only the third strike in police history. Among their twenty demands were a monthly increase of 3,500 intis and an allowance for "exposure to danger," a 48-hour work week, a commitment to the same salary for the same rank, the right to vote, the right to form a union, and the right to strike. After 48 hours an agreement was signed, but it was not accepted by the rank and file who took to the streets, commandeering buses and inducing police to stop work at key posts such as utilities. Rather than using military force, García prevailed by waiting and cutting off supplies to 3,000 police barricaded in a Civil Guard building. After four days the revolt ended; 383 police were tried and 39 officers were fired, including the heads of the Republican and Civil Guards. (*LAWR*, 18 June; *FBIS*, 18 June; *Resumen Semanal*, 5–11 June.)

Presumably, a major benefit of clear civilian control was to enable the government to more effectively pursue the continuing struggle against terrorism. Since García took office, terrorist activities have increased 65.3 percent, the estimated number of senderistas has grown to over 10,000, and attacks have taken place in 22 of the 24 departments. A state of emergency exists in six departments, which means over 50 percent of the population lives with restricted liberties. In two years, 54 APRA officials and a total of 105 civilian authorities have been murdered. (*CSM*, 15 October; *WSJ*, 9 October.)

The death rates for 1987 are particularly discouraging. Using the figures through November, the number of police and armed forces killed in political violence (177) will be higher than ever. Civilian deaths (514) will be higher than 1986 but down from every other year since 1983. The interesting figure is that the number of presumed senderistas killed (327) is much lower than every year since 1983. (*Resumen Semanal.*)

To the criticism that he lacked a coherent and effective counterinsurgency, García responded, "There is no short-term way to eliminate a force rooted in poverty, alienation, and leftist messianic fanaticism . . . [it] needs long-term cure" (*WP*, 18 April). His efforts in 1987 toward the long-term cure included improving the capacity of the military and the police, expanding legal initiatives, and using concentrated force.

The capacity of the armed forces and the police were definitely improved by the reorganization and better coordination of the eight intelligence networks. Assistance in equipment and training was received from Italy, France, Germany, and Israel in 1987. The creation of specially trained antiguerrilla groups appeared to provide dividends as more senderistas were captured and more bombs were detonated before doing damage than was previously the case. (*Resumen Semanal*, 27 February–5 March; *CSM*, 11 February; Lima Television, 30 May; *FBIS*, 1 June.)

On the legal front several new laws attempted to improve the prosecution of those charged with terrorist offenses and those military officers charged with torture, disappearances, and murder. For the IU the two were linked. The new antiterrorist law created more stringent punishment for terrorist crimes, but it also included pardon possibilities if those accused repented or cooperated with authorities. (Lima Panamericana Television, 27 February; *FBIS*, 2 March.) In March another law was passed to increase to twenty years the penalty for officers "derelict in duty" (*Resumen Semanal*, 27 March–4 April). Although the IU congressmen were pleased with the intent, they remained skeptical that the law would be implemented with any diligence. They also had reservations about the special tribunals created to hear charges of terrorism. The goals of speeding up the process and providing privacy to protect judges from intimidation, though laudable, could, they felt, be easily abused. (*LAWR*, 8 January.)

Most disheartening to the left, however, were García's bold strikes against suspected centers of subversion. On 13 February, during the early morning curfew, 4,000 police and military units entered one suburban and three Lima universities. They searched dorms and kitchens looking for evidence of subversive training and storage centers. Approximately 650 pounds of explosives, about 20 guns, and "great amounts" of leaflets were found. Under the eyes of public defenders brought by the police, 793 people were arrested; 449 were released in two days, and after two weeks fewer than 100, who either could not prove they were students or had false identification, were still detained. For the García administration this justified the invasion of the university's traditional autonomy. The president argued that "anything that has to do with terrorism must be fully investigated." The rectors of the universities, Barrantes and the IU, and the president of the Peruvian Supreme Court vigorously protested the "aggression," countering that the costs—one dead, three wounded, and the violation of university freedom—were not outweighed by the minimal evidence uncovered. (*Resumen Semanal*, 30 January–19 February; *LAWR*, 26 February; EFE, 13 February; *FBIS*, 17 February.) The IU called for the resignation of Interior Minister Abel Salinas amid fears that the university raid represented yet another step toward restricting democratic political life (AFP, 18 February; *FBIS*, 20 February).

IU members certainly felt greater constraints on their activities in 1987. The IU's main concern continued to be its ability to freely participate in Peruvian political life—that is, to speak, be heard, mobilize, and demonstrate. Therefore a great deal of attention was placed on those members of the IU who had been detained without trial after being picked up in massive sweeps for terrorists. Most of them have had histories of labor union or popular organizational activity. The IU congressmen who tried to visit those in jail were harassed, detained, and often denied visiting privileges. (*Resumen Semanal*, 23–29 January.)

After the negotiations for the amnesty fell through in August, the CDN of the IU demanded special attention be given to IU prisoners who were threatened by the senderistas at Lurigancho. The IU members consider themselves to be political prisoners and await amnesty; the members of Sendero Luminoso call themselves prisoners of war and reject the concept of amnesty (ibid., 4–10 September). Confusion on this point was compounded when the 1987 Amnesty International report charging the APRA government with deliberately covering up torture, murder, and secret burials in the June 1986 massacres referred to the senderistas as "political prisoners." This displeased all sides. (Ibid., 23–29 January; *LAWR*, 5 March; AFP, 27 February; *FBIS*, 3 March.)

One of the IU's major accomplishments in 1987 was the completion of an investigation of the prison massacres in which over 270 prisoners were killed. Despite García's promise to try those responsible for the "excesses" immediately after that event, little was done. An investigative commission did not get underway until a year later. The president was IU deputy Roland Ames, an independent with ties to progressive church groups (*Resumen Semanal*, 31 July–6 August). After four months of hearing extensive testimony and visiting the prisons, the commission issued a hard-hitting 285-page final report that placed responsibility on the president and the Council of Ministers for the blanket orders to crush the rebellion and on the military joint command and the chief of operations at each of the three prisons for disproportionate and excessive military action (ibid., 4–10 September, 13–19 November).

The APRA members on the commission bolted at the last minute. They wrote a "majority report" of six pages that exonerated the government and managed to get it passed by Parliament in a late-night session after the IU delegation had left. Even the conservative press denounced the APRA's behavior (*El Comercio*, 15 December; *Resumen Semanal*, 11–17 December). Although few people expected any military leaders to be brought to trial, observers praised the Ames Commission Report as a thorough, professional documentation of the events that will be a part of the historical archives (*Resumen Semanal*, 27 November–3 December).

International Views and Positions. The García administration's foreign policy continued its anti-imperialist, nonaligned orientation. In 1987 emphasis was placed on better relations with Latin American nations and on an independent stance in regard to the United States. Thus, García was prominent in the Contadora Support Group and at the Group of Eight meeting in Acapulco, Mexico.

The president visited Nicaragua, Mexico, and Uruguay during the year. In January he went with Barrantes and other congressmen to Nicaragua to attend the celebration of the new constitution and received that country's highest decoration, the Order of Augusto César Sandino. García's views were solicited by the Nicaraguan foreign minister before the Central American presidents' meeting in May. (Lima Channel 9 Television, 15 May; *FBIS*, 21 May.) Peruvian ties with Nicaragua are more than rhetorical. Peruvian youths participated in the International Youth Brigade that helped with the Nicaraguan coffee harvest, and the government sent 34,000 barrels of petroleum in September to help alleviate a scarcity (*El Nuevo Diario*, 9 January; *JPRS*, 4 May; *Resumen Semanal*, 4–10 September).

Relations with Cuba were mixed. On the one hand, the two nations signed their first economic accord to formalize stable commercial relations. They agreed to exchange Cuban grains and medical supplies for Peruvian industrial parts and mining equipment. (*Resumen Semanal*, 24–30 April.) On the other hand, the diplomatic flap regarding three refugees who have been in the Peruvian Embassy in Havana for seven years smolders unresolved. (Lima Panamericana Television, 11 February; *FBIS*, 11 February.)

Peru's economic situation continued to determine its international relations. Western banking and financial communities remained skeptical of Peru's ability to remedy its worsening economic situation, despite apparent moves to more orthodox policies. García's public position on the foreign debt was belied by private efforts in the last half of the year to reinstate Peru in the World Bank system for balance of payments support. This led to greater dissatisfaction in the PCP and IU as they claimed García was reneging on his 10 percent limit of debt repayment. (*LARR*, 8 October.)

Relations with the communist bloc remained friendly and were expanded in 1987. Because of the Ninth Party Congress, delegations of high-ranking party leaders from around the world traveled to Peru and the PCP leader was honored many times. In July del Prado traveled to East Germany to receive an honorary doctorate from the Superior School of Karl Marx in East Berlin. He was recognized for his half a century of struggle for the liberation of Latin American peoples. (*Unidad*, 27 July.)

The deputy chairman of the Supreme Soviet, Grant Voskanyan, headed a delegation that visited the Peruvian congress and met with García, high APRA officials, and members of the IU (*Resumen Semanal*, 27 March–2 April). Cultural exchanges and cooperation on radio and television broadcasting were agreed on by representatives of the Peruvian National Communication System and the USSR's state committee for special programs (Lima Television Peruana, 15 May; *FBIS*, 19 May). An important trade agreement was also made with the USSR in which Peru purchased five Antonov-32 military transport planes at $4.5 million each. These planes will replace models that Peru bought over a decade ago, and some of those earlier planes are to be sold to Cuba for $1 million each. (AFP, 26 May; *FBIS*, 27 May.)

Two delegations from the People's Republic of China visited Peru in 1987. The vice president of the National People's Congress, Huang Hua, spent six days in Peru. In meeting with García and the presidents of both houses of Congress, he emphasized their common views on world peace and joint development of the Third World economies. (Lima Radioprogramas del Perú, 18 May; *FBIS*, 20 May.) The next month the first visit ever by a Chinese foreign affairs minister was made. Wu Xueqian visited for three days, during which he discussed mutual positions on peace, disarmament, foreign debt, and the international economic order. The minister started talks that should increase the present rice-fishmeal trade between the two countries, and he received the keys to the city of Lima. (AFP, 7 June; *FBIS*, 10 June.)

With the debt and nonalignment as a motivation to increase and expand trade and diplomatic contacts, closer relations were evidenced this year with the Arab world. The Second Conference of the Federation of Palestinian Institutions in Latin America and the Caribbean (Coplac) was held in Lima, and a high-level Palestine Liberation Organization (PLO) delegation met with the foreign minister and representatives of the IU and the CGTP. Interest in the Palestinian cause was also expressed by Barrantes when he met with PLO chairman Yassir Arafat in Algeria in September. (*LAWR*, 17 September.)

The newest debt repayment deal to use payment-in-kind was arranged with the Czechoslovakian government. Czech technology will be used to build the Aguaytia-Pucallpa pipeline. In turn, the Czechs will purchase Peruvian computers, frozen fish, zinc discs, iron pellets, and leather goods to help reduce the debt. This year 500 computers will be exported with hopes that next year it will reach 1,500. Peru will receive one-third of the price in Czech goods, one-third in currency, and one-third in debt credits. It is anticipated that this arrangement will soon be expanded to the USSR, Hungary, and East Germany. (Lima Television Peruana, 3 April; *FBIS*, 8 April.)

Terrorist Activities. As Sendero Luminoso approached its seventh year of armed struggle against the Peruvian government, it was evident that the party had redefined its evaluation of the national reality and was adjusting its activities accordingly. Nevertheless, the political activity of Sendero Luminoso in 1987 was more overt, with a new emphasis on publicity, political operations, and traditional party activities. Much greater effort was made to compete for the attention of the mass organizations controlled by the IU and its constituents and the revolutionaries attracted to the MRTA. Public meetings were held at San Marcos University, posters appeared on Lima highways, and for the first time television and radio stations were seized to transmit the group's messages. The most important evidence of this theoretical change came from the party's central committee with the publication of a 110-page document that was widely distributed around the nation. The clandestine nature of the leadership, however, remained intact, and the health and whereabouts of founder and leader Dr. Abimael Guzmán is still a matter of speculation.

In September Sendero held its first plenary session. The report of the meeting had two themes: the optimistic conviction that its long-term victory was assured, and a severe self-criticism. From its orthodox Maoist orientation, the party had argued that the optimal guerrilla strategy for Peru was rural revolution to encircle the cities from the countryside. In the 1986 document, "To Develop the Popular War Serving World Revolution," it acknowledged that cities were "complementary" to rural mobilization, and in 1987 it recognized that urban organizing was essential to its overall goals. The emphasis of the self-criticism was to realize limitations in organizing the campesinos in the countryside. There had been unprecedented levels of migration from the highlands, in large part a reaction to the party's own activities, depriving Sendero of the very people it needs to launch a successful rural rebellion. In addition, the party was unprepared to reach out to the masses in the urban areas. (Lima, *Quehacer*, vol. 50, p. 58.)

In keeping with traditional communist party activity, Sendero's first plenary decided to hold its first national party congress. In preparation for this meeting, scheduled for 1988, five documents were circulated for discussion. They covered international policy, democratic revolution, military policy, construction of the instruments of revolution, and policy for the masses. (Ibid.)

Sendero defined new strategies for new problems, which meant taking its competition with the radical IU groups and the MRTA more seriously. The areas of most intense competition in 1987 were Lima and the Upper Huallaga Valley in the northeastern department of San Martín. In the capital, tactics turned more to selective assassination, and some efforts were made to justify actions in order to diminish the popular image of the group as demonic fanatics. In the countryside, Sendero confronted the MRTA head on in armed conflict. (Ibid.)

Sendero's overall goal remained that of destroying the current system through armed revolution. Its terrorist tactics continued to provoke popular denunciation yet showed few signs of letting up or being stopped by any government countermeasures. For the first time, bankers, businessmen (both domestic and foreign), and bystanders became victims. But the most frequent targets of Sendero's violence were APRA officials. On 30 January Dr. César López Silva, the APRA's secretary for general affairs, was killed in Lima. During the year eight mayors were assassinated, several attempts were made on President García's life, and two prominent APRA officials were murdered: Rodrigo Franco Montes, head of the ENCI, in August; and Nelson Pozo Garland, deputy organization secretary, in October.

The year started with a three-week wave of violence that was the worst ever in Peru. Within fifteen days there were two major power outages as towers in the Mantaro River were downed. During the blackout four banks and five political party offices were bombed, two textile factories were torched, and dynamite damage was sustained by the Indian Embassy and two television stations. (*Resumen Semanal*, 1–9, 10–15 January.)

In May another wave of terror hit. On the 2d three guards were killed at a hospital, and on the 4th fourteen high-tension towers were knocked out, producing a blackout in Lima and nine other departments. This was followed by dynamite attacks on twelve buildings in the capital, including the Korean Embassy. On the 5th the Bata-Rimac shoe factory was firebombed, causing over ten million intis damage and putting hundreds of people out of work. (Ibid., 1–7 May.) In November the Nissan plant was sabotaged, sustaining over $20 million in damage, which made it the worst such attack since García took office (*LAWR*, 3 December).

The region with the greatest activity in 1987 was the northeastern department of San Martín. Tocache province in San Martín produces 30 percent of the world's coca. Since 1983 the region has been occupied alternatively by guerrillas and the military, with the production of coca paste increasing under each. In early 1987 the area was controlled by the MRTA, but Sendero defeated that group in May. After a major campaign in July, the military reoccupied the area. The armed forces had maintained that there were 2–3,000 guerrillas; but after taking over, they revised this to a mere 30 and blamed drug traffickers for making it look like there were more terrorists. This may have been a tactical revision, since the United States government was helping with drug eradication but would not enter the area to deal with guerrillas. (EFE, 6 June; *FBIS*, 9 June; *NYT*, 23 August.)

The MRTA also underwent significant changes in 1987. The urban-based group proved itself persistent, if not successful, in operating in the countryside. Even after its defeat in June by Sendero, it had created liberated zones and a "rural popular army" of 50 in other areas of the San Martín department. In November, however, the military launched an attack of 500 troops with air support and pushed the revolutionaries into the Amazonas area. (*Resumen Semanal*, 6–12 November; *LAWR*, 12 November, 17 December.)

Meanwhile the MRTA pursued a conciliatory path toward the rest of the Peruvian left. Making known its desire for unity, it denounced "unilateral forms of struggle" and underscored the possibility of all forms, even electoral, to reach its goals. (*Cambio*, 5 September; *Resumen Semanal*, 25 September–10 October.)

The MRTA's criticism of its rival Sendero is similar to that of the legal left. It rejects the violence of assassination because, it argues, that gives the government legitimacy in its offensive (*Resumen Semanal*, 30 January–19 February). Concrete ties between the various radical parties of the IU and the MRTA are denied, but there is certainly a modicum of sympathy. IU senator Andrés Luna Vargas attended the funeral for an MRTA member who died in a confrontation with the military. (Ibid., 13–19 November.)

Whether the guerrillas move toward legal means of participation or split with the IU and take up arms will depend on how the IU defines itself in 1988. There is little doubt that the front will take on a more strident criticism of the government with Barrantes no longer at the helm. This may keep the radicals in the fold. But the independents and the PCP are still confident of their popular following, so it is unlikely that they would forgo the electoral arena. If for any reason that path were closed, however, it is quite likely the guerrilla movement would grow substantially.

Sandra L. Woy-Hazleton
Miami University

Puerto Rico

Population. 3,320,520
Party. Puerto Rican Socialist Party (Partido Socialista Puertorriqueño; PSP); Puerto Rican Communist Party (Partido Comunista Puertorriqueño; PCP)
Founded. PSP: 1971; PCP: 1934
Membership. PSP: 150; PCP: 125 (both estimated)
General Secretary. PSP: vacant; PCP: Franklin Irrizarry
Leading Bodies. No data
Status. Legal
Last Congress. PSP: Second, 1979; PCP: none known
Last Elections. 1984; PSP: 0.3 percent, no representatives
Auxiliary Organizations. No data
Publications. PSP: *Claridad* (weekly)

In 1987 the island enjoyed unprecedented prosperity with annual growth at about 4 percent and unemployment at 16.7 percent, down from 23 percent when the present governor, Rafael Hernández Colón, took office in 1984. With less than a year before the 1988 election, Hernández Colón and his Popular Democratic Party (Partido Popular Democrático; PPD) appeared increasingly sure of another victory. Even the leaders of the opposition New Progressive Party (Partido Nuevo Progresista; PNP) conceded that, barring a sharp economic decline or a major scandal, Hernández Colón and the left-of-center PPD would be in power until at least 1992.

The divisive issue of the status of the island—that is, should it remain a "Commonwealth associate" of the United States with an autonomous form of government, or should it become the 51st state?—was put on a back burner and is not likely to become a major topic in the 1988 election. Nor have the *independentistas*—Puerto Ricans who favor declaring the island an independent country, most of whom are members of the Marxist left—gained any strength. Forty-five percent of the voters support the Commonwealth status, 45 percent favor statehood, and 10 percent favor independence.

In 1987, as in previous years, the Marxist left played an insignificant role in the island's political life. The PSP, a pro-Castro group with some 150 members, was the main Marxist organization. The pro-Moscow PCP, with some 125 members, is closely associated with the Communist Party USA. Two Trotskyist parties, the International Workers' League and the Puerto Rican Socialist League, had even smaller memberships. Clandestine, terrorist, extreme-left organizations also gave sign of their existence. For reasons unfathomed by the police, five small bombs exploded in San Juan in May, hours before the appearance there of King Juan Carlos and Queen Sofía of Spain. The bombs caused no casualities and only minor damage; the police blamed terrorists for the action.

George Volsky
University of Miami

Suriname

Population. 388,636
Party. National Democratic Party (NDP); 25 February Unity Movement, or Standvaste (25FM), pro-military; Revolutionary People's Party (revolutionaire Volkspartij; RVP), pro-Cuban; Communist Party of Suriname (KPS), pro-Albanian.
Founded. NDP: 1987; 25FM: 1983; RVP: 1981; KPS: 1981
Membership. NDP: 2,000 (estimated); 25FM: largely assumed by NDP; RVP: 100 (estimated); KPS: 25 (estimated)
Leadership. NDP: Desire (Desi) Delano Bouterse (founder), Jules Wijdenbosch (chairman); 25FM: Harvey Naarendorp (general secretary, Organiz-

ing Committee); RVP: Edward Naarendorp, Glenn Sankatshing, Lothar Boksteen; KPS: Bram Mehr was executed in 1982, current leadership unknown.

Status. Restrictions on political parties were lifted in the fall of 1985. However, a political party must have support of 1 percent of the population in order to run for office.

Last Congress. NDP: First, 7 June; 25FM: First, 12 May 1984; KPS: First, 24 July 1981

Last Elections. 25 November; NDP received 10.4 percent of the vote.

Since the military coup that brought Lieutenant Colonel Desi Bouterse to power in February 1980, he has remained adept at maintaining power by alternating alliances with radical Marxist elements in the Surinamese society and the more moderate and democratic private sector. Bouterse was faced in 1987 with an economy paralyzed by a virulent guerrilla war that spread across the country and with the continuation of the cut-off of the $1.5 billion development package from the Netherlands, which was suspended after the execution of prominent democratic leaders in 1982. Popular discontent with his regime was manifest early in the year by students who conducted national protests in February and March and by the actions of the Jungle Commando, or Surinamese National Liberation Army, led by Bouterse's former bodyguard Ronny Brunswijk, conducted near the capital of Paramaribo and the rice-growing region of Nickerie.

With a deteriorating economy and internal unrest, Bouterse and the military were pressured into implementing their long-awaited return to representative government. After serious internal debates over the precise form of government, the Constitutional Commission headed by lawyer Eddy Bruma, a former adviser to the Chin A Sen government, produced a document outlining a complex multitiered executive and legislative structure that simply replaced a nonelected assembly with an elected one. Throughout the year, as the guerrilla war waxed and waned, the "old" political parties, now joined together in the United Front for Democracy and Development (UFDD), maintained pressure on Bouterse to honor free elections in November. At the end of the year Bouterse was still a commander of the armed forces, surrounded by a coterie of committed Marxist aides and cronies, even though the latest incarnation of his 25FM, the NDP, had failed dismally at the polls. The year ended with the new, democratically elected National Assembly struggling with Bouterse over the issues of a negotiated settlement to the guerrilla war and the degree to which the military will cede power to the new civilian government.

Domestic Affairs. The year-long insurgency began in the summer of 1986 after a military police search for the 25-year-old Ronny Brunswijk, a disaffected Bush Negro who had served as Bouterse's bodyguard, precipitated the mass murder of a number of Bush Negroes in Brunswijk's village. This military action by the government led to a full-scale uprising on the part of the country's 40,000 Bush Negroes, who have a history of rebellion against foreign forces. In the ensuing months the Surinamese National Army, said to number 5,300, conducted counterinsurgency campaigns that resulted in the flight of some 8,900 Bush Negroes and another 1,000 Amerindians to Saint Laurent in French Guiana; another 12,000 were internally displaced. The primary battlefield existed for most of 1986 and early 1987 between the bauxite mining town of Moengo and the Marowijne River border with French Guiana.

In February Bouterse issued orders that the Saramaka tribe had to evacuate their homelands, and as a consequence the tribe pledged to open a second front against the government to the south of Paramaribo in the area of the huge hydroelectric dam. By March Brunswijk's numbers had swollen to about 1,000 and his cadres were launching attacks on several fronts, including expanding their operations into western Suriname. A politically significant firefight in the Indian village of Bitagron resulted in the capture of Ewoud Leefland, one of the original plotters of the 1980 coup. In addition, the Jungle Commando cut off the only road linking Paramaribo with the Nickerie district, forcing the government to send foodstuffs to the city by smaller, slower, and more costly river and ocean transport. (*Caribbean Review,* Spring; *NYT*, 18 June; *San Francisco Examiner and Chronicle*, 25 October.)

Throughout the year the Suriname government charged that the French were allowing a 500-man mercenary army to mobilize on its soil in preparation for an invasion. The government also reported that Brunswijk met with former president Henk Chin A Sen and former prime minister Jules Sedney in Suriname in July; at the same time tensions between French Guiana and Suriname escalated to the point where French troops reinforced their positions along the border areas to prevent any cross-frontier raids by the Surinamese. Throughout the summer the guerrillas disrupted the electrical feeds to the capital and forced the closure of Surlaco's bauxite mines in Moengo by cutting it off from Paramaribo. (Paramaribo International Service, 16, 20 July; *FBIS*, 17, 21 July.)

The insurgency posed no real threat to the populated areas but retained its capability to sabotage economic installations at will. Because of this ability to close down the Moengo bauxite operations, government earnings from bauxite and alumina plunged from $238 million in 1986 to around $100 million in 1987. (*Caribbean Report*, 10 December.)

Throughout the year Bouterse faced a series of crises in government. In February, with the insurgency in full swing, a rash of protests hit Paramaribo led by secondary school and college students. The protests, which were brutally quelled by the military, spread throughout the capital, and demonstrators able to muster from 2,000 to 5,000 people were joined by bauxite workers who had been laid off because of war damage to the mines and processing plants. Besides the chronic shortages and economic hardships, the protesters were also reacting to Bouterse's shift to the left when he dissolved the Radhakishun Cabinet and replaced it with one headed by the former minister of interior affairs and a member of the 25FM, Jules Wijdenbosch. The appointment signaled a shift to the left through the re-emergence of radical RVP members to seats of power. (*Caribbean Review*, Spring; Paramaribo International Service, 17 February; *FBIS*, 18 February; *De Volkskrant*, 23 February; *FBIS*, 4 March.)

However, to counterbalance the internal changes, the Surinamese government sent Foreign Minister Henk Heidweiller on a tour of Europe, including Holland, to discuss the promised democratization process. Throughout the next several months, Suriname took several steps to assure foreign powers and the old political powers that elections would be held. (Hilversum International Service, 11 March; *FBIS*, 13 March; Paramaribo International Service, 19 March; *FBIS*, 20 March.)

In June Wijdenbosch was sent to the United States to meet with U.S. congressmen and the Permanent Council of the Organization of American States (OAS) about Suriname's democratization process. Paramaribo announced that Alcoa, the U.S. company that owns the country's bauxite industry, would ask both the U.S. Congress and the Department of State to use their influence to help bring an end to terrorist activities in eastern Suriname. During the Washington discussions it was announced by the high-level delegation accompanying Wijdenbosch that the sole condition for a return to civilian government was the end of the insurgency against the regime. On 30 June former president Chin A Sen announced his separation from the Free Suriname National Resistance Council (NRC) in Holland, which had been supporting the Jungle Commando amid suspicions of financial peculiarities. (*Latin America Weekly*, 23 July; Paramaribo International Service, 29 June; *FBIS*, 30 June.)

Within Suriname there was considerable controversy over the constitutional referendum to be held in September. The new constitution met with severe criticism from human rights organizations, from the Committee of Christian Churches (CCK), which brings together the Evangelical Moravian Brethren (EBG) and the Roman Catholic Church, and from among the old political parties that supported the referendum. The president's powers were so great that many Surinamese believed he should be elected directly and that the preponderance of executive power threatened to undermine the legislative powers of the National Assembly. But the most forceful criticism was directed at the constitutional position allotted the National Army led by Bouterse. Several articles in the constitution elevated the National Army to the role of "military vanguard" of the people that "is also involved in national reconstruction and the liberation of the nation." According to Article 178, the Military Authority (Militar Gezag) also has the task of "guaranteeing the conditions under which the Surinamese people can realize and consolidate a peaceful transition to a democratic and socially just society." In addition, the military retained legal power through the various decrees they had promulgated since 1980, which would remain in force. The critics also feared that the Council of State, which would include Bouterse, would in fact be the co-legislative and governing power in the new government. (*NRC Handelsblad*, 26 September; *FBIS*, 13 October.)

To prepare for the elections, Bouterse created a new party to represent the military, the NDP, which would assume priority over the older 25FM as the political arm of the National Army. The creation of the new party was in large part intended to assuage the army's network of civilian supporters after Bouterse announced that his 25FM would not contest the November elections. Viewing younger Surinamese as the potential base for his new NDP, Bouterse announced that Prime Minister Wijdenbosch, a creator of the 25FM, would assume the party chair. On 7 June approximately 5,000 people attended the formal announcement of the NDP while the leaders of the other parties boycotted the proceedings. (*NRC Handelsblad*, 13 April; *FBIS*, 22 April; Paramaribo International Service, 9 June; *FBIS*, 18 June.)

The old parties shook the government by setting aside their long-standing ethnic and political differences under a coalition banner, which suggested that the November elections might not be the charade orchestrated by Bouterse. At a rally of 60,000 people in downtown Paramaribo, they announced the formation of the UFDD. This alliance blends several traditional groupings: the largely Creole Surinamese National Party headed by independence era prime minister Henk Arron; the Hindustani-dominated Progressive Reformed Party led by perennial opposition leader Jaggernath Lachmon; and the Indonesian Peasants' Party led by Willy Soemita. The UFDD also achieved a reconciliation between the Kaum Tani Persuatan Indonesia (KTPI) and its rival, Pendewa Lima. Similarly, the Bush Negro party—the Association of Brotherhood and Unity—and the Moederbond trade union federation also joined the coalition. Fred Derby, the leader of the powerful C-47 trade union confederation, which includes the bauxite workers, formed his own Suriname Labor Party.

The military reacted badly to UFDD criticisms of its policies and requested Bouterse to resign from the government. After government ministers threatened to resign and bring the government down, UFDD leaders succeeded in securing Bouterse's signature on a pact, called the Leonsberg Agreement, that acknowledged the legitimate role of both the civilian political parties and the Surinamese National Army as well as Bouterse's intentions to honor the outcome of the elections.

Despite serious criticism of both the constitution and the manner in which the referendum vote was conducted, all political parties in Suriname urged their followers to vote "yes" in the 30 September referendum. According to the government, more than 120,000 voters turned out to approve the constitution, though turnout was low in the Marowijne district where the guerrillas hold sway. Nearly 90 percent approved the new constitution, and the UFDD saw the referendum as paving the way for free national elections in November.

The campaign for the election was dominated by Bouterse overruling both the Independent Elections Commission and the National Assembly in holding elections in three districts where a state of emergency had been declared. Throughout the campaign Bouterse claimed that the UFDD had secret communications with the Jungle Commando and was negotiating a cease-fire behind the military's back. Although opposition parties had feared that the ten seats in the war zone would provide the NDP with the necessary votes to block a UFDD election and force the creation of a government of national unity controlled by Bouterse, the large turnout in the elections brought the UFDD 40 out of the 51 seats, leaving 4 for Pendawa Lima, 4 for the leftist PALU party, and only 3 for the NDP. (*Latin America Weekly*, 10 December; *Carribbean Insight*, January 1988; Paramaribo International Service, 10 December; *FBIS*, 14 December.)

The landslide electoral triumph of the UFDD produced promises from the Jungle Commando for a cease-fire lasting until 1 January 1988 so that a dialogue between the new civilian government and the guerrillas could begin. However, the significance of the election will only be determined by the degree to which the military, especially Bouterse, allows the civilians to rule.

On 4 December the National Army elected five members to the Military Authority, the political arm of the army. Although only 20 percent voted, Bouterse and Chief of Staff Ivan Graanoogst won the poll. The three other members are prominent Marxists: Major Badressein Sital, Captain Charles Mijnals, and Lieutenant Lieuw Yen Tai, who is head of the military police. The council's first act was its public disapproval of the annual ceremony honoring the dead of 8 December 1982 and mounting a parade for their executioners. (Paramaribo International Service, 7 December; *FBIS*, 9 December.)

Foreign Affairs. Brazil remained the dominant force in Surinamese politics, especially as the insurgency remained an irritant to the regime. In a mid-September meeting with President José Sarney, Bouterse raised the issue of renegotiating his $3 million debt and securing military assistance and training from the Brazilian military. During the meeting with Sarney, Bouterse allegedly told Brazilians about the difficulties he had in re-equipping his armed forces due to an international boycott imposed by the United States and the Netherlands.

Although it was publicly denied by Brazilian authorities, a document by the Brazilian military existed that urged greater political and military cooperation with Suriname. The meeting was followed up by a visit in December by Graanoogst to discuss the training of Surinamese soldiers at the Brazilian military institutes in Rio de Janeiro. (Brasilia Radio Nacional da Amazonia, 11 September; *FBIS*, 14 September; *Folha De São Paulo*, 12 September; *FBIS*, 15 September; Paramaribo International Service, 2 December; *FBIS*, 3 December.)

In August both Graanoogst and Bouterse visited Libya. On a one-week visit to meet with Jerry Rawlings of Ghana, Bouterse stopped over in Tripoli on 22 August and was received by Moammar Khadafy as well as by members of the General People's Committee. (JANA, 5 August; *FBIS*, 12 August; Paramaribo International Service, 19 August; *FBIS*, 20 August; JANA, 22 August; *FBIS*, 24 August.)

The Soviet Union further strengthened its ties to the Surinamese labor movement, with which it has a four-year protocol of cooperation. Delegations of trade unionists, women, and parliamentarians from both the 25FM and the umbrella trade union coalition, Aafacsur, visited the Soviet Union for extended stays. (Paramaribo International Service, 4 February, 19 June, 14 October; *FBIS*, 5 February, 26 June, 15 October; *Izvestiia*, 16 September; *FBIS*, 22 September.) It was obvious through the year that Soviet strategy toward Suriname had shifted to support for the Suriname Labor Party and other manifestations of the vigorous labor movement in the country.

R. Bruce McColm
Freedom House, New York

United States

Population. 243,084,000
Party. Communist Party USA (CPUSA)
Founded. 1919
Membership. 15,000-20,000
General Secretary. Gus Hall
Political Bureau. Gus Hall, Arnold Bechetti, Jim West, Charlene Mitchell, James Steele, Louis Diskin, Lee Dlugin, James E. Jackson, Judith LeBlanc, Daniel Rubin, John Pittman
Status. Legal.
Last Congress. Twenty-fourth, 13–16 August, in Chicago, Illinois
Last Election. 1984 presidential, under 0.1 percent
Publications. *People's Daily World* (Barry Cohen, ed.), *Political Affairs* (Mike Zagarell, ed.)

The CPUSA is the leading Marxist-Leninist organization in the United States. Founded in 1919, the CPUSA achieved its greatest influence in the years from 1935 to 1950, gaining a significant role in the labor movement and a measure of influence within liberal and labor political circles in a number of states. The CPUSA reached its greatest organizational strength in the late 1930s with a membership of nearly 100,000. As the Cold War developed and domestic anticommunism increased following World War II, the CPUSA became isolated politically; it was driven from most labor unions and out of mainstream politics, and its leaders were prosecuted by the federal government. The 1956 revelations of Stalin's crimes by Soviet leaders, along with the suppression of the Hungarian revolution, prompted a number of party leaders and the bulk of its remaining members to leave the CPUSA. From a low point of a few thousand members in the late 1950s, the party has regained members slowly, showing its greatest growth in the last decade. Its membership in 1987 was about where it stood in the mid-1950s before its near disintegration.

Leadership and Party Organization. Gus Hall, age 77, has served as general secretary since 1959 and has led the CPUSA longer than any individual in its history; he is the longest tenured communist party leader in the world. Other prominent leaders are James Jackson (Central Committee secretary), James Steele (Legislative and Political Action Department director), Jim West (Central Review Commission chair), Lee Dlugin (International Department chair), Victor Perlo (Economics Commission chair), George Meyers (Trade Union Department chair), Sid Taylor (party treasurer), Simon Gerson (Legislative and Political Action Department chair), Charlene Mitchell (Peace and Solidarity Commission chair), Judith LeBlanc (acting national organization secretary), Rosalio Munoz (Commission on Chicano/Mexican American Equality secretary), and Pat Barile (financial secretary). Key state and local leaders include Scott Marshall (Illinois district organizer), Kendra Alexander (Northern California district chair), Evelina Alarcon (Los Angeles County Communist Party chair), Jarvis Tyner (New York district chair),

Maurice Jackson (Maryland, Virginia, and the District of Columbia organizer and CPUSA legislative representative), Sam Webb (Michigan Communist Party executive secretary), Joelle Fishman (Connecticut district organizer), Sandra Jones (Wisconsin district organizer), John Rummell (New Jersey district organizer), Rick Nagin (Ohio district chair), Elsie Dickerson (Eastern Pennsylvania–Delaware district chair), and Michael Bayer (Indiana Communist Party executive secretary).

Barry Cohen edits the CPUSA's newspaper, *People's Daily World* (*PDW*). The tabloid-style *PDW* is published five days a week, varies from twelve to thirty-six pages in length in a typical week, and often includes a Spanish-language section entitled *Nuestro Mundo*. It claims an average daily circulation of 70,000, with a few special issues running to 250,000. Mike Zagarell edits the party's monthly ideological journal, *Political Affairs* (*PA*). The party's various auxiliary organizations also publish journals aimed at specialized audiences. These include *Black Liberation Journal* (Charlene Mitchell, editor), *Jewish Affairs* (Herbert Aptheker, editor; Lewis Moroze, managing editor), and the Young Communist League's *Dynamic* (Elena Mora, editor).

The CPUSA Twenty-fourth National Convention on 13–16 August in Chicago was attended by 400 delegates and about 600 guests. Sixty percent of the delegates were under age 45, 40 percent had been members of the party for less than ten years, 43 percent were women, 21 percent were Afro-American, 4 percent were Chicano, 2 percent were Puerto Rican, 1 percent was Native American, 1 percent was Asian, and 33 percent were union members from 43 unions (*PA*, September/October). The convention elected a new Central Committee, National Council, and Central Review Commission. There have also been changes in the Political Bureau and Secretariat. Following established habit, the members of the new governing boards were not announced and actual membership is only apparent when the titles of various individuals change when they appear in the party press.

Domestic Party Affairs. At the convention Gus Hall spoke with satisfaction about his party's achievements since the last convention in 1983 and with considerable optimism for the future. The CPUSA has, indeed, made significant advances in recent years. After more than 30 years of isolation from mainstream politics, the party is regaining a foothold in liberal-left politics and in the labor movement.

There are a number of examples of the CPUSA's increasing reacceptance in mainstream American life. The CPUSA-aligned U.S. Peace Council, once shunned for its communist links and partisanship with the Soviet Union, has won acceptance by most of the major so-called peace organizations in the United States. Al Marder, a member of the board of the U.S. Peace Council and national coordinator of the CPUSA-backed Campaign for a People's Peace Treaty, sits on the board of the Connecticut Nuclear Freeze Campaign. Leo Cadwell, a long-time communist and member of the Washington State Communist Party committee, served on the national board of the nuclear freeze campaign until his death in November. *PDW* proudly reported on 30 April that a "thousand-strong contingent" walked behind CPUSA banners in the massive 25 April Washington demonstration put on by a coalition of the main peace and solidarity groups as well as a number of the more left-wing labor unions and religious figures. On 4 June *PDW* carried a guest column by David McReynolds, chair of War Resisters International and a major figure among established peace groups. McReynolds said that "one of the historic tragedies in the U.S. is that the division of the American left between the Socialists and the Communists has led us into seeing each other as the main enemy. That we have disagreements is true enough. But the main enemy we confront is the capitalist structure in this country and the arms race endangering the planet."

PDW has also reported on a number of public figures associating themselves with communist-linked public events, events that ten years ago, or even five years ago would have been avoided by almost all public figures. For example, the CPUSA preceded its Twenty-fourth Convention with a "People's New Agenda Rally." Danny Davis, alderman from Chicago's 29th ward and a prominent local politician, gave a welcoming address to the rally. The rally was attended by 2,000 people and was chaired by Charlene Mitchell (*PDW*, 15 August). At a *PDW* banquet in northern California (featuring the Soviet spokesman Vladimir Posner), the mayor of the City of Richmond gave a welcoming address and greetings were read from the mayors of San Francisco, Oakland, and Berkeley, the chair of the San Francisco Board of Supervisors, one Alameda County supervisor, and U.S. Representative Ron Dellums (ibid., 4 June). At a similar event in Cleveland, Ohio, greetings were sent by a city councilman and the president of the school board (ibid., 19 June). In July Edna Hayes, wife of U.S. Representative Charles Hayes, was one of 170 American delegates to the World Congress of Women in Moscow along with Maryann Mahaffey, a Detroit city council member (ibid., 22 July). Mahaffey is also on the advisory council of the World Peace Council. U.S. Representative John Conyers gave a welcoming address at a reception for delegates to the national conference of the U.S. Peace Council, and Detroit mayor Coleman Young sent a proclamation praising that council (ibid., 17 November).

Early in 1987 a number of memorials were held for Henry Winston, the CPUSA's national chairman who died in December 1986. In addition to numerous party spokesmen, appearances were made at these memorials by such public figures as former Manhattan Borough president Percy Sutton and an incumbent Alameda County (California) supervisor (ibid., 13 January, 12 February). It is also a sign of the growing acceptance of associating with the CPUSA that a principal of a public high school in San Francisco should appear at a Winston memorial and that *PDW* felt free to publicize it (ibid., 13 February). A similar example of the lack of controversy regarding communist-linked events can be seen even in the South, traditionally a region with strong anticommunist sentiments. The Fayetteville (North Carolina) *Observer-Times* on 25 July carried in its religious section a lengthy article, phrased in routine journalistic tones, about the favorable impressions of the World Congress of Women by the president of the Fayetteville Church Women United. The latter had been recommended to the Moscow congress as a delegate by the CPUSA-aligned Women for Racial and Economic Equality.

A major reason for the growing willingness of public figures and other noncommunists to associate with the party is the breakdown of the anticommunist consensus that once existed in U.S. society. Gus Hall pointed to this when he remarked that "today there is hardly any need to prove there is a decline in anti-Sovietism and anti-Communism. For anyone taking an active interest and involvement in the labor, peace and other people's movements, the evidence is plain to see. Along with it, redbaiting has lost its sting. This means that one of the most divisive tools of reaction and militarism has lost its potency for dividing the forces of peace, progress and democracy . . . This is a clear green light for boldly, more freely and more forthrightly joining the hands of Communists and non-Communists in the struggle for peace and democracy." (*PDW*, 6 August.)

Also contributing to the CPUSA's recent advances and its optimism for the future is its new leadership. Although Gus Hall and some of the party's other top leaders are veteran cadres who speak with the crude accents of CPUSA's lean years, much of its secondary leadership and its state and local leaders have been replaced by younger and more sophisticated figures. *PA* reported in its September/October issue that 75 percent of the CPUSA's state and district leaders are under 50, and, as noted earlier, the delegates to its Twenty-fourth Convention were relatively young and many had been in the party only a few years. Typical of the new leadership is Barry Cohen, 37. Cohen was a founder and student leader of the New Mobilization Committee Against the War in Vietnam at the University of Michigan in the late 1960s. He later became active in the CPUSA's Young Workers' Liberation League, joined the staff of *PA* in 1972, and became editor of *PDW* in 1987.

The party's long investment of time, effort, and concern in the black community also appears to be finally paying dividends. A good share of its new, younger leadership is black, such as James Steele. Black elected officials are among those mainstream public figures most willing to associate with CPUSA activities. In a lengthy *PDW* article Steele, citing the potential of the black vote and its progressive nature, announced that the party would give the election of blacks to public office priority. Steele also remarked that "the 23-member Congressional Black Caucus is the most progressive and consistently anti-Reagan political bloc in the Congress. It is an extension of the people's movement into the Congress." (*PDW*, 24 September.) The CPUSA strongly backed the re-election of Harold Washington (Chicago's first black mayor) and claimed an active role in the campaign that supported him (ibid., 26 March; *PA*, May). Steele called the coalition backing Washington a model for the "broad people's movement" (*PDW*, 17 March) the party wanted to build throughout the nation. (Mayor Washington's unexpected death was deeply mourned by the CPUSA.) The CPUSA also claimed a role in the election of Carrie Saxon-Perry as the first black woman to win the mayor's office in Hartford, Connecticut. At a Hartford celebration of the 68th anniversary of the founding of the CPUSA, a representative of the steering committee of People for a Change—the group that sponsored the election of Saxon-Perry and two victorious city council members—"paid tribute to the role of the Communist Party in building electoral unity" (ibid., 25 November).

Gus Hall's main report to the Twenty-fourth National Convention called for a continuation of recent party policies of working around and in the left wing of the liberal and labor movement. However, Halls' formulation appeared to call for communists to take a more aggressive and somewhat higher profile than in the past. He called for a "united working-class front, all-people's unity—and most important, unity in action" to defeat Reaganism. He called for communists and their allies to make the 1988 election "a pitched battle between the ultra-right and the all-people's front, and a referendum on the Reaganite conspiracy" and to devise "policies, programs, and slogans that will mobilize masses into an all-people's electoral front to defeat Reaganites." Hall announced that "slogans and tactics have to be looser, broader, and more flexible. The loosening up of our tactics must be based on our assessment of changing thought patterns."

In his report, Hall also spoke favorably of the anti-Reagan, progressive character of the major candidates for the Democratic Party's presidential nomination, saying that "this consensus reflects the tremendous pressure the forces of political independence are putting on the Democratic Party to field a nominee who can become the medium for the level of mass mobilization necessary to defeat the Republicans. If this consensus among the candidates continues to develop, it will help create a framework favorable for the nomination and election of candidates at least partially committed to the issues. This in turn would be conducive to the nominee becoming a vehicle through which the all-people's front, the forces of political independence in particular, could wage an all-out campaign against the Reaganites on all levels of the election." Hall devoted a section of his report to Jesse Jackson's candidacy, saying that "the more advanced of the independent forces [Hall's term for acceptable political tendencies]—inside and outside the Democratic Party—will tend to coalesce around Jackson's candidacy... Jackson's concept of a 'Rainbow Coalition' that includes labor and farmers and of a 'coalition of progressive Democrats' will also contribute to all-people's unity and political independence."

Despite the major emphasis in his report on working for unity among those hostile to Reaganism and his lengthy discussion of the Democratic Party presidential contest, Hall's report did call for fielding a communist presidential ticket in 1988 in a brief passage. However, three months later Hall and James Steele held a press conference to announce that the CPUSA probably would not run a communist ticket in 1988 (*NYT*, 20 November).

With regard to the labor movement, in his main report Hall said there were "fresh winds" and that "because of these changing thought patterns it is more difficult—and unnecessary—to speak of a right, a center, and a left... The thought patterns that were considered center in the past have now become the thought patterns of the bulk of the trade union membership and much of the leadership. And the broader left now occupies part of the domain also." Because of the declining power of the right (identified with AFL-CIO president Lane Kirkland and American Federation of Teachers leader Albert Shanker) in the labor movement, Hall called for a more aggressive stance by the left. He told the delegates that "it is necessary for a united left to give leadership to a united working-class front. This shift in tactics raises the importance of and makes it possible to work more within the trade union structure—local unions, central labor and state bodies. The united left forces can now think in terms of moving the whole trade union movement." (*PDW*, 14 August.) Hall de-emphasized the "center-left" strategy he articulated at the 1983 CPUSA convention and appeared to urge that left forces take a more forceful role commensurate with their greater strength.

Allied Organizations. Michael Myerson is executive director and Gus Newport, former mayor of Berkeley, California, is co-chairman of the U.S. Peace Council, the most active organization linked to the CPUSA. The Young Communist League (YCL) is headed by John Bachtell, its national chairman. At a National Student Conference on 28 March in New York City, the YCL claimed delegates from twenty campuses and announced that YCL members had been elected to student government posts at the University of Washington in Seattle and the University of Massachusetts in Amherst (*PDW*, 4 April). Bachtell later announced the formation of ten new YCL clubs but specified only Wright State University, the University of Massachusetts, and one in Tucson, Arizona (ibid., 7 August). The National Alliance Against Racist and Political Repression held its ninth national conference in Birmingham, Alabama, re-electing Angela Davis (a CPUSA Central Committee member) as co-chair and Frank Chapman as executive director (ibid., 12 November). The National Council of

American-Soviet Friendship (the Reverend Alan Thomson, director) is increasingly active; 100 delegates from 26 societies attended its fifth national convention in Minneapolis, Minnesota, and its new chair was the Tony award winning actor John Randolph (ibid., 23 June). Trade Unionists for Action and Democracy publishes a journal, *Labor Action*, but tends to keep a low profile.

International Views, Positions, and Activities. The CPUSA stridently supports the Soviet Union without deviation on all issues and in all arenas. One example of its devotion to the Soviet cause is that in 1987 the *PDW* printed 69 items attacking the ABC television miniseries "Amerika," which is about life in the United States after Soviet conquest. The CPUSA has dealt cautiously with the programs of *perestroika* and *glasnost'* announced by CPSU General Secretary Mikhail Gorbachev. Coverage of Gorbachev's program in the CPUSA press has been chiefly from official Soviet sources. Carl Bloice, a *PDW* associate editor and one of the CPUSA's rising young leaders, has been stationed in Moscow for most of 1987. His dispatches on Gorbachev's reforms tend to closely parallel official Soviet interpretations. There has been very little analysis by American communists about the implications of Gorbachev's reforms.

The most striking characteristic of the CPUSA's views on foreign affairs is the depth of its hostility to Israel. No nation, aside from the United States, is assailed as frequently in the *PDW* as is Israel. In 1987, 166 separate negative press items were carried by the *PDW* regarding Israel. This was an average of more than one every other issue. The stories range from lengthy denunciations of Israeli policies to brief news notes reporting some negative item about Israel. The language regarding Israel is often strident, as in the greeting sent by the YCL to a banquet of the Palestine Democratic Youth Organization. The YCL greeting stated that "Palestinian youth and the youth of the United States have a common and united enemy—the U.S. imperialist-zionist alliance. As youth we are the primary victims of this alliance." It also declared "the fascist Israeli prisons are packed with youth, tortured youth, including many whose only crimes are throwing stones at their oppressors." (*PDW*, 5 June.)

The CPUSA sent delegates to several communist conferences around the world. Gus Hall attended the Moscow celebrations of the 70th anniversary of the October Revolution and addressed a related gathering of 173 communist and Marxist-Leninist parties. Margrit Pitmen, a member of the CPUSA National Council, spoke to the Twenty-eighth Congress of the Danish Communist Party (CP) and the Eighth Congress of the Socialist Unity Party of West Berlin; Simon Gerson, a member of the Central Committee, represented the CPUSA at the Twelfth Congress of the Greek CP. Present as fraternal delegates at the CPUSA's Twenty-fourth National Convention were representatives of the Bulgarian CP, the Canadian CP, the Czechoslovakian CP, the French CP, the German CP, the Socialist Unity Party of Germany, the Greek CP, the Hungarian Socialist Workers' Party, the CP of India, the CP of Israel, the Mexican Socialist Party, the Mongolian People's Revolutionary Party, the Southwest African People's Organization (SWAPO) of Namibia, the Polish United Workers' Party, the Romanian CP, the CPSU, and the Socialist Unity Party of West Berlin.

Other Marxist-Leninist Organizations. Although small—less than 2,000 members—the Socialist Workers' Party (SWP) is the largest Marxist-Leninist body independent of the CPUSA. It was founded in 1938 and is the leading Trotskyist organization in the United States; Jack Barnes is the national secretary. The SWP publishes *The Militant* (*TM*), edited by Doug Jenness and Margaret Jayko; a sister Spanish-language paper, *Perspectiva Mundial*; and a theoretical journal, *New International*, edited by Mary-Alice Waters. The press run of *TM* is usually under 10,000, and on 13 March it reported only 1,658 long-term subscriptions.

The SWP and its youth group, the Young Socialist Alliance (YSA), were deeply involved in the antiwar movement of the Vietnam War era and achieved some influence in the student antiwar movement. In the last decade, however, the SWP and the YSA have rapidly lost strength. In 1984 older Trotskyists associated with the veteran SWP leader George Breitman (who died in 1986) left the SWP, formed the Fourth International Tendency, and have continued to publish the *Bulletin in Defense of Marxism*. Another group followed Peter Camejo, the SWP presidential candidate in 1976, into a body called the North Star Network (based in Berkeley, California).

The greatest success of the SWP in recent years has been in court. In a suit regarding FBI covert activity involving the SWP, U.S. judge Thomas Griesa in 1986 awarded the SWP and YSA $264,000 in damages. In a continuation of the suit in 1987, Judge Griesa barred the federal government from using most of the information it had collected on the SWP and YSA in any way. (*TM*, 20 August.)

In a frank speech to the Iowa district of the SWP, Mac Warren, SWP midwest regional field organizer, noted that in "the past decade the membership of the SWP had dropped by half. And while in the past year and a half the size has stayed about the same, we have no reason to expect it to go up right away" (*TM*, 9 October). In a parallel speech to a regional SWP meeting in Pittsburgh, Jack Barnes acknowledged the membership losses but asserted that the SWP was ready to grow (ibid., 20 March). The only significant toehold the SWP claims in the labor movement is in a few midwestern meatpacking locals of the United Food and Commercial Workers (UFCW) (ibid., 7 August). The SWP had been enthusiastic backers of the militant leadership of UFCW local P-9, a large meatpackers' union in Austin, Minnesota. P-9's strike against the Hormel company, however, was lost in 1986 and the militants were eliminated from the union by the UFCW in 1987. The most active campaign undertaken by the SWP in 1987 was the "Benjamin Linder Peace Tour." Ben Linder, an American volunteer in Nicaragua killed in a fight with anti-Sandinista *contras*, was the brother of John Linder, an active SWP member. John Linder has become a featured speaker at SWP events throughout the country.

The SWP is contemptuous of radicals who work within mainstream politics, and it regularly runs candidates for public office under its own banner. Under its current leadership the SWP has been less concerned with traditional Trotskyist ideology and is more attuned to radical feminism, gay rights, and similar counterculture themes than was either the old SWP or the CPUSA. It generally supports the Soviet Union, although it makes traditional Trotskyist criticism about the deformities of Soviet leadership. The SWP reserves its greatest enthusiasm for Third World communism and Marxism, such as that in Cuba (where it strongly supports Fidel Castro's recent re-emphasis on moral incentives), Nicaragua, Grenada before the assassination of Maurice Bishop, and Burkina Faso before the recent coup against Thomas Sankara. The SWP received fraternal greetings at its 1987 conferences from the government of Burkina Faso (pre-coup), SWAPO, the Socialist Bloc of the Dominican Republic, Radio Venceremos of the Farabundo Martí National Liberation Front of El Salvador, and the All Trinidad Sugar and General Workers' Union. (Ibid., 4 September.)

The Young Socialist Alliance (YSA; Rena Cacoullos, national secretary) held a convention in Chicago on 23–25 May. *TM* reported 569 people in attendance with 112 delegates from 55 cities. Fraternal delegates were present from the Maurice Bishop Youth Organization of Grenada, the African National Congress, SWAPO, and the Young Socialists of Canada. Greetings were also received from the Union of Young Communists of Cuba. The YSA publishes *Young Socialist*, edited by Marea Himelgrin. (Ibid., 12 June.)

Beyond the fading SWP, the most active Marxist-Leninist organization is the Communist Workers' Party (CWP), an organization best known for having five of its members killed in a gun battle with Nazis and Klansmen in Greensboro, North Carolina, in 1980. The CWP shifted its views away from violent Maoism in the early 1980s, however. Electoral politics, previously scorned, became acceptable, and in 1984 it announced a plan to "take over a great deal of the local apparatus of the Democratic Party." In 1985 the CWP changed its name to the New Democratic Movement and, under the leadership of Jerry Tung, its general secretary, set out to infiltrate the Democratic Party in New York City through an organization entitled the Asian-Americans for Equality. (The membership of CWP is largely Chinese-American.) By 1987 one of the group's members was on the New York State Democratic Committee, the Asian-Americans for Equality had obtained several million dollars in state and city funds for various projects, and the group had won a significant role in the Village Independent Democrats, a well-known political club in New York City. The CWP's activities became a matter of political controversy in a Democratic Party primary contest when they were made public in a New York newspaper (*Our Town*, 2 August).

Another group of note is a pro-Soviet body called Line of March that publishes *Frontline* (Irwin Silber and Max Elbaum, editors). Line of March is one of the few rival Marxist-Leninist organizations that the CPUSA publicly notices and chastises for ideological errors. *Frontline*, for its part, criticizes the CPUSA's "failure to acknowledge the material basis of opportunism in the workers' movement and its underestimation of the struggle required to unite the U.S. working class on an anti-racist, internationalist basis." Line of March calls on the CPUSA and other radicals to exploit the "left social democratic current" it sees in the labor movement and to adopt a more tolerant, broad left political stance. (*Frontline*, 8 June.) Line of March sees the CPUSA as weakening communist activity in liberal and left arenas by failing to develop an ideological analysis that accommodates such activity. In its view Gus Hall's talk about "forces for political independence," when in fact the CPUSA works within the mainstream labor movement and in and around the left wing of the Democratic Party, simply reflects CPUSA inability to unite theory to practice. *Frontline* editorially endorsed Jesse Jackson and his Rainbow Coalition campaign for the Democratic Party presidential nomination. (Ibid., 12 October.)

John E. Haynes
Washington, D.C.

Uruguay

Population. 2,964,052
Party. Communist Party of Uruguay (PCU)
Founded. 1920
Membership. 11,000 (claimed) (*Pravda*, 22 December 1987, p. 5)
General Secretary. Rodney Arismendi
Secretariat. Rodney Arismendi, Jaime Pérez, Alberto Altesor, Thelman Borges, Leopoldo Carlos Bruera, Ramon Cabrera, Feliz Diaz, Leon Lev, Esteban Valenti (*La Hora*, 23 December 1983)
Status. Legal
Last Congress. Twentieth, December 1970 (National Conference, December 1985; *WMR* indicated that the Twenty-first Congress would be held in the last quarter of 1987, but there has been no further data)
Last Election. November 1984; PCU ran with Frente Amplio coalition, 6 percent, no seats
Auxiliary Organization. Union of Communist Youth
Publications. *La Hora*; *El Popular*

This was a fairly quiet year in Uruguay. The economy continued to grow. Political speculation and maneuvering for the November 1989 election picked up steam, and the campaign to collect signatures for a referendum to overturn the amnesty law for the military that was passed in late 1986 culminated in the submission of over 634,000 signatures—80,000 more than is required by the Constitution. If the signatures are certified by Uruguay's electoral court, the referendum will undoubtedly be at the center of political events in Uruguay in 1988.

The Uruguayan economy expanded in 1987, although not at the 6.3 percent rate experienced in 1986. Best estimates are that the gross domestic product grew at 4.5 percent in the first half of 1987, with a slowdown exhibited in the second half. Inflation stood at 58 percent in 1987, down from 83 percent in 1985 and 70 percent in 1986. Unemployment fell to 8.3 percent in Montevideo by October, the lowest level in several years.

The most important economic news involved yet another refinancing of Uruguay's public debt with the major international commercial banks; this was completed in October. Some $1.8 billion in loans covering the 1985–1991 period were involved. Nevertheless, Uruguay will have to continue to devote over one quarter of its export earnings to service its total foreign debt of some $5.3 billion. With growth slowing, resentment over the price of financial respectability will only increase.

The amnesty bill for the military, officially known as the law renouncing the punitive intention of the state, was passed on 22 December 1986. The issue of its passage became the dominant political question of 1987 when groups opposed to the amnesty began a campaign to collect signatures for a referendum to overturn the law.

President Sanguinetti defended the amnesty law: "What is more just? To consolidate the peace of the country where human rights are guaranteed today, or to seek retroactive justice that could compromise that peace? It is a choice of values. I believe human rights trials would have been incompatible with peace and institutional stability" (*LAT*, 30 March).

The passing of the law absolving the military for any crimes committed during its eleven years in power alienated the left. The leftist coalition known as the Frente Amplio (Broad Front) spent much of 1987 collecting signatures for the referendum. However, the referendum petitions were about the only thing the left could agree on during the year. Friction between the PCU and a social democratic party, the Partido por el Gobierno del Pueblo (PGP) led by Senator Hugo Batalla, gave rise to rumors, subsequently denied, that Batalla might leave the Frente Amplio. The PGP held its first national convention in late November. The convention ratified the moderate socialist position of the group and reiterated the party's willingness to stay within the front despite strains with the communists.

Disunity also continued on the question of the admission of the former guerrilla organization, the Movimiento de Liberación Nacional–Tupamaros (MLN-Tupamaros), into the front. Now organized as a legal political movement claiming 4,500 members, the MLN-Tupamaros began to express frustration with the Frente Amplio's inability to make room for them. At the end of the year a harsh exchange took place between the communist biweekly *La Hora* and the MLN-Tupamaro weekly *Mate Amargo* when the MLN-Tupamaros attacked the narrowness and lack of imagination of the left (especially of the PCU) and called for the creation of a Frente Grande (Great Front) that would include all progressive forces in the society, including dissident Blancos and Colorados.

The Frente Amplio held its first national congress in early December; it was attended by some 2,200 delegates elected from 515 local base committees. All of the major parties that make up the front also held their own conventions during the year.

A special congress of the labor confederation known as the Interunion Workers' Plenum–National Workers' Confederation (PIT-CNT) met at the end of May and agreed to keep representation on its executive board based on the current individual union structure. At first glance this would seem to favor the noncommunist representatives, but a closer examination reveals that the communists expect to win several key union elections, which would then give them undisputed control of the labor federation.

The most significant activity of the PCU during 1987 was the promotion of a new generation of party leaders, including Esteban Valenti and Leon Lev. Long-time general secretary Rodney Arismendi hinted at retirement; his deputy, Jaime Pérez, is expected to be his successor.

Soviet foreign minister Eduard Shevardnadze visited Montevideo for three days in early October. In addition to confirming an agreement with Uruguay that would involve Soviet use of the port of Montevideo for resupplying its fishing fleet, Shevardnadze signed a cultural and scientific agreement with Education and Culture Minister Adela Reta. The most dramatic moment of his visit involved a demonstration by some 1,000 Uruguayan Jews outside the Soviet Embassy. Shevardnadze and the Soviet ambassador, Igor Laptov, left the embassy and engaged in an extended conversation with the demonstrators and their principal spokesman, Pedro Shofsky. In a clear display of *glasnost'*, Shevardnadze impressed the demonstrators with his accessibility, apparent concern for their complaints about the treatment of Soviet Jews and their inability to emigrate, and his willingness to follow up on individual requests.

After the Shevardnadze visit, President Sanguinetti reconfirmed his intention to visit Moscow in early 1988, a visit that had been postponed in June. Soviet general secretary Mikhail Gorbachev is expected to make a stop in Montevideo during a visit to Latin America scheduled to take place before the end of 1988.

Martin Weinstein
William Paterson College of New Jersey

Venezuela

Population. 18,291,134

Parties. Communist Party of Venezuela (Partido Comunista de Venezuela; PCV); Movement to Socialism (Movimiento al Socialismo; MAS)

Founded. PCV: 1931; MAS: 1971 (as splinter from PCV)

Membership. PCV: 4,000 (estimated)

Top Leaders. PCV: Alonso Ojeda Olaechea (general secretary); MAS: Pompeyo Márquez (president)

Politburo. PCV: 7 members: Alonso Ojeda, Jesús Faría, Pedro Ortega Díaz, Eduardo Gallegos Mancera, Trino Melean, Silvino Varela, Alí Morales. 3 alternates: including Luis Ciano and José Manuel Carrasquel

Executive Committee. MAS: 15 members: including Pompeyo Márquez, Freddy Muñoz (general secretary), Teodoro Petkoff, Victor Hugo de Paola, Mayita Acosta, Rafael Thielen, Leopoldo Puchi, Manuel Molina Peñaloza, Luis Manuel Esculpi

Central Committee. PCV: 65 members; MAS: National Directorate, 45 members

Status. Both legal

Last Congress. PCV: Seventh, October 1985;

MAS: Sixth National Convention, June–July 1985
Last Election. 1983; PCV: 3 of 195 deputies; MAS: 10 of 195 deputies, 2 senators
Auxiliary Organizations. PCV: Unitary Central of Venezuelan Workers (Central Unitaria de Trabajadores Venezolanos; CUTV), Communist Youth (Juventud Comunista; JC)
Publication. PCV: *Tribuna Popular*, Américo Díaz Nuñez, director

The nomination of presidential candidates for the December 1988 general election has been taking place against a backdrop of ongoing student protest and increasing violence along the border with Colombia. Three students have been killed and hundreds wounded in nationwide demonstrations that authorities claim are orchestrated by Red Flag (Bandera Roja; BR) guerrillas. Curiously, the BR is seldom mentioned in accounts of border warfare and kidnappings by Colombian guerrillas.

The PCV. The PCV congratulated the new leftist intellectuals' party, Moral Movement (Movimiento Moral), on its nomination of Edmundo Chirinos for president and said it will "study this candidacy carefully" (*Ultimas Noticias*, 18 November). The PCV has still not settled on a candidate, but Chirinos, rector of the Central University (Universidad Central de Venezuela), is among those it has been considering all year. Independent Reinaldo Cervini and Radical Cause leader Andrés Velásquez were also possibilities. According to Jesús Faría, the PCV had hoped for "a center leaning, independent candidate" who would unite all the left as well as other discontented sectors in a common program for the benefit of all Venezuelans; Faría continued to insist on a single candidate despite the "fascistoid" and "divisionist" decision of the MAS to exclude the PCV from its own "unity" slate. (*El Nacional*, 14, 16 June.)

PCV deputy Raúl Esté appeared at many of the student protests and joined in a congressional vote of censure against the interior minister for his heavy-handed repression of the demonstrations. With other leftist deputies Esté also signed a declaration blaming the government's "anti-popular economic policy" for the outbursts, not a "terrorist plan," which is "a lie fabricated not only to hide the profound social and economic discontent behind the disorders, but also to disqualify the struggle of legitimate leaders, intimidate the people, and justify repression" (ibid., 13 May). Silvino Varela, national organization secretary, also considers the conflicts a result of government failure to reactivate the economy, with the social sequels of unemployment, food shortages, and a crisis in public services (ibid., 18 May).

The Politburo praised Brazil's suspension of interest payments on its foreign debt and said that Venezuela, which will spend 34 percent of its budget in 1988 in debt payments, should join that stand in a show of Latin American unity. It further urged Venezuelan political parties, trade unions, and other public organizations to make a common stand in defense of national interests. (*WMR*, May.) Draft legislation on wage and salary increases presented by the CUTV did not pass, but other benefits defended by PCV legislators, such as a freeze on utility rates and some price controls, will be enacted in early 1988. CUTV honorary president Cruz Villegas received the Lázaro Peña Order from the Cuban Council of State in Havana and was later honored on his 70th birthday in Caracas at a rally organized by the directors of the four Venezuelan labor centrals. The PCV supported the winning independent slate in elections at the National Press Association (Sindicato Nacional de Trabajadores de la Prensa; SNTP).

The CUTV was among the sponsors of a Foreign Debt Conference in Caracas; delegates from 27 countries published a document condemning U.S. intervention in Nicaragua (ibid., 10, 28 April). Defense of Nicaragua had also been high on the agenda of the Second Conference of South American Communist Parties held in Lima in December 1986. The conference supported Soviet peace and arms control proposals and demanded an end to human and civil rights abuses in most South American countries (*IB*, April). A CPSU delegation invited by the PCV was headed by M. A. Knyazyuk, CPSU Central Committee member. The group toured Venezuela, met regional PCV committees, and discussed relations between the USSR and Venezuela and between the CPSU and the PCV (*Pravda*, 8 October; *FBIS*, 13 October).

The MAS. Teodoro Petkoff won the presidential nomination once again, defeating sectors represented by Pompeyo Márquez and Juvencio Pulgar that favored an independent candidate capable of unifying all opposition to the mainstream parties—that is, Democratic Action (Acción Democrática; AD) and the social christian COPEI. The MAS decision obeyed the reasoning that this ideal candidate does not exist and that it would be futile for the

MAS to give away its hard-earned recognition for anything less. Problems of identification also played a role. Since the MAS can be confused with both the PCV and AD, Petkoff thinks the national campaigns are necessary to reinforce the image of an "independent democratic socialism; not communist and not social democratic" (*El Nacional*, 16 February). Primaries for a leftist unity candidate had been discussed earlier and the MAS jumped the gun by naming Petkoff. It offered to enter him in a primary against an independent candidate, but this has not prospered.

As in 1983, the MAS campaign will apparently have outside support only from the Revolutionary Left Movement (Movimiento de Izquierda Revolucionario; MIR), but Petkoff believes that his position is still much stronger than that of a relatively unknown unity candidate would have been. Contributing to this is the "growing strength of party organization at state and local levels, its well known leaders and candidates, and effective presence in local struggles and movements" (ibid., 18 November). The MAS program will emphasize unemployment, foreign debt management, the environment, relations with Colombia, and government reform to reduce state centralism and bureaucratization (ibid., 20 July).

The MAS condemned AD's proposed electoral reforms—direct nominal election of municipal council members and creation of the post of mayor—because they do not go far enough (*Veneconomy*, 16 December). In addition, the MAS wanted direct election of governors, separation of presidential and parliamentary elections, and nominal election of state and national legislators, doing away with straight party ballots that are still color coded for illiterates.

In what some analysts see as a developing trend, independent candidates won most of the posts in the elections for deans in the Central University. The MAS, long the leading force in the university, lost that position to the more radical left of the independents (*El Nacional*, 23 May; *JPRS*, 24 August). The MAS holds one seat on the executive committee of the AD-dominated Venezuelan Labor Confederation (Confederación de Trabajadores Venezolanos; CTV), which controls about 90 percent of organized labor.

Pompeyo Márquez, together with other political leaders, backed President Jaime Lusinchi's refusal to negotiate under pressure from Colombia on the delimitation of areas in the Gulf of Venezuela. Colombia would like to take the dispute to the World Court, but Venezuela refuses since vital interests, such as petroleum shipments from Lake Maracaibo, are involved. To attract world attention and goad Venezuela into action, Colombia took a warship into Venezuelan waters, removing it two days later when the first goal was achieved. Tension has been high ever since (*El Nacional*, 13 May). On these border problems with Colombia, Petkoff said he would firmly defend national interests and promote bilateral commissions on the Gulf of Venezuela dispute as well as on narcotic traffic, contraband, and guerrillas (ibid., 20 July).

Other Marxist Parties. General Secretary Moises Moleiro and President Hector Pérez Marcano lead the MIR, which is a 1960 AD splinter. Originally Marxist-Leninist, the party has described itself since 1985 as socialist, revolutionary, and democratic. Moleiro's proposal for a fusion of the major leftist parties (see *YICA*, 1987) had been generally well regarded within the MIR, but considerable opposition to another Petkoff candidacy developed in 1987 as well as objections to exclusion of the PCV from the electoral alliance. Available reports on the November MIR-MAS alliance do not indicate any sizable desertion thus far from the MIR.

The People's Electoral Movement (Movimiento Electoral del Pueblo; MEP) discussed socialist mergers and presidential primaries during much of the year with no real result. The November assembly threw the party's support to the Moral Movement candidate, Edmundo Chirinos. The MEP likes the Moral Movement idea of providing a channel of expression for all those discontented with Venezuela's unsatisfactory democracy and, with their votes, installing a "meritocracy to restore the 1961 Constitution" (ibid., 9 February). The MEP has four deputies in the National Congress and two seats on the executive committee of the CTV. Officers are founder and president Luis Beltrán Prieto Figueroa (who recently received a peace prize from East Germany), vice president Jesús Angel Paz Galarraga, and general secretary Adelso González.

Guillermo García Ponce's New Alternative (Nueva Alternativa; NA) supported leftist independent José Vicente Rangel in the 1983 election but moved to the right in 1987, declaring its support for former Central Bank president Leopoldo Díaz Bruzual. NA alternate deputy Jesús María Pacheco walked out of the November convention with about half the delegates. Dissidents led by Radamés Larrazábal who left the PCV in 1986 formed their own party, the Revolutionary Patriotic Movement (Movimiento Patriótico Revolutionario; MPR). Larrazábal took the top post of general coordinator, and the political commission includes Noel Sirit, Simón Rodríguez, Hugo Guillén, Andrés Araujo, Elam Pacheco, Rafael Sivira, Federico Melo, and Franklin González. According to the new party, Simón Bolívar "is the leader of the Revolution," and "the creative application of Marxism-Leninism to national conditions is the guide for revolutionary action" (ibid., 23 February).

Larrazábal and Sirit attended an *El Nacional* round table with leaders of four other small leftist groups: Humberto Gómez and Eduardo Sanz of the Popular Anti-imperialist Movement (Movimiento Popular Anti-imperialista; MPA); Leticia Barrios of Colectivo Barricada; Alí Rodríguez of Revolutionary Tendency; and Freddy Cárquez of Progressive Front (Frente Progresista). None of the groups were identified, and neither they nor the MPR had decided on presidential candidates (ibid., 18 November).

Radical Cause (Causa R) launched the youngest candidate, its president and union leader Andrés Velásquez. The 17,000 member union of the state steel company, SIDOR, intervened five years ago when Radical Cause won a majority. Elections were finally called again in 1987 and Radical Cause again won; it will apparently be allowed to stay. In a recent interview, Velásquez had difficulty defining "radical democracy" but said party policy revolves around employment, health, education, and the foreign debt (ibid., 30 October). In the 1984 municipal elections Radical Cause elected five councilmen in the state of Bolívar.

Guerrillas. As proof of a subversive plan of destabilization behind the student riots, Interior Minister José Angel Ciliberto read two documents to Congress: first, a lengthy 1985 action plan of BR guerrillas calling for "immediate struggle, seizing of the political initiative," and rebuilding of the Américo Silva front; and second, a 1986 letter to Moammar Khadafy asking for help in mounting protests and organizing the masses against the "starvation policies of the government" (ibid., 14 May). For many observers the proof was too weak to justify the administration's severe repression, which included military trials for indicted offenders. "Hooded agitators" were undoubtedly active in the protests and well-known rabble rousing leftists were prominent, but critics felt the government's rhetoric on terrorist threats exacerbated the situation (ibid., 13 May).

At the same time as student riots were spreading, an undeclared civil war was in progress just across the border in northeastern Colombia, sometimes spilling over into Venezuela. On 12 June guerrillas of the Colombian National Liberation Army (Ejército de Liberación Nacional; ELN), Camilo Torres Front, attacked a Venezuelan national guard post at Sierra de Perijá, killing nine men who had been among eighteen detailed to destroy a coca plantation. An ELN open letter to Lusinchi in July said the attack was a reprisal for Venezuelan persecution of Colombian immigrant farm workers in the area. It offered to negotiate a nonagression pact with Venezuela, adding that the "Camilista Unión–ELN has no connection with narcotics traffic" (ibid., 7 July).

The security threat posed by the guerrilla forces was further aggravated by continued kidnappings of ranchers, a contraband of goods and food into Colombia that was emptying Venezuelan markets, massive contraband Venezuelan gold, and the two-week border closing during the worst of the Gulf of Venezuela incident.

Carole Merten
San Francisco, California

ASIA AND THE PACIFIC

Introduction

With the exception of North Korea, the leaders of the communist-ruled states of Mongolia, the People's Republic of China, and Vietnam continued to discuss reforms to revitalize their societies. In the Philippines, negotiations between the government and the communist party's New People's Army (NPA) broke down, and fighting between the two sides resumed. Also noteworthy is that a profile describing communist activity in the South Pacific Islands has been added this year.

Elsewhere in the region, some communist parties held their party congresses. A few communist parties registered minor gains to advance their influence and power; others lost ground; still others only maintained the status quo. Their activities can be briefly reviewed by classifying communist activity as follows: states with ruling communist parties; states with banned communist parties in opposition; and states with legal communist parties.

States with Ruling Communist Parties. The Chinese Communist Party (CCP) successfully put down large-scale student demonstrations in early January and suppressed debate and criticisms of party reforms with a campaign of its own: an anti-bourgeois liberalism drive to rid the CCP of overzealous critics. By spring the writer Wang Ruowang, the astro-physicist Fang Lizhi, and the journalist Liu Binyan had been expelled from the party. By summer nearly 400,000 college graduates and postgraduate students were being sent out to the grass roots for two years instead of being assigned to government agencies. Another one million were to spend the summer recess on compulsory work in factories, offices, and rural villages as part of a program to "remold their views."

Security organs continued to search out and arrest counterrevolutionaries throughout the country, many of leftist persuasion. Between late January and early June the authorities reportedly discovered 15,000 anticommunist posters in eleven counties of Sichuan province alone.

While dealing with criticisms from the right as well as the left, the CCP held its Thirteenth Party Congress in early November. Delegates approved a new slate of leaders for the Politburo and its standing committee; they also elected a younger, one-third membership to the Central Committee, cutting that body from 210 to 175 and reducing its average age by several years. For the first time since 1949 fewer people with military experience were in the Politburo and a new generation of leaders had replaced the "Long March" survivors. Deng Xiaoping, Chen Yun, Peng Zhen and others no longer held formal offices, but they still served as elder statesmen.

The Thirteenth CCP Congress upheld the party line set forth in late 1978—that is, reform to achieve modernization while adhering to the four cardinal principles: follow the socialist road; uphold the dictatorship of the proletariat; maintain the dictatorship of the communist party; and adhere to Marxism-Leninism and Mao Zedong thought. The new general secretary, Zhao Ziyang, admitted that China was still in the "primary stage of socialism" and that the road to modern socialism would be long and arduous.

The Chinese agricultural reforms suffered some setback. China had to import fourteen million tons of grain in 1987 at a cost of $1 billion, the largest annual grain import in this decade. Pork, vegetable oil, and sugar became so scarce in the cities, and raw materials for manufacturing firms were in such short supply, that the state had to reimpose rationing in December 1987 and reintroduce procurement pricing and delivery for some raw materials in early 1988.

In communist Vietnam the new "circle of five" leaders—who had replaced Truong Chinh, Pham Van Dong, and Le Duc Tho in late 1986—are now led by Nguyen Van Linh. They concentrated their efforts primarily on reshuffling personnel, ridding the party of inept and corrupt members, and building networks of supporters throughout the country. Although they discussed reform, few positive steps were initiated. The new leadership also stressed more openness (*cong khai*) in conducting party business and learning from previous mistakes.

The Mongolian People's Revolutionary Party, with some 88,000 members, responded to Moscow's call for reform by holding meetings to discuss how to bolster the sagging pastoral economy. The United States established diplomatic ties with Mongolia, the Soviets removed some troops from the country, and ties with China were slightly improved.

The Korean Workers' Party in North Korea continued to mobilize support for Kim Chong-il to succeed his father, Kim Il-song, as the heir apparent. North Korea planned to boycott the winter 1988 Olympic Games and all signs indicate that Pyongyang's athletes will not attend the September 1988 Olympic Games in Seoul. In January 1988 a young woman admitted to being a North Korean agent who had placed a bomb in a Republic of Korea (ROK) airplane over Burma in November 1987, destroying the plane and its 115 passengers. Meanwhile, North Korea refrained from participating in any serious negotiations with the ROK, instead trying to capitalize on the violence that frequently erupted in the south during the summer of 1987.

States with Banned Communist Party Opposition. In Indonesia the communist party remained inactive. In the spring approximately 653 members of the Marxist-Leninist faction of the Malaysian Communist Party surrendered to the government, leaving an undisclosed but greatly reduced number of guerrillas in that country's border area. In Thailand more defections from the communist party took place. Thai police also arrested a handful of leaders in Bangkok when they held a top level meeting to plan the Fifth Party Congress for October. In northern Burma the aging Burmese Communist Party leaders maintained a tight grip over party affairs, although there have been serious splits in that leadership. Similarly, the party's military force remained active despite failures in the past few years to re-establish its former foothold in central Burma.

In the Philippines the communist party and the NPA escalated their activities to destabilize the government's rule over this large group of islands. After rebel leaders broke off negotiations with the Aquino government, they resumed armed struggle. The NPA increased its attacks on government units and police as well as on private companies and plantations. The communist party dispatched "sparrow" squad units of assassins to kill government officials and their key supporters. Rebel forces also increased contacts with international support groups outside the Philippines. Late in 1987 the Aquino government reversed its policy of reconciliation with the communists and increased military and paramilitary activities against the NPA. Although the United States increased its economic and military aid to the Philippines, the widespread poverty that currently exists, the lackluster economy, and the prevailing social anarchy still make it impossible for the government forces to suppress the NPA. Scattered throughout the major islands and well entrenched in its base areas, the NPA is now a formidable force to be reckoned with.

The total population of the independent island states in the South Pacific, including Papua/New Guinea, is around 5.5 million. Although there is no communist party in this region, several formal Marxist groups exist in the French associated territory of New Caledonia. Over the past few years various student and youth associations in New Guinea, Fiji, Western Samoa, Nauru, Tuvalu, Palau, and Tonga have sent their representatives to youth and women's organizations in Eastern Europe and the USSR as well as to Australia for participation in pro-Soviet labor union activity. In March, when Soviet foreign minister Eduard Shevardnadze visited Canberra, Australia, he surprised his hosts by adding Tuvalu, Papua/New Guinea, and Tonga to the list of island nations that have shown interest in developing agreements with the Soviet Union. For example, the conservative Tongan minister for defense and foreign affairs, Crown Prince Tupouto, traveled to Moscow in February, reportedly to discuss another fishing agreement, although previously the Crown Prince had assured Australia that his country had no fish to sell to the Soviets.

States with Legal Communist Parties. The Bangladesh Communist Party held its Fourth Party Congress in April in Dhaka and endorsed the party line to promote "national democratic revolution." This line calls for the party to work with all "progressive liberal democratic forces" to topple the current regime. In New Zealand, communist-led front organizations whipped up support for Nicaragua and tried to oppose the new economic policies of the government to privatize social welfare and reduce budget deficits. Although they were unsuccessful in the latter effort, some of their members did win seats in the 1987 Council of Trade Unions elections. The small but vigorous Communist Party of Australia continued its effort to link with numerous dissident groups whose demands have so far been ignored by the Australian Labor Party. The communist party hopes to consolidate these groups into a new front organization that can oppose the government while rallying other splinter, dissident groups to its cause.

The Communist Party of Sri Lanka held its Thirteenth Party Congress in March and published appeals for the ethnic violence on the island to end. No leadership or policy changes occurred, but party members did elect a new Central Committee. In Japan the communist party celebrated the 65th anniversary of its founding in July and commemorated the 95th birthday of Sanzo Nosaka, chairman-emeritus of the party's Central Committee. In November the party held its Eighteenth Party Congress and endorsed the same line it has followed since the previous congress.

Soviet Activity in the Region. With words rather than deeds the Soviet Union continued its diplomatic initiatives to improve contacts with states in Asia and the Pacific. Late in the year Soviet diplomats met with Japanese foreign minister Sosuke Uno in Tokyo to state that Moscow would like to improve relations with Japan, but they offered no concessions on the Kuril Islands issue that might induce Japan to take those overtures seriously.

On 7 July the Mongolian People's Revolutionary Party hosted a congress for the purpose of initiating a campaign to make Asia and the Pacific Basin into a peace zone. All 21 communist parties of the region, except those from China (which was not invited), Japan, and North Korea, participated. Mikhail Gorbachev sent a message of greeting to the congress. The delegates discussed the means by which the region's communist parties and front organizations could promote nuclear-free zones and prevent the United States, Japan, and South Korea from strengthening their security ties.

Ramon H. Myers
Hoover Institution

Australia

Population. 16,072,986

Parties. Communist Party of Australia (CPA); Socialist Party of Australia (SPA); Communist Party of Australia–Marxist-Leninist (CPA-ML); Socialist Workers' Party (SWP); Association of Communist Unity (ACU); Socialist Labor League (SLL); International Socialists (IS); Spartacist League of Australia and New Zealand (SLANZ)

Founded. CPA: 1920; SPA: 1971; CPA-ML: 1964; SWP: 1972; ACU: 1985; SLL: 1972; IS: 1971

Membership. CPA: 1,000; SPA: 500; CPA-ML: 300; SWP: 400; ACU: 50; SLL: 100; IS: 100; SLANZ: 50

Leadership. CPA: Judy Mundey (president); SPA: Peter Dudley Symon (general secretary), Jack McPhillips (president); CPA-ML: Neil McLean (chairman); SWP: Jim Percy (national secretary)

Status. Legal

Last Congress. CPA: Twenty-ninth, 6–8 June; SPA: Fifth, September 1984; SWP: Eleventh, 2–6 January 1986

Last Election. 11 July; official government report says communist party polled 0.3 percent of national vote.

Publications. CPA: *Tribune* (weekly), *Australian Left Review* (quarterly); SPA: *Youth Voice* (monthly), *The Guardian* (weekly; Hannah Middleton, editor); CPA-ML: *Vanguard* (weekly), *Australian Communist*; SWP: *Direct Action* (weekly; Steve Painter, editor), *Resistance* (occasional); ACU: *Survey* (monthly; Bill Brown, editor); SLL: *Workers' News* (weekly; Mike Head, editor); IS: *Socialist Action* (monthly)

The re-election in July of the Australian Labor Party (ALP) prime minister Robert Hawke for a third term produced continuing despair among the various communist parties and their satellite organizations of the far left. Underlying the far left's frustration was the government's strong adherence to the ANZUS (Australia–New Zealand–United States) alliance, reflecting the fact that more than 70 percent of Australians support the security treaty with the United States (*WP*, 21 June). The various communist parties ran candidates during the June federal election, but the CPA polled a miserable 0.3 percent of the vote. The pro-Moscow SPA fared even worse, and the pro-Cuban SWP scored just 0.01 percent of the net Senate vote (*Federal Elections 1987, Legislative Research Service* Paper 6). Due to an aberration in the complicated Senate preference voting system, the anti-ANZUS Nuclear Disarmament Party (NDP), despite a decline in its vote from approximately 8 percent in 1984 to just over 1 percent, elected one senator from New South Wales.

This decrease in public impact was manifest not only in the demise of the NDP but also in falling attendances at combined far-left activities such as the Palm Sunday peace rallies. Moreover, their inability to influence core policies of the Labor government—such as support for the joint U.S.-Australian intelligence facilities at Pine Gap, Nurrungar, and North West Cape—led the various communist factions to form the Anti-Bases Coalition to oppose the ANZUS treaty by "direct action."

Another sign that the four major communist parties were trying to reconcile their differences was the National Left Fightback Conference in April, which was attended by members of the CPA despite the continuing adherence of its leading union cadres to the social contract with the ALP government. The conference itself was something of a disappointment. It was a meeting of the SPA, the SWP, and the China-aligned CPA-ML. They were joined by the Tomato Left (so described because they pelted reaffiliated delegates of the four moderate unions with tomatoes), including its ALP members such as George Crawford and Joan Coxsedge, and its non-ALP group led by Bill Hartley of the pro-Libyan Industrial Labor Party.

The CPA, CPA-ML, SPA, and SWP have also been talking about forming a new left party and to this end published an unprecedented joint statement in their official papers (*Vanguard*, 9 December; *The Guardian*, 9 December; *Tribune*, 9 December; *Direct Action*, 9 December). The statement resulted from a national conference on 28 November "where steps were taken to launch a new left party in 1988" (*Direct Action*, 12 December). An official in the Victoria branch of the CPA, Mike Evans, even suggested that the party may drop its name, but there was no sign that these four Marxist-Leninist parties will dissolve their own party apparatus. (*The Age/Sydney Morning Herald*, 24 July.)

The communists' political and electoral impotence vis à vis the ALP, their "lowest common denominator" activities against the U.S.-Australian facilities, and the lessening of international communist polemics between Moscow and Peking all doubtlessly contributed toward this phenomenon of unity. The image of *glasnost'* and *perestroika* in the Soviet Union and the more modern leadership style of Mikhail Gorbachev have led to a lessening of criticism and indeed a more open identification with the Soviets, especially by the Eurocommunist CPA and the pro-Havana SWP. Although it is true that the electoral impact of the communists has seldom been lower, the influence, especially of pro-Soviet elements in labor unions, continues to grow. Solidarity activity in liberation movements in the South Pacific on behalf of the Soviets has also become more important. Moreover, despite their marginal real political importance, communist views and campaigns receive wide coverage in the Australian media. For instance, *Australian Left Review* editorial board member David McKnight wrote a number of key anti-U.S. articles for the prestigious *Sydney Morning Herald*, one of which claimed the CIA was behind the coup in Fiji.

Soviet Activity. In 1987 the semiclandestine pro-Soviet activity of various communist parties and fronts was a high point in open and public relations between Australia and the USSR. The Australian government again expressed its concern over Moscow's political activities in the South West Pacific, endorsing the warnings of visiting Japanese foreign minister Kuranari that increased Soviet commercial and political activity could have a disturbing impact on the area (*FBIS*, 9 January). Eduard Shevardnadze was received cordially by the Australian government in March. However, he met with noisy opposition from Jewish, Afghan, and East European demonstrators (*FEER*, 12 March; *FBIS*, 3 March).

Australian minister for foreign affairs and trade Hayden and Shevardnadze exchanged frank remarks on their countries' interests in the South Pacific (TASS, 4 March; *FBIS*, 3 March). But official Australian concerns about the USSR's regional interest did not seem to be alleviated during the year. Hayden said "there is a surprisingly high level of Soviet-backed activity in South Pacific countries. Australian intelligence reports showed the Soviet Union was recruiting and funding local activists. This work was often done through third parties and Soviet representatives were not directly involved. . . Australia wanted to alert island countries to the problems that could arise if Soviet activities were not closely monitored." (*FBIS*, 10 August.)

This activity in the South Pacific was not only undertaken by pro-Soviet communist parties like the SPA and the New Zealand Socialist Unity Party (SUP) but also accounts for the intense Libyan activity in Australia and the region. Prime Minister Hawke expelled all Libyan diplomats and closed down the People's Bureau Embassy for interfering in domestic and regional affairs (*NYT*, 20 May). Libya's removal followed the widely publicized offers of training to Australian aborigines and South Pacific radicals at a specially convened Asia/South Pacific follow-up to the Third World Conference Against Zionism, Racism, and Imperialism (a World Peace Council offshoot) held in Libya in April. The Soviets went to great lengths to disparage Australia's concerns about Libyan regional activities. A senior Soviet diplomat in Canberra, Yuri Beleobrov, held a news conference to insist there was no reason to take exception to Libya (*FBIS*, 21 April).

Leading members of the Protestant churches and their Commission for Social Responsibility often attend regional and Eastern bloc meetings of the Christian Peace Conference (CPC). The Reverend Wes Campbell, executive director of the churches' peace network, attended a number of such meetings in 1987, and the Reverend Keith Suter of the United Church's Trinity Peace Centre hosted the CPC's chief, Karoly Toth, when he recently visited Australia.

The CPA. The CPA has been unwilling to unify with the other left parties, but faced with a decline in the party's political fortunes, its leaders now try to incorporate with other communist parties and amalgamate other radical groups, including women's, environmental, and antinuclear groups, to unify all elements to the left of the ruling ALP. The *Tribune* did not report the office bearers elected at the CPA congress in June. One explanation offered was that the CPA had already decided to participate in a new party of the left and did not want its national officers to overshadow its representatives in the leadership of the new party. The CPA remains committed to the Australian Council of Trade Unions' (ACTU) accord with the Labor government, and it is hard to see how this key policy can be knitted in with a common electoral program for the new left party. Indeed, one of the accord's principal advocates, Laurie Carmichael, a former national chairman of the CPA, was elected to the ACTU. This is the first time that a communist has held such a high-level position in Australia's peak union body. The CPA still retains significant influence in major labor unions such as those for metalworkers, Australian railways, and electricians, and through delegate affiliation it exerts significant influence in state and federal branches of labor councils and the socialist-left faction of the ALP.

The CPA is now far more muted in criticizing the Soviet Union. Leading cadres resumed their trips to that country, and the party weekly again accepted advertising from the Soviet Union's Progress Publishers (*Tribune*, 1 April, 18 February).

The year began with leading cadre Dennis Freney canvassing the possibility of liquidating the party organ, the *Tribune*, which has a circulation of some 3,000, along with other leftist periodicals; these would be replaced by a joint publication whose circulation he forecast at some 10,000.

The CPA's objective is to build an effective party. Its participation in both the Broad Left Conference in 1986 and the Fightback Conference in April 1987 have been steps toward that goal. Party veteran Eric Aarons, writing in the *Tribune*, says the way forward is through a process of renewal rather than staying the same, waiting for the tide to turn, or being subsumed by the ALP.

To advance the renewal process, the CPA argues that there is now space on the left of the spectrum beside the ALP for a new party to be active. Old doctrinaire socialist demands will fail. The new strategy calls for "intermediate" demands, presumably too hot for the ALP to handle but not so extreme as to alienate potential support. (*Socialist Action*, May/June.)

The CPA has focused its international work on solidarity with the New People's Army (NPA) in the Philippines. Its radio programs in Melbourne and Sydney, together with the party press, describe the exploits of the NPA. CPA representatives visited the NPA's training camp in Bataan to express solidarity, and the international representative of the Communist Party of the Philippines, Luis Jalandoni, visited Australia following his presence at the conference in Libya in April. CPA cadres still dominate in such peace front organizations as the Congress for International Cooperation and Disarmament (CICD), which outside of Victoria is called People for Nuclear Disarmament (PND).

The SWP. The SWP is probably the only new left party in the Western world to align with the Soviet bloc. Since it split from the Trotskyist Fourth International in 1985, the SWP has been closely tied to Havana. SWP cadres organize and join the annual work brigades in Cuba, and the party paper publishes verbatim excerpts from *Granma*, the Cuban communist organ (*Direct Action*, 4 February, 27 July, 9 September). The SWP also plays a leading role in the Australia-Cuba Friendship Association, but the function distinguishing it from the other communist parties is its principal role in solidarity fronts with the various Central American Marxist factions.

The SWP openly identifies with the Soviet Union, its congresses are attended by members of the pro-Moscow SPA, and since 1985 its youth section has attended Soviet-orchestrated congresses. But 1987 saw, for the first time, Soviet embassy officials from Canberra addressing public meetings of the SWP. To commemorate the 70th anniversary of the Bolshevik Revolution, the SWP organized a series of functions in all cities highlighted by a dinner at the SWP's Melbourne headquarters addressed by a Soviet diplomat and SWP national secretary Jim Percy. Leading cadres now go on study missions to the Soviet Union, and others participate in extreme-left delegations to Soviet front meetings in Third World countries like Libya (*Direct Action*, 28 January, 13 May). The weekly SWP paper reflects the Soviet line on disparate issues, enthusing over official Soviet doctrines of *perestroika* and *glasnost'* and describing the modern era as "the Soviet century" (ibid., 11 November). Regular ads appear for the Sandinista *Barricada*, the Soviet *Moscow News*, and the Cuban *Granma*. The SWP has minor influence in tramways' and clerical officers' unions but has returned to campus politics, playing a significant role in the revival of an extreme-left national student union.

The SPA. The SPA is the largest pro-Soviet party in the South Pacific and provides a reliable transmission belt for USSR foreign policy. Its influence has been reduced since most of its trade union officials left to form the ACU. It now produces a weekly newspaper and operates New Era bookshops in most states. The SPA gave continual emphasis to opposing what the extreme left of Australia calls the U.S. bases (which are in fact U.S.-Australian joint facilities, as there are no U.S. military personnel based there). Although it still maintains its own peace front, the Australian Peace Committee, the SPA's support for unity of the various communist parties began during 1987 with their support for the Australian Anti-Bases Coalition (*Guardian*, 28 January). Opposition to these key Western intelligence facilities is a lowest common denominator for the SPA and the other Marxist groups. The party lent its full support to bringing together 70 delegates in Adelaide to prepare nationwide protests (ibid., 25 February). Nevertheless, an October demonstration mobilized barely 1,000 activists and received disappointingly little publicity.

The SPA attacked various aspects of the Labor government's national unity policies. It published a special booklet attacking Defence Minister Kim Beazley's "White Paper on Defence," which the SPA said cast Australia in the role of "the new Pacific policeman" (*Guardian*, 25 March). In April the SPA took the lead in organizing rallies outside U.S. consulates protesting the U.S. air raid on Libya. Common interests with the pro-Cuban SWP were expressed by the continual advertisements that appeared in the SPA paper for the Fifth Australian Work Brigade to Cuba, organized by the Australia-Cuba Friendship Association, and the Fourth Work Brigade to Nicaragua, organized by the Resource and Action Committee of Latin America. These work brigades have numbered up to 100 people and include academics, unionists, public servants, and students who do not necessarily belong to any communist party but share the major passion of Australia's extreme left—anti-Americanism.

The SPA's solidarity work with pro-Soviet elements among immigrant communities from Greece, Uruguay, and the Arab world was evidenced by continuing publicity given to functions of the pro-Soviet faction in those communities (*Guardian*, 4 March, 24 July). In fact, the secretary of the Greek Orthodox community in New South Wales stood as the SPA candidate in the House of Representatives, and Habib Fares of the Lebanese community stood on the SPA Senate team in that state. The SPA also plays a leading role in the Australia–East Germany, Australia-Czechoslovakia, Australia-Poland, and Australia-Bulgaria friendship associations. (*Guardian*, 24 July.) The Australian federal elections saw the SPA stand Senate tickets in four major states: Queensland, South Australia, New South Wales, and Victoria (ibid., 8 July), while in further moves toward left unity they stood joint CPA-SPA tickets for the Senate in South Australia.

The party's international solidarity work in the South Pacific seems to have increased. Leading party cadres continued the pattern of overseas visits to the Eastern bloc and front organizations. Party chairman Peter Symon and *Guardian* editor Hannah Middleton attended the consultative meeting of communist parties in Mongolia in July (*Guardian*,

15 July), and Alan Miller, the Victoria state secretary of the SPA, returned in June from a study tour of East Germany, Hungary, and Czechoslovakia (ibid., 24 July). The Young Socialist League was represented at the first preparatory meeting for the World Festival of Youth and Students in Moscow in February (ibid., 18 February) and at the Fifteenth Congress of the International Union of Students in Havana (*Youth Voice*, December).

The party organization seems particularly strongly based in New South Wales and South Australia. As a lead up to the U.S.-Soviet summit and the anti-bases protests, the SPA played a major role in organizing the South Australian trade union peace conference attended by 170 trade union delegates and partially funded by the Australian government.

The ACU. Although it is one of the smallest in numbers of Australia's communist groups, the ACU is perhaps the most important because of the involvement of its members in the leadership of major unions. Among the major unions whose leaders are involved in the ACU are Pat Geraghty, federal secretary of the Seamen's Union of Australia; Barry Swayne, general secretary of the Miners' Federation; Stan Sharkey, assistant national secretary of the Building Workers' Industrial Union; and Bob Sharkey, assistant secretary of the New South Wales Teachers' Federation.

Whereas the pro-Moscow SPA retains some influence in the Australian Federated Union of Locomotive Enginemen, the ACU retains the allegiance of the bulk of pro-Soviet trade unionists. This may explain why the Eastern bloc, much to the annoyance of the SPA, invites both groups to important front meetings. Thus, ACU national secretary Pat Clancy and SPA national secretary Peter Symon both attended the same consultative meeting of the communist and workers' parties of the Asian-Pacific region, held in Mongolia 7–9 July. In fact Clancy, Australia's most important pro-Soviet unionist, died while on his return from this conference. A death notice from the ACU appeared on the front page of *Pravda* (24 July) and an obituary on page 4 (26 July).

The ACU still disagrees with the other communist parties about its support for the Labor government's industrial wage accord with the official trade union movement, and therefore it will probably not support the other communist parties' moves toward greater unity. Together with the SPA, the ACU is involved in the Australia-USSR Friendship Association.

The CPA-ML. The emergence in late 1986 of a new chairman of Australia's pro-Peking party, Neil McLean, brought a slightly more open style to Australia's most secretive communist party but saw no reversal of the CPA-ML's decline. McLean is one of the few student Maoists recruited during the Vietnam era to have stayed with the party. He has been an important cadre since his days as president of the communist-controlled and now defunct Australian Union of Students. McLean's ascension to leadership was taken seriously in China; he was officially received there in January (*FBIS*, 7 January).

McLean strongly supported the moves for left unity expressed by the Fightback Conference in April. In view of past attacks by the CPA-ML on Soviet "revisionism," this new turn in policy was marked by a remarkable toning down in criticism of the Soviets (but not the Vietnamese) and in a previously unthinkable exchange of articles on "left unity" with the pro-Moscow SPA. (*Vanguard*, 11 February.) McLean was prominently pictured with other communist faction leaders and other members of the extreme left at the Fightback Conference (ibid., 4 March). The CPA-ML is unusually close to two liberation movements: the Palestine Liberation Organization and the Pan Africanist Congress.

CPA-ML fortunes were not aided, however, when the Victoria state government seized $A2 million of assets from the CPA-ML's only trade union, the Builders Laborers Federation, led by the party's vice-chairman Norman Lesley Gallagher. The state and federal actions against its traditional union base have led the CPA-ML to attack the Hawke Labor administration, and it is its increasing isolation that explains this normally sectarian group's passion for "unity of the left."

Trotskyist Parties. The SLL, like its British parent, has split three ways following the row between its guru, Gerry Healey, and its most famous cadre, Vanessa Redgrave. The SLL continues to produce its newspaper, *Workers' News*, which is mainly filled with reports of inter-Trotskyist faction fights. The SLANZ is equally frenetic, appearing at left-wing demonstrations to denounce the other communists as heretics. The IS seems to have some presence in white-collar unions in Queensland, New South Wales, and the Australian capital territory, such as the Australian Clerical Officers' Association.

Michael Danby
Melbourne, Australia

Bangladesh

Population. 107,087,586
Party. Communist Party of Bangladesh (CPB)
Founded. 1948 (as East Pakistan Communist Party; banned in 1954; re-emerged in 1971 following the establishment of Bangladesh)
Membership. 5,000 (claimed; Calcutta *Statesman*, 1 May)
General Secretary. Muhammed Farhad until October; thereafter, Saifuddin Ahmed Manik
Secretariat. 10 members
Central Committee. 39 members
Status. Reportedly banned as of 14 November; current status uncertain
Last Congress. Fourth, 7–11 April
Last Election. 7 May 1986; CPB won 5 of the 300 contested seats in the parliament; an independent member of parliament later joined the CPB, giving it 6 seats in the 330-seat assembly; parliament was dissolved in December 1987.
Auxiliary Organizations. Trade Union Centre, Cultural Front, Chatra Union, Khetmozdur Samiti, Mahila Parishad, Jubo Union
Publication. *Ekota* (in Bengali)

In April, 900 CPB delegates met in Dhaka for the Fourth Party Congress. They endorsed a party line calling for a "national democratic revolution." Under this formula the CPB will continue to contest elections and coordinate antiregime activities as part of an alliance of "progressive, liberal democratic forces." Simultaneously, the CPB pledged to retain an "independent identity," exclusive of its tactical alliance with the Awami League. (Dhaka, *New Nation*, 8 April.) This two-track strategy recognized that the CPB lacked the organizational muscle to topple the government or win elections on the strength of its own following. Consequently, the party's call for what Central Committee secretary Ajoy Roy called a "united front of progressive forces" (*WMR*, August) was enthusiastically endorsed by the CPB congress.

As part of its strategy of forging links with left-wing, secular opposition parties, the CPB invited a wide range of Bangladeshi political parties to send observers to the party congress. Many of the opposition observers were long-time pro-Soviet Marxists. These included representatives from the National Awami Party, the Gana Azadi League, the Bangladesh Kirshak-Sramik Awami League (BAKSAL), and the Samyabadi Dal. The country's most prominent opposition leaders—the Awami League's Sheikh Hasina Wazed and the Bangladesh National Party's Begum Khaleda Zia—also attended the congress. Party organizers skillfully orchestrated local media coverage of the congress to project the image of a united opposition. General Secretary Farhad scored another public relations coup by circulating the CPB draft resolution among noncommunist intellectuals prior to the party congress; according to Farhad, the political manifesto adopted by the CPB incorporated over 100 suggestions put forward by nonparty members (Calcutta, *Statesman*, 1 May).

The Fourth CPB Congress also grappled with the perennial problem of promoting the party's ideological commitment to Marxism without offending the religious sensitivities of the nation's Muslim majority. Farhad maintained that the CPB was not anti-Islamic, as opponents claimed; the party, he said, only opposed "obscurantist forces" that acted on behalf of "international imperialism." In a significant departure from previous CPB formulations on the subject, the congress explicitly recognized that most Bangladeshis are pious Muslims, and so it welcomed Muslim support. Observers speculated that softening the party line on religion might induce the pro-Moscow National Awami Party to rejoin the CPB fold. In addition, the CPB hoped to counter the growing political threat posed by the Islamic fundamentalist party, the Jamiat-i-Islami. To signal the CPB's embrace of religious toleration, Farhad authorized local cadres to broadcast Koranic readings and allow party members to say prayers (Dhaka, *Holiday*, 13 February).

Predictably, the CPB congress rigorously criticized the "fascist and anti-people regime" of President Hussain Mohammed Ershad (Dhaka, *Bangladesh Observer*, 10 April). The CPB claimed that Ershad had subjected the country to "growing neocolonial bondage." According to CPB theoreticians, the regime was an unholy alliance between the army, "100 big capitalists," multinational corporations, and "an emergent class of comprador-bureaucratic freebooting capitalists" (*Statesman*, 1 May). The manifesto attacked Ershad for failing to alleviate economic hardships caused by massive floods, soaring inflation, and a mounting debt-repayment burden. To address these crises, the CPB proposed remedial measures that catered to the interests of selected CPB constituencies, such as workers, students, and peasants. CPB proposals included renationalizing firms that the regime sold to the private sector, lowering bus fares, and providing monetary incentives to farmers (*Bangladesh Observer*, 9 April).

Although the congress paid lip service to the revolutionary overthrow of the government, party leaders resisted pressures from militant cadres to withdraw from parliament and wage street demonstrations to force Ershad's resignation. The CPB acknowledged that the parliamentary and presidential elections that set the stage for the lifting of martial law in November 1986 were fraudulent. The CPB was unwilling, however, to forfeit its parliamentary seats—a stance that soon set the CPB apart from allied opposition parties urging an opposition withdrawal from parliament. As the opposition campaign to oust Ershad gathered momentum at the end of 1987, the CPB came under intense pressure to alter the party line laid down at the April congress.

On the international front, the CPB adhered faithfully to Soviet party pronouncements. CPB leaders had traveled to Moscow to iron out the party platform prior to the Fourth Congress (see, for instance, *FEER*, 3 April 1986). The final resolution railed against "U.S. imperialism" and endorsed Soviet arms control proposals—stands that the Soviet press noted with approval (*Pravda*, 8 April). The CPB took a benign view of Indian intentions in the region and blamed "imperialist forces and their local agents" for creating tensions in Indo-Bangladeshi relations. Delegations from 17 fraternal communist parties from around the world attended the session. For the first time, the Bengali-dominated Communist Party of India–Marxist sent a delegation to Dhaka (*New Nation*, 10 June). In line with Moscow's efforts to downplay its ideological differences with Beijing, CPB propagandists did not single out China for attack, although the CPB also did not invite the Chinese party to send a delegation to Dhaka.

Leadership and Organization. Party membership increased from the 3,000 members listed for the Third Party Congress in 1980 to 5,000 members in 1987. The 900 delegates who attended the congress represented 60 of Bangladesh's 64 districts and 300 of the country's 460 subdistricts (*Statesman*, 1 May). Party leaders cited these statistics to show that the CPB is a national political party—a claim that is impossible to verify in the absence of reliable statistics on party membership. Historically, the CPB appealed mainly to students and trade unions in large urban centers such as Dhaka, Chittagong, Mymensingh, and Rajshahi. CPB support in rural areas, where 75 percent of the population resides, has never been impressive.

Roughly two-thirds of the Fourth Congress delegates were under 35 years old, and the CPB seems to be trying to infuse new blood into the aging party structure. An occupational breakdown of the party's delegates showed that 25 percent were "workers and peasants" (including a handful of illiterate delegates), 13 percent were "teachers," 38 percent were "students," and 24 percent were full-time "party workers" whose source of income was not revealed. As with all Bangladeshi political parties, women play a peripheral role in the CPB. According to party statistics, only 20 of the 900 delegates were women. (Ibid.)

The CPB openly supports six front organizations that carry the party's message to targeted constituencies. In his report to the congress, Farhad claimed that the combined membership of all CPB fronts totaled 825,000. To highlight the party's outreach strategy in rural areas, Farhad noted that Khetmozdur Samiti, the CPB's peasant front, enrolled 200,000 new members during the six years since the last party congress. Other CPB fronts include the Trade Union Centre (workers), the Cultural Front (intellectuals), the Mahila Parishad (women), the Chatra Union (students), and the Jubo Union (youth). The CPB did not reveal membership statistics for any of these organizations. Internationally, the CPB participates in the entire spectrum of Soviet-sponsored fronts, such as the World Peace Council and the World Federation of Trade Unions.

The Fourth Party Congress endorsed a number of key leadership changes. Moni Singh, the elderly and infirm CPB stalwart who had guided the party since its earliest days as the East Pakistan Communist Party, was relieved of his party duties and accorded the honorary title "founding father." His position as CPB president was abolished. In practice, however, Farhad assumed Singh's mantle as party theoretician. Saifuddin Ahmed Manik became the second-ranking CPB official when the party congress assigned him the newly created position of assistant general secretary.

The congress also confirmed the selection of a ten-member Secretariat, the party's center of power. Secretariat members include Manazoorul Ahsan Khan, Mujahidul Islam Selim, Abdus Salam, Ajoy Roy, Nurul Islam, Matiur Rahman, Osman Ghani, Shams-ud Doha, Shahidullah Chowdhury, and Sankar Ghose (*Bangladesh Observer*, 12 April). Members of the CPB inner circle routinely affix their names to theoretical formulations put out by the party (see, for instance, *WMR*, August), but little else is known about these leaders. At least two secretaries, however, are Hindus, judging from their surnames. Only Farhad held a high party post in addition to a seat in parliament (*New Nation*, 11 November). The CPB congress also authorized an expansion of the Central Committee from 33 to 39 members.

In October Farhad traveled to Moscow for one of his periodic consultations at the Kremlin. While in Moscow, the 49-year-old general secretary suffered a heart attack and died (Dhaka Domestic Service, 10 October; *FBIS*, 15 October). From all outward appearances, Farhad's death did not precipitate a power struggle within the CPB; Assistant General Secretary Manik assumed the top position in the party. The CPB did, however, lose a parliamentary seat with Farhad's demise, and it faced the unpleasant prospect of having to campaign for his seat in a by-election tentatively scheduled for early 1988. Political events prevented the Ershad government from staging any elections, however, as Bangladeshi opposition parties mounted a broad-based and surprisingly effective campaign to force Ershad's resignation.

Domestic Political Developments. Although President Ershad engineered his own election as a civilian president and commanded a two-thirds majority in parliament, his ruling Jatiya Party did not have support in the country. Many Bangladeshis regard Ershad as a corrupt and lackluster leader bent on defending the army's political prerogatives against mounting opposition calls for free and fair elections.

Since Ershad's seizure of power in 1982 the CPB has been active in a broad-based opposition campaign to overthrow the regime. Throughout 1987 the CPB participated in an eight-party, left-of-center coalition headed by the Awami League (AL). A rival, seven-party opposition combine is headed by the Bangladesh National Party (BNP). Unlike the AL-led alliance, however, the BNP and its partners refused to participate in any election staged while Ershad was in power. To complicate the picture, two other opposition alliances incorporating an independent left-wing grouping and a collection of Islamic fundamentalist parties vied for influence. So long as the 23 parties that spanned four political alliances were divided, Ershad was reasonably confident that he could survive the opposition challenge.

Two events, however, served to unite Ershad's political opposition. In July and August the worst floods in decades inundated two-thirds of Bangladesh, causing massive economic dislocations. Opposition parties capitalized on the economic discontent caused by the disaster. For its part, the CPB organized peasant demonstrations demanding that the government institute a nationwide food-for-work program (*Bangladesh Observer*, 24 September).

The second event that compounded Ershad's political difficulties was the ill-considered District Council Bill that he submitted to parliament in July. Under provisions of the legislation, army personnel would serve on local administrative bodies. All opposition parties condemned the bill as an attempt by Ershad to institutionalize the army's political role in administering the country. Although Ershad soon withdrew the bill from consideration, the opposition used the unforeseen opportunity to its advantage. To the surprise of many observers, Sheikh Hasina and Begum Zia agreed to submerge their political differences and combine forces against Ershad. Their agreement to force new elections—and possibly trigger another army coup—put the CPB in a ticklish position. Although the CPB was anxious to capitalize on the public discontent over Ershad's leadership, party leaders feared the CPB could lose its parliamentary seats if fresh elections were held. Consequently, the CPB acted cautiously and called for Ershad's resignation without demanding elections (*FEER*, 27 July). On 21 July the combined opposition staged a three-day general strike that immobilized the country. Confident that the nation would rally behind its call for Ershad's removal from office, the 23 opposition parties awaited the end of the monsoon season to wage an all-out test of strength with the regime.

Faced with a potentially violent challenge to his authority, Ershad vowed to oppose the "politics of terrorism and hooliganism" (Dhaka Domestic Service, 19 November; *FBIS*, 20 November). Furthermore, Ershad claimed that "the army will not interfere as long as I am president" (*NYT*, 15 November). On 27 November the embattled president declared a state of national emergency. Under this constitutional device, Ershad suspended individual liberties, imposed press censorship, closed the universities, and banned strikes and demonstrations. Most key opposition figures languished under house arrest or in prison. The opposition stuck to its nonnegotiable demand that Ershad step down.

At year's end the political situation in Bangladesh remained a stalemate. Ershad scheduled national elections for February 1988. The opposition pledged to render the contest meaningless by refusing to field candidates. Observers speculated that if Ershad failed to negotiate a political settlement that would allow the country's precarious economy to resume functioning, the army might invoke martial law (*FEER*, 24 December). Although the CPB did not play a pivotal role in 1987's opposition campaign, moderate elements within the AL, the BNP, and the government itself share the fear that the CPB and its radical partners could be the main beneficiaries of a protracted political crisis (*FEER*, 26 November). Using his emergency powers, Ershad banned the CPB and two minor communist parties. It is not clear whether the ban will be lifted in advance of scheduled elections (Delhi Domestic Service, 14 November; *FBIS*, 16 November).

Foreign Affairs. The political turmoil in Bangladesh did not affect the country's external relations with either the Soviet Union or China. Bangladesh maintains cool but correct relations with the Soviets; Sino-Bangladeshi relations remained extremely cordial.

During the April party congress, CPB spokesmen pointed out to the press that the Soviets wished to improve bilateral relations with Bangladesh. Party spokesmen claimed that Mikhail Gorbachev's omission of Bangladesh from his July 1986 Vladivostok speech was not a slight but a "drafting oversight" (*Statesman*, 1 May). Five weeks after the conclusion of the CPB congress, Soviet deputy foreign minister I. A. Rogachev arrived in Dhaka for official talks. The two sides signed agreements covering shipping and air services (Dhaka Overseas Service, 23 May; *FBIS*, 26 May). Two-way trade, however, remains stagnant, totaling only $100 million per year (*New Nation*, 5 July). The Soviets also offered to assist Bangladesh in constructing a river bridge—a showcase project probably designed to counter Chinese assistance in building the Buriganga "friendship bridge" outside Dhaka.

In July Ershad paid an official visit to China, his first since becoming a civilian president (*Bangladesh Observer*, 5 July). Arriving at a time when India and China were exchanging harsh words over their long-standing border dispute, Ershad pledged that Bangladesh would be neutral in the event of a Sino-Indian confrontation (*FEER*, 30 July). The Chinese again signaled their support for Ershad in December when Bangladesh was paralyzed by opposition-led demonstrations. At the height of the crisis, Shah Moazzam Hussain, the deputy prime minister and head of Ershad's Jatiya Party, arrived in Beijing for consultations with Chinese party officials (Dhaka Domestic Service, 1 December; *FBIS*, 1 December).

Douglas C. Makeig
U.S. Department of Defense

Note: The views expressed in this article are the author's own and do not necessarily reflect those of the U.S. government or of any U.S. agency.

Burma

Population. 38,822,484
Party. Burmese Communist Party (BCP)
Founded. 1939
Membership. 3,000 (1979); estimated armed strength 8,000–15,000
Chairman. Thakin Ba Thein Tin (73, Sino-Burmese)
Vice Chairman. Thakin Pe Tint (71, Burmese)
Politburo. Thakin Ba Thein Tin, Thakin Pe Tint, Khin Maung Gyi (60), Myo Myint (63), Tin Yee (65), Kyaw Mya (72), Kyin Maung (65, Chinese) (Ages of officials: *FEER*, 4 June)
Central Committee. 29 members: Aye Hla, Aye Ngwe, Bran Ba Di, Khin Maung Gyi (secretary), Kyauk Mi Lai, Kyaw Mya, Kyaw Myint, Kyaw Zaw, Kyin Maung, Mya Thaung, Myint Min, Myo Myint, Ni Tu Wu, Pe Thaung, Po Ngwe Sai, Po Tint, Sai Aung Win, San Tu, Saw Ba Moe, Saw Han, Soe Hein, Soe Lwin, Thakin Ba Thein Tin,

Thakin Pe Tint, Tin Yee, Tint Hlaing, Tun Lwin, Ye Tun, Zaw Mai
Status. Illegal
Last Congress. Third, 9 September–2 October 1985
Last Election. N/a
Auxiliary Organizations. None identified
Publications. *People's Power* (*Pyeithu Ah Nar*) (Voice of the People of Burma [VOPB], 2 December; *FBIS*, 3 December). No copies have reached the West. The BCP broadcasts over VOPB, apparently located along the Sino-Burmese border inside Burma.

Western journalist Bertil Lintner of the *FEER* visited BCP-held territory in 1986–1987; his observations, along with the VOPB broadcast of the Central Committee Political Report to the Third Party Congress, provide a unique view of the BCP (even though the new Political Report lacks much of the illuminating detail of its 1978 predecessor; see *YICA*, 1981). Lintner's account provides the only firsthand Western contact to date with the BCP leadership and administration, though it fits well with previously available information. (The major part of Lintner's observations was published in *FEER* in two installments: "War in the North" on 28 May, hereafter cited as Lintner 1; and "The Rise and Fall of the Communists" on 4 June, hereafter Lintner 2.)

Leadership and Organization. Lintner's account includes biographic information for a group of BCP leaders, previously identified as members of the BCP Politburo (Lintner 2, p. 28); see, for example, the biography of Thakin Ba Thein Tin below.

Lintner characterizes the present top BCP leadership as "aging" and says there is no second line of younger cadre trained to take over because of a wide generation gap between the veteran leaders and "younger intellectuals" who joined the party in the 1970s (Lintner 1, pp. 50–51). These younger intellectuals were probably ethnic Burmese students, disenchanted by Rangoon's economic stagnation and the lack of jobs during the early- to mid-1970s. Such recruits may have contributed to more sophisticated BCP propaganda (particularly in the use of official Rangoon statistics in attacks on government policies) after the late 1970s.

Lintner notes a general shakeup of the BCP's civil and military structure in 1987 that included a consolidation of the old war zones and "bureaus" into regions. Yet neither the new regions nor the bureaus they reportedly supersede conform precisely to the BCP organization as reflected in the 1978 Political Report.

In December a VOPB broadcast indicated the publication of a BCP organ, *People's Power*, which takes its name from a party weekly published for several years in the late 1940s. Neither frequency nor format of the new publication are yet known. (VOPB, 2 December; *FBIS*, 3 December.)

VOPB broadcasts continue to be much weaker in strength than before the April 1985–January 1986 break in transmission (*YICA*, 1987). As a result, the incidence of unintelligible sections of broadcasts also continues to be higher than previously. Unintelligible or tentative words/passages noted by *FBIS* are designated in parentheses.

Party Internal Affairs. The major statement of party policy that reached the outside world during 1987 was the final portion of the Central Committee Political Report to the Third Congress, broadcast in four installments by the VOPB (21 December 1986, 31 January, 15 February, 8 March; *FBIS*, 9 January, 12, 18 February, 13 March). Besides implementing the "line and tasks laid down at the 1976 Central Committee plenary session as well as the resolutions of the 1984–1985 Central Committee plenary session," the BCP will implement the nine future programs, or "nine future tasks," defined as follows:

1. Completely eliminating right deviationism emerging within the party while at the same [time] correcting remaining left deviationism and maintaining vigilance to prevent its emerging again.
2. Keeping the military task as the central pillar and building the party, army, base areas, (?and the united front) (words indistinct).
3. Building party organizations so that they will be strong in all aspects—ideologically, politically, organizationally—and in their style of work while at the same time consolidating and extending the (words indistinct).
4. Building the People's Army, which is under the direct and absolute leadership of the party, into a stronger force and making it an army that can not only serve the people better but that also has a better and sharper military capability.
5. Systematically reorganizing and strengthening mass and class organizations, such as the peasants' unions and the women's unions, and taking steps to make farm workers and poor peasants (?accept) the leadership of the peasants' unions.

6. Systematically reforming people's administrative organs based on peasants' unions. Moves must be directed at making people's administrative organs into rural people's power organs that are based on the alliance of the poor and middle-class peasants.

7. Systematically and fruitfully carrying out under different regional conditions the agrarian revolution—the main axle of the people's democratic revolution; making the production movement a success; and (?building) strong base areas. At the same time, new base areas must be built systematically, gradually, and in a planned manner.

8. Remaining in close unity with all forces in the existing united front and endeavoring to unify with both the rural and urban patriotic forces, with which we have not yet established a united front today, on the basis of directing the fight at the common enemy—the military government—and with the objective of abolishing the BSPP [government] one-party dictatorship and establishing a multi-party democratic system.

9. Striving for closer unity among Marxist-Leninist parties on the basis of the principles of Marxism-Leninism-proletarian internationalism (words indistinct) complete equality, independence, mutual respect, and noninterference in the internal affairs of another party. (passage indistinct) (VOPB, 8 March; *FBIS*, 13 March.)

On strategy, the second of the future tasks reflects the continued de-emphasis of the "three banners" associated with the abortive BCP-government peace negotiations of 1981 (*YICA*, 1982). In a pre-anniversary commentary, the VOPB advocated welcoming the party's anniversary "by pledging to keep the armed struggle as the main form of struggle and correctly integrating it with other appropriate forms of struggle and carrying out the armed revolution through to the end . . . A violent revolution is the only means if the workers, peasants, and the oppressed classes are to seize power in Burma." The BCP is "flying high the victory banner of the revolutionary war." (VOPB, 16 August; *FBIS*, 18 August.) Thakin Ba Thein Tin himself, in his 48th anniversary message, declared that "The enemy must be destroyed by closely following the strategic and tactical lines of the People's War" (VOPB, 20 August; *FBIS*, 21 August).

Disagreement exists among some senior cadre on this emphasis on armed struggle, according to Lintner. Some cadre maintain "that the time is not yet ripe for war, arguing that, for the moment at least, it is better to work within the existing power structure." The chief advocate of this line was "the first political commissar of the BCP's northeastern base area," Than Shwe, who recently resigned from the Central Committee and then quit the party. (Lintner 1, p. 51.) Yet Than Shwe's Central Committee resignation must have come before the VOPB's 7 February 1986 broadcast describing the new committee, because his name was not included (*FBIS*, 12 February 1986).

A second policy split within the party, identified by Lintner, is that the "younger intellectuals" criticize the old BCP propaganda of the 1940s. Feudalism and imperialism are two major concepts that these younger party members claim are outdated (Lintner 1, p. 55), but the old party statements continue. For example, on 16 August the VOPB emphasized that the BCP's basic line has always been the eradication of imperialism, feudalism, and bureaucratic capitalism (*FBIS*, 18 August).

Such splits could be behind comments on errors within the party in the Political Report: "numerous wrong methods of thinking and working are hampering the work of making the party stronger. The errors are mainly right deviationism. But left deviationism also exists . . . Petty bourgeois thinking is being reflected within the party" (VOPB, 15 February; *FBIS*, 18 February). These concerns were repeated in the first of the future tasks. Lintner noted a rectification campaign "reportedly planned for 1987" that was to include a shake-up of BCP civil administration and an attempt to improve local cadre performance (Lintner 1, p. 50). The fifth and sixth future tasks appear to reflect such an intention in calling for reorganization of local mass organizations and the reform of local administrative bodies. It may also be reflected in the declaration in the preface to the first issue of *People's Power* that, to strengthen and consolidate the party, "On the basis of the policies laid down, party organizations in all departments and regions must be consolidated" (VOPB, 5 December; *FBIS*, 8 December). This phrasing appears to echo Thakin Ba Thein Tin's anniversary call that "All levels of party organizations must be united and consolidated so as to concentrate efforts on the military task" (VOPB, 20 August; *FBIS*, 21 August). The party chairman also called for resolute opposition to "selfish attitudes and outlooks and deeds which ignore the people's sufferings" (VOPB, 20 August; *FBIS*, 21 August), a veiled attack on administrative shortcomings.

Although the BCP has long been aware of developing problems in its local administration, the party seems to have made little progress in correcting them. Lintner notes that he found many local BCP administrative offices empty, and those local administrators he did find complained about the declining activity of the peasants unions, which had strongly supported the BCP. Schools in BCP areas are "few and far between," he notes, in contrast to the Kachin rebel areas, and most of those schools are not run by the BCP "but by villagers, Buddhist monks and, in the northern Wa hills, by Baptist church workers." BCP officials reportedly explained the situation as the result of a lack of funds and problems finding suitable teachers. Lintner's explanation is important: "Aside from its financial problems, the BCP's neglect in administering its northeastern base areas is related to its general attitude towards the region. Unlike the Kachin and other ethnic minority rebels, who seek autonomy from Rangoon for their own people in Northern Burma, the BCP views their northern base areas only as springboards from which to spread their influence and control throughout the country. Hence, drafting recruits appears to be the BCP's main preoccupation in the northeast" (Lintner 2, p. 29). Insofar as this is correct, it represents a devastating criticism of a party that, since 1975, has made its primary base in ethnic minority areas, on which it depends both for its own recruits and for rebel allies.

Although their criticism has not succeeded in changing BCP propaganda, the young intellectuals do influence the BCP's criticism of Rangoon's policies. For example, a 1 October VOPB broadcast cited government rice production statistics to demonstrate that production growth had fallen behind population growth and that export earnings had declined. In addition, the standard attack on "feudal landlordism" in ethnic Burmese areas was transformed into a detailed criticsm of the move of former hereditary rulers into local government administration in the minority-dominated Shan and Kachin states (VOPB, 4 January); this reflects a continuing, albeit inconsistent, increase in BCP sophistication. A more traditional line was the Political Report's attack on Rangoon's agrarian policies as intended to maintain "landlordism under different forms" and promote "exploitation under bureaucrat capitalism. The moves further impoverished farm laborers and poor peasants and only served the rich peasants and landlords" (VOPB, 21 December 1986; *FBIS*, 9 January).

Other government policies that came under attack included the Rangoon application for "least-developed country" status with the U.N. (in order to qualify for special economic assistance). According to the VOPB, this proved that "the BSPP military clique is economically bankrupt as well as politically isolated at home and abroad." Claiming widespread disunity among government forces, the VOPB noted reports of government detention of some 200 military personnel (VOPB, 16 August; *FBIS*, 18 August).

The government's 5 September announcement of the demonetarization of 25, 35, and 75 kyat banknotes was a particular target for BCP attack as clearly demonstrating "the selfishness, the flagrancy, and the vileness of the military government" (VOPB, 4 October; *FBIS*, 5 October). This action was "designed to rob peoples of all nationalities of their currency . . . Organizationally, the mask of socialism that had been put on has been uncovered, and the antagonism between the military government and the people has reached its peak. For them it is a time when national unity is at its lowest level, while the unity of the revolutionary forces has begun to flourish" (VOPB, 10 December; *FBIS*, 14 December). As with previous demonetarizations, it is probable that the BCP took some financial losses, along with ethnic rebels. Business at the Karen insurgent Thai border smuggling point of Mae Sot was said to be "reeling," although smuggling centers along the border of Thailand's Mae Hong Son province further north were little affected (Bangkok, *The Nation*, 7 September; *FBIS*, 8 September).

The drug trade has reportedly become financially important to the BCP since about 1979, compensating in part for the scaling down of aid from China. According to Lintner, shortly after the Third Congress BCP leaders decided to move against private opium trading, manufacture of low-grade heroin, and other illegal activities that had involved the local cadre. (Such measures presumably would not apply to party-sanctioned opium trading.) Punishment for party members involved in unauthorized opium trading, and even execution for possession of more than two kilograms of either low-grade or high-grade heroin, were said to be part of this year's rectification campaign. Lintner notes potential conflicts within the party apparatus and predictions by "local observers" that such measures would be abandoned to avoid party splits. (Lintner 2, pp. 32–33.) In contrast to this reported BCP crackdown on private drug trafficking, the Burmese government reported that the Third Congress adopted a three-year economic plan to smuggle opium and jade in order to finance purchases of weapons and medical supplies (*Bangkok Post*, 29 January, citing Rangoon, *Vanguard*, 28 January; *FBIS*, 2 February). The decision by the congress called for two party-operated refineries, at Panghsang and in the Kokang area, according to another report. Jade smuggling would be conducted in collaboration with Kachin rebels, and opium smuggling in cooperation with those in Shan. (Hong Kong, *South China Morning Post*, 25 February.) Another Burmese source dated BCP production of heroin back to 1980–1981, with chemicals and raw materials needed for refining obtained "across the western border of Burma" (a delicate reference to China) and sold into Thailand (Rangoon Domestic Service in Burmese, 15 July; *FBIS*, 16 July). Another accusation against the BCP came from a somewhat curious source. Long-time warlord and drug smuggler Mo Hein accused the BCP of refusing to pay "customs" duties on its opium and contraband caravans passing through his territory (*The Nation*, 25 May; *JPRS*, 29 June). BCP ties to Kachin rebels and continuing links with China assume additional significance with reports that drug smuggling routes are increasingly diverted away from Thailand (where law enforcement efforts have increased), through Kachin territory into India and Bangladesh, and through China to Hong Kong (*FEER*, 13 August). Rangoon did not use U.S.-supplied aerial eradication planes against opium growing areas under BCP control, according to one report (*FEER*, 12 November), probably due to Burmese fear of losing scarce aircraft to insurgent fire.

The Insurgency. The year was marked by two major events: an ethnic insurgent alliance leader who had opposed cooperation with the BCP was replaced, and government troops attacked BCP and Kachin insurgent positions in the Kachin and northern Shan states.

Lintner asserts that BCP armed strength has declined from a mid-1970s peak of some 23,000 to probably less than 10,000. He characterizes the BCP as a declining regular army that Panghsang must convert into a guerrilla force, asserting that training and operational deficiencies are reflected in high casualty figures in battles with the government. A "senior [BCP] officer" was quoted as saying that discipline within the BCP armed forces is at its lowest ebb since he joined the insurgency in 1948. Improved training was to be a major element in 1987's rectification campaign. (Lintner 1, p. 50.)

International Positions and Activities. On 31 October Beijing radio acknowledged the BCP Central Committee's greetings to the Chinese Communist Party (CCP) Thirteenth National Congress (Beijing International Service in Burmese; *FBIS*, 3 November). In spite of this, BCP-Chinese relations are stagnant. Although Chinese aid has never been completely terminated, it is much reduced from the mid-1970s, now primarily party-to-party financial aid and limited quantities of ammunition. (Lintner 2, p. 34.)

In spite of continued BCP-CCP links, Rangoon-Beijing relations appear good. Burma sent congratulations on the 38th anniversary of the founding of the People's Republic of China (Rangoon Domestic Service in English, 1 October; *FBIS*, 2 October). Seven Chinese delegations were reported in Rangoon at various times during the year, including Vice Premier Qiao Shi, a minister, and two vice-ministers.

Thai security investigated reports of "coordination" between the BCP and Thai communists, "understood [to be] so far limited to low-level contacts in the vicinity of the Lao-Thai-Burmese tri-border area" (*FEER*, 7 May). A "senior Thai military official" said that contacts between Burmese and Thai communists had increased since the beginning of the year, with BCP activities "frequently monitored" in the border area of central Mae Hong Son province, opposite the Kayah and northern Karen states. BCP elements were trying to persuade Karen villagers to support them, the official claimed. (*The Nation*, 8 June; *FBIS*, 8 June.) Thai police reportedly arrested nine BCP members at the house of a Chinese "former Kuomintang [KMT] leader" in Chiang Mai province on 30 December (*Bangkok Post*, 31 December; *FBIS*, 31 December). The arrests appear to substantiate an earlier assertion by Mo Hein of BCP connections with KMT remnants along the Thai-Burmese border (*The Nation*, 25 May; *JPRS*, 29 June). Besides smuggling drugs and other contraband and the search for allies in intra-insurgent conflict, a motive for BCP interest in Thailand probably continues to be the availability of black market arms. The Thai press has reported three seizures by highway police of illicit weapons in Surin, Kachanaburi, and Nakhon Sawan provinces, including 42 rockets, two semi-automatic rifles, over 22,000 rounds of ammunition, an M-79 grenade launcher with 30 rounds of ammunition, and 155 60mm mortar shells. This last item was believed part of a larger quantity of shells stolen from a Thai Third Army arsenal. (Bangkok, *Matichon*, 3 February; Bangkok, *Naeo Na*, 21 March; *Bangkok Post*, 20 March; *FBIS*, 3 February,

25, 26 March.) None of these shipments were reported destined for the BCP, but they probably represent a small proportion of the total weapons traffic.

Thai-Burmese relations reached their highest point this year, according to Thai army commander in chief Chawalit Yongchaiyut (*The Nation*, 28 July; *FBIS*, 28 July). Thai concern over BCP and other Burmese insurgent spillover into Thailand, which certainly at least partly coincides with Burmese government interests, probably encouraged intergovernmental exchanges. In 1987 these exchanges included visits to Thailand by the Burma army supreme commander General Saw Maung, Burmese prime minister U Maung Maung Kha, and Burmese government leader Ne Win (*Bangkok Post*, 1 December; *FBIS*, 1 December).

Biography. *Thakin Ba Thein Tin.* Thakin Ba Thein Tin was born in Tavoy in 1914; his father was a Chinese petty trader and his mother was ethnic Burmese. Thakin graduated from secondary school in 1931 and was admitted to Rangoon University, but he was unable to continue his studies "because his debt-ridden father could not afford university fees." Instead he entered nationalist politics, working full time for *Dobama Asiayone* from 1938. He joined the BCP a few months after its founding in 1939 and reportedly fought against the Japanese in 1945 in the Tavoy-Mergui area. He was promoted to the BCP Central Committee in December 1945 and joined the Politburo in 1946. He represented the BCP at the 1947 British Empire Communist Party Conference in London and accompanied then-party chairman Than Tun to the Second Congress of the Indian Communist Party in Calcutta in 1948. Thakin was sent to China as part of the BCP representation to the CCP in 1953, making Beijing his primary residence for the next 25 years. During this time he reportedly visited the USSR several times and traveled to Hanoi in 1963, until the deepening Moscow-Beijing split prevented further trips. He became BCP chairman in 1975, a few months after Than Tun's death in March of that year, and returned permanently to Burma in 1978. He resides at Panghsang (Wan Long), BCP party headquarters. (Lintner 2, pp. 29–30.)

Charles B. Smith, Jr.
U.S. Department of State

Note: The views expressed above are the author's own and do not necessarily represent those of the Department of State or the U.S. government.

Cambodia (formerly Kampuchea)

Population. 6,536,079. Average annual growth rate is 2.26 percent.

Major Parties.

• Khmer People's Revolutionary Party (KPRP)

Membership. 7,500 (*FBIS-Asia and the Pacific* [*AP*], 21 October 1985; *WMR*, February 1986)

Founded. 1951 (exact date uncertain)

General Secretary. Heng Samrin (b. 1934, former Khmer Rouge official and military commander; fled Cambodia 1977–1978 after an abortive revolt against the Pol Pot leadership; returned December 1978 with the invading Vietnamese army).

Politburo. 9 full and 2 candidate members: Heng Samrin (president, Council of State); Chea Sim (b. 1932, chairman, National Assembly; National Council of the Kampuchean United Front for National Construction and Defense); Hun Sen (b. 1951, chairman, Council of Ministers; prime minister; chairman, KPRP Foreign Relations Commission); Say Phuthong (b. 1925, secretary, KPRP Central Committee; vice-chairman, Council of State; chairman, KPRP Central Control Commission); Bou Thang (b. 1938, vice-premier; vice-chairman, Council of Ministers; vice-chairman, National Council of the Kampuchean United Front for National Construction and Defense); Chea Soth (b. 1928, vice-chairman, Council of Ministers; chairman, KPRP Central Committee Inspection Commission; chairman, KPRP Central Committee Emulation Council); Men Sam-An* (b. 1953, chairman, KPRP Central Organization Commission; member, KPRP Control Commission); Mat Ly* (b. 1925, vice-chairman, National Assembly; chairman, Kampuchean Federation of Trade Unions); Ney Pena* (minister of the interior); Chan Seng* (b. 1935, candidate member; vice-chairman, KPRP Control Commission; vice-chairman, Kampuchean Federation of Trade Unions); Nguon Nhel* (candidate member; secretary, Phnom Penh municipal KPRP committee).

**Indicates new members selected at the Fifth Party Congress.*

Secretariat. Heng Samrin (chief), Hun Sen, Bou Thang, Men Sam-An, Ney Pena

Control Commission of the Central Committee. Say Phuthong (president), Chan Seng, Sim Ka, Men Sam-An, Say Chhum, Mean Sam-An, El Vansarat

Central Committee. 31 full and 14 candidate members (for list of names, see *YICA*, 1987)

Status. Sole authorized political party in all areas of Cambodia controlled by the regime in Phnom Penh. As in other Marxist states, party and government are synonymous, and KPRP leaders serve concurrently as key officials in the governing apparatus of the People's Republic of Kampuchea. The KPRP has been heavily influenced by the Vietnamese Communist Party, and its present dynamics and key decisions remain under the tutelage of Vietnamese advisers.

Last Congress. Fifth, 13–16 October 1985 in Phnom Penh. Attended by 250 delegates from 22 subordinate party committees representing the provinces, municipalities, and armed forces in the People's Republic of Kampuchea.

Last Election. May 1981, National Assembly. The KPRP was unchallenged by any political opposition. Out of 148 candidates running for office, 117 were elected.

Auxiliary Organizations. Kampuchean Federation of Trade Unions (80,000 members); Kampuchean People's Revolutionary Youth Union (37,000 members); Kampuchean Revolutionary Women's Association (1.3 million members); Kampuchean Revolutionary Youth Association (80,000 members); Kampuchean Committee for the Defense of Peace; Kampuchean United Front for National Construction and Defense (KUFNCD), formerly called the Kampuchean United Front for National Salvation; Kampuchean Afro-Asian People's Solidarity Organization Committee; Kampuchean Center of the Asian Buddhists' Council of Peace

Publications. *Pracheachon* (People), semiweekly of the KPRP Central Committee, founded October 1985, circulation 37,000, editor in chief Som Kim Suor, deputy editor Pen Panhnha; *Kangtap Padevoat* (Revolutionary Army), weekly of the Khmer People's Revolutionary Armed Forces (KPRAF), editor in chief Ros Savanna, deputy editor Son Saramalay; *Phnom Penh*, weekly of the Phnom Penh municipal KPRP committee; *Kampuchea*, weekly of the KUFNCD, editor in chief Khieu Kanharit; *Neak Khousna*, monthly magazine. The official news agency is Sarpordamean Kampuchea (SPK), general director Em Sam-An, deputy directors Kit Kimhuon, Sum Mean, I Lon; SPK publishes *Daily Bulletin* in English, Khmer, and French, and *Angkor*, a monthly magazine, in Khmer. Other media are Voice of the Kampuchean People (VOKP) radio, general director Kim Yin, executive director Un Samon; and Kampuchean Radio and Television Commission, director Kim Yin, deputy directors Som Kim Suor, Van Sengli, Van Sunheng.

• Party of Democratic Kampuchea (PDK). Formerly the Kampuchean (or Khmer) Communist Party (KCP), which was the political instrument of the Khmer Rouge, who governed Cambodia harshly from April 1975 to December 1978, when they were driven from power by the Vietnamese invasion.

Founded. Traces its origins to the KPRP, founded in 1951. The KCP was replaced by the PDK in December 1981.

Membership. No data. The only large PDK mass organization known to be extant is the National Army of Democratic Kampuchea (NADK), a guerrilla force numbering 30,000–35,000 armed personnel. Most combatants, however, are probably not formal party members.

General Secretary. Pol Pot possibly still the dominant figure, in spite of his official retirement in August 1985. In late 1986 he was allegedly terminally ill in Beijing.

Secretariat. Possibly no longer functioning.

Control Commission. Possibly no longer functioning.

Politburo. Party organizations, except for the NADK, lapsed into inactivity when the KCP converted to the PDK (Floyd Abrams, *Kampuchea After the Worst: A Report on Current Human Rights* [New York: Lawyers' Committee on Human Rights, 1985], p. 182). A Supreme Military Commission of the NADK was reportedly disbanded with Pol Pot's retirement and may have held its final meeting in August 1985.

Central Committee. Possibly no longer functioning.

Status. The PDK represents the Khmer Rouge, which is the dominant partner in a tripartite anti--

Vietnamese front with the Khmer People's National Liberation Front (KPNLF) of Son Sann, and the National United Front for an Independent, Neutral, Peaceful and Cooperative Cambodia (Front uni national pour un Cambodge indépendant, neutre, pacifique et coopératif; FUNCINPEC) of Prince Sihanouk. The front took the name Coalition Government of Democratic Kampuchea (CGDK) in mid-1982. PDK authority extends to its refugee and insurgent camps along the border with Thailand and Laos and probably to a zone of control in the Cardamon Mountains of Koh Kong province in southwestern Cambodia.

Last Congress. Third (and last), 14 December 1975, in Phnom Penh.

Last Election. 20 March 1976, for the People's Representational Assembly of Democratic Kampuchea. Elected were 150 peasants, 50 workers, and 50 soldiers.

Auxiliary Organizations. Communist Women's Organization, headed by Khieu Ponnary, the wife of Pol Pot, was reportedly founded in July 1961. An Alliance of Democratic Kampuchean Youth was reportedly established in February 1962. Both organizations existed underground and may have been defunct since December 1978.

Publications. *Tung Padevoat* (Revolutionary Flag), official journal of the KCP; *Yuvechon nung Yuvanearei Padevoat* (Revolutionary Youths and Maidens), youth magazine of the KCP. Both publications are probably defunct. The PDK maintains a radio broadcasting station, the Voice of Democratic Kampuchea (VODK), that still operates clandestinely.

Leadership and Party Organization. *KPRP*. Party leadership and organization remained unchanged in 1987. Late in the year the Council of State of the KPRP-dominated People's Republic of Kampuchea appointed three new vice-chairmen of the Council of Ministers. In keeping with past custom, their names were not immediately announced. (*FBIS-EAS*, 29 October.)

PDK. The party remains one of the most secretive Marxist-Leninist movements in the world. Internal party organization remains unknown except that it has divided Cambodia into four semiautonomous, politico-military zones. Each of these zones is headed by a prominent Khmer Rouge leader: Ieng Sary, Khieu Samphan, Son Sen, and Ta Mok. Pol Pot remains a shadowy presence behind the scenes.

Domestic Party Affairs. *KPRP*. The Central committee of the KPRP held fourth and fifth plenums during the year. Attendees at the meetings expressed satisfaction at progress achieved toward the party goals set forth at the Fifth Congress in October 1985. They approved plans for a self-criticism campaign and the forthcoming summit conference of the Indochinese countries. They also noted with satisfaction the development of special ties with Laos, Vietnam, and the Soviet Union, and they made a plea for broader international support. (Berkeley, California, *Indochina Chronology* [*IC*], April–June *FBIS-EAS*, 22 July.)

During the year the KPRP-dominated National Assembly elected in 1981 held its twelfth and thirteenth sessions. Delegates heard reports from various ministries and welcomed new members chosen from six Cambodian provinces in a special by-election held in June (*FBIS-EAS*, 24 June, 14 July).

A number of domestic measures also hinted at some flexibility by the party and government in searching for an end to the eight-year war in Cambodia. In August Phnom Penh unveiled a new Policy on National Reconciliation to encourage the insurgents to rally to the republic. The full text statement had six points: (1) the policy noted that it was "aimed at uniting all Cambodians to construct an independent, peaceful and non-aligned Cambodia"; (2) the government was prepared to meet with other Khmer groups, excluding the Pol Pot faction of the PDK, to bring about national reconciliation; (3) the government invited overseas Cambodians to return home to contribute to national defense and reconstruction; (4) the government considered Cambodians who had served the Khmer insurgent factions to have been misguided and invited them to return home where they would be assisted to resume a normal life and to participate in the political process; (5) the government would welcome back armed combatants of the insurgent factions and would grant them citizenship rights; and (6) the government sympathized with the plight of the refugees in the camps on the Thai border and appealed to Bangkok to put an end to the use of such camps as insurgent and criminal havens and place them under international supervision. (*FBIS-EAS*, 27 August.)

Almost concurrent with this declaration was a KPRP list of former Khmer Rouge leaders who would be unacceptable to Phnom Penh in any future power-sharing arrangments with the Khmer insurgent factions. Named specifically for exclusion were Pol Pot and his wife Khieu Ponnary, Ieng Sary and his wife Ieng Thirith, and Nuon Chea, the former deputy general secretary of the KCP under Pol Pot. Conspicuous by their omission from the list, and therefore presumably acceptable to the Phnom Penh government, were Khieu Samphan and several lesser but hard-line Khmer Rouge leaders such as Son Sen, Ta Mok, and Ke Pauk. (*FBIS-EAS*, 14 August.)

PDK. The party continues to conduct its affairs in great secrecy from havens in southwestern Cambodia. No significant developments were reported to the outside world in 1987.

Military Issues. *KPRP*. The level of military activity in Cambodia decreased on all sides. Nevertheless, Western sources reported that the Khmer People's Revolutionary Armed Forces (KPRAF) was still lacking in training and motivation, with a high rate of desertion and a reluctance to engage the enemy. Military shortcomings were corroborated by the party organ in Phnom Penh, which declared that the "quantity and quality of our People's Revolutionary Army has yet to fully meet the demands of the revolution." Singled out for criticism was propaganda work that failed to arouse citizens "to the call for army service in defense of the fatherland." Cadres and party members also were denounced for insufficient zeal in meeting their responsibilities to promote recruitment in the armed forces. Local party committees were criticized for ignoring party policy on caring for military dependents and survivors—failing to provide for local training and education of new recruits and for the billeting and care of soldiers stationed in their areas. On the positive side, however, the party organ acknowledged that recruitment councils had been created at all levels in the People's Republic of Kampuchea down to the rice roots, and a number of localities were commended for meeting or exceeding their draft quotas. (*FBIS-AP*, 24 February; *FBIS-EAS*, 2 June, 24 November.)

Toward the end of the year units of the People's Army of Vietnam staged their sixth annual withdrawal from Cambodia. Two army divisions, comprising five brigades and supporting units, or a total of 20,000 personnel, were withdrawn. This reduced Vietnamese military forces in Cambodia to 140,000, down from 180,000 in the early 1980s. According to Vietnamese sources, the withdrawal was tied to the increased capability of the KPRAF to defend the Phnom Penh government. Some military observers viewed the pullout with skepticism, as simply a rotation of troops that would be replaced unobtrusively later by other units. (*FBIS-EAS*, 1 December.)

In the meantime, Plan K-5, the project conceived by Hanoi and Phnom Penh to erect fortifications and obstacles along the border with Thailand to impede the passage of guerrillas, was believed to be largely completed. According to information that could not be verified independently, Cambodian authorities, with the completion of K-5, had launched a new project codenamed S-85. This new undertaking placed an obligation on villages in zones of guerrilla activity to clear their areas of underbrush and erect obstacles and defensive works to deny the insurgents concealment or unimpeded passage. (*FBIS-AP*, 24 March.)

PDK. The NADK remained the strongest of the three insurgent forces fighting the continued Vietnamese occupation of Cambodia. It was well ensconced inside the country with some of its combat operations reported as far east as Kampong Cham, a province on the border with Vietnam. Vietnamese military sources, like their Western and ASEAN counterparts, conceded a decreased intensity of fighting during the year but singled out two areas of heavy NADK activity in the country: northeast of the Tonle Sap (Great Lake), and in Batdambang province, especially along Route 5 leading from Batdambang City to Phnom Penh. According to Vietnamese intelligence, an NADK headquarters was located in the triborder area of Laos, Thailand, and Cambodia. Another headquarters, or NADK zone, was the area between the Thai border town of Trat and Pouthisat (Pursat) astride Route 5. From this zone, insurgent units sallied forth to prey on villages and isolated enemy outposts south of the Tonle Sap and along Route 4 from Kampong Saom to Phnom Penh. (*FBIS-EAS*, 2 June.)

Around mid-year NADK units were detected retreating westward to the Thai border from provinces as far east as Stoeng Treng (Stung Treng) and Kracheh (Kratie). Western and noncommunist Khmer observers were at a loss to explain the movement but attributed it tentatively to steady Vietnamese military pressure and the loss of NADK supply depots in the interior of Cambodia. (*Asian Defence Journal*, October.)

Auxiliary and Front Organizations. *KPRP.* The mass organizations of the KPRP reported a number of activities during the year. In February the Kampuchean Revolutionary Women's Association held a national convention that set organizational goals for 1987. These goals included promotion of the emulation movement for women and consolidation of branch offices. Attendees were reminded of women's duty to persuade male relatives serving with the insurgent factions to rally to the cause of the regime in Phnom Penh. President Mean Sam-An, in a keynote address, reported proudly that 28,248 women had joined village militias and that 1,234 had participated in the construction of frontier fortifications on the Thai border (SPK/*Daily Bulletin*, 13 February).

In March the Kampuchean People's Revolutionary Youth Union held its second congress in Phnom Penh. It was attended by 300 delegates, including some representatives from friendly Marxist-Leninist states. In his keynote address, Council of State president Heng Samrin praised the accomplishments of the movement's youthful members in defense, agricultural, industrial, health, and educational pursuits. He acknowledged the importance of the organization in training young people for party membership and imparting to them the correct party ideology, declaring that "The youth union is a school of communism for the youth." Placing a high premium on party orthodoxy, he added that the organization had a duty to educate and train young people "so as to turn them into vanguard workers who execute the tasks of the revolution and, with absolute loyalty, carry on the revolutionary cause of the party and nation." The central committee of the youth union also took advantage of the second congress to unveil a new "three excellents" emulation campaign: excellent in combat and combat support activities, in production and work, and in study and self-training. (*FBIS-AP*, 9, 10 March.)

The KUFNCD feted its ninth anniversary in early December. In the celebration Chairman Chea Sim praised the role of the organization as "an immense force of every strata (sic) of people and masses to take part actively in every revolutionary movement for the cause of defending and building the fatherland gradually and through stages toward socialism" (*FBIS-EAS*, 3 December).

International and Regional Issues. *KPRP.* The most important development was the momentum achieved at the end of the year toward a political settlement to the war in Cambodia. This progress was brought about as a result of talks between People's Republic of Kampuchea (PRK) prime minister Hun Sen and Coalition Government of Democratic Kampuchea (CGDK) president Prince Norodom Sihanouk (on leave of absence May 1987–May 1988). Following nearly a year of political maneuvering and false starts, the two leaders finally met in a Paris suburb with the approbation of their mentors—the Soviet Union and Vietnam for the PRK, China and the ASEAN states for the CGDK. In the three-day discussions that followed, Hun Sen and Sihanouk sought a formula that would bring peace to their war-ravaged country. Reportedly the two leaders achieved considerable personal rapport in their dialogue.

In his notes on the discussions released to the press, Prince Sihanouk asserted that he had declined a high post in the administration of the PRK and stated that he would return to Phnom Penh only at the head of a nonaligned, quadrapartite government (the PRK, Khmer Rouge, and two noncommunist factions) that would have a multiparty, parliamentary system such as France. Sihanouk declared to Hun Sen that China, the Soviet Union, and Vietnam should be petitioned to end their dispute at the expense of Cambodia, which in turn should seek friendship with its neighbors Thailand and Vietnam and with the three great powers: China, the Soviet Union, and the United States. Hun Sen for his part assured Sihanouk that Vietnamese troops would leave Cambodia by 1990 and that Phnom Penh concurred on the need to involve all three insurgent factions in the quest for a political settlement.

In the joint communiqué that followed the talks, the two sides agreed that the Cambodian conflict needed to be settled politically, through negotiations among all Khmer parties concerned, in order to "rebuild an independent, democratic, sovereign, neutral and nonaligned Kampuchea." Both sides agreed to meet for further discussions in 1988 and, once an accord was reached by all the Khmer parties, to convene an international conference that would "guarantee the independence of Kampuchea, and peace and stability in Southeast Asia." (*FBIS-EAS*, 3, 4 December.)

Aside from the momentum for a possible political settlement to the war, the party and government in Phnom Penh pursued its ties with the 36 mostly Marxist-Leninist states and revolutionary movements that recognize the PRK. In March Phnom Penh played host to Soviet foreign minister Eduard Shevardnadze. The visit appeared short on substance; in its wake, however, the PRK and the USSR signed a protocol for cooperation in geological research and industrial cooperation and, later on, an accord by which Moscow would provide repair shops for agricultural machinery. This direct cooperation between Cambodia and the Soviet Union, without the intervention of Vietnam, continued in several sectors. Soviet experts worked on upgrading the port of Kampong Saom and repairing the Cambodian railway system. Soviet physicians worked at the Friendship Hospital in Phnom Penh, and 96 Soviet scholars and teachers were on the staff of the Cambodian School of Technology. In mid-1987 the Soviet-installed Intersputnik satellite in Phnom Penh went into operation. (*FBIS-AP*, 16, 19 March; *IC*, January–March; *FBIS-EAS*, 15 June.)

In addition to relations with the Soviet Union, the PRK maintained a lively exchange program with other Marxist-Leninist states. Party and government elites in Cambodia traded visits with their counterparts in Vietnam, Laos, Poland, Czechoslovakia, Hungary, Mongolia, Cuba, and Greece.

Relations with the United States continued to be nonexistent. Washington does not recognize the government in Phnom Penh on the grounds that it was placed in power by the invading Vietnamese in 1979, and it supports instead the two noncommunist factions of the CGDK. Phnom Penh over the years has reciprocated this distrust, although it has accorded courteous treatment on occasion to visiting U.S. scholars. In 1987 as in the past, the PRK in a pro-forma denunciation condemned "the U.S. imperialists, who stubbornly persist in accelerating the nuclear arms race and (in) striving to achieve the Star Wars program, which is causing tension throughout the world, seriously threatening world peace and mankind's survival." Having thus demonstrated rhetorically its solidarity with the Marxist-Leninist states, Phnom Penh denounced with considerably more acrimony an issue that was much closer to home—the joint Thai-U.S. military exercises, codenamed Cobra Gold 87. The party-controlled PRK media charged that the maneuvers, which involved about 5,000 Thai and U.S. troops in Thailand, "clearly proved that at no time have the (Bangkok and Washington) warmongers given up their ambition to snap at and swallow countries in Southeast Asia." The media also labeled the exercise "a dark, pernicious act that reflected the hostile policy of the Bangkok and Washington authorities in threatening the PRK and the three Indochinese countries." Whether these distortions really originated with the PRK government or with its Vietnamese mentors was a matter of speculation. Nevertheless, against a background of such hyperbole, PRK prime minister Hun Sen made a startlingly conciliatory declaration when he acknowledged that Cambodia held the remains of "a certain number" of Americans killed in the Vietnam War and was willing to return them if an official demand was made by the United States. Aside from the humanitarian aspects of the gesture, there could be little question that the gambit represented a bid for implied recognition of the PRK, a concession that Washington was not prepared to grant. Hun Sen's overture therefore went unanswered for the time being, although Washington lists 91 personnel—83 military and 8 civilian—as missing in Cambodia. (*FBIS-EAS*, 21 May, 17 July, 22 October.)

PDK. The PDK suffered a blow to its image in late April when Prince Sihanouk stepped down from his post as president of the CGDK for a one-year leave of absence. In explaining his abrupt move, Sihanouk laid the blame squarely on the Khmer Rouge, charging that they had attacked his own forces in the past and had committed human rights violations against other Cambodians. Khmer Rouge leaders appealed to Sihanouk to reconsider his decision, recognizing full well that the CGDK, of which they were the strongest component, had lost its most prestigious leader. Sihanouk held firm, but ultimately his temporary absence from the coalition had little impact on the U.N., which annually considers the question of the continued Vietnamese military presence in Cambodia. In the U.N. General Assembly session held in the fall of 1987, delegates once again called for an immediate end to the Vietnamese occupation of the war-ravaged country by a vote of 117 to 21, with 16 abstentions. For another year at least, the vote doomed the hope of the PRK to gain Cambodia's seat in the U.N. and left it occupied by the Khmer Rouge in the name of Democratic Kampuchea, the regime that has been defunct since 1979. (*FBIS-EAS*, 4 June; *London Times*, 16 October.)

Russell R. Ross
Library of Congress

China

Population. 1,072,330,000 (excluding Taiwan, July 1987) (China Central Television, 11 November; UPI, 11 November)

Party. Chinese Communist Party (Zhongguo gongchan dang; CCP)

Founded. 1921

Membership. 46,011,951 (including 2.4 million probationary members at the end of 1986; *Beijing Review*, 2–8 November)

General Secretary. Hu Yaobang (until 16 January); Zhao Ziyang (68; acting general secretary 16 January–2 November)

Standing Committee of the Politburo. 5 members: Zhao Ziyang, Li Peng (59; acting premier as of 24 November), Qiao Shi (63; first secretary, Central Commission for Inspection Discipline; member of Secretariat; vice-premier), Hu Qili (58; in charge of propaganda; member of Secretariat), Yao Yilin (70; vice-premier; minister, State Planning Commission)

Politburo. 17 full members: Wan Li, Tian Jiyun, Qiao Shi, Jiang Zemin, Li Peng, Li Tieying, Li Ruihuan, Li Ximing, Yang Rudai, Yang Shangkun, Wu Xueqian, Song Ping, Zhao Ziyang, Hu Qili, Hu Yaobang, Yao Yilin, Qin Jiwei. Alternate member: Ding Guangen

Secretariat. 4 full members: Hu Qili, Qiao Shi, Rui Xingwen, Yan Mingfu. Alternate member: Wen Jiaobao

Central Military Commission. Chairman: Deng Xiaoping; first vice-chairman: Zhao Ziyang; permanent vice-chairman and secretary general: Yang Shangkun

Central Advisory Commission. 200 members. Chairman: Chen Yun; vice-chairmen: Bo Yibo, Song Renqiong

Central Commission for Discipline Inspection. 69 members. First secretary: Qiao Shi; deputy secretaries: Chen Zuolin, Li Zhengting, Xiao Hongda

Central Committee. 175 full members and 110 alternate members (since 1 November)

Status. Ruling party

Last Congress. Thirteenth, 25 October–1 November

Last Election. 1987

Auxiliary Organizations. All-China Women's Federation, led by Kang Keqing; Communist Youth League of China (50 million members), led by Hu Jintao; All-China Federation of Trade Unions, led by Ni Zhifu; People's Political Consultative Conference (CPPCC), led by Deng Yingchao.

Publications. The official and most authoritative publication of the CCP is the newspaper *Renmin Ribao* (People's Daily), published in Beijing. The theoretical journal of the Central Committee, *Hongqi* (Red Flag), was published approximately twice a month. More influential in recent years, however, is *Liaowang* (Outlook), the weekly publication of Xinhua (the New China News Agency; NCNA), the official news agency of the party and government. The daily paper of the People's Liberation Army is *Jiefangjunbao* (Liberation Army Daily). The weekly *Beijing Review* (*BR*), published in English and in several other languages, carries translations of important articles, editorials, and documents from these three publications and from other sources. *China Daily*, the first English-language national newspaper in the People's Republic of China (PRC), began official publication in Beijing and Hong Kong on 1 June 1981. It began a New York edition in June 1983.

Domestic Affairs. The year began in an atmosphere of crisis, a direct consequence of student demonstrations that had erupted in December 1986, and continued on the first day of 1987 on Tiananmen Square in Beijing where the first students were arrested, if only temporarily. The crisis soon came to a head in mid-January, and important changes in the party leadership took place. The struggle between conservatives and reformers continued during the year as both sides jockeyed for desired policy and personnel decisions by the time of the party congress scheduled in the fall. The Thirteenth Party Congress proved to be another success for Deng Xiaoping and his reform program, but there were important concessions made to the conservatives within the party, even though most of the elders retired from prominent party posts. Although there were problems in the economy (such as inflation and rationing) the State Statistical Bureau indicated in an interview with Xinhua on 29 December that China's GNP will exceed $270 billion in 1987, up 9 percent from 1986. Industrial output reportedly increased 14.5

percent while agricultural output was up 4 percent. (*Honolulu Star-Bulletin*, 29 December.)

An important top-level conference on party life was held 10–15 January that began with a self-criticism by General Secretary Hu Yaobang. Hu admitted committing violations of the party principle of collective leadership and making serious errors on other important political principles, and accordingly submitted a request to resign his top post. The party life conference was followed on 16 January by an enlarged meeting of the Politburo, attended by eighteen Politburo members, two alternate members, four representatives from the Secretariat, seventeen leading cadres from the Central Advisory Commission, two members from the Central Commission for Discipline Inspection, and others. (*BR*, 26 January.) Bo Yibo reported to the meeting on the particulars of the preceding party life conference. Hu's resignation was accepted and Zhao Ziyang was named acting general secretary.

Also early in January, a campaign against "bourgeois liberalization" gathered momentum. Three prominent party intellectuals were soon removed from their positions and expelled from the party: the writer Wang Ruowang; the outspoken astrophysicist Fang Lizhi (who was vice-president of the elite University of Science and Technology in Hofei, Anhui); and the popular muckraking *Renmin Ribao* journalist Liu Binyan.

Zhao Ziyang, in a national address on 29 January (Chinese New Year), set important limits on the campaign against bourgeois liberalization, saying that it was to be limited to party members, focus on political principles, and not be carried out in rural areas nor allowed to influence economic construction and reform programs (text of speech in *BR*, 9 February).

There was for a time considerable conservative resistance to Zhao's injunction. The conservative *Beijing Daily*, which had been an object of derision by students, held that students should serve time working in the fields, in factories, and in the army, revealing that thousands of Beijing students had already spent their winter vacation on such assignments (Beijing, AFP, 13 February; *FBIS*, 17 February). On 4 February Zhu Houze, a reform-minded associate of Hu Yaobang, was replaced as propaganda department head by Wang Renzhi, the former deputy editor in chief of *Hongqi* (*BR*, 16 February).

Deng Xiaoping's response was cautious. On 16 February an important speech he had made at an enlarged Central Committee working conference of 7,000 in 1962 was publicly released in full, but without comment. The speech was on democratic centralism, which was described as a "fine tradition" of the party. Various interpretations were proferred. Some saw it implying criticism of Hu Yaobang for not having exercised sufficient collective leadership, while others believed it was meant to remove apprehensions about the threat of suppression of honest and frank minority viewpoints. (See, for example, Yau Shing-mu and Chan Wai-fong's article in the *Hongkong Standard*, 2 March; *FBIS*, 3 March; also Zhong Jiwen's article in *Renmin Ribao*, 4 March; *FBIS*, 5 March.)

A new enlarged edition of Deng Xiaoping's *Build Socialism with Chinese Characteristics* was also made available. Half of the 44 pieces included in that edition were recently given talks, as recent as January, and many were published for the first time. The volume indicated clearly two aspects of the party line since 1978: the open policy and the policy of reform on the one hand, and opposition to bourgeois liberalization on the other. (*BR*, 23 March.)

In March two Shanghai workers were given long prison terms for inciting crowds during the student demonstrations in Shanghai in December 1986. The two were among fourteen who were arrested during the demonstrations. (Beijing, AP, 22 March; *NYT*, 23 March.)

The fifth session of the Sixth NPC was held from 25 March to 11 April. Again the NPC demonstrated its increasing willingness to speak its mind regarding the performance of the State Council. It approved Premier Zhao's "realistic" report on the work of the government but criticized the government for not having taken prompter and more effective measures to solve certain problems in agricultural production, especially in grain production, and for neglecting the "fine tradition" of building up China through thrift and hard work. It also expressed concern regarding the large deficit in 1986 and the "long-standing" problem of over-extended capital construction. It urged the government to take effective measures to eliminate or reduce the deficit, to limit price hikes, to end the import of large numbers of cars, and to make efficient use of foreign currency.

It is interesting that the premier's government work report was revised in accordance with the suggestions put forward by the NPC. The following ideas were added:

> In recent years, we have been talking less about the principle of building up the country through thrift and

hard work. This is a lesson we have to learn.

Governments at all levels must take the initiative to ask the people's congresses and their standing committees to supervise their work.

Greater efforts should be made to guarantee sufficient acreage for grain crop production and to increase the per-hectare output. (*BR*, 20 April.)

Zhao's report on the work of the government consisted of four parts. The first reviewed the current domestic situation and basic tasks. The second affirmed the determination to persist in the "principle of steady, sustained economic development." The third stressed a determination to "deepen the reform of the economic structure and open wider to the outside world." The fourth emphasized the intention to "consolidate and develop political stability and unity." (Full text in *BR*, 20 April.)

On the final day of the NPC it was announced that Ruan Chongwu was replaced by Wang Fang as minister of public security. The urbane Ruan, who was close to Hu Yaobang, had acknowledged soon after his own appointment two years earlier that police misconduct was a problem. He was clearly intent on improving the image of the police. However, Wang, unlike Ruan, has had considerable experience within the security apparatus. The NPC also approved the appointment of Li Tieying, minister of the electronics industry, as head of the State Commission for Restructuring the Economy, a post previously held by Zhao Ziyang. (*LAT*, 12 April.)

By March and April the reformers began to reassert themselves generally and were unmistakably helped in this by Deng Xiaoping. Deng emphasized a hard line on matters such as democracy, student activism, bourgeois liberalization, and the pre-eminence of the party, but he continued to speak to the need for reforms and increasingly indicated his support of Zhao Ziyang and annoyance with some of the conservative detractors.

With Deng Xiaoping's backing, Premier Zhao gave an important speech on 13 May at a meeting of propaganda, media, and party school cadres at Huairen Hall in Zhongnanhai. He reportedly took the occasion to criticize systematically various views expressed by conservatives in recent months. That same evening an enlarged meeting of the Politburo was held at which Zhao criticized by name three prominent conservatives—Bo Yibo, Hu Qiaomu, and Deng Liqun—for leftist deviations. (Hong Kong, *Ching Pao*, 10 June; *FBIS*, 18 June.)

On 15 May the director and deputy director, Du Daozheng and Liu Gao, respectively, of the State Administration of News and Publications (which had been established in January) held a press conference to explain the reasons for the new agency. They held that ten years ago China's 75 publishing houses published 186 newspapers and 542 periodicals. Today, those figures are seven to ten times higher (446 publishing houses, 1,574 newspapers, and 5,248 periodicals), occasioning a problem for China, which was "short of good editors and paper." Hence, there was a need to "consolidate." It was agreed that the establishment of the administration did have "something to do with the struggle against bourgeois liberalization," even if it was not the only reason. (*BR*, 25 May.)

On 26 May the Central Party Guidance Commission met to evaluate and sum up its experience of the past three and a half years. At the meeting, Zhao Ziyang spoke of the need to adhere simultaneously to the four cardinal principles and to the general principles and policies of reform, opening to the outside world, and invigorating the economy. Bo Yibo, vice-chairman of the commission, gave the main report to the meeting (former general secretary Hu Yaobang had earlier been the chairman of the commission). Bo said the consolidation had been successful but was unbalanced since some party organs did not complete their work, and "some even did it superficially." Bo indicated that 33,896 persons were expelled from the party, including some high-ranking cadres. Ni Xiance, who had joined the party in 1966 and was removed as governor of Jiangxi province in October 1986, was referred to as an example. (Full report by Xinhua, 31 May; *FBIS*, 2 June; see also *BR*, 8 June.)

The *Renmin Ribao* reported on 25 May that the Secretariat of the Central Committee and the State Council had decided to readjust the country's cadre-distribution structure in order to strengthen the political science, law, and economic regulatory organizations. The decision was aimed, it was said, at keeping pace with the ongoing economic reforms and streamlining of government offices. (*BR*, 8 June.)

Li Shuxian was elected as a delegate to the Haidian district NPC (a district that includes Peking University) in a landslide victory, which was interpreted as an expression of sympathy and support after the expulsion from the party of her husband, astrophysicist Fang Lizhi (AFP, 4 June; *FBIS*, 4 June).

Just before his departure for Eastern Europe, Premier Zhao made the surprising disclosure (at the time) that Hu Qili would act in his stead in presiding over the Central Committee's Secretariat, although Hu would not use the "acting general secretary" title (Hong Kong, *South China Morning Post*, 4 June; *FBIS*, 5 June). Vice-Premier Wan Li filled in as acting premier during Zhao's absence.

Meeting with Stefan Korosec, member of the Presidium of the Central Committee of the League of Communists of Yugoslavia, on 12 June, Deng Xiaoping called for a speedup in reform. Deng again declared that the reform of the political structure would be one of the main topics at the upcoming party congress, the general purpose of which "is to consolidate the socialist system, the leadership of the Party and the development of the productive forces under that system and that leadership." To this end, the party had to be revitalized, made more efficient, and have the initiative of its grass-roots units stimulated. Deng noted that the average age of members of the CCP Central Committee "is higher than it is in the central committee of any other Communist Party in the world." (*BR*, 24 August.)

The 21st session of the Sixth NPC Standing Committee closed on 23 June after approving several documents and appointing three new ministers. Approved was the Sino-Portuguese Joint Declaration on Macao, which sets the resumption of China's sovereignty over Macao on 20 December 1999. Condolences were extended to relatives of the victims of the Greater Hinggan Mountains forest fire, which had raged between 6 May and 2 June, and blame was laid to the "mismanagement, slack discipline, and serious bureaucracy of the forestry leaders" for the fire. Vice-Premier Yao Yilin took over the State Planning Commission. The commission's former minister, Song Ping, had been earlier named head of the Central Committee's Organization Department. The former head of the latter department, Wei Jianxing, was appointed the first minister of the newly established Ministry of Supervision. This ministry will monitor the performance of government departments, government officials, and government-appointed factory managers. (*BR*, 6 July.)

On 1 July, the anniversary of the CCP, Deng Xiaoping's speech on "Reform of the Leadership Systems of the Party and State" originally given on 18 August 1980 was republished in all major Chinese newspapers. In 1980 the speech had been a clear call for political reform, so its republication on this symbolic date in the weeks just before the party congress was a significant reformist gesture. However, a close comparison of this printing of the speech with the version that had been published in the 6 July 1983 *FBIS* (*China Daily Report*) reveals that an additional paragraph was added. This new paragraph discusses the efforts to be made "to change the plant director responsibility system and the manager responsibility system under the leadership of the party committee," placing it under the "leadership and supervision of a joint committee composed of the plant management committee, the company's board of directors, and the integrated economic establishment." Similar consideration is to be given "to reforming the systems of responsibilities of school principals, academy presidents, and institute directors." The new paragraph says that "These reforms are aimed at enabling the party committee to get rid of routine affairs and concentrate its efforts on ideological and political work and organizational and supervisory tasks. This is not to weaken the party's leadership but is to improve and strengthen the party's leadership more successfully." (*FBIS*, 7 July.)

Another compilation of Deng Xiaoping's speeches (a total of 44 of them since December 1984) entitled *Fundamental Issues in Present-Day China* was published in June and was intended for wide distribution in the weeks before the party congress (including English, Russian, and Japanese editions). The two main themes of this new publication were, on the one hand, opposition to bourgeois liberalization, and on the other, adherence to the policies of reform and opening to the world. (See *BR*, 29 June, 13 July.) In addition, Xinhua announced on 1 July that a series of some 50 reference books on political structural reform published by Chunqiu Publishing House were to be made available within the following few days (Xinhua; *FBIS*, 8 July).

On 1 July a Hong Kong newspaper reported that most of the nearly 400,000 college graduates and postgraduates of the current class were to be sent to work at the grass roots for two years instead of being assigned to state organs. A recent national conference on coordination of plans for college graduates had reportedly established a policy to send graduates of the current class to the grass roots to reinforce the frontline of production. In addition, the number of graduates assigned to ten remote province and autonomous regions was to be increased by 30 percent over 1986. (Hong Kong, *Wen Wei Po*, 1 July; *FBIS*, 1 July.) Already, however, more than one million college students were on their way to spend the summer recess in compulsory jobs in factories, offices, and rural villages—as part, it was said, of a program to remold their views. This was the first mass migration of students for such purposes since the end of the Cultural Revolution. Students, on the defensive since the crackdown on their demonstrations in late 1986 and early 1987, were becoming notably cynical and were frequently accused by authorities of indiscipline and extravagances (see, for example, *NYT*, 5 July).

On 1 July tighter restrictions were announced on Chinese students going abroad for further study. Although these new restrictions had already been decided on in December 1986, their publication followed the return of a delegation to the United States that sought to persuade the U.S. government to compel Chinese students to return to China. The Chinese government also began to replace the system whereby 1.9 million college students have been provided grants of about 2,300 yuan ($622) each to cover the expenses of their education with a new loan system, which would require repayment of such financial assistance. State Education Commission vice-minister Lu Zhongde said that the change "is mainly aimed at motivating students to study hard, behave properly, and maintain their health." (*China Daily*, 29 June; *FBIS*, 2 July.)

The *China Legal News* reported on 6 July that police had arrested eleven "counterrevolutionaries" allegedly involved in a secret society attempt to seize power. Between 26 January and 8 June authorities discovered 15,000 anticommunist posters in eleven counties in Sichuan province. Zhang Jinsheng, the arrested alleged leader, confessed that he and his accomplices planned to stir up riots and bomb bridges around Chengdu. In his possession were 65 flags of a "people's republic of loyal people," dynamite, counterfeit money, printing machinery, and seals. (Beijing, AFP, 6 July; *FBIS*, 7 July.)

This manifestation of rebellious instability was echoed in Beijing itself, where bombs were detonated and bomb plots were discovered at various times throughout the year. Such a bomb exploded early on 17 July in the vicinity of the Chairman Mao Memorial Hall. In another incident, a person traveling from Northeast China to Beijing was found to be carrying an 80-page book on the "record of CCP crimes," which included plans that listed Deng Xiaoping as the number-one target for assassination. The apprehended person died during interrogation. On 27 July slogans such as "Down with the new gang of four of Peng Zhen, Bo Yibo, Hu Qiaomu, and Deng Liqun," "Expose and criticize crimes of the new gang of four who brought calamities to the country and the people," and "We want democracy and freedom not autocratic rule" were posted simultaneously in Chongwenmen, Xidan, and Dongsi in Beijing. The Public Security Bureau subsequently received an unprecedented phone call in which the caller claimed responsibility for the slogans on behalf of "the young vanguard of democracy, freedom, and progress." (Hong Kong, *Cheng Ming*, 1 August; *FBIS*, 5 August.)

Across the Taiwan Strait the government in Taiwan undertook two decisive actions on 15 July that were not without implications for Beijing. It abolished the 38-year-old Emergency Decree, which had been referred to as "martial law," and it removed restrictions from the possession and use of foreign currency by Taiwan citizens. On the following day the Taiwan government also lifted the ban on direct travel to Hong Kong and Macao by Taiwan citizens, a restriction that had been imposed on 28 April 1979 to prevent capital flight. The lifting of controls on foreign currency had immediate beneficial effect, and within a week the amount of Taiwan's foreign exchange holdings dropped from the record high of almost $62 billion to $60.7 billion. (Taipei, *The Free China Journal*, 20 July.) According to David Dean, director of the Taipei Office of the American Institute in Taiwan, the relaxation of foreign exchange controls will lead Taiwan to become an international banking, insurance, and marine industry center by the year 2002 (ibid., 27 July). Subsequently, on 14 October, Taiwan authorities announced permission for aging Taiwan citizens to visit relatives on the mainland. On the following day the Chinese government welcomed such visits. Indirect trade between the Chinese mainland and Taiwan was expected to reach $1.5 billion during the year. (*Renmin Ribao*, 14 November; *FBIS*, 18 November.)

On 20 July Zhao Ziyang met a group of middle-aged scientists and their families in Beidaihe, the famous summer resort near Beijing. This was the first time the Central Committee had invited intellectuals to spend a holiday there. (*BR*, 3 August.) But conservative leftists asserted themselves notably on 1 August by arranging for the expulsion of eight prominent intellectuals from the party. One of these, playwright Wu Zuguang, revealed that Hu Qiaomu had visited his apartment and told him to quit the party or be expelled. Hu read to him a party document accusing him of opposing the party leadership in the 1950s and publicly criticizing the 1983 campaign against spiritual pollution. The 70-year-old Wu, who had joined the party in 1981, agreed to resign. The other intellectuals ordered to resign were: Su Shaozhi, director of the Research Institute of Marxism-Leninism–Mao Zedong Thought; Zhang Xianyong, a member of the institute; Sun Changjia, deputy editor of *Science News*; Ge Yang, editor of *New Observer* magazine; Yu Haocheng, an editor at the Masses Publishing House; Li Honglin, a literary critic; and Yan Jiaqi, co-author of a controversial recent history of the Cultural Revolution. (See, for example, Jen Chien-pai's analysis in *Cheng Ming*, 1 September; *FBIS*, 8 September.)

On 17 August the China Social Survey System made public the results of the first nationwide surveys ever conducted by China's professional polling organization. The survey showed that 64.4 percent of the people questioned were satisfied with the current economic reforms and that 93.8 percent thought that it is necessary to carry out political reforms. (*BR*, 31 August.) In mid-August Chinese authorities agreed to repatriate 7,000 Vietnamese who had flooded into Hong Kong from China during the summer (London, *Financial Times*, 20 August). On 1 September regulations went into effect covering private enterprises that define who may start such businesses and how and that clamp down on fraud, overpricing, tax evasion, and other problems accompanying the rapid expansion of the 12 million private businesses in China (Peking, AP-Dow Jones; *Financial Times*, 20 August). In September Amnesty International reported that widespread torture persists in China and government efforts to end it are thwarted by the police and party officials (*NYT*, 9 September).

The Dalai Lama, speaking in Washington, D.C. on 21 September, rejected Chinese proposals that he return to Tibet, saying that he could better serve his people from abroad. He outlined a five-point peace plan that proposes: declaring Tibet a demilitarized zone of peace and nonviolence, halting the transfer of Chinese to Tibet, respecting the human rights and freedoms of the Tibetans, halting the production of nuclear weapons in Eastern Tibet and plans for dumping nuclear wastes, and conducting earnest negotiations on Tibet's future status and relations with China. (Washington, D.C., AP; *Honolulu Star-Bulletin*, 22 September.)

At least fourteen persons died and many policemen were seriously injured following pro-independence demonstrations and rioting in Lhasa on 27 September and 1 October. There were reports of Tibetan monks being arrested and beaten, and additional Chinese security forces arrived in Lhasa. (Lhasa, AP; *Honolulu Star-Bulletin*, 3, 5 October.) On 8 October fifteen journalists were expelled from Tibet, ostensibly for having gone there without permission (Chengdu, AP; *Honolulu Star-Bulletin*, 8 October). Subsequently, all travelers were ordered to leave Tibet within one week. Foreigners were warned not to get involved, and some who had photographed the demonstrations had their film confiscated. (Lhasa, AP; *Honolulu Star-Bulletin*, 9 October.) Chinese officials claimed that these disturbances were connected to the Dalai Lama's efforts to separate Tibet from China. (See, for example, *BR*, 12 October.)

The seventh plenary session of the Twelfth Central Committee met on 20 October. The plenum approved the key documents to be presented to the impending party congress. It approved in principle "general ideas on the reform of the political structure," the major points of which would be in the Central Committee's work report to the congress. It also accepted Hu Yaobang's resignation of 16 January from the general secretaryship and approved Zhao Ziyang's appointment as acting general secretary. Hu Yaobang was present at the plenum. (Xinhua, 20 October; *FBIS*, 20 October.)

The Presidium of the Thirteenth Party Congress met in the Great Hall of the People on 24 October. The Presidium elected 30 comrades to its Standing Committee, including Zhao Ziyang and Deng Xiaoping, and three deputy general secretaries of the congress: Qiao Shi, Song Ping, and Wen Jiabao. It approved the report of Qiao Shi, chairman of the credentials committee, on the 1,936 delegates who had been elected by secret ballot among multiple candidates. Included were 1,465 cadres (75.7 percent of the total) from various levels; 366 persons (18.9 percent representing economic, science and technology, culture and education, physical culture, and public health sectors; and 105 (5.4 percent) were combat heroes and model workers. As many as 1,152 delegates had college or higher education background (59.5 percent), and 1,139 were below the age of 55 (58.8 percent). There were 288 women delegates (14.9 percent) and 210 minority nationality delegates (10.8 percent). Also, 61 veteran cadres who joined the party before 1927 and who served in important leadership positions were specially invited delegates. (Xinhua in English, 24 October.)

The Thirteenth Party Congress was held from 25 October to 1 November. Among the unprecedented features of the congress was the attendance of about 300 foreign journalists at the opening and closing sessions. This was the first time Western journalists had been invited to a CCP congress, except for Soviet and East European correspondents who attended the Eighth Party Congress in 1956. The invited journalists included Soviet newsmen and correspondents from Taiwan. The Chinese media hailed the media access to the congress as an example of *kaifang*, the Chinese equivalent of Soviet *glasnost'*, or openness. (Beijing, UPI, 25 October.)

The congress was attended by 1,953 actual delegates representing a membership of 46,011,951, including 2,410 probationary members at the end of 1986; it was declared open by Deng Xiaoping at 9 A.M. on 25 October. Acting General Secretary Zhao Ziyang then took two-and-a-half hours to deliver the Central Committee's work report entitled "Advance Along the Road of Socialism with Chinese Characteristics." A draft of this report had been circulated to more than 5,000 party leaders in August and had seen several successive drafts. The report was subdivided into seven parts, each entitled as follows: historic achievements and the tasks of the present congress; the primary stage of socialism and the basic line of the party; the strategy of economic development; restructuring the economy; on reform of the political structure; strengthening party building while carrying out reform and the open policy; and striving to win victories for Marxism in China.

Zhao said that the central task of the congress was to accelerate and deepen China's reform, "a process which is irreversible and which accords with the will of the people and the general trend of events." He noted the great changes that had taken place in China in the nine years since the third plenum of the Eleventh Central Committee, whose line was upheld and would be further developed. There had been sustained, stable growth in the national economy. During the nine years China's gross national product, state revenue, and the average income of both urban and rural residents, roughly speaking, had doubled. He said that the overwhelming majority of the country's one billion people had secured a life with sufficient food and clothing, and people in some areas were beginning to become well-off. Job opportunities for 70 million urban residents had been created. In the countryside, 80 million peasants had shifted wholly or part-time from farming to industry. Market supplies had greatly improved. China had basically ended the situation in which there were acute and long-lasting shortages of consumer goods. There was a marked improvement with regard to the serious imbalance between major sectors of the national economy, which had gradually been set on a course of more or less coordinated development.

Zhao elaborated on the important ideological finding that had been under discussion for some time—that China "is now in the primary stage of socialism, and it will be for at least 100 years from the 1950s, when the socialist transformation of private ownership of the means of production was basically completed, to the time when socialist modernization will have been in the main accomplished, and all these years belong to this stage." He pointed out that "a correct understanding of this present historical stage" was "of prime importance as the essential basis on which to formulate and implement a correct line and correct policies." He explained that this is a specific stage China must necessarily go through while building socialism under conditions of backward productive forces and an underdeveloped commodity economy."

The basic line of the party in this stage, Zhao held, is: "To lead the Chinese people of all nationalities in a united, self-reliant, intensive, and pioneering effort to turn China into a prosperous, strong, democratic, culturally advanced, and modern socialist country by making economic development the central task while adhering to the four cardinal principles and persevering in reform and the open policy."

Zhao said that China's development strategy involved three steps, the first of which—doubling the GNP of 1980 and solving the problem of food and clothing—has already been largely accomplished. The second step would be to double the GNP again by the end of this century in order to enable the Chinese people to lead a more comfortable life. The third step would be to reach the per capita GNP level of medium-developed countries by the middle of the next century. This would enable the Chinese people to enjoy a relatively affluent life and provide a basis for further economic advance. For the present, it was important to succeed with the second step. In this regard, he outlined three major tasks: give priority to expanding scientific, technological, and educational undertakings; maintain a rough balance between total demand and total supply and rationally adjust and reform the structure of production; and open wider to the outside world, constantly expanding exchanges and cooperation with other countries.

As for restructuring the economy, Zhao asserted that the socialist economy in China is a planned commodity economy based on public ownership.

He said, "This is the theoretical basis for the reform of the economic structure." Even so, the reforms are to include the development of different types of ownership and are to allow the private sector to exist and develop, although public ownership will remain predominant. Zhao said that the main task is to change the managerial system of enterprises and to institute supporting reforms in the systems of planning, investment, allocation of materials, finance, monetary affairs, and foreign trade. Thus, China is to gradually establish a basic framework for a planned commodity economy. The socialist planned economy is to be a system that integrates planning with the market.

Political structural reform was included as one of the seven topics of the work report, rather than having been placed on the agenda of the congress as a separate, more prominent topic. Nonetheless, Zhao made the most of this opportunity, reaffirming that China is a socialist country under the people's democratic dictatorship and that its "basic political system is good." However, he conceded that "there are major defects in our system of leadership, in the organizational structure and style of work, which mainly find expression in over-concentration of power, a serious degree of bureaucratism, and feudal influences that are far from being eliminated."

He said that the purpose of reforming the political structure is "to promote what is beneficial and eliminate what is harmful and to build a socialist democracy with Chinese characteristics." He said that the long-range goal of the reform is to build a socialist political system replete with a high degree of democracy and a complete set of laws—a system that is effective and full of vitality. The immediate objective, he said, is to institute a system of leadership that will help to raise the efficiency, increase the vitality, and stimulate the initiative of all sectors of society.

The immediate objective, Zhao explained, was the separation of the functions of the party and the government, delegating powers to lower levels, reforming government organs, reforming the personnel system concerning cadres, establishing a system of consultation and dialogue, improving a number of systems regarding socialist democracy, and strengthening the socialist legal system. He also said that China would never introduce a Western system of separation of legislative, executive, and judicial powers and of different parties ruling the country in turn.

With regard to party building, Zhao called for being strict with party members. During the revolutionary wars, he said, party members had to go through the test of sacrificing their lives. "Today they must stand the test of holding office and working for reform and the open policy." Strengthening the party's collective leadership and democratic centralism, he said, should begin with the Central Committee and include: establishing a system of regular reporting by the Politburo Standing Committee to the Politburo, and by the latter to the Central Committee; increasing the number of Central Committee plenary sessions each year; and formulating work rules and a system for holding democratic meetings of the Politburo, its Standing Committee, and the Secretariat, so as to institutionalize collective leadership and place party leaders under more strict supervision and control.

Zhao called for adhering to the policy of making the ranks of the party's cadres more revolutionary, younger, better educated, and more professionally competent. "In our efforts to promote younger cadres to leading posts, we should now focus on members of the central leading bodies."

Zhao said that there have been two major historic leaps in the more than 60 years of integrating Marxism with practice in China. The first leap took place during the new democratic revolution, when the CCP found a road of revolution based on China's particular conditions and led the revolution to victory. The second took place after the December 1978 third plenum. After having analyzed both the positive and negative experiences of more than 30 years since the founding of the PRC and studying the experience of other countries and the world situation, the CCP, he said, had found a way to build socialism with Chinese characteristics, thus ushering in a new period of socialist development in China.

From 26 to 27 October the delegates were divided into 33 groups to discuss the report and the candidates for the Central Committee, the Central Advisory Commission, and the Central Commission for Discipline Inspection. The lists of names of these candidates were presented by the Presidium, which held its second meeting on 27 October to decide on the candidates and the electoral procedures. The candidates for the members and alternate members of the Central Committee and the members of the Central Commission for Discipline Inspection were to be decided by the results of preliminary elections—but there would be at least 5 percent more candidates standing for the preliminary elections than the number of full memberships in the Central Committee and the number of members in the Central Commission for Discipline Inspection. There were to be at least 12 percent more candidates standing for the preliminary election of alternate members of the Central Committee. As for the Central Advisory Commission, the election was to be conducted with an equal number of candidates and actual places. The meeting also endorsed the "lists of scrutineers [ballot counters], selected by the various delegations, for the preliminary elections and of the general scrutineers selected from among the scrutineers."

The resulting elections appeared to respond, at least in part, to the reformist calls for younger party leaders and for organizational streamlining. The Thirteenth Central Committee was smaller than its predecessor, with only 175 full members as compared to 210 in the former and only 110 alternate members as compared to 133. The new Central Advisory Commission had 200 members, a substantial increase from the former body's 162 members, reflecting the departure of many of the older cadres from the Central Committee. The new Central Commission for Discipline Inspection had 69 members.

Although most of the party elders did follow Deng Xiaoping into retirement from the Central Committee, what occurred seems to have been more a matter of "de-ossification" than the "rejuvenation" that was widely publicized. In fact, the average age of the 175 members of the Thirteenth Central Committee is 58.5 years, as compared to the 59.6 years of the 210 Twelfth Central Committee members at the time of their election. Moreover, since some 54 members of the Twelfth Central Committee, many of them in their late 40s and early 50s, were elected separately in 1985, the average age of the current Central Committee when its term expires will exceed that of the Twelfth Central Committee.

The new Central Committee, with only ten female members, remains heavily male-dominated. Provincial leaders, numbering 69, form the largest group. The central government group is second with 48 members. There are 32 military officers, only four fewer than on the 210-member Twelfth Central Committee. Proportionally, however, the military group is larger than that of the Twelfth Central Committee. A total of fourteen members of the party center working in Beijing are members of the new Central Committee. Only four members are from what may be described as the science and technology field. There is an increase from fourteen to sixteen in the number of minority nationality representatives. (*South China Morning Post*, 7 November; *FBIS*, 9 November.)

One surprise in the Central Committee election was that Deng Liqun, an arch conservative who had annoyed Deng Xiaoping in recent months, was not elected.

The congress also approved the reports of the Central Advisory Commission and the Central Commission on Discipline Inspection and the revision of several articles of the party constitution. Revisions of the party constitution included: limiting the number of members and alternate members of the Central Committee to be replaced or newly elected so that they do not exceed one-fifth of the respective totals of members and alternate members of the Central Committee; specifying the Secretariat as the "working body" of the Politburo and its Standing Committee, whose members are nominated by the latter body, subject to the endorsement of the Central Committee in plenary session; no longer requiring that the chairmen of the Military Affairs and Central Advisory commissions and the first secretary of the Central Commission for Discipline Inspection be members of the Politburo Standing Committee; no longer listing the people's communes as a venue of the ubiquitous primary party organizations; in enterprises and organizations where the responsibility management system is practiced, supporting the administrative leaders and concentrating on party ideological, political, and mass work; no longer requiring the formation of leading party members' groups in leading bodies but requiring that such leading bodies now be elected; and, similarly, leaving it to the Central Committee to determine whether party committees should even be formed in government departments that must exercise highly centralized and unified leadership, rather than simply determine the powers, functions, and tasks of such committees. (*BR*, 16–22 November.)

The new Thirteenth Central Committee held its first plenary session on 2 November. Zhao presided over the 173 members and 106 alternate members who attended, along with members of the Central Advisory Commission and the Central Commission for Discipline Inspection. The plenum elected the members of the Politburo, the Politburo's Standing Committee, the Secretariat, the Military Affairs Commission, the Central Advisory Commission, and the Central Commission for Discipline Inspection. Zhao delivered a speech at the end of the session (*BR*, 9–15 November.)

The Central Committee held its first work conference following the conclusion of the Thirteenth Party Congress. It decided on the division of work between the five Politburo Standing Committee members and on the functions and operations of the central departments, and it made general arrangements regarding next year's work. Zhao was to handle all-round work; Li Peng State Council matters; Qiao Shi party matters; Hu Qili propaganda, the work of the Secretariat, and routine matters; and Yao Yilin the economy. The Secretariat immediately carried out the transferring of responsibilities to its smaller successor body, and several former members quickly moved out of Zhongnanhai (*Wen Wei Po*, 10 November; *FBIS*, 10 November).

The Central Advisory Commission, enlarged now to 200 members, was seen as a likely source of conservative opposition to some of the plans of the reformers. Accordingly, on 4 November a report prepared by the Central Advisory Commission itself was issued, telling party elders who had recently retired to "stand at a distance from the direct handling of affairs" of the party and the state (*WP*, 5 November).

The final meeting of the 23d session of the National People's Congress (NPC) Standing Committee on 24 November accepted Zhao Ziyang's resignation as premier and accepted his suggestion of Li Peng as acting premier; accordingly, Li was appointed (Xinhua, 24 November; *FBIS*, 25 November). The 23d session also approved a Trial Village Law that contains 21 articles defining the character, functions, establishment, and tasks of the 948,000 village committees in China, as well as their relationship with the township people's governments. The law says that the village committees will be responsible for handling the public affairs and utilities of the village, mediating disputes among villages, assisting in maintaining public order, and reporting villagers' opinions and demands. The village committees will also support and organize villagers in promoting production, supply and marketing, credit and consumption, and provide services in production. (Ibid.)

It was reported in mid-November that Bao Tong, who was just elected to the Central Committee and was a close associate of Zhao Ziyang, was appointed to be political secretary of the Standing Committee of the Politburo. The political secretary is said to be in charge of secretary work of a nonroutine character. (*Wen Wei Po*, 19 November; *FBIS*, 19 November.)

On 19 November a People's Liberation Army (PLA) pilot defected to Taiwan with a MiG-19 (known as a J-6 in China) jet fighter. This was the sixth such defection to Taiwan since 1949; there have also been six similar defections to South Korea since 1950. (Taipei, AFP, 19 November; *FBIS*, 19 November.)

In late November General Yang Dezhi (77) was replaced by Chi Haotian (61) as PLA chief of staff, after having served in the post for seven years and overseeing substantial reductions in the size of the PLA. Similarly, General Yu Qiuli (73) was replaced as director of the General Political Department by Yang Baibing (age unavailable). Zhao Nanqi (in his 50s) was made director of the PLA General Logistics Department. Yang Shangkun, the permanent vice-chairman of the Military Commission, was made concurrently the commission's secretary general. Hong Xuezhi and Liu Huaqing are deputies to Yang. (Beijing, AP; *San Francisco Chronicle*, 28 November; *BR*, 7–13 December.)

For the first time in several years, pork, the favorite meat in China, was rationed in Shanghai, Tianjin, and Beijing. Already rationed were other foodstuffs in short supply, including rice, eggs, flour, and cooking oil. The pork shortage was attributed to the drop in grain production beginning in 1985 because of artificially low prices for grain. Subsequent higher prices for feed grain discouraged pig production. (*WSJ*, 2 December.)

On 7 December about 1,000 university students defied hundreds of policemen and marched through Beijing, protesting the killing of a student by a hooligan on the campus of the University of International Business and Economics two days earlier. This was the first such student demonstration since the nationwide demonstrations in early 1987. The immediate complaint was the inept handling of the matter by university officials. (*NYT*, 8 December.)

Auxiliary and Front Organizations. The fourth session of the sixth national committee of the CPPCC was held almost simultaneously with the fourth session of the Sixth NPC from 24 March to 8 April. Otherwise, the large national mass organizations appeared to be relatively quiescent. The party leadership gave some prominence to the satellite "democratic" parties during the year, "consulting" with their representatives along with other intellectuals primarily regarding the decisions of the Thirteenth Party Congress.

International Affairs. Despite some temporary uncertainty during the first three or four months of 1987 regarding the extent of the conservative impulse in China, the party leadership continuously underscored in both word and deed its commitment to economic reform and to the open-door policy as keys to economic development. Deng Xiaoping and other leaders emphasized this determination to various visiting foreign dignitaries and on prominent occasions. Top leaders also made well-publicized visits abroad. In March President Li Xiannian visited Bangladesh, Sri Lanka, Egypt, Somalia, and Madagascar. From 4 to 21 June Zhao Ziyang visited Poland, East Germany, Czechoslovakia, Hungary, and Bulgaria, despite his heavy dual responsibilities at home during a period of political struggle. Li Xiannian visited Europe (France, Italy, Luxembourg, and Belgium) from 7 to 23 November.

According to an official of the Central Committee's International Liaison Department on 24 October, the CCP has established or resumed relations with more than 130 foreign political parties since its Twelfth Party Congress in 1982. The party now has relations with 230 parties worldwide. (*BR*, 9–15 November.)

Earlier, on 11 February, however, a Foreign Ministry spokesman had indicated that "conditions are not yet ripe for a multilateral meeting of communist and workers' parties under the present circumstances." This was in response to Mongolia's invitation for a meeting of such parties in the Asia-Pacific region to take place in Ulan Bator. The spokesman held that "such a conference, if held now, can hardly yield any positive results." He said that "the most pressing issue concerning the maintenance of peace and stability in the Asia-Pacific region requires the parties concerned to take concrete actions in removing 'hot spots' and obstacles in this region." (*BR*, 23 February.)

Relations between the Israeli Communist Party and the CCP were re-established as a result of the visit to China of Israeli Communist Party general secretary Meir Vilner (*BR*, 13 July). However, on 1 July a Chinese Foreign Ministry spokesman said that diplomatic relations between China and Israel were "currently out of the question" (ibid., 20 July). Unofficial relations, however, have remained extensive for a number of years.

On 5 June China carried out its most powerful nuclear test ever at Lop Nor in Xinjiang province. This was the 33d such test since they began in 1964, and the first since 19 December 1984. (Paris, AFP, 5 June; *FBIS*, 8 June.)

On 23 September Foreign Minister Wu Xueqian spoke to the U.N. General Assembly on China's stand on key international issues, including disarmament, regional conflicts, and peace and development (full text in *BR*, 5 October).

On 29 October an agreement was signed to make the Bank of China's Great Wall card a member of Visa International (ibid., 9–15 November).

Relations with the USSR. Sino-Soviet relations continued to improve and expand during 1987. In early April Soviet ambassador to China Oleg Troyanovskiy said that he was sure the Soviet and Chinese communist parties would restore friendship in the future. He said that neither ideological differences nor border disputes were sources of quarrels between the two countries. He revealed that for the first time the Soviets would discuss Cambodia and Afghanistan at the tenth round of consultations scheduled to be held in Moscow that month. Troyanovskiy also said that an exchange of experience would help promote political and economic reforms currently underway in both countries. This assurance followed upon Soviet vice premier Nikolay Talyzin's agreement with Chinese officials during his visit to China in 1986 to exchange economic reform experience. (Beijing, Kyodo, 7 April; *FBIS*, 8 April.)

The first talks in nine years on the Sino-Soviet boundary were held in February in Moscow. A resumption of the talks had been facilitated by General Secretary Mikhail Gorbachev's agreement to a Chinese demand in 1986 to consider the mainstream of the border rivers to be the international boundary rather than the river bank on the Chinese side. A second round of boundary talks was held in Beijing, 7–21 August. Both sides agreed to continue the talks and to set up working groups to discuss specific matters relating to the alignment of the entire eastern sector of the boundary. (*BR*, 31 August; Beijing, AFP, 19 August; *FBIS*, 20 August.)

The foreign Ministry announced on 18 August that Yu Hongliang, formerly ambassador to Poland and Romania, would become ambassador to the Soviet Union, replacing Li Zewang who had held the post since February 1985. Yu had already served in Moscow as first and second secretary at the Chinese Embassy. (Beijing, AFP, 20 August; *FBIS*, 20 August.)

Despite the improving relations generally, the CCP did not send an official party representative to the celebration of the 70th anniversary of the Bolshevik Revolution, 2–3 November in Moscow, underscoring the continued situation in which formal interparty ties have not yet been restored. There was, however, a delegation from the Chinese-Soviet Friendship Society.

Relations with the United States. The U.S.-China relationship continued to bloom in 1987 despite uncertainties generated by the conservative resurgence in China early in the year, despite the continued improvement in Sino-Soviet relations, and despite occasional signs of strain.

On 30 January Lawrence MacDonald, an American, Beijing-based AFP reporter was expelled from China, according to the Chinese, "because of his recent activities that did not accord with his status as a journalist" (*BR*, 9 February).

Secretary of State George Shultz visited China in late February–early March, his third visit to China but the first in four years and reportedly his longest stay in a foreign country since becoming secretary of state. The visit provided the top-ranking U.S. official with the opportunity to determine for himself ramifications of the recent leadership change in China, although the visit had been arranged before the leadership crisis occurred. The visit also coincided with the fifteenth anniversary of the Shanghai Communiqué of 1972.

From 6 to 9 April a 35-member Chinese investment delegation attended the U.S.-China Symposium for Investment Opportunities in Washington, D.C., sponsored for the first time by the U.S. Overseas Private Investment Corporation and attended by more than 150 U.S. companies and organizations. Zhang Haoruo, vice minister of foreign economic relations and trade, noted that between 1979 and 1986 China signed foreign loan agreements totaling $28.9 billion, of which $20.7 billion had already been executed. He said that during this same period over 7,800 foreign investment contracts for equity or contractual joint ventures, wholly foreign-owned businesses, and offshore oil exploration projects had been established, involving a total of $19.1 billion of which some $6.6 billion had been executed. Zhang said that China would continue its efforts to improve the investment climate. (Washington, D.C., Xinhua, 6 April; *FBIS*, 8 April.)

Yang Shangkun, vice-chairman of the Central Military Commission, led a Chinese delegation on a visit to the United States 15–27 May and then went on to Canada for a twelve-day visit (*BR*, 1, 8 June).

Concern over Chinese sales of Silkworm missiles to Iran led finally to the restriction by the United States of the transfer of high-technology equipment to China. (See, for example, *FEER*, 5 November.) Such accusations were routinely denied by China throughout the year. On 4 November, for example, a Foreign Ministry spokesman dismissed such charges as groundless rumors and "really ridiculous" (*BR*, 16–22 November). Nevertheless, the Chinese soon announced that they were halting further Silkworm missile sales to foreign nations.

On 30 December the U.S. Department of State confirmed that two Chinese diplomats had been asked to leave the United States after engaging in what American officials said was espionage. One of the two men, an assistant military attaché, had been detained in Washington a week earlier after having accepted what he thought were classified documents of the National Security Agency from an undercover FBI agent. The two Chinese diplomats departed the United States within a week. (Washington, D.C., Combined News Services; *Honolulu Advertiser*, 31 December.)

Relations elsewhere. Sino-Japanese relations experienced a deepening of the rift that had begun in mid-1985 and that rapidly accelerated after the fall of Hu Yaobang, who had been generally well-disposed toward Japan. Chinese resentment over the trade deficit with Japan seemed to lead a number of concerns, including renewed apprehension regarding increased military spending in Japan. Japanese businessmen and journalists bore the brunt of this resentment, and some of them complained that Chinese authorities aimed to humiliate them during random personal inspections at the border. (Beijing, UPI, 10 May; *Honolulu Sunday Star-Bulletin & Advertiser*, 10 May.) In May a Japanese Kyodo newsman was accused of stealing state secrets and fabricating reports and was expelled from China (Beijing, AFP, 8 May; *FBIS*, 8 May).

The Chinese expressed their annoyance with the Japanese government's refusal to satisfy China's protest over the judicial decision in February to award the Kokario building in Kyoto, built with funds provided by a pre-1949 Chinese government, to Taiwan authorities. The Japanese government has held that its decision upholds the separation of powers among the three branches of authority in Japan, but China claims that such a position is tantamount to "creating two Chinas." (*BR*, 1 June.)

North Korean leader Kim Il-song visited China for the first time in five years from 21 to 26 May (*BR*, 1 June). In the meanwhile, unofficial relations between China and South Korea continued to develop promisingly. Officials at the Hongkong & Shanghai Banking Corp., the chief financier of Chinese–South Korean trade, estimated that the total trade between the two countries had exceeded $1.2 billion in 1986 (*WSJ*, 10 July).

The first round of border talks between the governments of China and Mongolia was held in Beijing from 19 to 27 March, reportedly in a friendly atmosphere (*BR*, 6 April).

One of the bloodiest encounters along the Sino-Vietnam border took place 5–7 January, involving an assault by the Chinese in division strength backed by heavy artillery. Hanoi claimed that about 1,500 Chinese were killed. Each side accused the other of initiating the action, but Western diplomats believe that China may have made the first move. A Chinese Foreign Ministry spokesman said that Chinese frontier guards had repulsed recent provocations by Vietnamese troops and claimed that the "battle achievements" that were announced by Vietnam were "sheer boasting aiming at deceiving the Vietnamese people and world opinion" (*BR*, 19 January). In April China accused Vietnam of occupying a disputed South China Sea island (Bojiao Island in the Nansha group, also known as the Spratly Islands), warning that China retained the right to recover its "sacred territory" (*Honolulu Advertiser*, 16 April).

China and Portugal initialed a joint declaration on the settlement of the Macao question on 26 March, restoring Chinese sovereignty over Macao on 20 December 1999 (*BR*, 6 April). The document was signed by Premier Zhao and Portuguese prime minister Anibal Cavaco Silva in Beijing on 13 April (ibid., 20 April).

Sino-Indian relations became tense during the year, continuing a souring that began in 1986. In February Deng Xiaoping reportedly repeated to visiting U.S. secretary of state Shultz a warning that he had related to U.S. secretary of defense Caspar Weinberger in October 1986 that China would have to "teach India a lesson" if that country did not stop nibbling at Chinese territory (*FEER*, 4 June). But in February India held a ceremony marking the establishment of statehood for Arunachal Pradesh (approved by the Indian Parliament in December 1986) in territory that is disputed between the two countries, which the Chinese government quickly protested (*BR*, 2 March; also *Liaowang*; *FBIS*, 2 April).

Subsequently, India amassed troops and conducted maneuvers along the Sino-Indian frontier. Apparently the two sides came very close to an outright military encounter in May. (*BR*, 4 May; *FEER*, 4 June.) Indian foreign minister N. D. Tiwari held talks with Chinese vice-foreign minister Liu Shuqing and also met with Acting Premier Wan Li in Beijing on 15 June. The Chinese maintained that, before negotiations could begin, both sides should strictly observe the line of actual control drawn on 7 November 1959. Liu is reported to have said that the only way "unpleasant incidents" are to be avoided "is for India to withdraw its military personnel who have crossed the line of actual control." Liu and Tiwari agreed to hold the next round of talks between Chinese and Indian officials in New Delhi within the next six months. (*BR*, 29 June.) Liu Shuqing led the Chinese delegation to the talks that began on 15 November (ibid., 23–29 November).

Stephen Uhalley, Jr.
University of Hawaii at Manoa

India

Population. 800,325,817
Parties. Communist Party of India (CPI); Communist Party of India–Marxist (CPM)
Founded. CPI: 1928; CPM: 1964
Membership. CPI: 479,000; CPM: 361,000
General Secretary. CPI: C. Rajeswara Rao; CPM: E. M. S. Namboodiripad
Politburo. CPI: Central Executive Committee, 9 members: C. Rajeswara Rao, Indrajit Gupta, Indradeep Sinha, Jagannath Sarkar, N. Rajasekhara Reddi, N. E. Balaram, M. Farooqi, A. B. Bardhan, Homi Daji; CPM: 10 members: E. M. S. Namboodiripad, B. T. Ranadive, M. Basavapunnaiah, Harkishan Singh Surjeet, Jyoti Basu, Samar Mukherjee, E. Balanandan, Nripen Chakravarty, Saroj Mukherjee, V. S. Achuthanandan
Central Committee. CPI: National Council, 125 members; CPM: 70 members
Status. Legal
Last Congress. CPI: Thirteenth, 12–17 March 1986, in Patna; CPM: Twelfth, 25–30 December 1985, in Calcutta

Last Election. 1984. CPI: 2.71 percent, 6 seats; CPM; 5.96 percent, 22 seats (out of 509 contested in 544-seat Parliament)

Auxiliary Organizations. CPI: All-India Trade Union Congress, All-India Kisan Sabha, All-India Student Federation; CPM: Centre for Indian Trade Unions, All-India Kisan Sabha, Students' Federation of India

Publications. CPI: *New Age* (Indradeep Sinha, editor), Indian-language dailies in Kerala, Andhra Pradesh, West Bengal, Punjab, and Manipur; CPM: *People's Democracy* (M. Basavapunnaiah, editor), Indian-language dailies in Andhra Pradesh, Kerala, and West Bengal

State assembly elections were held in Kerala (southwest) and West Bengal (northeast) during 1987. A communist-led front regained power in Kerala and another communist-led front significantly enhanced its position in West Bengal. In other state elections, however, the communists remained weak, underscoring the regional nature of Indian communism and its inability to build a firm base outside established areas of support.

The CPM. The CPM again demonstrated that it was far more successful electorally than the CPI. In the West Bengal and Kerala state assembly elections, where the communists did well, the CPM was the senior partner in left front alliances and was by far the biggest party in such fronts. The communists also did well in the village council elections in the northeastern state of Tripura, where they won 104 of the 167 contests. Tripura has a Bengali-speaking majority and its state assembly has a communist majority. However, neither communist party was able to do well outside these traditional bastions of strength. In the Haryana state assembly elections, for example, the communists were able to win only two of the 87 contested seats.

In all three states where the communists did well, CPM-led fronts dominated the political scene. In West Bengal and Tripura the leftist partners of the CPM performed poorly. This resulted in grumbling among them, especially on the part of the CPI, whose leaders complained that the party had not been fairly treated in the allocation of seats. In Kerala the CPM was by far the largest element in the left front, but it did not dominate as completely as in the other two cases.

The West Bengal state elections in March, held at the same time as the Kerala and Kashmir assembly elections, was an electoral triumph for the CPM and for the 73-year-old Jyoti Basu, who has been chief minister of the state continuously since 1977. The CPM won a landslide in rural West Bengal, where the party has built a well-honed organization based on an extensive land distribution program. The leftist coalition won 251 of 294 seats, and the CPM alone had a comfortable majority. However, the ruling Congress Party again outpolled the left front in Calcutta, West Bengal's major urban center. The CPM also lost some support in the northern Darjeeling district, where militants are fighting to carve out a separate Nepali-speaking state. Some 2,500 party cadre were reportedly forced to flee the district as a result of the violence. (*FBIS–South Asia*, 26 August.) CPM general secretary E. M. S. Namboodiripad went so far as to call the Nepali movement anti-national, although he did not rule out the possibility of a measure of self-government for the region (ibid., 8 January). The CPM accused Prime Minister Rajiv Gandhi and his Congress Party of playing to Nepali separatist sentiment. The left front, portraying itself as the defender of Bengali interests against an unfriendly center, may have gained support among the state's voters for its stand.

Encouraged by the magnitude of its victory, the CPM moved more quickly than before to form a state government. Within a week Basu selected most of his cabinet, reserving eight portfolios for himself. Laying down a firm line with the CPM's leftist partners, the appointments were made without the usual lengthy negotiations.

Basu emerged as the indisputable leader of the CPM's powerful West Bengal unit. The party organization under state general secretary Saroj Mukherjee has been unable to exert control over the legislative branch, which is in marked contrast to the power wielded by the organizational wing during the long tenure of Pramode Das Gupta, who died in the early 1980s. A more self-confident Basu also quickly asserted himself on the national scene. In the wake of the West Bengal victory he called for an alliance of left and democratic parties to oppose the Congress Party at the center and for a meeting of opposition chief ministers to discuss state/center relations. Basu has been among the more outspoken chief ministers demanding greater state control over the allocation of financial resources.

Basu's enhanced prestige might complicate the national CPM leadership's efforts to cooperate more closely with the CPI, because he tends to take a more pragmatic stance regarding cooperation with conservative parties than either the national leadership or the CPI and also because of his pragmatic economic policies within the state. In addition, the left wing of the CPM in West Bengal is likely to become more restive under another five years of Basu's leadership because the chief minister will probably continue his program of enforcing labor discipline in the state and encouraging joint public-private ventures in order to generate jobs in the state. (*NYT*, 24 March.) One of the most visible joint ventures is a large petrochemical complex in a Calcutta suburb involving the Goenka family, perhaps India's most successful capitalists.

In the state of Kerala the communists unseated the Congress Party-led United Democratic Front (UDF). Nevertheless, even though the CPM-dominated Left Democratic Front (LDF) increased its strength from 53 to 76 seats (of 138), it only gained 2 percent more of the popular vote than the UDF. The communist victory may have resulted from marginally greater support of Hindus worried by the increasing assertiveness of the large Muslim minority in the state. CPM general secretary Namboodiripad took a hard line against electoral alliances with any communal party, Hindu or Muslim. This stance led to a walkout by some CPM members in Kerala who considered it poor electoral tactics not to work out electoral arrangements with a faction of the Muslim League. Indeed, Namboodiripad's stand was part of a national effort by the CPM to portray communalism as one of the country's major dangers. Hindus might also have appreciated the communist opposition to the Muslim Women's Bill, legislation passed by Parliament at Gandhi's insistence to prevent the courts from ruling on traditional Islamic customs regarding divorce. Hindus all over India argued that Gandhi was "pandering" to the demands of obscurantist Muslim leaders.

The CPM has traditionally taken a negative view toward the Congress Party and, unlike the CPI, has never been involved in any fronts with it. But Gandhi's political troubles during the first half of 1987 presented the party with a dilemma. The CPM leadership calculated that the divisions within the Congress Party might lead to Gandhi's downfall. Should the party cooperate with the opposition to bring this about? Many CPM members believed that Gandhi's fall would result in an even more conservative substitute. The 13 July presidential elections were a litmus test of Gandhi's ability to hold the ruling party together. A loss might well have set the stage for his defeat, especially if President Zail Singh were the candidate. Singh might have been able to gain the support of a sufficient number of state assembly and parliamentary legislators—who elect the president—by drawing support both from Congress Party dissidents and from the opposition. Developments leading up to the presidential election indicate that the CPM's national leadership decided against participating in efforts to oust the prime minister.

The National Coordinating Committee—comprising both the CPM and the CPI—issued a statement on 30 April opposing the notion that the president possesses the constitutional power to dismiss the government and call for new parliamentary elections. This action distanced the communists from much of the political opposition, which backed this constitutional thesis. (*FEER*, 24 May.) Namboodiripad even indicated that the CPM could support the Congress Party candidate if that party met three conditions: specifically naming the "imperialist" countries destabilizing India; prohibiting multinationals from operating in India; and instituting a "genuine" land reform program (ibid.). Implementation of such conditions, however, would have involved a real leftward lurch that the Gandhi government was unwilling to make, even though the Congress Party's Working Committee had virtually subscribed to these proposals early in the year. The cautious communist stand, particularly that of the pro-Moscow CPI, may have been influenced by open Soviet praise of Gandhi. A pro-CPI journal reported that during Soviet leader Mikhail Gorbachev's visit to New Delhi in November 1986, he advised communist leaders not to confront Gandhi (*Patriot*, 27 December 1986).

In mid-June—when the effort to draft Singh was being actively discussed—the CPM national executive registered its formal opposition to a second term for Singh. The CPM leaders argued that the opposition had in principle agreed to a mutually acceptable candidate and that the CPM had already indicated its opposition to the incumbent. (*FEER*, 9 July.) Politburo member H. S. Singh told the press that calling for Gandhi's resignation made no sense because the prime minister still had a large parliamentary majority (*Telegraph*, 29 May). The CPM and the CPI backed V. K. Drishna Iyer, a retired judge with reportedly leftist leanings, and Iyer was nominated by a multiparty selection committee including Namboodiripad; the decision infuriated the Hindu-revivalist Bharatiya Janata Party. In the 13 July presidential poll, R. Venkataram, the Congress Party candidate, won by a vote of 740,248 to 281,550. The unity among the Congress Party legislators in the vote probably strengthened the self-confidence of Gandhi and indicated that communist support was no longer crucial.

Almost immediately after the presidential poll, the CPM and CPI made a virtually complete turnabout on Gandhi and his government. They began to demand his resignation and actively participated in rallies supporting V. P. Singh, who was trying to mobilize support for his anti-corruption campaign. Singh was drawing huge crowds in the Hindi-speaking area that is the base of his support. The communists' rather sudden enthusiasm for him may have been a calculated move to gain entry into the Hindi-speaking region where they have been weak. They may also have wanted to retain influence in a movement that might eventually replace Gandhi. The CPI, which suffered a major loss in support because of its backing of the Congress Party during the 1975–1977 state of emergency, probably wanted to avoid losing its legitimacy as an opposition party.

But many CPM cadre, particularly in West Bengal, probably disagreed with the national leadership's policy prior to the presidential vote. As early as March, West Bengal chief minister Basu was calling for joint opposition activity to exploit the crisis within the Congress Party (*FEER*, 30 July). Basu was the first speaker at a 19 April opposition rally calling for a united opposition response to Gandhi, even referring to the prime minister as a "liar" (*FBIS-South Asia*, 10 April). Nripen Chakravarty, CPI chief minister of Tripura, also spoke at the rally.

The communists' National Coordination committee met on 2 August, just weeks after the presidential poll, and called for the opposition parties to form a front aimed at forcing Gandhi to resign and to call for fresh parliamentary elections. The CPM was willing in principle to participate in a broad opposition front, whereas the CPI wanted to limit close cooperation to acceptable leftist parties. Perhaps responding to CPI wishes, four acceptable leftist parties (the CPM, CPI, Forward Bloc, and Rashtriya Socialist Party) met 16 August to forge a common strategy; they adopted V. P. Singh's anti-corruption theme as a key element in the campaign against Gandhi, though they did not recommend closer political ties with Singh. (*FEER*, 2 September.) The CPM's Central Executive Committee even encouraged dissident Congress Party legislators to bolt the party and thus hasten the downfall of the prime minister. Namboodiripad stated that the ruling party is not interested in carrying forward the "anti-imperialist tradition"; he even argued that the Congress Party was itself a cause of the country's instability. (*Link*, 23 August.) The CPM and CPI sponsored a massive 9 December rally in New Delhi demanding the resignation of Gandhi and fresh elections.

But the CPM, at least its national leadership, was opposed in principle to an opposition alliance. Politburo member H. S. Singh argued in May that such an alliance was not possible without a common program (*Telegraph*, 29 May). However, the party did lend support to Singh's anti-corruption drive. On 12 October it helped organize a large anti-communalism rally in Patna that featured V. P. Singh. Yet Singh was careful at that rally not to criticize directly either the Hindu-revivalist RSS or the Bharatiya Jana Sangh, organizations that provide important leg work in his drive to mobilize support in the Hindi-speaking states. This incident underscored his dilemma as he tried to turn his Jan Morcha organization into a viable political movement. The ideological left and the right possess the desired cadre and they each have important regional bases of support, but the ideologically opposed groups have refused to cooperate with each other and could reject Singh if he appeared to draw too close to one side or the other. Even the CPM, which will cooperate with a broader range of parties than the CPI, refuses to take part in any conclave involving the Bharatiya Janata Party. So far Singh has walked a fine line to maintain the support of both sides. This is made doubly difficult because both the communist left and the Hindu-revivalist right contain important elements that support Gandhi.

On specific domestic and foreign policy issues the two communist parties are not very different. Their differences tend to be over personalities and political tactics. In foreign policy they both tend to back Soviet policies and have praised Gorbachev's Asian policy announced in July 1986. After Gandhi's successful October visit to the United States, both parties blasted the Gandhi government for abandoning what they define as India's progressive foreign policy. The Soviets now regularly include the CPM in briefings conducted by visiting dignitaries.

The CPI. The CPI continued to play a junior role to the CPM in the leftist front state governments in West Bengal, Kerala, and Tripura. The party's legislative standing actually declined in elections held in West Bengal and Tripura, resulting in considerable grumbling about the larger communist party's fairness. Nonetheless, the National Coordination Committee met more frequently than in the past, and the two parties jointly sponsored a larger number of activities. There are important tactical differences between the parties. The CPI is more selective about the parties with which it will cooperate. A pro-CPI journal criticized the CPM's participation in "conclaves" with rightist parties (*Link*, 23 August). The CPI disagrees with the CPM's endorsement of a revolt within the Congress Party and with the CPM's thesis that the Congress Party is itself a cause of the country's instability. In short, it believes that the ruling party is still within the progressive camp.

General Secretary C. Rajeswara Rao spelled out his party's tactics at the CPI's 6 June National Council meeting (*New Age*, 14 June). He argued that religious communalism is the major cause of instability, pointing to the growth of the Hindu-revivalist RSS, Sikh militancy in Punjab, and Islamic fundamentalism in Kashmir. He claimed that the West is backing such forces to undermine Indian economic development and to change its progressive foreign policy. He maintained that the communists must guard against a mere rightist alternative to Gandhi. The bourgeois parties, he claimed, ignore the magnitude of the threats to Indian integrity. Therefore the only suitable alternative to Gandhi is to build a new front around the CPI and CPM. The election results in Kerala and West Bengal were perceived as a hopeful sign in this direction.

Regarding V. P. Singh, Rao argues that the CPI should assist him on the limited issue of corruption. He opposed more general political support to Singh, who he claims has adopted a "dull policy" on the key question of communalism. (*Hindustan Times*, 18 October.)

Despite the national CPI leadership's less hostile view toward the Congress Party, Rao continued to reject any close relationship with it. He had led a bruising party battle in the late 1970s to distance the CPI from the ruling party in an effort to restore its legitimacy as a viable opposition party after almost a decade of CPI cooperation with the Congress Party. There are important CPI elements who oppose this stand, and they could take comfort in the statements of Soviet leaders backing Gandhi. Rao dropped Mohit Sen and P. Pandiyan—two of the more prominent CPI leaders backing a closer relationship with the Congress Party—for opposing the offical party line. (*Patriot*, 27 December 1986.)

Although the foreign policies of the CPI and CPM are similar, the CPI tends to focus more on foreign policy issues and to vigorously defend the Soviet line. After Gorbachev's late 1986 visit, the National Council announced that the USSR will stand by India "in facing any threat," probably a response to those who fear that Gorbachev's new Asia policy diminishes the importance of India (*IB*, February). Regarding Moscow's new economic policies, Rao stated that the reforms will provide "huge opportunities and advantages of the socialist system" (TASS, 5 May).

Other Communist Parties. Small communist parties and groups exist on both the left and right of the CPM and CPI. On the right is the All-India Communist Party (AICP), established by S. A. Dange, a Lenin Peace Prize recipient who left the CPI in a disagreement over its decision to abandon the united front policy with the Congress Party. The AICP has been virtually ignored by the Communist Party of the Soviet Union (CPSU), perhaps because of its continued anemic electoral performance. Moreover, its separate existence is apparently in opposition to the CPSU's desire for a united Indian communist party. In 1986 the moderate Communist Marxist Party emerged in Kerala because the national leadership refused to sanction alliances with communal parties. It was excluded from the left front in the Kerala state assembly elections and won only 1 of the 70 seats it contested.

To the left of the CPI and CPM are a number of small and often antagonistic Maoist parties, often collectively called Naxalites—a reference to a district in West Bengal where radical communists tried to establish a rural base of operations in the late 1960s. Some of these parties have retained their revolutionary orientation and others have begun to operate by the rules of India's parliamentary system. Radical Naxalite activity is reported to be growing in West Bengal, Bihar, and Andhra Pradesh. Perhaps the most violent group is the People's War Group operating in the Telengana region of Andhra Pradesh. It has reportedly been involved in a number of direct encounters with the state police and has built a substantial support base by distributing land to the peasantry. (*Patriot*, 2 November.)

On 27 December Naxalites in Andhra Pradesh staged a dramatic kidnapping of eight senior bureaucrats—including the principal secretary of the state government—who belong to the elite Indian Administrative Service. In subsequent negotiations the state government agreed to release eight Naxalite prisoners. The militants and the government released their respective prisoners on 29 December. (*FBIS–South Asia*, 30 December.)

Walter K. Andersen
Alexandria, Virginia

Indonesia

Population. 180,425,534
Party. Indonesian Communist Party (Partai Komunis Indonesia; PKI)
Founded. 1920
Membership. 1,000–3,000, with less than 10 percent engaged in organized activity (*World Factbook*, 1987); 100–300 in exile
General Secretary. Pro-Moscow: Satiadjaya Sudiman; pro-Beijing: Jusuf Adjitorop
Leading Bodies. No data
Status. Illegal
Last Congress. Seventh Extraordinary, April 1962
Last Election. N/a
Front Organizations. None identifiable in Indonesia
Publications. *Tekad Rakjat* (People's Will), published abroad, no data on editor

Despite some official expressions of concern about a possible resurgence of communist infiltration, especially during this election year, and despite claims by exiled PKI leaders, there was little discernible activity by Indonesia's once-mighty communist party, banned since 1967. There was some unrest in the country, but it is not clear whether the PKI was involved.

Leadership and Party Organization. In February an official of Indonesia's Home Affairs Ministry put the number of members or supporters of the PKI at 1,410,333. This estimate, he said, was based on a 1955 registration process and the present number might actually be less. In any case, of that number 1,370,230 were to be allowed to vote in the upcoming election. The 40,000 barred from voting had failed to pass a security screening held in May 1986 (*Jakarta Post*, 12 February).

It remains difficult to determine what if any party organizational structure exists in Indonesia or abroad. Satiadjaya Sudiman, believed to be the general secretary of the party's smaller Moscow wing, remains its only visible leader. He continues to be a member of the editorial board of the *World Marxist Review*, to which he contributed several articles during the year, and he attended meetings in Prague and in Ulan Bator as the representative of the Central Committee of the PKI.

The only information about PKI leaders still in Indonesia came from an article by Sudiman identifying former PKI leaders whose execution was apparently imminent. They include Ruslan Widjajasastra, a labor leader who had been sixth in line in the party leadership; Sukatno, general secretary of the People's Youth Organization; Iskandar Subekti; and Acep Suryaman. It is not known if these executions, which Sudiman said were timed to occur before the 23 April elections to intimidate the population, took place (*WMR*, March).

Domestic Party Activities. Whatever PKI activities took place in Indonesia were not generally evident. Nevertheless, especially in the weeks leading up to the elections, government officials warned of a possible resurgence of communist activity. In February armed forces commander general L. B. Murdani said that former members of the defunct PKI were still actively subverting the government. He said that security offices had recently caught some of them, but gave no details. Former PKI members were active abroad, consolidating themselves and attempting to paint a bad image of the New Order, he said; "It is our task to detect their activities as part of national preparedness." (*Jakarta Post*, 18 February; *FBIS*, 24 February.)

In a lecture in Semarang a few weeks later, Major General Setiyana, the military region commander, spoke of efforts by leftist and rightist extremist groups to foil the elections by constitutional means as well as by force. Rightist extremist groups refers to Islamic fundamentalists, who have been showing increasing strength in Indonesia. Setiyana said that PKI leaders had infiltrated everywhere without being identified. He believed the PKI would continue to make a comback because of its unrelenting fighting spirit and would re-emerge at an appropriate time. "They are trying to infiltrate all social strata by covertly exploiting the intelligentsia. Their infiltration may occur within institutes of higher learning and the armed forces," he said. Facts show, he went on, that PKI remnants are trying to infiltrate student and youth groups to control campuses as well as to infiltrate religious and other social groups. He said there were indications that remnants of the PKI were hiding in Central Java and other regions. He asked the campuses to enhance their vigilance to avoid being infiltrated by irresponsible elements deliberately trying to destroy the New Order, and he urged security personnel to report to special officers the presence of unidentified persons in their neighborhoods. Setiyana warned that leftist and rightist extremist groups would destabilize the situation by instigating workers to strike, provoking young people to commit crimes and acts of banditry, spreading negative reactions to the fruits of development, and urging people not to vote. He urged rectors, lecturers, and students to prevent the campuses from "being turned into theaters for the extremist groups." (*Merdeka*, 6 March; *FBIS*; 13 March.)

Setiyana's remarks coincided with the arrival in Jakarta of the Soviet foreign minister and reportedly received serious attention for that reason (*Jakarta Post*, 10 March; *FBIS*, 20 March). There seemed to be a mixed reading in the Indonesian government over whether the communists posed a real threat to the elections. A few days after Setiyana's remarks, Lieutenant General Tri Sutrisno told an audience of military and civilian leaders in Bandung that he was not aware of any groups in the country wishing to disrupt the general election. In Jakarta General Murdani said that warnings about extremist threats during the coming elections did not mean that the security situation had deteriorated. (*Jakarta Post*, 10 March; *FBIS*, 20 March.)

In any case, the government sought to minimize opportunities for disruption during the election campaign by establishing careful controls. The main condition for candidates standing for election was that they be "environmentally and personally clean," a term meaning that the candidate and his family be clear of communist ideology (*Jakarta Post*, 18 February; *FBIS*, 24 February). Contestants were advised not to hold large rallies since they would be difficult to control. During the 25-day campaign, the five-day "cooling-off period," and election day itself, all conferences, meetings, workshops, and scientific research, and other activities involving large groups of people and government officials were to be postponed (*Jakarta Post*, 10 March; *FBIS*, 20 March). During the "cooling-off period" campaign activities were banned, newspapers prohibited from publishing political stories, and the armed forces were placed on alert (*WSJ*, 21 April).

Despite these bans, however, on the last official campaign day an estimated one million people showed up at an opposition rally in Jakarta, possibly the largest political gathering in twenty years (ibid.). There were stone-throwing incidents in various parts of the city; tension in the streets was high, and troops and riot police fired warning shots to break up the fighting. At a major rally of Golkar, the ruling government party, State Secretary Sudharmono offered his condolences to victims of the violent clashes that had taken place during the campaign period. A few days earlier the military command had officially confirmed the death the previous week of an opposition supporter in Klaten, a Javanese city (Hong Kong, AFP, 16 April; *FBIS*, 22 April).

This was, nevertheless, the most orderly and violence-free election since independence, although the campaigning revealed a strong undercurrent of dissatisfaction among young, urban Indonesians. Sarwono Kusumaatmadja, the young general secretary of Golkar, noted that the new generation of Indonesians—a majority of the population is now under age 30—is less concerned with "the old bogies of communism, extreme right, [or] extreme left" and more interested in "the intangibles: justice, fair play, democracy" (*WP*, 25 April).

Both within Parliament, where Golkar won its expected 70 percent of the vote, and outside of it, there were indications that the leadership and particularly the military were seeking to defuse opposition before it exploded in violence as in Korea. Nevertheless, there were at least three student protests in early November. The largest, in Ujung Padang, the capital of South Sulawesi, reportedly was a riot by thousands of students from several college campuses (*WP*, 6 December). The police chief in Ujung Padang said the rioting was serious enough to disturb public order, but in Jakarta General Murdani said that the unrest involved "a small group of people who refused to use safety helmets," which had been made mandatory for motorcycle riders. Murdani said the protestors had stoned and burned police vehicles, forcing the police to take stiffer measures, but he indicated that he was unaware of any possible political reason behind the rioting. (*Jakarta Post*, 3 November; *FBIS*, 16 November.)

One area in which the party claimed to be active in Indonesia was dissemination of the party paper, *Tekad Rakjat*. The founding and development of *Tekad Rakjat* was described in a survey of press organs of fraternal parties published in the *WMR*. In view of the situation in Indonesia, the article said, publication was begun abroad. The first issue appeared on 7 November 1967.

Initially the format was that of a typical magazine, but it was then reduced to pocket size, averaging 25 pages. Recently it was reduced to a single sheet with very closely printed text in order to make it safer to circulate and keep in Indonesia. It is printed in Indonesian, with some issues also printed in English "for the benefit of sympathizers in other countries." Ten years after it was founded, *Tekad Rakjat* began publishing an *International Monthly Bulletin*, carrying articles from the *WMR* in Indonesian. The journal's editorial staff "works under the party's direct leadership"; it carries analyses of current problems linked to the party's life and struggles, especially "the struggle for the unity of Indonesian Communists." The "Motherland" section reports on economic, political, and cultural developments in Indonesia. The section on international events includes reports on the international communist and working class movement, the national liberation movement, and the peace movement.

The links with readers are through party organizations and a readers' post, and the number of requests for additional copies "is prompting us to increase the journal's circulation . . . The paper is circulated chiefly among PKI members. Although it goes chiefly to workers, intellectuals and students, it is read also by people of other social groups" (*WMR*, August). There is no independent estimate available to indicate how wide a readership the journal has, but several years ago the Indonesian government had warned the population against this publication (see *YICA*, 1984).

International Views, Positions, and Activities. On the international scene the pro-Moscow wing of the PKI continued to be represented in the traditional gatherings that mark the communist calendar. The party continues to have a representative on the editorial board and editorial council of *Problems of Peace and Socialism*. A PKI representative attended a *WMR*-sponsored international symposium in Prague 19–21 May on the October Revolution and the "Main Problems of our Age" (*WMR*, July).

General Secretary Sudiman took part in the Consultative Meeting of Communist and Workers' Parties of the Asia-Pacific region, organized by the Mongolian People's Revolutionary Party. The meeting, held in Ulan Bator 7–9 July, was attended by delegations sent by 21 parties from eighteen countries. The meeting was one in a series focused on the problems of peace and security in the Asia and Pacific regions. (New Delhi, *People's Democracy*, 19 July.)

Sudiman also attended the symposium in Prague on the "U.S. Policy of Neoglobalism, the Military-Industrial Complex, Contemporary Militarism, and the Working Class" sponsored by the *WMR* Commission for General Theoretical Problems. He participated in the discussion on the question, "Can the military-industrial complex be bridled?" (*WMR*, September).

Sudiman had two articles in the *WMR*. In March he wrote an appeal to "all people of goodwill" to strengthen their solidarity with Indonesia's democrats and halt the Indonesian government's plan to execute another group of PKI members. The article, "Stop Executions and Free Political Prisoners," called on the government not only to call off the planned executions but also "to release all imprisoned patriots immediately and unconditionally." Sudiman had issued a similar appeal to no avail in 1986, when the first group of former communist leaders sentenced to death fifteen years earlier were executed (see *YICA*, 1987).

In the April issue Sudiman's article, "Against Japanese Militarism," stated that U.S. strategists have assigned Japan "the key role in knocking together" an anti-Soviet, anti-socialist bloc in the Asia-Pacific region. The Japanese government's decision to raise the limit on defense spending paved the way "to the unrestrained growth of appropriations for militaristic purposes." Indonesia had particular reasons for concern, because heavy Japanese capital investments in Indonesia of $5.2 billion and over 200 Japanese business projects were not only pushing out their foreign rivals but also ruining national entrepreneurs. "A large part of the Indonesian bourgeoisie with the mass petty proprietors linked to it" want the Indonesian government to bar Japan's economic expansion. Although the Japanese government has given its utmost support to this expansion, "diplomatic and political pressures on other countries, including Indonesia, do not always work," the article noted. "Could that be the cause of the nostalgia for the military strength which the Japanese ruling circles have been building up on an ever greater scale?" The lifting of the military spending limit was said to be a "sinister symptom" with serious consequences for Asia; it is linked to Japan's inclusion in NATO's military strategy, the extension of its sphere of military activity to a thousand miles, and its participation in the U.S. Strategic Defense Initiative.

Throughout the year the Indonesian government continued to strengthen its ties with Eastern bloc countries, not only economic ties but also endorsing with enthusiasm some of the political positions espoused by a series of high-ranking Soviet and East European visitors, including the bloc-approved Pacific Nuclear-Free Zone agreement. Although economic ties were also being strengthened with the People's Republic of China, old suspicions about Chinese assistance to the Indonesian communist party did not disappear. No diplomatic relations have existed with China since 1967, although trade was resumed in 1985. The use of Chinese characters is still forbidden in Indonesia. Indeed, Tai Chi—the Chinese gymnastics that have become something of a fad in Indonesia—aroused a Jakarta city councilman to suggest that they be banned because the exercises were reportedly followed by lectures in Chinese (*NYT*, 21 January). Although the Tai Chi issue was generally regarded as a joke, State Secretary Sudharmono said that the new cabinet to be appointed in 1988 would not alter Jakarta's current attitude toward China (Hong Kong, AFP, 17 April; *FBIS*, 21 April).

Jeanne S. Mintz
Washington, D.C.

Japan

Population. 122,124,293
Party. Japan Communist Party (Nihon Kyosanto; JCP)
Founded. 1922
Membership. 470,000 (*World Factbook*, 1987)
Central Committee Chairman. Kenji Miyamoto
Presidium Chairman. Hiromu Murakami
Central Committee. More than 200 members
Status. Legal
Last Congress. Eighteenth, 26–28 November
Last Election. July 1986; 9 percent of popular vote in House of Representatives, 12 of 250 seats in House of Councillors, 27 of 512 seats in House of Representatives
Auxiliary Organizations. All-Japan Student Federation, New Japan Women's Association, All-Japan Merchants' Federation, Democratic Foundation of Doctors, Japan Council of Students, Japan Peace Committee, Gensuikyō (Japan Council Against Hydrogen and Atomic Bombs)
Publications. *Akahata* (Red banner), daily circulation 550,000, Sunday circulation 2,500,000, total readership over 3,000,000 in addition to frequent special issues and a poster called *Akahata Photo News* published twice a month in 90,000 copies; *Gakusei shimbun* (Student newspaper), weekly; *Shōnen shōjo shimbun* (The boys' and girls' newspaper), weekly; *Zen'ei* (Vanguard), theoretical journal; *Gekkan gakushū* (Monthly studies), *Josei no hiroba* (Women's tribune), *Gurafu konnichiwa—nihon kyōsantō desu* (Hello, we are the JCP), *Asu no nōson* (The countryside tomorrow), *Bunka hyōron* (Cultural review), *Keizai* (Economics), and *Rōdō undō* (Workers' movement)—all monthlies; *Sekai seiji: Rompyō to shiryō* (International politics: critical reviews and materials), fortnightly

In 1987 the JCP celebrated the 65th anniversary of its founding in July, released an updated history of the party, and celebrated the 95th birthday of Sanzō Nosaka, chairman-emeritus of the Central Committee.

The party had some cause for optimism during the year. Its candidates performed so well in the August nationwide local elections that the JCP now has more representatives in local assemblies than at any time in its history. Central Committee chairman Miyamoto also announced an increased party membership and an enlarged readership of the party's newspaper, *Akahata*. But these gains are probably due to recent membership drives and campaigns to increase subscriptions to *Akahata*, and so they may be temporary.

On a less positive note, the JCP remained isolated from other political parties, all of which JCP leaders regard as anticommunist. Even cooperation with the Japan Socialist Party was infrequent, not only in elections but in antinuclear protests and support for disarmament. According to JCP leaders, all of the other parties were to some degree cooperating with the conservative Liberal Democratic Party; therefore the JCP is Japan's only "progressive party." Hence, the possibility of the JCP joining in a coalition in an effort to win control of the government seems more remote than ever.

JCP leaders were at odds with the Japanese media, labor unions, and the government of Yasuhiro Nakasone, as well as with Prime Minister Noboru

Takeshita, who assumed power in November. Relations remained bad with the People's Republic of China but showed continuing improvement with the Communist Party of the Soviet Union (CPSU). The JCP was active internationally and won points both at home and abroad for its work on the issue of nuclear disarmament.

The JCP remained a "Eurocommunist" party, claiming that it would come to power peacefully and through constitutional means. The Japanese public has little reason to question the veracity of this, though the party's image was sullied to some degree by activities of the Japanese Red Army and other terrorist and left-wing groups that are incorrectly associated with the JCP in the minds of many Japanese.

Party Leadership and Meetings. Kenji Miyamoto, at age 79, remained the JCP's top leader and party spokesman. Tetsuzō Fuwa, chairman of the Party Presidium, had a stroke in April and spent several months recuperating. In November at the party's Eighteenth Congress, Fuwa was elected to the newly created post of vice-chairman of the Central Committee. The move was apparently made to allow Fuwa to retain an important title even though he was no longer active in day-to-day party work. Hiromu Murakami, who had been acting Presidium chairman, became chairman.

The JCP held its sixth Central Committee plenum meeting 9–11 February at its headquarters in Tokyo. Miyamoto gave the opening address; Fuwa delivered a report for the Presidium and covered party work. The main issues discussed at this meeting were the JCP's opposition to the sales tax bill and preparations for nationwide local elections in April. Also discussed were Japan's "de-industrialization," mass political propaganda, increasing *Akahata* readership (setting a goal of a gain of 30 percent since the last elections), vitalizing party life, socialist countries' relations with Japan, and a number of other issues. (*Akahata*, 13 February.)

It was resolved to abolish the daily reporting system (from party branches to district committees), in order to overcome bureaucratism. Proposals were also made to combat "defeatism"—to prevent party members from leaving—and to increase readership of party decisions (which Miyamoto said was only 30–40 percent). (Ibid.)

The party's seventh plenum was convened on 30 May for four days, also at party headquarters. Miyamoto gave the opening address; Murakami delivered the Presidium report. The major issues discussed were the national sales tax (being promoted by Prime Minister Nakasone), secret arrangements and collusion with the United States to bring nuclear weapons into Japan, the wiretapping of party members, and the results of the April election. Three Central Committee members—Sueo Sasaki, Iwao Teramae, and Norio Nakamura—were elected to the Presidium. It was also resolved that the Eighteenth Congress would be held in November.

The Central Committee of the JCP held its ninth plenum 16–17 September, again in Tokyo. Miyamoto and other party leaders addressed the meeting. The meeting unanimously approved a draft resolution for the Eighteenth Congress, amendments to party rules, and the procedure for electing delegates to the congress. According to the draft resolution, the JCP had expended much effort in averting nuclear war and urging the elimination of nuclear weapons. This was cited as a plus in terms of the popularity of the JCP in Japan and its global reputation. In this context the party line was set regarding the upcoming talks between Soviet general secretary Mikhail Gorbachev and U.S. president Ronald Reagan on intermediate nuclear force (INF) weapons. The document also described the internal situation in Japan and difficulties in the party's relation with other political parties in Japan. (*FBIS*, 25 September.)

The JCP held its Eighteenth Congress for five days in November in Atami in Shizuoka prefecture. Miyamoto gave the opening address; Murakami gave the report of the Central Committee. Miyamoto reviewed the history of the party, past policies, the recent elections, and various issues and problems facing the party. Essentially, however, the policy line remained unchanged from the Seventeenth Congress.

The main successes reported by Miyamoto were the antinuclear movement and the April election victory (see below). Miyamoto noted that he had reported at the last congress that the "Appeal for Hiroshima and Nagasaki—for the total ban and elimination of nuclear weapons" had spread to 135 countries and had obtained the signatures of fifteen million people in Japan. Since then, he said, it has become active in 150 nations and has 27 million signatories in Japan. Nineteen million people, he reported, had just recently signed the appeal in Vietnam. He also reported optimistically that, at the World Conference Against Atomic and Hydrogen Bombs held in Japan in 1987, a call was made for one billion signatures—double the number of the

Stockholm Appeal. (*Akahata*, 26 November.) He went on to say that even though the INF agreement would eliminate only one class of weapons, it is good because it would "inspire people of the world." Finally, he reported, the Association for Non-Nuclear Government had formed in 24 of Japan's prefectures. (Ibid.)

In his Central Committee report, Murakami asserted that the U.S. arms buildup was the cause of the October stock market crash and that the elimination of nuclear weapons would strengthen the global economy. He went on to pledge support for the INF talks, but declared that they were not going nearly far enough. In that context he condemned "deterrence theory" and stated that 70 percent of the Japanese people, according to public opinion polls, do not believe the three nuclear principles (not building, no acceptance of, and no transport of nuclear weapons) are being adhered to. (Ibid.)

Regarding domestic issues, Murakami charged that the Takeshita government was carrying on the line of the Nakasone cabinet—resorting to *nemawashi* (maneuvering behind the scenes) and *kane-mawashi* (give and take of secret money). He also condemned the Japan Socialist Party's visits to the United States and the People's Republic of China, its shift to the right politically, its cooperation with the conservative Liberal Democratic Party, and its anticommunist policies. He expressed concern about the trade union movement, land prices, and the "plight" of the farmers. (Ibid.)

In formulating resolutions at the Eighteenth Congress, Miyamoto stated that the policy and line of the Seventeenth Congress had "proved correct." He pointed to the record victory of the JCP in the House of Councillors election in 1986, to the fact that in proportional representation constituency of the upper house the JCP's representation is the highest ever, and to the JCP's victories in the nationwide local elections in 1987. He stated that the party's criticism of the "general crisis" theory at the previous congress proved correct and delineated reasons why. (*Akahata*, 30 November.)

Resolutions or statements of future policy in regard to nuclear issues included: An antinuclear international united front is neither anti-imperialist nor anti-capitalist; elimination of nuclear weapons is the "urgent, central task" linked to preventing nuclear war and facilitating nuclear disarmament; and antinuclear peace movements, individuals, parties, and other groups who talk but do not act should not be included. The party also resolved to struggle against "hegemonism" and to defend the right of self-determination—in a pointed reference to the Chinese Communist Party. It resolved to oppose the Council on Tax Reform (which had "shut out" the JCP in discussions on the sales tax issue), the celebration of the emperor, and the resubmission of the State Secrets' Protection Bill. Finally, Miyamoto said the party would "struggle for progressive unity" in the trade union movement to prevent it from being turned into an "industrial patriotic association" under parties "supporting the establishment." (Ibid.)

Miyamoto was critical of the Coordinating Committee for Export Control to the Communist Bloc (COCOM) for closing its eyes to U.S. hi-tech sales to China yet censuring Toshiba for selling military-related technology to the Soviet Union. He charged, moreover, that the Japanese government and COCOM have restricted free trade. Miyamoto also said the JCP is resolved to struggle to impose "democratic control" over monopoly capital to "ensure that it fulfills its social responsibility" while advocating a reduction in fixed property taxes, more urban planning, and inheritance taxes on housing lots. (Ibid.)

In the report on party construction, JCP membership was put at 480,000, *Akahata* readership at over three million, and supporters at six million. The report, however, did note that the goal of four million *Akahata* readers set at the Twelfth Congress in 1973 had not been reached and was, in fact, below the peak of three and a half million. It was also reported that 19,000 new party members were recruited before the Eighteenth Congress and 450,000 new *Akahata* readers were added—both record lows; 80 percent of party branches recruited no new members until the recent recruitment drive. Miyamoto concluded that party construction lags behind what the JCP has been able to do in the international field. (Ibid.)

The report parenthetically noted that workers account for 65.6 percent of JCP membership, farmers 2.6 percent, working citizens 8.9 percent, and intellectuals 4.5 percent—"bringing together advanced people from all strata." Women, it said, make up 38.3 percent of membership, illustrating the "weight the JCP has always attached to the role of women." In age, the report said, members in their 30s constitute 36.8 percent, concluding that "the overwhelming majority of members are at the age of mental and physical maturity." (Ibid.)

Domestic Affairs and Issues. The major issues of concern to the JCP during 1987 were, broadly defined, economic and military. The party was also troubled about police wiretapping of party members. Relations with other political parties were not good, and that constituted a domestic problem for JCP leaders. Party support in Okinawa—a major stronghold for the JCP—waned, which was also of concern. The organization of a new national labor organization, comprising a number of labor unions, rejected ties or cooperation with the JCP; that weakened JCP labor support.

The paramount issue for the JCP during the year, particularly in terms of its campaigning for the April elections, was the 5 percent general sales tax promoted by Prime Minister Nakasone. JCP leaders contended that Nakasone had promised he would not introduce such a tax and that it would cause a net tax increase for 90 percent of wage earners. The JCP in particular opposed the tax because, as party spokesmen argued, it would be used for increases in the defense budget and would be offset by lower corporate taxes. The JCP also opposed terminating the tax exemption on personal savings accounts because it would hurt small and medium wage earners. (*Akahata*, 13 February.)

All of the opposition parties opposed the tax, though the JCP was not welcomed into any joint efforts. The party thus worked with the "Liaison Council of Various Circles Against the Introduction of Large-Scale Indirect Tax and Abolition of Tax Exemption on Small Savings" and the Tokyo conference (on the Spring Labor Struggle) led by a number of trade union organizations. The JCP also organized its own signature campaigns. It won considerable public suport on the issue, and this no doubt helped the party considerably in the April elections.

The JCP also railed against the "de-industrialization" of Japan, or the shifting of production facilities abroad and the heavy investment abroad by large Japanese companies. The party attributed this to the rising value of the yen, which was under pressure by the United States, and to the record accumulation of capital by Japanese companies in recent years. JCP leaders noted that bankruptcies of small companies had increased by ten fold since 1985, that unemployment was at a record 3 percent (predicting it would go to 6 or 7 percent) and that wages were going down, employees were being shifted to subsidiaries with lower pay, and many were being dismissed. In short, according to the JCP, the lifetime employment system in Japan has begun to collapse. (*Akahata*, 15 January.)

In drawing theoretical implications from Japan's and the world's economic situation, JCP leaders argued that Stalin's thesis of a "general crisis" of capitalism, because of the strength of the socialist bloc, was not accurate. Instead JCP leaders cited Lenin's thesis in *Imperialism* that world capitalism is growing but is unstable. The Sino-Soviet split and other problems among communist countries were additional reasons for rejecting Stalin's view in favor of Lenin's. JCP leaders concluded that revolutionary movements would be encouraged by the rapaciousness of world capitalism, global economic instability, and contention in the capitalist world. The party also argued that Japan, rather than becoming an independent force of imperialism, was even more controlled by the United States, as witnessed by Japan's growing military strength and the rise of the yen—both policies originating in Washington. (*Zen'ei*, May.)

The JCP continued its strong opposition to defense spending, arguing that it violates the Constitution, and criticism of the military alliance with the United States. This made the party unique among the political parties in Japan. JCP leaders protested that Japan had exceeded the 1 percent of gross national product limit on defense spending set by the Liberal Democratic Party. In this connection, Miyamoto compared Prime Minister Nakasone with Hitler and called his "1986 System" comparable to the Imperial-Rule Assistance Organization that produced Japanese fascism before and during World War II. He also said the State Secrets' Protection Bill proposed by the Nakasone administration is like the wartime General Mobilization Law. (*Akahata*, 1 January.)

The JCP strongly supported the Soviet Union's INF proposals and lauded the talks between Gorbachev and Reagan later in the year. Party spokesmen added, however, that the talks should go further. The JCP emphasized that Japan should be a nuclear-free area, that the Strategic Defense Initiative (SDI) should be condemned, and that Japan should not participate in the SDI effort. (*Akahata*, 4 March.) The JCP later proposed a nuclear weapons "zero" for Asia and the Pacific as well as for Europe—a policy it has espoused for some time. JCP leaders attributed the nuclear arms race—as well as nuclear testing and the arming of space—primarily to President Reagan. (Ibid.)

The JCP's relations with other political parties continued to be strained. This was reflected, for example, in few instances of cooperation in fielding jointly sponsored candidates in the elections. In mid-year Miyamoto charged that the Japan Socialist Party and Komeitō Party have "virtually accepted" the U.S.-Japan Security Treaty and the Japanese Self-Defense Forces and that all of the opposition parties have "accelerated their turn to the right" (*Japan Times*, 27 July). Later in the year Presidium Chairman Murakami declared that the JCP would not even seek cooperation from the Japan Socialist Party to achieve the abolition of nuclear weapons (*FBIS*, 3 December).

As another reflection of the JCP's difficulties and differences with other opposition parties, it was excluded in mid-year when the Japanese Private Sector Trade Union Confederation (Rengō) was formed from 62 labor unions with a total membership of 5.5 million and ties were established with the opposition parties (*Japan Times*, 21 November). Miyamoto admitted that this would strengthen the noncommunist opposition forces in Japan and condemned the movement to unify labor in Japan, saying that nearly three million workers are not committed to Rengō (ibid., 27 July). Miyamoto noted that it is the policy of the JCP to form a national labor organization with a distinct class character (ibid.).

In August the JCP filed a complaint with the Tokyo District Court alleging that the Kanagawa police had tapped the telephone of Yasuo Ōgata, head of the party's International Department (ibid., 11 August). Ōgata had complained earlier of bugging attempts, and the JCP had gone on record saying that the government has approved of spying on party officials. Ōgata's charge seemed to be based on concrete evidence, though it was uncertain if it involved top police officials or not. (Ibid., 5 August.)

The JCP staged protest rallies in Okinawa in the spring to commemorate the fifteenth anniversary of its reversion to Japan from the United States. Demonstrations were held near U.S. bases. The turnout, however, was not as good as expected, reflecting a conservative trend in a region of traditionally strong JCP support. This, in addition to opinion polls showing greater support among college students for the U.S.-Japan Security Treaty than in other parts of Japan, troubled JCP leaders. (Ibid., 16 March.)

Elections. Nationwide local elections were held on 12 April (for thirteen governors, forty-four prefectural assemblies, two mayors, nine municipal councils, and 26 other local government heads and assemblymen). The two days of balloting combined a total of 2,573 local elections for some 3,700 prefectural, mayoral, and town assembly posts and 830 heads of local government. (*FBIS*, 26 March.) The opposition, including the JCP, sought to redress the Liberal Democratic Party's victory in the dual national elections in 1986. The government's sales tax package was the biggest election issue, and opposition to it was the main plank of the JCP's campaign. JCP candidates charged in their campaign that the tax would be a burden to 90 percent of wage earners and would be used to finance U.S.-Japan military cooperation. (Ibid.)

In a prelude to this election, a House of Councillors by-election was held in Iwata prefecture in early March. The Japan Socialist Party candidate—with the support of the Democratic Socialist Party, United Social Democratic Party, and Komeitō Party—beat the Liberal Democratic Party candidate in a largely conservative area. The JCP fielded its own candidate, Yasuo Ushiyama, who won only 31,949 votes out of 659,309 cast. (Ibid., 10 March.)

However, in the April elections the JCP performed very well. In 44 prefectural assemblies it increased its representation from 88 (in 1983) to 121. In assemblies in cities with "special legal status" the JCP won 80 seats for an increase of six. In both categories the JCP ranked fourth in number of seats of all parties participating. (*Akahata*, 1 June.) This gave the JCP 4.5 percent of the seats in the prefectural assemblies and 12 percent of the seats in the assemblies of the major cities. The JCP also won a victory in the Fukuoka gubernatorial election. The jointly sponsored JCP–Japan Socialist Party candidate defeated the candidate supported by the Liberal Democratic Party, Democratic Socialist Party, and Komeitō Party in a hotly contested election. (Ibid.)

In the second phase of the election, the JCP increased its representation from 926 to 972 in ordinary cities, from 159 to 167 in Tokyo wards, and from 776 to 831 in towns and villages. In the ordinary cities the JCP ranked fourth among the parties in seats; in Tokyo wards it ranked third behind the Liberal Democratic Party and Komeito. In the towns and villages the JCP ranked first—though this was less than significant because independents hold the overwhelming majority of seats in the towns and villages. (Ibid.)

Tetsuzō Fuwa, who was Presidium chairman at that time, later noted that the JCP had "overcome its absence" in 144 assemblies at the city-town-village level. He also pointed out that the JCP had increased the total number of local assembly members to a record of 3,824. (Ibid., 3 June.) At the party's seventh plenum, Miyamoto boasted that only the JCP, among all of the parties, gained at every level. (Ibid.)

Miyamoto attributed the JCP election victory to "pioneering efforts" in the struggle for progress in Japanese society and to the JCP's stance on Nakasone's tax plan. He also credited increases in *Akahata* subscriptions, party work in educating the voters, and good campaigning. (Ibid.) The JCP was no doubt also helped by a lower voter turnout: 59.78 percent in the gubernatorial elections as compared to 63.2 percent in the previous election, and a decline of 1.8 percent in the prefectural assembly elections (*FBIS*, 13 April).

Although the election was clearly a victory for the JCP in one of Japan's three most important elections and the one said to be a harbinger of future political trends, the JCP did little more than recover from its losses in the previous national local elections. Miyamoto also expressed displeasure at the fact that 181 JCP incumbents lost—a very large number as compared to incumbent losses in other parties (*Akahata*, 3 June). Also not good news was the fact that there was little cooperation between the JCP and other opposition parties. Finally, there was friction in the party concerning how many candidates to field and whether the party should enter races where there was little chance of success. (Ibid.)

Auxiliary Organizations and Splinter Groups. The JCP supports or maintains strong ties with a number of affiliate organizations. (See previous volumes of *YICA* for additional details.) However, the JCP does not maintain ties with other communist organizations in Japan and is generally known to eschew any contacts with radical leftist groups, especially terrorist organizations, although links are often made by the media and therefore in the public mind, thereby damaging the reputation of the JCP.

One of the most important JCP-affiliate groups, Gensuikyō, sponsored a three-day peace conference in Tokyo during the summer. The meeting was attended by 300 participants, including representatives from 39 foreign countries and 75 international organizations. Atomic bomb victims related their experiences, and future antinuclear activities were planned. (*Japan Times*, 2 August.) Gensuikyō also held rallies in Hiroshima and Nagasaki and planned a "peace wave" movement to circle the earth in October during United Nations Arms Reduction Week (ibid., 11 August). A similar organization affiliated with the Japan Socialist Party that had often held joint meetings with Gensuikyō in the past remained alienated and held its own meetings in Hiroshima and Nagasaki at about the same time (ibid., 2 August).

The Japanese Red Army, which is not connected with the JCP but is frequently identified with it in the public mind, was in the news several times during 1987. In February a Greek newspaper, citing sources from Interpol, reported that the Japanese Red Army planned to attack a commercial airport in Europe. Fingerprints confirmed that several members of the group had visited Rome and Munich recently, and as a result Japan Airlines instructed its office to take greater security precautions. (*FBIS*, 9 February.)

In November Osamu Maruoka, number two in the Japanese Red Army leadership, was arrested in Tokyo. As a result police learned that the Japanese Red Army had sent messages to its sympathizers criticizing the Seoul Olympic Games and suggesting that terrorist acts might be committed there. Maruoka was in the process of making plans for a trip to South Korea and had in his possession a large sum of cash. It was also learned that Maruoka might have also been planning to somehow, perhaps through a hijacking or kidnapping, negotiate the release of Masashi Daidoji, member of the East Asian Anti-Japan Armed Front, a terrorist organization held responsible for a number of bombings of Japanese companies. (*Japan Times*, 26 November.)

Maruoka was also known to have been involved in the Lod Airport massacre in 1972. Based on that background, officials opined that he was planning some type of spectacular terrorist action to celebrate the fifteenth anniversary of that event. After Maruoka's arrest several of his accomplices or associates were also arrested, revealing efforts by Maruoka to establish a Japanese Red Army base in Okinawa. Further investigation revealed a possible Philippine connection, though a police raid there failed to result in any arrests. Nevertheless, the problem was considered serious enough for the Association of Southeast Asian Nations (ASEAN) to cut short by one day their meeting in Manila in early December. (Ibid., 25 November, 1, 4 December.)

In December Italian police arrested two members of the Japanese Red Army and charged them with rocket attacks on the U.S. and British embassies in Rome in June. No one was killed or injured in these attacks, but they did cause a disturbance at the time of an important annual summit meeting of leaders of seven Western nations. Responsibility for the attacks was claimed by a group called the Anti-Imperialist International Brigade. This group, which became known in May 1986 after claiming responsibility for attacks on the U.S. and Japanese embassies in Jakarta, Indonesia, is thought to be connected to the Japanese Red Army; some say it is that group's "guerrilla operation force." (Ibid., 5 December.)

All of this indicates that the Japanese Red Army, which has been relatively inactive since 1977, has become a threat again. Yet it has also been reported that the group may have split, which is confirmed by its own messages concerning becoming a "mass oriented" organization aimed at the being a left-wing unification group with anti-war, antinuclear, and anti–U.S.-Japan Security Treaty goals; or, terrorist-oriented members may have gone on their own. (*Japan Times*, 5 December 1987.)

International Views and Activities. The JCP remained an active party in terms of international contacts and conferences. Its international views and activities have been widely known in Japan and abroad. The party saw some improvement in relations with the Soviet Union during 1987; however, there was no improvement in relations with the People's Republic of China. The JCP sent a number of delegations to meet leaders of other communist parties and received a number of visitors in Tokyo.

In his New Year's message, Miyamoto denied that the JCP had provided arms to the New People's Army in the Philippines, charging that these rumors originated from a U.S. plot to complicate the issue of U.S. aid to the Nicaraguan *contras*. He asserted that the JCP has no relations with the Communist Party of the Philippines or the New People's Army, though he said he hopes "democratic forces will move ahead" in the Philippines. (*Akahata*, 1 January.) During the year the Polissario Front (Western Sahara) visited JCP officials in Tokyo. The party also said that it strengthened its ties with the African National Congress (South Africa) and the Sandinistas (Nicaragua).

In January Yoshitomo Kobayashi, representing the JCP, met with Nguyen Van Linh, general secretary of the Vietnam Communist Party. Linh said he "highly valued" the JCP's vanguard role in the "struggle against Japanese monopoly capital in collusion with U.S. imperialism," and he expressed solidarity between the two parties to consolidate and develop a new stage in the revolutions in each country. (*FBIS*, 30 January.)

In May the JCP and the Romanian Communist Party issued a jont declaration as a follow-up to talks between Miu Dobrescu and Miyamoto in August 1986. Miyamoto and Romanian Communist Party leader Nicolae Ceauşescu signed the declaration on behalf of each party. The declaration focused on the international situation, particularly the global arms race, and on global economic instability. Both sides called for intensified efforts to prevent nuclear war and for disarmament talks. Noting that the world "transverses a crucial period" and that the destructive potential of nuclear weapons is sufficient to destroy humankind scores of times, they pledged to support a "united international antinuclear front that will include all of the forces of peace and democracy and to take common action internationally." (*JPRS*, 25 June.)

The two leaders also noted that the foreign debt of developing countries had reached nearly a trillion dollars and that the widening gap between the poor countries and the developed countries "put in jeopardy not only national independence and sovereignty, but also the growth and stability of the world economy and the future of mankind." They proposed the implementation of a new international economic order and an international conference under U.N. aegis. (Ibid.)

In October Ceauşescu received a delegation of the JCP headed by Presidium member Hiroshi Tachiki in Bucharest. The two agreed on global problems and confirmed the correctness of the joint declaration in April. (*FBIS*, 7 October.)

In September Tachiki met with Erich Honecker, general secretary of the Socialist Unity Party of Germany, in East Berlin. The two discussed the nuclear arms race, disarmament, and the global situation generally. They stressed common interests in nuclear disarmament and their common views on the INF talks. (Ibid., 29 September.)

Several JCP delegations visited the Soviet Union during the year, reflecting warmer relations between the JCP and the CPSU. The JCP changed its position on one important issue relative to the Soviet Union: the Northern Islands controversy. The JCP had been the strongest critic among Japanese political parties of the Soviet Union not returning the islands to Japan. However, in his New Year's address Miyamoto stated that the islands would be used for military purposes by the United States and Japan if returned and, therefore, the security of the Soviet Union would be endangered. He went on to argue that the U.S.-Japan military alliance is an obstacle to successful talks on the issue. (*Akahata*, 1 January.)

In January an *Akahata* delegation visited Moscow and Leningrad. *Pravda* hosted the delegation led by Yoshinori Yoshioka, chief editor of *Akahata*. In June G. M. Korniyenko, first deputy head of the CPSU International Department, met with Miyamoto in Tokyo. The Soviet ambassador to Japan also attended the meeting. (*FBIS*, 23 June.) In October a JCP delegation visited Moscow at the invitation of the CPSU to discuss economic restructuring in the Soviet Union. TASS reported the meeting under the rubric of "interparty ties." (Ibid., 5 October.)

In addition to these meetings, the Soviet Union sent congratulations to the JCP on its 65th anniversary, and the JCP lauded Gorbachev's efforts to get rid of nuclear weapons, particularly the INF negotiations (ibid., 17 July, 18 November). In October, in commemoration of the 70th anniversary of the Bolshevik Revolution, *Akahata* carried a long article assessing relations between the JCP and the CPSU. The article delineated the reasons for past differences but noted that, since the December 1984 summit talk between Miyamoto and then-general secretary Konstantin Chernenko, the two had "put aside differences of opinion" and as a result relations had improved. The article mentioned some remaining disagreements but cited the parties' overriding concern with nuclear disarmament. The article concluded by describing the "main feature" of relations between the two as friendship and cooperation. (*Akahata*, 22 October.)

In contrast, relations between the JCP and the Chinese Communist Party (CCP) remained strained. JCP spokesmen declared that the struggle against hegemonism is essential to the defense of the right of self-determination and that there is a need to overcome interference derived from support for "parallel parties." JCP leaders stated that China had not apologized for its past interference in JCP affairs and thus there could not be rapprochement between the two parties. (Ibid., 1 January.) The JCP assailed Chinese leaders for advocating "mutual trust" with the Nakasone government and for supporting the U.S.-Japan Security Treaty and the Japanese Self-Defense Forces. It also attacked the CCP for its "anti-people" policy of supporting Japan's industrial structure adjustment "because of aid money Peking [Beijing] was receiving from Japan." (Ibid.) In March *Akahata* carried a long article delineating the history of relations between the JCP and the CCP; it chided China for, among other things, its "barbarous" attack on Vietnam in 1979, its support of Pol Pot, its collusion with the United States, and its erroneous "Three Worlds View" (of Mao) (*Akahata*, 30 March). In July *Zen'ei* carried a long, two-part article entitled "China's Foreign Policy Since the Cultural Revolution." It too was highly critical of Beijing, citing China's "betrayal" of scientific socialism, its abandonment of world revolution, its alignment with the United States, and its "hegemonism." (*Zen'ei*, July.)

Elsewhere the JCP blasted North Korea for trying to dictate policy on the Korean Peninsula and for demanding "blind obedience" to Kim Il-song. Party publications cited "barbarian hegemonism and anti-social offenses," such as violations of self-determination and North Korea's attitude toward the Olympic games. (*FBIS*, 9 November.)

Biography. *Hiromu Murakami.* Murakami, age 66, joined the JCP after World War II, during which time he had been an officer in the Japanese Imperial Army. During the period of U.S. occupation Murakami was active in union work. He was arrested on one occasion for involvement in a campaign against the closure of a school for Korean residents in Japan. In 1970 he became chairman of the JCP's Osaka prefectural committee. He became Acting Presidium Chairman following Tetsuzo Fuwa's stroke in April 1987 and was named Presidium Chairman at the close of the Eighteenth Party Congress in November. He is a member of the Japanese Lower House from the Osaka No. 3 constituency.

John F. Copper
Rhodes College

Korea:
Democratic People's Republic of Korea

Population. 21,447,977
Party. Korean Worker's Party (Choson Nodong-dang; KWP)
Founded. 1946 (a united party since 1949)
Membership. 2.5 million
General Secretary. Kim Il-song

Standing Committee of the Politburo. 3 members: Kim Il-song (DPRK president), Kim Chong-il (Kim Il-song's son), O Chin-u (minister of People's Armed Forces)

Politburo. Kim Il-song, Kim Chong-il, O Chin-u, Yi Kun-mo (DPRK premier), Pak Song-chol (vice president), Yim Chun-chu (vice president), Yi Chong-ok (vice president), Hong Song-nam, So Chol, Yon Hyong-muk, Kim Yong-nam (foreign minister), Ho Tam, O Kuk-yol, Kang Song-san, So Yun-sok; alternate members Kye Ung-tae, Chon Pyong-ho, Hyon Mu-kwang, Kim Pok-sin, Choe Kwang, Kang Hui-won, Cho Se-ung, Hong Si-hak, Chong Chun-ki, Yi Son-sil

Secretariat. Kim Il-song, Kim Chong-il, Kang Song-san, Yon Hyong-muk, Ho Tam, Kye Ung-tae, Hwang Chang-yop, Ho Chong-suk, Chon Pyong-ho, Chae Hui-chong, So Kwan-hui, Choe Tae-pok, Chi Chang-ik.

Central Committee. 145 full and 103 alternate members

Status. Ruling party

Last Congress. Sixth, 10–15 October 1980, in Pyongyang

Last Election. 2 November 1986. 100 percent participation reported for Eighth Supreme People's Assembly, all 706 candidates on the slate elected.

Subordinate and Auxiliary Organizations. General Federation of Trade Unions of Korea, Union of Agricultural Working People of Korea, Korean Democratic Women's Union, Socialist Working Youth of Korea, Friends' (Chongdogyo religion) Party, Korean Democratic Party, Committee for Peaceful Reunification of the Fatherland, many others

Publications. *Nodong sinmun* (Worker's daily), KWP organ; *Minju Choson* (Democratic Korea); *Kulloja* (The worker), party theoretical organ; *Choson inminkun sinmun* (Korean people's army news); many others. English-language publications include the *Pyongyang Times* and *Korea Today*; in Japan *The People's Korea* generally follows the North Korean line. The official news agency is the Korean Central News Agency (KCNA).

Leadership and Organization. Kim Il-song and his son, Kim Chong-il, continued to dominate North Korean politics. In particular, except for the period around Kim Il-song's birthday in April, the media paid increasing attention to the activities and thoughts of Kim Chong-il. A typical paean praised the "dear leader" as an "outstanding genius . . . unlike any of the present times" (KCNA, 13 October). In February the regime opened up the restored "Secret Camp" at Mt. Paektu, including the log cabin that is Kim Chong-il's official birthplace (Pyongyang Domestic Service, 11 February). Domestic media stressed that the future of the party and people depended on the "inheritance of unity," and on 16 February the younger Kim's birthday was celebrated with the expected pomp and obeisance. The media also acclaimed the 70th anniversary of the birth of Kim Chong-suk, Kim Chong-il's late mother and the object of her own personality cult (KCNA, 22–24 December; *Democratic People's Republic of Korea*, December).

Nevertheless, there were indications of concern within the leadership that the succession might not be smooth, and rumors that some senior officials believe Kim Chong-il is unfit (see *NYT*, 20 September). Quotations from the younger leader himself indicated the existence of problems. On 15 July, for example, *Nodong sinmun* devoted its first two pages to a speech he had given exactly one year before to a group of Central Committee members, "On Problems of Education in the Chuche Idea." The speech was also printed in the July issue of *Kulloja*, the KWP theoretical journal. Kim stressed the importance of "the monolithic ideology of our Party" and complained that some officials misunderstood this "perfect revolutionary theory." He criticized those who "are not firm in regarding the leader as the center of a social-political organism" and attacked some officials for "defeatism," implying they held doubts concerning the Kims' social and economic policies.

For the next several months the media referred to the importance of this speech, marking it as a significant event in the expanding public adulation of Kim Chong-il. On 14 September *Nodong sinmun* published a special article that not only extolled the speech but also carried a particularly strong demand for unquestioning loyalty to the leader. According to this piece, Kim could not be considered as merely the leading individual in the social body. "As physical life is impossible without parents, social and political life is unthinkable without the leader." The author warned that those who forgot about the leader's "benevolence" would not be considered "dutiful."

The public stress on party unity continued through the autumn. Special articles commemorated a 1976 Kim Chong-il call for political cohesion and "purity" (*Nodong sinmun*, 16, 22 October). Party members were warned against allowing the emergence of "factional elements." In a further indication of concern, the State Theatrical Company revived "Three Pretenders," a play about three ministers at a fictional Korean court who feign loyalty to the king while he is alive but contend for the throne once their master is dead. Each seeks outside support, and their rivalry leads to the disaster of foreign conquest. The play had been written in the 1920s, a time of "extreme factional strife in the nationalist movement and the early communist movement in our country." (*Democratic People's Republic of Korea*, November.)

Kim Chong-il maintained his interest in cultural affairs in 1987, apparently shaking off the effects of the embarrassing defections the year before of Sin Sang-ok and Choe Un-hui, the film director and actress. In one of his few (compared to his father) major public appearances, the junior Kim gave "on the spot guidance" at the State Theatrical Company in Pyongyang (KCNA, 21 March). In addition, his work was the major focus of the Sixth Congress of Korean Journalists, which was held in Pyongyang at the end of July. A speaker told the assembled delegates that "all the successes achieved in press activity are entirely the results of the wise leadership and warm care of dear comrade Kim Chong-il" (ibid., 29 July).

The younger Kim continued to promote people associated with his cultural policies. Choe Tae-pok, a relatively obscure alternate Central Committee member and head of the State Education Committee, was apparently rewarded for his role in the educational system. Choe moved from the State Education Committee to full Central Committee membership and was made a party secretary at a Central Committee plenum in December 1986.

Kim Chong-il continued to play little role in foreign affairs. Rumors that he would visit China or the Soviet Union proved false; in July the North Korean ambassador to China denied the rumor that the younger Kim had gone to Beijing earlier in the month (Xinhua, 27 July). For most of the year Kim Chong-il continued not to meet with foreigners or accept gifts directly from their hands.

Toward the end of the year, however, there were tentative signs that Kim Chong-il might become more active in this area. In November *Nodong sinmun* carried unusual quotes from the younger Kim on international topics (KCNA, 19 November). He urged the practice of *chajusong* (sovereignty) not only by Third World countries but also by states "that follow U.S. imperialism," perhaps implying interest in improved relations with developed capitalist states. Around the same time he issued greetings to some Third World politicians (KCNA, 11 November). On 20 November Kim and his father both received a visit from the outgoing Soviet ambassador to Pyongyang (Pyongyang Domestic Service, 20 November). Ten days later a North Korean delegation carried greetings from both Kims to Chinese leaders (Xinhua, 30 November).

Rumors in 1986 that the Seventh KWP Congress would be held the next year proved false. The congress should have been held by 1985 at the latest—according to party rules adopted in 1970—although a full ten years elapsed between the Fifth (1970) and Sixth (1980) Congresses.

A Central Committee plenum did meet in December 1986 and resulted in some leadership changes (KCNA, 30 December 1986). Yi Kun-mo, the new premier, and Hong Song-nam, the new first vice-premier, were elevated to the Politburo. Former premier Kang Song-san and former first vice-premier Yon Hyong-muk retained their Politburo slots and moved to the Secretariat. Choe Tae-pok and Chon Pyong-ho also became secretaries, replacing Kim Hwan and Pak Nam-ki, who were dropped. In October 1987 Hong Song-nam returned to his previous status as a vice premier and chairman of the State Planning Commission. Pak Nam-ki was removed from the latter and assigned to an unidentified post.(Pyongyang Domestic Service, 14 October.) Virtually the entire leadership turned out in November for local assembly elections (KCNA, 15 November).

Kim Chung-nin, who was dropped from the Politburo after the 1983 Rangoon bombing, reemerged in public as head of the KCNA in 1987. He made a few public appearances and led a delegation to the USSR in November (KCNA, 19 November, 2 December).

The question of institutional stability was complicated by generational changes in the KWP—an important metaphor, given North Korea's dynastic politics. A 15 September editorial in *Nodong sinmun* noted that revolutionary leaders were relinquishing their "positions on the frontline" to the new generation. The commentator complained that these younger leaders lack their elders' experience of "arduous struggle." Again, in early October, Pyongyang media stressed the importance of teaching the younger generation about the feats of Kim Il-song and other elder heroes (Pyongyang Domestic Service, 7 October). This could have been an indirect criticism of Kim Chong-il—the leader of the new generation—but more likely was a general call for greater productivity and sacrifice from party functionaries.

These comments came in the context of physical problems among older leaders. Rumors concerning the elder Kim's health continued to surface—and be disproved. Japanese press reports connected a two-and-a-half week absence (20 June–7 July) of the "Great Leader" from public view with rumors he had been incapacitated. Kim's meeting with Indonesian foreign minister Mokhtar on 7 July belied this story. (KCNA, 7 July.)

Defense Minister O Chin-u, 77, who was rumored to have suffered serious injuries in an automobile accident in 1986, was absent from public view from September 1986 until August 1987. Chief of Staff O Kuk-yol, 60, performed many ceremonial duties in O's place. O Chin-u finally reappeared on 20 August, when he paid his last respects at the bier of Central Committee member and veteran revolutionary fighter Pak Yong-sun; however, O was not reported to have attended the funeral (Pyongyang Domestic Service, 20 August; KCNA, 21 August). He next appeared in the company of Kim Il-song at the theater on 2 October and at the 40th anniversary celebration of the Mangyongdae Revolutionary Academy on 11 October (Pyongyang Domestic Service, 2, 11 October). He appeared well on the road to recovery by 22 October, when he met with his East German and Malian counterparts (KCNA, 22, 30 October). He met with new Chinese ambassador Yun Yezhan on 3 November and the next week saw outgoing Soviet ambassador Nikolay Shubnikov (KCNA, 3, 9 November). In December he saw the commander of China's Shenyang Military Region and the incoming Soviet ambassador, Gennadiy Bartoshevich (Xinhua, 14 December; KCNA, 28 December).

Pak Yong-sun was one of three Central Committee members to die in the late summer. Yi Kyong-son died in August, as did Minister of State Security Yi Chin-su. Kim Chong-il made a personal appearance at Yi Chin-su's bier on 24 August (KCNA, 24 August).

Domestic Developments: The Economy. The leadership has been dissatisfied with the country's lackluster economic performance. Kim Il-song admitted to a group of visiting Japanese legislators that North Korea's economic growth has been "slow" (Tokyo, *Asahi shimbun*, 2 June). So far, however, there have been no signs that Kim is ready to reform economic management.

Economic issues dominated the agenda of the twelfth plenum of the Central Committee on 28 December 1986 (Pyongyang Domestic Service, 28 December 1986). There was little evidence of any North Korean interest in economic reform along either Soviet or Chinese lines. The regime, in a typically orthodox manner, charged party cadres with the task of raising the workers' revolutionary spirit in order to attain greater economic accomplishments. One editorial proclaimed flatly that finding "reserves for increased production" depended on the revolutionary spirit of party functionaries (ibid., 24 July). On 13 February a *Nodong sinmun* special article warned that "departure from class principle is an act of abandoning the revolutionary banner." The regime's keynote themes, contained in the new economic plan, included no apparent stress on greater rank-and-file autonomy or a role for the marketplace in decisionmaking (KCNA, 22, 23 April). In October an article in *Nodong sinmun* warned against the "slightest" expression of illusion about imperialism and declared that North Korea would not compromise any "interests of revolution" (ibid., 4 October).

On the other hand, the regime called the alleviation of the country's food, clothing, and housing shortages "one of the most important tasks" of the Third Seven-Year Plan (1987–1993). The new plan—which had been delayed two years by problems in meeting the goals of the old one—was launched at the second session of the Eighth Supreme People's Assembly (SPA), held 21–23 April. In his lengthy report, Premier Yi Kun-mo repeated goals set at the first SPA session in December 1986 for annual production of many basic commodities. In addition, Yi declared that North Korea's foreign trade volume would increase 3.2 times, its industrial output 1.9 times, railroad freight traffic 1.6 times, and agricultural output 1.4 times, as compared to 1986.

Finance Minister Yun Ki-chang reported figures for 1986 expenditures and the 1987 budget plan. He reported a 1986 surplus of 142.4 million won, based on revenues of more than 28.5 trillion won and expenditures of less than 28.4 trillion won (KCNA, 22 April). Defense spending reportedly accounted for 14 percent of total spending. In 1987, according to Yun, the state expected to spend more than 30.3 trillion won. Yun declared that defense spending in 1987 would be 13.8 percent of total expenditures. The leadership reportedly planned to increase investment as follows: industrial construction by 8.6 percent; power industry by 10.5 percent; extractive industries by 8 percent; metal industry by 9.1 percent; agriculture by 6 percent; education by 5.8 percent; cultural affairs by 2 percent; public health by 6.5 percent; and scientific and technological development by 21.5 percent (KCNA, 23 April).

The size of this last figure reflected the leadership's desire—highlighted in the SPA law passed in support of the new Seven-Year Plan (KCNA, 23 April)—to seek in technological advancement a way to escape economic stagnation. Pyongyang media called for "preferential" efforts in scientific and technological fields and claimed that 4,000 new inventors had emerged since Kim Chong-il had published "On Further Developing Sciences and Technology" in 1985 (ibid., 4 November).

The regime demonstrated a particular interest in modernizing the agricultural sector. One editorial referred to the "ideological, technological, and cultural backwardness" of rural life and warned against the class distinctions between workers and peasants (*Nodong sinmun*, 23 October). The regime clearly believed that "industrialization" of rural life was a necessary prerequisite to alleviating North Korea's shortages of food, clothing, and housing.

Indications of economic problems surfaced with the defection to South Korea (via Japan and Taiwan) in January of eleven members of a family from Wonson (KCNA, 26 January). Kim Man-chol, a doctor and the group's leader, claimed that grain shortages are commonplace and that fish and pork rations are provided only on four public holidays (Hong Kong, AFP, 12 February). His mother-in-law claimed clothing rations were also scant; for example, North Koreans reportedly receive no more than two pairs of socks per year and can get new shoes only when they turn the old ones in. There is no evidence of widespread dissatisfaction with the economic situation, and Kim Man-chol admitted that North Koreans regard their plight as a "matter of course" (Yonhap, 27 February).

Nonetheless, reports of shortages appear plausible—even given the possibility that Kim Man-chol exaggerated the extent of the problem. A *Pravda* correspondent, after a visit to North Korea, wrote of "certain difficulties and complex problems" that persist in agriculture. He noted that the grain problem "still has not fully been resolved." (*Pravda*, 7 October.) There were indications in 1987 that supply problems were caused in part by the North's inadequate transportation system. A 21 July *Nodong sinmun* editorial spoke of the "strained state" of railroad transportation and complained that the effect of production increases could be negated by inadequate transportation. The editorial noted that solving the transportation problem was imperative if the Seven-Year Plan was to be implemented successfully, and it urged that new lines be constructed and the load capacity of existing ones be strengthened.

Economic problems were further complicated in July when—for the second year in a row—both Koreas were hit by typhoons. North Korea seems to have survived the storms better than those of 1986, judging from public praise for the performance of the country's irrigation and drainage system (KCNA, 5 August). No such praise had been given the year before.

Difficulties of a different kind were highlighted in September, when two Western bank syndicates declared North Korea in default on loans totaling $770 million. Creditors threatened to seize North Korean property, but they reportedly expressed hope Pyongyang would restore their faith by making interest payments. Some Hong Kong companies doing business with North Korea reportedly were considering halting further transactions because Pyongyang was falling increasingly behind in its payments. (*NYT*, 20 September.)

Despite its economic problems, the leadership showed no signs of reducing the priority placed on large, showcase construction projects. A 27 July *Nodong sinmun* article urged all economic sectors to supply materials and labor for these projects "preferentially and in a timely manner." In August General Yon Chong-won stated that soldiers being discharged under North Korea's peace initiative "should proceed to the grand Socialist construction sites." Having completed the Nampo Lock Gates (a tideland reclamation and navigation improvement project on the country's west coast), the regime turned its attention to expanding the Kimchaek Iron and Steel Works and building the Sunchon Vinalon (synthetic fabric) complex, the Sariwon Potash Fertilizer complex, and other projects (*Nodong sinmun*, 7 March). In addition, a high priority was assigned to the construction of facilities for the 1988 Olympic Games and the 1989 meeting of the World Federation of Democratic Youth.

International Views and Positions. North Korean foreign policy in 1987 was marred by South Korea's progress toward an unprecedented diplomatic and propaganda victory with the 1988 Olympic Games. On other fronts, the North launched a peace offensive designed to seize the diplomatic high ground regarding both the suspended North-

South dialogue and relations with the United States. North Korea–Soviet relations remained generally good, despite differences over economics and the Olympics. Kim Il-song's visit to China demonstrated his determination to balance relations with its giant communist neighbors, although problems in Sino–North Korean relations remained apparent. In addition, North Korea continued to place a high priority on good relations with Third World states.

By year's end, North Korea's attempts to prevent other countries from attending the 1988 Olympics seemed to be falling apart. Only Nicaragua, Ethiopia, and a few other countries were quoted in North Korea as joining Cuba in support of a boycott (KCNA, 25 March, 29 April). On 22 December, however, South Korean media claimed that 115 out of 167 national Olympic committees had already accepted invitations to participate in the games (Yonhap, 22 December). The Soviet Union, China, and the Eastern European countries all plan to participate.

Relations with South Korea. On 11 January new North Korean premier Yi Kun-mo and Defense Minister O Chin-u sent letters to their South Korean counterparts urging bilateral political-military talks, thus explicitly dropping the demand for U.S. participation (KCNA, 11 January). South Korean president Chun responded on 12 January, when he used the occasion of his New Year's message to urge the North to resume the dialogue without preconditions (Yonhap, 12 January). Pyongyang criticized the South's "insincere attitude" in relatively mild terms and virtually ignored Chun's comments (Pyongyang Domestic Service, 26 January). O and Yi repeated the North's offer on 30 January, suggesting the South respond in 20 days, or before the commencement on 19 February of the annual U.S.–South Korean joint military exercises (Team Spirit 1987). On 1 February the North Koreans linked their proposal to the much-discussed notion of a summit meeting between Kim and Chun, noting that holding a summit before the opening of political-military talks would mean "setting the cart before the horse" (*Nodong sinmun*, 1 February).

South Korea, which did not send a formal response to the first set of letters, answered the new ones. It repeated its demand for unconditional resumption of the dialogue and called in addition for "water resources" talks (Yonhap, 14 February). This latter point referred to South Korea's accusations that North Korea's Kumgangsan Dam project was designed to permit the North—through a deliberate breach in the dam—to inundate Seoul.

North Korea continued to offer concessions in return for political-military talks, even though it bridled at the mention of water resources and despite the beginning of Team Spirit on 19 February. On 3 March, in a major policy retreat, Yi and O sent a third set of letters to the South, offering to resume the dialogue simultaneously with the opening of political-military talks (Pyongyang Domestic Service, 3 March). On 17 March the South repeated its insistence on the resumption of economic and Red Cross talks (Seoul ignored preliminary parliamentary talks), but proposed that North and South Korean prime ministers discuss military subjects, water resources, and other topics (Yonhap, 17 March). This response proved effective; not only did the United States lend its expected support but even a Soviet commentator termed it "not bad" (Moscow International Service in Korean, 19 March).

North Korea apparently agreed. On 30 March a new letter from Yi to South Korean prime minister No Shin-yong accepted the offer of a prime ministers' meeting—though he did call for a preliminary discussion at Panmunjom on 23 April—and dropped the North's call for political-military talks. The North sidestepped the issue of dialogue resumption but indicated its willingness to discuss water resources. (Pyongyang Domestic Service, 30 March.)

South Korea, however, ignored the proposed 23 April meeting. It suggested instead that water-resources discussions begin on 6 May, with economic and Red Cross talks resuming six days later (Seoul, Reuters, 10 April). This was a skillful approach. Seoul pocketed Pyongyang's nonreference to political-military talks on 30 March without changing its baseline position on the dialogue, thus appearing to be forthcoming while scuttling the North's attempt to promote security discussions.

The North Koreans responded to the South's maneuver by shutting off this exchange of proposals. On 24 April—they presumably waited until the South did not show up in Panmunjom on the 23d—Yi Kun-mo denounced South Korea's stance and announced that the North would make no further concessions. He traced in detail the development of his country's proposals, alleging that the diplomatic record proved North Korean sincerity and South Korean duplicity. (KCNA, 24 April.) Further North Korean denunciations followed the joint communiqué of the annual U.S.–South Korean Security Consultative Meeting on 8 May.

The outbreak of riots in South Korea on 10 June strengthened North Korea's bilateral negotiating position, but the North went to some pains to avoid being blamed for South Korea's problems. Pyongyang, as it had after the assassination of South Korean president Pak Chung-hui in 1979, pledged not to meddle in the South's affairs. The North termed South Korean ruling party presidential candidate No Tae-u's 29 June call for direct elections a victory for popular struggle, but it warned South Koreans not to trust the ruling clique. (ibid., 21 July.) Pyongyang media published increasingly vicious attacks against No, linking him to Chun's "crimes" and claiming he "should no longer be left alive" (*Nodong sinmun*, 21 August).

Nonetheless—as during previous episodes of South Korean turmoil—Pyongyang implicitly cautioned South Korean students against self-defeating radicalism. The North Korean-run broadcasting station, Voice of National Salvation (VNS), urged students to give top priority to supporting the workers, who are "much more powerful than any other class." The VNS expressed support for the workers' "reformist movement" and economic demands, and it criticized students for failing to achieve class solidarity. (VNS, 8, 18 August.) This message was repeated when South Korean students returned to their campuses after the summer vacation (ibid., 3 August).

Domestic developments in South Korea almost certainly played a major part in the North's resumption of its peace offensive in August. By offering new concessions, Pyongyang may have hoped that South Korean opposition politicians, students, and workers would respond by pressuring the weakened Chun regime to make greater efforts to achieve national reunification.

Accordingly, on 23 July North Korea called for tripartite U.S., North Korean, and South Korean security talks in Geneva in March 1988. The North declared it would unilaterally discharge 100,000 troops and proposed reductions to 100,000 troops on each side by 1992. Pyongyang also demanded that the United States negotiate a parallel withdrawal of its forces—including nuclear weapons—from Korea. The North suggested that the Neutral Nations' Supervisory Force should monitor the reductions. (Pyongyang Domestic Service, 23 July.)

This proposal resembled its June 1986 call for tripartite political-military talks in that it represented a return to the tripartite format from the bilateral proposals offered earlier in 1987. In its content, the proposal drew from several previous proposals. The pledge to discharge 100,000 troops was reminiscent of Pyongyang's declaration in 1986 of its intention to withdraw 150,000 soldiers from the "front lines" to work on civilian construction projects.

South Korea's response to the new offer also contained well-worn themes. It proposed bilateral foreign ministers' talks in September around the margins of the U.N. General Assembly session in New York (Yonhap, 3 August). The South expressed its hope that foreign ministers' talks would lead to a prime ministers' meeting and to an eventual summit. Seoul agreed to discuss military tension reduction but also insisted that negotiations aim toward cross-recognition of the two Koreas by the major powers and simultaneous entry of both Korean states into the United Nations—positions that are anathema to the North. In addition, Seoul indicated again that "water resources" should be discussed, which suggests that the South was trying to elicit a negative reaction from the North.

The North Korean reaction on 6 August criticized South Korea's proposed agenda but agreed to foreign ministers' talks if U.S. secretary of state George Shultz attended (KCNA, 6 August). Pyongyang proposed either a tripartite preliminary meeting in August or parallel bilateral meetings between North Korean and U.S. officials in New York and North and South Korean officials in Panmunjom. The North agreed that a successful foreign ministers' meeting could lead to bilateral prime ministers' talks. Pyongyang implied that U.S. participation might not be necessary for all agenda items and made U.S. troop withdrawals the culmination, rather than a precondition, for North-South dialogue. This stance reversed Pyongyang's 1984 position that explicitly relegated the South Korean "puppets" to a second-class role in tripartite talks.

There is evidence that some in Pyongyang did not approve of their government's new troop-reduction offer. An article in *Nodong sinmun* on 9 August quoted a Kim Il-song declaration at a 1940 meeting of the Korean People's Revolutionary Army (KPRA): "Most important in preparing for the great event of national liberation is to preserve and accumulate the forces of the KPRA, the central force of the Korean revolution." The same article also stressed the 1940 decision to switch from large to small-scale unit activity. (KCNA, 9 August.)

South Korea ignored the nuances in North Korea's approach and reiterated its calls for bilateral talks (Yonhap, 13 August). The South also rejected North Korea's offer to hold bilateral vice-ministerial meetings on 23 September in advance of U.S. participation in the dialogue (KCNA, 28 August). Seoul, however, did not want to appear unwilling to open channels to Pyongyang, and on 17 September it announced that its diplomats thenceforth would be permitted to conduct "free" contacts with North Korean counterparts "at formal or informal functions around the world" (Yonhap, 17 September).

Meanwhile, North Korea repeated its call for force-reduction talks and backed off further from its insistence on initial U.S. participation. On September 24—one day after the date the North had proposed for North-South vice-ministerial talks—Pyongyang stated that a North-South foreign ministers' meeting could take place without U.S. participation. The North punctuated its offer with a claim that it had already discharged 30,000 troops, reducing its forces to 420,000 men. (KCNA, 10 September.) The United States and South Korea noted that this claim was unverifiable and stuck to their stated opinion that the North had over 800,000 people under arms.

The North shifted gears in November in order to take advantage of the South Korean presidential election campaign. Pyongyang supported those South Koreans who called for a politically neutral cabinet to oversee affairs until the election. In addition, Pyongyang expressed the hope that a new South Korean government would be more forthcoming on Korean issues, perhaps picking up on opposition leader Kim Tae-chung's claim that his election would permit an Olympics settlement and a renewed dialogue with the North (see Yonhap, 11 November). On 11 November a joint meeting of the Democratic Front for the Reunification of the Fatherland (DFRF) and the Committee for Peaceful Reunification of the Fatherland (CPRF) proposed that North and South resume their dialogue once a new government was installed in Seoul (Pyongyang Domestic Service, 11 November). The DFRF also urged South Korean opposition forces to unite behind a single candidate (ibid., 5 December). These front organizations pledged the North to permit officials of a new South Korean government to travel to the North for negotiations. In contrast to the Olympics issue—according to the Chinese press—the North made clear it would still deal with the current government if the latter accepted its proposals for tripartite talks (Xinhua, 11 November). On 14 December North Korea announced that 100,000 troops had been "demobilized" (KCNA, 14 December).

Both Kim Yong-sam and Kim Tae-chung responded by promising to deal with the North if elected president (*Korea Times* and *Korea Herald*, 19 November). The South Korean government, however, rejected this appeal, causing the North once more to question its negotiating sincerity (Pyongyang Domestic Service, 2 December).

The North was almost certainly disappointed in the outcome of the 16 December election, and it shared the general view that the opposition split was to blame for the South Korean government's victory. Initial North Korean commentary stressed charges of fraud and reports of protests (KCNA; VNS, 18 December), but the relatively orderly election aftermath undercut any hopes the North may have had for a South Korean implosion. Subsequent commentary criticized the "democratic forces" for not presenting a unified front to the electorate (*Nodong sinmun*, 19 December).

Several incidents late in the year reminded both sides—and their allies—that Korea remains a volatile troublespot. On 7 October the South Koreans accused North Korea of firing on and sinking one of their fishing boats (Seoul Domestic Service, 7 October). The North responded that the boat sank after attempting to ram a North Korean patrol craft (Pyongyang Domestic Service, 7 October). It was not clear whether this was merely another in the series of ad hoc confrontations or a deliberate attempt by either side to raise tensions in the wake of the Olympics imbroglio and the deadlock in North-South dialogue.

On 21 November the two sides traded recriminations over another shooting incident at the demilitarized zone (Pyongyang Domestic Service; Yonhap, 21 November). The South claimed Northern troops opened fire on a South Korean guardpost in central Korea, wounding one South Korean soldier. The North reported no casualties of its own, but claimed that South Korean "puppets" damaged one of its facilities. The North accused the South of another firing incident on 5 December (Pyongyang Domestic Service, 5 December).

Most serious was the apparent bombing of a Korean Airlines jet that disappeared near the Thai-Burmese border on 29 November with 115 people on board. Two passengers carrying Japanese passports who had debarked from that plane in the Middle East took cyanide when they were approached by authorities about the incident. International speculation centered on the Japanese Red

Army and on Chosen Soren, the organization of pro-Pyongyang Koreans living in Japan, as well as on North Korea itself. Chun and South Korean police authorities, predictably, suggested this terror could be part of North Korea's efforts to disrupt the Olympics. (Kyodo; Yonhap, 2 December.) Seoul threatened to break off talks about sharing athletic events with the North if it proved to be guilty of this crime (*Korea Times*, 4 December). The International Olympic Committee Executive Committee discussed the possibility of barring the North from the 1988 Olympics if it turned out to be responsible for the attack.

North Korean and Chosen Soren officials denied complicity (KCNA, 3, 4 December), comparing this incident to South Korean efforts in 1973 to blame North Korea for the kidnapping of Kim Tae-chung in Japan by the South Korean CIA. The North Korean Foreign Ministry bitterly criticized Bahrain for its "inexcusable" decision to extradite the surviving suspect to South Korea (ibid., 15 December). Pyongyang also complained that Japanese "reactionaries" were harassing Korean residents of Japan in reaction to accusations of the North's complicity in the aircraft bombing.

Relations with the Soviet Union and China. Differences over the Olympics marred North Korea's relations with both neighbors. In addition, there were signs of Soviet impatience with North Korea's economic problems. As noted above, a *Pravda* correspondent wrote of agricultural problems after a visit to the North. In addition, after his visit to Pyongyang in late 1986, Arkady Baksberg wrote that North Korea was going through "hard times" (*Literaturnaya Gazeta*, 3 December 1986). He portrayed a Pyongyang of empty streets and deserted shops, where citizens lacked decent footwear and adequate supplies of meat and bread. In place of taxis, middle-aged women carried baggage around town in bicycle trailers.

North Korea, for its part, expressed dissatisfaction with Moscow's attitude toward bilateral economic relations. Chong Song-nam, North Korea's minister of external economic affairs, called for the "restructuring" of Soviet–North Korean trade (*Izvestiia*, 18 October).

Still, the two sides continued to exchange high-level visitors. In 1987 the most important exchanges were as follows.

KWP alternate Politburo member Kim Pok-sin led a delegation to Moscow in February and held talks with Soviet premier Nikolai Ryzhkov (KCNA, 1 February). North Korean foreign minister Kim Yong-nam stopped over in Moscow in February on his way to New Delhi. Soviet media reported that the two sides discussed security issues and expressed mutual satisfaction with bilateral ties, but made no mention of the Olympics. (TASS, 25 February.) The Soviets and North Koreans reportedly discussed ways of further developing relations when KWP Central Committee secretary Hwang Chang-yop visited Moscow in March (ibid., 18 March). In May CPSU secretary for heavy industry Dolgikh and Navy commander admiral Chernavin spent six days in North Korea (KCNA, 11–16 May). In July a relatively low-level Korean People's Army delegation returned the 1986 visit paid by Soviet general A. D. Lizichev (Moscow, *Krasnaya Zvezda*, 23 July).

In October a North Korean Central Committee delegation visited Moscow to discuss heavy industry (*Pravda*, 23 October). Vice President Pak Song-chol was North Korea's chief representative at the celebration of the 70th anniversary of the Bolshevik Revolution (KCNA, 1 November). Soviet light industry minister Klyuyev visited Pyongyang in November (KCNA, 10 November), and North Korean Politburo member Cho Se-ung, party secretary in North Hamgyong province, visited Vladivostok (Pyongyang Domestic Service, 5 November). Later that month Soviet interior minister Vlasov visited Pyongyang, meeting with Minister of Public Security Pak Haek-nim and Premier Yi Kun-mo (KCNA, 25 November).

In December North Korea hosted the Executive Committee of the World Federation of Democratic Youth. Kim Il-song met with the delegates and spoke at a banquet in their honor (ibid., 9 December). Soviet vice-foreign minister Igor Rogachev, termed a "special envoy of the leadership of the Soviet Union," met with Kim Il-song in Pyongyang on 19 December, apparently to brief Kim on the U.S.-Soviet summit (TASS; KCNA, 19 December). Foreign Ministers Eduard Shevardnadze and Kim Yong-nam met in Moscow on 24 December. According to *Pravda* their talks took place in a "comradely and businesslike atmosphere," probably indicating differences of opinion, perhaps on the Olympics or the Korean Airlines disaster (*Pravda*, 24 December). North Korean media, by contrast, claimed the meeting had been held in a "warm and comradely" atmosphere (Pyongyang Domestic Service, 25 December).

In general the two sides continued to support each other's arms control and disarmament initiatives, but it was not clear whether coincident summer peace offensives meshed very well. North Korean media virtually ignored Mikhail Gorbachev's 21 July offer to scrap all SS-20 missiles in Asia. Gorbachev had dropped previous Soviet demands for withdrawal of U.S. nuclear weapons from South Korea (and elsewhere), but North Korea's proposal for tripartite security talks explicitly called for such withdrawals. Although the Soviets continued to issue ritual support for the North's earlier proposal for a Korean nuclear-free zone, it is possible the North was pressing a demand that Moscow had hoped to shelve pending an intermediate nuclear forces (INF) treaty.

Similarly, the North initially paid little attention to reports in September of an imminent U.S.-Soviet INF agreement. Pyongyang media praised Gorbachev's security message to the U.N. General Assembly, but withheld specific mention of his position on INF (KCNA, 26 September). In October the Japanese—but not the North Korean—press reported that Politburo member Ho Tam praised U.S.-Soviet INF negotiations and urged the United States to accept North Korea's own disarmament initiatives (Tokyo, *Mainichi shimbun*, 2 October). An article in *Nodong sinmun*—reprinted in *Pravda*—praised Gorbachev's security initiatives but contained no mention of INF (*Pravda*, 12 October). Pyongyang media did mention the U.S.-Soviet summit and welcomed the INF treaty in December. The North, however, warned that the world would not be safe until the United States removed its nuclear weapons from Korea (Pyongyang Domestic Service, 10 December).

Kim Il-song's visit to China in May seems to have been a protocolary success but probably did not narrow bilateral differences on the Olympics and other issues. Kim saw Deng Xiaoping, Premier Zhao Ziyang, and President Li Xiannian. The KCNA stated that his talks with Deng were held in a "comradely, sincere, and friendly atmosphere" but did not repeat Xinhua's characterization of the discussions as "very cordial and warm" (KCNA, 22 May; Xinhua, 22 May). As during previous visits, the two sides did not issue a joint communiqué. The statement issued by the KWP Politburo noted that the two sides "held unanimous views on all issues discussed" but did not include the Olympics among those topics (Beijing Domestic Service, 28 May).

Korean People's Army chief of staff O Kuk-yol followed Kim to Beijing in August (KCNA, 17 August). Wang Hai, commander of China's air force, visited Pyongyang later that month and met with Kim Il-song (Shanghai City Service, 3 September). In October, on the eve of the Thirteenth Congress of the Chinese Communist Party (CCP), Yang Hyong-sop, KWP Central Committee secretary and chairman of the SPA Standing Committee, met in Beijing with Zhao Ziyang (KCNA, 8 October). Chang Chol, North Korea's minister of culture, visited China later that month (Xinhua, 29 October).

Yi Kun-mo made his inaugural foreign trip as North Korea's premier to China from 9 to 14 November. He met Deng Xiaoping, Zhao Ziyang, Vice President Ulanhu, and Peng Zhen, chairman of the National People's Congress (Xinhua, 9–11 November). Yi's delegation included Minister of External Economic Affairs Chong Song-nam and Deputy Foreign Trade Minister Song Hui-chol, which led to press speculation that the North Koreans pressed China for help in repaying their overdue foreign debts (Reuters, 9 November).

The Chinese were more friendly than the Soviets toward the North's July troop-reduction proposal—perhaps a further indication that Pyongyang's initiative did not mesh well with Moscow's INF offer. Beijing termed Pyongyang's offer "an important proposal" for easing tension and expressed the hope it would help break the negotiating deadlock (Beijing, *Renmin ribao*, 23 July). In another positive development, China opened a consulate in the Northern port of Chongjin in July (KCNA, 1 July).

Despite these developments, Sino–North Korean relations in 1987 continued to show signs of strain. For example, China sent no message of greeting on the occasion of Kim Chong-il's birthday in February. In addition—in the context of criticizing Japan's role in permitting the Kim Man-chol group to defect to the South—North Korean media termed Taiwan (a transit stop for the defectors) a "third country" and referred to one of its ambassadors without using quotation marks (KCNA, 15 February). Both references, while well short of granting Taiwan legitimacy, were nonetheless unusual. According to Western press reports, North Korea was increasingly concerned about China's growing informal relationship with South Korea; trade between those countries in 1987 allegedly exceeded that between China and the North (*NYT*, 20 September).

Relations with Japan. North Korea continued to try to expand ties with Japan in 1987, but relations suffered from ups and downs in fishing talks and were marred by Tokyo's role in the February defection of the Kim Man-chol group. The defectors' boat drifted into Japanese waters after developing engine trouble, and—after conflicting reports of whether the group wanted to go to South Korea or stay in Japan—the government permitted it to proceed to South Korea via Taiwan. North Korea's response was predictably vitriolic; it temporarily cut off fishing talks. In a bizarre and possibly related development, North Korean media publicized the presence in North Korea of two Japanese fishermen who had been presumed killed in a sea accident in 1963 (Kyodo, 17 March).

Relations with the Third World. Vice President Yi Chong-ok, Foreign Minister Kim Yong-nam, and other officials conducted visits throughout Africa and Asia. They attempted to shore up North Korea's relations with important developing states and—apparently without much success—to garner Nonaligned Movement (NAM) support for Pyongyang's Olympic demands. The "South-South" NAM meeting, held in Pyongyang from 9 to 13 June, attracted delegates from 100 countries and organizations, but it was probably small consolation for the failure of North Korea's candidacy for the next NAM summit or foreign ministers' meeting.

David B. Kanin
Washington, D.C.

Laos

Population. 3,765,887
Party. Lao People's Revolutionary Party (Phak Pasason Pativat Lao; LPRP)
Founded. 22 March 1955
Membership. 40,000 (*WMR*, June)
General Secretary. Kaysone Phomvihane (67, Lao-Vietnamese, premier)
Politburo. 13 members: Kaysone Phomvihane, Nouhak Phoumsavan, Souphanouvong (president), Phoumi Vongvichit (acting president), Khamtai Siphandon, Phoun Sipaseut, Sisomphon Lovansai, Sisavat Keobounphan, Sali Vongkhamsao, Maichantan Sengmani, Saman Vi-gnaket, Oudom Khatti-gna (alternate), Chounmali Saignakon (alternate)
Secretariat. 9 members: Kaysone Phomvihane, Khamtai Siphandon, Sisavat Keobounphan, Sali Vongkhamsao, Maichantan Sengmani, Saman Vignaket, Oudom Khatti-gna, Chounmali Saignakon, Somlak Chanthamat
Central Committee. 51 full members, 9 alternate members
Status. Ruling and sole legal party
Last Congress. Fourth, 13–15 November 1986, in Vientiane
Last Election. 1975; all 46 candidates were LPRP approved
Auxiliary Organizations. Lao Front for National Construction (LFNC), Lao People's Revolutionary Youth Union, Federation of Trade Unions, Women's Federation, Unified Buddhist Organization
Publications. *Pasason* (The people), LPRP central organ, published in Vientiane (daily); *Alun mai* (New dawn), LPRP theoretical journal, published in Vientiane (quarterly); the official news agency is Khaosan Pathet Lao (Pathet Lao News Agency; KPL)

The LPRP leadership, which had been approved at the 1986 Fourth Congress, continued to rule. However, it did de-emphasize the party's "special relations" with Vietnam and urge greater activity in relations with the Communist Party of the Soviet Union (CPSU). A major preoccupation of the LPRP was its new economic policies designed to overcome the previous years of economic stagnation, attributed to following Vietnam's policies. The LPRP also approved foreign policy moves aimed at continuing to improve relations with China and the United States begun in 1986. Relations with Thailand were marked by repeated shooting incidents along the two countries' common border.

Domestic Party Affairs. The LPRP held its third plenum in January, reviewed the state plan and budget for 1986, and approved the plan for 1987. The gross national product had reportedly climbed 11 percent and labor productivity had increased by 8 percent. (Radio Vientiane; KPL, 2 February; *FBIS*, 2, 5, 6 February.)

In June the LPRP held its fourth plenum. The meeting addressed reform of the education system for the period up to 1990 and approved a new policy, previously proposed in 1985, that calls for dismantling the old price-setting mechanism and replacing it with a new price system. The new price system would try to freeze public sector spending and allow some prices to be set by the free market. But prices would also serve as economic levers to guide supply, demand, the purchasing power of money, and free-market prices. A new tax policy would facilitate developing consumer and export manufacturing and reorganize agricultural taxation. The Council of Ministers was instructed to expedite the new price and tax reforms. The meeting also heard a report on nationality relations that urged greater vigilance to thwart enemy propaganda aimed at harming national unity. In addition, it endorsed the moves toward national reconciliation in Kampuchea and expressed readiness for further talks by the Lao People's Democratic Republic (LPDR) with both China and Thailand. (KPL, 15 June; *Pasason* 17 June; *IB*, September; *FBIS*, 16 June, 1 July.)

The Supreme People's Council held its annual session 2–4 February, chaired by Sisomphon Lovansai. Other Politburo members in attendance were Kaysone Phomvihane, Phoumi Vongvichit, Khamtai Siphandon, and Sali Vongkhamsao. One report cited that the LPDR now counted 3,976 agricultural cooperatives covering 74 percent of peasant families and 65 percent of farmland. Other items of business included a ten-year-old effort to draft a constitution and an election law. (Radio Vientiane, 2, 5, 6 February; *FBIS*, 2, 5, 6 February.)

Auxiliary Organizations. The LFNC, the party's principal mass-mobilization organization, held its Second National Congress in Vientiane 9–11 September with 303 delegates in attendance. Acting President Phoumi Vongvichit replaced the ill Souphanouvong, and Bolang Boualapha and Chaleun Yiapaoheu became vice presidents. Permanent members are Mrs. Boun-gna Phitsavat, Khamtan Thepbouali, Bolivong Vondala, and Soulot Senkhamphon. The congress approved the appointment of a Central Committee made up of 94 members, of whom twelve are Buddhist monks and six are women. As for the ethnic composition of the Central Committee, there are 60 Lao Loum, 19 Lao Soung, and 15 Lao Theung. (Radio Vientiane; KPL, 9–16 September; *FBIS*, 14–16, 21 September.)

In his political report to the congress, Phoumi Vongvichit said that the LFNC had unified all tribes and classes on the basis of a worker-peasant alliance under the leadership of the party. The party also coordinated mass organizations in the fields of education and training, contributed to national defense, mobilized peasants to join collective organizations, and developed all-around agricultural production through irrigation projects, raising livestock, switching from slash-and-burn cultivation to rice growing, and maintaining and building roads. (Radio Vientiane, 9 September; *FBIS*, 23 September.) The congress also dealt with new rules for governing the LFNC, selecting its members, and formulating the principles and style of party work (KPL, 10 September; *FBIS*, 11 September).

Rice production suffered a double setback in 1987 due to drought in the north and flooding in the south. Drought was severe from May to July (when wet rice is planted and transplanted), particularly in Vientiane, Luang Prabang, Sayaboury, Oudomsai, Bokeo, Namtha, Phong Saly, Houa Phan, and Xieng Khouang provinces. Total rice production will probably fall 350,000–400,000 tons below the 1987 plan target of 1.57 million tons. (KPL, 12 August; *FBIS*, 14 August.)

International Views and Activities. The tenth anniversary of the signing of the 25-year Treaty of Friendship and Cooperation between the LPDR and Vietnam was marked on 18 July with only a perfunctory exchange of congratulatory messages and the announcement of the observance of a month of Lao-Vietnamese friendship (1–31 July). Although party and state messages sent to Hanoi carried the usual references to "special relations" between the partners to the treaty, and although Politburo member Sali Vongkhamsao made honorific mention of Ho Chi Minh in an interview with the Vietnam News Agency (VNA), there was no exchange of high-level party and government delegations, nor public statements by the LPRP about the war-cemented bond with the Vietnam Communist Party, as had been customary on past occasions. Public statements by the LPRP focused instead on Vietnamese economic aid projects.

The question of the border between the two countries, the settlement of which was one of the principal objectives of the 1977 treaty, received further attention in October when a supplementary protocol on the redelineation of the border in areas where it is marked by rivers and streams was signed in Vientiane by the joint Lao-Vietnamese and Vietnamese-Lao border committees. The preparatory work was said to have taken three months. Signing the protocol were Khamphon Boutdakham, deputy minister of interior and head of the Lao-Vietnamese Border Committee, and Nguyen Van Loi, head of the Border Committee of the Council of Ministers of Vietnam and head of the Vietnamese-Lao Border Committee. (Radio Vientiane, 19 October; *FBIS*, 19 October.) Loi spoke at a ceremony in Hanoi on 15 July at which "several Vietnamese offices and provinces" were honored with the friendship order of the LPRP. He was identified by the VNA as Luu Van Loi (VNA, 15 July; *FBIS*, 10 August).

In October a force of some 200 anticommunist Vietnamese was reportedly intercepted in southern Laos while attempting to make its way across the mountains into Vietnam to set up resistance bases. Radio Vientiane initially confused the identity of the intruders when they crossed the Mekong from Thailand in mid-July "because their uniforms, equipment, and ID cards were similar to ours." But in a series of clashes the intruding force was annihilated. These clashes in Saravane and Sekong provinces indicate that the intruders had managed to penetrate well into eastern Laos near the Vietnam border. The reported fighting took place at the height of the rainy season in weather made worse than usual by two successive typhoons in August. "The enemy elements sent into Laos were either annihilated or captured, and the rest surrendered." (Radio Vientiane, 27 October; *FBIS*, 27 October.)

The trial of the seventeen surviving intruders took place in Ho Chi Minh City in early December. The LPRP reported receiving an official letter from Vietnam requesting extradition of the captured individuals on 12 November, and it gave its favorable response on 24 November (KPL, 27 November; *FBIS*, 30 November). The same report made a rare reference to the "Vietnamese volunteer troops" in Laos, which had been in action against the intruders. There are an estimated 40,000 Vietnamese troops permanently stationed in Laos. (*NYT*, 24 November.) LPRP leaders were reported by reliable diplomatic sources to have been upset by Vietnam's publicly mentioning the intruders; they chose to ignore the fact that several of the anticommunist Vietnamese involved in the affair had U.S. citizenship.

On other Indochinese matters, the LPRP gave a favorable signal to the moves under way to effect national reconciliation in Cambodia, published a Foreign Ministry statement on 5 September stating, "This national reconciliation policy shows its constructive nature and constitutes an important step leading to the political settlement of the Cambodian problem" (Radio Vientiane, 7 September; *FBIS*, 11 September).

Party and government relations with the Soviet Union remained close in 1987. Soviet foreign minister Eduard Shevardnadze visited Vientiane 3–10 March. His visit was well publicized, but what was not made public was that a small bomb exploded in front of the Soviet Cultural Center in Vientiane on the morning of 9 March, killing one person and wounding another, an incident that embarrassed the LPRP. (Bangkok, AFP, 10 March; *FBIS*, 11 March.) Kaysone was in the Soviet Union for "a rest period" in the summer (TASS, 12 August; *FBIS*, 13 August), and he also led a party-government delegation to Moscow for the 70th anniversary of the Bolshevik Revolution (Radio Vientiane, 20 October, 12 November; *FBIS*, 20 October, 12 November).

Foreign Minister Oskar Fischer of East Germany visited Vientiane 11–14 March (Radio Vientiane, 11, 12 March; *FBIS*, 12, 13 March).

The LPRP's relations with China also grew closer, following moves toward their normalization initiated in 1986. LPRP first deputy foreign minister Kamphai Boupha reciprocated a Chinese visit to Vientiane by visiting Beijing 24–30 November. An atmosphere of "mutual understanding and frankness" surrounded the talks, a report said. "The Lao delegation was very glad to receive an assurance from the Chinese delegation that the Chinese side will not give support and assistance to the exiled Lao reactionaries . . . Afterwards, the two sides agreed in principle to exchange ambassadors, [and] to consult with each other on the trade relations between the two countries, including trade between provinces sharing the common border." (Radio Vientiane, 9 December; *FBIS*, 10 December.)

Despite several exchanges of delegations and statements expressing a desire for peaceful relations, the LPRP and Thailand were still unable to come to terms for mutual peaceful coexistence. The dispute about sovereignty over three villages on the Sayaboury-Uttaradit provincial border was still unresolved and was in fact complicated in 1987 by LPRP charges of illegal timber smuggling in the area. Tensions also flared at a number of other points along the border, leading in a number of instances to exchanges of gunfire. In spite of all this, the annual boat races on the Mekong downstream from Vientiane were held as usual in October, reportedly drawing a large crowd on both banks, including high-ranking officials of Vientiane and Nong Khai provinces. The Thai men's rowing team was victorious, but the Lao women's team won its races. (KPL, 5 October; *FBIS*, 6 October.)

In relations with the United States, the year was marked by the visit of LPRP deputy foreign minister Souban Salitthilat to Washington, D.C. 6–8 October (Radio Vientiane, 7 October; *FBIS*, 7 October). It paved the way for the first "Lao-U.S. technical meeting" held in Vientiane 11–13 November regarding certain specific steps to improve relations" (Radio Vientiane, 20 November; *FBIS*, 20 November).

The stage for these moves had been set by the visit to Vientiane 10–12 August by a U.S. delegation headed by National Security Council staff member Richard Childress; the delegation included Ambassador Shepard Lowman of the East Asia Bureau of the State Department and Ann Mills Griffiths, executive director of the National League of Families of POWs/MIAs (Radio Vientiane, 7, 11, 14 August; *FBIS*, 10, 11, 14 August). As a result of this meeting, the United States "reiterated its opposition to irresponsible private efforts to interfere in government-to-government cooperation" (Radio Vientiane, 12 August; *FBIS*, 13 August). It wanted more cooperation from the LPRP in the resolution of the MIA problem and in clamping down on reputed narcotics traffic from Laos.

Arthur J. Dommen
Bethesda, Maryland

Malaysia and Singapore

Population. Malaysia: 16,068,516; Singapore: 2,616,236
Party. Communist Party of Malaya (CPM); North Kalimantan Communist Party (NKCP)
Founded. CPM: 1930
Membership: CPM: fewer than 1,000 armed insurgents on Thai side of international border; estimated 200 full-time inside peninsular Malaysia; fewer than 100 in Sarawak
General Secretary. CPM: Chin Peng; NKCP: Wen Ming-chuan
Politburo. No data
Central Committee. No data
Status. Illegal
Last Congress. CPM: 1965 (last known)
Auxiliary Organizations. CPM: Malayan People's Army (MPA); Malay Nationalist Revolutionary Party of Malaya (MNRPM)
Publications. No regular periodicals known; CPM: Voice of Malayan Democracy (VOMD), clandestine radio station broadcasting from southern China.

The year 1987 marked a watershed for the Malaysian communists. In March and April virtually the entire Marxist-Leninist faction of the party laid down its arms, leaving only the 850 or so members of the pro-Beijing wing still operating in the border area. In Singapore, where no communist activity had occurred for many years, the authorities arrested 20 people for allegedly participating in a Marxist conspiracy. By year's end all but one of the detainees had been released.

Leadership and Party Organization. At the beginning of the year the CPM strength on the Malaysian-Thai border was estimated at between 1,500 and 2,000 active guerrillas. The Thai military's program of amnesty had successfully reduced the Communist Party of Thailand and the Muslim separatist forces to an insignificant number. By the end of 1987 the combined Malaysian-Thai operations along the border had wiped out all permanent CPM camps and reduced the guerrilla forces to scattered units of only five to ten men. (*Bernama*, 15 January; *FBIS*, 16 January; *FEER*, 12 February.)

In March and April, the approximately 850 soldiers of the CPM's 8th Regiment, including 653 members of the Marxist-Leninist faction, surrendered to Thai forces. Both Malaysian and Thai authorities saw this as the beginning of the end of a 40-year-long security problem. The mass defections have probably eliminated the Marxist-Leninist faction and the smaller Revolutionary Faction that split off from the pro-Beijing CPM in the late 1960s and joined the Communist Party of Malaysia (MCP) in December 1983. (*Bernama*, 4 June; *FBIS*, 8 June.) A spokesman for the guerrillas quickly pointed out that they had not surrendered but merely stopped their armed activities so they could "participate in economic reconstruction in southern Thailand" (Bangkok, *The Nation*, 9 May; *FBIS*, 11 May).

Chang Chung-Ming, the former leader of the Marxist-Leninist group, maintained a low profile after his surrender in April. His deputy, Chieu Chen, speaking for the group at a welcoming ceremony on 2 June, said that the 8th Regiment had surrendered because the CPM's 40-year armed struggle was futile. "We abandoned our struggle against Malaysia because we had to adjust to a new era," said Chieu, who had joined the CPM in 1948. "At the end of our lives, we want to farm peacefully here." (*Bangkok Post*, 3 June; *FBIS*, 4 June; *CSM*, 3 July.)

At the 2 June ceremony, the commander in chief of the Thai army, General Chawalit Yongchaiyuth, pledged to help the CPM defectors to lead a normal life. Although 70–80 percent of the defectors are believed to be of Malaysian origin, General Chawalit assured them they would not be sent back to Malaysia. Unlike Thailand, which had adopted a policy of blanket amnesty, the Malaysian government continued to require a case-by-case review with each defector subject to a program of social rehabilitation. All the defectors were accorded the formal title of "participants in nation-building," assuring them the same treatment as returnees from the Communist Party of Thailand. They were to be sent to resettlement villages along the border and allowed to keep some weapons. (Kuala Lumpur Domestic Service, 2 April; *FBIS*, 3 April; Hong Kong, AFP, 30 May; *FBIS*, 1 June; *FEER*, 11 June.)

Until their surrender, the insurgents had reportedly extracted $4–8 million a year in protection money and illegal taxes from local plantations and businesses. Many of the insurgent leaders allegedly had homes and businesses in Bangkok. One source said, "You'd be surprised at the number of times CPM leaders were right ahead of you as you waited to get off your plane in Bangkok from the south." With such an economic stake in Thailand, he said, "it is inevitable that they will want to enjoy their profits." (Hong Kong, AFP, 30 May; *FBIS*, 1 June.)

Shortly after the mass defection of the CPM's 8th Regiment, the Thai authorities issued an appeal to the remaining CPM guerrillas to follow suit. When initial negotiations failed to produce results, the Thai army mounted large-scale military operations in May against the insurgents' camps. Although the CPM's long-time general secretary, Chin Peng, remains in nominal command—the party's traditional New Year's greeting was issued in his name—he is old and ailing and believed to be in China. The CPM insurgents are apparently led by individual commanders pursuing independent policies. These conditions differ from the former CPM/Marxist-Leninist, in which even after surrender Chang Chung-Ming exercised undisputed authority; the Thai military, aware that other guerrillas are watching closely, have tried to accommodate Chang. (*FEER*, 18 June.)

The number of communist insurgents within the borders of peninsular Malaysia diminished during the year. In July the deputy home affairs minister reported to parliament that a total of 57 communists had surrendered in the past year, leaving only 158 insurgents still actively operating inside the peninsula (Kuala Lumpur Domestic Service, 6 July; *FBIS*, 7 July). The deputy prime minister noted early in the year that the enfeebled communist terrorist forces had changed their struggle and were becoming bandits (*Berita Harian*, 21 January; *FBIS*, 2 February). In Sarawak the chief minister reckoned that with the surrender of two communist terrorists in late August, only about 43 insurgents remained in the state's jungle area (*Berita Harian*, 1 September; *FBIS*, 16 September).

The Internal Security Department announced in May that it had "uncovered a Marxist conspiracy to subvert the existing social and political system" through "communist united front tactics." Sixteen persons were arrested on 21 May for alleged involvement in the conspiracy and were held under the Internal Security Act, which permits detention without trial. Vincent Cheng, a 40-year-old full-time Catholic lay worker, was said to have headed the conspiracy in Singapore. Tan Wah Piow, characterized by the authorities as a Marxist and former student agitator who had evaded military service and fled to Britain in 1976, was charged with being the mastermind behind the plot. (*Straits Times*, 27 May; *FBIS*, 29 May.) Four of the sixteen arrested were full-time church workers and six others were volunteers in various church groups (*Straits Times*, 3 June; *FBIS*, 9 June). On 20 June the government released four of those originally detained but arrested six new suspects said to have been implicated by the detainees.

The group was charged with executing a systematic plan to infiltrate and subvert church organizations and student and other groups to build a legal front as a cover for political sabotage. They were also said to have infiltrated the Workers' Party and to have formed their own front organization, the Third Stage, a theater group. The government claimed the conspirators had links with Filipino leftists, European Marxists, and Sri Lankan separatists. They were accused of organizing communist-style indoctrination sessions and producing publications to disseminate Marxist ideas and radicalize student and Christian activists. These, said the official government statement, are familiar united front tactics traditionally resorted to by communists in Singapore and elsewhere in preparation for a communist revolution. (*Straits Times*, 27 May; *FBIS*, 29 May; *NYT*, 21 June.)

In two days of television appearances, twelve of the sixteen detainees outlined the roles they had played in "an intricate network to subvert Roman Catholic organizations and student groups and use them to create widespread unrest beneficial to a communist takeover" (Singapore, Reuters, 30 June).

Tan, the alleged mastermind of the conspiracy, had served a one-year prison term for rioting before he fled to England. Now age 36 and studying law at Oxford, he denied that he is a communist. (*FEER*, 11 June.) The Singapore government speculated that Tan was a puppet in a larger, more dangerous game. Home Affairs Minister S. Jayakumar, in a speech entitled "The Marxist Conspiracy: An Unfinished Story and the Unseen Hand," said that Tan, Cheng, and the others in the group are "the first of a few" in a new phase of the battle with the communists. "If the CPM is not already behind this network and directing its activities, they would certainly have come into the picture if we had not taken early action," he said. However, numerous questions remained unanswered, he said, including what Tan's links were with the CPM. Who enabled Tan to establish contacts with CPM members in the People's Republic of China? Tan had told William Yap, one of the detainees, that he visited China in 1978 and had met CPM leaders. Whoever the real leaders behind Tan were, their tactics had changed, he noted. The communists had failed in their previous attempts and were trying again with new tactics and new guises. (*Straits Times*, 6 July; *FBIS*, 7 July.)

The arrests provoked protests by the Workers' Party and internationally by the European Parliamentary Union, members of the U.S. Congress, and several human rights organizations. Eleven of the detainees were to be held for a year but were released before the end of the year. Vincent Cheng was given two years' detention and remains in custody.

What apparently surprised many Singaporeans was that the long-dormant communist threat had reemerged as a movement not of mainly poor, secular, Chinese-educated cadres but of essentially middle-class, English-educated radicals who infiltrated church organizations and not the trade unions. Prime Minister Lee Kuan Yew summed up the reaction when he said, "How can there be new communists in our prosperous Singapore? Have we not left poverty behind us?" (Singapore, Reuters, 8 August.)

In late December the government dissolved a Christian ecumenical organization and ordered its five foreign executives to leave the country. The Christian Conference of Asia (CCA) was charged with using Singapore as a base to support "liberation movements" in other Asian countries and helping to fund procommunist movements. The government said the CCA had given financial support to Cheng. (ibid., 30 December.)

Domestic Activities. Seemingly unaffected by the decline in the party's strength, the CPM's traditional New Year's greeting over its clandestine radio station focused on the economic decline in the past year. It asserted that this decline was caused by the government's insistence on carrying out its New Economic Policy (NEP), "aimed at developing the bureaucrat and comprador capitalists and by its dependence on foreign capital and debts." The government's policies were charged not only with severely harming the economic and political rights of the people of all nationalities but also with preventing the nation from developing into a fully independent country economically and politically. Once again, the comrades in the party, its army, and the mass revolutionary organizations were exhorted to implement the call of the Central Committee in its 29 April statement on the party's special program for the present period (for details see *YICA*, 1986). The New Year's message ended with the standard appeal to all patriotic and democratic political parties, people's organizations, and leaders to broadly unite to establish a gigantic united front and a democratic coalition government. (VOMD, 31 December; *FBIS*, 5 January.)

Auxiliary and Front Organizations. The chairman of the MNRPM, Abdullah C. D., extended greetings in a broadcast, "Let Us Unite for Greater Victories." His address was directed more specifically to Muslim comrades and supporters but covered the same essential theme as the other party pronouncements, charging the government with responsibility for the ailing economy. Claiming that Federal Land Development Authority (FELDA) estate workers and land settlers lived as peasant slaves, heavily in debt for life, he said that the total number of FELDA settlers is now as many as 1,200,000 persons, or 20 percent of the total Malaysian population. The only economic policy that can improve living standards will materialize "when the patriotic and democratic forces in the country win their victory." Aimed at an audience not expected to be composed of party stalwarts, Abdullah's speech did not contain the usual reference to the CPM's April 1985 program. (VOMD, 31 May; *FBIS*, 1 June.)

The Central Committee of the Islamic Brotherhood Party of Malaya (Paperi) marked the prophet Muhammad's birthday with a broadcast exhorting its listeners to "spread the Islamic Patriotic Movement and end the iron-handed rule of the Barisan Nasional [the ruling coalition]" (VOMD, 5 November; *FBIS*, 9 November).

International Activities. There is no information about CPM or affiliated organizations' activities in international communist forums.

Jeanne S. Mintz
Washington, D.C.

Mongolia

Population. 2,011,066
Party. Mongolian People's Revolutionary Party (MPRP)
Founded. 1921
Membership. 88,150 (*Novosti Mongolii*, 29 May 1986; *FBIS Supplement*, 11 July 1986); 30.3 percent women, 69.7 percent men; 33.2 percent workers, 16.8 percent Agricultural Association members, 50 percent intellectuals
General Secretary. Jambyn Batmonh (61)
Politburo. 7 members: Jambyn Batmonh (chairman, presidium of Great People's Hural), Dumaagiyn Sodnom (premier), Bat-Ochirym Altangerel, Bujyn Dejid, Demchigiyn Molomjamts, Tserendashiyn Namsray, Bandzaragchiyn Lhamjab; 2 candidate members: Sonomyn Lubsangombo, Paavangiyn Damdin
Secretariat. 6 members: Jambyn Batmonh, Tserenpilyn Balhaajab, Paavangiyn Damdin, Bujyn Dejid, Demchigiyn Molomjamts, Tserendashiyn Namsray
Central Committee. 85 full members; 65 candidate members
Status. Ruling party
Last Congress. Nineteenth, 28–31 May 1986, in Ulan Bator
Last Election. 22 June 1986; of 370 seats in Great People's Hural, 346 or 93.5 percent went to members or candidate members of the MPRP
Auxiliary Organizations. Mongolian Revolutionary Youth League (over 200,000 members), Ts. Narangerel, first secretary; Central Council of Mongolian Trade Unions, B. Lubsantseren, chairman; Committee of Mongolian Women, L. Pagmadulam, chairwoman
Publications. *Unen* (Truth), MPRP daily organ, published Tuesday–Sunday; MONTSAME is the official news agency.

Leadership and Party Organization. The MPRP's top leadership was affected, but not significantly, by death and retirement. In July Tumenbararyn Ragchaa retired from the Politburo before the third plenum of the Thirteenth MPRP Central Committee and was replaced by Bandzaragchiyn Lhamjab, previously a candidate member. Paavangiyn Damdin, a secretary of the Central Committee, moved up to candidate membership on the Politburo. (MONTSAME, 30 June; *FBIS*, 2 July.) In September N. Jagbaral, a candidate member of the Politburo, died of liver cancer and by the end of the year had not been replaced.

Other key changes included the retirement of D. Tsebegmid, deputy chairman of the Council of Ministers, in May and his replacement by Bat-Ochirym Altangerel; in December Altangerel left the chairmanship of the Great People's Hural and was succeeded by L. Rinchin (MONTSAME, 12 December; *FBIS*, 14 December). S. Gungaadorj, who had been appointed minister of agriculture and livestock breeding in October 1986, was made a vice chairman of the Council of Ministers in October 1987, and C. Suren, a vice chairman of the Council of Ministers, was made minister of light and food industry (Xinhua, 11 October; *FBIS-PRC*, 13 October).

Domestic Affairs. Responding to Soviet leader Mikhail Gorbachev's call for reform, restructuring (*perestroika*), and openness (*glasnost'*), Mongolia's leaders followed suit. At the third plenum Batmonh stated that Mongolia would study the "rich experience of revolutionary restructuring" taking place in the Soviet Union and would "creatively utilize this in the socialist construction of our country" (MONTSAME, 30 June; *FBIS*, 1 July). Council of Ministers chairman Sodnom admitted in his report that Mongolia's economy had not developed sufficiently to achieve the per capita national income level of the East European countries (MONTSAME, 30 June; *FBIS*, 2 July).

A further example of potential Mongolian *glasnost'* (*il tod* in Mongolian) came in October when the MPRP newspaper *Unen* published an article showing that the productivity of pastureland in Mongolia had decreased by more than 60 percent over the past two decades. The advancing Gobi Desert and a plague of field mice and locusts caused the loss of millions of hectares of productive land each year. The article called for more environmental protection and observed that neither state nor local agencies were adequately equipped to deal with the problem. (MONTSAME, 8 October; *FBIS*, 13 October.)

Although Mongolian reforms have yet to approach the scale and scope of the Soviet Union, some results are evident. According to a *FEER* reporter, Mongolia plans to give provincial and town administrations greater autonomy in production matters. The reporter also interviewed the new president of the Mongolian Academy of Sciences, N. Sodnom, who said that the academy's research work would be more practical and efficient to serve the development of the national economy. (*FEER*, 10 December.)

Nevertheless, Mongolia continues to face serious economic difficulties. Although livestock production has improved, herds are still below the long-standing goal of 25 million head, and the survival number after birth was nearly one million below the target (*FEER*, 10 December).

Mongolia still depends heavily on Soviet aid and support. According to MONTSAME, 90 percent of the country's machinery and equipment and 100 percent of its oil and rolled ferrous metals come from the USSR (*FBIS*, 28 August). Over 80 percent of Mongolia's trade is with the USSR and only 16 percent is with close Soviet allies. During the current Five-Year Plan, the Soviets will provide economic and technical assistance for 500 agricultural, industrial, housing, and service projects (MONTSAME, 2 February; *FBIS*, 3 February).

In June elections were held for "local people's hurals" and "people's courts." A total of 15,967 deputies were elected, of whom 4,708 were women; 56.5 percent were MPRP members and the remainder were Youth League members or nonparty members (MONTSAME, 26 June; *FBIS*, 30 June).

Auxiliary Organizations. The Thirteenth Congress of the Central Council of Mongolian Trade Unions met in May. It elected new leaders, though B. Lubsantseren was re-elected chairman. Lubsantseren said that trade union members "consider it our sacred duty of honor and conscience to dedicate all our strength and ability to the cause of socialist construction of our motherland." Also striking a reformist tone, Lubsantseren called for developing "production democracy" and an economic criterion for production management. (MONTSAME, 15 May; *FBIS*, 20 May.)

In July Ulan Bator hosted the Consultative Meeting of Communist and Workers' Parties of the Asia-Pacific Region. Although China did not attend, citing the lack of party ties with the MPRP, many other ruling and nonruling parties sent delegations. Batmonh's keynote speech blamed the imperialists for threatening Asian peace and security, hailed Gorbachev's Vladivostok (June 1986) proposals, and claimed that the meeting would allow the parties to better learn one another's positions and thereby facilitate the struggle against war. The Soviet representative, Anatolii Dobrynin, also hailed this communist dialogue. (MONTSAME, 7 July; *FBIS*, 10 July.)

International Views and Affairs. Three key developments in Mongolia's foreign relations occurred in 1987: Mongolia established diplomatic relations with the United States; the Soviet Union, as a gesture to China, removed some of its forces from Mongolia; and Mongolia further improved its relations with China, including new agreements and a visit by a Chinese parliamentary delegation.

On 27 January Ulan Bator and Washington, D.C. announced the establishment of diplomatic relations. The two sides also signed a memorandum on facilitating diplomatic missions. (MONTSAME, 27, 29 January; *FBIS*, 28 January, 2 February.) According to one source, Ulan Bator's motive is to further buttress its claim of national independence, whereas Washington hopes to gain a useful site for monitoring the development of Sino-Soviet relations (*FEER*, 5 March).

The USSR announced that it would withdraw some of its troops from Mongolia on 15 January, and on 11 April the withdrawals began. The withdrawal of one motorized rifle division and several individual units was completed by 8 June. (Xinhua,

7 June; *FBIS-PRC*, 8 June.) A joint statement issued by the USSR and Mongolia following the visit of Mongolian foreign minister Durgersuren to Moscow on 3 February hailed the troop withdrawal as a "manifestation of the two fraternal countries' goodwill facilitating the strengthening of trust, mutual understanding, and goodneighborliness in relations among the states of the Far East and Asia as a whole" (MONTSAME, 3 February; *FBIS*, 4 February).

The Chinese, however, were less enthusiastic. A Chinese Foreign Ministry spokesman reiterated that all three obstacles to Sino-Soviet relations (China's demands that the USSR draw down its troops along the border and in Mongolia, withdraw from Afghanistan, and cease supporting the Vietnamese occupation of Cambodia) must be removed (AFP, 17 January; *FBIS*, 20 January). The spokesman subsequently asserted that not just some but all Soviet troops should be removed from Mongolia (AFP, 8 June; *FBIS*, 10 June). The Hong Kong communist press noted that the Soviets were removing only about 10,000 of their approximately 75,000 troops from Mongolia and that Soviet control of Mongolia would not be weakened (*Wen wei po*, 22 January; *FBIS-PRC*, 30 January). Another Hong Kong communist newspaper stated that, though withdrawing some troops was better than withdrawing none, the Soviet gesture toward China was still "far from adequate" (*Ta kung pao*, 17 January; *FBIS-PRC*, 20 January). A Japanese newspaper suggested that the withdrawals were not militarily significant since the forces were being relocated close to the Mongolian border and could be recommitted to Mongolia within two days (*Sankei shimbun*, 18 July).

Whatever the uncertainties about the Soviet troop-withdrawal gesture, a continuing trend of improvement in Sino-Mongolian ties was clearly evident. The consular treaty concluded between the two sides in August 1986 was ratified in January. On 6 June the two countries initialed a new agreement on handling problems along the border (Xinhua, 6 June; *FBIS-PRC*, 8 June). Ulan Bator and Beijing also concluded a new cultural exchange plan, a border trade protocol that signified expanding trade, a new scientific and technological cooperation agreement, and, together with the USSR, a new border railway protocol.

For the first time in more than two decades, a high-level Chinese delegation visited Ulan Bator. Headed by Peng Chong, vice chairman of the National People's Congress Standing Committee, the delegation met with top Mongolian leaders and restored parliamentary ties between the two countries. MONTSAME reported that Batmonh told the delegation that the MPRP "consistently pursues a line aimed at restoring and developing friendly relations" with China. (*FBIS*, 25 June.) In September a delegation from the Executive Committee of the Federation of Mongolian Peace and Friendship Organizations and the Mongolian-China Friendship Association, headed by D. Tsakhilgaan, visited Beijing and was received by Peng Chong (Xinhua, 29 September; *FBIS-PRC*, 29 September).

Mongolia continued its outreach to other countries. Durgersuren made official visits to Australia and Japan; he told a Japanese newspaper that his visit to Japan symbolized expanding relations in political, economic, cultural, and other fields (*Yomiuri shimbun*, 17 May). But the overwhelming emphasis continued to be on ties with the Soviet bloc. Besides traveling to Moscow to meet Gorbachev, Batmonh traveled in Eastern Europe to continue to build ties with several countries there. Afghan prime minister Ali Keshtmand traveled to Mongolia in July, and Ethiopian leader Haile Mariam Mengistu visited in November. A wide variety of other communist delegations visited Ulan Bator throughout the year.

The MPRP continued to adhere closely to Soviet positions on foreign policy issues. At the conclusion of the Gorbachev visit to Washington and the signing of an intermediate nuclear forces (INF) accord in December, for example, the Great People's Hural issued a statement praising the "tireless struggle and purposeful initiatives of the Soviet Union" in making such an agreement possible. The statement further asserted that the INF treaty would "add fresh impetus to anti-war and anti-nuclear movements in this part of the world." (MONTSAME, 12 December; *FBIS*, 14 December.)

William R. Heaton
Dumfries, Virginia

Nepal

Population. 17,814,294

Parties. Nepal Communist Party–Marxist (NCP-Marxist); Nepal Communist Party (Marxist-Leninist) (NCP-ML), with two pro-Beijing factions and three Maoist factions that support China's disgraced "Gang of Four"; Nepal Communist Party/pro-Moscow (NCP/M), with four factions; Janabadi Morcha (Democratic Front)

Founded. NCP-Marxist: 1949; NCP-ML: 1978; Janabadi Morcha: founded in 1980 as radical democratic organization but turned Che Guevarist in 1985

Membership. 10,000 (estimated), with pro-Beijing, Maoist, and Marxist factions acounting for almost 75 percent of members

Leadership. NCP-Marxist—Man Mohan Adhikary, Mrs. Sahana Pradhan (Pushpa Lal's widow); NCP-ML (pro-Beijing)—Radha Krishna Mainali, Mohan Chandra Adhikary; Nepal Workers' and Peasants' Organization: Narayan Man Bijukchhe "Rohit"; NCP-ML (Maoist)—Fourth Congress: Nirmal Lama; Mashal: Mohan Bikram Gharti; Bahumat Mashal: Kiran (pseud.); NCP/M—Rayamajhi faction: Dr. Keshar Jung Rayamajhi; Manandhar faction: Bishnu Bahadur Manandhar; Varma faction: Krishna Raj Varma; Tulsi Lal faction: Tulsi Lal Amatya; Janabadi Morcha (Che Guevarist)—Ram Raja Prasad Singh

Politburo. 9 members in NCP-Marxist; no data on other factions

Secretariat. No data

Central Committee. 35 members in NCP/M (Rayamajhi faction); 35 members in NCP-Marxist; no data on other factions

Status. Proscribed

Last Congress. 1961 (last pre-split congress); Monandhar faction: Fifth, date unknown (*WMR*, July)

Last Election. 1959; 7.5 percent, 4 of 109 seats

Auxiliary Organizations. NCP-Marxist: Nepal Progressive Student Union; pro-Beijing: All-Nepal National Free Student Union; pro-Moscow: Nepal National Student Federation, Nepal National Youth Federation. In addition, all the communist groups have shadow organizations within the government-sponsored labor and peasant organizations.

Publications. NCP-Marxist: *Naya Janabad* (New democracy), *Nepal Patra*; NCP-ML (pro-Beijing): *Barga Sangharsha* (Class struggle), *Mukti-Morcha* (Liberation front); NCP-ML (Maoist): *Mashal* (Torch); NCP/M: *Samikshya Weekly* (reflects views of all pro-Soviet factions). *Daily Diary Weekly* and *Dristi Weekly* regularly publish views of all communist factions.

Political developments in Nepal in the first half of 1987 were shaped by election campaigns for local Panchayats (assemblies). After nearly six months of intraparty discussions, Nepali Congress—to the surprise of many observers—decided to participate in the local elections (*Nepal Press Digest* [NPD], 23 February; *FEER*, 19 March). That party had boycotted national-level elections in 1986. The communists remained divided on whether to participate in Panchayat elections. All pro-Moscow groups, a pro-Beijing faction, and the Maoist Fourth Congress decided to participate, whereas the Maoist Mashal faction and the NCP-Marxist decided to abstain.

Elections were peacefully conducted in March and April, although bomb scares were reported in some areas. The election results came as a shock to Nepali Congress: it lost heavily in some 85 percent of the constituencies, including Biratnagar, the hometown of the party's late leader, B. P. Koirala (*FEER*, 30 April). The government-backed candidates won 65 percent, and communists belonging to different factions captured 20 percent of the local Panchayat seats (ibid.). The opposition accused the government of large-scale vote-rigging. A leftist legislator, Jagrit Prasad Bhetuwal, even displayed some ballots that had been marked before the election in favor of government-backed candidates in far eastern Nepal (*NPD*, 6 April). Nepali Congress volunteers kept vigil outside Kathmandu Town Hall for six days to ensure proper counting (*FEER*, 30 April). Some independent observers maintain that Nepali Congress's loss in the elections was mainly due to its long isolation from the masses after the royal takeover in 1960.

In the aftermath of the local elections, Nepal was rocked by two major scandals: the Chernobyl nuclear radiation of imported dairy products, and the arrests and prosecution of drug smugglers in high government positions.

King Birendra addressed the 38th session of the National Panchayat and laid out his government's policies and programs for the coming year. A group of legislators then attempted to table a no-confidence motion against the Council of Ministers. Leftist members continued to demand the introduction of a multiparty system. In an interview with a local weekly, Bhetuwal demanded the introduction of a Marxist-Leninist system, which, he believed, would free Nepali people from the domination of exploiters (*FEER*, 6 July). Another leftist member, Bhim Bahadur Shrestha, was suspended from the National Panchayat when he demanded the introduction of a multiparty system (ibid., 13 July). This suspension was deplored by all important politicians of Nepal.

In mid-November, in a move to cleanse the administration of corrupt officials, the Nepal government dismissed 162 officials from the civil service. This came as a follow-up action to the earlier arrest and conviction of nearly 100 persons on charges of drug trafficking, smuggling, and corruption. (ibid., 3 December.)

Relations with India remained uneasy for most of the year. India's provincial governments—Assam, Meghalaya, and Tripura—expelled thousands of Nepalis lacking valid work permits. The reaction in Nepal to these expulsions was one of anger. The Nepal government announced that aliens working in Nepal would also be required to obtain work permits (*NPD*, 6 April). This announcement was hailed by several Nepali newspapers (ibid., 13 April).

In addition, the newspapers continued to demand the extradition from India of Ram Raja Prasad Singh, one of the masterminds behind the June 1985 bomb explosions in Nepal (ibid., 25 May). The Nepal government also condemned India's airdrops of supplies to the Tamils of Sri Lanka (ibid., 6 June). Nepal welcomed the 29 July accord between those two countries (ibid., 27 July). India continued to ignore Nepal's peace zone proposal, and, inside Nepal, criticisms of the 1950 Indo-Nepali treaty and demands for its abrogation continued as usual (ibid.).

Relations with the People's Republic of China remained cordial in 1987. King Birendra visited that country in early September. Chinese leaders expressed their support for Birendra's wish to declare Nepal a zone of peace. (*FBIS*, 13, 14, 17 September.)

The Soviet Union showed its willingness to cooperate with Nepal in the development of water resources, but the Soviet ambassador, G. K. Scheglov, told the press that there had been no change in the Soviet position regarding Nepal's peace zone proposal (*NPD*, 26 January). The Soviet Union regards that proposal as essentially a regional problem and hence supports India's lead in the matter. Soviet deputy foreign minister Igor A. Rogachyov visited Kathmandu in late May and discussed matters of mutual interest with Prime Minister Marich Man Singh Shrestha (ibid., 1 June).

Relations with the United States remained good. A U.S. congressional delegation visited Nepal in early January. Senator Mark O. Hatfield, the leader of the delegation, described the visit as "extraordinary" (ibid., 12 January). King Birendra and President Ronald Reagan exchanged messages of congratulations on the occasion of the 40th anniversary of the establishment of diplomatic relations between Nepal and the United States (ibid., 27 April).

Romanian president Nicolae Ceauşescu and West German chancellor Helmut Kohl visited Nepal in March and July, respectively (ibid., 23 March, 20 July).

Leadership and Organization. Unity talks between several leftist groups continued throughout 1987. Two pro-Moscow factions—Amatya and Varma—were reported to have announced their formal merger (ibid., 1 June). The report, however, was contradicted by both leaders in a joint statement maintaining that many questions had yet to be settled (ibid., 8 June).

Two groups previously described as neutralist factions formally merged and assumed the name NCP-Marxist at a unity meeting held at the Indian city of Banaras (ibid., 22 June). The meeting elected Man Mohan Adhikary as general secretary and Mrs. Sahana Pradhan as secretary of the newly formed group. The meeting also elected a 35-member Central Committee and a 9-member Politburo. This party is to follow the Communist Party of India–Marxist's line, will not embrace either Beijing or Moscow, and will attempt to extend its contacts with both the Chinese and the Soviet communist parties. Adhikary visited Moscow and reportedly met with Soviet leader Mikhail Gorbachev during the year. (ibid., 25 May.)

The Fourth Congress faction formerly led by Mohan Bikram Gharti is now divided into three factions: the Fourth Congress, the Mashal, and the Bahumat Mashal. The leaders of these factions, respectively, are Nirmal Lama, Mohan Bikram Gharti, and Kiran (pseud.). Despite their differences, all three groups seem to follow Gharti's opinion regarding post-Mao China. They hold the view that true communism does not exist anywhere in the world, and they still put their faith in the thought and activities of China's disgraced Gang of Four. These factions reportedly have contacts with the Communist Party of the United States.

Another pro-Beijing faction, led by Narayan Man Bijukchhe "Rohit" and known as the Rohit group, functions under the name Nepal Workers' and Peasants' Organization; it is influential in the Bhaktapur district and surrounding areas. This group differs from other Maoist organizations in that it relies on legal or systemic means to promote its ideology and depends mainly on local and communal factors. It has one representative in the National Panchayat.

The NCP-ML, an offspring of the Indian Naxalite movement, has been particularly active in eastern Nepal since the early 1970s, when it launched a "class annihilation" movement against the "exploiting class." The ideological line of this group is not clear; it hovers around Maoism, Lin Biaoism, and the ideas of the Gang of Four. The leadership of the NCP-ML is considered immature by other communist factions. Nevertheless, this group enjoys a significant amount of influence among radical university students.

Janabadi Morcha, which made headlines in the summer of 1985 by exploding bombs in different parts of the country, is led by a lawyer and former national legislator, Ram Raja Prasad Singh. Morcha is violence prone, extremely antimonarchist, and Che Guevarist. The party's rank and file come from Nepal's Terai, and its headquarters are located in an undisclosed location in India. The group is reported to have split in 1987 (*NPD*, 22 June). A special court handed down verdicts against 96 persons arrested and prosecuted by the Nepal government in the aftermath of the 1985 bombings; Singh was sentenced to death in absentia (ibid., 1 June).

Domestic Party Affairs. The main issue of division in the communist parties since the mid-1950s has been the problem of identifying the main enemy and creating a united front against that enemy. Sino-Soviet disputes appeared to be the issue only in the mid-1960s, especially after the beginning of the Cultural Revolution in China. The Maoists belonging to the Fourth Congress and the Mashal factions regard the king and Nepali Congress as enemies of equal proportion and hence reject the idea of any form of united front with Nepali Congress. The NCP-ML, also known as the Naxalites, regards the monarchy as the primary enemy but rules out the possibility of a united front with Nepali Congress, which, it says, is a puppet of both international comprador capitalism and the reactionary Indian government. In 1986, however, the NCP-ML changed its line and participated in the political process; as a result, the government released its leaders—Radha Krishna Mainali, Mod Nath Prasrit, and Khadga Prasad Oli—from jail in October 1987. The NCP-Marxist appears to be guided more by the ideology of radical socialism than by Marxism-Leninism. Its program envisages the replacement of the Panchayat system with a democratic system rather than the overthrow of the monarchy. It advocates a broad-based united front of all progressive and democratic elements, including Nepali Congress, to achieve its objectives. In contrast, the pro-Soviet factions see different roads to democracy and hence advocate both covert and overt strategies.

Auxiliary and Front Organizations. Leftist student movements continued to remain anti-Indian in nature. They opposed expulsions of Nepalis from the northeastern states of India. Four leftist organizations—the Democratic Unity Forum, the Civil Rights Forum, the People's Rights Protection Forum, and the National People's Forum—appeared in 1987 and called for nationwide demonstrations and closing businesses to oppose those expulsions (*NPD*, 21 December). Violence broke out in several areas, and in southeastern Nepal one student was killed by police gunfire (ibid.).

International Views, Positions, and Activities. No change was recorded on international views and positions of the NCP factions. The Fourth Congress and both Mashal factions are critical of China and the Soviet Union. Differences of opinion exist on the issue of supporting or opposing the Gorkhaland agitation in northern West Bengal of India for a separate homeland for the people of Nepali origin. The Fourth Congress, Mashal, and Marxist-Leninist groups have expressed support for the Gorkhaland movement; pro-Moscow groups and the NCP-Marxist do not support that movement because of its separatist character.

The NCP-Marxist deplored India's sending of troops to Sri Lanka under an Indo–Sri Lanka accord, and it demanded their prompt withdrawal. Mashal maintained that the agreement had exposed the "expansionist character of the Indian reactionaries, as well as the capitulationist policy of the Jayawardene government." Other pro-Beijing and independent leftist leaders took it as the product of India's aggressive designs. (*NPD*, 10 August.) Pro-Soviet factions, however, welcomed the agreement as "a basis for the establishment of peace in Sri Lanka" (ibid.).

Dr. Keshar Jung Rayamajhi seems to have been abandoned by the Soviet Union, because there have been rumors in Nepal that the Soviets have shifted their support to Dr. Rayamajhi's dissenters—the Manandhar and Varma factions. In fact, Soviet embassy officials occasionally participate in the Varma and Manandhar meetings. There is no indication of any covert or overt Chinese support for the divided pro-Beijing groups.

Chitra K. Tiwari
Arlington, Virginia

New Zealand

Population. 3,291,600 (New Zealand Department of Statistics, June)
Parties. Communist Party of New Zealand (CPNZ); Socialist Unity Party (SUP); Socialist Action League (SAL); Workers' Communist League (WCL)
Founded. CPNZ: 1921; SUP: 1966; SAL: 1969; WCL: 1980
Membership. CPNZ: 50; SUP: 300; SAL: 100; WCL: 50 (all estimated)
Leadership. CPNZ: Harold Crook (secretary); SUP: George Jackson (national president); SAL: Russell Johnson (national secretary); WCL: Graeme Clark
Status. All legal
Last Congress. CPNZ: Twenty-third, 1984; SUP: Seventh, 26–27 October 1985; SAL: Eleventh, 26–31 December 1986; WCL: Third, June 1986, special national planning conference, September 1987
Last Election. 15 August (parliamentary), no representatives elected; 11 October 1986 (local government), no representatives elected
Auxiliary Organizations. SUP: Youth in Unity, Workers' Institute for Scientific Education (WISE), Peace Council New Zealand, New Zealand–USSR Society; SAL: Young Socialists, Socialist Forum, Latin America Solidarity Committee, Cuba Friendship Society, Committee for a Workers' Front, Nicaragua Must Survive Committee
Publications. CPNZ: *People's Voice* (bimonthly); SUP: *NZ Tribune* (bimonthly except for 8 June–27 August when it was published weekly as part of the 1987 New Zealand election campaign), *Socialist Politics* (every two months); SAL: *Socialist Action* (bimonthly), *Socialist Action Review* (periodically); WCL: *Unity* (every three weeks)

Domestic Affairs. Although the four New Zealand communist parties admire and support much of the Labour government's antinuclear and independent foreign policy, they have been aghast at its right-wing economic policies and its apparent intention to dismantle the traditional social welfare system. Fearful of a National Party victory that would reverse Labour's foreign policy, however, the communist parties reluctantly supported the Labour Party at the triennial elections to the New Zealand Parliament on 15 August.

The pro-Moscow SUP explained to its supporters that they should vote Labour and then work with the government to do what the SUP wanted, not only in foreign affairs but also in providing jobs, free health care, education, and cheap housing. The pro-Albanian, Stalinist CPNZ and the pro-Chinese WCL also did not field candidates in the election. The pro-Cuban SAL officially sponsored candidates for three of the 97 seats in the Parliament. All three were safe Labour seats: Christchurch Central (Dr. Felicity Brereton), Porirua (Peter Bradley), and Otara (Eugen Lepou). Brereton received 196 of the total 18,149 votes cast in Christchurch Central; Bradley 154 out of 15,881; and Lepou an even more derisory 77 out of 16,338.

Three other anti-Labour left-wing candidates, who tried to put together a broader support base, fared somewhat better. Joce Jesson, standing as a "Left Alternative" on a feminist, antiracist, peace movement, anticapitalist platform, polled 1,090 out of a total of 17,255 votes cast in Auckland Central. In Miramar, Vivian Walker, standing for the People First coalition, received 433 out of 20,177 votes. In Saint Albans the Socialist Alliance candidate, Dr. Geof Pearce, recorded 181 out of 20,831 votes.

Communists had more success in trade union elections than they did in the parliamentary arena. On 21 October the New Zealand Council of Trade Unions (NZCTU) was formally constituted. The NZCTU combined some 530,000 members in 70 private and state-sector affiliated unions. Previously, most private sector unions had belonged to the New Zealand Federation of Labour and most state employees to the Combined State Unions, the largest of which was the Public Service Association. The first president of the NZCTU is Ken Douglas, who is also national chairman of the SUP. Another leading SUP member, G. H. "Bill" Andersen, became a member of the NZCTU executive. The formation of the NZCTU coincided with the worldwide stock market crash, and Douglas used the occasion to launch a blistering attack on capitalism at home and abroad. The NZCTU will undoubtedly reflect a Marxist and a particularly though not exclusively SUP perspective and analysis.

The SUP. The SUP's work in the trade union movement will be assisted by the party's foundation of WISE. With the assistance of "two very generous donors," WISE acquired a conference center near Auckland as "a powerful educational base to widen the struggle for democracy, peace and socialism . . . Reasonably priced residential accommodation will be made available to all labour movement activists, youth, women, peace, Maori, and unemployed groups as well as all left parties" (*NZ Tribune*, 8 May).

Among the gatherings held at the WISE center was an SUP school in October attended by visiting Soviet professors Vorontsova and Nukhovich, and in November a special conference of the SUP's Auckland region was held to review forms of party branch organization and ways of raising funds.

The increased activity by the SUP throughout 1987 was indicated by the party's fighting fund, which at $43,060 at the beginning of November was some $8,000 higher than at the corresponding time the previous year.

The WCL. In September the WCL held a national planning conference to discuss, amend, and adopt a draft paper put forward at the third conference of the WCL in June 1986 and subsequently published in *Unity* (16 February).

The WCL, although supportive of international communism, pays less attention to foreign policy than does the SAL and is concerned more with what it sees as the three fundamental contradictions in contemporary New Zealand society: between capital and labor; between settler colonialism and indigenous Maori self-determination; and between the patriarchy and the women's liberation movement. Each of those issues is seen as having its own history and origin, though intertwined with the others.

The importance of cooperation and eventual organizational unity among communist parties and factions in New Zealand is stressed by the WCL, which laments that "there is no single or predominant revolutionary political organisation in Aoteroa [the Maori name for New Zealand] with deep roots throughout society . . . Relations between the various groups have generally taken the form of cooperation in mass movements around short-term demands, and ideological debate on everything else" (*Unity*, 16 February).

Seven major goals were adopted by the September planning conference: to build a united, national, left-progressive movement; to combat sexism, recruit more women, and hold a women's conference; to work for Maori self-determination; to influence as much as possible the health workers' unions; to increase political work among young people, especially students, because "education of educators is an urgent task"; to move the trade unions toward a class struggle position; and to encourage and support international socialist solidarity (*Unity*, 28 September).

The SAL. The National Committee of the SAL met in Auckland from 3 to 5 October to discuss "Internationalism and the working class today" with the emphasis on the significance for world politics of the political revolution unfolding in Cuba. Present were three foreign visitors: Mac Warren, a member of the Political Committee of the Socialist Workers' Party of the United States; Steve Penner, executive secretary of the Canadian Revolutionary Workers' League; and Ron Poulsen from Pathfinder Press, Australia.

In November the SAL opened a street-front bookstore in Auckland. The store specializes in socialist and revolutionary literature provided by Pathfinder Press New York, Pathfinder Pacific and Asia Press in Sydney, and the José Martí Publishing House in Cuba. The shop is also intended to be a center for political discussion and will add to the outlets for radical literature in Auckland already serviced by the SUP's Socialist Bookshop, which operates a thriving mail-order business, and the Combined Organisation for Relief Services Overseas (CORSO) shop, which stocks a wide range of socialist and radical papers and books.

The CPNZ. The tiny and aging CPNZ received a severe blow with the death in Auckland on 19 July of its chairman, Richard C. "Dick" Wolf. At the funeral service Wolf was described by CPNZ secretary Harold Crook as "a great ideological, political, and organisation leader of our Party."

Born in Auckland on 25 September 1906 to German immigrant parents, Wolf joined the CPNZ in the early 1930s. A plasterer by trade and president of the Plasterers' Union, Wolf illegally produced the party newspaper, *People's Voice*, during World War II. A strong Stalinist, Wolf rejected Moscow's leadership and supported the pro-

Chinese side in the Sino-Soviet conflict during the 1960s. In 1979, when the CPNZ broke with China and followed the Albanian line, Wolf was elected party chairman, and he held that position until his death. As of the end of the year, no successor had been announced.

Support for Nicaragua. New Zealand's four main socialist-communist parties devoted much of their work during the year to supporting the Sandinista government in Nicaragua. The Nicaragua Must Survive Committee raised $170,000 in 1986 and organized visits and conferences throughout 1987.

Some 370 people attended a large antiwar conference in Wellington on 17–19 July that focused on Nicaragua and anticolonialism in the Pacific. This South Pacific Conference for Peace and Justice in Central America was sponsored by the SUP, the WCL, the SAL, the Labour Party's Nicaragua Support Committee, CORSO, and the Wellington Trades' Council, whose secretary, Graeme Clark, is a WCL leader. All these organizations support the ad hoc Nicaragua Must Survive Committee and the Latin America Solidarity Committee.

The conference coincided with the eighth anniversary of the Nicaraguan revolution and included Alberto Gallegos, head of the Middle East, Asian, and South Pacific divisions of the international department of the Sandinista National Liberation Front of Nicaragua, and Antonio Hernandez, head of Asian and Pacific relations for the Farabundo Martí National Liberation Front and the Democratic Revolutionary Front of El Salvador.

Gallegos addressed the conference to explain the importance of the liberation struggles in Nicaragua, El Salvador, South Africa, Namibia, Palestine, New Caledonia, and Fiji in the ongoing campaign against U.S. imperialism. The conference also heard from a panel consisting of Dewe Gorodney (New Caledonia Independence Front), Eva Rickard (New Zealand Maori), and Quake Raddock (Fijian Labour Party).

Prior to the conference some speakers toured New Zealand, notably Glenda Monterrey, organizational secretary of the Sandinista Union Federation; Alicia Torrez Perez, Nicaraguan government office for women's affairs; Luis Jalandoni from the National Democratic Front of the Philippines; and Roberto Ortaliz, president of the Philippines Sugar Workers' Union.

Conference members decided to organize a national day of education and action on 16 October to focus the New Zealand public's attention on the "United States government's war against Nicaragua, solidarity with other liberation struggles in Latin America and the Caribbean, and support for a nuclear-free and independent Pacific" (*Socialist Action*, 4 September). This action would coincide with similar protests in Latin America and the Caribbean and would involve a speaking tour of New Zealand by Mirta Muniz, a member of the Cuban president's staff and delegate to Cuba's National Assembly, who would launch a book marking the twentieth anniversary of the death of Che Guevara.

The Day of Action on Central America involved several Labour members of Parliament (MP). In Christchurch Jim Anderton, MP for Sydenham and chairman of Parliament's Foreign Affairs and Defence Committee, addressed a gathering of some 150 people. In Wellington, where 200 marchers condemned the United States and praised the "positive achievements" of the Sandinista revolution, Sonya Davies, recently elected MP for Pencarrow and former vice president of the New Zealand Federation of Labour, was a speaker.

The success of the pro-Sandinista lobby in New Zealand was revealed at the governing Labour Party's annual conference in Auckland 6–8 November, when Minister of Foreign Affairs Russell Marshall announced that the New Zealand government would establish formal diplomatic relations with Nicaragua, probably through the New Zealand embassy in Mexico.

In December 1986 and January 1987 more than twenty New Zealanders spent six weeks picking coffee in Nicaragua as a sign of support and solidarity. The group was named the Harry Holland Brigade after the first leader of the New Zealand Labour Party, a theoretical Marxist fascinated by the Russian Revolution. A second work brigade spent six weeks in Nicaragua in December 1987–January 1988, and the project was extended to another group picking citrus fruit in Cuba at the same time.

Other International Activities. It was not coincidental that the Day of Action on 16 October was followed on 17, 18, and 19 October by a meeting in Auckland of the World Peace Council Bureau. The meeting was attended by delegates from some 50 countries, including the council's president, Ramesh Chandra of India; the president of the East German–based Women's International Democratic Federation; Freda Brown of Australia; Francisco da Costa Gomes, former president of Portugal; Luis

Echeverria, former president of Mexico; Olga Aviles Lopes of Nicaragua; and Vladimir Orel of the USSR.

On 21 October the SUP's newspaper, *NZ Tribune*, highlighted the attendance of Anderton and Davies by twice reproducing a photo of them at the top table with Chandra. Anderton's address to the World Peace Council was fully reported.

As usual, a large number of SUP members and others whom the SUP and the Soviet Union wished to influence visited the USSR during 1987. Marilyn Tucker, acting general secretary of the SUP, attended the World Congress of Women in Moscow in June accompanied by Shelley Hiha (Federation of Labour Maori Advisory Group and Clerical Workers' Union), Frena Brorens (Wellington Shop Employees' Union), and Pauline Tangiora (Maori Women's Welfare League). Tucker and Ken Douglas then went on to the Conference of Asian-Pacific Region Communists at Ulan Bator in Mongolia. Representatives of 21 parties discussed the twenty-first century as an age of economic and strategic opportunity in the Pacific.

Among others to visit the USSR during the year were Jan Farr, editor of the *NZ Tribune*, who in May attended a meeting in Moscow convened by *Pravda*; SUP Central Committee member Bernie O'Brien, who in June studied *perestroika* (restructuring); Ella Ayo, the veteran woman activist and party national vice-chairperson; and Peter Hall-Jones, a Wellington regional committee member who attended a preparatory meeting for the Thirteenth World Festival of Youth and Students. Acting General Secretary Marilyn Tucker and Central Committee member Bruce Skilton represented the SUP at the 70th anniversary celebration of the Bolshevik Revolution in Moscow in October.

The most prominent of the non-SUP persons to accept invitations to visit the USSR were Margaret Wilson, president of the Labour Party; Tony Timms, general secretary of the Labour Party; and Fran Wilde, Labour MP for Wellington Central and subsequently promoted to associate minister of foreign affairs. They visited Moscow, Leningrad, and Riga in January as guests of the Communist Party of the Soviet Union (CPSU). Both parties publicly praised each other's foreign policy.

Although New Zealand deputy prime minister Geoffrey Palmer and a New Zealand Parliamentary delegation led by Speaker Gerard Wall visited China in March and May, respectively, and although Prime Minister David Lange had also visited China in March 1986, New Zealand officials believe that such a visit to the USSR by Lange would be unwise before he has made official visits to the United States and Japan. It could possibly be misinterpreted in the context of the delicate situation between New Zealand and the United States over the former's banning of American nuclear-powered or nuclear-weapon-capable ships and the subsequent suspension of the ANZUS treaty.

Perhaps because of the importance New Zealand places on its export trade to the USSR, neither of those countries made a serious issue out of the expulsion by the New Zealand government in April of Sergei Budnik, counsellor at the Soviet embassy in Wellington, for undisclosed activities "not in accord with those of a diplomat." Unlike 1980, when New Zealand's expulsion of Soviet ambassador Vsvelod Sofinsky led to the expulsion of New Zealand's ambassador and four years when neither country was represented at that level in Moscow or Wellington, the Soviet reaction to Budnik's expulsion was muted. The USSR retaliated only by expelling the New Zealand embassy's maintenance man, and the matter was quickly forgotten.

Soviet visitors to New Zealand during 1987 included a Soviet trade delegation in April led by Gleb Simonenko, Professor Bella Vorontsova (an expert on the history of the CPSU), and Professor Edward Nukhovich (a political economist); Dr. Vladimir Ivanov, head of the Pacific Studies Department of the USSR Academy of Sciences, who visited Auckland briefly in October on his way back to Moscow after two months at the Australian National University in Canberra; and in November a three-member delegation of Soviet politicians led by Rafik Nishanov, vice-chairman of the USSR Supreme Soviet.

Barry Gustafson
University of Auckland

Pakistan

Population. 104,600,799
Party. Communist Party of Pakistan (CPP)
Founded. 1948
Membership. Under 200 (estimated)
General Secretary. Ali Nazish
Status. Illegal

Last Congress. First, 1976 (clandestine)
Leading Bodies. No data
Publications. None

In 1987 the political opposition's boycott of the government—a boycott that had been ongoing since 1985—fell apart after President Zia ul-Haq lifted martial law. The major opposition party, the Pakistan People's Party (PPP), led by Benazir Bhutto, as well as several smaller parties decided to participate in the new political order by running a candidate in a September parliamentary by-election and participating in the November local elections held in all four provinces.

The major opposition parties, responding positively to the liberalizing trend, now speak of a "bridge to democracy." Prime Minister Mohammed Khan Junejo's ruling Pakistan Muslim League (PML) and the larger opposition parties busied themselves during 1987 with organizational matters, such as holding internal party elections to develop a grass-roots structure able to mobilize support for the next general elections in 1990. Although some of the leaders of the smaller parties belonging to the Movement for the Restoration of Democracy (MRD) and some nonaffiliated leftist groups such as the CPP have continued their boycott policy, they have had only partial success.

Party Affairs. Although the CPP is formally banned and not a constituent of the MRD, it supported those parties in the MRD advocating a continued boycott of the new political order. The tiny CPP exercises a negligible influence on its own, though Marxists outside the party play some role among the PPP's militant left (not its dominant faction). Indeed, Bhutto has kept the party on a centrist course and has been criticized by the left in her party. The leftists in the PPP were particularly disturbed by her comment in early 1987 that the USSR seemed insincere about a settlement of the Afghan situation. (*FEER*, 23 April.) There are also Marxists among the leftist constituents of the MRD: the Quami Mahaz Azadi, the Pakistan Socialist Party, the Pakistan Progressive Party, and the Awami National Party (ANP). The CPP adheres faithfully to the foreign policy line of the USSR and is invited to various international conclaves sponsored by pro-Soviet communist parties and groups. It was represented, for example, by a Politburo member at the July meeting on Asia-Pacific security hosted by the Mongolian communist party. (*FBIS–EAS*, 14 July.)

Foreign Affairs. Relations between Pakistan and the USSR were again dominated by the issue of Soviet troops in neighboring Afghanistan. The USSR, perhaps seeking Pakistani backing for a Soviet withdrawal on the best terms possible, went out of its way to signal a desire for better relations. In his 28 November 1986 press conference in New Delhi, Soviet leader Mikhail Gorbachev had been careful to make conciliatory statements regarding Pakistan. Soviet ambassador to Pakistan Abdul Rakhman Ogly Vezirov reportedly reminded his Pakistani interlocutors "constantly" of Gorbachev's statements (*Indian Express*, 17 December). Communist Party of the Soviet Union (CPSU) Secretariat member Anatolii Dobrynin visited New Delhi in May and publicly stated that Indian fears of Pakistan's nuclear weapons program were exaggerated (ibid.). Inder Malhotra, a prominent Indian journalist, wrote that Soviet officials referred nostalgically to their country's mediation of the 1965 war when Moscow maintained good relations with both South Asian states (*Times of India*, 20 February). On his return from early February talks in Moscow, Pakistani foreign minister Sahabzada Yaqub Khan said he was impressed by the Soviet desire for better relations (*FBIS–South Asia*, 13 February).

The year started with a high-level Soviet mission to Islamabad led by First Deputy Foreign Minister Anatolii Kovalev, whose major purpose was to exchange views regarding the Soviet Union's "new gestures" on the Afghan situation (ibid., 20 January). These new gestures undoubtedly related to the timetable for the withdrawal of Soviet troops, which is the only unresolved issue at the U.N.-sponsored indirect talks between Pakistan and Afghanistan. The withdrawal question was the major topic at the two sets of indirect talks during 1987: 25 February–9 March and 7–10 September. At the first session, the Afghan representatives reduced the withdrawal timetable from four years to eighteen months, whereas Pakistan agreed to increase it from four to seven months (*State Department Report*, no. 173, December). At the second meeting, the Afghans reduced the withdrawal timeframe to sixteen months, whereas the Pakistanis increased it to eight (ibid.). The two sides still have some way to go on this key question. They have yet to reach a consensus on the controversial issue regarding an interim government in Kabul that would supervise the transition to a popularly elected government. This issue has not yet been on the agenda at Geneva, though it will probably be a major question during future meetings there. Despite the unresolved problems, at the end of 1987 President Zia told a German television journalist, "I think we can trust Gorbachev when he says the Soviet Union intends to leave Afghanistan" (*FBIS–South Asia*, 29 December). Moreover, on the contentious question of an interim government, Zia noted, "I think we can convince the Mujahidin . . . that such an interim government should also include those in power today" (ibid.). This may be difficult, because much of the Mujahidin leadership is adamantly opposed to the involvement of anyone associated with the present Kabul regime in an interim political arrangement.

Despite the repeated Soviet references to better relations, Moscow was not above applying pressure to get its way. The acts of terrorism, perhaps with Soviet involvement, increased. The number of Afghan air incursions at the border resulted in a substantially larger number of deaths and injuries in 1987 than in 1986. (*State Department Report*, no. 173, December.) In addition, there were reports of Soviet military helicopters "straying" into Pakistani air space (*FEER*, 20 October). In early October two Soviet gunships made a forced landing in Pakistan some 50 kilometers from the border; Pakistan immediately returned the crew to the USSR as a goodwill gesture (*FBIS–South Asia*, 7 October). Afghan diplomats, with Soviet support, launched a campaign to undermine backing for the annual Pakistani resolution at the United Nations calling for the immediate and complete withdrawal of foreign forces. Nevertheless, in November at the U.N. General Assembly, 123 nations, the largest total to date, voted for the resolution.

In contrast to the tensions that have often marked Pakistani-Soviet relations, Islamabad's ties with Beijing remained a cornerstone of Pakistan's foreign policy. China is viewed as a valuable ally that has stood by it for over two decades. It remains a major source of military equipment. Premier Zhao Ziyang in his June visit reaffirmed Chinese support for the Pakistani position on the Afghan question.

Walter K. Andersen
Alexandria, Virginia

Philippines

Population. 58,100,000 (*Asia 1987 Yearbook*)
Parties. Communist Party of the Philippines (Marxist-Leninist) (CPP); Communist Party of the Philippines (Partido Komunista ng Pilipinas, PKP)
Founded. CPP: 1968; PKP: 1930
Membership. CPP: 15,000 (estimates range from 10,000 to over 30,000); PKP: 200
Leadership. CPP: Benito Tiamson (chairman), Rafael Baylosis (general secretary); PKP: Felicismo C. Macapagal (general secretary)
Central Committee. CPP: 29 members, including Benito Tiamson, Rafael Baylosis, Ignacio Capegsan, Jose Luneta (deputy general secretaries), Saturnino Ocampo, Antonio Zumel, Benjamin De Vera, Romulo Kintanar, Luis Jalandoni, Rondel Echaniz, Wilma Austria Tiamzon, Francisco Pascual, Tomas Dominado, Salvador Bas, Sotero Blamas, Arturo Tabara, Antonio Cabanatan, Juanito Rivera, Armando Liwanag, Santiago Santaromana, Ericson Baculinao; PKP: Felicismo C. Macapagal, Alejandro Briones, Jesus Lava, Jose Lava, Merlin Magallona
Status. CPP: Illegal; negotiations to legalize the party were started in December 1986 but halted in February; PKP: legal
Last Congress. CPP: Ninth, January; PKP: Eighth, 1980
Last Election. 11 May 1987, legislative
Auxiliary Organizations. CPP: New People's Army (NPA), National Democratic Front (NDF). The NDF, which has an international affairs office in Athens, Greece, includes the Association of Revolutionary Workers, Association of Nationalist Teachers (KAGUMA), Christians for National Liberation (CNL), Nationalist Youth (KM), and the Organization of Nationalist Women. The Filipino Peoples Committee (KSP), based in the Netherlands, represents "people's organizations in the Philippines." Other organizations thought to be influenced by the CPP include Bayan (Nation; from Bagong Alyansang Makabayan or New Nationalist Alliance); May First Movement (KMU); Movement of Attorneys for Brotherhood, Integrity, and Nationalism (MABINI); Movement of

Philippine Farmers (KMP); and the Nationalist Health Association (MASAPA). PKP: National Association of Workers (Katipunan), Philippine Committee for Development, Peace, and Solidarity (PCDPS)

Publications. CPP: *Ang Bayan* (The nation), monthly; NPA: *Pulang Bandila* (Red flag), bimonthly; NDF: *Liberation*, monthly; *Taliba ng Bayan* biweekly; *NDF-Update*, bimonthly, published in the Netherlands; *Ang Katipunan*, irregular, published in Oakland, California; PKP: *Ang Komunista*, irregular

In 1987 the CPP and NPA changed tactics and leadership, signaling an escalation of violence in their twenty-year-old insurgency, according to one detailed analysis. "All indications are that [CPP] moderates have been replaced by hardliners intent on regaining the momentum lost when former president Marcos was ousted by Corazon Aquino." (*FEER*, 17 December.)

Five major changes occurred during 1987 in the escalating civil war in the Philippines. Rebel negotiators of the NDF broke off cease-fire negotiations with the Aquino government and resumed armed struggle to achieve power. Hostilities intensified as rebel forces increased selective assassinations against government armed forces and police; these were carried out in urban as well as rural areas; they included threats and attacks on U.S. military personnel. Rebel forces also increased their contacts with international support groups. The Aquino government, after shrill and sometimes violent opposition and coup d'état attempts from right-wing groups, reversed its earlier policy of reconciliation with the rebels and started military and paramilitary actions against rebel groups and their suspected supporters. The United States increased its support for the new Aquino government counterinsurgency program with stepped-up military assistance and Central Intelligence Agency (CIA) covert operations. However, there were numerous indications of persistent massive poverty and abuses by military and paramilitary forces—the basic forces at the roots of the rebellion.

After a decade of rapid expansion, the communist insurgency was slowed in 1986 by the broad-based reformist movement that had forced Ferdinand Marcos into exile and propelled Corazon Aquino and her People Power coalition into a new government after fraudulent elections and a civil disobedience campaign. Initially, Aquino pursued a policy of reconciliation with the rebels, despite some contrary views in her cabinet and the military. On 10 December 1986 a 60-day cease-fire began, ending over seventeen years of hostilities between government forces and communist guerrillas. Government and rebel representatives began negotiations over highly contentious issues, including the legalization and demilitarization of the CPP and NPA, amnesty for the rebels, power-sharing by the CPP in the new government, redistribution of wealth and power concentrated during the Marcos years, and the status of U.S. bases in the Philippines. In February 1987 the cease-fire talks broke down and hostilities resumed. In the aftermath of the dramatic rise of the Aquino government, the CPP undertook a major overhaul of leadership and strategy. (*NYT*, 29 May.)

The NPA. The NPA is a political and propaganda force as well as a fighting force. Its first objective, according to its basic document, is to help recruit and train communist party members; second, to carry out agrarian reforms; third, to build rural bases or guerrilla fronts and to engage in armed struggle; and fourth, to help mobilize support for the NDF. Most NPA members are not soldiers; they are political workers, social workers, agricultural advisers, paramedics, and teachers. They work in rural barrios and poor urban centers, in factories and on plantations, in churches, and even in government offices.

The rebel strategy is summarized in the party slogan, "Centralized Leadership and Decentralized Operations." The CPP Central Committee formulates general policies and guidelines. The local committee or guerrilla front has flexibility to experiment with different tactics for implementing general policy. As a result, guerrilla fronts have been created in almost every ethnolinguistic and geographic region of the country.

Fom a total force of a few thousand armed guerrillas in 1980, the NPA has grown to probably over 23,000 regulars and a larger number of part-time irregulars. The NPA force estimates range from 16,500 according to the Pentagon to 32,000 according to the NPA (see also *CSM*, 6 January). These forces were operating on as many as 60 fronts around the country, including occasional company level (200–300 men) operations. The NPA reportedly has shadow governments in 10–15 percent of the country's villages. Some level of NPA activity now exists in almost all of the country's 73 provinces. (ibid.; *FEER*, 17 December.)

The NPA has significantly increased its operations in urban areas. A spate of apparent assassinations by the communists in May caused the army to form "special action units" that would assist the Manila police, according to General Fidel Ramos. At least twenty soldiers and policemen were killed during a two-week period in May. The military has confirmed that at least seven of these killings had been communist assassinations, Ramos said. (It was believed that criminals sometimes covered their tracks by imitating the rebels' notorious three-man "sparrow" units.) The Manila killings marked a departure from the guerrilla war that the communists had long waged in the countryside. In March two men who depicted themselves as members of the NPA said the rebels had killed sixteen officials in Manila since February but only about fourteen over the previous three years. (*WP*, 7 June; see also *NYT*, 7 September.)

Military statistics show that 103 people, most of them policemen and soldiers, were killed in 97 insurgency-related shootings in Manila in the first ten months of 1987. The average annual casualty rate in previous years was nine. Manila police estimated that there were 1,200 armed insurgents operating in Manila and that 28 neighborhoods were "infested" with the insurgency (*NYT*, 1 January). Another report found that more than 150 people, mostly government troops and police, were killed by communist "sparrow" squads in Manila in 1987 (MacNeil-Lehrer Report, 5 January 1988; see also *FEER*, 26 November).

The NDF. The NDF is the political front created and led by the CPP. It has developed significant support among some radical Christian groups, labor organizations, student groups, and others. NDF influence is evident in Bayan, a legal opposition coalition founded in April 1985 that grew out of the Coalition for the Restoration of Democracy, which emerged after the murder of Benigno Aquino in 1983. Bayan now encompasses elements of the Marxist left plus cause-oriented groups and traditional nationalist politicians, academics, and even businessmen. A conflict over leadership structure and the role of CPP supporters led to the departure of important supporters, including Agapito "Butz" Aquino—the brother of Benigno—and Jose Diokno, an elder statesman of Filipino nationalism.

In areas where guerrilla fronts have been established, the NDF functions as the provisional local government. It provides a regular exchange of material benefits for political support. It collects taxes, implements land reforms, organizes public works and schools, and administers "revolutionary justice." The NDF has been able to spread its anti-Marcos and anti-U.S. views among both radical and moderate opposition groups, from rural areas to urban areas. The NDF represented the armed insurgents in negotiations with the Aquino government.

Government Response. In order to defuse the persistent insurgency, Corazon Aquino began her term by fulfilling her campaign pledges of political reconciliation. Her first proclamation was to abolish the government's power to detain people without charge, a practice that Marcos had used widely in purported cases of subversion, sedition, and conspiracy.

Over 500 political prisoners were ordered released by the government, despite some objections from top military officials. These included Jose Maria Sison, founder of the CPP and a former English professor at the University of the Philippines, and Bernabe Buscayno, also known as Commander Dante, son of a poor farm family and reportedly the former head of the NPA. Both had been imprisoned for nearly ten years. Also released were Alexander Birondo, alleged chief of the Armed City Partisans in Manila, and Ruben Alegre, who had been captured in a shoot-out with police in Manila in 1985. Although the official CPP is still illegal, Sison, Buscayno, and other Filipinos have now organized a new legal leftist party, the People's Party (Partido ng Bayan). It has the support of the KMU, a leftist labor federation that claims to have about half a million members, the largest in the country.

Aquino's economic goals aimed to reduce the country's poverty, unemployment, and underemployment, an essential task to defuse the communist insurgency. Finance Minister Jaime Ongpin called his economic program "private enterprise with a social conscience." It gave top priority to increasing domestic food production and only secondary importance to export promotion.

Land reform, however, was not addressed by the Aquino government. This is a crucial challenge to the government, especially in the economically depressed sugar-producing regions of Negros and Panay islands and northern Mindanao, where the NPA and CPP continue to be active. Firefights and general strikes occurred with regularity before the election and continued up to the cease-fire of December 1986. Shadow governments have continued to operate in the hinterland villages.

Cease-fire Negotiations. On 4 January, at the start of substantive cease-fire talks, NDF chairman Antonio Zumel said the two sides were "poles apart" in their proposals; he said he had little hope that the insurgency could be solved at the negotiating table (*NYT*, 6 January). The two sides agreed in principle to talk about "food and freedom, jobs and justice." Half of the cease-fire period was taken in attempting to reach agreement on an agenda for negotiations.

The talks gave Aquino's government a chance to win popular support away from the guerrillas and to organize a comprehensive counterinsurgency program. Her cabinet approved a $50 million rebel rehabilitation program, but it was not implemented during the 60-day cease-fire.

Some observers, however, saw the cease-fire as a strategic advantage for the communists. "They will use the new 'democratic space' to expand their political contacts among centrist elements, recruiting new members, and trying to further infiltrate the government, and developing foreign connections both for future material and ideological support" (*CSM*, 6 January). Hence, "both the communists and the military see the cease-fire as an opportunity for war, not peace" (ibid.; see also Taipei, *Issues and Studies*, November).

The rebels took the opportunity of the cease-fire to hold a party congress and to broaden their international contacts. The NDF maintains an office in Utrecht, the Netherlands, where Luis Jalandoni, a former Roman Catholic priest, works with Sixto Carlos, a former political prisoner. The NDF has good informal ties with the Dutch Labor Party and formal recognition from the governing Pasok Party in Greece. The NDF is reported to be preparing a petition to the U.N. Human Rights Commission in Geneva about alleged human rights violations. The front also arranged "exposure visits" to Manila by various European and Australian parliamentarians, journalists, and trade unionists. Two Salvadoran rebels visited Manila and five NDF members visited Cuba during the cease-fire period (*FEER*, 26 March). A Japanese United Red Army member was reported to be in the Philippines late in the year (*Japan Economic Newswire*, 5 December).

Moscow and Beijing appear to have little influence on the Filipino rebels; however, fraternal relations with communist parties in power have been pursued with the Soviet Union, North Korea, and Vietnam. "We are now in the process of seeking and establishing relations with the ruling parties in Eastern Europe and elsewhere," said a CPP bulletin in July (*Ang Bayan*, 7 July; see also *FEER*, 17 December; *San Francisco Examiner*, 29 November).

During the cease-fire period the government was also preoccupied with the Muslim rebellion and lingering resistance from pro-Marcos groups. The government and Muslim rebels signed a pact on 4 January under which the Muslims agreed to give up their demands for a separate state, beginning a process to end the fourteen-year insurgency in which more than 60,000 people had been killed. The agreement was reached in talks in Jidda, Saudi Arabia, between the Moro National Liberation Front (MNLF), led by Nur Misuari, and a government team headed by Agapito Aquino. The talks were held under the auspices of the Organization of the Islamic Conference. Misuari agreed to drop the MNLF's demand for a separate state and accept autonomy, although he disagreed with the form of autonomy proposed in the draft constitution. The MNLF signed two agreements, one of which would allow residents of five islands in the southern Philippines to vote on the issue of autonomy from the government in Manila. Christians and Muslims alike would vote on autonomy for the islands of Mindanao, Palawan, Basilan, Tawitawi, and Sulu. Programs for economic and social development for the region were proposed in the agreement (*NYT*, 7 January).

The Moro Islamic Liberation Front, a separate Muslim rebel group led by Hashim Salamat, carried out a number of attacks on Mindanao to protest its exclusion from the peace talks. Some fourteen attacks were reported from 13–14 January, in which one person was killed and as many as seventeen wounded. Targets included the provincial capitol in Maganoy, the capital of Maguindanao province, and businesses, private homes, bridges, and power pylons. Two battalions of army troops were airlifted to Mindanao 14 January to crush the rebels (ibid., 15 January).

Deposed president Ferdinand Marcos was foiled in a plan to return from exile in the United States to the Philippines, where dissident soldiers had attempted a coup on 27 January. The soldiers had seized a suburban Manila broadcasting complex but failed in their attempts to take over military installations and the main power company. They did not end their rebellion until learning that the scheme by Marcos had failed. Colonel Oscar Canlas claimed that the soldiers merely wanted a tougher government line against communism and communist guerrillas. General Ramos, chief of staff of the armed forces, ordered the arrest of four high-ranking officers linked to the attempted coup. Thirteen officers and 359 soldiers of lower ranks were detained, pending investigation of charges linked to the uprising. But other observers said the chief of staff had to contend with the widespread feeling among officers and the ranks that the rebels were "merely principled anticommunists." Some of the officers implicated in the coup attempt (such as Brigadier General Jose Maria Zumel and Colonel Rolando Abadilla) were highly placed in the Marcos government and had also been involved in the so-called Manila Hotel incident, a military uprising organized by Marcos backers in July 1986 (ibid., 28 January, 1 February).

The worst incident of political violence during the cease-fire period was a clash in which government troops killed eighteen left-wing protesters on 22 January. Security forces fired into a crowd of left-wing demonstrators marching on the presidential palace in Manila. It was the first such attack on civilians in the eleven months Corazon Aquino had been president, and outrage over the dead and wounded dealt what observers agreed was the harshest blow so far to her policy of national reconciliation. The gunfire killed 18 people and left 96 wounded. The crowd numbered 10,000 and included a large number of peasant farmers marching for land reform. There was no attempt to parley as the demonstrators approached, and the bridge's customary barbed-wire barrier was not there to hold them back. Their front ranks surged against the Philippine Constabulary, some 300 of whom had been stationed at the bridge with riot shields bearing the words "maximum tolerance"—Aquino's announced policy toward public demonstrations. Some protesters carried makeshift clubs and lead pipes, and rocks and bottles began to sail from the crowd as the police gave ground. The answering shots were said to have come mainly from marines ranked behind the police. Reports differed on whether the soldiers first opened fire into the air or with their weapons already trained on the protesters. But some of the bodies showed bullet wounds in the head, indicating they had been shot with intent to kill, and at least one victim had been shot in the back. Most of the bodies lay only yards from the police line. A pastoral letter read 25 January by Jaime Cardinal Sin, Roman Catholic archbishop of Manila, blamed government inaction on land reform for the deaths. In addition, five of the seven members of the government human rights commission resigned that day (*NYT*, 23 January; *WP*, 26 January).

The cease-fire between the government and communist rebels ended 8 February after the communists ruled out an extension of the 60-day truce. But discussion had never moved past wrangling over an agenda. Among the issues dividing the two sides were rebel demands for the government to "reform and reorient" the military, for political recognition of the NDF, and for "meaningful" land reform. The NDF negotiators had suspended the bargaining 22 January before formally ending the talks 30 January. The negotiators at first cited death threats made against them, but on terminating the talks they pointed to the earlier slaying by government troops of eighteen left-wing protesters. Both the government and the rebels accused each other of bad faith, a charge the NDF repeated 7 February in a statement reiterating claims that the government had engineered the truce simply to weaken the rebel ranks with offers of amnesty. The government had not yet launched a planned full-scale rehabilitation program, but by one count some 1,000 rebels had surrendered during the truce to accept government forgiveness and aid. The government planned to seek individual talks with regional groups belonging to the insurgents (*NYT*, 8 February).

For their part, conservative critics of the government said rebel leaders had seized upon the truce merely to regroup forces and spread the communist message. A thorn in conservatives' sides was the free-conduct passes issued 50 rebel officers, permits that gave communist leaders the unprecedented chance to make their case freely on television and in the press. The military and the Aquino government had been driven further apart as impatience with the cease-fire grew among officers and the ranks. (*CSM*, 5 February.)

Violations of the truce were charged by both the rebels and the military. One of the most serious to be alleged was a purported attack by rebels in Kalinga Apayo province on 6 February. Five soldiers were said to have been killed. The day after the cease-fire ended, the military launched several so-called hot pursuit operations against the rebels. Soldiers and communists clashed near Lupao on Luzon Island on 10 February. The military issued an initial fatality toll of one soldier, two civilians, and eleven rebels. Subsequently, General Ramos ordered an investigation into the apparent slaying of seventeen civilians by soldiers. Some local newspapers had called the 10 February incident a "massacre." The target of the dawn attack was a small community on the outskirts of Lupao, a town some 90 miles north of Manila. The poverty-stricken cluster of homes lay at the foot of the Sierra Madre hills, haven to many of the guerrillas. The military considered the village to be friendly to the communists. After a brief gun battle with rebels, who managed to slip away, the soldiers had systematically shot villagers and burned down some of their homes, surviving civilians said. One soldier died. The local press and Lupao's acting mayor insisted that almost all the fatalities had been civilian. The Lupao official said the dead included an elderly couple and six small children. (*NYT*, 14, 17 February.)

After the Cease-fire. In the weeks after the end of talks, Aquino pressed her campaign for individual cease-fires with regional groups within the communist movement. She had also offered amnesty to the insurgents, announcing 28 February that "full and complete" forgiveness would be extended to all rebels who surrendered within the next six months. In sketching the program's outlines, Aquino said she would set up "national reconciliation and development" centers that would give former insurgents "the means and training to resume productive roles in society." Officials added that rebels would be paid for the arms they surrendered and that those who feared reprisal would be relocated. But analysts said the government seemed to have arrived at a strategy of stepping up military force while offering economic incentives for surrender (*NYT*, 1 March).

General Ramos said that the Aquino government badly needed a comprehensive anti-insurgency program. Not usually known as a critic of Aquino, Ramos had often acted as a broker between her government and elements in the military impatient for a harder line against the communists. Ramos also made public his order for the dismantling of "so-called fraternal organizations" within the armed forces. The order, which set a 16 March deadline, said the "proliferation" of the groups had caused "divisions." Chief among the organizations were the Guardian Brotherhood and the Reform the Armed Forces Movement (RAM). Members of each of the groups had taken a hand in coup attempts against Aquino. The Guardian Brotherhood mainly drew on enlisted men, whereas RAM was composed of reform-minded young officers. Linked to former defense minister Juan Ponce Enrile, RAM had figured in the 1986 overthrow of Marcos and in negotiations to gain leniency for soldiers involved in the January 1987 coup attempt. RAM had been founded to fight the cronyism fostered in the military under Marcos. (*LAT*, 19, 23 February.)

Sharp differences between the Aquino government and the military over counterinsurgency policy were evident in both electoral politics and "the parliament of the streets and barracks." President Aquino's fledgling government received a vote of confidence 2 February when Filipino voters overwhelmingly approved a draft constitution for the new political system. Early returns indicated a majority upwards of 87 percent. Turnout among the 25 million registered voters was heavy, and pro-constitution majorities were recorded in almost every region of the country, with the significant exception of voting areas around military bases. Of those among the 250,000-member armed forces who cast votes, only about 60 percent backed the constitution. The air force was the only service to have registered a majority of "no" votes, but anti-constitution majorities had been recorded at such key facilities as Villamor Air Base and Camp Aguinaldo itself. Balloting passed peacefully, with little of the fraud or intimidation that Filipino voters had become used to before Aquino's eleven-month presidency. Communist rebels interfered in a few areas, but most appeared to sit out the occasion. Those against the charter included Bayan and the KMU on the left, as well as Marcos supporters and former defense minister Enrile. (*NYT*, 3 February; *LAT*, 4 February; *CSM*, 5 February.)

Aquino survived an apparently premature assassination attempt by disgruntled military elements on 18 March. Four days later Aquino told graduating military cadets that military victory and not compromise would end the country's communist insurgency and the rebellions by other extremist forces. Speaking at the Philippine Military Academy in Baguio, the president asserted that the "answer to the terrorism of the left and the right is not social and economic reform but police and military action." Aquino said she had sought to settle matters peacefully: "God knows I have tried. But my offers of peace and reconciliation have been met with the most bloody and insolent rejections by the left and the right." The 18 March blast, which occurred during graduation rehearsal ceremonies, had killed four people and wounded as many as 47 others. The military said it was detaining an unidentified army captain, three enlisted men, and six civilians as suspects. (*LAT*, 23 March; *WP*, 23 March.)

The week of the blast was reported to be one of the bloodiest since the end of the communist peace talks and the cease-fire that had accompanied them. Clashes between the rebels and soldiers were said to have claimed 108 lives that week. The Defense Ministry estimated that at least 350 people had died in insurgency-related violence since the end of the cease-fire. Early in March officials said the rate of deaths was lower than at the same time in 1986 but that a higher proportion of the casualties were soldiers (*LAT*, 18 March). Military-civilian relations were tested again on 18 April when military rebels made an attempt to free soldiers imprisoned for the failed January coup. Loyal government troops put down the revolt at Camp Bonifacio in Manila. (*NYT*, 18 April.)

Political Violence. On 16 March Aquino ordered the dissolution of "all private armies and other armed groups," but the next day the government issued a "clarification" saying "no immediate steps" were required to carry out the order. The country's new constitution bans private armed forces. Human rights advocates accused such groups of preying upon innocent civilians. But many in the military welcomed the bands as allies in the fight against the stubborn communist insurgency. Aquino's personal military adviser, retired brigadier general Jose Magno, had made known his admiration for the Civilian Home Defense Force, a 40,000-member militia that was the only group specifically named in the president's 16 March order. On 29 March Aquino told a campaign crowd in Davao City that unarmed vigilante groups were a legitimate example of the "people power" that had helped propel her into office. Aquino said that civilians would be encouraged to organize into patrols that would deny the rebels freedom of movement but would carry only such traditional weapons as machetes. (*LAT*, 17 March; *NYT*, 23 March; *CSM*, 1 April.)

By one count there were 260 private armed bands in the Philippines (*NYT*, 4 April, 27 December). These ranged from the private armies of warlords to the jungle religious sect commonly known as Tadtad (*Chopchop* in Tagalog). The first and most celebrated of these was Alsa Masa (Arise, masses), a band that dominated Agdao, a slum district in Mindanao Island's Davao City. The group contained more than half of the estimated 13,000 anticommunist vigilantes in the country, according to a confidential government survey reported in the press. The NPA had left Agdao and Davao as a whole in late 1986, a few months after the formation of Alsa Masa. (*CSM*, 23 March; *LAT*, 3 April.)

A bullet fired by unknown assailants grazed Bernabe Buscayno the night of 8 June. The former head of the NPA communist fighting force had been driving from a Manila television station when, witnesses said, he was fired on by gunmen wearing fatigues. Buscayno, 42, had left the communists in 1986 and led a leftist slate in the May 1987 legislative elections. (*NYT*, 9 June.)

Unidentified gunmen killed local government secretary Jaime Ferrer outside his home in the Manila suburb of Paranque on 2 August. He was said to be the first cabinet official in Philippine history to be assassinated. The swift attack and escape by the handful of men resembled the killings recently mounted in Manila by the three-man "sparrow" units of the communist NPA. The group had publicly marked Ferrer for assassination, but neither it nor any other group took responsibility for the slaying. Once in the post, Ferrer had campaigned vigorously for creation of unarmed vigilante units to fight the communists. He had also ordered local officials to campaign for the government's candidates in the May congressional elections. His insistence on a good showing for the government slate was said by some to have fostered widespread voter fraud. (*NYT*, 3 August.)

Despite last-minute government concessions, labor groups went ahead on 26 August with strikes and demonstrations that had been planned to protest recent price increases. The protests, which had been called as a general strike, were led by the leftist labor organization known as the KMU. The KMU groups had also been in the forefront of demonstrations from 21–24 August, including a protest on the fourth anniversary of the assassination of Benigno Aquino. The KMU had hoped to bring two million people into the streets of Manila 26 August, and though press reports put the actual number of demonstrators in the "thousands," strikes by transport workers disrupted—but did not cripple—business in Manila. Telephone operators, teachers, students, and some factory workers also joined the strike. A crowd of 5,000–6,000 marched on the presidential palace in Manila chanting, "Cory Aquino, puppet of the Americans." Protests were also held in Cebu City, the Philippines' second-largest city, and in other provincial towns. The protests over oil prices were the latest manifestation of growing discontent with a perceived lack of progress by the Aquino government after eighteen months in power. The left-wing *Malaya* referred to "the people's growing disenchantment with the regime" and said that "questions unasked before will have to be answered." The centrist *Daily Inquirer*, a strong supporter of Aquino, warned of "signs of a new cronyism" like that which plagued the regime of deposed president Marcos. (*CSM*, 26 August.)

The most serious attack against the Aquino government was launched by mutinous Philippine soldiers and began in Manila in the early hours of 28 August. Fifty-three people—twelve government troops, nineteen rebels, and twenty-two civilians—died in the fighting, according to government figures. Hundreds of others were wounded, including the president's son. The United States reportedly told mutiny leaders that all U.S. military aid would be cut off if the coup succeeded (for a chronology of civilian-military relations, see *NYT*, 30 August).

Political instability surged again in late September when Aquino reshuffled her cabinet and removed her closest adviser, Executive Secretary Joker Arroyo. The military had been pressing for the removal of Arroyo and of another adviser considered to be a leftist, special legal counsel Teodoro Locsin. Arroyo, considered by many Filipinos to be second in power only to the president, had been increasingly condemned as a leftist by military and business leaders in the wake of the attempted coup. The military had accused Arroyo of interfering with its efforts to put down the revolt and of being too lenient toward the communist insurgents (*NYT*, 10 September). Vice President Salvador H. Laurel left his cabinet post as foreign minister on 16 September, citing "basic, fundamental differences" with Aquino's policy toward the communist rebels. Laurel announced he would open an anticommunist publicity campaign nationwide (ibid., 17 September).

A top leftist leader was shot to death 19 September in Quezon City, near Manila. Leandro Alejandro, general secretary of the left-wing Bayan coalition, was shot repeatedly in the head by gunmen firing from a passing vehicle. Alejandro was the second Bayan leader slain in the past year. (*LAT*, 20 September.)

On 20 October Aquino warned that the government would use force if necessary to break a series of nationwide strikes that was disrupting the Philippine economy. "I will not allow an unruly minority to use the rights of labor . . . to achieve a communist victory," she declared. The KMU began the nationwide strikes 12 October to protest low wages. A spokesman for the movement said the strikes affected 250,000 employees in 3,871 factories and businesses. The labor unions were pressing for a ten-peso increase in the daily minimum wage. Some business and military officials believed that the wage issue was a secondary concern of the KMU; they maintained that the movement had close ties to the CPP and that its ultimate goal was to destabilize Aquino's presidency (*LAT*, 21 October).

Relations with the United States. The U.S.-Philippine military-bases agreement comes up for review in 1988 and for possible renegotiation in 1991. In anticipation of this and of the continued polarization of Philippine politics, U.S. officials have begun to make detailed contingency plans in order to relocate Navy and Air Force units from the Philippines to Guam, Okinawa, and other Pacific locations. The United States has also leased 18,000 acres on the Mariana Islands of Tinian and Saipan for possible replacement of Philippine facilities. The Pentagon also began considering hiring shipyards in Singapore and South Korea to replace Philippine facilities.

During her September 1986 state visit to the United States, Aquino had said she would keep all her options open for the bases until the renegotiations. However, one major change occurred when the new constitution was approved in February 1987. It would allow for legislative and popular referenda on the continued presence of U.S. bases in the Philippines in addition to the previous method of renegotiating through executive agreement.

Richard L. Armitage, the U.S. assistant secretary of defense for international security affairs, said 17 March that the Aquino government placed too much trust in "symbolic political acts" to stop the rebels and that it had "regrettably failed" to develop a comprehensive counterinsurgency program. Accordingly, Armitage said, the communist rebels had swelled their fighting ranks by 9 percent under the Aquino regime. Their armed membership now totaled 24,430, he said, and the number of villages that felt their influence had increased by 21 percent, to some 8,200 communities. Armitage made his criticisms in testimony before the U.S. House Foreign Affairs Subcommittee on Asian and Pacific affairs. The hearings dealt with the $260 million in aid sought by the Reagan administration for the Philippines. (*WP*, 18 March.)

An apparent aid mix-up added to the disgruntlement. In September 1986 President Reagan had promised $10 million in emergency medical aid, a promise that his aides described as a symbol of his commitment to the Aquino government. But Philippine records said that only $2.75 million of the aid had arrived as of 24 February. Some of the aid that did arrive included heavy ski parkas and boxes of aspirin labeled as tuberculosis medicine. (*LAT*, 25

February.) State Department officials had painted a more optimistic picture of the situation earlier in the hearings. The departing U.S. ambassador to the Philippines, Stephen W. Bosworth, said he had "a good deal of confidence" in Aquino's ability to handle the rebels (*NYT*, 22 March).

Philippine-U.S. relations were complicated by a 23 March *Newsweek* report that the CIA was poised to mount a multimillion-dollar covert activities operation against the Philippine communist insurgents. The news account said the alleged project would involve "undercover political activities" and intelligence-gathering, including overflights "if necessary." The alleged operation, the existence of which President Aquino denied, was said by *Newsweek* to have been authorized by President Reagan in the first covert activities finding that he had signed since the Iran arms deals had become public.

J. Antonio Carpio, director of the Philippines National Bureau of Investigation, said that "our country would be converted into another Vietnam" if the United States took direct action against the insurgents (*NYT*, 12 April). Shortly thereafter, a U.S. Defense Department official criticized Aquino by saying she was far too reluctant to use counterinsurgency tactics against the communists. The official, George Talbot, said that both the Aquino government and the U.S. State Department mistakenly favored building up Philippine conventional forces and were hostile to the idea of the United States training Philippine forces in counterinsurgency. He added that the United States was "not now involved in any meaningful way in countering insurgency in the Philippines" and that it had no plans to become so involved. (*WP*, 28 April.) Reports of CIA support for vigilante groups persisted, however (*NYT*, 26 May). In addition, the United States delivered ten helicopter gunships to Manila for anti-rebel use on the eve of U.S. secretary of state George P. Shultz's visit to the Philippines (*NYT*, 12 June).

Shultz conferred with officials in the Philippines during his 13–17 June visit that was one of several stops on a regional tour. The Philippines visit was Shultz's third since Corazon Aquino had come to power there in 1986. He met with Aquino in Manila and officially signed over $176 million in aid. The sum was an installment of the $413 million that the United States had earmarked for the Philippines for 1987. The armed forces' share of the aid was $50 million, only half as much as the Reagan administration had asked the U.S. Congress to provide for the military. Shultz offered warm praise for Aquino during a 13 June talk with reporters. Her government had done "quite a job" with the economy, Shultz said, and the "professionalization" of the military was "proceeding well." He said the country's communist insurgency "must be tackled in more military terms," but he defended Aquino's earlier attempts to negotiate with the rebels. He said the talks, broken off in January, had bought time for the army to improve and had helped solidify Philippine opinion behind the antiguerrilla struggle. Shultz also endorsed the use of private citizens to fight the rebels. He said on 16 June that the citizen bands were apparently "organized within the framework of governmental authority" and were not "free-floating vigilante groups" (*NYT*, 17 June).

The first known terrorist attacks against U.S. servicemen in the Philippines in more than ten years took place on 28 October when three servicemen, one of whom was retired, were shot to death in a series of attacks near Clark Air Base. The attacks appeared to have been coordinated. A Philippine businessman was also killed in one of the attacks, and a fourth U.S. airman was fired upon but escaped injury. The attacks were carried out within fifteen minutes of each other in different areas of Angeles City. All the attacks occurred within two miles of the air base. Gunmen suspected of being communists had shot and killed two Philippine soldiers, two policemen, and one local politician in separate attacks 27–28 October in Manila (*CSM*, 29 October). Responsibility for the attacks near Clark Air Base was later claimed by Saturnino Ocampo, an NDF spokesman and former cease-fire negotiator. He said the servicemen were killed "as a matter of policy," according to an NDF decision in June to attack U.S. military personnel because of the increase in U.S. support for the Philippine army's campaign against the rebels. "All U.S. military and civilian officials and personnel involved in the implementation of the total war program are to be targets for attack," Ocampo said (*NYT*, 13 November; *CSM*, 24 November).

Apprehensions of violence threatened to postpone or relocate the mid-December meeting of the heads of state of the Association of Southeast Asian Nations (ASEAN) (*FEER*, 3 December). With extraordinary security precautions, the meeting took place without incident, "a symbolic triumph over security threats to the Aquino government" (ibid., 24 December).

Both the rebels and the government called for a holiday truce on Christmas and New Year's Day. The truce was soon violated by several rebel attacks, according to military reports. Some of the killings were also related to campaign violence against mayors and pro-administration candidates for the 18 January 1988 local government elections (*NYT*, 27 December 1987; 3 January 1988).

David Rosenberg
Middlebury College

South Pacific Islands

Populations. Federated States of Micronesia (FSM): 73,200; Fiji: 727,902; Kiribati: 66,441; Marshall Islands: 36,000; Nauru: 8,748; New Caledonia: 145,000; Palau: c. 12,000; Papua/New Guinea (PNG): 3,563,743; Solomon Islands: 301,180; Tonga: 98,689; Tuvalu: 8,329; Vanuatu: 149,652; Western Samoa: 175,084

Papua/New Guinea. Most political parties in PNG are regionally or personality based. PNG has no formal communist party, Moscow-aligned or otherwise, but as with the other island states, it has seen a continuing and now increasing level of activity by the Soviet fronts. PNG's unions, which are generally one of the best-organized social forces in these developing island states, have for years been invited to World Federation of Trade Unions (WFTU) congresses and regional meetings, with varying degrees of success for the USSR. The pro-Soviet, Sydney-based Committee for International Trade Union Unity (CITUU) and the WFTU's regional arm, the India-based Asia Oceania Trade Union Organising Committee (AOTUOC), have been particularly active in PNG.

Pro-Soviet unionists from the New Zealand Federation of Labor and the Australian Movement seem to have more success in influencing PNG unions at meetings of the Pacific Trade Union Community to adopt unilateralist and nuclear-ship banning policies. However, Melanesian antinuclear sentiment is primarily motivated by opposition to French nuclear testing in the South Pacific. It is difficult to credit Soviet-front activity with much success in this area, since former prime minister Michael Somare supported the pro-ANZUS stance of Australian prime minister Robert Hawke. Hawke maintained that the visits of allied U.S. warships would not be constrained by the regional treaty known as SPNFZT (South Pacific Nuclear Free Zone Treaty).

Because nearly all parliamentarians and members of the bureaucratic elite are recruited directly out of the major university, the University of Papua New Guinea, in the capital Port Moresby, the Soviets have been diligent in cultivating student leaders. The PNG Student Representative Council is affiliated with the Prague-based International Union of Students (IUS). Gabriel Ramoi, a former student leader who is now a member of Parliament, had caused some dissension by offering tickets to the 1985 Moscow meeting of the World Festival of Youth and Students (WFYS); he subsequently became communications minister in Prime Minister Paias Wingti's first government. PNG youth and student leaders have received increased attention from Moscow, such as an invitation to the Eighth International Seminar on the Problems of Peace in the Pacific in June 1986 as well as to bureau meetings of the WFDY and IUS in Prague and Budapest, respectively, in November 1986. According to *Youth Voice* (January 1987), the newspaper of the youth section of Australia's tiny pro-Soviet communist party SPA, a student leader "representing" PNG also attended a regional conference of the WFDY in Hanoi. On 6–8 February 1987 PNG student and youth leaders traveled to Moscow for the first preparatory meeting of the thirteenth WFYS, to be held in North Korea (Socialist Party of Australia, *The Guardian*). PNG trade union and women's organizations are also cultivated at Soviet-orchestrated conferences in Australia, such as the Sydney meeting addressed by World Peace Council (WPC) leader Romesh Chandra entitled "International Peace Conference on the Pacific and Asian Regions."

It is difficult to judge whether Moscow's cultivation of youth leaders has had long-term effects. Both the current Wingti government and the previous Somare administration were publicly pro-Western. Perhaps the worst that can be said is that a view of moral equivalence between the United States and the Soviet Union appears to be developing in elements in the PNG polity. This is evidenced by recent claims by Prime Minister Wingti that his country is considering broadening ties with Moscow; in addition, Foreign Minister Aruru Maitabe stated that it was not in his country's interests to be party to superpower rivalries and therefore PNG would consider joining the Nonaligned Movement (*FBIS*, 24 August, 4 September).

Fiji. Independent since 1970, Fiji experienced two military coups and a partial return to civilian rule in 1987. Ostensibly these bloodless putsches were based on ethnic Fijian concern that immigrant Indians dominated the deposed Labour Party/National Federation coalition government. Coup leader Brigadier Rabuka also cited his concern that Fiji was moving away from its obligations to the Western alliance. He was referring to the intended policy of the deposed Labour Party that would have banned nuclear-armed or -powered ships from entering Fijian waters. As in the case of New Zealand this would have effectively barred the U.S. Navy.

Although Moscow seemed to play no role in Fiji's political turbulence, that island state, too, has been targeted by a range of Soviet fronts. The University of the South Pacific (USP) Student Association, which trains island leaders not only from Fiji but also from all the smaller independent island states, is affiliated with the International Union of Students (IUS). Through this IUS connection, students at the USP receive scholarships in the Eastern bloc; for example, following an IUS meeting with USP student leader Poloma Komiti, two students were given scholarships to Moscow and Warsaw (*Fiji Sun*, 18 August 1986). Fijian—particularly Indian Fijian—student leaders have, since independence, attended the Soviet-orchestrated WFYS, including the four preparatory meetings. Previous bans on Soviet officials entering Fiji were circumvented by sending in Australians or New Zealand members of the pro-Soviet communist parties.

Pro-Moscow unions have long been present in Fiji, leading to a split in the Fiji trade union movement as early as 1972. Apisai Tora led five unions into a labor federation that was affiliated with the WFTU. This rival to the Fiji Trade Union Congress has since collapsed, but this did not prevent Krishna Datt (president of the Fiji Teachers' Union) or Mahendra Sukhedo (secretary of the National Union of Municipal Workers) from attending as observers the Eleventh World Congress of the WFTU in East Berlin in 1986. Datt is a Fijian vice president of the World Peace Council and since 1985 has been secretary of the Fiji Labour Party. He was foreign minister briefly until deposed by the military coups in May 1987.

Apisai Tora, the former labor radical and leader in the ethnically Fijian Taukei nationalist movement, was installed as minister for Fijian affairs in the Rabuka government. He is said to be one of the forces behind the military government's opening of links with the Soviet Union and China (*CSM*, 27 October). The U.S. State Department has accused regional media of a Soviet-style disinformation campaign alleging that U.S. intelligence services, led by U.S. ambassador to the United Nations Vernon Walters, were involved in the Fiji coups. Moscow's involvement in spreading this story has been extensively documented. (*Australian Bulletin*, 18 August; *IPA Review*, November.)

The Solomon Islands. Independent since 1978, the Solomon Islands have several political parties and 38 elected members of Parliament. The islands have witnessed peaceful and democratic changes of government and provide an example of the smooth transition to democracy that is possible in these new states.

Nevertheless, the largest union—the Solomon Islands National Union of Workers—is affiliated with the WFTU and takes a leading role in anti-U.S. posturing in the Pacific Trade Union Community. The union's leader, Joses Tuhanuku, and its vice president, Peter Bennet, attended the 1986 East Berlin WFTU congress. In an article attacking the U.S. labor movement for allegedly "using external money to try and dominate the islands of our area and trade unions," an Australian cited the Solomons unions as an example of the sort of organization that ought to be defended by the left (*WMR*, June).

New Caledonia. An overseas territory of France, New Caledonia has a 46-member, directly elected territorial assembly, has four regional congresses, and is represented in Paris by a senator and two deputies. A referendum in 1987, whereby just under 60 percent of the population voted to remain with France, will probably not see an end to troubles between the majority and the indigenous Melanesians (Kanaks) who wish to see the territory independent (*ND*, 5–6 September). This conflict gives considerable scope for radicalization, although the two quasi-Marxist parties—Palika and Opoa—have made few popular inroads. The Kanak nationalist movement, the FLNKS, does have a radical wing, the FULK, which has attempted to increase links with Libya and to a lesser extent with the Soviet Union. Both moderate and radical Kanak supporters in the New Caledonian trade unions attended the 1986 WFTU congress and both are regularly invited to WPC and IUS regional gatherings. The FULK faction has gone a step further, to the chagrin of France and the larger Melanesian faction headed by FLNKS leader Jean Marie Tjiabou. Since 1984, the FULK has been attending World Congresses to Condemn Zionism, Racism, and Imperialism, originally held in conjunction with the WPC. Delegates from New Caledonia attended the World Conference on Zionism/Fascism held in Tripoli in March 1985. Uregei, the radical "foreign minister" of the FLNKS, has been to Libya several times. The official Kanak representative in Australia, Jean Peu, a member of the FULK faction, defied Canberra by attending the Tripoli terrorist summit in early 1986. This precipitated a split in the FLNKS after the Australian government barred Peu's re-entry into Australia. The dominant group of the New Caledonian nationalists forbade further Libyan ties. These Libyan conferences have become annual events and are reportedly orchestrated by East German security personnel (*Pacific Defense Reporter*, September 1986; *Social Action*, July).

Of more concern is the number, now totaling 36 FULK cadres, who have received paramilitary training in Libya. FULK leader Yann Celene Uregei said "the FULK had been assigned as the permanent representative in Tripoli of the Asian and Pacific progressive parties that attended a conference of revolutionary movements" in Libya in April 1987 (*FBIS-EAS*, 9 September). Uregei was dropped as FLNKS foreign spokesman in September, but it is widely believed that he will soon be reinstated.

Vanuatu. On 30 November the South Pacific's most radical government was narrowly re-elected in the third free election since independence in 1980. Father Walter Lini's government has entered into a fishing agreement that will allow port access to Soviet fishing vessels, and it will look at Aeroflot landing rights in 1988. Unlike other South Pacific countries, Vanuatu maintains diplomatic relations with Cuba, Nicaragua, and the Soviet Union and is a member of the Nonaligned Movement. Vanuatu is also a key focus for an alliance of regional anti-Western leftists called the Nuclear-Free and Independent Pacific (NFIP).

Where Vanuatu really earned its radical stripes, however, was in the Lini government's dalliance with Libya. Not only did Lini send a message of support to Colonel Moammar Khadafy following the April 1986 U.S. air strike on Tripoli terrorist bases, but he also sent some members of his governing party to Libya for paramilitary training. Indeed, it was not until Australia—the dominant power in the region—closed down the Libyan People's Bureau in Canberra that the Lini government reconsidered its position. The Australian move focused South Pacific attention on Libyan designs in the region; only then did the Lini government drop plans to open an official Libyan outpost and send an additional 50 party cadres to Colonel Khadafy for training. Furthermore, Lini turned away two Libyans when they appeared on his island uninvited at the same time as a visit by the U.S. ambassador to the United Nations, Vernon Walters. Lini, although crippled with a stroke, beat off—at least temporarily—a challenge by the secretary general of the ruling Vanuaku Pati, Barak Sope. The radicalism of Sope, who, to the concern of many, still walks around Port Vila with Libyan-trained bodyguards, is not unique in the party.

Lini's sister Hilda flew to New Zealand in July to participate in a South Pacific Conference for Peace and Justice in Central America. This important meeting brought together radicals to support the Nicaraguan Sandinistas and the Marxist-Leninist guerrillas in El Salvador.

In the future, the opposition Labour Party may be a moderate swing factor in garnering moderate Anglophones, if Sope, "the Libyan candidate," succeeds Lini as leader of the Vanuaku Pati. Despite the fact that Ephraim Kalsakau attended the WFTU East Berlin Congress, the Vanuatu Labour Party and trade union movement are strongly opposed to alliances with Moscow and Libya.

Relations with France remained icy. Paris cut millions of dollars of foreign aid and withdrew 30 technicians from Vanuatu following the expulsion of its ambassador and three other diplomats (*FBIS*, 3, 10 November).

Kiribati. Formerly the Gilbert and Ellice Islands, Kiribati is a functioning democracy with a 36-member House of Assembly. It achieved brief international notoriety in 1985 for signing a fishing agreement with the Soviet Union, but Prime Minister Tabai refused the Soviets landing rights and did not renew the agreement when they failed to agree to the previous high price per ton of tuna caught. Although Barry Tebau, assistant general secretary of the Kiribati Trade Union Congress (KTUC), attended the 1986 WFTU congress, his federation is a member of the International Confederation of Free Trade Unions (ICFTU), and the KTUC is strongly opposed to the docking of Soviet vessels in their country. Kiribati youth and student leaders attended the 1985 WFYS in Moscow and are now being more intensively cultivated by being asked to bureau meetings of the IUS and World Federation of Democratic Youth (WFDY) (*Youth Voice*, January).

Western Samoa, Nauru, Tuvalu, Palau, and Tonga. Youth and student representatives from all of these countries have attended meetings of Soviet youth and women's fronts, but there is minimal Marxist activity. The general secretary of the politically moderate West Samoan Public Service Association attended the 1986 WFTU congress, and the Soviets have claimed to be interested in rehabilitating the 80 percent of Nauru devastated by phosphate mining. None of these activities seem to have much impact, although there appears to be a Soviet focus on Palau both in disinformation and in Soviet-front activity. On 13 March *Pravda* attacked U.S. attitudes toward this tiny island and the plebiscite that narrowly failed to attain the 75 percent vote necessary to enter a Compact of Free Association with the United States. Speculation about the future of U.S. bases in the Philippines and the relocation of such facilities on Palau probably explain this verbal attack.

During his March visit to Canberra, Soviet foreign minister Eduard Shevardnadze stunned Australian ministers by adding Tuvalu, PNG, and Tonga to the list of island nations that have shown interest in agreements. The conservative Tongan minister for defense and foreign affairs, Crown Prince Tupouto'a, was in Moscow in February, reportedly discussing another fishing deal, although the crown prince had previously assured Australia that his country had no fish to sell to the Soviets.

Michael Danby
Melbourne, Australia

Sri Lanka

Population. 16,406,576
Parties. Communist Party of Sri Lanka (CPSL, pro-Moscow); Lanka Sama Samaja Party (LSSP, Trotskyist); People's Liberation Front (Janatha Vimukthi Peramuna; JVP, Maoist)
Founded. CPSL: 1943; LSSP: 1935; JVP: 1968
Membership. CPSL: 5,000 (estimated); LSSP: 2,500 (estimated); JVP: unknown
General Secretary. CPSL: Kattorge P. Silva; LSSP: Bernard Soysa; JVP: Rohana Wijeweera
Politburo. CPSL: 11 members, including Kattorge P. Silva, Pieter Keuneman (president)
Status. CPSL, LSSP: legal; JVP: illegal
Last Congress. CPSL: Thirteenth, 22–26 March
Last Election. 1977, parliamentary: CPSL, 2.0 percent, no seats (1 member elected in by-election); LSSP, 3.6 percent, no seats; JVP, did not contest. 1982, presidential: CPSL, did not contest; LSSP, 0.9 percent; JVP, 4.2 percent
Auxiliary Organizations. CPSL: Federation of Trade Unions (24 affiliated unions), Public Service Workers' Trade Union Federation (100 affiliated unions), Communist Youth Federation, Kantha (women's) Peramuna; LSSP: Ceylon Federation of Labour (16 affiliated unions), Samasamaja Kantha Peramuna, Youth League
Publications. CPSL: *Aththa* (newspaper; B. A. Siriwardene, editor; circulation 28,000)

The ethnic conflict between the Sinhalese and Tamils again dominated Sri Lankan society in 1987. However, the year was marked by a series of events that appeared to change the nature of the conflict and the role of Sri Lanka in it. The most important was the signing of a peace agreement between President Junius Richard Jayawardene of Sri Lanka and Prime Minister Rajiv Gandhi of India on 29 July. The signing of the peace accords set in motion a backlash among extremist elements in the majority Sinhalese community that resulted in a new threat to the Sri Lankan government. Throughout these events the CPSL and its allies—the LSSP, Mahajana Eksath Peramuna, and Sri Lanka Mahajana Party—called for a negotiated resolution of the conflict. The CPSL claimed that the conditions of the peace accords were largely based on their position in the conflict. The party's Thirteenth Congress in March was dominated by its desire to resolve the ethnic violence before meaningful change could occur in the society. The congress did not make any major changes in the CPSL leadership, though it did elect a new central committee.

The ethnic conflict appeared to alter the role of the Communist Party in Sri Lankan politics. The peace accord called for an end of fighting by the "tiger" guerrillas and the establishment of a provincial council uniting the Eastern and Northern provinces. The Indian government was required to enforce the accord and to station troops in the Tamil areas in the north and east of the island. These troops were to ensure that the Tamil tigers surrendered their arms and that the Sri Lankan government did not attack the Tamils. The united provincial council, which had been a stumbling block to the signing of the accords, called for a referendum to be held in the Eastern province to determine if the two provinces would continue with a united council or establish two separate councils. This referendum was to be held within one year of the signing of the accords.

The treaty, which was never signed by the Liberation Tigers of Tamil Eelam (LTTE) leadership, was undermined when the LTTE refused to give its weapons to the Indian peacekeeping troops. The LTTE had become the dominant tiger group after militarily defeating the other major tiger groups, including all of the Marxist tiger organizations, in 1986 and early 1987. Battles between the LTTE and the Eelam People's Revolutionary Liberation Front (EPRLF) continued into March and occurred again in September after the EPRLF had turned in their weapons. The only other remaining tiger organization with a military capacity was the Eelam Revolutionary Organization of Students (EROS). EROS has preferred bomb attacks, and in 1987 it established an alliance with the LTTE. In October the Indian peacekeeping troops attacked the LTTE, but their military actions were strongly criticized for causing many civilian casualties. By the end of the year they controlled most of the Jaffna Peninsula and the Eastern province but still had not defeated the LTTE.

The Sri Lankan government claimed that the Soviet Union was arming the LTTE. Some Western press sources briefly reported these charges (CBS Evening News, 1 June), but the government did not provide any evidence of Soviet support. The LTTE leadership continued to focus on ethnic issues, though this did not stop pro-Soviet Tamils within the LTTE from trying to forge closer ties with the Soviet Union. The Soviet Union denied them aid and instead increased its support for the Sri Lankan government. In August a Soviet team worked on the Mahaweli irrigation project, to which the Soviet government had pledged over $2 million.

Sinhalese rioting in Colombo and elsewhere followed the announcement of the July accords. After the riots had ended, the country was faced with a new insurgency. A Sinhalese extremist group, the JVP, began attacking government officials; by the end of the year it had been responsible for killing over 150 government officials and workers. Its attacks included an attempted assassination of President Jayawardene in Parliament on 18 August and the assassination of the leader of the ruling United National Party, Harsha Abeywardene, on 23 December.

The JVP had been responsible for a youth-led Maoist insurrection in 1971 that caused several thousand deaths and nearly toppled the government of Sirimavo Bandaranaike. The imprisoned leader of that insurrection, Rohana Wijeweera, was released from jail by Jayawardene in 1978. He ran for president in the 1982 presidential elections before going underground when his party was banned after the 1983 anti-Tamil riots. Since that time he has developed a network of supporters among high school- and university-aged youths, who now back his efforts to topple the government. However, his movement has become factionalized. At least one splinter group has established ties with one of the tiger organizations, the Popular Organization for the Liberation of Tamils. The main JVP group professes a Marxist ideology but is disowned by the Soviet Union. This group, led by Wijeweera, has taken an anti-Tamil, Sinhalese-chauvinist stance and incited young Sinhalese to oppose the signing of the peace accords. This egalitarian movement espouses extreme nationalism, and some critics say it professes Pol-Potism—that is, the policies of the former Cambodian leader, Pol Pot (*Island*, 14 June). The CPSL opposes the JVP, but its support among young people has eroded as more youth leave for the JVP. The JVP now threatens the government as well as the traditional leftist leadership of the CPSL and LSSP in Sri Lanka.

Robert C. Oberst
Nebraska Wesleyan University

Thailand

Population. 53,645,823
Party. Communist Party of Thailand (CPT)
Founded. 1942
Membership. 250; 500–1,000 armed strength (estimated)
General Secretary. Thong Jaensri (unconfirmed; possible pseud.)

Politburo. 7 members: Thong Jaensri (general secretary [?]), Waithoon Sinthuwanich, Sin Dermlin, Prachuab Ruangrat, Nop Prasertsom, Virat Angkathavorn, and Vinai Permpoonsap
Status. Illegal
Last Congress. Fourth, March and April 1984, clandestine
Last Election. N/a
Auxiliary Organizations. No data; all organizations reportedly dissolved
Publications. *Thong Thai* (Thai flag), *Prakai Fai* (The flame), both intermittent underground publications

In 1987 the military continued to dominate Thai politics. Prime Minister Prem Tinsulanond, a former army commander in chief, owed his position to the military. General Chawalit Yongchaiyut, the probable successor to Prem and current army commander-in-chief, became the most outspoken Thai leader on security, development, and state reforms. Because Thailand was not threatened from outside or from within, the Thai military needed to justify its large budgets and pivotal role in politics. "Development" served that end. The military's active participation in rural development programs ensured more control over local officials who had become increasingly dependent on the military for their resources.

The military suffered an embarrassment when some 70 Thai soldiers were killed at the Chong Bok pass near Thailand's border with Laos and Cambodia. These troops had attacked Vietnamese soldiers in areas inhabited by rebel forces from Cambodia.

Prem's government is based on a four-party coalition and has an elected majority in the House of Representatives. Prem became prime minister in 1980 and is Thailand's longest-ruling elected leader. The administration remained stable despite factionalism within the Democratic Party, a major backer of the coalition. Members of the military, monarchy, and bureaucracy continued to support the Prem administration.

Thailand's economy continued to have a steady growth rate. In 1987 the decline in world oil prices reduced the trade deficit, and economic growth in real terms reached 5 percent.

Little is known about the CPT: the party has gone underground, party publications are intermittent and uninformative, CPT membership fell from some 12,000 in 1976 to 250 (500–1,000 armed supporters) in 1987, no party congress has taken place since 1984, and the leadership of the CPT has been decimated.

The demise of the CPT stems from four main developments: the effective counterinsurgency strategy of "politics over military" and government planned economic development in Thailand's impoverished provinces; the ending of aid to the CPT from China and the Soviet Union; the schism within the party leadership between pro-Soviet and pro-China members; and the amnesty program that led to the defection of thousands of party members, including most of the students and intellectuals who joined the movement in 1976.

General Chawalit continued to be Thailand's major spokesman on communist issues. Despite the success of the counterinsurgency policy and the almost complete decimation of the CPT, Chawalit repeated his view that the CPT remains the nation's primary security threat.

A series of coordinated raids in Bangkok 21–22 April resulted in the arrest of eighteen CPT members, including four of the seven Politburo members: Waithoon Sinthuwanich (Comrade Karb), Sin Dermlin (Comrade Prawat), Prachuab Ruangrat (Comrade Sayam), and Nop Prasertsom. Other members arrested were Wibul Jenchaiwat (Comrade Thung), a Central Committee member in the Northeast, Chao Pongsunthornsathit (Comrade Poon), and Chidchanok Soponparn (Comrade Sueb), who is an aide of Waithoon. The three Politburo members still at liberty are: party general secretary (?) Thong Jaensri, who is believed to be based at the CPT's headquarters in the south; former party general secretary Virat Angkathavorn, who is ill in China; and Vinai Permpoonsap, who has not been seen since 1984. Thus these arrests effectively demolished the party's capacity to reverse the past five years of decline. The members were arrested when they allegedly met to plan a fifth party congress for October.

In addition to the four Politburo members, the police also reportedly arrested one Central Committee member, one member of a southern provincial party committee, and a CPT military commander (*Bangkok Post*, 25 April). All were held for interrogation.

General Chawalit denied that the arrests contradicted the prime ministerial order that granted amnesty to CPT members. He argued that those arrested were hard-core leaders who had not voluntarily defected. Chawalit noted that the CPT has moved its subversive activities from rural to urban areas. That perception is indeed confirmed by the

Fourth Party Congress resolution to abandon armed struggle in rural areas in favor of fomenting conflict in the urban areas. But such urban subversion had been dealt a severe blow in 1984 when 23 party leaders, including Central Committee members in charge of the urban strategy, were arrested. The arrest of eighteen more members in April 1987 could only weaken the party's urban efforts.

The Thai-Malaysian border has long been an area of tension between the two nations and a potential threat to Thai security. The outlawed Communist Party of Malaya (CPM) has carried out terrorist acts inside the Thai border for four decades. The CPM consists of Thai nationals, mostly of Chinese origin, who were born in Thailand but identify with Malaysia. After the CPT was virtually wiped out in the south, the Maoist CPM became the major focus of Thailand's Fourth Army Regional Command. Although the estimated 1,500–2,000 CPM insurgents never posed a serious threat to Thai security, they used jungle bases in Thailand's southernmost provinces to harass the Thais.

In March and April some 850 soldiers, making up the CPM's 8th Regiment, surrendered to the Fourth Army. Among them were 653 members of the CPM's Marxist-Leninist faction, which has been influential among the Chinese living in Thailand's Betong district, bordering Malaysia. They received amnesty and land like that given to CPT defectors. The Thai government played down the surrender because it did not want to jeopardize negotiations for the return of the remaining insurgents. These defectors are now called "participants in nation-building."

The disintegration of the CPM-ML ended a major insurgency problem in the south. But the remaining Maoist CPM members have not ended their operations. In October the Thai army announced it would shift to military operations if political negotiations failed.

In March Crown Prince Maha Vachiralongkorn met Deng Xiaoping during a state visit to China. China sold Thailand 50 T-69 medium tanks at 10 percent of their market value.

Conditions along the Thai-Cambodian border remained tense because of the 260,000 refugees, who comprise three groups: supporters of former prime minister Sihanouk, followers of anticommunist leader Son Sann, and members of the Khmer Rouge. Thailand will not take these refugees, and other countries are no longer willing to accept large numbers of them.

To strengthen the kingdom's counterinsurgency operations, Prime Minister Prem replaced General Chawalit as director of the Internal Security Operation Command (*FEER*, 5 March). This personnel change represents the government's intention to stress political rather than military means to combat the CPT.

Clark D. Neher
Northern Illinois University

Vietnam

Population. 63,593,000
Party. Vietnam Communist Party (Dang Cong San Vietnam; VCP)
Founded. 1930 (as Indochinese Communist Party)
Membership. 1.9 million (Indochina Archive estimate, December 1987); 20 percent women; ethnically, almost entirely Vietnamese; average age in mid-50s; 40 percent *ban co* (poor peasant); 25 percent peasant/farm laborer; 15 percent proletariat; 20 percent other
General Secretary. Nguyen Van Linh (b. 1915)
Politburo. Nguyen Van Linh, Pham Hung (b. 1912), Vo Chi Cong (b. 1912), Do Muoi (b. 1917), Vo Van Kiet (b. 1922), Le Duc Anh (b. 1910?), Nguyen Duc Tam (b. 1920), Nguyen Co Thach (b. 1920), Dong Sy Nguyen (b. 1920?), Tran Xuan Bach, Nguyen Thanh Binh, Doan Khue, Mai Chi Tho (b. 1922), Dao Duy Tung (alternate)
Secretariat. Nguyen Van Linh, Nguyen Duc Tam, Tran Xuan Bach, Dao Duy Tung, Tran Kien, Le Phuoc Tho, Nguyen Quyet, Dam Quang Trung, Vu Oanh, Nguyen Khanh, Tran Quyet, Tran Quoc Hoang, Pham The Duyet
Central Committee. 124 full and 49 alternate members
Status. Ruling party
Last Congress. Sixth, 15–18 December 1986
Last Election. 19 April, Eighth National Assembly, 98.8 percent, 496 seats, all VCP-endorsed (*Indochina Chronology*)
Auxiliary Organizations. Vietnam Fatherland Front (Huynh Tan Phat, chairman), Ho Chi Minh

Communist Youth Union (Ha Quang Du, general secretary)

Publications. *Nhan Dan* (The people), VCP daily, Hong Ha, editor; *Tap Chi Cong San* (Communist review), VCP theoretical monthly; *Quan Doi Nhan Dan* (People's army), army newspaper

The year 1987 was one of presentiment for Vietnam. It began with a pervasive sense of anticipation throughout society that the year would bring significant change to the lives of the Vietnamese, especially economically. Within the VCP there was the expectation that measures were about to be put into place that would purify the conduct of internal affairs and enhance the role of the individual within the party. Among foreign observers of the Vietnamese scene a strong belief existed that 1987 would prove to be the year of the thaw in Vietnam, when the long-delayed, frequently predicted, but continually postponed systematic change in the party/state structure would finally begin. These expectations came in the wake of the December 1986 Sixth Congress, which, while in session, had seemed so momentous in nature. Speeches and resolutions at that congress left the widespread belief that 1987 would be a seminal year—when there would be a generational transfer of political power, bringing in a new national leadership; when there would finally emerge clear socioeconomic policies designed to move Vietnam out of the bicycle age and into the computer age; and when new foreign policies would be unveiled to end the sterile condition of Vietnam's regional isolation.

Little evidence at year's end justified this sense of anticipation. Nor did 1987 prove to be a year of obviously profound events. Even so, and despite the absence of major overt developments, the presentiment remained. There were subterranean shiftings whose full meaning could only be dimly assessed. It could well be that historians may come to fix 1987 as a watershed year, one that turned Vietnamese society in a new direction. In any event, the anticipatory mood remained undiminished, and the new year began with the expectation that 1988 would bring important change to Vietnam and its people.

For everyone in Vietnam the year was marked by a concern for things economic. Inflation ravaged the system at perhaps its worst rate ever, chiefly the result of efforts to establish a new wage-scale arrangement—one that eliminated subsidies and payments in kind—which pumped billions of new dong into the economy. Vietnam remained essentially on the socialist world dole, in debt to the ruble bloc by about $6.2 billion; hard currency imports amounted to about $1.5 billion versus $550 million in exports. Additional incentives introduced into the agricultural sector were designed to improve the contract system installed in 1979, permitting higher profits to be taken on above-quota agricultural production and certain tax benefits. These measures appeared to be slowly showing an effect. Grain production in 1986 had been 18.5 million metric tons (MT) as compared to 18.2 million MT in 1985. The 1987 crop was estimated at 18.1 million MT by most experts (and as low as 17 million MT by some), but the drop was attributed to natural causes such as drought, typhoon flooding, and insect infestation—not state policies. Industrial production continued to increase slowly but not enough to meet minimal needs. Factories were still operating at about 50 percent capacity due to lack of raw materials, shortage of spare parts, and poor management. The plan announced in 1985 to liberalize the industrial sector so as to tap lucrative Vietnamese émigré sources of investment capital and technical assistance remained only a plan on paper. The new investment code, whch had been expected to be unveiled in June, was further delayed and had not been issued by year's end. Beyond this there was a growing belief among outsiders that an export-led, high-technology strategy was not appropriate for Vietnam. Even Soviet advisers were believed to be telling the Vietnamese economic planners that such a strategy is not merely a matter of opportunities, capital, subsidies, and tariff reductions, but would require high-quality product design, quality control, and slick packaging in order to compete even within the region.

Much of the year was devoted to implementing the instructions set down by the Sixth Congress, which mandated that the economic sector (1) increase production of food, consumer necessities, and export goods on something of an emergency basis; (2) reorient economic development away from a Stalinist heavy-industry model and toward a strategy emphasizing agricultural and light-industry development, with emphasis on water conservation and electric power projects; (3) decentralize to some extent the state's central management function by extending limited autonomy and planning authority to the provincial level and to the individual enterprise, which would require a more flexible transportation and communication system and a better tax system; (4) end or vastly reduce the state's subsidy system of payment in kind, a holdover from the war, and replace it with a flexible cash payment system, one that also factors in differentials as incentives; and (5) introduce a more efficient cost-accounting and statistical system to better monitor production and to increase productivity.

The emphasis, as party chief Nguyen Van Linh repeatedly asserted during the year, was on increasing production of food, consumer goods, and export commodities. This, he said, represented the "key to the settlement of Vietnam's socioeconomic problem" (address to party cadres, 27 October).

Neither the Sixth Congress instructions nor Linh's advice was new. Some of it dated back in official form to 1979. The intent had long been to reduce state intervention in the economy in a limited way. The purpose from the start was to solve the more pressing short-run economic problems and eventually to launch the country onto the path of true economic development. Nor did the instructions and advice represent a basic or philosophic change in economic thinking. Central planning and the spirit that doctrine represents, not the marketplace, would remain the society's chief economic beacon. The party and its cadres would continue an ubiquitous presence, intruding as required even into technical economic decisionmaking and remaining one of the chief impediments to rapid economic progress in Vietnam.

Despite the measures ordered by the Sixth Congress and progress made during the year, the basic dilemmas remained—between economic need and ideological imperatives; between party and state; and between domestic programs and foreign policies. Radical reform of the economy involving an overhaul of the party/state system called for reduction of the socioeconomic costs being extracted, particularly in external relations. The party leadership was impelled to seek some sort of settlement in Cambodia, to reach a modus vivendi with China, and to make friendly gestures to ASEAN, Japan, and the United States in the pursuit of economic aid. Set against this was the fact that the leadership's position was not fully secured. The Linh faction had to deal with still-powerful conservatives who, though not flatly opposed to the reforms he proposed, did question their pace and scope, fearing that precipitous actions could usher in unanticipated secondary effects. Externally, Hanoi's problem remained whether to retreat from overextended positions such as the Cambodian occupation so as to facilitate domestic programs, or to defend those positions by making minimal concessions and retreating only inch by inch. Increasing the difficulty of decisionmaking here was ambiguity in assessing the cost of regional accommodation—that is, in determining precisely what would be involved in an acceptable Cambodian settlement, or what exactly China would demand for marked improvement in relations.

Leadership and Party Organization. The year began with disarray in the upper levels of both party and state leadership, which is a relatively unknown phenomenon in the Hanoi governing circle. Much of this disarray, but not all of it, had sorted itself out by year's end. What remained was to reshuffle the second level of party and state bureaucracy, after which would come implementation of the new and hopefully more successful economic policies, at best a slow and lugubrious process.

The changes in party leadership effected by the Sixth Congress, together with state leadership changes made by the newly elected Socialist Republic of Vietnam (SRV) Eighth National Assembly in June, amounted to the start of a generational transfer of political power in Hanoi.

The basic political construct remained—that is, Chinese-based factionalism, collective leadership, and Marxist-style consensus politics. But within this structure emerged a new political lineup as most of the old guard passed from the scene and was replaced by younger, if not young, men. The major power holders who moved to the forefront were a new "circle of five": Nguyen Van Linh, Pham Hung, Vo Van Kiet, Le Duc Anh, and Vo Chi Cong. Of slightly less powerful rank but in newly strengthened positions were Nguyen Co Thach, Mai Chi Tho, and possibly Lieutenant General Dong Khue and Dong Sy Nguyen. A "southern predominance" emerged in the new lineup; virtually all of the major figures had long and intimate career associations in the South or were themselves southern. This meant a leadership that would understand southern ways and be better able to mobilize the economic potential represented by the South. There was also a rise in influence of what might be called special interest groups, such as science and technology sector cadres, economists, party provincial secretaries, and the military.

The reshuffle left three of the party's major figures—Truong Chinh, Pham Van Dong, and Le Duc Tho—in the anomalous position of being out of party office but still "historic leaders," as *Nhan Dan* (8 January) described them. They were named to the newly created posts of "consultant to the Politburo" with the duty of advising it on "strategic questions" concerning economic, social, political, military, and diplomatic matters. With the convening of the new National Assembly in June the three apparently relinquished all state positions, though they clearly remained an influence in Hanoi politics.

Most of the personnel changes during the year were on the state rather than on the party side. A 16 February Council of State directive ordered a far-reaching reorganization at the ministerial level, one that involved both institutional change and personnel replacement. Senior General Van Tien Dung was dropped as defense minister and replaced by Senior General Le Duc Anh. Foreign Minister Nguyen Co Thach was promoted to the additional post of deputy prime minister. Mai Chi Tho was named minister of interior. Thirty-one out of 39 SRV ministries were affected, and reorganization of the cabinet involved nineteen ministries and commissions. The three ministries of Food, Agriculture, and Food Industry were combined into a single Ministry of Agriculture and Food Industry. The two ministries of Power and Mines and Coal were merged into a single Ministry of Energy. The two ministries of Labor and War Invalids and Social Welfare were merged into a Ministry of Labor, War Invalids, and Social Welfare. Newly established was the Ministry of Information, which absorbed the Vietnam Radio and Television Commission. The Commission for the Protection of Mothers and Children was absorbed by the Ministry of Education. The General Department of Job Training was absorbed by the Ministry of Higher Education and Vocational Training. The General Geological Department was renamed the General Department of Mines and Geology. Newly established was the Commission for Economic Relations with Foreign Countries.

The elections on 19 April saw a record number of Vietnamese voters go to the polls to elect the Eighth SRV National Assembly. A total of 496 persons were chosen in 167 constituencies from a slate of 829 candidates. It was the first general election since 1981 and was more open and offered greater choice than previous elections. All the top leaders running for assembly seats were elected. A Central Elections Council communiqué of 18 May said the new assembly included 88 women, 55 persons under age 35, and 70 members of ethnic minorities. By occupation it listed 123 intellectuals, 105 farmers, 100 political cadres, 91 workers, and 49 military personnel.

State officials elected by the Eighth National Assembly 17–18 June included the following. In the State Council: Vo Chi Cong (president), Nguyen Huu Tho, Huynh Tan Phat, Le Quang Dao, Nguyen Quyet, Dam Quang Trung, Nguyen Thi Dinh (vice presidents), Nguyen Viet Dung (general secretary). In the National Assembly: Le Quang Dao (chairman), Tran Do, Hoang Truong Minh, Huynh Cuong, Phung Van Tuu, Nguyen Thi Ngoc Phuong (vice-chairpersons). In the Council of Ministers: Pham Hung (chairman), Vo Van Kiet, Nguyen Co Thach, Dong Sy Nguyen, Vo Nguyen Giap, Nguyen Khanh, Nguyen Ngoc Triu, Nguyen Van Chinh, Doan Duy Thanh, Tran Duc Luong (vice-chairman), Nguyen Khanh (general secretary). In the National Defense Council: Vo Chi Cong (chairman), Pham Hung (vice-chairman), Le Duc Anh, Nguyen Co Thach, Mai Chi Tho (members). In the Council of Nationalities: Dam Quang Trung (chairman). On the People's Supreme Court: Pham Hung (president). In the Supreme People's Prosecutor's Office: Tran Quyet (president).

During 1987 the party leadership, as if by tacit agreement, abandoned its great doctrinal dispute of the postwar years. This dispute had long been labeled by outsiders as "Ideologue versus Pragmatist." It was essentially an argument over models of economic development and best methods for solving various sociopolitical problems and, beyond these, over how far Marxism-Leninism can be bent before it breaks. It seemed clear at year's end that the dispute no longer obtained, at least for the moment. Many outsiders pronounced this a victory for the pragmatists. In actuality it was more that the dispute had metamorphosed into a new set of arguments over the nature and pace of changing policies in the economic sector and their meanings for national security and foreign affairs. The pragmatists became "renovationists" (and might fairly be called "reformers"), whereas the ideologues became ultracautious pragmatists (and might be termed "conservatives"). What separated them primarily was the question of orthodoxy in economic change, specifically the degree of willingness to scrap long-standing doctrine to fit new needs. The reformers were more willing to innovate, experiment, and take risks in the economic sector. The conservatives saw the reformers as pressing programs that did not fully take into account the effect these would have outside the economic sector. The shift of power from conservatives to reformers was not as decisive as many had initally anticipated. Earlier it had been widely believed that the reformers were taking full control, that Vo Van Kiet would become prime minister and Le Duc Tho a major power wielder. A counter view was that the reformers still faced formidable opposition from the conservatives and that the best they could hope for would be a political compromise. And that is what happened, with the appointment of conservative Pham Hung as prime minister and reformer Vo Chi Cong as president of the State Council, and with the departure of Le Duc Tho. It was a compromise forced on reformer Nguyen Van Linh, and its chief significance was that he could not move as rapidly in making policy changes as he would like.

Linh himself, in his first full year at the helm, was still very much a man on trial, still in the process of establishing and proving himself, still carving out a leadership role within the party, and still defining his powers in the state sector. He was busy both solidifying his position within the never-ending factional power struggle and pressing his economic and social reforms. Most of his daily activities during the year resembled those of a candidate in the midst of an election campaign. Tirelessly he stumped the country, speaking chiefly to party gatherings. His message, in what came to be called the "Linh fever," was candid and hopeful: things have not gone well for Vietnam in the past decade; it need not be this way; socialist doctrine, which is to say Leninism more than Marxism, has the answers; the party is the only proper guiding instrument; it is simply a matter of putting dogma and institution together in the right mix; and we must maintain our "ideological optimism." As with any new administration, there was a need on Linh's part to assert control. He did this by moving upper-level party and state officials in and out of positions in a general reshuffle and with rhetoric asserting his determination to make sweeping policy changes. By all evidence, his political methods seemed to work. At year's end Linh appeared to be the man in charge.

Domestic Party Affairs. Giving focus to internal party develoments during the year were two plenums (of the Sixth Congress): the second plenum 1–9 April, and the third plenum 20–28 August. Linh chaired both, gave the opening and closing addresses at the second, and gave the major address at the third. His speeches, as well as the plenums themselves, were largely given over to domestic economic matters. The second plenum was chiefly devoted to what was termed the distribution-circulation problem, meaning specific difficulties involving wage scales, price controls, regulations governing domestic and foreign trade, availability of credit, and efforts to increase agricultural production and improve productivity in both agriculture and industry. Linh's assessment of what was wrong economically in Vietnam was blunt and candid: never before has inflation worsened so fast, never have prices increased so steeply and unexpectedly, never have the lives of the people become so difficult; inflation now runs at 1,000 percent per annum; Vietnam cannot prolong forever extensive use of the state budget to cover production losses, which amount to billions of dong per year and which have doubled the national deficit in five years; underlying this is the fact that the average Vietnamese conception of what is socialism is simplistic and unrealistic. Such was his assessement.

Linh's second plenum speech stressed "lack of focus" in economic thinking, which appeared to mean an absence of consensus as to what should be the proper economic model in addressing distribution and financing problems. As a result, he said, these two sectors were "tense and confused." The third plenum agenda was somewhat broader in scope; in effect it was a review of the performance of the economy in implementing the "urgent policies and measures" ordered by the Sixth Congress in 1986. The intent of the party leadership, it was clear from both plenums, was to learn from past mistakes and to rectify earlier, unworkable policies. Since the leadership in recent years has tended to dodge this responsibility, it could be said the plenums represent progress. However, the rhetoric of the plenum resolutions was largely exhortative rather than analytical, and what emerged was not new policies so much as an assertive determination to slog on with existing policies, hoping to hone them, improve them, make them work better.

The spirit of change introduced by Nguyen Van Linh during the year was often described as *cong khai* (openness), resembling the concept of *glasnost'* as introduced in the USSR. Editorials in party journals during the year explained that openness was an integral part of the process of changing the "style of party leadership" and that within the general society it would help limit "negative manifestations" (a code term for antisocial behavior). The all-encompassing term used to describe this campaign of change was *canh tan* (renovation). Party journals emphasized that renovation required eliminating the rising tide of party corruption. It also involved renovation of cadre attitude, poetically described as "abandoning the old ways of flags, lanterns, trumpets, and drums." More to the point, renovation justified full use of revolutionary violence against "those whose self-serving misdeeds sabotage Vietnamese society in alliance with imperialism and expansionism-hegemonism" (*Quan Doi Nhan Dan*, 15 February).

An important party conference was staged in Hanoi in early January by the Central Committee Organizing Department, chaired by the department head (and Politburo member) Nguyen Duc Tam. The session mapped out overall internal party activity for the year. It scheduled a series of regional party conferences, arranged for intensified self-criticism sessions, set up special provincial-level cadre training sessions, and ordered extensive rice roots–level reorganization work. Meeting at the same time in Hanoi was the Organizing Department of the Central Control Committee, whose members have responsibility for overseeing party members and cadre conduct and for supervising investigation of misbehavior of party members (such as corruption, theft of collective property, "bearing grudges," and "usurping land"). Control cadres also settle charges, complaints, and "denunciations" brought by party members, and in general have disciplinary authority over rank and file members and lower-level cadres. These two conferences set in motion a nationwide party "militancy" drive, more commonly termed the anticorruption or "purification" drive; it was officially launched 3 February, on the 57th anniversary of the founding of the party. Old Guard figure Do Muoi was made general overseer of all "control" activity within the party, in effect becoming czar of party morals as he had once been czar of Hanoi's wartime economy.

The party's purification drive was a highly significant undertaking that could eventually have far-reaching effect. It was an intense, ambitious, ideologically oriented campaign to restore party cadre self-confidence, return the party as an institution to its previous high standards of performance, and polish its badly tarnished image among the general public. The official purpose of the campaign was cast in highly ideological but rather vague terms: "to purify and enhance the militant strength of Party organs and efficiency of the State machinery; to purify social relations; and to implement social justice" (Politburo resolution, 15 September). A theme stressed in the campaign was that the reason for Vietnam's current poor condition was that the transformation to socialism was still incomplete. Because of this, only "weak socialist relationships" existed, which permitted "spontaneous capitalist influences" and corruption to assert themselves.

The party press was soon filled with advice on how the party could lift itself by its ideological bootstraps. There was much castigation of individual miscreants and luridly reported descriptions of various, often ingenious, wrongdoings.

The media reported on many disciplinary actions taken by lower-level party units. These ranged from official warnings to expulsion from the party. The Hanoi City party announced that in the first six months of the year 695 members had been disciplined, including 163 expulsions. Vinh Phu province, with about 70,000 members, expelled 848 and took lesser disciplinary measures against another 3,200 in March. Similar reports came from throughout the country. Extrapolations from these provincial-level announcements indicate that nationwide about one member in 35 was disciplined and one in 140 expelled. It is believed that some 200,000 members have been purged from party roles since 1980. Where a reason is given for expulsion, it is usually either corruption or "opportunistic behavior," meaning use of party position for personal gain. Meanwhile, party recruitment efforts continued intensively, especially among the young. About 60 percent of new members admitted during the year were under age 30; 40 percent were women.

The enthusiasm with which the press attacked party misbehavior drew a cautionary note from party theoreticians who warned that purification must not be pursued at the price of undermining party unity. The party's main strength, they said, lay in its solidarity, which must be preserved at all costs. Do Muoi, for his part, also trod lightly. He spoke to a May conference of control cadres on the mechanisms and methods to be employed in the purification drive. But it was a technical rather than exhortative address, essentially uncritical of the party. His theme was that control cadres should do a better job of policing the party but should work with great care. Nguyen Van Linh contributed to the campaign with a speech at the Nguyen Ai Quoc Higher Party School on 6 May in which he described an ideal cadre's intellectual, moral, and technical abilities. An evaluation of the campaign came on 12 September with a Politburo resolution that was generally grim in tone. It asserted that at best a good start had been made in purifying the party and that the campaign would necessarily continue at least until 1989.

In February the party published the revised *Statutes of the Communist Party of Vietnam*, commonly known as the party by-laws, the basic legal document for the party as an institution in Vietnam. The new version consists of 62 articles divided into twelve chapters, as opposed to 59 articles and eleven chapters in the 1976 version. The new document remains essentially the same as the earlier versions, though there is some tightening of language having to do with enforcing party discipline. A separate chapter has also been added on the party and the armed forces that specifies in more detail than in past versions the organization and function of the party within the People's Army of Vietnam (PAVN). (English text of the *Statutes* published by *FBIS*, 11 September.)

Front Organizations. Vietnam's mass organization, the Vietnam Fatherland Front (VFF), observed its 57th anniversary in Hanoi on 14 November in ceremonies presided over by its honorary chairman, Hoang Quoc Viet, and the chairman of the VFF Central Committee Presidium, Huynh Tan Phat. Earlier in the year the VFF had organized the National Assembly elections. The VFF and the National Assembly are the chief instruments for mobilizing and harnessing political activities in Vietnam outside of the party.

The Fifth Congress of the Ho Chi Minh Communist Youth Union was held in Hanoi 26–30 November and was attended by 750 delegates (representing 4.2 million members) as well as by representatives of 24 foreign parties and youth organizations. Ha Quang Du was elected first secretary along with a nine-member Secretariat and a 150-member Central Committee.

The Sixth Vietnamese Women's Congress was held in May in Hanoi under the gavel of Vietnam Women's Union president Nguyen Thi Dinh; it was attended by 1,000 delegates and foreign visitors. Speakers cited the prominent place of women in Vietnamese affairs: 7 on the VCP Central Committee, plus 6 alternates (out of 173); 108 members of the National Assembly (22 percent of the total); 16 in ministerial posts; and 200 department heads. Women's leadership in the party clearly increased at the local level—18 percent at that level, in contrast to a 5 percent increase of women on the Central Committee.

International Positions. Virtually no change occurred during the year in Vietnamese foreign affairs. In part this appeared to be due to a preoccupation in Hanoi with leadership change and economic troubles, and in part to a sort of resignation among Hanoi foreign policymakers that they had at the moment few options for change that could bring improvement.

The war in Cambodia slogged on amidst continual rumors that some sort of settlement was in the offing. Nothing had developed, however, by year's end. The vice–foreign ministers from Vietnam, Cambodia, and Laos went to Moscow in early January for a two-day "exchange of views" with Soviet leaders. The press communiqué issued 9 January made no direct reference to Cambodia, but it was believed that Soviet officials had urged the Indochinese officials to find a resolution to the Cambodia problem. The PAVN staged its annual partial withdrawal from Cambodia in November, the sixth since it invaded in 1979. PAVN strength in that country after withdrawal was estimated to be about 135,000.

The Sino-Vietnamese border war erupted sporadically during the year, with intensive clashes reported in early January, late May, and again in December. In between these open conflicts, the cold war continued.

Vietnam's dominant, even overpowering, relationship continued to be with the USSR. It remained, as in the past decade, a relationship built on Vietnamese dependency and perceived Soviet opportunism. Although relations were close and generally workable, there were indications of Moscow's restiveness over the continuing malaise in the Vietnamese economic sector and the price this was extracting from the USSR. A Soviet-Vietnamese conference at the Central Committee level was held in Moscow 5 January, chaired by Soviet Politburo member Yegor Ligachev with SRV deputy foreign minister Vo Dong Giang as the ranking Vietnamese. The conference discussed ways to "strengthen and heighten the efficiency of Soviet-Vietnamese cooperation." Out of it came the "common task" of raising Vietnamese consumer goods production during the current Five-Year Plan by 15 percent and exports by 70 percent over the previous plan, with Soviet assistance.

The highlight of the year in Soviet-Vietnamese relations was the visit 18–21 May to Moscow by Nguyen Van Linh and his entourage. It was marked by a whirlwind round of talks, banquets, document-signing ceremonies, and visits to symbolic Moscow tour stops. Ligachev hosted the group. Linh met privately with General Secretary Mikhail Gorbachev, who also hosted a banquet. There were seven Vietnamese in the delegation, including economic aid specialists. The bulk of the working sessions were apparently devoted to discussions of bilateral relations, especially economic—that is, spending the $2 billion that Moscow sends annually to Vietnam. Also discussed was Cambodia; the two sides agreed that a political solution is the only answer, providing it is "within prevailing realities."

Four economic agreements were signed, involving increased production of light-industry goods in Vietnam; production of electronic and technical electrical equipment in Vietnam; coconut oil production and processing; and tea production, the latter two commodities for export to the USSR. Prior to the visit, on 7 May, the Politburo, in a pointedly well-publicized meeting in Hanoi, discussed the problem of "renovating and improving the efficiency" of Vietnamese-Soviet economic relations and "profoundly reviewing mistakes and shortcomings by various echelons and sectors as regards awareness and guidance in effecting cooperation."

Biography. *Pham Hung.* In June Pham Hung was named chairman of the SRV Council of Ministers, the office equivalent of prime minister in Vietnam and most important of all state posts. He also retained his seat on the Politburo, which he has held since 1957. Thus, at age 75 Pham Hung had reached the political pinnacle in Vietnam, climaxing a journey begun in the late 1920s when, at the age of 18, he embraced Marxism-Leninism. Now he stood alone, the last of the Old Guard, the last survivor of the original "inner circle," and the last of the charter members of the Indochinese Communist Party still in office.

From the earliest days in the party Pham Hung was regarded by his superiors—and later by his subordinates—as tough, competent, and reliable, a skilled covert organization man and careful apparat administrator. As he rose through the ranks and was assigned a wide variety of tasks, he was hardened by the fires of experience. He became highly knowledgeable in cadre management, political mobilization, and internal security matters. At the same time he gained a reputation among his peers as a hard-line conservative, a firm-minded, but never fanatical ideologue. Others were motivators; Pham Hung was a mobilizer.

Pham Hung was born in the Mekong Delta village of Long Ho in Vinh Long province on 11 June 1912. His original name was Nguyen Van Thien; later he took his party name, Pham Hung (his code name was Hai Hung). Pham Hung's family could be called village gentry, since they owned land and had social status in Long Ho village. He attended secondary school in My Tho and reportedly studied law at the University of Hanoi (although he apparently never graduated). He joined a proto-Marxist organization known as the Vietnam Revolutionary Youth League in the late 1920s. When the Indochinese Communist Party was formed in 1930, he became a charter member. According to his official biography, he was jailed by the French from 1931 to 1945; however, French records list him as having been jailed twice: 1931–1936 and 1939–1945. The first incarceration was for complicity in the death of a French official during violent May Day 1931 demonstrations in My Tho; he was released under the 1936 general amnesty ordered by the united front government that had assumed power in Paris. The second jailing came as part of a French roundup of all known radicals in Indochina the day after World War II started. Pham Hung was incarcerated on the prison island of Poulo Condore, where he met and began a lifelong relation with Le Duan; both were released after the Allied victory in 1945.

Pham Hung spent the Viet Minh War doing underground work in the South, serving under the party's apparat chief for the South, Le Duan, and his deputy, Le Duc Tho. Later in the war he replaced Tho (who returned to Hanoi) and at one point held three posts: party cadre administrator for the South; behind-the-scenes manager of the united front organization Lien Viet; and political commissar of the southern Viet Minh troops. These were important party posts, although the South itself during the war was something of a military backwater. In the Geneva Accords period, 1954–1955, Pham Hung and General Van Tien Dung served on a PAVN military liaison team to the International Control Commission supervising the accords. In late 1955 he was ordered back to Hanoi.

In the period between wars, Pham Hung held a series of state posts, the most important being deputy prime minister (appointed in 1958), which meant he was acting prime minister when Prime Minister Pham Van Dong was out of the country. Most of his work dealt with agriculture, trade, and fiscal matters, although he kept an interest in southern affairs as a National Assembly delegate working with the assembly's National Reunification Commission. He had become a party Central Committee member in 1951, a Politburo member in 1957, and a Politburo Secretariat member in 1960.

The war in the South, begun in 1959, gradually grew more intense and complex, particularly after 1964 with the arrival of the U.S. ground forces. When the party chief in the South, General Nguyen

Chi Thanh, was killed in a B-52 raid, a successor was required who could meet the challenge by converting guerrilla war into a war of military-political strategy. This required a person of experience and skill, someone capable of coordinating major covert mobilization and motivation programs. Pham Hung was the obvious choice.

Virtually all Hanoi public references to Pham Hung ceased after 1966. He did not run for re-election to the National Assembly in 1971. It is now known that he moved to the South in early 1967 and set up party headquarters on the border just inside Cambodia opposite the Vietnamese province of Tay Ninh. There he installed himself as the general secretary of the People's Revolutionary Party (PRP), as it was officially called—privately it was known as the Southern Branch of the Lao Dong Party. The PRP Central Committee at the time was also known informally as the Central Office (of the Lao Dong Central Committee) of Vietnam. It was the party's instrument within the united front institution, the National Liberation Front of Vietnam (informally, Viet Cong); this front controlled the military force in the South, the People's Liberation Armed Forces (PLAF). Pham Hung surfaced in Saigon at the end of the war and was officially identified as general secretary of the party Central Committee Office for South Vietnam and PLAF political commissar. In his duty Pham Hung worked closely with another long-time party figure in the South, Nguyen Van Linh.

In the postwar era Pham Hung's most important assignment was minister of interior (1980), which made him responsible for internal security in Vietnam. Much of his daily activity appears to have concentrated on internal security matters in the South. He was also named vice-chairman of the Council of Ministers in 1980 and was re-elected a deputy to the sixth and subsequent national assemblies. The Eighth National Assembly in 1987 elected him chairman of the Council of Ministers.

Pham Hung was regarded as a member of the Pham Van Dong faction in Hanoi party politics since Dong was in effect his mentor. On occasion Pham Hung would also ally himself with the Le Duan faction in its doctrinal infighting with the Truong Chinh faction. Rumor in Hanoi maintained that Pham Hung's arch personal rival in upper-level party politics was To Huu. Reportedly, he was in serious political trouble in the immediate postwar days for advocating a "go slow" policy in the South and opposing the punitive policies that were adopted. Although a reputation for being "soft" on the South may have hurt him earlier, by the early 1980s it had become a political asset as the South came to be regarded as the best hope for leading Vietnam out of the economic wilderness.

Pham Hung's writings are fairly extensive, consisting chiefly of short, technically oriented articles on state management and administrative problem-solving. He coauthored a book with Le Duan, *Revolutionary Line for the South* (1958). Very little is known about Pham Hung's private life. He is believed to have married in 1952.

Douglas Pike
University of California, Berkeley

EASTERN EUROPE AND THE SOVIET UNION

Introduction

The 70th anniversary of the Bolshevik Revolution in November attracted delegations to Moscow from approximately 100 communist and workers' parties; some 40 revolutionary-democratic and national liberation movements; another 30 socialist, social-democratic, and labor parties (including the Socialist International, the Indian National Congress, the Center Party of Finland, and the Greens); and others. (*Pravda*, 19 January 1988.) The sessions were informational. CPSU general secretary Mikhail S. Gorbachev painted an optimistic future, ending his speech with these words: "We are traveling to a new world, the world of communism. We shall never deviate from this path." (Moscow TV in *FBIS*, 3 November.) Neither China nor Albania sent representatives to the celebration.

An interview with Gorbachev appeared in a December issue of the Chinese communist weekly *Liaowang* in which the Soviet leader mentioned a possible summit meeting with his counterpart (*Izvestiia*, 11 January 1988). A spokesman for the regime in Beijing rejected this suggestion. Hence, for the time being, there will be no party-to-party relations between these two neighbors. The same applies to the Albanian communists.

The Soviet Union. At the October 1987 plenum of the Central Committee, the resignation for health reasons of Geidar A. Aliev from the Politburo was accepted. Boris Eltsin, candidate Politburo member and first secretary for the Moscow city party organization, reportedly attacked the CPSU leadership for being slow to implement *perestroika*. His dismissal from the Moscow position followed. (*Pravda*, 12 November.) Earlier plenary sessions of the Central Committee had ousted Kazakhstan party boss Dinmukhamed A. Kunaev from the Politburo in January and promoted Aleksandr Iakovlev and Nikolai N. Sliunkov to full members in June.

At the latter plenum, Agriculture Secretary Viktor P. Nikonov became a member, and the new defense minister, Colonel General Dmitrii Yazov, a candidate for membership on the Political Bureau. Most, if not all, of these men appeared to be protégés of the general secretary. His power position had seemingly become consolidated within the short period since his election in March 1985 as CPSU leader. Whether this assessment remains accurate may be confirmed by the 19th national party conference, which opens on 28 June 1988.

Demonstrations (by Kazakhs at the beginning of the New Year over the replacement of CPSU leader Kunaev by an ethnic Russian; at midyear by Crimean Tatars from Central Asia, where 400,000 had been deported in 1944; and in all three Baltic republics of Lithuania, Latvia, and Estonia on the anniversary of the Nazi-Soviet pact in August) gave the USSR a bad press. Protests by Jews as well as ethnic Germans, and perhaps intercessions by high-ranking U.S. officials, resulted in substantially larger numbers of Jews and Germans being allowed to leave the USSR.

The more liberal interpretations of the right to emigrate may involve the Soviet drive to influence West European public opinion. Signing the treaty to ban all intermediate- and shorter-range nuclear missiles in December 1987 made Gorbachev more popular than President Ronald Reagan in some Western countries, and both shared Man of the Year honors in *Time* magazine.

Nevertheless, the Soviets were not inclined to back away from regional objectives. They dismissed a U.S. suggestion, made at the December 1987 summit in Washington, D.C., that USSR military assistance to Nicaragua be stopped (*NYT*, 4 February 1988). Even in the case of Afghanistan, the envisaged withdrawal over a twelve-month period of USSR troops would begin only 60 days after an agreement had been signed and guaranteed by the United States (*Pravda*, 11 January 1988). In effect, it was hoped that continuing foreign policy successes would cover Moscow's difficulties at home.

Soviet-U.S. relations continued to be affected by the continuing use of disinformation against the United States, especially throughout the Third World. Despite pledges by top leaders to end such "active measures," a report planted by the KGB in the *Ghanaian Times* was picked up from Accra and sent out that same day over the worldwide English service of TASS. It alleged that the United States had delivered chemical weapons to and exchanged information about bacteriologic warfare with the Republic of South Africa. (TASS release in *FBIS*, 9 January 1988.)

Numerous blatant anti-American propaganda themes are also being channeled via communist front organizations, which are directed from the international department of the CPSU Central Committee apparatus under Anatolii F. Dobrynin (*Problems of Communism*, no. 2, 1988), who spent almost 25 years as Soviet ambassador to the United States. The objectives remain to unite communists with others and to make USSR foreign policy objectives look respectable.

Soviet propaganda themes, disseminated by the fronts during the year under review, included demands that the United States stop nuclear tests and Strategic Defense Initiative research outside the laboratory. Much more emphasis centered on the Far East and the southwestern Pacific, especially regarding establishment of nuclear-free zones (*WMR*, September 1987). Another theme revolves around the so-called New International Economic Order, which would redress the imbalance in wealth between capitalist and underdeveloped countries.

Eastern Europe. No mention is ever made, however, about USSR exploitation of its client states through the Council for Mutual Economic Assistance (CMEA). These economies are harnessed in support of a comprehensive fifteen-year program for scientific and technical progress, adopted in December 1985, with the goal of narrowing the East-West technology gap. It appears from Soviet press reports that little, if any, progress has been made (*Pravda*, 18 September; *Izvestiia*, 10 October). The so-called direct links between production units in the USSR and Eastern Europe frequently remain on paper only.

CMEA members, nevertheless, agreed to a collective concept for an international socialist division of labor that will apply during the period 1991–2005 and also assist their Third World affiliates: Cuba, Mongolia, and Vietnam. Power engineering will be overhauled, with the nuclear aspect to be given priority (*Neues Deutschland*, 14 October). The latter may not be easy to implement after Chernobyl, with public protest most recently having forced the USSR government to abandon construction of a nuclear power plant near the Black Sea (*NYT*, 28 January 1988).

Another basic problem concerns the fact that more than 80 percent of Soviet hard currency earnings come from exports of energy. The low world market prices for oil and natural gas have reduced that type of income from more than 20 billion rubles each year before 1981 down to about 13 billion rubles in 1987. The official USSR government newspaper (*Izvestiia*, 10 October) admits that the country has become a "raw materials appendage" of the capitalist world.

The military dimension of intrabloc relations is conducted through the Warsaw Treaty Organization (WTO). No change in the number of Soviet troops, stationed throughout Eastern Europe, has taken place. The WTO political-consultative committee met in East Germany toward the end of May. It repeated all earlier Soviet proposals for intermediate-range nuclear forces, START, mutual and balanced force reduction (MBFR), test ban, ASAT, strict adherence to the anti-ballistic missile treaty, chemical weapons, and a nuclear-free zone. This last one supposedly originated with General Wojciech Jaruzelski in Warsaw and suggests it apply to a 300-kilometer strip of land across Central Europe (*WMR, Information Bulletin*, August).

The MBFR talks in Vienna entered their fifteenth year, without any sign of a possible agreement. The nineteen delegations (twelve NATO and seven WTO) appeared to be winding down their activities, in view of parallel discussions toward a mandate for a new set of negotiations. These might include all 35 Helsinki Final Act signatories and expand the geographic area covered from the Atlantic to the Urals, instead of Central Europe alone.

Warsaw Pact military exercises continued as before, with NATO observers attending when more than 17,000 troops were involved. The East even provided visitors with binoculars, although some of the exercises appeared to have been rehearsed. NATO officers were forbidden the use of dictaphones or video cameras. During USSR-Czechoslovak maneuvers, they could not even see the combat units. Other experiences appeared to be less restrictive.

The foregoing economic and military constraints have an impact on Soviet–East European relations. Leaders from all six client regimes gave speeches during the 70th anniversary of the revolution in early November at Moscow. Their content indicates that Hungary and Poland support deep reforms. In between, the Bulgarian and Czechoslovak leaders paid only lip service to acceleration of restructuring. The East Germans never even mentioned these slogans, and the Romanians went so far as to implicitly reject some of the economic reforms as not being applicable.

Only four of the East European leaders (Jaruzelski, Erich Honecker, Todor Zhivkov, and Nicolae Ceauşescu) stood with the CPSU Politburo members on top of Lenin's tomb during the 7 November parade. Gustáv Husák and János Kádár had returned to Czechoslovakia and to Hungary, respectively, perhaps because of poor health.

In his speech given five days earlier at the Kremlin before a joint session of the CPSU Central Committee and the USSR Supreme Soviet, Gorbachev enumerated six principles for intrabloc relations: unconditional equality, responsibility of the ruling party for its country, concern for the cause of socialism, respect for one another, voluntary cooperation, and peaceful coexistence.

This unity in diversity must proceed within the communist orbit, however, and all reforms will be confined within the one-party system. That is no problem for the older leaders. Only one of these, namely Husák (74) from Czechoslovakia, was succeeded by the hard-liner Miloš Jakeš (63). In Hungary, Károly Grósz may be the heir apparent to party leader Kádár (75). It is yet unclear who will succeed Zhivkov (also 75) in Bulgaria, Ceauşescu (69) in Romania, and Jaruzelski (only 64) in Poland. All but the last man have been in power between 22 and 32 years. Gorbachev clones may emerge in some of these countries as future communist leaders, although this too depends on whether the CPSU general secretary survives.

Richard F. Staar
Hoover Institution

Albania

Population. 3,085,985

Party. Albanian Party of Labor (Partia ë Punës ë Shqipërisë; APL)

Founded. 8 November 1941

Membership. 147,000 regular party members; 39.8 percent workers; 29.5 percent cooperativists (peasants); 31.3 percent white-collar workers. Women constitute 32.2 percent of the membership. (*Zeri i popullit*, 4 November.)

First Secretary. Ramiz Alia

Politburo. 13 full members, many of whom occupy other high government positions as well: Ramiz Alia (first secretary, president of the republic, commander-in-chief of the armed forces), Adil Çarçani (prime minister), Besnik Bekteshi (deputy premier), Foto Çami, Lenka Çuko, Hekuran Isai (deputy premier, minister of internal affairs), Hajredin Çeliku, Rita Marko (deputy chairman of the Presidium of the People's Assembly), Pali Mishka, Manush Myftiu (deputy premier), Prokop Mura (minister of defense), Muho Asllani (party chief of Shkodër), Simon Stefani (secretary); 5 alternate members: General Kiço Mustaqi (deputy defense minister, chief of the General Staff), Llambi Gjegprifti (mayor, Tiranë district), Vangjel Çerava (deputy premier), Qirjako Mihali (party chief, Durress district), Pirro Kondi (party chief, Tiranë district).

Secretariat. Five members: Ramiz Alia, Foto Çami, Lenka Çuko, Simon Stefani, Hajredin Çeliku

Central Committee. 85 members, 46 alternate members

Status. Ruling party

Last Congress. Ninth, 3–8 November 1986, in Tiranë

Last Parliamentary Elections. 1 February 1987, all 250 candidates of the Democratic Front. Only one ballot was declared invalid. (*Zeri i popullit*, 3 February.)

Auxiliary Organizations. Albanian Democratic Front, Nexhmije Hoxha, chairwoman; Central Council of Trade Unions (UTUA), approximately 610,000 members, Sotir Koçallari, chairman; Union of Labor Youth of Albania (ULYA),

Mehmet Elezi, first secretary; Albanian War Veterans, Shefque Peçi, chairman; Pioneers of "Enver"

Main State Organs. Council of Ministers (24 members, including 2 members without portfolio, Alfred Uçi and Ajet Ylli, who serve as chairmen of the Committee for Culture and Art and the State Committee for Science and Technology, respectively (*Zeri i popullit*, 21 February).

Publications. *Zeri i popullit*, daily organ of the Central Committee of the APL; *Rruga ë partisë*, monthly theoretical organ of the Central Committee of the APL; *Bashkimi*, daily organ of the Democratic Front; *Puna*, weekly organ of the UTUA; *10 Korik* and *Lluftetari*, biweekly organs of the Ministry of Defense (circulated in the armed forces); *Nendori*, literary monthly, organ of the Albanian Writers' and Artists' League; *Laiko vema*, daily organ of the Greek minority. The Albanian Telegraphic Agency (ATA) is the official state news service.

The Albanian Communist Party was founded on 8 November 1941 in Tiranë on the initiative of the Comintern acting through the Yugoslav Communist Party and Josip Broz Tito. Two Yugoslav emissaries, who subsequently spent most of the war in Albania supervising the newly founded organization, impressed on the small number of Albanian communists the need to unite on a nationwide basis and to assume the leadership of the antifascist struggle. The problems that the Comintern faced in Albania were twofold: (1) the self-proclaimed Albanian communists were thoroughly tribalized, and (2) there were only a handful to begin with. In fact, at the first meeting of Albanian communists in Tiranë, under the supervision of Tito's emissaries (Miladin Popović and Dušan Mungoša), a total of fifteen individuals represented communist groups of Korçë, Shkodër, and a Tiranë youth organization. After acrimonious debates that lasted several days, the Albanian Communist Party was founded and a seven-member Central Committee elected. The provisional Central Committee consisted of Enver Hoxha, Qemal Stafa, Koçi Xoxe, Tuk Jakova, Kristo Themelko, Ramadan Çitaku, and Gjin Marku. (Hoxha, *Kur lindi Parti* [When the Party Was Born], p. 220). It is worth noting that all the original members of the Central Committee except Hoxha were either purged or executed. Only one, Qemal Stafa, was killed in action.

Hoxha, the son of a mullah from Gjoricastër with close ties to the royal family of Zog, was elected first secretary as a compromise. Because of persistent bickering between the Korçë and Shkodër groups, the two Yugoslav supervisors achieved a consensus that no leader of any existing group could be named first secretary. Hoxha, who had moved to Tiranë from Korçë, had no solid base and thus, in the opinion of the Comintern agents, was qualified to assume the post of first secretary.

One characteristic of the Albanian Communist Party is its instability at the top. Major purges have been undertaken either to reorient the country's foreign policy or to even scores between contending leaders. Thus in 1948, Koçi Xoxe and Pandi Christo (along with several hundred of their followers) were eliminated. Following the purges, Albania entered the Soviet bloc and became a vociferous critic of Titoism. In 1961, after several top members of the Politburo, including a pregnant woman, were executed, Hoxha turned against Moscow's "modern revisionism" and became an ardent supporter of Mao's "true" Marxism-Leninism. Fifteen years later, Hoxha eliminated his top aide and longtime bodyguard, General Beqir Baluku, minister of defense, as a traitor, along with the chief of the armed forces, Petrit Dume. Their purge was followed by Albania's break with Peking, which was not as total as its break with Yugoslavia and the Soviet Union in that Albania and China retained diplomatic relations. In 1981 Hoxha turned his wrath against his longtime competitor, Mehmet Shehu, prime minister for 28 years, who was accused of being a triple agent. Shehu's purge, ironically, was followed by a further opening to the West, a policy that Shehu had favored all along.

The post-Hoxha leadership of the Albanian Communist Party has made its transition to power without major shake-ups but with obvious uncertainties about its direction. A reduced militancy in pronouncements and unusual degree of candor in alleviating "errors" seem to characterize the Alia leadership style. The changes at the top party levels thus far, however, do not suggest any distinct pattern and merit further observation before one can state with assurance that Alia is in full control of the party and state apparatus. Yet there is an apparent urgency on the part of Alia to shore up support for his policies, which are still characterized by continuity rather than innovation.

The beginning of Alia's drive to broaden his support at the local level indicates a long-range approach to power consolidation. He and other top party leaders traveled the country in early spring to underscore the importance of "electing the proper people" to base, regional, and city party organizations (*Zeri i popullit*, 28 May). Local elections of party officials usually determine the composition of higher party organs, and the Tenth APL Congress might be the decisive point in Alia's quest to consolidate his power (*WMR*, August, p. 43).

Several changes in top positions offer a contradictory picture of the workings of the party hierarchy, for some cases seem to be demotions, while others look like rehabilitations. Çerava, the young nonentity who was elevated to the Secretariat in the wake of the post-Shehu purges (*YICA*, 1983, pp. 241–242), lost that position and was shifted to the post of deputy premier, one of Çarçani's four deputies, with Bekteshi the de facto number two man in the executive branch (ATA, 20 February; *FBIS*, 3 March). Çerava's place in the Secretariat was assumed by Çeliku, who had to relinquish his post as minister of industry and mines (ATA, 19 February; *FBIS*, 19 February). The assumption of a Secretariat post by Çeliku could have been interpreted as a promotion except that his ministry was singled out by Alia for serious shortcomings in production and for poor management (ATA, 11 July; *FBIS*, 19 July). Given Alia's sharp criticism of the performance of the Ministry of Industry and Mines, Çeliku's elevation to the Secretariat can only be explained as the product of forces beyond Alia's control that played a role in determining the composition of that critical body. (Alia's criticism was indeed pointed. "Things are not going too well in oil extraction," he stated at the Tenth Plenum of the Central Committee, "we have placed responsibility on the leading comrades in the Ministry of Energy and in the districts where oil and gas are being extracted" [ibid.].) Veteran of many posts, Petro Dode's reappearance on the scene suggests a regrouping of sorts. Dode, who earlier had been criticized for "excessive zeal" in eliminating private plots (*YICA*, 1987, p. 262), had served as chairman of the state planning commission, party chief of Shkodër, and deputy premier and was perceived as a key Shehu supporter, returned as chairman of the People's Assembly. Indications are that Dode was viewed by the Alia group as a problematic planner, and, to some extent, the failures of the sixth Five-Year Plan were laid at his doorstep, which may explain why he was replaced by Niko Gjizari. Dode's reappearance in a position of high visibility, receiving foreign guests and parliamentarians, supports the notion that some form of regrouping by diverse but not necessarily pro-Alia forces, perhaps under the tutelage of Hoxha's widow, is taking place (*RAD Background Report*, no. 16, 9 February). Finally, Isai, minister of internal affairs and the only man dropped from the Secretariat after the Ninth Party Congress, was also elevated to the post of deputy premier (ATA, 20 February; *FBIS*, 3 March). Although an ideologue in search of an orientation, Isai has made a habit of speaking on economic matters and supports the expansion of the private plots (*RAD Background Report*, no. 33, 10 March). In sum the postelection reshuffling of party and executive posts suggests weaknesses in Alia's position, for on the one hand there is the return of Dode, who two years ago opposed private plots and private livestock herds, but on the other hand, there is the elevation of Isai, who now openly supports them, "provided the products of the plot" are not sold in the open market (ibid.). Rounding out the situation is an apparent gain in stature by Asllani (party chief of Shkodër), who was given a high decoration at the young age of 50 (ATA, 17 October; *FBIS*, 19 October), and Bekteshi, who is now the number two man in the cabinet, a key Politburo member, and a known Hoxha supporter. On the periphery of these upper-echelon maneuverings stands Kondi, party chief of Tiranë and a known Stalinist, who started his own daily, *Tiranë*, the first new organ under the control of a regional party chief (ATA, 16 July; *FBIS*, 16 July).

Whereas the Alia team members seem to be jockeying for position, the Hoxha cult is being cultivated by his ardent supporters, especially his widow. On the anniversary of his death, the entire Politburo, the cabinet, and the leaders of the mass organizations visited Hoxha's gravesite and paid homage to "his genius" (ATA, 11 April; *FBIS*, 14 April). The publishing houses of Tiranë continue to issue and reissue Hoxha's collected works (now standing at volume 56) and the first volume of his diaries (ATA, 4 August; *FBIS*, 6 August). The popularity of the Hoxha cult makes the establishment of an Alia cult difficult, if not impossible. In the long run, this may be to Alia's advantage since Albanian society is long overdue for a pragmatic approach to its problems.

Domestic Politics. As usual the domestic agenda of the APL was dominated by economic issues and problems in productivity. The Third Plenum of the Central Committee was concerned about the market supply of essential goods, namely, agricultural products and protein foods (ATA, 23 April; *FBIS*, 27 April). As in the previous year, "bureaucratism" was singled out as a major problem hampering economic growth and smooth market supply (*Zeri i popullit*, 11 April). To overcome this, Alia and his party cadres sought to introduce some flexibility and pragmatism in management. Newspapers and journals emphasized the same theme on numerous occasions. "Styles and methods of work are not set once and for all," the party organ stated in a major editorial. "They change, they develop, and are enriched in accordance with new conditions and tasks" (ibid.).

To deal more effectively with economic issues, the Politburo of the party, speaking through the prime minister, reorganized the cabinet and brought on board new faces, most of them with economic training. The new Albanian cabinet now consists of 24 members, including four deputy premiers (one more than before). Çarçani and two of his deputies have economic-engineering training, one is an agricultural specialist, and one (Isai) is the product of Marxism-Leninism. Dropped from the post of deputy premier was Mihali, who was first appointed to that position in 1980 (*RAD Background Report*, no. 33, 10 March; ATA, 20 February; *FBIS*, 3 March). The Ministry of Light Industry and Food, headed by the widow of anti-Moscow architect Hysni Kapo, was divided. Vito Kapo kept her rank as minister of light industry, but the mayor of Elbassan, Jovan Bardhi, assumed the post of minister of food industry. The ministers of public services and public health were also replaced, along with the minister of education and culture, Tefta Çami. Skender Gjinush, a newcomer, replaced Çami in her position, but the ministry is now divested of its "cultural jurisdiction." Instead, a Committee for Culture and Arts was established, headed by Alfred Uçi who was given cabinet rank. Similarly a Committee on Science and Technology was created and its chairman, Ajet Ylli, was also given cabinet rank (ibid.).

Parliamentary Elections. On 1 February 1987, general elections for the 250 seats of the People's Assembly were held. The Democratic Front, headed by Nexhmije Hoxha, played a key role in spearheading the "electoral campaign" and in selecting all candidates. Alia was nominated and elected from district 21 of Tiranë, Hoxha's electoral district since 1946. Not surprisingly, all 1,830,653 eligible voters cast their ballots for the Front candidates. Only one vote was declared invalid "in accordance with Article 38 of the Law on Elections to the People's Assembly" (*Zeri i popullit*, 3 February). The composition of the parliament indicates an effort to rejuvenate the leadership and to bring educated young people into higher rank. According to the ATA (20 February), about 32 percent of the deputies were elected for the first time, 84 percent of whom have some form of higher education. In the new assembly 48 percent of the deputies are under the age of 40, another 42.8 percent are 40 to 60, and only 7.2 percent are over 60 (*Izvestiia*, 18 March; *Zeri i popullit*, 3 February). Thus, the Eleventh Legislature of the Albanian Socialist People's Republic commences work with an improved educational makeup and a relatively younger image, reflecting substantial turnover. A total of 97 deputies were elected for the first time, and 66 members of the assembly are women, an increase compared with the Tenth Legislature.

Auxiliary and Mass Organizations. The Tenth UTUA Congress was held in Tiranë on 25 June. Delegations from 26 Third World countries, Vietnam, Cambodia, and splinter communist groups from Great Britain, Denmark, and Spain attended. A communist delegation funded by the socialist government of Greece also attended the proceedings of the congress, and in true Marxist fashion, it praised the achievements of Albanian labor (ATA, 23 June; *FBIS*, 26 June). The main address to the congress, delivered by Koçallari, chairman of UTUA, included an exhortation to the working class to implement the "decisions of the Ninth APL Congress" (ATA, 25 June; *FBIS*, 29 June). The proceedings were followed by all members of the Politburo, and the congress was addressed by Çarçani, Alia, and other high-level party and cabinet officials. All admonished the working class to be more productive and to assist the party in curbing "bureaucratism" (*Zeri i popullit*, 27 June). Alia's speech went beyond economic matters to cover a wide range of issues with an emphasis on foreign policy. Taking advantage of the many foreign delegations present, Alia expanded on Albania's foreign policy philosophy of no relations with the superpowers but supported the idea of "multilateral or bilateral meetings as long as they do not lower the people's vigilance" (*Puna*, 26 June).

The Democratic Front was preoccupied for the first part of the year with the preparations for the general elections and the selection of candidates for the 250 seats in the People's Assembly. Its chairwoman, Nexhmije Hoxha, participated in numerous other activities and, on occasion, would express views on foreign policy issues as well. Thus she welcomed Greek prime minister Andreas Papandreou's "correct policy" in terminating the state of war with Albania (*Zeri i popullit*, 16 September), for she saw this as a vindication of her husband's policy vis-à-vis Greece.

The Ninth ULYA Congress was held on 20 October and, like the UTUA Congress, included delegations from numerous Third World countries and splinter Marxist groups (ATA, 20 October). The congress was addressed by Çeliku, a member of the Politburo and the Secretariat, as well as by other high-ranking officials (ATA, 24 October; *FBIS*, 24 October).

Alia addressed the congress in its closing day and exhorted its youth to orient their studies toward science, avoid foreign influences, and be vigilant against remnants of old bourgeois thinking. Elezi was re-elected first secretary of the ULYA, along with a fifteen-member Central Committee and an eleven-member Auditing Committee (*Zeri i rinise*, 25 October, p. 2). Many of the members of the ULYA Central Committee are also high party members, suggesting that nepotism is alive and well in "socialist" Albania.

Social Issues. Gradually but unmistakably, signs of impatience with the past are appearing in Albanian society. With Hoxha gone from the scene, the notion of change seems to have infected some top party members, among them the academician Çami, who is a key member of the Secretariat and the Politburo. In a major address before the Academy of Sciences, published in the theoretical organ *Rruga ë partisë* (no. 4, April 1987), Çami advocated needed changes in scientific research in social sciences and economics, two areas that have been stifled by orthodox clichés of Marxism-Leninism, and argued in favor of change "as long as the people's authority and its democratic nature are preserved." Once these things are secure, "other things can and must be changed when it becomes necessary, so long as it does not affect [adversely] the foundations of our socialist system" (ibid.; *RAD Background Report*, no. 90, 4 June).

Çami returned to the same themes in a speech at the October Plenum of the Central Committee meeting, in which he admitted that the Soviet "openness onslaught" had an impact on Albania and recommended that "changes" be made in all aspects. As he stated, "everything must be subjected to the test of practice; the criterion of practice must be the only criterion of truth." What remains unchanged, he said, "are our basic principles and general laws" (*Zeri i popullit*, 9 October; *RAD Background Report*, no. 200, 28 October). A more pointed criticism of the current state of the social-intellectual life of the country came from Professor Hamid Beqeja, a psychologist at the University of Tiranë. In a major article in *Zeri i popullit* (7 April), Professor Beqeja attacks those who believe that the "youth is going to the dogs" and who forget that many of the same pessimists "attempt to conceal their own failings with their political record, family histories, or long experience and become the reason for stagnation and deadlock in the process of our work" (*RAD Background Report*, no. 82, 21 May). In a more recent article, Professor Beqeja went even further on matters of intellectual freedom and the proper upbringing of youth. His analysis, entitled "On Broad View on Learning, Thinking and Creative Activity" (*Zeri i popullit*, 14 November), criticizes mechanical or "rote" learning because it depends on memory but even more because "it petrifies and standardizes thought, encourages pedantry, dogmatism and even conformism; it leaves no room for a conscious personal standpoint, for discussion and the clash of opinion, and least of all for the conflict which learning the truth requires" (ibid.). Obviously such thoughts, which sound Jeffersonian, would have been impossible if the distinguished scholar had no political patrons. Çami, himself an academician, could be the promoter of this Albanian-type *glasnost'*.

Judging from recurring references in the Albanian press, the authorities continue to have difficulties in containing the youth, a group that defies not only ideological training but even the law. "Antisocial" tendencies run the gamut from espousal of religious beliefs to outright thuggery. In an interview with Reuters, Professor Beqeja, also a prolific writer on youth matters, admitted that while "institutional religion does not exist, religious consciousness does; we cannot stop that through legal means" (Reuters, 30 April). But pervasive disregard for "socialist property" and outright theft manifest themselves throughout the country, often taking such perverse forms as hacking down trees in state parks (*Zeri i popullit*, 3 October; *Rruga ë partisë*, no. 9, September, pp. 25–32).

Cultural degeneration and lack of imagination among artists and writers also came under severe criticism during an extended plenum of the Union of Albanian Writers and Artists (*Zeri i popullit*, 24 March). Dritero Agolli, chairman of the union, decried the complacency toward mediocrity and the tendency of local writers' organizations to reward such mediocrity by granting extended leave to aspiring authors and artists for creative thinking without considering whether they are capable of producing what they promise (*Drita*, 15 February). The low level in the cultural life of the country, according to a major article in the party daily, is related to "passive and mechanical study," which "having been cultivated in childhood and at school, the disease of standardized, uncreative learning and thinking continues in adult life" and often "assumes the most fossilized and conservative character" (*Zeri i popullit*, 14 November). This kind of self-criticism is new in Albania and will not be easily contained.

The Economy and Its Problems. The Albanian economy lumbered along during 1987 without resolving its critical problems of plant modernization, increased productivity, and market demands. The year started off with promises of incentives to spark productivity, but these incentives were calculated so as to make little difference to the workers or peasants. For example, exceeding a quota by 1 percent may qualify a worker for an increase, but then quality is thrown in as a measurement (*Zeri i popullit*, 15 January), which has nothing to do with the amount of work put in by a worker. Thus, in coal extraction, the Btus of the product are taken into account for worker remuneration. However, the authorities seem to be moving away from past efforts to keep the gap between manual and white-collar labor as narrow as possible (ibid.).

The deputy minister of finance, Robert Koli, placed some of the blame for poor economic performance on the lack of adequate economic training, a deficiency that begins in the schools (*Zeri i popullit*, 27 February). Despite three related legislative decrees aimed at improving productivity, the government still complained that a "harmony between moral and material incentives" has not been found. What the government does not admit, however, is that the incentives, as stated above, were basically a sham. For example, according to *Zeri i popullit*, "those who work underground in copper and pyrite mines, fulfill their expected norms, and are never absent without a cause will be given a bonus of up to 2 percent of each 1 percent of output above plan, *depending on the proportion of copper in the ore*" (ibid.).

Another perennial problem is the inability of Albanian economic enterprises to keep their accounts straight. The party daily decried the "wall of imprecise accounts" despite the "party's instructions to managers and economic institutions to take measures to prevent euphoric and imaginary accounting" (*Zeri i popullit*, 14 November).

Although Albania has insisted all along that its economic system is immune to the tribulations of capitalist and revisionist economies, Gjizari, chairman of the state planning commission, and Prime Minister Çarçani both stressed the need to "become better acquainted with and to make proper use of circumstances in the world economy and the world markets" (*Zeri i popullit*, 17 May). Acquaintance with world market conditions complements political moves toward more pragmatic relations with the outside world. Perhaps the fundamental problem of productivity is to be found in the high expectations set by the Ninth Party Congress, which, for industry at least, decided that about 74 percent of the growth in production will be attained through fuller use of existing plants and equipment (*Zeri i popullit*, 15 May). However, existing equipment and plants are obsolete and spare parts, scarce.

Notwithstanding all the efforts by the lower apparatchiks to put forth as good an image as possible, the economy was in serious trouble, according to Alia's report to the Tenth Plenum of the Central Committee (ATA, 11 July; *FBIS*, 15 July). Alia candidly admitted serious shortcomings and made no pretense of hiding errors. His language was indeed blunt. "Compared with last year," he stated, "national revenues have shown an absolute decline." He placed the blame on poor management, the central department, inadequate organization, and lack of discipline and control. Oil, chrome, and agricultural production, all important hard currency earners, have declined, Alia stated. "The chrome industry has placed us in an unexpected situation due to its deficits. The planned extraction of chrome is tens of thousands of tons short" (ibid.). He zeroed in on the Ministry of Industry and Mines, which "ignored the problems" for too long and failed to make needed investments to improve the conditions of the plants.

There were no meaningful departures in budgetary allocations for 1987. The state budget foresees an income of 9.350 billion leks (an increase of only 50 million leks from 1986) and expenditures of 9.3 billion leks. Like last year, a surplus of 50 million leks is expected (*Zeri i popullit*, 22 February, pp. 1, 6). National defense recovered 200 million leks more than last year, and there is a small increase in the budget for the maintenance of the administrative apparatus. The bulk of state expenditures (5.076 billion leks) goes toward the development of industry, agriculture, transportation, and other areas that

Alia stated needed urgent modernization. Allocations for cultural and social programs have been reduced by approximately 100 million leks (ibid.).

Foreign Relations. The process of expanding contacts with the West and Third World countries, initiated by Prime Minister Shehu in 1976, continued during 1987 and apparently acquired a pattern of stability and endurance. Diplomatic relations were established with the Philippines (ATA, 13 June), Uruguay (ATA, 15 October), and Bolivia (ATA, 25 August), and Tiranë's ties to Iran seem to get closer (*Zeri i popullit*, 20 October). However, two important events support the notion that Albania is feeling quite confident with its policy of gradual opening and careful expansion of ties with noncommunist European countries.

First, on 28 August, the Greek minister of foreign affairs, Karolos Papoulias, a smooth apparatchik in Papandreou's regime, recommended to the cabinet that the state of war between Greece and Albania be terminated unilaterally (*Kathimerini*, 29 August). Although the opposition leader, Constantine Mitsotakis, immediately announced that he is not bound by the government's decision if he comes to power since it was reached in an unconstitutional manner in that the president of the republic and parliament were not consulted as required by the constitution, the last international anomaly caused by World War II came to an end. The Tiranë regime welcomed the "realistic" approach of the Greek government and made vague promises about further expanding relations between the two countries (*Zeri i popullit*, 16 September).

This upswing in Greek-Albanian relations culminated in a visit by Papoulias to Tiranë, accompanied by the minister of national economy, Panayote Roumeliotes; the minister of culture, Melina Mercouri; the minister of environment, Evangelos Couloumbis; and the general secretary of the ministry of foreign affairs, Constantinos Yeorgiou (ATA, November 18; *FBIS*, 19 November). The Greek delegation signed eight different agreements but made no progress on a Greek request for permission to travel to Albania by private automobiles or a ferry boat connection linking Corfu and Sarandes. During their stay in Albania the members of the Greek delegation visited several areas inhabited by the Greek minority, and Papoulias met with his former communist classmates of Pogoniani high school, close to the Greek-Albanian border, where Papoulias was first exposed to Marxism.

Second, relations between Albania and the Federal Republic of Germany were normalized in a pompous manner on 15 September, after three years of demands by the Albanian government for war reparations (*CSM*, 17 September, p. 12). Foreign Minister Hans-Dietrich Genscher traveled to Tiranë to open the West German embassy, which is temporarily housed in the Hotel Dajti (ATA, 23 October; *FBIS*, 26 October). Currently, Great Britain and the Soviet Union are the only major European powers without diplomatic relations in Tiranë. Pragmatism forced Tiranë to abandon its war reparations claim in the hope that West German investment toward plant modernization would be forthcoming. To that end, Franz-Josef Strauss, the Bavarian premier and famous anticommunist, ventured to Tiranë to get a head start in future investments (ATA, 16 November; *FBIS*, 17 November). Strauss was received by all major figures of the Albanian government as a "friend" of the country (ibid.). As evidence of his "friendship," the Bavarian premier issued an "authorization of disposal" of six million marks, a sum the Albanian government can use to purchase goods of its choice in West Germany, "except weapons and police vehicles" (Hamburg DPA, 16 November; *FBIS*, 17 November).

Relations between Albania and the superpowers seem frozen for the time being. Alia's speech at Vlorë on the 75th anniversary of Albanian independence and the speech of the prime minister on the same occasion leave little room for optimism (ATA, 28 November; *FBIS*, 30 November). The November speech was a reaffirmation of earlier statements, which were even tougher vis-à-vis the Soviet Union and the United States. For example, Alia's speech to his constituents of district 210 in Tiranë made no distinction between the United States and the Soviet Union as far as their "motives toward" Albania are concerned. "American imperialism has always been present in all the military pressures against Albania, in all political onslaughts and economic blockades," Alia stated (ATA, 29 November; *FBIS*, 2 February). Leaving no doubts about the future, he continued, "the Albanian people and their Party of Labor will never take a step toward rapprochement with the United States" (ibid.). As far as the Soviet Union is concerned, Alia stated that "it constitutes as great a danger to our country, to peace and to freedom of the peoples, as U.S. imperialism does. No pressure, flattery, or circumstance can cause our party to deviate from the line hitherto tested," he concluded (ibid.).

Despite the tough talk, however, the Albanian leadership during the past year has improved its state-to-state relations with all Soviet allies in East Europe and signed trade protocols with them. There was a similar expansion in relations with all NATO countries, except Great Britain and the United States. Negotiations are progressing with Great Britain to find a resolution for the return of Albanian gold (estimated at $70 million) and a face-saving method to pay reparations for the Corfu incident of 1946, when two British destroyers were sunk by mines allegedly laid by Albania (*CSM*, 17 September).

Albanian-Yugoslav relations followed the ups and downs of previous years, with Tiranë taking the offensive against Belgrade's military measures in Kosovo and the alleged repression of Albanian cultural life (*Drita*, 26 July; *Zeri i popullit*, 23 October). Despite the persistence of polemics carried out by the press on each side, Tiranë announced that it will participate in a multilateral conference to be held at Belgrade in February 1988, provided that this meeting is prepared carefully and with a "defined agenda in order to avoid anything unexpected and lead to the improvement and development of bilateral and multilateral relations of the Balkan countries" (ATA, 17 October; *FBIS*, 19 October).

Relations with Turkey continued at the pace and frequency of previous years. Commencing with a visit by the speaker of the Turkish grand assembly, Necmentin Karaduman, Ankara and Tiranë sought to build on their "traditional" good relations, which apparently are based on their shared Muslim culture (ATA, 20 March; *FBIS*, 23 March). Aware of the state of Greek-Turkish relations, the Tiranë regime is always careful to keep Ankara apprised of its contacts with Athens. Thus, a day after the Greek delegation, headed by Foreign Minister Papoulias left Albania for Greece, Deputy Foreign Minister Sokrat Pliaka flew to Ankara, where he was received by Prime Minister Turgut Ozal and Foreign Minister Vahit Halefoglou (ATA, 24 November; *FBIS*, 26 November).

Italian-Albanian contacts continued at a slower pace during 1987. Relations between the two countries are affected by Italy's refusal to turn over to Albanian authorities a six-member Albanian family that sought asylum in the Italian embassy at Tiranë in 1985 (*YICA*, 1986, p. 263). The year began with Albania seizing two Italian fishing boats, which allegedly violated its territorial waters during Albanian military maneuvers. The eight-member crews were put on trial in the city of Vlorë and given suspended sentences of four to ten months (*FBIS*, 9 January; ANSA in English, 9 January). The two captains were initially sentenced to one year in prison, only to have this reduced by the Albanian Supreme Court to suspended sentences and release (ATA, 13 January; *FBIS*, 13 January). In a similar incident during 1963, the crews were returned without trial after a fifteen-day detention. The Albanian position on critical issues that affect the world in general and the Middle East in particular is at odds even with militant Third World movements with which the country fraternizes.

The theoretical journal *Rruga ë partisë* (no. 10, October) as well as the daily organ *Zeri i popullit* (3 April) rejected the whole idea of disarmament as "evidence of superpower cynicism." A senior commentator, Bardhyl Cani, viewed general security as a Soviet imperialist theory and policy, which if accepted would mean negation of the idea of national security. "On the political plane," he argued, "the idea of general security is openly contrary to the security, sovereignty, and independence of all countries; the Soviet revisionists have come out openly against national security" (*Zeri i popullit*, 3 April). Myftiu, deputy premier and Politburo member who gave the keynote address on the festivities marking the October Revolution, mocked Gorbachev's policy of *perestroika* as a desperate attempt to improve his country's image abroad that was badly damaged by its "abandonment of Marxism-Leninism." The "new" Moscow policy, Myftiu stated, is aimed at "fooling the imperialists too, who believe that opening up the Soviet Union would mean the kneeling of the Soviet society, when the latter has in mind to improve and create a strong economy as a means of achieving its imperialist goals" (ATA, 7 November; *FBIS*, 9 November; *Rruga ë partisë*, no. 10, October, pp. 67–76).

In the Middle East conflict, the Albanians seem to have opted for Iran because of the greater opportunity to attack U.S. imperialism. Further evidence of that is the exchange of visits between the two countries and the warm greetings exchanged by Alia and Iran's president on the latter's national day (*Zeri i popullit*, 20 October).

Party Relations. A total of 26 procommunist delegations attended the Tenth Congress of the UTUA in Tiranë, reflecting Albania's ties with Third World and Marxist splinter parties in Europe. There were no party-to-party contacts with Eastern Europe or the Soviet Union during 1987, but an Albanian delegation attended the congress of the

Vietnamese Communist Party (ATA, 18 April; *FBIS*, 7 May). A group headed by Dode also visited Cambodia to support the Vietnamese incursions into that country and, ironically, placing Albania on the same side as Moscow (ATA, 5 May; *FBIS*, 7 May). Despite the lack of official contacts between Tiranë and Moscow, the Soviet press continued to give full and favorable coverage to events and "achievements" in Albania. Alia rejected all this publicity as devious flattery (ATA, 28 November; *FBIS*, 2 November).

Nikolaos A. Stavrou
Howard University

Bulgaria

Population. 8,960,749

Party. Bulgarian Communist Party (Bŭlgarska komunisticheska partiya; BCP)

Founded. Bulgarian Social Democratic Party founded in 1891; split into Broad and Narrow factions in 1903; the Narrow Socialists became the BCP and joined the Comintern in 1919.

Membership. 932,055. According to information presented at the Thirteenth Party Congress in April 1986, 44.36 percent of the members are classified as industrial workers, and 16.31 percent are classified as agricultural workers (BCP Central Committee Report to the Thirteenth Congress, Bŭlgarska telegrafna agentsiya, 5 April 1986; *FBIS*, 8 April). Bulgaria no longer publishes data on ethnic minorities; ethnic Turks and Gypsies, the two largest minority groups, are believed to be underrepresented in the party in proportion to their numbers in the general population.

General Secretary. Todor Khristov Zhivkov (b. 7 September 1911)

Politburo. 11 full members: Todor Zhivkov (chairman, State Council), Chudomir Alexandrov (b. 1936), Georgi Atanasov (b. 1933, prime minister), Milko Balev (b. 1920, member, State Council), Ognyan Doynov (b. 1935), Dobri Dzhurov (b. 1916, minister of national defense), Grisha Filipov (b. 1919), Pencho Kubadinski (b. 1918, member, State Council; chairman, Fatherland Front), Petŭr Mladenov (b. 1936, minister of foreign affairs), Stanko Todorov (b. 1920, chairman, National Assembly), Yordan Yotov (b. 1920); 6 candidate members: Petŭr Dyulgerov (b. 1929, chairman, Central Council of Trade Unions), Andrey Lukanov (b. 1938, minister of foreign economic relations), Stoian Markov (b. 1942), Grigor Stoichkov (b. 1926, deputy prime minister), Dimitŭr Stoyanov (b. 1928, minister of internal affairs), Georgi Yordanov (b. 1931, minister of culture, science, and education)

Secretariat. 9 members: Chudomir Alexandrov, Milko Balev, Grisha Filipov, Emil Khristov (b. 1924, member, State Council), Stoyan Mikhailov (b. 1930), Dimitŭr Stanishev (b. 1924), Vasil Tsanov (b. 1922), Yordan Yotov, Kiril Zarev (b. 1926)

Central Committee. 194 full and 145 candidate members

Status. Ruling party

Last Congress. Thirteenth, 2–5 April 1986, in Sofia; next one scheduled for 1991.

Last Election. 8 June 1986. All candidates ran on the ticket of the Fatherland Front, an umbrella organization (4.4 million members) comprising most mass organizations. Fatherland Front candidates received 99.9 percent of votes cast. Of the National Assembly's 400 members, 276 belong to the BCP and 99 to the Agrarian Union; 25 are unaffiliated (most of these are Komsomol members). The Bulgarian Agrarian National Union (BANU, 120,000 members) formally shares power with the BCP and holds 3 of the 27 seats on the State Council; has places in the ministries of justice, public health, and social welfare; and fills about one-sixth of the people's council seats. BANU leader Petŭr Tanchev's post as first deputy chairman of the State Council makes him Todor Zhivkov's nominal successor as head of state.

Auxiliary Organizations. Central Council of Trade Unions (CCTU, about 4 million members), led by Petŭr Dyulgerov; Dimitrov Communist Youth League (Komsomol, 1.5 million members), led by Andrey Bundzhulov; Civil Defense Organization (750,000 members), led by Colonel General Tencho Papazov, provides training in paramilitary tactics and disaster relief; Committee on Bulgarian Women (30,000 members), led by Elena Lagadinova, stimulates patriotism and social activism.

Publications. *Rabotnichesko delo* (*RD*; Workers' Cause), BCP daily, edited by Radoslav Radov;

Partien zhivot (Party Life), BCP monthly; *Novo vreme* (New Time), BCP theoretical journal; *Otechestven front* (Fatherland Front), front daily; *Dŭrzhaven vestnik* (State Gazette), contains texts of laws and decrees. Bulgarska telegrafna agentsiya (BTA) is the official news agency.

The Soviet examples of *glasnost'* and *perestroika* had a powerful impact on Bulgaria during the year. Campaigns against alcoholism and corruption were pursued, and the media exposed abuses of power and shortcomings in economic and political life, although at a lower level of intensity than their USSR counterparts. According to party leaders, Bulgaria was entering a period of transition from "power on behalf of the people to power through the people," and major reforms were introduced to allow for greater economic and political "self-management." The full impact of these reforms was not yet clear when the year ended.

Leadership and Party Organization. Zhivkov gave no sign that he felt threatened by the new environment that has emerged in many of the communist-ruled countries of the world since Gorbachev came to power in the USSR. Zhivkov pursued a vigorous schedule, delivering a number of major addresses on Bulgaria's reform program and making several trips abroad, including a five-day visit to China. In West Germany he told a correspondent from *Die Welt* (5 June) that, having abandoned alcohol and tobacco and taken up jogging, he might live to be 120 and that he planned to remain in power since Bulgaria "had not found anyone better."

Although no changes were made in the membership of the Politburo or Secretariat during the year, large-scale shake-ups in economic and political administration had a major impact on the party at all levels. At a BCP Central Committee plenum 28–29 June, Zhivkov called for a broad series of economic and political changes, including the creation of a "Bulgarian Association of Commodity Producers" to act as a "coordinating body" for the management of the economy (*RD*, 29 July; *FBIS*, 5 August). Two months later, however, the National Assembly adopted a different scheme of reorganization. It abolished the four councils (economic, social, intellectual development, and agriculture and forests) that were created last year (see *YICA*, 1987). It also eliminated the post of first deputy prime minister and six of the seven deputy prime ministerships and disbanded several economic committees. In their place, the assembly approved the creation of five new ministries: agriculture and forestry; public health and welfare; culture, science, and education; economy and planning; and foreign economic relations. In the personnel shifts that accompanied this reform, the biggest loser appeared to be Politburo member Doynov, who had headed the old Economic Council. At the July plenum Zhivkov criticized the council for failing to overcome bureaucratic obstacles to reform, and Doynov was given no new position when the council was abolished. The new Ministry of the Economy and Planning is headed by Stoyan Ovcharov, who was almost unknown at the time of his appointment. Reportedly about 45, Ovcharov was trained at Moscow in the field of biotechnology. His previous post was that of first deputy chairman of the State Committee for Science and Technological Progress under candidate Politburo member Markov. Although a party member, Ovcharov was not even a candidate member of its Central Committee. His elevation over Doynov and Markov represented a sensational advance and will probably be followed by promotion in the party hierarchy. Late in the year he was returned to the National Assembly in a by-election.

Other shifts were less dramatic. Aleksi Ivanov was appointed minister of agriculture and forestry. He had previously been chairman of the Council on Agriculture and Forests. Politburo member Yordanov, who had headed the Council on Intellectual Development, was appointed minister of culture, science, and education. Lukanov, who had been a first deputy prime minister, became minister of foreign economic relations. And Radoi Popivanov, a member of the Agrarian Union, was named minister of public health and welfare (RFE, *Situation Report*, 21 August).

On 17 March it was announced that Yotov would leave his post as editor in chief of the party daily (*RD*) to "concentrate entirely on his responsibilities as a member of the Politburo and party Secretariat" (BTA, 17 March; *FBIS*, 19 March). In his memorandum on the January CPSU Central Committee plenum and its significance for Bulgaria, Zhivkov criticized *RD* for its "cautious and delicate attitude" toward exposing the shortcomings of party and government organs. However, the appointment as editor in chief of Radov, Yotov's deputy editor since 1981 but only a candidate member of the BCP Central Committee, did not suggest that major policy changes would follow, and indeed the paper continued to show restraint in its treatment of problem areas.

Mitko Grigorov, a former Politburo member who was once considered a possible successor to Zhivkov, died on 6 September. Grigorov had been chief of the party's ideological sector until purged by Zhivkov in 1966. He subsequently received a number of diplomatic posts and in 1974 was made a deputy chairman of the State Council, signifying his substantial rehabilitation (RFE, *Situation Report,* 16 September).

The winds of change in the party blew strongest at the district level, beginning with a shake-up of the Sofia City BCP Committee. Last year Anastasi Donchev was appointed its first secretary following severe criticism of the committee's past performance (see *YICA,* 1987). Even after his appointment criticism continued, and Zhivkov on at least two occasions singled out the Sofia leadership for failing to make the capital a showplace for national technological development and for demonstrating a conservative, "patriarchal" atmosphere. On 24 March CPSU Politburo member Mikhail Solomentsev visited Sofia, delivering an address on "the politics of restructuring" to the city's party leadership. On the following day Donchev was suddenly dismissed and replaced by Ivan Panev, first secretary of the district party committee in Plovdiv. Panev, born in 1933, had gained a reputation for dynamic leadership in Plovdiv, Bulgaria's second-largest city, and had been included in the five-man delegation that represented Bulgaria at the Twenty-seventh CPSU Congress in 1986. Donchev was appointed first deputy chairman of the State Committee on Research and Technology, an important position but clearly inferior to his previous post. Panev was replaced in Plovdiv by Panteley Pachov, who had led the municipal party committee (BTA, 25 March; *RD,* 20 March; *FBIS,* 26 March; RFE, *Situation Report,* 20 May).

At the end of 1986 Zhivkov sharply criticized the administrative structure of the country. He complained that Bulgaria's 28 districts pursued "feudal" policies, aiming at economic self-sufficiency without regard for national needs, and that they had developed entrenched, conservative bureaucracies that stifled initiative at the lower level. In February representatives from the district party committees and people's councils of Russe and Razgrad signed an agreement committing the two districts to a program of integration in the "material, social, and intellectual spheres" that would apply until the year 2000, and Veliko Turnovo and Gabrovo districts formed a similar relationship in June.

During the summer these rather modest experiments were superseded by a comprehensive reform of district and local government. On 7 July the National Assembly declared that municipalities would become "self-managing communities" and indicated that they would be given greater economic independence and increased political power vis-à-vis the district authorities (*RD,* 8 July; *FBIS,* 14 July). This was followed on 21 August by legislation that replaced the system of 28 district governments with nine consolidated regions (*oblasti*). With the exception of the Sofia City *oblast,* which is identical to the old district, the *oblasti* were formed by consolidating districts into regions roughly equal in territory and population. The new *oblasts,* named for their regional centers, were Burgas, Khaskovo, Lovech, Mikhailovgrad, Plovdiv, Razgrad, Sofia, Sofia City, and Varna. This reform, which was adopted with almost no advance publicity, caused consternation in some of the district capitals that had been placed in subordinate positions. Neshka Robeva, a member of the National Assembly and the trainer of Bulgaria's world champion rhythmic gymnastics team, voted against the bill in protest against the "degradation" of her native Russe, which had been made a part of the Razgrad *oblast.* This is the first known case in communist Bulgaria of a negative vote being cast in parliament.

Although the legislation stated that the consolidation of the districts would take place gradually over the course of the year, the Politburo announced a decision to proceed with the consolidation at once and appointed "temporary" *oblast* party committees and people's councils, which amounted to a virtual coup d'état directed against the district leaderships. Only about one-third of the members of the district party committees and people's councils were appointed to positions at the *oblast* level. Politburo member Chudomir Alexandrov, who is in charge of cadres, said that most of the displaced officials would most probably find work at the local level or in economic enterprises. For most of them this would appear to be a demotion (RFE, *Situation Report,* 16 September).

In a further elaboration of the territorial reform, Zhivkov stressed the importance of multicandidate elections "at all levels," and the first of these, for positions on the local and *oblast* people's councils, were expected to take place in February 1988 (*RD,* 20 November; *FBIS,* 1 December). In his report to the July plenum, Zhivkov stated that the adoption of the principle of self-management in the economic and administrative spheres would require changes in the constitution. He suggested specifically that the State Council, which seems never to have become much more than an honorific body, ought to be abolished and that the National Assembly should become "a collective working body of self-management." A commission was appointed to prepare amendments to the constitution for consideration during 1988 (Press release of the Bulgarian Embassy in Washington, D.C., 28 July).

In a move against "pomposity, megalomania, and needless extravagance," the Politburo decreed a reform of party imagery and state rituals. The intention was to do away with slogans and billboards on buildings and along roadways and to restrict the display of portraits and busts to government buildings. Moreover, no portraits or busts of living political leaders, Bulgarian or Soviet, are to be displayed. The flag and national emblem are to provide the primary symbols in parades and on patriotic occasions. The decree also stated that decorations and medals will in the future be given only for merit, rather than because of the age or position of the recipient, and several categories of awards were abolished (RFE, *Situation Report*, 21 August). The Politburo also abolished the privileges enjoyed by certain categories of applicants for admission to educational programs. Particular schools or courses of study are the gateway to successful careers, and it has long been the practice to give preference to the children of "active fighters against fascism and capitalism" and to holders of certain decorations. According to the Politburo decree, educational admissions will now be determined exclusively by grades and the needs of regions and enterprises. If actually carried out, this reform would strike at an important mechanism that the elite uses to ensure the well-being of its sons and daughters, which is strongly resented by ordinary citizens (BTA, 21 August; *FBIS*, 24 August).

Internal Affairs. *Glasnost'.* In its evaluation of the January CPSU plenum and its significance for Bulgaria, the BCP Politburo stated that candor and freedom of criticism must play a central role in restructuring. But while the Bulgarian regime has enthusiastically embraced economic and administrative reform, it has lagged behind the Soviet Union in encouraging a policy of openness in the media. Zhivkov and other party leaders called throughout the year for an intensified struggle against "negative phenomena," a term that includes corruption and abuse of power by party or state officials. The party daily reported that Georgi Vutev, a candidate member of the BCP Central Committee and a former deputy minister of foreign trade, had been given the maximum sentence of fifteen years in prison for accepting bribes and for "currency crimes" (*RD*, 17 January; *FBIS*, 21 January). Later in the spring, the party press commented with some sympathy on a work stoppage that occurred at a machine-building plant in Mezdra. The reporter wrote that although the factory management had not violated any laws, it had shown insensitivity to the legitimate concerns of the workers (*RD*, 5 May; *FBIS*, 13 May). At a party plenum in November, Zhivkov suggested that *RD* should be the organ of the whole party, not just of its Central Committee, and that it should not fear to take positions in opposition to the party leadership (*RD*, 20 November; *FBIS*, 1 December).

Opposition to *glasnost'* was also discernible. In an interview with the *Financial Times* of London (10 March), Politburo member Alexandrov said that Bulgaria had sufficient openness in its media and had nothing to learn on that subject from the USSR. Lalyu Dimitrov, chairman of the Committee for Television and Radio, was abruptly dismissed in August amid criticism that Bulgarian television was insufficiently positive and that it "rummaged for weaknesses and mistakes as an end in itself" and frequently portrayed the economy as being on the verge of collapse. Dimitrov's successor, Lyubomir Pavlov, has had a career in the party's cultural bureaucracy (BTA, 20 August; *FBIS*, 21 August).

As in the USSR, members of the creative intelligentsia provided the most evident support for greater freedom of expression, although their views were often presented in abstract terms. A striking exception to this tendency, however, was provided by the well-known writer Evtim Evtimov, editor of *Literaturen front*, who was quite specific in calling for the party to publish the complete stenographic record of the April 1956 plenum that began Bulgaria's de-Stalinization process, the complete records of the investigation and trial of Traicho Kostov, and the records of the 1942 interrogation of Anton Ivanov by Bulgarian authorities. Each of these events is surrounded by a cloud of myth in party tradition, and the first two involved party leaders, including Zhivkov, who are still on the scene (*Literaturen front*, 15 October; *FBIS*, 26 October).

The appointment of Lyudmil Staykov as director general of the film industry in January was welcomed by film directors and critics. Staykov, who has directed some of the best-known Bulgarian films, is the first director general in fifteen years actually to come from the film industry. His predecessors were criticized for managerial heavy-handedness and for not being open to different ways of thinking. It was also admitted that in the past many films "had not been allowed to reach their audience" by the authorities (RFE, *Situation Report,* 31 March).

Economy. According to the government's report, Bulgaria's domestic net material product grew during 1986 at a rate of 5.5 percent, substantially exceeding the target of 4.0 percent. Much of this growth came in the agricultural sector, which increased output by "over 10 percent," reflecting recovery from a severe drought that had caused a sharp drop in output in 1985. Industry saw its best performances in coal mining (up 10.2 percent) and machine building (up 9.3 percent). Energy production remained a problem owing to lower water levels that reduced hydroelectric production, to delays in nuclear power expansion, and to outdated technology in many thermoelectric plants. Electricity production grew by only 0.5 percent in 1986 and remained well below 1983 and 1984 levels (*RD,* 30 January; RFE, *Situation Report,* 31 May). In October the government issued a series of directives to the population aimed at conserving household consumption of electricity to avoid blackouts during the winter months (RFE, *Situation Report,* 20 November).

In keeping with the new system of economic management, no plan was adopted for 1987. Rather, the National Assembly approved the Ninth Five-Year Plan (for 1986–1990) and left it to the Council of Ministers to work out the annual implementation. The five-year plan itself called for a 30 percent increase in domestic net material product (as opposed to the 20 percent increase achieved in 1981–1985) and for substantial structural changes. Priority will be given to development in the fields of electronics and robotics, biochemistry, electric transport systems, laser technology, and optical electronics. These priorities clearly reflect Zhivkov's goals of carrying through the "scientific-technical revolution" in Bulgaria and becoming competitive with advanced Western states (*RD,* 23 December 1986).

Since the first form of the "new economic mechanism" was introduced at the end of the 1970s, Bulgaria has repeatedly experimented with different techniques and organizational arrangements intended to stimulate initiative from below and to introduce at least some degree of market principles. In an address to a BCP plenum held at the end of 1986, Prime Minister Atanasov admitted that previous reforms had not had the desired effect owing to their limited implementation, the confusion at lower levels, and the lack of a positive attitude on the part of economic managers who were reluctant to abandon old habits. Atanasov announced that, in the future, the state would continue to be responsible for the overall management of the economy, but it would exercise its control indirectly through taxes, interest rates, credits, control of foreign currency, and the placing of direct orders with enterprises, rather than by assigning specific plan targets. Within this framework, enterprises would be free to contract with suppliers and to plan their own output but would be subject to market discipline, implying that inefficient producers would be allowed to fail. Atanasov also envisioned the formation of trusts and "associations of a new type" that would assist in planning and financing through a "dialogue" with the enterprises. Apparently taking a page from the Hungarian experience, Atanasov stated that there would be a "radical increase" in the role of commercial banks, which would participate extensively in the activities of the trusts and enterprises. Finally, he stated that prices would be set on the basis of international markets and that Bulgarian producers would have to adjust to these, although there would be a period of transition during which state subsidies to noncompetitive enterprises would continue (*RD,* 23 December 1986; *FBIS,* 6 January; RFE, *Situation Report,* 13 February).

In his memorandum on the January plenum of the CPSU Central Committee and its significance for Bulgaria (Sofia Domestic Service, 18 February; *FBIS,* 27 February), Zhivkov stressed the need for pressing forward with the implementation of economic reforms, complaining that too often in the past party initiatives had been allowed "to fall into oblivion." On 29 April the National Assembly published a declaration transferring socialist property to labor collectives for management. Although the implications of this transfer remain unclear, it seemed intended to instill among the workers a greater sense of control over economic decision-making on the lower level (RFE, *Situation Report,* 20 May).

Dissent. Open expressions of dissent in Bulgaria have been rare in recent years, but in March the U.S. delegation to the Helsinki review conference in Vienna presented an appeal from a group of six Bulgarians calling for "human rights and fundamental freedoms." The appeal proposed the creation of a permanent intra-European commission to monitor the way in which each country signatory to the Helsinki Accords provides for such basic rights as freedom of movement, emigration, access to objective information, and free choice of work and to expose those regimes that signed the accords only as a "diversionary maneuver." A Bulgarian delegate to the conference described one signer of the appeal, Grigor Simov Bozhilov, as "mentally unbalanced." It was later reported that Bozhilov had been sentenced to three years internment in a village near the Romanian border. The French newspaper *Le Quotidien de Paris* (2 April) published a telephone interview with another signer, Eduard Genov, who was described as a 41-year-old stonemason. He stated that he had signed the appeal "because of the repression that State Security has imposed for years."

The same French newspaper (13 March) and French television also called attention to the case of a 50-year-old mechanic, Dimitur Penchev, who had been periodically persecuted for political offenses since the early 1960s. According to these reports, Penchev was being held without trial and threatened with prosecution for espionage. The Bulgarian journal *Anteni* (6 May) accused the French media of spreading "absurd allegations" and of seeking to damage Bulgaria's reputation. (RFE, *Situation Report,* 20 May.) Nevertheless, after continued remonstrances in the French press and from the labor union *Force Ouvriere,* Penchev was released and allowed to emigrate. He and his family arrived in Paris during July.

A number of protests against Bulgaria's treatment of its Turkish minority came from within the country and from Bulgarian Turks who had managed to emigrate. According to their stories, Bulgaria continued to imprison individuals who insisted on retaining their Turkish identities. The Bulgarian press rejected these claims (Amnesty International, *Bulgaria: Continuing Human Rights Abuses Against Ethnic Turks,* July 1987).

Acquired Immunodeficiency Syndrome (AIDS). In March the Ministry of Public Health announced the first death from AIDS in Bulgaria and at the same time stated that blood tests conducted on "high-risk groups" had turned up an additional 22 carriers of the virus. Nineteen of those infected, including the fatality, were said to be foreigners resident in the country, while the three ethnic Bulgarians were reported to be hemophiliacs who had received contaminated blood products. The ministry reported that some unspecified measures against AIDS had been taken as early as 1983, but these had not been given much publicity. Bulgarians were reassured that an AIDS epidemic was unlikely in the country since the principal high-risk groups, homosexuals and intravenous drug users, were "extraordinarily rare."

After the ministry's announcement the press began to discuss the disease more openly, informing the public that it could not be transmitted in food or water or by normal social contact but recommending abstention from promiscuous sexual activity by both homosexuals and heterosexuals. The use of condoms was also recommended, but these are believed to be in limited supply and of poor quality.

Measures adopted by the government to control the spread of AIDS included testing donated blood and organs and the compulsory testing among high-risk groups. The press continued to repeat the Soviet-inspired disinformation that AIDS was created by military genetic engineers in the United States, but testing in Bulgaria was focused on students from African countries, where the disease has already reached epidemic proportions. An amendment to the law on resident foreigners stated that anyone found capable of spreading a contagious disease would be deported without delay. Later in the year the national news agency of Zimbabwe reported that two students from Zimbabwe and one from Zambia had been sent home from Sofia in accordance with this law. (RFE, *Situation Report,* 20 May.)

Further testing discovered several more Bulgarian carriers of the AIDS virus, including at least one who had come down with the disease. Most of these were again described as hemophiliacs, but it was admitted that one was a homosexual and another a prostitute. On 1 July the newspaper *Trud* published a sharp attack on the Ministry of Health for its slowness in carrying out measures to protect the population and for its reluctance to disseminate detailed information about the disease. According to *Trud* there were widespread, irrational fears about the disease that were fueled by distrust of the ministry's statements. Perhaps in response to this criticism, later in the summer the ministry began the broad distribution of a pamphlet on AIDS that was straightforward and frank in its presentation. Stating that *glasnost'* in the discussion of the disease must be one of the principal weapons in fighting it, the pamphlet described the nature of AIDS, its etiology and recent spread, and the measures to combat it being undertaken around the world. It also warned that each citizen should be aware that the fate of others may rest on his or her sexual self-control. (Dr. Valentin Dimov, "AIDS: Fear and Hope," published as an insert to the journal *ABV,* 21 July.)

Auxiliary Organizations. Early in the year Zhivkov announced that the process of restructuring would be extended to the country's mass public organizations. He again emphasized this theme at the Tenth Congress of Bulgarian Trade Unions held 7–10 April, stating that the economic and social changes now in progress required the unions to adopt new functions and forms of organization. Trade union chairman Dyulgerov, a candidate member of the Politburo, followed with a speech containing a long section of self-criticism. In the past, he stated, the trade union council was too heavily bureaucratized and too focused on conveying centrally assigned tasks to the workers in their brigades or enterprises. He added that some comrades had raised the question of whether under socialism workers required the "protection" of trade unions but that life had shown there was indeed a need for it. In conclusion, he proposed a number of structural changes that the congress subsequently adopted. These called for trade union bodies to be elected "from the bottom upward." They would form "voluntary associations," which would replace the current thirteen central committees governing the various trade union branches. At the conclusion of the congress, Dyulgerov was re-elected chairman (*RD,* 11 April; *FBIS,* 17 April; RFE, *Situation Report,* 20 May).

Zhivkov also spoke on the need for restructuring at the Tenth Congress of the Fatherland Front that was held during 14–16 May. The reports of Politburo member Kubadinski, chairman of the Front, and other leaders called attention to numerous shortcomings in national life, including the poor quality of consumer goods, inadequate health services, low birthrate, and environmental pollution. The demoralization of youth was also stressed, with speakers expressing alarm at the growing influence of religion, the admiration of Western fashions and music, and the desire to mimic "the bourgeois way of life." Kubadinski proposed no actual changes in the structure or composition of the Front, although he did call for it to establish a consumers' council to promote improvements in quality and to ensure "the strict observance of prices." Such a council actually existed in the mid-1960s but quickly faded from the scene. Retired General Slavcho Trunski, a partisan hero who spent years in prison as a Kostovite in the 1950s and is now a member of the Front's presidium, warned that the Front should not be given tasks that properly belong to administrative authorities with the power to act. He added that for all the talk of restructuring, entrusting a grab bag of reforms to the Front would lead to "formalism, weariness, and indifference" on the part of local organizations. At the conclusion of the congress, Kubadinski was re-elected chairman (BTA, 14 May; *FBIS,* 26 May; BTA, 16 May; *FBIS,* 22 May; RFE, *Situation Report,* 24 June).

In the weeks before the Fifteenth Congress of the Komsomol, held 25–27 May, Bulgaria's youth organization was severely criticized in the press. *Anteni* (20 May) reported approvingly that approximately two thousand students in Stara Zagora had organized a peace demonstration independently of the Komsomol because they were disgusted with the "formalism and sloganeering" of Komsomol officials. It was also proposed that the Komsomol be converted into a vanguard organization like the BCP with membership confined to dedicated activists or that it be broken up into separate organizations targeted at particular age or social groups (*Narodna mladezh,* 16 May; *Otechestven front,* 21 May). The congress did not accept these proposals but did adopt a new constitution that established four councils—for secondary school students, university students, young workers, and young scientists and academics—and authorized local Komsomol units to establish clubs devoted to sports or special interests. These measures were intended to bring the Komsomol closer "to the real interests and concerns of youth." The congress re-elected Bundzhulov as first secretary. Among the 236 Central Committee members elected was Evgeniya Zhivkova, the 21-year-old granddaughter of Todor Zhivkov and daughter of Lyudmila Zhivkova (*RD,* 26 May; *FBIS,* 1 June; BTA, 25 May; *FBIS,* 2 June; RFE, *Situation Report,* 8 July).

International Affairs. Although issues of domestic reform held center stage throughout the year, visits by Zhivkov to China and to West Germany marked significant improvements in relations with both East and West.

The Soviet Union. The extent to which Bulgaria's internal reforms are being pushed by the USSR remained unclear. According to some speculation, Mikhail Gorbachev was dissatisfied with the slow pace of change in Bulgaria and asked Zhivkov to resign at next year's party conference

(*Eastern Europe Newsletter,* 28 October). Similar rumors, however, circulated before last year's party congress and proved groundless. It is also possible that Zhivkov, as he had in the days of Khrushchev, was calling on Soviet support to overcome conservative resistance inside the BCP.

Zhivkov and other members of his Politburo were frequent visitors to the USSR during the year, and several CPSU Politburo members visited Bulgaria, most frequently to discuss "problems of restructuring." In April, Prime Minister Atanasov led a Bulgarian delegation to Moscow to discuss implementation of the treaty linking Bulgarian and Soviet economic development through the year 2000 (*Pravda,* 28 April). Zhivkov met with Gorbachev in Moscow during May, on his way back from China, and in October to "brief the Soviet leader on the course of restructuring in Bulgaria." On international issues Bulgaria, as usual, emphasized its full support for USSR positions.

Other East European and Balkan Countries. Bulgaria's relations with Turkey continued to be bad in consequence of the forced Bulgarianization of the Turkish minority that was carried out in 1984 and 1985. Halil Ibishev, a former member of Bulgaria's National Assembly who defected last year, published a long interview in Turkey in August describing the repression directed against the Bulgarian Turks and stating that he had been "forced" to sign a letter to the Turkish prime minister denouncing Turkey's protests (RFE, *Situation Report,* 9 September). At the end of August Prime Minister Turgut Ozal accused Bulgaria of treating the Turkish minority "like slaves" and said that the situation "would soon change" (Ankara Domestic Service, 22 August; *FBIS,* 24 August). The Bulgarian government reiterated its position that there are no Turks in Bulgaria, only Turkicized Bulgarians who are now reclaiming their Bulgarian heritage, and reminded the Turkish government that the days of the Ottoman Empire had ended (Press release of the Bulgarian Embassy in Washington, D.C., 31 August).

Turkey's international campaign in defense of the Turkish minority in Bulgaria had limited success, partly because of Turkey's own poor record on minority rights and partly because Bulgaria enjoys good relations with several Muslim states. A delegation from the Islamic Conference Organization visited Bulgaria in June, met with representatives of Bulgaria's Muslims, and remained noncommittal (RFE, *Situation Report,* 24 June). In October Syrian president Hafiz al-Assad met with Zhivkov in Sofia, where the two leaders discussed improving economic relations and their harmony of views on most international questions (Damascus Television Service, 23 October; *FBIS,* 26 October). Earlier in the year Zhivkov paid a brief visit to Algeria, meeting with President Chadli Benjedid and addressing the Algerian parliament. The two leaders expressed their agreement on most foreign issues, the record of good relations and cooperation between their countries, and the belief that the future would bring even further improvements (*RD,* 24 April; *FBIS,* 30 April).

Prime Minister Andreas Papandreou of Greece paid a state visit to Bulgaria in July, where he joined Zhivkov in calling for the Balkans to be made free of nuclear and chemical weapons. The two leaders are also believed to have discussed the possibility of reducing the number of troops stationed along their frontier, a move that would allow Greece to redeploy forces to its Turkish border (BBC, Caris 86/87, 15 July).

Romanian president Nicolae Ceauşescu and his wife visited Sofia in October, and the usual expressions on unity and cooperation were issued. Parts of Zhivkov's speech dealing with restructuring were censored in the Romanian press (*Scinteia,* 10 October; *FBIS,*15 October).

China. Last year no Chinese delegation attended the BCP's Thirteenth Congress. In May Zhivkov made a week-long visit to China, meeting with Deng Xiaoping and other officials and concluding several economic and cultural agreements. The two countries plan to double their volume of trade over the next five years. Deng hailed Zhivkov as "an old fighter and revolutionary," and Zhivkov expressed "great interest" in China's current economic experiments. Zhivkov's visit was the fourth by an East European leader in recent months and seemed to be part of a developing rapprochement between China and the Soviet Union's East European allies (BBC, Caris 42/87, 12 May). A Chinese parliamentary delegation visited Sofia in September to follow up the improvement in relations and called for more extensive cooperation (BTA, 22 September; *FBIS,* 2 October).

Western Europe and the United States. In recent years Bulgaria has acquired a sinister reputation in the West owing to its alleged links with international terrorism and the drug trade and its persecution of the Turkish minority. Last year the collapse of the case for a "Bulgarian connection" in Mehmet Ali Agca's attempt on the life of Pope John Paul II opened the door to some improvement in relations, and the Bulgarian government took steps to improve its image. Along with traditional efforts to further cultural exchanges, the regime adopted stronger measures to curtail the flow of drugs across its territory. These won the public acknowledgment of President Reagan and were also praised by the U.S. ambassador in an interview published by the mass-circulation journal *Pogled* (26 January).

Italian foreign minister Giulio Andreotti visited Sofia 13–14 February for talks that focused on improving economic relations. In 1981 Italy was Bulgaria's third-most-important trading partner in the West, after West Germany and Switzerland, but, in the wake of the accusations of Bulgaria's participation in the attempted assassination of the Pope, trade between the two countries was disrupted. Italian imports from Bulgaria dropped by more than 50 percent while exports to Bulgaria also fell sharply. During 1986 trade between the two countries approached the 1981 level, and Andreotti signed a long-term agreement on scientific and economic cooperation aimed at continuing the expansion. Bulgaria is particularly interested in gaining access to Italian technology and in establishing joint ventures, while Italy is expected to increase its purchases of Bulgarian foodstuffs and raw materials. (RFE, *Situation Report,*31 March.)

In September 1984, in the wake of the deployment of new U.S. missiles in West Germany, the USSR sent heir-apparent Gorbachev to Sofia to force Zhivkov to cancel a planned visit to Bonn. Since that time both Bulgaria and West Germany have indicated their desire to remain on good terms, and on 2 June Zhivkov flew to Bonn for a four-day visit, meeting with President Richard von Weizsaecker, Chancellor Helmut Kohl, and other prominent German politicians. During this visit Zhivkov called for closer trade relations between the EEC and CMEA, the approval of Bulgaria's application to join the General Agreement on Tariffs and Trade, and improved bilateral economic, scientific, and cultural cooperation. Zhivkov also discoursed before various German groups on Bulgaria's economic and administrative reforms and measures to protect the environment and toured the Volkswagen plant at Wolfsburg, which he hailed as a model from which Bulgarians could learn much. The visit was unquestionably a public relations success and led to agreements on various aspects of economic cooperation and to expanding the number of Bulgarian students in German universities. West German leaders pressed for Bulgaria to approve the opening of a branch of the Goethe Institute in Sofia, and Zhivkov pledged to consider it. (RFE, *Situation Report,* 24 June.) In July, on the eve of a visit by West Germany's foreign minister, Bulgaria stopped jamming the Bulgarian-language broadcasts of *Deutsche Welle.* Follow-up talks between economic officials proceeded to lay the groundwork for the development of joint ventures (BBC, Caris 97/87, 11 August).

United States deputy secretary of state John Whitehead visited Sofia 3–6 February, meeting with Zhivkov and several other officials. Although this visit seemed to produce little besides an exchange of views, Whitehead was the highest-ranking U.S. official ever to visit Bulgaria (BBC, Caris 12/87, 4 February).

John D. Bell
University of Maryland, Baltimore County

Czechoslovakia

Population. 15,581,993

Party. Communist Party of Czechoslovakia (Komunistická strana Československa; KSČ)

Founded. 1921

Membership. 1,705,490 (*Rudé právo*, 3 September)

General Secretary. Miloš Jakeš

Presidium. 11 full members: Ladislav Adamec (deputy prime minister), Vasil Bil'ák, Petr Colotka (deputy prime minister), Miroslav̌ Zavodil (chairman, Revolutionary Trade Union Movement), Gustáv Husák (president of the republic), Alois Indra (chairman, Federal Assembly), Miloš Jakeš, Atonín Kapek, Josef Kempný, Jozef Lenárt, Lubomír Štrougal (federal prime minister); 6 candidate members: Jan Fojtík, Josef Haman, Vladimír Herman, Miloslav Hruškovič, Ignác Janák, František Pitra

Secretariat. 9 secretaries: Miloš Jakeš, Mikulá Beno, Vasil Bil'ák, Jan Fojtík, Josef Haman, Josef Havlín, Karel Hoffman, František Pitra, Jindřich

Poledník; 3 members-at-large: Zdeněk Hořeni, Marie Kabrhelová, Miroslav Zavadil

Control and Auditing Commission. Jaroslav Hajn, chairman

Central Committee. 135 full and 62 candidate members

Status. Ruling party

Last Congress. Seventeenth, 24–28 March 1986, in Prague; next congress scheduled for 1991

Slovak Party. Communist Party of Slovakia (Komunistická strana Slovenska; KSS); membership: 436,000 full and candidate members; Jozef Lenárt, first secretary; Presidium: 11 members; Central Committee: 91 full and 31 candidate members

Last Election. 1986, 99.94 percent, all 350 National Front candidates; 66 percent of seats reserved for KSČ candidates

Auxiliary Organizations. Revolutionary Trade Union Movement (Eleventh Congress, April 1987), Cooperative Farmers' Union, Socialist Youth Union (Fourth Congress, October 1987), Union for Collaboration with the Army, Czechoslovak Union of Women, Union of Fighters for Peace

Main State Organs. The executive body is the federal government, which is subordinate to the 350-member Federal Assembly, composed of the Chamber of the People (200 members) and the Chamber of the Nations (150 members). The assembly, however, merely rubber-stamps all decisions made by the KSČ Presidium and Central Committee.

Publications. *Rudé právo*, KSČ daily; *Pravda* (Bratislava), KSS daily; *Tribuna*, Czech-language ideological weekly; *Predvoj*, Slovak-language ideological weekly; *Život strany*, fortnightly journal devoted to administrative and organizational questions; *Práce* (Czech) and *Práca* (Slovak), Revolutionary Trade Union Movement dailies; *Mladá fronta* (Czech) and *Smena* (Slovak), Socialist Youth Union dailies; *Tvorba*, weekly devoted to domestic and international politics; *Nová mysl*, theoretical monthly. Československá tisková kancelář (ČETEKA) is the official news agency.

The KSČ developed from the left wing of the Czechoslovak Social Democratic Party, having coopted several radical socialist and leftist groups. It was constituted in Prague and admitted to the Communist International the same year. Its membership in the Comintern, however, was an uneasy one until in 1929 the so-called bolshevization process was completed and a leadership of unqualified obedience to the Soviet Union assumed control. During the First Czechoslovak Republic (1918–1939), the KSČ enjoyed legal status, but it was banned after the Munich Agreement. After the war, it emerged as the strongest party in the postwar elections of 1946, although it did not poll a majority of votes. In February 1948, the KSČ seized all power in a coup d'état and transformed Czechoslovakia into a communist party-state of the Soviet type. The departure from Stalinist practices started later in Czechoslovakia than in other countries of Central and Eastern Europe, but it led to a daring liberalization experience known as the Prague Spring of 1968. A Soviet-led military intervention by five Warsaw Pact countries in August of the same year ended the democratization course and imposed on Czechoslovakia the policies of so-called normalization—a return to unreserved subordination to the will of the Soviet Union and the emulation of the Soviet example in all areas of social life. Unqualified obedience to the Soviet power center, however, need not be identical with the pursuit of the present conservative, antireformist course; this became obvious in 1987.

Party Internal Affairs. Although 1987 did not see any major regular events on either the party or the state level—the KSČ national congress and parliamentary elections had been held in 1986—party life did not lack dynamism or surprises. This resulted from developments in the Soviet Union and the continuing crisis in the KSČ itself. Of the two, the most stimulating was the impact of the reforms initiated in the USSR by Mikhail S. Gorbachev. The Soviet example had an unsettling effect on Czechoslovakia; for the second time in its postwar history, the KSČ appeared to lag behind its Soviet mentor. A similar situation had developed in the second half of the 1950s when Antonín Novotný reluctantly and slowly adopted de-Stalinization. The situation in 1987 was complicated by the fact that those in power had been installed by the USSR in 1969, after the Soviet military occupation.

Another element in the crisis was the need to replace Gustáv Husák, aging party boss. This change, of course, could also adjust Czechoslovak internal policies to those of the Soviet Union. Informed observers in the West had known since 1985 that Jakeš was the most favored candidate. He passed as a "centrist" and, therefore, seemed more acceptable to the conservatives. Prime Minister Štrougal's trip to Moscow in November provided some grounds for rumors that he might be a favorite of the Kremlin. This uncertainty persisted until shortly before the end of the year.

The KSČ Central Committee met in three plenary sessions during 1987. The fifth one since the Congress, held 18 March, decreed some changes in the party's governing bodies, but none indicated an impending shift in the policy. The meeting accepted the resignation, for health reasons, of Josef Korčák, Presidium member and prime minister of the Czech republic. He was succeeded in both functions by Adamec. Another member of the Presidium, Hoffman, became one of the eight secretaries but relinquished his responsibility as chairman of the trade unions. In the latter post he was replaced by Zavadil who also became a Secretariat member (*Rudé právo*, 19, 20 March). On the same occasion, Husák explicitly endorsed intensification, and acceleration—to which he previously had made rather reserved references (*YICA*, 1986) and announced that systematic efforts would be made to attain these goals. Another important objective of the Soviet reform, "openness" or *glasnost'*, was downplayed in Husák's presentation but received more emphasis in the government report given by Štrougal to the Federal Assembly one week later (*Rudé právo*, 25 March).

Many expected a more pronounced shift in the direction of reforms to occur after Gorbachev's visit to Prague in April. However, it seemed as if the conservative course, with the reforms limited strictly to management of the economy, would reassert itself. Some hard-liners, such as Bil'ák, had argued that the ongoing changes in the USSR could be "misused by the antisocialist forces in Czechoslovakia" (Radio Hvězda, 10 February). Fojtík claimed that the emphasis on "openness" in the Soviet reform program did not mean as much an obligation to provide more information and to allow more criticism but rather "an enhancement of the Leninist character of the party" (*Rudé právo*, 13 February). On another occasion, he declared that the restructuring of the economy and the society was necessary but that it had to be closely watched. "The party," said Fojtík, "must retain initiative in this process; the initiative must not be allowed to pass to individuals or pressure groups." One of the conditions for the success of such a reform was that the present party leadership should remain in control (ibid., 12 June). The conservatives took great pains to make it clear that adoption of the Soviet course must never bring back the Prague Spring of 1968, although even this was re-evaluated by party spokesman Bil'ák, who conceded that in 1968 the reforms were "necessary but they in the end profited the enemy of socialism" (*Pravda*, Moscow, 12 February).

The Sixth Plenum did not bring any changes in the party leadership. The main point on the agenda concerned the Czechoslovak economy, and it was characteristic of the conflicting views on the whole reform that no final document relative to this subject could be adopted at this session, although it had been discussed in various commissions since March (*Rudé právo*, 7 November). No draft was ready for approval at the plenum the following month, and all material was sent back for amendments. Notwithstanding this, the Seventh Plenum entered KSČ history when it accepted Gustáv Husák's resignation for reasons of health. The Central Committee appointed Jakeš as general secretary, which seemed to be in tune with the middle-of-the-road position on economic and social reforms. For the same reason, Western observers felt that this appointment was a temporary compromise (*WSJ*; *Frankfurter Allgemeine Zeitung*, 18 December). An unwritten rule during the past twenty years had been that the four most important posts in the party and in the state—the president of the republic, the chairman of the Federal Assembly, the federal prime minister, and the party general secretary—should be divided between the Czechs and the Slovaks, the two main ethnic groups. With Jakeš general secretary, three of these key positions are now held by Czechs. It is thus speculated that Premier Štrougal (a Czech) might soon step down; and indeed, he admitted that nineteen years may be too long a tenure (DPA, Prague, 21 January 1988). Štrougal stated that "there is no alternative to reforms," which now "must be pursued at the fastest possible rate."

An important, long-term KSČ problem has been renewing its rank and file. In proportion to the population, the KSČ is one of the largest communist parties of the world. Directives for recruiting new members stress the need to include "young people from the industrial sector," for too large a proportion are middle-aged, white-collar employees (32 percent). Only about a third are 35 or younger (*Pravda*, Bratislava, 4 September). Another, more subtle preoccupation involves the "scientific-technological revolution" and the increased role of the market in planned economic reforms, which are likely to increase the prestige of professional and managerial occupations to the detriment of the political sector. Because this might make party membership less desirable, the elites might be outside of immediate KSČ control. Twenty years ago, this contributed to the Prague Spring, officially referred to as a "crisis development in the party and society" (*Život strany*, no. 17).

Domestic Affairs. Among the public issues is the threat to the environment. Czechoslovakia is one of the most polluted countries of Central and Eastern Europe. Ecological concerns, however, are of only recent date. In many places, the contamination of rivers and groundwater reserves has assumed alarming proportions (*Rudé právo*, 6 February). There is also uneasiness about the security at nuclear plants, especially after the disaster at Chernobyl. In response, the government negotiated various agreements for the protection of the environment. Documents about cooperation in ecological matters were signed with the Federal Republic of Germany (Radio Hvězda, 8 May) and Austria (*Rudé právo*, 18 July). Government spokesmen nevertheless admitted that measures for protecting the environment were either inadequate or improperly implemented (Radio Prague, 8 October; *Rudé právo*, 20 October).

Another topic that elicited strong response was the new legislation on abortion, in effect from 1 January. It virtually leaves the decision about interruption of pregnancy in the hands of the affected woman. Not unlike the West, this issue deeply divides the citizens. Even among civil rights activists, who otherwise have displayed strong solidarity and mutual support, opinions are in sharp conflict. After a large group petitioned against the legislation, some Charter '77 signatories opposed the petition as incompatible with the notion of freedom. Both groups later became objects of police investigation (RFE-RL *Situation Report*, no. 1, 17 January). The new law, however, was also criticized by some health experts. A leading Slovak gynecologist, Dr. Olga Blaskova, deplored in press interviews that the number of abortions among girls 14 to 15 years old had increased by 150 percent since the implementation of the new legislation (*Nové slovo*, 20, 21 May).

Although the country has become much more homogeneous, the Hungarian-speaking population in southern Slovakia continued to voice various grievances. Official media claimed that "untroubled coexistence between the Slovaks and the ethnic Hungarians in Czechoslovakia had been promoted with success" (Radio Hvězda, 11 April). Government spokesmen pointed out that the Hungarians fared much better than their kin in Romania or Yugoslavia (Radio Budapest, 11 April).

A source of pride to Czechoslovak communists has been that their country is one of two truly developed and industrialized states in the Soviet bloc. Yet development has also had its price: regardless of the socialist mode of ownership, Czechoslovakia experiences a number of problems that are typical of all advanced industrial societies. Among these, crime continued to preoccupy both the authorities and the public, who felt that the crime rate was on the rise. Corruption, too, was widespread at all levels of the state administration. About half the perpetrators of criminal acts were young people between 15 and 29. Large cities showed a 36 percent increase in the crime rate over the six years ending in 1987, while the average national crime rate grew by 8 percent. Many crimes against property concerned objects of public ownership, such as equipment or material belonging to enterprises (*Rudé právo*, 26 June; *Večerní Praha*, 12 June). A sensational trial of ten defendants before the regional court in Bratislava lasted a week and exposed a whole ring of embezzlers of public funds who were able to engage in illegal activities because they catered to influential officials, including the federal minister of engineering and the federal planning office chairman (Czechoslovak Television, 30 June).

Alcoholism and fatal road accidents among the young continued to keep the police and the courts busy. The government made plans to open a network of centers for the treatment of narcotic addicts (Radio Prague, 16 August). The perennial problem of prostitution remained unsolved, even 40 years after introduction of the communist socioeconomic system and has developed into more "modern," refined forms. Many educated women, wives of the country's elite, engage in prostitution as a source of additional income, often belonging to call girl rings. This problem is complicated by the spread of venereal disease and AIDS (Radio Prague, 1 June; *Večerní praha*, 18 September). An advisory center on AIDS was opened in the capital (Radio Prague, 1 October).

Responding to the pressure of public opinion, and in line with the current Soviet call for "openness," the presidium of the federal assembly urged the government to expedite the draft of new regulations on citizens' complaints (ibid., 19 October). The USSR examples of introducing the secret ballot and of several candidates running for the same office in local elections also attracted attention. Media recorded this interest and raised the possibility of adopting the same approach (Radio Hvězda, 24 February). Many KSČ members inquired why their party could not do as the CPSU had done. In an extensive article, the party daily explained that the secret ballot had been foreseen by the KSČ statutes and that it was up to each party unit to make use of this provision (*Rudé právo*, 22 April).

The noncommunist majority of the population exhibited reserved optimism toward the reform movement in the Soviet Union and hoped that some of its momentum would affect Czechoslovakia. The visit of the CPSU general secretary in April had been awaited with keen interest, but many of these expectations ended in disappointment. Gorbachev neither "deposed" the KSČ rulers nor did he explicitly rehabilitate the 1968 reformist course. Nevertheless, he missed no opportunity to emphasize the need for a thorough reform of the USSR system, which implicitly but unmistakably extended to all regimes in the Soviet orbit. His professed goal of "drastically broadening democracy and reorganizing socialist society" (Radio Prague, 11 April) was widely appreciated in Czechoslovakia. The number of people who filled the streets of Prague and Bratislava to see Gorbachev greatly exceeded those of any previous such visit. Demand for Soviet newspapers and USSR television programs (available via satellite transmission) have increased substantially since the beginning of *glasnost'*. When the Czech translation of Gorbachev's book *Restructuring: New Thinking for Our Country and the World* appeared in December, people stood in line to buy it. The volume had two reprints within a month; by the following month, some 95,000 copies had been sold (ČETEKA, in English, 13 January 1988). This surge of interest in Soviet affairs did not seem to please the official representatives. At the congress of the Czechoslovak-Soviet Friendship Society in November, the spokesman for the KSČ Presidium warned the delegates that the sudden popularity of all things Soviet "need not be an unequivocally positive phenomenon."

At the same time, mistrust continued unabated toward any sign of public sympathy for the West. When a group of Czechoslovak citizens submitted a request to the Interior Ministry for permission to establish a Society of Friends of the United States, *Svaz přátel USA* (the title is a variant of the name that the present Czechoslovak-Soviet Friendship Society bore before 1939: *Svaz přátel SSSR*), the request was denied on 19 June.

On the other hand, the year saw a distinct shift in the official assessment of the First Czechoslovak Republic. On the occasion of the 50th anniversary of the death of its first president, T. G. Masaryk, the KSČ party organ carried a commemorative editorial that was much more objective and balanced than earlier presentations of his work (*Rudé právo*, 14 September). A great majority of the readership welcomed this approach to Masaryk as politician and thinker, as well as the recognition of his merits, while a few argued that the official party organ should not publish such articles. For the first time in many years the pilgrimage of about 200 of Masaryk's admirers to his grave in Lány took place unhindered by the police, who did not even appear on the scene (AFP, Prague, 13 September).

Economy. Czechoslovakia shares all the major economic problems of the USSR and other bloc countries. Thus, improving the performance of the system was the most important objective. Reforms in other areas—democracy and "openness"—were presented as the prerequisites for success in the economic area. The terms *restructuring*, *intensification*, and *acceleration*—all taken from the Soviet vocabulary—had previously been used in official reports and pronouncements; but their application had been rather timid, and their desirability, ambivalent. Most top party officials considered the idea of economic reform—not to mention political and cultural reforms—too closely linked to the liberalization of 1968, which they had been called on to stop and reverse. Among a minority willing to follow the Soviet example was Prime Minister Štrougal, who criticized, at a meeting of party and government economic experts, the continuing "extensive" approach to economic planning and management as a burdensome heritage of the Stalinist past and argued that it was necessary to reform "not only the economic base but also the entire superstructure, and in principle all other spheres of social life" (*Rudé právo*, 28 January). Other leaders were more reluctant, for only in the fall did Husák acknowledge that "the entire socialist world is seeking a new system of economic and political management and the democratization of society" and that all opposition to this quasi-universal movement was pointless (ibid., 16 October). A month later, Husák had to relinquish his key post in the party, but the choice of his successor—an obvious compromise—seemed to indicate that in matters of reform the KSČ was not yet prepared to abandon its cautious attitude.

The economic difficulties that the propounded

reforms are to help overcome are not so acute or visible as those in Poland or Romania; there has not been even a drastic increase in consumer prices, like those in neighboring Hungary. Czechoslovak workers are assured of a stable, modest income that can buy a limited number of articles of not too high quality but that is sufficient to satisfy basic needs, which may in itself inhibit a more powerful reform drive. Yet the performance of the economy in 1987 was indisputably substandard. Despite continuing capital investment, efficiency did not improve in line with the plan. Labor productivity remained significantly below target. Unused products—merchandise unsold due to low demand (often caused by bad quality)—increased by 18 billion korunas (U.S. $3 billion).

Statistical figures published in the middle of the year showed that the planned "intensification" (an increase in quality and efficiency) had largely remained on paper. As in the past, the consumption of energy and raw materials clearly exceeded the plan. Material costs, instead of decreasing by 0.16 percent, rose by 1.49 percent. As a consequence of these failures, the growth in national income equaled a mere 2 percent, while the plan had foreseen 3.1 percent (*Hospodářské noviny*, no. 30, 24 July). Another important long-term target has been the radical shift from the use of fossil fuels to more modern sources of energy such as hydroelectric and nuclear power; the former should decrease by 50 percent and the latter increase fivefold by the year 2020 (*Plánované hospodářství*, no. 2, 1985). Should these objectives be reached, the image of Czechoslovakia as a smokestack industrial giant would change thoroughly. On the side of light industry production, a new model passenger car, the "Škoda 781," should start rolling off the assembly lines in 1989 and recapture some of the West European and Third World markets that were lost during the 1950s. This may prove to be more difficult than imagined, especially because of keen competition from Yugoslavia and South Korea.

Development of the retail trade was unsatisfactory, continuing a trend that had started several years earlier. It seems doubtful that the increase of 50 percent in personal consumption, planned for the year 2000, will be achieved. The number of retail stores again decreased. There is one supermarket for every 67,800 people in Czechoslovakia, compared with one to 5,000 in Sweden and Switzerland. An average Western supermarket carries 200,000 items, whereas the largest one in Prague displays only half that. As a remedy, economic experts recommended the introduction of full accountability of enterprises, substantial increases in profit margins, and flexible prices. Furthermore, large department stores and supermarkets will compete with small private shops and the so-called fringe enterprises operated by collective farms. Although the volume of sales by the latter category more than doubled over the last five years, amounting to more than 16 billion korunas (U.S. $2.75 billion), it could not compensate for the failing state-owned sector (*Zemědělská ekonomika*, no. 7, 1986). Moreover, any further expansion of the private and cooperative sectors in retail trade must overcome the resistance of conservative elements in the party and the government; this is one of the many difficulties encountered by "restructuring." The KSČ Presidium decided that, beginning in 1988, licenses would be issued to organizations and individuals willing to open catering businesses. It also announced that "better use will be made of people taking on second jobs" (Radio Prague, 13 July). The impact of this measure, however, will depend largely on the performance of the state-owned sector because private firms and restaurants have to rely on the national enterprises for their daily supplies. The professed intention to make better use of workers who "moonlight" seems just a belated acknowledgment of an extremely large "gray economy"—a phenomenon that is endemic in the orbit of "real socialism."

Culture, Youth, and Religion. The contrast between the need for change and the obstacles to meaningful change is also a part of cultural life. Young people were especially aware of this contrast. They felt frustrated and generally refused to identify with the establishment. Official media were shocked by an opinion survey that found that "the majority of young people are preoccupied with their own private concerns, while the involvement in social issues and responsibilities is rated at the bottom of their list of priorities" and that the younger the respondents, the more "social and moral values constantly decline and skepticism about the purpose of the youth organization increases" (*Život strany*, 3 January). The organization in question was the only one allowed, the Czechoslovak Socialist Youth Union (SSM), which held congresses of its Czech and Slovak branches and its national congress, during the late summer and early fall. On these occasions, KSČ spokesmen stated that "restructuring" and the idea of a social reform in general are subjects of great interest among the youth, who often "get impatient waiting for practical steps which would bring about the desired change" (*Rudé právo*, 3 October). Some speakers, including KSČ Presidium member Štrougal, called for a thorough revision of the methods by which the SSM worked and advised that the role of any youth organization in forming the character of future generations should not be overestimated (Prague Radio, 9 September). Similar reservations were also expressed at the Fourth National Conference of the Young Pioneers' Organization (PO SSM), which works with school children from 7 to 14 years of age. Although membership figures of these Young Pioneers are impressive (about 75 percent of all eligible individuals belong to the PO SSM), the state-sponsored body offers little to satisfy its followers' needs and interests (*Mladá fronta*, 22 June; *Tribuna*, 10, 17 June). The life-style that most appeals to young people is that of the West, especially its dress and entertainment, rather than the life-style of some future "new socialist man." Western music, especially jazz, is an important component of this pattern. The regime has fought a losing battle against jazz, the most recent phase of which is the "jazz section affair." The authorities dissolved the jazz section of the Czechoslovak Union of Musicians, probably frightened by its size and the scope of initiative. With several thousand members and publishing a periodical with a circulation of more than 100,000, the supervisors of culture probably felt that a social organism of those dimensions and popularity could not be effectively controlled. The jazz section, however, refused to disband and appealed to the U.N. Educational, Scientific and Cultural Organization (UNESCO) for help, invoking the registration of the Union of Musicians and thus the jazz section, with the U.N. In the end, the main spokesmen for the section were arrested and brought to trial. However, because of the UNESCO involvement, the affair became an international issue. Several civil rights organizations in the West protested to the Czechoslovak government. The five defendants were eventually sentenced to relatively light prison terms; the presiding judge explicitly acknowledged that the intentions of the jazz section officials had been "serious and honorable" and that "they were experts in their professions" (*CSM*, 5 March; *NYT*, 12 March). It appeared that in this phase of the battle against Western music the regime would be the loser.

National conventions of three cultural organizations—the Third Congress of the Czechoslovak Writer's Union, the Fourth Congress of the Union of Dramatic Artists, and the Ninth Congress of the Union of Journalists—were held during 1987 and reflected the uneasy climate of a system that desperately sought to prevent all change. In the past, meetings of the Writers' Union had often been marked by nonconformist attitudes of the delegates and had even been precursors of important events in the political sphere but not this time. Jakeš, the main speaker at the congress, who later became KSČ general secretary, emphasized the right of the party to regulate literary activities rather than the right of the author to express his or her views (*Rudé právo*, 15 May). The congress of the Union of Dramatic Artists (theater, cinema and television) became a sensation thanks to Miloš Kopecký, a distinguished national artist, who called on the KSČ and state leadership "to resign honorably before you are forced out of office in disgrace." He said that the men at the helm offered no hope because they had "the past under their skin and in every pore, nerve, and fiber of their bodies" (*Rudé právo*, 7 May; *Der Spiegel*, 25 May). His appeal was explicitly rejected by chief ideologist Fojtík (*Rudé právo*, 12 June), who returned to this subject later as the key speaker at the Union of Journalists' Congress. He stressed that the party remembered well the experiences of 1968, when "all the press was seized and abused by the right wing" and that "no one—abroad or at home" should speculate that the process of restructuring could become "a repetition of post-January 1968 politics" (*Nové slovo*, 9 July).

The antireligious campaign and restrictions on churches continued, although official voices called for "good normal relations," especially with the Roman Catholic church and the Vatican (ČETEKA, 5 October). However, it is not easy to establish such relations under the present conditions. The Catholics, by far the largest group, have suffered 40 years of harassment and obstruction by the regime. One serious obstacle to religious freedom is the state's refusal to confirm the appointees of the pope to the growing number of vacant bishop and archbishop seats. Only 3 out of 13 such positions have a permanent incumbent. The Greek-Catholic diocese in eastern Slovakia is also administered by a provisional ordinarius (*Frankfurter Allgemeine Zeitung*, 22 January 1988). Other continuing grievances included restrictions on and interference with religious education, insufficient opportunity to train young clergymen, deliberate delays in issuing permission for newly ordained priests to carry out their duties, and obstruction of spiritual meetings conducted by laymen. These and other complaints were included in a lengthy memorandum sent by Primate Cardinal Tomášek to Milan Klusák, the minister of culture for the Czech Republic (*Informace o Chartě '77*, no. 8, 3 July; Reuters, Prague, 3 July). The restrictions of religious life were not limited to the Catholic majority. Smaller Protestant churches and denominations have also been the objects of persecution. In the summer of 1987, Pastor Jan Dus of the Evangelical Church of the Czech Brethren was released from a long detention (AFP, Prague, 3 August).

On the more hopeful side, it was encouraging to Christians of all creeds when Mother Teresa, on her way from Częstochowa in Poland, stopped in Slovakia to participate in the 1987 pilgrimage to Šaštín. About 40,000 people took part in this event (*Katolícke noviny*, 21 June). Some interpreted Mother Teresa's visit as an indication that Pope John Paul II might be allowed to come to Czechoslovakia in the near future. The lack of support for official policies in matters of religion was demonstrated again when a group of Czechoslovak believers, represented by Father Václav Malý, lodged a protest on 18 September with U.N. secretary general Javier Pérez de Cuéllar against awarding the title "Messenger of Peace" to *Pacem in Terris*, the proregime organization of Catholics banned by the Vatican in 1982 and repeatedly disavowed by Cardinal Tomášek. The protest letter emphasized that *Pacem in Terris*'s real goal was "to camouflage the stark reality of the violent persecution and restriction of the church's activity." Nevertheless, several high-ranking foreign politicians and diplomats who in the course of the year visited Czechoslovakia were allowed to meet with the primate. These meetings were reported by the official press agency and the media. These included Austrian foreign minister Alois Mock (AP, Prague, 17 July) and West German foreign affairs minister Hans-Dietrich Genscher (*Rudé právo*, 28 November).

Dissidence. The most important civil rights group, Charter '77, held its 10th anniversary in 1987. Only 240 members signed the original charter document, but a decade later there were more than 1,300 signatories. During this period, 26 people served as spokespersons, which took more courage than to sign because it could mean loss of employment and police harassment, if not imprisonment. On 1 January this responsibility was assumed by Jan Litomiský, Libuše Šilhanová, and Josef Vohryzek. Litomiský, known for his earlier work in the Committee for Defense of Unjustly Persecuted, had spent three years in jail as a result of this work and was later placed under special police supervision for another two years (*Informace o Chartě*, no. 1). From 1977 until the end of 1986, the Charter group issued no fewer than 197 documents, each dealing with a specific human rights issue or with a subject of public interest such as the environment, alcoholism, and so on. It also sent open letters to government representatives and communiqués to the domestic and foreign press and has been distributing regular bulletins about its own activities (*Informace o Chartě*). To mark its 10th anniversary, the group appealed, in a document released on 1 January, to the Czechoslovak public to stand up for democratic reform and civil rights. Although it made no explicit reference to the current debate about the reform of the economic and political system, it clearly indicated that the time may now be propitious for a concerted action with the purpose of bringing about a substantial improvement of the situation (*Charter Document*, no. 1, as reported by Reuters, Prague, 1 January). The group also issued statements on the critical housing situation in the capital city (ibid. no. 8, 30 January), on problems of the environment (*Charter Document*, no. 33, April), and on the 19th anniversary of the Soviet-led invasion of Czechoslovakia (ibid. no. 47, 1 August).

An ad hoc group of fifteen journalists and civil rights activists, independent of Charter '77, circulated an appeal to the Czechoslovak media urging them to take advantage of the current search for openness (*glasnost'*) in the Soviet Union (AFP, Prague, 17 February). As could be expected, hints by the dissidents about the USSR example proliferated as the date of the visit to Prague by Gorbachev neared. A large number of individuals made written representations to the prominent Soviet guest even before he arrived, including an open letter from the former KSČ first secretary Alexander Dubček, which drew particular attention. The samizdat Czechoslovak publications commented extensively on the possible effects of Gorbachev's visit on the internal matters of the Czechoslovak communist party and on conditions in general. Some took a rather optimistic position, but others were more sober and critical. Milan Huebl, a former communist journalist known for his conflict with Novotný in 1965 over the issue of the political trials of the 1950s, called those who expected Gorbachev to disavow Husák "incurable romantics" and urged them to "come down to earth from cloudland!" Gorbachev's visit, to be sure, did not vindicate the optimists, but the feeling prevailed that "things had begun to move, albeit slowly and clumsily" ("Reconstruction or Changing Clothes?" Prague, April; A.Z., "Gorbachev's visit as Reflected in Independent Publications," Prague, July).

Other foreign visits might have given the dissidents new hope. These visits of politicians and diplomats from the West resulted in unexpected opportunities to meet with representatives of human rights groups. John C. Whitehead, U.S. deputy secretary of state, while in Prague saw not only Cardinal Tomášek but also two Charter spokespersons, Litomiský and Anna Šabatová (AP, Prague, 2 February). Timothy Renton, deputy foreign secretary of Great Britain, arrived shortly afterward and also met with the Charter leadership (Reuters, Vienna, 3 February). Austrian foreign minister Mock, during his official visit, talked with Václav Havel, a prominent dissident playwright who had been imprisoned for political reasons (AFP, Prague, 18 July). Havel had just received the prestigious West European cultural Erasmus Prize but decided not to go to Brussels in person for fear the regime might not let him return home, as it had done with several other dissidents. Instead he sent his award address to the awarding institution; it was later translated into all major languages. Last but not least, in November West German foreign minister Genscher received Jiří Hájek, the former minister of foreign affairs in the 1968–69 government at the German federal embassy in Prague. Hájek had been the first and best-known spokesman of Charter '77 when it was constituted ten years earlier (AFP, Prague, 26 November). Foreign observers and Western media noted a dinner at the U.S. embassy given by Ambassador Julian Niemczyk for the leaders of Charter '77 that included playwright Havel (AP, Prague, 25 September). The guests came and left unhindered. These gestures of lenience on the part of the authorities, whatever may have been their motivation, were at sharp variance with the harsh treatment of dissidents who, in the past, had made attempts at contacting prominent Western visitors.

Foreign Affairs. High-ranking government representatives from the West and the East visited Czechoslovakia, and state officials in their turn traveled to many parts of the world. U.S. deputy secretary of state Whitehead spent three days in Prague on his tour of Central and Eastern Europe. He met with KSČ Presidium member Bil'ák and Foreign Affairs Minister Bohuslav Chňoupek, with whom he discussed economic relations and human rights (AP, Prague, 2 February). Czechoslovakia was also the host to British deputy foreign secretary Renton, who met with Prime Minister Štrougal and other cabinet members and who gave an interview that was reproduced unabridged, despite a "frank discussion of controversial issues" (*Rudé právo*, 3 February). Finnish president Mauno Koivisto visited shortly afterward. The following month, Indian foreign minister Narayan Datta Tiwari came to Prague and held talks with President Husák, Štrougal, Chňoupek, and Federal Assembly chairman Indra. He also met with a group of Czechoslovak journalists to whom he gave an interview (Radio Hvězda, 2 April). Austrian federal chancellor Franz Vranitzky stopped in Prague on a "private" trip and met with Štrougal (*Rudé právo*, 27 April). Australian foreign minister Bill Hayden met with Chňoupek and Štrougal in Prague (ČETEKA, in English, 18 May). The foreign minister of Argentina, Dante Mario Caputo, saw Husák at the end of the same month (*Rudé právo*, 2 June). Greece was represented by Foreign Minister Karolos Papoulias, who came for a short official visit (ibid., 4 July). An important event was the arrival of King Juan Carlos of Spain a few days later. In his speech at the gala dinner the king emphasized close contact with and the support given to the Spanish people by the First Czechoslovak Republic during the civil war in the 1930s. The royal couple also went to Bratislava, where they were guests of the government of the Slovak Republic (*Pravda*, Bratislava, 9 July). A week later, Prague hosted Austrian foreign minister Mock on his two-day visit. On this occasion, Mock was received by President Husák (AP, Prague, 17 July). Iranian deputy premier Ali Reza Moayeri also stopped during his tour of Central and southeastern Europe (Radio Prague, 26 August). The list of foreign visitors from the West and the Third World was concluded by Genscher, foreign affairs minister in the Federal Republic of Germany, who came for a three-day visit and met with President Husák, as well as with his counterpart, Chňoupek (*Rudé právo*, 28 November).

Among the visits paid by Czechoslovak officials to Western and nonaligned countries was Foreign Minister Chňoupek's stay in Vienna for the Helsinki follow-on conference, where he spoke at the plenary session of the conference and reviewed matters of common interest with Austrian foreign minister Mock (Radio Prague, 31 July). A government delegation visited Syria (ČETEKA, in English, 24 August) and Foreign Minister Chňoupek traveled to

Belgium (Radio Prague, 16 September). From Brussels he continued to New York and attended the 42nd session of the U.N. General Assembly (ibid., 18 September). In the same month a group from the Federal Assembly, led by Indra, traveled to Ottawa where it met with the members of the Canadian parliament (ČETEKA, in English, 25 September). Deputy Prime Minister Jaromír Obzina paid a two-day visit to France (Radio Prague, 29 September). After Foreign Minister Chňoupek fell ill in New York, First Deputy Foreign Minister Jaromír Johanes replaced him at the head of the Czechoslovak delegation to the U.N. General Assembly. During his stay, Johanes also met in Washington, D.C., with Deputy Secretary of State Whitehead (ČETEKA, in English, 2 October). After his return from France, Obzina traveled to West Germany to continue the exchange of views on protection of the environment (Radio Prague, 7 October).

As for diplomatic contacts with the communist-ruled states, the most important was the visit by Soviet minister of foreign affairs Eduard Shevardnadze, who spent three days talking with President Husák, Prime Minister Štrougal, and Foreign Minister Chňoupek. The main topics were the current U.S.-Soviet negotiation on reduction or elimination of intermediate-range nuclear missiles (*Práce*, 5 February). After many years of rather cool relations with the People's Republic of China, two top-ranking Chinese visitors arrived: Foreign Minister Wu Xuequian (Xinhua Press Agency, in English, 8 March) and, four months later, Prime Minister and party leader Zhao Ziyang was received by President Husák and other members of the government (Radio Prague, 11 June). First Deputy Prime Minister Ion Dincă and party secretary Ion Stoian accompanied Romanian party boss Nicolae Ceauşescu to Prague, where they were guests of President Husák (Radio Prague, 11 May). Abdul Wakil, foreign minister of Afghanistan, followed a week later (ČETEKA, in English, 17 May). Prime Minister Branko Mikulić of Yugoslavia was in Czechoslovakia at the end of the same month (Tanjug, in English, 26 May). Hungarian Deputy Prime Minister Judit Csehak also arrived in Prague for an official visit (Radio Prague, 10 September).

On the Czechoslovak side, Foreign Minister Chňoupek went to Budapest for a "working visit" (Radio Budapest, 14 July). Prime Minister Štrougal was an official guest of the Hungarian government at the invitation of his counterpart, Károly Grósz; he also was received by party leader János Kádár (Radio Prague, 31 August). President Husák, accompanied by Foreign Minister Chňoupek, traveled to Yugoslavia, where he held talks with President Lazar Mojsov and party leader Boško Krunić (Tanjug, in English, 23 September).

Foreign Trade and Debt. The problems that Czechoslovakia faced in the sphere of foreign trade in 1987 were typical of all countries of the Soviet bloc, but they assumed a specific form and urgency determined by endemic conditions. Managers of the economy had hoped that Czechoslovakia would become a creditor in hard currency. This proved to be too optimistic. Compared with other countries of Central and Eastern Europe—with the exception of Romania—the Czechoslovak debt in convertible currencies appears rather modest and has even declined during the last few years. However, in 1987, instead of decreasing further, it increased considerably. From $3.1 billion gross ($2.3 billion net) in 1986, it reached the level of $4 billion gross ($3 billion net) in 1987. Czechoslovakia even considered taking out additional loans of at least $200 million from Western banks (*Financial Times*, London, 1 June). Yet the foreign debt in itself would not be out of the ordinary, especially if the potential of the economy is taken into account; what has prevented balancing of foreign payments is the orientation of the country's exports. About 80 percent of Czechoslovak products are exported to the USSR and the countries of the CMEA (the "ruble zone") where they are sold for "soft," nonconvertible currencies. In 1987, the volume of the trade with hard currency partners diminished further, which poses another serious problem: the ability of Czechoslovak industry to produce articles for export depends on imports of many raw materials; these can usually be bought only with convertible currency. Still another problem has been the quality of industrial output. Among the goods manufactured for export in 1987, as many as 20 percent were below world standards (*Rudé právo*, 29 January). What seems to be needed is not so much an increase in the volume of exported goods—Czechoslovakia in 1986 exported products worth 40 percent of its national income (*Hospodářské noviny*, 11 July)—but rather a drastic reorientation of its trade. Whether this will be possible, or even seriously attempted in the wake of the "restructuring" process, remains to be seen. Closely connected with the problem of balancing payments has been the more general question of currency convertibility within CMEA. These currencies are not even mutually convertible, although the Hungarian forint, especially before the price increases of December 1987, enjoyed a form of de facto convertibility in the West. This question was raised by Prime Minister Štrougal at the 43rd CMEA session in Moscow, where he pleaded for "organic links between the CMEA national currencies and the convertible ruble." Jaromír Matějka, from the office of the federal prime minister, said in an interview with the trade union daily that the "ultimate goal" was the convertibility of the koruna but that reaching this goal would depend, above all, "on foreign currency reserves, as well as on a realistic exchange rate vis-à-vis the hard currencies" (*Práce*, 1 October).

Further progress was made during the year in the area of joint economic ventures with Western enterprises, although the extent and variety of this cooperation still could not compare with those developed by other bloc countries (for example, Hungary). Foreign firms were invited to participate in modernizing Czechoslovak industry. No comprehensive new legislation relative to these joint enterprises appeared in 1987, although certain basic principles were laid down by the government. Only a Czechoslovak citizen may head a joint venture. The enterprise must pay the same taxes and make the same contributions to social security as the domestic firms, but the profit tax is more lenient; it is capped at 50 percent, while the national enterprises can be taxed up to 75 percent. The after-tax profit is divided according to shares in the venture and can be repatriated in the respective country's currency. It is expected that the number of these joint ventures will increase when the restructuring program is implemented (Štrougal interview with DPA in *Frankfurter Allgemeine Zeitung*, 21 January 1988).

Among the economic and trade negotiations with other countries, there were also talks with the European Economic Community aiming at a bilateral agreement (ČETEKA, in English, 22 July). French foreign trade minister Michel Noir arrived to discuss trade relations (Radio Prague, 24 August), and the U.S.-Czechoslovak Economic Council held its seventh session in Prague (Radio Prague, 14 September). The Mixed Czechoslovak–West German Commission for Economic, Industrial, and Technical Cooperation convened for its eleventh session (DPA, Prague, 30 September), and Tunisian planning and finance minister Ismail Khelil came to discuss economic cooperation (Radio Prague, 7 September). Foreign Trade Minister Shane Korbeçi made the first official visit from Albania since the end of the 1960s, when all relations were broken with the USSR and its allies. A new trade agreement was signed by Korbeçi and his counterpart, Minister Bohumil Urban (ČETEKA, in English, 21 September). Cooperation in the field of trade with the People's Republic of China, which had been interrupted for many years as a consequence of the Sino-Soviet rift, was renewed during the second half of the 1980s. The Czechoslovak-Chinese Commission for Trade and Scientific-Technological Cooperation held its third session (Radio Prague, 27 September). Earlier in the same week, talks were held between Czechoslovak and Chinese representatives on cooperation in the power industry (ČETEKA, in English, 23 September). A protocol on trade and payments with Vietnam was signed the same day. President Husák signed a long-term program of economic and scientific-technological cooperation with Yugoslavia on 22 September.

In the field of economic and trade relations with the USSR, negotiations during 1987 were affected by the restructuring programs being initiated or implemented in the two countries. In October, Prime Minister Štrougal discussed the implications of restructuring for all CMEA countries with Oleg Bogomolov, director of the Institute for Economics of the World Socialist System (Radio Prague, 6 October). Nine days later, the same subject was examined by Bogomolov and Jakeš, the KSČ Presidium member who soon afterward became KSČ general secretary. On 7 October, Soviet automobile industry minister Nikolai Pugin arrived in Prague to examine the possibility of developing a joint model of a passenger car that could be produced after 1990 (TASS, 7 October). Trade with the Soviet Union, which represents 44 percent of the total Czechoslovak turnover, was not without problems. Complaints about the deteriorating quality of Czechoslovak goods have multiplied of late; footwear seemed to be particularly defective (*Večerní Praha*, 12 June). The Soviets also appeared to be increasingly uneasy about the structure of these exchanges, with the USSR delivering almost exclusively raw materials and energy, while Czechoslovak exports consist mainly of finished products (Radio Hvězda, 31 March). Soviet concern about the structure of foreign trade has been in line with the economic objectives of Gorbachev's reform program, as presented at the Twenty-seventh CPSU Congress in 1986. The USSR wishes to substantially improve its position in the world markets as a developed industrial state. This pressure may oblige Czechoslovakia to consider exporting its manufactured goods to other parts of the world.

International Party Contacts. Relations and exchanges with the CPSU, always the most important contact of the world communist movement, were in 1987 more than ever the focus of attention. Much of this concentrated on one particular event, namely the visit of the CPSU general secretary. The possible impact his visit could have on developments in the KSČ stimulated a number of prognoses and theories, as did the circumstances of the visit itself. Gorbachev's arrival, for example, had originally been scheduled for 6 April and had been postponed, literally at the last minute, after foreign journalists had received an extensive briefing and after hundreds of members of the SSM and the PO SSM had been dispatched to the airport. This gave rise to speculation of all kinds. Officially, the delay was explained as being due to a cold (TASS, 6 April; Radio Prague, 7 April). This explanation was later dropped from the news, which only further whetted the curiosity of the public. Some commentators conjectured that the postponement might have been caused by a division of views within the CPSU leadership as to the wisdom of Gorbachev's visit to Czechoslovakia—a markedly sensitive spot in the socialist universe—at that point in time. Others believed that Gorbachev intended to mention in his talks with the KSČ officials the possibility of complete withdrawal of the Soviet troops, which, in the eyes of his critics and opponents in the Kremlin, was tantamount to a rehabilitation of the 1968 Prague Spring. In terms of this theory, Gorbachev had to renegotiate the agenda, which would account for the three-day delay (*La Repubblica*, Rome, 8 April).

No sensational changes in the KSČ or in the government occurred immediately after Gorbachev's visit. Yet the speeches and the various communiqués issued by the Soviet guest on the one hand and by his Czechoslovak hosts and their press organs on the other hand confirmed the dissonance between the two in their approach to economic and social reforms. Gorbachev clearly stated his belief "that transformations in all spheres of Soviet life" would also be "in the interest of the other socialist countries" (Radio Prague, 9 April). The subsequent "unreserved endorsement" of the restructuring project by KSČ leaders and the change in the highest executive office of the party at the end of the year proved that what Gorbachev had in mind was a complete realignment of Czechoslovakia to the USSR course.

The disharmony of views between KSČ conservatives and Gorbachev came to the fore when the new KSČ general secretary was appointed in December. The party central daily, rendering into Czech the congratulatory telegram sent by Gorbachev to Jakeš, translated the Russian word "renewal" (*obnovlienie*) of socialism in Czechoslovakia into the Czech term for "strengthening" (*upevnění*). That this had been deliberate and not just an inadequate translation became evident from Jakeš cabled reply. Referring to Gorbachev's message of good wishes, Jakeš also used the *upevnění* instead of *obnovlienie*. Thus, the team in control saw its most important task as consolidating the status quo rather than innovations of any kind (TASS, in English, 17 December; *Rudé právo*, 18 December).

Another possible conflict on important issues between the CPSU and KSČ leaderships occurred in Moscow during the celebration of the 70th anniversary of the October Revolution, where Soviet media acknowledged the receipt of a letter sent to Gorbachev by Dubček to mark the occasion. Husák and the KSČ delegation must have perceived this as an affront and also been irritated by statements of Soviet historians and journalists—among them Georgi Arbatov—at a news conference in Moscow the same week about the necessity to re-evaluate the Soviet-led invasion of Czechoslovakia in August 1968 (*NYT*, 10 November). As a gesture of protest, Husák did not appear on the official tribune at Red Square during the traditional parade, and the Czechoslovak delegation left the Soviet capital before the end of the festivities. Some commentators wondered whether this incident had not been the actual motive for Husák's resignation from his function as general secretary at the next session of the Central Committee (RFE-RL, Munich, *Czechoslovak Situation Report*, no. 18, 22 December).

The KSČ participated in the meeting of the party secretaries in charge of international and ideological affairs in Warsaw during 22–23 January (*WMR*, March). It was also represented at the meeting of CMEA secretaries for agriculture in Moscow, 10–11 February (ibid., April). In January, a delegation from the Communist Party of Greece led by General Secretary Kharilaos Florakis came to Prague and was received by KSČ Presidium member Bil'ák (*WMR*, March). A delegation of the ruling "fraternal" party from Benin, headed by Politburo member Martin Dohou Azonhiho, also visited Czechoslovakia (Radio Prague, 20 August). KSČ secretary Havlín traveled to Moscow for a working visit (TASS, 15 September). A KSČ delegation went to Helsinki at the invitation of the Communist

Party of Finland (ČETEKA, in English, 21 September), and President Husák awarded the Order of Friendship to Pieter Keuneman, chairman of the Sri Lanka Communist Party, on his 70th birthday (*Rudé právo*, 3 October). KSČ secretary Pitra went to Bucharest at the invitation of the Communist Party of Romania (Radio Prague, 12 October). Simultaneously, a study delegation of the KSČ traveled to Belgrade (Tanjug, 12 October). Later, Zdeněk Hoření, KSČ secretary and editor in chief of the main party daily, *Rudé právo*, made a working visit to France. It was a follow-up to a previous visit by a KSČ delegation to Paris in November 1986 (*WMR*, February). Hoření was received by Politburo member Maxime Gremetz, with whom he discussed possibilities of further cooperation between *Rudé právo* and *L'Humanité* (ČETEKA, in English, 23 October). The Central Committee of the KSČ sent greetings to the national conference of the People's Democratic Party of Afghanistan (*Pravda*, Bratislava, 19 October).

The KSČ maintains regular contacts with twelve communist movements in Western Europe and on the North American continent, as well as with "fraternal" parties in industrialized capitalist countries. This information was contained in a special document released by Prague in the summer of 1987 that acknowledges with satisfaction that "a major breakthrough has recently been achieved in relations with the Japanese Communist Party." It also reports "signs of improvement in relations with some of the communist parties with whom relations were broken off or deadlocked in the past over fundamental differences of approach to a number of issues" (*WMR*, August). The "fundamental differences" to which the document refers have in most cases been disagreements over the Soviet military intervention in Czechoslovakia, which took place twenty years ago, and the suppression and persecution of the reformist partisans in the KSČ by the present party leadership. It may well be that the endorsement of the Soviet program of "restructuring" by the KSČ has somewhat eased the tension with its critics in the world communist movement. However, more significant changes must occur in Czechoslovakia before a "fraternal" party such as the Communist Party of Italy (conspicuously missing from the twelve parties listed in the document) will consent to resume regular relations with the KSČ.

Zdeněk Suda
University of Pittsburgh

Germany:
German Democratic Republic

Population. 16,610,265

Party. Socialist Unity Party of Germany (Sozialistische Einheitspartei Deutschlands; SED)

Founded. 1918 (SED, 1946)

Membership. 2,324,386 members and candidates (*Neues Deutschland* [*ND*] 3 July); 58.1 percent workers, 4.8 percent peasants and farmers in cooperatives, 22.4 percent intelligentsia, 14.7 percent others (*ND*, 18 April 1986)

General Secretary. Erich Honecker (75)

Politburo. 22 full members: Erich Honecker (chairman, State Council), Hermann Axen (71), Hans-Joachim Böhme (56; first secretary, Halle regional SED executive), Horst Dohlus (62), Werner Eberlein (67; first secretary, Magdeburg regional SED executive), Werner Felfe (59; member, State Council), Kurt Hager (75; member, State Council), Joachim Herrmann (59), Werner Jarowinsky (60), Heinz Kessler (67; defense minister), Günther Kleiber (56; deputy chairman, Council of Ministers, and permanent representative to CMEA), Egon Krenz (50; deputy chairman, State Council), Werner Krolikowski (59; first deputy chairman, Council of Ministers), Siegfried Lorenz (56; first secretary, Karl-Marx-Stadt regional SED executive), Erich Mielke (80; minister of state security), Günter Mittag (61; deputy chairman, State Council), Erich Mückenberger (77; chairman, Central Party Control Commission), Alfred Neumann (78; first deputy chairman, Council of Ministers), Günter Schabowski (58; first secretary, East Berlin regional SED executive), Horst Sindermann (72; deputy chairman, State Council, and president, People's Chamber), Willi Stoph (73; chairman, Council of Ministers, and deputy chairman, State Council), Harry Tisch (60; member, State Council, and chairman, Free German Trade Union Federation); 5 candidate members: Ingeborg Lange (60), Gerhard Müller (56; first secretary, Erfurt regional SED executive), Margarete Müller (56; member, State Council), Gerhard Schürer (66, deputy chairman, Council of Ministers, and chairman, State Planning Commission), Werner Walde (61; first secretary, Cottbus regional SED executive)

Central Audit Commission. Kurt Seibt, chairman (79; president, GDR Solidarity Committee)

Secretariat. 11 members: Erich Honecker, Hermann Axen (international relations), Horst Dohlus (party organs), Werner Felfe (agriculture), Kurt Hager (culture and science), Joachim Herrmann (agitation and propaganda), Werner Jarowinsky (church affairs, trade, and supply), Egon Krenz (security affairs, youth, and sports), Ingeborg Lange (women's affairs), Günter Mittag (economics), Günter Schabowski (East Berlin)

Central Committee. 165 full and 57 candidate members (1986)

Status. Ruling Party

Last Congress. Eleventh, 17–21 April 1986

Last Election. 8 June 1986, 99.94 percent of vote, all 500 seats won by National Front candidates

Auxiliary Organizations. Free German Trade Union Confederation (FDGB), 9.5 million members, Harry Tisch, chairman; Free German Youth (FDJ) 2.3 million members, Eberhard Aurich, first secretary; Democratic Women's League of Germany (DFD), 1.5 million members, Ilse Thiele, chairwoman; Society for German-Soviet Friendship (DSF), 6.3 million members, Erich Mückenberger, president

Publications. *Neues Deutschland*, official SED daily, Herbert Naumann, editor in chief; *Einheit*, SED theoretical monthly; *Neuer Weg*, SED organizational monthly; *Junge Welt*, FDJ daily; *Tribüne*, FDGB daily; *Horizont*, foreign policy monthly. The official news agency is Allgemeiner Deutscher Nachrichtendienst (ADN).

The activist foreign policy of the German Democratic Republic (GDR) toward the West, after finally receiving Moscow's endorsement, could claim some significant successes in 1987, including the first official trip of an East German head of state to the Federal Republic of Germany (FRG). In regard to domestic matters, however, several clear differences with the Soviet Union emerged, and the question of whether the GDR's long-standing economic and social policies should continue unchanged seemed much more debatable than in recent years. Honecker thus faced the CPSU leadership with decidedly mixed emotions, confident that his main foreign policy initiatives had found acceptance, perhaps even emulation, but also apprehensive that Soviet-style "restructuring" and "openness" might force the SED to abandon the gradualist approach to institutional change that he prefers.

Leadership and Party Organization. Although Honecker maintained a vigorous political schedule and showed no signs of ill health, his advancing years nevertheless provoked speculation about a successor. Krenz, long thought to be Honecker's favorite, still appeared to be heir apparent, but his relative youth and inexperience may not be acceptable to a majority of Central Committee members. Two other possibilities found frequent mention: Schabowski, who has made an unusually rapid rise to the inner circle of power and has conspicuously supported Honecker, and Felfe, who has headed agriculture for the past six years and also maintained a high profile in important party matters. Honecker has apparently taken care to balance the top leadership along a variety of lines, including pragmatists and ideologues as well as centralists and spokesmen for regional interests. Very likely this transfer will not occur before the Twelfth Party Congress in 1991, but when the change does occur, the SED seems better positioned than other Eastern bloc states for an orderly succession (RFE-RL *Research*, 3 January, 25 February).

The Central Committee plenum in December saw only minimal changes. The composition of the Politburo and the Secretariat remained unaltered, while two names were added to the Central Party Control Commission: Horst Heiser as a full member and Peter Karweina as a candidate member (ADN, 16 December; *FBIS*, 17 December). In the rounds of party elections and conferences held between 2 March and 26 April, the stability of the SED rank and file also seemed confirmed, with more than three-quarters of the local leadership returned to office. At the same time, an effort was made to raise the educational level and to enlist more women and young people (*ND*, 6 May; *JPRS*, 25 June).

Most unexpected was the departure of Markus "Mischa" Wolf, 64, the head of the foreign intelligence agency (*Hauptverwaltung Aufklärung*) within the Ministry of State Security. Not only the longest serving intelligence head of any Warsaw Pact country but also widely acknowledged to be among the best spy masters in the world, Wolf was considered likely to succeed Mielke as minister of state security. Although the official explanation stated that Wolf was leaving active service "at his own request," speculation in the West centered on reasons of health or deep-seated personal differences with Mielke that had denied Wolf entry into the Central Committee and hence barred a ministerial appointment (ADN and DPA, 5 February; *FBIS*, 6 February; *Deutschland Archiv* [*DA*], March).

In a move that seemed to indicate the party's desire to exercise even greater control over intelligence activities, Werner Grossmann, 65, a major general in the state security forces, was named as Wolf's successor; unlike Wolf, he is not a deputy minister but is responsible to Rudolf Mittig, the deputy minister of state security (*Die Welt*, 23 June). Mittig, who became a full Central Committee member last year at the Eleventh SED Congress, now seems the most probable successor to Mielke, who is 80 and in poor health.

Domestic Affairs. *Social and Political Affairs.* Almost as soon as Honecker's planned visit to the FRG was announced came the declaration of a general amnesty that would free all prisoners except those sentenced for "Nazi and war crimes, crimes against humanity, espionage, or murder" (ADN, 17 July; *FBIS*, 20 July). When the amnesty concluded on 12 December, East German officials reported that 24,621 persons had been released from prison and that proceedings had been stopped against 2,741 people held in custody (ADN, 13 December; *FBIS*, 14 December). The freed political prisoners were given the opportunity to apply for exit visas to the FRG, presumably because the SED wanted to avoid the situation that followed the last amnesty in 1979, when many persons were rearrested for attempting to flee the GDR (*Die Welt*, 16 December; *FBIS*, 16 December).

In related moves, East Germany also declared the abolition of the death penalty and the creation of a second court of appeals at the highest level (ADN, 17 July; *FBIS*, 20 July). Given the fact that the death penalty had not been imposed or carried out since 1979, it appeared that the GDR was more concerned with offsetting criticism of its human rights record by becoming the first Warsaw Pact country to end capital punishment officially. Similarly the appellate court, which had been urged by long-time Honecker confidant Wolfgang Vogel on behalf of other East German lawyers, spelled little fundamental reform of a legal system in which judges remain bound by the dictates of the party (*DA*, August).

The problems the GDR confronts among its youth found dramatic expression when police attempted to bar thousands of rock fans from eavesdropping on a series of concerts held on the western side of the Brandenburg Gate. Not since 1977 had an incident of this magnitude occurred. Chanting "The wall must go!" and "Gorbachev! Gorbachev!," more than 3,000 demonstrators clashed with GDR security forces before the three-day unrest was brought to a halt (*NYT*, 10 June). The East German news agency, however, flatly denied that the confrontation had taken place, attributing reports to "the fantasies of some Western correspondents who traveled across the border motivated by sensationalism" (ADN; *FBIS*, 9 June). Also rejected were West German charges that a cameraman and other reporters had been obstructed in violation of a 1972 treaty and subjected to excessive force (*ND*, 11 June). Later in the year the Berlin Wall received added fortifications, especially near the Brandenburg Gate (*Frankfurter Allgemeine Zeitung*, 19 December).

That the SED recognized an estrangement with its youth seemed confirmed by a report of meetings between aides of Education Minister Margot Honecker and teachers throughout the country. Complaining of a growing disrespect for the FDJ and disinterest in the party press, including the daily *Junge Welt* (Young World) with its more casual and contemporary format, the ministry officials called upon teachers to make a more concerted effort to combat these tendencies among the youth (*Der Spiegel*, 20 April; *FBIS*, 28 April). A tacit admission of this problem could be detected in the removal of many restrictions on travel to the West for young people. Occurring quietly in the wake of the June demonstrations, these policy changes lowered age requirements and made it possible under certain conditions to visit friends, not just relatives (*Frankfurter Rundschau*, 18 July; *FBIS*, 20 July).

Contending that only 0.02 percent of those who made a Western trip in 1986 did not return, GDR officials apparently felt that emigration pressure could be offset by a less restrictive travel policy. In fact, reports throughout the year confirmed a sharp decrease in the number of exit permits issued and the prospect of a new policy that will extend the waiting time for potential emigrants to a minimum of three years (*Foreign Report*, 30 April; *Der Spiegel*, 19 October; *Die Welt*, 19 August). One notable exception, however, involved Lieutenant General Manfred Grätz, deputy defense minister; his son became the first immediate relative of a high-ranking military official permitted to leave for the FRG (ibid., 8 April; *FBIS*, 9 April).

A growing trend of the past decade has made the Evangelical church a key vehicle for registering social and political discontent. A number of obstacles thus had to be cleared before GDR Protestants were permitted to hold their congress, for the first time, in East Berlin. Security authorities feared that the final session might be augmented by day visitors from the West and become uncontrollable, but Honecker, wanting to make the celebration of Berlin's anniversary as all-embracing as possible, overruled them (*Der Spiegel*, 2 February; *FBIS*, 3 February). It then took negotiations between church and SED officials before financial and logistical support from the state was forthcoming.

The Protestants, however, faced a sharp division within their own ranks, as grass roots groups expressed increased resentment at the church hierarchy for its concessions to the government. In particular, anger at the cancellation of a "peace workshop" at this year's meeting resulted in a circular calling for an unofficially constituted "congress from below" to run parallel to the official one. Although all three sides made compromises and kept the 24–28 June assembly from open eruption, the dynamics of the situation are quite unstable and beyond any easy resolution. Indeed, a synod of the Federation of Evangelical Churches held in Görlitz in mid-September revealed again the strong impulse of some participants to pressure the SED to greater liberalization as well as the reluctance of the main Protestant leadership to jeopardize its delicate relationship with the state. Heino Falcke of Erfurt aroused much controversy when he sought official endorsement of a petition entitled "A Rejection of the Practice and Principle of Delimitation" that criticized the contradiction between the foreign policy of détente pursued by the GDR and the curtailed contact imposed on its citizens. Despite Falcke's lack of success, the final resolution did contain a call for more "dialogue and openness in society" and for a social service alternative to compulsory military service. SED response was noticeably muted (RFE-RL *Research*, 10 July, 28 September).

The willingness of the Evangelical church to permit nonreligious peace and environmental activists to operate under its aegis has further complicated matters for the church leadership. A raid on the East Berlin Zion Church in late November by GDR security forces resulted in the arrest of two secularist protesters and the confiscation of printing and mimeographing equipment, along with material termed "hostile to the state." Although the two men were released several days later, numerous persons outside East Berlin with similar views were questioned by police authorities and placed under a travel ban. The church organized a vigil to express its displeasure and reaffirmed its commitment to "speak up on behalf of any person who is seriously threatened" (*Die Welt*, 26–28 November). Nevertheless, at a meeting of leading Protestant officials several weeks later, concern was voiced that such groups exclusively pursuing their own aims could imperil the church-state relationship that has evolved over the past ten years (ibid., 19 December).

The first nationwide convention in the GDR helped the small and declining Roman Catholic population feel less isolated. The attendance in Dresden far exceeded expectations, attracting nearly 100,000 members to the final "day of pilgrimage." But hopes that Pope John Paul II would be permitted to attend were dashed when Honecker specified a papal stopover in East Berlin as a condition, forcing the pontiff to cancel (ANSA, 28 March; *FBIS*, 31 March). The SED maintains a distant relationship with Catholic leaders, and the church has been reluctant to become involved with social and political issues. More willing this year to acknowledge the laity's desire for "participation" in society, Joachim Cardinal Meissner nevertheless continued to affirm the limits that a Christian must accept. The 10–12 July gathering held only religious observations, although potentially more assertive roles were suggested by a series of small working groups meeting in closed session. After helping with some of the arrangements, state authorities watched the proceedings quietly and attentively, for little has been done to establish for Catholics the procedural framework that regulates Protestant activities (*DA*, September; RFE-RL *Research*, 15 July).

The Tenth Congress of the GDR Writers' Union held 24–26 November produced sharp criticisms of government publishing restrictions. In a speech evoking strong applause, Günter de Bruyn insisted that it was the union's task to "render oppression from the permission-to-print practice less oppressive and ultimately scrap it altogether." He also read a letter from Christa Wolf that not only urged unlimited publication of literary works but criticized the union for its reluctance to support authors who fell prey to the censors. The movement to reevaluate the works of Friedrich Nietzsche was endorsed by union president Hermann Kant and poet

Stephan Hermlin. At the same time, a majority of the nearly 300 delegates still showed some ambivalence about easing restrictions on freedom of expression and adamantly rejected a proposal to depart from the planned program for a more open and spontaneous discussion. It also seemed clear that, by permitting Western journalists to attend the plenary sessions for the first time, the SED was attempting to prove its willingness to tolerate criticism as long as it stayed within prescribed limits (DPA, 25 November; *FBIS*, 27 November; *NYT*, 28 November; RFE-RL *Research*, 4 December).

The importance of ideological motivation within the military was underscored by a meeting of leading cadres from the National People's Army (*Nationale Volksarmee*; NVA), the GDR border troops, and the civil defense forces at which Politburo member Krenz emphasized fulfillment of the class assignment outlined by the Eleventh SED Congress (*ND*, 6 March; *FBIS*, 19 March). A publication of the East German Defense Ministry likewise urged that NVA exercises "assume a military-political situation that corresponds to the class conflict between socialism and imperialism" and simulate the most realistic conditions of warfare (*Informationen*, no. 5). The general fitness of the army received acknowledgment when, under the auspices of the 1986 Stockholm agreement on confidence-building measures, representatives from 22 nations observed large-scale NVA troop exercises and accorded high marks to their preparation and execution (*ND*, 15–16 April).

Economic Affairs. Although the East German regime could again claim the most successful economy of the Eastern bloc states, there were indications of weakness in several areas. According to the Politburo report delivered to the Central Committee plenum in December, the agricultural sector appeared to have fared the best and, in spite of adverse weather conditions, could boast the largest grain harvest on record. Less impressive was the fact that the produced national income through November grew by only 4 percent, falling below the 4.4–4.7 percent rate projected by the five-year plan adopted in 1986. In this context, the Construction Ministry was singled out for sharp criticism, allegedly for having failed to prevent delays in new equipment and plant expansion. The report further stated that, despite an increase of 4.5 percent in the net monetary income of the population and a large rise in the value of goods purchased, there had been shortages of numerous consumer items ranging from furniture and washing machines to certain articles of clothing and footwear. Also noteworthy was the candid admission that 37 percent of East Germany's forests had suffered severe damage and were in need of urgent attention (*ND*, 16 December; *FBIS*, 21 December).

The chronic energy shortage of the GDR loomed as a large problem in 1987 because of the bitterly cold European winter. In January power cuts left residential areas without heat and electricity for days, and, with reduced supplies causing shorter factory hours and some closings, industrial production fell behind schedule during the first quarter and only began to recover toward midyear. Not only was the press unusually forthright in reporting how the population coped with the situation, but SED Politburo members visited factories and mines to boost worker morale. Even Honecker, in his address to the regional secretaries, came close to conceding that a major problem existed (*ND*, 7 February; *FBIS*, 10 February).

The desire to improve the balance of trade, as well as the USSR's decision to export less oil to its allies, has led the GDR to depend on its domestic supplies of lignite, which met more than 80 percent of the country's electric and heating needs the previous year. The disadvantages of brown coal, however, were never more apparent. Vulnerable to the freezing temperatures because of its high water content, it proved exceedingly difficult to excavate (the use of dynamite by the military was reported in some instances) and transport. Moreover, much of the severe air pollution in various parts of the FRG could be traced to the lignite power plants concentrated primarily in the districts of Cottbus, Halle, and Leipzig. With the current five-year economic plan projecting the use of lignite to rise to 335 million tons by 1990, with mining procedures growing more costly and complex, and with the price of Soviet oil averaging more than world market prices, the vice president of the GDR Committee of the World Energy Congress stated that no long-term solution to the country's energy dilemma had been found (*DIW Wochenbericht*, 12 March; *JPRS*, 22 May; *IWE Tagesdienst*, 24 March; *JPRS*, 28 April; RFE-RL *Research*, 6 March).

For the present, the SED implored the industrial sector to reduce consumption, as the Carl Zeiss Jena VEB proclaimed the motto "Full Production with Less Energy" and the Leipzig Gear Works pledged to cut 5 percent of its electric usage in 1987 (*ND*, 6 May; *JPRS*, 25 June). In addition, one result of Honecker's FRG visit was to advance discussions about connecting a power grid that would allow the GDR to purchase electricity from West Germany and other European suppliers (*WSJ*, 11 September).

Whatever the problems, outward confidence in the economic course charted by the 1986–1990 plan remained undiminished at year's end. In his financial report to the People's Chamber, Prime Minister Stoph again stated that "comprehensive intensification" provided the means to increase production in all areas of the economy (ADN, 18 December; *FBIS*, 21 December). Honecker's address to the Central Committee plenum stressed even more emphatically the ability of the existing giant industrial monopolies or combines (*Kombinate*) to develop "key technologies," thus excluding the need for any major reform (*ND*, 17 December).

Foreign Policy. *Intra-German Relations.* Overshadowing all other events was the long-awaited, first-time visit of an East German party leader and head of state to West Germany. Since full diplomatic recognition is still lacking, the FRG called the trip a "working visit" instead of a "state visit," thereby diminishing some of the ceremonial trappings, but the extensive media coverage of the five-day event by both Germanies more than compensated for the distinction. Between 7 and 11 September, Honecker made stops in four West German states, including his hometown of Wiebelskirchen in the Saarland, and conferred with Chancellor Helmut Kohl, President Richard von Weizsäcker, important political leaders and parliamentary groups, and a number of prominent bankers and industrialists.

The fundamental issue separating the two states—the FRG's insistence on a united Germany and the GDR's adherence to a "two-state theory"—tended to be confirmed by official statements from both sides, especially Honecker's assertion that "socialism and capitalism are as incompatible as fire and water." His ambiguous remarks in his native village in the Saarland (the "borders are not as they should be" and "the day will come when the borders will not separate us any more, but will unite us, just as the border between the GDR and Poland unites us") provoked much attention and a variety of interpretations but did not indicate any basic shift in policy (*FBIS*, 15 September).

The talks thus concentrated on matters of interstate travel, trade, and economic cooperation. As the number of GDR residents under 65 who visited the FRG increased from 66,000 in 1985 to 573,000 in 1986 and to more than 866,000 in the first eight months of 1987, the Bonn government specifically sought to keep this trend in motion, even when it meant supplying additional subsidies to GDR visitors because of the drain on East Germany's hard currency. Kohl also pressed Honecker to abolish the order for border guards to shoot would-be defectors on sight. The East German leader made no explicit concessions, although this practice, according to the testimony of several former border guards, appeared to be temporarily suspended when important state visits or political elections in the FRG were taking place (*DA*, January; *Die Welt*, 12 August; *FBIS*, 13 August).

Both Germanies showed a keen interest in reviving trade, which had fallen by 9 percent in 1986, but the inability of East German goods to compete in the FRG makes any substantial change doubtful in the near term. Despite its solid financial rating, the GDR expressed no desire to receive more credits along the lines of the 1984 agreement. More revealing were signs that Honecker had overcome his reluctance to enter joint venture projects and was now willing to "open up new fields of economic cooperation." Three accords, in fact, were signed that will lead to greater cooperation in the areas of scientific and technological research, environmental planning, and nuclear safety. More specifically, East German researchers and technicians will have greater access to West German universities and will also be involved in more than two dozen joint projects, ranging from physics and production technology to research on the acquired immunodeficiency syndrome (AIDS). The final communiqué mentioned the possible establishment of an economic commission designed to bring East German combines into closer contact with small and medium-sized enterprises in the FRG (*ND*, 9 September; RFE-RL *Research*, 17 September; *WSJ*, 11 September).

In the spirit of the cultural accords signed in the spring that set up exchanges of art exhibitions and television programs, Honecker consented to ease restrictions on the importing of printed materials and audio- and videocassettes (*NYT*, 1 November). Another long-standing problem was solved when the two Germanies agreed to exchange several hundred works of art that had been displaced by World War II (*Informationen*, no. 21).

By the time this historic event ended and Kohl had accepted Honecker's invitation to visit East Germany in 1988, it was difficult to recall that the year had begun on a more acrimonious note. During his re-election campaign, Kohl charged that the GDR was keeping "2,000 of our fellow countrymen as political captives in prisons and concentration camps" (DPA, 4 January; *FBIS*, 5 January). The GDR Foreign Ministry quickly issued a blunt denial, but no full-scale counterattack was launched. *Neues Deutschland* preferred instead to print a selection of letters written to Honecker by FRG citizens who were upset at their chancellor's behavior (*ND*, 24 January). In commenting on the West German election results, however, the East German press took particular note of the CDU/CSU setback, asserting that the "slanderous" attacks on the GDR had backfired, and expressed satisfaction that FRG foreign minister Hans-Dietrich Genscher would be able to continue with his self-proclaimed "new phase of détente" toward the East (*ND*, 27 January).

The celebration of the 750th anniversary of Berlin's founding, understandably, became a politically charged occasion for the two Germanies. Although joint ceremonies were never a real possibility, the question arose whether West Berlin mayor Eberhard Diepgen and Honecker should attend festivities in each other's sector of the city. Showing keen interest in accepting Honecker's invitation to go to the East in October, Diepgen issued a counterinvitation to the East German leader to attend the West Berlin ceremony planned for late April. In the end, however, Honecker declined, citing a letter written by Diepgen in 1986 that urged West German state premiers not to take part in official ceremonies in East Berlin (ADN, 13 April; *FBIS*, 14 April). No doubt the prime reason could be found in the differing claims about the status of the city. For Diepgen to appear officially in the eastern sector would add legitimacy to the GDR's proclamation of East Berlin as its capital, just as Honecker's presence alongside the West German chancellor could be interpreted as acknowledgment of a special political relationship between West Berlin and the FRG. Since the USSR and the GDR view the western sector as a "separate political entity," it seems likely that Soviet pressure and, perhaps, some misgivings in the SED led Honecker to jettison this quid pro quo offer.

To reaffirm the allied commitment to West Berlin, French president François Mitterrand, U.S. president Ronald Reagan, and Queen Elizabeth II of Great Britain made official stops in the city during the late spring. Not to be upstaged by festivities on the other side of the wall, East Berlin was the site of more than 1,000 exhibitions, meetings, and cultural events throughout the year, including an international convention of mayors from 168 cities (with the exception of Frankfurt, the twelve most populous cities of the FRG were represented) (*ND*, 2 June). Besides undergoing some remarkably lavish renovation, especially in the "old town" area near the Nikolai Church, East Berlin was officially dubbed "a place for peace" in order to evoke the historical struggle between the forces of "progress" and "reaction" during the past 750 years and also to mesh with current SED slogans about world peace (RFE-RL *Research*, 13 March).

Courtship of the Social Democratic Party (SPD) of West Germany continued with visits to the GDR by Oskar Lafontaine, Hans-Jochen Vogel, and Karsten Voigt and with further discussions about a nuclear-free corridor in central Europe (*ND*, 13 March, 16–18 May; ADN, 23 July; *FBIS*, 24 July). Honecker and Vogel agreed to the establishment of a joint SED-SPD working group on security questions, and, by late November, it had convened in East Berlin to discuss conventional arms reduction (ADN, 27 November; *FBIS*, 2 December). A meeting in Bonn between the FDJ and the FRG's Young Socialists took up the nuclear disarmament theme and laid plans for a series of international youth conferences (East German Television, 10 February; *JPRS*, 12 February).

A new plateau of understanding between the SED and the SPD was reached with the release of the joint statement entitled "The Battle of Ideologies and Common Security." Prepared by representatives of each party and made public just before Honecker's FRG visit, the seventeen-page document stated that the danger of nuclear annihilation necessitated a "new thinking" about international problems: "war as a method of politics" must be eliminated, confrontation between different political systems should be restricted to nonviolent forms, and more areas of mutual agreement need to be sought. The full text was quickly reprinted in *Neues Deutschland* (*ND*, 28 August), and a roundtable discussion with the negotiators from each party was broadcast live on state television. At the same time, East German commentators cautioned that the document did not imply "ideological convergence" and that the eventual "victory" of socialism over capitalism remained as certain as ever. Honecker later referred to it as a practical expression of peaceful competition between different social systems, denying that it connoted "a standstill in ideological conflict" (*ND*, 6 October; *FBIS*, 9 October). Although some specific passages such as the removal of "hate images of the enemy" run counter to the practices of the regime and might be seized upon by domestic opposition groups, the document represented a step forward in Honecker's campaign to legitimate the SED within the FRG (RFE-RL *Research*, 8 September).

Westpolitik. Because the U.N. figures prominently in the GDR's repeated call for a "coalition of reason and common sense" as well as in its quest for greater international recognition, the elevation of Deputy Foreign Minister Peter Florin to the presidency of the Forty-second General Assembly was greeted with no small feeling of accomplishment (*ND*, 16 September; for biographical portrait, see *NYT*, 22 September). Similarly, the visit of U.N. secretary general Javier Pérez de Cuéllar to East Berlin in mid-June not only resulted in a world peace award for Foreign Minister Oskar Fischer and an honorary doctorate for the secretary general but also conveniently coincided with the anniversary of the 1953 uprising (*ND*, 16–17 June).

Another key element of GDR foreign policy is the stress on "common European interests," specifically the cultivation of both neutral and NATO member countries. Most notable in this respect were Honecker's first official trips to the Netherlands and Belgium, which brought the total number of NATO countries visited by the GDR leader to five. His June stay in The Hague included discussions with Queen Beatrix, Prime Minister Ruud Lubbers, and other government leaders and was dominated by the issue of arms control. Besides stressing the importance of nuclear disarmament, Honecker conceded that a "certain imbalance" in conventional weapons between NATO and the Warsaw Pact existed but offered nothing more specific than the proposal that both sides reduce their forces by 25 percent. Lubbers pressed the East German leader on human rights abuses and the "unnatural" division of Europe, but Honecker deflected the charges by recalling the warm hospitality he had experienced in Holland during the "antifascist" struggle of World War II. Although the GDR was primarily seeking greater political recognition, trade and economic cooperation, which had fallen from its high point in 1984, also had definite importance; a new agreement on scientific, technological, and industrial exchanges for the coming year was concluded (*ND*, 3–7 June; RFE-RL *Research*, 26 June).

Despite enthusiastic press coverage of meetings with King Baudouin, Prime Minister Wilfried Martens, and other top government representatives, Honecker's trip to Belgium in October had a somewhat anticlimactic tone and did not break much new ground. Belgium, the first NATO country to establish diplomatic relations with the GDR, was already bound by extensive agreements, mostly economic, and an earlier meeting between Honecker and Martens had secured Belgian participation in a joint East German-Czechoslovak initiative regarding a European chemical-free zone and a ban on numerous chemical weapons. In addition, Honecker no longer had any reason to lobby for an FRG visit as he had in the Netherlands (*ND*, 13–16 October; *DA*, January).

The GDR also remained attentive to its interests outside the NATO sphere. Austrian chancellor Franz Vranitzky, who went out of his way to praise his country's relationship with the GDR, received a stream of officials including Politburo member Mittag, Foreign Trade Minister Gerhard Beil, and Foreign Minister Fischer (*ND*, 10 April, 3 June, 21 August; ADN, 5 May; *FBIS*, 6 May). Repaying Honecker's visit of 1984, Finnish president Mauno Koivisto held top-level consultations in East Berlin that resulted in several bilateral accords, including the first agreement between East Germany and a Western country abolishing visa requirements for travelers to the GDR (East German citizens still must request permission to travel to Finland) (*ND*, 2 October). Geopolitical considerations help explain the intense interest shown toward Cyprus. A Cypriot parliamentary group met with GDR prime minister Stoph and People's Chamber president Sindermann in East Berlin; Cypriot president Spyros Kyprianou received a military delegation in Nicosia headed by GDR defense minister Kessler; and Cypriot foreign minister Georgios Iakovou consulted with Honecker in East Berlin (*ND*, 6–8 April, 23 May, 30 June). One tangible result was an agreement expanding the use of port facilities for East German ships (ibid., 30 July).

President Yasuhiro Nakasone became the first Japanese head of state to visit the GDR since diplomatic relations were established in 1973. Honecker no doubt felt especially gratified, for Nakasone included the GDR in a limited European itinerary after Mikhail Gorbachev's trip to Japan was canceled. Trade between Japan and East Germany, which has been steadily decreasing since its high point in 1983, probably has too many major hurdles to overcome to be revived by the new agreements. Far more potential lies in expanded cultural exchanges, with Nakasone's frequent invocation of

"German culture" reinforcing the GDR's already favored position among East European countries. Nakasone left his East German hosts briefly for an excursion into West Berlin lest his trip be seen as undermining the official four-power status of the city (*ND*, 15 January; *DA*, February). Diplomatic momentum was maintained later in the year by Sindermann's trip to Tokyo and by the visit of a Japanese parliamentary delegation to the GDR (*ND*, 26 March, 18 June).

Relations with North America, in contrast to Europe and Japan, had much less precedence, although Charles Joseph Clark became the first Canadian foreign minister to visit the GDR and although new treaties expanding economic cooperation were announced later in the year (ibid., 7 May, 29 October). John C. Whitehead, U.S. deputy secretary of state and the highest-ranking American official to visit the GDR, held talks with Honecker and other party officials as well as with Protestant and Jewish representatives (ADN, 10–11 November; *FBIS*, 12 November).

Third World. In Latin America, Cuba and Nicaragua remained the key points of East German contact. Politburo member Kleiber met with Fidel Castro in Havana, and Politburo member Carlos Rafael Rodríguez went to East Berlin to confer with Honecker and conclude a protocol implementing the current five-year economic agreement (*ND*, 28 March, 22 October). In addition, Aurich led an FDJ contingent to a Cuban communist youth congress in Havana, and Defense Minister Kessler received a Cuban military delegation for consultations (ibid., 2 April, 6 October).

At the Moscow celebration of the 70th anniversary of the Bolshevik Revolution, the leader of the Nicaraguan ruling party, Daniel Ortega, had a well-publicized meeting with Honecker (*ND*, 4 November). Earlier in the year Ortega had received a GDR parliamentary delegation, while a Sandinista agitprop study group went to East Berlin for orientation and instruction (*ND*, 29 April, 13 June; *FBIS*, 23 June). In addition, members of the Sandinista army, led by the head of the political section, made an inspection tour of NVA home troops and installations (ADN, 27 July; *FBIS*, 29 July). Nicaragua and the GDR also signed an agreement calling for an improved postal and telecommunications system (*ND*, 17 March). To follow up last year's trip by Politburo member Axen, Deputy Foreign Minister Bernhard Neugebauer undertook a lengthy tour of Latin America with stops in Mexico, Argentina, Uruguay, and Brazil (ibid., 6–15 April). Uruguay concluded an expanded trade treaty with the GDR and also dispatched Foreign Minister Enrique Iglesias to a meeting with Honecker in East Berlin (*ND*, 9 July, 1 September).

Ethiopia, Mozambique, and Angola continued to be the main East German interests in sub-Saharan Africa. Ethiopian relations were maintained by numerous party and ministerial exchanges throughout the year, including visits by Sindermann, Seibt, and Dohlus to Addis Ababa and by Ethiopian foreign minister Berhanu Bayih to East Berlin (ibid., 2, 25, 29 April, 12 September). A new treaty of cooperation to 1990 was signed, and trade between the two states was projected to rise by 60 percent (*ND*, 5 March). The GDR further pledged to continue its medical assistance and to complete the construction of 268 new settlements for more than 300,000 persons by the end of the year (ibid., 29 April). Kleiber led a group of SED Central Committee members for talks with FRELIMO (Front for the Liberation of Mozambique) president Joaquim Chissano in Maputo, while Honecker received a military delegation headed by the Mozambican defense minister, who extended his gratitude for the cadre training supplied by the GDR (*ND*, 13 March, 1 September). Also in Maputo an agreement was concluded for increased medical assistance and exchanges, including the services of GDR doctors in Mozambican hospitals (ibid., 2 April). Relations with Angola were highlighted by the extension of a $100 million credit to be used in the period to 1990 for the purchase of equipment, trucks, and consumer goods (ADN, 9 January; *FBIS*, 12 January).

The 75th anniversary of the African National Congress (ANC) was marked by special commemorations in East Berlin and Potsdam and by a telegram from Honecker to ANC leader Oliver Tambo expressing solidarity "with the oldest and most experienced liberation movement on the African continent" and calling once again for the release of Nelson Mandela (*ND*, 8, 12, 22 January). A "solidarity shipment" of relief supplies for the ANC reportedly arrived the following month in Luanda (ibid., 13 February). Later in the year, Tambo was received by Honecker and awarded the "Great Star of People's Friendship" (*ND*, 11 November).

In the Middle East, Kessler led a military delegation to Damascus to meet with Syrian president Hafiz al-Assad and to inspect the country's armed forces (ibid., 21 May). A trip to Tunis by Foreign Minister Fischer resulted in meetings with Tunisian president Habib Bourguiba and with Yassir Arafat, whose re-election later in the month as head of the PLO was greeted by the GDR delegation in attendance as well as by a telegram from Honecker (*ND*, 2, 3, 27–28 April; *FBIS*, 5 May). Iranian prime minister Mir-Hussein Musavi, after visiting East Berlin last year, received GDR chemical industry minister Günther Wyschofsky in Teheran to discuss increased economic cooperation (*ND*, 6 July).

A region of lesser priority with fewer cultivated interests, South and Southeast Asia was still not ignored by the GDR, as Foreign Minister Fischer made a lengthy tour with stops in Sri Lanka, Laos, Cambodia, Vietnam, and Indonesia (ibid., 5–17 March). In addition, Thai foreign minister Siddhi Savetsila met with Honecker and other officials in East Berlin for talks about expanded economic and cultural ties (*ND*, 19 May).

International Party Relations. No question fueled greater and more sustained interest in 1987 than the SED's attitude toward the changes under way in the USSR. The first outward indication of any differences of opinion was shown by the East German press coverage of the CPSU Central Committee plenum in January; *Neues Deutschland* uncharacteristically printed only a summary of Gorbachev's opening speech, omitting his unfavorable references to the Brezhnev era and his stern criticism of many current CPSU officials (*ND*, 28–30 January). Just a few days later Soviet foreign minister Eduard Shevardnadze made his first visit to the GDR and met with Honecker, Foreign Minister Fischer, and Prime Minister Stoph. Official coverage underscored the common foreign policy objectives of the two states, and more praise was heaped upon the performance of the East German economy, not just by the SED but also by Shevardnadze, who maintained that the GDR's "achievements have inspired us" (ibid., 3–4 February). Shortly afterward, without referring specifically to the Gorbachev program, Honecker reassured a gathering of regional party secretaries about the state of the GDR economy and asserted that there was no reason "to remain silent about our progress, or even our successes" (ADN, 7 February; *FBIS*, 10 February).

The first direct utterance by a senior SED official came from Hager, the party's chief ideologist, in an interview conducted by the West German magazine *Stern* and reprinted in its entirety in *Neues Deutschland*. He reinforced the theme sounded by Honecker that each socialist society must act in accordance with its own distinctive needs and stage of development. Then, after stressing the continuity of SED policy since 1971, Hager summarized his party's position by asking, "If your neighbor decides to put up new wallpaper, would you feel obliged to follow suit?" (*Stern*, 9 April; *ND*, 10 April). Although taking note of the interview, the Soviet press chose to omit any reference to Hager's tart question (*Pravda*, 15 April; *FBIS*, 28 April).

Probably worried that his own long silence might be misinterpreted as a rift with Moscow, Honecker became increasingly forthright later in the year about the "restructuring" under way in the Soviet Union. Before two different groups of Western journalists, he acknowledged his sympathy for Gorbachev's extensive program and even conceded that some mistakes had been made in developing a socialist society in both the Soviet Union and the GDR. Still he showed no indication of altering his fundamental position—that the economic modernization of East Germany had already been instituted in the early 1970s and that the GDR will continue to find answers to its problems in a more gradual and circumscribed manner (*ND*, 29 September, 13 October; RFE-RL *Research*, 15 October).

The SED, however, remained conspicuously quiet about the noneconomic ramifications of Gorbachev's policies. Lacking an official German equivalent, the word *glasnost'* appeared only when a speech of the CPSU general secretary was quoted, even though the East German population was well-informed on this subject through Western radio and television reports. Admittedly, it would have been most unwise for Honecker to state publicly that the SED is less afflicted by the maladies that are plaguing the CPSU, however valid the assertion. Nevertheless, no one doubted that a reform of party election procedures and an open airing of problems, as well as a less oppressive cultural policy, run completely counter to the way that the SED has constructed its "socialist democracy" (*DA*, March; RFE-RL *Research*, 6 March).

The SED joined its East European allies in a display of unanimity with Gorbachev's foreign policy initiatives when the Warsaw Pact summit conference convened in East Berlin during 28–29 May. At the same time, some possible misgivings about Honecker's active pursuit of relations with the FRG could be detected, especially in the final communiqué, which singled out West Germany for its "revanchist activities," a reference that was notably missing from East German commentaries on the meeting (*DA*, June). General Wojciech Jaruzelski's appearance in East Berlin less than a week after Honecker's return from the FRG emphasized the particular reservations felt by Poland about any change in the divided status of Germany. Whether Polish fears were allayed by the joint statement of Jaruzelski and Honecker, which affirmed the inviolability of the present borders as well as respect for the 1970 treaty between Poland and the FRG, remained open to doubt (*ND*, 17 September).

Less problematic were relations with other bloc states. In late September, Honecker visited Bulgaria for meetings with party leader Todor Zhivkov, signing a new agreement for long-term economic cooperation and endorsing the Bulgarian call for a nuclear- and chemical-free zone in the Balkans (ibid., 24–25 September). Following Stoph's trip earlier in the year, Honecker journeyed to Bucharest in late October to confer with Romanian chief Nicolae Ceauşescu. Since both men are viewed as the Warsaw Pact leaders most resistant to Gorbachev's domestic program, they made a special point in their communiqué of stressing the "committed work" and "rich initiatives" of the CPSU general secretary (*ND*, 27 February; ADN, 29 October; *FBIS*, 29 October).

Last year's much-publicized visit to the People's Republic of China by Honecker was reciprocated this year by party leader Zhao Ziyang, who on arrival in East Berlin proclaimed that these top-level exchanges "heralded a completely new stage" in relations between the two states. Although the agreement for economic cooperation concluded last year was reaffirmed, the revival holds more immediate benefits for the Chinese, especially since the plants set up in China in the 1950s by the GDR badly need rehabilitation. That the Chinese market will constitute more than 1 percent of East Germany's foreign trade before 1990 appears most unlikely (*FS-Analysen*, no. 4, 1986; *JPRS*, 16 April). It was therefore not surprising that the remarks of Zhao and Honecker laid particular stress on the resumption of party ties after a hiatus of more than two decades (*ND*, 9–11 June).

Jefferson Adams
Sarah Lawrence College

Hungary

Population. 10,613,000

Party. Hungarian Socialist Workers' Party (Magyar Szocialista Munkáspárt; HSWP)

Founded. 1918 (HSWP: 1956)

Membership. 870,992 (Thirteenth HSWP Congress Report, 1985); 30.5 percent women (average age 46.0); 42.6 percent industrial workers; 7.8 percent collective farm workers; 42.4 percent intellectuals and white-collar workers; 7.2 percent other occupations. Some 80.3 percent of members have joined the party since the 1956 revolution.

General Secretary. János Kádár (75, worker)

Politburo. 13 members: György Aczél (70, intellectual), János Berecz (56, historian), Judit Csehák (47, physician), Sándor Gáspár (70, worker), Károly Grósz (57, worker), Csaba Hámori (39, technical intelligentsia), Ferenc Havasi (58, worker), János Kádár, György Lázár (63, technical intelligentsia), László Maróthy (45, technical intelligentsia), Károly Németh (65, worker), Miklós Óvári (62, educator), István Szabó (63, farmer)

Secretariat. 9 members: János Kádár (general secretary), György Lázár (deputy general secretary), János Berecz, György Fejti (41), János Lukács (52), Miklós Németh (39), Miklós Óvári, Pál Lénárt (61), Mátyás Szürös (54)

Central Committee. 107 members (listed in *JPRS*, 17 May 1985)

Status. Ruling party

Last Congress. Thirteenth, 25–28 March 1985

Last Election. June 1985; 387 seats (35 national list, 352 multicandidate constituencies). Approximately 70 percent of deputies are HSWP members.

Auxiliary Organizations. Patriotic People's Front (PPF), secretary general, Imre Pozsgay; Communist Youth League (CYL), 913,300 members, first secretary, Csaba Hámori; National Council of Trade Unions (NCTU), 4,399,000 members, chairman, Sándor Gáspár; National Council of Hungarian Women, chairwoman, Mrs. Lajos Duschek.

Publications. *Népszabadság* (People's Freedom),

HSWP daily, editor, Gábor Borbély, deputy editor, Péter Rényi; *Társadalmi szemle* (Social Review), HSWP theoretical monthly, editor, Valéria Benke; *Pártélet* (Party Life), HSWP organizational monthly; *Magyar hírlap* (Hungarian News), government daily, editor Dezsö Pintér; *Magyar nemzet* (Hungarian Nation), Patriotic People's Front (PPF) daily, editor, István Soltész; *Népszava* (People's Word), NCTU daily, editor, László Fodor. The official news agency is Magyar Távirati Iroda (MTI).

The Hungarian section of the Russian communist (Bolshevik) party was established in March 1918 in Soviet Russia by Béla Kun (1886–1939) and a few other Hungarian prisoners of war captured during World War I. The Party of Hungarian Communists (*Kommunisták Magyarországi Pártja*) was founded in November 1918. Kun was the dominant leader of this party, which proclaimed the Hungarian Soviet Republic on 21 March 1919. The communist dictatorship lasted 133 days, from March to August.

During the interwar period the party was outlawed in Hungary, and the great majority of Hungarian communists lived in exile in the Soviet Union, Czechoslovakia, and Western Europe. Only a few hundred communists were involved in the underground movement inside Hungary. But with the Soviet "liberation" and the backing of the Red Army, the Hungarian Communist Party (HCP) reemerged as an important actor in domestic politics. Although the party—under the leadership of the Muscovite communist Mátyás Rákosi (1892–1971)—won no more than 17 percent of the votes in the free 1945 elections, it successfully dominated key government positions (in the Ministries of Defense, Interior, Education, and so on) and thus was able to exert a disproportionate influence in the coalition government. As a result of Soviet support and coercive tactics, the HCP gradually acquired control, and by 1948 Hungary had become a totalitarian one-party state, emulating the Stalinist model.

Between 1948 and 1954, the state was characterized by a terrorist dictatorship in the political and socioeconomic spheres. Rákosi's purge trials incarcerated Hungary's primate, József Cardinal Mindszenty, and liquidated alleged Titoist Minister László Rajk. The New Course of 1954–1955, led by moderate communist Imre Nagy (1896–1958), attempted to correct some of the mistakes and injustices of the preceding years. De-Stalinization encouraged the increase of popular opposition, which could not be halted even by Nagy's replacement in 1955. Following the outbreak of the revolution on 23 October 1956, the communist party was dissolved and Nagy headed a multiparty government that eventually announced Hungary's withdrawal from the Warsaw Pact. On 25 October, János Kádár (b. 1912) became the leader of a new communist party, the HSWP. The Nagy government was overthrown by the Soviet Army on 4 November 1956.

Since the end of the revolution, the HSWP, firmly aligned with the Soviet Union, has ruled unchallenged. Following a few years of repression, Hungarian domestic politics have become increasingly liberalized and there have been persistent efforts to reform the country's failing economy since 1968 when the New Economic Mechanism was introduced. Hungary, a member of the CMEA and the Warsaw Pact from their inceptions, has in recent years taken limited measures aimed at political democratization and further economic reforms. It has become clear, however, that these piecemeal reforms must be replaced by systemic economic *and* political changes to salvage the ailing economy and the demoralized society. Since the early 1980s, Hungary has been characterized by serious economic and social crises.

Party Affairs. Perhaps the most important political development in 1987 was the HSWP's realistic evaluation of Hungary's economic crisis and its changes in leadership. The party's "leading role," especially in directing the economy, has further eroded. Questioning of the HSWP's sociopolitical role by increasingly vocal intra- and extraparty elements has been also noteworthy.

The 23 June meeting of the HSWP Central Committee (CC) ended with major personnel changes in the leadership of the HSWP and of the government. The most significant outcome of the reshuffle is, however, the lack of change in the top position of general secretary. In spite of his advanced age and reportedly failing health, Kádár who, during the fall session of the parliament somewhat jocularly admitted his responsibility for erroneous decisions in the past, shows no sign of relinquishing his position, remains the general secretary of the HSWP. Moreover, although Kádár consented to the removal of HSWP Deputy General Secretary Károly Németh, who was little more than a ceremonial entity, he replaced him with Lázár, who has been the lackluster prime minister of the country for more than a decade. Thus, the top party policymaking posts remained under the firm control of Kádár and his closest longtime associates. But there was some movement at the governmental executive levels. Grósz, relieved from his position as the first secretary of the Budapest HSWP Committee, became the new chairman of the council of ministers (prime minister). He was replaced by Havasi, another Politburo member, and Havasi's post as CC secretary for economic policy was filled by Miklós Németh, the deputy head of the CC economic policy department. Pál Losonczi retired from his ceremonial position as chairman of the Presidential Council and also relinquished his seat in the Politburo. Losonczi's post in the Presidential Council was filled by Károly Németh, who had been deputy general secretary of the HSWP since the Thirteenth HSWP Congress (1985). The two vacancies in the Politburo created by the retirement of Losonczi and István Sarlós were filled by deputy prime minister Csehák and CC Secretary Berecz, who is responsible for ideology and propaganda matters. István Horváth, who has been CC secretary since 1985, was given the post of deputy prime minister. His successor in the party position is Fejti, who was first secretary of the Borsod County HSWP Committee. Another new member of the CC Secretariat is Lukács, who was first secretary of the Baranya County HSWP Committee. Thus the question of succession still remains very much open. Generally Grósz and Berecz are considered to be the frontrunners, but the names of Pozsgay and Szürös are also frequently mentioned.

According to Pintér, the editor of the government daily, these personnel changes indicate regrouping, rejuvenation, and freshening (Budapest Television, 28 June; *FBIS-Eastern Europe*, 29 June). Many Hungarian and Western critics view these changes with skepticism, for although the country's social and economic problems need speedy and comprehensive remedies, it is questionable whether the newly appointed leaders will be able to make significant differences. Major political reforms should accompany systemic changes in the economy for Hungary to re-emerge from its present crisis; nevertheless, both Grósz and Berecz, the probable successors to Kádár, have asserted their adherence to the prevailing political system. In fact, Grósz has called for even tighter party direction of the economy for the sake of efficiency (RFE *Research*, 30 June). Grósz, considered a pragmatic politician committed to the continuation of the economic reform, it appears, would also like to see the emergence of a government more independent from the HSWP and more representative of the entire population. Personnel changes gave an opportunity to a number of younger cadres, but most of the older leaders—along with Kádár—were able to hold on to their positions, among them Politburo members Aczél, Gáspár, and Óvári.

A joint declaration in four major samizdat periodicals by the "democratic" opposition blamed Kádár for avoiding the changes needed for real economic and political reforms. According to the declaration, the personnel changes only shifted people around so as not to leave anyone who was in favor of democratic reform in a position of power. Most notable, perhaps, is Pozsgay's continued omission from the Politburo. The popular Pozsgay has allegedly been at odds with Kádár, who reportedly disapproves of the former's liberal views. The opposition also bemoaned the fact that the decisions were made behind closed doors and publicized only two days later, even though they had been reported earlier by the Western press (RFE *Research*, 22 July).

HSWP activities in 1987 were dominated by Hungary's critical economic situation. The changes in leadership also signaled discontent with the performance of party and governmental bodies under whose supervision the national economy continued to function poorly. The 2 July session of the HSWP CC implicitly acknowledged the party's responsibility for the deteriorating economic situation but failed to provide any specific remedies. Instead the session delineated wide parameters that the new government might want to observe.

By 1987 some of the party's leaders realized that the HSWP has lost the confidence not only of a large segment of the population but also of an increasing proportion of the party membership. According to a senior party official, HSWP members are doubtful about the social situation when "discussions and debates within the party have often failed to yield the desired results." Furthermore, "there is also a rather large group of people in our party who do not take part in implementing our decisions, and there are even some who actually hinder their implementation." (*Pártélet*, no. 2.) Nevertheless, the majority of top party leaders still seems to believe the myth of overwhelming popular support for their policies. As CC Secretary Horváth asserted in the beginning of the year, "the great majority of Hungarian society is committed to the tasks of socialist construction, and accepts our party's strategy and tactics as they pertain to our own domestic conditions" (*Társadalmi szemle*, no. 1).

One fundamental contradiction that needs to be resolved in contemporary Hungary is that the regime demands increasing economic sacrifices from the citizenry yet has been reluctant to significantly expand political participation. There are a few members within the HSWP leadership, however, who are acknowledging the question of political reform. Pozsgay, a member of the HSWP CC, the general secretary of the PPF, and the most outspoken supporter of political liberalization, has allegedly been at odds with Kádár and would like to see interest groups emerge that have real autonomy and that propagate the withdrawal of the party from its present relationship to the state and society. According to Pozsgay, real party democracy should be upgraded and the time people hold top positions should be limited (*CSM*, 13 October). It appears that Pozsgay's opinion—which is a thinly veiled attack against Kádár's 31-year tenure—is shared by a number of party officials. Some admit that Kádár is out of control and that there is a "healthy"—if rather invisible—opposition to Kádár's continuing rule within the HSWP. Hungary needs a new beginning, but, according to a senior official, for the 75-year-old Kádár "it's hard to begin again" (*CSM*, 23 September). The question of enhanced political pluralism was addressed at the 11 November session of the HSWP CC. Instead of concrete proposals, however, the CC merely "decided" that within the party a more lively debate and discussion were desirable (Budapest Radio, 14 November; *FBIS-Eastern Europe*, 19 November).

Government and Mass Organizations. The political importance of the government, the Hungarian parliament, and various auxiliary organizations—for decades totally subordinated to the HSWP's "leadership"—has become perceptibly enhanced, as these bodies have demonstrated somewhat more independence from the HSWP in their assertions and activities. One dominating political theme in 1987 has been the acknowledged need for expanded political participation, with CC member Pozsgay already claiming that the "legislative and controlling functions of the government have been restored." Although this statement appears to be an exaggeration, it is certain that recent developments point toward more freedom for the government from the interference of HSWP directives. Pozsgay suggested that in the future "the party should act merely as trustee of the values of socialism, and coordinator of the ways and means leading to socialism" (MTI, 23 October).

Grósz's new government faces possibly insurmountable problems, especially in the economic realm. Nevertheless, what set the fall session of the National Assembly apart from its past meetings was a straight and realistic evaluation of Hungary's economic problems and a more direct dialogue between the country's leaders and the deputies in parliament. The Hungarian public was allowed, for the first time, to view the parliamentary session live on television. In his speeches to the National Assembly, Grósz dealt primarily with the economic crisis but did not fail to address the growing tension within Hungarian society. He admitted that the political mood of the country has deteriorated in recent years and acknowledged the persistence of "extremist views" within society. The fall session of parliament was followed by an unprecedented press conference held by Grósz, who said he wished that the National Assembly had more control over the government (RFE *Research*, 3 October).

In the fall a newly established governmental body, the Parliamentary Secretariat, commenced its basic task of promoting contacts and the flow of information between the Council of Ministers and the National Assembly. In the view of the National Assembly deputies, this permanent body will ease the increased "appetite" of delegates for information (*Magyar hírlap*, 17 October). Notwithstanding some favorable developments, deputies in parliament are still far from satisfied. Many object to the new interpellation rules, which regulate questions from the floor to members of the government by requiring deputies to submit their questions and comments three days in advance to the responsible parliamentary committee, and to the short meetings (two to three days) of the assembly. Some outspoken deputies have suggested a more definitive role for parliament in legislative activities. According to the present regulations, the Presidential Council can repeal a law without the knowledge and approval of the National Assembly. Some deputies called for restrictions on the legislative activities of the Presidential Council (*Magyar nemzet*, 3 December).

All three major auxiliary organizations have adopted policy lines independent of the HSWP, a marked difference from their previous subservience. The PPF, the communist umbrella organization under the leadership of Pozsgay, has become an outspoken critic of the party. In July, for instance, the PPF submitted a "strictly confidential"—later leaked—document (Recommendation for the Reform of Public Life) to the leadership. According to the report, 30 years of change in Hungary have barely touched the media, which receive almost daily instructions from the government. An opinion poll found that 40 percent of those asked did not know the meaning of the word *reform*, although it has been a predominant term in the Hungarian political vocabulary for the past two decades (*The Independent*, 24 July; *FBIS-Eastern Europe*, 27 July). The PPF also has a growing interest in youth policies and supports the new *Jövönk a tét* (Our Future Is at Stake) action program of the CYL. The PPF contends, however, that the CYL should not be the only opportunity for youths to participate in public life and has attempted to provide a forum for youths who are not CYL members.

The increasing alienation of Hungarian youth from communist organizations has manifested itself in the severe drop of CYL membership. For example, in one year the membership of vocational and secondary students in the CYL decreased by 20 percent (*Köznevelés*, 22 May), and membership figures have dropped for all strata of Hungarian youth. The CYL leadership, in its quest for increased cooperation from its membership, has been supportive of the HSWP economic resurgence program but did publish its own program of economic recovery. In July, the CYL CC made its proposals public before forwarding them to the HSWP CC and the Council of Ministers. The CYL's suggestions elicited a cool response from the HSWP. According to these proposals, badly needed economic reforms must take precedence over social and political considerations. The document also called for political liberalization and increased democracy within the HSWP. Even if abruptly squelched by the party elite, the emergence of the CYL as a political pressure group pushing the HSWP toward meaningful reforms has been an unexpected development for the Hungarian public and for the League's own membership (RFE *Research*, 22 July).

During 1987 Hungary's largest social organizations, the trade unions, have also displayed some independence from the official party line. The need for a more democratic trade union movement in which the leadership pays increased attention to the membership's will, in direct opposition to the opinion of Chairman Gáspár, was voiced by NCTU general secretary Tibor Baranyai. According to him, the "trade union movement must have an independent concept on a national, professional, regional, and plant level" (Budapest Television, 7 January; *FBIS-Eastern Europe*, 9 January). The NCTU reluctantly agreed to the party's program of economic recovery, which spells out lower living standards, potentially substantial unemployment, and other predicted economic developments that are expected to considerably worsen the situation of Hungarian workers. According to Gáspár, the veteran NCTU chairman, none of the measures proposed by the HSWP and the government are likely to appeal to workers. Although the NCTU accepted the need for most of the proposed measures, it did not give the economic recovery program its enthusiastic support. Gáspár vehemently opposed the raising of the retirement age, an idea discussed by the leadership in its attempt to offset the financial burden of a rapidly aging population (BBC *Research*, 14 July).

Economic Affairs. In 1987 Hungary's economic situation continued to deteriorate. The problems of the country's economy were addressed with increasing candor by the party and state leadership. Favorable developments, however, have not been reported to date, and the difficulties of the economy have been adversely affecting the Hungarian sociopolitical situation. Today at least 40 percent of the country's population lives below the subsistence level (*Insight*, 23 November).

According to economic experts, Hungary has to alter its entire view and think in terms of the economy's place in the global system. These experts contend that the country's economy has been unable to adapt to the changing circumstances of the world, a shortcoming that needs urgent remedy. The economy should aim in particular for the growth of hard currency exports, which have shown a steady decline in recent years, and Hungarian enterprises should realize that improved quality and reduced costs are more important than increased quantities. (*Heti világgazdaság*, 28 March).

In May the draft of the HSWP's economic program, which was intended to pave Hungary's way out of its economic crisis and toward long-term prosperity, was unexpectedly rejected by the Hungarian Academy of Sciences; the academy contended that it was a communiqué rather than a serious proposal. Even Lenárt, himself an academician and the party chief in charge of science, failed to rise to its defense (*NYT*, 24 May). This action marks a departure from the general practice of automatic approval of the party's proposals by social institutions.

In spite of earlier criticisms the new prime minister introduced his much-awaited economic program during the fall session of the National Assembly.

The government's proposals were unanimously approved by the assembly and can best be characterized as a cluster of comprehensive austerity measures. According to the program the next few years will be a stabilization (or consolidation) phase during which the most important goals are (1) to balance the annual budget, (2) halt the increase of foreign debt, (3) to increase productivity, and (4) to counterbalance rapidly growing social tensions. The government is predicting a stabilization period of three to six years, which will be followed by a ten- to fifteen-year full development stage. In Grósz's view, the ability to create harmony between short- and long-term goals will be of the utmost importance (*Magyar hírlap*, 20 August; *FBIS-Eastern Europe*, 27 August). In the stabilization stage, consumption is to be reduced by 6 to 8 percent and inflation is expected to rise above 15 percent annually. An important feature of the new program is the 1 January 1988 introduction of the first Western-style, value-added, comprehensive personal taxation system in a communist country. The tax law was approved by parliament following a lively debate.

The new regulations reduce the maximum level of taxes for enterprises from 90 to 70 percent. According to some observers, however, the failure of the enterprise tax law is that it does not encourage firms to improve their production and productivity (RFE *Research*, 3 October). Personal income taxes will increase progressively with earnings to the maximum level of 60 percent for those earning more than 600,000 forints (about $12,000 at the official exchange rate). There will be no taxes levied on annual incomes of 48,000 forints (about $960) or less, and thus personal income taxes, introduced to raise state revenues, will not affect a substantial part of the population. (Approximately 70 percent of Hungary's pensioners will be exempt from taxes.) It is estimated that of the six million people with incomes in Hungary (4.8 million of whom are wage earners), approximately 3.5 million (58 percent) will pay personal income tax in the future (RFE *Research*, 15 June). Further decentralization is another feature of the government's new economic program. Enterprises will be allowed more independence, and control over their activities will be substantially eased. Increasing profits and exports (especially hard currency) should be the primary concerns of enterprises.

According to the new program, enterprises that are consistently "producing" losses will be liquidated. During 1986, the state paid out approximately 25 percent of the total state budget to subsidize inefficient economic units. In September, a law was passed that specifically provided for the winding down of nonviable enterprises, not fewer than 400 of which would qualify for liquidation. In one case bankruptcy proceedings were begun in the spring, but the persistence of the authorities in the implementation of the new law is doubtful because of its political implications. In the view of some observers the first phase of the stabilization period would result in unemployment for up to 150,000 people, and, if the program were strictly adhered to, it could spell unemployment for at least a quarter of a million workers (*CSM*, 5 March). Even with the introduction of public utility work and retraining programs for unemployed workers, the social and political effects of such large-scale unemployment are difficult to foresee.

A related feature of the government's austerity program is a series of drastic price increases for virtually all commodities. Although rising prices are familiar phenomena to the population, the price increases already in effect and those expected to take place in the near future are beyond the Hungarians' worst dreams. Major price increases already were put into effect in January, April, and July of 1987. Further, as of 1 January 1988, the prices on 60 percent of consumer goods are forecast to be raised by authorities. As a result of these reports, hoarding has become prevalent among a population already pessimistic about the future.

Despite considerable governmental effort, Hungary's foreign debt situation also has continued to deteriorate. The new prime minister admitted that Hungary, with its $16 billion gross hard currency debt, is one of the most heavily indebted nations in the world (*L'Humanité*, 24 October; *FBIS-Eastern Europe*, 3 November); Hungary's per capita hard currency debt is by far the highest among CMEA countries. It currently devotes 45 percent of its export income to financing the foreign debt (*WSJ*, 19 November). Nevertheless, Hungary thus far has serviced its debts in a respectable fashion. It appears that foreign creditors continue to have confidence in the recovery of the Hungarian economy, witnessed by the granting of new loans and credits. On 22 July, the Hungarian National Bank (HNB) signed a contract for $400 million in credit with 39 foreign banks and received another $150 million from the International Reconstruction and Development Bank toward the structural reorganization of Hungarian industry. During the new prime minister's October visit to West Germany, Grósz not only received a one billion Deutsche Mark loan—underwritten by the West German government—but also gained some much-needed support for Hungary in its negotiations with the European Economic Community for more favorable terms of trade, particularly the reduction or elimination of some especially disadvantageous tariffs and quotas. In late November, Deputy Prime Minister József Marjai negotiated with the World Bank and the United States for $350 million in loans and new technology. Throughout the year Hungary has actively solicited not only financial sources of relief but also various forms of economic cooperation with Western partners, particularly joint ventures with U.S. firms. By the end of 1987, there were more than 100 enterprises operating in Hungary with Western capital involvement of Austrian, Swedish, and West German companies, although Japanese and American interest in such undertakings has noticeably increased recently.

To ease Hungary's economic crisis, on 1 January 1987 a reform of the Hungarian banking system was introduced. Hungary now has a two-tier system in which the central bank (HNB) ceased to function as a credit bank. During January, five chartered general credit banks were established to serve the banking needs of customers and organizational subdivisions. The authorities expect this new system will help the HNB to discharge its bank-of-issue function more effectively and to influence the new commercial banks with its tools of monetary policy and regulation (*Külgazdaság*, no. 1). At the same time, the introduction of five competing banks was expected to improve service. So far, however, no drastic changes have taken place. The new banks have problems such as inadequate facilities and capital and have not been free of state interference. Nevertheless, these new financial institutions have not become "specialized branches" of the HNB (as was feared by many experts), and the new banking system appears to be a solid basis to build on.

Improving the balance of Hungary's foreign trade figures prominently in the government's new economic program. Although the country's economy depends heavily on foreign trade, its performance has been deteriorating. According to Grósz, during the consolidation phase the government will maintain financial solvency by achieving an export surplus equivalent to 3 or 4 percent of the annual national income (RFE *Research*, 3 October). This is an ambitious task, given that Hungary has had a negative trade balance, particularly in hard currency trade, in recent years. The reduction of imports can only be attained at the expense of the individual consumers since the government's first priority is the injection of new Western technology into the economy. The state has been trying to convince its Western partners to buy more Hungarian goods; Western leaders are generally sympathetic toward Hungary's economic problems but contend that the condition of expanded trade relations must be based on the improved quality of Hungarian goods.

Hungarian leaders have not been entirely content with the country's economic relationship to the CMEA. Some experts, most notably Rezsö Nyers, an HSWP CC member and the "father" of the Hungarian economic reforms, have been openly critical of the country's unfavorable links with the communist bloc. According to these critics, export structures within the CMEA are extremely outdated, the replacement of products is sluggish, and technological efficiency is underdeveloped. Moreover, product specialization is, in many cases, a mere formality; it only represents a method by which certain product shortages are remedied (*Népszabadság*, 1 August). Within the CMEA, Hungary has been calling for reforms for years and hopes that with a reform-minded Soviet leader it will receive more favorable response.

Although the new tax law is expected to hit Hungary's developing private sector hard, the leadership has reiterated the need for small ventures in the Hungarian economy. A greater scope for private economic activities was encouraged by the government's action that allowed private enterprises to hire a maximum of 30 employees, including family members. Beginning 1 January 1988, private ventures with corporate status will also be possible (*Népszabadság*, 3 October; *FBIS-Eastern Europe*, 8 October). Agriculture, which was adversely affected by the weather in 1987, remains the strongest sector in the Hungarian economy. Small-scale private producers continue to enjoy the regime's support.

Social and Cultural Affairs. By East European standards, Hungarian authorities continue to be relatively tolerant toward the small but active "democratic opposition." Nevertheless, various human rights violations frequently occur. The police routinely raid apartments where underground publications are mimeographed and stored, samizdat material is confiscated on a regular basis, and publishers and editors often receive heavy fines. There are no reports of lengthy prison sentences, however. Another common form of repression is the denial of passports to members of the opposition who are invited to visit Western countries. In March, for instance, Miklós Vásárhelyi, a historian and press spokesman for Nagy during the 1956 revolution, was not allowed to lecture in Rome, even though his services were requested by the Hungarian Ministry of Culture (*NYT*, 13 March). Similar treatment was meted out to dissident activists János Kis and Miklós Haraszti (in both cases compromise solutions allowed them to leave Hungary, albeit some time after the conferences they were to participate in had been held.) In July, a secret Politburo document on the activities of the Hungarian political opposition made its way to the West. The contents of this document did little for Hungary's reputation as a more "liberal" communist country, admitting, as it did, the increased societal influence of dissent and calling for more repressive measures against both individuals and institutions involved with oppositional activities (RFE *Research*, 22 July).

On 15 March, the anniversary of the 1848 revolution, some 1,500 Hungarians marched peacefully in Budapest. Such demonstrations in the past had been marked by police intervention, roughing up and detaining "ringleaders," but in 1987 the authorities remained surprisingly calm, notwithstanding calls from speakers for the rehabilitation of Nagy and even for the withdrawal of Soviet troops from Hungary (*NYT*, 16 March). For the second time in two years, some 150 leading Hungarian intellectuals met in the village of Lakitelek to discuss the political, social, and economic situation of the country. Among the several speakers was Pozsgay, the PPF general secretary. In an interview published by *Magyar nemzet*, Pozsgay evaluated the debates favorably, although he pointed out that while the intent of the individuals present was honorable, there was no complete agreement among debaters about how to deal with Hungary's difficulties. The communiqué issued at the end of the meeting was published in the PPF daily and called for a comprehensive reform of political and social organizations and the establishment of an independent democratic forum that could be the organ for continuous, public dialogue between the citizens and the authorities (*Magyar nemzet*, 14 November). Perhaps the event that most signaled the frustration of the population with the regime was the burning of two factories in the provincial city of Szombathely. According to Western reports, which Hungarian media denied, arsonists started the fires in protest against the drastic summer price increases. Although the rescue work of fire brigades was impeded by thousands of enraged people, police did not interfere. Similar incidents reportedly took place in several other Hungarian towns (*Kurier*, 12 August; *FBIS-Eastern Europe*, 13 August).

For much of the first half of 1987, the crisis of the Hungarian Writer's Union (HWU), which began the previous year, persisted. The animosity between the HSWP and the HWU started when the November 1986 meeting of the HWU voted into power an executive committee that contained almost no members from the official party slate. As a result, many writers loyal to the regime—including László Gyurkó, Kádár's unofficial biographer, and Minister of Culture Béla Köpeczi—resigned from the HWU, and the dissolution of the HWU by the authorities was feared. This situation was resolved during a 23 March meeting between HSWP and HWU officials, who reached a compromise whereby one elected official was removed from the HWU presidium and three "loyalists" were admitted to the HWU executive committee. Since HWU officials are not appointed but elected, those resigning had to be persuaded rather than be dismissed. Under tremendous pressure, József Annus—the deputy editor of the literary monthly *Tiszatáj* that was suspended in 1986—agreed to relinquish his seat in the HWU presidium (RFE *Research*, 18 May). *Tiszatáj* reappeared in March 1987 with a new editorial board approved by the government.

During 1986 and 1987, the NCTU not only failed to represent the financial interests of the new writers' trade union in debates over the new Hungarian taxation system but also rejected the claim for preferential treatment. To counteract the lackluster NCTU efforts, in January 1987 a separate trade union for writers was established to help defend the interests of writers, poets, and journalists. The chairwoman, the noted author Erzsébet Galgóczi, stated that one of the union's most important tasks was more effectively guiding the financial interests of its membership (*Élet és irodalom*, 27 February). Debates have long surrounded the tax burden on artisans, and the chairwoman vowed to negotiate with the authorities for a fair taxation system applied to writers. In spite of the new trade union's efforts, the taxation rate on writers was doubled, and a frustrated Galgóczi resigned in protest against what she called taxation without representation (RFE *Research*, 30 October).

Church-state relations continue to be evaluated favorably by both sides. Roman Catholic primate

László Lékai died in June 1986, and a new primate, László Páskai (59), was named by the Holy See; on 25 April, more than 12,000 people attended his enthronement in a colorful open-air ceremony in the historic city of Esztergom. During the ceremony Páskai pledged to further improve church-state relations, which are troubled by the continued existence of Hungary's critical Catholic "basic communities" and an increase in the number of young men objecting to military service on religious grounds. Although the church hierarchy sides with the regime on these issues, the local parish priests, privately at least, appear to be supportive of the "renegades." Anti-Semitism is again evident in Hungary and, although a previously taboo subject, did receive some publicity in 1987. A number of reports and essays discussing the complexity of the issue have been broadcast and published by the media. The government also allowed Americans to finance and build a statue in Budapest commemorating Raoul Wallenberg—the Swedish diplomat who saved thousands of Hungarian Jews from the Nazis and then disappeared into Soviet captivity. The government's relatively good record in its treatment of the Hungarian Jewry was attested to by the World Jewish Congress holding its July meeting in Budapest, the first time it had done so in a communist country.

Hungary's various social ills also have received increased attention. The country still has the highest suicide rate in the world, and the spreading use of illegal drugs finally prompted the authorities to face the problem instead of continuing to build walls of evasiveness. After persistent calls for government action from the public, the Anti-Alcoholism State Committee formed a drug subcommittee. A National Institute for Alcohol Research—a scientific research arm of the Health Ministry—was also established and began operation. Care facilities for patients suffering from alcohol-related diseases were increased (*Magyar hírlap*, 30 January). However, the number of criminal cases also rose significantly. From 130,000 publicly prosecuted crimes in 1980, the figure for 1986 exceeded 180,000. Crimes against property account for the largest part of this increase (*Népszava*, 19 August; *FBIS-Eastern Europe*, 21 August).

Foreign Affairs. One basic tenet of Hungarian foreign policy is that small nations contribute to security and cooperation among all nations. Hungary assumed an active role in the past, maintaining the East-West dialogue and broadening international relations. According to Szürös, the HSWP's CC secretary in charge of foreign affairs, the main objective of Hungary's foreign policy is to promote international conditions that favor the country's internal development (*Pártélet*, no. 3). In 1987, Western relations were dominated by economic diplomacy. The most important aim of official visits was to maintain Hungary's reputation as a relatively liberal communist regime, for the leadership seems to believe that a favorable Western perception of Hungary is a precondition for developing economic relations with capitalist states. The visit of CC Secretary Szürös to the United States reflected Hungary's desire to improve relations, and while there, Szürös repeatedly stressed that Hungarian political and economic reforms will be continued.

In September, Hungary and Israel signed an accord to re-establish limited diplomatic relations between the two nations after 20 years. According to the agreement, an Israeli interest section with five diplomats will be stationed at the Swiss embassy in Budapest, while five Hungarian envoys will work at the Swedish embassy in Tel Aviv. Although the Hungarian leadership emphasized that there will be no change in its foreign policy toward the Middle East, Arab sources expressed their displeasure with the accord. Furthermore, a Kuwaiti newspaper charged that, in return for the diplomatic agreement, the World Jewish Council had promised the Hungarian government financial assistance to ease its economic crisis (RFE *Research*, 3 October).

Prime Minister Grósz's first Western trip took him to West Germany, where he was received by Chancellor Helmut Kohl and other top federal and provincial leaders. Grósz evaluated his visit very positively, emphasizing "the great deal of sympathy toward our homeland, a great deal of interest, and readiness to help and support us" (Budapest Radio, 10 October; *FBIS-Eastern Europe*, 13 October).

Other important visits to the West by Hungarian politicians included those of Politburo member Aczél to Spain and Italy, Kádár's trip to Sweden in April, Deputy Prime Minister Csehák's visit to Norway in June, and Presidential Council president Károly Németh's meetings in Brazil during November. Visits to Hungary by Western statesmen included those of British foreign secretary Sir Geoffrey Howe in March, Danish prime minister Poul Schlüter in April, Canadian foreign minister Charles Joseph Clark in May, Dutch foreign minister Hans Van Den Broek in September, and Queen Margrethe II of Denmark in October.

Communist Affairs. The HSWP supports the renewed dialogue between the superpowers and evaluates the new developments in the Soviet Union positively. Although Hungary remains a loyal ally of the USSR and still follows the Soviet foreign policy line, some leaders have voiced dissatisfaction with certain aspects of Hungary's membership in the Warsaw Pact and especially in the CMEA, referring to "various forms and mechanisms of cooperation" that do not always reflect the changes that have taken place in the global economy and in world politics the last decade (*Pártélet*, no. 3).

In April, CPSU Politburo member Egor K. Ligachev visited Budapest and spoke highly of Hungary's economic reforms, stating that the USSR can learn from the Hungarian experience. Ligachev said that the Soviet leadership was especially interested in Hungary's experience of relaxing the direct control by the communist party and central planning offices over the activities of individual enterprises. He indicated that the Soviet leadership would also draw on Hungary's introduction of multiple candidates for parliamentary elections (*LAT*, 26 April). In July, Grósz visited Moscow on his first trip abroad as prime minister and held talks in a "cordial and comradely atmosphere" with Nikolai Ryzhkov, his Soviet counterpart, and CPSU leader Mikhail Gorbachev; these meetings focused on bilateral economic relations. The USSR leaders expressed their conviction that greater bilateral trade, increased cooperation in joint ventures, and closer industrial links would be beneficial for both states. Grósz went out of his way to praise the CPSU's program of renewal and "restructuring," which he said was of "historical and revolutionary significance" (RFE *Research*, 11 August). In November Kádár led the Hungarian delegation to Moscow to celebrate the 70th anniversary of the Bolshevik Revolution.

Relations between Hungary and China became closer during 1987. In June, Chinese Communist Party general secretary Zhao Ziyang was the first Chinese party leader ever to visit Hungary. During talks with Hungarian leaders, both parties expressed mutual interest in each other's economic reforms. As the Chinese leader asserted, "We are ready to learn from one another" (*Népszabadság*, 19 June). In October, Kádár visited China for the first time in 30 years at the invitation of Zhao Ziyang. In his speech to Chinese leaders Kádár expressed his party's great satisfaction with the improvement of Hungarian-Chinese relations. He pointed out that Hungary and China share identical views on major issues that decide the destiny of the world. He further stated that relations among communist parties and countries should be developed on the basis of equality, independence, mutual respect, and noninterference in internal affairs (*Xinhua*, 11 October; *FBIS-China*, 13 October). Chinese and Hungarian sources alike evaluated Kádár's trip very positively and referred to it several times as the "meeting of close friends."

Hungary's relationship to Romania, which has been characterized by much tension and animosity, took a turn for the worse in 1987. At the center of the disagreement is Romania's treatment of the approximately two million Hungarian nationals living (primarily) in Transylvania. Although the Hungarian leadership had been reluctant to raise the issue until the mid-1980s, in the last few years partly as a result of public pressure, Hungary has voiced its concern over Romania's Hungarian minority in several national and international forums. In early March, Hungary supported a Canadian proposal on the rights of minorities at the Vienna Conference on Security and Cooperation in Europe. (Significantly, this was the first time that a Warsaw Pact member had supported a NATO country on a human rights issue.) Romania fiercely attacked the appearance of a three-volume history of Transylvania published by the Hungarian Academy of Sciences in late 1986 and edited by Minister of Culture Köpeczi. Romanian authorities denounced the publication as a work of "chauvinism, fascism, and racism." According to some Western sources, the USSR is annoyed by the undisguised tension between the two countries, but it does not plan to act as a mediator, according to Hungarian party officials (*NYT*, 21 May). In an interview Köpeczi asserted that relations between Hungary and Romania are "cool," and since discussion of the Transylvanian problem began, "the situation has steadily deteriorated" (*La Repubblica*, 12 February). In contrast, Hungary's relationships with other communist countries have developed to the satisfaction of all.

Zoltán Barany
University of Nebraska at Lincoln

Poland

Population. 37,726,699

Party. Polish United Workers' Party (Polska Zjednoczona Partia Robotnicza; PZPR).

Founded. 1918, Communist Workers' Party; 1948, PZPR

Membership. 2,129,002 full and candidate members in 20,270 primary party organizations: workers, 38 percent; farmers, 9 percent; intellectuals, 53 percent; women, 27 percent; young people, 7 percent; pensioners, 17 percent

First Secretary. General of the Army Wojciech Jaruzelski

Politburo. 14 full members: Kazimierz Barcikowski, Józef Baryła, Józef Czyrek, Jan Główczyk, Czesław Kiszczak, Zbigniew Messner, Alfred Miodowicz, Włodzimierz Mokrzyszczak, Zygmunt Murański, Marian Orzechowski, Tadeusz Porębski, Florian Siwicki, Zofia Stępién, and Marian Woźniak; 5 alternate members: Stanisław Bejger, Manfred Gorywoda, Janusz Kubasiewicz, Zbigniew Michałek, and Gabriela Rembisz

Central Commitee. Approximately 200 members and 70 alternates. 10 secretaries of the Central Committee: Józef Baryła, Henryk Bednarski, Stanisław Ciosek, Kazimierz Cypryniak, Józef Czyrek, Jan Główczyk, Zbigniew Michałek, Tadeusz Porębski, Andrzej Wasilewski, and Marian Woźniak.

Status. Ruling party

Last Congress. Tenth, July 1986

Last Election. 1985. The regime claimed that 78.81 percent of eligible voters participated; independent sources estimate the vote at only 60 percent.

Auxiliary Organizations. United Peasant Party (ZSL); Democratic Party (SD)

Publications. *Trybuna ludu* (*TL*), party daily; *Nowe drogi* and *Ideologia i polityka*, party monthlies; *Życie partii*, fortnightly party organ; *Żołnierz wolności*, army daily; *Tygodnik powszechny* and *Słowo powszechne*, Catholic publications. Polska Agencja Prasowa (PAP) is the official news agency.

The contradictory nature of the Jaruzelski regime in Poland has its origin in the military takeover of 13 December 1981. Threatened by the support shown to the independent trade union Solidarity, the desperate communist regime overreacted and applied full military repression against this popular movement that sought peaceful social and economic change. This harsh, suppressive reaction was coupled with a flow of government propaganda concerning the August 1980 agreement between the union and the regime, which committed both parties to socioeconomic reforms.

The specter of a Soviet invasion had initially provided the regime with a justification for its repressive military rule in Poland. Soon, however, the capacity of Polish communism to reform itself and to take the initiative for the liberalizations demanded by society became preconditions for its legitimacy. To establish a necessary minimum of popular support and to ensure its very survival, the communist regime has had to carefully consider changing its methods of governing. The ruling elite must demonstrate both that it is responsive to the real movement of Polish society toward democratization and that the official communist ideology continues to be relevant. Therein lies the contradictory character of the Jaruzelski government. The essence of "socialist renewal" (intrasystem reforms in Poland) is to promote change in the basic organization and control of society within the framework of a rigid communist monopoly of power.

The regime in Poland concluded that the socioeconomic structure of the country and the current level of political awareness have rendered the old micromanagement counterproductive. Communist authorities have traditionally overextended themselves trying to regulate every minute aspect of social and economic life. In consequence, the PZPR has wasted its resources on trivial issues and even jeopardized its position of leadership in society. There has emerged a recognition that there is and will be an inevitable wave of spontaneous economic and social change in Poland with or without government encouragement. Therefore, the regime has come to the conclusion that the PZPR monopoly of the political system will be preserved and perhaps even enhanced by a partial withdrawal of the regime from direct control via administrative fiat. The new approach to maintaining absolute political control is to encourage genuine social and economic activism within acceptable limits. A popular reorganized economy, including private enterprise, must be confined within the framework of the politically communist-dominated state. In the jargon of Marxism-Leninism, transformation of the state would be limited to the form of control over the society and its superstructure, while the communist model would be left untouched.

Moreover, this "socialist renewal" should be a revolution "from above," initiated and directed by the PZPR. Spontaneous, grass roots movements of the working class are still regarded as dangerous initiatives, which, bereft of the guiding role of the party, would most likely "degenerate" into movements opposed to total communist political control. The PZPR has not abdicated its selfish political ambitions; it has only agreed to put a more acceptable face on the old centralist political style. The new political structure would ostensibly permit free political, social, and economic activities but only within the impenetrable framework of the communist state.

In effect, the PZPR is once again trying to subjugate indigenous social initiative and pretending to be the driving force behind change. The Jaruzelski regime is basically a Stalinist model communist state, which modifies its character only to the extent necessary to accommodate inevitable movement toward political, economic, and social liberalization. If communist political power is to be consolidated and sustained, the government must accommodate a politically assertive society that is demanding a more efficient and rational organization of the state. However, these accommodations will be largely superficial, measured segments in carefully selected areas, with virtually no compromise of the principles of the PZPR hegemony. The reforms offered by the regime are no more than a tactical, and perhaps temporary, retreat from complete control of the entire socioeconomic milieu. Such maneuvers will permit a continued hold on the reins of political power during volatile periods of unrest. General Jaruzelski is an advocate of reforming communism by giving it a new and improved form rather than replacing it with participatory democracy. In the final analysis, the regime is acting on behalf of Soviet world communism, with the preservation of the regime in Poland as the principal objective. The achievement of this objective determines the scope of permissible change. Behind the announced desire to revise the communist state lies the traditional belief in the infallibility of the party and its loyalty to Moscow.

Yet the regime's commitment to reform is the key to its legitimacy. Since World War II, and especially following the introduction of martial law in Poland, there has been an explicit division between the society and the authorities—"we" and "they." Polish society is united in its rejection of the communist government as a totally isolated and alien force. Since this force was imposed from the outside, it cannot understand or represent national needs and aspirations. The communist state in Poland is viewed as inherently incompetent, opposed to accepted national values, in conflict with cultural heritage, and, finally, incapable of reforming itself. The great majority of Poles contend that the preservation of the national identity, necessary for eventual independence, requires total opposition to the state. Since the existing communist state contributes so little to Polish national aspirations as envisioned by the people, nationalism is promoted through both active and passive resistance to official policies. Political apathy and negative attitudes toward work are forms of the struggle against the communist regime, wherein short-term gains under communism are sacrificed for the sake of future freedom and prosperity. (That Polish citizens have adopted the policy of passive resistance against communism is reflected by government policies in 1987.) Despite hardships and poverty, the majority of Poles remain uninterested in economic reforms and greater output lest such achievements strengthen the hated regime. Such subversive attitudes, of course, render the state ineffective and irrelevant, with little or no influence on its people. The restoration of a legitimate government becomes impossible, which complicates, if not precludes, an economic recovery and a political revitalization. Poland is actually in a state of bloodless civil war that will ultimately bring full independence, followed by socioeconomic progress, or the loss of identity of the Polish nation altogether. The idea of an indefinite partnership between the communist state and the alienated people is highly unlikely, as demonstrated by a population continuing to boycott official appeals for votes and work.

The Party. An important PZPR objective in 1987 was to overcome the obstacles against communist influence on the workers and youth. The party has consolidated and strengthened itself in recent years; however, this internal reorganization, plus a will to project influence, has failed to produce tangible results. The PZPR "front line" has had little effect on society as a whole. For example, state economic enterprises successfully resisted governmental economic reforms. At the same time the younger generation remained fascinated by religion and elated at the prospects of emigration to the West in search of a "normal" life (*Tygodnik powszechny*, 14 December 1986).

In fact, the PZPR is desperate to achieve "confidence on the part of the working class, a credibility and an authority in the eyes of working people," as admitted by the PZPR first secretary, Jaruzelski (*Polityka*, 10 January). To obtain such authority and confidence involves a radical change in the image of the party as a foreign agent on Polish soil, with special stress on public understanding and respect for the specific circumstances concerning the origins and development of the communist system. Of course, these explanations are designed to deflect criticisms of the system itself.

The task of delivering Polish society to the side of the regime to support the acceleration of official economic reforms is now assigned to the primary PZPR organizations. At the Fourth Plenum of the Central Committee (22 May), General Jaruzelski initiated the grass roots approach to political struggle by ordering all 20,000 primary party organizations to take over the "daily struggle for genuine normality, for implementing all that is modern and efficient, and for promoting [a] wholesome social atmosphere including all the constituent parts of our life as a society, from smallest to the largest" (*TL*, 23–24 May).

The current younger generation is maturing in confusing and difficult times of economic deprivation, with a weakened system of values. The prevailing attitude of the young is to detach themselves from bitter reality. Lack of basic opportunities has resulted in disillusion and disappointment. As long as the country is unable to extricate itself from political and economic crisis, Polish youth is not likely to support the communist system.

The official view is that the younger generation is not disappointed with the political system, only with the speed of recovery. To address this problem, the Politburo instructed basic party units and other organizations to focus on the development of "civil militancy" among young people. The Politburo ordered its units to combat ideological indifference, reluctance to assume social commitments, and failure to develop a consumers' attitude toward life among young people. The PZPR would like to make its "socialist renewal" revolution in Poland, using the energy of young people to carry out economic and political programs designed by the authorities. Young people are being placed in top positions throughout the social organizations and economic enterprises to demonstrate the outstanding opportunities provided by Jaruzelski's *perestroika*. Since 1982 Poland has had a Ministry for Youth Affairs headed by a person not yet 30 years old. His success is frequently cited as an example of what can be accomplished by ambitious, loyal, and "militant" individuals.

However, the PZPR is unwilling or unable to admit that its Soviet ideology, martial law detention camps, and suppression of normal living standards are the primary reasons behind the passive resignation of the young. Government programs designed to meet the aspirations of youth have the self-serving ideological objective of promoting communism. Vital popular demands like public housing, however, are sorely neglected. The regime has succeeded in creating a "paper reality" of numerous resolutions and so-called youth laws. These paper plans have, so far, brought no improvements in living standards, in the quality of education, or in the quality of professional life. Like every other social program in Poland, the one for youth suppresses spontaneous initiative. Moreover, the authorities obviously intend to promote goals that strengthen the communist regime and that set in place systems that will influence the generation born after World War II to embrace communism. The regime, for obvious reasons, is also motivated by a fear of this younger generation, which during Solidarity times was in elementary school. These youths must be diverted from anticommunist political thinking and activism, which in several years' time could fuel another uprising.

There is also a body of data that sees the young people in Poland as uninterested in "socialist construction" because they are keenly intent on emigration. According to a recent poll carried out by the Institute for Research into Young People's Problems, more than 87 percent of the respondents want to travel abroad, some 11.7 percent wish to leave Poland permanently, and 15.2 percent would stay abroad for an indefinite period. This means that every fourth youngster wants to leave the country for good. The dominant reason to emigrate is economic: 71.5 percent of young people are motivated by the prospect of higher living standards in leading industrial countries. About 33.3 percent would like to leave Poland for ideological-political reasons. (The great majority of prospective emigrants does not consider leaving Poland to be in conflict with its patriotic obligations [*Polityka*, 17 October].)

Emigration to the West has become a major social problem because it drains the nation's work force. It is estimated that more than 250,000 Poles have left the country in search of a stable, higher living standard. The situation has reached such alarming proportions that the Episcopate appealed to young people, arguing that "escape from the difficulties of everyday life and the search for an easier existence alone" should not be a sufficient reason for emigration (RFE *Research*, Poland, 8 October).

Using the slogans "POP Facing Man" (POP is the acronym for the primary party organization) and "open-style," the Fourth Central Committee Plenum defined the PZPR's principal mission as service to the people. The regime became alarmed by the popular inclination toward internal emigration (the individual's passivity and indifference to regime goals) and real emigration. To redress these negative attitudes, and to head off the possibility of another Solidarity-like revolt in the near future, the PZPR promised "sensitivity toward people's problems and concerns" in the "struggle for the younger generation."

> One will not succeed in winning over the generation that will be middle-aged when the 21st century begins, if all one has to offer is small-scale stabilization and half-measures. We will attract this generation if we go all out, unequivocally, for what is modern, for an efficient and rational organization of life and if we manifest a genuine readiness to meet half-way the bold initiatives, ideas, and innovations. (*TL*, 23–24 May.)

The Fifth Central Committee Plenum met on 8 October and focused its attention on the second stage of the economic reform. Seeing it as the highest form of social consultation, this plenum approved the idea of a nationwide referendum on the stimulation of economic activities through accelerating the pace of price increases. Higher prices, according to the official line, would create the permanent foundation for economic equilibrium and would eventually result in a substantial improvement in living standards.

The second stage of the reform, according to the official plan, has five basic objectives: (1) reorganization of the management system, (2) higher productivity, (3) encouragement of innovation and managerial flexibility, (4) international division of labor, and (5) greater satisfaction of citizens' needs, including improvements in the quality of services. Achievement of these benefits was to be facilitated by higher prices for basic consumer goods because the first stage of economic reform had failed to ensure the money market balance on the domestic market. So far, the regime has used both rationing and relatively moderate price increases, which fueled inflation and encouraged speculation. (Warsaw Domestic Service, 8 October; *FBIS-Eastern Europe*, 9 October.)

The initiative of holding a nationwide referendum on the implementation of the second stage of economic reform, which would include exceptionally high price increases, was coupled with the vague promise of further democratization of political life. The PZPR decided to seek a vote of acceptance for the unpopular price increases that might easily trigger major social unrest. Asking the people to accept yet another economic sacrifice in a sharp rise in the cost of living, the party added the carrot of democratization. In the referendum approach it gave the regime a chance to retreat if its policies were rejected by the people. Thus, the referendum would serve as proof of a new democratic orientation of the PZPR and as an invitation to a partnership between the regime and the people. Premier Messner described the referendum as "a natural fulfillment of the policy of renewal, the enrichment of democracy, and an example of citizens' participation in the governing of the state" (ibid.).

The PZPR continues to harbor the illusion that its rule is synonymous with progress and freedom. Oblivious to its perversion of the original ideas of Marxism and the dictatorial nature of communism, the party likes to project the image of being a vanguard of the people—a popular leadership that has corrected all past mistakes and is now developing its "revolution within the revolution," or "second revolution." Political concepts that dominate communist thinking have not changed since Lenin and his Bolsheviks seized power in Russia. The essence of political control, from the communist perspective, has little to do with the consent of the governed; it simply follows from the ideological "correctness" of the party line. The party calculates what can be successfully imposed on the society it controls rather than reacting to what the people would like to achieve. The people are perceived as a mob, yet to be blessed with the correct communist, ideological "consciousness" and, therefore quite dangerously, an easy target for "anticommunist demagogues." Like other Leninist organizations, the PZPR is highly critical of any spontaneous political activity and ever aware of the danger of "degeneration" into an "antisocialist" direction, as in the case of Solidarity. Solidarity demonstrated to the communists the political and organizational potential of society. Now, at a time of serious socioeconomic crises, the PZPR's political strategy is to capture the public's desire for reform and turn it to the regime's purposes. If successful, the party would not only disarm the opposition but, once again, would identify itself with socioeconomic progress. Currently, the Jaruzelski regime has adopted the appealing slogan of a Polish form of "socialist pluralism," which it presents as a modernized version of the "united front" to attract popular support. The 1987 referendum on economic reform and "democratization" was the first step toward establishing such a form of pluralism.

By putting forward this program, the PZPR hopes to marry its political line to the expectations of the society. Solidarity has been pointedly excluded from all reforms. Stressing "militancy" and faithful adherence to the August 1980 agreement, the PZPR claims itself the true revolutionary leader of the labor union movement. Exclusion of an independent Solidarity from the reform movement means that the party would welcome socialist pluralism as long as its own monopoly of power continues. The communist idea of socialist pluralism in Poland includes no provision for the legalization of Solidarity, for free elections, or for independent political parties.

The Sixth Central Committee Plenum, on renewal of socialist democracy and economic reforms, was an official review of the state of the Polish political and economic system. The main thrust was to encourage popular support for the national referendum on higher prices and "democratization." In its report to the plenum, entitled "The Deepening of Socialist Renewal—Condition for Accelerating Poland's Development," the Politburo painted a wholly positive picture of renewal and promised even more dramatic improvements once the new program of reform was approved by the nationwide referendum.

The report was a lengthy propaganda statement addressed to the nation as well as to leaders in Moscow. It pledged that the PZPR would follow the "road of expansion of civil rights" and claimed that the "scope of change implemented over the recent years in favor of democratization and law and order is unequalled in the history of Poland." The report stressed the "humanistic goals of socialism" and reinforced Politburo commitment to the expansion of democracy and economic, social, cultural, and educational rights. It also stressed its support for the expansion of self-management and for the new law on social organizations that would permit registration of independent political clubs.

The PZPR advanced a new slogan of national reconciliation with the opposition and with those who left its ranks after it imposed martial law against Solidarity. The principle of "it does not matter where you are coming from; what matters is what you are doing today and where you are going" provides a platform for social mobilization. The report continues,

> The essence of Polish socialist pluralism lies in respecting the range of motivations stemming from various world philosophies and points of view. Socialist pluralism consists of identifying and bringing together the different interests and confronting them in a national dialogue. The goal of this exercise is then to transform these divergent interests into a driving force of development for the benefit of the nation and the socialist fatherland. Its limits, that cannot be overstepped, are the Polish reason of state and the constitutional systemic order . . . attempts to use the broadening democratic liberties for anti-systemic purpose must not be belittled. (Warsaw PAP, in English, 17 November; *FBIS-Eastern Europe*, 23 November.)

This last provision of the PZPR program is a paraphrased version of the Soviet constitutional principle that limits the purpose of civil rights to enhancing the interests of the regime.

The ambiguity and vagueness of the socialist pluralism model advanced at the Sixth Plenum was further compounded by the strong emphasis on ideology and by the conclusion that "the more socialism there is in Poland, the stronger, the more just and sovereign she is. Socialism is all the more full and rich, the better it addresses Polish conditions and expresses the will and striving of our people." Finally, the report equated the Polish road to socialism "with the Soviet reconstruction, as well as the goals which many other communist and workers' parties have." For these reasons, the ideological concept of socialist pluralism in Poland is not new or extraordinary. Under difficult conditions, the communist regime has become more tolerant of independent political and economic activity. Social unrest has forced adjustments in the style of governing to strengthen the role of the PZPR as the dominant political force.

However, Jaruzelski's "democratization" is too restricted and narrow to satisfy the political aspirations of the people. Social ombudsmen, a consultative council, and wider parliamentary participation of noncommunists are just cosmetic changes, given that the regime has stubbornly refused to legalize any independent organization—Solidarity above all.

The Church. Church-state relations are far from the "constructive coexistence" claimed by General Jaruzelski during his welcome for Pope John Paul II as the state of affairs between these two most influential institutions. The pope's visit to his native land, the third since his election to the papacy and the second since martial law, was welcomed by the regime as a measure of its legitimacy. However, as a Vatican priest observed, "The Government has had nothing to give the people except price increases and shortages, and so a well-organized papal visit serves as a gift to the people and as a propaganda tool in the outside world" (*NYT*, 8 June).

For the church, the week-long papal pilgrimage had religious and patriotic significance, for Pope John Paul did not go to Poland to popularize communism. As a matter of fact, the visit brought few tangible benefits to church-state relations and most likely contributed to a deepening of the cleavage between the regime and the people. For the church, the visit was intended to consolidate the Episcopate's position as a political force in a country where more than 80 percent of people are practicing Catholics, including 90 percent of the high school students, and to bring about a rebirth of the nation. The pope, however, failed to endorse any official policies and refused to assist the government in moving the country out of its political deadlock.

At the meeting with General Jaruzelski in the royal castle of Warsaw, the pope disclosed the central purpose of his visit—to deliver a powerful message on the relationship between human rights and peace. Referring to the Human Rights Charter of the U.N. as an "unambiguous" expression of the "surge of consciences," he said that,

> This document constitutes . . . the very framework of the U.N. organization, whose aim is to guard the peaceful coexistence of nations and states throughout the world . . . If you want to keep peace, remember about man, remember about his rights, that are inalienable, as they result from the very humanity of every human being. Also remember his right to religious freedom of expression. (Warsaw Domestic Service, 8 June; *FBIS-Eastern Europe*, 9 June.)

In another speech at the Catholic University in Lublin, the pope condemned the materialistic outlook of communism because it "allow[s] man to be reduced to an object" (*Słowo powszechne*, 10 June).

In his sermons the pope did not hesitate to advance the ideas of Solidarity, although he never mentioned the union specifically. "In the name of mankind and of humanity, the word 'solidarity' must be pronounced," the pope said to shipyard workers in Gdynia; diverting from the written text he asked, "what is solidarity? It is a way of living that respects differences between people. It means unity in numbers. This is solidarity. This is pluralism." He concluded that "the world cannot forget it. This word is your pride." (*NYT*, 12 June.)

Supporting and encouraging the opposition, Pope John Paul met privately with Lech Wałęsa, leader of the outlawed union. The pope also told newly ordained priests to follow the example of Father Jerzy Popieluszko, the young priest brutally murdered in 1984 by three Polish secret policemen. At this point the pope directly challenged Poland's primate, Józef Cardinal Glemp, who, as a gesture to the authorities, had played down the popularity of Father Popieluszko. In general, the cardinal had sought to avoid airing politically sensitive issues in exchange for greater tolerance of the social activities of the church and the expected establishment of formal diplomatic relations between the Vatican and Warsaw. The pope, on the other hand, strongly endorsed the militant anticommunism of Father Popieluszko and presented him as a role model for other Poles to follow. Appealing directly to the people, over the heads of government and the Episcopate, the pontiff legitimized opposition to communism. "The Pope Is with Us" read a Solidarity banner displayed during a demonstration marking the 7th anniversary of the August 1980 agreement (*NYT*, 1 September). The pope's words and symbolic gestures had enormous impact on the nation. "We don't live in a free country" read the statement of the banned union, "and our voices cannot always be heard and, therefore, the pope spoke about us and to us and—as he himself underlined—for us" (ibid., 15 June).

The beatification of Karolina Kózka, the eighteen-year-old girl who in 1969 was killed while resisting rape by a Russian soldier, was perhaps the pope's most symbolic act during his 1987 visit to Poland. "She gave her young life, when it was necessary to give it," stated the pope, "to defend her dignity as a woman, to defend the dignity of a Polish peasant girl" (*NYT*, 11 June). The symbolism of relations between Poland and Russia is apparent to every Pole.

In sum, the pope's visit had a confrontational character. He extolled the political and moral values of Solidarity and favorably contrasted Christianity with Leninism. The regime in Warsaw did not receive public approval of its social and economic policies and was pointedly instructed by the pope to respect human rights in conceiving and pursuing public policies. The moral authority of the "People's Poland" was openly questioned in public and, in effect, Jaruzelski's disrespect for human rights and his unwillingness to legalize Solidarity were interpreted as acts of war against humanity. The outlawed Solidarity, with its emphasis on political freedom and social equality, was presented by the pope as representing universal human rights that every political ruler should respect.

The regime press gave the pope's visit a positive review. For example, *Trybuna ludu* commented that "cooperation between the church and the state was enriched with further positive experience during the preparations for the visit and during the visit itself" (*TL*, 13 July). However, the visit failed to provide a new impulse to improve relations. Moreover, the establishment of formal diplomatic ties between the Holy See and Warsaw, a step that would advance the legitimacy of Jaruzelski's regime, was never under consideration. The East European policy of the Vatican is founded on the moral authority of the Roman Catholic Church and on the assumption that carefully orchestrated, consistent pressure on unpopular regimes will lead to eventual emancipation from communism, with the long-term aim of outlasting the regime. An angry Polish official accused the pope of intending to establish a theocratic state in Poland and concluded "I fear the Khomeinization of Poland" (*CSM*, 19 June). General Jaruzelski noted cynically that the pope "cannot take Poland's problems with him" to the Vatican (*WP*, 26 July).

The church in Poland is indeed on the offensive. Communist authorities are visibly weak and have no realistic solution to the deepening socioeconomic crises. The regime's lack of legitimacy and resources has created an enormous vacuum in internal politics that is rapidly being filled by the church in its expanding social role. As a patron of the so-called Third Polish Republic, an underground society, the church is active in education, cultural life, and the economy. Churches not only are providing places of worship but are also promoting and housing cultural events like exhibitions, theater performances, movies, and lectures. According to official sources, the church is teaching Polish history in an effort to train the leadership of a future independent Poland (*TL*, 8 January).

The pilgrimage of John Paul II to Poland was a significant event because of his teachings on moral, national, and social matters. He called attention to universal human rights and reminded the regime about the natural laws that should be respected by political power. He strengthened the religious and patriotic convictions of the Poles and focused national attention on human dignity and the rights of the individual as prerequisites for peace and prosperity. The social implication of his message is that the people have "inalienable" rights to organize themselves, independent of the authorities; to establish social institutions; to conduct economic activities; and to develop their own cultural life. His teaching neither endorsed nor supported any particular form of government; however, he carefully avoided any reference to reconciliation between the people and the regime. Moreover, he told the Polish people to take certain initiatives into their own hands, for only by such initiatives would they achieve solidarity in spirit, harmony in pursuit of religious and national goals, and the conquest of lethargy and pessimism. A Catholic writer concluded that the pope's "call aims at awaking the will in each of us to realize and build dignity in each and everyone" (*LAT*, 2 August; *JPRS-Eastern Europe*, 30 October). When translated into political language, the pope did not ask the Poles to struggle against communist authorities but to ignore their rulers and form their own associations and communities. He saw in Poland a future fellowship of men and women working together for the common good.

The immediate result of the pope's visit was a U.S.-funded program to allow the church to import farm machinery for private farmers. This is seen as the first move toward establishing an agricultural fund that would use the money from the sales of imported equipment to finance water and sewage projects. Today the church has more than $28 million at its disposal, and if the government grants the foundation independent legal status, the church could assume the principal role in the development of Polish agriculture. Professor Witold Trzeciakowski, who heads the church agricultural committee, observed that, "I think the government has finally realized that without the initiative of the people, they will not achieve any of their goals in the economy. And after the visit of the pope, they understood that without cooperation with the Church they cannot get out of the current crisis." (*WP*, 26 July.)

The Opposition. Adam Michnik, a leading member of the Social Self-Defense Committee, summarized the current political strategy adopted by the opposition in an interview with *Avanti* (Rome) on 31 March, where he said that the struggle taking place in Poland concerns the rebuilding of the civilian society, specifically involving a "pluralism in public life, a share in the ownership of the means of production, the right to self-management and monitoring, the freedom of expression, the right to legality as the real regulator of interpersonal relations." Thus, the opposition is planning for the "postcommunist" society and promoting the establishment of pluralistic institutions. It is, however, determined to avoid violence that could lead to war with the USSR or a forceful intervention by Soviet armed forces. Michnik went on to explain:

> We in Poland are trying to create faits accomplis. This is why we often say that we are struggling not for power but for a different kind of society. We are creating it through our activities—by creating an independent structure, publishing houses, libraries, independent student unions, independent associations, and so forth. We do not know what form postcommunist society will take. I assume it will be a society based on two values—civil freedom and social justice.

Jacek Kuroń, another well-known opposition leader, argues that Solidarity has three distinct strategies: (1) an "everything or nothing" policy of extreme pressure or total inaction until more favorable conditions for struggle emerge, (2) a "dialogue" with the regime, and (3) "a policy of accomplished facts." Under the current political circumstances in Poland and the current military situation in Europe, Kuroń favors dialogue combined with the effort to structurally alter the socioeconomic reality in Poland.

The political actions of Solidarity reflect this new philosophy, as the union continues to search for a program that would avoid confrontation with the authorities. The union is ever mindful that involvement in provocative demonstrations not only triggers repressive reactions but may lead to serious violence. Solidarity would never win "through armed combat but through development," observed Chairman Wałesa (in *Neue Kronen Zeitung*, 3 October; *FBIS-Eastern Europe*, 6 October). As the "conscience of the nation," the union provides for continuous idea exchange and stimulates and directs national development in its process of grass roots democratization. Without waiting for "permission" to organize society in a democratic, self-governing fashion, the "underground Solidarity" provides the ideological umbrella and example of how to practice pluralism.

Solidarity today has become a point of reference for Polish society. The authorities destroyed its national organization, but the union's ideas, its political concepts, live on and serve as an example. The eventual evolution of the communist system includes a danger that society could lose the ability to govern itself. Such a civil breakdown is to be prevented by an aggressive program of strengthening voluntary associations of people—people who freely accept responsibility for popular national values and economic well being. All changes in Poland must take place peacefully. "No stones and no clubs, we must win with wisdom," summarized Wałęsa (AFP, Paris, *FBIS-Eastern Europe*, 21 August).

This deradicalization of Solidarity, evident in the peaceful, evolutionary, long-term program, has rendered the issues of legalization of the union and confrontation with the authorities of secondary importance. Opposition to the communist regime has become more subtle, less visible, and less dramatic. This form of temporary accommodation with the government does create an impression of an aging Solidarity, declining in popularity and lacking an action plan. However, Wałęsa states his hopes and fears as follows: "If one organizes a strong underground group, one risks an equally strong counteraction by the regime. In my view, one can do more if one lives and works normally in broad daylight, as I and many others do." (*Neue Kronen Zeitung*, 3 October.)

Younger and more radical activists, however, ridicule Solidarity's peaceful methods, pointing to the crashing defeat the union suffered when martial law was imposed. These forces, frustrated by inaction, passivity and the inability to overcome the political and economic stalemate, search for more active and heroic means to struggle with communism. Thus militant attitudes are generated accompanied by keen hopes for immediate results. Several radical groups have entered the Polish political scene, including the pacifist Freedom and Peace Movement, the radical Fighting Solidarity, and the Greens, who combine environmental concerns with political claims and actions.

The Freedom and Peace Movement, the most active and visible opposition group in Poland, practices an "open-door" political program that stresses creative flexibility regarding the forms of opposition it will exert against communism. This movement also has an effective network of connections with similar groups in Hungary, Czechoslovakia, and the West. These credentials, combined with zeal and energy, make this movement effective in public confrontation with the authorities. The Freedom and Peace political platform promotes human rights, peace, and a better environment and opposes the death penalty. So far these activists have forced the authorities to shut down a toxic plant in Wrocław; publicized the Wehrmacht soldier Otto Schimek who, during World War II, was sentenced to death for his refusal to participate in mass executions; and achieved a new law permitting conscientious objectors to perform alternative duty in lieu of normal military service (*Dziennik Polski*, London, 23 June).

The political program of Fighting Solidarity has strong Marxist overtones. Calling for the defense of the working people against "exploitation," the leading members of this group insist on "intensification" of the struggle with communist authorities (*JPRS-Eastern Europe*, 26 February). The only methods employed by the Fighting Solidarity are strikes, demonstrations, and boycotts; yet the official communist propaganda depicts its members as desperate terrorists and CIA agents.

Meanwhile, the Confederation of Independent Poland (KPN), a political movement searching for restoration of independence and alliance with the Ukrainian Republic and Lithuania, issued its political declaration. Speaking at a press conference in the British parliament, Leszek Moczulski, founder and leader of the group, enumerated six KPN principles:

1. Equal rights and responsibilities for all citizens, regardless of their philosophy, religion, political beliefs, origin, language, race, nationality, sex, social status, or affiliation
2. The freedom for all to have their own humanist values, philosophy, faith, and beliefs, not only within their own company but also in institutions of public life such as government offices, the mass media, schools, higher schools, cultural establishments, and others
3. The freedom to speak out for one's beliefs including the freedom to criticize, make demands, and use technical means to do so
4. The freedom to come together in free philosophical, religious, ideological, political, social, professional, community, ethnic, and cultural associations
5. The freedom to choose one's own government representatives in accordance with the principle of national sovereignty through truly free, public, equal, direct, and secret voting
6. An independent state that is genuinely free from any outside decisions and that completely preserves sovereignty and state territorial and economic integrity. (*Dziennik Polski*, London, 14 February.)

Another threat to Solidarity comes from the conciliatory policy of the regime designed to co-opt some better-known members of the union into government-sponsored institutions and associations. Talks between government representatives and selected individuals representing the opposition are publicized "to gain a degree of respectability for official actions and institutions," explains analyst Jan B. de Weydenthal (RFE *Research*; *RAD Background Report/186*, 14 October). "This objective is even more important at a time when any form of support from or acceptance by the opposition is invaluable for ensuring public acquiescence to the government's economic program" (ibid.). The union, however, has rejected cooperation with the authorities until its legal status is formalized.

The political carrots offered by General Jaruzelski came side by side with a new and perfected selection of sticks. The 1986 amnesty freed all political prisoners and resulted in the lifting of U.S. economic sanctions imposed in protest against martial law. The Polish government then proceeded with a revision of the criminal code that gave internal security forces the judicial authority to hear cases involving illegal possession of printing materials and illicit journals, membership in illegal organizations, participation in illegal meetings, and so on. This "decriminalization," "depoliticization," and decentralization moved political offenses to the local administrative level, which was a dual advantage for the regime. First, the regime is no longer embarrassed by a large number of political prisoners, and second, it has a new array of painful economic penalties from which to choose. For example, the government may now confiscate an automobile, often valued at three years' salary or more. Sentences are imposed instantaneously, "without attracting international attention and without giving the accused the right to a full defense" (*NYT*, 25 February).

The more militant activists continue to be accused of terrorism. The press and other media frequently report detention of individuals from these outlawed groups, who are repeatedly accused of being terrorists. Official accounts include elaborate lists of weapons allegedly found in numerous hideouts, and quite often the authorities claim to have discovered bombs, grenades, machine guns, and chemical weapons. An instruction manual allegedly was found that identified security services and civil militia officials and their families, including makes of cars, addresses, and personal descriptions. These reports are most likely fabricated and intended to deter people from taking part in activities sponsored by the opposition.

Nevertheless, after six years of martial law, Solidarity continues to fight and enjoys enormous popularity at home and abroad. At least 25 percent of the Polish labor force still pay dues to the underground union. Quite frequently, individual enterprises petition the regime to legally recognize the union. Frequent strikes and demonstrations are additional evidence of the popularity and vitality of the union and, hence, the regime's vulnerability.

The Referendum. When martial law was imposed six years ago, General Jaruzelski justified it as necessary to prevent a Soviet invasion and to quickly arrest the rapidly advancing economic crises. Perhaps martial law was the only way to spare the country from another foreign occupation; however, Jaruzelski's junta has been unable to produce the minimum necessary economic reforms that would put Poland on its feet. Several times the regime came up with grandiose schemes that would cure all political, social, and economic ills, including the establishment of the Patriotic Movement for National Rebirth. This program of economic reforms would increase the role of market forces, create new trade unions independent of the authorities, and establish ombudsmen with broad powers and the immunity necessary to deal effectively with cases concerning the protection of citizens' rights and liberties.

These steps had two objectives: to inspire the people to support the regime and forget Solidarity and to improve performance of the economy. This national referendum on the future of Poland's economic and sociopolitical life was to be the strategic turning point toward economic prosperity and democracy. Only once, 40 years ago, had the Poles been asked to vote; then it was on a referendum on the nationalization of the means of production and the incorporation of the Oder-Neisse territories.

The authorities presented the referendum as an extraordinary event that would permanently alter the political and the economic system. As one Polish official stated,

> The referendum will be a form of deciding the most important, existential affairs for Poland and for Poles. Let Polish citizens be managers in the fatherland. The essence of our statehood is expressed by the principles of pluralistic partnership and corresponding partnership of the working people in ruling the state. (Warsaw Domestic Service, 23 October; *FBIS-Eastern Europe*, 26 October.)

At the same time, the regime made it clear that the purpose of the referendum was to approve a program of "rapid" or "radical" reform designed to bring immediate and spectacular results in two or three years. Failure to win sufficient popular support for the official *perestroika* would neither discourage nor affect its content. In case of public disapproval, the government would only decelerate the rate of price increase and "gradually" restructure the economy. The choice presented to the public was limited to the form rather than the direction and the nature of change.

This point was made clear by a Polish official who explained that,

> the referendum questions are not about the implementation of the reform and about its detailed mechanisms. They are about the speed of the reform, about whether we want to implement it more quickly in order to reap the resulting advantages, and whether we want to abandon small steps that stretch efforts over many years. (*TL*, 24–25 October.)

The referendum became an integral part of the so-called second stage of the economic reforms program that envisioned the following steps:

1987—An essential change in the functional scope and organizational structure of the central economic administration (which is going on now) and the possibility of developing new ventures in various sectors and fields of the economy

1988—A step forward in balancing the Polish economy and increasing the role of the market, an acceleration of increase in supply, and an increase of trade with foreign countries

1989—Coming closer to an economic balance, clear progress in normalization of the currency rate, and arrangement of pay systems

1990—Achievement of a balance between supply and demand for production and investment goods and consumption goods and arresting the rate of price increases to some 7 to 9 percent annually

1991—A balance in current payments in trade with foreign countries and the basis for beginning to reduce the foreign debt

1992 and beyond—Full normalization of the payment situation, which will make stable, further economic growth possible and convertibility of the Polish złoty on the world currency market. (PAP, Warsaw, October; *FBIS-Eastern Europe*, 28 October.)

Political preparations for the referendum began in October, including a major shake-up and reorganization of the government. The total number of ministers was reduced from 26 to 19, and the number of central agencies, from 16 to 8. Also, the number of deputy premiers dropped from five to three. Approximately 3,500 bureaucrats were dismissed. (*NYT*, 25 October.)

This general overhaul of the central bureaucracy was to convince the public how serious and determined the PZPR was to implement the new economic program. The successful fulfillment of the economic reforms, however, incurred such costs as a 110 percent increase in the price of food, fuel, and other basic commodities and a 57 percent inflation rate for at least one year, and it was feared that this highly unpopular measure might provoke major national unrest similar to the riots and demonstrations in 1970, 1976, and 1980. The regime calculated that, using the referendum, it could win public acceptance of another decline in the standard of living, a good possibility since this economic initiative was coupled with a vague promise to democratize political life in Poland. The regime felt these steps to be unavoidable in order to restore the economic equilibrium. Sacrifices would be necessary to develop realistic prices that reflect actual production costs. The regime sought to discontinue the enormous subsidies for some basic food items and to integrate Poland into the world economy, thus stimulating financial discipline.

Polish voters were asked to answer yes or no to two questions formulated by the authorities:

1. Are you in favor of the full realization of the program presented to the Sejm on the radical healing of the economy, which aims at the clear improvement of society's living conditions knowing that this requires passing through two or three difficult years, full of rapid changes?

2. Are you in favor of the Polish model for the profound democratization of political life, the aim of which is to strengthen self-government, widen the rights of citizens, and increase citizens' participation in governing the country?

Affirmative responses to both questions were presented as magical and expedient cures to a long list of economic and political problems. Higher prices, according to official sources, would check inflation, strengthen the currency, increase the standard of living, open new job opportunities, increase housing construction, improve education and medical care, provide for better protection of the environment, stimulate exports, and break down production monopolies. Political changes envisioned by the referendum included acceleration of "socialist renewal," more political freedom, "strengthening of civil rights and adherence to the law," "enrichment of the forms of socialist pluralism," and "widening the areas of dialogue and national accord." The objectives of the referendum were vague, meaningless, and deceptively phrased. For example, the people were not even asked their opinion about changing the constitution.

Skepticism about the referendum and the effectiveness of economic reforms prevailed among major socioeconomic groups from the moment this new initiative was pronounced. After all, price increases had been the only method employed by the regime to cope with the economic crisis, and for almost twenty years they have produced no positive result. The "eat less work more" formula for economic recovery was never popular, and now there is evidence to prove that it does not work.

First of all, reducing the number of bureaucrats did not reduce bureaucratic control over the economy. Two key industries—coal mining and energy production—were excluded from the reorganization. Moreover, the principal cause of inefficiency, PZPR control over the economy, was preserved. The communist concept of economic reform does not mandate a reduction of the party's role in management of the economy. Significantly, the proposed economic reform program has been founded on two contradictory principles. Woźniak, a Politburo member and Central Committee secretary, explained that the reforms would be an integral part of the socialist renewal and are expected to achieve two mutually exclusive goals:

> The first objective of this program is to stimulate initiative and the enterprising spirit in all sectors and units of the economy, to remove barriers, and to strengthen that which boosts effectiveness.
>
> The second objective is to transform the management system in order to strengthen the strategic functions of the socialist state and expand self-management activities so as to switch from bureaucratic centralism to independence and responsibility as soon as possible.

The real meaning of the reforms, Woźniak continues "is to make a breakthrough in the effectiveness and efficiency of the *realization* of programs and decisions" (*TL*, 24–25 October). Clearly, the PZPR is searching for more effective methods of exercising its monopoly of power.

Second, the regime's decision to disguise another price increase and press for its public approval without support from other sociopolitical groups was evidence that the government hoped that the Polish people had forgotten that it was General Jaruzelski and his junta who crushed the grass roots democratic movement in Poland. Proceeding alone, Jaruzelski expected to pre-empt Solidarity and the church by adopting elements of their program and then formulating the questions in such a manner that opposition would appear unpatriotic and self-defeating. The church response was to adopt a neutral position, in effect, refusing to endorse the government's program. Solidarity, however, was under pressure to express its position and, avoiding a choice between yes or no, recommended a boycott of the referendum.

Accusations directed against the regime included charges that the "Polish model of democratization" proposed by the authorities was vague and "of a solely propaganda nature" (*LAT*, 27 October). The fundamental question of political power, the essence of pluralism in Poland, was carefully excluded from public discussion and voting. "I just wonder that one significant question was not mentioned," stated Wałęsa. "Do the Poles want to breathe socialist air?" He concluded that the referendum was just "a waste of time." (Ibid., 25 October.)

Wałęsa presented Solidarity's position on the referendum in an interview for the Spanish publication *Ya*.

> We—the people in Solidarity—were and are in favor of a referendum. We were and are in favor of effecting reforms. What we cannot do is to pretend that we are effecting reforms or that we are holding a referendum. This referendum which the government is preparing is a parody. The first question in the referendum says: "Do you want to have a better situation in two years' time?" Who can say that he does not want to be better off in two years' time? Of course we want to be better off. The second question says: "Do you want to have more democracy?" Of course the Polish people want more democracy. And all this is costing the Polish people over one billion złoty. It is not worthwhile to spend that fortune in order to ask these questions. This referendum is a waste of money. For these reasons we are opposed to the referendum. Because we also wonder: What will the government do when it feels stronger? Nor do we know what the government will do when we are richer. It is a dangerous situation.
>
> For a referendum to be honest it must fulfill three conditions. First, the people must have influence, or rather, participation concerning the questions' substance and their form. Second, the people must have the opportunity to supervise the vote counting. Third, the people must have participation in the actual holding of the referendum. If these minimum conditions do not exist, it is very difficult to believe in any referendum. That is why I emphasize that we are in favor of a referendum and of effecting reforms, but not in favor of this referendum and these reforms. (*Ya*, 22 November; *FBIS-Eastern Europe*, 14 December.)

"Democratization" under the communist system has become a device for strengthening PZPR rule. Explained a Polish political scientist,

> What is happening is a defense of the party's more important role—that of the sole dominant political force—by giving up some of its decisionmaking powers in some areas. That means other forces will now be allowed to participate, but only if they first recognize the supremacy of the party. (*WP*, 19 November.)

The referendum was another test for Solidarity, for support by only 51 percent of all those eligible to vote would make both propositions binding. According to official data, provided by the Central Commission for the Referendum, only 63.8 percent (17.6 million) of those eligible had voted on 30 November. Even according to official data, it was the lowest turnout in the history of communist Poland. Only 44 percent supported the economic proposition, and only 46 percent voted in favor of the political liberalization program. The next day, a government press spokesman admitted that the regime had failed to acquire the support necessary for a "rapid" implementation of the reforms. He attributed low attendance to "the announced information about the scale of wage and price rises and about the social costs of the change." (PAP, Warsaw, 30 November; *FBIS-Eastern Europe*, 30 November.)

The actual degree of participation in the referendum may never be known, but rough estimates by the opposition claim that a maximum of 30 percent of all eligible voters cast their ballot. Particularly significant and a new development, the opposition claims, was the lack of support from members of the PZPR and the government apparatus, including the armed forces and the security forces. These, the privileged elites in any communist society, have a strong record of loyalty to the system but now appear to be disillusioned with the internal situation in Poland. A popular perception sees Jaruzelski's iron fist showing signs of fatigue and losing support from those who only six years ago joined him to impose martial law. This immediately encouraged the opposition to press harder, demanding legalization of Solidarity groups in individual enterprises and public institutions. Social assertiveness in Poland is again on the rise, confronting the regime with the dilemma of democratization versus a repressive crackdown.

The authorities presented the results of the referendum as a success, despite the fact that attendance was about 10 percent lower than during the last parliamentary elections in 1985. The number of people who ignore the authorities has increased, an indication of the declining influence of the regime. Political impasse in Poland continues, but it is doubtful that General Jaruzelski understands the absolute necessity of dialogue with the people and their true representatives. Without Solidarity's support, he and his junta can police the country but are unable to rule effectively. Nothing short of meaningful democratization including the legalization of Solidarity by name (not just ambiguously defined as "opposition clubs") could inspire the Poles to accept economic austerity in anticipation of better times in the future. The referendum vote showed a lack of public confidence in a system that is inherently incapable of reforming its most debilitating feature.

The Jaruzelski regime also failed to offer tangible concessions or satisfy the public's demand for self-determination. Never before has the government in Warsaw operated in an international environment more receptive to fundamental, structural changes in the archaic system of political power still practiced by communist-ruled states. Preoccupied with their own domestic and international problems, Soviet leaders left Warsaw to solve Poland's chronic economic and political malady. This insecurity, preoccupation with tactical maneuvers, and Jaruzelski's instinctive fear of Moscow are the primary barriers to real reforms in Poland. The referendum, another of Jaruzelski's tricks that did not work, was a victory for the opposition and a vindication of its nonviolent strategy of resistance. Solidarity's declaration on the referendum told the regime once again that,

> The population wants radical political and economic reforms, but does not have any faith in the leadership and its representatives. Freedom of association and trade-union pluralism have to be created in order to overcome the crisis of confidence and save the country from going under. Economic and political reforms form a unity, for a state organized along totalitarian lines cannot have a rationally managed economy with market mechanisms. (DPA, Hamburg, 6 December; *FBIS-Eastern Europe*, 7 December.)

The Polish economy suffers from stagflation, low productivity, low levels of technological sophistication, depreciation of national assets, a very low degree of integration with the foreign market, high consumption of energy, and imbalance between the demand and supply. The first stage of economic reform has resulted in minor improvements in managerial efficiency and labor productivity. However, overall structural difficulties persist.

The second stage of the economic reform involves another large price increase, a notorious way of income draining that has become a communist cure-all approach to the economy. The rapid increase in prices (more than 100 percent), according to the official expectation, would in a relatively short period of time create sound conditions for better management, ignite individual ingenuity, and increase productivity and the quality of goods. How this "thrift" strategy, designed to reduce the standard of living, would help eliminate shortcomings, restore market forces, terminate the state monopoly on foreign trade, produce currency convertibility, and achieve rapid growth of national income has never been clear. What is beyond doubt, however, is that the regime has no plans to change its political methods and control of economic operations. No "restructurization" has ever been seriously considered by the party, which jealously guards its hegemony over economic lives in Poland. For this reason, the country's lasting economic crisis has no realistic prospects for modernization or stabilization. In the opinion of a Catholic publication,

> One cannot see any real circumstances that would signify that prosperity will occur after this period (two to three years)—at least no one is informing us about them. So the assurances about progress in the 1990s, nonbinding in any case, are not convincing anyone and the government officials are incapable of mobilizing anyone to anything. (*Tygodnik powszechny*, 1 March.)

Janusz Onyszkiewicz, the press spokesman for Solidarity, described price rises as "the usual and often repeated attempt to weigh society down with the costs of maintaining an irrational and ineffective economic system" (*NYT*, 31 March).

The standard of living in Poland is one of the lowest in Europe and continues to decline. The average monthly wage (about 12,000 złotys) pays for such routine items as food for two people but does not cover household necessities, rent, and other expenses. About 60 percent of wages in Poland are below this minimum. (*Tygodnik powszechny*, 1 March; *JPRS-Eastern Europe*, 12 May.) This data, however, does not show the income generated by a huge subterranean economy, for it is a well-documented phenomenon in Poland that household expenditures substantially exceed reported income.

The housing situation is tragic. In 1981–1985 about five apartments per 100 individuals were made available for occupancy. Only about 79 percent of the urban population and 38 percent of the rural population have basic plumbing in their homes. It is estimated that there are 113 households per 100 dwellings and 2.1 million people waiting for cooperative apartments, including 162,000 waiting for state-allocated housing and 388,000 waiting for work-supplied housing. The mortality rate in Poland has increased from 9.9 percent per 1,000 in 1980 to 10.3 percent in 1985. (*Życie gospodarcze*, 26 July; *JPRS-Eastern Europe*, 28 October.)

In 1987, the economy registered a moderate "statistical" growth. The gross national product rose about 5 percent, and the per capita increase in national income should be more than 4 percent. The value of socialized industry's "sold" production increased by 3.4 percent, and the highest rate of increase was attained by industries specializing in electrical engineering, precision instruments, and engineering (*Rzeczpospolita*, 1 September). Wages in the socialized sector of the economy increased by 21 percent instead of the planned 13 percent, 500 billion złotys more than expected. In the private sector, agricultural production income increased 43 percent, although only 24 percent was anticipated. Inflation continues at approximately 30 percent, 10 percent above wage increases reported by the public sector and 10 percent below wage increases in the private economy. Productivity per employee rose slightly to more than 4 percent.

However, the prevailing attitude is that the "people do not want to work." Social fatigue in Poland is high. Wages are low and markets so poorly supplied that, as one observer noted, "getting a good place at the right time in the line for meat can be more profitable for a large family than earning a little money during that time" (*Tygodnik powszechny*, 1 March; *JPRS-Eastern Europe*, 12 May).

If the official statistics are correct, in 1987 industrial production in Poland exceeded that of the previous year, just before the economic crisis. However, in eight years the population grew by more than two million, meaning that industrial production per capita is still far below the 1978 level. Also, in 1987 Poland again had a budget deficit amounting to 298 billion złotys. This is substantially lower than the anticipated 418 billion, but it is still unlikely that the regime will be able to balance the budget in 1988, especially since the 110 percent price increase was voted down in the November referendum (PAP, Warsaw, 7 December; *FBIS-Eastern Europe*, 10 December). Following the defeat, the Polish authorities decided to postpone the price increase on food but to move ahead with 150 to 200 percent increases in the cost of rent, utilities, fuel, and transportation (*WP*, 6 December).

Polish indebtedness to Western countries reached $33.5 billion at the end of 1986 and grew substantially in 1987 due to changes in exchange rates on the international currency markets. Decline in the value of the dollar meant that Polish obligations in West German marks increased when marks were converted to dollars. Poland may have suffered up to $3 billion in additional losses during the last three months of 1987. Furthermore, Polish indebtedness to Soviet bloc countries is about seven billion transfer rubles.

The servicing of Poland's foreign debt continues to be a major problem. The country's trade surplus with the West was about $1.6 billion (same as 1986), but the 1987 debt service charges exceeded

$6 billion. This year Poland again devalued its currency by 16.7 percent, from 200 złotys to 240 per dollar (*WSJ*, 3 February). The unofficial, black market value of the dollar increased from approximately 800 złotys in 1986 to 1,400 złotys in 1987.

In conclusion, no progress has been made toward solving Poland's political stalemate or dealing with its economic imperatives. The country is drifting aimlessly, facing the danger of another dramatic confrontation that could be provoked by even a minor incident. The regime will not share its power with the people, who get even by refusing to work. Moods of discouragement and apathy have intensified as people realize that the country is in a political and economic trap and that the regime has no plausible strategy for national revival and full utilization of Poland's natural and human resources. On the contrary, the current rulers have been systematically avoiding every chance to build social consensus, with their every move dictated by an unyielding determination to preserve the PZPR's absolute monopoly of power. This selfish motive permeates socioeconomic programs formulated by the authorities, and thus these programs inevitably breed popular distrust and skepticism. The absence of democratic institutions checking political power and of self-regulating economic mechanisms are formidable barriers to a socioeconomic renaissance. As long as the regime of General Jaruzelski is committed to defend these barriers, Poland is headed toward catastrophe.

Foreign Affairs. Today the regime in Warsaw is no longer burdened by the stigma of martial law and international isolation, which technically ended with the removal of all U.S. sanctions. This newly acquired freedom was greatly enhanced by the improvement of U.S.-Soviet relations and by Mikhail Gorbachev's *glasnost'*, which could be used to secure new credits and to compensate for domestic socioeconomic failures. For the second time in its post–World War II history, Poland returned to international activism, stressing the political importance of smaller states in Europe rather than the priority of superpowers. Poland's foreign policy is still an extension of the Soviet one; however, in assuming a more independent and visible role, Warsaw has the opportunity to promote its own interests both in the East and in the West.

Virulent anti-Americanism, prompted by Warsaw at the beginning of the 1980s, has dissipated, together with Poland's subservient fidelity to Moscow. The regime in Warsaw continues to be a Soviet ally, but its foreign policy pronouncements are more balanced and optimistic toward the United States and West Germany. For example, the Poles carefully avoided involvement in such highly controversial issues as the war in Afghanistan, and their center of attention shifted outside the Soviet bloc. Following martial law, less-developed states were the only international partners of Warsaw, but the Polish regime has now shifted its foreign policy attention back to the European arena. With extraordinary fervor, energy, and unusual publicity, Poland has proceeded to rebuild bilateral relations with Italy, Great Britain, West Germany, France, Spain, Greece, and other West European states, thereby implying that relations with these states reflect the proper prestige and worldwide importance of Poland on the international scene. The authorities also want to create the strong impression that the highly industrialized democracies are natural economic partners.

These new aspirations of Poland found expression in the proposal to reduce the number of Soviet bloc tanks in exchange for cuts in NATO's offensive air power. With this initiative, known as the Jaruzelski Plan, Warsaw assumed the leading role in regional disarmament politics as it tried to bypass the deadlock that developed at the Mutual and Balanced Force Reductions (MBFR) talks in Vienna. In Jaruzelski's words, "We know the West believes that there is a preponderance of the Warsaw Pact in tanks. We believe that the NATO countries have a predominance in certain kinds of aircraft, especially bombers. The first step could be taken with these two categories." (*WP*, 12 November.)

When viewed in perspective, the plan is just one element in a whole spectrum of arms reduction proposals offered by the East. Moscow, the sole nuclear power in the Warsaw Pact, advanced proposals regarding strategic, regional, and battlefield nuclear arms control. Poland, the second largest member of the Pact, took over responsibility for reduction of conventional weapons in Europe. In effect, Warsaw assumed the role of spokesman for the bloc with regard to nonnuclear forces in Europe.

The Jaruzelski Plan, according to Polish sources, is not a duplication of the MBFR talks, which focus on troops rather than weapons, but is complementary to Soviet proposals, includes no preconditions, aims at prevention of a sudden attack along the East-West line in Europe, and represents an entirely new concept of disarmament. The Western leaders' reactions, however, were not too enthusiastic, as they pointed out that implementation of this plan would undermine the U.S. military commitment in Europe and that the Polish scheme does not take the unequal geographic depth of each bloc into account (*Życie Warszawy*, 6 July). Finally, expecting NATO's stronger emphasis on conventional weapons after the intermediate-range nuclear forces agreement between the superpowers, the immediate political purpose of the Jaruzelski Plan is to blunt NATO's proposals with a carefully prepared and well-advertised peace initiative.

The Soviet decision to delegate such an important international undertaking to Warsaw confirmed that Moscow has a renewed interest in Poland as a communist-ruled country and ally. General Jaruzelski is closely linked with Soviet leader Gorbachev on such policies as *glasnost'*, *perestroika*, and improved relations with the West. The Poles point out that there is an absolute unity of Polish and USSR views on fundamental issues of international politics. "Equally there is conformity of the policy of socialist renewal and reform in Poland with the Soviet strategy of restructuring. And this harmony in Polish-Soviet relations enables Warsaw to act more independently," said Polish foreign minister Orzechowski. (*Nova mysl* [Prague], 26 May; *FBIS-Eastern Europe*, 20 August.)

As always, the Russians extracted concessions for their tolerance of Poland's international activism and liberal politics at home. In April Warsaw and Moscow concluded a treaty on cooperation in ideology, science, and culture that constitutes another step in the Soviet policy of constructing direct links between institutions, including economic enterprises, scientific research organizations, educational institutions, and propaganda centers. The Soviets acquire direct access to the major and now self-managing socioeconomic institutions in Poland, monitoring and influencing their activities. This process reflects a new USSR strategy of controlling East European satellites. These direct links are advantageous for furthering Moscow's planned economic integration of the bloc, for these states are currently constructing numerous expensive projects in the USSR in exchange for future deliveries of fuel and raw materials.

The new Polish-Soviet understanding also noted that there are "white spots" in the officially sanctioned history of Soviet-Polish relations. Apparently, both countries are inclined to search for mutually acceptable interpretations of such events as the liquidation of the Polish Communist Party in 1938 combined with the execution of 15,000 Polish communists. Carefully constructed interpretations are also needed for the 1939 Nazi-Soviet Pact to invade and partition Poland, the Soviet massacre by the NKVD of 15,000 Polish officers, the deportation of 1.6 million Poles in the areas occupied by the Red Army during 1939–1941, and many other painful events. (During July Polish authorities discovered a grave near the Soviet border with the remains of men, women, and teenagers executed by Soviet troops in 1945. According to local residents, hundreds of their relatives were taken away on Russian trucks and disappeared.) Michael Kaufman, the *New York Times* correspondent in Poland, noted that "the discovery, tersely announced by the Polish state radio today, could prove a test of the joint Polish-Soviet declaration of eagerness to clarify and reveal tense aspects of recent history" (*NYT*, 16 July).

The Catholic publication *Przegląd katolicki* (23 August) suggested in addition to "the reinterpretation of tragic events, which continue to trigger nasty emotions," the process of filling "blank spots" in Polish-Soviet relations should include information on Polish ideological dogmatism (Stalinism) and intellectual life in Poland. Equally significant would be free access to data on social and economic developments and better opportunities "to popularize on a massive scale" findings revealed by social studies.

The first effect of *glasnost'* on these relations was Soviet willingness to catalog and protect monuments of Polish culture located in the USSR. Also significant, was Moscow's permission to develop cultural contacts with the more than 1,150,000 Poles still living in the western parts of the Ukrainian Republic, Belorussia, and Lithuania (*Polityka*, 25 July).

Poland's relations with its Eastern bloc neighbors have rarely been good examples of friendly or "fraternal" ties, for East Berlin and Warsaw have developed considerably different forms of communism. East Germany is probably the most orthodox satellite state, completely loyal to Moscow, whereas Poland is at the other end of this spectrum. The economic system in East Germany works relatively well and continues to function according to the old Stalinist principles in contrast to the Poles, who experience one sociopolitical turmoil after another, forcing East Germany to subsidize the Polish economy. Also, the Germans resent the territorial changes after World War II, when Poland acquired the Oder-Neisse lands, which are rich in natural resources, and the Poles resent East German eagerness to restore a Sovietlike system in Poland during the 1980–1981 crisis. Both countries are competing for second place status (after Moscow) in the bloc.

One fundamental concern of Polish foreign policy is to keep Germany divided and to discourage any movement, however minor, that could keep the idea of unification alive. Warsaw did not hide its satisfaction when the 1984 visit of East German leader Erich Honecker to West Germany failed to materialize. In September 1987, when Honecker finally traveled to Bonn, the Poles played down the significance of the visit by giving it minimum press coverage. The Poles moreover stressed that "the unification of Germany is not on the agenda in the historically anticipated future" (*Rzeczpospolita*, quoted in *NYT*, 7 September).

Immediately after Honecker's return to East Germany, General Jaruzelski went for a brief "working visit" to East Berlin. The joint communiqué on the Jaruzelski-Honecker talks highlighted the issue of the long-term program of economic cooperation between the two countries, but made no reference to the political situation in Europe and relations between East Germany, West Germany, and Poland. Specifically, the communiqué stated that,

> [B]oth the GDR and the PPR [Polish People's Republic] are striving for further developments in relations with the FRG on an equal basis, in accordance with the generally recognized norms of international law and respecting the territorial and political realities on the continent. In this they will be guided by the 21 December 1972 treaty on relations between the GDR and the FRG, by the 7 December 1970 treaty on normalization of relations between the PPR and the FRG, and by the principles of the CSCE [Conference on Security and Cooperation in Europe] Final Act. (*FBIS-Eastern Europe*, 22 September.)

On paper, at least, Warsaw received assurances on the permanent status of its western border and the division of Germany into two states.

The keen sensitivity of both countries to the territorial issue was illustrated by the dispute over the boundary in the Bay of Szczecin. Poland refused to recognize the extension of East German territorial waters into the bay and decided to test the German position by organizing a boat race in the disputed zone. The East German navy interrupted the event, and the question of delimiting territorial waters with East Germany is to be negotiated by both governments.

Poland's policy toward Western Europe has several elements. The regime in Warsaw is anxious to liquidate all remnants of isolation, to secure new credits, and to frustrate the West German claim to a dominant role in Europe. Reporting to the Polish parliament (Sejm), Foreign Minister Orzechowski explained that Poland is guided by three objectives: stabilization, democratization, and Europeanization:

> Stabilization denotes respect for borders, the promotion of mutual trust, and refraining from undermining the balance of forces that ensures Europe's peace. Democratization denotes, inter alia, respect for the CSCE Final Act's 10 principles and an increase in the role of medium-sized and small countries in consolidating security and promoting disarmament and the infrastructure of cooperation. Europeanization is a symbol of a comprehensive new approach toward the affairs of our continent—strengthening the awareness that our fate is the same, countering divisions and eliminating whatever intensifies divisions, and emphasizing common interests and dangers regardless of differences.

These principles express the essence of Polish interest in Europe, with Warsaw demanding more freedom to maneuver combined with a Western commitment to refrain from supporting internal opposition in Poland. The Polish regime would like to have a free hand in domestic affairs, assuming that any attempt to undermine its position threatens the balance of power in Europe. In effect, the Polish government is promoting a new interpretation of the CSCE Final Act that implies Western obligation to support communism in Eastern Europe. Such a position transforms the Helsinki Accords into a holy alliance pledged to incarcerate social progress. The principle of Europeanization reveals the long-standing Polish desire to overcome the division of the continent that pushed the country into Soviet control. Elimination of the U.S. presence from Europe and an attempt to discourage unification moves in Western Europe are also included in this point.

General Jaruzelski's visit to Italy, his first official travel to the West since martial law, launched Poland's Western policy in 1987. Apart from the political significance of the visit, the Polish leader secured Italian support for the modernization of the domestic automobile industry. Poland expects to receive $200 million to start production of a new automobile designed by Fiat. This new Italian-Polish cooperation will eventually result in a long-term $1.5 billion deal. Another goal of the visit involved discussions with the Vatican concerning the re-establishment of diplomatic relations (*NYT*, 13–14 January).

In November General Jaruzelski arrived in Greece for an official three-day visit. Other contacts with Western Europe were limited to the foreign minister level and usually resulted in the opening of bilateral dialogue on numerous political and economic issues. French and Danish foreign ministers came to Warsaw, and Polish foreign minister Orzechowski traveled to London. British prime minister Margaret Thatcher has agreed to visit Poland in 1988. Poland also hosted Japanese prime minister Yasuhiro Nakasone.

The past year marked a turning point in Polish-American relations. At the end of January, Deputy Secretary of State John C. Whitehead visited Warsaw to discuss lifting the remaining economic sanctions. His schedule included meetings with General Jaruzelski, Wałęsa, and Cardinal Glemp. Both the church and Solidarity appealed for removal of sanctions, and Polish leaders reassured the United States that the political dissidents who were released under the 1986 amnesty would not be rearrested. Lifting of U.S. economic sanctions has been contingent on improvement of the human rights situation in Poland.

President Ronald Reagan formally removed all economic sanctions and most important, reinstated the most-favored-nation trade status for Poland on 19 February, opening the way to an exchange of ambassadors between the two countries (*NYT*, 20 January). Economic relations and scientific exchange are also expected to intensify, but Poland should not be expected to quickly regain those markets that were lost because of the sanctions. The present level of Polish trade with the United States is about $255 million, and the immediate impact of the most-favored-nation status would involve only an extra $50 million in hard currency earnings for Poland.

Polish reaction to the U.S. announcement on the lifting of sanctions was positive but restrained. Characterized as "pragmatic sluggishness," the policy was said to have moved "from restrictions to realism" (*TL*, 10 March). The Poles have also reiterated their totally unsubstantiated claims that in five years U.S. sanctions cost Poland $15 billion in economic losses and that the United States would not compensate Poland for these damages (Warsaw Domestic Service, 19 February).

The Polish government could not admit that the sanctions were effective and that the United States has succeeded in practicing a "dual" policy toward Poland. Western nations continue to deal with the regime in Warsaw but render full support and recognition to Solidarity and the church as the spokesmen of the Polish nation. When visiting Poland, Western leaders routinely schedule meetings with Wałęsa and Cardinal Glemp. Without a doubt, the West has recognized the pluralistic nature of Polish society, and its foreign policy gives expression and encouragement to this trend. The United States has, de facto, recognized pluralism in Poland.

The regime eventually opened its prisons and decided to tolerate the political activities of the opposition. Polish dissidents expressed gratitude for U.S. support of their "programs and ideas," but they also welcomed the U.S decision to restore normal relations with Poland. Speaking on behalf of Solidarity, Wałęsa said that "the decision taken by President Reagan is a consistent continuation of his policy of supporting the interests and aspirations of the Polish nation" (*NYT*, 20 January).

The official Polish assessment of U.S motives was quite different, however:

> The United States views Europe primarily from the point of view of its own interests and the state of its relations with the USSR. That is how it has always been and always will be. This means certain domestic situations in the socialist countries are used as tools for the United States' own purpose.

In the official Polish judgment,

> Right now relations between both sides (that is, US and the USSR) are dominated by the disarmament problem. Ronald Reagan is on the defensive against Mikhail Gorbachev's initiative and is not engaging in ideological confrontation. Against this background, the trip by Deputy Secretary of State John Whitehead to Poland, Czechoslovakia, and Bulgaria is an expression of Washington's desire to revive, and in Poland's case restore, bilateral relations with USSR allies. (*Życie Warszawy*, 17 February.)

Following the visit to Warsaw by Deputy Secretary Whitehead, a return visit to Washington was scheduled in early March by Czyrek, the Central Committee secretary for international affairs, who is generally regarded as second in command to General Jaruzelski. Also a six-member delegation of Polish parliamentarians arrived in the United

States in June. Although these officials were inclined to express their views on a number of political issues, the emerging pattern of Polish-American relations indicates that Warsaw would prefer to limit contacts with the United States to economic matters. Normalization of mutual relations did not bring both governments closer on political issues—it just "normalized" Polish economic ties with the United States. All Warsaw wants from the United States is money.

Commercial motives behind the Polish government's interest in good relations with the United States were explicitly pronounced by an interview with Czyrek, where he defined normal Polish-American relations as, "creating instruments that would enable us to obtain trade loans instead of paying cash for purchases; securing guaranteed loans . . . to promote long-term cooperation; and reaching agreement on the principles of utilizing such international fiscal mechanisms as the IMF [International Monetary Fund], the World Bank, and the Paris Club. (*Życie Warszawy*, 11 March.)

Political differences between Poland and the United States and the "dualism" in U.S. policy toward Poland were clearly visible in July when the U.S. Congress appropriated $1 million to support Solidarity. Accepting the money, the union pledged not to use these funds for its own political purposes but for the support of social projects, especially health care. The union established a special seven-member board in charge of the foundation responsible for the distribution of the American aid. Wałęsa described the acceptance of U.S. aid as "a patriotic gesture" and expressed gratitude to the American people (RFE *Research*, vol. 12, no. 37, 18 September). The government spokesman in Poland, however, declared that acceptance of the U.S. grant by the "illegal structures of underground Solidarity" proved the guilt of that illegal Polish organization.

> This is the end of the legend that the leaders of Solidarity are acting for Polish interests and that they are independent fighters for a good cause. The heads of the former Solidarność have decided to commit political hara-kiri simply for money. A million dollars is nothing for the U.S. Government. It is a tip. But for several dozen or several hundred leading underground Solidarność activists, this sum, taken at the black market rate of the dollar, is a billion złotys. (*FBIS-Eastern Europe*, 29 July.)

Despite such condemnations, the authorities did not interfere with Solidarity's acceptance and distribution of the U.S. aid.

The highest point of Polish-American relations in 1987 was reached in early October during Vice-President George Bush's visit to Poland. The political ramifications of the vice-president's visit were numerous, ranging from his opening of his own presidential campaign to General Jaruzelski's eagerness to host well-known visitors for the sake of international publicity. The vice-president was the highest-ranking U.S. official to visit Poland since President Jimmy Carter visited Warsaw in 1977.

From the beginning the trip was planned as two visits, one with Polish officials and another with the Polish people. After a cool and restrained reception by General Jaruzelski, the vice-president was enthusiastically welcomed by the Polish people. Popular reaction to his arrival was fervent and spontaneous. He was welcomed by Wałęsa and other leaders of the opposition and then received by Cardinal Glemp. Vice-President Bush made numerous public appearances in Poland, the most dramatic of which were his unexpected speech from the balcony of Saint Stanisław Kostka's Church in Warsaw, where he stood next to Wałęsa and addressed an excited crowd, and again at the grave of Father Jerzy Popieluszko. He was closely followed by U.S. television, and the public scenes from Poland were "regarded by Bush campaign strategists as a masterpiece of political theater" (*WP*, 4 October).

The only substantive element of Bush's visit involved a message to Jaruzelski that the lucrative Polish economic relations with the United States will be contingent on respect for human rights. In exchange for the regime's tolerance of the political opposition, Vice-President Bush promised General Jaruzelski help in rescheduling Poland's foreign debt payments and in Poland's access to new credits. In his televised address to the Polish people, the vice-president stated,

> I can tell you what has worked in our country and in many other countries. It is respect for human rights. It is the right to form independent and self-governing organizations for many purposes, including the protection of workers' interests. It is an economic system that encourages people to reach their full potential.

In the end, the visit was a fine U.S. gesture to the Polish people and an event during which all parties involved gained a little extra publicity. But the Bush visit produced few, if any, substantive changes in Polish-U.S. relations. The United States, however, did resume high-level contacts with the Polish government and the representatives of the Polish people, and the vice-president's visit was the best proof that the international campaign in defense of human rights can produce positive results.

Arthur R. Rachwald
U.S. Naval Academy

Romania

Population. 22,936,503

Party. Romanian Communist Party (Partidul Comunist Român; PCR)

Founded. 8 May 1921

Membership. 3,640,000 (31 December 1986). Party members make up 23 percent of the adult population and 33 percent of the employed population. About 34 percent of the PCR are women, up from 22 percent in 1965, and half of all new members are women. The PCR social composition is 65 percent workers, 15 percent peasants, and 20 percent intellectuals and others. (*Cronica* [Iasi], 8 May; *WMR*, June.)

General Secretary. Nicolae Ceauşescu

Political Executive Committee (PEC). 19 full members, 7 of whom are members of the Permanent Bureau: Nicolae Ceauşescu (PCR general secretary; president of the republic; chairman, National Defense Council; chairman, Supreme Council on Socioeconomic Development), Emil Bobu (Central Committee [CC] secretary for party organization; chairman, Council on Problems of Economic and Social Organization), Elena Ceauşescu (first deputy prime minister; chairwoman, National Council of Science and Instruction), Constantin Dăscălescu (prime minister), Manea Mănescu (vice-president, State Council), Gheorghe Oprea (first deputy prime minister), Gheorghe Rădulescu (vice-president, State Council); other full members: Virgil Cazacu, Lina Ciobanu (deputy prime minister), Ion Coman (CC secretary for military and security matters), Nicolae Constantin (chairman, PCR Central Collegium), Ion Dincă (first deputy prime minister), Miu Dobrescu (chairman, Central Council of the General Confederation of Trade Unions), Ludovic Fazekas (deputy prime minister), Paul Niculescu, Constantin Olteanu (member, State Council), Gheorghe Pană (chairman, Committee for People's Councils' Affairs), Ion Păţan, Dumitru Popescu (rector, Ştefan Gheorghiu PCR Academy); 23 alternate members: Ştefan Andrei (deputy prime minister), Ştefan Bîrlea (chairman, State Planning Committee), Nicu Ceauşescu (PCR first secretary, Sibiu County), Gheorghe David (minister of agriculture), Suzana Gâdea (chairwoman, Council of Socialist Culture and Education), Mihai Gere (chairman, Council of Working People of Hungarian Nationality), Maria Ghitulica, Nicolae Giosan (chairman, Grand National Assembly), Neculai Ibanescu (deputy prime minister), Mihai Marina, Ilie Matei, Vasile Milea (minister of national defense), Ioachim Moga, Ana Mureşan (minister of domestic trade; chairwoman, National Council of Women), Elena Nae, Cornel Pacoste (deputy prime minister), Tudor Postelnicu (minister of internal affairs), Ion Radu (CC secretary; chairman, Central Council of Workers' Control of Economic and Social Activities), Ion Stoian (CC secretary for international relations), Iosif Szasz (vice-chairman, Grand National Assembly), Ioan Totu, Ion Ursu (vice-chairman, National Council of Science and Instruction), Richard Winter.

Secretariat. 10 members (with assumed areas of responsibility): Nicolae Ceauşescu (general secretary), Radu Balan (unknown), Vasile Bărbulescu (agriculture), Emil Bobu (party organization), Ion Coman (military and security matters), Silviu Curticeanu (chief of staff), Constantin Mitea (propaganda and media), Ion Radu (the economy and control of party and state bodies and staff activity), Ion Stoian (international relations), Gheorghe Tanase (cadres)

Central Committee. 265 full and 181 alternate members

Status. The PCR is the only legal political party in Romania.

Last Congress. Thirteenth, 19–22 November 1984, in Bucharest; next congress scheduled for 1989

Last Elections. 17 March 1985; of the 15,733,060 registered voters, 15,732,095 (97.8 percent) voted for candidates of the Socialist Democracy and Unity Front (SDUF). Next elections are scheduled for 1990.

Auxiliary Organizations. The SDUF, the PCR's political front organization selects local and national government officials, Nicolae Ceauşescu, chairman; Manea Manescu, first vice-chairman; Tamara Maria Dobrin, chairwoman of the executive bureau. General Confederation of Romanian Trade Unions (7 million members), Miu Dobrescu, chairman of the Central Council; Union of Communist Youth (Union Tiniteretul Comunist [UTC], 4 million members), Ioan Toma, first secretary. National Council of Women, Ana Mureşan, chairwoman; Councils of Working People of Hungarian and German Nationalities, Mihai Gere and Eduard Eisenberger, respective chairmen

Publications. *Scînteia*, PCR daily (except Monday), Ion Mitran, editor in chief; *Era socialistă*, PCR theoretical and political biweekly; *România liberă*, SDUF daily (except Sunday); *Lumea*, foreign affairs weekly; *Revista economică*, economic weekly. Agerpres is the official news agency.

The PCR was founded in Bucharest on 8 May 1921, after splitting from the Social Democratic Party over the question of affiliation with the Communist International. For the next three years the PCR was subject to police harassment and restrictions on its activities, and in April 1924 it was outlawed. Even before the ban, the PCR was unsuccessful in attracting support. In 1922 its membership was reported to be 2,000, and the highest estimate during the interwar period was only 5,000.

Many factors contributed to its failure to win support. During the first decade of its existence, the PCR suffered from a highly fractionalized leadership, and it was a full decade before Moscow was able to establish control. The most serious obstacles were the party's subservience to the Soviet Union and its hostility to Romanian national aspirations. After World War I, Romania acquired Bessarabia from Russia and Transylvania from Hungary, both of which were inhabited by large ethnic Romanian populations but also present were significant numbers of minorities. The Soviet Union refused to accept the loss of Bessarabia, and the PCR was forced to adopt policies favoring its return. The hostility of the Hungarian minority to Romania's annexation of Transylvania was a source of instability that the Soviets wanted to exploit. The PCR was thus required to support "national self-determination" for Transylvania (that is, its separation from Romania), which placed the PCR squarely at odds with Romanian national aspirations. As a result, the small PCR was dominated by ethnic minorities and had little appeal to Romanians.

The party came to power as a result of Romania's occupation by the Red Army during the final year of World War II. The Soviet occupation forces required the inclusion of the insignificant PCR in successive coalition governments. With the support of Soviet troops and with PCR control over a core of militant forces in the major population centers, the party gradually seized the dominant role in the coalition government. It acquired additional credibility when it won the support of Dr. Petru Groza, a political leader who had participated in Romanian governments during the 1920s. The PCR-dominated regime, with the help of the occupying Soviet army, suppressed the traditional political parties and "won" the elections of 1946. When it was fully in power, the PCR banned all other political parties. The final stage was the merger of the PCR with the remnants of the Social Democratic Party. The new organization—the Romanian Workers' Party (Partidul Muncitoresc Român, PMR)—was the only legal political organization. The leaders of the former Social Democratic Party took a minor role in the new organization, and the communist leaders quickly completed their total domination of the PMR and the country.

During this period, the communist leadership was involved in a bitter internecine struggle between two principal factions. The "Muscovites," who spent most of the interwar years in Moscow, were led by Ana Pauker and Vasile Luca, while the "nativists," most of whose members spent those years in Romania, were headed by Gheorghe Gheorghiu-Dej. In 1952 Gheorghiu-Dej gained the upper hand, purged his opponents, and established uncontested control over the party.

Although ethnic Romanians came to play the dominant role in the party's leadership, particularly after the purge of the Jewish Pauker and the Hungarian Luca, the party was still dominated by the Soviet Union and continued to be seen by most Romanians as an alien institution inimical to Romanian interests. Gheorghiu-Dej carefully followed the accepted Soviet pattern, and Romania became a model Stalinist satellite. Agriculture was collectivized, which further alienated the peasantry, and a program of Stalinist industrialization was implemented at considerable economic and personal cost. Party control was established over intellectual and cultural life, which assumed the drab uniformity of "socialist realism."

After Stalin's death in 1953 and Nikita Khrushchev's rise to power in the Soviet Union during the mid-1950s, Gheorghiu-Dej began to take steps that ultimately led to important economic and political differences with the Soviet Union and to a redefinition of the relationship between the PCR and the Romanian people. Initial USSR efforts toward the economic integration of Eastern Europe in the late 1950s and the early 1960s were stubbornly resisted by Gheorghiu-Dej. Although the Soviet proposals had a certain economic rationale, the PCR doggedly continued to pursue a Stalinist policy of economic nationalism and proceeded to construct a series of heavy-industry projects that the USSR strongly opposed.

The differences between the Soviet Union and China in the early 1960s gave the Romanians the opportunity to expand their autonomy from the USSR in interparty affairs. This reached its high point in the April 1964 "statement" of the PCR Central Committee, which asserted the sovereignty and independence of each communist party and affirmed the principle of noninterference of parties in each other's internal affairs. This foreign policy provided an opportunity for the party to develop genuine national support.

These policies were initiated under the leadership of Gheorghiu-Dej, PCR leader from 1945 until his death in 1965, but they have been continued and extended by his successor, Ceauşescu, who has dominated the PCR and Romania since 1965. His rise during his long association with Gheorghiu-Dej began at the end of World War II. His full confirmation in power came, after the death of Gheorghiu-Dej, at the Ninth PCR Congress (at which the PMR was renamed the PCR). In international relations, Ceauşescu continued the autonomous policies that began under Gheorghiu-Dej. The high point of these international policies came in 1967–1968, when Romania continued to maintain diplomatic relations with Israel as the rest of the Soviet bloc severed all diplomatic ties, established diplomatic relations with West Germany before the USSR approved *Ostpolitik*, and moved much closer to the nonaligned bloc. Ceauşescu's vigorous denunciation of the Soviet-led invasion of Czechoslovakia in August 1968 marked the apogee of Romanian defiance of the Soviet Union but also emphasized the limits of deviance. Although the PCR under Ceauşescu has continued to pursue an international policy that reflects a degree of autonomy from the Soviet Union, it has also carefully avoided pushing that policy to the point of provoking military intervention. Although USSR threats and other actions have established clear limits to his foreign policies, Ceauşescu's international policies remain the principal source of his legitimacy with the Romanian people.

Between 1965 and 1971, at the same time that he achieved the greatest flexibility and autonomy in international relations, Ceauşescu pursued a certain liberalization in the economy and in cultural policy. Since the early 1970s, however, he has pursued a rigid, centralized economic policy involving substantial investment in heavy industry and limited production of consumer goods. This, plus lack of investment and poor organization in agriculture, has contributed to periodic food shortages and growing popular dissatisfaction. Under Ceauşescu's economic policies, Romania incurred substantial foreign debts and repaying them has been difficult. A massive effort to cut imports and expand exports to repay all foreign obligations by 1990 has contributed to the economic hardship. In the cultural and educational sphere, Ceauşescu has demanded rigid ideological consistency.

Ceauşescu has maintained his control over the party through strict concentration of power in his own hands. He has prevented the development of any internal centers of opposition by shifting subordinates from one position to another and by giving important positions to family members and to long-trusted associates. Although the PCR has maintained a degree of autonomy from the Soviet Union, it has lost much of the popular support, authority, and legitimacy that it won during the 1960s as a consequence of Ceauşescu's mismanagement of the economy and his rigid, Stalinist domestic policies.

Leadership and Party Organization. As genuine popular support for Ceauşescu and the PCR has waned, the party leader has encouraged artificial rituals of personal adulation. His 69th birthday was no exception, as journalists and public figures sought to outshine one another in paeans of praise (*Scînteia*, 25–27 January). The party leader's home village of Scornicesti contains a memorial house and a museum and has become a national pilgrimage site with almost religious overtones. Now that his wife, Elena, has also been beatified, she too is given lavish praise on her birthday (*Scînteia*; *Romania liberă, 6, 7, 8 January; Lumea*, no. 2, 8 January), and her village has also become a model commune (RFE, *Romanian Situation Report*, 3 September).

Ceauşescu's reliance on his family has been a principal means of maintaining his grip on the party. His wife, Elena, is a full member of the PEC as well as first deputy prime minister and chairwoman of the National Council of Science and Instruction. The most important post she holds, however, is head of the PCR cadres' commission, which oversees all party personnel matters. The youngest son of the couple, Nicu Ceauşescu, is an alternate member of the PEC and for several years served as first secretary for the UTC. In October, he was appointed PCR first secretary of Sibiu County. There is no doubt that the career change represents his father's continuing efforts to promote his son's career. In recent years, the party leaders of Romania's 40 counties have been trusted key officials of Ceauşescu's regime (RFE, *Romanian Situation Report*, 6 November). Other members of Ceauşescu's family that hold key party and government positions include his brother Lieutenant General Ilie Ceauşescu, who is deputy defense minister responsible for party control of the armed forces; Nicolae A. Ceauşescu, another brother, who is head of the cadres department at the Ministry of Internal Affairs; and Ion Ceauşescu, a third brother, who is first vice-chairman of the State Planning Committee and a member of the Council of Ministers. It is significant that most of the family members in key positions are responsible for personnel. During CPSU general secretary Mikhail Gorbachev's visit to Bucharest in May, he criticized the "nepotism" of the Brezhnev era in the Soviet Union in terms that were clearly intended to draw a parallel with Ceauşescu's practice in Romania (*Scînteia*, 27 May). At year's end, however, the PCR remained firmly under the family's thumb.

In addition to relying heavily on members of his family, Ceauşescu has continued his policy of rotating individuals in and out of party and government positions. During the year many ministers, county party first secretaries, and other officials were moved from one position to another. The Yugoslav news agency (Tanjug, 12 September), reporting the round of government changes, noted that since March 1985 (the date of the last parliamentary elections) "there have been over twenty government reshuffles including changes in the key departments of defense, finance, foreign trade, and foreign affairs." At a CC plenum reviewing party activity the previous year, Ceauşescu defended his policy: "Rotation must be considered normal. No one should feel that being transferred from one activity to another is an expression of lack of confidence. On the contrary: going from one activity to another equivalent, higher, or even lower activity is a sign of appreciation and an expression of confidence." (*Scînteia*, 29 March.) The principal benefit of such rotation is that it prevents PCR officials from establishing a solid geographic or organizational base from which to challenge the incumbent party leader. The only constituent for aspiring PCR officials is Ceauşescu.

Domestic Party Affairs. In contrast to the political and economic reforms being pursued by the Soviet Union and the other countries of Eastern Europe, Ceauşescu maintained and vigorously defended his own dogmatic, antireformist policies. In a speech on his birthday, he was critical of efforts at "socialist renewal" and "perfecting socialism" (a veiled criticism of Soviet leader Gorbachev's reforms), and he was equally critical of those within the PCR who wanted a "quieter, more comfortable life" (*Scînteia*, 27 January). Even toward the end of the year, at the National Party Conference called to review economic progress, he defended his highly centralized system of economic planning and said that "problems of economic development" can not be left "to the vagaries of supply and demand—so-called market socialism" (*Scînteia*; *WP*, 15 December). A Yugoslav periodical suggested that the Romanians were facing "Albanianization"—that is, the PCR was resolutely rejecting democratization or liberalization in the same way as were the super-orthodox and isolated leaders of Albania (RFE, *Romanian Situation Report*, 6 March).

A massive effort to reduce foreign indebtedness has contributed to Romania's economic problems. Since 1981, foreign obligations have dropped from an estimated $10 billion to just over $5 billion. Hard currency imports have been drastically reduced, and Romanian exports that will earn foreign exchange or that can be bartered for Soviet oil have increased. In 1986, for example, one quarter of all meat imported by the USSR came from Romania.

The Romanian people have paid a heavy price for Ceauşescu's continued economic dogmatism and his crash program to cut the foreign debt. Severe energy shortages have resulted in strict government rationing of natural gas and energy during the coldest months of the year (*Scînteia*, 7 February, 11 November), and in major cities streets are unlighted at night to conserve electricity. Long lines for food are common, and there is little variety in the poor-quality foodstuffs available. Meat, fruit, and vegetables are scarce or nonexistent. Furthermore, the shortages are not a new phenomenon but have been a fact of Romanian life for the past six years, and stringent laws prohibit hoarding. Amnesty International reported that five Romanians were given death sentences for stealing meat (*WP*, 17, 24 August).

There have been only limited signs of unrest under these extremely trying circumstances in large part because the party and internal security organs have kept a tight reign on dissent. During November, however, several thousand workers in the industrial city of Brasov ransacked the city hall instead of voting in municipal elections to protest harsh living conditions, a second month of pay cuts for nonfulfillment of the plan, and the prospect of another winter of food and energy shortages. There were reports of student support for the workers. The military and secret police quickly moved in, and a number of workers were arrested. A mass meeting at the plant produced pledges of support for fulfilling the plan goals, and previous shortcomings of the plant management were criticized. (RFE, *RAD Background Report*, no. 231, 4 December; *NYT*, 22 November; *WSJ*, 30 November.)

The serious labor unrest in Brasov forced the PCR to make some concessions. On 11 December, at the suggestion of Ceauşescu, the PEC approved an immediate 50 percent advance payment to Romanian workers of the 1987 profit-sharing fund, with the remainder to be paid during the first half of 1988 when all accounts have been balanced (*Scînteia*, 12 December). At the national party conference just a few days later, Ceauşescu announced that basic wages would increase by 10 percent between the summer of 1988 and 1990. He also promised improvements in the supply of meat and consumer goods. On the same occasion, however, he defended the PCR's centralized planning and strict control over economic and social life (*WP*, 15 December).

As the demonstrations in Brasov indicate, conditions are ripe for popular unrest. Ceauşescu and the PCR have shown a willingness to use the full repressive force of the police, the military, and the security organs to maintain order. Under these circumstances isolated outbursts are likely, but a more general uprising is unlikely. Although there have been signs of discontent within the PCR against Ceauşescu's policies, there is no focal point for opposition to rally around.

Auxiliary and Front Organizations. There were no unusual developments involving the PCR's principal auxiliary organizations during 1987. The SDUF took the lead in local elections in November that selected deputies for municipal, town, and commune people's councils. There were 117,349 individuals nominated for the 57,584 positions, which means that in about 80 percent of the races there were two persons running for the same position. Of the 16,931,841 Romanian citizens who cast ballots, 98.3 percent voted for the SDUF candidates (*Scînteia*, 16 November).

The Central Council of the General Confederation of Romanian Trade Unions held a plenary meeting in February at which Ciobanu was released as chairwoman because she had been appointed minister of light industry. Dobrescu was selected chairman of the Central Council. The UTC celebrated its 65th anniversary at a gala festivity in Bucharest, which was addressed by PCR general secretary Ceauşescu (Radio Bucharest; *FBIS*, 21 March). The party leader's son Nicu was first secretary of the organization, which gave it particular prominence, and it was called to mobilize young people for fulfillment of plan objectives and PCR policies. In October Nicu was rotated into another party position and Toma, a secretary of the CC of the UTC, was named first secretary to replace him (Agerpres, 13 October). The Councils of Working People of Hungarian and German Nationalities were mobilized in response to criticism of Romania's human rights policy, in particular to its treatment of the Hungarian minority. (For more details, see international activities, below.)

International Activities. *Relations with the Soviet Union and the CPSU.* The first foreign policy concern, as always, pertains to relations with the Soviet Union. The new CPSU general secretary, Gorbachev, has sought to ensure domestic calm and compliance in Eastern Europe. In May he made an official trip to Romania—the last East European country he visited since becoming CPSU leader in March 1985. Leonid Brezhnev was the last general secretary to have visited Bucharest, in 1976. The delay appears to have been deliberate because Ceauşescu was the last East European leader to pay his respects after Gorbachev had been named CPSU leader. Although Gorbachev was received with appropriate honors, the welcome was polite but not particularly warm. The photograph in *Pravda* (26 May) showed both Gorbachev and Ceauşescu, grim-faced. Furthermore, before, during, and after the visit, the Soviet press published critical reports on conditions in Romania, including some surprisingly explicit details of daily hardships (*Izvestiia*, 24 May). Gorbachev criticized frankly, though indirectly, Romania's unwillingness to expand cooperation with CMEA and undertake Soviet-style economic reform. In a speech in Bucharest that was broadcast live, Gorbachev extolled his policies of "restructuring," "openness," and "democratization" and implicitly criticized Ceauşescu's domestic policies (*Scînteia*; *Pravda*, 27 May). The hand-picked audience of PCR activists applauded Ceauşescu wildly but sat in stony silence when Gorbachev described his own policies, and Ceauşescu reportedly looked impatiently at his watch (*NYT*, 27 May).

The PCR Political Executive Committee unanimously approved the results of the visit and praised the agreements for economic cooperation, but the CPSU Politburo merely "analyzed" the visit and gave it significantly less praise than Gorbachev's earlier visit to Czechoslovakia (RFE, *Romanian Situation Report*, 21 July). The PCR continued its usual relationship with the Soviet Union—pursuing its own policies and accepting economic cooperation when it benefits Romania and does not involve a loss of Romanian control over the process. The PCR theoretical journal published a series of articles defending the party's right to pursue its own development strategy in the face of "globalist theories" (*Era socialistă*, no. 11, 10 June). Furthermore, Romania continued its selective participation in Soviet–East European meetings. For example, in November, Ceauşescu was in Moscow for the 70th anniversary of the Bolshevik Revolution, but he did not attend an 11 December summit in East Berlin, at which Gorbachev reported on his meeting with President Reagan.

Despite reiteration of the familiar rhetoric on economic cooperation, however, trade between Romania and the Soviet Union has undergone a substantial increase in recent years, growing by 23 percent during 1986. By the end of that year it was 47 percent above the volume of the previous two years. During the same period trade between the USSR and the other states of Eastern Europe increased only 7 percent. Imports of Soviet energy, raw materials, and industrial technology were balanced by increased Romanian exports of machinery, steel, and food products. Romania had been the only East European country to receive increased Soviet oil deliveries since 1984 and has become the USSR's largest supplier of oil- and gas-drilling equipment and of electric transformers. Although trade increases of this magnitude are not expected to continue over the entire 1986–1990 plan period, Soviet-Romanian trade is projected to increase by 70 percent during that time (RFE, *Romanian Situation Report*, 22 April). Despite the significance of these changes in trade, Romania continued the rhetoric of opposition to economic integration. At a meeting of CMEA prime ministers in Moscow during October, Romanian prime minister Dăscălescu implicitly rejected Soviet proposals for further integration of the CMEA economies (Agerpres, 13 October). In the long run, however, these significant changes in trade patterns may severely undermine that policy.

International Problems over Romania's Treatment of Its Hungarian Minority. One of the most serious foreign policy issues that arose during 1987 was Romania's violation of human rights, in particular the treatment of the Hungarian minority in Transylvania. The issue, which was raised at the Vienna follow-up meeting to the Conference on Security and Cooperation in Europe (CSCE) was the major issue in Romania's deteriorating relations with Hungary and a factor behind the decision of the U.S. Congress to revoke Romania's most-favored-nation (MFN) status. Furthermore, the issue had serious domestic political ramifications. The Hungarian minority numbers from two to two-and-a-half million, with most living in territories that were part of Hungary until 1918. (The precise number is in dispute because official Romanian statistics generally minimize the number of Hungarians.)

Romania was criticized for its treatment of the Hungarian minority at the Vienna CSCE review conference, which had begun in the fall of 1986. The British, Belgian, and U.S. delegations were explicit in citing Romanian violations. On 12 December 1986, the Hungarian delegate raised the treatment of Hungarian minorities in neighboring states, although Romania was not mentioned by name (*Magyar nemzet*, Budapest, 13 December 1986). A few weeks later, the Protestant and Roman Catholic churches in Hungary explicitly and publicly criticized Romania's assimilation policy toward its Hungarian minority (*Die Presse*, Vienna, 30 December 1986; RFE, *Hungarian Situation Report*, no. 1, 31 January).

In response, the PCR Political Executive Committee instructed the Romanian delegate in Vienna to oppose raising the minority question and strongly rejected the discussion of the "so-called human rights issue and the false issue of nationality" (Agerpres, 14 January). The Romanian delegate in Vienna said that discussion of the Hungarian minority question was interference in Romania's internal affairs (*Scînteia*, 7 February). In response Mátyás Szürös, the Hungarian party CC secretary for foreign relations, criticized Romania's forced assimilation of Hungarians and emphasized that minority issues do have international aspects (Radio Budapest; *FBIS*, 9 February). In an interview with the Italian daily *La Repubblica* (12 February), Hungarian minister of culture Béla Köpeczi also criticized Romanian treatment of the minority in Transylvania.

The PCR responded by mobilizing its auxiliary organization for ethnic Hungarians. On 27 February Ceauşescu addressed a joint plenum of the Councils of Working People of Hungarian and German Nationality. The intensity of his rhetoric was striking. He denounced "the revival of Horthyist, fascist, and even racist theses by reactionary imperialist circles," even "in some of our neighboring countries." He also attacked the scholarship in the three-volume *Erdely Tortenete* (*History of Transylvania*), edited by Köpeczi (*Scînteia*, 28 February). The Council of Working People of Hungarian Nationality adopted a resolution sharply criticizing "attempts of reactionary circles to incite nationalist, chauvinistic, irredentist, and revanchist manifestations" (*Scînteia*, 4 March).

Within days of the mass meetings in Romania, the Hungarian delegate in Vienna announced that his government was cosponsoring proposals supporting minority rights that had been put forward by Canada and Yugoslavia—the first instance of a Warsaw Pact country sponsoring a Western human rights proposal. Meanwhile, the polemic continued on several fronts. To mobilize ethnic Romanian support and to ensure that the Hungarian minority understood the PCR position, the Romanian-language and Hungarian-language press in Romania published a barrage of articles defending the PCR's position, and Romanian historians and journalists launched another major attack on *Erdely Tortenete* (*History of Transylvania*) (RFE, *Hungarian Situation Report*, 3 April, 18 May). The dispute even prompted a Romanian sympathizer in Athens to place a full-page advertisement in *The Times* of London criticizing the Hungarian position (*WSJ*, 4 May). Hungarian historians and government officials, meanwhile, rebutted the Romanian charges. Even Hungarian party leader János Kádár, when questioned about the problem at a press conference during an official visit to Sweden in April, confirmed the existence of significant differences over the issue but expressed the hope that Hungary and Romania could reach an understanding on the issue (RFE, *Hungarian Situation Report*, 18 May).

The controversy escalated to the point that, during his visit to Romania in May, CPSU general secretary Gorbachev urged the Romanians to follow the principles of Leninist national policies in the context of his call for strengthening friendship among peoples (*Scînteia*, 27 May). A few days after Gorbachev left Bucharest, an effort was made to resolve the differences by sending to Budapest a high-level PCR delegation composed of Bobu, the highest-ranking PCR official after Ceauşescu, and Stoian, CC secretary for foreign relations. They met with a Hungarian delegation of equally high rank. The press statements issued at the end of the talks indicated how far apart both sides still were. The Hungarians' statement openly and frankly discussed their disappointment when Romania was unwilling to make improvements in its treatment of the Hungarian minority and stressed the Hungarian view that such improvement was necessary to fulfill commitments made by Ceauşescu during his last meeting with Hungarian party leader Kádár in 1977 (Radio Budapest; *FBIS*, 5 June). The Romanian statement did not even mention the Hungarian minority issue, consistent with the Romanian position that the matter is an internal affair (Agerpres, 5 June).

CPSU Politburo member Egor Ligachev, when asked during a visit to Budapest if the USSR would have to intervene in the dispute, expressed the hope that Romania and Hungary could work out their differences. Soviet foreign minister Eduard Shevardnadze also expressed the hope that a bilateral solution to the problem could be found (AP, 18 June). Romania and Hungary continue to go their separate ways on the issue, and the Soviet Union does not seem anxious to push the two disputants to a resolution at this time. The problem continues to be a source of tension between Romania and Hungary, as well as an important added source of domestic instability in Romania.

Relations with Other Communist-ruled States and Communist Parties. With the exception of Hungary, relations between Romania and the other members of the Warsaw Pact followed the pattern of Romania's relations with the Soviet Union. The other East European states were anxious not to be more friendly than the Soviet Union was, but Romania sought to demonstrate that relations were cordial. Highlights during the year included a visit by Ceauşescu to Bulgaria for meetings with Todor Zhivkov (*Scînteia*, 10 October) and visits to Romania by East German party leader Erich Honecker (*Neues Deutschland*, 29, 30 October) and by Prime Minister Willi Stoph in February (*Neues Deutschland*, 26, 27 February). Ceauşescu also hosted

Boško Krunić, the president of the presidency of the Yugoslav League of Communists, for an official visit (*Scînteia*, 23, 24, 25 July) and paid a return visit to Yugoslavia himself during 12–14 November. The PCR continued its long-standing policy of maintaining cordial relations with nonruling communist and leftist parties. Romanian officials were sent to represent the PCR at party congresses around the world, and anniversaries important to obscure parties elicited a warm message of congratulations from the PCR general secretary.

Relations with Third World Countries. After the "socialist countries," Romania gives second place in its foreign policy priorities to the Third World, continuing its active policy in relations with the nonaligned countries in an effort to continue to be identified with that group. Ceauşescu's favorite method of diplomacy is a personal visit with foreign heads of state, which bolsters his prestige at home and puts him in the diplomatic spotlight. Ceauşescu, accompanied by his wife, Elena, made a four-nation tour of nonaligned Asian countries—India, Bangladesh, Burma, and Nepal—in March. Consistent with the policy of maintaining good relations with all parties in conflict, Ceauşescu made a brief stopover in the Pakistani capital en route to Delhi to balance the trip to India. Romanian media gave considerable attention to the state protocol of the visits. For example, it reported in some detail about the Ceauşescus and the king and queen of Nepal riding in gilded, horse-drawn coaches through the streets of Kathmandu in a welcoming parade. There were no important new political developments to come from the trip, but it provided an occasion for the Romanian media to emphasize Ceauşescu's role as world statesman.

The Ceauşescus hardly had a chance to unpack their bags from the Asian trip before they were off again, this time to Africa for state visits to Angola, Zaire, and the Congo from 28 March to 3 April. As with his Asian trip, completed just the week before, Ceauşescu did not break any new ground. Third World heads of government to visit Romania included Somalian president Mohammed Siad Barre in June; Ethiopian president Haile Mariam Mengistu in November; the chairman of the Republic of the Sudan, Sayed Ahmed El Mirghani, in October; and the president of Burma, U San Yu. Prime Minister Dăscălescu sought to encourage foreign trade with visits to Cairo in June and to Tunisia and Morocco in September.

The Arab States and Israel. Romania's policy of maintaining friendly ties with both the Arab states and Israel and its interest in playing the role of broker in the Middle East conflict was again underscored during the year. Ceauşescu, who received some of the credit for bringing about the Camp David meetings between the leaders of Israel and Egypt in 1978, met with Palestinian and Israeli leaders several times during the year. In June the chairman of the Palestine Liberation Organization, Yassir Arafat, was in Bucharest; in August, just before his visit to Moscow, Arafat met with Ceauşescu for the 20th time since 1974 (*Scînteia*, 6 June, 12 August). A few days later, Ceauşescu met with Elias Freije, the Christian Arab mayor of Bethlehem, who has close ties to King Hussein of Jordan. In an attempt to win Israeli support for an international Middle East peace conference, Ceauşescu invited Israeli prime minister Yitzhak Shamir to Bucharest for a three-day visit in August. Shamir, however, was not willing to accept such a proposal, as he made clear at a news conference on his departure for home (RFE, *Romanian Situation Report*, 3 September).

The United States and Western Europe. Romania's economic relations with the United States suffered important setbacks during the year. First, in January, the U.S. government removed Romania from the duty-free generalized system of preferences because of Romania's disregard for the rights of its workers. (During 1987 this might have cost Romania as much as $150 million in lost exports to the United States.) The second major setback was the bipartisan action of the U.S. Congress to suspend MFN status for six months and possibly longer. Congress objected to human rights violations in Romania, including limitations on religious freedom, restrictions on emigration, and policies toward the Hungarian minority (U.S. Congress, House of Representatives, Committee on Foreign Affairs, *United States–Romanian Relations and Most-Favored-Nation [MFN] Status for Romania*, 30 July). The effect of the action is difficult to calculate. Trade with the United States during 1986 gave Romania a surplus of $588 million, with exports to the United States of $838.8 million and imports of $250.9 million. Commerce Department officials estimated that loss of MFN status could cost Romania $300 million a year (*NYT*, 27 June). The loss could be particularly difficult since Romania is in the midst of a major campaign to reduce its foreign indebtedness. Romanian reaction was extremely negative. An offical commentary on the Senate vote to deny MFN called it a "hostile act" (Agerpres, 27 June). Earlier Ceauşescu had told a group of visiting U.S. businessmen that "religion, human rights, and other such matters are solely of Romanian jurisdiction" and "human rights issues are not related to MFN status" (Agerpres, 24 March).

The themes of Balkan cooperation and a nuclear-free zone there were revived in July when Greek prime minister Andreas Papandreou paid a one-day visit to Bucharest. Ceauşescu, in a continuing effort to balance relations, paid an official visit to Turkey in October, during which a long-term agreement for commercial, economic, and technical cooperation was signed. Although both visits emphasized Romania's continuing interest in fostering Balkan cooperation, no major developments came about as a result of these efforts.

Robert R. King
Washington, D.C.

Union of Soviet Socialist Republics

Population. 281,700,000 (TASS, 13 February); 284,008,160 (CIA, July)

Party. Communist Party of the Soviet Union (Kommunisticheskaia Partiia Sovetskogo Soiuza; CPSU)

Founded. 1898 (CPSU, 1952)

Membership. 19,037,946, as of the Twenty-seventh CPSU Congress (*Politicheskoe samoobrazovanie*, April); workers and farmers, 40.6 percent; women, about 34 percent in district, city, and regional committees

General Secretary. Mikhail S. Gorbachev

Politburo. (Unless otherwise indicated, nationality is Russian; first date is year of birth, second is year of election to present rank.) 13 full members: Mikhail S. Gorbachev (b. 1931, e. 1980), Viktor M. Chebrikov (b. 1923, e. 1985, chairman, Committee for State Security [KGB]), Andrei A. Gromyko (b. 1909, e. 1973, chairman of the Presidium [president], Supreme Soviet), Egor K. Ligachev (b. 1920, e. 1985), Viktor P. Nikonov (b. 1929, e. 1987), Nikolai I. Ryzhkov (b. 1929, e. 1985, chairman [prime minister], Council of Ministers), Vladimir V. Shcherbitsky, Ukrainian (b. 1918, e. 1971, first secretary, Ukrainian Central Committee), Eduard A. Shevardnadze, Georgian (b. 1928, e. 1985, foreign minister), Nikolai N. Slyunkov (b. 1929, e. 1987), Mikhail S. Solomentsev (b. 1913, e. 1983, chairman, Party Control Committee), Vitali I. Vorotnikov (b. 1926, e. 1983, chairman, Russian Soviet Federated Socialist Republic [RSFSR] Council of Ministers), Aleksandr N. Yakovlev (b. 1923, e. 1987), Lev N. Zaikov (b. 1923, e. 1986, first secretary, Moscow city party committee) NOTE: Chebrikov and Ryzhkov were listed in Soviet sources as Ukrainian before their appointments to chairs in the KGB and to the party Secretariat, respectively, in November–December 1982; they have since been listed as Russian. 5 candidate members: Piotr N. Demichev (b. 1918, e. 1964, first deputy chairman of the Presidium [vice-president], USSR Supreme Soviet), Vladimir I. Dolgikh (b. 1924, e. 1982), Yuri F. Solovyev (b. 1925, e. 1986, first secretary, Leningrad oblast party committee), Nikolai V. Talyzin (b. 1929, e. 1985, first deputy chairman [first deputy prime minister], Council of Ministers), Dmitrii T. Yazov (b. 1923, e. 1987, minister of defense)

Secretariat. 11 members: (* indicates members of Politburo): *Mikhail S. Gorbachev (general secretary), *Egor K. Ligachev (ideology and personnel), *Viktor P. Nikonov (agriculture), *Nikolai N. Slyunkov (economy), *Aleksandr N. Yakovlev (culture and propaganda), *Vladimir I. Dolgikh (heavy industry), Aleksandra P. Biryukova (b. 1929, light industry), Anatolii F. Dobrynin (b. 1919, international affairs), Anatolii I. Lukyanov (b. 1930, police and security organs), Vadim A. Medvedev (b. 1930, ruling communist parties), Georgii P. Razumovsky (b. 1936, cadres)

Central Committee. 307 full and 170 candidate members were elected at the Twenty-seventh CPSU Congress. The Central Committee is organized into 21 departments; key department heads include Anatolii F. Dobrynin (international), Nikolai I. Savinkin (b. 1913, administrative organs), Ivan I. Skiba, Ukrainian (b. 1937, agriculture), Nikolai E. Kruchina (b. 1928, administration of affairs), Georgi P. Razumovsky (party organizational work [cadres])

Status. Ruling and only legal party

Last Congress. Twenty-seventh, 25 February–6 March 1986, in Moscow

Last Election. Supreme Soviet, 4 March 1984; more than 99.9 percent of vote for CPSU-backed candidates, all 1,500 of whom were elected; 71.4 percent of elected candidates were CPSU members.

Defense Council. The inner circle of the leadership concerned with national security affairs; only the chairman is publicly indentified. Chairman: Mikhail S. Gorbachev; probable members, as of 1 January 1988: Andrei A. Gromyko, Egor K. Ligachev, Aleksandr N. Yakovlev, Marshal Dmitrii T. Yazov. Possible members or associates: Nikolai I. Ryzhkov, Viktor M. Chebrikov, Anatolii F. Dobrynin, Marshal Sergei F. Akhromeyev (b. 1923), the chief of staff and first deputy minister of defense.

Government. 110 members of the Council of Ministers, including two first deputy chairmen (first deputy prime ministers), 10 deputy chairmen (deputy prime ministers), 15 ex officio deputy chairmen (prime ministers of the Union republics), 58 ministers, and 24 chairmen of state committees. Key members of the government not identified above include Vsevolod S. Murakhovsky, Ukrainian (b. 1926, first deputy chairman, Council of Ministers, and chairman, State Committee for the Agroindustrial Complex), Boris L. Tolstykh (b. 1935, deputy chairman for science and technology, Council of Ministers), Aleksandr V. Vlasov (b. 1932, minister of internal affairs), Lev A. Voronin (b. 1928, deputy chairman, Council of Ministers and chairman, State Committee for Material and Technical Supply).

Auxiliary Organizations. Communist Youth League (Kommunisticheskii Soiuz Molodezhi; Komsomol), 42 million members, led by Vladimir Mironenko, Ukrainian (b. 1953); All-Union Central Council of Trade Unions (AUCCTU), 132 million members, led by Stepan A. Shalayev (b. 1929); Voluntary Society for the Promotion of the Army, Air Force, and Navy (DOSAAF), led by Admiral Georgi M. Egorov (b. 1918), more than 65 million members; Union of Soviet Societies for Friendship and Cultural Relations with Foreign Countries

Publications. Main CPSU organs are the daily newspaper *Pravda* (circulation more than 11 million), the theoretical and ideological journal *Kommunist* (appearing 18 times a year, with a circulation over 1 million), and the semimonthly *Partinaia zhizn'*, a journal of internal party affairs and organizational matters (circulation more than 1.16 million). *Kommunist vooruzhennykh sil* is the party theoretical journal for the armed forces, and *Agitator* is the same for party propagandists; both appear twice a month. The Komsomol has a newspaper, *Komsomolskaia pravda* (6 days a week), and a monthly theoretical journal, *Molodaia gvardiia*. Each USSR republic prints similar party newspapers in local languages and usually also in Russian. Specialized publications issued under supervision of the CPSU Central Committee include the newspapers *Sovetskaia Rossia*, *Selskaia zhizn'*, *Sotsialisticheskaia industriia*, *Sovetskaia kultura*, and *Ekonomicheskaia gazeta* and the journal *Politicheskoe samoobrazovanie*. TASS is the offical news agency.

Following a period of unprecedented leadership instability in the first half of the 1980s, the USSR appeared to settle down to a strong, long-term direction of its affairs with Gorbachev's March 1985 election as general secretary of the CPSU. During the remaining months of 1985, Gorbachev moved to swiftly consolidate his personal power, a drive climaxed by the December ouster of Viktor Grishin, one of his principal opponents, as head of the Moscow city party organization. At the Twenty-seventh CPSU Congress in February 1986, this thrust for dominance continued, and several choices of the general secretary, notably Dobrynin and Yakovlev, were installed in key posts on the party Secretariat.

Gorbachev would need all the personal authority he could muster, in view of his ambitious program to correct long-standing deficiencies of Soviet society and to strengthen the USSR's position in the world. He had inherited a society beset with multiple crises. Abroad, the correlation of forces seemed to be turning against the USSR, and his predecessors had led the country into a diplomatic isolation that belied its superpower status. At home, problems of low productivity, technological lag, and general inefficiency were compounded by rampant alcoholism, corruption, and loss of confidence in the system among the populace. Domestic decay was so pronounced that the USSR no longer served as a viable model for even the most backward Third World country.

Gorbachev's solution for the ills of the USSR was contained in the twin concepts of *perestroika* (restructuring) and *glasnost'* (openness or publicity). *Perestroika* was intended to affect all areas of the society, reinvigorating Soviet life and providing a new sense of national purpose. It involved a change of attitudes among leading cadres of all institutions and broader participation of the masses in decision-making, but the most important emphasis was on reorganization of the economy to render it more efficient and to close the technological gap with the West. *Glasnost'* was viewed as necessary for the success of *perestroika*, publicizing the shortcomings of officials, providing the climate for the freer exchange of technical knowlege, and enlisting popular support for regime goals.

Perestroika and *glasnost'* also applied to foreign affairs. Gorbachev quickly seized control of the policymaking mechanisms, and, following the appointment of Shevardnadze as foreign minister in July 1985, a more open, less bellicose style became apparent in the conduct of diplomacy. Restaffing of the Central Committee's International Department and a radical reorganization of the foreign ministry followed in 1986. Meanwhile, new priorities were set and former inflexible positions were abandoned as Gorbachev moved vigorously on a variety of fronts to end Soviet isolation and alter negative images of the USSR.

The early impression was of movement rather than of clearly defined goals; it was not clear how far Gorbachev would or could go with *perestroika* or how much of a "thaw" would be permitted. Nevertheless, there were indications that the country had been shaken out of its longtime lethargy and that a momentum had been achieved that would facilitate further change. But both *perestroika* and *glasnost'* were brought into question by the explosion at the Chernobyl nuclear power plant in April 1986. *Glasnost'* failed its first major test: details of the disaster were withheld for a week, and Gorbachev remained silent on the subject for eighteen days. Serious questions were raised about the ability of the unwieldy Soviet economic structure to handle modern technology, and outsiders were appalled by the apparent callousness of the Soviet leadership to the effects of radiation on other countries.

Chernobyl slowed the momentum of *perestroika*, but the leadership managed a fair recovery at home and abroad. The stalemate at the Reykjavik summit in October, however, left the foreign policy initiatives that constituted a key component of Gorbachev's program in doubt. Meanwhile, events were in motion that would escalate tensions over the new leader's reform program during 1987.

Dinmukhamed Kunaev was ousted as leader in Kazakhstan in December, foreshadowing a massive drive against corruption in that central Asian republic. Andrei Sakharov's return to Moscow was followed by a selective release of political prisoners in the new year.

In January, the KGB chief upbraided a subordinate for abuse of power on the front page of *Pravda*, and in the following month the head of the security agency in the Ukraine was removed. The full flower of *glasnost'* came when previously banned and controversial works were allowed to be published. The leadership showed that it meant business on the economic front by appointing 1,500 inspectors to supervise quality control in factories. Plans for the economic reform were firmed up, and the completed package was approved by the Central Committee and the Supreme Soviet in June. Meanwhile, the leadership displayed even greater flexibility in its push for an arms control agreement with the United States.

But there were storm clouds on the horizon. The appointment of an ethnic Russian as Kunaev's successor had triggered riots in Kazakhstan, bringing to the surface the problem of nationalities. Despite Chernobyl, the overall performance of the economy in 1986 had been impressive, although economic growth dropped to the near-zero level during the first half of 1987. The leadership was embarrassed again when a young West German landed a small private plane in Red Square on Border Guards' Day in May. Gorbachev was able to turn the incident to his immediate domestic political advantage, but the episode touched a nerve, displaying inefficiency in the armed forces and leaky frontier defenses.

Most troublesome for Gorbachev was the reaction against his reform program, which seemed to extend from the top leadership down to the factory floor. Gorbachev had perhaps been more successful than any previous leader in consolidating his power at an early stage, but, the more he succeeded in extending his apparent organizational control, the more resistance he encountered to his reform program, witness his increasingly sharp statements about the opposition. Party "second secretary" Ligachev was widely viewed as the rallying point for "conservative" elements opposed to either the objectives or the pace of *perestroika* and *glasnost'*. In Gorbachev's favor was the lack of cohesion among the resisters; those in the hierarchy dubious about reform could not consistently agree on either issues or personnel. But the general secretary was also pressured from another side, as impatient reformers pressed for a renovation of the economy and the society.

The debate within the leadership came to a head at the October Central Committee plenum when the outspoken Moscow party chief, Boris Eltsin, delivered a broadside against the leadership for slowness in effecting reform, with Ligachev as the apparent main target. This evidence of disarray in upper political circles came on the eve of the 70th anniversary of the Bolshevik Revolution and a few weeks before the U.S.-Soviet summit on arms control, a most inopportune time for Gorbachev. Eltsin was ousted from his position at a Moscow party meeting during which Gorbachev delivered a stinging rebuke to his erstwhile supporter. A few days earlier, Gorbachev appeared to pull back from his advanced positions with a speech at the 70th anniversary celebration that disappointed the reform-minded at home and public opinion abroad. Although Gorbachev called for a critical re-evaluation of Soviet history, he denounced Trotsky, declined to rehabilitate Nikolai Bukharin, defended Joseph Stalin's brutal collectivization of agriculture, and upheld the Nazi-Soviet pact that opened the way for World War II. At the same time, Gorbachev insisted on continuing reform at its present pace and chastised his critics on both the right and the left.

Although Gorbachev had been quite successful in extending his personal authority, he had launched his broad, unsettling program of change before his power was fully consolidated, thus perhaps incurring greater political risks than any previous Soviet leader. Many Western observers concluded that Gorbachev badly needed a major success at his December summit with U.S. president Ronald Reagan to shore up his domestic position for the challenges ahead.

Leadership. The January, June, and October plenums of the CPSU Central Committee made changes in the central leadership favorable to General Secretary Gorbachev. At the January plenum Kunaev, ousted as party leader in Kazakhstan a month earlier, was dropped, as expected, from Politburo ranks. No other change was made in the full membership, which was reduced to eleven members. However, Gorbachev protege Yakovlev, Central Committee secretary for propaganda, was elected as a candidate member. Moscow party chief Eltsin was again denied promotion to full membership, possibly due to the opposition of Ligachev, with whom Eltsin had crossed swords at the Twenty-seventh CPSU Congress on privileges of the party elite and other matters.

A holdover from the Leonid Brezhnev era, Mikhail Zimianin (72), Central Committee secretary for culture, retired from the Secretariat. Zimianin had been one of the conservative officials who attempted to put the brakes on *glasnost'*, and it was probably no accident that his retirement was followed by several months of remarkable relaxation on the cultural front.

Two secretaries were added, bringing Secretariat membership to twelve. Slyunkov was transferred from the party leadership of Belorussia, presumably to direct economic planning and the civilian sector of the economy, the function performed by Ryzhkov before his appointment as prime minister in October 1985. Slyunkov had worked under Ryzhkov in Gosplan from 1979 to 1983, and the prime minister's influence was probably crucial to Slyunkov's co-option into the leadership of the central party apparatus.

Lukyanov (56), head of the General Department since 1985, was also added to the Secretariat (*Pravda*, 29 January). One of Lukyanov's functions in his new post was that of supervisor over the Department of Administrative Organs, which oversees the KGB. Lukyanov, a fellow law student with Gorbachev at Moscow State University in the early 1950s, owed his position in the central party apparatus to the general secretary. Lukyanov's appointment represented a major effort by Gorbachev to check the power of the security agency; the dismissal, in February, of the head of the Ukrainian branch of the KGB (see below) indicated that Lukyanov was vigorously pursuing his mandate.

Gorbachev, in the early days of his leadership, relied heavily on the KGB and its head, Chebrikov, but the unprecedented denunciation of a subordinate by Chebrikov in a January *Pravda* article indicated that the honeymoon was over. Rising tensions between the general secretary and the KGB, or at least some elements of that massive, complex organization, may have provided the necessary backdrop for more obvious opposition to Gorbachev's plans in upper leadership circles during the year.

An attempt to discredit Gorbachev in early spring bore KGB footprints and lent credence to rumors of a rift between the party leader and the upper levels of the security agency. A videotape, probably made with a hidden camera by a KGB agent during the Gorbachevs' October 1985 visit to Paris, circulated in Moscow showing Raisa Gorbacheva shopping with her American Express gold card in the boutiques of Pierre Cardin and Yves Saint-Laurent (AP, 4 April). The tape's relatively free circulation in the Soviet capital seemed possible only with the blessing or connivance of the secret police.

Reports of other conflicts within the leadership surfaced during the following months. Nevertheless, when the Central Committee assembled again in June, Gorbachev scored even more impressive gains than he had at the January plenum. Yakovlev and Slyunkov were promoted from candidate to full Politburo membership, and Nikonov, 58, party agriculture secretary, was also made a full member without going through candidate status. Colonel General Yazov, 64, minister of defense, named to that post in May, displaced ousted Marshal Sergei Sokolov as a candidate member of the Politburo. Kunaev, the discredited former leader of the Kazakhstan Communist Party, was expelled from the Central Committee (*Pravda*, *NYT*, 27 June). Moscow party chief Eltsin again failed to win promotion from candidate to full Politburo status, perhaps exacerbating those frustrations that would explode at the Central Committee plenum in October. The previously understrength Politburo now had fourteen full members.

Yakovlev, Nikonov, and Yazov were all clients of Gorbachev, and these promotions certainly strengthened the hand of the general secretary in the party's ruling body. In view of the past association between Slyunkov and Ryzhkov, the prime minister's influence was probably also enhanced. The June plenum also emphasized the striking disparity in organizational power and the ability to control appointments between Gorbachev and "second secretary" Ligachev, reputedly leader of the "conservative" opposition to the general secretary. No client of Ligachev had been added at either level of the Politburo or to the Secretariat since his assumption of the number two post in the party.

Gorbachev's seemingly clear-cut victory at the June plenum did nothing to discourage speculation, at home or abroad, concerning the stability of the leadership. The party chief was not seen in public from 7 August to 29 September, and the Moscow rumor factory worked overtime guessing that either he or his wife was suffering from a serious ailment or, more likely, that he was in political trouble. Certainly a summer vacation of 53 days was long, even by the standards of Gorbachev's physically infirm predecessors. But the general secretary reappeared on 29 September looking tanned and rested and explained that he had been working at his retreat in the Crimea on a book about *perestroika* (*LAT*, AP, 30 September). The book duly appeared, in both Russian and English editions, later in the year.

Others in the hierarchy apparently took advantage of Gorbachev's absence to slow the movement for change and perhaps to organize more conservative elements for further efforts to contain *perestroika* and *glasnost'*. Ligachev, who since the Twenty-seventh CPSU Congress had been the most outspoken advocate of caution on the reform front, spoke out even more critically of excessive relaxation in cultural matters (*Uchitelskaia gazeta*, 27 August). At a meeting commemorating the 110th anniversary of the birth of Felix Dzerzhinsky, founder of the Cheka, Chebrikov was restrained in his references to *perestroika*, describing the reforms as merely "long-range plans." On cultural matters, Chebrikov charged that the USSR's opponents in the West were pushing some writers, filmmakers, and others toward "demagoguery and nihilism" and were encouraging the "blackening" of some periods of Soviet history (*CSM*, 14 September). KGB chiefs customarily deliver hard-line speeches at Dzerzhinsky fetes (see Yuri Andropov's at the 100th anniversary of the secret police founder's birth in 1977), but Chebrikov's speech was scrutinized closely for clues on the current domestic political situation. He apeared to be solidly behind Ligachev on the controversial issues.

Another reputed opponent of Gorbachev's policies, Geidar Aliev, was dropped in October from the Politburo at the Central Committee plenum "in connection with his retirement on health grounds" (TASS, 21 October; *NYT*, 22 October). Aliev had reportedly been a supporter of Gorbachev at the outset of the latter's tenure, but, after being passed over for the premiership in October 1985, Aliev evidently played a steadily diminishing role in major policy matters. During 1987, government sectors for which he was responsible, including transport and consumer goods, had been sharply criticized by the media and by Gorbachev. There were reports that Aliev had suffered a heart attack earlier in the year, and his wan appearance lent some credence to the official account of his retirement. But considerations of health have rarely been the real reason for departures from the leadership, and most Western observers were inclined to view his "resignation" as the result of his emergence as a consistent critic of the Gorbachev reform program. In any case, Aliev was certainly not an enthusiastic supporter of the general secretary, and his exit was seen as likely to strengthen Gorbachev's position in the Politburo.

The big news from the October plenum, however, was divulged in the week following the meeting. Confronting widespread rumors of a serious verbal battle among party leaders, Lukyanov told a press conference that Eltsin had expressed views at the meeting with which other Central Committee members did not agree and that Eltsin had been asked to resign as party chief of Moscow and as a nonvoting member of the Politburo (AP, 31 October). Official discomfiture over the incident was indicated by TASS instructing Soviet news media not to carry Lukyanov's remarks (*CSM*, 2 November).

Glasnost' does not extend to meetings of the Central Committee; the only confirmed information about such proceedings is that disseminated by officials. Although the subsequent meeting of the Moscow city party committee was reported in detail, officials steadfastly refused to provide specifics about the 22 October debate or to allow publication of Eltsin's speech. But Soviet sources told Western reporters that Eltsin criticized the slowness of reform, said that *perestroika* had reached a dead end and that Ligachev was obstructing its progress, and concluded that he "especially did not want to work in Moscow any more" in view of the obstacles posed for his renovation efforts there by members of the upper leadership.

One report had Eltsin charging that Gorbachev's associates had created a new "cult of personality" around the leader, but Eltsin vigorously denied making any such assertion (AP, 3 November). Another account suggested that Eltsin's biggest mistake was the alleged inclusion of Raisa Gorbacheva in his criticisms (*Time*, 7 December).

Pravda (22 October) listed Eltsin as the first speaker at the plenum; it is not clear whether he had been scheduled to address the committee. Ligachev was listed as the second speaker; he reportedly delivered a stinging response to Eltsin. There were no reliable reports on the remarks of most other speakers, but the general tenor of their contributions was said to have been highly critical of Eltsin. *Pravda*'s list evidently followed the order of actual debate since it was not arranged alphabetically. KGB head Chebrikov was listed sixteenth. He is reported to have defended Ligachev and severely criticized Eltsin for, among other things, talking too freely with Western reporters about negative aspects of Soviet life.

Eltsin's fate was put on hold until after the major celebrations in early November. At the commemoration of the 70th anniversary of the Bolshevik Revolution and the annual 7 November parade in Red Square, Eltsin took his place with other candidate Politburo members, and many Western observers concluded that the storm had blown over. But at a meeting of the Moscow city party committee four days after the festivities, Eltsin was fired as Moscow party leader amid a torrent of abuse, with Gorbachev in the forefront. Eltsin was condemned for "political adventurism," for "splitting the Politburo," and for promoting a "big-boss syndrome." Gorbachev told the meeting that "Comrade Eltsin has put personal ambitions before the interests of the Party"; Eltsin responded with contrite self-criticism, agreeing that ambition was one of his worst characteristics and that he had allowed it to cloud his judgment (*Pravda*, 12 November). Some Western journalists described the Moscow atmosphere surrounding the Eltsin affair as reminiscent of Stalin's purge trials of the 1930s. This was perhaps an exaggeration, but the harsh treatment of Eltsin seemed likely to discourage the open discussion of issues supposedly encouraged under *glasnost'*. It was ironic that Eltsin was subjected to exactly the same sort of public humiliation that he had dealt out to his predecessor, Viktor Grishin.

One week after Eltsin's dismissal, he was appointed first deputy chairman of the USSR State Committee for Construction, a troubled government sector subjected to its second reorganization in a little more than a year (*Izvestiia*, 19 November). Whatever the position of the various hierarchs on Eltsin's earlier disgrace, the provenance of his rescue from oblivion seemed clear. It was Prime Minister Ryzhkov who saved his fellow member of the Kirilenko-led Sverdlovsk machine from a bad end by installing Eltsin in a government job under Ryzhkov's supervision.

Western interpretations of the episode differed markedly. Some analysts concluded that the startling chain of events had wounded Gorbachev severely in the Kremlin political game and that conservative elements in the leadership had won a signal victory. According to another appraisal, Gorbachev, outraged by Eltsin's conduct, had willingly led the charge against him. Eltsin's 21 October speech was surely a serious violation of party protocol and highly embarrassing to the general secretary as he prepared for the 70th anniversary celebration and for the December summit with U.S. president Reagan. TASS provided some supporting evidence for this version when it revealed that Eltsin had told Gorbachev during the summer that he might resign and that Gorbachev had urged him to wait until after the November celebrations before making a decision. Finally, some sovietologists argued that Gorbachev had skillfully recovered from a bad situation by taking the initiative and sacrificing Eltsin, thus putting his own house in order and proving that he did, after all, possess "iron teeth."

The thesis of artful maneuvering by Gorbachev was consistent with the appointment of Eltsin's successor, but that move could also justify other interpretations. Named as Moscow city party first secretary was Central Committee secretary Zaikov, the former head of the Leningrad party organization and reportedly a consistent supporter of Gorbachev in the Politburo. Under Zaikov, *perestroika* could proceed in Moscow without the fanfare of the flamboyant Eltsin. However, it was quite possible that Ligachev had encouraged the transfer of Zaikov to get the party's number three man out of the Secretariat. In the new distribution of power among the leaders, much would depend on the identity of Zaikov's successor as defense industry overseer. For the short run, the move of Zaikov from the Central Committee building on Old Square to the nearby Moscow city party headquarters seemed certain to elevate Yakovlev, Gorbachev's closest associate in the upper echelons of the party, to the position of third-ranking Central Committee secretary.

The future of the reform movement was rendered more problematic by Gorbachev's long speech marking the 70th anniversary of the Bolshevik Revolution, which generally evoked disappointment among advocates of more advanced reform positions within the USSR, emigres, and Westerners, who looked to the new leader in Moscow as the standard-bearer of a real transformation of the Soviet system. Gorbachev warned against both "conservative forces" who will seek "to discredit *perestroika* and provoke dissatisfaction among the people" and "the pressure of the overly zealous and impatient." On arms control, he said that a treaty to ban intermediate-range nuclear missiles "is very important in itself" and pledged further efforts toward "concrete results in reducing strategic offensive armaments and barring weapons from outer space—the key to removing the nuclear threat" (*Pravda*, 3 November).

The address, widely expected to include a radical reappraisal of Soviet history comparable to that of Khrushchev's secret speech at the Twentieth CPSU Congress in 1956, was a great disappointment to liberal opinion at home and abroad. Gorbachev did declare that Stalin had committed "enormous and unforgivable crimes" and promised that a campaign to rehabilitate his victims would resume. However, Stalin's victims were said to number in the thousands, far fewer than generally accepted estimates, which are in the millions. The party leader made no move toward rehabilitation of Bukharin, which many dissidents regard as the touchstone of any genuine effort for a historically accurate review of Soviet history. In fact, the speech included some criticism of Bukharin, that pioneer Bolshevik theoretician who was killed on Stalin's orders in 1938, as well as a ritualistic denunciation of Trotsky. Gorbachev also defended Stalin's collectivization of agriculture, and this stance figured to inhibit any later attempt to organize the farm sector more rationally. Furthermore, Gorbachev's endorsement of the 1939 Nazi-Soviet pact had negative implications for the vocal demands of Baltic nationalities for a new look at the record of Stalin's repressions in the three northwestern republics. Gorbachev's speech was so restrained that its vetting by Ligachev seems plausible; the "second secretary" had repeatedly discouraged an unlimited reopening of the historical record. But Gorbachev himself had not been entirely consistent on the reappraisal of Soviet history.

Whether or not the speech constituted a real point of departure was debatable. But the events of October and November clearly had a chilling effect on Soviet intellectuals and young technocrats, many of whom were Gorbachev's most ardent supporters in the face of determined opposition by entrenched bureaucrats and of endemic skepticism among the masses. This reaction, no longer considering the new leader a knight in shining armor but merely another Soviet politician, was confirmed by the soundings of Western correspondents. Nevertheless, Gorbachev's reform program had not been reversed, and the immediate future of his leadership depended less on popular attitudes than on the configuration of power in the hierarchically organized Soviet system, where Gorbachev had more impact during his first three years in office than had any previous Soviet leader in a comparable period. Wholesale turnover at various levels in party and state had broken up old regional and bureaucratic aggregations of power. Gorbachev's position in the party was firmly grounded in an "organizational tail" including at least four of the twelve most important regional organizations in the Russian Republic, as his clients headed the key southern regions of Krasnodar, Stavropol, Rostov, and Volgograd. Most Secretariat members were Gorbachev's personal choices, and his associates Lukyanov, Razumovsky, Dobrynin, Yakovlev, and Nikonov were in charge of the crucially important functional areas of police, cadres, foreign affairs, propaganda, and agriculture. But nearly 60 percent of the members of the Central Committee were holdovers from the Brezhnev era, and there were indications that this body was playing a far more active role than usual in determining policy. Historically, periods of increased influence for the Central Committee have come only when the Politburo was unable to present a monolithic facade, and many Western observers considered the thirteen-man Soviet "cabinet" a weak link in Gorbachev's structure of political support.

The Politburo probably does not contain a cohesive "opposition" bloc. Given the authority of the general secretary, outright resistance to him by a bloc of members is dangerous and likely to lead to a showdown, as in the conflict between Khrushchev and the "antiparty" group in 1957. Moreover, pressures for internal consensus are likely to produce shadings of difference rather than overt competition. Nevertheless, public statements by members indicate that some are enthusiastic about Gorbachev's program and that some have reservations; it is the relative weights of the hierarchs involved that intrigues Western analysts. Ligachev, with protocol rank as the number two man in the party, was generally recognized during the year as the most important "conservative" in the Politburo.

Early in the year, shifting functional assignments within the Secretariat appeared to sharply diminish Ligachev's role in party affairs, leading to speculation that Gorbachev was skillfully chipping away at the bureaucratic foundations of the former's influence. The responsibility of Lukyanov for the police and of Dobrynin for foreign affairs and the emergence of Yakovlev as the most prominent spokesman on ideological matters all pointed in this direction. Further, there were indications that Razumovsky reported directly to Gorbachev on matters of party organization. However, during the spring, Ligachev presided over meetings in fields such as transport and agriculture, far removed from his previously recognized areas of supervision, suggesting that he had assumed a much broader overseer function. But the extreme weakness of his party organizational ties, when compared with Gorbachev's, would have made his growing intransigence on certain policy matters a risky business without sustenance from other influential Politburo members. By early fall, it appeared that this necessary support was mainly obtained from Chebrikov and the KGB.

Shevardnadze and Yakovlev were identified by Western analysts as the only enthusiastic devotees of *glasnost'* and *perestroika* among Gorbachev's Politburo colleagues. Zaikov was thought to be highly supportive of the general secretary, and Nikonov was a nondescript client. Gromyko, now reduced to a sinecure holder, was certainly no enthusiast of radical change, and Shcherbitsky publicly acknowledged, at least implicitly, his disagreements with the general secretary. Vorotnikov and Solomentsev, elected prior to Gorbachev's assumption of the leadership, probably regarded Gorbachev as indebted to them for his election and very likely retained a large measure of independence.

Ryzhkov was generally regarded as quite cautious on *perestroika*. Although the prime minister and Slyunkov, his former close associate, could not be placed along the ideological spectrum with any confidence, the old Kirilenko wing of the party (the premier's power base) had clearly sustained a major setback in the Eltsin affair. The presence of Ryzhkov and Ambassador to France Yakov Ryabov, Eltsin's other prominent fellow graduate of the Sverdlovsk machine, as speakers at the tumultuous 21 October meeting of the Central Committee emphasized the embarrassment of the erstwhile clients of Kirilenko. More important, the ouster of Eltsin from his party position removed the premier's foothold in the Moscow city party organization.

All of this seemed to leave the general secretary in a relatively weak position within the party's ruling body. But there were crosscurrents that made relationships among the hierarchs highly complex, and these perhaps facilitated Gorbachev's ongoing drive for organizational power even as controversy over policies intensified. Whatever their positions on *glasnost'*, Solomentsev and Vorotnikov had been vigorous practitioners of discipline and opponents of corruption. Shcherbitsky held on, probably thanks to support from Chebrikov, his onetime protege in Dnepropetrovsk, despite continual predictions of his political demise. But a solid bloc of the three supposed conservatives was not in the cards; it was Ligachev's severe condemnation of the performance of the Ukrainian party organization that rendered Shcherbitsky's position most precarious. Aliev, before his "retirement," had been a natural candidate for a bloc of "conservatives" seeking to slow down reform, a bloc presumably headed by

Ligachev. But the critical interventions by the "second secretary" in areas for which Aliev was responsible suggested that Ligachev may have personally led the charge against the ruthless and charming Aliev.

At year's end, the composition of the Politburo and the complexity of relationships within it would appear to leave the general secretary far more vulnerable on policy than on tenure in office. But it seemed clear that further progress in his reform program hinged on a much broader and deeper consolidation of his personal power position. As Gorbachev approached the 3d anniversary of his accession, the supreme paradox of his leadership remained: although Gorbachev advocates democratization of party, state, and society, both his program and his political future depend on the establishment of something approximating one-man rule.

Party Policies, Organization, and Personnel. Meetings of the Central Committee during the year endorsed the main outlines of Gorbachev's plan for reform of the economy, but there were disparities between the leader's rhetoric and the plenum outcomes on other matters, particularly intraparty democracy. The Politburo had worked out compromises on economic matters that perhaps fell short of Gorbachev's maximum objectives, but issues relating to control of society by the inner core of the *nomenklatura* were too controversial to be resolved in this manner. The first plenum of the year had been originally scheduled for November 1986; the postponement was attributed by Western analysts to growing discord among Politburo members on fundamental questions of *glasnost'* and *perestroika*.

The January plenum endorsed plans for continuing to restructure government ministries and plans for democratization and heightened worker participation in the organization of individual enterprises (*Pravda*, 31 January). However, the plenum only gave a vague approval to the concept of intraparty democracy, and its resolutions omitted any reference to earlier Gorbachev suggestions for secret ballot, multiple-candidate elections for party posts (*LAT*, 30 January). Gorbachev, in his opening address to the plenum, indicated that such changes would not violate the fundamental principle of democratic centralism, according to which decisions of higher bodies, including those on personnel, are absolutely binding on lower ones (TASS, 27 January; *Pravda*, *WP*, 28 January). The question of how the contradictory practices of co-option and election by secret ballot could be combined was left unanswered. But, apparently, even the possibility of looser central control was anathema to Ligachev and other "conservative" members in the leadership. Fears that even a modest dose of democratization might endanger the elite's monopoly of power intensified a few weeks later with the announcement of the results of multicandidate Soviet elections (see below).

The plenum also failed to impose a mandatory retirement age. Such a requirement had been broached before the Twenty-seventh CPSU Congress, and Gorbachev kept the issue alive, reportedly proposing an age limit of 70 for all party and state officials. Some Soviet sources privately identified this controversy as a major reason for the Central Committee meeting delay.

Other than personnel questions, the major focus of the January plenum was on economic plans and performance. Gorbachev and other speakers noted a slow start in restructuring the economy (*Pravda*, 27, 31 January). A party conference on agriculture before the plenum had dealt severely with poor performance on Ukrainian farms, presumably increasing the pressures on Shcherbitsky (*NYT*, 24 January).

The June plenum approved the comprehensive design for restructuring of the economy through 1990, a plan formally put into effect by the Supreme Soviet a few days later (see below). The Central Committee at its June meeting also scheduled the Nineteenth All-Union Conference of the CPSU to convene in Moscow on 28 June 1988 (*WMR*, September).

Substantive issues were overshadowed at the October plenum by the Eltsin affair. TASS (20 October) reported that Gorbachev's report dealt with the 70th anniversary of the revolution and "some current tasks." Earlier, Soviet officials had said that Gorbachev planned to seek Central Committee approval for a crash program to increase the availability of food and other consumer goods (*NYT*, 22 October).

Despite the intense concentration on cadre performance at the January plenum and in the official press throughout the year, turnover in midlevel positions generally slowed after the massive replacement drive of Gorbachev's first two years in power. However, at lower levels renewal continued at a steady clip as earlier midlevel appointees carried out cadre renewal in their departments and regional organizations. After Slyunkov was transferred to Moscow in January, the vacancy in the Belorussian leadership was filled by Efrem Sokolov, first secretary of Brest *obkom* (*Sovetskaia Belorussia*, 3 February). Sokolov formerly served as head of the agriculture department of the Belorussian Central Committee.

Lukyanov's elevation to the Secretariat in January created an opening in the position of head of the General Department, which was filled in May by Valerii Boldin, a personal assistant to General Secretary Gorbachev (*RL Research*, 9 July). Georgii Smirnov, another personal assistant of Gorbachev, displaced the veteran ideologist Anatolii Egorov as head of the Institute of Marxism-Leninism. A further expansion of the party leader's influence over the central apparatus came with the ouster of Oleg Rakhmanin, the hard-line proponent of bloc subordination to Moscow, as first deputy head of the Central Committee department for liaison with parties of the socialist countries. He was replaced by Georgii Shakhnazarov, a supporter of innovation in both foreign and domestic affairs (*The Political Quarterly*, April–June).

Exceptions to the general slowdown in midlevel cadre turnover were found in central Asia. Gennadi Kolbin, whose appointment as first secretary of the Kazakhstan Communist Party in December 1986 had set off rioting in Alma Ata, moved to purge middle-level appointees closely connected with the Kunaev leadership. Overall, the new appointments seemed designed to produce more of a balance between Russians and Kazakhs, reflecting a measure of distrust of the latter, who were usually strongly supportive of the old order favoring their nationality.

Sagidulla Kubashev (60), a Kazakh who had served as first secretary of Semipalatinsk *obkom* since October 1982, was named second secretary of the Kazakhstan party, thus restoring the balance between Russians and Kazakhs in the two top posts (Alma Ata Domestic Service, 19 January; *FBIS*, 13 January).

The effects of a widespread purge were also felt in the other central Asian republics, and the changes were often associated, as in Kazakhstan, with charges of corruption. Uzbekistan's first secretary, Inamzon Usmankhodzhaev, was sharply criticized at a plenum of the republic Central Committee in April for not having done enough to produce necessary changes (*RL Research*, 10 April).

Major changes in the Ukrainian party organization were tied to specific issues but resulted in a weakening of First Secretary Shcherbitsky's position; they also appeared to give Gorbachev something of a foothold in the Ukraine. The first major change was part of the fallout from the scandal over the arrest and detention of the journalist Viktor Berkhin by the KGB in Voroshilovgrad in the fall of 1986: Boris Goncharenko, the first secretary of Voroshilovgrad *obkom* since 1973, was fired (*Pravda*, 15 February) and replaced by Ivan Lyakhov, a 51-year-old Russian, who was head of the Organizational Party Work Department of the Ukrainian Central Committee (Radio Moscow, 27 February). Lyakhov had previously served as secretary and second secretary of the Ivano-Frankovsk party organization in the western Ukraine. In 1983, Lyakhov succeeded Skiba as head of the Ivano-Frankovsk *obkom* when the latter moved to Moscow as deputy head of the CPSU Central Committee Agriculture Department (*RL Research*, 2 March). Lyakhov is apparently a client of Skiba, who is a close associate of Gorbachev and who now heads the Central Committee Agriculture Department.

Lyakhov's place in the cadres department was taken by Anatolii Ivanovich Kornienko (49), first secretary of Ternopol *obkom* since February 1983 (ibid., 4 May). Before 1983, Kornienko served as head of the Ukrainian Komsomol and was a subordinate of Boris Pastukhov, head of the All-Union Komsomol, who probably recommended him for the Ternopol post. Pastukhov, presently ambassador to Denmark, is believed to have been closely associated with Gorbachev during the latter's rise to power.

In mid-February, at the Sixth Congress of the Ukrainian Union of Journalists, Shcherbitsky had referred to "instances of an incorrect attitude toward articles in the press" in both Dnepropetrovsk and Lvov (*RL Research*, 4 May). On 17 March, Dnepropetrovsk first secrtary Vladimir Boiko was removed "for permitting serious shortcomings in work" (*Pravda*, 18 March). It was later revealed that the charges against Boiko included "various violations and abuses involving law enforcement agencies" (*Radianska Ukraina*, 21 April; *RL Research*, 4 May). Boiko was succeeded by Vladimir A. Ivashko, ideological secretary of the Ukrainian Central Committee. Ivashko's place in the republican Secretariat was taken by Yuri Yelchenko (58), first secretary of the Kiev city party committee, who accompanied Gorbachev on a trip to East Europe in 1986. Yelchenko's successor in Kiev was a 51-year-old Ukrainian, Konstantin Masyk, an inspector of the CPSU Central Committee since October 1986.

Viktor Dobrik, first secretary of Lvov *obkom*, was ousted on 20 March and succeeded by Yakiv

Pogrebniak, industrial secretary of the Ukrainian Central Committee since 1971 (*Radianska Ukraina*, 26 March; *RL Research*, 4 May). A housing scandal in the city of Lutsk caused the dismissal of Volyn *obkom* first secretary Zinovii Kovalchuk in June (*Pravda Ukrainy*, 12 June). A further change in the Ukraine involved the transfer of Andrei Girenko from first secretary of Kherson *obkom* to first secretary of the Crimean *obkom*. His place in Kherson was filled by M. M. Kushnirenko, Kherson *obispolkom* chairman (*Pravda Ukrainy*, 24 June; *FBIS*, 14 July).

Throughout the party the "new style of work," discipline, and the role of cadres in restructuring were emphasized. Numerous editorials and meetings of party organizations stressed these themes, identifying those units that had met or failed to meet the required standards. In the aftermath of the January plenum on personnel, a front-page *Pravda* editorial (31 January) lamented "serious omissions in the activity of control organs both within the party and within the state" and said that "the decisive criterion for assessing cadres is their attitude toward restructuring and their real actions to implement it." On the eve of the Central Committee plenum in June, another front-page *Pravda* editorial praised the strengthening of labor discipline in Tataria and Krasnoyarsk and in Sverdlovsk, Kuibyshev, Chelyabinsk, and Taluga oblasts. Yet in the following month the CPSU Central Committee severely reprimanded party and other organizations in Kuibyshev oblast for shortfalls in housing, transportation, energy, and other public services (Moscow Domestic Service, 21 July; *FBIS*, 23 July). In September, the Central Committee severely reprimanded the Kaliningrad party organization for shortcomings in agricultural production (*Sovetskaia Rossia*, 30 September).

Following the installation of Yazov as defense minister in May, the armed forces stepped up the campaign to restructure the military. A front-page editorial in *Krasnaia zvezda* (10 October) charged that some communists in the armed forces "have let themselves go, have forgotten the notion of military obedience, subordination, courtesy, and a seemly external appearance."

Moscow party chief Eltsin kept up a steady drumfire of exhortation and criticism directed at party cadres before his ouster in November. The February plenum of the Moscow *gorkom* carried out replacements of leading personnel (*Moskovskaia pravda*, 22 February). Yet at the next plenum, in May, Eltsin emphasized "shortcomings" that remained and spoke of the need for intensified self-criticism among holders of top posts (Moscow Domestic Service, 30 May; *FBIS*, 5 June). Despite Eltsin's vigorous efforts during his almost two years as Moscow party head, at the time of his departure most officeholders in the city, apparently holdovers from the Grishin era, had not responded well to the first secretary's reformist zeal.

A largely overlooked obstacle to restructuring the party was the "dead souls" in the Central Committee. By the beginning of the year, sixteen people had been removed from posts normally carrying Central Committee membership, in addition to five pensioners elected at the Twenty-seventh CPSU Congress. These people presumably had nothing to lose by opposing Gorbachev's plans, and the ranks of the "newly discontented" would only have increased if the proposal for a mandatory retirement age were to be adopted (*RL Research*, 12 January). But the real problem was the possibility of inhibiting the midlevel cadre renewal needed to implement the reform program. With four years until the next party congress, substantial dismissals might alienate a large bloc of "dead souls," who could resist reform efforts until the next full reconstitution of the Central Committee. This may account for the relatively slow midlevel cadre turnover since the Twenty-seventh CPSU Congress.

Law and Government. The Central Committee approved in January plans that would give voters a choice of candidates in general elections to local government bodies (*NYT*, 29 January). The first multiple-candidate elections, for 2.3 million deputies to 52,000 district, city, and regional soviets, were held on 21 June in the fifteen republics (*Pravda*, 29 June). Previously, the CPSU was thought to have a strong majority on most councils, but 57 percent of newly elected deputies in the Russian republic were reported to be nonparty members (TASS, 28 June).

Three days before the Soviet elections, the USSR Supreme Soviet Presidium issued an amnesty decree to mark the 70th anniversary of the October Revolution. The decree provided no punishment or prosecution for combat veterans, winners of awards or medals, pregnant women, women with underage children, men over 60, women over 55, and certain categories of invalids (*Izvestiia*, 19 June). Not included were persons charged or convicted for the Chernobyl disaster and the Black Sea ship collision of summer 1976 or those convicted for "spying, contraband, treason, and banditry" (TASS, 19 June; *FBIS*, 23 June).

The Supreme Soviet enacted two important laws at its June meeting. For the first time, citizens were granted the right to appeal actions of public officials that violated their citizens' rights. The new law was expected to be used mostly by workers to file job-related complaints against employers. Party secretary Razumovsky said that citizens who file unfounded complaints will be liable for court costs and possible slander suits. He also revealed that complaints related to national security would be prohibited, which apparently precludes complaints by persons denied the right to emigrate on grounds of their access to secret information. It is not clear whether immigration officials are covered by the law (*NYT*, 1 July). The Supreme Soviet also gave formal sanction to the package of proposals on the economy endorsed by the Central Committee at its June plenum (see below).

There were more changes in the ministerial structure during the year. The Supreme Soviet Presidium announced in July that it was combining four ministries into two new ones in the continuing effort to simplify the unwieldy governmental structure. Aleksandr Yezherskii (72) was appointed to head the new ministry of agricultural and tractor machine building, and Vladimir Velichko (50) was named as chief of the new ministry of machine building for animal husbandry and fodder production (TASS, 20 July; *FBIS*, 21 July). A new "super ministry" for construction was set up for that sector of the economy, which was still beset with chronic problems (*Izvestiia*, 19 November).

The USSR State Committee for Science and Technology, a key organization in economic restructuring that had come under fire from Gorbachev during 1986, was given a new chairman. Guri Marchuk was shifted to the presidency of the USSR Academy of Sciences and replaced by Tolstykh, an electronics engineer who had served as deputy minister of the electronics industry since December 1985 (*Izvestiia*, 8 February; *RL Research*, 11 February). In the Ukraine, the republic's veteran premier, Aleksandr Lyashko (72), retired and was replaced by Vitalii Masol (59), chairman of the Ukrainian state planning commission (*Izvestiia*, 12 July).

Grishin, the former longtime party boss of Moscow, gave up his last official post in July when he resigned from the USSR Supreme Soviet "at his own request" (TASS, 14 July; *WP*, 15 July). Viktor Dementsev retired as chairman of the USSR State Bank Board and was succeeded by Nikolai Garetovskii (*Pravda*, 21 October).

Party leader Gorbachev took advantage of a bizarre incident in May to shake up the leadership of the armed forces. Mathias Rust, a nineteen-year-old West German amateur pilot, flew a light plane over western Russia and landed in Red Square. The episode was doubly embarrassing because it coincided with Border Guards' Day. Amid a barrage of criticism aimed at the military, particularly the air defense forces and the border guards, the Politburo met hurriedly and decided on major changes in the high command. Marshal Sergei Sokolov (75), defense minister since September 1984, was replaced by Colonel General Yazov (64), armed forces personnel chief since January and former commander in the Far East.

Yazov, a strong advocate of restructuring in the military, was evidently Gorbachev's favorite general and, reportedly, the general secretary's choice for the post. Yazov, who was apparently being groomed for eventual succession to Sokolov, was promoted over more senior officers to the top post on the heels of the scandal wrought by the young German's spectacular flight. The head of the air defense forces, Chief Marshal of Aviation Aleksandr Koldunov (63), was also fired for "negligence and lack of control over his units" (TASS, 30 May; AP, 31 May).

Economy. *Perestroika* was designed mainly to cure the sluggishness of the Soviet economy and to close the technological gap with the West. Gorbachev, describing the situation as critical, pushed the leadership for economic renovation, and the January and June plenums of the Central Committee approved major measures of economic reform. But opposition mounted to changes in economic mechanisms, and indications were that Gorbachev did not get all he wanted on restructuring of the economy.

At the beginning of the year, the outlook appeared promising for *perestroika* advances. Despite the Chernobyl disaster, performance of the economy during 1986 had been impressive. The official plan fulfillment report for 1986 showed the following increases: national income, 4.1 percent; gross industrial output, 4.9 percent; gross farm output, 5.1 percent; investment, 8 percent. All represented substantial increases over average figures for the years 1981–1985 (*Pravda*, 18 January). Soviet officials attributed the good showing mainly to success in the drive for greater labor discipline, particularly the campaign against alcoholism.

Despite the upsurge in agricultural production, the farm sector remained a major concern of the leadership. Agriculture was the one area where significant short-run results could be achieved during a period of economic reorganization, and the gains to date had not been sufficient to provide a balancing asset against possible short-run losses in other sectors. Moreover, agricultural performance by region had been highly uneven. A conference on 23 January brought together party and government agricultural cadres from all the union republics to discuss introduction of the latest methodology, removal of organizational bottlenecks, and "problems of radically improving party leadership of the agroindustrial complex development in the interests of the timely and complete fulfillment of the country's food program" (ibid., 25 January).

Gorbachev told the conference that "the whole of the 11th five-year plan period was a wheelspin" and that "we have been stalled since 1972, especially since 1975." His remarks seemed to confirm that Gorbachev had not been in favor of the major agricultural policies adopted during the latter part of the Brezhnev era and that, as the party secretary for agriculture, he had been unable to push through any innovative proposals of his own. Party secretary Ligachev's much more specific remarks directed scathing criticism at the Ukraine. He said that party officials in the republic had been "intolerably slow" in reorganizing agriculture along the new agrobusiness lines in which managing crop production is combined with processing and distribution. Further, he noted the striking turnaround in grain production: the Ukraine, once the country's "breadbasket" and source of excess grain, had become a consumer of grain produced in other regions (TASS, 24 January; *NYT*, 25 January).

The January plenum of the Central Committee was devoted primarily to personnel questions, some of which related directly to the economy. The Central Committee approved Gorbachev's proposal in broad outline without endorsing specific proposals. One of these, which was incorporated less than two weeks after the plenum on the Draft Law on the State Enterprises and was formally adopted by the Supreme Soviet in June (*Izvestiia*, 1 July), said that all supervisory personnel up to the level of enterprise director are to be elected by the labor collective, which will be responsible for monitoring the entire economic activity of the enterprise. This supposedly provides for a radical democratization of industry. However, the draft law also provided that the party organization of the industry will direct the activities of the collective and its self-management bodies (*Pravda*, 8 February; *RL Research*, 27 February).

Early experiments with the democratization scheme found major difficulties on the government side. The press reported cases of the electoral process being sabotaged by government agencies and enterprise bureaucrats. At the Transport Construction Research Institute in Moscow, all staff-nominated candidates withdrew under pressure from the authorities, 85 percent of the employees were declared ineligible to vote, and an executive selected by the government became the new director (*NYT*, 29 May).

Meanwhile, other economic reforms were put into effect, also with disappointing early results. Limited quality control in the civilian sector of the economy was introduced 1 January, as inspectors similar to those responsible for military production began their work. The inspectors were assigned to independent commissions of the USSR State Committee for Standards (Gosstandart) and were to supervise output of 1,500 enterprises belonging to 28 different ministries. The sale of goods not bearing the acceptance commission's stamp of approval is prohibited. Nearly all tractors and combines, most television sets and refrigerators, 70 percent of automobiles, and more than half of all machine tools are covered by the new quality control (*RL Research*, 24 March).

A slowdown in economic growth during the first half of the year was generally attributed by officials and economists to the negative impact of the new control system on gross output. Gross production was up only 1 percent in the first quarter (*Ekonomicheskaia gazeta*, April) and fell even lower during the second quarter; the USSR appeared headed for a negative economic growth rate. Even though some improvement was anticipated as the new system gained fuller acceptance, it appeared that economic indexes would show much lower increases for the year than the unsatisfactory ones of the previous five-year plan.

New regulations went into effect in January to break the monopoly over imports and exports held by the Ministry of Foreign Trade, to vastly expand foreign trade, and to promote importation of Western technology. Twenty-one other ministries and 72 state enterprises were permitted to arrange their own dealings with the outside world and to set up joint ventures with noncommunist firms (TASS, 6, 13 January; *FBIS*, 7, 14 January). Hundreds of Western firms rushed to explore opportunities under the new rules but found that doing business in the USSR was still difficult.

Bureaucratic resistance to reform, turf battles within ministries, lack of understanding by Soviet officials of capitalist business practices, and uncertainty over the new regulations frustrated Western and Japanese negotiators. The outsiders' basic aim—to make and sell products within the USSR—conflicted with the Soviet aim of absorbing foreign investment and expertise to make export products that would earn urgently needed hard currency (*WSJ*, 17 July).

Following repeated criticisms of the long-standing tendency to level income without regard for productivity, a new wage policy was introduced in February. Individual enterprises are to set actual wage rates within the limits of the new guidelines; a portion of any increased revenue can be set aside for distribution as wages. The difference between the lowest and highest wage groups is to be increased to 80 percent from the previous 58 percent. Quality work is to be encouraged by a wage differential of up to 24 percent for the highest quality, plus another differential of up to 12 percent for productivity. Existing wage supplements are to be abolished, except those for excellent performance or for particularly important work. Any supplement will be limited to 50 percent of the basic wage, and salaries of engineers may rise up to 45 percent compared with a permitted increase of up to 25 percent for industrial wages (*Pravda*, 17 February; *NYT*, 8 March).

The new regulations reportedly increased disaffection among workers, who were already disenchanted with earlier drives widely characterized as "more work for less vodka." The favorable treatment for the previously severely disadvantaged engineers did not accord with rank-and-file notions of democracy. Most important, the absence of the previously expected automatic bonus was a shock to men on the assembly line as, indeed, it was intended to be. The supposed attitudes in the workplace were confirmed by the practice, new for the Soviets, of public opinion polling. Professor Vilen Ivanov from the Sociological Research Institute at the USSR Academy of Sciences reported that in one Moscow factory, 62 percent of the workers questioned said that the only effect of restructuring so far was greater work pressure (BBC Caris, 6 May).

The June plenum of the Central Committee approved a package of proposals for economic reform, some of which were merely firmed-up plans approved earlier. Economist Abel Aganbegyan confirmed that some disagreements had been expressed at the meeting (*LAT*, 27 June; *RL Research*, 30 June). The Central Committee resolution, notable for its lack of detail, gave a go-ahead signal for the program of restructuring and summarized general goals. The overall plan envisions a high degree of independence for individual enterprises, with central planning agencies responsible for the setting of long-range goals and "normative planning." Enterprises are to be responsible for their own supply and credit arrangements and will be evaluated on the basis of profit and loss (*Pravda*, 27 June).

Further economic reforms aroused fears among officials and the populace about bankruptcy, unemployment, and price increases. In March, an apparently symbolic and exemplary bankruptcy of a major enterprise involved a Leningrad construction trust that was shut down, temporarily displacing 2,000 employees, because it had fallen behind its delivery schedules, overrun cost limits, and produced substandard work (*WSJ*, 27 March). The Leningrad closing raised afresh workers' fears of unemployment, which provided conservative opponents of reform with a powerful weapon in the ongoing debate on restructuring. Clearly, there would be at least fractional unemployment with the implementation of reform, and a cardinal feature of the scheme was the removal of secure tenure in existing jobs. Gorbachev repeatedly denied that there would be Western-style unemployment under the reform program. Under increasing pressure from conservative critics, he was impelled, in a June local Soviet election speech, to provide a general assurance against "unemployment." He said "that will not do" and reminded his listeners that they were guaranteed jobs. "We have a stable society," he said. "That is what makes it stable, because these are fundamental matters: people are protected, today and for the future" (Soviet Central Television, 21 June; *RL Research*, 23 June).

There were indications that price reform, considered essential for a rational reordering of the economy, would soon be initiated. Economist Anatolii Deriabin reported that a price-setting reform was being studied by the USSR State Committee for Prices. A basic principle of such a reform, he said, would be preservation of working people's living standards. Deriabin noted that prices for bread had not changed since 1954, meat and dairy products, since 1962, and rent had remained unchanged since 1928 (TASS, 17 September; *FBIS*, 24 September).

Two weeks after the Deriabin report, Gorbachev made the first general announcement about price reform in a statement on nationwide television. Speaking in Murmansk, he informed the Soviet public that price increases on a wide range of basic foodstuffs were under consideration and would likely be introduced soon. He reassured those on low or fixed incomes. Pensions, student grants, and payments to those with large families would, he said, be adjusted to take account of price increases for basic staples (Soviet Television, 1 October; *RL Research*, 14 October).

A flood of decrees, criticisms, and reorganizations during the second half of the year pointed up the intensification of problems as reform proceeded. As it became increasingly obvious that short-run incentives were lacking elsewhere, quantitative and qualitative improvements in food supply took on greater urgency. Two party-government decrees called acceleration in the growth of food production "the pivotal goal of party policy" and deplored delays in reorganization of the agricultural complex. Full introduction of intrafarm-contracted production assignment and remuneration was scheduled by the end of 1988, and additional support for the "individual sector" of production and its fuller integration with the general economy were mandated (*Pravda*, 25 September).

A report spotlighting serious shortcomings in the machine-building industry stated that earlier gains in the RSFSR machine-building complex had been lost by a sharp turndown during 1987. More than 60 percent of enterprises were said to be failing to fulfill targets with regard to the "basic indicator," deliveries of equipment to clients and customers (*Sovetskaia Rossia*, 15 September). A Council of Ministers' resolution in July provided for the "fundamental restructuring of material and technical supply" and issued a stinging criticism of Gossnab. According to the resolution, "USSR Gossnab has not devoted the necessary attention to improving the economic mechanism, has relied primarily on administrative methods of management, and has not made sufficient use of economic accountability principles in organizing its activity" (*FBIS*, 6 October). In a further reorganization, the union-republic ministry of nonferrous metallurgy was converted to an all-union ministry (Moscow Domestic Service, 3 October; *FBIS*, 6 October).

During the year, a growing sense of economic emergency was conveyed by the escalating rhetoric of General Secretary Gorbachev. In numerous statements during the final months of the year, Gorbachev fleshed out the critical situation that he had outlined with a startlingly negative theoretical formulation at the midyear Central Committee plenum: "We more and more have come to understand that the need for *perestroika* is called into existence by the accumulated contradictions in the development of society, which, having gradually built up and having failed to find a prompt resolution, have acquired an essentially precrisis form" (*Pravda*, 26 June).

At year's end, the USSR appeared to have temporarily lost further ground in its struggle to catch up with nonsocialist economies. Western economists considered the odds against the USSR's improving its relative economic position greatly via *perestroika* to be large. However, Gorbachev's critics had failed to offer viable alternatives for the urgently required revitalization of the Soviet economy.

Glasnost'. Deemed by Gorbachev as essential for the success of restructuring, *glasnost'* was carried to unprecedented lengths during the first half of the year. Both old and new issues were subjects of open debate, and the failings of the Soviet system were exposed as never before. *Glasnost'* had a beneficial effect on the USSR's image abroad, but this was not its primary intended purpose.

The policy proved even more controversial than *perestroika* because conservative elements viewed it as more threatening to the regime. Gorbachev himself seemed to recognize that there were limits beyond which *glasnost'* might be precarious and thus took the position that the central authorities must retain ultimate control of the process and that criticism of top leaders could not be tolerated. During the second half of the year, there were signs that the "thaw" might give way to a less permissive atmosphere. Nevertheless, despite growing obstacles, *glastnost'* survived.

Following Andrei Sakharov's return from internal exile in December 1986, a less repressive policy on domestic control seemed to be developing. Early in January one of the more remarkable events in Soviet history occurred when KGB head Chebrikov, in a front-page *Pravda* article (8 January), announced the firing of one of his subordinates, the security chief in Voroshilovgrad in the Ukraine, for arranging the false arrest of a journalist. There was no known precedent for such a denunciation of a KGB field officer in the official press, and it was generally assumed that Chebrikov's role in the affair could not have been voluntary. The article was shortly followed by a "minipurge" of the Ukrainian

KGB, including the republic chairman of the organization.

Sakharov emerged from exile as a proponent, in the main, of Gorbachev's policies, and his release may have been partially designed to garner support for the leadership from the creative and scientific intelligentsia. Sakharov was allowed an unusual degree of freedom to speak his mind, and he soon made it clear that, although he endorsed the general direction of regime policy, he retained his intellectual independence. During a forum on arms control in February—his first appearance at a major government-sponsored function since his return from Gorky—Sakharov appealed for more civil liberties in the USSR and for an easing of emigration restrictions (*NYT*, 15 February).

Secretary Yakovlev reportedly had been a major force in the encouragement of *glasnost'* since his return to the Central Committee apparatus in 1985, and the relaxation of information flow and cultural expression became far more pronounced following his elevation to candidate Politburo rank in January. Yakovlev was certainly not a Western-style liberal, and foreign observers noted that his earlier writings revealed a deep-seated hostility toward the United States and a distorted image of U.S. life. But samizdat and other sources identified Yakovlev as the main protagonist for opening up the Soviet system in a way that was almost revolutionary compared with previous practices. As *glasnost'* proceeded, it became increasingly obvious that Yakovlev's advanced positions were being challenged by the party's "second secretary," Ligachev, and the checkered pattern of cultural reform during the year seemed to reflect a tug of war between these two powerful members of the ruling central elite.

The effects of *glasnost'* were felt in the relatively free dissemination of information about events inside the USSR and their candid assessment, which was the hallmark of *glasnost'* during Gorbachev's first two years in power and became even more pronounced in early 1987. An informal "do-it-yourself" censorship in the media, with tacit recognition of certain limits, replaced the former rigid bureaucratic controls. Abuses in the Soviet system were widely publicized, previously taboo topics were examined in depth, and a lively discussion of some issues was encouraged.

The Soviet public was treated to a more realistic depiction of life in the West, particularly the United States. Westerners had more access to Soviet society, although there were some hints of a "Potemkin village" approach to select, welcomed foreigners. Previously banned works appeared on film and in print, and Soviet history was subject to a limited, and controversial, reassessment.

Tatiana Zaslavskaia, silenced during Konstantin Chernenko's tenure, emerged as a leading advocate of *glasnost'* in academia. She published a lengthy article in *Pravda* (6 February) that was sharply critical of the state of sociology and of the suppression of vital information about Soviet society. Zaslavskaia noted that the first 100 professional sociologists in the USSR will graduate in 1989, whereas in the United States 260 sociology faculties annually produce 6,000 specialists. Her sharpest criticism was reserved for the dearth of data on social problems. She said that in the USSR data are not published on the prevalence of crime, the frequency of suicide, the level of alcohol and drug abuse, or the ecological situation in various cities and regions, "although these phenomena are traditional subjects of statistics in economically developed countries." The USSR's best-known sociologist also charged that "data on migrations between regions and between the city and the countryside have disappeared from the press."

Filipp Ermash's dismissal on 28 December 1986 and his replacement by Aleksandr Kamshalov as head of Goskino, the state committee on cinematography, were followed by the release of previously banned films including Tengiz Abuladze's *Repentance*, an allegorical attack on Stalinist repression, and two starring the late unorthodox poet and songwriter, Vladimir Vysotsky (AP, 25 January).

Previously unpublishable works such as Anatolii Rybakov's *Children of the Arbat*, a graphic account of Stalinist terror, appeared in print, as did the writings of deceased emigres, including Vladimir Nabokov. The "thaw" stopped short, however, of allowing the works of living emigres such as Aleksandr Solzhenitsyn to be published. Boris Pasternak, reviled as "anti-Soviet" during the Khrushchev era, was accorded a posthumous rehabilitation.

Valentin Rasputin, whose book *Fire*—a depiction of social collapse in a Siberian village—was the first literary work of the Gorbachev era, gained new prominence as a spokesman for environmental causes. His articles on the state of Lake Baikal reportedly had the support of fellow Siberian Ligachev. Rasputin, who is not a member of the communist party, received two of the USSR's highest awards, Hero of Socialist Labor and the Order of Lenin (*CSM*, 19 March).

Despite the toleration shown to Rasputin, Viktor Afanasiev, editor in chief of *Pravda*, complained at a meeting of Soviet journalists in March about limitations on coverage of environmental issues as well as lack of candor in reporting on the space program. He disclosed that criticism could now be directed at authorities in the union republics, government ministers, and regional party leaders (*NYT*, 23 April). Foreign affairs and the top echelon of the CPSU, however, were still off-limits.

In general, the new official openness concerned only those matters the central authorities wanted brought to public attention, such as corruption in regions targeted for purges, labor indiscipline, and the campaign against alcoholism. Results of a ten-year study on drug abuse in Georgia were reported by the press (*Zaria vostoka*, 20 February), in line with the new official confrontation of certain social problems and with the crackdown on various forms of deviance in the southern republics. Revelations about reactions to the war in Afghanistan also became more candid. *Komsomolskaia pravda*, which in the previous year had revealed the phenomenon of "Afghantsy"—disillusioned veterans who frequently form violence-prone gangs—devoted space in its weekly supplement to letters and commentaries about apathy and resistance among Soviet youth toward participation in the war (*Sobesednik*, no. 1; *RL Research*, 14 January).

The reappraisal of Soviet history, a key feature of *glasnost'*, was mostly done through fiction and press articles, but in March it was announced that new textbooks would carry more realistic views of Soviet history from the revolution forward. Little restraint was evident in criticisms of the Brezhnev era, but reassessment of Stalin's time was a more sensitive matter. *Moscow News* published Lenin's deathbed letter denouncing Stalin (UPI, 15 January), and the spate of newspaper interviews, historical extracts, and magazine essays that followed called for a more rational and realistic retelling of Soviet history. But there were also counterattacks that explicitly or implicitly defended Stalin and his close associates.

Reacting to items critical of Soviet history, Ligachev sought to apply the brakes in a speech in March. He warned Soviet historians not to abuse current freedoms by writing of the country's past as nothing but seven decades of mounting mistakes, failure, and disappointment (*Chicago Tribune*, 29 March). Despite Gorbachev's frequent calls for historical truth, the general secretary maintained a certain reticence about Stalin. In July Gorbachev told Soviet editors that "I think we shall and should never be able to pardon or justify what happened in 1937 and 1938," but he did not mention Stalin by name and added that "we cannot tolerate a lack of respect toward the generations" that endured the earlier trials (*Pravda*, 15 July).

The hoped-for rehabilitation of Bukharin was widely considered a touchstone on Stalinism among members of the intelligentsia. Fedor Burlatsky, a prominent advocate of *glasnost'*, published a one-act play sympathetic to Bukharin (*Literaturnaia gazeta*, 22 July), and the 70th anniversary of the October Revolution was expected by many in Moscow to be the occasion for rehabilitation of this famous victim of Stalin's purges. But Gorbachev's mild praise for Bukharin fell far short of full rehabilitation, and his treatment of Stalin also disappointed the more vocal defenders of historical reappraisal.

Moscow News, under its vigorous new editor Egor Yakovlev who succeeded Gennadi Gerasimov in August 1986, became the most outspoken media organ in defense of more openness. Many important news items concerning the USSR could be found in no other publication. One of its more sensational articles was a condemnation of the Sinyavsky-Daniel trial of the 1960s by Vladimir Simonov, a commentator on foreign affairs (*Moscow News*, no. 8). That *Moscow News* emerged as the vanguard of *glasnost'* suggests the limited impact of the "thaw." A weekly newspaper published by the Novosti Press Agency, it is aimed mainly at foreigners and is available in several languages, with a Russian-language circulation of 250,000 copies, all sold in the capital (*NYT*, 7 March).

The monthly theoretical journal of the Komsomol, *Molodaia gvardiia*, took the position of principal media countercritic to *Moscow News*. An article by Vyacheslav Gorbachev, deputy editor of the journal, criticized *Moscow News*, *Literaturnaia gazeta*, *Sovetskaia kultura*, *Nedelia* (a weekly supplement to *Izvestiia*), and the weekly magazine *Ogonek* for orienting their publications "to the philistine morals which more often are compatible with the lack of spirituality and consumerism of Western mass culture." Editor Gorbachev quoted Ligachev's January speech in Saratov in which the "second secretary" charged that "elements of mass bourgeois culture have begun to penetrate into society, literature, and art." The article also cited the March meeting of the Writers' Union of the Russian Republic as proof that Soviets are not satisfied with the approach taken by some of the more open publications (*Molodaia gvardiia*, no. 7, July).

The March meeting of the Writers' Union criticized some of the publications mentioned in the *Molodaia gvardiia* article for stories dealing with such previously taboo subjects as prostitution, drug abuse, vagrancy, and police brutality. The Writers' Union especially censured *Moscow News* for publishing an article critical of establishment writer Vasili Belov and also cited a passage from Ligachev's Saratov speech in which he urged greater respect for traditional Soviet literature.

While party leaders Gorbachev and Ligachev did not offer public criticism of each other, the differences in their viewpoints were readily apparent, and the struggle was clearly joined between their more vocal devotees. At a plenum of the Board of the USSR Journalists' Union in June, Ivan Laptev, editor in chief of *Izvestiia*, denounced the new trends in the Soviet press and charged that "people who are a long way from serious scholarship" had "with unprecedented force, started to express their views, which are often subjective." He said that journalists, while criticizing specific errors of officials, had often slipped into criticism of "socialism as a system" (*Sovetskaia kultura*, 20 June).

Ligachev visited the offices of *Sovetskaia kultura*, one of the offending publications, and delivered a speech to the editorial staff. Although ostensibly supporting *glasnost'*, he dealt a hard-line rebuke to many of its practitioners. "Ultimately," he said, "the genuine value of a work of art is ensured by the combination of profound party ideological commitment and artistic merit. They form a single, inseparable whole. Unfortunately, there have been quite a few examples which indicate a departure from this principle." Ligachev continued,

> On the whole, the process of democratization, openness, and self-criticism is moving in the right direction. But as was to be expected, the waves of restructuring and renewal have also washed up some scum and debris. "Energetic" people who sometimes try to supplant our spiritual values with their own ideas and intentions have emerged (*Sovetskaia kultura*, 7 July; *FBIS*, 10 July).

Gorbachev, accompanied by Yakovlev, addressed a meeting of "leaders of the mass media and the creative unions," a few days after Ligachev's visit to *Sovetskaia kultura*, but this speech was not reported in the official press until mid-July. It was here that the general secretary deplored the events of 1937 and 1938 without naming Stalin. Gorbachev also sharply criticized the March RSFSR Writers' Union meeting, characterizing its outcome as "impermissible." In view of what transpired at the March conclave, this came close to an open break with Ligachev. Gorbachev may also have had the cultural conservatives in mind when he asserted that "it is not necessary for the party and mass media alike to synchronize their watches all the time." But he also appeared to warn media people across the Soviet ideological spectrum that there were limits to *glasnost'* and that these limits had at least been approached:

> If extremes have made their appearance anywhere—incidentally, they have and we have seen them—that happened nevertheless in the framework of the struggle for socialism, to improve it, in the framework of a struggle which was in the interests of the people.
>
> But if they start seeking out and tossing us values outside of the limits of the interests of the people and beyond the limits of socialism, then the Central Committee will publicly subject this to criticism, make an appraisal and will, in the framework of democracy and *glasnost'*, also express its position on a question of principle. (*Pravda*, 15 July.)

These controversies appeared to affect only a small segment of the Soviet population, but a by-product of *glasnost'*, the flourishing of informal groups, touched a much wider audience. According to the Soviet press, there are more than 100,000 rock music groups; other informal groups are devoted to sports, literature, pacifism, and computer-related activities. Of more concern to the authorities are groups devoted to the preservation of historical monuments and the environment, "law and order" and "Afghantsy" vigilante groups, "punks," hippies, and "Lyubery" (the name is derived from the Moscow suburb of Lyubertsy), who oppose "noxious Western influences" on young people and reportedly beat up "punks" and hippies (*RL Research*, 11 June). On at least one occasion during the year, tensions between informal groups flared into major public disorder. In February there was a demonstration in Moscow by some 500 secondary and vocational school students aged 14 to 17 who carried slogans denouncing the "Lyubery" (Moscow World Service, 23 February; *FBIS*, 24 February).

Another demonstration by 400 members of Pamyat (memory) in May embarrassed the Soviet leadership. Pamyat, which is said to have about 1,000 members, and Otechestvo (fatherland), a similar group based in Sverdlovsk, were originally official organizations devoted to the preservation of cultural monuments. They have turned out to be havens for rabid ultranationalists, apparently with some hidden support in official circles. Pamyat, especially, has displayed a blatant anti-Semitism.

The May demonstration confronted the leadership with a difficult decision: the commitment to *glasnost'* versus the avowed distaste for what the group represented. In the event, *glasnost'* temporarily prevailed. Ostensibly gathered at the Kremlin wall to demonstrate against rejection of a religious motif for a war memorial on Moscow's Poklaniie Hill, Pamyat demanded and was granted a meeting with Eltsin. In their exchange with Eltsin, Pamyat members complained about permissiveness and alcohol and drug use and warned about "cosmopolitanism," a Stalinist code word for Jewish influence. Eltsin told them that "we shall have to think over," giving the group official status (*NYT*, 26 July). A month before the Eltsin encounter, Pamyat demonstrated its clout by seizing control of the Moscow section of the official All-Russian Society for the Preservation of Historical and Cultural Monuments (*RL Research*, 26 August). The ultranationalists were also reported to have a widely circulating samizdat that spread propaganda about a Zionist and Masonic conspiracy working to obliterate Russian culture (*Foreign Report*, 2 July).

The May demonstration by Pamyat evidently convinced the party leadership that the group was too dangerous to be ignored, and a major press campaign against the ultranationalists was launched. One article indicated that senior party officials in Moscow had twisted arms to obtain space for the group's meetings and noted Pamyat opposition to official policies, such as allowing Jewish emigrants to return to the USSR and permitting ousted officials to retire on pensions (*Komsomolskaia pravda*, 22 May). Other articles played up the group's history of anti-Semitism, as well as a report that a Pamyat leader had been committed to a mental institution in the late 1970s in connection with the death of his wife (*WP*, 24 May).

Glasnost' enjoyed a spectacular run during the first half of the year, but signs accumulated of an impending slowdown. The speeches of Ligachev and Gorbachev in July, the thrusts by Ligachev and Chebrikov toward a more restrictive policy during Gorbachev's absence in August and September, and the general secretary's 70th anniversary speech with its mixed treatment of Stalin all discouraged the more zealous advocates of *glasnost'*. Most ominous of all for the "liberal" intelligentsia was the firing of Eltsin, who had the most visible public profile of a *glasnost'* defender than any Soviet official except Gorbachev.

Yet, despite the rising political temperature, the USSR did not appear on the verge of a return to a cultural ice age. Unofficial practitioners of *glasnost'* maintained vigorous activity. The first issue of *Glasnost'*, an unofficial journal of news and opinion and the first privately controlled periodical to be published openly, appeared in July after its organizers failed to obtain official permission to publish. The journal is edited by Sergei Grigoryants, a literary critic released from prison earlier in the year after serving four years for his work on a clandestine human rights publication (*NYT*, 26 June). Despite official harassment, Grigoryants and his associates continued, and by late fall, most copies were being printed abroad. *Glasnost'* was the first publication to report on demonstrations protesting the dismissal of Eltsin, and its issues later in the year contained lists of political prisoners and their status and reports on unofficial political groups (*Newsweek*, 14 December).

Two other unofficial journals appeared during the summer, again after both had been denied official permission to publish. *Ukrainskii vestnik* (Ukrainian Messenger) reappeared on 5 August after a fifteen-year hiatus due to the imprisonment of its editor, Vyacheslav Chornovil, for publishing the journal. Shortly thereafter, *Vybor* (Choice), a Moscow-based philosophical and literary review of Russian Christian culture edited by Gleb Anishchenko and Viktor Aksyuchits, made its debut (Paris AFP, 8 September; *FBIS*, 10 September).

In August, a meeting of 47 unofficial groups was held on party premises in Moscow, and in September seven representatives of unofficial groups supporting *perestroika* gathered in the capital to discuss their future political activities. Boris Kagerlitskii, spokesman for the seven, announced that the groups hoped to "put forward their own candidates in elections to government bodies." Facilities for the September meeting were provided by Novosti, leading to charges that the groups had been co-opted by the authorities (Paris AFP, 8 October; *FBIS*, 9 October).

Despite the uncertainty produced by the Eltsin affair, official purveyors of *glasnost'* persevered. In the first week of December, *Moscow News* published Sakharov's latest call for the release of political prisoners, an exhibition of the works of Marc Chagall opened at Moscow's Pushkin Museum, and preparations for the publication of Pasternak's *Doctor Zhivago* were continuing. Despite Gorbachev's backpedaling, the more avant-garde official journals continued to chip away at Stalin's image. Among many articles critical of the dictator's excesses was one in *Literaturnaia gazeta* (9 December), which announced that the first Soviet biography of Stalin since his death in 1953 will be completed in 1988. Another article by demographer Mark Tolts charged that Stalin altered census data in the 1930s to hide the millions of deaths that resulted from poor harvests and his rapid industrialization and forced collectivization of agriculture (*Ogonek*, 21 December).

Nationalities and Dissent. Long regarded by many Western observers as the most serious, long-range Soviet problem, discontent of nationalities became an urgent, immediate concern during the year as smoldering resentments against Russian domination erupted in demonstrations and violence. In the past, the natural isolation of ethnic groups from each other had enabled the regime to compartmentalize ethnic tensions and avoid a general crisis. But in the era of *glasnost'*, with events reported in the media, there appeared to be a spillover effect as news of overt protest by one group encouraged another to challenge the system. Behind the scenes, the upsurge of protests by ethnic groups may have provided the best ammunition for conservative critics of *glasnost'*.

An uneasy phase in nationality relations was ushered in by the December 1986 rioting in Alma-Ata, when Kazakh students violently protested the firing of Kunaev as republic party first secretary and the installation of Gennadi Kolbin, a nonresident Russian, as his successor. The leadership in Moscow had evidently viewed the republic's leading institutions and its Kazakh minority as being so closely tied to the corrupt Kunaev leadership that it was necessary to bring in an outsider to manage a thoroughgoing purge. But the appointment of an ethnic Russian with no experience in Kazakhstan demonstrated an extraordinary insensitivity to minority sentiments, an attitude probably traceable to the fact that most members of the new leadership in Moscow had spent their entire careers in the Russian republic.

Early accounts of the rioting in Alma-Ata attributed the disturbances to "hooligan" elements, but the reporting shortly became more sophisticated, targeting Kazakh officials as the real force behind the rioting. After the new year, an official report claimed that such officials had roused Kazakh students from their dormitories on the night of 17 December, excited them by alcohol and drugs and nationalist slogans, and urged them to march on the city's central square. However, underlying blame was attributed to patterns of ethnic segregation in the local universities and resulting tensions between Kazakhs and Russians, which university administrators and Komsomol officials had allowed to fester (*Komsomolskaia pravda*, 9 January).

K. Rakhmetov, alleged ringleader in the rioting and a Komsomol secretary at Kazakh State University, was sentenced to seven years in prison (*Kazakhstanskaia pravda*, 11 January; *FBIS*, 21 January), and other convictions followed. A massive purge of party and government cadres ensued to eliminate corruption in the republic. But the pattern of replacements was also designed to reassure the Russian inhabitants, who had long grumbled about Kazakh domination of major institutions (*RL Research*, 28 January). Various actions of the new leadership in the cultural sphere seemed geared to a campaign to repress manifestations of nationalism. In January, the head of the Kazakh Writers' Union urged ideological workers and writers in the republic to combat "vulgar, philistine nationalism" (*Trud*, 14 January; *FBIS*, 16 January). At the Kazakh Writers' Congress in May, which was addressed by Kolbin, the emphasis was on the "internationalist education of the working people" (Alma-Ata Domestic Service, 23 May; *FBIS*, 5 June). A resolution of the CPSU Central Committee in July charged that the former leadership and many party committees in Kazakhstan "have committed serious mistakes in implementing the nationalities policy and have substantially relaxed the work on the working people's international and patriotic education" (*Pravda*, 16 July).

At the January plenum of the Central Committee, Gorbachev maintained the hard-line approach that had been apparent in the leadership's reaction to the events in Alma-Ata. Some difficulties in national relations were charged to actions of previous leaderships; according to Gorbachev, "the negative phenomena and deformations we have been combating have also manifested themselves in the sphere of relations between nationalities." The "enhancement of internationalist education" was the main remedy for situations like the one in Kazakhstan. "It is especially important," Gorbachev said, "to save the rising generation from the demoralizing effect of nationalism" (ibid., 28 January).

Jewish dissidence has long constituted a special case in Soviet nationalities policy. A week after Gorbachev's firm remarks on nationalism to the

Central Committee, Jewish protesters erupted in spectacular fashion at the Arbat shopping mall in central Moscow. Protesters carried placards demanding freedom for Josef Begun, a Jewish activist imprisoned since 1983 on a charge of spreading anti-Soviet propaganda. The Kremlin announced on 10 February the release of 140 political prisoners, but Begun was not included. After a week of demonstrations, plainclothesmen moved in to break up the protest, beating protesters and Western journalists and smashing cameras (AP, 13 February).

TASS the same day accused Western journalists of orchestrating the demonstration and said that police stepped in to prevent violence between protesters and "passersby." The timing of this brutal assertion of police power was particularly unfortunate for the Kremlin, coming as it did on the eve of an international "peace" forum in Moscow that attracted hundreds of Western scientists, politicians, and celebrities. Moreover, Sakharov, following his release from exile in December, resumed his public campaign for the release of all dissidents, while supporting the main outlines of Gorbachev's reform program.

Three days after the police assault on demonstrators and journalists and two days after an announcement that the Begun case was closed, the Kremlin switched gears and ordered the release of Begun (*WP*, 16 February). The reversal came amid reports of rising tension between Gorbachev and the KGB. According to the Moscow rumor factory, Gorbachev overruled the KGB on the release of Sakharov in December, on the Berkhin affair in January, and on the Begun matter.

The leadership may not have been united on questions of *glasnost'* and dissidence, but there was apparently no discord on how to deal with the Jewish minority. The backlog of requests by Jews for emigration has allowed the Kremlin to use the applicants as pawns in international politics, easing restrictions as a "concession" when the leadership seeks improved relations with the West. The tactic was again successful during 1987, with the Soviet drive for accords with the United States, the USSR's effort to improve its image in Western Europe, and the tentative moves toward rapprochement with Israel accompanying an upsurge in emigration.

Western officials in Vienna reported in early September that about 800 Soviet Jews were arriving each month, compared with 945 for all of 1986. Ethnic Germans also benefited from the relaxation: during the first eight months of the year 7,127 had received visas, against 397 in a comparable period in 1986 (*CSM*, 9 September). During September and October, the Soviets granted permission to leave to more than a dozen prominent "refuseniks," including Begun, Ida Nudel, and Vladimir Slepak. The 59-year-old Slepak, who had been sentenced to five years of internal exile in 1978 for displaying a banner from his balcony demanding permission to go to Israel, had been waiting seventeen years (AP, 14 October).

Encouraged by the policy of *glasnost'* and by the apparent success of the Jewish demonstrators, the Crimean Tatars mounted a major campaign for redress of their grievances stemming from Stalin's forced deportation in 1944 of 400,000 Tatars to central Asia. The campaign featured appeals to the Supreme Soviet and enlisting support among Soviet cultural figures and audiences abroad. Evgenii Evtushenko was the most prominent endorser of the Tatars' demands. Meeting with a slow response from officials, the Tatars in July resorted to direct action; on 6 July, about 80 Tatars demonstrated in Red Square to draw attention to their principal demand—permission to return to the Crimea. On 9 July, a commission was set up under the chairmanship of Soviet president Gromyko to study the Tatars' complaints. The Tatars were unimpressed. Their spokesman, Dr. Fuat Albiamitov, cited past broken promises, and on 23 July about 100 Tatars demonstrated near CPSU headquarters in Moscow (Paris AFP, TASS, 23 July; *FBIS*, 24 July), demanding to see Gorbachev "personally."

Russian crowds were generally hostile to the demonstrators, but the police were remarkably restrained. Some Western diplomats speculated that the Tatars' Muslim faith linked the protests to the touchy situation in central Asia and accounted for the Kremlin's moderation on the issue. Police restraint was again evident on 25 July, when more than 300 Tatars staged a more disruptive demonstration in Red Square (*NYT*, 26 July). After 24 hours, the demonstrators dispersed when their leaders accepted an offer of a meeting with Gromyko relayed by interior minister Aleksandr Vlasov (*FBIS*, 27 July).

Rejecting Gromyko's call for their return to central Asia, Tatar leaders said they were "not satisfied" with the outcome of their meeting with Gromyko and vowed to continue demonstrating (Paris AFP, 28 July; *FBIS*, 29 July). On 29 July, a generally sympathetic article in *Moskovskiie novosti* explicitly tied the issue to *glasnost'* and spoke of the danger of "extremist approaches." On the following day, the Tatars staged another demonstration, this one in Pushkin Square. Official reporting grew harsh; TASS termed the demonstrators a "group of extremists" with "incendiary slogans." The police finally took decisive action, forcing the protesters to move to Ismailovo Park and warning individual members that they would be prosecuted if they remained in Moscow. Dissident sources reported that leaders of the protest were being forcefully removed from Moscow and sent back to central Asia (*WP*, 31 July).

In a patterned response that was becoming familiar, the Soviets blamed the United States for the explosive confrontation. U.S. embassy first secretary Shaun M. Byrnes was shown on Soviet television talking with three Tatar activists in Ismailovo Park; he and other U.S. diplomats were accused of instigating the street demonstrations. Embassy spokesman Jaroslav Verner called the charge "absurd" and said that it showed the limits of *glasnost'* (*LAT*, 31 July).

The Tatars subsequently held a series of rallies in central Asia and planned a protest march to the Crimea in October to coincide with the 67th anniversary of the founding of their autonomous republic in the Crimea. The march, scheduled to last for eleven days and end in the Crimean town of Simferopol, was broken up on its second day, four miles from its starting point, the Caucasian port of Taman (Paris AFP, 8 October; *FBIS*, 9 October).

With Tatar protest apparently under control, the commission headed by Gromyko finally issued its report on 15 October. A bland document that avoided the main issues, the report called for measures to meet the "cultural demands" of the Tatars and for more exact determination of "the rules of domicile and residence" in the Crimea. However, the report implied that the latter recommendation was based on the importance of the Crimea as a vacation area, not on the grievances of the Tatars. The commission noted that it had received some 10,000 letters calling for "resolute action" to curb the activity of "extremist-minded persons" among the Crimean Tatars (TASS, 15 October; *FBIS*, 16 October).

The most extensive protests were demonstrations in the Baltic states that continued into November. On 14 June demonstrators laid flowers at a monument in Riga to commemorate Latvians who were deported in 1942 to the Soviet Union. Encouraged by the mild police response, demonstrators turned out in all three Baltic capitals on 23 August, the 48th anniversary of the Nazi-Soviet pact, to protest the USSR's seizure of the states in 1940 and its distortion in official Soviet accounts of the period. Some 500 demonstrators reportedly gathered in Vilnius, and more than 5,000 gathered in Riga (AP, 23 August). TASS (23 August) charged that the protest in Tallin was "instigated by the Voice of America, the subversive Free Europe and Liberty radio stations." But Latvian television reportedly gave objective coverage to the demonstration in Riga, and an official commentator criticized the police (*CSM*, 27 August).

A series of disorders related to nationalism followed in Estonia, beginning with an anti-Russian demonstration on 23 August at a volleyball match between U.S. and Soviet teams in Tallin that was televised throughout the USSR. In October, there were at least two major disturbances motivated by nationalism that were reported in the official press (*FBIS*, 12 November). On the anniversary of Latvia's independence in November, more than 8,000 turned out in Riga for a demonstration that was suppressed by the police (*WSJ*, 19 November).

Issues related to nationalism also appeared in other republics. Participants at a session of the presidium of the Board of the Ukrainian Writers' Union on 10 February criticized the "second-class" status of the Ukrainian language in various institutions of the republic, especially schools, and demanded repeal of legislation that makes study of the native language voluntary (*Literaturna Ukraina*, 12 March; *RL Research*, 24 March). In a move certain to arouse widespread resentment among predominantly Muslim central Asians, the government of Tadzhikistan announced a propaganda campaign to persuade women in the republic to have fewer children (*Kommunist Tadzhikistana*, 20 January; *RL Research*, 2 February).

Estimates varied on the number of dissidents still imprisoned in the USSR, but of those released during the year, political prisoners were a definite minority. Moreover, there were signs that, behind a facade of *glasnost'*, the mechanisms of the police state were operating much the same as before. Vladimir Titov, a dissident released from a psychiatric hospital on 9 October, said that the use of punitive psychiatric treatment in Soviet hospitals had not changed despite recent public criticism of such practices in the Soviet press. "There are no changes," Titov said, "on the contrary, it's getting nastier" (*NYT*, 21 October). In November, "Press Club *Glasnost'*," an independent human rights group, reported that KGB agents and uniformed police had beaten and kidnapped activists in a "widespread campaign of repression" as the

Reagan-Gorbachev summit drew near (AP, 27 November).

At year's end, the pressures that had yielded a rather erratic approach to questions of human rights and dissent, particularly those related to nationalism, posed the threat of a "scissors crisis" for Gorbachev's reform program. If *glasnost'* proceeded largely unchecked, nationalist agitation seemed certain to accelerate, and such discord would surely give added weight to hard-line demands for a return to more rigid controls and a suspension of the processes of "democratization."

Auxiliary and Front Organizations. Activities of auxiliary organizations during the year concentrated mainly on the various campaigns initiated by General Secretary Gorbachev. The All-Union Women's Conference, attended by 1,200 delegates, was held at the Kremlin in January under the direction of Valentina Tereshkova, head of the Soviet Women's Committee. The conference adopted plans for a network of women's councils to promote the "active drawing of women into the public and political life" and for a World Women's Congress to be held in Moscow during June 1988. The slogan of the congress will be "no nuclear weapons by the year 2000: peace, equality and development for all" (TASS, 30 January; *Izvestiia*, 2 February).

The Eighteenth Congress of the USSR Union of Journalists, held in Moscow during 14–16 March, was dominated by *glasnost'*, but much of the formal work of the congress seemed aimed at setting bounds for "openness" by the press. Although most speeches reflected conservative or cautious approaches, Aleksandr Bovin, political commentator of *Izvestiia*, sharply criticized foreign reporting by Soviet journalists, saying that it was still dominated by "standard formulas" (*Sovetskaia kultura*, 17 March; RL *Research*, 24 March).

The All-Union Komsomol, already reeling from a steady drumbeat of criticism, heard additional strictures at its Twentieth Congress, held at Moscow during April. In his opening speech to the congress, First Secretary Viktor Mironenko said that the Komsomol had suffered an almost complete loss of authority and that the organization still suffered from bureaucratic methods, although more than 3,000 officials had been fired during the previous four years (*Pravda*, 16 April). CPSU general secretary Gorbachev, speaking on the second day of the congress, also charged that the Komsomol had become enmeshed in bureaucracy but said this was partially due to denial of independence for the youth organization by superior organs. His speech was largely an attempt to rally support of young people for his reform program, and he maintained that the success of *perestroika* would depend on the attitudes and actions of Soviet youth (ibid., 17 April).

The All-Union Voluntary Sobriety Society claims 14 million members who are active in some 450,000 primary organizations and hundreds of "sobriety clubs." On the occasion of the 2d anniversary of the society's founding, it was credited with a major role in the antialcohol drive that resulted, according to official reports, in cutting consumption of alcohol by half, increasing average life expectancy, and changing "previously ingrained views on drunkenness as an inevitable and insurmountable phenomenon" (Moscow Domestic Service, *FBIS*, 25 September). However, later society reports printed in the official press spoke of serious backsliding after early gains in the campaign, with even Sobriety Society branch chiefs being brought to police sobering-up stations.

International Views, Positions, and Activities. The search for a breakthrough arms accord with the United States dominated the USSR's foreign relations during the year. Not only was this the centerpiece of Moscow's world policy, but it was closely linked to key objectives of Gorbachev's domestic program. When he assumed power in 1985, Gorbachev appeared to have a mandate to reverse unfavorable trends in the global "correlation of forces." The biggest stumbling block to such a recovery on the international front was the multifaceted decline at home, and Gorbachev repeatedly stressed that the ultimate purpose of *perestroika* was to enable the USSR to continue to function as a great power.

Given the urgent requirements of domestic economic renovation, there was pressure to transfer resources from the military to the civilian sector of the economy, but continued high levels of international tension would likely lead to increases, in both absolute and relative terms, in Soviet arms expenditures. Thus a resumption of détente centered on arms control measures could be vital for *perestroika*, and Gorbachev evidently sold other members of the Soviet leadership on this linkage.

Determination of the main lines of USSR foreign policy was not, however, simply a by-product of domestic crisis. The military component of the "correlation of forces," acknowledged by the Soviets to be the principal factor in the rise to superpower status, turned out to be, in many respects, counterproductive. The installation of SS-20 missiles targeted on Western Europe, a gamble for regional supremacy in the "correlation of forces," provoked the Western response of the Euromissiles and the strongest cohesion of the NATO alliance in three decades. The invasion of Afghanistan resulted in the immediate scuttling of the last vestiges of détente and alienated much of the Third World, particularly the Arab-Muslim countries. The Soviet thrust for expanded influence in key areas of the Third World through support of proxies, a successful gambit in the 1970s, turned sour as U.S. aid, under the impetus of the Reagan administration's drive to halt the succession of cheap victories for Moscow, flowed to the USSR's opponents. Virtually everywhere the Soviets had made gains in the 1970s, "freedom fighters" stubbornly contested Moscow's clients at an increasing cost to the USSR.

The flawed reliance on military power increasingly isolated the USSR from other actors in the international arena, which was compounded by Soviet belligerence and ineptitude in relations with the outside world. By the time Gorbachev came to power, this isolation was complete enough that a continuation of the prevailing course was untenable. The adoption of new methods, strategies, and tactics in the Soviet approach to world affairs seemed imperative.

A fresh approach to diplomacy became evident with the appointment of Shevardnadze as foreign minister in July 1985 and was confirmed by personnel changes in 1986. In March Dobrynin, generally considered as the ablest Soviet world diplomat, came from Washington to assume command of the Central Committee's International Department. During the summer, a thoroughgoing reorganization of the foreign ministry was effected, reportedly supervised by Dobrynin. During the course of the year, virtually all key embassies and many lesser ones had their incumbents displaced by new men, mostly more competent and more professional than their predecessors. A new style was manifest in the execution of policy, personified by Gorbachev himself—more flexible, superficially convivial, and highly sensitive to the impact of public opinion in the democratic countries. The new team proved extraordinarily proficient in the manipulation of "peace" issues, in contrast to the heavy-handed bungling of Gromyko.

The new approach was aided immensely by the impression that monumental changes were afoot within the USSR where the image was conveyed of a society being rapidly transformed so that it no longer posed the same threat to the free world. The new leader's splashy entry into the realm of international politics epitomized the fresh approach and new image of the USSR, and he became an invaluable foreign policy asset. During the summer of 1987, public opinion polls in Europe showed Gorbachev to be more popular than Reagan, and surveys in the United States at the time of the Washington summit in December confirmed that the Soviet leader's appeal extended to the American public as well. Above all, the revolution in Soviet diplomacy established a credibility for the Kremlin among Western publics that was truly remarkable in view of the Soviets' recent record in both domestic and foreign affairs.

However refreshing the new style, its significance lay in the establishment of preconditions for realistic dealing with questions of substance. On the general direction of policy, two schools of thought appeared in the Soviet leadership, represented by Gorbachev's two principal advisors, Dobrynin and party secretary Yakovlev. Dobrynin, the principal vehicle for Soviet-American diplomacy during the heyday of détente, considered superpower relations as the crucial aspect of Soviet foreign policy. Yakovlev, on the other hand, expressed in print his view that superpower relations should be downplayed and that concentration should be on the upgrading of the Soviets' world position through amelioration of relations with Western Europe and the other "borderlands" on the USSR's periphery. Gorbachev's contribution appears to have been a synthesis of these opposing views. It seemed possible to have it both ways. Such an outcome could be sought through the medium of arms control negotiations, and the sine qua non was arms reductions in central Europe.

The Soviets had treated Star Wars as the supreme issue of international politics for nearly three years up to the Reykjavik summit, and, indeed, they could not afford a protracted race for space in view of the USSR's technological disadvantage, despite the early Soviet lead in development of space weaponry. The Reykjavik summit broke up over the issue of the U.S. Strategic Defense Initiative (SDI), but this was a case of Gorbachev going for the whole ball game. In the drawn-out interplay leading to an agreement, he had to probe for an opening that might permit him to attain maximum aims. But SDI was, at worst, a distant threat, one that might well be dissipated by U.S. domestic political processes, and such an eventuality could be promoted by a demonstration of the decreasing necessity for the program.

The Soviets' real and overriding objective was central Europe. The U.S. side, aware of this, held top card and played it skillfully.

The Soviet installation of SS-20 missiles had been the biggest blunder since the Cuban missile crisis. The NATO response left the USSR under the nuclear gun as never before and with a position in the strategic balance inferior to that of ten years earlier. The paramount importance of the removal of this threat led Gorbachev in 1987 to drop the side issue of SDI and accept Reagan's "zero option," which had first been widely considered as an empty U.S. bargaining ploy. Obscured for much of the year by the usual diplomatic verbiage, this was the essential fact: once the "zero option" had been agreed on, achievement of an agreement was largely a diplomatic mopping-up operation.

In December at the Washington summit, Reagan and Gorbachev signed the first agreement to eliminate a whole category of weapons. The treaty was also remarkable in that both sides could plausibly advertise it as a victory. The pact amounted to total achievement of the objective set by the NATO alliance in 1979 when the Euromissile program had been made contingent on the presence or absence of Soviet intermediate-range missiles targeted on Western Europe. For the Soviets, it involved elimination of the perceived threat posed by the Euromissiles and wiped the slate clean on the serious miscalculation of an earlier leadership.

Like the Cuban missile crisis, which resulted in legitimation of the communist foothold in the Western Hemisphere, recovery from this blunder could have desirable long-range consequences. The perception of the USSR as a superpower committed to nuclear disarmament could further a Soviet-European diplomatic strategy and have a beneficial effect on relations with the rising powers of East Asia as well, although, objectively, the overall relative power of the USSR was at least as great as before. Some critics of the accords thought the "Soviet threat" was increased by the superpower agreement. A potential benefit of the agreement might lie in the long-sought "uncoupling" of U.S. and West European defenses, a prospect stressed by conservative opponents of the agreement in the United States. Much would depend on the negotiations expected to follow the Washington summit on conventional forces, space weaponry, and long-range strategic arms.

It seemed more than coincidental that the breaking of the arms control impasse closely followed the further sharp reduction of military influence on Soviet policy. After the young West German amateur pilot Rust flew across western Russia in May and used Red Square as a landing strip, Gorbachev had shaken up the defense ministry, putting his favorite general, Yazov, in as defense minister. Although Chief of Staff Marshal Sergei Akhromeyev was treated to a remarkable tour of the secret corridors and recesses of the Pentagon, the generals played a decidedly secondary role at the summit. Military officers did, however, play an important technical advisory role in the negotiations immediately before the summit.

All aspects of foreign policy were now firmly under party control, emphasized by the conspicuous proximity of Dobrynin and Yakovlev to Gorbachev at various meetings and public appearances in Washington. Within the party, basic foreign policy decisions appeared to have a consensus not prone to the fissures that were obvious in domestic affairs. The results of the summit seemed likely to strengthen Gorbachev's hand in treatment of other important international problems.

Among the more important of these was Afghanistan, a touchstone for improvement of Soviet relations with China, the Arab-Muslim countries, and the Third World generally. No progress on the issue was reported at the summit, but the often-rumored Soviet pullout from Afghanistan seemed finally to be imminent. Unable to win the war, the puppet regime in Kabul was going to some lengths to distance itself from Moscow, and the Soviets were reportedly proceeding with their own timetable for winding down the intervention. But details of a face-saving solution for a final withdrawal remained to be worked out.

The Soviets maintained and even increased support for Third World footholds other than Afghanistan but toned down backing for controversial non-Marxist regimes in Libya and Syria in the interest of other important objectives. Meanwhile, Moscow courted influential, non-Marxist countries such as Mexico, Brazil, and Kuwait using diplomatic, economic, and other means to expand influence in developing regions.

Although some incidents, deriving primarily from Soviet aggressiveness, frequently marred relations with particular countries outside the bloc, there was generally a much less abrasive posture by Moscow and a more cooperative attitude, less colored by ideology. This changed stance extended to such formerly divisive issues as terrorism and the Persian Gulf. But the Soviets showed no inclination to renounce long-standing regional goals and seemed as determined as ever to play a major role in the Middle East. With this end in view, Moscow made significant progress in thawing the once-glacial relations with Israel.

The Soviets turned a new face to the world under Gorbachev. With radical changes in style and tactics, they sought to dispel the image of a threatening colossus and to replace it with one of a trusting and trustworthy member of the world community. There were indications that large sections of the world audience had been captivated by the dazzling break with traditional practices. But concessions made by the Soviets on several fronts in no way implied a retrenchment in the USSR's aspirations for a continuing superpower role.

On the contrary, Gorbachev and his associates clearly aimed for enhanced Soviet influence in the world during a period of probable upheaval at home. The revamped Soviet foreign policy apparatus pursued goals by more economical means, in line with the similar thrust in domestic policy, and successes could be expected to have a stabilizing effect on the unsettled internal political situation.

At the end of the year, Soviet gains in foreign affairs appeared quite impressive. In a very short time, the USSR had emerged from stark isolation to resume a central role in the world political arena. But a further expansion of that role would require resolution of complex issues, and the way ahead was fraught with difficulties. The Soviet-U.S. rapprochement was conditioned by the inability of the superpowers to maintain the tenuous polarization that had undergirded general peace for more than four decades.

A redistribution of world power was slowly evolving that would evoke new issues that could not be resolved by the joint efforts of the USSR and the United States. But for the near future, Soviet-U.S. relations seemed likely to continue as the hinge of Moscow's general policy. In the superpower era, relations between Moscow and Washington had proceeded in a staccato rhythm, alternating between détente and confrontation, ultimately propelled by domestic politics on both sides. Given its critical domestic situation, the USSR needed more than a temporary respite in its competition with the United States. But doubts lingered in the West as to whether the image and reality of the USSR under Gorbachev corresponded to the current version of détente.

Arms Control. In the aftermath of the Reykjavik summit, the atmosphere during the early weeks of the year did not seem conducive to agreement. The Soviet media regularly blasted the United States for the failure to achieve a dramatic breakthrough on nuclear arms, citing Reagan's stubborn insistence on Star Wars as the principal obstacle. In a major development, the USSR announced on 26 February that it had resumed nuclear testing after a nineteen-month moratorium because of the U.S. refusal to follow suit (TASS, 26 February; *NYT*, 27 February).

Washington reacted with studied indifference to the Soviet resumption of tests but responded with intense negotiations in Geneva after a Gorbachev speech at the beginning of March. The Soviet leader accepted in principle the "zero option" and proposed that all USSR and U.S. medium-range missiles be removed from Europe, with each side retaining 100. The Soviets would be allowed to deploy theirs in Soviet Asia, and the Americans, in the United States. Significantly, the speech contained no demand for a simultaneous accord on space-based defenses. The U.S. negotiators at Geneva welcomed the change in the Soviet position but raised the issues of verification and short-range missiles (*WP*, 23 March). Three weeks after the Gorbachev speech, White House chief of staff Howard Baker said on U.S. television that the superpowers were drawing closer to an arms control agreement and that he "would not be surprised" to see a Reagan-Gorbachev summit in Washington before the end of the year (UPI, 23 March).

On the same day as the favorable Baker assessment, the former chief Soviet negotiator at the Geneva talks, Viktor Karpov, said that U.S. reservations on Pershing II and cruise missiles meant that the United States was attempting to back out of an agreement. "There are more and more indications," he said, "that the United States does not want the elimination of European-based medium-range nuclear missiles" and added that "the so-called zero option was a bluff from the very start." However, he reiterated the Soviet willingness to accept the "zero option": "We are prepared to eliminate all of our medium-range missiles in Europe, to scrap all the SS-20s, whose number is 243, together with their launching pads" (*Izvestiia*, 22 March).

In Geneva, U.S. chief negotiator Max Kampelman pressed for a global "zero option" that would entail no SS-20s or shorter ranger intermediate-range nuclear forces (INF) missiles anywhere in the USSR. During U.S. secretary of state George Shultz's visit to Moscow in mid-April, Gorbachev conceded the point and agreed that all INF missiles would be eliminated throughout the USSR (*Pravda*, 16 April).

The following week some Western European officials openly expressed doubts about such a deal, worrying that elimination of nuclear weapons on the continent would leave their countries in the precarious position of facing Soviet superiority in conventional weaponry. In a blistering commentary, the Soviet press agency accused the NATO countries of stepping back "from their own proposals," and Ligachev told a visiting U.S. delegation that whether the Soviet arms proposals are translated into reality "depends entirely on the United States" (TASS, 17 April; AP, 18 April).

Ligachev's challenge, however, was not entirely in accord with the facts. The Soviet delegation at Geneva, headed since January by First Deputy Foreign Minister Yuli Vorontsov, continued to advocate "zero option" for Europe only, a position earlier rejected by the United States and supposedly superseded in Gorbachev's talks with Shultz. This aroused speculation that Gorbachev's move might have been entirely his own and that the Politburo had failed to endorse it. On this view, when Ligachev made his 17 April "take it or leave it" comment, he was challenging the United States to return to the unacceptable negotiating situation obtaining before 15 April.

After Vorontsov finally got around to making the new Gorbachev proposal, the talks in Geneva went more smoothly, concentrating on details of verification. But public comments by negotiators for both sides in late July and early August indicated that there were still obstacles to an INF agreement. Moreover, the multiple negotiations going on in Geneva apparently produced some confusion.

It was unclear whether there would be an agreement on long-range strategic arms and whether, or how, such a pact might be linked to INF and Star Wars. On 31 July, the Soviet side presented a draft treaty calling for the superpowers to cut their long-range nuclear arsenals in half, but it linked an accord to limits on the U.S. Star Wars system. U.S. Arms Control and Disarmament Agency director Kenneth Adelman called the proposal unacceptable because it did not limit the USSR land-based missiles. He accused the Soviets of "stonewalling" in their insistence on significant reductions in SDI (AP, 1 August).

Shevardnadze and Kampelman evidently cut the Gordian knot by concentrating on an INF deal when the Soviet foreign minister came to Geneva to address the 40-nation Conference on Disarmament in the first week of August. Shevardnadze told reporters that a medium-range agreement "is almost elaborated." He said that "a great many outstanding questions do remain. But they are not insurmountable." (Ibid., 6 August.)

Shultz and Shevardnadze subsequently settled the main points at issue between the two sides, and it was announced that Gorbachev and Reagan would meet at Washington in December to sign an INF treaty (*NYT*, 19 September). At the end of October, Reagan announced at a press conference in Washington, with Shultz and Shevardnadze present, that 7 December had been set as the opening day of the meeting (*WP*, 31 October). However, many details remained to be worked out, and the two sides were pressed to meet the deadline. Soviet and U.S. negotiating teams flew together across the Atlantic on the eve of the summit to put the final touches to the treaty while en route (NBC News, 7 December).

The treaty, signed on 8 December, requires destruction of all missiles that can strike targets 300 to 3,400 miles from their launch sites and withdrawal (but not destruction) of the approximately 3,800 warheads and their guidance mechanisms. The most important weapons are the Soviet SS-20s and the U.S. Pershing-2 and ground-launched cruise missiles (AP, 8 December). The treaty also provides for verification by the two sides of each other's missile destruction and for unprecedented on-site and short-notice inspection of production facilities (*NYT*, 10 December). Once details of the pact were released, critics immediately complained that most of the covered missiles are mobile and that some resemble others outside the affected class, making compliance difficult to ensure (AP, *WP*, 8, 9, 10 December).

The two sides failed to arrive at definite agreement for long-range weapons, but, at a press conference before his departure from Washington, Gorbachev reported that progress had been made. He said that a sublimit of 4,900 for intercontinental ballistic missiles and air-launched cruise missiles within a broad ceiling of 6,000 had been agreed on and that the United States had indicated willingness to set limits for long-range missiles launched from submarines (NBC News, 9 December).

U.S. officials said that the two sides remained divided over how many intercontinental ballistic missiles could be heavy missiles. They also reported that the United States preserved the right for broad testing under the SDI but agreed to adhere to the 1972 anti-ballistic missile (ABM) treaty for a period of time yet to be negotiated. Gorbachev acknowledged that the ABM treaty permits research and development and "if necessary, tests" authorized by the pact (AP, 11 December).

White House spokesman Marlin Fitzwater said that the two leaders agreed to hold another summit, their fourth, in Moscow during the first half of 1988 (*NYT*, 11 December). A U.S. administration official said that "it might be possible with hard work" to have a strategic arms pact ready for signing at Moscow but that a summit would be held whether or not a pact is ready (UPI, 11 December).

On his return to Moscow, Gorbachev told a nationwide television audience that "it is far too early to speak about a drastic turn in our relations" and disagreed with Reagan's assessment that SDI would no longer block progress on negotiations to cut both sides' long-range nuclear missiles by 50 percent (Moscow Television, TASS, 14 December).

Other U.S.-Soviet Relations. The USSR campaign to favorably influence U.S. public opinion continued in high gear throughout the year. Prominent Americans were welcomed to Moscow, and the Soviets went to some lengths to display their new openness, including a tour of the controversial Krasnoyarsk radar facility for a visiting U.S. congressional delegation. Soviet-U.S. television exchanges became commonplace, culminating in an hour-long interview of Gorbachev by Tom Brokaw on NBC television shortly before the summit. In May, the U.S. embassy in Moscow reported that the Soviets had stopped jamming Voice of America broadcasts into the country for the first time in seven years (*WP*, 26 May).

The general tone for friendlier contacts was set by Gorbachev in early February when he met for three hours in the Kremlin with a group of prominent Americans, sponsored by the Council on Foreign Relations. The visitors included former Secretaries of State Henry Kissinger and Cyrus Vance, former Secretary of Defense Harold Brown, former Ambassador to the United Nations Jeane Kirkpatrick, and six others (TASS, 3 February). The Americans declined to discuss details of their conversation with Gorbachev, but several said they had been impressed by his grasp of international relations and his vigorous presentation. The group subsequently met with Sakharov (*NYT*, 4 February).

The promotion of *glasnost'* did not, however, entirely dispel the old image of Soviet abrasiveness; several ugly incidents produced minor strains in U.S.-Soviet relations. In May, the USSR charged that four U.S. diplomats (Earl Irving, Stephen Young, Allen Westrom, and Clifford Hart), had tried to instigate trouble in Central Asia earlier in the year by offering to help Kirghiz students fight against ethnic Russians (TASS, 6 May). A U.S. embassy spokesman characterized the charges as "absurd," "disinformation," and "slander" (AP, 7 May).

In June, the Novosti Press Agency published a report that Americans were using "war gases" in developing countries. Charles Wick, head of the U.S. Information Agency, in Moscow for the opening of the "Information USA" exhibit, met with Novosti head Valentin Falin to complain. Wick said the meeting ended abruptly after Falin read off a list of alleged U.S. "ethnic warfare" atrocities, including its treatment of American Indians, experiments on Japanese in World War II, responsibility for "epidemics now sweeping Nicaragua and Cuba," and development of a gas used in Africa that is deadly to blacks but not harmful to whites. Wick also complained that although the Soviets had stopped jamming Voice of America broadcasts, they were still trying to interfere with Radio Free Europe and Radio Liberty (*LAT*, 6 June).

New Politburo member Viktor Nikonov led a delegation of Soviet agricultural officials on a tour of America's midwestern farm belt in October. The delegation, particularly its leader Nikonov, acted more like Vyshinsky and Molotov than ambassadors of goodwill and *glasnost'* and left several U.S. congressmen angry about what they called the delegation's rude and insulting behavior.

At one stop, Nikonov responded to a toast by a U.S. businessman with a lecture that the meeting should be used for business, not eloquence. The delegation walked out on a presentation by an Iowa farm economist, and when officials of the Chicago Board of Trade expressed hopes for increased U.S.-Soviet trade, Nikonov replied with a tirade against the capitalist system (Knight-Ridder newspapers, 13 October).

Western Europe. The impending superpower arms agreement also dominated Soviet relations with West European countries during the year. In official circles of the NATO governments, there were strong reservations about the removal of the Euromissiles, and considerable pressure was exerted by Washington, particularly on Bonn and London, to induce the allies to go along with the proposals. Following the signing of the INF treaty, West Europeans generally welcomed the new atmosphere, and anti-nuclear activists staged jubilant celebrations. Official reaction was mixed.

Gorbachev stopped in London on his way to Washington for a talk with British prime minister Margaret Thatcher, a move resented in Washington as a possible attempt to split the NATO alliance (*NYT*, 8 December). Gorbachev's visit may have had a reassuring effect on the dubious Thatcher; she publicly hailed the treaty as "a marvelous Christmas present." But she also emphasized the need to hold on to 4,000 or so nuclear weapons not covered by the treaty to compensate for the USSR's superiority in conventional forces (*LAT*, 12 December). A week after the Washington summit, Britain and France announced plans for joint development of an air-launched missile, and their spokesmen insisted, despite Soviet complaints, that the new weapon would not undermine the superpower INF treaty (*NYT*, 15 December).

Volker Ruhle, defense spokesman for West German chancellor Helmut Kohl, said that "all the remaining land-based systems will now be exclusively on German soil." That, he argued, violates the alliance's doctrine of risk-sharing. Conservative critics in France spoke of "another Yalta," and President François Mitterrand called the treaty "not much" but nevertheless "important" (*LAT*, 12 December).

The advent of *glasnost'* and Moscow's European strategy did nothing to slow Soviet industrial espionage, and more spy rings were uncovered during the year. In the first week of April, France expelled three USSR diplomats (AFP, 3 April). No reason was given for the expulsions, but they were assumed to be related to the arrests of seven people accused of gathering information on Europe's Ariane space rocket and other technology for a Soviet bloc country. In retaliation, the USSR expelled four French diplomats and two French businessmen (AP, 5 April).

Norway expelled a Soviet diplomat and two USSR trade mission delegates in July; they were accused of working for the KGB to gather industrial intelligence on high technology. Moscow responded by declaring two Norwegian diplomats persona non grata. Despite the resulting diplomatic tension, Norwegian foreign minister Thorvald Stoltenberg said that an official visit by Soviet premier Ryzhkov, set for January 1988, would go ahead as scheduled. Stoltenberg also said that no Norwegians were suspected of wrongdoing in the case (AP, TASS, Beijing Xinhua, 31 July; *FBIS*, 4 August).

Norwegian citizens were found to be involved in two other espionage scandals uncovered later in the year. The state-owned Kongsberg Vaapenfabrikk arms firm was found by the Norwegian police to be involved in a decade-long pattern of illegal high-tech sales, which helped the USSR in the construction of nuclear weapons and naval vessels. Five other firms in Italy, West Germany, Britain, and France were identified as participants in the illegal sales. The Norwegian investigation was started after the discovery that Kongsberg and Toshiba Corporation of Japan had sold computerized milling tools to the Soviets, a transaction that allowed the USSR to develop quiet submarine propellers capable of evading U.S. navy surveillance (*WP*, *NYT*, 22 October).

Soviet relations with Sweden, strained in recent years by submarine incursions into Swedish waters and clandestine *spetsnaz* visits, improved somewhat as Moscow made gestures to lower the diplomatic temperature. In February, the USSR allowed sixteen Soviet citizens to join their families in Sweden (AP, 6 February). During the summer, the USSR made a turnaround on the disputed waters of the Baltic. Soviet deputy foreign minister Valentin Nikiforov presented to Swedish premier Ingmar Carlsson a proposal that would allow Sweden to take more than half of the "white zone" previously claimed by the USSR (*Insight*, 6 July).

Soviet premier Ryzhkov visited Austria in July and concluded agreements on cross-Danube trade between the USSR and Austria, supplying of natural gas after the year 2000, and civil aviation (*Pravda*, 10 July). Ryzhkov also pushed for Austrian participation in the recently authorized joint economic ventures (TASS, 10 July; *FBIS*, 14 July).

While the Soviets sought to develop new relationships throughout the region, the key country remained West Germany, which was crucial both for an INF accord and, as the USSR's number one trading partner in the West, for technological imports sorely needed by the Soviet economy. In July, West German president Richard von Weizsäcker and foreign minister Hans-Dietrich Genscher were welcomed to Moscow for talks with Gorbachev, Shevardnadze, USSR president Gromyko, and Secretary Yakovlev. A protocol was signed putting into effect treaties signed during April and May on scientific and technical cooperation in various fields. In his welcoming speech, Gromyko emphasized Gorbachev's favored themes of "our common European home" and a "single historical destiny" (*Pravda*, 7 July). But it was clear that many obstacles existed in regard to West Germany's place in Gorbachev's European strategy. The talks covered a broad range of sensitive issues, including arms reductions, and the Soviet media described the conversation between Gorbachev and Weizsäcker as "frank" (Moscow Domestic Service, 8 July; *FBIS*, 10 July).

Two incidents marred the initially cordial atmosphere at the Moscow talks. Genscher expressed "astonishment" about the censorship of Weizsäcker's speech in response to Gromyko. *Pravda* (7 July) omitted the West German president's statements about better emigration opportunities for ethnic German Soviet citizens and about the division of Germany. On the final day of the meetings, Gromyko handed Weizsäcker a list containing fifteen names of alleged war criminals wanted by the USSR and said to be living in West Germany. Nevertheless, assessment of the Moscow talks by the two principal West German participants was upbeat.

Weizsäcker described the talk with Gorbachev as "intensive, serious, open, and trusting" and affirmed that there would be a meeting between Gorbachev and Chancellor Kohl. No date was set for such a meeting, but it was expected to take place in early 1988. Genscher said that a desire on both sides for a "cardinal improvement" in relations was the decisive result of the Moscow talks and came out against those doubting the sincerity of the Soviet policy of restructuring and openness (Hamburg DPA, 7 July; *FBIS*, 10 July).

Although President Weizsäcker had insisted in Moscow on acceleration of ethnic German emigration, the USSR's improved record in this matter was a factor both in the scheduling of the talks and in the ensuing softer diplomatic tones. By August, a total of 5,432 ethnic Germans had been allowed to leave the USSR, more than seven times that for all of 1986 (BBC Caris, 5 August).

Behind the scenes, Yuli Kvitsinsky, USSR ambassador to Bonn and a veteran of the Geneva arms negotiations and fluent in German, worked effectively to sell Moscow's case on INF and prepared the ground for the next step in Soviet–West German rapprochement. Dobrynin spent six days in Bonn during October at the invitation of the Social Democratic Party and met with Chancellor Kohl. Dobrynin, the highest-ranking Soviet official to visit Bonn since 1983, reportedly thanked Kohl for his willingness to eliminate West Germany's 72 Pershing IA missiles and confirmed a November conference between Shevardnadze and Genscher to discuss a 1988 meeting between Kohl and Gorbachev. But Dobrynin threw cold water on hopes for a radical Soviet turnaround on questions of the division of Germany. Rumors had been flying for weeks of a changed Soviet stance on the status of the two German regimes, including the possibility of dismantling the Berlin Wall, and this speculation had been fed by comments of mid-level Soviet officials. At a Bonn press conference, Dobrynin, saying that he was speaking for the CPSU Central Committee, asserted that Moscow's position on Berlin and the "German question" was unchanged and that speculation and "fantasies" should be stopped (*Frankfurter Allgemeine Zeitung*, 9, 13 October; RFE *Research*, 22 October).

The Soviets maintained the heightened level of contacts with West Germany for the remainder of the year, including consultations with Genscher in Bonn immediately following the Washington summit.

In the final week of the year, Franz-Josef Strauss was welcomed to Moscow, where he met with Gorbachev. Strauss, the leader of the Bavarian Christian Social Union and once scorned by Moscow as a reactionary militarist, said that a "new political era" has begun for the USSR and West Germany. Strauss strongly advocated increased business dealings between the two countries but gave a mixed review of the Soviet-American INF treaty (*LAT*, 31 December).

Eastern Europe. Moscow devoted a great deal of attention to the East European bloc, concentrating on building support for its arms control initiatives, which were highly popular in the region. In East Germany and Czechoslovakia, there was hope that arms accords would result in removal of the Soviet missiles stationed in those countries. For the region as a whole, the prospect of reduction in conventional forces holds out hope for lessening of the USSR military presence in the northern tier of states and in Hungary. Such an outcome would probably lessen direct Soviet influence in the region, as would various other aspects of Gorbachev's European strategy.

For the present, Soviet domestic reform complicated Moscow's relations with old-line leaders of the East European regimes, who resist any spillover of *perestroika* and *glasnost'* into their societies. Unable to control the flow of events in the region, the Soviets projected a posture of noninterference in domestic affairs, while attempting to maintain military and economic cohesion.

There were indications of more flexible approaches to various issues by the Soviets and the bloc countries. A slight but noticeable cooling toward terrorism and hostage-taking was noted by Western experts. The USSR and Bulgaria evidenced a rhetorical shift on the issue, and some East European countries cut back the number of diplomats from Middle Eastern countries associated with terrorism, such as Libya. Hungary was reported to be actively cooperating with Western governments in tracing international terrorists (*CSM*, 20 March).

Gorbachev and General Wojciech Jaruzelski, meeting in Moscow during April, called for seeing the "truth in its entirety" about Soviet-Polish history (*NYT*, 27 April). This was welcomed in Poland, particularly in regard to the projected opening of long-secret files (*CSM*, 29 May). However, expectations about greater historical openness were considerably diminished by Gorbachev's defense of the Nazi-Soviet pact at the time of the 70th anniversary celebration of the October Revolution.

Meetings between representatives of CMEA and the European Economic Community were directed toward expansion of trade between East and West, with major emphasis on badly needed imports of technology to the Soviet bloc. The Political Consultative Committee of the World Trade Organization issued a strong endorsement of the establishment of "normal" relations between CMEA and EEC (TASS, 8 June; *FBIS*, 12 June).

Within the bloc, the overriding issue for political leaders was the possible effect of Soviet internal developments on their own regimes. No one gave more than lip service to the Soviet reforms, and there was much outright opposition to any application of the Gorbachev program in the other countries. Hungary, which had long ago carried out more sweeping economic reforms than those scheduled in the USSR, stepped up its repression of dissidence as did Czechoslovakia, which in February prosecuted five jazz enthusiasts for publishing uncensored materials. Even Poland, whose leader Jaruzelski has developed extremely close relations with Gorbachev, gave no indication of emulating any part of the Soviet leader's domestic program (*NYT*, 5 April), although committed to a Polish version of "restructuring." In East Germany, Margot Honecker, education minister and wife of Socialist Unity Party head Erich Honecker, published an article in the party youth newspaper denouncing "naive attempts to liberalize communism" (*Foreign Report*, 2 July).

Although Gorbachev evoked much popular enthusiasm on his travels in the bloc countries, he apparently had little impact on political leaderships. His April visit to Prague was postponed for three days, officially charged to a "slight cold" but attributed by Western observers to disagreements within both the Soviet and Czechoslovak leaderships over Gorbachev's reform program. When he made his rescheduled visit, Gorbachev defended the Soviet domestic reforms but stressed that the CPSU was not calling upon other socialist countries to copy the Soviet experience (*Pravda*, 11 April). The Czechoslovak leadership had been particularly sensitive about the Soviet domestic program because many veterans of the Prague Spring viewed it as similar to the crushed liberalization drive of Alexander Dubček in 1968. On the most important issue, that of a possible withdrawal by some of the 80,000 Soviet troops in Czechoslovakia, Gorbachev said nothing during his Prague sojourn.

A May visit by the Soviet leader to Bucharest left unchanged the USSR's relationship with the highly independent Romanian regime. Romania's president, Nicolae Ceauşescu, wished the Soviets "bigger successes" in their reform program but said that Romania had already achieved success in the "broadening and improvement of the democratic framework" and "democratic management" of its economy (ibid., 26 May). Internally, the Ceauşescu policies on domestic control were diametrically opposed to those of Moscow, and the Romanian leader displayed his aversion to *glasnost'* on the eve of the Gorbachev visit by denying entry to six Western correspondents and by expelling two others (*NYT*, 26 May). Toward year's end, Ceauşescu decisively ruled out any economic reforms similar to those proposed by Gorbachev in a four-hour speech to a Romanian party conference (AP, 14 December).

The Soviet leader moved on from Bucharest to a two-day summit meeting of Warsaw Pact leaders in East Berlin. Gorbachev and Raisa received an exceptionally warm welcome from the crowds, but his meeting with Honecker apparently left relations unchanged with that prickly ally. The only result of the summit was ritualistic endorsement of Soviet arms control proposals (*WP*, 29 May; *Pravda*, 29, 30 May).

Although Eastern bloc leaders invariably praised Soviet initiatives, there was uneasiness about the possible long-range implications of Gorbachev's European strategy, and the Kremlin was obliged to issue reassurances against any radical Soviet approach to the German question. On the eve of Honecker's visit to Bonn, *Pravda* (6 September) warned against West German hopes that the trip was a forerunner of eventual German reunification. "The division of Germany is reality," the newspaper asserted in its commentary, adding that "political realities demand that Bonn should cast off the ballast of obsolete ideas." The commitment to a divided Germany was made firmer in the following month, when party Secretary Dobrynin publicly issued a strong denial in Bonn to rumors concerning a change in Soviet policy on the "German question" (see above).

Perhaps making a virtue out of necessity, Gorbachev appeared to renounce the Brezhnev Doctrine. Speaking to a gathering of representatives from leftist, socialist, and communist parties in Moscow, the general secretary indicated that the USSR would no longer seek to dictate domestic policy to its allies. Gorbachev said that "a more sophisticated culture of mutual relations among progressive forces" was needed to take into account "diversity of experience." He criticized the inflexible approach to doctrine and intrabloc relations, characterizing previous policy as marked by the "arrogance of omniscience" (*Pravda*, 6 November).

In a move that suggested a coordinated reappraisal of the Brezhnev Doctrine, the new head of the Institute of Marxism-Leninism, Georgii Smirnov, spoke with reporters and suggested that historians take a new look at the Soviet invasion of Czechoslovakia in 1968. However, when Miloš Jakeš replaced Gustáv Husák as Czechoslovak party leader in December, a congratulatory telegram from Gorbachev indicated that the new leadership in Prague would be expected to follow the domestic social and economic policies of the USSR. Gorbachev said,

> We are confident that the Central Committee under your leadership will ensure the fulfillment of wide-scale tasks facing the party in the field of further development and renewal of socialism on Czechoslovak soil, the restructuring of the economic mechanism, the democratization of the public and political life of the country (AP, 17 December).

China. So long as Soviet perceptions of China emphasized a possible military "threat" and the potential of a three-way linkage of the People's Republic of China (PRC), Japan, and the United States versus Soviet "hegemonism," Moscow's options were limited and concentrated on outflanking Beijing through military power and alliances with other communist regimes. In recent years, China has moved toward a more independent diplomatic position and has de-emphasized military strength to concentrate on domestic economic reform. This has made feasible a Soviet turn to the more flexible tactics preferred by the new leadership in Moscow. But a rapprochement with China could not be produced by soft words and "open" diplomacy; it depended on substantive moves on the three major irritants for Beijing: the Soviet military concentration along China's northern borders, Afghanistan, and the Vietnamese occupation of Cambodia. During the year, some progress was made in assuaging PRC concerns on these issues, without alienating Moscow's allies. But all of the issues were complex and difficult to resolve; moreover, there remained ideological and other impediments to a full normalization of relations with the PRC.

Progress was most evident on matters of China's northern borders. Early in the year, the USSR and Mongolia reached agreement on a partial withdrawal of Soviet troops from the latter country (*Far Eastern Economic Review*, 22 January; *Pravda*, 3 February). Moscow reportedly obtained Mongolian approval of the move in exchange for its blessing on the establishment of diplomatic relations between Ulan Bator and Washington. But Mongolian resistance apparently accounted for limitation of the pullout to one motorized rifle division and several smaller units, rather than the "substantial part" promised by Gorbachev in his July 1986 Vladivostok speech. However, Beijing welcomed the move as a possible first step to the loosening of the Soviet hold on Mongolia (*Far Eastern Economic Review*, 5 March).

Sino-Soviet border talks resumed in Moscow on 9 February, and another round in Beijing followed during August. Provisional agreement was reached on demarcation of the Sino-Soviet border along the Amur and Ussuri rivers (TASS, 21 August; *Pravda*, 22 August). The middle of the main navigational channel will form the boundary line, thus conceding Damanskiy island to the PRC, in accord with Gorbachev's offer in his July Vladivostok speech of the previous year.

Indications of a probable wind down of the Soviet intervention in Afghanistan and in Cambodia were also welcomed in Beijing, but it appeared that much more evidence would be required for PRC leaders to discount the threat of Soviet "hegemonism" in the Far East.

In other areas, improvement in USSR-PRC relations was marginal but steady. The two countries signed an agreement providing for repair of five Soviet vessels in Chinese shipyards (TASS, 25

June; *FBIS*, 29 June). USSR media reported progress in fulfillment of the 1985 agreement on Soviet assistance in the building and renovation of power plants in China (Moscow Radio, 19 June; *FBIS*, 29 June). The following month, a delegation from the All-China Federation of Trade Unions visited Minsk and Kiev and expressed satisfaction with the resumption of contacts between Soviet and Chinese trade unions (TASS, 3 July; *FBIS*, 16 July). A first-ever agreement was signed on a business exchange between USSR and PRC book publishers (*Sovetskaia kultura*, 30 June). Border trade during 1986 was reported to have reached a value of more than 30 million rubles, a fourfold increase over 1983 (TASS, *FBIS*, 20 January).

The main Soviet concern, however, was clearly the long-range potential of China as a world power rivaling the USSR. China's impressive economic growth rates, its adaptability to advanced technology, and the strong momentum generated by its economic reform program contrasted starkly with the ills of the Soviet economy. Any successes achieved in the Chinese modernization program would tend to accentuate the irrelevance of the Soviet model of development for the Third World, already so obvious to elites in developing countries that it constituted a serious liability for Soviet foreign policy. The Chinese economic reform attracted much interest among Soviet economists, but the official press in Moscow reacted cautiously. A lengthy report by three Soviet correspondents on the PRC economic reform acknowledged that the program helped in solving "the most immediate problems of China's economy" but stressed its "contradictions and negative aspects" (*Izvestiia*, 17 January).

Japan. The slow warming trend in relations between Moscow and Tokyo came to an abrupt halt during the summer over revelations of Soviet industrial espionage. The uncovering of the illegal export of high-technology machine tools by the Toshiba Corporation to the USSR and charges that Soviet embassy officials were involved in a spy case at the U.S. Yokota air base strained relations between the two countries.

At midyear, the USSR foreign ministry charged that Japan was conducting an anti-Soviet campaign and warned that Moscow would take retaliatory measures if the Japanese continued the campaign (Tokyo Kyodo, 11 June; *FBIS*, 12 June). In the following month, Soviet leader Gorbachev said that he had postponed a possible visit to Tokyo because of "dark clouds" over the relationship between the USSR and Japan.

Matters came to a head in August. Moscow expelled the Japanese defense attaché, Nobuhiro Tokeshima, for allegedly acquiring secret trade-related information; this marked the first time since World War II that a Japanese government official had been expelled from the USSR. At the same time, the head of Mitsubishi Corporation's office in Moscow, Takao Otani, was charged with spying while traveling in Odessa and ordered to leave the country.

Tokyo retaliated by expelling Soviet trade representative Yuri Pokrovskiy because of his alleged involvement in the theft of diagrams used for flight management systems and circuit diagrams for a sophisticated computer part from Tokyo Aircraft Instrument Company (*WSJ*, 21 August). For their part, the Soviets continued to play up the involvement of two Japanese firms in an alleged 1985 attempt to carry an automated center for collecting intelligence across the USSR in a railroad container, which the Soviets implied was done in conspiracy with U.S. government agencies (TASS, 25 August; *FBIS*, 26 August).

Southeast Asia and the South Pacific. Soviet foreign minister Shevardnadze made another goodwill tour to Vietnam, Cambodia, Laos, Thailand, Indonesia, and Australia. The trip reflected the new pattern of USSR interests in Southeast Asia and the South Pacific: resolution of the conflict in Cambodia, upgraded contacts with the ASEAN countries, and solicitation of Australian support for a nuclear-free zone in the south Pacific (primarily barring U.S. nuclear-armed vessels from ports in the area) (RL *Research*, 2 March).

Some evidence of early returns on Shevardnadze's trip was apparent in late spring. Thailand's foreign minister, Sitthi Sawetsila, returned Shevardnadze's visit by traveling to Moscow for talks with the USSR foreign minister (TASS, 11 May; *FBIS*, 12 May). At midyear, it was announced in Djakarta that Indonesia would explore the possibility of Soviet assistance in the launching of a communications satellite and that the Indonesians would not rely upon U.S. financial and technological help in the next stage of their space program (Moscow Domestic Service, 23 June; *FBIS*, 24 June).

Nguyen Van Linh, general secretary of the Vietnamese Communist Party, visited Moscow, and recent tensions in relations between the allies were markedly absent. The emphasis was on the socialist "division of labor," and several accords were signed dealing with trade in consumer products and the production of light industrial goods (*Pravda*, 18, 20, 22 May). Gorbachev and other Soviet officials evidently did not pressure Linh for a quick solution to the conflict in Cambodia (*Far Eastern Economic Review*, 4 June). However, later in the year, the Soviets apparently pushed harder, and the DRV made some moves toward disengagement. In August, representatives of the USSR and of Laos, Cambodia, and Vietnam met in Phnom Penh and proposed a "political solution" to the Cambodian problem, a "national reconciliation policy" involving all factions except Pol Pot and other Khmer Rouge leaders. The communiqué issued at the conclusion of the meeting said that the four nations fully supported an offer of citizenship for refugees, émigrés, or guerrillas who rallied to the Vietnamese-backed government (Reuters, 29 August).

Malaysia's prime minister Mahathir bin Mohamed visited Moscow during the summer for talks with Gorbachev, Shevardnadze, and First Deputy Premier Vsevolod Murakhovsky. A number of minor agreements were signed, two of which dealt with maritime transport and the avoidance of double taxation (*Izvestiia*, 6 August).

India. Soviet relations with India, somewhat questionable during the early days of Rajiv Gandhi's leadership, continued on an upbeat note following the euphoria generated by Gorbachev's visit to Delhi in November 1986. Gandhi returned the visit by going to Moscow the following summer and was warmly received by the Soviet leadership (*Izvestiia*, 4 July). The major result of the visit was the signing of a comprehensive long-term program for scientific and technical cooperation. On his return to Delhi, Gandhi gave high marks to his negotiations with Gorbachev and other Soviet leaders. He praised Soviet efforts to defuse tensions in the Persian Gulf area and said that in Moscow the USSR and India had reaffirmed their commitment to the Delhi Declaration on nuclear disarmament and nonviolence (TASS, 4 July; *FBIS*, 13 July).

Prime Minister Ryzhkov also visited India for talks with Gandhi. Questions of economic cooperation were paramount, with the concept of joint enterprises figuring prominently in the discussions (*Pravda*, 25 November). Agreements were signed for construction of an oil refinery in Karnale and a thermal power station in West Bengal, to be financed by a Soviet credit of 12 million rupees (Moscow Television, 26 November; *FBIS*, 27 November). Gandhi strongly endorsed the projected INF treaty between the United States and the USSR and joined Ryzhkov in opposing "the militarization of outer space."

Afghanistan. There were fresh signals at the beginning of the year that Moscow wanted to disengage from its military involvement in Afghanistan but not at the price of a major loss of its influence or total replacement of the satellite regime. Soviet foreign minister Shevardnadze and Central Committee secretary Dobrynin journeyed to Kabul at the beginning of the year for talks with the Afghan leader (TASS, 5 January; *Pravda*, 6 January), supposedly to flesh out accords reached by Gorbachev and Najibullah in December.

The talks at Kabul closely followed Najibullah's call for a ceasefire to start 15 January and a coalition government of "national reconciliation." Guerrilla leaders in Pakistan dismissed the offer as "meaningless" (*CSM*, 6 January).

On his return to Moscow, Shevardnadze said that a political settlement in Afghanistan was near (TASS, 7 January; AP, 8 January) and appeared to soften the Soviet stance on troop removal. The Soviets had proposed a four-year timetable for withdrawal, against the three or four months demanded by Pakistan in negotiations. Western diplomats, skeptical of Moscow's claimed greater flexibility, felt that there would be little more than a token removal of forces (*NYT*, 8 January).

Najibullah indicated that his government and the USSR had agreed on a timetable for the withdrawal, but it was not made public (*NYT*, 21 January). Meanwhile, the stalemated war appeared to be turning against the communist regime. Western diplomats in Kabul estimated Soviet-Afghan aircraft losses at one a day; ten planes and helicopters were reportedly shot down in the first week of February by the guerrillas, who were using U.S.-supplied Stinger surface-to-air missiles (AP, 12 February).

Although both Moscow and Kabul continued to speak of a negotiated settlement, there were contradictory signs. The Soviets were reported to have recently stepped up economic measures designed to draw Afghanistan closer to CMEA along with an acceleration of cultural links, particularly bloc support for Kabul radio and television (*Foreign Report*, 14 May).

Najibullah claimed successes for "national reconciliation" and said that the policy was in no way a sign of weakness. He asserted that more than 4,000 rebel representatives had joined the commissions for reconciliation (*Pravda*, 14 May). The following month Najibullah declared that the Kabul regime intended to extend its moratorium on combat operations but noted that the leadership did not harbor illusions that the undeclared war would end at once when it launched the idea of national reconciliation (TASS, 3 June; *FBIS*, 4 June).

Moscow media reports during the summer painted a realistic picture of Soviet failure in Afghanistan. A series of articles in the magazine *Ogonek* spoke of poor morale and desertion among some Afghan units, described tough fighting between elite Soviet troops and the guerrillas, and implied that large areas of Afghanistan were under guerrilla control (*CSM*, 21 July).

A senior U.S. administration official reported that the insurgents had killed or wounded 250 to 300 Soviet *spetsnaz* soldiers and shot down fifteen Soviet and Afghan aircraft during the first two weeks of June (*WP*, 11 July). After fierce hand-to-hand fighting with the special forces, the rebels reportedly turned back a column of 5,500 Soviet troops. After a two-month cutoff, the guerrillas were again receiving U.S. Stingers; deliveries rose to the rate of 100 per month. Additionally, Britain was supplying Blowpipe antiaircraft missiles and sending instructors to train the guerrillas in their use (*Insight*, 3 August). The Soviet-DRA military position continued to deteriorate, and late in the year even the government headquarters in Kabul could not be secured against the rebels.

The negotiations recessed in March and resumed in September at the request of the Afghan government, amid reports that the USSR was now willing to withdraw its forces within one year (*WP*, 6 September). Najibullah subsequently endorsed a one-year withdrawal and said that it had been negotiated with the USSR. He also made symbolic gestures to Muslim sentiment, denied an intention to establish communism in Afghanistan, and gave the appearance of disengaging from the Moscow connection (*Time*, 14 December). In November, Moscow sustained a major diplomatic defeat when the U.N. General Assembly, by a vote of 123 to 19, called for immediate withdrawal of Soviet forces from Afghanistan.

Despite public indications of a sense of urgency, Moscow was hanging tough on Afghanistan in the final weeks of the year. Two Soviet preconditions for withdrawal—inclusion of the People's Democratic Party in an interim government and cessation of all U.S., Chinese, and other foreign military support for the rebels—remained as obstacles in the negotiations. A senior U.S. administration official said that Moscow had been following a "calculated policy of loose talk" for months but that the words had not been accompanied by deeds (*CSM*, 20 November). In his interview with Brokaw before the Washington summit, Gorbachev gave a new dimension to *glasnost'* by claiming that the Soviets had intervened in 1979 at the invitation of the Afghan government (NBC, 2 December). Regional issues were discussed at the summit, but no progress toward a settlement in Afghanistan was reported.

Middle East. USSR policy in the region was even more pragmatic, as Moscow pursued the twin objectives of participation in the Middle East peace process and gaining influence in the Persian Gulf area. Playing down ties with forces linked to terrorism, such as Syria, the Palestine Liberation Organization (PLO), and Libya, the Soviets developed formal and informal contacts with non-Marxist actors, such as Israel, Kuwait, and Saudi Arabia. Gains were limited by the contradictory goals of diplomatic targets and by the Soviet desire not to be excluded from influence in the region. This delicate balancing act provided clear evidence of the increased diplomatic competence among practitioners of USSR foreign policies.

At the start of the year, the Soviets issued a strong call for resolution of the Iran-Iraq conflict and said that its continuation "is being used by the imperialist forces to increase their military presence in the Persian Gulf and create conditions for interference in the internal affairs of states in the area" (*Pravda*, 9 January). Two days later, in a press conference at the U.N., chief Soviet delegate Aleksandr Belonosov blamed Teheran for continuing the war and characterized Iran as an aggressor nation that should be deprived of arms deliveries (*NYT*, 12 January).

Displaying a definite tilt toward Iraq, the Soviets continued to push for a negotiated settlement of the war and linked the Teheran regime to forces opposed to the USSR elsewhere. In two separate statements the Soviet government accused Iran of "taking an inflexible position on the conflict with Iraq," "wrecking all attempts to settle the disputes between the two countries peacefully at the negotiating table," colluding with the U.S. imperialists who sought to "drown the Sandinista revolution in blood," and prolonging the war in Afghanistan by support for the "Afghan criminals" (TASS, 8 May; *FBIS*, 11 May). The USSR reportedly collaborated with Saudi Arabia in promoting a 26 April meeting in Jordan that brought together two of the Arab world's bitterest foes, Syrian president Hafez al-Assad and Iraqi leader Saddam Hussein. The achievement was clearly marginal; only days after the meeting, Damascus signed an agreement with Teheran for the supply of one million tons of Iranian oil to Syria in the coming year (*CSM*, 11 May).

The Soviets joined Arab efforts to isolate Iran diplomatically and also forged ties with an Iraqi supporter in the gulf. Worried by the increased involvement of the United States in the Persian Gulf, the USSR agreed to charter three of its oil tankers to Kuwait and keep oil supplies moving through the Gulf. The presence of the Soviet flag, however, was no guarantee for Kuwaiti shipments; on 6 May Iranian gunboats for the first time attacked and damaged a Soviet merchant ship (*NYT*, 7 May).

The USSR's response to this and later attacks on vessels flying the Soviet flag was mild. Although eager to prevent a U.S. monopoly on protection of the shipping lanes, the Soviets clearly did not want war with Iran or a total breakdown of their tenuous ties with Teheran. The restraint paid off two months later when First Deputy Foreign Minister Yuli Vorontsov negotiated a deal in Teheran that reportedly provided for construction of a railroad linking the USSR with Iran and for conversion of an existing gas pipeline for shipment of oil (*NYT*, 5 August; *CSM*, 12 August). There was some doubt among Western analysts about the feasibility of such a conversion project but, if carried out quickly, it would lessen Iran's dependence on the Persian Gulf and reduce its strategic vulnerability vis-à-vis Iraq and the Western powers.

Despite dealings with Teheran, Moscow maintained its primary commitment to Iraq and indicated willingness to consider a U.N. arms embargo against Iran. In December an article published in a party journal in Armenia, but not reported in Moscow, contained a violent denunciation of the Ayatollah Khomeini and his entourage. Calling Khomeini a "fanatical and stubborn figure," the article accused the Ayatollah and his lieutenants of waging war against Iraq only to preserve their power and cover up their "total incompetence" in social and economic development (*Kommunist Armenii*, 19 December; *LAT*, 26 December).

An eight-member USSR consular team arrived in Tel Aviv at midyear, ostensibly to handle questions related to Soviet property in Israel (*NYT*, 14 July). Both the USSR and Israel officially played down the contact, emphasizing the low level of business to be transacted. The Soviets temporarily suspended the jamming of Israeli broadcasts to the USSR on the day following arrival of the team but resumed interference two days later (ibid., 17 July). The following month, Israeli premier Shimon Peres' chief political aide, Nimrod Novick, met with Soviet Middle East expert Vladimir Tarasov to discuss a possible international peace conference for the region, and Israeli officials said that the two countries had agreed to set up regular political contacts (AP, 18 August).

In line with the objective of participation in a peace process involving Arab forces and Israel, the Soviets continued to push for Arab unity and reportedly solicited support for the USSR's overtures to Israel. Karen Brutents, deputy head of the Central Committee's International Department, met with Syrian president Assad in Damascus (*Pravda*, 9 February), and Soviet representatives were quite active at the subsequent meeting of the Palestine National Council (PNC) in Algiers. First Deputy Foreign Minister Vorontsov talked with PLO chairman Yassir Arafat, and General Secretary Gorbachev met with Assad in Moscow (*Foreign Report*, 30 April). A Supreme Soviet delegation journeyed to Damascus in June for meetings and again stressed the importance of a general peace settlement in the Middle East (TASS, 17 June; *FBIS*, 23 June). The various meetings made no appreciable contribution to achievement of Soviet objectives in the region.

The USSR generally took a more aloof attitude toward forces linked with terrorism and continued to hold Libya's Moammar Khadafy at arm's length. However, Moscow signaled its intention of maintaining links with the Libyan strongman. In March, candidate Politburo member Yuri Solovyev was dispatched to Tripoli for talks with Khadafy (*Pravda*, 4 March).

The continuing importance of the Soviet foothold in South Yemen was emphasized when Gorbachev met Yemen Socialist Party leader Ali Salim al-Biedh in the Kremlin on 10 February. The talks dealt with "questions of bilateral relations" and the importance of Arab unity for the Middle East peace process (ibid., 11 February). But when Libyan foreign minister Gaballah Azouz Talhi passed through Moscow in May, there was little fanfare and he did not meet with Gorbachev (*NYT*, 24 May).

The Soviets continued to make slow progress in improvement of relations with Egypt. USSR ambassador to Cairo Gennadi Zhuravlev announced in

September that an agreement would be initialed shortly on trade exchanges in 1988 between Egypt and the USSR and said that contracts had been signed on modernization projects valued at $100 million (Cairo MENA, 22 September; *FBIS*, 23 September).

Africa. Overshadowed by major initiatives elsewhere, Soviet activity in Africa south of the Sahara was devoted to maintaining influence in Ethiopia, Angola, and Mozambique and improving ties elsewhere without any major investment of resources. The USSR continued to be chief supplier of arms and military training for the African National Congress (ANC), whose ranks include members of the South African Communist Party (SACP). The upsurge of violence in South Africa made the country a promising target for revolutionary upheaval, but indications that the USSR favored a negotiated political settlement evidently diminished Soviet influence with influential black militants. However, some success was apparent in Zimbabwe, where previous relations had been chilly because of Soviet support for the losing group (the Zimbabwe African People's Union [ZAPU]) in the country's liberation war. A Supreme Soviet delegation headed by Deputy Premier Pavel Gilashvili visited Angola, Botswana, Tanzania, Zambia, and Zimbabwe during March (*Africa Confidential*, 15 April). The announcement in the last week of the year of plans for a coalition government including Joshua Nkomo offered hope for a further normalization of relations between the USSR and Zimbabwe.

Soviet personnel led a massive military buildup of government forces in Angola. In April, U.S. officials in Luanda reported round-the-clock deliveries by hundreds of military planes carrying equipment and Cuban and Angolan troops to bases near rebel-held territory in the southeast. The Soviet aim was to crush the U.S.-backed National Union for the Total Independence of Angola (UNITA) rebels and free Angolan forces to support the independence movement in neighboring Namibia (*CSM*, 7 April). However, excesses of the Soviet fishing fleet were a source of tension between the USSR and Angola, and a major shakeup of Angolan diplomatic personnel was reportedly aimed at improving relations with West European countries such as France, Portugal, and West Germany and even with the United States (*Africa Confidential*, 17 May).

Ethiopia's continuing importance to Moscow was indicated by the dispatch of Lev Zaikov, Politburo member and (at the time) number-three man on the Secretariat, to Addis Ababa as chief Soviet representative at the 13th anniversary celebration of the Ethiopian revolution (TASS, 11, 14 September; *FBIS*, 15 September). A Supreme Soviet delegation headed by A. A. Mokanu, deputy chairman of the Presidium, visited Congo (Brazzaville) in midyear. Talks with Congolese leaders stressed the two countries' opposition to South Africa's policy in Namibia (*Izvestiia*, 10, 11, 16 July).

Joaquim Alberto Chissano, chairman of FRELIMO (Mozambique Liberation Front) and president of the People's Republic of Mozambique, was welcomed to Moscow for meetings with Gorbachev, Shevardnadze, Dobrynin, and other Soviet officials. The talks reportedly again emphasized joint opposition to policies of the Pretoria regime and strongly condemned South Africa's occupation of Namibia, its maintenance of apartheid, and its operations against the "frontline" states of southern Africa (*Pravda*, 7 August). Chissano's predecessor, Samora Machel, had been killed in October 1986 in the crash of a Soviet Tupelov passenger aircraft. USSR propaganda continued to claim that the crash was caused by a false radio signal beamed by Pretoria agents from the South African side of the Mozambique border, although evidence uncovered by an investigating team pointed to poor aircraft maintenance and pilot error as probable causes (*Informafrica*, June).

Latin America. The Soviets were unusually active in the region during the year, stepping up contacts with countries largely ignored in the past. Some initiatives were related to problems involved in maintenance of the Marxist regime in Nicaragua. But Soviet diplomacy played down revolutionary goals and used a highly pragmatic approach. The main objective seemed to be that of laying the foundations for long-term Soviet influence in the region on a very businesslike, nonideological basis, with the general goal of making the USSR's presence felt on every continent as proof of its superpower status. For the short run, the USSR exploited the possibilities of undercutting U.S. influence in the region by taking advantage of various tensions between Washington and Latin American states, being careful not to appear provocative.

In February, Yuri Pavlov, the Soviet ambassador to Costa Rica, went on a "private" visit to Guatemala, which had cut diplomatic ties with the USSR after the overthrow of Jacobo Arbenz in 1954, and talked with Guatemalan officials, reportedly discussing Central American peace-seeking efforts. That same month a Panamanian legislative mission, headed by Efrain Diaz, president of the National Assembly, visited Moscow, apparently for soundings about the establishment of diplomatic and commercial links. Yuri Visaslov, USSR commercial attaché for Central America stationed in Costa Rica, traveled in May to Honduras to discuss possible purchases of sugar; the national sugar industry had been adversely affected by cuts in U.S. import quotas (*Latin American Regional Reports*, 16 July).

Mexico is a more important target. The country was often mentioned as an alternative supplier of oil to Nicaragua, because of cutbacks in Soviet deliveries. The matter was discussed in a 14 May meeting in Mexico City between Nicaragua's vice-president Sergio Ramirez and Mexican officials. However, there remained two problems for such transactions: Nicaragua's failure to pay for earlier shipments and the necessary conversion of Nicaraguan refineries (*WP*, 4 June). Despite the critical situation for Moscow's Central American ally, there was reportedly no mention of oil during the visit by Mexican foreign minister Bernardo Sepulveda to Moscow.

Sepulveda spent a week in Moscow, receiving the sort of reception usually accorded to representatives of great powers. He met with Gorbachev, Shevardnadze, and Gromyko; Gorbachev disclaimed any interest in encouraging "socialist revolutions" in Latin America and said that he did not want to meddle in Latin relations with the United States. Soviet press reports indicated that the talks stressed Mexico's role in the Contadora peace effort in Central America and the need to promote access of Third World products to markets in developed countries (*Pravda*, 7 May; *NYT*, 25 May).

Foreign Minister Shevardnadze made a trip to several Latin American countries during September and October, becoming the highest-ranking Soviet official ever to visit that continent. The trip, which included stays in Argentina, Brazil, and Uruguay, with a stopover in Cuba, had few tangible results but reportedly paved the way for a visit by Soviet leader Gorbachev to Latin America in 1988. The foreign minister went to some lengths to avoid creating the impression that his visit was aimed at undermining U.S. influence in South America, and he told a Buenos Aires news conference that his tour was not meant to harm the interests of "third countries" (Reuters, 3 October; *RL Research*, 11 October). The talks with South American officials apparently were mainly concerned with commercial matters. In Buenos Aires, Shevardnadze was received by Argentine president Raul Alfonsin; in addition to discussions on trade, the Soviet foreign minister signed agreements on cultural exchanges and consular relations (*Izvestiia*, 5 October).

The USSR remained the major supplier of military hardware and other materials to the Sandinista regime in Nicaragua, which was participating in peace talks involving other Central American governments and the United States. On 25 October, Nicaraguan defense ministry official Roger Miranda Bengoechea defected to the United States, disclosing plans for a massive military buildup with Soviet help. The defector was kept under wraps until the U.S.-Soviet summit had been concluded, and U.S. officials were apparently dubious about his revelations. But three days after the end of the summit, Nicaraguan defense minister Humberto Ortega confirmed the story, saying that Nicaragua planned to double its active duty and reserve armed forces to 600,000 men by 1995 and equip them with advanced Soviet fighter planes, missiles, and artillery (*NYT*, 13 December).

Reacting to the Ortega statement, U.S. national security adviser Lieutenant General Colin Powell and President Reagan told reporters that Gorbachev, during the summit meetings, had offered to suspend Soviet military aid to the Sandinistas in exchange for a similar action by the United States vis-à-vis the *contras* (AP, 14, 15 December). In Managua, the defense minister's brother, President Daniel Ortega, denied that the military buildup had been approved by his government, saying that it was only a recommendation by army officials (*WP*, 15 December). Whatever the validity of the conflicting stories from Nicaraguan sources, the incident served to dispel some of the euphoria in Washington of the Reagan-Gorbachev summit.

Chronic strains in the relationship between Havana and Moscow were perhaps even more evident than usual. On the Cuban side, the heavy burden of serving as the USSR's surrogate in Africa and Central America risked domestic unpopularity for the Castro regime. For the Soviets, the pressures involved in keeping their oldest ally in Latin America afloat were felt keenly during a time of economic stress within the USSR. Tensions between Fidel Castro and the Soviet leadership reportedly increased during the year. However, Castro received a warm welcome in Moscow, where he figured prominently in the anniversary celebrations, appearing alongside Prime Minister Ryzhkov at the 7 November parade (Knight-Ridder newspapers, 8 November).

International Party Contacts. The general absence of rhetoric on "world revolution" and "national liberation," the lessened cooperation with certain radical forces in the Third World, and the moves toward normalization of relations with "bourgeois" regimes on many fronts all suggested a downgrading of nonruling communist parties in the application of Soviet foreign policy. However, the CPSU maintained a steady level of contacts with nonruling parties as well as regular exchanges with parties of established "socialist" regimes. Far from discounting ties with fraternal parties, the CPSU appeared to give added emphasis to such links. The new course in Soviet policy at home and abroad provided an atmosphere conducive to dealing with ideologically disparate elements in the splintered world communist movement.

Changes in personnel in the CPSU's foreign policy establishment also proved to be a positive factor in more flexible relations with both ruling and nonruling parties. Dobrynin, head of the International Department, applied the same pragmatic approach that had been so successful in his role as star player in superpower politics to his task of dealing with communist parties. He was unfettered by the ideological baggage that had encumbered his predecessor, Boris Ponomarev, who was simultaneously the CPSU's principal spokesman for "proletarian internationalism" and its chief representative in relations with parties that rejected Moscow's leadership. Within the bloc, the replacement of Konstantin Rusakov and Oleg Rakhmanin by Vadim Medvedev and Georgii Shakhnazarov in the top posts of the Central Committee department for liaison with ruling communist parties provided a similar shift from dogmatism to pragmatism. The new team in Moscow appeared to give somewhat greater emphasis to international meetings of CP representatives, while concentrating on key figures and movements in bilateral contacts.

Three major conferences of specialists representing the ruling bloc parties were held during the year. Central Committee secretaries for ideological and international affairs of "Socialist Commonwealth" CPs met in Warsaw, 22–23 January (*WMR*, March); CP agriculture secretaries of the CMEA countries met in Moscow, 10–11 February; and the CPSU's Institute of Marxism-Leninism held an ideological conference of the bloc parties' "think tank" scholars in Moscow, also during February (ibid., April).

Dobrynin represented the CPSU at a consultative meeting of the communist and workers' parties of the Asia-Pacific region, held in Ulan Bator, Mongolia, 7–9 July, and attended by delegations of 21 parties from eighteen countries. The conferees endorsed Soviet initiatives on nuclear arms and proposals for an Asian-Pacific "zone of peace" in accord with CPSU General Secretary Gorbachev's Vladivostok speech of July 1986 (TASS, 9 July; *FBIS*, 13 July).

Perhaps the international gathering with the greatest long-range significance was the conference of representatives of leftist, socialist, and communist parties held in Moscow in early November. Addressing the meeting, Gorbachev apparently renounced the Brezhnev Doctrine, severely criticized previous Soviet handling of relations with bloc countries, and stressed the importance of the "diversity of experience" of socialist regimes (*Pravda*, 6 November).

The personal diplomacy of General Secretary Gorbachev figured prominently in party contacts within the bloc, just as it did in the wider realm of great power politics. Gorbachev conferred with Czechoslovak CP leader Husák in Prague (ibid., 11 April), traveled to Bucharest for talks with Romanian party head Ceauşescu (*Pravda*, 26 May), and met with Honecker in East Berlin (ibid., 29 May). The visit to East Berlin also included a summit meeting of Warsaw Pact leaders that endorsed Soviet arms control proposals (*Pravda*, 30 May).

CPSU relations with the East European parties were complicated by the resistance of hard-line bloc leaders to any imitation of Soviet domestic reforms and by the popularity of Gorbachev and his policies among the masses in the other bloc countries, a phenomenon that tended to undercut popular support for the regimes. This spillover effect may have been a major factor in the December changeover in leadership of the Czechoslovak party. This effect also appeared to be quite important in Romania. As the internal crisis expanded in that country, Western diplomats in Bucharest reported that Gorbachev had applied more direct pressures on the leader of the Romanian party, severely criticizing Ceauşescu and his policies in private conversations during the May visit (AP, 28 December). Jaruzelski continued to be Gorbachev's favorite East European leader and was warmly received during an April visit to Moscow. At that time Jaruzelski hailed the "internationalist bond between the Polish United Workers' Party and the CPSU" (*Pravda*, 22 April).

Bulgaria's Todor Zhivkov was the only other bloc leader who gave strong public endorsement to Gorbachev's domestic policies. Following his meeting with Gorbachev in Moscow, the Bulgarian media stressed agreement between the CPSU and the Bulgarian Communist Party on "further promoting and deepening socialist democracy" (Sofia BTA, 21 October; *FBIS*, 22 October). Earlier, CPSU secretary Biryukova had conferred with Zhivkov in Sofia on the implications of restructuring for the two countries (Moscow Domestic Service, 16 July; *FBIS*, 17 July).

During the summer, several prominent CPSU figures—candidate Politburo member and Leningrad *obkom* first secretary Yuri Solovyev (*Pravda*, 12 June); K. N. Mogilnichenko, deputy chief of the CPSU Organizational Party Work Department (ibid., 12 July); and Central Committee secretary and Politburo member Aleksandr Yakovlev (TASS, 7 August; *FBIS*, 10 August)—visited East Germany for talks with party officials. USSR foreign minister and Politburo member Shevardnadze met with party leaders in Belgrade on the last stop of a tour that also included Bulgaria and Hungary (TASS, 20 June; *FBIS*, 23 June).

A meeting between Gorbachev and Ali Salem al-Biedh, head of the Yemen Socialist Party, in the Kremlin emphasized the importance of Arab unity for the Middle East peace process (*Pravda*, 11 February). Other meetings with leaders in power similarly emphasized Soviet regional goals or featured attempts to smooth over old differences. Central Committee secretary Zaikov's visit to Addis Ababa apparently avoided the tensions that had colored relations between the Soviet and Ethiopian parties in recent years (TASS, 11, 14 September; *FBIS*, 15 September).

Relations with the Afghan party were dominated by concern of CPSU leaders about possible disengagement from Afghanistan and the policy of "national reconciliation." Najibullah, head of the People's Democratic Party of Afghanistan, met with Gorbachev, Shevardnadze, and Dobrynin in Moscow (TASS, 19, 20 July; *FBIS*, 20 July). Earlier, Shevardnadze and Dobrynin had seen Najibullah in Kabul (*Pravda*, 6 January). When Vietnamese general secretary Nguyen Van Linh visited Moscow for talks with Gorbachev and other CPSU figures, the emphasis was upon the "socialist division of labor" and issues of regional peace and security, instead of Vietnam's poor record on utilization of Soviet aid, which had been a major concern in previous years (ibid., 18, 20, 22 May).

Relations with nonruling parties frequently could be tied to particular Soviet foreign policy goals. CPSU party control committee chairman Mikhail Solomentsev headed a delegation to the 12th Congress of the Communist Party of Greece, which strongly approved the peace initiatives of the Soviet Union and other socialist countries (TASS, 16, 18 May; *FBIS*, 20 May).

Karl Vaino, first secretary of the Estonian party, led the CPSU delegation to the 21st Congress of the Finnish Communist Party (*Pravda*, 13 June).

The tensions that have sometimes marked relations between the CPSU and the French Communist Party seemed to be totally absent, when Gorbachev and French Communist Party (PCF) leader Georges Marchais met in Moscow. Marchais highly praised the CPSU's domestic reform plans and pointed out that the PCF was the only party in France that strongly resisted plans for a French military buildup agreed upon by President Mitterrand and the conservative government (ibid., 5, 14, May; *WMR Information Bulletin*, July).

The new flexibility of the CPSU was quite evident when Secretary Yakovlev led a delegation to Spain. Yakovlev met with both Ignacio Gallego, general secretary of the Communist Party of the Peoples of Spain and Gerardo Iglesias, head of the Communist Party of Spain (*Pravda*, 11, 13 March).

Although the CPSU sought good working relationships with parties that had displayed a high degree of independence in the past, it did not neglect longtime adherents of "proletarian internationalism" and consistent followers of the Moscow line. General Secretary Alvaro Cunhal of the Portuguese Communist Party was received by CPSU General Secretary Gorbachev in Moscow on 29 December 1986 (*WMR*, March). Secretary Georgii Razumovsky headed the CPSU delegation to the 26th Congress of the Austrian Communist Party (*Pravda*, 1 April); and old warhorse Gus Hall, general secretary of the Communist Party of the USA, met with Secretary Dobrynin in Moscow (ibid., 21 September).

Brutents, deputy head of the International Department, led the CPSU delegation to the Fifth Congress of the Communist Party of Lebanon (*Pravda*, 9 February). The CPSU sent greetings to the Fourth Congress of the Moroccan Party of Progress and Socialism, hailing the party as "a prominent detachment in the anti-imperialist Arab movement" (ibid., 17 July).

Candidate Politburo member Nikolai Talyzin led a delegation that participated in celebrations marking the 10th anniversary of the Treaty on Friendship and Cooperation between the USSR and Mozambique and met with FRELIMO head Chissano (*Izvestiia*, 31 March). Meanwhile, in Moscow, Secretary Dobrynin and FRELIMO secretary Jorge Rubelo signed an agreement on links between the two parties during 1987 (TASS, 30 March; *FBIS*, 2 April). Chissano later visited Moscow for talks with Gorbachev, Shevardnadze, Dobrynin, and other officials (*Pravda*, 7 August).

Vadim Bakatin, first secretary of the Kirov *obkom*, led the CPSU delegation to the 13th Congress of the Communist Party of Sri Lanka (TASS, 22 March; *FBIS*, 23 March). The CPSU delegation attending the Fourth Congress of the Communist Party of Bangladesh was led by N. Y. Klepach, chief editor of *Politicheskoe samoobrazvanie*, and V. P. Baidakov, a senior official of the International Department (*Pravda*, 13 April).

Pointing up the importance of the communist beachhead in Central America, the Soviets sent a high-level parliamentary delegation, headed by candidate Politburo member Eltsin, to Nicaragua for a three-day visit. Eltsin conferred with Sandinista leader Daniel Ortega and other officials. National Assembly president Carlos Nuñez called the delegation's stay in Managua the most important Soviet visit to Nicaragua to date (*WP*, 8 March). The Eltsin group stopped in Havana on its return trip to Moscow. The Soviet press reported that the meeting between Eltsin and Cuban leader Castro was held in "a warm and fraternal atmosphere" (TASS, *FBIS*, 6 March). Castro was singled out as a special guest of honor at the Moscow celebration of the 70th anniversary of the October Revolution (Soviet Television, 7 November; *Pravda*, 8 November).

Biographies. *Aleksandr Nikolaevich Yakovlev.* Born 2 December 1923 of peasant parents in Yaroslavl, Yakovlev is an ethnic Russian. He served in the army during the war and joined the CPSU in 1944. Following his graduation from the Yaroslavl Pedagogical Institute in 1946, he became a professional party worker, concentrating on ideology and propaganda. He served as a CPSU lecturer and newspaper department head in Yaroslavl and in 1953 became a staff member of the CPSU Central Committee.

Between 1960 and 1965, Yakovlev served as chief of the Propaganda Department's broadcast section and as a member of the editorial staff of the ideological journal *Kommunist*. In 1965, he was named deputy head of the Propaganda Department but lost that job in 1953 over a Brezhnev-era controversy on "openness." Sent into political "exile" as ambassador to Canada, he established a reputation in Ottawa as an unusually spontaneous and flexible Soviet diplomat.

Reportedly greatly impressing Gorbachev during the latter's visit to Canada in 1983, Yakovlev was brought back to Moscow in 1984 to become head of the Institute of World Economics and International Relations. In 1985, he was named head of the CPSU Propaganda Department and in March 1986, at the conclusion of the Twenty-seventh CPSU Congress, Yakovlev was elected as a secretary of the Central Committee in charge of domestic and foreign propaganda. In this post, he was reputedly the chief architect of the policy of *glasnost'* and apparently became General Secretary Gorbachev's closest associate in the leadership.

In January Yakovlev was elected a candidate member and in June a full member of the CPSU Politburo. By the time of the latter promotion, he had assumed a wide range of responsibilities, served as a major spokesman on ideological questions, and been one of Gorbachev's principal advisers on foreign policy. Yakovlev accompanied the general secretary to both the Reykjavik and Washington summit meetings.

Yakovlev was a member of the Central Auditing Commission of the CPSU, 1971–1976, and has been a full member of the Central Committee since the Twenty-fifth CPSU Congress in 1976. Since April 1984, he has served as a member of the Commission on Foreign Affairs of the USSR Supreme Soviet's Council of Nationalities.

(Sources: *Pravda*, 27 June; *NYT*, 27 June; *RL Research*, 6 February; Boris Lewytzkyj [ed.], *Who's Who in the Soviet Union*, Munich, 1984, p. 121.)

Raisa Maksimovna Gorbacheva. Raisa Maksimovna Titarenko was born in 1932 in Rubtsovsk, Altai *krai*, the daughter of a railway engineer. When her family moved from Siberia, they settled in the town of Stavropol, in the Kuban. She studied at Moscow State University from 1951 to 1955 and, in early 1954, married fellow student Mikhail Sergeevich Gorbachev, who was a native of Stavropol *krai*.

Raisa Gorbacheva worked as a teacher in Stavropol, 1955–1978, and from 1978 to 1985 was a lecturer in Marxisn-Leninism at Moscow State University. Primarily trained as a philosopher (Marxism-Leninism) in Moscow, she subsequently studied sociology at the Stavropol Teachers' Training Institute and became a pioneer in Soviet sociological research. In 1967, Gorbacheva was awarded the degree of candidate of philosophical sciences (the equivalent of a Ph.D.) by the Moscow State Pedagogical Institute. Her dissertation, on changing attitudes and interests of the peasantry in Stavropol *krai*, employed methods of survey research that would not be generally employed in the USSR until nearly two decades later.

Accompanying her husband on trips to Western Europe in the 1960s, Raisa Gorbacheva gained an acquaintance with the West that would serve her well when she became "first lady" of the USSR. The Western media discovered her on a December 1984 official trip to Britain and labeled the Gorbachevs the "Gucci comrades" for their stylish appearance and engaging personalities. After Mikhail Gorbachev's election as general secretary of the CPSU, Raisa accompanied him on an official visit to Paris in October 1985 and to the summit meetings in Geneva (November 1985), Reykjavik (October 1986), and Washington (December 1987).

Obscured by her celebrity status, the role of Raisa Gorbacheva in the new Soviet approach to the world is an important one. She is regarded as the most powerful spouse of a Soviet political leader since Lenin's wife, Krupskaya, and Mikhail Gorbachev told interviewer Tom Brokaw in December 1987 that he discussed all political and social issues with her (a reply deleted for the Soviet audience). Controversial within the USSR, partially because the Soviets are accustomed to virtual invisibility of their leaders' wives, she has been an important figure in the new "open" diplomacy within the bloc. During 1987, she figured prominently in the reception of Poland's leader Jaruzelski and made public appearances in Bucharest and East Berlin before enthusiastic crowds, with whom she mixed freely.

Raisa Gorbacheva's most important public function has been that of goodwill ambassador to the Western world, and her contribution to the softening of the Soviet image abroad, a vital aspect of the changed Soviet foreign policy strategy, has been considerable. Limited in the overt role she can play within the USSR by the traditionalist attitudes of a male-dominated society, she is believed to have quietly promoted the fledgling discipline of sociology. A member of the CPSU, she is reputed to be a rather orthodox Marxist, despite her image as a person of Western tastes and style.

(Sources: *L'Unita*, 9 April 1985; Zhores A. Medvedev, *Gorbachev*, New York, 1986, pp. 47, 58, 63; *Pravda*, 22 April; *NYT*, 10 December; *Time*, 4 January 1988.)

Aleksandra Pavlovna Biryukova. Born 25 February 1929, Biryukova, an ethnic Russian, joined the CPSU in 1956. A 1952 graduate of the Moscow Textile Institute, she subsequently held various positions in the textile industry, rising to the rank of chief engineer of the Moscow collective combine "Trekhgornaia manufaktura" in 1963.

From 1968 to 1986, Biryukova served as a secretary and member of the Presidium of the USSR Central Council of Trade Unions and also filled the post of the organization's deputy chairman during the latter part of that period. At the first meeting of the Central Committee elected by the Twenty-seventh CPSU Congress, she was named a secretary of the CPSU Central Committee, with responsibility for light industry and consumer affairs. She thus became the highest-ranking woman in the Soviet political system since 1961, when Ekaterina Furtseva lost her positions on the Politburo and the Secretariat at the Twenty-second CPSU Congress.

During 1987, Biryukova delivered a major speech to Azerbaijan party and government cadres in Baku, in which she severely criticized the economic performance of the republic, and represented the CPSU on a trip to Bulgaria, where she met with Bulgarian party leader Zhivkov and other officials to discuss issues of economic restructuring.

Biryukova was elected as a candidate member in 1971 and as a full member in 1976 of the CPSU Central Committee and was re-elected to full membership at the Twenty-sixth and Twenty-seventh CPSU Congresses.

(Sources: *RL Research*, 1 April 1986, 6 February; Boris Lewytzkyj [ed.], *Who's Who in the Soviet Union*, Munich, 1984, p. 50; *FBIS*, 16 June, 18 July.)

Dimitri Timofeevich Yazov. Born 8 November 1923 in Yazovo, Omsk oblast, Dimitri Yazov is an ethnic Russian of peasant origins. He joined the Soviet army in 1941, was commissioned as an officer in 1942, and was wounded during the war. He remained in the army as a regular officer and graduated from the Frunze Military Academy in 1956 and the General Staff Academy in 1967.

Rising steadily through the ranks, Yazov was

promoted to colonel in 1965, to major general in 1970, and to colonel general in 1984. His major assignments have included command of Soviet forces in Czechoslovakia (1979–1980) and of the Central Asian Military District (1980–1984). In February 1984, he was given command of the Far East Military District.

A prolific writer for military journals, Yazov was already recognized as an expert on personnel questions before his promotion to colonel general. His writings dealt with matters of training, morale, and combat readiness. These interests and his frankness about the state of discipline in his own command reportedly greatly impressed General Secretary Gorbachev on the latter's visit to the Soviet Far East in July 1986. When Yazov was reassigned to Moscow as deputy minister of defense for personnel in January 1987, it was generally believed that the promotion was due to the influence of Gorbachev.

In the shakeup of the high command on 30 May, Yazov was named defense minister, replacing Marshal Sergei Sokolov. As defense minister, Yazov has led a campaign to extend certain aspects of *perestroika* to the armed forces, with major emphases on improved discipline and more efficient utilization of resources.

Yazov was elected a candidate member of the Central Committee at the Twenty-sixth CPSU Congress in 1981 and was re-elected at the Twenty-seventh CPSU Congress in 1986. At the Central Committee plenum, 26 June 1987, he attained full Central Committee membership and was elected a candidate member of the Politburo.

(Sources: *Krasnaia zvezda*, 16 January; *Pravda*, 31 May, 27 June; *Problems of Communism*, July–August; *RL Research*, 30 May 1982, 1 April 1986.

R. Judson Mitchell
University of New Orleans

Yugoslavia

Population. 23,430,830

Party. League of Communists of Yugoslavia (Savez Komunista Jugoslavije; LCY). The LCY is the only political party in the Socialist Federal Republic of Yugoslavia (SFRY). However, there are party organizations in each of the six republics—Slovenia, Croatia, Bosnia-Hercegovina, Montenegro, Macedonia, and Serbia—and in the two autonomous provinces—Kossovo and Vojvodina—as well as within the Yugoslav armed forces (JNA).

Founded. April 1919, as the Socialist Workers' Party of Yugoslavia; disbanded and replaced by the Communist Party of Yugoslavia (CPY) in June 1920. The CPY took the name League of Communists of Yugoslavia at the Sixth Party Congress in November 1952.

Membership. About 2,150,000

President of the Presidium. Milanko Renovica (59), a Serb from Bosnia-Hercegovina, replaced in June by Boško Krunić (58), a Serb from the autonomous province of Vojvodina.

Secretary of the Presidium. Radiša Gačić (49), a Serb from Serbia (first half of a two-year term). At this time there are 7 appointed executive secretaries: Slobodan Filipović, Marko Lolić, Vukašin Lončar, Boris Muževič, Stanislav Stojanović, Uglješa Uzelac, and Ljubomir Varošlija. The number of executive secretaries varies as needed.

Presidium. 23 members representing the republics, autonomous provinces, and the LCY organization in the Yugoslav armed forces. Fourteen members of Presidium hold that job between party congresses. However, there are 9 ex officio members who take part in Presidium meetings by virtue of their positions as presidents of their own territorial League of Communists (LC) or as head of the JNA party organization. Since these presidencies rotate on different schedules—sometimes on a one-year, sometimes on a two-year basis—the makeup of the ex officio members can change within any given year. Members: Slovenia, Stefan Korosеč and Franc Šetinc; Croatia, Ivica Račan and Stipe Šuvar; Bosnia-Hercegovina, Ivan Brigić and Milanko Renovica; Montenegro, Marko Orlandić and Vidoje Žarković; Macedonia, Milan Pančevski and Vasil Tupurkovski; Serbia, Dušan Čkrebić and Radiša Gačić; Kossovo, Kol Shiroka; Vojvodina, Boško Krunić. Ex officio members: Slovenia, Milan Kučan; Croatia, Stanko Stojčević; Bosnia-Hercegovina, Milan Uzelac; Montenegro, Miljan Radović; Macedonia, Jakov Lazarovski; Serbia, Slobodan Milošević; Vojvodina, Djordje Stojšić; Kossovo, Azem Vlasi; party organization in the army, General Georgije Jovičić.

Central Committee. 165 members: 20 from each republic, 15 for each of the two autonomous provinces, and 15 for the army's party organization.

Status. Ruling party
Last Congress. Thirteenth, June 1986
Last Elections. 1986. The Yugoslav parliament has two chambers: a 220-member Federal Chamber and an 88-member Chamber of Republics and Provinces. Elections are conducted by the Socialist Alliance of the Working People of Yugoslavia via a complex delegate system. In May, Marjan Rožić (Slovenia) became president of the assembly; Živan Marelj (Vojvodina) became vice-president. The term of office is one year but may change if constitutional amendments are adopted.
Auxiliary Organizations. The Socialist Alliance of the Working People of Yugoslavia (Socjalistički savez radnog naroda Jugoslavije; SAWPY) is an umbrella mass organization that includes all major political/social organizations as well as individuals. SAWPY provides the political machinery for conducting elections and mirrors the tensions of the LCY. There is also the Confederation of Trade Unions of Yugoslavia (Savez sindikata Jugoslavije; CTUY) and the League of Socialist Youth of Yugoslavia (Savez socijalističke omladine Jugoslavije; LSYY).
Governmental Bodies. An 8-member collective state presidency was elected in May 1984 for five-year terms. The president and vice-president serve for one year, and these positions rotate among the membership. In May 1987 Lazar Mojsov (67), from Macedonia, became president of the SFRY; Hamdija Pozderac (Bosnia-Hercegovina) became vice-president (in September Pozderac resigned and was replaced by Foreign Minister Raif Dizdarević). Other members of the presidency are Slovenia, Stane Dolanc; Croatia, Josip Vrhovec; Kossovo, Sinan Hasani; Montenegro, Veselin Djuranović; Vojvodina, Radovan Vlajković; and Serbia, Nikola Ljubičić. LCY president Boško Krunić met with the state presidency as an ex officio member. Day-to-day government is in the hands of a 29-member Federal Executive Council (FEC) selected for four years and headed by Prime Minister Branko Mikulić (59). There are two vice-premiers: Miloš Milosavljević and Janez Zemljarič. Among the most important federal secretaries are Budimir Lončar, foreign affairs; Admiral Branko Mamula, defense; Dobroslav Ćulafić, internal affairs; and Svetozar Rikanović, finance.
Publications. Main publications of the LCY are *Komunist* (weekly) and *Socjalizam* (monthly); SAWPY's main publication is *Borba*, a daily newspaper with Belgrade and Zagreb editions. Other major dailies include *Politika*, *Večernje novosti*, *Politika ekspres* (Belgrade), *Večernji list*, *Vjesnik* (Zagreb), *Delo* (Ljubljana), *Oslobodjenje* (Sarajevo), and *Rilindja* (Priština). Prominent weeklies are *NIN* (*Nedeljne informativne novine*; Belgrade) and *Danas* (Zagreb). The boldest youth newspapers are the Slovene Youth Organization weekly, *Mladina*; the Maribor student weekly, *Katedra*; and the Belgrade weekly *Student*; much controversial religious material appears in the biweekly Catholic journal, *Glas koncila* (Zagreb). Tanjug is the official news agency.

Leadership and Party Organization. In 1987 the party leadership that was elected at the June 1986 LCY Thirteenth Congress searched for ideological unity and economic stabilization amid rising ethnic tensions, skyrocketing inflation, and increasing demands for political reform. With the average age of the 23-member presidium in the early 50s and the 165-member Central Committee in the mid-40s, this collective leadership represented a generational change.

There were few organizational surprises. On 30 June, Krunić took over as LCY president of what is perhaps the world's most elaborate quota system. According to the established rotation schedule for top officials of the Yugoslav federation from 1986 to 1994, the new president had to come from the autonomous province of Vojvodina (Tanjug Domestic Service, 30 June; *FBIS*, 7 July). As party president, Krunić achieved the appropriate territorial division of power; however, he is ethnically Serbian as was his predecessor, Renovica (Bosnia-Hercegovina). Secretary Gačić, a Serb from Serbia, had another year to serve; thus, Serbs continued to hold the two top party positions. The ethnic balance existed not at the top of the party but in an interlocking party-government leadership where the president of the eight-member state presidency was Macedonian (Lazar Mojsov) and the prime minister was a Croat from Bosnia-Hercegovina (Mikulić).

Western Yugoslav watchers were divided on the ideological implications of the 58-year-old Krunić's election. Some considered him a hard-liner, while others pointed to his statement that party unity can be achieved "only through the expression of different views" (*Nedeljna Dalmacija*, Split, 18 January; RFE *Research*, 7 August) and his open support for Mikhail Gorbachev's *perestroika* as a "democratizing" force in Soviet society (Tanjug, 18 February;

RFE *Research*, 7 August). In any case, the one-year rotating mandate of the LCY president substantially reduces the potential impact of his political-ideological preferences.

The consequences of the short mandate were reinforced by an overwhelming agenda. According to LCY secretary Gačić, before the end of the year the Presidium needed to examine economic trends, adopt a program to implement the Ninth Central Committee Plenum on Kossovo, evaluate the changes in the law of associated labor, draft a program for stopping the emigration of Serbs and Montenegrins from Kossovo, persuade those who had emigrated to return, and brief the Central Committee on a regular basis. In the meantime the party Central Committee was slated to discuss realizing "legality and constitutionality," deciding on appropriate forms of ideological-political training, evaluating the proposed constitutional amendments, and coming up with workable economic development policies (Tanjug Domestic Service, 19 July; *FBIS*, 21 July).

Predictably this ambitious agenda fell short of realization. Although the top of the Yugoslav political hierarchy agreed on the problems, they could not agree on solutions. Presidium member Dr. Šuvar (Croatia) set the tone of the debate on the LCY's need to restore credibility with a call to purge all "corrupt, rapacious, and irresponsible persons" to create a more united party as a prerequisite for dealing with the ongoing economic-political crisis (*Komunist*, April; BBC, 13 April). Questions were immediately raised as to whether those seeking "to cleanse" (euphemism for purge) the LCY were merely seeking a quick fix for endemic socioeconomic weaknesses. Was this call for "cleansing" simply "a substitute for incompetence or lack of will to change the social situation more thoroughly?" (*Borba*, 24 April; *FBIS*, 29 April).

Responses at the April "ideological plenum" underlined the difficulties. Šuvar presented a hard-hitting, polemical opening address. (Tanjug Domestic Service, 28 April; *FBIS*, 5 May.) Kučan, the head of the Slovene party organization, characterized attempts to repress differing views as a sign of the party's weakness and rejected demands for what he considered an "ideological holy war." Conversely, Uzelac, his counterpart in Bosnia-Hercegovina, attacked "vacillation" in the LCY struggle against anticommunism and nationalism (BBC, 29 April). Although Uzelac denounced the idea of democratic and dogmatic regions in Yugoslavia, the contrast between his own view and the Slovene position was evident.

Radovan Radonjić, chairman of the Central Committee commission for ideological effort, summed up the debate in an interview entitled "We Agree that We Do Not Agree" (*NIN*, 10 May; *JPRS-Eastern Europe Report* 87-106, 10 July). Although Radonjić's proposal—that an action program be adopted, which, if not implemented, would force the entire Presidium and Central Committee to resign—did not survive, he was "encouraged" that the plenum agreed to set forward the disputed issues so they could be openly discussed by the Central Committee and the public. In short, the "ideological plenum" admitted the disagreements at the top of the party as a necessary step toward resolving them.

The struggle for ideological unity continued into July. Šuvar's press conference on the documents of the "ideological plenum" shifted the emphasis from achieving unity at the top to "ideological work. . . as an every day activity for which the basic LCY organizations are most responsible" (Tanjug Domestic Service, 23 July; *FBIS*, 29 July). He complained that basic LCY organizations were stagnating, spending more time "lamenting the fate of socialism" than attending to their ideological tasks. Šuvar's remarks on the need for invoking "public party responsibility" against those who do not stick to party policy or those who interpret it "in a biased way," left the impression of yet another attempt to operationalize democratic centralism. When questioned about the reaction of the Serbian party, however, he objected to "territorialization of opinions" and suggested that such differences should be resolved in the forthcoming constitutional changes.

For those impatient with the cumbersome machinery of collective leadership, this looked like blaming the lowest level of LCY organization for inaction and using the constitutional amendments as another delaying tactic. Conversely, for those committed to decisionmaking via consensus, it was a crucial part of the process that requires that everyone keep talking until a common denominator is found. No matter how one interprets the results of the ideological plenum, agreeing to disagree at the top of the party undoubtedly sent conflicting signals to those LCY organizations that Šuvar wanted to see engage in ideological struggle and did not bode well for the scheduled November plenum devoted to theoretical work and ideological training.

The uncertainties of party work; the mountain of political, ideological, and economic problems; and the avalanche of criticism and self-criticism of LCY leadership made recruitment difficult. In fact, the decline was less than might have been expected. Using the figures of then–party president Renovica, the year began with more than 2,150,000 LCY members, with workers representing about 30 percent (*Borba*, 1 January; *FBIS*, 2 January). According to the data presented to a Serbian Central Committee session in April, Serbian party members in Serbia proper dropped by 2.3 percent in 1986, the Vojvodina party was down by 3.1 percent, and Kossovo party membership went up 1.7 percent (*Politika*, 23 April; *JPRS-Eastern Europe Report* 87-103, 30 June). This partially confirmed earlier reports of declines in membership in Serbia, Croatia, Slovenia, and Vojvodina and of increases in Bosnia-Hercegovina, Macedonia, and Kossovo (*Politika*, 13 January; *FBIS*, 29 January).

Perhaps more worrisome in terms of organizational demographics, LCY membership among the group aged 18 to 27 had declined by 10.4 percent since 1980 (RFE *Research*, 4 June). Indeed, a reported 75 percent of the Serbian party organizations did not admit new members in 1986. To cope with this problem, the Presidium opted for a sliding scale on which LCY membership dues would range from .20 to 3 percent of the member's income. This move came into force during July with the stipulation that the new dues were to be assessed by December 1988 at the latest. In practical terms it meant that 71 percent of the party would pay a reduced fee, 18.4 percent would stay at the same rate, and 10.6 percent would face increases, particularly in some sections of the Slovene LCY and the party organization in the armed forces (Tanjug Domestic Service, 2 June; *FBIS*, 2 June).

Thus throughout 1987 the LCY tried to establish general guidelines for tackling the country's deepening political-economic crises. The Ninth LCY Central Committee Plenum during 26–27 June reversed the stand of the 1981 plenum on Kossovo, which minimized the danger of provincial riots, and agreed that Kossovo was an all-Yugoslav problem. But within that context the plenum walked a fine line between condemning "growing escalation of Albanian separatist nationalism" and warning against "all nationalism" as dangerous. A commission was set up to investigate Fadilj Hodza, the former head of the Kossovo party and a former member of the Yugoslav collective state presidency, and his responsibility for Albanian nationalist activities.

The differences the plenum was attempting to resolve marked its sessions. For example, the opening speech by Montenegrin Orlandić strongly attacked "illegal activities of counterrevolutionary forces" in the region. He called on the Kossovo LCY committee to determine political accountability and to throw the rascals out. Vlasi, head of the Kossovo party, protested against victimizing all Albanians for the nationalist excesses of a few (*Politika*, 27 June; RFE *Research* 29 June).

The attempt to sort out federal, republic, and provincial responsibilities for the unhappy situation in Kossovo was tangled in LCY efforts to subdue what some viewed as "excessive" freedom of the press in the form of "local orientations" focused on neighboring nationalisms rather than Yugoslav unity (*Večernje novosti*, 9 December 1986; RFE *Research*, 22 January). However, those "local orientations" had powerful regional protectors. In Serbia, the attitude towards Albanian nationalism and whether it was paired with Serbian nationalism became the dividing line in a power struggle between Milošević, the head of the Serbian LCY, and Ivan Stambolić, Serbian republic president. The Serbian LCY was badly split, and what had been a federal media policy problem also reflected republic political struggle.

Thus, when Dragiša Pavlović, the head of the Belgrade LCY committee, criticized the "extremism" of some newspapers in their Kossovo coverage (*Borba*, 11 September; RFE *Research*, 22 October), he was objecting to their politics as much as to their reporting. Pavlović opposed the increasingly hard-line majority of the Serbian LCY in his assessment of the relative dangers of Albanian and Serbian nationalism; it was not a popular position and would cost him his job. General Miloslav Djordjević, another voice of moderation, was booed when he tried to speak about Serbian nationalism to the republic Central Committee session at the end of the month (*Danas*, 13 October; *FBIS*, 15 October).

These political differences fed the disagreements about the role of the media on the road to political reform and economic stabilization. A unified federal, republic, and provincial media policy was simply not possible. There was official ambivalence to a Yugoslav version of *glasnost'*, but republic and provincial politicians continued to defend their own political turf in the emerging tug-of-war over proposed constitutional amendments.

Meanwhile the party faced another challenge to its tenuous leading role—issue-specific social movements advocating the causes of ecology, feminism, pacifism, and the like. Frequently lumped together as "alternativists," these social movements dovetailed with republic resistance to federal authority in the form of the "Slovene syndrome" (*Vjesnik*, 18 April; *JPRS-Eastern Europe Report*-092, 11 June). Party response, as on other escalating pressures, was divided. Some defended these movements as spontaneous, self-managing contributions to society; others feared them, insisting that the claim to ideological neutrality masked anticommunist intentions (*Borba*, 24 December 1986; *FBIS*, 7 January).

Not surprisingly, the magnitude of the problems and the seeming inadequacy of proposed solutions raised questions about the need for a radical overhaul of the complex political machinery and consensual principles of operation. Although the top leadership had dismissed demands for an extraordinary LCY congress in March, by September calls for such a congress re-emerged in the context of financial scandal and ethnic violence (*Večernje novosti*, 11 September; RFE *Research*, 1 November). Many had come to feel that the Titoist solution was simply not the answer.

Domestic Affairs. The year 1987 was a brutal one for Yugoslav policymakers. Prime Minister Mikulić squandered his political capital on a series of unworkable economic packages that one frustrated government planner described as "trying to cure AIDS [acquired immunodeficiency syndrome] with Band-Aids" (*WP*, national weekly edition, 14 December). Mikulić was under mounting pressure to have his government resign, while Mojsov, the head of the state presidency, collapsed during his report to the Federal Assembly on the latest draconian austerity program designed to ward off economic disaster. Mojsov was reportedly treated at Belgrade's military hospital and returned to finish his speech (Tanjug, in English, 19 October; *FBIS*, 19 October). But the incident underlined the high-stress nature of his job and his political commitment, as well as the unpleasant economic realities that had become the fundamental political dynamic in Yugoslavia. In 1987 Yugoslav politics were the politics of economics, with demands for political and economic reform as inseparable as Siamese twins.

The Economy. Officially Yugoslavia's medium- and long-term hard currency debt amounted to $17.8 billion at the end of 1986 (Tanjug, in English, 14 September; *FBIS*, 15 September). When short-term debts were added, the figure climbed to between $19.2 and $19.7 billion, "roughly $20 billion." Against this is some $2 billion owed to Yugoslavia, although that debt, largely on the part of Third World, nonaligned allies, is not easily collectible.

Debt servicing was the albatross of the Yugoslav economy. Prime Minister Mikulić, notwithstanding his plummeting political popularity, should be credited with holding down the debt level and indeed contributing to the six-year trend which reduced it by $1 billion. This international fiscal responsibility, however, had disastrous consequences for the domestic economy.

Hard currency debts have to be serviced in foreign exchange. To do so requires making exports competitive, devaluing the dinar, and tolerating domestic inflationary pressures. As money becomes less valuable, workers demand higher wages and enterprises insist on higher prices, which sets off still more demands for higher wages. Thus as the year progressed, the economy was gripped by a runaway inflation over which the government had lost control.

FEC vice-president Milosavljević, in his defense of the October anti-inflationary program to the Federal Assembly, admitted that by the third quarter inflation had reached 168 percent, with projections for a staggering 220 percent by the beginning of 1988 (Tanjug Domestic Service, 14 November; *FBIS*, 16 November). If so, inflation more than doubled during the year, giving Yugoslavia the highest rate in Europe.

With an estimated 16 percent unemployment (roughly 1.3 million Yugoslavs of the 6.5 million employed in the socialist sector), Yugoslavia ranked second in this category behind Spain, which had to cope with a 20 percent jobless rate (interview with LCY member Korosec, Tanjug Domestic Service, 13 September; *FBIS*, 17 September).

As the inflation/unemployment vise closed, the Mikulić government re-evaluated its debt-servicing policy in an effort to bring domestic relief. Declaring a "foreign liquidity" crisis, Yugoslavia began negotiating with its foreign creditors to reschedule the hard currency obligations at a less damaging level. The proposal would reduce the annual amount of foreign currency exchange used for debt payments from 46 to 25 percent. The assumption is that funds would thereby be available to spend on Western imports, which, in turn, would provide domestic competition and drive prices down. The cost of such a solution involved negotiating yet another standby agreement with the International Monetary Fund (IMF) at the price of the October anti-inflationary program—price hikes and wage freezes.

IMF negotiations got under way throughout the fall amid another wave of predictable strikes and worker protests. Mikulić's efforts to adjust wages to correspond to actual productivity were less than successful. According to LCY Presidium member Šuvar's report to the April CC plenum, in 1986 there had been 927 work stoppages involving some 93,000 workers (Tanjug Domestic Service, 28 Apri; *FBIS*, 5 May). Within weeks of the February wage freeze, about 1,000 enterprises and some 150,000 workers were taking part in intermittent strikes. There was no clear end in sight for the strikes set off by the October wage freeze, but it was evident that exceptions would be negotiated on a case-by-case basis. For example, the 5,000 Macedonian foundry workers who marched on the regional assembly in Skoplje were promised that their wages would be raised to the average wage in foundries throughout Yugoslavia (*NYT*, 18 November). Such exceptions underlined the government's difficulties in convincing Yugoslav workers to pay the cost of economic stabilization and weakened the credibility of the anti-inflation program in the eyes of foreign creditors.

This tension between the demand for internal fiscal responsibility necessary for the foreign credits needed to keep the economy afloat and the imperatives of enterprise came into focus when the December 1986 bankruptcy law went into force in July. In August some 1,600 Montenegrin construction workers became the first casualty of this move, which was designed to force Yugoslav enterprises to balance their books or go out of business (*NYT*, 19 August). The new law gave enterprises operating at a loss six months to get their finances into shape or face bankruptcy proceedings.

Evidence that the government intended to enforce the bankruptcy law was meant to frighten Yugoslav managers into better business habits. Even symbolic bankruptcies sent the message that Prime Minister Mikulić believed that enterprises should make a profit and that workers' wages should reflect productivity. Given that an estimated 7,000 enterprises employing something like a fourth of the Yugoslav labor force were among those creating losses instead of profits (BBC, 28 August), rigid enforcement would put another million Yugoslavs on the unemployment roll and destroy the economy, not save it.

The government's internal economic woes went beyond enterprises operating at a loss. At the end of August a financial scandal involving a major agroindustrial empire, Agrokomerc, in Bosnia-Hercegovina revealed a staggering level of intraenterprise banking debts and political wheeling and dealing that involved the top leaders of the country. Agrokomerc came under investigation for having issued perhaps as much as $900 million (U.S.) worth of unsecured promissory notes in local currency to carry out development plans for which it could not generate federal support. As many as 63 banks appear to have lent money without proof of collateral. The Bank of Bihač may go bankrupt, and the others are in varying degrees of financial trouble. Vice-president of the state presidency Pozderac, facing charges of being the Agrokomerc protector, resigned his post in September, claiming that he knew nothing about the irregularities. Some 42 members of the LCY were expelled. Fikret Abdić, the president of the enterprise, was arrested, while as many as 130 party members face either criminal charges or LCY discipline (*WSJ*, 14 September). And that may not be the end of the matter.

Like Vice-President Pozderac, Prime Minister Mikulić's home base is in Bosnia-Hercegovina, and although he was not part of the close family ties between the Pozderac clan and the luckless Mr. Abdić, there are questions as to what the prime minister knew and when he knew it. Whether or not there was evidence of a direct connection, and despite Mikulić's record of having opposed using federal funds for Agrokomerc development (*Borba*, 14 September; *FBIS*, 17 September), suspicions of a connection continued.

Some considered the Pozderac resignation a positive political sign (Tanjug Domestic Service, 13 September; *FBIS*, 14 September) because it was the first example of a top official taking responsibility and implied the possibility of accountability within the highest party-government circles. Notwithstanding the economic consequences of what the Yugoslav social accounting service estimates at nearly $8.5 billion of unsecured enterprise credits (RFE *Research*, 1 November), as the penalties of Agrokomerc mismanagement continue to come down from courts and LCY disciplinary bodies, undoubtedly the temptation of other Yugoslav enterprises to ignore the two-year old law against solving their cash flow problems by borrowing from one another or local banks without collateral seemed less attractive.

In this manner the Agrokomerc scandal increased the clout of the bankruptcy law and the law against unsecured borrowing, sharpened these administrative instruments in the campaign for fiscal responsibility, and made it harder for republic/provincial politicians to look the other way. It remained to be seen whether the Mikulić government could pull off the political and fiscal balancing act needed to restore ailing enterprises, establish fiscal restraint, and create the business norms essential for any genuine market socialism. Not all the obstacles on the road to economic stabilization flowed from flawed policies. Federal incentives for small private businesses, for example, frequently received little support from communal officials, and less progress was made in developing this alternative form of employment as a result. Actual credits bore little relation to the government's monetary policy.

The October anti-inflation program faced severe criticism in regional assemblies, and the Yugoslav press acknowledged that the entire Slovene delegation voted against passage (*NYT*, 15 November). However, the package was adopted by both houses of the Federal Assembly, which meant that prices shot up and that the dinar was devalued another 24.6 percent, bringing the new exchange rate of the National Bank of Yugoslavia to almost 1,300 dinars to the dollar (Tanjug, in English, 17 November; *FBIS*, 17 November). In these circumstances, Mikulić managed to keep the long-suffering Yugoslav workers from revolting and foreign creditors from jumping ship, which were accomplishments in themselves. They also may have helped the prime minister in his struggle to stay in his job by emphasizing the difficulties that faced potential challengers as well as the problems of mobilizing support.

Not all economic indicators were negative. There had been a good harvest. Exports were up, especially with hard currency markets, and industrial production increased by 2.6 percent for the first half of the year (*Politika*, 14 August; *FBIS*, 20 August). These economic rays of hope aside, discrepancies between spiraling wages and prices among republics and the autonomous provinces exacerbated already explosive ethnic tensions. This was particularly true in Kossovo, where average personal income rose only 76.9 percent compared with the Slovene increase of 115 percent (Tanjug, 9 September; *FBIS*, 10 September), while even official inflation surpassed 120 percent.

The National Question. Karl Marx had little patience with southern Slav nationalism. He assumed it was incompatible with socialism—a false consciousness that would disappear in proper socialist societies where class identities would replace national aspirations. Marx expected the national question to land on the rubbish heap of history. In Yugoslavia that expectation proved to be wishful thinking rather than scientific socialism. In his commitment to ideological solutions, Marx underestimated the tenacity of historical political cultures.

Interwar Yugoslavia, failing to achieve multiethnic integration, collapsed into a Serbian dictatorship. Subsequent wartime atrocities deepened ethnic hatreds, and communist Yugoslavia inherited a hornet's nest of ethnic strife and animosity. The founding myth of partisan solidarity on which postwar Yugoslavia was built came out of the shared struggle to throw out the German occupier and reunite the country. The corollary was Tito's pledge of liberty and equality for all nations of Yugoslavia.

The national question was thus institutionalized in the form of Yugoslavia's federal political system. The tension between nation and class became a fundamental political dynamic, and the need to draw the line between national rights and counterrevolutionary activity, a perpetual policy problem. Throughout the 1980s the autonomous province of Kossovo within the Republic of Serbia has been the key arena of conflict.

Kossovo. In 1987 there was a dramatic ethnic confrontation between the Albanian majority, now estimated at 85 percent of the population, in Kossovo (*NYT*, 1 November) and the declining Serb-Montenegrin minority of roughly 200,000. For the Albanians the issue is one of numbers and fairness. Why should 500,000 Montenegrins have their own republic and not 1.5 million Albanians? Yet for the eight million-plus Serbs in Serbia proper as well as for those living in the province, it is unthinkable that the heart of historic Serbia, the seat of the Serbian church, should be cut away. To do so would violate Serbia's territorial integrity.

After the fall of Serbian strongman Aleksandar Ranković in 1966, the ethnic Albanians have moved step-by-step into power in the province party, policy-making bodies, the judiciary, schools, and factories. The Slavic power elite that controlled the province under Ranković has been replaced by an Albanian power elite. This de facto home rule has reduced the once-dominant Serb-Montenegrin minority to a psychological and political subordinate status. In the best of circumstances that would have been a painful adjustment but combined with incidents of harassment by resentful Albanians seeking an ethnically pure province in lieu of the unattainable republic, it became a question of physical security for the individuals involved and a political crisis for provincial, republic, and federal policymakers alike.

Marches on Belgrade and protests and petitions demanding protection for the Slav minority became the norm. In June Kossovar protesters demonstrated outside the Ninth LCY Central Committee Plenum in aid of defusing Albanian nationalism, containing the Serbian backlash, and stopping the emigration of Serbs and Montenegrins who had decided that Kossovo was no longer a safe or desirable place to live. For the first time Belgrade residents joined the demonstrators. The Gypsies even got into the act with a blunt statement to the Socialist Alliance of Kossovo that Gypsies were "the most endangered" of all Kossovo minorities (*Večernje novosti*, 21 June; RFE *Research*, 29 June).

The Ninth Plenum admitted that "counterrevolutionary activities in Kossovo" and the spillover of the province's ethnic hostilities into national politics had become the "gravest and deepest political problem of both Kossovo and the whole of Yugoslavia" (*Politika*, 28 June: RFE *Research*, 7 August). Although the 22 proposals put forward included suggestions for bilingual education, family planning, and economic development, they could in no sense be considered an action program, for the plenum stopped short of assuming federal responsibility for implementation. By placing that responsibility squarely on the Kossovo provincial LCY organization, the federal party adhered to the principle of republic/provincial autonomy that has shifted the balance of power away from the center in post-Tito Yugoslavia; but, in so doing, it intensified anxiety and frustration among those Serbian communists who were convinced that the Kossovo party organization was a hotbed of Albanian nationalism unable and unwilling to protect the Kossovar Slav population or to prevent it from packing up and getting out.

Ethnic passions were further inflamed when a twenty-year-old Albanian conscript ran amok with a machine gun in the Paračin military barracks in southern Serbia. When the shooting stopped, four soldiers were dead and five wounded. The gun-happy conscript reportedly committed suicide. Given that two of the dead and three of the wounded were Sunni Muslims, the killings did not appear to be premeditated ethnic violence. However, the incident accelerated already deteriorating Serb-Albanian relations. Some 10,000 demonstrators protested at one victim's funeral in Belgrade. Serbian nationalists elsewhere in the republic vandalized Albanian-owned shops. Arrests were made, and a Croatian member of the LCY presidency warned against "repressive measures" in the irrational, passion-ridden atmosphere (*NYT*, 15 September).

In just that atmosphere Pavlović, head of the powerful Belgrade LCY, attempted to calm emotions and spoke of the dangers of Serbian as well as Albanian nationalism (*Borba*, 14 September; *FBIS*, 8 October). His statesmanlike appeal cost him his job. Charging that Pavlović was soft on Albanian counterrevolutionary separatism, Milošević pandered to the Serbian backlash with a "policy of the hard hand" and declared his determination to deal with antisocialist forces "even if they call us Stalinists" (*NYT*, 1 November). The barracks killings thus contributed to a political climate in which Serbian party president Milošević succeeded in outmaneuvering a key rival.

Milošević's attitude did not bode well for federal efforts to contain interethnic hostilities. His language and political style were confrontational and his political agenda lacked new solutions. Meanwhile, the disgrace and expulsion of Hodza, former vice-president and Kossovo politician, from the Council of the Federation, an advisory body to the Yugoslav collective presidency, over a tasteless joke at a meeting of reserve officers in Prizren during November 1986 illustrated the bizarre, Byzantine nature of Serbian/Kossovo politics. Reportedly Hodza suggested that one means of dealing with rapes in the province would be to legalize prostitution. But, of course, Albanian women would not be involved in such a thing, so by implication he had insulted Serbian womanhood. Since there were no reporters present, his remarks were rumor until almost a year later when they appeared in Serbian newspapers, ostensibly based on handwritten notes taken at the meeting. Serbian women in Kossovo were outraged and took to the streets to defend their honor. The repercussions spread all the way to the LCY Presidium, which went on record as understanding the protests of the Serbian women balanced by the opinion that the incident was being manipulated by Serb/Montenegrin nationalist attacks against the unity and equality of Yugoslavia's nations as well as attacks "aimed at other socialist values" (Tanjug Domestic Service, 20 October; *FBIS*, 21 October).

As a precaution the central authorities sent a

detachment of 380 federal riot police to the province (BBC, 26 October). Their presence was largely intended as a deterrent and perhaps to preempt Milošević's next move. It was unlikely that these troops would be used to disperse Serb/Montenegrin protests or be particularly effective in stopping individual acts of Albanian harassment of the Slav minority. The resort to federal riot police also indicated a lack of confidence in the province authorities. With or without an active role, the police ran the risk of becoming targets, thereby making the federal government more vulnerable to repercussions of Kossovar ethnic politics. In an environment where 258 of the country's political prisoners in 1986 were Albanians (RFE *Research*, 29 June), where unemployment was roughly triple the national average (54.4 percent) (RFE *Research*, 4 June), and where the standard of living was the lowest in Yugoslavia, it was asking for trouble.

Yet, one must keep the rhetoric surrounding Kossovo in perspective. Notwithstanding warnings of the "Lebanonizing" of Yugoslavia, the country is not Lebanon. Albanians from Tirana do not play the role of either Syria or Israel. There is no equivalent to the political role of the Palestine Liberation Organization (PLO), nor have Yugoslav authorities done anything as damaging as Indira Gandhi when she sent the Indian army into the Golden Temple to rout out Sikh extremists. Those who criticize the federal LCY for, at the Ninth Plenum, insisting that the Kossovo province party put its house in order tend to forget the lessons of history. Unless the federal LCY was willing to opt for virtually endless martial law, it had little choice. The politics of accommodation, of keeping everyone talking, of containment are ambiguous and frustrating. Only the alternatives in Yugoslavia as all around the world are worse.

The Slovene Syndrome. Although the idea of a Slovene syndrome was rejected as "unacceptable and harmful" by Jože Smole, president of SAWPY (Tanjug Domestic Service, 6 April; *FBIS*, 23 April), there were discernible differences between Slovenia and the other Yugoslav republics, mostly having to do with internal Slovene politics as well as with Slovene positions on all-Yugoslav political and economic issues. Indeed, the two components of the Slovene syndrome fed on one another, for the republic's liberal media policy tolerated a level of criticism and diversity of opinion that horrified hard-line Serbian politicians. Not surprisingly, in Serbia, Slovene commentaries pointing to Serbian nationalism as an historical dimension of the Kossovo crisis were condemned by Serbs as politically insensitive and unsupportive.

Whereas the nationalism of Kossovar Albanians breeds on province poverty and political frustration, Slovene nationalism is an unintended consequence of good fortune. Slovenia is the most Western, liberalized, economically prosperous, and ethnically homogeneous republic in Yugoslavia. Some 1.7 million Slovenes, roughly 8 percent of the country's population, produce 18 percent of the gross national product (Slovene premier, Dušan Sinigoj, *NYT*, 13 July). There is virtually no unemployment in Slovenia; the per capita income is roughly double the national average.

Nonetheless, the Slovenes have a range of economic complaints. Their policymakers and enterprise managers alike chaffed at the foreign currency laws that force them to send foreign currency earned by Slovene exports or tourism to the federal government and then petition to get back what they need to continue producing for export. Matjaž Kmecl, a member of the Slovene LCY presidency, graphically underlined Slovene dissatisfaction with his claim that Slovene exports to hard currency markets were 25 percent of the Yugoslav total, while subsidies to their southern neighboring republics (Bosnia-Hercegovina, Macedonia, Montenegro) and the province of Kossovo take 20 to 30 percent of the Slovene national product (*NYT*, 13 July). Whether or not his figures can be disputed, the perception existed that federal regulations hampered the Slovene ability to export and that contributions to the less developed regions of Yugoslavia drained the Slovene economy.

Slovene economists criticized the slow progress toward market socialism and the government's economic management. Korošec, the Slovene representative on the LCY presidency, hammered at the necessity to eliminate economic and ideological obstacles in order to promote the small businesses that would contribute to economic stabilization (*Borba*, 23 October; *FBIS*, 17 November). The low opinion of Prime Minister Mikulić's most recent anti-inflation program was reflected by the entire Slovene delegation in the Federal Assembly voting against it (*NYT*, 15 November).

Politically, the Slovenes advocated an expanded role for SAWPY, multicandidate elections, insisted that religious belief should not be a criterion for cadre policy, and tolerated alternative groups and social movements viewed with suspicion elsewhere in Yugoslavia. These positions led to fears that what

Slovene analysts considered unacceptably "centralist" constitutional amendments would erode the republic's internal political autonomy and disadvantage it economically (*Politika*, 18 March; *FBIS*, 7 April).

Another aspect of Slovene political culture—a long-standing disinclination of young Slovenes to become professional soldiers or to take advantage of the educational opportunities offered by the military academy—brought about increasingly acrimonious exchanges with spokesmen for the Yugoslav armed forces. This lack of enthusiasm for a military career was not new but combined with a movement for a civilian alternative to military service, it became more of a sore point with the military establishment. The issue took center stage in midsummer when France Popit, the president of Slovenia, bluntly suggested that the army should take responsibility for the lack of interest in a military profession rather than blaming society as a whole (*Delo*, 6 July; RFE *Research*, 30 September). The army weekly retorted that "attacks on the army influenced some young people" and took a slap at the insular nature of Slovene politics by claiming that "the army is more 'Yugoslav' than republic oriented" (*Narodna armija*, 6 August; RFE, ibid.).

As expected, dissent was an integral part of the Slovene syndrome in 1987, as Slovene politicians simultaneously attempted to defend and contain the outspoken student press, pacifist tendencies, and the contribution of alternative social groups to socialist development.

Dissent. In the Yugoslav context of ongoing political struggle and with the ambiguity of the rules of the political game, dissent is pervasive. Indeed, much of what is characterized as "opposition" and referred to in the same breath with dissent (RFE *Research*, 16 March) can be seen as legitimate in-system debate over the nature of political and economic reform. (To have true dissent requires agreed-on public policy to dissent from.) Throughout 1987 a wide spectrum of Yugoslav politicians and ordinary citizens were deeply dissatisfied with the functioning of their political system and generally agreed that the "Titoist solution" needed to be improved on; hence, the proposed constitutional amendments. Yet equally deep disagreement existed between those who wanted to repair the machinery of rotating collective rule based on decisionmaking by consensus and those who considered it hopeless.

Polemical rhetoric ran high, and yet much was acceptable that formerly would have been unthinkable. The Slovene student paper *Katedra*, associated with the University of Maribor, published an interview with the prominent political dissident Milovan Djilas that was the first to appear in Yugoslavia since he broke with the party in the 1950s, thus ending a 34-year "conspiracy of silence" (*NYT*, 27 March). The interview followed the return of Djilas' passport in January and, more important, came on the heels of Prime Minister Mikulić's interview with the German weekly (*Der Spiegel*, 23 March; *FBIS*, 24 March) in which he called Djilas "a first-class traitor" to his country.

This did not mean that everything was acceptable. Within the month after the Djilas interview went to press, *Katedra*'s acting chief editor Miran Lesjak resigned, reportedly under official pressure (BBC, 9 July). Subsequently, the Maribor student paper was banned for "insulting" Vice-President Pozderac (before his involvement in the Agrokomerc scandal led to his resignation), the LC, the militia, and the justice organs (*Borba*, 23 July). From the Maribor magistrates' court's point of view, *Katedra* had gone too far. The most offensive article in question was the open letter to Vice-President Pozderac from Dr. Vojislav Sešlj concerning his imprisonment on charges of counterrevolutionary activity stemming from his unpublished works that call for a reform of the country's federal institutions. From one perspective this was an attack on the undemocratic, hard-line stance of republic authorities in Bosnia-Hercegovina and thus constituted Slovene efforts to meddle in the affairs of its southern neighbor. From another angle, the Sešlj-Pozderac hostility resembled a personal vendetta elevated to interrepublic politics.

The incident underlined the trial-and-error nature of establishing a coherent media policy and the difficulty of sorting out dissent from freedom of expression. Meanwhile courts continued to ban articles and publications that were too critical of federal and republic officials. Explicit attacks on Tito's memory remained taboo, while "offending the reputation" of the collective presidency or the Federal Assembly took the eighteenth issue of the satirical humor magazine *Berekin* off the newsstands (Tanjug Domestic Service, 6 November; *FBIS*, 9 November).

In an attempt to defend the media and the academic community against what appeared to some as arbitrary, repressive government tactics, a Solidarity Fund movement was organized in 1986 to raise money for Dušan Bogavac, an editor of *Komunist* who was fired for printing articles critical of government policies. By spring 1987 the group had some 600 journalists, writers, and professors but was generally ignored until a draft of a proposal seeking legal recognition to coordinate the activities of those who wanted to eliminate "ideological, political, economic, and any other kind of repression" circulated in Belgrade (*LAT*, 1 March). Accusations followed that the Solidarity Fund amounted to an embryonic opposition party, and some journalists who had joined the organization were expelled from the Belgrade municipal LCY committee (Tanjug, in English, 13 March; *FBIS*, 16 March).

Throughout the year a variety of nationalist, religious, and media dissenters contributed to the ranks of what Amnesty International put at roughly 500 Yugoslav political prisoners. Reportedly more than half of those imprisoned were Albanian nationalists. The crimes ranged from terrorism to rude remarks about Tito (BBC, 30 July). The treatment of these political prisoners was a dispute that intensified throughout 1987, beginning with charges growing out of the widely publicized 1986 case of Dobroslav Paraga, who sued Croatian authorities on the grounds that his treatment in prison (where he spent four years for advocating the freeing of all political prisoners) had wrecked his health and left him unable to work. Croatian officials countercharged that Paraga "spread false information." Although the former political prisoner was given another six-month suspended sentence for his pains, conditions at the island prison (Goli Otok) came in for widespread criticism, and the fate of political prisoners became a media issue.

Concern was expressed not only in the more radical Slovene student press, where it could have been expected, but also in mainstream Yugoslav newspapers. During May and June, *Borba* published a series of twenty articles on prison conditions throughout the country. The generally favorable assessment was flawed by the authors' lack of access to penal institutions in Kossovo, where one presumes a substantial number of the Albanian political prisoners are jailed (BBC, 30 July). Nonetheless, this was by no means a whitewash, for when it came to Goli Otok *Borba* flatly labeled the isolation cells "inhuman" and recommended that the island prison be shut down.

Unofficial human rights organizations joined the press in calls for an investigation of the treatment of political prisoners. The matter was taken up by the Federal Secretariat of Justice, although results of that investigation have yet to be published. However, the Croatian National Assembly decision to close Goli Otok "for economic reasons" beginning in December 1987 and targeted for completion by the end of 1988 was undoubtedly not a coincidence (*Danas*, 15 September; RFE *Research*, 30 September).

Dissent was by no means the extreme of the Yugoslav political spectrum. There were also clandestine political organizations that were not part of the in-system dialogue but were explicit opposition groups with aspirations of Albanian separatism or a return to greater Serbia. It was this end of the spectrum that caused concern among the Yugoslav military leadership and that brought the army back into the political arena.

The Army. Party-army relations have been symbiotic ever since the national liberation struggle that gave birth to communist Yugoslavia in 1945. Organizationally speaking, the army was the womb of the party, for comparatively few ideologically experienced prewar party members survived the war and those who did had fought to throw out the German occupiers. Thus the Club of 1941 was seasoned in combat and bonded to the military with ties that went beyond ideological principles. With the Soviet-Yugoslav split, those bonds strengthened, and in 1971 Tito made no bones about his willingness to use the army to whip a "nationalistically minded" party back in line if need be (*Borba*, 23 December 1971). The implication was that the army was the guardian of the revolution and, if necessary, would be used against wayward elements within the party itself.

Western commentators speculated that the answer to post-Tito Yugoslavia was a military coup long before the godfather of Yugoslav communism died in 1980 (*Financial Times*, 25 May 1971). It was in these circumstances that the party organization in the JNA was brought into the post-Tito power-sharing arrangement. The president of the JNA party organization sits on the LCY Presidium along with the presidents of the republic/province organizations. Fifteen places in the 165-member federal Central Committee are reserved for communists in the military, that is, representation equal to that of the autonomous provinces. In short, the Titoist solution attempted to facilitate party-army relations by dealing the army in, not out, of politics. By 1987, however, the strains of the politics of scarcity had affected civil-military relations, and when Prime Minister Mikulić responded that

Yugoslavia would defend its constitutional system by "all means including the military" in his interview with a West German correspondent (*Der Spiegel*, 23 March; *FBIS*, 24 March), the role of Yugoslav soldiers in politics again took center stage.

A series of acrimonious exchanges between Slovene media and military spokesmen took place over such issues as the military budget, Slovene distaste for military service, demands for a civilian alternative, and the value of issue-specific political movements in a communist society. The Slovene literary journal *Nova revija* drew attention to an article by Marko Milivojević, a Yugoslav author living in Britain, that suggested that a Polish solution (martial law) might be the only way to solve Yugoslavia's prolonged economic and political crisis. The article, largely a foil for Slovene objections to any such military management, raised the specter of Serbian chauvinism, and then concluded that it would be disastrous to place the more economically advanced parts of the country under the political domination of the less economically developed Serbs. The army weekly, *Narodna armija*, responded sharply that such an analysis unjustly accused JNA officers of "dogmatism, juntaism, and centralism" (BBC, 26 August).

Within a matter of days the Paračin barracks killings would underscore the deadly mix of nationalist emotions, barracks life, and access to military weapons. Defense Minister Mamula took the occasion to speak out. According to his figures, between 1981 and 1987 some 216 illegal organizations with 1,435 Albanian nationalist members had been uncovered in the JNA. These organizations (or individuals, the text of his speech was unclear) had committed offenses ranging from stealing weapons and poisoning food to inciting nationalist incidents and plotting armed rebellion with the intent of deserting to join the ranks of the "counterrevolution" in Kossovo. (*Borba*, 24 September; *FBIS*, 1 October.) Mamula warned that there was no way of knowing whether there were other potential nationalist time bombs among the 3,792 Albanian conscripts currently fulfilling their military obligations in the JNA.

The defense minister catalog of the military leadership's complaints included (1) slander about the army's putschist ambitions, (2) attempts to disqualify the army politically, (3) attacks on the military budget, (4) pressure for a civilian alternative to military service, and (5) efforts to damage the army's reputation with society. More generally, Mamula spoke about the imperative for the LCY to clarify its character and tasks and to assume the role of the forerunner in needed changes. He insisted that until the LC could carry out its role in society "we could not expect any serious progress in resolving the present crisis." Although Western analysis of Mamula's speech captured the urgency of his plea that the LCY get organized (*The Economist*, 3 October), there was a tendency to overlook the fact that he did not offer concrete suggestions as to how to proceed. The defense minister instead referred to "numerous bright spots in the determination of the nations and nationalities of Yugoslavia, the working class and youth to change the situation for the better." He called on the LC to place itself at the head of this democratic energy evidenced by the grass roots. In doing so, he rejected the possibility of a "so-called third [by implication noncommunist] Yugoslavia."

Despite Defense Minister Mamula's sober assessment, his tone differed markedly from those Third World military leaders who assume that the secret of good governance is to throw out their civilian colleagues and issue the proper orders. One side benefit of having the military integrally involved with the Yugoslav political process has been the lack of illusions among top military leaders about easy answers. Although the Yugoslav armed forces might come to see themselves as the vanguard of the party if LCY politics became paralyzed by nationalist, sectarian polarization, the coup scenario appears unlikely.

The arena of political struggle in which Yugoslav soldiers in politics will have to develop their political strategy is in their stand regarding proposed constitutional amendments. Yugoslavia in 1987 was a direct reflection of the constitutional principles adopted in 1974; and although the draft amendments have been adopted by the Federal Assembly (Tanjug, in English, 18 August; *FBIS*, 19 August), it remains to be seen whether this attempt to make the Yugoslav political system more workable becomes a solution or just another part of the problem.

The Draft Constitutional Amendments. A working group headed by former Vice-President Pozderac proposed 29 amendments to the 1974 constitution. These amendments then passed to the Assembly Constitutional Commission, which forwarded them to its federal chamber. By the end of September the proposed amendments had been accepted by the LCY Presidium. The process then shifted to public discussion and debate in republic and province assemblies before the draft returns to the Federal Assembly for final approval, expected around April 1988.

Highlights of the draft amendments include direct election by Yugoslav workers of communal, republic, and province assemblies as well as the federal chamber of the National Assembly. There was no mention of multicandidate elections. However, there are changes designed to encourage foreign investors and changes to make it attractive for Yugoslav citizens to invest in socialist sector enterprises. The ten-hectare limit on privately owned farm land per family is projected to increase. It is also proposed that the presidents and vice-presidents of the Federal Assembly and the presidents of the two assembly chambers abandon yearly rotation for a four-year term with no right of re-election (Tanjug, 4 August; *FBIS*, 5 August).

Among the most controversial suggestions are those intended to give federal authorities more control over a united market and to weaken the stranglehold of decisionmaking by republic/province consensus. In the forthcoming public debate one can expect the lines to be drawn between the Serbian drive for increased unity and the jealously guarded autonomy of the northern republics and the two autonomous provinces (BBC, 20 August). Seasoned observers of Yugoslav politics could say only that the proposed amendments would be debated with sound and fury, and what that would signify in April 1988 remained to be seen. In the meantime, the president of Vojvodina predictably raised objections to companion changes for the Serbian constitution (*Politika*, 5 August; *FBIS*, 12 August).

Auxiliary Organizations. Throughout 1987 a deepening economic crisis and the government's attempt to enforce a realistic relationship between worker productivity and wages dominated trade union activity. As with many other aspects of Yugoslav politics, the Slovenes were the most outspoken. In March the republic council of the Slovene Trade Union Federation denounced the FEC's "administrative measures," such as the new accounting procedure and the intervention (read, wage freeze) law. The council was unhappy that these measures had been taken without consultation and stressed that the consequences would be borne by the FEC and that the government should not assume the trade unions would solve the problems the FEC had created in associated labor organizations (*Borba*, 19 March; *FBIS*, 23 March). Croatian trade unions objected that it was "illogical and unacceptable" for the government to freeze wages and then within a few days allow prices to rise (Tanjug Domestic Service, 23 March; *FBIS*, 27 March). In short, Yugoslav trade unions largely supported striking workers and insisted that the charges of lack of accountability should be leveled at those responsible for causing strikes rather than at the workers taking part in them (Tanjug Domestic Service, 18 June; *FBIS*, 19 June).

Trade unions demanded amendment of the bankruptcy law in order to provide a uniform criterion throughout the country on what to do when workers lost their jobs. They agreed that there was a need to support enterprises with "realistic prospects" but worried that there was no "restructuring" program or money targeted for such programs (Tanjug, 20 July; *FBIS*, 21 July). These concerns focused on the plight of the workers, and thus it would be incorrect to consider the trade unions as conduits of party/government policy into the working class. On balance, the trade unions were openly critical of the prime minister's attempted solutions if not his philosophy.

The thrust of trade union complaints was taken seriously. Although the trade unions (like the government) were better at posing questions than finding answers, some strides were made in the area of consultation. Prime Minister Mikulić and Zvonimir Hrabar, president of the CTUY, agreed to a working meeting between the FEC and the council presidium of the Trade Union Federation to examine the present economic crisis with particular attention to living standards (Tanjug Domestic Service, 27 August; *FBIS*, 31 August). The seriousness of the occasion could be seen in the high level of participants: Krunić, president of the LCY Presidium; Milojko Drulović, president of the federal conference of the Socialist Alliance; and Milan Pavić, president of the Yugoslav Chamber of Economy.

The joint communiqué of the FEC and the Trade Union presidium stressed the need for better price control and stricter enforcement of bankruptcy laws and called for reducing "unproductive costs" with specific reference to a reduction in the number of management employees. However, this joint assessment did not extend to agreement on who should pay the cost of needed economic changes on the road to stabilization. As might have been expected the prime minister's anti-inflation program that again sharply raised prices met with scant enthusiasm.

Predictably the tensions and divided priorities

that sapped party/government decisionmaking ability spilled over into the workings of the broad-based SAWPY. With a lack of unity at the top, the SAWPY task of coordinating the political activities to carry out the economic stabilization program stalled.

Stojan Dimovski, the secretary of the SAWPY federal conference, admitted that the alliance lacked sufficient "unity and perseverance" to agree on and implement practical solutions (Tanjug Domestic Service, 20 May; *FBIS*, 21 May). He combined this criticism of SAWPY with the statement that before the Socialist Alliance could meet the challenge of providing "a new quality in our political life," the LCY must transform itself and get in touch with the working class as a whole whether or not the workers were party members. The Socialist Alliance must also "establish its own identity and autonomy" regardless of whether workers belonged to the communist party or were SAWPY members and must put more energy into defending the workers' constitutional rights and duties.

Although in general the federal SAWPY conference supported the need for constitutional amendments (Tanjug, in English, 24 March; *FBIS*, 31 March), there was considerable disagreement among republic/province branches of the Socialist Alliance as to what would be acceptable. Reportedly, Smole, the president of the Slovene SAWPY conference, publicly stated that on some proposed constitutional changes Slovenia would "not give an inch," thereby setting off yet another controversy over what he had said at the cultural meeting in Maribor (Tanjug Domestic Service, 21 October; *FBIS*, 22 October).

Meanwhile the Serbian SAWPY organization responded to Serbian LCY pressure to place the Belgrade media under control. In the process Ivan Stojanović, the director of *Politika*, was removed, and the editorial policy of *NIN* came under attack for its sharp criticism of "Stalinist methods" at the Serbian plenum in September (Tanjug Domestic Service, 12 October; *FBIS*, 13 October). In short, republic/province SAWPY organizations were whipsawed between the country's political/economic crisis and the imperatives of regional politics.

Nonetheless, the SAWPY education commission provided some interesting statistics on the problem of illiteracy. According to this report, Yugoslavia still had an illiteracy rate of 12 percent, with one citizen out of ten over the age of ten illiterate. As with other indicators of economic/political development, Slovenia and Kossovo were at opposite ends of the spectrum: 1 percent illiteracy in Slovenia compared with 18 percent in Kossovo, where, although some progress was noted, there was concern about "new sources" of illiteracy due to girls dropping out of primary schools (*Borba*, 24 March; *JPRS-Eastern Europe Report* 87-064, 22 April).

Throughout much of the year the Yugoslav Socialist Youth Federation was virtually paralyzed by its inability to elect a new president. In July the Slovene candidate was rejected (*Politika*, 17 July; *FBIS*, 22 July), and the outraged presidium of the Slovene youth organization called for the dissolution of the federal youth presidium over the issue (*Politika*, 2 October). By the end of the month a new president, Milan Janjić, was finally elected but "without regard for the previously established rotation order" (Zagreb Domestic Service, 28 October; *FBIS*, 29 October). These difficulties largely flowed from conflict over controversial proposals of the Slovene youth association, such as using the money set aside for the youth festival in honor of former president Tito's birthday to meet pressing social needs and a civilian alternative to military service.

Indeed the Slovene youth organization was among the more vocal proponents of an emerging Slovene national program, strongly attacked by the Serbian press (*Borba*, 23 February; *FBIS*, 5 March), which was the basis for the stereotypical Slovene syndrome that Smole objected to (Tanjug Domestic Service, 6 April; *FBIS*, 23 April). Concern for the Slovene republic's autonomy also was expressed by the Slovene Writers' Society, which held a five-hour public forum on the proposed constitutional amendments that explicitly called on the Slovene assembly to defend Slovene national interests (*Politika*, 18 March; *FBIS*, 7 April).

On the federal level the Yugoslav Writers' Association made little progress in healing a two-year-old split. The association complained about the lack of funds, but as with the youth federation the more serious problem was an inability to agree on leadership. The Serbian candidate for president was not acceptable. In protest the Serbian association sent a single representative instead of a delegation. The presidium of the Yugoslav Writers' Association rejected his letter on Kossovo and refused to put it on the agenda, thereby underlining the extent to which nationalist sentiment divided Yugoslav intellectuals as well as politicians. (Tanjug Domestic Service, 20 June; *FBIS*, 23 June.)

Foreign Policy. Notwithstanding the pressures of debt servicing and foreign policy imperatives set by the country's position in the international political economy, Yugoslav nonaligned initiatives continued to occupy a substantial amount of Foreign Minister Dizdarević's time and attention throughout 1987. Part of this activity flowed from Yugoslav commitments made at the Eighth Nonaligned Summit (1986) in Harare, Zimbabwe. The Yugoslav foreign minister took part in a special ministerial conference of the Nonaligned Movement's coordinating bureau (Tanjug Domestic Service, 10 March; *FBIS*, 11 March). In April he was back in Harare for a meeting of the Nonaligned Committee on the Middle East; in June he attended an extraordinary ministerial conference of nonaligned countries devoted to South-South cooperation in Pyongyang, North Korea. Dizdarević stressed that these efforts were in no way designed to "reduce or replace" economic cooperation with developed countries (Tanjug Domestic Service, 9 June; *FBIS*, 12 June). There was an impressive stream of nonaligned dignitaries that visited Belgrade, including representatives from Cambodia, Cyprus, Algeria, Oman, the United Arab Emirates, Egypt, Turkey, Libya, and Nicaragua. Nonalignment was on the agenda during President Mojsov's tour of Latin America, which took in Peru, Argentina, Mexico, and Cuba, and was central to LCY President Krunić's trip to Zimbabwe, which also dealt with bilateral relations and the situation in southern Africa (Tanjug Domestic Service, 17 November; *FBIS*, 20 November).

By midsummer there were signs of a thaw in the twenty-year chill between Yugoslavia and Israel. President Mojsov reportedly met with Israeli Foreign Minister Shimon Peres in Geneva, and the president of the World Jewish Congress, Edgar Bronfman, visited Belgrade. Yugoslav commentary was favorable. The reference that it was premature to discuss diplomatic relations with Israel signaled that such relations were at least under consideration (BBC, 28 July).

Combined with Yugoslav efforts to bring about a meeting of foreign ministers from Balkan countries (Tanjug, in English, 9 July; *FBIS*, 10 July), these tentative steps toward normalization of Yugoslav-Israeli relations could position Yugoslavia to assume the role of Middle Eastern peacemaker. Such a move would enhance Yugoslav international prestige, to say nothing of the potential economic benefits. If mishandled, however, Yugoslav efforts to reestablish ties with Israel could bring about an Arab backlash with high economic costs. Yet if the unofficial reports of PLO-Israeli meetings in Belgrade (Tanjug, in English, 28 July; *FBIS*, 29 July) were correct, Yugoslav-Israeli contacts should be seen as a facilitation rather than as an abandonment of the Palestine-Arab cause.

Overall Yugoslav relations with the Soviet Union and other East European countries continued on an even keel during 1987. Economically this was a mixed blessing, for trade with the CMEA countries accounted for nearly half of Yugoslav foreign trade (Tanjug, in English, 18 May; *FBIS*, 22 May). For the most part these were not hard currency–producing exchanges, and, indeed, a $1.5 billion trade surplus with the Soviet Union amounted to what Prime Minister Mikulić characterized as an "interest-free loan" to Moscow (*Borba*, 26 August; RFE *Research*, 16 September). Economic strains aside, Yugoslav-Soviet relations flourished in the wake of LCY president Renovica's visit to Moscow in December 1986. Soviet foreign minister Eduard Shevardnadze came to Yugoslavia in June to discuss key questions of bilateral relations. The Yugoslavs supported USSR efforts to achieve an agreement on eliminating medium- and short-range weapons from Europe. The Soviet foreign minister, in turn, praised the nonaligned movement as "an authoritative force" in world affairs (*Pravda*, 21 June; *FBIS*, 22 June).

His visit was followed by a meeting between Yugoslav defense minister Mamula, who was vacationing in the USSR, and his Soviet counterpart, Colonel General Dmitrii Yazov that included discussions of interarmy cooperation. Mamula also had talks with the chairman of the USSR State Committee for Foreign Economic Relations on questions of military economic contacts between Yugoslavia and the Soviet Union (Tanjug, 7 July; *FBIS*, 8 July).

Given the brief reports of these meetings, there was no way to assess whether they had been more successful than the economic talks with the chairman of the presidium of the Soviet Chamber of Industry and Trade at the end of August. Western observers correctly characterized those economic discussions as more promise than performance (RFE *Research*, 16 September), while the Yugoslav media did not consider the offer to help build a Belgrade subway as a first priority (*Večernji list*, 28 August). Prime Minister Mikulić combined his complaint about carrying the Soviet debt with concern at the decline in the absolute amount of trade between the two countries, which had dropped from $7 billion in 1985 to $5 billion in 1986 (*Borba*, 26 August; *Večernji list*, 28 August).

Still, expectations swirled around the planned visit of CPSU leader Mikhail Gorbachev, anticipated at the end of the year and shifted to the beginning of 1988. Unconfirmed media reports spoke of a major declaration to be signed with "permanent and principled political content" (*Politika*, 27 November; *FBIS*, 30 November). This visit had substantial political implications, for whether or not Gorbachev's *perestroika* had less than positive implications for Soviet-Yugoslav economic interactions, the CPSU leader's tolerance for socialist pluralism substantially legitimized Yugoslav autonomy. That Moscow might actually learn from other communist parties was implemented by party and academic consultations on the theme of "Socialism and Democracy" involving Yugoslav and Soviet social scientists meeting at the Soviet Academy of Social Sciences in Moscow (*Pravda*, 25 June; *FBIS*, 8 July).

Relations with Yugoslavia's East European neighbors were also active. In February LCY President Renovica visited Hungary. In May Prime Minister Mikulić was in Czechoslovakia, and President Gustáv Husák returned the visit to Yugoslavia in September. Uncharacteristically for Prague, the joint Yugoslav-Czechoslovak communiqué expressed appreciation of the "positive role of the Nonaligned Movement" (ČTK, in English, 23 September; *FBIS*, 24 September). In October a delegation of the East German People's Chamber led by Horst Sindermann, a Socialist Unity Party (SED) Politburo member, came to Yugoslavia, as did the secretary of the Hungarian Communist Party, Mátyás Szürös. Romanian president Nicolae Ceaușescu was greeted effusively in mid-November. Notwithstanding continued feuding over the fate of the Bulgarian Macedonian minority, the 1987 trade protocol with Bulgaria agreed to a trade turnover of $350 million, up 12 percent from the 1986 figure. Relations with Poland did not appear to progress, most likely due to the crises endemic to both the Yugoslav and the Polish economies.

As expected, rhetorical statements hoping to improve Yugoslav-Albanian relations could not survive the deeply rooted Yugoslav belief that the anguish of Kossovo could be traced directly to Tirana's interference in province affairs. At the same time Yugoslav mistrust met Albanian convictions that the rights of Kossovar Albanians were ignored in favor of a "Serb clan" that imposed its will on the province (BBC, 13 July). Given that the family of Albanian leader Ramiz Alia originally came from Kossovo, it is perhaps not surprising that little political improvement followed the September 1986 meeting of Yugoslav-Albanian foreign ministers at the U.N. Still, economic relations were marginally better, showing a 9.8 percent trade increase in 1986 over the 1985 level with a total $92.7 million trade turnover (*Borba*, 6 March; *FBIS*, 13 March).

Meanwhile, Yugoslav political and economic contacts with China increased at both the federal and the republic level. In January the Serbian LCY hosted members of a Chinese delegation from Heilongjiang Province, signed a number of business contracts, and discussed expanding opportunities for economic, scientific, and technical cooperation between the Serbian republic and the Chinese province. Serbian party president Milošević accepted the Chinese invitation for a return visit (*Borba*, 16 January; *FBIS*, 21 January).

Vukašin Micunović, an LCY Central Committee member, led a Yugoslav delegation to China in search of firsthand information on Chinese reforms in February (Beijing Xinhua, in English, 13 February; *FBIS*, 17 February). In July the mayor of Beijing visited Belgrade to take a look at Yugoslav reforms and technological achievements. This mutual admiration led to a positive assessment of the Chinese Thirteenth Party Congress by Yugoslav commentators as "a victory for reformers" (*Borba*, 3 November; *FBIS*, 12 November). To the extent that the Chinese congress focused on modernization rather than democratization, it reflected the hopes of some for Yugoslavia's own internal reform efforts.

With respect to intracommunist politics, the LCY kept up an active round of bilateral meetings and dutifully attended fraternal party congresses ranging from Finland to Morocco. As one could see in the coverage of LCY president Renovica's meetings with the Italian party leadership in Rome, the focus tended to parallel the Yugoslav government's foreign policy priorities rather than targeting interparty concerns (Tanjug Domestic Service, 18 May; *FBIS*, 20 May). Krunić, Renovica's replacement, subsequently addressed a meeting of 180 communist, worker, socialist, social democratic, labor party, and national liberation leaders who took advantage of the 70th anniversary of the Russian Revolution in Moscow to exchange opinions "on the problems of the contemporary world" (Tanjug Domestic Service, 5 November; *FBIS*, 6 November). Krunić re-emphasized long-standing Yugoslav principles such as mutual respect for differences and the right of each party to decide its own sociopolitical direction. Within a context of increasing international interdependence, he stressed the need for democratization of social relations, tied that need firmly to the reform process in socialist countries, and pointed to the contribution of the nonaligned movement to making the world safe for democracy—a world "without hegemony on any pretext." His remarks should be considered a preview of Yugoslav positions during the scheduled visit of CPSU leader Gorbachev.

Yugoslavia's relations with the West inevitably focused on the imperatives of the country's roughly $20 billion hard currency debt. A refinancing accord with fifteen Western governments and Kuwait was reached in Paris at the end of March. This second stage of funding included refinancing 84 percent of the principal due for repayment between May 1987 and March 1988 (Tanjug, in English, 31 March). Throughout the year complex negotiations continued as Yugoslavia moved to go back under a standby agreement with the IMF to provide the necessary credibility for desired debt rescheduling with the Paris Club and commercial banks. The optimistic assessment was that such rescheduling would allow 80 percent of imports and prices to be liberalized within two years.

Improving conditions for joint ventures was also high on the list of Yugoslav economic diplomacy vis-à-vis the West. Prime Minister Mikulić made some progress in that direction in the form of an agreement to avoid double taxation of Yugoslavs working in West Germany during his two-day visit to the Federal Republic of Germany (FRG) (*Politika*, 27 March; *FBIS*, 1 April). On the U.S. side, Chronar Corporation announced an agreement to build a $12 million photovoltaic panel manufacturing plant in Split to be completed by mid-1988 (*WSJ*, 12 March).

Joint ventures and debt rescheduling also appeared on the agenda of Foreign Minister Dizdarević's meeting with his West German counterpart (Tanjug Domestic Service, 15 July; *FBIS*, 16 July). That further liberalizing opportunities for foreign capital investment and other private investment appeared prominently in the proposed 29 constitutional amendments testified to the government's seriousness in this regard (Tanjug, in English, 18 August; *FBIS*, 19 August).

On the whole, the Yugoslavs expressed satisfaction at West German readiness to improve economic cooperation, and the two governments appeared in agreement on such issues as the need to hold an international conference on the Middle East and a successful resolution of the Vienna Conference on Security and Cooperation in Europe (CSCE) meetings. The decision of the Bavarian government to introduce "discriminatory" AIDS control measures that affected Yugoslav citizens wishing to stay in Bavaria province longer than three months (Tanjug, in English, 4 June; *FBIS*, 5 June) remained unresolved, although the FRG foreign minister assured the Yugoslavs that he would take the matter of abolishing such measures up with Bavarian authorities (Tanjug Domestic Service, 15 July; *FBIS*, 16 July).

Simultaneously Yugoslav interior secretary Ćulafić met with his West German colleague, Friedrich Zimmermann, and agreed on further cooperation between the two security services to prevent international terrorism (Tanjug, in English, 15 July; *FBIS*, 16 July). There appears to have been an agreement on military cooperation because the West German security council approved the sale of 100 Tornado engines to Yugoslavia, which would assist the Yugoslavs in building their own jet fighters (Paris AFP, in English, 9 August; *FBIS*, 10 August).

Throughout the year European policy was divided between efforts to shore up the Yugoslav position vis-à-vis the European Economic Community, neutral and nonaligned networking related to the ongoing Vienna CSCE in Europe, and attempts to protect the status of and benefits from Yugoslav workers and minorities in neighboring countries. All three issues were on the agenda during talks with the Austrian secretary general for foreign affairs, Thomas Klestil, in Belgrade (*Wiener Zeitung*, 17 July; *FBIS*, 21 July) and with the Netherlands' foreign minister, Hans Van Den Broek (Tanjug Domestic Service, 10 November; *FBIS*, 12 November).

The search for joint ventures and expanded economic ties extended to Asia as well as Europe. In January the secretary for foreign trade, Nenad Krekić, toured the Philippines, Thailand, and Bangladesh as head of a Yugoslav economic delegation. More important, Prime Minister Mikulić discussed setting up joint ventures with a delegation of officials and businessmen led by the chairman of the Japanese society for promoting the machine building industry. (Tanjug Domestic Service, 18 May; *FBIS*, 19 May.)

As for the United States, the newly appointed Yugoslav ambassador, Živorad Kovačević, began his job under relatively auspicious economic circumstances in that Yugoslav exports to the United

States had increased by roughly 40 percent during the first half of 1987 as compared with an increase of 23 percent of U.S. imports to Yugoslavia, thereby making some progress at reducing a $200 million trade deficit with Washington (speech by Ambassador Kovačević at Cleveland State University, 21 August). This was on top of a $1.25 billion trade turnover in 1986. Politically the relationship remained sound. When the new ambassador presented his credentials, President Reagan restated the U.S. position that Yugoslavia's independence and nonaligned status are important to European peace and stability. He predicted that "the atmosphere of friendship, mutual respect and understanding" between Yugoslavia and the United States "is sure to continue" (Tanjug, in English, 20 July; *FBIS*, 21 July).

Robin A. Remington
University of Missouri at Columbia

Council for Mutual Economic Assistance

A Hungarian analyst recently asked, "Is the CMEA still water or are there some currents flowing?" (*Ötlet*, 5 March; *JPRS-East Europe Report*, 12 May). If the numerous outspoken criticisms of CMEA voiced by prominent public officials in the member states (including Mikhail Gorbachev) offer any indication, then little "still water" surrounded this organization in 1987. Indeed, a Yugoslav source accurately observes that disagreement over how, if at all, to reform—or "restructure," to use Gorbachev's vernacular—the CMEA has caused "sparks to fly within the organization" (*Borba*, 16 October).

Comprehensive Program. Much of the controversy in 1987 centered on the status of the Comprehensive Program. This program, adopted at the 41st session of the CMEA in December 1985, represents Gorbachev's ambitious attempt to narrow the East-West technology gap by promoting joint efforts in research, design, and production among CMEA states in five priority areas (electronics, automation, nuclear power, new materials and technologies, and biotechnology) through the year 2000. The Comprehensive Program designates leading or chief coordinating organizations (all of which, to date, are located in the USSR) to supervise the work of newly established international associations, joint enterprises, and direct links between producers in different countries to fulfill sundry research projects, topics, and targets. All participants are endowed—at least in theory—with broad powers of decisionmaking and execution within their respective areas of competence under the Comprehensive Program. (For details of the Comprehensive Program, see *Izvestiia*, 22 March 1986.)

Numerous commentaries in official media make it clear that the Comprehensive Program has failed to realize its goal. (Typical examples of this contention appeared in *Izvestiia*, 10 October and *Pravda*, 18 September.) Most fundamentally, the price system employed by the CMEA, in which prices are determined administratively and do not reflect actual costs, does not encourage joint ventures such as those envisaged by the Comprehensive Program. Blunt criticism of the present price system was commonplace—according to Lubomír Štrougal, prime minister of Czechoslovakia, reform of the price system "will largely determine the success" of efforts to restructure CMEA (*Rudé právo*, 14 October).

To achieve this end, officials of all European members of CMEA except those from East Germany and Romania now call for the increasing utilization of world prices—prices determined by the dictates of supply and demand on international markets—in intra-CMEA trade. (See, for example, the remarks by Premier Nikolai Ryzhkov of the USSR at the 43rd session of the CMEA, TASS, 13 October.) The ultimate goal of this policy would be to make the national currencies of the CMEA states and the transferable ruble (an accounting unit employed in intra-CMEA trade) freely convertible with one another and with Western currencies. The achievement of full convertibility would provide CMEA states with an objective and uniform standard—world prices—with which to assess the overall costs and determine the profitability of their economic activity. However, central planners and other advocates of centralized control of the economy, fearing a diminution of their power, typically resist the introduction of currency convertibility.

The imperatives of central planning clash with other aspects of the Comprehensive Program, in particular those provisions that devolve decision-making and executive powers on the leading organizations and that establish international associations, joint enterprises, and direct links between producers, all of which remain largely unimplemented. The leading organizations in 1987 were leading in name only. They possess no independent sources of financing, remain subordinate to higher administrative units whose orders they must obey, and exercise no authority over participants in the Comprehensive Program attached to different ministries and departments in the USSR (let alone in other CMEA states). Not surprisingly under such circumstances, the leading organizations display a helplessness in the fulfillment of their duties (*Pravda*, 6 July).

Similarly, the ministries and departments responsible for the creation of international associations, joint enterprises, and direct links between producers have exhibited passivity and inertia in their work (ibid., 26 July). By the end of 1987, only twelve international associations and seven joint enterprises had been established under the Comprehensive Program.

The creation of direct links—at least numerically—appears more extensive. Six hundred such arrangements existed in 1987 between production units in the USSR and Eastern Europe in accordance with agreements that the USSR concluded with all other European members of CMEA except Romania (*Voprosy ekonomiki*, no. 10). However, these links typically exist only on paper and often represent little more than the relabeling of previously existing forms of cooperation (*Pravda*, 28 September).

The 43rd (Extraordinary) Session of CMEA. If the official designation of this session as "extraordinary" sought to emphasize the significance of proposals that would issue from its deliberations, then the CMEA is guilty of rhetorical excess. The session did agree, inter alia, to elaborate a Collective Concept of the International Socialist Division of Labor for the Years 1991–2005 to establish special comprehensive programs for multilateral cooperation in aid and trade to assist the less developed non-European members (Cuba, Mongolia, Vietnam) of the CMEA, to streamline the CMEA organization by eliminating superfluous bureaucratic structures, and to promote joint efforts to dramatically overhaul the power engineering sector and develop the nuclear power industry at priority rates of speed (communiqué reported by TASS, 14 October).

Premier Štrougal of Czechoslovakia, in his speech to the session, bluntly asserted that the participants failed to agree to a specific program of action to mitigate the most pressing problems confronting the CMEA. The final communiqué, he added, simply listed "a number of tasks that we intended to deal with several times before, but which we, in fact, have not even begun to tackle." Štrougal appeared equally unimpressed with the proposals that the session did adopt. To facilitate agreement, he contended, the "individual provisions were reaching a progressively higher level of generalization, which inevitably weakened the concreteness and effectiveness of the measures being prepared." (*Rudé právo*, 14 October.)

These remarks apply especially to the crucial issue of reform of the price mechanism. Prime Minister Károly Grósz of Hungary—a prominent proponent of such reform—accurately observed that the communiqué represented no qualitative breakthrough regarding this issue and that its relevant provisions contained few concrete elements (MTI, 13 October; *FBIS*, 14 October). Reportedly, East Germany, Romania, and Vietnam were the principal states responsible for this circumstance (*Rudé právo*, 19 October; RFE *Background Report*, no. 208, 5 November).

The communiqué reaffirmed the primacy of central planning over decentralization and direct links between producers. The relevant provision stated that it was deemed necessary to continue to pursue this work under the leadership of the central planning agencies of the council's member countries. This formulation echoed the remarks at the session by the heads of both the East German and Romanian delegations (*Neues Deutschland*, 14 October; *Scînteia*, 15 October.)

No participant at the session publicly opposed the initiative to provide increased assistance to Cuba, Mongolia, and Vietnam. However, several speakers, including Prime Minister Zbigniew Messner of Poland and Prime Minister Štrougal of Czechoslovakia, stressed the limited capacity of their economies to provide aid and emphasized that trade with these countries must be mutually beneficial (*Trybuna ludu*, 14 October; *Rudé právo*, 14 October). In contrast, a Soviet official has argued that the non-European CMEA states are so underdeveloped that mutual advantage cannot apply in trade with them and that, in effect, trade is a disguised form of aid (Moscow Radio, 22 May; *FBIS*, 5 June).

Trade between the USSR and Eastern Europe also was a subject of discussion. According to Premier Ryzhkov, several aspects of this trade concern the Soviet Union: (1) fuels and raw materials comprise too large, and machinery and other processed goods too small, a share of Soviet exports to Eastern Europe; (2) Eastern Europe exports its higher quality goods to the more competitive capitalist, rather than the less competitive socialist, market; (3) the value of Soviet exports to Eastern Europe—primarily because depressed prices on the world energy market have reduced comparable prices in CMEA trade—has virtually stagnated since 1985. (Prime Minister Grósz provided a good summary of Ryzhkov's views over Budapest radio 14 October; *FBIS*, 15 October.) In Ryzhkov's opinion, the development of trade and overall economic ties in the CMEA will become even more complicated if such conditions are not soon mitigated (TASS, 13 October).

These views elicited a mixed response among the Eastern Europeans. For example, Prime Minister Grósz, after promising that Hungary would do everything in its power to stimulate trade with the Soviet Union, asserted that above all Hungary needed increased exports of fuels and raw materials—and not machinery, as Ryzhkov had proposed—from the USSR (Budapest Radio, 14 October; *FBIS*, 15 October). Prime Minister Constantin Dascalescu of Romania reiterated this position even more forcefully. He contended that, despite an agreement that the USSR reportedly made at the 39th session of the CMEA in 1984 to increase deliveries of fuels and raw materials to Romania, this issue remains very topical (*Scînteia*, 15 October).

Finally, conflict emerged over whether the unanimity principle—wherein unanimous consent is required for the adoption of a proposal—should govern all decisionmaking in the CMEA. Ryzhkov, presumably reacting to the considerable opposition (both overt and covert) to many Soviet proposals at the session, believes it should not. States not prepared to participate in a particular project should not hinder others from reaching accord, Ryzhkov asserted (TASS, 13 October). Romania, not surprisingly given its history of opposition to many Soviet-sponsored CMEA initiatives, was the most ardent supporter of the unanimity principle. Abrogation of this principle, Prime Minister Dascalescu warned, would adversely affect the interests of the member states and could even create dangerous consequences for the very existence of the organization (*Scînteia*, 15 October).

CMEA-EEC Relations. CMEA and the European Economic Community (EEC) in 1987 continued negotiations toward the promulgation of a joint declaration that would establish diplomatic relations between the two organizations and provide a framework for their mutual cooperation in trade, transportation, the environment, and sundry other multilateral projects. The USSR, in the person of CMEA secretary general Viacheslav Sychev, first proposed the joint declaration in 1985. Both political and economic considerations motivated this initiative. These considerations, inter alia, included a desire to enhance the political status of the CMEA, to exert greater control over Eastern Europe by establishing a common bargaining position in the CMEA toward the EEC, and to derive economic benefits through concessions on trade and participation in multilateral scientific and technological endeavors such as the West European Eureka program. (For details, see RFE *Background Report*, no. 98, 16 June.)

The two sides met in Geneva during 18–20 March to discuss the joint declaration. According to a TASS release, the parties conducted the meeting in a "good and business-like atmosphere" and were able to achieve certain progress in specifying their stands and in drawing them closer together (TASS, 20 March). However, they failed to reach agreement, primarily because the CMEA would not include in the joint declaration the so-called territorial application clause affirming the status of West Berlin as an integral part of the EEC.

Shortly thereafter, government officials (including Sychev) and private citizens from both Eastern and Western Europe met in Hamburg for informal discussions regarding CMEA-EEC relations. Reportedly, the participants were optimistic that the two organizations would soon establish official ties. However, disagreement arose when discussion turned to several controversial subjects, including above all the Western ban on the export of security-related technologies and equipment to the CMEA states (DPA, 24 March).

Similar informal talks took place in October between a ten-member Soviet delegation that included no CMEA officials and members of the European parliament. At a press conference, the head of the Soviet delegation, Lev Tolkunov, chairman of the Council of the Union in the Supreme Soviet, stated that the USSR now accepted all conditions demanded by the EEC for the establishment of official relations with the CMEA (RL, no. 414, 16 October). If accurate, this statement means that the USSR will accept the inclusion of the territorial application clause regarding the status of West Berlin in the joint declaration. Tolkunov, however, may have meant that the Soviets would accept the proposal advanced by several members of the European parliament, especially those from the Social Democratic Party of West Germany, who proposed that the joint declaration not include the territorial application clause but that the CMEA states in an exchange of letters with the EEC would acknowledge that they took note of the status of West Berlin. (RFE *Background Report*, no. 191, 21 October.) By year's end, the EEC had not accepted this proposal.

Bilateral relations between several CMEA states, especially Hungary, and the EEC showed some improvement. In April, the EEC council charged its commission to negotiate a ten-year agreement on trade and overall economic cooperation with Hungary. The charge also confirmed EEC willingness to view the Hungarian economy as different from other CMEA states. A Western source speculated that the outcome of negotiations could be highly favorable to Hungary, including a substantial easing of restrictions on the import of Hungarian goods into the community (ibid.).

Developments in bilateral relations with other CMEA states were more limited. The EEC council did instruct the commission to negotiate a new cooperative agreement with Romania that would expand considerably the scope of the existing agreement concluded in 1980. However, Romania requested a delay in the start of these negotiations. (Ibid., no. 98, 16 June.)

The commission also conducted two rounds of negotiations in July and December with Czechoslovakia on the conclusion of a bilateral agreement. The commission stressed that any such agreement would be far more restricted in its scope than those agreements contemplated with Hungary and Romania. At a less formal level, the commission held exploratory talks with Bulgaria and Poland. Poland reportedly seeks—but the commission is not yet prepared to conclude—an agreement with the EEC similar in scope to the one now envisaged with Hungary. (RFE *Background Report*, no. 191, 21 October.)

Depressed prices on the world energy market continued to be of primary concern to the Soviet Union in its relations with EEC states. As in previous years, the USSR derived more than 80 percent of its earnings of hard currency from exports of energy to capitalist, principally EEC, countries. Consequently, the persistence of low world market prices for oil and natural gas throughout the 1980s has substantially reduced Soviet hard currency earnings and, concomitantly, the capacity of the USSR to import Western technologies and machinery essential to modernize its economy. In the period of high world prices for energy before 1981, the USSR exported commodities to the West valued at upward of twenty billion rubles annually; in 1987 their respective value barely exceeded thirteen billion rubles. These circumstances prompted sharp criticisms from participants in a seminar held recently under the auspices of the USSR Academy of Sciences. A paradoxical situation has developed, one participant warned, wherein the USSR "with an advanced scientific sector and a powerful industry is playing the role in international economic relations of a 'raw materials appendage' of the developed states." (*Izvestiia*, 10 October.)

In sum, the past year witnessed considerable conflict within, blunt criticism of, and a host of pressing problems still unresolved by the CMEA. Whether the CMEA will merit a similar assessment in 1988 poses a question of keenest interest to observers of economic and political life within the member states.

John M. Kramer
Mary Washington College

Warsaw Treaty Organization

The Warsaw Treaty Organization (WTO), established in 1955, continued under Soviet control with no signs of diminishing effectiveness under Mikhail S. Gorbachev's policy of *perestroika* (restructuring) leading toward "new relations." The general secretary considered the pact's 1985 twenty-year extension as a crucial event, and the USSR leadership participated actively in WTO conferences and bilateral discussions to achieve cooperation and "harmonization of the initiatives in international affairs" (Mikhail Gorbachev, *Perestroika: New Thinking for Our Country and the World*, New York: Harper & Row, 1987). The sizable Soviet military presence in Eastern Europe continued, but Soviet medium-range nuclear weapons in the German Democratic Republic (GDR) and the Czechoslovak Socialist Republic (ČSSR) were to be eliminated under the December 1987 U.S.-USSR treaty. Moreover, multilateral negotiations on conventional forces that directly involve East European countries gave Eastern Europeans hope for both their own and Soviet reductions. Military leaders were concerned about shortcomings in training and combat effectiveness and felt that ideological work needed to be restructured.

Military Developments. There was no perceptible change in the number of intermediate-range ballistic missiles: 441 highly mobile SS-20 launchers with 1,323 warheads, 270 of which were deployed for striking targets in Western Europe; and in the western USSR, 112 older SS-4s were being retired. Aircraft categories remained essentially the same. (International Institute for Strategic Studies, *The Military Balance, 1987–1988*; Department of State, *Special Report*, no. 197, July.)

Interestingly, and perhaps significantly, for the first time *Voiennyi vestnik* (Military Bulletin) published numerical information on Soviet medium-range missile launchers. According to the journal, as of 1 January the Soviet Union had 355 of these, including 112 SS-4s and 243 SS-20s. (Radio Moscow, 4 December; *FBIS*, 8 December.) These last figures are far below Western estimates.

Increases in ground forces were minor. The USSR Defense Ministry announced its intention to withdraw one full-strength motorized rifle division and several separate units from Mongolia during April–June (TASS, 15 January; *FBIS*, 15 January). Reports of one unified army corps in the Belorussian Military District and another in the Far East appeared more certain. There were substantial increases in T-80 main battle tanks with their reactive armor capability, in mechanized infantry combat vehicles, in armored personnel carriers, and in reconnaissance vehicles. The air defense system was also being modernized. The number of high-performance MiG-29 and MiG-31 air force fighters showed rapid increases. The navy experienced the slowest improvement. (*The Military Balance, 1987–1988.*)

Non-Soviet WTO members registered no significant military change. Modernization was proceeding but at a slower pace than in the Soviet Union. The GDR activated the AT-5 antitank missile, and the ČSSR doubled the number of its Su-25 close-support aircraft. The Polish army added an impressive number of T-72 tanks, and its navy, a new Kilo-class submarine, the first in Eastern Europe. Polish naval aviation received one squadron of MiG-21s and another of Mi-14 antisubmarine warfare helicopters. The air force began replacing its Su-7s with Su-22s. (Ibid.)

Hungary added to its T-72 tank inventory. Bulgaria increased its military personnel, tanks, and Scud surface-to-surface missiles, but its navy remained operationally in poor condition; evidence indicated a squadron of Frogfoot, and reconnaissance units had new MiG-25s and Su-22s. Romania decreased its army slightly. Soviet military forces in the GDR (380,000), Poland (40,000), the ČSSR (80,000), and Hungary (65,000) were basically unchanged. (Ibid.)

Political Consultative Committee (PCC). Comprised of communist party leaders, the PCC is formally the highest governing body of the WTO and serves as a forum for proposing and endorsing Soviet policies. Before the 28–29 May session in East Berlin, several proposals were made by the Eastern Europeans, including Poland's Jaruzelski Plan and the GDR-ČSSR initiative for a 300-kilometer nuclear-free corridor in Central Europe. On 8 May Polish first secretary Wojciech Jaruzelski made a proposal for withdrawal of weapons from four East and five West European countries and for adoption of defensive military doctrines (PAP, 20 May; *FBIS*, 22 May). Moscow endorsed the plan (*Pravda*, 11 May).

The PCC communiqué called for abandonment of nuclear deterrence and for direct discussions with NATO on the reduction of conventional forces and tactical (battlefield) nuclear weapons. The communist leaders enumerated practical steps for nuclear disarmament: an immediate summit agreement on the elimination of all U.S. and Soviet medium-range missiles in Europe, including those in the GDR and the ČSSR; the elimination of Soviet and U.S. tactical missiles in Europe; an agreement for a 50 percent reduction in Soviet and U.S. strategic weapons within five years; negotiations on further reductions and elimination of all nuclear weapons; a ban on nuclear weapons tests; strict adherence to the antiballistic missile (ABM) treaty; and an agreement banning antisatellite systems and weapons.

The PCC called for the elimination of chemical weapons, reduction of armed forces and conventional armaments in Europe, and creation of nuclear-free zones. The communist leaders declared that the disarmament measures would be guaranteed by an effective system of verification, including on-site inspection. They favored the follow-up Conference on Security and Cooperation in Europe (CSCE) forum, now in Vienna, for such negotiations.

The PCC participants expressed interest in a possible Soviet-Afghan agreement on withdrawal of Soviet troops from Afghanistan. Regarding intrabloc relations, they called for greater dynamism in foreign policy cooperation and strict adherence to the principles of equality and joint responsibility. Accordingly, the PCC set up a multilateral group for current reciprocal information and a commission on disarmament. (*IB*, August.) With a new commission on disarmament the East European regimes should have a greater role—or at least a formal one—in arms control, a development they welcome.

The PCC issued a separate document on defensive military doctrine, claiming that WTO members will never begin hostilities unless attacked, will never be the first to use nuclear weapons, and have no territorial claims against any other state. The document pledged such principles as respect for independence and noninterference in internal affairs, citing six goals that were essentially included in the communiqué. In addition, the PCC proposed consultations with NATO on its military doctrines.

Significantly, the document admitted to existing imbalances and asymmetries in specific types of armaments and services of armed forces and proposed discussions for removing them to achieve lower troop levels. The talks, conducted by experts, could be held in Warsaw or Brussels or alternate between these cities. (Ibid.) The admission of disparities had been made earlier by Gorbachev; WTO officials had previously maintained that approximate parity existed and declined to exchange disaggregated data, although the West had provided credible evidence of asymmetries (Department of Defense, *Soviet Military Power 1987*; NATO, *NATO and the Warsaw Pact: Force Comparisons*, 1984).

NATO welcomed the WTO acknowledgment of disparities as a move toward admission of superiority in armed forces and armaments that might lead to positive steps toward reductions. However, Federal Republic of Germany defense minister Manfred Woerner perhaps expressed the Western consensus on the PCC arms control proposals when he called them "completely unsensational" (*Die Welt*, 1 June; *FBIS*, 1 June).

Foreign Ministers. The first meeting in 1987 of WTO Foreign Ministers' Committee was held 24–25 March in Moscow. Discussions centered on arms control, with the committee giving full support to Gorbachev's position on intermediate-range nuclear missiles. The ministers issued a communiqué (*Izvestiia*, 26 March) and a separate statement on a chemical weapons ban (TASS, 26 March; *FBIS*, 27 March).

The foreign ministers' meeting on 29 October in Prague covered numerous subjects. According to the communiqué, Foreign Minister Eduard A. Shevardnadze informed his colleagues about the 22–23 October U.S.-USSR talks in Moscow. Not surprisingly, the East Europeans gave complete support to Soviet policies, including the not-yet-concluded treaty on medium-range nuclear weapons, future reductions of strategic offensive weapons and conventional forces, interpretation of the anti-ballistic missile (ABM) treaty, nuclear testing, dissolution of military blocs, chemical weapons, regional conflicts, military doctrine, and nuclear and chemical weapon–free zones.

The committee cited as essential the realization of human rights and emphasized that all states must strictly respect national independence, sovereignty, and noninterference in the internal affairs of other countries. The ministers voiced serious concern over unnamed Western representatives proposing deployment of other nuclear and nonnuclear weapons as compensation for the elimination of U.S. nuclear weapons from Europe and over "the creation of new structures." They proposed reductions of armed forces and tactical nuclear and conventional weapons in Europe as well as of military expenditures, through the CSCE process. (ČETEKA, 29 October; *FBIS*, 30 October.)

A separate statement was issued on increasing the efficiency of the Geneva Conference on Disarmament, referring to the 40-member U.N. Conference on Disarmament (CD). Established in 1979, the CD has been concerned with arms control and, in recent years especially, a chemical weapons convention. Adequate verification has been a concern of the West. The foreign ministers suggested major efforts on prohibition and destruction of chemical weapons. To achieve "real results" at Geneva, they proposed using a more intensive timetable at the conference, relying more on experts and scientific centers, and holding meetings at the foreign minister level during crucial moments to create a positive impulse. Also, the committee considered expanding, with the CD "becoming a permanent universal instrument of talks on disarmament." (TASS, 30 October; *FBIS*, 2 November.)

Over the years Western positions on arms control issues have been well defined. Among the problems with WTO proposals has been acceptance of effective verification, especially on-site inspection. The Soviet Union, with the largest stockpile of chemical weapons in the world, had not even admitted having any until March (Department of State, *Special Report*, no. 171, 19 November). Government spokesman Friedhelm Ost said that West Germany welcomed the positive assessment the eastern foreign ministers made on arms control, adding that developments had been achieved because of NATO cohesion, persistence, and purposefulness (DPA, 30 October; *FBIS*, 2 November).

The Mutual and Balanced Force Reductions (MBFR) Negotiations. During the year the NATO-WTO negotiators on MBFR held three rounds of talks, with the 467th Plenary Session of Round 43 concluding on 3 December. These negotiations on conventional armed forces began in October 1973. The twelve NATO and seven WTO representatives continued to discuss their proposals of 5 December 1985 and 20 February 1986, respectively (see *YICA*, 1987). The Western position was that the WTO had not responded constructively to a major proposal. Both sides did agree there was a stalemate, for, among other things, they differed widely on verification, with the West demanding more stringent measures. The East insisted on including armaments in an agreement, while the West preferred reductions first in armed forces personnel, where the WTO has a substantial superiority as well as enjoying geographic asymmetry. Moreover, the Eastern suggestion for a symbolic "modest agreement" as a way of breaking the stalemate was rejected by Western negotiators as a dangerous one. NATO believed that opportunities would be lost for concluding an agreement of real substance and also for considering possible future conventional arms control negotiations in an expanded geographic area (*MBFR Press Transcript*, January–December).

Atlantic to the Urals. On 12 December 1986 the NATO council issued a declaration on conventional arms control that proposed East-West discussions to establish a mandate for negotiations on conventional arms control covering Europe from the Atlantic to the Urals. This Brussels Declaration suggested new negotiations "to eliminate existing disparities . . . and establish conventional stability at lower levels" with "an effective verification regime" (text in Department of State, *Bulletin*, March).

The discussions on formulating a mandate for such negotiations began on 7 February in Vienna with seven WTO and sixteen NATO representatives. Parallel to this and the MBFR negotiations, the third follow-up meeting of the CSCE—the first two had been in Belgrade and Madrid—began on 4 November 1986, also in Vienna, to review the implementation of commitments. On behalf of the WTO members the Soviet Union submitted on 22 June a draft to the group of 23 that combined short-range nuclear weapons with conventional weapons. This proposal reflected the PCC's June 1986 Budapest appeal (see *YICA*, 1987) and its East Berlin communiqué of May.

On 10 July the West presented a major security proposal within the framework of the CSCE process: (1) resume negotiations among all 35 CSCE member states to build on and expand the results of the Stockholm Conference on confidence- and security-building measures and (2) resume autonomous negotiations among the 23 NATO-WTO members to achieve conventional stability in Europe at lower force levels (*Twenty-third Semiannual Report* by the President to the Commission on Security and Cooperation in Europe on the Implementation of the Helsinki Final Act, 1 April 1987–1 October 1987). By year's end progress had been limited. The most serious problems involved the WTO attempt to incorporate tactical nuclear (battlefield) weapons and tactical strike aircraft with ground forces and the definition of the force zones and arms reductions (*Krasnaia zvezda*, 2 September).

Military Council and Defense Ministers. At its 24–26 September meeting in Prague, chaired by USSR Marshal Viktor G. Kulikov, the commander in chief of WTO Joint Armed Forces, the military council reviewed the year's combat training results and outlined tasks for the next twelve-month cycle.

In a statement, the council said that new tasks were established with regard to the document on the Warsaw Pact's military doctrine, announced at the PCC conference in May. This meeting, which had debated other aspects of joint armed forces activities, "confirmed its unity of opinion on all discussed issues." (ČETEKA, 26 September; *FBIS*, 1 October).

The 24–26 November session of the Defense Ministers' Committee was attended by the seven pact defense ministers, as well as Marshal Kulikov and USSR Army General Anatolii Gribkov, chief of staff for the Joint Armed Forces. According to the communiqué, the ministers discussed questions of troop training in their armed forces and outlined possible improvements. The committee emphasized that WTO military doctrine, formulated in the PCC East Berlin document, clearly reflected the defensive character of their countries' military strategy and facilitated a WTO-NATO dialogue as well as building trust in Europe. The doctrine's task was to prevent nuclear and conventional war but keeping armed forces and armaments at levels necessary for defense and "for repulsing possible aggression."

The committee gave unanimous approval to the almost-completed U.S.-USSR medium- and short-range missile accord as a "first real step toward destroying nuclear arsenals" while retaining a balance of armed forces and armaments at a lower level. The ministers favored early agreement on a 50 percent reduction in strategic offensive weapons and at least a ten-year observance of the ABM treaty. Finally, they defined measures for expanding WTO military cooperation, for strengthening the unity of their military forces, and for maintaining combat readiness to ensure security. (*Pravda*, 27 November.)

At a reception hosting the ministers, Romanian president Nicolae Ceauşescu expressed his country's need to cut military expenditures. He emphasized that preserving and strengthening the defensive capability of the army will be achieved within rational limits. He said the army would participate in Romania's socioeconomic development. (Radio Bucharest, 26 November; *FBIS*, 27 November.) The TASS report on the reception neglected to mention these comments by Ceauşescu (TASS, 26 November; *FBIS*, 27 November).

Military Exercises. Under the Helsinki Final Act of 1975 the WTO record on implementation of prior notification of military exercises had been poor (see *YICA*, 1987). Of the 27 large-scale maneuvers during 1975–1986, observers were invited to only 8. The Stockholm Conference adopted a document, effective 1 January, obligating the 35 signatories to announce at least 42 days in advance all military exercises involving 13,000 or more troops and at least 300 tanks and to invite observers from all signatory states when maneuvers comprised more than 17,000 men. Also, notification is to be given one year in advance for activities involving at least 40,000 troops and two years for those with more than 75,000 men (*Twenty-second Semiannual Report*, 1 October 1986–1 April 1987.)

Notifiable calendars were exchanged on 15 December 1986. The WTO announced 25 military activities for 1987—16 national and 9 multilateral. The Soviet Union forecast its participation in 18 of these—11 by its own forces—and an activity involving 40,000 troops scheduled for September 1988. Also, WTO states submitted two voluntary notifications. No Romanian military activities required notifications. Bulgaria had the poorest record, conducting two notifiable military exercises during 1987, in May and August. Its "Balkan 87" exercise lacked the required information (number of divisions), and the starting date changed. (*Twenty-third Semiannual Report*.)

Although reserving definitive judgment, the president's report considered WTO implementation of notification to be "encouraging." Some technical difficulties were experienced by all participating states, but the "Eastern practice met the letter and, in some cases, the spirit" of Stockholm. The Soviet exercises were the first since 1978 at which U.S. observers witnessed activities on USSR territory. (Ibid.)

The Stockholm provision for on-site inspection was invoked on two occasions. During 28–30 August the United States inspected a Soviet military activity near Minsk; on 10–12 September, the United Kingdom inspected a GDR-USSR exercise near Cottbus. Although some questions arose over restricted areas and technical problems, both Washington and London "were satisfied with the conduct of the inspections." (Ibid.) This was the first U.S. on-site inspection of a Soviet military exercise, and the United States considered this successful event as "a step in the process of improving openness and building confidence and security in Europe" (Department of State, *Special Report*, no. 171, 19 November). (For experiences of observers, see end of section.)

The following review of national and WTO exercises, although not exhaustive, provides some measure of understanding of these activities. Maneuvers in WTO countries, as elsewhere, are intended to enhance a country's or the Warsaw Pact's military preparedness. This objective is understood and thus not always cited.

The ČSSR conducted a division-level tactical exercise during 2–6 February in the western region near Marianske Lazne to improve combat in winter conditions. With 17,500 troops participating observers were invited from the CSCE countries. (Radio Prague, 25 January; *FBIS*, 27 January.) Twenty-three accepted, sending 43 observers (TASS, 30 January; *FBIS*, 5 February). During 9–13 March, Poland conducted the "Opal 87" multilevel divisional maneuvers in the northwest Pomeranian Military District that involved about 18,000 soldiers; 150 tanks; 130 antitank weapons; 100 artillery guns, mortars, and rocket launchers; and twelve helicopters. Warsaw informed all CSCE signatories. "Opal 87" was the first Polish army exercise in eleven years to which foreign observers were invited; 22 countries accepted. (PAP, 4, 10 March; *FBIS*, 5, 11 March; Radio Warsaw, 12, 13 March; *FBIS*, 13, 16 March.)

A joint exercise was held during 25–30 March in the GDR comprising 23,500 troops from the Group of Soviet Forces in Germany (GSFG), 1,500 troops from East Germany's National People's Army (NVA), 500 tanks, and tactical aviation. The maneuvers were conducted in the area of Gardelegen, Magdeburg, Wittenberg, Luebben, and Brandenburg. The exercise was led by Colonel General Valerian Belikov, commander in chief of the GSFG. In addition to field training, the aim was to "deepen the brotherhood between the two armies." Twenty states sent observers, including West Germany, the first time that uniformed officers from the Bundeswehr officially met with NVA officers on East German territory. Lieutenant General Gerhard Kunze, deputy chief of the NVA main staff, said this represented a "change from confrontation to détente and disarmament in Europe." (ADN, 25 March; *FBIS*, 26 March; *Neues Deutschland* [*ND*], 24, 30 March.)

During 10–16 April the NVA held national exercises with 17,000 troops in the Cottbus-Wittenberg-Torgau-Goerlitz region. The purpose included coordination between ground and air forces. Observers from 22 CSCE signatory countries attended. (DPA, 24 March; *FBIS*, 30 March; ADN, 10 April; *FBIS*, 13 April.) A Hungarian-Soviet command and staff exercise took place in Hungary during 12–18 June under the command of Marshal Kulikov. Only minor telecommunications and traffic control military units participated; the aim included "improving cooperation and intensifying brotherhood in arms." (MTI, 5, 12 June; *FBIS*, 8, 19 June.) Some 15,000 GSFG and NVA troops conducted maneuvers in the Brandenburg-Magdeburg-Wittenberg-Golssen area during 21–28 June. They were led by Colonel General Belikov, and all CSCE members were informed. (ADN, 10, 19 June; *FBIS*, 11, 22 June.)

Prague invited foreign observers for the second time during 1987, proving, said Lieutenant General Jiri Brychta, first deputy chief of the general staff, the ČSSR's determination to implement the Stockholm document. Thirty-five observers from eighteen countries witnessed the 15–21 July maneuvers involving 17,000 troops—16,500 from the Soviet Union and 500 from the ČSSR. This exercise included 300 tanks, 250 antitank guided missile launchers, 140 of the 100-mm cannon, 12 rocket launchers, and 21 helicopters. Conducted in northern Bohemia, the training was directed by Colonel General Viktor Yermakov, commander of the Central Group of Soviet Forces in the ČSSR, and intended to improve ground-air coordination. (ČETEKA, 8, 9, 10, 16 July; *FBIS*, 10, 14, 17 July.)

A joint East German–USSR exercise was held during 26–30 July in the Gardelegen-Magdeburg-Templin-Neustrelitz-Wittstock area. Some 25,000 GSFG and NVA troops employed 500 tanks, another 500 antitank missile launchers on armored carriers, 300 artillery guns, 36 multiple-rocket launchers, 30 fire-support helicopters, and twenty transport helicopters. The exercise, directed by Lieutenant General Rushchenkov, commander of one GSFG army, was observed by representatives from 21 countries. Rushchenkov said that foreign observers obtained an objective picture of the defensive nature of the exercise. (ADN, 26, 27, 30 July; *FBIS*, 27, 28, 31 July.)

The "Druzhba (Friendship) 87" exercise, involving East German, Polish, and USSR troops, took place during 27–31 July in northwest Poland. Its purpose was to improve cooperation among WTO troops in a coordinated defense system. The 13,000 soldiers were led by General Wojciech Baranski, chief of the Polish army combat training board. Observers included General Florian Siwicki, Polish minister of national defense, Marshal Kulikov, and Colonel General Horst Stechbarth, deputy minister of national defense and chief of GDR ground forces. Warsaw informed the Stockholm signatories. (Radio Warsaw, 27 July; PAP, 19, 31 July;

TASS, 31 July; *FBIS*, 20, 27 July, 3 August.) The initial forecast indicated 18,000 troops but was later reduced to 13,500, thus removing the requirement to invite observers (*Twenty-third Semiannual Report*).

Soviet troops of the Red Banner Carpathian Military District staged an exercise during 17–22 August in the Rava-Russka–Yavorov-Gorodok-Nesterov region of the Ukraine. With 18,000 ground troops and airmen participating, Moscow invited the 35 CSCE signatories; 24 states sent observers. (TASS, 10, 19, 22 August; *FBIS*, 13, 24 August.) A joint Hungarian-Soviet exercise was held during 1–6 September in the Transdanubian region, with more than 14,000 troops participating. Budapest informed all CSCE states. The maneuvers were led by Colonel General Aleksei A. Demidov, commander of the Soviet Group of Southern Forces in Hungary. (MTI, 21 July, 6 September; Radio Budapest, 1 September; *FBIS*, 22 July, 2, 8 September.)

A joint GSFG-NVA exercise was conducted during 6–12 September in the area of Ludwigsfelde, Wittenberg, Cottbus, and Wilhelm-Pieck-Stadt Guben. Up to 14,000 soldiers, led by a GSFG army commander, took part. CSCE signatories were informed. (ADN, 27 August, 6, 12 September; *FBIS*, 28 August, 8, 14 September.) During 22–27 September, the Soviet Union held maneuvers in the Transcaucasus, inviting CSCE observers. In this and the 17–22 August exercise, Moscow complied with the provisions of the Stockholm agreement "but did not go beyond its minimum requirements," as observation of personnel and tanks was limited. (*Twenty-third Semiannual Report*.)

The Hungarian "Basalt 87" tactical maneuvers were conducted with 8,000 troops 25–30 October in the Transdanubian military reservation. According to Budapest, the exercise was prepared "in the spirit of increased confidence and openness." Although the number fell short of 13,000, Hungary informed CSCE signatories of the maneuvers, which involved 120 tanks, 49 artillery weapons, 32 helicopters, and 24 airplanes. (MTI, 28 October; *FBIS*, 30 October).

Both NATO and WTO members played an active role in observing each other's exercises. Western observers had a positive but reserved reaction. They experienced friendly receptions, warm hospitality, interesting discussions, some troop contact, and were given binoculars by their WTO hosts. However, WTO notifications included no geographic coordinates of where troops were to deploy, "interpretative questions" arose over detailed information, and some exercises appeared rehearsed for the observers' benefit to indicate compliance (*Twenty-third Semiannual Report*).

NATO officers required greater access—for example, to more command posts—to verify the number of troops and equipment in the field, normally given to WTO observers at NATO maneuvers (DPA, 29 March; *FBIS*, 30 March). Western officers were forbidden to use dictaphones or video cameras, and actual observations of some exercises were too limited for a valid assessment. Conditions varied from country to country, with non-Soviet WTO countries, especially the GDR, more positive than the USSR. For example, at the 15–21 July USSR-ČSSR maneuvers Western observers were unable to view the combat units and were monitored by hidden listening devices. In contrast, at the "Opal 87" Hungarian exercise, Western observers were allowed more than was required. (*Twenty-second Semiannual Report*; *Twenty-third Semiannual Report*; Reuters in *The Philadelphia Inquirer*, 5 August.)

Postsummit Developments. Following his summit meeting with President Ronald Reagan, Gorbachev stopped over in East Berlin on 11 December to brief WTO communist leaders, as well as foreign affairs and defense ministers. Inexplicably, President Ceauşescu was not present but sent as his plenipotentiary representative Foreign Minister Ion Totu (*Pravda*, 12 December). Gorbachev received the expected enthusiastic welcome, and his allies "fully supported and highly praised the results" of the Washington summit. They characterized the U.S.-USSR treaty as "a step of historical dimension" and a "victory of realism and reason." According to the statement on the meeting, the assembled leaders expressed "profound gratitude" to Gorbachev for his efforts leading to the "first real results in nuclear disarmament, testimony to the effectiveness of the new political thinking." (Ibid.)

The treaty was of special significance to the GDR and the ČSSR, on whose territories Moscow maintains nuclear weapons. The treaty requires the Soviet Union to dismantle these facilities. The statement noted the expressed readiness of East Germany and the ČSSR "to facilitate the implementation of the treaty" (ibid.). At the meeting, the ministers of foreign affairs of East Germany, the ČSSR, and the USSR signed an agreement on inspections in conjunction with the U.S.-USSR treaty (in *ND*, 12–13 December).

The WTO leaders also noted that the U.S.-Soviet treaty would facilitate progress in other areas—chemical weapons, nuclear testing, and "reducing the armed forces and conventional armaments in Europe from the Atlantic to the Urals." Accordingly, the communist party heads affirmed their readiness "to resolve the problems of asymmetries and imbalances." (*Pravda*, 12 December.) Reductions of conventional forces are of particular importance to East Europeans, especially East Germany, Poland, the ČSSR, and Hungary, where the Soviet Union maintains substantial armed forces, as noted above.

Differences Within the WTO. The year witnessed continuity and change. Strains within the alliance continued, ranging from traditional nationalism to food shortages and high prices, resulting in general dissatisfaction and unrest. Gorbachev's policies of *glasnost'*, *perestroika*, and "new thinking" were resisted by some leaders—for example, East Germany's Erich Honecker and Romania's Ceauşescu—partly because they were afraid of unleashing internal forces that they would be unable to control. Open protests by Romanian workers in Brasov over shortages and working conditions indicated the gravity of unrest.

Gorbachev gave new meaning to the formulation "strengthening unity and cooperation" by his personal approach toward his allies, as he involved their leadership in larger bilateral and alliance activities. He was changing Moscow's style of control from dictatorial dominance to collaborative compliance. After years of failure, Honecker made an unprecedented visit to West Germany during 7–11 September, despite his reservations about Gorbachev-style reforms.

The Soviet leader encouraged—and even pressured—East European economic restructuring to assuage popular dissatisfaction and to assist his own reforms. With healthier economies, the Eastern Europeans would be more capable of undertaking a greater share of WTO military expenditures. The least capable was Romania, which continued its frugal military policy during 1987. Hungary was again preparing to take the lead in economic experimentation beginning with the new year. The first political leadership change since Gorbachev became head of the CPSU occurred on 17 December in the ČSSR with the replacement of General Secretary Gustáv Husák (nearly 75) by 65-year-old Miloš Jakeš. However, expectations were not high, despite the critical need for reform. Suggestions that Gorbachev's policies resembled those of Alexander Dubček, who had been deposed by a Soviet-led WTO invasion of Czechoslovakia in 1968, were rejected by both Prague and Moscow.

The WTO military establishments were not immune to *perestroika*. Serious shortcomings exist in numerous areas, including training, discipline, and equipment, and the reliability of Moscow's allies has been eroding steadily. *Perestroika* is designed to overcome these problems and "enhance combat readiness of troops and naval forces." Required is a new dynamism in political-ideological propaganda work to impart "new quality to patriotic and [in view of the U.S.-USSR treaty] international education." (*Krasnaia zvezda*, 10, 13 December.) As to prospects for reductions of conventional forces, the chief of a directorate in the USSR armed forces general staff, Colonel General Nikolai Chervov, declared that Moscow is willing to assess ways to eliminate imbalances "but not to upset the overall correlation of forces which is currently approximately equal" (Bratislava *Pravda*, 8 December).

In the conclusion of his book *Perestroika*, Gorbachev explains that the term means "progressive development, a fundamental change." *Glasnost'* and *perestroika*—more hope than reality in the Eastern Europe of 1987—seem to promise less oppression and more tolerance. However, skepticism in Eastern Europe remains. There is frustration and resignation born of knowledge that, as in the past, the Soviet Union will not permit systemic changes in their economies or any fundamental political or military deviation.

John J. Karch
Falls Church, Virginia

International Communist Organizations

WORLD MARXIST REVIEW

The *World Marxist Review* (*WMR*), the Soviet-controlled international communist theoretical monthly, is the only permanent institutional symbol of unity for the world's pro-Moscow and independent communist parties (see *YICA*, 1984 for a fuller treatment). At the end of 1986, Lubomir Hanak became the new Czech "executive secretary" (deputy chief editor) of the magazine, assisting Soviet chief editor Aleksandr Subbotin (Prague, *Rudé právo*, 6 December 1986). The other "executive secretary" is the Soviet Sergei V. Tsukasov. The number of communist parties represented on the magazine's editorial council remains at 69 (the "vanguard revolutionary democratic" Yemeni Socialist Party brings the total to 70) (*WMR*, November).

The quarterly *Al Nahj* (*The Way*), an apparent Arab extension or counterpart of the *WMR*, has become increasingly active. Whereas the *WMR* calls itself "the theoretical and information journal of the communist and workers' parties throughout the world," the *WMR* describes *Al Nahj* as "the journal of the communist and workers' parties of the Arab countries" (ibid.). Another authoritative source describes *Al Nahj* as a "theoretical organ" (East Berlin, *Neues Deutschland*, 30 July). Its editor, Fakhri Karim, is probably the same Fakhri Karim who is a member of the Iraqi Communist Party Central Committee (Rome, *L'Express*, 13 June 1982). Both *Al Nahj* and the *WMR* sent delegates to the July congress held by the (communist) Party of Progress and Socialism in Morocco (Casablanca, *Al Bayane*, 19 July), and the two magazines cosponsored a symposium in Nicosia entitled "Religion Is for God, the Homeland Is for All," apparently some time in the middle of the year (*WMR*, August). The *WMR* also participated in a conference sponsored by *Al Nahj* in Damascus 30 September–1 October called "The October Revolution and the Renewal of the World" (ibid., November).

FRONT ORGANIZATIONS

Control and Coordination. The Soviet-line international communist front organizations that have been operating since World War II are counterparts of organizations established by the Comintern after World War I, and their function is the same: to unite communists with persons of other political persuasions in order to support, strengthen, and lend respectability to USSR foreign policy objectives. Moscow's control is evidenced by the fronts' faithful adherence to the Soviet policy line as well as by the withdrawal patterns of member organizations (certain pro-Western groups withdrew after the Cold War began, Yugoslav affiliates left following the Stalin-Tito break, and Chinese and Albanian representatives departed as the Sino-Soviet split developed).

The Communist Party of the Soviet Union (CPSU) is said to control the fronts through its International Department (ID) (U.S. Congress, *The CIA and the Media*, 1978, p. 574), and ID sector chiefs have been publicly involved with front affairs—Yuliy F. Kharlamov in the World Peace Council (WPC) and Grigori V. Shumeiko in the World Federation of Trade Unions (WFTU) and the Afro-Asian People's Solidarity Organization (AAPSO) (Washington, D.C., *Problems of Communism*, September–October 1984). Such officials appear to operate, however, through the Soviet national affiliate, which usually has a representative at the front's international headquarters for on-the-spot direction. This person is usually a member of the front's Secretariat, but in some cases he or she may be a vice president (*YICA*, 1981).

Aside from the CPSU's indirect influence on the various fronts through the ID, there is also more direct coordination. First, since at least 1979, these fronts, defining themselves as "closely coordinating" international nongovernmental organizations, have met together periodically with the apparent intention of formulating a joint policy (the last such meeting was hosted by the WFTU at Prague in September [Prague, *CPC Information*, 30 September]).

Second, the WPC, the largest and most important of the international fronts, provides positions on its main bodies for the leaders of most of the fronts so they can interlock with one another. For example, ten are represented on the current WPC presidential committee (Helsinki, *New Perspectives*, no. 6), and two others had such representation in the past (ibid., no. 5, 1979 and no. 3, 1986). In addition, at least during 1983–1986, the International Association of Democratic Lawyers (IADL) maintained an organizational slot on the WPC proper while the president of the World Federation of Teachers Unions (FISE) was a member of its Sri Lankan delegation (WPC, *List of Members, 1983–1986*, pp. 162, 129).

Finally, the *WMR*, the Soviet-dominated policy guidance organ of nearly 70 communist parties, coordinates with the Problems of Peace and Democratic Movements Commission that is oriented toward the international fronts (Washington, D.C., *Problems of Communism*, November–December 1982). The July issue of the *WMR* notes an undated Prague seminar held by this commission on "Developments of the Peace Movement in the 1980s and the Communists" as well as a May symposium sponsored by the magazine, also in Prague, on "The October Revolution and the Main Problems of Our Age," which included representatives of the WPC, the WFTU, the Women's International Democratic Federation (WIDF), the World Federation of Democratic Youth (WFDY), AAPSO, and the International Union of Students (IUS)—the six most important international fronts (*YICA*, 1984)—along with 51 communist parties and four "revolutionary democratic" movements (ibid.). The year 1987, moreover, saw an unusually high number of front leaders —the IUS president, the secretaries general of the WPC and the International Organization of Journalists (IOJ), and vice presidents from the WIDF, the WFTU, and AAPSO—publish articles in the *WMR*. Representatives of the *WMR* have also participated in these front meetings, although one cannot tell how often (*YICA*, 1987).

The *WMR* is, of course, not considered with the fronts because it is (with one recent exception) fully communist in composition, whereas the fronts cover the spectrum, from such organizations as the WFTU (a plurality of whose affiliates are communist organizations) to the WPC (whose leadership has a fairly good balance of communists, socialists, "revolutionary democrats," and "independents") to the basically noncommunist Christian Peace Conference (CPC).

Techniques. Nineteen eighty-seven stands out as a year in which the Soviets seemed less apprehensive about appearing to dominate front activity than about maintaining tighter control, saving money, and exercising more direct influence. This was most obvious in the overuse of Moscow as a meeting site (where Soviet control could be relatively easily exercised, where hard currency expenditures could be kept to a minimum, and, of course, where the dynamic and attractive leader Mikhail Gorbachev could have an excuse to participate directly). But 1987 meetings had, for the most part, to have been planned in 1986 or even earlier, and the unusually open directions that Yuri Zhukov gave at the April 1986 WPC meeting and that Viktor Afanasiev gave at the October 1986 IOJ congress suggest that Moscow may have decided to increase efficiency at the expense of credibility within a year of Gorbachev's accession to power (U.S. Department of State, *Soviet Influence Activities*, 1987, pp. 1–2; Prague, *The Democratic Journalist*, January). An example of such preplanning is that Moscow had been decided on as a site for the June 1987 World Congress of Women (WCW), the largest front meeting of the year, and its attendant Ninth WIDF Congress by the time of the March 1986 WIDF bureau meeting (East Berlin, ADN, 23 March 1986). Havana was a meeting site second only to Moscow during 1987, but it appears that the Cubans were even less subtle about their role. (See *YICA*, 1986 for a description of the six Havana conferences held in 1985 on the Latin American debt and the role that Castro played in them.)

The lack of concern by the international fronts and their Soviet and Cuban affiliates that they might be too closely identified with those conferences that they have traditionally sponsored for their own members plus a wide circle of less committed persons was most obvious in the holding of such meetings back-to-back with official front ones. Although a common pattern in the past, during 1986 it looked as if the fronts were moving away from it: both the WPC and the WFTU, though in different ways, went to great lengths to separate themselves from their respective major "nonofficial" meetings—the World Congress Devoted to the International Year of Peace and the Eleventh World Trade Union Congress (see *YICA*, 1987).

As noted above, Moscow was the scene of the WCW in June and the Ninth WIDF Congress, which followed immediately. The two meetings were so closely intertwined that the WIDF president served as the WCW president; the WIDF secretary general, as the WCW secretary; and the Soviet Women's Committee president (soon to become a WIDF vice president), as the WCW vice president (East Berlin, *Women of the Whole World*, no. 3). Moscow was also the site of an IOJ presidium bureau meeting in March, where the Moscow connection was emphasized by the fact that the Union of Journalists in the USSR had held its Sixth Congress immediately preceding it. Other international front meetings held in Moscow during the year were the first International Preparatory Committee meeting for the WFDY-IUS 1989 World Youth Festival (February) and the Tenth Congress of the WFTU's Trade Union International of Chemical, Oil and Allied Workers (October).

International front leaders also flocked to Moscow during the year for meetings of Soviet national affiliates. Secretary General Ibrahim Zakariya led a WFTU delegation to the Eighteenth Congress of the (Soviet) All-Union Central Council of Trade Unions (February); among the reported 188 foreign trade unions present at that meeting were probably the bulk of the WFTU's 92 affiliates

(Prague, *Flashes from the Trade Unions*, 13 March). The president and secretary general of the IOJ were present at the aforenoted Sixth Congress of the USSR Union of Journalists (March), and one assumes that the rest of the IOJ top leadership was also there because the IOJ presidium bureau meeting followed immediately (Prague, *IOJ Newsletter*, no. 7). An incomplete listing of the foreign delegations to the Soviet Komsomol Twentieth Congress (April) shows that roughly two-thirds of the youth organizations represented on the WFDY bureau sent delegates, so members of the WFDY top leadership were probably also included (Moscow, *Komsomolskaya pravda*, 14, 16–17 April; Budapest, *WFDY News*, no. 11–12, 1986). Finally, the president and secretary general of AAPSO attended the Soviet Afro-Asian committee's meeting on "Great October in the Affairs of Restructuring" (September–October), and "prominent social and political figures from the countries of Asia, Africa, and the Near East" said to have been present may have included a number of AAPSO vice presidents (ibid., 1 October).

Havana was the scene of the second-most-important front meeting of the year, the Fifteenth IUS Congress, held just before the wider-ranging Havana world student conference, "Learning to Work Together for a Better Future" (November). Another back-to-back combination in that city was the meeting of youth organizations of Latin America and the Caribbean (April) and the Fifth Congress of the Communist Youth of Cuba that immediately preceded it. May included two more international front meetings in Havana: the Thirty-third Congress of the International Radio and Television Organization (OIRT) and the annual CPC conference for Latin America and the Caribbean.

Other back-to-back meetings involving international front activity held in places other than Moscow or Havana were the IUS Executive Committee meeting/IUS-UNESCO International Student Round Table on "The Role of the University in the Development of Society" (Addis Ababa, January); "Education for Peace" conference/FISE Administrative Committee meeting (Athens, May); Thirteenth Mongolian Trade Union Congress/ "Peace, Development, and Hope of Working People in Asia and the Pacific" conference (Ulan Bator, May); meeting of Latin American WPC affiliates/ Latin American human rights seminar (Guayaquil and nearby Quito, May); Asia-Pacific student peace meeting/IUS-ESCAP student seminar (Ulan Bator, June).

The year also saw less concern than usual about open Soviet and/or front connections in activities outside the scope of the traditional fronts or their affiliates (the following three examples were second attempts at techniques that had been successful in the past). First, by early 1987 a Copenhagen Framework for Peace and Disarmament apparently had been set up as a follow-on to the October 1986 World Congress Devoted to the International Year of Peace, even though the Danish press had gone to great length to point out that meeting's Soviet and WPC connections (London, *Economist Foreign Report*, 5 February; *YICA*, 1987). This Copenhagen framework parallels the International Liaison Forum of Peace Forces, set up to continue the work of the 1973 World Congress of Peace Forces in Moscow, and involves holding the wide-ranging Vienna Dialogues every few years. Second, a meeting of nearly 1,000 important personalities "For a Nuclear Free World, for the Survival of Humanity" was held in February. It had even fewer connections with any known front, but it met in Moscow, was addressed by Gorbachev, and was participated in by the top CPC leadership's subdivision that deals with religious "personalities" (Prague, *CPC Information*, 10 March; U.S. Department of State, *Soviet Influence Activities*, 1987, pp. 19–20). The parallel here was the meeting with more than 1,000 "personalities" outside the normal front framework to discuss the Latin American foreign debt in July–August 1985; it had been held in Havana and addressed by Castro (*YICA*, 1986). Third, a group of Soviet and American lawyers, outside the IADL framework, met in New York in August to form an International Organization of Lawyers Against Nuclear War (Moscow, TASS, 30 August; *FBIS*, 1 September). It is even more transparently a Soviet front effort than the parallel International Physicians for the Prevention of Nuclear War (IPPNW) was when it was started in 1980 by a core of Soviet and American doctors except that the IPPNW looks more and more like a Soviet-oriented front. In 1987, for example, the IPPNW received extensive and favorable publicity by the WPC's *New Perspectives* in connection with its May–June meeting in Moscow, and the *World Student News* implied an indirect IPPNW connection with the IUS by virtue of their joint connection with the International Federation of Medical Student Associations (Helsinki, *New Perspectives*, no. 5 and no. 6; Prague, *World Student News*, November; *Yearbook of International Organizations*, 1986/87, entry BB1970).

A new technique of the WPC, the other fronts, and the less obvious pro-Soviet organizations was the Global Peace Wave on 24 October. This involved a wide variety of activities in some 50 countries—"demonstrations, rallies, peace relays, ship cruises, pickets, and collection of signatures under various appeals . . . church bell ringing, human chains and peace concerts, radio and TV programs, and demonstrations by children and youth"—somehow all focused on 12 noon (local time) that day (Helsinki, *Peace Courier*, no. 11).

Themes. Just as some of the techniques used by the fronts during 1987 showed more than normal connections with the Soviets, so did many of the propaganda slogans. "Toward the Year 2000 Without Nuclear Weapons" was the theme of the aforenoted WCW (June), which the Tenth Congress of the International Federation of Resistance Movements (FIR) had used in May. This slogan had been put forth by Gorbachev in his speech on 15 January 1986 and had been endorsed by the Women's congress by the time of the March 1986 WIDF Bureau meeting in East Berlin (East Berlin, ADN, 23 March 1986).

Subsidiary themes, prominent during 1986 and carried over into early 1987, included the cessation of nuclear testing and the Strategic Defense Initiative (SDI) research. These two were, of course, specifically directed against the United States. When Gorbachev dropped the SDI ban as a condition for negotiating a removal of Euromissiles (statement of 28 February), support for these negotiations replaced both the nuclear testing and the SDI themes as the main propaganda line in this category. (The change was noted as early as the Vienna Dialogue [mid-March] sponsored by the WPC-related International Liaison Forum—Helsinki, *Peace Courier*, no. 4). In fact, when the October agreement to hold a summit meeting was concluded, it almost immediately became the number one emphasis of the WFTU's concurrent general council meeting in Bucharest (Prague, *Flashes from the Trade Unions*, 13 November). Gorbachev's admission on 30 November that the USSR was also engaged in SDI research, incidentally, should put that subject "on the back burner."

As for geographic coverage, 1987 saw perhaps a greater emphasis on the Far East and southwest Pacific than on any other part of the Third World (Latin America being the one area that might have come close). This emphasis seems to go back to Gorbachev's 28 July 1986 Vladivostok speech, generally interpreted as inaugurating a new Soviet emphasis on the area and cited as furnishing guidelines for the "*first* consultative meeting of representatives of the communist and revolutionary democratic parties of Asia and the Pacific region," held at Ulan Bator in July 1987 (*WMR*, September; Ulan Bator, MONTSAME, 7 July; *FBIS*, 10 July). A further Soviet connection was indicated by the new first deputy chairman of the Soviet Afro-Asian Committee, the presumed Southeast Asian specialist Vladimir Tolstikov, stating at that organization's June plenum that more attention must be given to Asia at the apparent expense of Africa and, possibly, the Middle East. (Washington, D.C., *Problems of Communism*, September–October 1984; Moscow, *Aziia i Afrika segodnia*, June). The most obvious manifestation of this regional emphasis was the large number of front meetings devoted to Asia during the year:

First Southeast Asian Student Forum (IUS-League of Filipino students)	Manila (March)
"Peace, Development, and Hope of Working People in Asia and the Pacific" conference (apparent spin-off from the congress of the WFTU-affiliated Mongolian trade union federation)	Ulan Bator (May)
Asia-Pacific Trade Union Seminar on Women (WFTU-related Asian and Pacific Trade Union Coordinating Committee [APTUCC] and Vietnamese Federation of Labor)	Haiphong (May)
"Trade Union Education in Asia" conference (WFTU-affiliated All-Union Central Council of Trade Unions)	Tashkent (June)
Asia-Pacific Student Meeting and IUS-ESCAP Students' Seminar	Ulan Bator (June)
Asia-Pacific Trade Union Seminar on Young Workers (WFTU-UNESCO)	Hanoi (July)
Second Conference of Trade Unions of the Asian and Pacific Countries (APTUCC)	Manila (August)
International Conference on Denuclearization, Peace and Anti-Imperialist Solidarity in the Asian and Pacific Region (AAPSO)	Pyongyang (September)
Asia-Pacific Trade Union Seminar on Social Security (All-Union Central Council of Trade Unions)	Alma Ata (September–October)
Joint Youth Action for a Peaceful Indian Ocean and a Nuclear Weapon	Bombay (October)

Free Asia-Pacific (WFDY/All-India Youth Federation/All-India Students' Federation)	
WPC Presidential Bureau Meeting (focused on Asia-Pacific region)	Auckland (October)
International Trade Union Conference on Solidarity with the Workers and People of (South) Korea (WFTU?)	Prague (November)

Slightly more than half of this activity had been in the trade union field, so it was only fitting that the capstone in the Far East should come with the announcement in the 4 January 1988 *Bangkok Post* that a group of "veteran labor leaders" affiliated with the "Revolutionary Council" would invite the WFTU to set up a regional center in Bangkok and that four Thai labor unions had agreed to apply for WFTU membership. (Up until now, there has been no Thai affiliation or any other official WFTU activity in this conservative country.)

The Latin American meetings mentioned in the previous section were in the context of Havana as a site and back-to-back conferences in other places. And the WPC-promoted October Buenos Aires conference on the South Atlantic as a "zone of peace" did, of course, link South America to western Africa. What few international front meetings were held in Africa and the Middle East appear to have occurred early in the year, including the two aforementioned IUS sessions in Addis Ababa in January, a WIDF–British Assembly of Women meeting on apartheid in London that same month, a WPC-AAPSO conference on the Iran-Iraq war in Cairo in February, and a WPC-related conference on Cyprus in Sofia in April.

Other front themes could not be so openly or immediately linked to direct Soviet inspiration. Aside from a momentary emphasis on nuclear-free zones in general (the subject treated by the WFTU-related Dublin Committee in May and by the IADL in June), and the WPC-promoted conference on the South Atlantic as a "zone of peace" (Buenos Aires, October), most of these additional emphases centered on Third World economies: most specifically, the New International Economic Order (to redress the imbalance in wealth between the developed *capitalist* counries and the underdeveloped ones) together with its subsidiary themes concerning alleged misdeeds of transnational corporations and the injustice of the debt that had been incurred by the Third World. These three items were the subject of resolutions coming out of the aforenoted WFTU General Council meeting in October and were also the major emphases of the Fifteenth IUS Congress in Havana. The debt issue had been treated at a trade union conference participated in but not sponsored by the WFTU in Campinas near São Paulo in May, while an antitransnational corporation theme had been prominent in a Dublin Committee meeting during June. Front propaganda links this package to the peace and disarmament motif, with the line that the reduction of arms expenditures would make it possible for more aid to be given the Third World (Prague, *Flashes from the Trade Unions*, 13 November; Geneva, *Pax et libertas*, September; Prague, *World Trade Union Movement*, October).

The WCW in Moscow also considered the development issue, the meeting's subtitle being "For Peace, Equality, and Development." A reading of the materials coming out of the meeting, however, gives the impression that it was third after peace and equality (East Berlin, *Women of the Whole World*, no. 3; Geneva, *Pax et libertas*, September; Prague, *World Trade Union Movement*, October). Women's rights thus appear to have had a relatively greater emphasis than the equivalent trade union rights at the aforenoted WFTU general council meeting, where women's rights appeared to rank third after peace and development (Prague, *Flashes from the Trade Unions*, 13 November). (The WFTU did, however, appear to play the major role in setting up an International Center for the Defense of Trade Union Rights in Prague in November.) The possible student equivalent—"education a right and not a privilege"—appeared to have received even less attention at the aforenoted two Havana student conferences (Havana, *Granma*, 20 November; *Granma Weekly*, 29 November).

Personnel. Huang Jang Yop (North Korea) and Abdallah Hurani (Palestine) were newly noted as WPC vice presidents during 1987. Huang merely replaced another North Korean, while Hurani returned to a position that he had held until 1983 but that remained vacant during the interim (Helsinki, *New Perspectives*, no. 3, 1983 and no. 6, 1987). The Palestinian representation on the WPC Presidential Committee went from two to six during the year, an increase not matched by any other delegation and for which no explanation was forthcoming (ibid.). Jesus Reyes Arencibia became the WPC's new Cuban secretary during the year (ibid., p. 1), and a West German secretary was added in the person of Tobias Thomas (Helsinki, *Peace Courier*, no. 11). Romesh Chandra (India) and Johannes

Pakaslahti (Finland) remained WPC president and secretary general, respectively.

Similarly, while Sándor Gáspár (Hungary) and Ibrahim Zakariya (Sudan) remained, respectively, president and secretary general of the WFTU, Miroslav Zavadil was elected the organization's new Czech vice president and Mario Navarro its new Chilean secretary during 1987 (Prague, *Flashes from the Trade Unions*, 13 November). No replacement has yet been named for WFTU's Australian vice president Ernest Boatswain, who resigned for unknown reasons (London, *Economist Foreign Report*, 26 November). Again, although President Freda Brown (Australia) and Secretary General Mirjam Vire-Tuominen (Finland) remained in place through the WIDF's Congress in June, Zoja Pukhova (USSR), Nirupama Rath (India), and Fatima Aoufi (Algeria) emerged as new vice presidents (East Berlin, *Women of the Whole World*, no. 3). Also, Prima Loomba and Irene Karska (countries unknown) were noted as WIDF secretaries for the first time (WCW, *Preliminary List of Participants*).

President Walid Masri (Lebanon) and Secretary General Vilmos Cserveny (Hungary) remained in their WFDY positions as did President Josef Scala (Czechoslovakia) and Secretary General Giorgios Michaelides (Cyprus) for the IUS. But Burkhard Herrmann and Gaston Grisoni (countries unknown) were noted as IUS secretaries for the first time during 1987 (Prague, *World Student News*, no. 4, p. 22, and no. 6, p. 25). For the AAPSO, in December Murah Ghalib (Egypt) was nominated for president to replace the deceased Abd-al-Rahman Sharqawi (Egypt) (Cairo, *Al Ahram*, 20 December) while Nuri Abd-al-Razzaq Husayn (Iraq) remained as secretary general. Several AAPSO vice presidents have been newly identified: Abdallah Hurani (Palestine—see above also under WPC), Mahmud Abd-al-Fattah (West Sahara), Pascual Luvualu (Angola), Yohannes Gebre Selaisse (Ethiopia), Dr. Victor Agadzi (Ghana), Vladimir Tolstikov (USSR), Hamid Mohtat (Afghanistan), K. M. Shepande (Zambia), Ali Amir Muhammad (Tanzania), Vaseduv Acharya (India), and Abu al-Shamat (Syria) (14th AAPSO Council Session, Moscow, 14–17 May 1986; Pyongyang, Korean Central News Agency, 25 September; *FBIS*, 29 September).

There were three major 1987 changes in the smaller fronts: Gerard Montant (France) became the new secretary general of the FISE; Sakari Kiuru (Finland), the new president of the OIRT; and the chairmanship of the Berlin Conference of European Catholics remained vacant upon the death of Otto Hartmut Fuchs (East Germany) (Prague, *Flashes from the Trade Unions*, 10 July; Prague, *IOJ Newsletter*, no. 11; Prague, *CPC Information*, 21 April). Also, Leonard Wells (UK) is the new deputy secretary general of the World Federation of Scientific Workers (WFSW), Albino Ribeiro Cardoso (Portugal) a new IOJ vice president, and Vladimir Artemov (USSR) and Herbert Geerhardt (East Germany) were newly noted as secretaries of the IOJ and FISE, respectively (London, *Scientific World*, no. 3; Prague, *Democratic Journalist*, no. 9; Prague, ČETEKA, 24 July; *FBIS*, 27 July; Prague, *Flashes from the Trade Unions*, 13 November). The other top officers of these organizations apparently remained the same: FISE president Lesturuge Ariyawansa (Sri Lanka), OIRT secretary general Gennadij Codr (Czechoslovakia), WFSW president Jean-Marie Legay (France) and secretary general Stan Davison (UK), and IOJ president Kaarle Nordenstreng (Finland) and secretary general Jiri Kubka (Czechoslovakia). The same can be said for Asian Buddhist Conference for Peace (ABCP) president Kharkhuu Gaadan and secretary general G. Lubsan Tseren (both, Mongolia), CPC president Karoly Toth and secretary general Lubomir Mirejovsky (Czechoslovakia), IADL president Joe Nordmann (France) and secretary general Amar Bentoumi (Algeria), International Institute for Peace president Georg Fuchs (Austria), and Organization for Solidarity of the Peoples of Africa, Asia, and Latin America president Susumu Ozaki (Japan, but no information since 1984) and secretary general Rene Anillo Capote (Cuba).

Finally, the Tenth Congress of the FIR (May) resulted in the publication of its complete set of new officers, including

Presidential Board. President: Arialdo Banfi (Italy). Vice presidents: Marcos Ana (Spain), Vladimir Bonev (Bulgaria), Jean Brack (Belgium), Otto Funke (East Germany), Marton Ispanovits (Hungary), Jozef Kaminski (Poland), Helge Kierulff (Denmark), Spyros Kotsakis (Greece), Alexei Maressiev (USSR), Frantisek Miseje (Czechoslovakia), Andrei Neagu (Romania), Joseph C. Rossaint (East Germany), Ludwig Soswinski (Austria), Mario Venanzi (Italy), Robert Vollet (France)

Secretariat. Secretary general: Alix Lhote (France). Deputy secretary general: Zygmunt Bieszczanin (Poland). Secretaries: Kurt-Julius Goldstein (East Germany), Ilia Kremer (USSR), Isacco Nahoum (Italy)

(Source: Unie Resistance Service d'information, *Xe Congres Statutaire de la FIR*, pp. 52, 59).

Wallace H. Spaulding
McLean, Virginia

THE MIDDLE EAST

Introduction

The continuing disaster of unresolved wars, both civil and international, dominated Middle East politics during 1987. In Afghanistan, between Iran and Iraq, in Lebanon, between Israel and most Arab states, in the territories occupied by Israel since 1967, and within the ruling remnants of the Yemeni Socialist Party of the People's Democratic Republic of Yemen (PDRY)—the debilitating if not devastating force of these conflicts remained evident. For Soviet policy, invigorated by *glasnost'*, this turmoil presented tantalizing opportunities simultaneous with profound dilemmas. On the one hand, Moscow's priority is to achieve credibility as a respectable establishment power in the region. On the other hand, the Soviet Union also desires to control events in Afghanistan, to gain special strategic advantage in Iran, to solidify and perhaps expand its military position in the PDRY, to remain supportive of both legal and illegal Marxist parties throughout the region, and to retain maximum cooperation from both Iraq and estranged neighboring Syria.

Afghanistan represents the principal Soviet dilemma. Although Moscow has carefully avoided classifying the ruling People's Democratic Party of Afghanistan (PDPA) as communist or even socialist, a Soviet military withdrawal that abandoned the PDPA to slaughter by guerrilla groups would create dangerous implications for both the imperial and revolutionary dimensions of Soviet policy. Perhaps the Soviets are counting on the long-range evolution of the young Afghan cadres being educated in the USSR to eventually form a cohesive and viable Marxist party that can wrest control from the Islamic-oriented groups likely to dominate Afghanistan in the post-Soviet era. This prospect seems so thin a reed that it creates doubt over the reality of a definitive and sustained Soviet military abandonment of Afghanistan.

The PDPA's ideological identification with Moscow has been as complete as its dependence for existence on in-country Soviet forces. Recent PDPA efforts to achieve a more nationalist and Islamic image have provided merely a veneer. Equally unsuccessful have been the PDPA's continued efforts during 1987 to draw opposition groups into the government. Nor have determined efforts by PDPA general secretary Najibullah to consolidate his power in the party notably reduced the factionalism that has traditionally debilitated party strength. Purges within the party, including the firing of eleven Central Committee members and four alternates, and wider efforts to gain strength such as doubling military salaries in June to reduce mass military defections and draft dodging appeared to have little effect (Radio Kabul, 17 October; *FBIS*, 28 June, 2 July, 19 October).

The Iranian communist Tudeh Party celebrated its 46th anniversary in October, and although ruthlessly suppressed within Iran it nonetheless claimed an increase in the number of party cells and in publishing activity during the year (*Tudeh News*, 14 October). These are impossible to verify, but the claims are plausible in relation to Iran's deteriorating economic conditions and growing public disillusionment with the war. Nevertheless, the personal popularity of Khomeini makes unlikely any widespread receptivity to the Tudeh call for communist revolution as well as for a "constituent assembly to provide a new constitution . . . [and] remove all theocratic rule" (Radio of the Iranian Toilers, 6 March; *FBIS-NES*, 9 March).

Tehran's brutal repression of the Tudeh extended in March to its ally, the Fedayeen-e Khalq, when the minister of information and security announced that 80 percent of the group's Iran cadres had been smashed because of spying on the military, sabotage, and cooperation with the Tudeh (Tehran Domestic Service, in Persian, 18 March; *FBIS-NES*, 19 March). Apart from this kind of repression, the Marxist left in Iran is severely weakened by a factionalism that is thought to divide the movement into at least twelve factions (*Middle East Report*, September-October). Until this situation changes, then, Soviet aspirations in Iran, at least on the surface, will focus on gaining status with the Islamic government.

Soviet opportunities increased during the latter

part of the year as Western navies virtually blocked Tehran's strategy of intimidation against the Gulf Cooperation Council (GCC) states, beginning with Kuwait. Heavily publicized economic agreements between Tehran and Moscow followed high-level Soviet missions to Iran. The most dramatic of these agreements involved plans for joint shipping ventures in the Caspian Sea, for converting Iran's gas export pipeline to the USSR for oil shipment, and for the resumption of major Soviet economic projects in Iran, obviously to involve a sharply increased Soviet presence. All the projects appeared to be a logical outgrowth of Iran's increasing diplomatic and geographic isolation. Yet because they also seem so clearly designed to create sufficient concern among the Western powers to induce relaxation of naval pressure and discourage diplomatic efforts toward an arms embargo, there is room to question whether they will ever move beyond the planning stage.

This ambiguity in Soviet Persian Gulf policy was a hallmark rather than the exception. Intensive Soviet diplomatic activity in the Gulf climaxed in April with the visit of Deputy Foreign Minister Vladimir Petrovsky, who called on Iran to end the war yet made reassuring visits to Gulf Arab states and proposed an international conference to protect Gulf shipping. The USSR maintained a steady supply of weapons to Iraq while assuring that the arms pipeline from East European states to Iran remained open. Toward the end of the year frustration by the Iraqis and the GCC states mounted as the Soviets continued to stall on implementation of U.N. Security Council Resolution 598, which committed that body to the enforcement of an arms embargo on Iran in the absence of a cease-fire.

For the Iraq Communist Party (ICP) the war's continuation meant even greater isolation from the Arab political mainstream of Iraq and greater identification with Kurdish separatists as well as increased dependence on Iran for the arms, logistics support, and safe haven provided to weaken Iraq. This unenviable position for the ICP was emphasized by its exclusion from the meeting in Tehran of the various Iraqi opposition groups late in the year (*The Middle East*, March). As in Afghanistan, Iranian support remains principally channeled to Islamic opposition groups. The ICP, therefore, remains isolated with the Kurdish separatists, who are uninterested in a communist revolution that would unite all Iraq; their isolation from most non-Kurdish Iraqis is heightened by their dependence on the national enemy Iran.

Mirroring the ICP's and the Afghan PDPA's struggle for legitimacy, the Yemeni Socialist Party (YSP) of the PDRY maintains power despite crippling factionalism and loss of its core leadership, both in part legacies of the January 1986 civil war. Soviet analysts of the region could hardly be encouraged about Moscow's long-range prospects in Afghanistan by the fate of the Marxist YSP's twenty years in power: a PDRY society still dominated by regional and tribal loyalties and a badly divided YSP leadership comprising party nonentities and technocrats in place of the exiled or murdered party veterans. But despite these handicaps, and despite signs of Islamic agitation stimulated by Saudi and Iranian propaganda and PDRY workers returning from abroad, the Soviet position in Aden seems secure. Moscow has extensively re-equipped the PDRY army since 1986 and assigned scores of advisers to YSP organizations to help party viability in part by discrediting the predecessor regime. This close Soviet identity with the current PDRY regime was not without regional costs. North Yemen, Ethiopia, Saudi Arabia, and many of the other GCC states maintain close ties with the previous regime, and the harsh prison and death sentences for its members announced by Aden late in the year generated a new wave of ill will.

Distinct from these problems of ruling Marxist parties or of the draconian state repression for most of the illegal parties of the region, national elections in Egypt for the People's Assembly provided an interesting trial for the Marxist left in a reasonably democratic contest. Although the Egyptian Communist Party (ECP) is illegal, the new election law permitted its members to run as independents. Overall, Egypt's opposition parties had grounds for charges that the government stacked the deck against them—by allowing only seven weeks for campaigning, by dominating radio and television time, and by various harassments. Specifically, the government conducted two pre-election crackdowns against the ECP and its newspaper, *al-Intisar*; it reportedly detained and sometimes sentenced readers found with a copy (*WMR*, September). But it is also true that other opposition parties were subject to similar harassments, such as the government's arrest of many Islamic radicals throughout Egypt two days before the elections on charges they intended to use arms to disrupt the voting process (*Middle East Report*, July-August).

The main legal left party in Egypt, the National Progressive Unionist Party (NPUP) exerted a major though apparently unsuccessful effort to distinguish itself from ideological association with the four communist candidates, none of whom obtained more than 700 votes. Three of the candidates—a renowned labor and human rights lawyer, a veteran of the communist movement since the 1940s, and a prominent intellectual since holding a position in Nasser's Arab Socialist Union—were widely known in their districts. The NPUP apparently suffered not only because of its association with communists and consequent supposed anti-Islamic and pro-Moscow inclinations, but also because it received just 2.2 percent of the total vote in 1984 and so by virtue of the 8 percent minimum rule remained precluded from representation in the People's Assembly.

In contrast, the alliance of the Islamic-nationalist Socialist Labor Party, the Muslim Brotherhood, and the right-wing Socialist Liberals Party won 17 percent of the vote and 35 assembly seats. The Muslim Brotherhood as a religious organization was precluded from formal participation in elections, but its presence within the alliance was clearly a principal source of votes. The success of Islamic groups in Egyptian university elections during 1987 mirrors this trend (*Middle East Report*, July-August). Despite widespread accusations of election abuses by government and the generally controlled atmosphere governing Egypt's politics, the message of an Islamic upsurge and a weakening of the communist-linked left was clear.

This trend, of course, was not confined to Egypt. In Lebanon the rapid growth of Shiite religious movements following the Israeli invasion of 1982 has resulted in declining influence for the Lebanese Communist Party (LCP) and the Organization of Communist Action in Lebanon (OCAL). As former allies of the Palestine Liberation Organization (PLO) for tactical reasons, both the LCP and OCAL fortunes suffered as the PLO dispersed, its power displaced throughout southern Lebanon by the Amal and Hizb Allah Shiite militias. The total and ferocious commitment of these militias against the re-establishment of PLO authority in their territory combined with religious fervor against atheists (particularly by the Hizb Allah) has resulted in waves of LCP and OCAL assassinations.

In February an alliance of communist and Druze forces took the offensive against Amal in Beirut, which suggested to Amal that the two Moscow-linked groups had Soviet backing. Druze leader Walid Jumblatt's speech at a rally for the LCP's 66th birthday three weeks before had urged revival of a united leftist front. Karen Brutents, the senior Soviet Middle East specialist, was present at the rally (*WP*, 18 February). But the offensive was not successful, and the following month there were reports that nine LCP leaders had been killed in Beirut and south Lebanon (*NYT*, 4 March); further assassination of officials occurred in March, including two Central Committee members and a well-known writer and professor of philosophy (*WMR*, April).

Growing unrest on the Israeli-occupied West Bank and Gaza Strip saw an apparent effort by the Palestine Communist Party to preserve ties with the PLO. In January Politburo member Na'im Ashhab cautioned against U.S. and Israeli attempts to weaken the PLO's role as representative of the Palestinians (*WMR*, January). The Communist Party of Israel (CPI) has long backed full equality for the Arabs in occupied territories and has offered to join any groups working to restore Arab lands (*WMR*, January). Yet the CPI also apparently sees the PLO as an essential element in the peace process. During November a CPI delegation met in Moscow with PLO chairman Yassir Arafat and reportedly conveyed a message back to the Israeli government that the PLO now accepts U.N. Resolution 242 and all other U.N. decisions on the conflict (*CSM*, 19 January 1988).

Morocco's legal Party of Progress and Socialism (PPS) resumed publication of its daily newspaper, *al Bayane*, in January following a two-month government-imposed suspension caused by General Secretary 'Ali Yata's declared intention to criticize both foreign and domestic government policy. With both French and Arabic editions and a circulation of 10,000, *al Bayane* is the only communist party daily newspaper published in a noncommunist African country. In a move unique in the Arab world, the PPS elected its first female member, Amina Lemrini, to the PPS Politburo (*al Bayane*, 21 July). Although the PPS failed in its attempt to create a coalition of left parties including Morocco's major opposition party, the Socialist Union of Popular Forces, by November the PPS had succeeded in cooperating with three other parties to oppose the government's development program for 1988–1992 and the government's 1988 budget (ibid., 29 December).

With the end of the long Habib Bourguiba era in Tunisia on 7 November, the Tunisian Communist Party (PCT) soon met with the major opposition in Tunisa, the Movement of Democratic Socialists, and noted similar viewpoints as well as the need for a broad national dialogue (*al-Tarik al-Jadid*, 28 November–4 December). The PCT held its first legal congress since 1962 in June. Over 150 delegates attended, together with representatives of all legal Tunisian opposition parties and Labor unions (*al Bayane*, 24 June). In addition, twenty delegations from other communist parties in the world, national liberation movements such as the PLO, and a Soviet delegation participated (*Pravda*, 13 July).

James H. Noyes
Hoover Institution

Afghanistan

Population. 14,183,671; refugee flow plus wartime casualties have reduced significantly a population that in 1978 was thought to number about 17 million.

Party. People's Democratic Party of Afghanistan (Jamiyat-e-Demokrati Khalq-e-Afghanistan, literally Democratic Party of the Afghanistan Masses; PDPA). The party has two mutually antagonistic wings: Parcham (Banner) and Khalq (Masses).

Founded. 1965

Membership. Officially 185,000 (Radio Kabul, 18 October; *FBIS*, 23 October), of whom about 13,000 are women (*Kabul New Times* [*KNT*], 15 June). The total figure includes candidate members (about half) and is greatly inflated. A maximum probable figure for full members is 40,000, of which only a fraction can be considered reliable (*YICA*, 1987). Of the members who joined since 1982 (almost 75 percent of the currently claimed membership), 58 percent were under age 30 and 18.3 percent said they were workers, 26.5 percent peasants, 3 percent craftsmen, and 36.9 percent intellectuals (*KNT*, 25 October).

General Secretary. Lieutenant General Najibullah, also known as Dr. Najib, Mohammed Najibullah, Mohammed Najibullah Ahmadzai, and variations (see *YICA*, 1987).

Politburo. 14 members: Najibullah, Sayed Mohammed Gulabzoi (43, Pashtun, minister of interior), Najmuddin Akhgar Kawiani (38, head of the Central Committee International Relations Department) (*KNT*, 10 June), Sultan Ali Keshtmand (52, Hazara, intellectual, prime minister of the Republic of Afghanistan), Suleiman Laeq (58, Pashtun, writer, minister of tribes and nationalities), Dr. Haider Masoud (full-time party worker) (Bakhtar, 15 March; *FBIS*, 17 March), Niaz Mohammed Mohmand (Pashtun, economic expert, head of Revolutionary Council Permanent Commission for Budget and Planning) (Radio Kabul, 3 January; *FBIS*, 5 January), Nur Ahmad Nur (51, Pashtun, intellectual, full-time party worker), General Mohammed Rafi (42, Pashtun, minister of defense), Abdul Zaher Razmjo (late 30's, secretary, Kabul city party committee), Abdul Wakil (41, economics teacher, foreign minister), General Mohammed Aslam Watanjar (42, Pashtun, minister of communications), Lieutenant General Ghulam Farouq Yaqubi (Pashtun, minister of state security), Dr. Saleh Mohammed Zeary (51, Pashtun, medical doctor, Revolutionary Council Presidium member); 4 alternate members: Mir Saheb Karwal (Pashtun), Farid Ahmad Mazdak (Tajik, secretary, Democratic Youth Organization of Afghanistan), General Nazar Mohammed (53, Pashtun, minister of defense and first deputy prime minister), Shahnawaz Tanai (38, Pashtun, chief of the General Staff of the armed forces)

Secretariat. 12 members: Najibullah, Mir Saheb Karwal, Najmuddin Akhgar Kawiani, Haider Masoud, Niaz Mohammed Mohmand, Nur Ahmad Nur, Saleh Mohammed Zeary, Mohammed Anwar Isar (secretary, Nangarhar Province Party Committee), Mohammed Daoud Razmyar (head, Central Committee Economic Department), Mohammed Khalil Sepayee (secretary, Herat Province Party Committee), Mohammed Sharif (secretary, Balkh Province Party Committee), Ahmad Nabi (secretary, Kandahar Province Party Committee). (Note: The names of the above secretaries of provincial party committees date from 1986 [*KNT*, 12 July 1986], whereas the fact that the persons [unnamed] holding those positions were members of the Central Committee Secretariat was announced only in late 1987 [*KNT*, 18 October]; it is possible that one or more of the provincial secretaries were replaced between 1986 and 1987.)

Central Committee. 102 full and 68 candidate members

Status. Ruling party

Last Congress. First, 1 January 1965, in Kabul; National Conferences, 14–15 March 1982 and 18–19 October 1987

Last Election. Local council elections were held from 1985 to 1987, usually by a unanimous show of hands and never by secret ballot. It was claimed that over 86 percent of the population had elected some 24,000 representatives, of whom 17.5 percent were "former opponents." The promulgation of a political parties law in late 1987 and the subsequent formation of rump parties may herald a new round of "elections" at some future date. Membership in the RC, the ostensible ruling legislative body that now contains a large number of nonparty figures, continues to be by PDPA appointment.

Auxiliary Organizations. National Front (NF), formerly known as the National Fatherland Front, claims 120,000 members and 730,000 "collective members" (Bakhtar, 16 January; *FBIS*, 20 January), Abdul Rahim Hatef, chairman; Extraordinary Commissions for National Reconciliation, claims over 100,000 members in 3,000 branches (*Literaturnaya Gazeta*, 16 September; *FBIS*, 17 September), also headed by Hatef; Central Council of Trade Unions, claims 300,000 members, Abdus Sattar Purdeli, president; Democratic Youth Organization of Afghanistan (DYOA), claims 200,000 members, including 46,000 girls, Farid Ahmad Mazdak, first secretary; Central Council of High Tribal Jirga, 154 members, Haji Mohammed Chamkani, chairman; Women's Council of Afghanistan (WCA, formerly All-Afghanistan Women's Council [AAWC]), claims 55,000 members (*KNT*, 17 June), Masooma Esmati Wardak, chairperson (Bakhtar, 22 June); agricultural and consumer cooperatives, 486 groups with 74,550 members (Bakhtar, 8 April; *FBIS*, 8 April); Council of Religious Scholars and Clergy, Ghulam Sarwar Manzoor, chairman; Artists' Union, Mashir Jamal, chairman; Economic Advisory Council; various militias ("groups for the defense of the revolution"); Union of Cultural Personalities, 2,000 members; Union of Journalists, 1,832 members; Union of Writers, Ghulam Dastaghir Panjsheri, president; Union of Artisans; Association of National Entrepreneurs; Chambers of Commerce and Industry, Mohammed Hakim, general president; Peace, Solidarity, and Friendship Society, Habib Mangal, president. For the larger groups the above statistics, like those for PDPA membership, are unquestionably inflated and involve a good deal of double counting.

Publications. *Haqiqat-e-Enqelabe Saur* (The Saur revolution truth), Central Committee daily organ in Dari and Pashtun, Bareq Shafiee, editor in chief; Bakhtar, official news agency, Sarwar Yuresh, chief; *Haqiqat-e-Sarbaz* (The soldier's truth); *Darafsh-e-Jawanan* (The banner of youth), Pashtu and Dari daily, circulation 70,000 per week (*KNT*, 26 May); *Dehqan* (Peasant); *Kabul New Times* (*KNT*), English-language daily, Mohammed Seddiq Rahpoe, editor; *Storai* (Story), DYOA monthly; *Peshahang* (Pioneer), monthly; *Zindaqi Hezbi* (Party life), biweekly, Abdul Rahim, editor. In all, 28 magazines and 43 newspapers are published. The regime maintains a radio station and has a limited television network.

Background. In 1967, two years after its founding, the PDPA split into opposing Parcham and Khalq wings. Both kept the PDPA name and both were loyal to Moscow, but each maintained a separate organization and recruitment program. Khalq, led by Nur Mohammed Taraki, the PDPA's founder, depended for support on the relatively poor rural intelligentsia and recruited almost solely among the Pashtuns, the dominant (40 percent) Afghan ethnic group. Parcham, more broadly representative ethnically, was urban-oriented and appealed to a wealthier group of educated Afghans. It was led by Babrak Karmal, son of an Afghan general. Both groups focused their initial recruitment efforts on intellectuals, media employees, and especially teachers. When Mohammed Daoud overthrew the Afghan monarchy in 1973, the Parchamis at first collaborated with him and were obliged to refrain from aggressive recruiting. The Khalqis, however, remained in opposition and began an intense recruitment campaign among the military in preparation for the PDPA coup that was to follow five years later. During this period, the Khalqis moved from numerical parity with the Parchamis to significant superiority.

Under Soviet pressure, Parcham and Khalq formally reunited in mid-1977, and their combined strength was enough to overthrow Daoud and establish the Democratic Republic of Afghanistan (DRA) in April 1978. They almost immediately fissioned again, however, with Taraki sending the most prominent Parchamis into diplomatic exile as ambassadors and jailing or demoting most of those who remained in Afghanistan. When a Parchami plot to unseat Taraki was discovered in the summer of 1978, the ambassadors were recalled but disobeyed the order and fled into exile in Eastern Europe.

Meanwhile, popular resistance to Khalq's

rigorous Marxist-Leninist rule grew rapidly and soon threatened to topple the new regime in spite of massive Soviet military aid. In September 1979, the Soviets attempted to force another artificial reconciliation between Parcham and Khalq, but their plan to place all the blame for the schism on Taraki's deputy, Hafizullah Amin, backfired when Amin himself seized power and murdered Taraki. Amin, however, could not pacify his rebellious people, and on 27 December 1979, Soviet troops invaded, shot Amin, and restored the Parchamis to power. Babrak (he affected the surname Karmal, meaning either "friend of labor" or "Kremlin," for political purposes) became the new leader and tried to heal the breach with the Khalqis on the one side and with the Afghan population on the other. In neither effort was he successful, and in May 1986 he suffered the first of several demotions from power. His successor, Najibullah, performed no better, and the regime maintained a tenuous hold on power only in a few main Afghan towns during daylight hours, thanks to a Soviet presence that slowly swelled from 85,000 combat troops in 1980 to about 120,000 by the end of 1984. Since that time the strength of the Soviet force has remained fairly constant. A marginal decrease in 1986 was offset by a marginal increase in 1987 (U.S. Department of State, *Afghanistan: Eight Years of Occupation*, Special Report No. 173, December 1987).

Since the Soviet invasion of Afghanistan in 1979, the PDPA has not technically been a communist or even a socialist (in the Soviet lexicon) party but merely the ruling party in a country undergoing the "national democratic stage of revolution." Unlike the avowedly socialist PDPA ideologues of 1978–1979, party spokesmen since the invasion have gone through contortions to avoid using the terms socialist and socialism when referring to Afghanistan. In 1987, for example, party spokesmen claimed that the PDPA had never been socialist or had even had socialism as an ultimate goal. Nevertheless, the total devotion and subservience of the party to Moscow's interpretation of Marxism-Leninism is unmistakable.

During 1987 the Afghan state, the PDPA's main front organization, and the party leader all modified their names. The Democratic Republic of Afghanistan became the Republic of Afghanistan (RA) (*KNT*, 29 November), the National Fatherland Front became the National Front (Bakhtar, 16 January; *FBIS*, 20 January), and General Secretary Najib reverted to his original, more religious name of Najibullah, "because the RC [Revolutionary Council] thought I should go by my full name" (TASS, 4 October; *FBIS*, 5 October). Although these changes could all be written off as merely cosmetic, they reflected an apparently genuine effort by the PDPA to "restructure all spheres of life in Afghan society" (*NYT*, 27 January, quoting Najibullah), in order to preserve at least part of its own fragile hold on power.

In the process, the PDPA may have broken new ground for a ruling Marxist-Leninist power when it repeatedly asserted its intention to share real political power with the opposition. Most of the suggested reforms remained in the realm of theory, however, if only because anticommunist hostility prevented any cooperation between the central government and the vast majority of Afghan citizens.

The reason for trying to launch the reforms, which at least in theory would seriously dilute PDPA power, was almost certainly the prospect of a possible Soviet withdrawal of its military occupation forces. If this were to occur under present circumstances, it would leave the PDPA at the mercy of a vengeful Afghan populace. The attempt to achieve some kind of "coalition government of national unity" could thus be interpreted as a desperate effort by the PDPA to achieve legitimacy before it is too late. The unanswered question remained whether the USSR would be willing actually to withdraw its forces regardless of the consequences for the PDPA. Clearly, the PDPA is taking the threat of such a withdrawal seriously, and the sweeping changes and proposed changes during 1987 must be viewed in that context.

Party Leadership and Organization. In 1987 Najibullah consolidated his hold on power by eliminating some opposition elements and securing his own "election" as chief of state and president of the RA. For the previous year, the acting head of state had been a fellow-traveling noncommunist, Haji Mohammed Chamkani, who held the ceremonial post of acting chairman of the Revolutionary Council (RC). When the position became important in late 1987, Chamkani was abruptly demoted and became only one of several deputy chairmen behind Najibullah and Nur Ahmad Nur, the first deputy chairman.

In the foreign ministry alone, Najibullah removed some 96 supporters of deposed party leader Babrak Karmal (UPI, 4 October). In the PDPA Central Committee apparat he fired a leading functionary in each of ten departments for "incompetence and lack of party discipline" (Radio Kabul, 17

September; *FBIS*, 18 September). Later, he fired eleven Central Committee full members and four alternates, promoting or appointing ten new full members and three alternates in their place (Radio Kabul, 17 October; *FBIS*, 19 October). Babrak himself was sent off to the USSR "at the invitation and advice of doctors" (*NYT*, 5 May), following a large, spontaneous demonstration for him during the Revolution Day festivities in April and subsequent Chinese reports that he had been arrested (U.S. Department of State, *Afghanistan: Eight Years of Occupation*, Special Report no. 173, December; *NYT*, 4 May). Three bomb explosions in Kabul immediately after his departure were ascribed to his disgruntled supporters (*NYT*, 13 May). When Najibullah himself dropped from sight for three weeks during a projected "short" trip to the USSR, rumors of his own political demise were quick to spread (*NYT*, 8 August), but were dissipated on his return.

The factionalism that has dogged the PDPA since its founding remained a basic weakness in 1987. The second party conference, originally scheduled for August–September, was postponed until late October in part because several local party groups tried to elect Babrak as a delegate (DoS, *Eight Years*). At the conference, Najibullah warned that the party had to achieve unity or face loss of its "leading role." He demanded that all sign a pledge of unity or face expulsion from the party, and he termed factionalism "treachery" that calls for severe punishment (Bakhtar, 19 October; *FBIS*, 19 October; Radio Kabul, 18 October; *FBIS*, 20 October). He acknowledged that some party leaders were spreading "doubt, panic, and pessimism" while others were indulging in "nepotism, and sometimes even revenge" (DoS, *Eight Years*). Politburo member Saleh Mohammed Zeary, in castigating pro-Babrak elements a short time later, claimed that the phenomenon of factionalism was confined to the middle and upper party ranks, but there is no evidence to support the claim; the system of party patronage is such that new members automatically adopt the factional preferences of their mentors.

These statements doubtless referred not only to the new split between pro-Babrak and pro-Najib elements in the Parcham branch of the party but also to the traditional rivalry between its Parcham and Khalq wings. Najibullah, however, seems to have taken some extraordinary steps to mollify the Khalqis. It was clear from questions put to him in May that many jailed members of the last (1979) Khalqi Central Committee had been released. The questions seemed to reflect hostility from both Parchamis, who did not like seeing their rivals at large, and Khalqis, who wondered why those freed were not reinstated in the Central Committee (*KNT*, 13 May). No names of formerly prominent Khalqis have been published, but according to the exile rumor market at least three (Ghorbandi, Jauzjani, and Wali) were released, whereas at least three more (Hashemi, Katawazi, and Sooma) were still in prison as of June. The failure to mention those pardoned by name probably reflects an ongoing debate within party circles as to the wisdom of releasing them. Even if the pardon becomes generally acceptable, the rigidly socialist Khalqis can be expected to oppose what they see as Najibullah's betrayals of conventional Marxism-Leninism.

Organizationally, the topmost PDPA levels were expanded: in place of eleven full and five alternate Politburo members, there were now fourteen and four, respectively, and the Secretariat was expanded from eight to twelve members. For the first time, secretaries of four major provinces were seated on the Central Committee Secretariat, a reflection of the party's perceived need to get in touch with grassroots Afghanistan. According to a Soviet account, PDPA Politburo members were required to spend 20 out of any 30 working days in the provinces (*Literaturnaya Gazeta*, 14 October), but that target figure appears to have little relation to reality.

The Politburo and Central Committee lost two old party stalwarts in the persons of Anahita Ratebzad and Mahmoud Baryalai, both intimately associated with ousted party leader Babrak Karmal. Ratebzad also lost her position as head of the Peace, Solidarity, and Friendship Society. The unofficial head of the Khalq party faction, Minister of Interior Sayed Mohammed Gulabzoy, was elevated from alternate to full Politburo membership, and Najmuddin Akhgar Kawiani, Haider Masoud, and Niaz Mohammed Mohmand became the other full members. Among the alternates, only Shahnawaz Tanai was a newcomer.

There was also some shuffling of responsibilities. Kawiani lost his key position as head of the Central Committee Organizational Department in order to take over the International Relations Department, a spot perhaps now more important as the USSR appeared to be reassessing its commitment to the PDPA. Kawiani's organizational duties may have been taken over by Masoud, who had previously been shifted from media responsibilities to the deputy slot in the Organizational Department.

As in previous years, the PDPA claimed a continued expansion of total membership, though at a somewhat lower rate of increase than in 1986 and, particularly, in 1985. A proposal to do away with the requirement for probationary membership (*KNT*, 25 October) was a sign of the party's continued preoccupation with growth. Yet the party also claimed to have expelled over 5,000 members, many for "opportunism" or "violations of the constitution" (ibid., 21 June).

In 1986 four parties that may have existed in name only were merged with the PDPA (*YICA*, 1987). In late 1987, two of these suddenly reachieved an independent existence in order to form the first non-PDPA elements in a coalition government. The loss of their inconsequential membership had no apparent effect on the PDPA's membership strength.

Domestic Affairs. The essence of the PDPA's domestic policies during 1987 was the continuation and intensification of the "broadened base" campaign that was started in late 1985. The intention of the policy was to achieve PDPA unity and discipline and to promote support for the government among noncommunist elements of the Afghan people. As originally conceived, the policy probably envisioned a small, tightly knit party making all essential decisions behind the scenes while a figurehead coalition government (and possibly a figurehead leader) provided a cover of democratic respectability. The PDPA (and the Communist Party of the Soviet Union [CPSU]) hoped to achieve by such political means the victory that was being denied them militarily.

If that was the original intent, events during 1987—including a militarily much more effective resistance—seemed to convince the PDPA itself that a more genuine approach to reform was needed. As Najibullah acknowledged, "it has become clear that we cannot solve our issues through sheer use of force" (UPI, 14 July). Nevertheless, he was obliged to keep trying to strengthen his military forces, weakened through mass desertions and draft dodging. In June he doubled military salaries (Radio Kabul, 28 June; *FBIS*, 2 July), but this had no visible effect on improving combat capabilities. His admission that 92 percent of the army's "volunteers" came from Kabul indicated that the capital was the only area under full regime control (AP, 23 June). Periodic exhortations to increase recruitment in the countryside and to improve military capabilities until the army "becomes an independent force capable of handling any combat task" were telling indirect admissions that neither goal had been attained (*KNT*, 15 June).

The drive for "national reconciliation," inaugurated in 1986, became a ubiquitous slogan during 1987 in spite of opposition by hard-line elements within the PDPA and total rejection by the resistance. One of the first concrete manifestations of national reconciliation was Najibullah's call for a cease-fire to begin on 15 January. The term was ill chosen. Not only did it became the starting signal for a series of Soviet and RA military operations against the resistance, but the resistance itself also rejected the call for a truce and launched its own offensives. Throughout 1987 military activity by all participants intensified to progressively higher levels, and casualties mounted accordingly. Nevertheless, in July and again in November Najibullah renewed the cease-fire for additional six month increments, with the last to expire on 15 July 1988 (Radio Kabul, 30 November; *FBIS*, 2 December).

A second reconciliation element was an amnesty for some political prisoners and a call for refugees to return home. Hassan Sharq, an old but unacknowledged communist, was made minister of repatriation affairs (Radio Kabul, 27 June; *FBIS*, 28 June). Both the amnesty and the claims of success by the repatriation commissions were misleading. The amnesty applied to only a limited number of prisoners, and the claimed rate of repatriation was greatly exaggerated. Even taken at face value, the claim that some 83,000 persons had returned to Afghanistan between January and October (Bakhtar, 1 October; *FBIS*, 2 October) would have no more than balanced the number of new refugees in Pakistan, who were arriving at the rate of 8,000–10,000 per month during 1987, and 8,200 in the first two weeks of December alone (*San Francisco Chronicle*, 15 December). In October a Western source placed the number of returnees at only about 800 (*The Independent*, 12 October).

Yet another aspect of the regime's effort to gain support was its emphasis on religion. Official proclamations began with religious invocations, the government sponsored an international Koran reading contest (won by an Afghan) (*KNT*, 24 May), and Najibullah stated that the government had allocated 2 billion afghanis (about $40 million at the official rate of exchange) for various religious purposes. He also announced the appointment of 426 "prayer leaders" in the army and 420 more in the police. The leader himself professed great piousness, a claim that was, however, seriously jeopardized by his wearing shoes while at prayer in a mosque (*NYT*, 26

January). When challenged by conventional party ideologues, he acknowledged that the PDPA's support for religion was contrary to "scientific revolutionary theory" but was a practical political necessity for the time being because most Afghans were believers (*KNT*, 13 May). The party's endorsement of religion was, in effect, a temporary tactic of expedience.

Land reform, undertaken by previous Afghan communist leaders with universally bad results, was essentially turned on its head during 1987. Previously, the maximum allowable acreage per family was 30 *jeribs* (about 15 acres), but this was raised to 100 *jeribs* (50 acres). Even this limit could be exceeded by vineyards or orchards whose owners had contracts with the state, by holdings considered "holy places," by landlords who had proven "cooperative with the state," and in "certain other cases" (Radio Kabul, 5 November; *FBIS*, 6 November).

Private enterprise was also encouraged. Generous bank loans were made available to entrepreneurs, a plastics factory seized in 1986 was returned to its owner, and private businessmen were awarded various medals, orders, banners, and honorary certificates by the RC (*KNT*, 14 April, 21, 26 May). The government made a point of conceding that 80 percent of the $3 billion economy, including almost all agriculture, was in private hands (*NYT*, 15 May), and in November Najibullah stated that Afghanistan's future economy would not be on a socialist but on a "mixed" basis (Radio Kabul, 30 November; *FBIS*, 2 December).

In the political field, the regime abandoned its system of zonal administration (Radio Kabul, 18 October; *FBIS*, 23 October) and undertook a program of local self-rule. Najibullah boasted in October that Kabul had established "peaceful control" over some 2,300 villages in the first ten months of the year (TASS, 11 November; *FBIS*, 12 November), but it appeared that this amounted to little more than an agreement by villagers to pay lip service to the central government. In February 65 percent of the "liberated" villages were under nonparty local control, and by December this had grown to 76 percent (Radio Kabul, 10 December; *FBIS*, 11 December). As spelled out by Najibullah, any villages opting to join the government might keep its old system and leaders; in return for its pledge of loyalty, the government would remove all Soviet and Afghan army units from the area, leaving behind only *Sarandoy* (ministry of interior police) and a local militia to keep order (*KNT*, 15 June).

By late June the government was claiming control over 8,600 villages, but the accompanying claim that fourteen districts and four provinces were being run by former members of the opposition cast doubt on the extent of its authority. By September Soviet forces had allegedly been withdrawn from "inhabited areas of the Hazarajat," leaving the Hazaras free to run their own local affairs, and at year's end they claimed to have removed their forces from thirteen provinces (Bakhtar, 3 December; *FBIS*, 3 December). At that time, elections for self-rule had been held in more than 6,000 villages (TASS, 2 December; *FBIS*, 2 December).

A political parties law drafted during the summer was promulgated in November, and five parties promptly registered, but none was in opposition. In addition to the PDPA there were the Revolutionary Organization of the Workers of Afghanistan, the Organization of the Workers of Afghanistan, the People's Islamic Party of Afghanistan, and Peasants' Justice Party of Afghanistan (*Pravda*, 29 November). Najibullah also suggested that a "bourgeois" party might be formed later.

As an enticement to resistance leaders—and as a maneuver to split their ranks—the regime first offered a few minor ministerial portfolios to the three nonfundamentalist resistance groups. When this failed to produce results, the offer was expanded to include 23 key executive positions, and it was ultimately extended to all seven members of the Peshawar-based combined resistance front (Radio Kabul, 30 November; *FBIS*, 2 December). The offer did not, however, include the presidency or the key ministries of interior, defense, or security (*Izvestiia*, 23 July; *FBIS*, 24 July). By year's end, five ministers were supposedly nonparty, but all were known as fellow travelers.

In addition, both Soviet and official Afghan media raised the possibility of a role for the exiled Afghan king, Zahir Shah, in a future coalition government that would include both communists and resistance representatives. In December a U.N. envoy, Diego Cordovez, opened negotiations with the king, a resident of Italy, on his possible role in a transitional government while the Soviet forces were being withdrawn (*NYT*, 11 December).

Many of these initiatives were embodied in a new constitution that was adopted unanimously on 29 November by an assembly packed with regime supporters (*NYT*, 29 November). In a vain effort to increase the document's legitimacy, Najibullah insisted that it did not "reflect the ideas of the PDPA" (Radio Kabul, 30 November; *FBIS*, 3 December).

The proceedings were marred by a resistance rocket attack that placed four rounds near the meeting hall and by gunfire from a turncoat resistance leader angered at having been denied entrance to the convention (*Financial Times*, 9 December).

Throughout the year there were contradictory signs about the role of the PDPA in any future government. The question of whether the PDPA would indeed be the "guiding force" or whether it would be just one of many equal parties was raised by Najibullah at the constitutional convention, but he dodged the issue by declaring that a "third, compromise position" on the question had been adopted (Radio Kabul, 30 November; *FBIS*, 3 December). The PDPA intention was clearly to hold onto as much power as possible, but both Soviet and Afghan media emphasized that not just "token" but "real power sharing" was the only solution (*KNT*, 15 June; TASS, 14 June; *FBIS*, 15 June). Najibullah reserved for himself the position of president under the new constitution, a post that gives him sweeping powers, but it was intriguing that he lost his absolute veto power in the document's final draft; he can now be overruled by a two-thirds majority of the National Assembly (Radio Kabul, 2 December; *FBIS*, 4 December).

There was also an intensified effort to distance both the PDPA and the RA from socialism. This became especially noticeable at the end of 1987 when Najibullah told a party audience, "Our revolution is not a proletarian or socialist revolution. I stress, comrades, that our revolution is not a proletarian or socialist revolution" (Radio Kabul, 18 October; *FBIS*, 23 October). This statement was replayed verbatim in Soviet media (Moscow Television, 25 October; *FBIS*, 26 October). Later, he denied that the PDPA was a communist party and requested that he personally no longer be referred to as "comrade" (Radio Kabul, 30 November; *FBIS*, 2 December). The denials of communist affiliation were probably designed mainly to salvage some popularity for the PDPA, but they also served a role in confirming Moscow's lack of obligation to protect the RA and/or PDPA under the Brezhnev Doctrine of defending socialism wherever it is threatened. The growing Soviet doubt about the PDPA's ability to rule was revealed starkly in a comment that was not repeated in Afghan media: ". . . the progressive vanguard of [Afghan] society is still not able on its own to choose the path of national development" (*Pravda*, 17 October; *FBIS*, 28 October).

Despite the revolutionary nature of the reform proposals and measures, the regime's military, economic, and political performance during 1987 was poor, and its future prospects appeared bleak. In the field, regime troops performed badly and continued to desert to a resistance whose morale and capabilities were greatly enhanced by the availability of improved antiaircraft weapons. Despite a 17 percent rise in private sector output, the economy continued its downward spiral. Inflation was running at 20–30 percent per year, and it was estimated that per capita income had fallen from $195 in 1979 to about $140 in 1987. Private investment in the economy had fallen from 10 percent in 1985–1986 to 1 percent in 1986–1987. Politically, the regime was impotent, and the resistance refused to have any dealings with it. In November the disintegration of regime morale was exemplified by the defection to the resistance of Najibullah's own brother. At year's end, many other leading families associated with the regime were discreetly sending large sums of money out of the country, enrolling their children in overseas schools, and otherwise preparing for a hasty departure in the event of a Soviet withdrawal (*London Times*, 2 December).

Front and Auxiliary Organizations. In mid-January, at the second congress of the National Fatherland Front, that organization's name was changed to the National Front (NF), and the formation of 217 new branches was announced. Nevertheless, Najibullah excoriated the organization for poor work. Buried in the proceedings was the information that the PDPA would no longer direct the work of the NF, whose present subordination was left unclear (Radio Kabul, 15 January; *FBIS*, 20 January). The NF's main duty was listed as helping to carry out national reconciliation (Radio Kabul, 24 April; *FBIS*, 29 April).

The executive organs for national reconciliation were the so-called Extraordinary Commissions, a name that coincides with that of the first Soviet secret police (CHEKA). The Afghan commissions were established by (and presumably subordinate to) the RC, and their duties were ostensibly to oversee the peaceful sharing of political power at the local level. They were to include not only PDPA functionaries but also clergymen, tribal leaders, other prominent nonparty figures, and even members of the armed opposition. By October it was claimed that 3,200 commissions had been set up. Their supposedly peaceful role was contradicted in a Moscow report that a combined Soviet/RA military offensive against a resistance group took place on "special instructions of the Supreme Extraordinary Commission for National Reconciliation" (Moscow Television, 19 April; *FBIS*, 20 April).

The statistics on agricultural cooperatives were ambivalent. Although 45 new cooperatives were claimed in 1987, there appeared to be a net decrease from 1986 of 188, from 674 to 486. Their total membership was 74,550 (Bakhtar, 8 April; *FBIS*, 8 April).

Pre-existing and new unions did not figure prominently in official media during the year. In line with the new policies on private enterprise, the Politburo called for establishment of national congresses of traders and private entrepreneurs in February. The Union of Creative Intellectuals held its second congress in March, and in June it was revealed that the Union of Cultural Personalities numbered 2,000. At the same time the Union of Journalists boasted 1,500 members.

Some confusion attended the women's front, whose name was changed in 1986 from the Democratic Women's Organization of Afghanistan to the All-Afghan Women's Committee (AAWC). It then became the Women's Committee of Afghanistan in mid-1987, only to revert to AAWC by year's end. Despite a change in leadership, membership remained static between 1986 and 1987.

Except for the national reconciliation commissions, it was a relatively slow year for PDPA fronts across the board.

International Views, Positions, Activities. The focus of PDPA attention abroad during 1987 was the question of Soviet support, without which neither the party nor the regime it ran could survive. Most of the decisions on this subject were being made in Moscow, which bore ultimate responsibility for PDPA/RA policies. The "national reconciliation" slogan around which most of the RA's policies revolved in 1987 was first coined by Mikhail Gorbachev in his famous Vladivostok speech in July 1986; since then it has become a watchword in a number of other Third World Marxist-Leninist regimes.

Party relations with the CPSU continued to be good. Najibullah was invited to the October Revolution ceremonies, from which he made several broadcasts to Afghanistan. His major speeches at home were reported faithfully by Soviet media. Some 9,000 civilian advisers and 20,000 dependents continued to augment the 115,000–120,000 Soviet combat troops on duty in the country (*NYT*, 24 January; *WP*, 13 May).

Similarly, relations with Moscow's firmest supporters in Eastern Europe, East Germany, and Czechoslovakia appeared to be warm. *Neues Deutschland* carried frequent sympathetic stories about the PDPA and RA. Likewise, Mongolia and Afghanistan continued their cordial relationship with several exchange visits of party officials. Relations with other Warsaw Pact nations were more subdued, but there was a community of interest with Vietnam and Cambodia, whose mutual relationship bore close similarities to that of the USSR and RA. Kabul also retained cordial relations with other Soviet client states, such as South Yemen and Angola, as well as with Libya.

Soviet moral support for Afghanistan was backed by significant economic aid, including $220 million in development assistance and $405 million in commodities during 1987 (DoS, *Eight Years*). Fifty million rubles were extended as credit to the private sector and 30 million more were allocated for education, mass media, and communications. According to Afghan sources, one billion afghanis of Soviet aid ($20 million at the official rate) were gratis, in the form of foodstuffs and "primary goods" (Bakhtar, 7 December; *FBIS*, 8 December). Administration of the aid was designed to improve the Soviet and RA image in the countryside, much of which had been devastated by Soviet air and ground offensives. Propaganda units of the army, as well as representatives of the police and "security units" (presumably secret police), were supposed to have responsibility for distributing 75 percent of the goods allocated to the RA, leaving the remainder for local organs to handle (Radio Kabul, 5 February; *FBIS*, 9 February). The Soviet forces also passed out large quantities independently. Charges of embezzlement and profiteering, made in both the Soviet and Afghan media, tarnished the intended image of generous patronage, however.

Moscow also seemed bent on tightening its trade ties to Kabul. In March an agreement was reached to set up two joint stock import-export companies, Aftorg and Afento, in which the Afghan side would invest 60 percent and the Soviet side 40 percent of the 200 million afghani ($4 million) initial capital. The agreement was supposed to result in a trade of Afghan commodities for Soviet consumer goods (Bakhtar, 11 March; *FBIS*, 12 March). In addition, direct Afghan trade with Soviet Central Asian republics was also to rise, and a special organization for cooperation with Soviet Central Asian republics was to be set up under the Council of Ministers (*KNT*, 15 June). In all, the USSR was responsible for 65 percent of Afghanistan's foreign trade (*Arab*

News, 11 October). The RA was still not a member of the Council for Mutual Economic Assistance (CMEA), but it could now make multilateral CMEA agreements instead of being restricted to bilateral agreements as before (TASS, 30 January; *FBIS*, 2 February).

In an effort to improve its image abroad, the RA launched a diplomatic offensive during the summer, sending emissaries to 66 foreign lands (*NYT*, 13 September). Later, Kabul would boast of its diplomatic recognition by 82 countries, but its expectations of favorable economic relations and moral support for its national reconciliation policies did not materialize.

The seventh round of proximity talks in Geneva between RA and Pakistani representatives had two sessions during 1987. The first was postponed at the request of the RA but finally undertaken from 25 February to 10 March. While the talks were being conducted, there were numerous air and artillery strikes on Pakistani territory from the RA side of the border, raids that caused over 150 deaths (*NYT*, 31 March). The motivation appeared to be intimidation of the Pakistanis, but the raids ceased when Pakistan threatened to break off negotiations. At the end of this round, the gap between the Pakistani insistence on a short timetable for a Soviet withdrawal and the Afghan (Soviet) demand for an extended one had narrowed to six months versus eighteen months. In August the Afghan side called unexpectedly for a resumption of the talks, but after several days of wrangling the two sides succeeded only in narrowing the gap to eight versus twelve months.

Both the diplomatic offensive and the call for talks appeared to be connected wth an unprecedented RA/Soviet effort to pressure the U.N. General Assembly into moderating its annual condemnation of the Soviet occupation. The effort failed when the United Nations voted 123 to 19, with 11 abstentions, in favor of the resolution. This was one more vote than the record-breaking 122 in favor in 1986 (*NYT*, 11 November).

Soviet concern with the future of Soviet Afghan relations was reflected in two unconventional statements of policy at the end of 1987. In discussing the new Afghan constitution, the official RA press made it clear that whatever the constitution, international agreements took precedence over it. The significance of this statement was emphasized when the government later declared that the 1921 Soviet-Afghan Friendship Treaty would remain valid in perpetuity (Radio Kabul, 30 November; *FBIS*, 2 December). It is probable that Article II of this treaty, which binds both sides "not to enter into any military or political agreement with a third State that might prejudice one of the Contracting Parties," is the key feature in Soviet eyes. So far, no reference has been made to the far more restrictive and binding friendship treaty of 1978, perhaps because the latter agreement—unlike that of 1921—has a provision for termination by either side on the tendering of a written notification six months in advance.

Biographies. During 1987 there seemed to be an effort to portray both the PDPA and the RA as somewhat more under collective leadership than in previous years. Although Najibullah remained the undisputed party leader and continued to enjoy far more press coverage than any other figure, the three individuals noted below gave keynote addresses or served as primary spokesmen for party and state policies on specific occasions. All three are PDPA veterans. (More complete biographic details on all three may be found in Anthony Arnold, *Afghanistan's Two-Party Communism: Parcham and Khalq* [1983].)

Nur Ahmad Nur was born in 1937 in Kandahar and claims to have joined the PDPA even before its founding congress. He sided with Babrak Karmal at the time of the original Parcham-Khalq split and has remained loyal to the Parcham faction ever since. In the first PDPA government (1978) he was briefly a member of both the Politburo and Secretariat, as well as being minister of interior, before being sent into diplomatic exile with the other ranking Parchamis. On his return to Kabul in 1980 on the coattails of the invading Soviet army, he again became a member of both the Politburo and Secretariat. He was also a deputy chairman of the RC Presidium but without any known substantive responsibilities. In early 1984, possibly as a result of a falling out with Babrak, he left suddenly for the USSR with his entire family, remaining there largely incommunicado for twenty months. His return to Kabul in September 1985 occurred at a time when the Soviets were clearly beginning to cast about for some successor to the ineffective Babrak. Following the June 1987 plenum, Nur was given responsibility for answering party workers' questions about party policy, and at the October party conference he gave a keynote address on changes in the party rules (*KNT*, 25 October).

Abdul Wakil, another recent prominent party spokesman, has had a career that parallels Nur's in many respects. Born in 1947 in Kabul, Wakil also claims to have joined the party before its official founding, upon graduation from Habibia high school in 1964. As a student in the Faculty of Economics at Kabul University in the 1960s, he was jailed for "political acts" twice before his graduation in 1971. Between 1971 and 1978 he was a Parchami activist. After the PDPA coup in 1978, he was briefly general secretary of the ministry of foreign affairs before joining the diplomatic exodus of Parchamis that year. He was named minister of finance under Babrak in 1980 and was also a member of the Central Committee. In August 1984, however, he was abruptly posted as ambassador to Hanoi. He was recalled in December 1986 to take over the ministry of foreign affairs in Kabul, where he was also named to the Politburo. In 1987 he made numerous trips abroad and returned to give full, published accounts of them, as well as to speak about other party matters (*KNT*, 26 May).

Dr. Saleh Mohammed Zeary was born in Kandahar in 1937. In the course of his PDPA career, which began with the founding congress, he has lived up to his nickname of "Quicksilver," acquired when he was still a high school student. He is an intelligent man, having led his class for seven years at Kabul University's medical school in the 1960s, and he is the only PDPA Politburo member to have retained his seat on that body under all Khalqi and Parchami leaders since 1978. After the Soviet invasion, despite his longstanding allegiance to Khalq, he became a Central Committee secretary and was soon named to head the fledgling National Fatherland Front, a job he lost to Abdul Rahim Hatef in May 1985. His high party standing in 1987 became clear when he delivered a party conference keynote address on the need for unity (*KNT*, 25 October).

Ruth and Anthony Arnold
Novato, California

Algeria

Population. 23,460,614
Party. Socialist Vanguard Party (Parti de l'avant-garde socialiste; PAGS)
Founded. 1920 (PAGS, 1966)
Membership. 450 (estimated)
First Secretary. Sadiq Hadjeres
Leading Bodies. No data
Status. Proscribed
Last Congress. Sixth, February 1952
Last Election. N/a
Auxiliary Organizations. No data
Publications. *Sawt al-Sha'b* (Voice of the people), issued clandestinely at infrequent intervals; editor unknown

Background. The Algerian Communist Party (Parti communiste algérien; PCA) was founded in 1920 as an extension of the French Communist Party. It has existed independently since October 1936. Although the PCA participated in the nationalist struggle against France, it was proscribed in November 1962, only four months after Algerian independence. In 1964 dissident left-wing elements of the legal National Liberation Front (FLN) joined with communists from the outlawed PCA to form the Popular Resistance Organization. In January 1966 this group was renamed the Socialist Vanguard Party. No regular party congress has been held since 1952, although the PAGS has held at least one national conference (in 1969) and in July 1981 held a meeting at which a ten-point general platform was adopted. Barely tolerated by the Algerian government, the PAGS is recognized in the communist world as the official Algerian communist party.

Leadership and Party Organization. Although the precise membership of the PAGS Politburo and Secretariat is not known publicly, prominent members of the party—in addition to Sadiq Hadjeres—are believed to include Larbi Bukhali, a former party secretary general; Bashir Hadj 'Ali; Ahman Karim; and 'Ali Malki. Both Hadjeres and Malki have contributed to the *World Marxist Review* and the *Information Bulletin* on behalf of the PAGS.

Domestic Party Affairs. The PAGS has generally viewed the regime of President Chadli Benjedid, which has ruled Algeria since early 1979, as opportunist and reformist compared with the more militant regime of Houari Boumediene (1965–1978) (see *YICA*, 1983). The party opposes what it views as "the slide to the right" that has occurred in Algeria under the Benjedid regime. In the PAGS's view, this slide to the right has involved liberalization of the economy, weakening of the strong state sector established under the Boumediene regime, worsening of the living conditions of the working class, a housing shortage, and a growing gap between official institutions and the masses (see *YICA*, 1987).

Operating in a hostile political climate and without legal standing, the PAGS prudently opted to maintain a low profile during 1987. The party did not take any public positions of note on either domestic or international issues. Instead, the PAGS continued to focus its energies on the mass organizations of the ruling National Liberation Front (FLN). PAGS members worked to gain influence among the leadership of the National Union of Algerian Youth, and the party maintained its efforts to place cells in factories to compete with the units of the General Union of Algerian Workers, the government-sanctioned labor union.

International Views, Positions, and Activities. The PAGS favors a foreign policy that would confirm positions that brought Algeria to the forefront of the Nonaligned Movement. These positions include effective support for national liberation struggles in Palestine, South Africa and Namibia, the Western Sahara, and elsewhere; promotion of a new world economic order; elimination of the indebtedness of exploited Third World nations; and increased cooperation and solidarity with the world socialist system in the struggle for peaceful coexistence and against the arms race.

In the spring, Malki attended an international seminar in Prague on "The Developments of the Peace Movement in the 1980s and the Communists." The seminar was organized by the *World Marxist Review* Commission on the Struggle for Peace and Democratic Movements. Seminar participants, who represented 21 communist parties on the journal plus three guests, noted that the struggle against the nuclear threat is entering a new phase; they analyzed the make-up of the peace movement today as a form of public stand and action and noted its breadth, massiveness, pluralism, flexibility, and ability to recruit new forces; they stressed the great importance of broader involvement of the working class and stronger ties with the trade unions for successfully advancing the peace movement; and they noted that forces of the peace movement have yet to exert an influence on political structures. (*WMR*, July.)

Relations with the Soviet Union. In 1987 Algeria continued its pattern of exchanging high-level visits with the Soviet Union. A Soviet parliamentarian delegation led by the vice president of the Soviet Supreme Presidium, Arnold Ryuytel, visited Algeria 7–10 June. The delegation held talks with members of the Algerian People's National Assembly on 8 June. (Algiers, Domestic Service in French, 8 June; *FBIS*, 9 June.) That same day the delegation met with Mohamed Cherif Messaadia, an important member of the FLN Politburo and leader of the FLN Central Committee Permanent Secretariat. During this meeting, Messaadia voiced Algeria's deep concern over the growing tension in the Mediterranean and the Persian Gulf; spoke in favor of an early settlement of the bloody Iran-Iraq war; pointed out that the United States is relying on its strategic ally, Israel, in its efforts to prevent a comprehensive Middle East settlement; and stated that Algeria is in favor of national reconciliation in Chad within the framework of the Organization of African Unity and without any foreign interference. (*Izvestiia*, 10 June; *FBIS*, 19 June.) Following this meeting, Ryuytel was received by Algerian prime minister Abdelhamid Brahimi (Algiers, Domestic Service in French, 8 June; *FBIS*, 9 June). On 10 June the Soviet delegation met with the Algerian minister of culture and tourism and the vice minister of cooperation in foreign affairs (*Izvestiia*, 12 June; *FBIS*, 19 June).

A Soviet delegation led by S. Mukashev, deputy chairman of the Supreme Soviet Presidium, visited Algeria 4–8 July to attend the 25th anniversary celebrations of Algerian independence. During its visit the delegation held meetings with Messaadia and Rabah Bitat, chairman of the Algerian People's National Assembly. (*Pravda*, 9 July; *FBIS*, 23 July.) At the end of August a Soviet military delegation led by Colonel General Kudurov visited Algeria (Algiers, Domestic Service in French, 31 August; *FBIS*, 4 September). In the other direction, an Algerian delegation headed by Sadek Zouaten, member of the FLN Central Committee Permanent Secretariat, visited Moscow in mid-September. The delegation represented Algeria at an international meeting held by the Associations of Friendship with the Soviet Union to mark the 70th anniversary of the October Revolution. (Algiers, Algerian Press Service in Arabic, 15 September; *FBIS*, 16 September.)

In late September a Soviet delegation visited Algiers in order to implement decisions made during President Benjedid's March 1986 visit to Moscow, where a long-term and multifaceted program of bilateral cooperation was arranged (see *YICA*, 1987). On 20 September the general secretary of the General Union of Algerian Workers, Tayeb Benlakhdar, and the president of the Central Council of Soviet Trade Unions, Stepan A. Shaleyev, signed a protocol of agreement and a joint communiqué. The protocol of agreement focused on enhancing cooperation in the field of education, training, and international cooperation, whereas the joint communiqué reviewed Algerian-Soviet relations as well as economic, social, and political issues. (Algiers, Algerian Press Service in English, 20 September; *FBIS*, 21 September.) The next day the Algerian minister of energy, chemical, and petrochemical industries, Belkacem Nabi, conferred with the chairman of the Soviet State Committee for Foreign Economic Relations, Konstantin Katushev. They reviewed Algerian-Soviet relations in the energy, chemical, and petrochemical work fields and explored possibilities of developing bilateral relations in these areas. An agreement was reached to form joint working groups to study development opportunities further, especially in the fields of chemistry and petrochemistry. On 22 September an expanded Algerian-Soviet working session was held under the joint chairmanship of the Algerian finance minister, Abdelaziz Khellef, and Katushev. (Algiers, Domestic Service in Arabic, 22 September; *FBIS*, 23 September.) The two sides discussed questions of economic, technical, and trade cooperation, and they reached accords on the further development and expansion of bilateral cooperation. (*Izvestiia*, 28 September; *FBIS*, 29 September.)

The Soviet delegation also had meetings with the Algerian prime minister, the ministers of heavy industry and light industry, and the deputy minister for cooperation at the foreign ministry. A number of specific agreements were signed as a result of the talks. These agreements specified deliveries of Algerian goods to the Soviet market and the Soviet side's participation in the installation of a number of establishments in Algeria. (Ibid.)

At the end of September another Soviet delegation visited Algeria. This delegation, led by Mr. Trushin, first deputy minister of internal affairs, met with Messaadia. The two sides reviewed relations between the Communist Party of the Soviet Union (CPSU) and the FLN and ties of cooperation in certain fields. (Algiers, Domestic Service in Arabic, 29 September; *FBIS*, 30 September.)

In early November Messaadia led an Algerian party and government delegation that visited Moscow to attend the celebration of the 70th anniversary of the October Revolution. On 6 November the delegation met with a Soviet delegation headed by Anatolii F. Dobrynin, secretary of the CPSU Central Committee. The two sides expressed satisfaction at the high level of Soviet-Algerian cooperation. (*Pravda*, 9 November; *FBIS*, 12 November.)

In addition to Algeria's relations with the Soviet Union, the Benjedid regime also received two visits during 1987 from high officials from the People's Republic of China (PRC). From 31 May to 2 June, Wu Xueqian, Chinese Communist Party Politburo member and PRC foreign minister, held talks with a number of Algerian officials. Wu exchanged views on disarmament, an end to the Persian Gulf war, and especially the Middle East; he stated that the latter issue was the specific reason for his visit to Algeria. (Algiers, Algerian Press Service in Arabic, 31 May; *FBIS*, 1 June.) From 3 to 7 September, PRC commerce minister Zheng Tuobin headed a Chinese delegation to the third session of the Algerian-Chinese joint commission (Algiers, Algerian Press Service in English, 3 September; *FBIS*, 4 September).

John Damis
Portland State University

Bahrain

Population. 464,102
Party. Bahrain National Liberation Front (NLF/B)
Founded. 1955
Membership. Unknown but believed negligible
Chairman. Yusuf al-Hassan al-Ajajai
General Secretary. Saif ben Ali
Governing Committee. (Now possibly Politburo):

Ali Naji Abdallah, Aziz Mahmud, Badir Malik, Aziz Ahmad al-Mudhawi, Jasim Muhammad, Abdallah Ali al-Rashid, Ahmad Ibrahim Muhammad al-Thawadi

Status. Illegal

Last Congress. Unknown

Last Election. N/a

Auxiliary Organizations. Bahrain Peace and Solidarity Committee (affiliated with the World Peace Council and presumably with the Afro-Asian Peoples' Solidarity Organization), Democratic Youth League of Bahrain (affiliated with the World Federation of Democratic Youth), National Union of Bahraini Students (affiliated with the International Union of Students), Women's Organization of the NLF/B (affiliated with the Women's International Democratic Federation), Federation of Bahraini Workers (affiliated with the World Federation of Trade Unions)

Publications. *Al-Jamahir* (The masses), *al-Fajr* (The dawn)

Protests against the arrests of some eighteen NLF/B members increased during late 1986 and continued into early 1987 as the main subject of propaganda by and about the organization. The protests had been one of the main subjects treated by the October 1986 meeting of so-called Arab East communist parties in which the NLF/B participated (Prague, *IB*, February, March). The January 1987 *World Marxist Review* carried an article on the subject by one Said Ali entitled "Stop the Campaign of Terror in Bahrain." The February anniversary statement of the NLF/B used the protests as its centerpiece (*WMR*, November), and *Pravda* on 18 March replayed the theme. After that, and for reasons unknown, the campaign reverted to the same low level as in the past (see *YICA*, 1987).

The NLF/B also participated in the Arab East communist parties' meeting in August that called for the removal of U.S. forces from the Persian Gulf and a cessation of the Iran-Iraq war (*Pravda*, 31 August). As usual, it was the one group at the meeting without the term communist party in its title (ibid.). For the first time, however, the NLF/B did seem to be moving toward a communist party structure. One Muhammad Ali was cited as an NLF/B Politburo member when attending the December French Communist Party congress (*L'Humanité*, 3 December), and one Tahar Ali Muhammad was labeled an NLF/B Central Committee member while attending the congress of the Moroccan Party of Progress and Socialism in July (Casablanca, *al-Bayane*, 19 July). The old Governing Committee (see *YICA*, 1987) appears to be out.

An NLF/B general secretary was noted for the first time when one Saif ben Ali was so listed twice in late October: once at the Nicosia Third Conference of Communist and Workers' Parties of the Eastern Mediterranean, Near and Middle East, and Red Sea, and once at the Moscow October Revolution 70th anniversary celebrations (Athens, *Rizospastis*, 22 October; *Pravda*, 31 October). Since communist parties or their equivalents can have a general secretary, a chairman, or both, this does not necessarily mean that the NLF/B's previously cited chairman, Yusif al-Hassan al-Ajajai, has been dropped (see *YICA*, 1987). In fact, he is probably the Yusif al-Hassan who represented the organization at the Nicosia symposium "Religion Is for God, the Homeland Is for All" that was co-sponsored by the *World Marxist Review* and *al-Nahj* (the Arabic communist theoretical quarterly) at some time prior to August (*WMR*, August).

Still other members were noted abroad in what appeared to have been an unusually active year for the NLF/B in this respect. Ali Naji Abdallah apparently attended the Greek Communist Party congress in May (*Rizospastis*, 9 May). Later that same month an unnamed representative of the NLF/B attended another *World Marxist Review* forum, this one in Prague and entitled "The October Revolution and the Main Problems of Our Age" (*WMR*, July). Four members of the NLF/B's Women's Organization attended the Moscow World Congress of Women in June. Finally, and most unusually, in mid-November an NLF/B delegation visited Afghanistan, allegedly as a guest of that country's government rather than of its sole and ruling party (Kabul, Bakhtar, 15 November; *FBIS*, 17 November).

Wallace H. Spaulding
McLean, Virginia

Egypt

Population. 51,929,962

Party. Egyptian Communist Party (al-Hizb al-Shuyu'i al-Misri; ECP)

Founded. 1921; revived in 1975

Membership. 500 (estimated)

General Secretary. (Apparently) Farid Mujahid

Politburo. Michel Kamil (chief of foreign relations), Najib Kamil, Muhammad Magdi Kamal (representative to the *WMR*); other names unknown

Secretariat. No data

Central Committee. Farid Mujahid, Yusuf Darwish; other names unknown

Status. Proscribed

Last Congress. Second, early 1985 (possibly 1984)

Last Election. N/a

Auxiliary Organizations. Union of Egyptian Peasants; others unknown

Publications. *Al-Intisar* (Victory), main ECP newspaper, published about nine times a year; *al-Wa'i* (Consciousness), deals with intraparty issues; *Hayat al-Hizb* (Party life), primarily concerned with party work. In the recent past, Egyptian communists in Paris published *al-Yasar al-Arabi* (The Arab left).

Background. The Egyptian communist movement remains as splintered as ever. Besides the ECP, several groups have surfaced during recent years. These include the Revolutionary Current (which has probably not overcome the devastation caused by arrests and confiscation of its archives and equipment at the end of 1986) (see *YICA* 1987, p. 430), the Egyptian Communist Party–8 January, the Egyptian Communist Workers' Party, the Popular Movement, the Armed Communist Organization, the Egyptian Communist Party–Congress Faction, a Trotskyite communist organization called the Revolutionary Communist League, and the Revolutionary Progressive Party. It is possible that some of these are merely descriptive labels rather than formal names of organizations, and it is not known whether there is any relationship between these groups and the ECP (or, in most cases, whether they continue to exist. All indications point to the relative insignificance of communist groups in comparison with the threat to the regime posed by militant religious movements or by the military (on the latter possibility, see Robert Springborg, "The President and the Field Marshal: Civil-Military Relations in Egypt Today," Washington, *Middle East Report*, July–August, pp. 5–16).

Leadership and Party Organization. Little is known about the ECP's leadership and organization. Few party officials have been mentioned in available publications. Official statements by ECP leaders published abroad are mostly anonymous. The names most often mentioned are Politburo members Michel Kamil, obviously because of his position as the party's chief of foreign relations, and *WMR* representative Muhammad Magdi Kamal. All indications point to the typical pattern of "democratic centralism," albeit in a rudimentary form resulting from the group's small membership and clandestine character.

Domestic Party Affairs. No information is available on meetings of party organs during the year. However, it is known that, following a decision by a conference of opposition parties on 5 February to participate in the upcoming elections for the People's Assembly (parliament), the ECP reached a decision to enter the elections and to present a party platform. Party candidates Nabil Hilali (south Cairo), Mubarak Abduh Fadil (north Cairo), and Mahmud Amin al-Alam (Giza) were designated to contest three of 48 single-member districts—technically as independents, since the party is banned, but actually in coordination with the National Progressive Unionist Party (NPUP). (The other 400 seats were filled on the basis of proportional representation, involving party lists.) A fourth communist candidate ran in Gharbiyyah province. No communist candidate's vote exceeded 700. (Beirut, *al-Safir*, 5 March; *FBIS*, 10 March; *Middle East Report*, July–August, pp. 17–22, 29.)

At least two crackdowns by the government against the ECP occurred prior to the 6 April general elections. One "group of extremist communists" was arrested on 3 March and accused of involvement in a "scheme to exploit the country's current democratic climate" by launching "an extensive agitation and incitement operation among the masses" through distributing massive quantities of antigovernment pamphlets. With search warrants issued by the Supreme State Security Prosecution, the state security police seized large amounts of printing equipment and "instigative" materials that "express[ed] a Marxist outlook that rejects religious values and spiritual teachings." (MENA, 3 March; *FBIS*, 4 March.) Similarly, governmental authorities arrested a ten-man "communist ring . . . on the charge of printing inflammatory leaflets inciting citizens to elect [PCP] candidates." The arrested individuals were said to be members of the NPUP. One of them, Ahmad Sayyid Hasan, was a journalist working for the NPUP newspaper, *al-Ahali*. (MENA, 4 April; *FBIS*, 6 April.) Most of the detainees were soon released, one exception being Mu'tazz Mahmud Zaki al-Hafnawi, an engineer in whose residence were found the printing equipment and leaflets calling for nonpayment of foreign debts, accusing the private sector of plunder, and calling for the right of workers to strike and of citizens to demonstrate (MENA, 4 April; Paris, AFP, 5 April; *FBIS*, 6 April).

According to Kamal, the ECP newspaper *al-Intisar* appears "on average, nine times a year" and "has appeared uninterruptedly for almost 14 years" despite "continued reprisals" and poor printing facilities. He said that anyone found with a copy of the newspaper in his possession is detained by the police and that several people who had copies of it were sentenced to three years in prison during 1986. He added that "a broad network of correspondents—party members in different regions and organisations . . . supply the paper with news." Besides *al-Intisar* and the more specialized party newspapers, *al-Wa'i* and *Hayat al-Hizb*, Kamal explained that "several [unnamed] legal periodicals and newspapers" are the under the party's "control" and, despite not being able to "appear on behalf of the ECP," they "circulate widely" and influence "the progressive public in general." (*WMR*, September.)

In another statement, Kamal opined that "objective conditions for change have matured" and announced that "the aim is to turn the ECP into a mass party, to step up activities among workers and peasants" (ibid., February).

The ECP election platform ("The Path of Struggle for Free and Democratic Society") announced that, though its "final aim" is "a socialist system and building of a communist society," the road "is long and difficult" and that the first priority would have to be "liberating the country from the manacles of reaction and counter-revolution, from dependence on and capitulation to U.S. imperialism and Zionism." Despite what it called "conditions of a police state" and the "possibility of crude interference in the course of the elections and falsification of its results," the platform called on the people to vote and urged that, though "real changes" will come only through "mass actions and the class struggle," the campaign could be one manifestation of the struggle.

The platform's alternative to "economic dependence" and "plunder by foreign and local capital and a parasitic bourgeoisie" specified the need for resisting controls by such organizations as the International Monetary Fund and the International Bank for Reconstruction and Development; for a "many-sided planned socio-economic development" designed to improve the life of the masses; for eliminating foreign capital from the banking system; for limitation of imports to "vital necessities"; for nationalization of "major industries, banks, insurance companies, big local and foreign capital, foreign trade, and the contractor sector"; for protecting and regulating the private sector in order for it to serve "the cardinal socio-economic interests of the entire people"; for suspending payment of the foreign debt; for continuing to subsidize foodstuffs; for ending "customs and tax privileges for foreign investors and big Egyptian capitalists; for decreased spending on security services and adjusting military spending; for "development of economic and trade relations with the USSR and other socialist countries, [and] with non-aligned states"; and for creating "a big cooperative sector."

There was also a call for "the creation of a free, democratic civil state" in which "the masses could legitimately participate." Specific demands included terminating the state of emergency; permitting political parties and other organizations to be created and legalizing the Arab Socialist Union and the ECP; ending censorship and detention of journalists; ending prosecution and imprisonment on political grounds; establishing the right to strike, ending torture, and bringing to trial those who have practiced torture; guaranteeing freedom of religion; establishing a parliamentary type of government; and writing "a new democratic constitution." (*IB*, no. 14.)

Kamal wrote of the mass media's having been "handed over to reactionary elements and CIA agents" and of a government controlled by "the parasitic sections of the Egyptian bourgeoisie." He maintained that though "the scale of resistance" has forced President Husni Mubarak to make some improvements," this has not affected the regime's "overall character." (*WMR*, February.)

Auxiliary and Front Organizations. Little information has come to light about any auxiliary organizations of the ECP. Under current conditions, it seems safe to assume that children's and youth organizations do not exist. In the past, the party was actively concerned with organizing primarily students and workers. According to Kamal, "The Left" made significant gains in union elections during 1983, but those who were elected were prevented from taking their seats. He also reported that the Union of Egyptian Peasants, with several thousand members and branches in every province, is sponsored by his "comrades," and he stated that the party's aim is to become "a mass party, to step up activities among workers and peasants, the main base of support for transformations to come." He also spoke of the goal of setting up a "national democratic front" to include "the nascent Nasserist Arab Socialist Party" as well as communists and the NPUP and of the existence of "temporary alliances with other opposition forces" for specific purposes. (Ibid.)

Much more important than the ECP or any other communist organization is the broad, legal leftist opposition front, the NPUP, whose general secretary is long-time Marxist Khalid Muhyi al-Din. (For a biography of Muhyi al-Din, see *YICA*, 1984.) Its deputy general secterary is Rif'at al-Sa'id. Some of the members of the NPUP are Marxists; others are Nasserites or other opponents of the non-socialist pro-Western direction of the regime. The NPUP, which put its membership at 170,000 in 1985, publishes the weekly newspaper *al-Ahali* (edited by Muhyi al-Din), whose circulation ranges from 75,000 to 100,000 (*Middle East Report*, July–August, p. 20). The party received only 3.8 percent of the total vote in 1984 and 2.2 percent in 1987; in each case, application of an 8 percent rule prevented it from getting a proportionate share of the seats. Neither did any NPUP candidates win in the single-member districts; despite Muhyi al-Din's known popularity in his home district and the victory that seemed imminent as the count proceeded, the final tally showed him among the losing candidates (ibid., p. 22).

NPUP spokesmen blamed their big defeat on official interference in the election and in the count. Calling the government's actions "a disaster," one spokesman reported poll watchers being beaten and kicked out by the police and ballot boxes being prematurely closed (*CSM*, 7 April). There is no dispute that corruption and manipulation, as well as arrests of party supporters and other kinds of interference during the campaign, contributed to the low NPUP vote; in addition, the party's lack of influence in the rural power structure put it at a special disadvantage (in comparison with other opposition parties) in resisting dishonest electoral practices (see ibid., pp. 23–30, for further details and analysis).

The ECP platform called on the people to vote for the NPUP ticket (*IB*, no. 14). But despite its cooperation with ECP candidates running as independents, there was an NPUP effort to differentiate itself from the communists and to stress its own non-Marxist character (ibid., p. 21). The NPUP's opponents, however, succeeded in reinforcing its image of being "dominated by Communists who are subservient to Moscow and hostile to religion" (ibid., p. 22). On the other hand, some young leftists deem the party to be "hopelessly caught up in the past, and autocratically run by the older generation" (ibid.).

International Views, Positions, and Activities. There were few available reports of international activities. Kamal was the ECP representative at a *World Marxist Review* symposium of communist party leaders held in Prague on "U.S. Policy of Neoglobalism, the Military-Industrial Complex, Contemporary Militarism, and the Working Class" (date unspecified) (*WMR*, September). He also participated in a seminar on "The Developments of the Peace Movement in the 1980s and the Communists" in the same city (date again unspecified) (ibid., July).

The party platform stressed the "cause of liberation of Egyptian . . . [and] other Arab lands" and the Palestinians' right of self-determination and the need to mobilize "to further general struggle against Zionism and imperialism." Specific demands included "measures to wreck the Camp David accords" and the "separate deal with Israel"; ending "political, economic, and military dependence on U.S. imperialism," particularly the "special relations with the U.S." and its military presence; revising "all international agreements concluded . . . after May 15, 1971"; "all-out support to" the Palestine Liberation Organization; promotion of "All-Arab unity"; resisting "Arab reaction"; "creation of an all-Arab national-patriotic progressive front"; ending inter-Arab conflicts and the Iraq-Iran war, with withdrawal to "internationally recognized borders" and support for "the creation of democratic foundations in" Iraq and Iran; and establishment of "fraternal relations" between Egypt and the Sudan. The platform further called for an Egyptian foreign policy devoted to "anti-colonialism and anti-imperialism" and with a restoration of Cairo's role in the Nonaligned Movement; supporting "peaceful coexistence" and actions against nuclear weapons in Europe, the Middle East, and the Mediterranean as well as against "the 'star wars' programme"; and developing "relations of friendship and cooperation with the socialist countries, primarily the Soviet Union," which has been shown to be "a friend of our country and the mainstay of its struggle for liberation and development." (*IB*, no. 14.)

Glenn E. Perry
Indiana State University

Iran

Population. 50,407,723
Party. Communist Party of Iran (Tudeh Party)
Founded. 1941 (dissolved May 1983)
Membership. 1,000–2,000 hardcore members; 15,000–20,000 sympathizers.
First Secretary. Ali Khavari
Leading Bodies. No data
Status. Illegal
Last Congress. 1986, National Conference
Last Election. N/a
Affiliated Party. Fedayeen-e Khalq (majority)
Publications. *Rahe Tudeh* (Tudeh path), *Mardom* (People) and *Tudeh News* (in English)

Domestic Affairs. As contrasted with 1986, the year 1987 appeared to bode well for the Tudeh Party. Although it had held a national conference in 1986, the party had suffered from the endemic problem of factionalism, which led to the expulsion of six members and alternate members of the Central Committee (see *YICA*, 1987). In 1987 only one member of the Central Committee was "suspended," ostensibly for "disregard for organizational principles," for the divulging of party secrets, and for "the rejection of the National Conference." In reality he was purged, like the other six in the previous year, for demanding greater independence for the party from Moscow and for "co-operation with the factional group expelled from the Party" in 1986 (*Tudeh News*, 4 February). In assessing its own 1986 successes, the party implied that its National Conference had been held in Iran and had "served to defeat the Islamic Republican regime's treacherous conspiracy aimed at obstructing our Party's activities." More important, the party claimed that in the previous year there had been "an increase in the number of Party cells inside Iran and also in the number of bulletins published by the various sections of the Party" (ibid., 15 April).

This important claim was not confined to the successes of the party in 1986. On the occasion of its 46th anniversary, on 2 October 1987, the party stressed the expansion of its cells inside Iran by stating: "Despite the increasing pressure of the regime's repressive organs, the number of Party cells has increased throughout the country and the quality of their work has risen to new heights" (ibid., 14 October). This ostensible growth of communist cells inside Iran presumably reflected the ever-deteriorating socioeconomic conditions of the country. The party partly blamed the regime's stubborn commitment to the "export of the Islamic Revolution and the imposition of the Supreme Parliament of the Islamic Revolution in Iraq" for the worsening social and economic situation in Iran (ibid., 22 July). But it assigned even greater blame to "the all-embracing aggravation of the structural crisis facing our society and the political instability of the present regime" (ibid., 4 February). The real source of this "structural crisis," the Tudeh party believed, was economic in nature. "The Islamic economy has not and does not exist. It is no coincidence that eight years after the revolution, the Islamic economy has emerged as a form of dependent capitalist system under the Islamic guise" (ibid., 8 July).

In fact, the Tudeh Party considered the sociopolitical situation so disastrous that in 1987 for the first time it combined its usual crusade for a communist revolution with a plan for a "Revolutionary and Democratic State" in Iran. The plan was launched on 6 March, calling for "a constituent assembly to provide, compose, and approve a constitution and determine the foundations for a new system of government" that would dissolve the reactionary state apparatus, obviate all forms of theocratic rule, and respect all religions and sects. Based on "the voluntary unity of all masses of the Iranian nation," such a government's hallmark would be its "consultative assembly, the highest source of state authority." It would be "responsible for legislation, selection of the cabinet, and inspection of performances" (Radio of the Iranian Toilers, 6 March; *FBIS-NES*, 9 March). The establishment of such a government would result in the abolition of "all present repressive and inquisition organs," the release of all political prisoners, and guarantees for freedom of opinion, religion, speech, trade unions, and strikes. It would provide for universal suffrage and guarantee "the right of independent worker trade organizations to unions and federations." The announcement of this new plan accompanied the promise of further details for the establishment of a revolutionary and democratic government.

While the Tudeh Party was dreaming such dreams in 1987, the Fedayeen-e Khalq (majority), its only ally, suffered a major setback. From the Tudeh Party's perspective, this alliance "was the most important event [since the February revolution of 1979] in laying the foundations of a united proletarian movement in our homeland" (*Tudeh News*, 4 March). The Tudeh Party stressed this importance on the occasion of the Fedayeen-e Khalq's sixteenth anniversary in February; it did not anticipate the severe crackdown by the Khomeini regime on its erstwhile ally less than a month later. According to a statement of 18 March issued by the Ministry of Information and Security of Iran, "some 80 percent" of the Fedayeen-e Khalq "has been smashed." The ministry's official statement revealed for the first time that the Khomeini regime, although it kept this group under surveillance, had tolerated it since March 1981 because it had managed to convey the impression that it supported the Islamic republican system. But when in 1985 the group "officially declared its true positions aimed at overthrowing" the Iranian government, the Khomeini regime began to attack the organization by destroying its "resources, equipment, and high-ranking cadres," a process that was 80 percent completed by March 1987.

In attempting to overthrow the Khomeini regime, Fedayeen-e Khalq was said to have actually spied on "military bodies" and tried to sabotage war operations by forging documents, attempting to undermine "productive enterprises," and encouraging and cooperating with "criminal and terrorist groups, particularly in Kurdistan." It was accused of having supported and collaborated with "the traitorous Tudeh Party" in an effort to revive its networks (Tehran Domestic Service, in Persian, 18 March; *FBIS-NES*, 19 March).

The external activities of the party in 1987 included ritualistic pronouncements made on major historical occasions in the communist movement. One such occasion was May Day. In April the central committees of the Tudeh Party and Fedayeen-e Khalq (majority) issued a joint communiqué in which they greeted the solidarity of workers worldwide and lamented the "Iranian workers and toiling people" whose representative organizations—the Tudeh Party and Fedayeen-e Khalq—had suffered "savage and brutal onslaught" at the hands of the "repressive regime" in Iran (*Tudeh News*, 13 May). Other examples of the party's external activities in 1987 included a delegation that attended the Eighth Congress of the Socialist Unity Party of West Berlin from 15 to 17 May and a delegation that attended the Twelfth Congress of the Communist Party of Greece in Athens from 12 to 16 May (ibid., 24 June).

As usual, the Tudeh Party's rhetorical flourish was reserved for the anniversary of the October Revolution in the Soviet Union. The party's Central Committee remembered gratefully that the new government of "the workers and peasants [of the USSR] recognized the right of Iran to self-rule" and that, among other things, the new Soviet government unilaterally invalidated the 1907 agreement dividing Iran between Britain and tsarist Russia (ibid., 25 November). Presumably this historical gratitude of the party to the Soviet Union for upholding Iran's independence may explain its longstanding compliance with the Soviet line in world affairs and particularly in 1987 with respect to every major position that Moscow adopted on the Iraq-Iran war and on the wider question of the protection of oil shipments in the Persian Gulf.

Foreign Relations. Unlike any other year in the relations of revolutionary Iran and the Soviet Union, 1987 witnessed unprecedented developments in the political as well as economic and technical fields between the two countries. In the political field, no real common interests in 1986 had sufficient weight to counterbalance the serious strategic, ideological, and political differences that divided the two countries. By contrast, in 1987 at least the appearance of common interests in the Persian Gulf gave rise to a new political rapprochement between Tehran and Moscow. Closer ties between the two capitals advanced so far that by the end of the year the Iranian foreign minister was compelled by his critics to explain Iran's foreign policy behavior. Asked if these closer political relations did not contradict the Islamic Republic's "neither East nor West" policy, Foreign Minister Ali Akbar Velayati replied that the "objective of the slogan is the negation of alien domination and not snapping of communication." "Nowadays," he added, "negating political relations with other countries means negating identity of the countries" (Tehran, Iran News Agency [IRNA], in English, 2 January; *FBIS-NES*, 4 January).

In a real sense, the foundation of progress in Soviet-Iranian economic and technical relations was established in 1986 when, after nearly a year of exchange of visits between Tehran and Moscow, the two capitals signed a comprehensive economic cooperation protocol on 11 December and ended the six-year suspension of activities by the Soviet-Iranian Permanent Commission for Joint Economic Cooperation. Although even before the signing of this protocol, and as early as August 1986, agreements on hydrocarbon issues had been announced, the resumption of the export of Iranian natural gas to the Soviet Union was still being discussed in 1987. Both sides were still examining "the technical issues involved" (Tehran, *Keyhan*, in Persian, 5 April; *FBIS-NES*, 15 April). For a while the natural gas issue was even sidetracked by the idea of using the gas pipeline for oil transportation. According to the Iranian oil minister, talks had been held between Iran and the Soviet Union about transferring 700,000 barrels of oil a day from Iran to the Black Sea via Baku, to be sold on foreign markets pending the construction of an oil pipeline that would later make it possible to use the existing pipeline for the export of gas (Tehran Domestic Service, in Persian, 8 August; *FBIS-NES*, 10 August).

This idea was prompted by the serious interruption of Iranian oil exports through the Persian Gulf as a result of heavy Iraqi attacks on tankers carrying Iranian oil. The same pressure seemed to have resurrected the idea of oil drilling in the Caspian Sea, a concept that had been around for decades. In 1987 more Iranian technicians began preliminary work on oil drilling, for which the Soviet Union was to supply some of the needed equipment. Progress of a more substantial nature was made in the hydrocarbon field in 1987 as a result of an agreement on oil and petroleum products. Iran agreed to supply 100,000 barrels of oil a day by pipeline from the south to the Caspian coast; from there the crude would be transported on Soviet tankers to the Baku refinery. In return, Iran would receive from the Soviets petroleum products, such as gasoline and diesel fuel, equal to the amount of Iranian crude. These products would be shipped across the Caspian and then sent by rail to Jolfa. (Tehran, *Keyhan*, in Persian, 3 December; *FBIS-NES*, 1 December.)

Because of geographic proximity, cooperation in regard to transport and transit had often appeared attractive to the Soviets and Iranians, but in 1987, partly because of the increased threats to Iranian oil exports moving through the Persian Gulf, this area of cooperation got a definite boost. The two sides signed a new protocol at the end of a meeting held 12–19 November, resolving "problems concerning improvement of air and railway transportation" and discussing a series of issues pertaining to the transportation of cargo from the Soviet Union to Iran as well as to the transit of cargo from Soviet territory to Iran. They also agreed on a joint shipping route between the port of Baku and Iranian ports (Anzali and Nowshahr) (Moscow, in Persian, to Iran, 28 November; *FBIS-SOV*, 1 December).

If these agreements actually materialize, their results will mark a new chapter in the history of Soviet-Iranian transport-transit relations. According to the Iranian ambassador to the Soviet Union, Naser Nobari-Heyrani, the relevant protocol specifies that Iran will be allowed to sail two cargo ships of its own through the Black Sea and through Soviet waters to the Caspian, whereas "previously, goods have been carried only by Soviet ships." "Under the agreement," he added, "from now on shipping in the Caspian will be a joint venture and Iranian ships will share the transportation of goods across the Caspian with Soviet ships." According to Ambassador Nobari-Heyrani, another agreement was reached by which ultimately the Iranian port of Sarakhs in the north would be linked with the Iranian port of Bandar Abbas in the south. The Iranians would provide technicians and the Soviets would furnish equipment. The Iranian ambassador believed that all this "indicates substantial growth and expansion in the routes linking the two countries and the volume of goods in transit between the two nations." (Tehran, *Keyhan*, in Persian, 3 December; *FBIS-SOV*, 17 December.)

Although the economic protocol of 11 December 1986 provided the legal and general framework, and the unprecedented increase in the disruption of Iranian oil exports through the Persian Gulf in 1987 provided the impetus for the conclusion of these more specific agreements, the real drive behind the Soviet-Iranian economic and technical rapprochement was political in nature.

Soviet-Iranian political relations went through two phases: between January and July, and between July and the end of 1987. The first phase was expected to lead rather quickly to improved Soviet-Iranian relations as a result of the visit of Iranian foreign minister Ali Akbar Velayati to Moscow on 13–14 February. Velayati met with Soviet foreign minister Eduard Shevardnadze; with the chairman of the Presidium of the USSR Supreme Soviet, Andrei Gromyko; and with the chairman of the Council of Ministers, Nikolai Ryzhkov. Although the talks involved some economic and technical issues, they were overwhelmingly concerned with political differences between the two countries over the Iraq-Iran war and the Soviet occupation of Afghanistan. On his return to Tehran, Velayati characterized his talks as "frank and detailed." With respect to the Iraq-Iran war, he complained to the Soviet officials that their arms supplies to the Iraqi regime "are used to cause bloodshed in towns, to bomb populated areas, and to commit war crimes."

Regarding Afghanistan, he is said to have reminded the Soviet officials that "the only solution is for the foreign troops to leave [Afghanistan] and for a nonaligned country to be formed based on the consensus and beliefs of the Muslim Afghan people." Though appreciative of the "positive decision" of the Soviets to withdraw their forces from Afghanistan, he told them that they "should accelerate the implementation of their decision before the United States, some other country, or some foreign forces take advantage of the situation and begin interfering in this sensitive region's affairs." (Tehran Domestic Service, in Persian, 14 February; *FBIS-NES*, 18 February.)

The Soviets characterized their talks with Velayati as "businesslike and frank," revealing their differences with the Iranians over the Iraq-Iran war and Afghanistan. The Soviets drew Velayati's attention "to the fact that dushman rebel groups waging an armed struggle against the Afghan people are sent from Iranian territory." Gromyko said that the "limited contingent of Soviet troops will be withdrawn from Afghanistan when a political settlement...has been reached." With respect to the Iraq-Iran war, he told Velayati bluntly: "Our evaluation of this war and your views on it do not agree. This mainly applies to the question of what should be done. Common sense tells us that the main attention should be devoted to the future and not the past, to ways of bringing the war to an end. It is not in the interests of your people that the number of graveyards filled with war dead increase. We believe that a more sensible solution must be sought—in other words, ways to end this war. We repeat what we have said to the Iranian leadership on more than one occasion: Even one day of war is worse than 5 years of negotiations." (Moscow, TASS, in English, 13 February; *FBIS-SOV*, 19 February.)

Despite Velayati's visit to Moscow, the chill in Soviet-Iranian political relations continued in 1987 for months before the second phase began in July. On 22 July two U.S.-flagged Kuwaiti oil tankers accompanied by three U.S. warships ushered in the beginning of the building up of a 33-ship U.S. force in the Persian Gulf. Not until half a year had elapsed since Velayati's visit to Moscow did a high-ranking Soviet official first show up in Tehran. Soviet deputy foreign minister Yuli Vorontsov arrived in Tehran on 12 June, ostensibly to follow up on the outcome of Velayati's visit, but actually to forge common cause with Iran in opposition to the burgeoning American and West European armada in the Persian Gulf. He expounded in lengthy talks with Iranian officials on the "deep concern" of the Soviet Union over the "moves and instigations by the United States in the Persian Gulf" and invited the powerful speaker of the Iranian Parliament, Hashemi-Rafsanjani, to visit Moscow. Expressing satisfaction with the expansion of mutual relations, Hashemi-Rafsanjani said: "If the two sides make an effort, we could have more cooperation than ever before." (Tehran Domestic Service, in Persian, 14 June; *FBIS-NES*, 15 June.)

After the U.S. government's decision on 7 March to reflag eleven Kuwaiti ships had been made public, one might have expected an earlier Soviet move to take advantage of the Iranian dissatisfaction with that decision. But the Soviets first had to overcome their anger over the alleged Iranian attack on a Soviet freighter, *Ivan Koroteyev*, on 6 May and the subsequent mining of one of the three Soviet tankers, *Marshal Chuikov*, leased to Kuwait. By the end of July both the start of the U.S. naval escort of Kuwaiti oil tankers and the death of hundreds of Iranian pilgrims in Mecca seemed to have played into Soviet hands. The Iranians charged that the Mecca incident was instigated by the United States, and the Soviets expressed sympathy. In his talk with President Ali Khamene'i on 3 August, Soviet deputy foreign minister Vorontsov categorically condemned the U.S. military presence in the Persian Gulf region and said, "Moscow's firm stance regarding the Persian Gulf is for all foreign ships to leave the region, and it still insists on this policy" (Tehran Domestic Service, in Persian, 3 August; *FBIS-NES*, 4 August).

Although President Khamene'i and other Iranian leaders expressed satisfaction with Vorontsov's statement, they suspected that the Soviets were trying to take advantage of the dangerous situation in the Persian Gulf to undermine Western power and influence while projecting their own. What Vorontsov was telling the Iranians in Tehran had been announced by the Soviets first on 3 July. At that time, they combined their call for the withdrawal of "all warships of states not situated in the region" with an attack on the United States, charging that Washington "would want to exploit the present alarming situation to achieve its long-harbored plans of establishing military-political hegemony in this strategically important area" (*NYT*, 4 July). As a matter of fact, the suspicion of Soviet motives led the Iranians to reject the Soviet bid to play the role of peace broker in the Iraq-Iran war in June when, during his visit to Iran, Vorontsov proposed a peace conference in Moscow to seek an end to the war (ibid., 3 July).

The Soviet efforts to court Iran by exploiting the angry Iranian confrontation with the United States in the Persian Gulf were complicated by other factors. The Soviet and U.S. interests in ending the Iraq-Iran war seemed to converge, and that was partly why Moscow supported the U.N. Security Council Resolution 598 of 20 July. But the Soviet interest in wooing Iran prompted the Kremlin to insist that the U.N. general secretary be given more time to implement that resolution before an arms embargo was imposed on Iran. The United States saw this Soviet position as a stalling ploy, as did the Arab states, which tried to pressure the Soviets to soften their support for Iran. So long as the U.N. general secretary's peace-making efforts appeared to be making some progress, the Soviet Union resisted both U.S. and Arab pressures on it to prod Iran toward a negotiated peace settlement. But after the general secretary told the Security Council on 10 December that its authority was being undermined by Iran's refusal to accept its cease-fire call, indicating that he felt it was time to impose an arms embargo, the Soviet attitude toward Iran appeared to change.

The Soviet Union supported the U.N. Security Council statement of 24 December that, in effect, threatened to impose an arms embargo on Iran, although the council also called on the general secretary to pursue negotiations with both Iran and Iraq (*WP*, 15 December). Another indication of a hardening Soviet attitude toward Iran was a "businesslike and frank" conversation between Gromyko and Nobari-Heyrani. According to a TASS report, Gromyko "emphasized the importance of an undelayed implementation of the U.N. Security Council's Resolution 598" and hinted at an arms embargo, saying that "if the resolution is not implemented, the question of further steps toward ensuring the implementation of the decisions adopted by the Security Council might be put on the order of the day" (Moscow, *Pravda*, in Russian, 5 December; *FBIS-SOV*, 7 December).

Yet the real Soviet position remained an enigma as 1987 drew to a close. Although the Soviets were hinting and acting as if they were moving toward a decision in favor of an arms embargo on Iran, they seemed to hedge in proposing a new U.N. force with "teeth." This proposal had the appearance of improving on the original Soviet call for a U.N. force that would replace the Western navies. But the statement by Soviet deputy foreign minister Vladimir F. Petrovsky that "we are proposing now not only to discuss and review the question of a second resolution with regard to an arms supply embargo but also to discuss the question of the creation of U.N. naval forces" left the impression that the Soviets were in effect making the arms embargo decision contingent on the creation of such a U.N. blockading force, perhaps as a new ploy to delay an arms embargo decision against Iran (*NYT*, 29 December). Besides, the Western press suspected that Iran had struck a secret deal with the Soviet Union, which, if true, would make the Soviet public positions vis-à-vis Iran both within and outside the United Nations a real smokescreen. The outlines of the deal were reportedly clear to some Western and Arab diplomats in Paris. According to these diplomats, Iran "cut its support for Afghan guerrilla forces and stopped stirring up religious sentiment among Moslems inside Soviet Central Asia, while the Soviet Union has reciprocated by helping stall a vote in the Security Council on sanctions against Iran" (*WP*, 2 December).

There was nothing murky about Iran's attitude toward the Soviet Union, despite what could be called its "kaleidoscopic foreign policy." Revolutionary republican, like conservative monarchical, Iran has used the Soviet card whenever it has been expedient. The revolutionary government first used it during the hostage crisis in order to counter Western pressures resulting from the imposition of U.S. and West European diplomatic and economic sanctions. But after those pressures ended and the revolutionary regime smashed the Tudeh Party (ironically with the intelligence aid of the CIA and a KGB defector), it secretly bought arms from the West for eighteen months to continue its war against the Iraqi Baathist regime, which was mainly armed by the Soviets.

R. K. Ramazani
University of Virginia

Iraq

Population. 16,970,000
Party. Iraqi Communist Party (ICP)
Founded. 1934
Membership. No data
First Secretary. Aziz Muhammad (63, Kurd, worker)

Politburo. (Incomplete): Zaki Khayri (77, Arab/Kurd, journalist), Fakhri Karim
Status. Illegal
Last Congress. Fourth, 10–15 November 1985
Last Election. N/a
Auxiliary Organizations. No data
Publications. *Tariq al-Sha'b* (People's road), clandestine

Background. Since breaking with the Baathist government of Iraq in 1979, the ICP has led a hunted, underground existence. Virtually all of its activity in Iraq is directed toward conducting or supporting armed rebellion in the Kurd-populated areas of the northeast. Many ICP leaders live abroad; most prominent among them is First Secretary Aziz Muhammad.

Leadership and Organization. The available information does not give a clear picture of the state of affairs within the ICP. For reasons of security, and probably also because of logistical and organizational weakness, the ICP says little about itself, and few of the hardy journalists who get into northern Iraq mention it in their reports. Since losing their radio station in fighting with Patriotic Union of Kurdistan (PUK) guerrillas in 1983, the Iraqi communists have depended on their Kurdish allies to broadcast propaganda or news items. The latter made little mention of the ICP in 1987.

Domestic Affairs. The ICP's goal of a broad national front of all groups opposed to the Baathist regime was no closer in 1987 than it had been three or four years before. The ICP remains in the Democratic National Front with the Kurdish Democratic Party of Iraq (KPD/I) and some smaller organizations. The KDP/I is clearly the dominant force in the front (*Le Monde Diplomatique*, October 1986). Moreover, it has cooperated for the past year with the PUK, a sometime opponent of the ICP, and both are heavily dependent on Iran for arms, logistical support, and safe haven. Iran assembled a reported 400 Iraq oppositionists in Tehran for a four-day conference on the Iraqi People's Cooperation in late December 1986. Speeches by Iranian leaders emphasized the Islamic nature of the opposition movement. (Radio Tehran, 27 December 1986; Iran News Agency [IRNA], 29 December 1986; *FBIS*, 29, 30 December 1986.) Kurdish groups attended, though the ICP was not represented (*The Middle East*, March).

Working in cooperation with the opposition groups has never been easy for Iraqi communists. The ICP continues to stick to its three-point slogan of "overthrowing the dictatorship, . . . democracy for Iraq, and genuine autonomy for Iraqi Kurdistan" (*WMR*, November 1986). The KDP/I agrees with the goal of Kurdish autonomy and overthrowing the Baathists, but the PUK has gone beyond seeking autonomy to advocate Kurdish independence and even the breakup of Iraq. A PUK spokesman asserted that the Iraqi communists are not part of the Kurdish movement but only use it "to promote the cause of communism in Iraq" (*Le Monde*, 16 April; *FBIS*, 30 April). The ICP does in fact consider itself an Iraqi party, not merely a Kurdish one, despite the concentration of resources in Kurdistan and the prominence of Kurds in the leadership. Party documents are published in Arabic. (*WMR*, September.)

The Iraqi regime's overwhelming priority is to end the war with Iran without bowing to Iranian demands that the Baathists leave power. Thus, the ICP's position is at odds with that of the vast majority of Iraqis. Many Iraqis do not like President Saddam Hussein; most respect the security apparatus; but virtually all view the prospect of Islamic government as abhorrent and so support their government against Iran. Since 1980 the ICP has blamed Iraq for starting the war, and though it assigns blame to Iran for carrying it on, it puts greater stress on the Baghdad government's responsibility for continuing the conflict. ICP first secretary Aziz Muhammad wrote that "*the government has its own reasons for not ceasing the carnage.* The regime . . . is afraid of the people's vengeance for its destructive gamble . . . The Iraqi ruling circles set a course toward a steady escalation of hostilities and . . . are constantly seeking to spread the conflict" (*WMR*, September, emphasis in the original).

In a 1 July message to the U.N. general secretary, the ICP Central Committee said: "The ICP considers . . . that our Iraqi people . . . refuse to believe the Iraqi government's claims to the effect that it is working to end the war" (*IB*, October). This statement recalled that "the ICP denounced the Iraqi government (in 1980) for unleashing the war," and among the nine points of its program to halt it, the seventh calls for "Exposure of those guilty of launching the war, their international condemnation and prosecution" (ibid.). This almost precisely matches the Iranian demand for punishment of the aggressor. It is not likely to win the ICP much credit with Iraq's leaders or citizens, who see Hussein as a bulwark against rule by mullahs. Aziz Muhammad's insistence that the ICP continue a policy of total opposition to what has become a national struggle was a factor in the defections and expulsions from the party leadership in the mid-1980s. (*YICA*, 1987.)

International Relations. The ICP continues to be active in international communist activities. It is a regular participant in the eight-member group of Communist and Workers' Parties of the Arab East; the other members are the communist parties of Jordan, Saudi Arabia, Syria, Palestine, Lebanon, and Egypt as well as the National Liberation Front of Bahrain. Representatives of these parties have met annually since 1982, issuing statements on matters of common interest. They urged Arabs and "their progressive and patriotic forces to work for more solidarity with fraternal Syria" in the face of a campaign against it by imperialism and Zionism (*IB*, January). The January meeting of the group heard a report by Aziz Muhammad on the situation in Iraq and on the war. The representatives believed that Iran's refusal to stop fighting "contradicts the interests of the Iraqi and Iranian peoples" and so plays into the hands of U.S. imperialism and Zionism. (*IB*, April.)

External activities of the ICP leadership got little coverage, apparently due to a reduced level of activity. Aziz Muhammad was reported less frequently than in previous years as traveling and having contacts with ruling or fraternal communist parties. In addition to attending the January meeting of eight Arab communist parties, he visited the People's Democratic Republic of Yemen in April, where he was received by Ali Salim al-Bid, general secretary of the ruling Yemeni Socialist Party. Muhammad spoke at the 70th anniversary celebration of the Bolshevik Revolution in Moscow (*Sovietskaya Rossiya*, 3 November; *FBIS*, 12 November). The ICP representative to *World Marxist Review* received brief mention in the July and October issues of that journal.

Soviet-Iraqi relations were generally good through the year. Iraqi foreign minister Tariq Aziz made two visits to Moscow, and First Deputy Prime Minister Ramadan went there in July. The leaders of the two countries exchanged cordial messages on the fifteenth anniversary of the Friendship and Cooperation Treaty. The USSR sent Deputy Foreign Minister Yuli Vorontsov to Baghdad in June and October. The seventeenth session of the joint Iraqi-Soviet committee on economic, scientific, and technical cooperation met in Baghdad in September.

More significant, however, were Soviet moves directly relating to the Iraq-Iran war. The USSR continued to be the principal supplier of military goods to Iraq, and overall its actions and positions favored the Iraqi side. Soviet naval vessels in the Persian Gulf protected Soviet tankers chartered to Kuwait. An official statement on 8 January called for an end to the war on terms basically the same as Iraq's—that is, "mutual respect of the sovereignty, territorial integrity, noninterference in the internal affairs of each other," and return to prewar borders. (*Pravda*, 9 January; *Soviet Union and the Middle East* 12, no. 1:6.) The USSR protested when, in mid-year, Iran detained a vessel carrying Soviet arms to Iraq via Kuwait; the vessel was promptly released, and no others were stopped (*NYT*, 27 December).

The Soviet Union joined in the unanimous passage of U.N. Security Council Resolution 598 on 20 July but later espoused an interpretation of it very close to that of Iran, to the public displeasure of the Iraqi foreign minister (London, *al-Hawadith*, 23 October; *FBIS*, 29 October). In addition, the Soviets held talks with Iran on improving economic relations. By December the Soviet effort to improve ties with Iran seemed to have run its course. Moscow was aware of how adversely Iraq's Arab neighbors had reacted to Iranian use of force against shipping and to its fostering a riot during the pilgrimage in Mecca, and so Moscow took steps to repair the cracks in relations with Arab states that Soviet-Iranian connections had caused.

John F. Devlin
Swarthmore, Pennsylvania

Israel

Population. 4,222,118 (not including territories occupied in 1967)

Party. Communist Party of Israel (CPI); also called New Communist List (Rashima Kommunistit Hadasha; RAKAH)

Founded. 1922

Membership. 2,000 (estimated)

General Secretary. Meir Vilner (68; member of the Knesset [parliament])
Politburo. 9 members, including Meir Vilner, David (Uzi) Burnstein, Benjamin Gonen, Wolf Erlich, Emile Habibi, David Khenin, Tawfiq Tubi (deputy secretary general and member of the Knesset). 4 alternates.
Secretariat. 7 members, including Meir Vilner, Salibi Khamis, David Khenin, Jamal Musa, Tawfiq Tubi
Central Committee. 31 members, 5 candidates
Status. Legal
Last Congress. Twentieth, 4–7 December 1985
Last Election. 23 July 1984; 3.4 percent of the vote (with the Democratic Front for Peace and Equality [DFPE]), total number of seats in the legislature: 120
Auxiliary Organizations. Young Communist League, Young Pioneers, Democratic Women's Movement
Publications. *Al-Ittihad* (Emile Habibi, editor); *Zo Ha-Derekh* (Meir Vilner, editor); *al-Jadid* (Samih al-Qasim, editor); *Information Bulletin, Communist Party of Israel*

Background. The disappearance by the late 1970s of the Israeli Communist Party (Miflaga Kommunistit Isra'elit; MAKI) left RAKAH as the undisputed communist party of Israel and the internationally recognized successor to the pre-1965 communist organizations. With Arab nationalist parties not permitted (although the joint Arab-Jewish Progressive List for Peace [PLP] emerged in 1984 to espouse the cause of Palestinian self-determination and thus to compete for the Arab vote), RAKAH has served mainly as an outlet for the grievance of the Arab (Palestinian) minority. Almost all of the party's vote—at least 85 percent—comes from the Arab population (the CPI-dominated DFPE got about 50 percent of the Arab vote in 1977, 38 percent in 1981, and 34 percent in 1984). The DFPE has dominated most Arab town councils since the 1970s.

Leadership and Party Organization. The organization of the CPI is typical of communist parties in general and is described by party leaders as being based on the principle of "democratic centralism." The congress normally meets at four-year intervals and chooses members of the Central Committee, the Central Control Commission, the Presidium, and the Secretariat. There are also regional committees, local branches (90), and cells. Cells are based on both residence and place of work. Politburo member David Khenin reports that "there are very many small enterprises at which it is practically impossible to form party cells" (*WMR*, May). The CPI is said to be the best organized political party in Israel, which gives it an important advantage in its rivalry with the joint Arab-Jewish Progressive List for Peace (PLP) for Arab votes.

Citing his party's growing membership (which has increased by 30 percent since 1981), Khenin singles out its "most significant achievement" as being gains among "young people, particularly students." He said that in some local organizations young people are in the majority and that half of the delegates to the Twentieth Congress in 1985 were less than 30 years old, adding that "The party continues to give priority attention to young people." He also reported that the party includes increasing numbers of intellectuals, with 32 percent of the delegates at the congress having a higher education and 31 percent a secondary school education. He said that the percentage of women in the party is increasing, but "slowly"; that there are "very few Arab women in our ranks, but even here there is visible progress"; and that both women and youths are gaining more "leadership posts." Although he reiterated the Twentieth Congress's statement that "Our principal task . . . is to strengthen our links to the working class," he noted the existence of "many objective difficulties," including the "inadequate class consciousness," which he described as "the Achilles heel of the Israeli working class movement." (Ibid.)

Although perhaps 80 percent of the members of the CPI are Arabs, Jews predominate in the top party organs. In recent years, the Jewish general secretary has been balanced by an Arab deputy general secretary. Khenin claimed that his party's success extends even to Jewish students, who had been "extremely reactionary" until recent years (ibid.). Although the party has been noted as a nearly unique arena of Arab-Jewish amity, there are reports of dissatisfaction on the part of Arabs because of their inadequate representation at the top.

Domestic Party Affairs. The Central Committee met on 6–7 February, and General Secretary Meir Vilner delivered a report (Moscow Domestic Service, 9 February; *FBIS*, 11 February). No information is available on other meetings of party organs during the year.

Vilner described the two largest blocs in the National Unity government—the Labor Alignment and the Likud—as differing only "on tactics" and as being united "on a common platform hostile to the working class" (*WMR*, November 1986). Politburo member Benjamin Gonen wrote of the government's "unprecedented assault on the working people's rights" in the form of the "'economic austerity regime'" in effect since 1985, which has caused a "steep decline" in wages, mass unemployment, and other conditions detrimental to the working class (ibid., January).

Gonen, who is one of the DFPE representatives on the Executive Council of the Histadrut (General Federation of Labor) and chairman of his faction in that body, described the Histadrut's leadership as having "an undisguisedly nationalistic, Zionist orientation." He said that instead of representing the true interests of the workers, it has repeatedly been used to urge them "to bear with the actions of entrepreneurs and the authorities to bring down the working population's standard of living" and to mobilize "mass support" for aggression. Histadrut enterprises were described as having "no influence whatever on the capitalist character of the relations of production" since they are "capitalist in all respects" and exploit their workers exactly as do other enterprises. He called for strengthening DFPE influence in "trade unions and workers' committees" and for changing "the Histadrut's policies and class character." (Ibid.) Vilner wrote of "state-monopoly capitalism [that] has built a powerful military-industrial complex, which now dominates the economy"; singling out the Histadrut's role in armaments production, he noted that peace would create a "crisis" for such "armaments monopolies" (ibid., November 1986).

Vilner spoke of discrimination against the Arab population and about the "threat to democratic freedoms" and the increased "risk of fascism" (Moscow Domestic Service, 9 February; *FBIS*, 11 February). He described racists as stirring "chauvinist, anti-Arab feeling" by "set[ting] unemployed Jews... against Arab working people, contending that the latter are responsible for the dearth of jobs." He referred to discrimination against Arabs in terms of jobs and the allocation of government funds for various purposes, and he noted the recent "marked growth of the influence of semi-fascist parties like Tehiya and Kach" as well as the increased activities of "fundamentalist religious groups." He accused the government of "act[ing] hand in glove with these groups, often seeking their support" and of "us[ing] chauvinistic, racist campaigns to enforce anti-labour socio-economic programmes, enact reactionary laws, and restrict democratic freedoms." He cited his party's demand for "full equality for the Arabs" and ending takeovers of their land. (*WMR*, November 1986.)

Auxiliary and Front Organizations. The CPI dominates the DFPE, which includes two noncommunist partners: the Black Panthers (an Afro-Asian or Oriental Jewish group protesting discrimination by Jews of European origin) and the Arab Local Council Heads. In addition to its delegation in the Knesset, the DFPE is particularly well organized in Arab towns and villages.

The CPI sponsors the active Young Pioneers and the Young Communist League. According to Khenin, "Considerable influence is exercised among the Arab populaton by the Young Communist League, the Democratic Women's Movement, and other progressive organizations in which the Communists participate"; he indicated that the Young Communist League plays "a large role in replenishing our ranks," with 40 percent of the party's new members during the past six years coming from that organization, which "has grown by 12 percent" and "has 73 locals, and 70 percent of its members are students" (*WMR*, May). He also spoke of "progressive organizations" in which communists participate in Israeli universities (ibid.). At least in the past, the CPI sponsored or actively participated in the Committee Against the War in Lebanon, There is a Limit (an organization calling on Israeli servicemen to refuse to serve in Lebanon), Mothers Against the War, Soldiers Against Silence, Women for Peace, the Committee for the Defense of Arab Land, the Israel-USSR Friendship Movement, the Israeli Association of Anti-Fascist Fighters and Victims of Nazism, and Arab student committees (which its members have long dominated at some universities).

International Views, Positions, and Activities. Central Committee member George Tubi participated in a *World Marxist Review* conference in Prague (no date given) (ibid., September).

An Israeli women's delegation, including members of the CPI and other parties, visited the USSR in June (Jerusalem Domestic Service, 18 June; *FBIS*, 18 June). Another delegation to Moscow included secretaries of four parties, including Vilner (Jerusalem Domestic Service, 17 June; *FBIS*, 18 June). Vilner and Deputy General Secretary Tawfiq Tubi were in Moscow in November to participate in the celebration of the 70th anniversary of the October Revolution and in a colloquium; they met with senior Soviet officials, who were said to convey a message to the Israeli government (Tel Aviv, *Ha'aretz*, 8, 14 November; *FBIS*, 12, 13 November). After his speech at the celebration, Vilner was "approached by representatives of countries," including Syria, that have no diplomatic ties with Israel (*Ha'aretz*, 8 November; *FBIS*, 12 November). He also spoke at a meeting of workers of Moscow oblast organizations and institutions (*Pravda*, 5 November; *FBIS*, 12 November).

There were several contacts with East European leaders during the year. George Tubi met with Bulgarian Communist Party Central Committee member Dimitŭr Stanishev in Sofia in April (Sofia Domestic Service, 4 April; *FBIS*, 8 May). A Communist Party of Czechoslovakia delegation headed by Michal Stefanák met with a CPI delegation headed by Khenin in Tel Aviv later in the same month (Prague, *Rudé právo*, 24 April; *FBIS*, 26 May). A Polish Communist Party delegation visited Israel in June as guests of the CPI (Jerusalem Domestic Service, 17 June; *FBIS*, 18 June). A CPI delegation headed by Vilner and including Central Committee members Ali Ashur and Leon Zahavi met with Socialist Unity Party of Germany general secretary Erich Honecker in Berlin in August (East Berlin, ADN International Service, 14 August; *FBIS*, 17 August).

After a 25-year break in relations between the CPI and China, a CPI delegation headed by Vilner and also including George Tubi visited Beijing in July at the invitation of the Chinese Communist Party. Chinese Politburo member Hu Qili, at a meeting with the delegation, praised the CPI's opposition to aggression and support for "a reasonable solution to the Middle East issue" and declared that "now the two parties have smoothly normalized their relations" (Beijing, Xinhua, 4 July; *FBIS*, 6 July). Vilner, too, reported that the two sides had "agreed to resume normal friendly contacts"; he said the talks had covered "a broad range of political and ideological questions" and that "their positions coincided or were similar on many of the issues . . . though [they] differed on some of the others" (*WMR*, September). There was speculation in Israel about whether "this invitation [is] tantamount to a Chinese signal to the Israeli Government" (Jerusalem Domestic Service, 16 June; *FBIS*, 17 June). According to Vilner, Beijing was not ready for the establishment of relations with Israel, but moves by the latter toward holding a Middle East peace conference might make it more amenable (*Jerusalem Post*, international edition, 18 July).

There were several contacts with the Palestine Liberation Organization (PLO) during the year. A delegation organized by the CPI and including Politburo member David Burnstein and Charlie Biton, the Black Panther member of the DFPE's Knesset delegation, met with PLO officials in Budapest in June (Tel Aviv, *Yedi'ot Aharonot*, 7 June; *FBIS*, 8 June; *Jerusalem Post*, international edition, 27 June). Biton met with PLO chairman Yassir Arafat in Geneva in September and received peace proposals to be conveyed to the Israeli government (*CSM*, 15 September). The first official meeting of delegations representing the CPI and the Executive Committee of the PLO took place in Moscow at the time of the celebration of the 70th anniversary of the October Revolution (*Neues Deutschland*, 19 November).

Statements by CPI leaders deplored all aspects of Israel's foreign policy. Vilner described Israel as "now a U.S. henchman not only in the Middle East but in other regions as well—Central America and Africa." He singled out Israel's performance of "the most villainous and sensitive assignments," such as "supplying military hardware to fascist dictatorships." He also spoke of reports of Israel's possession of nuclear weapons and "of secret collaboration in this area with South Africa and of joint tests of nuclear weapons." Denying that the United States is a friend, he called for the restoration of Israel's independence. (*WMR*, November 1986.)

"Anti-Sovietism" was repeatedly condemned by CPI spokesmen. Speaking in Moscow, Vilner declared that "we have always been in solidarity with the Soviet Union" and spoke of that country's "immense achievements in domestic policy and the international arena," adding that "restructuring and *glasnost'* in your country are shaking the world" (*Pravda*, 5 November; *FBIS*, 12 November). On another occasion, he declared that "Soviet policy is, in its entirety, aimed at safeguarding peace, preventing a nuclear-missile collision on the Earth and in outer space, negotiating a disarmament agreement, and moving from confrontation to détente" (*WMR*, November 1986).

On the Arab-Israeli conflict, Khenin blamed "the Israeli aggression of 1967" for "sharply aggravat[ing] the situation in the region" and called for "an end to the occupation and annexation of Arab lands, . . [and] the right of the Palestinian people to self-determination and the creation of their own independent state alongside the state of Israel" (ibid., May). Vilner insisted that "the only way" to reach a peace settlement is through "an international conference under the aegis of the United Nations. The Labor Alignment's recent support "with some reservations" for holding an international conference was described as flawed in its rejection of PLO participation and its insistence instead on participation by "Quislings included in the Jordanian-Palestinian delegation," in its insistence that the conference should meet briefly and then make way for direct talks between this delegation and Israel, and in its provision that the USSR's participation would be conditional on restoration of diplomatic relations with Israel (ibid., September). He deplored the "iron fist" policy in the occupied territories, where "even the most elementary human rights are flouted," and the growing "spirit of extreme brutality" that makes many Israelis "see the occupation, the shooting of demonstrators in the West Bank, and the torture and assassination of Arabs as quite commonplace and normal" (ibid., November 1986).

With demonstrations and riots directed against the Israeli occupation forces reaching the proportions of a major revolt in December, and with numerous Palestinians killed or arrested, specific statements by CPI spokesmen were not available at the time of this writing.

Other Marxist Groups. For information on the Israeli Socialist Organization (Matzpen) and groups that have broken away from it, including the Revolutionary Communist League, see *YICA*, 1982 and 1984.

PALESTINE COMMUNIST PARTY

Population. 4,500,000 (estimated) Palestinians, including 853,060 in the West Bank (including East Jerusalem), 558,729 in the Gaza Strip, 717,760 in Israel (*CSM*, 27 December), and more than 1.4 million in Jordan (East Bank) (estimated)
Party. Palestinian Communist Party (al-Hizb al-Shuyu'i al-Filastini; PCP)
Founded. 1982
Membership. 200 (estimated)
General Secretary. (Presumably) Bashir al-Barghuti (journalist)
Politburo. Sulayman al-Najjab, Na'im Abbas al-Ashhab; others not known
Secretariat. No data
Central Committee. Dhamin Awdah, Mahir al-Sharif, Sulayman al-Nashshab, Ali Ahmad, Mahmud al-Rawwaq, Na'im Abbas al-Ashhab, Mahmud Abu-Shamas, Mahmud Shuqayr; others not known
Status. Illegal, but tolerated to a large extent in Israeli-occupied areas
Last Congress. First, 1984
Last Election. N/a
Auxiliary Organizations. Progressive Workers' Bloc (PWB)
Publications. *Al-Tal'iyah* (The vanguard), weekly newspaper, Bashir al-Barghuti, editor

Background. With the approval of the Communist Party of Jordan (CPJ), the PCP was organized in February 1982 (for the evolution of the PCP, see *YICA* 1987, p. 443). The party was to include communists in the Gaza Strip and the West Bank, members of the PCO in Lebanon, and all Palestinian members of the CPJ, except those living in Jordan, that is, on the East Bank.

Leadership and Party Organization. Relatively little is known about the organization of the PCP. The First (constituent) Congress met in 1984 and adopted a program and rules for the party, as well as selecting the members of the Politburo, Secretariat, and Central Committee. Several non-PCP sources refer to Barghuti as the party's leader, but there is no evidence that he is necessarily the general secretary.

Palestinian Affairs. The PCP has been particularly active in the Israeli-occupied territories, but its activities extend to the Palestinian diaspora as well, though not to Jordan. Neither does it compete with the CPI in Israel proper. The party is evidently based in Damascus.

The PCP is illegal in the occupied territories, but—although concern for security sometimes leads to crackdowns (and there have been reports of individuals arrested at times for possessing communist literature)—it is in fact generally tolerated. Barghuti, who was once imprisoned by the Jordanians and was subjected to house arrest by the Israelis during the early 1980s, now edits the weekly party newspaper, *al-Tali'ah*, in East Jerusalem. The PCP also publishes a monthly magazine, *al-Kitab* (The writer) (Dov Shinar, *Palestinian Voices: Communication and Nation-Building in the West Bank* [1987], p. 41). Such materials, as well as publications of the CPI, are openly distributed in East Jerusalem, which Israel has annexed; though banned elsewhere in the West Bank, these publications are in fact quite accessible to anyone coming to East Jerusalem (ibid., p. 66). There were reports in the past of another PCP newspaper, *al-Watan* (Homeland), which is presumably published outside the occupied territories.

Before 1987 the PCP was not represented in the Palestine National Council (PNC), the Executive Committee, or other organs of the PLO, which is an umbrella group for the main organizations in the Palestinian national movement. However, it was actively involved with other Palestinian organizations (see *YICA*, 1987). It was one of five Palestinian factions that reached agreement on holding the eighteenth session of the PNC in Algiers in April in order to restore unity after a four-year rift (*NYT*, 18 March). Then the PCP was one of eight factions that participated in a preparatory meeting in the Algerian capital in mid-April (*Izvestiia*, 14 April; *FBIS*, 16 April), prior to the PNC session that began on 20 April. The PNC satisfied PLO chairman Yassir Arafat's critics, including the PCP, by abrogating the 1985 accord with Jordan and by deciding to restrict contacts with Egypt (see *Middle East Report*, July–August). In addition, the PCP finally obtained representation in the PNC and the Executive Committee; Politburo member Sulayman al-Najjab now sits on the latter body. A statement by the PCP Central Committee on 26 April—the only meeting of a party organ during the year on which any information is available—proclaimed this restoration of Palestinian unity to be "one of the most glorious victories for our people since . . . 1982" (*IB*, July). Central Committee member Mahmud Shuqayr declared that the previous lack of PCP representation had been "a flaw in the structure of the PLO" and that its representation on the Executive Committee was "the final step toward the restoration of Palestinian national unity" (*WMR*, October).

PCP spokesmen stressed the importance of the PLO as the overall framework for the Palestinian movement. Shuqayr insisted that "dialogue, debate, and the efforts to overcome differences should be conducted within the organization and not outside" (ibid.).

But there were many expressions of discontent with the non-Marxist groups that dominate the PLO. A joint communiqué issued by the PCP and the Communist Party of Jordan (CPJ) warned of the dangers posed to unity by "rightist forces" in the organization (*IB*, May). Shuqayr, speaking of the "PLO leadership" as expressing "the interests of the national bourgeoisie," complained of its "inclination toward appeasement" that had been thwarted only by an enemy "looking for complete surrender" (*WMR*, October). Politburo member Na'im Ashhab pictured the "bureaucracy" in various Palestinian forces after 1982 as having schemed "to preserve their own positions and comfortable life." He said that the "notorious 'Reagan plan' was concocted" in light of the "class character of the Palestinian national movement's leadership." (Ibid., January.)

PCP spokesmen warned against U.S. and Israeli schemes to subvert the PLO's role as the sole legitimate representative of the Palestinian people. Ashhab spoke against the tacit Israeli-Jordanian agreement to establish a system of shared rule in the West Bank and Gaza Strip. (Ibid.)

Ashhab identified five objectives of "Zionist colonization" plans: seizure of Arab land, establishment of Zionist settlements, ousting the Palestinian population, binding the economy of the occupied areas to Israel, and destroying the Palestinians' cultural heritage (ibid., June).

At the time of this writing, no information was available on possible PCP involvement in the uprisings in the Gaza Strip and West Bank in December.

Auxiliary and Front Organizations. The PWB, which is closely tied to the PCP, has long dominated the General Federation of Trade Unions in the occupied areas (see *YICA*, 1986, 1987). Union leaders have often been detained or put under town arrest. There were complaints during 1987 that the military authorities were blocking union activities and that union leaders were regularly being put under town arrest and union offices searched while troops tried to stop union elections in Gaza (*Jerusalem Post*, international edition, 27 June). PWB leader George Hazboun, who was subjected to town arrest in the past, was detained without charges or trial on 3 June for a three-month period, a matter about which Amnesty International expressed its concern (Washington, D.C., *Friends of Palestinian Prisoners*, December).

There is little information on other auxiliary organizations, though PCP involvement with student and professional groups has been reported in the past.

The PLO is in effect a government in exile, though it does not call itself that. Its supporters and its leadership span the political spectrum, and the inclusion of a PCP representative in its Executive Committee, which is analogous to a cabinet, would seem at least technically to qualify it as a popular front despite the peripheral role of the communists in the organization. The PLO's dominant component, Fatah, might itself be called a united front, since it avoids ideology in favor of pursuing a national cause. It contains some Marxists but is dominated by centrists like Arafat. Small groups like the Popular Front for the Liberation of Palestine and the Democratic Front for the Liberation of Palestine—both of which are represented in the PLO—are Marxist but are not considered communist.

The Palestine National Front was organized in 1973 as an alliance of communists and others in the occupied territories. It gained some brief importance but withered before the end of the decade (see *YICA*, 1985).

Al-Najjab called the restoration of the PLO's unity at the recent PNC session "the first fundamental step toward developing the PLO as a front" and stated two basic principles for strengthening this unity, namely "loyalty to the national consensus program" and—apparently meaning more communist representation—the guarantee of "proportional representation of the forces participating in these mass organizations" (London, *al-Tadamun*, 11 July; *FBIS*, 14 July). Shuqayr clarified that, during the struggle for liberation, "the main yardstick of one's commitment . . . is not one's views—right-wing, left-wing or moderate—but whether one is a patriot" (*WMR*, October).

International Views, Positions, and Activities. The PCP was one of eight communist parties of the Arab world that had issued a joint statement calling for solidarity with Syria on 27 October 1986 (*IB*, January). PCP and CPJ delegations met and issued a communiqué early in January (*IB*, May). Al-Najjab, together with representatives of non-communist Palestinian organizations, attended a meeting in Moscow on 4–5 April (*Pravda*, 7 April). The USSR is said to have "worked hard to reconcile" Fatah and "the Damascus-based factions," including the PCP (*CSM*, 27 April). Ashhab led a PCP delegation to Prague in May and held meetings with Vasil Bil'ák of the Communist Party of Czechoslovakia Presidium (Prague, ČETEKA, 22 May; *FBIS*, 28 May). Al-Najjab was a member of a PLO delegation that visited Moscow in response to an invitation by Foreign Minister Eduard Shevardnadze in June (Sanaa, Voice of Palestine, 21 June; *FBIS*, 22 June). No information is available on international contacts during the latter half of the year.

PCP statements repeatedly supported Syria. The joint statement of the PCP and CPJ called for "solidarity with the struggle by the Syrian people against the virulent anti-Syrian campaign by imperialist quarters" (*IB*, May). Shuqayr stated his party's belief that the recent PNC session had created "the objective background for restoring these [PLO-Syrian] relations" (*WMR*, October). The PCP-CPJ statement "condemned continuing aggression by the [Lebanese Shiite] Amal movement and the isolationist 'Lebanese army' against Palestinian camps in Lebanon, aided by outrageous raids by Israeli warplanes against these camps" (*IB*, May) but did not mention Syrian support for Amal. The two parties also "voiced solidarity with the Iraqi Communist Party and other democratic forces victimized by the dictatorial policy of the Iraqi rulers, whose continuation will bring still more tragedies to the fraternal Iraqi people" (ibid.). They condemned U.S. arms sales to Iran and "the criminal complicity by the Saudi reactionaries in these shipments" (ibid.). There were other statements unfavorable to "reactionary regimes" such as that of Saudi Arabia, to their "pressure" on the PLO, and generally to the extent to which "right-wing, reactionary circles have gained the upper hand on the Arab scene" (*WMR*, October).

Few available PCP statements dealt with the international scene beyond the Middle East. The joint PCP-CPJ statement "support[ed] consistent Soviet moves and peace initiatives" (*IB*, May). Shuqayr emphasized the importance of "fraternal relations with our friends on the international scene, first and foremost with the Soviet Union and other socialist countries, who have always selflessly assisted and resolutely supported the just cause of the Palestinians" (*WMR*, October). The United States was blamed for the failure of the Reykjavik summit, for its "steadily closer" alliance with Israel, and for its desire to "destroy the PLO" (*IB*, May, July; *WMR*, January). Shuqayr spoke of "the inevitable collapse of the racist colonial regime" in South Africa (*WMR*, January).

Glenn E. Perry
Indiana State University

Jordan

Population. 2,794,000 (excluding the West Bank and East Jerusalem)
Party. Communist Party of Jordan (al-Hizb al-Shuyu'i al Urduni; CPJ)
Founded. 1951
Membership. Accurate estimate not available
General Secretary. Dr. Ya'qub Zayadin
Leading Bodies. No data
Status. Proscribed
Last Congress. Second, December 1983
Last Election. N/a
Auxiliary Organizations. None
Publications. *Al-Jamahir*, *al-Haqiqa*

Background. The 1967 Israeli occupation of the remainder of Palestine and the consequent rise of an independent Palestinian resistance based largely in Jordan provided impetus for the re-emerging of oppositional political forces in that country. The CPJ enjoyed a period of relative toleration by the regime, interrupted by occasional repression (for detailed background, see *YICA* 1987, pp. 446–47). Following the rift between King Hussein and Yasir Arafat in February 1986, and the U.S. aerial raid on Libya in April of the same year, student demonstrations at one of Jordan's universities (al-Yarmouk), in which many people were killed and injured, provided an opportunity for the government to crack down on the party. The government arrested the entire leadership of the CPJ in May 1986, blaming it for the student protests. The 17 leaders were released on 4 September 1986, but the Party remained officially banned.

Party Internal Affairs. The CPJ Central Committee met in late December 1986 and elected Dr. Ya'qub Zayadin as the party's general secretary. Zayadin had been acting as assistant general secretary since the party was reunited in 1986; he succeeded Fa'iq Warrad, who resigned for health reasons. The Jordanian and Palestinian communist parties met in January 1987 and issued a joint communiqué decrying attempts to water down the Arab consensus on the question of Palestine and to generate alternative structures for a Palestinian settlement (*IB*, May).

Domestic Attitudes and Activities. The CPJ leaders have consistently denounced the Jordanian regime for following a "course aimed at suppressing democracy and civil rights and liberties" (*IB*, April). The Central Committee's December 1986 report stated that "the Rifai Government, more than any previous one, is tightening the screws on general human rights and freedoms" (*IB*, May).

The Central Committee has described Jordan as a consumerist society dominated by a parasitical bourgeoisie that relies on remittances from the Persian Gulf and by a bureaucratic bourgeoisie that creates state enterprises. The tensions between these two, as well as the growing number of indigenous and foreign laborers deprived of the benefits of social legislation and trade unions provide the CPJ with the opportunity to mobilize support among workers, students, women, and youth. Jordanian communists are represented in the General Secretariat of the Alignment of Popular and Trade Union Forces and in the newly established Committee of Political Parties and Organizations.

International Affairs. In October the CPJ, together with other Arab communist parties, issued a statement expressing solidarity with Syria after the United States and Great Britain withdrew their ambassadors and accused Syria of supporting terrorism. The statement said that "the situation of incitement and threats against Syria and the Arab Liberation forces is redolent of the atmosphere on the eve of the 1956 tripartite aggression against Egypt. Similarly, slander is being used against Syria's patriotic anti-imperialist line and resistance to the aggressive policy of the U.S. and Israeli Zionists to bring our region to heel and force the Arabs into accepting the Camp David deal" (*IB*, January).

The Central Committee's December 1986 report emphasized that Jordan's political crisis has been "compounded by acute economic crisis, with stagnation and repression rife in various economic sectors—industry, agriculture, tourism, transport, and construction; output is declining and the market has immensely shrunk." It added that "the treasury is being depleted, the budget and trade deficits are rising, exports are falling, foreign currency reserves have dwindled to a very precarious level, [and] foreign debt is rapidly growing." (*IB*, May.) The party's organ, *al-Haqiqa*, published an important article in March decrying U.S. interference in Jordan's internal affairs. It cited two studies by the Agency for International Development that urged Jordan to abandon state sector enterprises and subsequently privatize them. The measure was seen as a move to increase Jordan's dependency on the United States by seeking to submit the "local market to international capital interests" and create a "blind allegiance to the system of international capitalist division of labor." (*IB*, July.) Among the sectors targeted for privatization, the article mentioned the Public Transportation Department, the Telephone and Telegraph Department, and the Alia Civil Aviation Department.

Relations between the Soviet Union and Jordan continued to be limited to ceremonial visits that were often concluded with joint statements endorsing the need for an international settlement of the Palestine question.

The Soviet vice president of the Supreme Soviet Presidium, Vladimir Orlov, visited Jordan at the head of a parliamentary delegation in March, and the chairman of the Jordanian-Soviet Friendship Society, Bahjat al-Talhouni, visited the USSR in June. It was also announced that King Hussein was scheduled to visit the Soviet Union.

Naseer H. Aruri
Southeastern Massachusetts University

Lebanon

Population. 3,320,522
Party. Lebanese Communist Party (al-Hizb al-Shuyu'i al-Lubnani; LCP); Organization of Communist Action in Lebanon (Munazzamat al-'Amal al-Shuyu'i; OCAL)
Founded. LCP: 1924; OCAL: 1970
Membership. LCP: 14,000–16,000 (claimed); 3,000 (*NYT*, 4 March); OCAL: 1,500 (author's estimate)
General Secretary. LCP: George Hawi; OCAL: Muhsin Ibrahim
Politburo. LCP: 11 members
Central Committee. LCP: 24 members
Status. Legal
Last Congress. LCP: Fifth, 3–5 February 1987 (*IB*, May); OCAL: First, 1971
Last Elections. 1972, no representation
Auxiliary Organizations. LCP: Communist Labor Organization, World Peace Council in Lebanon, and a number of labor and student unions and movements
Publications. LCP: *al Nida'* (The call), daily, 'Abd al-Karim Muruwwah, publisher; *al-Akhbar* (The news), weekly; *al-Tariq* (The road), quarterly. OCAL: *al-Hurriyya* (Freedom), weekly, Muhsin Ibrahim, publisher.

Background. Both the LCP and OCAL (for more information, see *YICA*, 1987, p. 450) have participated in Lebanon's civil war and continue to play active roles in the country's political affairs. Nonetheless, since the Israeli invasion of 1982 and the resulting decline in the influence of the PLO in Lebanon, both organizations have found themselves increasingly on the political and military defensive. The ascendancy of Shi'ite movements, such as the Amal Movement and the Party of God (Hizb Allah), has been the chief cause of a palpable decline in the influence of the LCP and the OCAL. Furthermore, the ranks of both parties have been decimated by scores of assassinations carried out by Shi'ite militants, in particular.

Leadership and Organization. George Hawi has served as the LCP's general secretary since 1979, and Muhsin Ibrahim has led the OCAL since its foundation in 1970.

Formal authority in the LCP is vested in the 24-member Central Committee, which, in turn, elects the 11-member Politburo. A current list of the Central Committee membership could not be located, and it is possible it has not been published for reasons of physical security.

The party congress, theoretically the highest organ of the LCP, is supposed to convene every four years, but the LCP has held only five congresses since 1924. The Fifth Congress was held 3–5 February in the Lebanese Shouf mountain town of Baaklin, a preserve of the predominately Druze Progressive Socialist Party (PSP), a long-time ally of the LCP. The preliminary report of the LCP Central Committee had been published in July 1986 (see *al-Nida'*, 6 July 1986), and a plenary planning meeting of the committee had been held on 6 November 1986 (*IB*, April).

The congress met amidst rumors that Hawi, who has been criticized for subservience to Syria, would step aside, perhaps in favor of 'Abd al-Karim Muruwwah, one of two deputy general secretaries. In addition, a venerable Syrian communist, Khaled Bakdash, reportedly accused Hawi of failing to maintain party unity and regulations (*al-Dustur*, 26 May 1986). In the current climate of rampant religious factionalism, some observers have concluded that the replacement of Hawi, who is a Christian, with a Shiite Muslim like Muruwwah might attenuate some of the visceral enmity facing the LCP; however, this is a disputable proposition. The assaults on the LCP spring not simply from the sectarian identity of its leadership but from its espousal of an ideology that its adversaries find absolutely unpalatable and an alliance with Palestine Liberation Organization (PLO) and pro-PLO elements that is perceived as threatening by the Shiite Amal movement especially.

Despite the widely circulating rumors and reports, Hawi was re-elected as general secretary. Muruwwah and Nadim 'Abd al-Samad were reelected as deputy general secretaries.

The congress was attended by 350 delegates, of whom 85 percent were men. The average age of the delegates was 35, and average tenure in the party was 15 years. Fifty-four percent of the delegates had been directly involved in the fighting that has wracked the country since 1975, and 33.5 percent had been detained by Israel, Lebanese government authorities, or one of the belligerent Lebanese militias. A remarkable indicator of the extensive swath the conflict has cut is the report that 14 percent of the delegates were from families that had suffered the loss of a member; similar statistics would apply to almost any sample of Lebanese families, regardless of their political predilections. The class and social profiles of the delegates were as follows: blue- and white-collar workers, 40 percent; farmworkers, 5 percent; small landowners, 3.5 percent; students, 10 percent; teachers, 19 percent; intellectuals, 11 percent; professionals, 8 percent; and artisans, 3.5 percent. (*IB*, May.)

Reports on the congress were broadcast on the Voice of the People radio, a new clandestine station (*FBIS*, 4 February).

The USSR was represented at the Fifth Congress by Karen N. Brutents, the deputy head of the Communist Party of the Soviet Union (CPSU) Central Committee International Department. The USSR sent a long message (*Pravda*, 3 February) calling for an end to internecine fighting and the uniting of all groups to face Israel's imperialist-backed aggression (*World Affairs Report*, February). Delegations from Czechoslovakia, Romania, and Vietnam were also among those in attendance. Arab speakers included the leader of the PSP, Walid Jumblatt (*FBIS*, 4 February), and 'Abdallah al-Ahmar representing the Syrian Baath Party (*al-Baath*, 5 February).

The LCP maintains a well-organized and centrally controlled network of clandestine local cells; in turn, these are organized into districts and regions. Hawi indicated that the LCP resisted intraparty pressures to abolish the "underground structure" and channel the party into "legal mass work." He asserted that by maintaining secrecy the LCP has managed to frustrate U.S., Israeli, and Arab reactionary designs to eliminate the communists (*WMR*, November 1985). Both the LCP and OCAL maintain well-armed "self-defense" paramilitary units that participate actively in street battles and other "military operations."

In late 1987 rumors circulated indicating that the LCP was split into two factions, one supporting Hawi and the other supporting Central Committee member George Batal and Deputy General Secretary Muruwwah. In October a stormy meeting was purportedly held at the LCP headquarters, precipitated by reports that Hawi might have mishandled $3 million in funds. The Soviet ambassador allegedly intervened, persuading both sides to move the debate out of the public view. (*FBIS*, 4 November.)

Domestic Views and Activities. Like the three preceding years, 1987 was brutally punishing for the LCP. The party was viciously attacked by the Shiite Muslim Amal movement and the pro-Iranian Hizb Allah. For Amal, the LCP not only continues to be a competitor—albeit a less important rival than in years past—for Shiite recruits, but it is also a long-time ally of the PLO, which Amal has battled for nearly a decade. Above all else, Amal is dedicated to ensuring that the PLO and its Lebanese allies do not succeed in re-establishing the armed state-within-a-state that existed before 1982 and that led to much grief, especially in southern Lebanon.

For the militants of Hizb Allah, and for many adherents of Amal as well, it is the espousal of atheistic and heretical communism that anathematizes the LCP. According to LCP sources, Shiite clerics in south Lebanon delivered a *fatwah* (an authoritative interpretation of religious responsibility) that urged the killing of all communists (*NYT*, 4 March, citing *al-Nida'*). Especially in the current circumstances, such edicts are taken quite seriously among the Shiites and further enflame existing anti-LCP enmity. Muruwwah confirmed this information and indicated that the *fatwah* extended to Palestinian and Lebanese nationals who had been educated in communist countries (*al-Dustur*, 30 March). An Amal official acknowledged the decrees but admitted his inability to bring a close to anticommunist violence (*FBIS*, 5 March).

The year was marked by the assassination of a number of party officials and members. Nur Tuqan, an LCP official, was killed in the al-Shiyah suburb of Beirut (*FBIS*, 26 February). At least two Central Committee members were killed in West Beirut: the well-known writer, Husain Muruwwah, aged 78; and a professor of philosophy at the Lebanese University, Dr. Hassan Hamdan, aged 46 (*FBIS*, 18 February, 18 May). Hamdan and Muruwwah were both Shiite Muslims. Ironically, in his posthumously published article, "A Study of Islamic Organizations," Muruwwah denigrated the political plan of the "'revolutionary Islamic' alternative" that equates socialism with imperialism and promotes a "third road." In his prophetic words, "The obvious impracticality of this plan does not make it less dangerous to the struggle of the patriotic, progressive democratic forces for the national democratic programme of a radical and revolutionary transformation of the existing socio-political system." (*WMR*, April.) In March it was reported that nine LCP leaders had been killed in Beirut and in southern Lebanon (*NYT*, 4 March).

The bloodiest assaults began 15 February when Amal and Hizb Allah joined forces to attack the LCP in West Beirut. The Shiite offensive included attacks on the offices of the LCP organ, *al-Nida'*, and on the party headquarters, the only remaining LCP center in either Beirut or the southern suburbs of the capital (*Pravda*, 3 March; *IB*, June). The PSP went to the aid of its ally, bringing to an effective close the uneasy PSP-Amal alliance. One report indicated 32 LCP members were killed and 17 were kidnapped during the fighting, which was most intense from 15 to 18 February (*NYT*, 4 March), whereas another put the total casualties at 180 people killed and 380 wounded (*WP*, 20 February). The February fighting precipitated the introduction of 7,000 Syrian troops into West Beirut, an act that was "strongly welcomed" by the LCP (*FBIS*, 2 March; *IB*, June).

In July the LCP joined twelve other parties, including Amal, the PSP, and the pro-Syrian wing of the Baath Party, to form the Unification and Liberation Front, which affirmed Syria's policy line in Lebanon (*NYT*, 24 July; *FBIS*, 22 July). There is no evidence to suggest that the new front, like its defunct predecessors, was any more than a cosmetic gesture. The anodyne statement announcing the creation of the front commits each member to abolishing sectarianism in Lebanon, implementing equal opportunity, affirming Lebanon's special relationship with Syria, and resisting the Israeli occupation of Lebanese territory, but it cannot mitigate the deadly hostility that confronts the LCP.

Notwithstanding the pummeling it has suffered, the LCP maintains an active role in attacking the Israeli presence in South Lebanon. In 1982 the LCP, in cooperation with the OCAL and the Arab Socialist Action Party, created the Lebanese National Resistance Front (NRF). The NRF had achieved notable military successes against the Israeli army and its Lebanese proxy forces in south Lebanon (*al-Nida'*, 6 July 1986); however, its resistance activities in 1987 were restricted to those sections of the South lying outside of the Amal movement's control. Yet where the LCP does operate in the South it seems to enjoy popular support, a good local supply network, and a highly motivated and well-trained cadre of men; thus, it would be an error to presume that the LCP has been wholly supplanted in the South or in Lebanon in general.

Despite the fact that the LCP took pains to castigate the "Palestinian right wing," thereby aligning itself with Syria and against Yassir Arafat, it has still found itself at odds with Amal, which simply rejects the LCP's position that the Palestinians have a political role to play in Lebanon's "national democratic revolution" (ibid.). The LCP called for an end to the Amal assaults on the Palestinian camps in Lebanon (*IB*, July) and emphasized its view that the Palestinians have a lawful right to fight from Lebanese territory (*IB*, May), a position that puts it squarely at odds with Amal.

International Views and Contacts. The LCP remains a strong and consistent supporter of the Soviet Union. The party "emphasizes the great role the Soviet Communist Party is playing in the area of consolidating the unity, power, and status of the system of socialist countries" (*al-Nida'*, 6 July 1986). Yet this has not prevented the USSR from maintaining regular contact with the LCP's most significant political rival, Amal (see *FBIS*, 24 September, 5 October).

The LCP joined seven other regional parties in a statement applauding Mikhail Gorbachev's proposals put forward at the Reykjavik summit in 1986 and calling for resistance to the "fraudulent propaganda campaigns" of the United States and its NATO partners. In particular, the U.S. (and its allies') efforts to "fight terrorism" were singled out as slanderous of Syria and reminiscent of the 1956 aggression against Egypt. (*IB*, January.)

Deputy General Secretary Samad traveled to Bulgaria in March, where he was received by Dimitŭr Stanishev, secretary of the Bulgarian Communist Party (BCP) Central Committee (*JPRS*, 30 March), and again in November, when he was met by a BCP Politburo member (*FBIS*, 6 November). Deputy General Secretary 'Abd al-Karim Muruwwah led an LCP delegation to Beijing, which was met by Hu Qili, member of both the Politburo and the Central Committee of the Chinese Communist Party (*FBIS*, 17 September). Rafic Samhoun, LCP Central Committee member, participated in two symposia in Prague (*WMR*, July, September). In August Hawi met with members of the French Communist Party (PCF) in Paris. Georges Marchais, PCF general secretary, and Hawi "stressed the need for a comprehensive solution to the Middle East conflict guaranteeing Israel's withdrawal from all of the occupied territories, recognition of the Palestinian people's national rights, including their right to an independent state, the participation of the PLO . . . in any peace negotiations, and the need to end the military escalation in the Persian Gulf and the war between Iraq and Iran, in accordance with the U.N. Security Council resolution" (*L'Humanité*, 20 August).

Publications. The principal LCP publications are the Arabic-language daily newspaper *al-Nida'*, the weekly *al-Akhbar*, and the quarterly *al-Tariq*. The party also publishes the weekly *Kanch* (The call) in Armenian. These organs contain articles on Lebanese political and socioeconomic issues, international and Arab politics, and Marxist-Leninist ideology; they often disseminate the news of illegal communist parties in the Middle East, although in recent years their publication or distribution has been disrupted because of the prevailing insecurity in Beirut. The OCAL publishes the weekly *al-Hurriyya* jointly with the Democratic Front for the Liberation of Palestine, a component organization of the PLO. Both the LCP and the OCAL also publish booklets and pamphlets.

Auxiliary Organizations. A number of Lebanese communist and communist-dominated organizations have been mentioned in the news media from time to time; among these, the more significant seem to be the Communist Labor Organization, the Organization of Arab Communists, the Revolutionary Communist Party (Trotskyist), the Lebanese Communist Union, the World Peace Council in Lebanon, and various friendship committees with East European countries.

Augustus Richard Norton
United States Military Academy

Note: Views expressed in this article are those of the author, and do not necessarily represent the position of the U.S. government or any of its components.

Morocco

Population. 23,361,495
Party. Party of Progress and Socialism (Parti du progrès et du socialisme; PPS)
Founded. 1943 (PPS, 1974)
Membership. 3,000–5,000 (estimated)
General Secretary. 'Ali Yata
Politburo. 13 members: 'Ali Yata, Ismail Alaoui, Mohamed Ben Bella, Abdeslem Bourquia, Mohamed Rifi Chouaib, Abdelmajed Bouieb, Omar El Fassi, Thami Khyari, Abdallah Layachi, Simon Lévy, Mohamed Moucharik, Abdelwahed Souhail, Amina Lemrini
Secretariat. 4 members: Mohamed Rifi Chouaib, Omar El Fassi, Mohamed Moucharik, Abdallah Layachi
Central Committee. 71 members
Status. Legal
Last Congress. Fourth, 17–19 July 1987, in Casablanca
Last Election. 14 September 1984; 2.3 percent (official figure; estimate, less than 1 percent), 2 out of 306 seats
Auxiliary Organizations. No data
Publication. *Al-Bayane* (daily), French and Arabic editions; 'Ali Yata, director

Background. The Moroccan Communist Party (Parti communiste marocain), founded in 1943 as a branch of the French Communist Party, was banned by the French protectorate in 1952. After three years of open operations in independent Morocco, it was again banned in 1959. It was renamed the Party of Progress and Socialism (PPS), which was granted legal status in 1974. In the 1976 municipal elections, the PPS won thirteen seats on the city council of Casablanca. It participated in the Moroccan national elections in the spring of 1977 and won one seat in Parliament. In the last municipal elections, held in June 1983, the PPS won only two seats on the Casablanca city council. In Morocco's last parliamentary elections, held in September 1984, the PPS won two seats in Parliament, where the party is presently represented by Yata and Alaoui.

Leadership and Party Organization. The PPS's Fourth National Congress, held in July, re-elected 'Ali Yata as general secretary of the party, re-elected 56 of the 65 members elected to the Central Committee by the party's Third National Congress in 1983, and elected fifteen new members. The congress also elected a thirteen-member Politburo, which included the twelve men who had composed the previous Politburo plus Amina Lemrini, the first woman ever elected to the PPS Politburo. At the conclusion of the congress, the Central Committee elected a four-man Secretariat (including one new member, Politburo member Abdallah Layachi, who replaced Yata), a six-man Political Control Commission, and a four-man Financial Control Commission. (*al-Bayane*, 21 July.)

Domestic Party Affairs. Under the slogan, "With the people, for the triumph of the national cause, for democratic and social change," the PPS held its Fourth National Congress in Casablanca 17–19 July. This congress followed months of preparatory work by local PPS congresses in several Moroccan cities and by the Central Committee. About 1,300 PPS delegates participated in the congress, which was also attended by representatives of all major Moroccan political parties. Thirty-two foreign delegations were in attendance, including representatives from the communist parties of the Soviet Union, the People's Republic of China, seven East European countries, four West European countries, eight Arab countries, and four Asian countries. (Ibid., 19 July.) Yuri A. Sklyarov, chief of the Communist Party of the Soviet Union (CPSU) Central Committee Propaganda Department, headed a two-man Soviet delegation. Following the congress, Sklyarov met with Yata and other PPS leaders; he also had meetings in Rabat with leaders of two other Moroccan opposition parties. (Moscow, *Pravda*, in Russian, 23 July; *FBIS*, 12 August.) The ambassador of the People's Republic of China to Morocco led the Chinese Communist Party (CCP) delegation. The communist parties of Afghanistan, Nicaragua, and Cuba declined invitations to attend.

The Afghanistan issue was deliberately left off the congress agenda, presumably to avoid offending the Soviet Union. Nonetheless, several speakers angered the Soviet delegation by calling for an end to Soviet occupation of Afghanistan.

The PPS congress passed resolutions that declared the party's unequivocal support for Morocco's territorial claims to the Western Sahara and the Spanish-held enclaves of Ceuta and Melilla; criticized the Moroccan government's economic and social policies, including moves toward privatization and the liberalization of the economy, and rejected the recommendations in those directions of the World Bank and the International Monetary Fund; called for the release of Moroccan political prisoners and the return of those exiled; supported an international conference for the Middle East and backed the Palestine Liberation Organization (PLO) as the sole legitimate representative of the Palestinian people; and supported U.N. efforts to end the Persian Gulf war (*al-Bayane*, 20 July).

In his closing address on 19 July, General Secretary Yata spoke to other leaders of Moroccan political parties. He called for "an enlarged national anti-imperialist union" based on a coalition of the left in order to deal with pressing national issues. Yata condemned "sectarianism" and "ostracism" in favor of an approach by which all parties would "respect the opinions of others." He expressed his party's willingness to strengthen ties with the Socialist Union of Popular Forces (USFP), Morocco's major opposition party. (Ibid., 24 July.)

The PPS was encouraged by the speech delivered at the congress by USFP leader Abderrahim Bouabid. In his speech Bouabid said that Yata's report constituted the working base for the creation of a "progressive national front based on a medium-term program." He noted that the two parties' positions were almost identical and pledged to begin a dialogue with the PPS. The USFP leader saw no obstacle to the unification of democratic forces. (Ibid., 19 July.)

In the weeks following the July congress, the PPS broadened its call for a coalition from a popular front to a national front. The USFP Central Committee declared its party's interest in broad cooperation on basic national issues. The USFP responded to the PPS that it was open to dialogue but that it was absolutely necessary to specify the points, for good intentions by themselves are not enough. In the USFP view, each party would retain its individual character and its own positions on key popular questions. (Ibid., 4–5 October.)

The PPS then sent letters to several political parties in which it adopted the USFP's positions on five basic issues as its own. When PPS and USFP delegations met in August, disagreement emerged over the breadth and composition of the coalition. By this time, the PPS had returned to the position of its party congress in July, when it had launched the more narrow appeal to the USFP for the unification of "all patriotic and progressive forces." The PPS was not prepared to form a coalition with certain parties and unions, whereas the USFP favored joining forces with all who would support its basic platform. The PPS did not refuse a broader coalition but instead left open the option of pursuing the question further with the USFP leadership, though by the end of the year it had not done so.

Renewed efforts to form a broad coalition produced results at the parliamentary level in November. Encouraged by the USFP, the centrist Istiqlal Party cooperated for the first time with the PPS, and the PPS cooperated for the first time with the extreme left-wing Organization for Democratic and Popular Action (OADP). The four parties coordinated their positions in opposition to the government's five-year development program for the period 1988–1992. In December a unified stand among all these parties contributed to a parliamentary majority opposed to the government's 1988 budget.

In explaining the PPS vote against the 1988 budget, Yata declared in Parliament on 26 December that the government had presented "a weak contradictory budget, incapable of introducing the least progress or improvement . . . an austerity, deficit, stagnation budget." He complained that the budget lowered state investments and placed false hopes on the private sector to play the role of the driving force of development. Yata argued that the budget did not provide any measures to deal with growing and spreading unemployment and that it created no new jobs, although tens of thousands of young Moroccans needed work to assure their existence and future. (Ibid., 29 December.)

The PPS amendments to the 1988 budget bill were based on three main arguments. First, genuine economic development cannot take place without recognizing the demands of an enlargement of the domestic market and thus a noticeable improvement of workers' purchasing power. For this reason, the PPS proposed measures intended to produce a general salary increase of 60 percent. Second, austerity should not be imposed at the cost of investment but should apply instead to material and other expenses. The party thus called for an across-the-board cut of 5 percent in all ministry budgets. Third, because local industry needs to be protected, the PPS called for an increase in import duties to a minimum of 75 percent. (Ibid., 18 December.)

In the parliamentary debate on the education budget, Politburo member Ismail Alaoui presented his party's views on the serious problems of Moroccan education. One major source of these problems was that the expansion of education took place too quickly. This expansion should have combatted illiteracy in all age groups, which requires more schools and competent teachers. A second major source was the need to assure a quality education, which requires modernizing teaching methods. Alaoui predicted that the government's underfinanced education policy would lead to "the deterioration of the level of instruction, the deprivation of a large number of children of their right to go to school, and the granting of worthless diplomas." He warned that the government's proposed policy of relying on the private sector as an "alternative solution" would only lead to an impasse in education.

At several points during the year, the PPS protested the arrests of party members by local officials of the Ministry of Interior. In November seven party members in Tetuan province were arrested on "arbitrary" charges (ibid., 25 November). That same month the PPS protested the arrest and jailing, "under false and insignificant pretexts," of three party members in the province of Sidi Kacem (ibid., 28 November). Two weeks later another protest was lodged against the "arbitrary arrest" on 11 December of three party members by the same provincial official of the Ministry of Interior in Sidi Kacem province. In this instance, the three men were arrested on the pretext that the PPS was prohibited in the province. (Ibid., 13–14 December.)

The PPS daily newspaper, *al-Bayane*, resumed publication on 11 January following a suspension of more than two months. The newspaper had been suspended "indefinitely" on 31 October 1986 after Yata, who is also the director of *al-Bayane*, declared that henceforth the journal would criticize the government's foreign policy as well as its domestic policy. In November 1986 the National Moroccan Press Union protested and petitioned to the Ministry of Information for a lifting of the suspension. With a combined circulation of 10,000 for its French and Arabic editions, *al-Bayane* is the only communist party daily newspaper in a noncommunist country in Africa.

International Views, Positions, and Activities. During its Fourth Congress, the PPS stated that it had serious differences with the Soviet Union's positions on Afghanistan, Algeria, and the People's Republic of China. These differences, however, did not prevent the PPS from sending a two-member delegation led by Yata to Moscow to attend the International Party Congress held there by the CPSU on 4–5 November to celebrate the 70th anniversary of the October Revolution (ibid., 12 November). In December Politburo member Thami Khyari represented the PPS at the Twenty-sixth Congress of the French Communist Party (ibid., 11 December).

A few days later a PPS delegation headed by Secretariat member Layachi attended the Congress of Arab Opposition Parties held in Tripoli, Libya, 12–14 December. Along with other Moroccan opposition parties represented at that congress, the PPS lobbied in favor of a position on the Western Sahara issue supportive of Morocco, a positive evolution on this issue. The congress accepted unanimously the idea that it would be intolerable to admit the creation of a new state that would only impede the realization of Arab unity. The final resolution cited the necessity of respecting international decisions recommending the organization of a referendum in the Western Sahara to decide its future and end the bloodshed. (Ibid., 16 December.)

In a speech in Parliament on 25 December related to the foreign affairs budget, Yata stated the PPS's major views on foreign policy. In terms consistent with the party's position since 1974, he reaffirmed that for Moroccan foreign policy the most important question "remains the achievement of our territorial integrity." (Ibid., 27–28 December.) He then went on to discuss the four main "axes" of Moroccan foreign policy: North Africa; the Middle East; Africa; and East-West relations and disarmament.

Concerning North Africa, Yata asserted that Moroccan-Algerian relations are the key to the regional balance of power. He hailed as a positive step the 4 May meeting among King Hassan, Algerian president Chadli Benjedid, and Saudi King Fahd because this meeting helped to lessen tensions from the "prefabricated and artificial conflict over the Sahara." At the same time, improvement in this critical bilateral relation comes from internal evolution and transformation within Algeria. Yata called on the government to take more unilateral initiatives to promote unity among North African states and to welcome any serious effort in that direction. He argued for the need to go beyond criticisms of past Algerian policies and to support every improvement in Moroccan-Algerian relations. Improvement in these relations would help, on the one hand, to find a final solution to the Sahara conflict and, on the other, to open positive perspectives toward the achievement of North African unity. This unity would have a far-reaching effect in enabling the North African states to cope with the protectionist trade measures of the bloc of industrialized Western countries and the enlargement of the European Economic Community.

Concerning the Middle East, Yata argued that the organic relation of developments there to the rest of the Arab world required Moroccan foreign policy to work for the cause of the Palestinian people—the core of the Middle East conflict—and to support their just struggle. At the same time, it is necessary to support Arab union by struggling against dissensions and divisions in the Arab world. In the PPS view, Moroccan foreign policy ought to follow an orientation that is "anti-Zionist, anti-imperialist, and especially opposed to American imperialism." Yata called for the unconditional support of the Palestinian people in their struggle for the creation of an independent state with Jerusalem as its capital. He applauded King Hassan's efforts to organize an extraordinary summit of the Organization of the Islamic Conference's Higher Committee for the Liberation of al-Quds, the so-called Jerusalem Committee. The PPS leader hoped that this positive initiative would help raise Arab and Islamic solidarity to its highest level. This would be useful in putting pressure on the Zionists and their allies to accept the holding of an international Middle East peace conference under U.N. auspices, with the participation of members of the Security Council and all concerned parties, led by the PLO.

Yata also stated that the Gulf war constitutes a great danger for peace in the Middle East and weakens the energies of the countries in the region. In the PPS view, Morocco ought to adopt realistic and balanced positions destined to achieve peace and end the war between Iraq and Iran. At the same time, Morocco ought to work for the withdrawal of foreign naval fleets from Gulf waters, make every effort to convince the two warring parties to accept U.N. Resolution 598, and put pressure on those who refuse to end the war.

Turning to Africa, Yata asserted that Morocco needs to work untiringly to recover the place that it has lost among African states. He noted with approval Morocco's rapprochement with several sub-Saharan African countries. In the PPS view, this approach must now be broadened to all members of the Organization of African Unity (OAU), no matter how dogmatic or uninterested. The government must make efforts to convince African states of the justice of the Moroccan cause of territorial unity. At a time when recent developments have weakened the "mercenaries," Moroccan diplomacy should become more active and pass to the offensive to reveal the "deceitful campaign of the so-called Polisario." Yata argued that it is imperative to dislodge the Polisario from the OAU, so that Morocco could now reclaim its rightful place. This would enable the OAU to respect legitimacy and international credibility and to play its full role, which consists of serving African causes and coping with the crucial problems that threaten these causes. The PPS remains convinced of the possibility of achieving great victories in the African area if Moroccan foreign policy respects the principles of nonalignment and frees itself from all foreign dependence.

In the area of East-West relations and disarmament, Yata reaffirmed that the Washington summit in December between Mikhail Gorbachev and Ronald Reagan and the agreement to eliminate the category of medium-range missiles are among the most important positive events that the contemporary world has known since the end of World War II. The summit and the agreement came at a critical time when international tensions had reached a high level, especially in view of "the stubbornness of the United States and the obstinacy of its President to pursue the arms race and to install a nuclear system in space." Thus the agreement came as a great victory, not only for the Soviet Union and the United States but equally for all supporters of peace in the world. In addition, in the PPS view, this agreement opened new perspectives for reconciliation and international coexistence and confirmed that the possibility of eliminating nuclear arms is not an impossible act. The PPS also considers that the agreement is of historic importance and scope because it serves all of humanity, including the countries of the Third World and especially the countries of North Africa, which are quite near the medium-range missiles installed in Western Europe. This judgment is supported by the fact that the recent missile agreement will inaugurate a new era of security and peace.

Yata concluded by asserting, as he has so often in the past, that Moroccan foreign policy ought to be based on effective nonalignment, especially the refusal to adhere to any alliance. Thus the PPS totally opposes the military maneuvers in which Morocco participates jointly with forces of the Atlantic Alliance and especially with the United States, as recently happened in the Mediterranean Sea. Finally, the party is wholly against transplanting U.S. bases from Spain to Morocco, because such an operation could only be detrimental to Morocco.

John Damis
Portland State University

Saudi Arabia

Population. 14,904,794
Party. Communist Party of Saudi Arabia (CPSA)
Founded. 1975
Membership. Number unknown but believed negligible
General Secretary. Mahdi Habib
Other Spokesmen Noted Since 1979: Abd-al-Rahman Salih, Salim Hamid, Abu Abdallah, Muhsin Abdallah, Hamad al-Mubarak (Politburo member)
Status. Illegal
Last Congress. Second, August 1984
Last Election. N/a
Auxiliary Organizations. Saudi Peace and Solidarity Committee (affiliate of the World Peace Council and, apparently, the Afro-Asian Peoples' Solidarity Organization), Saudi Democratic Youth (affiliate of the World Federation of Democratic Youth), Workers' Federation of Saudi Arabia (associate member of the World Federation of Trade Unions), Democratic Women's League of Saudi Arabia (affiliate of the Women's International Democratic Federation)
Publication. *Tariq al-Qadyhin* (Path of the laborers)

General Secretary Mahdi Habib's article in the March issue of the *World Marxist Review* appears to have been the most comprehensive statement of CPSA domestic policy published in English during the year; it reiterated the call of the June 1986 Central Committee meeting "to put an end to the absolutist administration and establish a national democratic government that would be independent of world imperialism politically and economically." Perhaps a more moderate position was taken, however, in Habib's subdivision of the party's main enemies into better and worse components. He singled out the wing of the "ruling clan" headed by King Fahd as the more despotic and noted that there is unrest among "a fairly large section of the big bourgeoisie" (*WMR*, March). He then listed almost every other group as being a potential ally of the CPSA—that is, "workers, peasants, Bedouin masses, revolutionary intellectuals, petty bourgeoisie, and influential groups of the national bourgeoisie" (ibid.).

As in the past, Saudi Arabia's integration into the world capitalist system and the drop in world oil prices were assigned ultimate and immediate blame, respectively, for the country's present economic difficulties (ibid.). Although alleged overexpenditure on the military and security forces was again stressed, other budgetary "miscalculations"—such as the overemphasis of commerce, services, and the like at the expense of agriculture and nonpetroleum industrial production—were also mentioned (ibid.). The government was again pictured not only as economically inept but also as socially and politically repressive, with particular attention given to the status of women (ibid.). A short article by one Saad al-Almri in the February issue of the *World Marxist Review*, incidentally, played up the repression angle and noted that a human rights committee functioning inside the country is publicizing and agitating on the issue (see also *YICA*, 1987).

The CPSA Central Committee meetings from which documents were published during the year appear to have concentrated on foreign policy. The December 1986 meeting covered the whole Middle East: for example, the Iran-Iraq war, the Persian Gulf situation, and the Palestine and Lebanese crises. It put the United States, Britain, Israel, Iran, and the conservative Arab governments in one camp and the USSR, Yemen, the Palestine Liberation Organization (PLO), Syria, Libya, the Lebanese "patriotic movement," and the "peoples" of the Arabian Peninsula in the other (Prague, *IB*, October). It also described the alleged U.S. effort to dominate the Gulf area; called for the defense of South Yemen, Syria, and the "Lebanese people's cause"; advocated the building up of the PLO; and demanded the cessation of both the Iran-Iraq war and Amal attacks on Palestinian camps in Lebanon (ibid.). The June 1987 meeting document carried the same general line but was more narrowly focused on the U.S. presence in the Gulf and on blaming Iran for its hostilities with Iraq; it called for U.S. withdrawal and (again) a cessation of the war (Toronto, *IB*, September). These latter two points were made again in an August meeting of Arab East communist parties (including the CPSA) that was presumably held in Beirut (*Pravda*, 31 August).

Saudi communists were also moderately active elsewhere. Hamad al-Mubarak took part in a Nicosia symposium entitled "Religion Is for God, the Homeland Is for All," which was cosponsored by the *World Marxist Review* and *al-Nahj* (the Arab communist theoretical quarterly) at some time prior to August (*WMR*, August); he also represented the CPSA at the December congress of the French Communist Party (*L'Humanité*, 3 December). Muhsin Abdallah represented the party at the *World Marxist Review*'s May conference in Prague entitled "The October Revolution and the Main Problems of Our Age" (*WMR*, October). It is not known which of these men, if either one, is the CPSA's representative on the *WMR*'s Editorial Council.

The most important event of the year appeared to have been the admission of the Democratic Women's League of Saudi Arabia to the Women's International Democratic Federation (WIDF) at the latter's June congress in Moscow (*Women of the Whole World*, no. 3). Two members of this Saudi organization had attended the World Congress of Women, which immediately preceded the WIDF congress in the same city (World Congress of Women, *Preliminary List of Participants*, p. 36).

Wallace H. Spaulding
McLean, Virginia

Syria

Population. 11,147,763
Party. Syrian Communist Party (al-Hizb al-Shuyu'i al-Suri; SCP)
Founded. 1924 (as a separate party in 1944)
Membership. 5,000 (estimated)
General Secretary. Khalid Bakhdash (75); deputy general secretary, Yusuf Faysal (61)
Politburo. Khalid Bakhdash, Yusuf Faysal, Ibrahim Bahri, Khalid Hammami, Maurice Salibi, Umar Siba'i, Daniel Ni'mah, Zuhayr Abd al-Sammad, Ramu Farkha, Ramu Shaykhu (list of names not necessarily complete or up-to-date)
Secretariat. No data
Central Committee. Nabih Rushaydat, Muhammad Khabbad, Issa Khuri, R. Kurdi, A. W. Rashwani; other names unknown
Status. Component of the ruling National Progressive Front (NPF)
Last Congress. Sixth, July 1986
Last Election. February 1986; 8 out of 195 (presidential election in 1985)
Auxiliary Organizations. No data
Publication. *Nidal al-Sh'ab*

The Party of the Lebanese People, founded in 1924, was one of several Marxist or quasi-Marxist groups that appeared in Syria and Lebanon during the early 1920s. It united with two other factions in 1925 to form the Communist Party of Syria and Lebanon (CPSL). The Syrian and Lebanese parties separated in 1944, soon after the two countries were officially proclaimed independent, but they maintained close ties with each other.

The CPSL and the subsequent SCP underwent alternate periods of toleration or legality and of suppression. The SCP often emphasized nationalism and reform and played down revolutionary ideology. It gained a considerable following and a membership that may have reached 10,000 by 1945. The party became quite influential between 1955 and 1958 but suffered a serious blow with the creation of the United Arab Republic and the subsequent suppression. Seemingly no longer a serious threat and following a foreign policy that often paralleled that of the Baathist regime, it gained quasi-legal status after 1966 and finally joined the Baath-dominated NPF in 1972.

The Syrian communist movement has undergone several schisms in recent years. Riyad al-Turk, who was chosen general secretary of one breakaway group in 1974, has been imprisoned without trial since 1980 and subjected to beatings and torture. Three members of the proscribed Communist Party Political Bureau have been imprisoned without trial since 1981. Yusuf Murad, a former member of the SCP Central Committee, formed another group, the Base Organization, in 1980. There is no recent information on any of these groups.

Leadership and Party Organization. Little is known about the dynamics of the SCP's leadership except that General Secretary Bakhdash has long been the dominant figure. There have been some divisions among the top leadership; for example, Politburo member Ni'mah (now a representative of the SCP on the Central Command of the NPF) broke with the party temporarily during the early 1970s. There were also some reports of dissent within the party during 1986. No information is available on meetings of party organs during the year.

Domestic Party Affairs. The few available statements on domestic matters during the year indicate continuing distaste for the socioeconomic aspects of the Baathist regime. Thus in a speech delivered in Moscow, Bakhdash spoke of Syria's "great economic difficulties" and contrasted the condition of "the workers, peasants, and working masses" with that of "the parasitic bourgeoisie and the bureaucratic apparatus" who are becoming "increasingly rich." Seeming to imply that his party's alliance with the Baath is the result of Moscow's wishes, Bakhdash added, "If we proceeded only from our innermost wish in formulating our policy, we would be in opposition. We have repeatedly declared this quite frankly." (Moscow, *Sovetskaia Rossiia*, 4 November; *FBIS*, 6 November.) In a statement at a symposium in Prague, Politburo member Hammami praised military spending by "progressive regimes" for resisting "imperialist aggression" but added that this "has also negative effects both on national economic progress and on class struggle. The ruling patriotic bourgeoisie tries to quench the flames of that struggle with an arms build-up." (*WMR*, September.)

Auxiliary and Front Organizations. Little information (none of it current) on auxiliary organizations is available. The SCP presumably participates in such groups as the Arab-Soviet Friendship Society, the Syrian Committee for Solidarity with Asian and African Countries, the National Council of Peace Partisans in Syria, and the Syrian-Bulgarian Friendship Society.

The present Syrian regime is officially based on the NPF, which includes the SCP, the Arab Socialist Party, and the Socialist Union, in addition to the dominant Baath Party, which is non-Marxist. This does not mean that the SCP has any significant influence but rather that it has for the time being more or less abandoned revolution in favor of a largely formal vote. The quiet role of the regime's partner also conforms to the wishes of the USSR, whose foreign policy tends to parallel Syria's in many respects. An article by V. Peresada in *Pravda* on 17 April (*FBIS*, 22 April) praised Damascus's staunch anti-imperialist policy as the primary reason for its prestige in the Arab world, which is disproportionate to the size of its population and territory, and—in contrast to the views of Bakhdash that were cited above—singled out the country's "progressive" social and economic policies "in the working people's interests," adding that "cooperation between the ruling party and other [NPF] parties . . . is a characteristic feature of internal political life."

However, Damascus and Moscow are far from being in accord on all foreign policy issues, including Syrian support for Shiite Lebanese Amal forces battling with the Palestine Liberation Organization (PLO) and with other factions friendly to the USSR, such as the Lebanese Communist Party. The USSR was said to be "particularly annoyed" with Syria during the year over this matter (London, *Foreign Report*, February). Another source of discord is Syria's conflict with Iraq and its support for Iran in the Iran-Iraq War. According to "Arab diplomatic sources," Arnold Ryuytel, deputy chairman of the Supreme Soviet Presidium, dealt at length with the need for reconciliation with Iraq during his talks with Syrian officials in June (Abu Dhabi, *al-Ittihad*, 19 June; *FBIS*, 22 June).

The SCP has had eight seats in the Syrian parliament since the 1986 elections, and there are two communists in the cabinet. The SCP is also represented in the central leadership of the NPF.

As usual, during 1987 there were numerous exchanges of visits between delegations of Syrian state and Baath party officials and delegations of state and communist party officials from the USSR. President Hafiz al-Assad headed a delegation that visited Moscow during 23–25 April and held talks with General Secretary Mikhail Gorbachev. The delegation included Hammami, the SCP member of the NPF central leadership, and Ni'mah, the deputy premier for economic affairs and SCP Politburo member. (Damascus, *Syria Times*, 27 April.) In February, Karen Brutents, deputy chief of the International Department in the CPSU Central Committee, held talks in Damascus with Baathist assistant general secretary Abdullah al-Ahmar on relations between the two parties (Damascus Domestic Service, 2 February; *FBIS*, 3 February).

A delegation from the USSR's Supreme Soviet visited Syria in June (*Izvestiia*, 18 June; *FBIS*, 19 June). Konstantin Katushev, chairman of the USSR State Committee for Foreign Economic Relations, headed a delegation to Damascus in June that concluded agreements on economic and technical cooperation (Damascus Domestic Service, 19 June; *FBIS*, 22 June). A delegation of Syrian military officers visited Moscow on 9–14 June (Moscow, *Krasnaia zvezda*, 17 June; *FBIS*, 22 June). Interior Minister Muhammad Ghabbash led a delegation to Moscow in July (Damascus Domestic Service, 26 July; *FBIS*, 27 July). A delegation led by Yuli Vorontsov, first deputy foreign minister of the USSR, was in Damascus in August (Damascus Domestic Service, 1 August; *FBIS*, 3 August). A Soviet trade delegation led by Vladimir Burmistrov, the first deputy minister of foreign trade, attended the opening ceremonies of the Damascus International Fair later in the same month (Damascus, Sanaa, 17 August; *FBIS*, 19 August). A Baath party delegation also visited the USSR in August (Damascus, Sanaa, 25 August; *FBIS*, 25 August), as did another delegation led by People's Assembly speaker Mahmud al-Zu'abi (Damascus Television Service, 25 August; *FBIS*, 26 August). Yuri Yelchenko of the CPSU Central Committee headed a delegation that participated in a seminar on the October Revolution in Damascus in September and was received by al-Ahmar (Damascus Domestic Service, 30 September; *FBIS*, 5 October). A delegation headed by Yuri Khomenko, deputy chairman of the USSR State Planning Committee, held talks on industrial and technical matters with Syrian officials in Damascus in October (Damascus Domestic Service, 3 October; *FBIS*, 5 October). Nikolai Vasileyev, the Soviet minister of land reclamation and water resources, visited Syria in October (Damascus

Domestic Service, 28 October; *FBIS*, 30 October). A delegation representing "socialist and democratic Syrian parties" participated in the celebration of the 70th anniversary of the October Revolution (Damascus Domestic Service, 4 November; *FBIS*, 6 November).

A highly publicized symbol of Syrian-Soviet cooperation was the presence of a Syrian in a Soviet space flight in July. Syria continued to obtain large quantities of the Soviet Union's most advanced weapons. The two countries have been bound to each other by a treaty of cooperation since 1980.

Syrian-Soviet cooperation is not necessarily related to the official existence of the "national front" government in Damascus. Its basis is purely pragmatic, not ideological, and informed observers seem to be unanimous in rejecting the idea that Syria is a Soviet satellite.

There were also exchanges of visits with socialist countries other than the USSR. President Assad visited Romania for talks with President Nicolae Ceauşescu in November (*FBIS*, 1 December). Isam al-Qadi, a member of the Syrian-backed Baathist National (pan-Arab) Command, visited Sofia for talks with Bulgarian officials in January (Damascus Domestic Service, 21 January; *FBIS*, 18 March). Foreign Minister Abd al-Halim Khaddam met with Chinese leaders in Beijing during the same month (Beijing, Xinhua Domestic Service, 13 January; *FBIS*, 14 January). Delegations of both the Korean Worker's Party and the Vietnamese Communist Party were in Damascus during February for talks with their Baathist counterparts (Damascus Domestic Service, 8 February; *FBIS*, 9 February). A Bulgarian delegation visited Damascus in April (Damascus, Sanaa, 12 April; *FBIS*, 13 April). Heinz Kessler, German Democratic Republic (GDR) minister of defense and member of the Socialist Unity Party of Germany Politburo, held talks with President Assad in May (*Neues Deutschland*, 21 May). There were visits to Damascus in August by North Korean vice-premier and foreign minister Kim Yong-nam (Damascus Domestic Service, 1 August; *FBIS*, 3 August); Poland's Tadeusz Mlynczak, chairman of the Polish Democratic Party (Damascus Domestic Service, 2 August; *FBIS*, 3 August); a Cambodian People's Revolutionary Party delegation led by Yos Son, chairman of the party's Foreign Relations Committee; and a Czech delegation headed by Deputy Premier Svatopluk Potac (Damascus Domestic Service, 26 August; *FBIS*, 26 August). Delegations from the GDR and Bulgaria were in Damascus at the end of September (*Syria Times*, 1 October).

As for nonruling communist parties, President Assad received a Lebanese Communist Party delegation headed by General Secretary George Hawi on 21 January (Damascus, Sanaa, 21 January; *FBIS*, 22 January). In February, Ali al-Tijani al-Tayyib Babikar, a member of the Sudanese Communist Party Central Committee, met with al-Ahmar and discussed ways to promote the relationship between their two parties (Damascus, Sanaa, 8 February; *FBIS*, 9 February). Muhammad Harmel, general secretary of the Tunisian Communist Party, was in Damascus in September and met with al-Ahmar (*Syria Post*, 1 October).

International Views, Positions, and Activities. Hammami, who, in addition to his other offices, is the SCP representative on the *World Marxist Review* editorial council, participated in an international symposium sponsored by that publication on the "U.S. Policy of Neoglobalism, the Military-Industrial Complex, Contemporary Militarism and the Working Class" in Prague (*WMR*, September). He also participated in a *World Marxist Review* conference in Prague on the October Revolution (*WMR*, October).

The SCP was represented at a meeting of eight communist parties of the Arab world in October 1986 (*IB*, January). The eight parties issued a joint statement condemning the United States for thwarting the "concrete realistic proposals" made by Gorbachev at the Reykjavik summit meeting with President Ronald Reagan and for dashing the hopes of "the peoples of the world." The USSR was described as the leader of "the forces of global peace and freedom." A call was issued "for greater resistance to the aggressive policy of the United States and its Israeli ally, abetted and directly promoted by Arab reaction." The statement gave special attention to "the perilous build-up in the campaign mounted by imperialism and Zionism against Syria and the Arab liberation movement" and called for "solidarity with fraternal Syria." (*IB*, January.)

An article by Hammami in the *World Marxist Review* (October) dealt with Israeli expansionism and stressed the annexation of the Golan Heights as "a glaring violation of international law" made possible by "unlimited U.S. support" and Egypt's "truckling policy." Hammami also dealt with the anti-Israeli demonstrations held in the Golan Heights in April, which he called a pretext for further repression. He called for Palestinian self-determination, leading to an independent state under PLO leadership, and specified that an international peace conference is "the road" to this solution.

Glenn E. Perry
Indiana State University

Tunisia

Population. 7,561,461
Party. Tunisian Communist Party (Parti communiste tunisien; PCT)
Founded. 1934
Membership. 2,000 (estimated); PCT claims 4,000
Composition. Unknown
General Secretary. Muhammad Harmel (58)
Politburo. 9 members
Secretariat. No data
Central Committee. 22 members
Status. Legal
Last Congress. Ninth, 12–14 June, in Tunis
Last Election. 2 November 1986; boycotted by PCT
Auxiliary Organization. Tunisian Communist Youth
Publication. *Al-Tariq al-Jadid* (New Path), weekly

The PCT was founded in 1920 as a branch of the French Communist Party and became independent in 1934. The banning of the PCT in 1963 formalized a single-party state under the direction of the Destourian Socialist Party (PSD). In July 1981, the government lifted the ban on the PCT, ending the party's eighteen-year period of clandestine existence. The PCT was the only opposition party allowed to operate openly from July 1981 to November 1983, when President Habib Bourguiba legalized two other opposition parties (see *YICA* 1984).

Leadership and Party Organization. The PCT's Ninth National Congress in June re-elected Harmel as general secretary. It elected an enlarged nine-member Politburo to replace the six-member Politburo elected by the Eighth Congress in 1981 and a 22-member Central Committee to replace the 12-member Central Committee elected in 1981. (Moscow, *Pravda*, 16 June.) Harmel contributed an article to the September issue of the *World Marxist Review*, and Politburo member Muhammad al-Naf'a has also occasionally contributed to the *Review*.

Domestic Party Affairs. The PCT held its Ninth National Congress in Tunis 12–14 June. This was the party's first legal congress since the Seventh Congress in 1962, which was held before the PCT was banned by the Bourguiba government in 1963. (The Eighth Congress was held in February 1981, five months before the government lifted the ban on the party.) One hundred fifty-two PCT delegates participated in the congress, which was also attended by representatives of all legal Tunisian opposition parties and labor unions. (*al-Bayane*, 24 June.) About twenty delegations from other communist parties and national liberation movements, including the Palestine Liberation Organization, also attended. Victor I. Smirnov, a member of the CPSU Central Committee and second secretary of the Communist Party of Moldavia, headed the Soviet delegation. (*Pravda*, 13 July.)

The congress delegates approved a Central Committee report presented by General Secretary Harmel, which analyzed Tunisia's economic crisis and criticized the government's reform program that "far from remedying the economic structural crisis ills, is adding still new ones" (*IB*, September). The report blamed the International Monetary Fund (IMF) for its eagerness to pressure domestic demand both in consumption and in investment. It denounced the IMF's long-term intentions of advancing capitalism; liberalizing the economy by eliminating controls on prices, imports, and exports; deregulating industry and services; and revising Tunisian labor law to allow employers more advantages. The report rejected the private sector, profit, and market laws as the solution to the country's economic crisis and advocated rescheduling debt repayment as an emergency measure. (Ibid.)

In addition, the congress adopted a new party charter to govern the party's current legal operation. It also passed a resolution on peace and disarmament that implicitly backed Soviet peace initiatives, a resolution of solidarity with national liberation movements, and several resolutions to build up the party's organization and forge a broad democratic front in the country. (*IB*, September.)

In March the PCT took a position against that month's major government crackdown against Islamic fundamentalism within Tunisia, which the government attributed to support from Iran. Along with other Tunisian opposition parties that are critical of Islamic fundamentalists, the PCT urged the government to conduct a dialogue with the Islamic Tendency Movement (MTI), a mainstream Islamic political organization. This followed the arrest of the MTI leader and three weeks of government security actions against Islamic fundamentalists throughout Tunisia. (*CSM*, 31 March.) As is the case with all other important political groupings in the country, PCT members belong to the Tunisian League of Human Rights (founded in 1977), the oldest and most effective human rights organization in the Arab world; the party is represented on the league's 25-member executive board (ibid., 27 April).

Along with other opposition papers, the PCT weekly, *al-Tarik al-Jadid*, was allowed to resume publication in October, thus lifting a suspension imposed in May 1986 (see *YICA*, 1986). In the newspaper's first issue of the year, the party strongly criticized the Bourguiba government's economic policy, arguing that purchasing power within the country, in decline since 1983, was being ravaged. This situation, caused by the long freeze on salaries and the 1986 devaluation of the Tunisian dinar, requires an increase in salaries and bonuses much greater than the 5 percent approved by the government. (*al-Tarik al-Jadid*, 31 October–6 November.)

The PCT also protested the government's continuing harassment of the labor union movement. In the party's view, this harassment was intended to prevent labor representatives from participating in negotiations and to substitute government committees for union representatives, which prevent workers from expressing their demands and defending their rights. The PCT argued that this confirmed that the government takes decisions without considering that wage earners are part of production. To solve the labor issue, the party called for respect of democratic rules and the legality, independence, and representative function of the union.

The most important change in Tunisian politics since independence in 1956 occurred on 7 November when Prime Minister Zine el-Abidine Ben Ali deposed Bourguiba, Tunisia's 84-year-old president for life who had ruled and dominated the country for the 31 years since independence from France. Acting with the concurrence of the vast majority of senior government officials and opposition leaders, Ben Ali moved quickly and effectively after a medical commission had declared Bourguiba mentally and physically incompetent. The new president, who had the backing of the army and the police, continued to serve as minister of the interior. After the deposition, Ben Ali promised to liberalize political laws to allow more freedom for parties, end some press censorship, and run an open and democratic government. (*NYT*, 10 November.)

The party responded immediately to the change of government. Even before knowing the details of the new government's program for more democracy, the PCT Central Committee issued a statement on 7 November, the day of Bourguiba's deposition. Discussing the "mixed record" of the Bourguiba years, the statement stressed that "the negative practices, choices, and orientations led to a very serious crisis and to a very dangerous deterioration of the situations in all levels, including the way of managing state affairs." (*al-Tarik al-Jadid*, 14–21 November.) It welcomed Ben Ali's announcement that there was a need to involve the Tunisian people in the management of the country, to provide a democratic environment, to adopt political pluralism, to give legitimacy to law, to eliminate injustice and oppression, and to find a peaceful solution to the issue of presidential succession. The PCT then called for a genuine break with the old infallible mentality, with the phenomenon of one-man rule, and with the monopoly of opinion and decisionmaking by a single party, organization, or person. At the same time, the party called for measures to purify the political and social atmosphere, to declare a general legal pardon, to ban all unjust laws and decisions, and to eliminate injustice imposed on workers to allow them to benefit from their legal and, especially, union rights.

A few days later, the party newspaper offered a more detailed analysis of the change in government. It joined other political parties and labor unions in expressing the positiveness of the change and applauded Ben Ali's statement of the necessity to remove government officials who abuse their power and mismanage public funds. The PCT warned, however, that statements and promises are not enough to move the country from a situation full of dangers to a new situation of improved political life based on political pluralism. The ideal would be to abandon Tunisia's recent past while preserving and improving on its positive elements. The party specifically cited the need to renew and improve the national media as the worst example of those who praise leadership because they want to stay in power. It called on the new government to end nepotism and to make the Tunisian labor movement more active so that it can play its full role in a free and independent context. The PCT expressed its readiness to participate in building among all concerned elements a new relationship based on dialogue, exchange of views, and mutual respect.

The PCT Central Committee met again on 21–23 November to examine further the country's new political situation. A statement issued at the conclusion of these sessions noted the "positive substance" of the new government's first steps. The statement also acknowedged the need to mobilize the efforts of all the country's national forces to eradicate negative aspects of the past in all areas. (Moscow, *Pravda*, in Russian, 27 November; *FBIS*, 1 December).

As a first step in this direction, a PCT delegation met on 24 November with a delegation from the Movement of Democratic Socialists, the major opposition force in Tunisia. The two delegations noted the similarity of their parties' viewpoints on the positiveness of the democratic orientation of the change in government and on the necessity of a complete national dialogue to lead to the mobilization of all those concerned by this positive change. (*al-Tarik al-Jadid*, 28 November–4 December.)

Two days later, Harmel met with Hedi Baccouche, the new prime minister in the Ben Ali government. The meeting was the occasion for a general discussion of a broad range of issues as an introduction to a full dialogue between the government and the political parties. The party newspaper described the meeting as "frank and serious." Consistent with the Central Committee's statement of 7 November, the meeting encouraged the continuation of national dialogue in order to deepen the consideration of all existing affairs.

International Views, Positions, and Activities. Harmel led a two-member PCT delegation to Moscow to attend the international party congress held there 4–5 November by the CPSU to celebrate the 70th anniversary of the October Revolution (ibid., 31 October–6 November). During a meeting with the Soviet Academy of Agricultural Science on 4 November, Harmel delivered a speech praising the progress of the present Soviet generation in advancing the goals of the October Revolution. He stated that the PCT follows the policy of *perestroika* (restructuring) with great interest. (*al-Tarik al-Jadid*, 7–13 November.)

John Damis
Portland State University

Yemen:
People's Democratic Republic of Yemen

Population. 2,351,131
Party. Yemeni Socialist Party (al-Hizb al-Ishtirakiya al-Yamaniya; YSP)
Founded. 1978
Membership. 31,000 (including candidate members)
President of the Presidium of the Supreme People's Council. Haydar Abu Bakr al'Attas (elected November 1986)
General Secretary. 'Ali Salim al-Bayd (elected 7 February 1986)
Assistant General Secretary. Salim Salih Muhammad (elected 7 February 1986)
Politburo. 11 members: Salih Munassar al-Siyayli, Salim Salih Muhammad, Haydar Abu Bakr al-'Attas, 'Ali Salim al-Bayd, Yasin Sa'id Nu'man, Muhammad Sa'id 'Abdullah, Sa'id Salih Salim, Fadl Muhsin 'Abdullah, Abdullah Ahmad al-Khamiri, Salih 'Ubayd Ahmad, Muhammad Haydara Masdus. 3 candidate members: Haytham Qasim Tahir, Sayf Sa'il Khalid, Salim Muhammad Jubran.
Central Committee. 77 members
Status. Ruling party
Last Congress. Fourth, 20–21 June
Last Election. 1986; all candidates YSP approved
Publication. *Al-Thawra*, YSP Central Committee weekly

The People's Democratic Republic of Yemen (PDRY)—also known as South Yemen, Southern Yemen, or (as is preferred by its government) Democratic Yemen—has pursued a path of "scientific socialism" in domestic policy and close alignment with the Soviet Union and other Eastern bloc countries in foreign affairs. The YSP, heir to the independence-winning National Liberation Front (NLF), is the only legal party in the state and has had no significant opposition since independence in 1967. The party itself, however, has been riven with factionalism and infighting. Internal power struggles reached climaxes in 1969, 1971, 1978, 1980, and the civil war of January 1986.

The constitution (adopted in 1970) specifies that the Supreme People's Council (SPC) is the highest authority. Elections to the council were first held in 1978, and members are elected for five-year terms. The SPC elects the president and eleven to seventeen members of the Presidium, to which the SPC's authority is delegated when the SPC is not in session. The SPC also elects the prime minister and his cabinet and the members of the Supreme Court.

As in other socialist states, real power rests within the party. During the 1970s, several efforts were made to transform the ruling NLF into a true Marxist organization, and several other small legal parties were incorporated into it. Neither the Popular Democratic Union, a local communist party founded in Aden in 1961, nor the Vanguard Party (Baathist) had seriously challeged the NLF for power. The First Congress of the YSP was held in October 1972 following the ouster of the party's moderates, and another was held in October 1980 after the defeat of the ultraradical faction. The Third Congress took place in October 1985 amid considerable tension, and the Fourth Congress had to be postponed until June 1987 because of continuing fundamental differences.

Successive struggles for supremacy within the party have eliminated factions from both the right and the far left, as well as most of the original party leaders who fought in the war for independence. In January 1986, the country's pragmatic leader, 'Ali Nasir Muhammad (al-Hasani; prime minister, 1971–1985 and president, 1980–1986), sought to preserve his deteriorating authority by eliminating his doctrinaire left-wing rivals. Although his supporters managed to kill four of the last five prominent founding members of the party including former President and former party leader 'Abd al-Fattah Isma'il (al-Jawfi; ousted from power in 1980), 'Ali Nasir's opponents eventually won the resulting civil war. 'Ali Nasir, the fifth of these historic leaders, was forced to flee with his supporters; he maintains homes in the Yemen Arab Republic (YAR, North Yemen), Ethiopia, and Damascus. Documents introduced in court during 1987 put the cost of the January 1986 fighting at $115 million and the lives lost at 4,330.

The remaining nucleus of the Adeni regime, reduced to party lightweights and relatively unknown technocrats, has followed a pragmatic course and pursued many of 'Ali Nasir's policies, especially in foreign affairs, while refusing any dialogue with the exiled president. The effectiveness of the PDRY's leadership continued to be challenged by a variety of potentially serious divisions.

Internal Divisions. Despite twenty years of efforts to create a Marxist society, tribal and regional loyalties and enmities were still ingrained, as the 1986 fighting clearly illustrated. Although a number of Hadramis rose to high positions, including President Haydar Abu Bakr al-'Attas, Prime Minister Yasin Sa'id Nu'man, and YSP general secretary 'Ali Salim al-Bayd, the last round of fighting seems to have narrowed the struggle for effective power to the contending tribes of al-Yafa' and al-Dali'. Leaders of North Yemeni origin declined in number and influence.

Ideological differences remained endemic. The intensity of dispute abated, as did the violent climate of confrontation between opposing factions prevailing before 1986, thanks to the death and/or exile of many long-standing personal rivals. The continuation of policies of economic liberalization introduced by 'Ali Nasir, such as the acceptance of private sector initiatives in agriculture and fisheries to offset unproductive cooperatives and the encouragement of Western investment, were attacked by doctrinaire party members. Determination of the proper balance between central authority and local autonomy was also a matter of dispute.

A renewed emphasis on adherence to Marxist-Leninist principles, with the assistance of Soviet advisers assigned to party organizations, served to both debunk the previous regime and legitimize the present regime. From another angle, South Yemen is not immune to an Islamic resurgence fueled, in part, by Iranian and Saudi propaganda and by workers returning from abroad; so far, such activities have been easily controlled.

Another division was between party stalwarts and the younger, better-educated technocrats. The purges through the years and the 1986 decimation have attenuated the ranks of party cadres and left party leadership in the hands of lesser-known individuals. Technocrats such as President al-'Attas and Prime Minister Nu'man were admitted only recently to the higher echelons of government and party. To some extent, these lines parallel those between the remaining hard-liners, who wish to maintain the radical internal policies of former President 'Abd al-Fattah Isma'il and to consolidate ties with the Soviet Union, and the pragmatists, who emphasize development and the need for foreign aid from the Arab oil states.

Continuing tensions in the PDRY ruling establishment were indicated by an interview with ʻAli Nasir Muhammad in November. He identified five "traitors" to him (by implication, moderates losing ground in the Aden power struggle): President Haydar al-ʻAttas, who broke off contact with ʻAli Nasir during the January 1986 fighting when he saw he was losing; Prime Minister Yasin Saʻid Nuʻman, who changed sides during the fighting for "personal reasons"; ʻAbd al-ʻAziz al-Dali, who also changed sides during the fighting for "personal reasons," remained foreign minister because of his ties to both sides but found his position in Aden to be increasingly precarious (he lost his Politburo seat in early September); Muhammad Haydara Masdus, who had urged ʻAli Nasir to make a "decisive move" but switched when the fighting turned against ʻAli Nasir; and Salih Munassar al-Siyayli, who pulled off the remarkable switch of serving for five years as ʻAli Nasir's head of security to serving as minister of interior in the new regime. Nevertheless, Siyayli continued to face accusations of sympathy for the losing side.

Although 1987 ended with the uneasy balance between competing factions intact, there were other indications that the position of the pragmatists was being eroded. Hard-liners in senior positions appeared to find common cause with the many young party people in the provinces and army garrisons who were committed Marxists, popularly known as al-Fattahiyin (followers of the late ʻAbd al-Fattah Ismaʻil). The cabinet was reshuffled on 4 November: ʻAbd al-Qawi Muthanna Hadi was named minister of installations and housing, and Dr. Ahmad Nasir al-Danani replaced Mahmud Saʻid Madhi, accused by some of being an ʻAli Nasir supporter, as minister of finance. On 28 December the Central Committee promoted the three candidate members of the Politburo to full member status and added three new candidate members. Among the latter was Colonel Haytham Qasim Tahir, the increasingly powerful first deputy defense minister, army chief of staff, and a former follower of ʻAbd al-Fattah Ismaʻil—rumor had it that the Soviets would support him in a military takeover to put an end to intraparty rivalries.

General Party Congress. The strains in the Aden regime during 1987 were bound up with two potentially disruptive events. The first of these was a general party congress. Although the previous congress had been held in October 1985, the severe disorder in party ranks—bloated by the recruitment of supporters by various factions—made convening a new congress necessary. At the same time, the contentious issues of what to do about the thousands of exiles and the matter of reconciliation forced postponement of the congress until more than a year after the civil war. Much of the dispute appeared to have been settled in the rounds of local and regional party elections that preceded the Fourth YSP Congress 20–21 June 1987. The 345 delegates quickly dismissed 26 full and candidate members of the Central Committee for their involvement in the 1986 events and then appointed 25 individuals to candidate membership in the Central Committee. It appeared that an anticipated hard-liner/pragmatist clash had been avoided, at least for the moment.

One product of the congress was detailed analysis of the party's course from 1978 to 1987. Ostensibly critical of both right-wing and far-left "opportunists," the document castigated ʻAli Nasir Muhammad for deviating from party doctrine, for changing the party's class composition to infiltrate loyal supporters and fellow tribesmen, and for condoning corruption. The liberalization measures adopted at the 1985 congress were described in the document as a necessary capitulation to the right-wing's deviations to avoid an armed clash.

Relations With ʻAli Nasir Muhammad and His Supporters. A second potentially explosive issue pitted those who favored reconciliation with the January 1986 exiles against those who rejected their return. The regime claimed that ʻAli Nasir's supporters were continuing to provoke incidents; it reported an exchange of gunfire and the interception of a booby-trapped vehicle in Shabwa governorate in February and the capture of an armed group of infiltrators in Shabwa in May. These efforts were said to be the work of former Minister of State Security Ahmad Musaʻid Husayn. Defections from Aden continued as well. In early January, Moscow was said to have prevented some 300 military officers in the Soviet Union from joining ʻAli Nasir's forces in Sanaa (the YAR capital), and ten students at a military college in Baku reportedly were expelled to Aden after voicing opposition to the Aden regime. The deputy minister of justice (the former dean of Aden University's law faculty) defected to Sanaa via Moscow on 11 October.

At the same time, rumors of reconciliation talks between ʻAli Nasir and the Aden government continued to circulate. Kuwait, through its minister of state for foreign affairs, conducted an intensive mediation effort in February and March. 'Attas publicly acknowledged this effort, as well as previous Sudanese and subsequent YAR ventures, while denying press reports that he had met with 'Ali Nasir in Sanaa in September. 'Attas continued to insist that negotiations must be limited to the return of refugees under the general amnesty and that there could be no reconciliation with 'Ali Nasir.

From exile, 'Ali Nasir returned the harsh rhetoric of the Adeni regime, claiming the economy was in disarray and that Aden did not wish the refugees to return because they would upset the balance of power. The number of refugees has been estimated variously at 30,000 (by YAR President 'Ali 'Abdullah Salih), 35,000–60,000 (by other unidentified YAR officials), 85,000 (by YAR Deputy Prime Minister and Foreign Minister 'Abd al-Karim al-Iryani), and 200,000 (by 'Ali Nasir). President 'Ali 'Abdullah Salih put the total emigration from the PDRY to North Yemen over the years at 400,000. In a follow-up to the October 1986 exit from the Ethiopian embassy in Aden of 'Ali Nasir's son and six other compatriots, the PDRY government admitted in October 1987 that three South Yemenis still remained in the embassy.

The hard-liners in Aden, led by YSP assistant general secretary Salim Salih Muhammad and Minister of State Security Sa'id Salih Salim, opposed the amnesty and insisted on a show trial to punish their 1986 opponents. The quarrel had mixed results. Between January 1986 and June 1987, the Aden government claimed to have released all 5,000 of its admitted detainees. At the same time, however, the hard-liners succeeded in forcing the trial of 142 individuals, 48 of them in absentia.

The trial was completed in October but sentencing was postponed reportedly because of disagreements over the sentences. On 13 December, death sentences were announced for 'Ali Nasir and 34 supporters, including 16 of those in detention in Aden; another 85 defendants and "fugitives" were given prison sentences of five to fifteen years. A full amnesty was proclaimed for all others. The death sentences were announced despite pressure from North Yemen and other Arab states, and five people reportedly were executed on 29 December, including the former air force commander and the former head of 'Ali Nasir's personal guards. A number of sentences, including some death sentences, subsequently were reduced.

Foreign Affairs. Relations with the Soviet Union appeared to be gradually improving, although indications continued that Moscow was not entirely convinced of the long-term stability of the present PDRY regime. YSP General Secretary 'Ali Salim al-Bayd visited Moscow frequently; Mikhail Gorbachev, his host at a state dinner in February, noted the "tragic events" of January 1986 and expressed confidence in the ability of the YSP "to rectify mistakes that had been made." In reply, al-Bayd praised Soviet-Yemeni friendship and promised that "we shall spare no effort to solve the refugee problem." He returned to Moscow in October for a vacation, and gave a speech at the Kremlin on 3 November before a meeting of the CPSU Central Committee and the Supreme Soviet on the occasion of the 70th anniversary of the October Revolution.

Other PDRY civilians making the trek to Moscow were YSP assistant general secretary Salim Salih Muhammad in July, a delegation from the armed forces political directorate in the same month, and Prime Minister Yasin Sa'id Nu'man in September on his way to Prague. Soviet visitors to Aden included a CPSU Central Committee member who attended the YSP congress in June; the deputy director of the Middle East and North African office in the Soviet foreign ministry in August; the chairman of the Azerbaijan Soviet Socialist Republic (SSR) in September; the president of the Georgian SSR, who attended independence celebrations in November; and the deputy chief of the CPSU Central Committee's International Department in December.

Not surprisingly, military cooperation also continued, given the PDRY's total arms dependence on the Soviet bloc and Moscow's desire to exploit Aden's key location in the region. The USSR appears to have extensively re-equipped the PDRY army since the 1986 fighting. The PDRY defense minister held consultations in Moscow in May, the Soviet deputy minister of defense and commander of ground forces went to Aden in April, and a Soviet military delegation attended the 15th anniversary celebrations of the founding of the PDRY air force and air defenses at the end of September.

In the economic arena, the discovery of oil was the principal focus of attention. Strikes in three commercial oil fields ('Iyad West, 'Iyad East, and Amal) in the Shabwa governorate, not far from North Yemen's new oil fields in the Ma'rib area, were announced on 15 April. The Soviet Union's Technoexport handled the concession on a service contract for the PDRY government. The promise of oil production appeared to prompt the sending of an economic delegation headed by Soviet deputy premier and chairman of the State Planning Committee Nikolai Talyzin to Aden in March, followed by the Soviet minister of geology and the deputy chairman of the State Committee for Foreign Economic Relations in April. By June, tanker trucks were supplying the Aden refinery with 10,000 barrels per day (b/d) of crude oil, which meets part of the PDRY's domestic consumption of 15,000 b/d.

PDRY deputy prime minister and minister of energy and minerals Salih Abu Bakr ibn Husaynun held talks in Moscow on exploitation of the Shabwa oil resources in July, and on 28 July he signed a comprehensive agreement for joint exploitation of the PDRY's oil resources. The Soviet deputy ministers of petroleum industry and geology led a follow-up delegation to Aden in September. By the latter part of the year, ambitious plans were being made to complete an export pipeline from the Shabwa fields to the coast at Bir 'Ali or Bal Haf, with a spur pipeline to the Aden refinery, by early 1989. Exports of 100,000 b/d were projected for 1989, rising to as much as 500,000 b/d in subsequent years; it is impossible to gauge the validity of these projections. Beginning in 1986, Soviet assistance was also present in the production of gold from mines in al-Mukalla governorate.

Other PDRY-Soviet economic cooperation was displayed in fisheries, with the Yemeni-Soviet Committee for Marine Fisheries meeting in Aden in March and with the two countries' fisheries ministers signing an economic and technical cooperation protocol on 1 December that dealt with training, development of fishing cooperatives, development of Aden's fishing port (which opened in November 1987), and establishment of a fisheries complex on Socotra Island. In addition, under the terms of an accord for the exchange of commodities signed by the PDRY minister of industry, trade, and supply in Moscow in April, the Soviet Union agreed to export equipment, tools, spare parts, and industrial raw materials during the period 1987 to 1990 in exchange for rubber sandals, oils, and manufactured goods from the PDRY. Another protocol on marine transport and civil aviation was signed in Aden on 25 September, and the Soviet Union agreed in November to help develop a building-materials industry.

Other Soviet bloc visits to Aden included a Polish delegation in early February and a Czech deputy foreign minister and a military delegation later that month. The PDRY prime minister went to Prague in September, and a military delegation led by Defense Minister Salih 'Ubayd Ahmad visited Syria, Hungary, Czechoslovakia, and East Germany in October. Ties with Bulgaria seemed to mushroom: two Bulgarian party delegations made their way to Aden in March, and another senior Bulgarian official came in May. Cooperation protocols were signed between PDRY and Bulgarian friendship societies in April and between the two countries' youth leagues in July. The director of the SPC religious affairs department told the Bulgarian press that his visit in September had convinced him that Bulgarian Muslims enjoyed full freedom of religion.

Contacts with regional Marxist parties and states were maintained as well. In March, General Secretary al-Bayd met his Iraqi Communist Party counterpart in Aden. The secretary of the Afghanistan party's Central Committee attended the YSP congress in June, and an Afghanistan minister of state visited in August. Al-Bayd attended the 13th anniversary celebrations of the Ethiopian revolution in September; the commander of the Ethiopian air force returned the visit in October.

In other foreign affairs, Foreign Minister 'Abd al-'Aziz al-Dali visited Tehran in January and Djibouti at the beginning of July, the Somalian foreign minister visited Aden shortly afterward, and an SPC delegation went to Damascus in September. The minister of culture and information stopped in Kuwait in September to announce the PDRY's support for Kuwait's security. The deputy chief of staff visited Libya in September, the Iranian foreign minister arrived in October, and a Syrian Baath Party delegation attended the 20th anniversary celebrations of PDRY independence in November.

Given the country's perilous trade deficit, diminishing foreign aid, and steadily declining remittances from an estimated 100,000 workers abroad, the oil discovery could not have come at a better time. The third five-year plan, postponed until 1987 because of the civil war and emphasizing agriculture and fisheries, depends on foreign donors for about 50 percent of its financing, with the Soviet Union providing about 60 percent of that total. In May the Soviet Union said it was rendering aid to the PDRY in 1987 on 40 basic projects and themes and had more than 2,000 Soviet specialists working in the PDRY. Areas of assistance included geology, power engineering, agriculture and irrigation, fishing and fisheries, construction, transport and communications, the training of national cadres, and education and health care. Altogether about 6,000 Soviets are thought to be in South Yemen.

Denmark's recent commitment to provide $19.7 million in project aid makes it the largest Western donor. Kuwait, long a provider of various sorts of assistance, agreed on 20 January to double Kuwait Petroleum Company's commitment of 20,000 b/d of oil to be refined in Aden for a total of 30,000 b/d of Kuwait oil. Other crude oil for refining is provided by Iran (50,000 b/d), the Soviet Union (12,000 b/d), and Qatar (thought to be 10,000–20,000 b/d). In addition to Technoexport, eight oil companies are engaged in exploration in the PDRY, including Kuwaiti public and private sector companies in the Hadramawt and near Bal Haf.

Relations with Oman continued to deepen, as illustrated by the border talks and an exchange of visits by the two countries' foreign ministers. Repercussions over an accidental clash between South Yemeni and Omani border forces in October, which saw at least one soldier killed and others taken prisoner, were avoided in part because of the mediation of United Arab Emirates president Shaykh Zayid. President al-'Attas toured the Arab gulf states in March. 'Ali Nasir admitted that hundreds of his young supporters received scholarships to Libyan universities; there were rumors that some were fighting for Libya in Chad.

Although both the YAR and the PDRY proclaimed their desire to unify Yemen, there was little substantive progress in this area during 1987. The presence of the many armed refugees from the south in the YAR continued to be a stumbling block in north-south relations but was seen by the YAR as a counter to the continued presence in Aden of the anti-YAR National Democratic Front. A border skirmish between the two countries in January resulted in a trip to Sanaa by the PDRY chief of staff; matters were straightened out by the removal of some observation posts. Full-scale unity talks got under way in Sanaa on 21 July when al-Bayd made his first visit to the north since the 1986 civil war. Four days later, he returned to Aden without the release of any statement, a sign that no agreement had been reached. Meetings between the two Yemeni presidents were also arranged in Sanaa in September and during the Arab summit in Amman in November. Various discussions were held by oil officials and military from the two countries, indicating the importance of those two concerns.

In December, YAR president 'Ali 'Abdullah Salih pleaded unsuccessfully for leniency in the Adeni treason trials and vowed to ask Soviet help in pressuring a stay in executions. Former YAR president 'Abdullah al-Sallal, in a cable to al-Bayd signed "Your Father," added his voice to his successor's humanitarian appeal. Danielle Mitterrand, wife of the French president, was among those appealing for mercy. 'Ali Nasir reacted by claiming that the sentences had closed the door on mediation efforts to achieve Yemeni unity.

J. E. Peterson
Washington, D.C.

WESTERN EUROPE

Introduction

What was an auspicious beginning for Western Europe's communist parties at the beginning of this decade has steadily deteriorated. The Eurocommunist movement of the 1970s culminated in an electoral victory in France in 1981 that, without doubt, represented a major challenge for the West. The French Communist Party (PCF) joined a coalition government with the French Socialists, led by François Mitterrand, and occupied four cabinet posts in one of the most important countries on the continent. Two years later the *World Marxist Review* concluded that "the ideas advanced by Europe's communists meet the innermost interests of the people" (November 1983). The principal segments of French industry had been nationalized, including the leading banks of France, and the PCF was a legitimate party of government.

By 1984, however, the apparent cohesion of Europe's communist parties was clearly disintegrating and being replaced by interparty strife. In that year the PCF resigned from the coalition when the French government was forced to curtail its program of socialization, which had greatly weakened France's economy. By the beginning of 1987 it was far from clear what role the PCF would play in the future; indeed, in 1986 the party polled only 9.8 percent of the vote to the French National Assembly, its poorest performance in 60 years.

The PCF's strongest counterparts in Western Europe fared no better. Party leadership changed hands in Italy in 1984 for the first time in twelve years, and in 1986 the party held its first extraordinary congress since 1945 to discuss an uncertain future. The Spanish Communist Party, rent by divisiveness and struggles for control, split into three different competing communist factions in 1986, and during 1987 they proved unable to reconcile their differences. Voter confidence was clearly shaken. In each of the seven national elections held in Western Europe in 1985, the communist parties received fewer votes than they had in previous elections. In the four national elections held in 1986 this record continued, and in 1987 the communist parties of Italy, Finland, Iceland, and Portugal suffered significant losses.

The experience of the PCF in France adversely affected both the fortunes of its counterparts elsewhere in Europe and the confidence of the voters in the ability of the communist parties to govern. By 1987 strong leadership in the West European communist movement was noticeably absent. Whatever appeal Marxism-Leninism offered in 1981 had declined markedly, and the French challenge to the West had been transformed into a challenge to the communist parties to explain what constructive role they could play in their respective countries in the future.

Along with the erosion of "popular credibility and trust that they need to become more than minority forces" (Kevin Devlin, "The Decline of Eurocommunism: Downhill from the Summit," *RAD Background Report*, no. 60, 13 April 1984), Europe's communist parties also saw "the idea of socialism" fade. This was evident not only in Great Britain, where Prime Minister Margaret Thatcher has been reversing "the trend of 35 years of progressive socialism" since 1979, but also in France, where conservative Prime Minister Jacques Chirac was elected in 1987 at the same time that France's socialist President Mitterrand continued in the office he has held since 1981. It thus seemed clear by the end of 1987 that a return to the marketplace of competition, incentive, and free enterprise had a vastly greater appeal than the ephemeral promises of socialism. (See Joseph C. Harsch, "Fading Socialism," *CSM*, 18 June.)

During the year, 12 of Western Europe's 23 parties were represented in their respective parliaments—Cyprus, Finland, France, Greece, Iceland, Italy, Luxembourg, Portugal, San Marino, Spain, Sweden, and Switzerland. With the exception of San Marino, party members held no cabinet posts for the fourth consecutive year. Eleven national elections were held during 1987 (four were held in 1986, seven in 1985, one in 1984, and ten in 1983) in Belgium, Denmark, Finland, Great Britain, West

Germany, Iceland, Italy, Malta, Portugal, Switzerland, and Turkey.

For the first time in this decade the Italian Communist Party (PCI; formerly, the strongest party in Western Europe) was displaced in Italy's national elections. The PCI received 26.6 percent of the vote and won 177 of 630 parliamentary seats (1986: 29.9 percent; 198 of 630 seats). Of the remaining parties with legislative representation, Cyprus held the highest percentage of seats based on votes received (27.4), followed by San Marino (24.3), Iceland (13.2), Portugal (10.0), Finland (9.4), Greece (9.9), France (9.8), Sweden (5.4), Luxembourg (4.9), and Switzerland, for which no data is available. The eleven parties without legislative representation held between 0.01 (Great Britain) and 1.2 percent (Belgium) of their respective parliamentary seats based on votes received. Two reasons for this poor performance were anticipated in 1985 by Aleksandr Zinoviev, who was expelled from the Soviet Union in 1978:

> If the Western Communists want to survive and to continue to have any influence over the masses, they are doomed to repudiate Marxist ideology. Their future, if they are to have a future, is in any case bleak indeed. They must either follow the dictates of Moscow or break up. There is no other choice; they must be either pro-Soviet or anti-Soviet. (Kevin Devlin, "Zinoviev Sees Bleak Future for Western Communist Parties," *RAD Background Report*, no. 61, 2 July 1985.)

By the end of 1987 Western Europe's communist parties were caught in a dilemma: if they do not "change their ideology and their slogans" (ibid.) they have no appeal to the so-called working classes they claim to represent, and if they do make the changes Zinoviev describes they lose their credibility, as the PCF eloquently proved in the French elections in 1986. To put it another way, they must "either reassert their traditional philosophy, at the risk of losing more support, or move toward the social democratic center, at the risk of losing their identity" (William Echikson, "West Europe's Communists Running out of Steam," *CSM*, 2 October). This dilemma is compounded by the realities of life under communism in Eastern Europe and the Soviet Union, according to Juoko Kajonoja, general secretary of the Stalinist minority within the Finnish Communist Party: "[Europeans] see Gorbachev as a good guy and Reagan as a bad guy, but they still don't like the Soviet Union . . . In their view, the Soviet Union is an oppressive place, where no one can travel and everyone is poor" (ibid.).

The alternative, in the view of Oiva Björkbacka, secretary of information of the moderate wing of the Finnish Communist Party, is "to construct a 'new left,' reaching out to the new 'white-collar proletariat' along with antinuclear activists, feminists and ecologists . . . alliances should be struck with mainstream socialist parties that share communist views on issues from disarmament to ecology" (Echikson, *CSM*, 2 October). This conclusion was echoed by representatives of the communist parties of Italy, Belgium, Denmark, West Germany, Great Britain, and Sweden who, in October, advocated creation of the Euroleft, a phrase coined by the Communist Party of Italy in an interview conducted by *World Marxist Review* (October). Gianni Cervetti, a member of the Italian Communist Party leadership and chairman of the communist faction in the European Parliament, defined it as follows:

> We see the Euroleft as a composite entity comprising, first and foremost, the traditional parties of the working class and democratic movement with all their differences and in all their diversity, as well as other major movements—trade union, cooperative, peace, environmentalist and women's—together with the youth associations and cultural organizations.

Finnish party member Björkbacka expanded on this approach with a conclusion that will surely be the source of debate in 1988: "To achieve practical results, we must take part in governments in a capitalist country like Finland. We won't be able to dictate the goals of such a government when we represent only one-third of its support. We will have to compromise." (ibid.) Under Mikhail Gorbachev's leadership there is every indication that the Soviet government shares this view. According to Finnish diplomat Max Jacobson, "The Soviets understand the big change taking place in Europe and have no illusions about a rise of communist support in Europe. They want to improve their relations with Europe as it is, and that means downplaying ideology and improving state-to-state ties." (Echikson, *CSM*, 2 October.)

If past experience is any indication, however, the idea of the Euroleft is likely to meet the same fate as Eurocommunism and is unlikely to generate enthusiastic response from Europe's socialist parties. In straightforward terms there is little that Western Europe's communist parties can offer their respective voters that is economically or politically attractive, and cloaking their ideology in nationalist colors by advocating compromise is very likely to produce both confusion and uncertainty instead of "unity in diversity."

Developments within the PCF illustrate the latter point. Following the PCF's decision to withdraw from the French government in July 1984, the party formally abandoned support for a Union of the Left in 1985. But this decision did not eliminate dissent within the party or generate increased support from the French electorate. In an effort to restore unity to the party, Secretary Georges Marchais announced in 1986 that he would not be the PCF's candidate in the presidential elections set for May 1988, but his decision could not minimize the impact of the 1986 legislative elections, the worst electoral defeat suffered by the PCF since 1945. On the contrary, the party's defeat produced reformist demands for an extraordinary party congress to be held in 1987 before the French presidential elections in 1988.

In 1986 the PCF Central Committee rejected demands for an extraordinary party congress and focused criticism on Mitterrand's Socialist Party (PS) for "doing everything possible to break" the PCF and for governing in such a way as to "give in to the economic crisis, unemployment, and austerity, and justifying the existing capitalist order." (*YICA*, 1987). The resulting debates within the party

> included charges that Stalinism had returned to plague the PCF, public demands for the resignation of Marchais, and an analysis by former PCF spokesman, Pierre Juquin . . . in which he argued that the party's decline was due to the leadership's refusal to make the appropriate analysis of, and adjust strategy to, fundamental changes in French society (ibid.).

This prompted André Lajoinie, chairman of the PCF caucus in the French National Assembly, to accuse Juquin of "ultimately aiming to preserve capitalism" (*YICA*, 1987).

The rancor intensified in 1987 as party leaders struggled with the grim prospect of leading a strife-torn PCF into the presidential elections. Disaffected party leaders and functionaries—including at least one former minister and several Central Committee members—finally bolted from the party or from party offices, many of them rallying to the alternative communist presidential candidacy of Juquin. General Secretary Marchais and Politburo "conservatives" forced Juquin's expulsion from the party at almost the same time that the Twenty-sixth Congress, called in December earlier than expected, met to ratify Marchais's handpicked presidential candidate, Central Committee secretary Lajoinie. The party's leadership persistently deflected demands for open debate from self-styled "renovateurs" by emphasizing party unity as an exigency of the election campaign. The effort of Juquin's faction to coerce Marchais to permit a debate with the PS about the failure of the leftist coalition government between 1981 and 1984 failed, and Marcel Rigout, former minister of vocational training in the defunct Union of the Left government, resigned from the Central Committee. His departure, as well as that of other party members, prompted *l'Humanité* director and Politburo member Roland Leroy to attack Rigout for failing to distinguish between dissent within the rules of democratic centralism and for criticisms that clearly ran counter to the effort of the Twenty-fifth Congress "to turn the PCF into a substitute for the PS" (*l'Humanité*, 28 January). As the year progressed the party became increasingly concerned that the Juquin and Lajoinie candidacies would divide the party in half at a time when communist voter support remained at or below the disappointing electoral performance of 9.8 percent in 1986. Leadership efforts to mobilize the party's diminished strength for the presidential election, and for legislative elections that could follow, culminated in the Twenty-sixth Congress held in early December. The congress re-elected Marchais as general secretary for a seventh term and returned all members of the Politburo. But this ostensible show of unity was misleading, for at the end of the year the party was more divided than at any time since 1984. Indeed, prospects for continued party division and for a poor electoral showing in 1988 seemed foreordained.

The Communist Party of Italy (PCI) intensified its efforts to cultivate the idea of the Euroleft that was initiated in 1986 by party parliamentary leader Giorgio Napolitano, who argued "that the old differences between the communists and the socialist movements are not sustainable" (*YICA*, 1987). But these efforts did not produce electoral success in 1987. In the June parliamentary elections the PCI suffered what party Chairman Alessandro Natta called a "serious defeat" (*L'Unità*, 26 June). The loss of 21 seats in the Chamber of Deputies was the worst showing since the 1960s and exerted a negative impact on all areas of PCI activity. The immediate consequence was Natta's decision to propose Achille Occhetto as deputy general secretary of the PCI, a position that had been vacant since 1972 when Natta's predecessor, Enrico Berlinguer, was promoted to general secretary after serving for three years as Luigi Longo's deputy. Natta's nomination of his successor was not unanimously affirmed by the party's Central Committee (the vote was 194 in favor and 41 opposed); indeed, it was unprecedented for a personnel choice of such magnitude to be debated and sharply contested in the public eye. In addition, party membership declined from 1,551,000 in late 1986 to 1,505,000 at the end of the annual recruitment drive on 26 November (ibid., 13 December). This represented a continuation of the downward slide that began after 1977, when membership reached a high of 1,814,000.

For the remainder of the year the PCI was preoccupied with putting its political house in order, focusing on the party program approved in Florence in 1986. In a party plenum held in late July, Natta stressed that the PCI's political profile, or "image," had become "blurred" in the public mind as a result of the changes in its ideological and international posture over the past decade. He therefore called on the party to work out an explicit "program and platform for the renewal of society" that would clearly convey to Italian voters what the PCI meant by a "democratic alternative" (*L'Unità*, 29 July). In response to criticism that the party had failed to resolve "the great contradiction between minimalist reformism and reformism of the great transformations" (ibid.), Natta endorsed "the results that we laboriously achieved in Florence" regarding the strategy of building "an alternative signifying a change in government policies and in the country's leadership groups" through "unity on the Left."

As the year ended it was clear that the PCI would face a major struggle in 1988 to recover its declining popularity among the Italian electorate. First and foremost, however, would be a concerted effort within the PCI to unify the party's position on the future course of Italian politics. This point was made clearly in Occhetto's first report as Natta's deputy before a party plenum at the end of November. He enjoined the PCI to concentrate not on "polemics between the communists and the socialists" but on efforts to introduce stability to the Italian system of coalition government. Addressing the party's left wing, he emphasized the need for "structural transformations" of Italian society that would go beyond "the old Keynesian compromise" and rejected "acritical [sic] ruptures" with communist tradition even though certain discontinuities were necessary. His primary point was to pacify critical elements within the PCI, while emphasizing a constructive approach for dealing with the negative aspects of the permanent jockeying for power within successive coalition cabinets. Occhetto termed this "the crisis of the Italian political system," but there was no indication that the party would provide a solution in 1988.

Since 1977 the Spanish Communist Party (PCE) has enjoyed legal status and until 1981 was the leading proponent of Eurocommunism under the leadership of Santiago Carrillo. Gerardo Iglesias succeeded Carrillo in 1982, at the age of 37, and continues to serve as general secretary of the party. Between 1983 and 1987 Iglesias attempted to heal internal party wounds, but he did not succeed in establishing the PCE as an influential political party. The party, fragmented into three main parties in addition to several smaller groups, is one of the most divided in Europe. Pro-Soviet dissidents, led by Ignacio Gallego, withdrew from the Eurocommunist PCE in 1983 to form the Communist Party of the Peoples of Spain (PCPE). The third group, led by Carrillo, was formed after he was displaced as general secretary in 1982 (he formally resigned from the PCE in 1986). Initially calling it the Board for Communist Unity, Carrillo officially formed the Workers' Party—Communist Unity (PT-UC) in 1987.

Iglesias sought during the year to heal differences between the three parties by emphasizing a new climate of unanimous goodwill toward the Soviet Union and by continuing conciliatory overtures to the other parties. In September Iglesias proclaimed that the efforts at rehabilitation were successful and that the party crisis was over (*WMR*, September); however, it was also announced that the major object of discussion at the party's Twelfth Congress, scheduled for February 1988, would be steps to achieve reunification of all communist groups in Spain. Thus, although both Carrillo and Gallego remained suspicious as well as critical of the PCE, there were definite indications that the party split into pro-Soviet and Eurocommunist factions may be on the mend in 1988. In view of the party's weakness for the most of this decade, no other alternative is available if the PCE wishes to exert any significant influence on Spanish political life in the future.

Alvaro Cunhal has served as general secretary of the Portuguese Communist Party (PCP) since 1961 (he is 73 years of age), and the party claims a membership in excess of 200,000. The PCP, controlled by an aging leadership, remains one of the most Stalinist, pro-Soviet parties in Western Europe. The year was highlighted by domestic developments that very likely will affect the debate on the future leadership and direction of the PCP when it convenes its Twelfth Congress, scheduled for March 1988. In April the minority government of Prime Minister Aníbal Cavaco Silva was overturned by a vote of censure in the assembly. But instead of appointing a left-wing coalition to replace it, President Mário Soares called for new elections in July. This decision was vigorously opposed by the PCP, which insisted that the parties disposed to support a "democratic" government held a comfortable majority; the president's decision, it therefore concluded, represented support for the right. The reason for the PCP's opposition was illustrated by the election results. The party received, in coalition with "many independent democrats," 10 percent of the vote and 30 of 250 Assembly seats, which amounted to a major defeat (1985: 15.5 percent and 38 of 250 seats). Cunhal justified the PCP's relative isolation from Portugal's political parties by explaining that the communists "resolutely defend the interest of workers . . . against capitalist exploitation" (*Avante!*, 20 August; *FBIS*, 24 August). But Portugal's voters apparently did not agree, and the result is almost certain to be acrimonious discussion concerning the party's future in 1988.

In Cyprus, Greece, Malta, San Marino, and Turkey, the communist parties exert little significant influence on the conduct of domestic or foreign affairs. The Communist Party of San Marino (PCS) is an extension of the Italian Communist Party, just as the country's other political parties are extensions of their Italian counterparts. Between 1978 and 1986 the PCS formed part of a governing coalition that excluded only the Christian Democrats (DCS). In 1986, the party (which received 24.3 percent of the vote in 1983) and the DCS (42.1 percent in 1983) formed a coalition for the first time. In a government (Congress of State) that consists of three secretaries of state and seven ministers of state, the PCS has the secretaryship for internal affairs and the ministries for education and culture, industry and handicrafts, transport and communications, and tourism and commerce.

The Communist Party of Malta (CPM), founded in 1969, did not participate in a general election until May 1987. The result was disastrous. Of a total of 236,169 votes cast, the CPM received 119 and the party general secretary, Anthony Vassallo, received just 13. The party, pro-Soviet in orientation, plays a marginal role in Maltese political life but maintains extensive party contacts with communist parties throughout Europe and with the Soviet Union. The Maltese government has significantly increased cultural and economic agreements with the USSR during the past several years, which prompted former Deputy Ambassador to the U.N. from the United States Charles Lichenstein to conclude in late 1986 that "the democracies in the West must view with growing concern Malta's drift towards the Soviet sphere. This compromises Malta's stability and the security of the Mediterranean region." (The *Times*, Malta, 7 December 1986.)

The Communist Party in Turkey (TCP) is proscribed, the only communist party in this position in Western Europe. In Cyprus the Progressive Party of the Working People (AKEL) is supported primarily by the Greek Cypriot majority, which comprises approximately 80 percent of the island's estimated population of 670,000 and is proscribed in the Turkish Republic of Northern Cyprus. Party membership is claimed to be 12,000, and AKEL holds 15 of 56 seats in the Cypriot parliament, having garnered 27.4 percent of the vote in the national elections of 1985. In the May municipal elections, held for the first time since 1953 when Cyprus was still a British crown colony, AKEL received 32.5 percent of the Greek Cypriot vote and the office of mayor in nine of the eighteen cities on the southern part of the island; it thus enjoys a broad opportunity to influence local politics. Party leadership remains in the hands of Ezekias Papaioannou (79 years of age), who has served as general secretary since 1949; the average age of party leaders is over 65.

The extent to which this may lessen AKEL's appeal to younger voters as the party develops its campaign for the presidential elections scheduled for February 1988 is unclear. Since 1982 AKEL has supported President Kyprianou, head of the Democratic Party, but AKEL announced in midyear that it intends to support the independent candidate Yeoryios Vasiliou in 1988. Whether this decision will adversely affect the party's political fortunes will be determined to a large extent by younger voters.

The Communist Party of Greece (KKE) remains divided among the pro-Soviet and Eurocommunist factions into which it split during the period of military government in Greece (1967–1974). The pro-Soviet KKE has an estimated membership of 42,000 and won 13 of 300 parliamentary seats in the 1985 national elections. The Eurocommunist faction, known as KKE-Interior, underwent a major reorganization at its congress held in Athens in April but emerged divided into two major factions. One group, led by Leonidas Kyrkos, which seems to enjoy relatively greater support, adopted the title Greek Left, and the other, led by Giannis Banias, retained the title KKE-Interior and added the subtitle Renovating Left.

The KKE is headed by general secretary Kharilaos Florakis, and its domestic and foreign policy views often parallel those of Andreas Papandreou's governing Panhellenic Socialist Movement (PASOK). Relations between both party leaders remain cooperative, although KKE is vehemently anti-American and opposes the presence of U.S. military bases in Greece. In addition, the party rejects the austerity measures introduced by Papandreou in 1985 designed to strengthen the Greek economy. The party is plagued by a generation gap between those who control the leadership and the younger generation that gained prominence during the period of military dictatorship. Thus, at the party's Twelfth Congress held in May, its declarations urged compromise and cooperation among "democratic and progressive forces" of the left. Whether such cooperation will actually materialize is not yet decided. But PASOK is declining in popularity among the Greek electorate, and KKE estimates that during the year its following increased from approximately 10 to 15 percent, mostly from voters dissatisfied with PASOK's more conservative economic policies. This may mean that when the next national elections are held in Greece, presumably in 1989, the electoral outcome, if PASOK is weakened, will place the KKE in a strong bargaining position if the New Democratic Party does not win a majority. Whether this development occurs will depend to a large extent on the performance of the Greek economy during 1988 and on the unity of the left.

The Communist Party of Great Britain (CPGB) continued to decline in influence. The CPGB has never been one of Britain's major parties, and at its peak in 1942 the membership was only 42,000. Indeed, since 1980 its membership has dropped by 50 percent, and in 1987 stood at less than 10,000. In Great Britain's general election held in June the party received 0.1 percent of the vote (6,078 votes). It has not been represented in the British Parliament since 1950, but does have one member, Lord Milford, in the House of Lords.

The party's influence is exercised primarily through the country's trade union movement, but this, too, is diminishing. In fact, the party argues that "the whole character of the working population as a class has changed. Unless the hard left can come to terms with that it will find itself marginalised" (BBC Central Talks and Features, Milada Haigh, "British Communists: A Dying Species?" 6 January). The BBC's Haigh argues convincingly that if the party continues to lose members "as it has done since 1980, by 1994 there will be nothing left of it at all" (ibid.). Although this is unlikely to occur, the party is divided between those who seek a more realistic approach toward influencing British politics and those who adhere to a strongly pro-Soviet and Marxist-Leninist position. Indeed, the party's leadership, controlled by the moderate Gordon McLennan, argues that "Marx's classical working class . . . is a declining minority. If Britain's Communist party is to survive . . . it must adapt and seek support among a broader range of interest groups." (BBC, Haigh, "British Communists," 6 January.)

The Communist Party of Ireland (CPI) has never taken an active role in Irish political life. It is not represented in Parliament, although it did participate in local and national elections in 1987. What little support it does enjoy is found in Dublin and Belfast. During the year the party focused on the continuing political division of the country and on Ireland's economic problems. The CPI views the United Kingdom as an imperialist power that gains economically from holding Ireland in a subordinate position. It opposes terrorism in Ireland and believes that Irish unification can be achieved only through bodies promoting working-class solidarity and thus overcoming the divide between Protestants and Catholics.

The communist parties of Belgium, Denmark, the Netherlands, and Luxembourg played marginal roles in the political affairs of their respective countries during the year. The Communist Party of Luxembourg (CPL) won 2 of 64 parliamentary seats in 1984. Party leadership remains in the control of the Urbany family, which founded the CPL in 1921. The CPL was led until 1977 by Dominique Urbany, who remained honorary chairman until his death in 1986. His son, René Urbany, is the party's current leader (60 years of age), and he continues to follow a strongly pro-Soviet line.

The Communist Party of Denmark (DKP) received 0.9 percent of the vote in the country's national elections held in September (in 1984, 0.7%) and holds no seats in the Danish parliament. It has been represented in parliament since 1979, when its vote fell below the 2 percent minimum required for proportional representation. The year 1987, however, saw more change than usual on the leftwing of Danish politics. The party's chairman of ten years, Jørgen Jensen, died in April on the eve of the

Twenty-eighth DKP Congress. His successor is 32-year-old Ole Sohn, and undoubtedly the advent of a new generation of leadership increased public interest in the party. While the parliamentary elections gave the socialists a net gain of three seats, a parliamentary majority continued to support conservative Prime Minister Poul Schlüter. But the independent Marxist Socialist People's Party gained 6 seats (to 27) and almost 15 percent of the vote, and a new group of radical socialists, the Common Course Workers' Party, gained 2.2 percent of the vote, providing a net gain to radical socialist parties of 5 seats and a total of 17 percent representation in parliament. The DKP did not benefit directly from these developments, but new leadership, combined with the general election results, may provide the party with a much needed infusion of energy in 1988 even though it is almost certain to remain a peripheral observer and critic of Danish political affairs.

The Belgian Communist Party (PCB) membership is estimated at 5,000 in a country with a population of almost 10 million. For the first time since 1925 the party received only 1.2 percent of the vote in 1985 national elections and lost its two parliamentary seats. This pattern continued in the national elections held in December 1987 in which the PCB lost even more ground—so much so that *Drapeau Rouge* in three issues (15, 18, 19–20 December) of interviews with party Chief Louis Van Geyt agonized over the loss but without even once referring to the actual vote percentage for the PCB, which apparently is too small to list separately in any of the major publications (such as *NYT*, *Facts on File*, or *FBIS*).

The party's new course, adopted at the Twenty-fifth Congress in April 1986, emphasized that the party would be passed by if it did not respond to the "evolution of the working class" reflected in the "scientific and technological revolution and the 'transnationalization' of capital" (*YICA*, 1987). In an effort to be responsive to changing conditions, the party declared throughout the year that regional economic differences would require varying approaches in Flanders, Brussels, and Wallonia but within the framework of a federalized party structure. These efforts, however, did not produce measurable results in 1987, and the party's poor performance at the polls in December foreshadowed continued stagnation in 1988.

The Communist Party of the Netherlands (CPN) claims a membership of 27,000, but estimates place this number at approximately 12,000. The party exercises little influence over the political life of the Netherlands and holds no seats in the country's parliament. The most recent party congress, originally scheduled for 1987, was held in early December of 1986. Principal party leaders were re-elected, thereby reaffirming the decision to follow a strategy of renewal and cooperation with other forces on the left, including feminists and pacifists. As a result of cooperative efforts the CPN was able to elect 1 member to the 75-member upper house in 1987; however, this victory was of little practical significance. Despite broad endorsement of Mikhail Gorbachev's promises of *glasnost'* and *perestroika* among the left in the Netherlands, expectations were few that the CPN would be able to increase its popular support in 1988.

In the Nordic countries of Iceland, Norway, Sweden, and Finland, communist party activity, while extensive, nevertheless exerted a minimal impact. The People's Alliance of Iceland (PA) has an estimated membership of 3,000 in a country with fewer than 250,000 inhabitants. Founded in 1968 as the successor to a line of leftist parties dating back to 1930, it occupies the left wing of Icelandic politics. Marxist in orientation, it has participated in coalition governments on a regular basis. Since 1983, however, its political fortunes have declined. The PA's electoral setback in national elections held in April was the second in a row and occurred despite a strong showing in 1986 local elections. The PA received 13.4 percent of the vote and 8 of 63 seats in parliament (1983: 17.3 percent and 10 of 60 seats). This weak showing was particularly significant in view of the success of the radical Womens' Alliance, which doubled its representation to six seats and 10.1 percent of the vote. The PA's dismal electoral performance rekindled intraparty strife, which has plagued the party continuously since 1983. The immediate result was that party Chairman Svavar Gestsson announced that he would not be a candidate for re-election. His replacement by Olafur Ragnar Grimsson, a political scientist at the University of Iceland, reflected criticism of the PA by party members as "stagnated, boring and undemocratic." This public criticism may be a sign of a relatively open, pluralistic, and lively party, but the PA will face a difficult path in 1988 as it seeks to regain the respect of the electorate at the same time that newer radical parties are increasing their popularity.

The Norwegian Communist Party (NKP) competes for popular support with several other parties on the left, especially the Socialist Left Party (SV) formed by former members of the NKP in the mid-1970s. It has no representation in the Norwegian parliament (the SV has 6 of 157 seats) and remains a staunchly pro-Soviet, Stalinist party. NKP chairman Hans Kleven endorses SV chairman Theo Koritzinsky's advocacy of both a united front of left-wing parties in Norway and the concept of joint election lists with the SV. But the NKP remains one of the weakest communist parties in Western Europe and shows no indication of increasing its political support. At its Nineteenth Congress in April the NKP adopted a new party program that underscored its adherence to Marxism-Leninism and "proletarian internationalism" at a time when many of its counterparts in Western Europe were seeking to de-emphasize ideology in an effort to broaden their electoral bases by endorsing the vague but alluring concept of the Euroleft. The uncertainty concerning the proper path was illustrated by outgoing chairman Kleven's ambiguous conclusion that "Marxism needs neither renewal nor modernization but can always be developed further, adding new analyses and conclusions based on life's experiences" (*Friheten*, 23 April). Symptomatic of the dilemma in which many of Western Europe's communist parties found themselves was the declaration in the party organ *Friheten* (30 April) that was a classic example of seeking to have it both ways:

> Our strategy for Socialism is based on an alliance of the working-class parties that is able to unite all those who are objective opponents of monopoly capital and imperialism in the struggle to limit the power of monopoly capital and expand democracy. This struggle must take place both inside and outside parliamentary organs . . . The Social Democrats are our most important alliance partners on all the major political issues today. We must accomplish the task of developing a constructive and comradely cooperation with the Social Democrats while at the same time maintaining our fundamental criticism of their policies.

Whether the NKP recognized the contradictions in the latter conclusion was not elaborated. But the contradictions are there and undoubtedly contribute to the lack of credibility encumbering party pronouncements. It is possible that new party Chairman Kare Andre Nilsen (42 years of age) will be able to bring new life to the NKP, as well as respect, but this task will be virtually impossible to accomplish during 1988.

The Left Party Communists (VPK) in Sweden received 5.4 percent of the vote in national elections held in 1985 and continue to occupy 19 of 349 parliamentary seats (1982: 5.6 percent and 20 of 349 seats). Throughout the first half of the year, the VPK debated policy and personnel decisions to be made at its Twenty-eighth Congress in May, and a great deal of attention was focused on the leadership of party Chairman Lars Werner who, as chairman since 1975, has served longer in this position than any of his predecessors. The primary reason for this attention is that national elections will be held in September 1988, and thus the decisions taken at the party's congress would affect the 1988 campaign. The congress voted to retain Werner as chairman, but the presence of his two deputies, critical of what they consider to be weak leadership, will virtually assure bickering within the VPK in the new year. Indeed, one of Sweden's leading newspapers concluded that "Werner does not have a grip on the party machine. The conflicts within the VPK will continue . . . A divided and paralyzed VPK has little chance of reversing a falling membership trend, of winning support among today's young, or even of running an effective election campaign." (*Dagens Nyheter*, 27 May). Division within the party suggests that Sweden's Social Democrats may not be able to count on undivided support from the VPK in 1988. If this proves to be the case, it will not only affect the fortunes of the Social Democrats but is very likely to adversely affect the popularity of the VPK among Sweden's electorate.

The internal affairs of the Finnish Communist Party (SKP) have been dominated by factional strife since 1969 when the party adopted a "reformist" program, despite opposition from pro-Stalinists within the party. In 1985 an extraordinary party congress urged adoption of a new party program, Socialism with a Finnish Face, but the congress was boycotted by the Stalinist wing led by Taisto Sinisalo. In 1986 SKP party chairman Arvo Aalto made public a draft of a new program to be presented to the party's congress scheduled for June 1987. According to Aalto, the proposed program reflected the intention to expand "international activity, not Eurocommunism . . . the west European communist parties which operate in similar social circumstances [must be] seen as natural and intimate collaborators with the SKP" (*Kansan Uutiset*, 24 January 1986). The Stalinist wing of the party (SKP-Y) elected a "shadow" party leadership in April 1986, which was a copy of the SKP with Sinisalo as chairman. He insisted that the newly elected officials were the true leaders of the SKP and the legitimate heirs to the Twentieth SKP Congress

(1984) because the Aalto-led party is assertedly "revisionist" and has allegedly deserted Marxist principles.

This rift, according to Aalto, has alienated 150,000 supporters and 20,000 party members. Thus, as 1987 began, every sign suggested that the party would experience a turbulent year. Public opinion polls indicated both parties were suffering a loss of popular support, and national election results in March confirmed this prognosis. The SKP received only 9.4 percent of the vote and 16 of 200 parliamentary seats (1983: 14 percent and 27 of 200 seats), and the SKP-Y received 4.3 percent and 4 seats. Neither Aalto nor Sinisalo were elected. Following the elections the party was more divided than at any previous time. At the SKP-Y's First Congress in June, which organizers claimed was the SKP's Twenty-first Congress, differences developed over whom the party should support in the upcoming presidential election and whether the party should drop the fiction that it was the legitimate SKP. Sinisalo was re-elected party chairman and proposed party General Secretary Juoko Kajanoja as its presidential candidate. The congress also called upon the SKP to cancel its proposed party program as a prelude to reunification of the two communist parties and to form an electoral coalition for the 1988 presidential campaign.

The SKP congress was held one week after the SKP-Y congress and Aalto was re-elected chairman. The congress emphasized party renewal and announced that 20 of the 50 Central Committee members were newly elected, that the average age was 43, and that 22 members were women. The party's program was regarded as Eurocommunist (Euroleft) both in its description of Finnish socialism and in its disassociation of the party from the Communist Party of the Soviet Union (CPSU) (*Uusi Suomi*, 12 February). But despite efforts of both parties to improve their popular image, they remained outside the mainstream of political life. The future of both parties was cloudy at the end of the year, and no clear indications existed to suggest how the parties would fare in 1988 nor whom they would support in Finland's presidential elections.

The Communist Party of Austria (KPO) and the Swiss Labor Party (PdAS) occupy roles of negligible importance in the political affairs of their two countries. The KPO is not represented in the Austrian parliament and received only 0.72 percent of the popular vote in the last national elections (1986). The party is pro-Soviet and adapts its domestic and foreign policy positions to echo those expressed by the CPSU. Thus, throughout the year party Chairman Franz Muhri extolled the virtues of *glasnost'* and condemned Austria's coalition government of the (conservative) People's Party and the Socialists as a procapitalist government of the privileged. In Switzerland the PdAS received less than 1 percent of the vote in national elections in 1987. The party, pro-Soviet in allegiance, has long suffered a lack of support among younger voters, which accounts for a major change during the year at its Thirteenth Congress held in February. The party sought to rejuvenate its leadership by electing Jean Spielmann (43 years of age) as the new general secretary, replacing Armand Magnin. Replacement of members of the party's Central Committee has altered the age distribution there as well: 39 percent are under age 40, and 26 percent are between 40 and 50. Although outgoing party leader Magnin stressed the need to appeal to a broader segment of the Swiss population, it is doubtful that the party will be able to introduce the flexibility necessary to generate enthusiasm for Unity of the Left in 1988.

The Socialist Unity Party of West Berlin (SEW), according to its own estimate, has 7,000 members out of a population of approximately 1.86 million in the western sectors of the city. The party has been without representation in the city's parliament since its establishment in 1969. The SEW plays little part in the city's political life, is dependent financially on the East German Socialist Unity Party of Germany (SED), and mirrors the views and positions of that party. In a city divided by the Berlin Wall and surrounded by mine fields, the party does not appeal to the citizens of West Berlin, who have defended their freedom successfully since 1945. Indeed, the party slogan—With the SEW for Peace, Work, Democracy, and Social Progress—for its Eighth Congress in May had a hollow ring for the city's electorate.

In the Federal Republic of Germany (FRG) the German Communist Party (DKP) is not represented in the Bundestag and received only 0.5 percent of the vote in national elections in January. Party headquarters are located in Düsseldorf, and the party opened an office in Bonn in September 1985. DKP membership is claimed to be in excess of 50,000.

The party's loyalty to East Germany and to the Soviet Union reduces its electoral appeal to almost zero. It consistently points to the Soviet Union as the model of "real socialism" to be emulated. The CPSU is seen as the vanguard party of the communist movement, and hence the DKP's motto is "To learn from the Soviet Union means to learn to be victorious." The DKP and its East German counterpart, the SED, consistently support the foreign and defense policy objectives of the Soviet government; DKP leader Herbert Mies and SED chief Erich Honecker received the Lenin-Peace Prize in 1987 in Moscow. Gorbachev's leadership, however, is causing problems for the DKP.

On the one hand, Gorbachev's calls for *glasnost'* have been avidly embraced by the DKP's rank and file, who have long been restless over the "lack of possibilities for intra-party influence and participation," according to party author Erasmus Schöfer (*Der Spiegel*, 7 September). Party Chairman Mies admitted in a May 1987 interview with the DKP party organ, *Unsere Zeit* (Our Time), that "there is hardly another topic on which so many party functions and with such a large number of participants have been held over the past several years . . . The sympathy for the changes in the Soviet Union is unanimous." (*Unsere Zeit*, 20 May.) Mies recognized that "the attractive power of existing socialism has been growing" under Gorbachev, who, polls indicate, enjoyed greater popularity in the FRG in 1987 than did President Ronald Reagan. Gorbachev's welcome disarmament proposals present the DKP with "fresh opportunities in . . . our united action and alliance policy" and have "made it easier for Communists to act as respected and equal partners in the peace movement and other democratic movements. Not least important . . . is the possibility of using the growing sympathy for Soviet policy to spread the influence of the DKP as the party of socialism." (ibid.)

On the other hand both the DKP and the SED are seeking to control, if not dampen, the enthusiasm caused by the "strong impulses" coming from Moscow. In *Unsere Zeit* Mies cautioned that in a capitalist country like the FRG "there can be no imitation of the Soviet approach" and that the DKP must be careful "not to throw the baby out with the bathwater." One must not "reduce the splendid history of the Soviet Union . . . to economic and moral problems." Thus, the party has resorted to censorship to try and silence support for the reform impulses from Moscow. When party poet and member of the 94-member party executive committee Peter Schütt wrote a poem in early 1987 with the lines, "after decades of radio silence, the red star is again sending signals," he was admonished by chief party ideologue Willi Gerns not to publish the poem; it was subsequently published in the *Frankfurter Allgemeine Zeitung*. (*Unsere Zeit*, 20 May.)

In 1988 the DKP will continue "to broaden extra-parliamentary action, its policy of alliances and unity of action, and to enhance on this basis its own political role as a mobilizing and motive force, and increase its membership" (*IB*, May). But its support among the German population is so minimal in a country where the difference between democracy and communism looms so large that the DKP is unlikely to play a role of electoral importance in the future. However, its appeal for "peace" is a call well understood by Germans, and thus the DKP will continue to extol the virtues of the peaceful intentions of Soviet leaders in contrast, for example, to the efforts of Western leaders to develop a credible strategic defense. What effect this effort will have on the mainstream of political life in the FRG is uncertain, but the DKP's role will continue to be clearly defined as a mobilizing force for disarming the NATO alliance that has preserved peace in Europe since 1945.

Dennis L. Bark
Hoover Institution

Austria

Population. 7,569,283
Party. Communist Party of Austria (Kommunistische Partei Österreichs; KPO)
Founded. 3 November 1918
Membership. 15,000 (1986 estimate)
Party Chairman. Franz Muhri (b. 1924)
Politburo. 12 members: Walter Baier, Willi Gaisch, Michael Graber, Franz Hager, Anton Hofer, Hans Kalt (secretary of Central Committee), Franz Muhri, Otto Podolsky (Vienna party secretary), Irma Schwager, Walter Silbermayr (secretary of Central Committee), Susanne Sohn, Ernst Wimmer
Secretariat. 2 members: Hans Kalt and Walter Silbermayr
Central Committee. 72 members
Status. Legal
Last Congress. Twenty-sixth, 25–28 March 1987, in Vienna

Last Election. Federal, 23 November 1986, 0.72 percent, no representation

Publications. *Volksstimme* (People's Voice; Michael Graber, editor), KPO daily organ, Vienna; *Weg und Ziel* (Path and Goal; Erwin Scharf, editor), KPO theoretical monthly, Vienna

In 1987 the KPO held its Twenty-Sixth Party Congress and also saw some economic recession, primarily in the nationalized sector. The recession seemed, as in 1986, something to be exploited by the KPO. Having shown a slight improvement in the federal elections of 1986, the party held its own in 1987 in the provincial election in Burgenland (4 October) and added 0.58 percentage points to its vote in the provincial and municipal elections in Vienna (8 November). In the Vienna election, the KPO gained in each of the 23 districts, with a total vote of 1.72 percent and more than 2 percent in the four northeastern districts. The only district where the party failed to poll 1 percent was the downtown district, where its 73 votes almost tripled its vote share.

Detailed results are now available on last year's federal election, which show that, although the KPO did not poll 2 percent of the vote in any of Vienna's districts, it did so in twenty of Austria's myriad of municipalities (ten in lower Austria and six in Styria). Those in lower Austria (around Vienna or in depressed communities) tend to be small, whereas those in Styria—including Leoben, its second city—are the seats of nationalized mining or steel-producing enterprises.

Although none of the KPO candidates won a seat in the 1986 federal election, the following is a profile of the 297 candidates who showed up on the candidates' lists. Given the party's avowed feminism, it is surprising that only 27 percent of the communist candidates were women. The candidates' ages break down into 9 percent in their twenties, 31 percent in their thirties, 23 percent in their forties, 17 percent in their fifties, 19 percent in their sixties, and 2 percent in their seventies. The candidates' occupational self-classification presents an interesting picture. The largest group, 26 percent, were white-collar employees, followed by workers (15 percent), retired persons (13 percent), and tradespeople (12 percent). Housewives and public servants each made up 5 percent of the candidates, and teachers and journalists, 4 percent each. Students and miscellaneous academics each made up 2 percent. The groups contributing 1 percent each were accountants, salespersons, university teachers, social workers, professional engineers, businessmen, lawyers, secretaries, nurses, and declared party employees. There were no declared unemployed.

Leadership and Organization. As a prelude to the Twenty-Sixth Party Congress (Hotel Bohemia, Vienna, 25–28 March), *Volksstimme*, between the middle of January and the middle of March, printed dozens of discussion contributions made by various party members to the Central Committee's set of projected resolutions. At the congress, Kalt, chairman of the Central Committee's finance commission, reported moderately increased revenues, with sharp increases from bequests and major contributions (*Volksstimme*, 28 March). Prominent guests from Eastern bloc parties attending the party congress included Georgi Razumovsky, secretary of the Central Committee of the Communist Party of the Soviet Union (CPSU) (*Volksstimme*, 29 March). Erich Honecker addressed the party congress in writing (*Volksstimme*, 29 March).

Elections at the party congress expanded the Central Committee from 64 to 72 members. Gustav Loistl, Karl Reiter, and the veteran Erwin Scharf retired from the Politburo, and Reiter also retired from the Secretariat. New Politburo members are Baier and Sohn (*Volksstimme*, 31 March); Gaisch was added later (*Volksstimme*, 10 April).

In his address to the party congress (*Volksstimme* supplement, 28 March), Chairman Muhri announced that the KPO's 1984 program continues to serve the party's needs. After praises for *glasnost'* and the international policies of the USSR, Muhri attacked Austria's new Great Coalition between the conservative People's Party and the Socialists as a procapitalist government of the privileged. He recognized the merits of Austria's Greens Party (represented in Parliament for the first time) and regretted that conservatism prevented it from making common cause with the KPO. He warned against the strengthening of the liberal national Freedom Party under its new leader, the populist Jörg Haider (a "demagogue," according to Muhri). All Muhri had to say about the election of Kurt Waldheim as president of Austria was that it represented a rightist trend. Muhri's final speech (*Volksstimme*, 1 April) emphasized the KPO's role in opposing privatization and Austria's association with the European community. The party congress's proclamation (*Volksstimme*, 3 April) is mostly a diatribe against the coalition government.

The KPO's May Day proclamation (*Volks-*

stimme, 28 April) inveighs against retrenchment, the governing coalition, and the social partnership, and supports the new peace initiative of the Soviet Union. On 18 June, *Volksstimme* announced the publication of *Beiträge zur Geschichte der KPO* (*Contributions to the History of the KPO*), which updates to 1984 a party history with a chapter by Wimmer. All authors are, according to *Volksstimme*, communist historians.

Domestic Party Affairs. As in 1986, attempts at privatization or reduction of nationalized enterprises were again the chief domestic target of the KPO. The attack began with a *Volksstimme* (15 January) remembrance of the first anniversary of demonstrations in upper Austria and Styria against reduction of the activities of VOEST-Alpine, Austria's major nationalized steel firm. On 21 February, Muhri took a strong stand against any reduction or privatization of VOEST (*Volksstimme*, 22 February).

In regard to VEW, a conglomerate of smaller nationalized steel plants, Richard Ramsner, secretary of the lower Austrian KPO, said that the dimissal of 2,000 workers was a betrayal (*Volksstimme*, 20 March). *Volksstimme* (10 April) claimed that a communist city councillor was the only one fighting to maintain the VEW plant in the Styrian city of Murzzuschlag. On 27 April, Muhri warned that the coalition government was about to decide on a massive program of privatization that would cost jobs (*Volksstimme*, 28 April). The fight in defense of nationalized industries was the focus of the party congress of the upper Austrian KPO (*Volksstimme*, 19 May). The Communist Trade Union Federation (GLB) issued a strong letter against privatization (*Volksstimme*, 2 July). Earlier the KPO, including Muhri, took a firm stand against the planned cessation of bicycle and moped production in line with the sale of the nationalized Puch works to Fiat-Piaggio (*Volksstimme*, 22, 25 February).

Volksstimme (8 January), in headlines, reported that unemployment in 1986 averaged 5.2 percent and in December, 6.8 percent (comparable 1985 figures: 4.8 percent and 6.3 percent). In the 18 January *Volksstimme*, Kalt claimed, in some detail, that the coalition government planned to have 100,000 additional unemployed by 1990 (1986 average: 150,000). On 26 June, Muhri and Hofer (GLB chairman) presented an eight-point program to improve Austria's employment situation (*Volksstimme*, 27 June).

In late January (*Volksstimme*, 30, 31 January), the leadership of the KPO attacked the coalition pact of the Socialists and the People's Party. There were two targets. First, Muhri predicted an increase in unemployment through privatization and reduction of activity of nationalized enterprises. Second, he expressed apprehension about the appointment of Alois Mock, leader of the People's Party, as foreign minister. Mock, he said, would support Reagan's aggressive policies and force Austria into a policy of increased armaments. When the coalition presented its budget on 25 February, the KPO emphasized that, far from reducing the deficit, it would help big business and sacrifice jobs (*Volksstimme*, 26 February).

In early March, Vienna's KPO women went on a policy offensive (*Volksstimme*, 1, 5 March), with Otto Podolsky, the Vienna KPO chairman, pointing to the increasing militancy of communist women in Vienna. Socialist Vienna was accused of discriminating against women, particularly when it came to the granting of emergency social assistance. The conference also took stands against antiabortion efforts and compulsory acquired immunodeficiency syndrome (AIDS) testing. The women of the Trade Union Congress met in early June (*Volksstimme*, 3, 4, 7 June). Eva Kaiser of the Chemical Workers' Union coined the slogan that "women have heads not only for hairdos." Earlier in the year, Sohn attacked plans of the People's Party to entrench marriage and family in the Austrian constitution and to make abortion more difficult (*Volksstimme*, 25 January).

On 13 January, the Austrian Broadcasting Commission found that the KPO had been discriminated against in the November election when Muhri was not invited to the Austrian Broadcasting Company's "press hour" (*Volksstimme*, 14, 16, 22 January). The KPO blamed the party's slight gains in the election on this discrimination.

Volksstimme (23 June) triumphantly announced that the communist composer Walter Kubizek had received the Kery prize, named after the former socialist governor of Burgenland. The story went on to say that Kery had been enraged when he saw the composer, informally dressed in red, arriving to accept the prize.

The KPO's position vis-à-vis President Waldheim, after the United States put him on the "watch list" for his activities as an intelligence officer in the Balkans, is characterized by the 6 May headline of *Volksstimme*, "The Dilemma." During the following months, *Volksstimme* fought a two-front war against Waldheim and his U.S. accusers.

On 19 May, Wimmer made a comprehensive report on domestic policy to the KPO's Central Committee (*Volksstimme*, 23 May). In this report, he pointed to the contradiction between capitalist production and the interests of capitalist property. He ascribed the distancing of former Chancellor Bruno Kreisky from the Socialist Party to the efforts of Chancellor Franz Vranitzky and Vice-Chancellor Mock to satisfy the demands of capitalist property. Wimmer wondered to what extent the Trade Union Congress would be able to follow the government's direction. His broad criticism reports that Austria has been selected by Pope John Paul II to become the example of reactionary Catholicism and that it is also being prepared for membership in the capitalist European community.

International Views. Erwin Scharf used the Congress of the Austro-Soviet Society to praise Gorbachev's new thinking on international cooperation (*Volksstimme*, 28 January). He emphasized Austria's duty as a neutral state to stand for peace and disarmament. He derided those who equate *glasnost'* with the Prague Spring of 1968. The 9 April *Volksstimme* accused the Austrian government of undermining neutrality by advances to the European community.

The KPO decide to fight privatization as a danger to Austria's independence. *Volksstimme* of 1 May quoted Muhri as saying that selling some especially profitable public enterprises to foreign capital "borders on high treason." On 3 July, *Volksstimme* headlined similar remarks of Muhri with "Austria's Independence in Danger!"

On 10 July, *Volksstimme* proudly announced that, in the early 1990s, the Soviets would take an Austrian into space. When Vienna police broke up a demonstration against Franz-Josef Strauss's visit to the Opera Ball (because of plans in Bavaria for a nuclear plant and AIDS tests for foreigners), the KPO claimed that Strauss was importing Bavarian police methods to Austria (*Volksstimme*, 28 February, 1 March).

Much of the KPO's international activity was in the defense area, where it made common cause with various groups against the stationing of Swedish-made fighter planes in Styria (*Volksstimme*, 22 January, 4 March). In March, Silbermayr demanded a plebiscite on the fighter planes (*Volksstimme*, 18 March). The Styrian KPO (*Volksstimme*, 19 March) coined the slogan *Arbeitsplätze statt Abfangjäger* (jobs instead of fighter planes).

International Activities. On 9 March, Otto Horn participated in a discussion "Austria-GDR Relations—an Example in Europe?" (*Volksstimme*, 11 March). Soon thereafter *Volksstimme* (3 April) reported a congratulatory telegram from Gorbachev to Muhri on Muhri's re-election as party chairman. On 30 June, Schárf reported in *Volksstimme* on communications from West European communist parties regarding a possible peace conference. Scharf criticizes these parties, especially Spain's, as *Eurolinke* (Euroleft) but emphasizes that the Portuguese party under Alvaro Cunhal keeps international communist unity.

In July, Prime Minister Nikolai Ryshkov of the USSR used his official visit to Austria to meet with Muhri, Kalt, and Hans Steiner (*Volksstimme*, 12 July). In November, Muhri led a KPO delegation consisting of himself, Silbermayr, and Steiner on a visit to Moscow. In a meeting with Anatolii F. Dobrynin, a dialogue on the work of the CPSU and the KPO took place (*Pravda*, 14 November).

Eastern Business. *Volksstimme* of 5 May reported that twenty possibilities of joint Austrian–Soviet enterprises were under discussion. Ryshkov's visit to Austria led to substantial Soviet orders from VOEST (*Volksstimme*, 10 July). On 30 October, *Die Presse* reported a joint venture of J. M. Voith AG, a cellulose and paper plant in St. Pölten, lower Austria, with Soviet enterprise. Two weeks later (9 November), *Die Presse* reported an agreement of economic and scientific-technological cooperation between VOEST and the USSR.

Frederick C. Engelmann
University of Alberta

Belgium

Population. 9,873,066
Party. Belgian Communist Party (Parti communiste de Belgique; Kommunistische Partij van Belgie; PCP/KPB)
Founded. 1921
Membership. Under 5,000

Leadership. President: Louis Van Geyt; vice president: Claude Renard; Flemish president: Ludo Loose; Francophone president: Robert Dussart

Politburo. 14 members: Louis Van Geyt; Pierre Beauvois, Robert Dussart, Marcel Levaux, Jacques Moins, Jacques Nagels, Claude Renard, Jules Vercaigne (Francophone); Jan Debrouwere, Jos De Geyter, Miel Dullaert, Roel Jacobs, Ludo Loose, Jef Turf (Fleming)

National Secretariat. Marcel Couteau, Robert Dussart, Daniel Fedrigo (Francophone); Miel Dullaert, Roel Jacobs, Ludo Loose (Fleming)

Francophone Bureau. Didier Bajura, Pierre Beauvois, Marcel Bergen, Marcel Couteau, Robert Dussart, Daniel Fedrigo, Michel Godard, Marcel Levaux, Rosine Lewin, Maurice Magis (son), Jacques Moins, Jacques Nagels, Susa Nudelhole, Claude Renard, Jean-Marie Simon (Liège), Jules Vercaigne, Josiane Vrand

Flemish Bureau. Jos De Geyter, Filip Delmotte, Miel Dullaert, Roel Jacobs, Ludo Loose, Dirk Vonckx, Georges De Clercq, Claude De Smet, Hugo De Witte, Bernard Claeys, Tejo Cockx, Willy Minnebo

Central Committee. 72 members

Status. Legal

Last Congress. Twenty-fifth National, 18–20 April 1986. Second Francophone, 7–8 June 1986. Second Flemish, 7–8 June 1986

Last Election. 13 December 1987, negligible, no representation

Publications. *Drapeau Rouge*, daily party organ in French, Pierre Beauvois, editor; *Rode Vaan*, Dutch-language weekly, Jef Turf, editor

Background. The PCB/KPB has been at best a marginal political force in Belgium since 1945. Initially, after World War II, there were a few years where the party enjoyed minimal electoral successes, but from the 1950s into the mid-1980s, even low-level victories were substantially diminished. In the October 1985 election that gave birth to Martens VI—the sixth center-right mixed ministry coalition led by Wilfried Martens, the Flemish Christian Democrat—the Belgian communists lost two seats in the chambers and one in the senate. The consequences of this further reduction in the PCB/KPB appeal and drawing power included elaborate 1987 debate and discussion and some limited reorienting and restructuring of this small party.

The December 1987 election results did not alter this PCB political impotence (*NYT*, 15 December). When compared with the 1985 election, the communists continued to lose voters not just to language parties and peace and disarmament groupings but also to the ecological Greens of the AGALEV.

Domestic Affairs. In a partial and belated reaction to nearly a generation of regionalized politics in Belgium, the PCB has recently stumbled into an ambivalent political strategy of compromise. The party continued to put ideology over language and culture in an absolute sense until 1986. Although it remained at year's end basically federal in organization, with central institutions proclaiming policy for both of the Belgian-language communities, the PCB/KPB slowly and haltingly displayed some evidences that it might alter its traditional class-based strategy as nonresponsive to the more paramount language and ethnic divisions in the nation. The Twenty-fifth Party Congress of 1986 adopted some federalization principles that implied not only two formal wings to the party but also a greater receptivity to "individual region issue responses" (*Le Soir*, 10 December, 1986). There were, nevertheless, clear indicators that the real absence of structural adaptation would continue, with the party rhetoric emhasizing working-class themes and the "transnational capital" enemies. If any break in this continuum appeared on the horizon, it was in the north-south, Fleming-Walloon and economically sound and strong versus economically weak and depressed bifurcation of Belgium as it was reflected in the PCB/KPB. Traditional Marxist-Leninist notions and solutions persisted more strongly in the crisis-ridden Walloon south, with Flemish communists of the north demonstrating a stronger proclivity to "forge progressive and cooperative alliances" not only among the economically and socially unfortunate elements of society but also on those problems unique to certain regions and peoples. In the north, there was among communists a greater desire to regionalize the PCB in its entirety. Since the francophone portion of the PCB/KPB was still predominant (roughly three to every one Flemish-speaking), this regionalization process was curtailed by not only demographic but economic factors. For more than a generation, the waning industrial facilities of Liège, Charleroi, Namur, Mons, and Brussels have meant stronger left-wing political strength in the south as a whole.

Another important variable in the politics of communism in Belgium was the low level and fragmented nature of any Euroleft coalition, lacking even multiple common interests. Domestic and foreign policy issue differences between socialists and communists continued to exist, and, in fact, the PCB/KPB diversities were also mirrored in the schism and cleavages within the Parti Socialiste (PS) and its two language wings. Beyond some significant general critiques of austerity-oriented Martens Belgium that the PS and PCB shared, constant bickering and often outright hostility between noncommunist and communist left characterized the Belgian scene (*Drapeau Rouge*, 23 October). Additionally, there was the difficulty that contemporary terrorism bequeathed to the PCB. The 1984–1985 bombings attributed to an independent terrorist group called the Fighting Communist Cells resulted in a public outcry that appeared to give the PCB an undeserved but extremely bad image.

Some of the left opposition common cause and criticism of the government did play a major role in the collapse of Martens VI in October. The immediate issue was the Fourons/Voeren affair (see *YICA*, 1987), as it had been in October 1986 when Martens offered to resign and the king refused (*NYT*, *CSM*, 20 October). But the confrontation in the Flemish village on the linguistic frontier concerning its francophone mayor was surely only the tip of the iceberg of troubles that the Martens' coalition faced by fall 1987. The fragile truce collapsed on 15 October over the reluctance of the mayor to not only speak Dutch in Dutch-speaking Flanders but also to submit to a test of his Flemish language capability and to step down when a September 1986 court ruling directed him to do so (*Drapeau Rouge*, 17–18 October). The linguistic controversy was worsened for the government by the sharp left attacks on the Martens' economy recovery program. The PCB/KPB had opposed the "social war" of the government and its extensive reduced budget, saying that they would both end the liberal welfare state of 50 years duration in Belgium and further marginalize the Belgian working class (*Drapeau Rouge*, 24–25 October). In tandem with the PS, the communists assaulted Martens' call for wholesale privatization of public service and social program cuts, particularly in education and health.

One privatizing effort that particularly attracted PCB wrath was the project to move Zaventum, the Brussels airport, from a public facility to a private one, to be called the Brussels Airport International Company (*Drapeau Rouge*, 25 March, 12, 16 July). Another result of the public-private conversion process for the PCB was the supposed involvement of such "notables" as Etienne Davignon, the former Belgian minister of economic affairs and now head of a major Belgian bank, who were alleged to be the outright beneficiaries of these transfers of power (*Drapeau Rouge*, 24 June).

The double-digit Belgian unemployment (more than 13 percent) was also a subject of significance in the PCB opposition to such Martens measures as pay cuts through wage controls, the denial of state subsidies for industrial redevelopment, and even the absence of youth training programs in the Martens recovery agenda (*Drapeau Rouge*, 17–18 October). An alternative communist recovery scheme, which created a "new society" and called for "social renewal," found the answer in new jobs, a minimum income, and a reduced work week. Given the budget deficit and the Martens call to reduce government expenditures, the PCB/KPB often split with the PS on economic recovery measures, most frequently citing the socialist right-wing practice of compromise politics rather than opposition based on principle. The communists furthermore alienated an important political element when they attacked the accommodation position of the Socialist Trade Union Federation (*Drapeau Rouge*, 12 September).

Foreign Policy. Again in 1987 there was a strong relationship between cardinal domestic and foreign policy issues for the PCB/KPB. The party program of social and economic renaissance was closely linked to disarmament and peace. The manifestation of 25 October (*desarmer pour developper*) gave clear evidence of this attempt to associate PCB/KPB international perspectives with national economic circumstances. Van Geyt, the PCB president, said that "only advancement to disarmament will eventually make it possible to save funds so necessary for economic development and social progress." Criticisms of the militarization of space through Strategic Defense Initiative ventures (supported in some Western European nations) were tied to not just the "ultramilitaristic Reagan policy and its arms monopoly interests" but to the "transnational invasion and penetration of Belgium" (*Drapeau Rouge*, 24–25 October). Transnational Capitalism (TNC), said the communists, should be controlled by the state, which would decide on all key investments and insist on the profits being reinvested in the national economy to promote growth. So too, said the PCB, should the state prohibit sudden enterprise closures, making their fate part of long-term national planning. This battle against the Martens *néoliberalisme* emphasized the complicity of the government with such Belgian-based TNCs as Ford, Volvo, Citroen, Michelin, Bell,

Philips, GM, and Siemens (*Drapeau Rouge*, 31 May).

One example of PCB/KPB interpretation that intertwined social ideology, economic problems, and foreign policy attitudes was the assessment of the Heysel tragedy of 1985. During the summer trial in Brussels of 26 British soccer fans for their part in the soccer match violence that resulted in 39 deaths, the PCB called the British "hooligans" but stressed the point that these were "marginalized and unemployed youth, manipulated by the extreme-right British ruling elite and its political culture" (*Drapeau Rouge*, 14 July).

Disarmament seen in the widest context was not simply the communist advocacy of the Mikhail Gorbachev–intermediate-range nuclear forces (INF) treaty approach throughout the year but the promulgation of a more extensive *option zéro globale* and the escape from the dominance of U.S. and transnational corporations. The foreign policy of the PCB/KPB moved from its anti-Euromissile stance of the early 1980s into a position of strong support for a superpower agreement on the denuclearization of Europe and coupled this INF proponent posture with revamping and reorienting NATO (*Drapeau Rouge*, 19–20 September).

Nuclear arms reductions increasingly appeared to become in 1987 the essential mobilizing issue for the PCB/KPB. The Central Committee stated its position when it called for Europe's small- and medium-sized nations to step up their calls for the elimination of nuclear weapons on the continent and accentuated this demand when Belgium chaired the governing bodies of the European community in the first six months of 1987. The Belgian communists focused on the Martens government when they demanded that Belgium pursue a more independent foreign policy and actively support the creation in Central Europe of a nuclear-free corridor and ultimately a nuclear-free zone comprising both Germanies, the Benelux and Scandinavian states, plus Poland, Czechoslovakia, and Hungary. Clearly the linkage between overcoming the socioeconomic crisis and diminishing national defense expenditures was drawn over and over again, with little attention given to the vast implications for NATO conventional force build-up or the consequences of redirected burden sharing for nations with lingering economic malaise like Belgium (*Drapeau Rouge*, 3 March, 24–25 October).

Accelerating superpower disarmament and extolling Gorbachev became interrelated joint goals of the PCB/KPB during the year. The admiration and support of both the international policy and the domestic reforms of the Russian leader became a centerpiece of PCB discussion (see *WMR*, October and the statement of Turf). Hubert Cambier, the longtime *Drapeau Rouge* correspondent in Moscow, communicated continuous and even escalating praise of domestic *perestroika* and a European nuclear arms pact, but his reports more often centered on the general secretary's pressing for greater East-West dialogue and increased cooperation (*Drapeau Rouge*, 22 May, 12 July).

When the two communist leaders of East Germany and Hungary, Erich Honecker and János Kádár, visited Belgium 13–15 October and 16–17 November, respectively, the PCB/KPB pronouncements for building confidence and multilateral "trans-European" cooperation were at their strongest. These state visits did encourage joint ventures between "progressive left" states, both economic and cultural, but argued strongly for a principled U.S.-USSR agreement on first the European abolition of intermediate- and shorter-range weapons and then substantial reduction of all strategic weapons (*Le Soir*, 20 November). Therefore, a consistency between the past and present existed for communists in lumping together various foreign policy goals, such as the autonomy of Belgium (and Western Europe) from the United States and transnational titans, further cooperation between socialist and capitalist Europe, and solidarity with the Third World. The primary objective of the party in Belgium in this year, however, became the steadfast and unyielding primary push for nuclear disarmament (*WMR*, October).

Pierre-Henri Laurent
Tufts University

Cyprus

Population. 683,651 (80 percent Greek; 18 percent Turkish)

Party. Progressive Party of the Working People (Anorthotikon Komma Ergazomenou Laou; AKEL)

Founded. 1922 (AKEL, 1941)

Membership. 12,000 (estimated); 67 percent industrial workers and employees, 20 percent peasants and middle class, 24 percent women, 30 percent under 30 years old; all from Greek Cypriot community

General Secretary. Ezekias Papaioannou

Politburo. 13 members: Ezekias Papaioannou, Andreas Fandis, Dinos Konstantinou, G. Katsouridhis, Khambis Mikhailidhis, Andreas Ziartidhis, Khristos Petas, Kiriakos Khristou, Mikhail Poumbouris, G. Khristodoulidhis, A. Mikhailidhis, G. Sophokles, Dhonis Kristofinis

Secretariat. 3 members: Ezekias Papaoiannou, Andreas Fandis (deputy general secretary), Dinos Konstantinou (organizing secretary)

Status. Legal

Last Congress. Sixteenth, 26-30 November 1986; extraordinary, 20 December, to endorse Vasiliou as presidential candidate

Last Election. 1985, 27.4 percent, 15 of 56 seats

Auxiliary Organizations. Pan-Cypriot Workers' Federation (PEO), 45,000 members, Andreas Ziartidhis, general secretary; United Democratic Youth Organization (EDON), 14,000 members; Confederation of Women's Organizations; Pan-Cyprian Peace Council; Pan-Cyprian Federation of Students and Young Professionals; Union of Greek Cypriots in England, 1,200 members (considered London branch of AKEL); Pan-Cypriot National Organization of Secondary Students; Cypriot Farmers' Union

Publications. *Kharavyi* (Dawn), AKEL daily newspaper; *Demokratia*, AKEL weekly; *Neo Kairoi* (New Times), AKEL magazine; *Ergatiko Vima* (Workers' Stride), PEO weekly; *Neolaia* (Youth), EDON weekly

Since the establishment of the Republic of Cyprus in 1960, the AKEL has consistently proven to be the island's best-organized grass roots political party. This was certainly true in past parliamentary elections but was even demonstrated at the local level in the May 1986 municipal elections, the first since 1953, when Cyprus was still a British Crown Colony. The returns gave the AKEL 32.5 percent of the total Greek Cypriot vote, and today the communists hold the office of mayor in nine of the eighteen cities in the southern part of the presently truncated Republic of Cyprus. Among the Greek Cypriots, therefore, "the positions won by AKEL are giving it broader opportunities for influencing domestic policy, protecting the interests of the working people, and reinforcing its links to large sections of the population" (*WMR*, May).

Although the AKEL is not officially banned in the northern sector of the island (called since November 1983 the Turkish Republic of Northern Cyprus [TRNC] by the Turkish Cypriots), the communists have never attempted to establish an overt presence there. Although there may have been card-carrying communists among the Turkish Cypriots before 1960, the number today is probably insignificant. The same observation may be made about Turkish Cypriot membership in the AKEL labor front, the PEO, which flourishes in the southern half of the de facto partitioned island. There are two left-wing political parties in the TRNC: the Turkish Republican Party (CTP) and the smaller communal Liberation Party (TKP), both of which operate legally. The daughter of Ozker Ozgur, the CTP chairman, was granted a full scholarship to Prague University, the first ever given to a Turkish Cypriot student. The CTP also sponsors the Revolutionary Youth Organization (DGD), whose members have attended conferences in Bulgaria and the Soviet Union. The CTP publishes AKEL propaganda in its party newspaper, *Yeni Duzen* (New Order) and is known to agree with the communist line on the Afghanistan question.

Leadership and Organization. The AKEL is reputed to be a tightly controlled apparatus, structured along the principle of democratic centralism. The highest body is the congress, which is convened every four years. The Sixteenth Congress was held in 1986 and coincided with the 60th anniversary of the first party congress of the founding Communist Party of Cyprus (CPC). All of the officials of the governing hierarchy are elected at the party congress. Papaioannou, the 79-year-old careerist who has been general secretary since 1949, was re-elected in 1986, as were most of the gerontocracy that has ruled the AKEL for decades. At the Sixteenth Party Congress, delegations "from 33 fraternal parties" were in Cyprus to observe the AKEL proceedings (*WMR*, March).

Significant changes were made during the year in the editorial staff of *Kharavyi*, the AKEL daily newspaper. The chief editor, Andreas Kannaouros, was replaced by former manager Andonios Khristodoulou, and the chief commentator of the newspaper, Stavros Angelidhis, was succeeded by Kipros Kourtellaris, a member of the staff. One noncommunist source alleged that the changes were "connected with internal disputes concerning

Mikhail Gorbachev's *glasnost'* and *perestroika* policies or about the party's support for the independent presidential candidate, Yeoryios Vasiliou, in the 1988 election" (*Cyprus Mail*, 7 November). It was not clear why these staff changes were made in the first instance, but the AKEL Central Committee, in its usual slavish manner, declared unequivocally "that the party leadership had from the very start supported the *glasnost'* and *perestroika* launched by the Soviet Communist Party" (ibid.).

Domestic Party Affairs. General Secretary Papaioannou published a long article during the year in which he wrote the following: "The situation on our domestic front, given the conditions of the antioccupation, anti-imperialist, liberation struggle, is not what it should be." Consequently, the class struggle between labor and capital "is not the most important duty" at this time when Cyprus is in the struggle "for liberation and independence." (*WMR*, March.) The communist leader lamented the "disappointing experience of cooperation between AKEL and the Democratic Party," headed by President Spyros Kiprianou, which "materialized in 1982." He noted that communist "history teaches that the policy of alliances . . . is correct and imperative beyond any doubt, provided it is based on principles and lessons that we learn from the experiences of the past." Thus an alliance may be short or long term as long as it provides the "means to attain a specific goal" (ibid.). It was surely with these slogans in mind that Papaioannou announced in a midyear speech that the AKEL would support Vasiliou, the independent candidate, in the 1988 presidential elections. Although Vasiliou's platform "is not identical with AKEL's on all points," there is sufficient concurrence on the "principal questions of policy and tactics in struggling for a Cyprus solution, on nonaligned foreign policy, and on fundamental issues of social and economic policy" (Nicosia Domestic Service, 10 July). Choosing to oppose incumbent President Kyprianou, whom the AKEL helped to elect five years earlier, was the most significant decision the communists in Cyprus made in domestic affairs during the year.

In the same speech in which the AKEL general secretary endorsed the independent presidential candidate, Papaioannou saw fit to reiterate the communist positions in favor of "the withdrawal of Turkish troops and settlers, dissolution of foreign bases, return of all refugees and determination of the fate of missing persons" (*WMR*, March). He further stressed the need to convene an international conference under the auspices of the U.N. and, with the support of the Soviet Union, to solve the Cyprus question. Although it has been the AKEL's policy repeatedly to ask for such an international conference, the Cypriot communists claim that the obstacle is "Western imperialist circles" that are afraid such a move "will give the Soviet Union the right to have a say in the Cyprus question at a time when Cyprus is in the sphere of influence of the West" (*IB*, February).

When the Swedish government stated in midyear that its troops would leave the U.N. Peacekeeping Force in Cyprus at the end of 1987, a report surfaced that they would be replaced by Polish troops. This caused an immediate objection by the U.S. State Department "even though Polish troops had served with various U.N. peace missions in the past" (*Kharavyi*, 4 July). In a rare display of humor, the communist newspaper then quoted from the right-wing Cypriot journal *Alithia* (Truth), whose editor suggested that the United States should gladly accept the participation of the Polish contingent because "one should not rule out the possibility that for the first time an entire military contingent might defect to the West—something that I think has never happened" (ibid.). The communist writer ended his piece with this sarcastic comment: "Admittedly these Americans are very stupid. They could have never thought of such a thing, they are so foolish. It seems that the State Department needs better advisers."

After the government of Cyprus signed the long-awaited European Economic Community Customs Union Agreement in October, the AKEL criticized the government because "this agreement is the start of new hardships for the suffering Cypriot people." The communists direly predicted that the agreement would bring about "the destruction of the Cypriot economy, annihilation of agricultural population, a rise in the cost of living and unemployment, enslavement of the economy to international monopolies, undermining of the country's nonaligned foreign policy, and creation of a dangerous complication in the Cyprus issue." In conclusion, the AKEL demanded "that before the agreement is implemented there be a referendum so the people might decide" (Nicosia Domestic Service, 20 October).

International Views, Positions, and Activities. It is the AKEL position that because of the determinants of history, the geographic location, and its small size, Cyprus is "more exposed to foreign policy issues" than are many other countries (*WMR*, March). In addition, "the external and internal aspects of the Cyprus problem are so interwoven that it is virtually impossible to separate them." The security of Cyprus is linked to the security of its "neighbors and to peace in the region of the Mediterranean." The communists are, therefore, concerned about "NATO bases" on Cyprus that are "a mere half-hour's flight" from the southern borders of the USSR. The presence of the U.S. Sixth Fleet and U.S. "provocations against Libya and Syria," which could bring about a larger war, also trouble the AKEL leaders, who insist on "a return to a policy of détente." The communist goal of world peace can only come about if there is "the destruction of nuclear arsenals," the elimination of the U.S. Star Wars initiative, and the prevention of "a fresh escalation of the arms race by imperialism" (ibid.).

The AKEL again expressed "its total solidarity with and support for the Cuban people and its great leader, comrade Fidel Castro" (*IB*, February). In addition, the AKEL gave its encouragement to "the liberation struggles of other Latin American countries," specifically Nicaragua, El Salvador, and Chile, as well as to the Palestinians, the Namibians, and the mainland Turks, who are now living under "a camouflaged dictatorship" (ibid.). The communists in Cyprus reaffirmed that they are guided by "the healthy and invincible principles of Marxism-Leninism and proletarian internationalism" (*IB*, February).

In February, Cypriot President Kiprianou made his country's first state visit to Cuba, accompanied by members of the AKEL. In April, the chief of the Soviet ministry's first European department visited President Kiprianou in Cyprus, and "particular attention was paid to promoting the idea of an international conference on Cyprus" (Nicosia Domestic Service, 4 April). In May, a seven-member Soviet trade delegation came to Cyprus at the invitation of the Cyprus Chamber of Commerce and Industry "to further strengthen and develop bilateral economic ties" (ibid., 3 May). The premier of Czechoslovakia, Lubomír Štrougal, made a state visit to Cyprus in May and promised "that the close links of friendship and cooperation between the two countries will strengthen and expand even further" (Nicosia Domestic Service, 21 May). At the same time, Hungary's deputy foreign trade minister was invited to visit the Twelfth International Cyprus State Fair and expressed the desire "to further promote and expand Cypriot-Hungarian cooperation in the commercial, economic, and other fields" (ibid., 23 May). AKEL member Christoforos Ioannides visited Prague to attend a symposium on the "U.S. Policy of Neoglobalism, the Military-Industrial Complex, Contemporary Militarism and the Working Class" (*WMR*, September). Lastly, AKEL general secretary Papaioannou led a delegation to Moscow "at the invitation of the CPSU in order to participate in celebrations marking the 70th anniversary of the October Socialist Revolution" (Nicosia Domestic Service, 1 November).

T.W. Adams
Washington, D.C.

Denmark

Population. 5,130,260
Party. Communist Party of Denmark (Danmarks Kommunistiske Parti; DKP)
Founded. 1919
Membership. Under 10,000 (estimated, including youth and student fronts)
Chairman. Ole Sohn
General Secretary. Poul Emanuel
Executive Committee. 16 members: Ole Sohn, Ib Nørlund, Poul Emanuel, Bernard Jeune, Kurt Kristensen, Dan Lundstrup, Freddy Madsen, Anette Nielsen, Bo Rosschou, Frank Aaen (editor of *Land og Folk*), Anker Schjerning, Rita Sørensen, Inger Rasmussen, Sten Parker Sørensen, Harry Osborn (last 6 are new), 1 vacancy
Secretariat. 6 members: Ole Sohn, Poul Emanuel, Frank Aaen, Bo Rosschou, 1 vacancy
Central Committee. 50 members, 17 candidate members
Status. Legal
Last Congress. Twenty-eighth, 16–19 April 1987
Last Election. 8 September 1987, 0.9 percent, no representation
Auxiliary Organizations. Communist Youth of Denmark (Danmarks Kommunistiske Ungdom; DKU), Ole Jensen, chair; Communist Students of Denmark (Danmarks Kommunistiske Studenter; KOMM.S.), Poul-Erik Bjørn Nielsen, chair
Publications. *Land og Folk* (Nation and People), daily circulation 6,500 weekdays and 13,000

weekends; *Tiden-Verden Rund* (Times Around the World), theoretical monthly; *Fremad* (Forward), DKU monthly

The year 1987 saw more change than usual on the left wing of Danish politics, which for once included the DKP. Ten years of lackluster leadership by the affable Jørgen Jensen ended with his death at age 66 in April, on the eve of the Twenty-eighth DKP Congress. (His retirement had been expected at the congress.) A dual leadership emerged, with 32-year-old activist Sohn as chair and 47-year-old trade unionist Jan Andersen, vice-chair. Andersen's sudden death in July made the new "team leadership" experiment a brief one. The congress and a new generation of leaders raised public interest in the DKP. Periodic political polling, a Danish habit, revealed that, for the first time in years, the DKP's standing exceeded 1 percent. The sudden 8 September parliamentary elections caught most parties unaware. The DKP polled just under 29,000 votes (0.9 percent), a scant improvement of 5,846 votes over 1984. The DKP has not been represented in parliament since October 1979, when its vote fell below the 2 percent minimum required for proportional representation in the 179-seat unicameral Folketing (parliament).

The September parliamentary elections produced considerable changes in the party lineup. Sixteen parties fielded candidates, with six Marxist parties (including the DKP) running to the left of the reformist Social Democratic Party (SDP). Eight parties actually won seats in the new parliament, but the real issue is the balance between the two basic blocs: socialist and nonsocialist. Although the socialists had a net gain of three seats, a majority still backed conservative Prime Minister Poul Schlüter. The SDP lost two seats (from 56 to 54), and, following the disappointing election, Anker Jørgensen, its leader for the past fifteen years, resigned. The new SDP chair (and thus the presumptive alternative prime minister) is 44-year-old Svend Auken, a veteran parliamentarian, former labor minister, and political scientist.

Other changes on the left were more dramatic. The independent Marxist Socialist People's Party (Socialistiske Folkeparti; SF) gained 6 seats (bringing its total to 27) and almost 15 percent of the vote. Its advance, long heralded by the polls, reopened the question of its participation with SDP in a socialist coalition government or, as in 1966–1967 and 1971–1973, as a supporting party.

The Left Socialist Party (Venstresocialisterne; VS) torn by internal strife, lost their three remaining seats (two had previously defected to the SF) as their vote fell to a meager 1.4 percent. In contrast, a colorful new contingent of radical socialists entered parliament with the boss of the Seamen's Union, Preben Møller Hansen, at the helm. Composed mostly of former communists and current union activists, the new group, called the Common Course Workers' Party (Arbejderpartiet Faelles Kurs; CCP), gained 2.2 percent of the vote, enough to receive the minimum of four seats. The net gain of radical socialist parties was thus five seats.

Schlüter's minority government can no longer govern solely with the aid of the centrist Radical Liberals. The ultraconservative Progress Party, strengthened with the release from prison (for tax evasion) of its colorful leader, Mogens Glistrup, could provide the necessary votes, but the Radical Liberals will not join such a constellation. Schlüter's alternative is to seek pragmatic cooperation with the SDP, which seemed to be succeeding in December when the SDP supported, for the first time in five years, the national budget. What this will mean for the socialist bloc is uncertain.

The election occurred at a time of growing economic uncertainty. Rapid growth and falling unemployment in 1985–1986 had weakened Denmark's precarious balance of payments. The government had been forced to enact austerity measures (the so-called potato cure), which ended economic growth, increased unemployment to more than 8 percent by the end of the year, but reduced the balance of payments deficit to 60 percent of the 1985 level.

Foreign and security policies have been issues of strife between the socialist opposition and the government. The SDP can count on the Radical Liberals (normally supporters of the government) and the other leftist parties to oppose and harass the government. Since 1982 this has forced the government, against its will, to frequently resist NATO policies. Prime Minister Schlüter has chosen not to make foreign and security policy issues matters of confidence for his government, and in 1987 there was some domestic political "détente" on the issue, reflecting international improvements in East-West relations.

Thus with 17 percent of the vote and the parliamentary seats, the radical socialists may have considerable impact on the SDP replacing the weakened nonsocialist coalition. The issue for the new SDP leader, Svend Auken, is whether to seek pragmatic compromises with the center right government and risk losing more votes to the increasingly attractive SF or whether to force a political showdown only months after assuming the leadership of the country's largest party. If the next election confirms the current division, the SDP would then have to try to govern with radical socialist support, an experiment that ended disastrously in 1967 and 1973. The DKP remains remarkably irrelevant to all of this.

Leadership and Organization. Change is rarely on the program of the DKP, but when death and consistent failure confront its stolid cadres, even they respond. The Twenty-eighth Congress had been expected to produce some changes, particularly at the top. Jensen's retirement was expected, and Sohn and Andersen were already seen as successors. Both men had typical DKP backgrounds. Sohn rose quickly through the DKU into the Semi-skilled Workers' Union (SID) politics in the Jutland town of Horsens. In 1980 he was elected to the party Central Committee and three years later, to the Executive Committee. In 1982–1984 he sat on the town council. Andersen's Copenhagen background in the Metal Workers' Union was similar to Jensen's, but Andersen's prominence stemmed from leadership in the Shop Stewards' Movement (Formandsinitiativet), which periodically organized radical union activities (wildcat strikes and demonstrations) against state intervention in labor relations (*Nordisk Kontakt*, no. 7). His sudden death in July ended what might have been an interesting experiment in pluralism at the top of the DKP.

The party's highest authority is the triennial congress. The Central Committee is elected at the congress, and it, in turn, elects the party's Executive Committee (Politburo), chair, secretary, and other posts. Despite the attendance of some 460 delegates at the 1987 congress, which showed greater openness, the DKP functions fully in the Leninist model of a self-perpetuating elite. In recent years the Central Committee has met from four to six times annually. During noncongress years, the party holds an annual meeting. Such meetings, typically held in the early autumn, reaffirm the general party goals as set at the congress and are occasions for the party to use media coverage to make known views on domestic and foreign affairs. Despite the party's weakness, media coverage is surprisingly good.

The Twenty-eighth Congress was more interesting for intraparty changes than for new political positions. The national press wondered whether Mikhail Gorbachev's *glasnost'* would be felt across the Baltic. The congress was preceded by general discussion of openness in the party press *(Land og Folk)*, but the selection of new leadership and the party's program seemed very much in the Leninist tradition. The creation of the new post of deputy chair ensured that there would be room for both Sohn and Andersen at the top. For years, chief ideologue Nørlund was recognized as the number two man in the party. Not surprisingly he and his "old guard" colleagues were not pleased by changes in the DKP *(Information*, 15 April). Several changes were made at the congress in the composition of the 50-member Central Committee and in the party's bylaws, but they were trivial and did not change the practice of "democratic centralism."

Other young Executive Committee members are likely to challenge Sohn's leadership if the party's position does not improve shortly. Aaen, the political editor of *Land og Folk* and a former communist student leader, is a vigorous activist and a new member of the Executive Committee. Jens Bonde Nielsen, a leader of the anti-European Community Popular Movement and a member of the European Parliament, is another prominent member of the younger generation. It is interesting that he did not make the new Executive Committee as his name had been mentioned the year before as a possible candidate for chair. His "European" activities might be difficult to combine with a prominent party post.

The DKP's problem is not attracting energetic and talented activists but holding them inside a rigid, hierarchical, and Stalinist apparatus when many more promising opportunities may be found in the Danish left wing.

Domestic Affairs. With no parliamentary seats and greatly reduced representation in local government, the DKP was mainly a peripheral observer and critic of Danish domestic affairs. The surprisingly easy collective bargaining agreement of March and April, in part because trade unions have been decentralized to individual sector unions, deprived the DKP of one of its few remaining sources of influence: activism within the trade union movement. Communist and other labor militants such as the late Andersen and the late Hansen have staged dramatic confrontations over the years (without notable success). The labor movement remains, nonetheless, a principal area of action.

Although industrial labor relations, particularly for the skilled workers' unions, were generally fruitful and peaceful, public sector and unskilled workers continued to lose economic ground. Hospital doctors, in whose union DKP elements and others have become increasingly militant, undertook periodic action for improved pay and, especially, reduced duty hours. The DKP assiduously courts public employees, but so do the other radical socialist parties, with considerably more success.

The possibility of socialist alternative government was backed by all of the leftist parties in principle, but only for the SF was the issue entirely germane. The DKP supported the alternative, but its program, reaffirmed at the April congress, showed little new thinking. The DKP criticizes the nonsocialists for their various austerity programs and is skeptical about various wage earner fund ("economic democracy") proposals currently in fashion among Nordic social democratic parties. True to its history, the DKP calls for "nationalization" of large industrial and financial concerns. Also alive are DKP proposals for shorter working hours (without reductions in wage demands), increased taxation of the private sector, restoration of automatic cost-of-living raises, and restrictions on the movement of capital in and out of Denmark. Meanwhile public spending on defense is to be cut sharply while social spending leaps ahead (*Land og Folk*, 21 April). Although several West European communist parties claim to be a radicalizing force of the larger reformist social democrats, the DKP is of no interest to the Danish SDP except indirectly through struggles in certain labor unions (*WMR*, May).

Following the DKP's failure to make electoral headway in the September national elections, the issue of cooperation with other radical socialist parties arose again. Such collaboration has never been characteristic of the DKP. With the VS now also outside parliament, the issue of an electoral alliance seemed germane, especially since the prognosis was for another election sooner rather than later. Pointing to such an alliance in the Popular Movement (PM) against the European Community (EC), Sohn felt that both the DKP and VS could benefit from supporters who no longer risked throwing away their vote. Sohn's comments that the VS was on its last legs, with its left wing heading to the DKP and its right toward the SF cannot have warmed interparty relations (*Politiken Weekly*, 18 November).

Foreign Affairs. The revival of East-West détente in the wake of the November 1986 Reykjavik summit and the apparently successful conclusion of the intermediate-range nuclear forces treaty a year later produced a domestic security policy détente in Denmark. The DKP, whose fortunes have always been closely tied to world affairs, has had few initial gains from either the domestic or the international thaw. Changes in Soviet foreign policy present few problems for the DKP; their support for the USSR is consistent and complete. Moreover, foreign affairs gives the DKP a mechanism for mobilizing groups that would not otherwise have much interest in the party's program.

The peace movement is a recurring target of DKP activity, even though many peace issues enjoy broad support across the Danish political spectrum. DKP executive committeeman Schjerning spearheads the party's activities within the peace movement. The DKP perspective, of course, is to give the USSR full credit for any arms control progress and the United States and its allies (especially NATO in the abstract) blame for any tensions or failed negotiations. The October 1986 Copenhagen Peace Congress, which was dominated by European communists, formed the background for much DKP international affairs propaganda. Although some of the issues favored at the congress and by the DKP enjoy noncommunist support—the proposed but nebulous Nordic Nuclear Weapons–Free Zone is the most prominent—the party has little direct influence in the domestic security policy debate (*WMR*, January, June).

The anti-EC role of the DKP has been another area of pragmatic cooperation. As noted, Jens Bonde Nielsen, a communist, is one of the leaders of the PM against the EC and sits in the European Parliament. In the parliament the PM delegation of four (Denmark has sixteen seats) sits with the Communist and Allied Groups bloc. The PM, along with other Danish EC opponents, has been quiescent since their defeat in the February 1986 national referendum, which approved Danish accession to the Single European Act. PM activist Else Hammerich campaigned unsuccessfully for a similar referendum in Ireland. Her carpetbagging activities brought disparaging remarks from the voluble Danish foreign minister, Uffe Ellemann-Jensen.

International Party Contacts. Funerals and party meetings bring foreign attention, and thus 1987 was a busy year internationally for the DKP. The Soviet delegation at the Twenty-eighth Congress was headed by Boris Pugo, a high-ranking official of the Latvian party. In his speech to the congress, Pugo reiterated Soviet offers for the reduction of political tensions and weapons in Europe

(TASS, 14, 17 April). The German Democratic Republic (GDR) and its ruling Socialist Unity Party of Germany (SED) have had especially close ties to the DKP in the past decade. Chairman Jensen died in the GDR, where he had gone for medical treatment. The SED was also represented prominently at the congress. Shortly after his election, DKP chair Sohn had extensive talks in Berlin with Hermann Axen, a member of the SED Politburo, who has taken a continuing interest in Nordic affairs. Not surprisingly they found themselves in complete agreement on all current European issues (*Neues Deutschland*, 14 July).

Delegates and greetings from many foreign communist parties at the April DKP congress indicate that despite its political weakness, it is still accorded the honors appropriate to its continuing commitment to "proletarian internationalism" (that is, loyalty to the USSR and its allies) (*Land og Folk*, 21 April).

Other Marxist/Leftist Groups. The DKP is only one of several left-wing parties currently active in Danish politics. The September elections showed that the SF is by far the most powerful of these groups. Originally a splinter from the DKP (in 1958), the SF has steadily gained ground despite a decade of internal splits and electoral setbacks between 1968 and 1977. Ever since it won its first parliamentary representation in 1960, the SF has sought to push the SDP leftward. In 1966–1967 and 1971–1973, SF votes kept the Social Democrats in power. The first experiment in formal SF-SDP collaboration (the so-called Red Cabinet) ended when the SF's left wing split off to form the VS. Such collaboration with the Marxist left has worried SDP moderates, and in 1973, several right-wing Social Democrats abandoned their party to form the Center Democrats. Following the SF's advance in December 1981, it appeared that another effort would be made at collaboration, but necessary support from the VS and centrist groups was absent. Throughout the 1987 parliamentary and electoral debates, both the SF and the SDP sought to denote their differences without excluding political collaboration. At its summer annual conference, SF declared that it would not pose ultimatums on the SDP in either domestic or foreign affairs. The goal was to replace the Schlüter government (*Nordisk Kontakt*, no. 8). Veteran SF chair Gert Petersen stressed similar themes during the brief election campaign (*Politiken Weekly*, 3 September). Grass roots SF activists worry that the party's romance with the SDP will pull it again to the right. Meanwhile SDP leftists find the collaboration attractive (*Politiken Weekly*, 15 April; *Nordisk Kontakt*, no. 6).

The traditional SDP centrist allies, the Radical Liberals, have continued to support the Schlüter government's domestic program but have joined with the SDP (and occasionally the SF) on foreign and security policy issues. New SDP Chair Auken's decision to work out a budget compromise with the government in December suggests that he does not consider a formal or informal coalition with SF an immediate alternative.

The SF program is at least part of the problem. It is decidedly socialist, pacifist, and Marxist, even as it emphasizes Danish values and rejects foreign socialist models. SF's bargaining starts with five main conditions: adjustment of unemployment insurance and other social benefit payments to make up for inflation and cuts since 1982, a reduction in the standard working day to seven hours (without wage cuts), compulsory employee profit sharing and codetermination (economic democracy), fiscal and monetary policy free from EC interference, and declaration of Denmark as an unconditional nuclear weapons–free zone.

The SF is explicitly non-Leninist in both its internal party governance and its attitudes toward Danish parliamentary democracy. Its earlier feuds and schisms (especially when assuming indirect government responsibility) have faded under the experienced leadership of its veteran chairman, Gert Petersen. It has captured nearly a sixth of the parliamentary vote, exhibited substantial strength in local and regional government, and gained strength in the labor movement (especially among public sector and academic employees). With over 10,000 members (more than doubling in the past decade), the SF is an attractive alternative to dissatisfied SDP and other leftists. It offers a "soft" and democratic form of Danish Marxism and democratic-socialist alternatives without reference to or apologies for unsuccessful experiences elsewhere.

The VS is much weaker, and with its 1987 electoral disaster the party's future is again in doubt. Several of its original founders, like Preben Wilhjelm, have become inactive. Its pragmatic "realist" wing has drifted mainly into the SF, while its "opposition" Leninist wing may find a reinvigorated DKP attractive. The party has been through numerous crises in its twenty-year history. Moribund parties have remarkable longevity in Denmark, especially as the number of "protest" voters seems to be a significant portion of the modern Danish electorate. Whenever a party can signal its sympathy for discontent, renaissance is possible.

Such discontent may explain the gains made by Hansen's CCP. Hansen's party program, which he wrote, is similar to DKP's without ties to Moscow. He favors increased social expenditures on youth and older people financed by compulsory savings of interest paid to large bond holders (*Nordisk Kontakt*, no. 9). What may better explain Hansen's success is the overtly anti-immigrant tone of the CCP campaign in August. Denmark has had an exceptionally liberal refugee law and received thousands of refugees, the merit of whose cases has not always been apparent to the average citizen. South Asian and especially Middle Eastern refugees have been the most controversial. Despite her reputation for tolerance and liberality, Denmark is still a relatively homogeneous society that guards its ethnic identity. The CCP and the right-wing Progress Party both stressed "closing the door" and harsher control of "refugees of convenience," topics deemed impolite by the leaders of other political parties. Hansen's provocative and irregular behavior in the staid Danish parliament had at first some entertainment value, but his immoderation has cost his little clique whatever credibility it originally had. Nevertheless, its votes may come to count for the socialist ranks.

Less important are three small sects: the nearly defunct Communist Workers' Party (Kommunistisk Arbejderparti) a "Maoist" relic that has not run in the past three parliamentary elections; the International Socialist Workers' Party (Internationalen Socialistisk Arbejderparti; SAP), the Danish branch of the Trotskyist Fourth International, which received 1,800 votes in September; and the latest leftist group, the Marxist-Leninist Party (Marxistisk-Leninistisk Parti; MLP), whose pro-Albania line attracted fewer than 1,000 votes in September.

The SAP has only minimal support, but its newspaper, *Klassekampen* (Class Struggle), is well informed on Danish leftist politics as well as on the international Trotskyist movement. Even the MLP publishes a newspaper, *Arbejderen* (Worker), and a theoretical journal, *Partiets Vej* (The Party's Way). Its program is similar to other extreme leftist groups.

Two new parties, the Greens (De Grønne) and the Humanist Party (Humanisterne), were on the parliamentary ballot, but only the Greens registered any strength: nearly 45,000 votes but less than similar parties in Western Europe or than expected by polls. Neither is a Marxist party, but they are likely to appeal to some of the same voters.

Danish electoral laws make it possible to run nationally for parliament with only about 20,000 signatures, and Danes willingly sign such petitions. A major incentive to undertake even a hopeless parliamentary campaign is the free and generous radio and television time allowed all electoral parties. The sectarian Marxist groups are too small to have any political significance and are eclipsed by the possibility of a SDP-SF alternative government.

Neither the DKP nor other Danish leftist parties have direct ties to parties in the autonomous territories: Greenland and the Faeroe Islands. Greenland politics are fairly tumultuous, with the May election producing a majority for the governing left-wing coalition between the Forward (Siumut) socialists and the Eskimo leftist nationalists (Inuit Atassut). The election was occasioned in part by the vigorous discussion of U.S. plans to modernize its large radar installations in Thule. Leftist critics of the bases saw the construction of Phased Array Radars as a violation of the 1972 antiballistic missile treaty (Strategic Arms Limitation Talks I). Greenland premier Jonathan Motzfeldt accepted U.S. and Danish government assurances that the radars did not violate any international treaties (*Nordisk Kontakt*, no. 9; *Politiken Weekly*, 17 June).

Eric S. Einhorn
University of Massachusetts at Amherst

Finland

Population. 4,939,880

Party. Finnish Communist Party (Suomen Kommunistinen Puolue; SKP); runs as the Finnish People's Democratic League (Suomen Kansan Demokraattinen Liitto; SKDL) in parliamentary elections; "shadow" Finnish Communist Party or Finnish Communist Party-Unity (Suomen Kommunistinen Puolue-Yhtennaisyys; SKP-Y) runs as the Democratic Alternative (Demokraattinen Vaihtoehto; DEVA) in parliamentary elections

Founded. SKP: 1918; SKP-Y: 1986

Membership. SKP: 20,000; SKP-Y: 16,663 (both claimed)
Chairman. SKP: Arvo Aalto; SKP-Y: Taisto Sinisalo
General Secretaries. SKP: Esko Vainionpää; SKP-Y: Jouko Kajanoja
Politburo. SKP: Arvo Aalto, Esko Vainionpää, Arvo Kemppainen (vice-chair), Helja Tammisola (vice-chair), Aarno Aitamurto, Tatjaana Huhtala, Reija Käkelä, Erkki Kauppila, Timo Laaksonen, Tanja Lehmuskoski, Mirja Ylitalo; SKP-Y: Taisto Sinisalo, Yrjö Häkanen (vice-chair), Marja-Liisa Löyttyjärvi (vice-chair), Jouko Kajanoja, Pirkko Turpeinen, Mikko Kukoppa, Urho Jokinen, Ilmari Nieminen, Pentti Salo, Eino Kaajakari, Markku Kangaspuro, Seppo Ruotsalainen, Erkki Susi
Central Committee. Both SKP and SKP-Y: 50 full and 15 alternate members
Status. Both parties: legal
Last Congress. SKP: Twenty-first, 12–15 June 1987, in Helsinki; SKP-Y: First, 5–7 June 1987, in Espoo
Last Election. 1987, SKP: 9.4 percent, 16 (11 actual communists) of 200 seats; SKP-Y (DEVA front): 4.3 percent, 4 of 200.
Auxiliary Organizations. SKP: Finnish Democratic Youth League (SDNL); Finnish Women's Democratic League (SNDL); SKP-Y: Revolutionary Youth Organization
Publications. SKP: *Kansan Uutiset* (daily); *Ny Tid* (Swedish-language weekly); SKP-Y: *Tiedonantaja* (daily); (all published in Helsinki).

From the time it was legalized at the end of World War II until 1983, the SKP, operating through its front party the SKDL, was a major political force that frequently participated in government coalitions. Differences between the more doctrinaire and the more nationalistic communists, which had existed since the party was formed on 29 August 1918, flared into its present factional framework when Arne Saarinen was elected party chair in 1966 and the party adopted a more reformist program in 1969. The hard-line Stalinists (sometimes referred to as "Taistoists" after their leader, Taisto Sinisalo, or the "minority" as opposed to the "majority" or "moderates") walked out in 1969 and formed separate organizational units. Pressure from the CPSU prevented a complete split between the two intransigent groups until 1986.

In 1985, a special congress, dominated by the moderates under Aalto, the new party chair, authorized the SKP central committee to expel party units for disloyalty. In 1985 and 1986, the SKP purged the Stalinists and a "third-line" group, led by former Chair Kajanoja, that had linked with the Stalinists. In 1986 the minority formed a new party apparatus that exactly mirrored the SKP but denied that it constituted a new party. Minority leaders claim devotion to the principle of "unity" of the communist movement and say their new organizations constitute the true SKP because the Aalto-led party is "revisionist" and has deserted Marxist principles.

Party Leadership and Party Organization. In 1987, the Finnish communist movement paid the price, both in political influence and in parliamentary representation, for its split into two parties. For the first time since World War II, the communists found themselves outside the mainstream of Finnish politics. At the beginning of the year public opinion polls indicated that both parties were suffering a loss of popular support, and it was questionable whether the SKP-Y ("shadow" party) would win any representation in the upcoming 15–16 March parliamentary election (*Hufvudstadsbladet*, 6 March). Nevertheless, battling between the two continued as SKP-Y leaders sought to overcome the charge that they were the spoilers by saying that the SKP should repeal its expulsion of the Stalinists and that the two should cooperate in the ongoing election campaign.

Both front parties, the SKDL and the SKP-Y's DEVA, concentrated on economic issues in their electoral campaigns. The SKDL's platform was moderate; it sought more and better-priced housing, a 35-hour work week, better working conditions, national control of banks, and "fairer" taxes (*Helsingin Sanomat*, 10 March). Presenting the platform on 4 February, SKDL chair Esko Helle asked the Finnish society to adopt new values for more equitable income distribution; to accept "common responsibility for other peoples, nature, the world, and the future; and to work actively on behalf of peace, more broadly based democracy, and the nurturing of our national culture." The campaign warned that ongoing structural change in Finnish industry would cause vast unemployment (*Kansan Uutiset* 18 February; *JPRS-Western Europe Report* (WER) 87-021, 20 March).

DEVA concentrated more on the unemployment issue, but its platform was broader in sweep. It set goals of ending the arms race and achieving disarmament, removing unemployment and legally restricting dismissals from jobs, protecting the environment; cooperating internationally on a basis of national equality, and extending democracy to all peoples (*Helsingin Sanomat*, 22 February). DEVA chair Kristiina Halkola sought to dispel the notion that DEVA was only a front for the SKP-Y; she said her party was ready to cooperate with other socialist parties and the Greens, who, she claimed, shared many of DEVA's objectives (ibid., 16 February).

The blurring of ideological differences between the two parties was noted by *Hufvudstadsbladet* (19 February). It said that the Stalinists' attempt to quickly adapt to Mikhail Gorbachev's changes in communist dogma made it difficult to understand what the SKP-Y stood for. It was even harder to characterize DEVA policy. Both the SKDL and the DEVA were trying to imitate the Greens movement, which was gaining in popularity. The paper observed that DEVA was competing with the Greens in efforts to represent civic movements, while the SKDL maintained that care of the environment should be a "central criterion" of all national policy and that economic growth is "not a goal in itself."

SKDL and SKP leaders were able to rally more support during the campaign, but in the 15–16 March election the SKDL still lost votes compared with those cast for "moderate" SKDL candidates in the 1983 election. The DEVA share was about the same as what Stalinist candidates won in 1983. The SKDL received 9.4 percent of the 1987 vote compared with 14 percent in 1983; if the 4.3 percent cast for DEVA is added, the sum is just 0.3 percent short of the 1983 figure. But because of the electoral system and SKDL electoral strategy, that party received sixteen of the 200 Eduskunta seats compared with the seventeen it held before the election (after the ouster of the Stalinist deputies), whereas DEVA got only four seats, compared with the ten deputies representing it before the election. (In comparison, the Greens more than doubled their vote, also receiving four seats—a gain of two.) Five of the sixteen SKDL deputies were not communists (two of the remainder were "free-thinking" intellectuals), so the number of communists in the new Eduskunta, counting the four DEVA deputies, was only fifteen. Neither Aalto nor Sinisalo were elected; Halkola also did not gain office (*Hufvudstadsbladet*, 30 March). Jarmo Wahlström, close to Aalto, was elected head of the SKDL parliamentary group, and Vappu Sailynoja (socialist), vice-chair. Ensio Laine was named leader of the four-man DEVA delegation.

After the election *Kansan Uutiset* (17 March) said that SKDL losses were not unexpected and that, under the circumstances, the outcome was a good result. Aalto called on SKP and SKDL supporters not to let down after the election but at this crucial juncture to gird for battle through the upcoming party congress and new party platform. A "vision" must be created that could counter the rightward trend in the society. (*Kansan Uutiset*, 24 April; *JPRS-WER*-87-070, 25 August.)

Noncommunist opinion could not agree on how the communists had fared or on the election's consequences for their future. *Hufvudstadsbladet* (30 March; *JPRS-WER*-87-052, 16 June) thought the communist share of the vote was not bad considering the low turnout of voters and the fact that the Social Democrats had lost 100,000 votes; it was noted that the Social Democrats had not benefited from communist losses. The editorial concluded that DEVA, whose basic appeal rested on Finland's relatively high unemployment rate, was now solidly on the political scene with voter support from over the entire country, in contrast to the previous concentration of Stalinists in certain districts. *Helsingin Sanomat* (23 March), however, believed that DEVA had barely survived, pointing to the fact that it had not achieved representation in ten electoral districts. That paper raised the question of whether hard-line Stalinists would now gradually disappear.

The Stalinist spirit was upbeat, particularly in view of the fact that DEVA had won more votes than pre-election polls had indicated. DEVA chair Halkola declared the election outcome a "victory" because of a fighting DEVA spirit that the struggle against heavy odds had created (*Tiedonantaja*, 31 March; *JPRS-WER*-87-070, 25 August). However, the SKP-Y's First Congress on 5–7 June at Espoo (a Helsinki suburb), which organizers claimed was the SKP's Twenty-first Congress (*Hufvudstadsbladet*, 4 June), was a fractious affair. Differences appeared over whom the party should support in the upcoming presidential election and whether the party should drop the fiction that it was the legitimate SKP. Uusimaa District representatives, led by Markus Kainulainen, again made a motion to consider forming a new party, and, when it was not brought to a vote, twenty walked out in protest. In late November, this faction, made up of representatives of the Uusimaa and Helsinki districts, met "secretly" in Espoo and selected a "central council" to organize a new party (*Hufvudstadsbladet*, 22, 23, 25 November; *FBIS*, 30 November; *Neue Zuricher Zeitung*, 29/30 November). This action led some to conclude that the left was being splintered to the point of paralysis (*Hufvudstadsbladet*, 26 November).

Helsingin Sanomat (16 May) said there had been a movement before the meeting to replace Sinisalo as party chair with Esko-Juhani Tennilä, who wanted to get away from the old factionalism, but, just before the congress met, Tennilä announced his support of Sinisalo (*Helsingin Sanomat*, 19 May). Little resistance to Sinisalo's re-election was offered at the congress. The greatest struggle occurred over the presidential issue. Sinisalo attacked former SKDL chair Kaveli Kivistö, whom many delegates wanted to support, as having been a driving force in the SKDL's ouster of Stalinists and proposed Secretary General and former SKP chair Kajanoja as the Stalinist candidate. The names of Tennilä and Laine were put forth as contenders, but Kajanoja was approved. Tennilä was named to the Politburo, but he reportedly refused to accept the post. Löyttyjärvi, one of Tennilä's close associates, was named one of two vice-chairs. Ten new members were elected to the 50-member central committee, which now includes 11 women; 9 of the 15 deputy members are new. Kajanoja was re-elected general secretary and Häkanen, vice-chair, alongside Löyttyjärvi. (*Helsingin Sanomat*, 6, 8, 9 June; *JPRS-WER*-87-076, 25 September.)

Sinisalo's lengthy political report expressed Marxist-Leninist views (although dressed up as "new thought" in international affairs), called for "good and fraternal cooperative relations with all our fraternal parties," claimed the Finnish-Soviet "peace" policy meant Finland could not be a neutral, urged formation of a Nordic nuclear weapons–free zone, demanded a "radical reorientation of Finland's policy to support independence movements" and "freedom from the domination of supranational capital" of Third World countries, opposed Finnish membership in European organizations (such as the European Community) that excluded the USSR, and proposed Finnish financing of increased trade with the Soviet Union. On disarmament, he asked that Finland give an example to other countries by unilaterally reducing its army and shortening the period of conscript training. Addressing the question of "the structural crisis of the economy," he called for expanding "participation of workers in economic and social decision-making, administration, and planning." Finally, after saying "we strive for the unification of communist forces in Finland," Sinisalo endorsed the creation of a DEVA youth association and the formation of a women's organization. (*Hufvudstadsbladet*, 6 June.)

The congress called again for the SKP to cancel its proposed new party program and rules as a prelude to reunification of the two communist parties, formation of electoral coalitions between the two parties for the 1988 presidential race, and cooperation between the two in several areas—peace activities, fostering closer relations with the USSR, and efforts to achieve economic and social goals of workers. In an apparent concession to the SKP (and a step away from its own principle of democratic centralism), a statement was adopted that said unity of the communist party did not "presume the complete sameness of opinions or the hiding of differences of opinion." (*Hufvudstadsbladet*, 6, 8 June; *FBIS*, 16 June; *Pravda*, 6, 8 June; *FBIS*, 15 June; *Tiedonantaja*, 5 June; *JPRS-WER*-87-080, 15 October.)

Despite protestations of the congress, the non-communist press characterized its actions as divisive. *Helsingin Sanomat* (9 June) said the Stalinists were "still living their own separate life" unaffected by changes in the Soviet party and claimed that the congress had further undermined communist unity by continuing to construct new organizations.

In contrast, the SKP congress, held 12–15 June, one week after the SKP-Y's, seemed a model of solidarity. It was forced again to expel former Stalinist-controlled party units. The Helsinki Court of Appeals on 11 June upheld a lower court ruling that the SKP's central committee expulsion in 1985 had violated party bylaws by not giving enough notice of certain changes in the bylaws needed for the expulsion. The new expulsion occurred under the authority granted the party congress by the old rules. (Predictably, the new expulsion was also challenged in the courts [*Hufvudstadsbladet*, 24 November].) Aalto and Vainionpää were re-elected, and Aitamurto, who had been named vice-chair of the Central Organization of Finnish Trade Unions (SAK), was replaced as one of the vice-chairpersons by Kemppainen, the head of the Lapland District, who had led the fight to oust the Stalinists. As proof of party renewal, SKP leaders pointed to the fact that 20 of the 50 Central Committee members were new, that the average age had dropped to 43 (from 44), and that 22 were women. One new member was Tutta Tallgren, an instructor at the SKP's Sirola Institute who had been a close associate of Kajanoja, head of the "third-line" and now general secretary of the SKP-Y. Her naming was held up as proof that those who returned to the party would not face discrimination. (*Helsingin Sanomat*, 11, 14, 15 June; *Kansan Uutiset*, 13, 15, 16 June; *JPRS-*

WER-87-072, 4 September; *Hufvudstadsbladet*, 13, 14 June.)

Aalto's political report said disarmament was a key to resolving international disputes; praised Gorbachev for the progress made in reaching agreement with the United States on reducing intermediate-range missiles and applauded his reforms in the USSR; urged more Finnish initiatives in the foreign policy area while asserting that the most important civic task of communists was to cultivate closer relations with the USSR; pointed to SKP efforts to develop relations with fraternal parties on a basis of mutual respect, citing the recent restoration of relations with the Chinese party; announced that the SKP was prepared to unconditionally cooperate in the international workers movement with other groups such as the Social Democrats in promoting democracy and social advancement; said society should control banks, insurance companies, and large industrial enterprises by an overseer committee of owners, workers, and the state; and claimed that the SKP was ready to cooperate politically with the Social Democrats "in all connections" with a view to establishing a coalition of workers' parties, Greens, and center parties. He acknowledged that the SKP had suffered from previous government participation without showing much progress in realizing its goals, being slow to recognize the significance of the environmental issue, delaying restructuring the party and the membership, and not working hard enough for equality of the sexes and recruitment of the youth. (Helsinki International Service, 12 June; *FBIS*, 15 June.)

The political declaration of the congress supported the themes of Aalto's address, stressing the need to give unions the right to participate in company decisionmaking, electing company management, and interpreting labor agreements. It also called for transferring the state's bureaucratic power to elected officials of the national government and decentralizing much of the power to regional and local governments; rejecting closer ties with western international organizations, such as the European Community (EC), that would weaken Finland's neutrality, international position, or workers' power; and increasing support for President Mauno Koivisto's proposal to construct confidence-building measures among naval powers in the waters around the Nordic area.

A party study, published on the eve of the congress, showed that only 4 percent of SKP members were under 30, while 34 percent were pensioners. Workers, including agricultural workers, made up 45 percent, and white-collar workers, 20 percent. About 78 percent had attended elementary school or adult education courses, compared with 45 percent in the population as a whole. (*Hufvudstadsbladet*, 31 May; *FBIS*, 9 June; *Kansan Uutiset*, 30 May; *Kommunisti*, 6–7.) According to a survey for the National Board of Commerce and Industry, more DEVA supporters had more higher education than the SKDL supporters—23 compared with 8 percent. A Gallup poll showed that only 17 percent of SKDL supporters were under 30, compared with 20 percent of Social Democrats and 59 percent of Greens (*Uusi Suomi*, 26 July).

The SKP congress also adopted a new party program, the party's third, which replaced the 1966 one. The final version of the new program differs markedly from the first draft, written in 1986 (see *YICA*, 1986), evidently as a result of rank-and-file criticism of the first version. Approved by the Central Committee on 9 February and later released to the public, the program was regarded as Eurocommunist in nature (*Uusi Suomi*, 12 February), both in its description of Finnish socialism and in its disassociation of the party from the CPSU. Although committed to the traditional communist view of utopian socialism in much of its description, the final version dropped the description of the party as "a Marxist revolutionary party" and instead characterized the SKP as a "revolutionary, communist party" of the working class movement. It said that party activity is guided by "those principles whose basis Marx, Engels, and Lenin laid down and the tradition of social struggle inspired by them" and that the SKP "adapts and develops Marxist theory" according to Finnish conditions. Finland is described as a "capitalist society" and a "bourgeois democracy," which had made considerable achievements. But this progress has been at the price of reducing the power of the people, alienating Finns from work, and ruining the environment. The program states that the "most important elements of the framework for socialism are now ready" but leaves vague how socialism is to be reached. It says that the government structure should remain unchanged but that power now held by "capitalists" should be transferred to government. Some traditional themes were repeated; for instance, it states that "banks, insurance companies, large industrial enterprises, and energy production will belong to society" and that "local organs of self-government" will create economic units to carry out "industrial and construction activity, handle distribution and delivery of goods, and produce other services." "Self-administration" on regional, factory, shop floor, and industrial levels should direct the economy.

In contrast to the first draft, whose longest section was on international affairs, the final version devoted only 5 of 36 pages to that subject. What drew the most attention was the omission of the first draft's statement on proletarian internationalism, thought to have been added to the first draft to appease the CPSU. The final version does not mention proletarian internationalism at all. The only reference to SKP-CPSU relations is made in a discussion of the SKP's cooperation with all fraternal communist and workers' parties; the only direct statement is the comment that "the cooperation of the SKP and CPSU solidify for their part the friendly relations of Finland and the Soviet Union." At the same time, the program keeps the first draft's emphasis on the "unconditional equality" and "independence" of each party and the requirement for "noninterference in the internal affairs of other parties." Relations with fraternal parties are now portrayed as "natural," not "close" as in the first version. Socialist practice in communist countries is said to suffer from the "suffocating effects" of their bureaucracies (a statement that clearly parallels what Gorbachev had said about the situation in the USSR). Although the importance of the 1948 treaty of Friendship, Cooperation and Mutual Assistance (FCMA) with the USSR is described as the basis for Finnish-Soviet relations, the meaning of that pact is presented in terms similar to the official formulation of the Finnish foreign office. Finnish-Soviet relations are described as serving "as an example" of the "peace-loving neutral foreign policy carried out by our country."

The program criticizes the United States at length and by name; an entire section is devoted to "Imperialism Gives Rise to the Threat of War." The United States is said to subordinate Europe and Japan, strive for military superiority, and limit high-technology exports to socialist countries. Also "the United States finances, trains, and arms groups of saboteurs in several countries which have reached the road of national independence and progress."

The new program aroused considerable attention. *Uusi Suomi* (12 February) said it "is a great leap in the direction of accepting Finland's democratic state system and disassociation from the centrally directed, dogmatic Stalinism," although the analysis of existing conditions is internally contradictory. *Helsingin Sanomat* (12 February) remarked that "the SKP has taken such a vigorous step in the direction of the worker movement's reformist line that there may be something in it for the SDP [Social Democratic Party] to think about." *Hufvudstadsbladet* (15 June) believed the program combined "a socialist Finland with democratic planning of the national economy." *Tiedonantaja* (18 June; *JPRS-WER*-87-072, 4 September) hostilely characterized the program as departing from Marxism-Leninism and representing an "opportunistic practical policy," which deviated from "the basic judgments of the international communist movement."

Domestic Party Affairs. The 15–16 March election confirmed the worst fears of communist leaders, but at the same time its outcome offered opportunities to increase communist popular support. Aalto in particular had warned that the continued trend to the right in Finnish politics together with the split in communist ranks might push the Social Democrats, who had led recent governments, to turn to the National Coalition Party (Conservatives) instead of the SKDL for cooperation in the future. The Social Democratic Party (SDP) electoral program, which called for increased children's allowances and tax reform, led *Kansan Uutiset* (5 March) to comment that there was nothing in the program that would rule out Conservative participation in government since it did not conflict with Conservative populist policy. The paper added caustically that the platform themes did not spring from "traditional reform endeavors" of the workers' movement. *Suomen Sosialdemokraattinen* (5 March), the principal SDP spokesman, concluded that the comments of both the SKP and SKP-Y press on the platform were so negative that they ruled out any chance to rally leftist forces after the election. Illka Suominen, Conservative chair, expressed the belief that the SDP had moved surprisingly closer to the same objectives the Conservatives sought; the National Coalition executive had agreed to raise children's allowances (though not as much as the SDP wanted), and the party also supported tax reform (*Uusi Suomi*, 5 March).

Independent *Helsingin Sanomat* (9 March) concluded that the SKDL and DEVA campaigns were outside the mainstream of political debate, which was mainly concerned with who would be in the next government. The Social Democratic–Conservative race for the leading electoral position attracted the most interest. On the eve of the election, *Kansan Uutiset* (10 March) announced that the SKDL was the only "realistic alternative" to the growing power of the capitalists and to current government policies.

The SDP lost 100,000 votes in the election compared with the 1983 poll, and the Conservatives came within three seats of SDP representation (53 compared with 56 out of 200 seats). Voter turnout was relatively low, a factor that was generally believed to have hurt the parties on the left, whose share of the vote dropped to 37.9 percent, the lowest point since World War II (Helsinki Domestic Service, 16 March; *FBIS*, 17 March). The centrist electoral coalition parties—consisting of the Center, Swedish People's, Christian League, and Liberals—received the largest portion of the vote, although the Center Party gained only slightly. Center Party leaders took it for granted that party Chair Paavo Väyrynen would lead the next government; the party proposed him for the prime ministership before the president made his wishes known. Refusal of the Social Democrats to consider an SDP-Center-Conservative coalition surprised no one, but Koivisto's choice of Harry Holkeri, the Conservative presidential nominee, to sound out the possibility of SDP-Conservative cooperation shocked Center Party leaders. In the last days of Holkeri's negotiations, which culminated in formation of a "red-blue" (or "red-black") coalition on 30 April under Holkeri's leadership, Center Party leaders tried to prevent their isolation by dropping their insistence that Väyrynen head the next government. Väyrynen warned (Center Party press, 15 April) the Conservatives that cooperation with the Social Democrats would increase the latter's "supremacy." The small Swedish People's and Rural parties were added to the new coalition. Outgoing Prime Minister Kaleva Sorsa (who resigned as chair of the SDP) took the post of foreign minister.

The idea of Social Democratic–Conservative cooperation upset leftist groups in the SDP (*Helsingin Sanomat*, 27 April) and in the communist parties. Both SKDL and DEVA leaders publicly opposed Conservative entry into the government (*Tiedonantaja*, 22 April; *JPRS-WER*-87-070, 25 August), and the SKDL called for tighter "left-wing cooperation to improve social justice, equality and the opportunity for citizens" to influence social development (*Kansan Uutiset*, 9 April; *JPRS-Western Europe Report*-87-056, 25 June). During the negotiations, DEVA called on all "progressive" forces to prevent consummation of the negotiations (*Helsingin Sanomat*, 13 April). Esko Helle said (*Kansan Uutiset*, 15 April) that the Sorsa decision to cooperate with the Conservatives was "short-sighted," placing desire for power above principle, and the SKP Politburo warned that it would strengthen the big capitalists (*Hufvudstadsbladet*, 16 April). *Suomen Sosialdemokrattinen* (16 April) defended the Social Democrats from SKP-SKDL charges (made in banner newspaper headlines) that the Social Democrats were leading the country into an alliance of labor and capitalism; it claimed that the Social Democrats would not agree to a coalition until they could be sure that the workers would have a greater say in economic life and more safeguards for keeping jobs. Sorsa made the same assurance in a statement to the Congress of the Central Federation of Trade Unions (SAK).

In mid-April, the Social Democrats and Conservatives agreed on a government program of full employment, tax reform, more aid to families with children, a reform of working life, and direct election of the president (all papers, 16 April). *Kansan Uutiset* (16 April) heavily criticized the Social Democrats, saying their new line was not liked by SDP trade unionists because the Conservatives represented employers and big business. It thought that the SDP leaders' dislike of Väyrynen could not be the only reason for this step, and that SDP leaders were directing the party away from the worker movement. Aalto in a speech said the move would not bring more power to the working class and that reforms to change society's foundations could not be carried out with the Conservatives (*Kansan Uutiset*, 17 April). *Tiedonantaja* (22 April; *JPRS-WER*-87-070, 25 August) complained that the communist split and the accommodating attitude of the moderates had smoothed the way for the SDP action.

There was also sharp reaction on the right. The Confederation of Finnish Industries (STK) disliked taxes on dividends and environmental regulations, while *Uusi Suomi* (30 April) remarked sourly that Social Democratic "hegemony" would be perpetuated.

When the coalition took office on 30 April, its historical significance was generally recognized. Holkeri said he hoped "red-blue" cooperation would close the 1918 "trenches," a reference to the fact that Finnish politics had been deeply affected by allegiances to conflicting sides in the Finnish civil war. The SKDL and SKP issued a joint statement saying that the new government program was an "unfeeling" proclamation of "casino capitalism," intended to tie Finland more firmly to international capitalism, and that the decision of the Social Democratic Party to endorse the program was another step toward its becoming a party of the well-to-do (*Kansan Uutiset*, 30 April). Aalto, speaking of the coalition's goal of carrying out labor reform, said the "road to hell is paved with good intentions" (*Helsingin Sanomat*, 3 May), and Sinisalo remarked that the coalition was "dangerous and detrimental to the whole country" (*Uusi Suomi*, 3 May).

SKDL chair Helle put out feelers for SKDL-DEVA cooperation in the parliamentary opposition (*Helsingin Sanomat*, 17 May), and the SKDL and DEVA parliamentary delegations combined to put the new government to its first test in early June. Pointing to recent dismissals and layoffs in industry, they put forward an interpellation asking what measures the government intended to take to counter the negative consequences of structural change. They also stated that the government's international policies were increasingly directed toward the West. Prime Minister Holkeri responded to the last point by declaring that trade policy was aimed at all points on the horizon; its only guide was Finnish national interest. (*Helsingin Sanomat*, 27 May; *Hufvudstadsbladet*, 11 June.) SKDL and DEVA leaders sought to gain the cooperation of the other opposition parties, including the Center Party, in making coordinated attacks on the coalition. This placed the Center Party in a dilemma over long-term strategy—whether to join the communists, its former coalition partner, or to seek the cooperation of center-right groups. (*Uusi Suomi*, 29 April; *JPRS-WER*-87-061, 7 July.) The general feeling was that the Center Party was moving to the right, filling the place the Conservatives had held. This shift was making it difficult for the Center Party to continue to represent small farmer and worker interests. (*Uusi Suomi*, 29 September.)

In the fall, the two communist parties returned to the attack, trying to get united opposition support to prevent the government from delaying implementation of a law intended to protect worker job security (*Hufvudstadsbladet*, 14 September). But only the Christian League and the Greens came to a meeting called by DEVA to plan action on the issue (ibid., 19 September). This demonstrated the tenuous nature of Stalinist-moderate cooperation: at the same time that Sinisalo called for formalized cooperation with the SKP, he heavily criticized SKP leaders (*Helsingin Sanomat*, 15 September). The government's budget, presented in mid-September, renewed cries in both communist camps that the government was moving to the right and favoring higher income groups (*Kansan Uutiset*, 16 September; *Helsingin Sanomat*, *Uusi Suomi*, *Hufvudstadsbladet*, 23 September). A proposal to appropriate funds to construct a new air defense system was especially criticized (*Kansan Uutiset*, 1 September; *Helsingin Sanomat*, 9 September). In late October, SKDL and DEVA (with the Christian League) joined in a Center Party interpellation calling on the government to increase maternity and sick leave allowances, unemployment subsidies, and national pensions. The government easily won a vote of no confidence.

The parliamentary election had been heavily colored by party jockeying for the upcoming presidential election, scheduled for 31 January–1 February 1988, despite the efforts of Koivisto, who had refused to announce his candidacy for re-election before the parliamentary election had taken place. However, Holkeri (later to be prime minister) and Väyrynen (then foreign minister) were already avowed candidates for the Conservative and Center parties, respectively. The question for the communists was whether to run their own candidates or whether to support Koivisto as the SKDL had done in 1981. SKDL general secretary Vainionpää opted for running Kaveli Kivistö, who had been the SKDL candidate in 1981, as the best way to get out the SKDL vote; at the same time, the party should make sure that Koivisto did not lose to Holkeri or Väyrynen in the electoral college (*Helsingin Sanomat*, 6 April). SKP and SKDL newspapers commissioned a poll that showed that Kivistö also had support in other parties, especially the Greens and DEVA (*Kansan Uutiset*, 4 June). On 11 June, the SKDL council decided not to formally nominate Kivistö, although it left the option open if Kivistö and his backers so desired. The object was to allow a broad coalition of groups to rally behind Kivistö (*Helsingin Sanomat*, 14 June; *JPRS-WER*-87-072, 4 September). A campaign organization headed by Dr. Erkki Haahti of the Greens and including SKDL chair Helle was then formed (*Kansan Uutiset*, 21 July). On 12 September, it was formally launched under the name Action 88. Kivistö called for a more active foreign policy to promote peace, economic equality, and protection of the environment. (*Hufvudstadsbladet*, 13 September.) Koivisto announced his candidacy for re-election on 12 October, and a special campaign organization, Pro-Koivisto, was also formed to draw support from a broad spectrum.

After a protracted struggle, on 13 June DEVA's advisory committee chose Kajanoja, already endorsed by the SKP-Y after similar infighting, as the DEVA candidate. DEVA chair Halkola had previously declared for Kivistö (*Helsingin Sanomat*, 11 June; *JPRS-WER*-87-079, 13 October), and some members of the advisory committee wanted to investigate the possibility of forming a DEVA-SKDL electoral coalition behind Kivistö. But that proposal received only some twenty votes, and Kajanoja was selected by about 80 votes. (*Hufvudstadsbladet*, *Helsingin Sanomat*, 14 June; *JPRS-WER*-87-072, 4 September.) A political resolution was adopted calling for a broad front to work for "peace and our country's independent, democratic development." It said movement toward the West, under the influence of large capitalist groups, should be stopped and a president elected who would take risks to establish a nuclear-free northern Europe and support Soviet peace initiatives. (*Tiedonantaja*, 23 June; *JPRS-WER*-87-072, 4 September.)

Väyrynen, kicking off his campaign on 24 August, made his main theme the "defense of Finnish independence." He stressed the "threat" of integration into international organizations (aimed mainly at the Council of Europe and the EC), a theme dear to the communists. Kajanoja launched his campaign on 30 August, accusing the government's foreign policy leadership of damaging relations with the USSR by not acting more forcefully to increase Finnish-Soviet trade. He warned against rightist influence on foreign policy (*Hufvudstadsbladet*, 31 August.) Polls in November indicated that Kajanoja's popular support had dropped to nearly 0 percent, partly because so many DEVA followers favored Kivistö; this situation led to speculation that DEVA was on its last legs (*Hufvudstadsbladet*, 26 November). Kivistö, in his first speech on 1 November, supported Väyrynen's anti-international line, wanted top priority to be given protection of Finnish workers, and called for a more "humanitarian" policy of receiving refugees (*Hufvudstadsbladet*, 2 November).

In the trade union field, unemployment and discontent with the new government and industry plans for restructuring were credited with a decline in support for Social Democratic trade union leaders and a rise in support for the moderate communist leadership. Chief issues concerning trade unions were more worker say in business firm decisions, higher pay for low-paid workers, and a 35-hour work week. In the election of delegates to the Construction Workers' Union, the communists' greatest stronghold, the moderate communist share of the vote rose by about 5 percent to two-thirds, Social Democratic support dropped, correspondingly, to 22 percent, and the Stalinists remained the same at some 11 percent. Aitamurto, the moderate communist chair of the union, left his post, succeeding Olavi Hänninen as the SAK's second chair. In turn, Aitamurto was succeeded by Pekka Hynonen, also a moderate communist, as union chair. Stalinists were again kept out of leadership positions, and the SKP held 20 of 25 executive committee seats and 40 of 51 executive council seats. (*Kansan Uutiset*, *Hufvudstadsbladet*, 11 March; *Helsingin Sanomat*, *Hufvudstadsbladet*, 18 May.)

Communist strength also rose in the powerful Metal Workers' Union at the expense of the Social Democrats. The latter held only a bare majority of delegates in the election to that union's 13–16 December congress, while their share of the vote actually dropped to less than half. The combined moderate and Stalinist vote was only 2 percent behind the SDP, but the moderates, whose strength was three times that of the Stalinists, continued to cooperate with the Social Democrats, who led the union. (*Hufvudstadsbladet*, 14, 30 May and 24 October.) At the congress, Per-Erik Lundh (SDP) was reelected chair and Veikko Lehtonen (SKP), vice-chair.

Auxiliary and Front Organizations. The new party and political situation posed critical problems for front and auxiliary organizations and even threatened their survival. The SKDL itself came under pressure; one new SKDL parliamentarian said Aalto should consider an "honorable" withdrawal as SKP chair because the SKP had become "fossilized" (*Kansan Uutiset*, 19 May; *Helsingin Sanomat*, 19 May; *JPRS-WER*-87-071, 2 September). At its council meeting on 24–25 October, General Secretary Reija Käkelä said that the SKDL and the SKP should review the ties between the two organizations and that the SKDL should perhaps change its name in an effort to create a new leftist orientation as a counterweight to the political trend to the right. SKP, SKDL, and the SKDL Parliamentary Group leaders could set up a joint executive to plan and carry out policies of the day. SKDL and SKP organizational ties could thus be loosened while the unity of the movement's struggles on such issues as unemployment, taxation, and social policy could be kept. SKP members could also be members of SKDL. Käkelä said that politics were changing so radically that cooperation with the Social Democrats must be regarded from a new leftist viewpoint and be increased if not put foremost. Käkelä added that the SKDL should become more active and take a leading role in adopting new policies. A leftist orientation meant among other things "a great personal renewal and a reform of our movement." (*Hufvudstadsbladet*, 25 October.) Aalto said later that Käkelä did not mean that the SKP should leave the SKDL; he was merely throwing out suggestions for debate. That debate should wait until after the presidential election, when the results of the Kivistö movement could be judged. (*Helsingin Sanomat*, 26 October.)

These remarks aroused wide attention; one noncommunist newspaper (*Uusi Suomi*, 26 October) said they reflected the crisis of the far left. A *Hufvudstadsbladet* editorial (27 October) believed that Action 88, the promising start of the Kivistö organization, had awakened great enthusiasm and that Käkelä was seeking to move the SKDL out from under the SKP's shadow and attract a broad spectrum of socialists, communists of all stripes, leftist sympathisers outside parties, and "green" intellectuals. The aim was to create a more free-wheeling movement, perhaps on the model of the Socialist People's Party in Norway. Käkelä's suggested name League of the Left—SKDL for the new organization was reminiscent of the Swedish communist party name: Party of the Left—the Communists. The editorial concluded that although the needs of the time had drawn forth this proposal, it had little likelihood of being adopted or succeeding. Action 88 was having trouble getting off the ground, according to the polls, and would wilt when the presidential election was over and Kivistö resumed his provincial governorship. In the final analysis, Käkelä's proposal faced a fatal contradiction: in the editorial's opinion, the SKDL would cut loose from the SKP while still depending mainly on communists for its support.

The socialist organization within the SKDL applauded Käkelä's proposal for SKDL reorganization (*Hufvudstadsbladet*, 29 October; *FBIS*, 6 November). The socialists at their third congress on 24 May at Turengi elected Tuomo Molander as their delegation's chair, replacing Ele Alenius. Reija Saarinen was named vice-chair. Kalevi Suomela and Paivi Heinonen were named chair and vice-chair of the executive board. The question of whether the organization would continue in the SKDL was left undecided. Ecology and peace were the chief themes. (*Hufvudstadsbladet*, *Kansan Uutiset*, 25 May.)

The SKP youth league, SNDL, completed its expulsion of Stalinists by ousting some 500 local sections in May (*Tiedonantaja*, 19 May; *JPRS-WER*-87-068, 13 August; *Helsingin Sanomat*, 20 May). The youth organization of DEVA, the Red Council, at its founding meeting at Oulu on 4 October took the name Revolutionary Youth Organization. Markku Kangaspuro was elected chair; Asmo Koste and Sanna Koivisto, vice-chairs; and Tapani Piri, general secretary. Komosol, the African National Congress, and Czech, Danish, and Swedish organizations sent representatives (*Helsingin Sanomat*, 5 October). Before its formal organization, the Red Council was invited by the Committee of Youth Organizations of the Soviet Union to send representatives to the Moscow youth festival over the head of the Finnish festival committee (*Hufvudstadsbladet*, 7 August; *FBIS*, 14 August). The Socialist Students' Union (SOL), which belonged to both the SKDL and DEVA, seemed less dominated by the Stalinists and backed Kivistö for president (*Helsingin Sanomat*, 5 October).

DEVA also came under stress in late November, when the Kainulainen faction made plans to organize a third party with a new name (*Hufvudstadsbladet*, 25 November). *Hufvudstadsbladet* (26 November) believed continued splintering was changing the nature of the communist movement and affecting the entire political scene.

The communists were active on the peace front, but participation was less than in 1986 and often alongside other political elements. The organization Committee of 100 created an independent "citizens' committee" on security policy matters to plan for national defense in the 1990s. Jorma Hentilä (SKDL) was a member of the latter committee, along with representatives of the Social Democrats, Center Party, and Liberals (who were represented by Archbishop Mikko Juva). (*Kansan Uutiset*, 13 December 1986.) The Finnish Peace League and the International Peace Bureau convened a symposium in January on Women and the Army (ibid., 22 January). The Finnish Nuclear Test Ban Committee sent a delegation to Washington in March bearing a petition signed by members of all parliamentary groups except a tiny right-wing one asking President Ronald Reagan to stop U.S. nuclear tests (ibid., 24 March). In April, *Kansan Uutiset* (4 April) publicized an appeal to the U.S. ambassador in Helsinki asking that the United States stop financing wars in El Salvador and Nicaragua; it was signed by student organizations, the Latin America Solidarity Committee, the Finno-Nicaraguan Society, and the Christian Student League.

In late November, the Finnish-Soviet Society elected new leadership. Provincial Governor Ahti Pekkala (Center Party) replaced Martti Miettunen as chair, and SKDL Parliamentary Deputy Heli Astala and Tapani Mörttinen (Conservative) were elected vice-chairs. Of the 50 central board members, 15 were Social Democrats, 15 SKP/SKDL, 5 DEVA, 10 Center Party, 3 Swedish People's Party, and 2 Conservatives. The SKP/SKDL contingent included Aalto, Kivistö, and Vainionpää; the DEVA, Sinisalo; the Swedish People's Party, Professor Jan-Magnus Jansson; and the Conservative, Prime Minister Holkeri. Paavo Lipponen (SDP) was named board chair. (All papers, 28, 29, 30 November.)

International Views, Positions, and Activities. During this crucial year, the two communist parties anxiously awaited signs that Moscow favored one over the other, but Soviet and CPSU leaders continued to deal more with the Finnish Social Democrats and to downgrade their contacts with the communists. Premier Nikolai Ryzhkov, during his official visit to Finland of 6–9 January, treated the two equally, as did Presidium Chair Egor Ligachev in November 1986 by receiving delegations from each party on his last day in Helsinki. The morale of the minority communists was bolstered when Soviet civic organizations invited a DEVA delegation for a five-day stay in Moscow just after the Ryzhkov visit. The eight-member delegation was headed by DEVA Chair Halkola and included Kajanoja, Parliamentary Deputy Sten Söderström, Professor Yrjö Makinen (who was both an elected official of the Greens in Turku and a member of the DEVA presidium), and Lahja Kivinen of the Socialist Workers' Party (STP) (*Hufvudstadsbladet*, 8 January.) The CPSU also invited DEVA deputy Tennilä, in his capacity as chair of the SKP-Y Lapland district, to visit Moscow and Murmansk on 9–11 March to discuss increased cooperation between the inhabitants of the Murmansk area and Lapland (*Hufvudstadsbladet*, 27 February).

The Finnish press (*Helsingin Sanomat*, 18 June) was quick to note that the CPSU sent an official delegation, headed by Karl Vaino (a Central Committee member and leader of the Estonian Communist Party), to the SKP congress (*Izvestia*, 13 June, *FBIS*, 22 June). In contrast, CPSU representation at the SKP-Y congress was unofficial and led by a lower-ranking communist officer, Central Committee candidate member, Peter Yakovlevich Slezko, who urged the Finnish communists to reunite (ibid., 11 June). However, Vaino told the Finnish radio (Helsinki International Service, 13 June; *FBIS*, 17 June) that the CPSU regarded the two parties equally. Sinisalo, Kajanoja, and Kajanoja's wife spent summer holidays in the USSR, and in August the CPSU arranged joint seminars with representatives of both the SKP and the SKP-Y on current international and bilateral issues (*Helsingin Sanomat*, 7 August; *Kansan Uutiset*, 21 August). The twenty-member SKP delegation, led by Vainionpää, included Kemppainen, who had previously been refused a visa to the USSR (*Kansan Uutiset*, 21 August). By the end of the year, CPSU softening toward the SKDL became evident when SKDL chair Helle was invited to head a delegation to Moscow on 14 December. One paper (*Helsingin Sanomat*, 9 December) said this was the first time in 25 years that an SKDL delegation would visit Moscow.

The SKP and SKP-Y were invited to send delegations to Moscow to help celebrate the 70th anniversary of the October Revolution in early November; Aalto headed the SKP delegation, which included SKDL general secretary Käkelä, and Sinisalo headed the SKP-Y delegation together with SKP-Y general secreatry Kajanoja (*Hufvudstadsbladet*, 16 October). Moscow radio (Moscow International Service, 4 November; *FBIS*, 6 November) reported that Sinisalo spoke to Soviet "workers." At that celebration, a meeting of the attending communist parties was called, and Gus Hall exhorted the divided parties to unite. Afterwards, the SKP-Y sent a letter to Aalto proposing unofficial consultations, citing the Hall speech (*Helsingin Sanomat*, 12 November). Aalto remarked that there were no obstacles in principle to businesslike discussions, but feared the letter was merely an effort to raise SKP-Y's prestige (*Kansan Uutiset*, 12 November). The two parties held separate meetings to celebrate the anniversary later in Helsinki (*Pravda*, 24 November; *FBIS*, 30 November).

Representatives of other parties were also guests of the CPSU. A Center Party delegation led by then Foreign Minister Väyrynen was hosted in early December 1986, and Ligachev received Väyrynen. A communiqué said that Finnish foreign policy "has remained consistent and unchanged" (*Helsingin Sanomat*, 6 December 1986). In July, a delegation headed by the new Social Democratic Party secretary, Ulpu Iivari, and including Center Party vice-chair Martti Pura, visited Mosocw (*Helsingin Sanomat*, 1 July). Another Center Party delegation, led by party Secretary Seppo Kaariainen, was the guest of the CPSU and held talks 10 –11 October during a seven-day stay in the USSR (*Hufvudstadsbladet, 13 October). The CPSU agreed that a high-level group would return the visit in 1988 (*Helsingin Sanomat*, 18 October).

Social Democratic Party secretary Iivari said in an interview (*Suomen sosialdemokrattii*, 25 August) that cooperation between his party and the CPSU would grow; the two parties planned a joint seminar as part of the 70th anniversary celebrations of Finnish independence and the October Revolution. Vladimir Feodorov of the CPSU International Department and Yuri Krasin of the Soviet Institute of Social Sciences attended the closed seminar in Helsinki. Krasin said the Social Democrats and the communists should cooperate to oppose neoconservatism. (*Helsingin Sanomat*, 14, 15 November; *Pravda*, 18 November; *FBIS*, 30 November.) At the seminar, the new Finnish Social Democratic Party chair Paasio declared that his party and the CPSU were ready to continue their dialogue, and Sorsa advocated greater international cooperation to exploit the Arctic areas and construct confidence-building measures between military forces in northern waters. (*Suomen Sosialdemokraattinen*, 16 November.) Paasio and Iivari represented the party at the Moscow celebration on 2 November. Ulf Sundqvist, president of the Finnish Workers' Savings Bank and a former Social Democratic Party secretary, was also a guest of honor (*Helsingin Sanomat*, 4 November). From Eastern Europe, a Polish communist party delegation led by Central Committee member Ernest Kucza, was the guest of the Social Democrats in early May (Warsaw PAP, 8 May; *JPRS-Eastern Europe Report*-87-087, 4 June).

The decline of the Finnish communists proved no hindrance to improvement in Finnish-Soviet relations as Gorbachev's *glasnost'* policy unfolded. The Ryzhkov 6–9 January state visit, concerned principally with trade matters, ended with a communiqué that was somewhat more forthcoming in recognizing Finnish neutrality. It said that the Soviet Union valued President Koivisto's proposal for confidence-building measures in the northern maritime region and was itself seeking to restrict extensive military exercises in the Nordic area. (All papers, 10 January.) *Helsingin Sanomat* (12 January) wrote that events during the visit disclosed that both sides were "deeply satisfied" with the present state of affairs. Soviet minister of railways Nikolai Konarev headed a delegation to Helsinki to celebrate the 39th anniversary of the FCMA pact in early April, and Koivisto attended a reception at the Soviet embassy (*Kansan Uutiset*, 30 March; *Helsingin Sanomat*, 8 April).

The defeat of the left in the Finnish parliamentary election on 15–16 March and the establishment of the "red-blue" coalition based on the Conservatives and Social Democrats did not disturb those relations. Finnish communist fulminations against Conservative membership in the government had no echo among the Soviet leaders or press. For instance, *Tiedonantaja* (24 April; *JPRS-WER*-87-061, 7 July) charged that while the foreign policy stance of the Conservatives had changed, that party still represented "big capital, greater dependence on the West, and conservatism" and that its leadership of the government could not help but affect Finnish foreign policy. But Prime Minister Holkeri's declarations on taking office that he would follow the traditional "Paasikivi-Kekkonen line" of friendship toward the USSR called forth an article in *Izvestia* (9 May) describing Holkeri positively. The article stated that the Conservatives had changed their foreign policy and now relied on friendship toward the USSR. It also commented that Conservative domestic policies were now realistic and widely supported. (*Helsingin Sanomat*, *Uusi Suomi*, 10 May.)

During a visit to Stockholm on 23 June, Foreign Minister Sorsa said that the traditional term *Paasikivi-Kekkonen line* to describe Finland's policy (of friendship) toward the USSR should be replaced by the term *Finland line* because more than 90 percent of Finns supported it and it did not change with governments. (All papers, 24 June.) Hostile reaction arose immediately and ran the spectrum from former Foreign Minister Väyrynen of the Center Party to Sinisalo. Even Conservative Party vice-chair Jouni J. Sarkijarvi said the traditional terminology was natural because it indicated that foreign policy is set by the president, not parliament or the government (*Helsingin Sanomat*, 25 June). Despite some support for Sorsa, conservative circles tried to play down the issue, saying that the two terms could be used interchangeably (*Hufvudstadsbladet*, 25 June). Soviet foreign ministry official Yuri Deriabin, in a statement to a local Finnish newspaper (*Keskisuomalainen*, in Jyvasklya, 15 July), opposed Sorsa's suggestion, averring that the old terms were used in the USSR and that the names of Paasikivi and Kekkonen had political and historical significance. Deriabin's remarks were believed to express official Soviet thinking; he was thought to be the author behind the pseudonym of Yuri Kommisarov, who wrote on occasion for Finnish publications (*Hufvudstadsbladet*, *Uusi Suomi*, 16 July). (For instance, Kommisarov was quoted in *Uusi Suomi* [17 February] as approving Koivisto's foreign policy stance.)

It was in this atmosphere that Prime Minister Holkeri made his first major foreign policy speech before the Paasikivi Society on the first anniversary of Kekkonen's death. He had previously disassociated himself from Sorsa's proposal (*Helsingin Sanomat*, 27 July; *JPRS-WER*-87-075, 18 September). In his speech, he described Finland's foreign policy as indivisible, having become universal after all six major parties had supported Urho Kekkonen in the 1979 presidential election. Holkeri avoided the terms *Paasikivi-Kekkonen line* or *Finland line* and spoke of a *national line.* He said that, while that line was permanent, "we ourselves have an opportunity to define our interests and the policies required by those interests at any given time." Addressing Center Party and leftist criticism of Finland's closer relations with the EC, Holkeri declared that those closer relations were an example of looking after Finland's interests just as Kekkonen had done when he sanctioned joining the European Free Trade Area (EFTA) and making a free trade agreement with the EC while maintaining Finland's independent decisionmaking authority. (*Helsingin Sanomat*, *Hufvudstadsbladet*, *Uusi Suomi*, 4 September.) *Pravda* (5 September) quoted his speech.

Finnish exchange visits with Eastern Europe and the USSR grew during the year to a crescendo during the celebrations of the 70th anniversary of the October Revolution and Finnish independence. President Koivisto made three-day official visits to Czechoslovakia in late April (*Helsingin Sanomat*, *Uusi Suomi*, 24 April) and to East Germany 29 September–1 October (*Neues Deutschland*, 29, 30 September, 2, 3, 4 October). Trade was the main topic in both cases.

Starting 4 October, Koivisto was the official guest of Gorbachev during a week-long stay in the USSR. He was accompanied by his wife and cabinet members representing the four government parties—Foreign Minister Sorsa, Trade and Industry Minister Illka Suominen (Conservative), Education Minister Christoffer Taxell (Swedish People's Party), and Communications Minister Pekka Vennamo (Rural Party)—as well as representatives of the major trade union and employer federations. His party also included opposition figures: Martti Miettunen, the chair of the Finnish-Soviet Society (Center Party) and Erkki Kivimäki, that society's vice-chair (SKP).

On the eve of Koivisto's visit (1 October), Gorbachev made sweeping proposals during a speech in Murmansk. He endorsed creation of a Nordic nuclear weapons–free zone, long associated with former President Kekkonen, and confidence-building measures at sea, which Koivisto had suggested in 1986. As Ligachev had done during his visit to Helsinki in November 1986, Gorbachev offered to act as "guarantor" of a nuclear-free zone and withdraw Soviet submarines containing ballistic missiles from the area, called for NATO and Warsaw Pact consultations on restricting the size of naval exercises in the region, and proposed limiting antisubmarine warfare weapons and banning naval activity in straits and shipping lanes. These proposals created little stir since they had previously been discounted as posturing. But Gorbachev also took up economic and cultural issues: he asked for joint regional development of mineral resources, creation of a scientific council to study ethnic and cultural issues, the opening of Arctic shipping lanes to the Far East, and establishment of a regional council to protect the area's environment. (Moscow Television Service, 1 October; *FBIS*, 2 October.) These latter proposals struck a responsive cord in Finland, Sweden, and especially Norway, where development and protection of the Arctic area were political issues.

Koivisto issued a statement before his departure applauding Gorbachev's suggestions, and the two leaders discussed them during talks in Moscow (*Hufvudstadsbladet*, 7 October; *FBIS*, 20 October). A lengthy communiqué issued at the end of the visit stated that "the Finnish side welcomed the proposals" and added that "on the Finnish side, satisfaction was expressed with the constructive nature of the Soviet side's thoughts" on the issue. (*Pravda*, 12 October [second edition]; *FBIS*, 13 October.) But the Murmansk proposals did not dominate the visit. Koivisto stressed Finnish neutrality; in a statement to Moscow television, he said a spirit of trust and cooperation marked Finnish-Soviet relations. (All papers, 5 October.) For his part, Gorbachev, at a dinner honoring Koivisto, sought neutral nation support for the Soviet proposals to have the countries that participated in the Conference on Security and Cooperation in Europe (CSCE) examine the relative strength of the European alliances' conventional arms and hold a CSCE human rights conference in Moscow. (Ibid.)

A minor flap over the comuniqué arose in Finland when a major paper (*Helsingin Sanomat*, 12 October) claimed that Koivisto had tried to change the traditional phraseology describing Finnish neutrality and had been rebuffed. Another paper (*Hufvudstadsbladet*, 13 October) noted that the ongoing presidential election campaign might account for such charges. Koivisto told Finnish television (25 October) that he had merely sought to alter the style of the communiqué and deprecated the importance of communiqués, remarking that they were used only with the USSR (*Hufvudstadsbladet*, *Helsingin Sanomat*, 27 October). Predictably, Center Party leader Väyrynen came to the defense of traditional communiqués later in October at a seminar he had organized to celebrate the anniversary of the FCMA treaty (*Helsingin Sanomat*, 28 October). Another controversy arose when Soviet embassy counselor Albert Akulov, speaking at a Paasikivi seminar on 25 November, hinted that the USSR would take preventive action if Cruise missiles were fired over Finland. He later tried to say that of course the USSR would respect Finnish neutrality, but *Helsingin Sanomat* (3 December) replied by quoting his previous statements verbatim.

Koivisto returned to Moscow on 1 November to speak before the jubilee session of the CPSU Central Committee on 2 November, as part of the October Revolution anniversary (Moscow Television Service, 2 November; *FBIS*, 3 November). He was accompanied by Foreign Minister Sorsa, who represented the Socialist International in his capacity as vice-chair of that organization. The chairs of the Social Democratic, Center, and the two communist parties were also present. (*Helsingin Sanomat*, 31 October and 2 November.) Koivisto made a brief address to the session, praising Finnish-Soviet relations and Soviet "peace initiatives." (All papers, 3 November.) On 5 November, Koivisto spoke at anniversary celebrations at the House of Culture in Helsinki. Soviet vice-premier Vladimir Gusev headed the Soviet party that took part in the Helsinki ceremonies and talked with Prime Minister Holkeri (Helsinki Domestic Service, 4 November; *FBIS*, 5 November). At a press conference on 6 November, Gusev invited Finnish journalists to tour the naval base of the Soviet northern fleet at Severomorsk (all papers, 7 November). Holkeri was invited to Leningrad for a three-day official visit starting 29 December to participate in ceremonies celebrating Finland's 70th independence anniversary (Helsinki Domestic Service, 30 December; *FBIS*, 31 December).

There were many exchange visits by lower-ranking officials during the year, with trade usually the main topic of conversation. Prime Minister Holkeri's first foreign guest was Hungarian deputy prime minister Joszef Marjai, who spent five days in Finland during May, principally discussing trade matters (*Hufvudstadsbladet*, 5 May). In June Finnish parliamentarians hosted a six-day visit of Soviet parliamentarians; a joint communiqué supported all "realistic attempts to further debate, improve international security, and strengthen peace" and said that the Finns "greatly appreciated" Lenin's signing the decree that granted Finnish independence (*Izvestia*, 19 June; *FBIS*, 22 June; *Helsingin Sanomat*, 19 June). During 16–22 August, Hungarian Lt. General Lajos Morocz, state secretary of the Hungarian Defense Ministry, was the official guest of General Jaakko Valtanen, commander in chief of Finnish defense forces (*Hufvudstadsbladet*, 16 August). Valtanen visited Moscow briefly on 26 May and met with the Soviet defense minister, Marshal Sergei A. L. Sokolov (ibid. 27 May). In October, the Finnish Center for Promoting Tourism sponsored a seminar at Oulu which was attended by the director of Sputnik, the Soviet youth travel agency; in 1986, some 40,000 Soviet citizens had visited Finland, outnumbered only by Swedes (*Helsingin Sanomat*, 9 October). In the organized labor field, Finnish trade union federations sent a joint delegation, led by SAK chair Pertti Viinanen, to attend the All-Union Central Council of Trade Unions congress in Moscow (*Kansan Uutiset*, 20 February).

Finnish-Soviet relations in 1987 centered mainly on trade relations and problems. Because of the barter nature of trade agreements, the continued imbalance in Finland's favor (Finland's surplus in 1986 was five billion markka) created fear that Finnish exports would be forced to still lower levels. Paper, chemical, metal, and agricultural products were especially affected. During his visit, Ryzhkov plumped for joint Finnish-Soviet economic ventures, announcing that the first would be a Finnair-Soviet agreement to modernize the Hotel Berlin in Moscow. (Actually, the Finnish firm Sandolin formed the first joint venture with the Estonian Estkolkhozstroy [Administraiton for Construction of Collective Farms] on 11 June to produce wood protection agents [*Uusi Suomi*, 12 June; *JPRS-WER*-87-075, 18 September].) Ryzhkov signed a trade protocol for 1987 that introduced flexible quotas, as well as agreements for space research cooperation and for reporting of industrial accidents (the last was clearly an effort to overcome Finnish disgruntlement with the damage done in Finland by the Chernobyl accident).

Ryzhkov's efforts brought Finnish praise; *Uusi Suomi* (12 January) said Finland was being used as a testing ground for joint economic ventures. On the other hand, Center Party chair and former Foreign Minister Väyrynen continued to criticize Prime Minister Sorsa's handling of trade relations (*Kansan Uutiset*, 11 March). Aalto in turn criticized Väyrynen for trying to use Finnish-Soviet trade as a "political football" (ibid., 13 March).

The meeting of the Commission for Finnish-Soviet Economic Cooperation in Helsinki on 10 February, which Soviet deputy premier Vladimir Kamentsev, Soviet cochair of the commission, attended, tried to spur a project for joint exploitation of the Kola peninsula (Helsinki Domestic Service, 10 February; *FBIS*, 11 February). In April, as imported Soviet oil seemed likely to be restricted, pessimism rose that Finnish construction projects in the USSR—including a video recorder plant, a diskette station plant, a dairy (in Riga), an institute for biochemistry, and a circus in Moscow—would suffer. The Finnish surplus had exceeded the limit of the bilateral clearing account of 300 million rubles by one-third. An increase in Soviet oil imports in May eased this fear somewhat (*Helsingin Sanomat*, 2 June). In August, Sorsa (by then foreign minister but still Finnish cochair of the Commission for Finnish-Soviet Economic Cooperation) led a delegation to Moscow in an effort to balance the trade, or at least hold a reduction in Finnish exports to 10 percent. About 40 percent of the accumulated Finnish surplus of $1.1 billion was deposited in a special interest-bearing account in Moscow; holding the remainder was costing the Bank of Finland $44 million a year. (*Helsingin Sanomat*, 13 August; *JPRS-WER*-87-077, 29 September.)

A special delegation to handle bilateral negotiations was established under Trade and Industry minister Suominen. Finnish exports were believed to be lagging behind those in 1986 (*Uusi Suomi*, 1 September). During the official Koivisto visit to Moscow, Sorsa signed an extension of the long-term economic cooperation agreement for five years to the year 2000, Suominen signed a new tax agreement, and Education minister Taxell, an agreement on cooperation in science, art, and culture. More Soviet oil would have to be imported than ever before if balance were to be achieved; contracts let to Finns had already exceeded the 1988 quota. Nevertheless, joint ventures continued to be arranged; the Finnish firm Nokia Oy negotiated in October with the Soviet Ministry of Electrical Industry to produce copper wire for telephone cables. By the end of the year, some nine ventures were being planned or had started. In late October an agreement was reached to aid modernization of Soviet forestry and wood-processing industries (*Hufvudstadsbladet*, 23 October). In August Rautaukuukki Oy contracted to deliver 1,900 railcars to the USSR in 1988 (*Helsingin Sanomat*, 13 August; *JPRS-WER*-87-077, 29 September).

Negotiations on the balance issue continued into late December. Soviet officials said that the Finns would either have to reduce sales of consumer and agricultural goods or agree to postpone Soviet payments for ships and project construction exports. Finnish exporters were willing to accept postponement if interest were paid and exchange rate fluctuations accommodated. But the Finnish government and the Bank of Finland did not approve this course because of the burden it would place on liquidation of the special interest-bearing account in the Soviet Foreign Trade Bank required during the period 1989–1991. However, the Finnish government gave way somewhat when Suominen and Soviet foreign trade minister Boris Aristov signed the 1988 protocol in Moscow on 22 December. Payments for Finnish ship deliveries could be postponed until 1989 through provisions that compensated shipbuilders for extra costs and foreign currency risks. The protocol maintained current trade levels but again allowed flexible quotas on Finnish exports because of uncertain world oil prices. Re-exports of Soviet oil were also permitted in an effort to balance the trade. Finnish imports of coal, coke, natural gas, chemicals, timber, food products, and machinery and equipment were to be increased.

Both communist parties applauded closer Soviet-Finnish relations and urged more progress, particularly in the trade field. Sinisalo and other SKP-Y leaders still tried to claim that Soviet leaders were not satisfied with the pace of trade relations or with Finnish government attempts to place Finnish neutrality above Finnish obligations under the 1948 FCMA Pact but found no response in the USSR or Finland. Both parties praised Gorbachev for his disarmament proposals (*Kansan Uutiset*, 13 March), and their criticism of the United States mitigated slightly as a U.S.-Soviet agreement on intermediate-range nuclear forces neared. But attacks on the United States over such issues as Nicaragua and El Salvador continued unabated (*Kansan Uutiset*, 4, 14 March, 23 September). Top priority was placed on the peace theme in propaganda activities. The Gorbachev Murmansk initative was enthusiastically welcomed, and greater urgency was given the campaign for a Nordic nuclear weapons–free zone. Pressure was applied on the Finnish government to hasten the report of the five Nordic governments' high-level expert committee on the creation of such a zone. The communists gave strong support to the Nordic council on such issues as the zone proposal and attempts to form concerted Nordic actions against South Africa (*Kansan Uutiset*, 24 February).

The SKP continued its effort to draw closer to the other European communist parties. Aalto reportedly met often with Lars Werner, chair of the Swedish party (*Kansan Uutiset*, 6, 28 February). In February, Alessandro Natta, general secretary of the Italian party, was a guest of Aalto and held two-day talks with the SKP and the SDP leaders in Helsinki (AFP, 13 February; *FBIS*, 17 February).

Outside Europe, Aalto, accompanied by Erkki Kauppila, chief editor of *Kansan Uutiset*, and Jarmo Wahlström of the SKP Central Committee, visited China in January and talked with top Chinese officials. This visit was the first since 1960 and reopened relations between the two parties.

F. Herbert Capps
Bethesda, Maryland

France

Population. 55,596,030

Party. French Communist Party (Parti communiste français; PCF)

Founded. 1920

Membership. 604,282 (*L'Humanité*, 3 December)

General Secretary. Georges Marchais

Politburo. 23 members: Georges Marchais, Charles Fiterman (propaganda and communication), Jean-Claude Gayssot (party organization), Maxime Gremetz (foreign affairs), André Lajoinie (president of the communist group in the National Assembly), Paul Laurent (liaison with party federations), Gisèle Moreau (women's activities and family politics), Gaston Plissonnier (coordination of the work of the Politburo and Secretariat), Gustave Ansart (president of the Central Commission of Political Control), François Duteil (urbanism, environment, and consumption associations), Claude Billard (party activity in business and immigration), Pierre Blotin (education of communists), Guy Hermier (intellectual, cultural, educational, and university affairs), Philippe Herzog (economy), Francette Lazard (director of the Marxist Research Institute), René Le Guen (science, research, and technology), Roland Leroy (director of *L'Humanité*), René Piquet (president of the French communist group in the European Parliament), Madelaine Vincent (local communities, elections), Henri Krasucki (secretary of the General Confederation of Labor), Louis Viannet (Mail Workers' Federation), Antoine Casanova (director of the review *La Pensée*), Jackie Hoffmann (women's issues)

Secretariat. 7 members: Maxime Gremetz, Jean-Claude Gayssot, André Lajoinie, Paul Laurent, Gisèle Moreau, Gaston Plissonnier, Charles Fiterman

Central Committee. 145 members

Status. Legal

Last Congress. Twenty-sixth, 2–6 December 1987; next congress planned for 1990

Last Election. 1986, 9.8 percent, 35 of 577 seats

Auxiliary Organizations. General Confederation of Labor (CGT); World Peace Council; Movement of Communist Youth of France (MCJF); Committee for the Defense of Freedom in France and the World; Association of Communist and Republican Representatives

Publications. *L'Humanité* (Paris: Roland Leroy, director; daily national organ), *L'Echo du centre* (Limoges, daily), *Liberté* (Lille, daily), *La Marseillaise* (Marseille, daily), *L'Humanité-Dimanche* (Paris: weekly), *La Révolution* (Guy Hermier, director; weekly publication of the Central Committee), *La Terre* (weekly), *Cahiers du communisme* (monthly theoretical journal), *Europe* (literary journal), *Economie et politique* (economic journal), 5 journals published by the Marxist Research Institute; 4 monthly magazines; other periodicals on sports, children's themes, and the like, and books on political, economic, and social topics published by Editions sociales, the PCF publishing house in Paris.

The French Communist Party's hemorrhage of dissident leaders and public support intensified in 1987 as party bosses struggled with the grim prospect of leading a strife-torn PCF into presidential elections. Disaffected party leaders and functionaries—

including at least one former minister and several Central Committee members—finally bolted from the party or from party offices, many of them rallying to the alternative communist presidential candidacy of one-time PCF spokesman Pierre Juquin. General Secretary Marchais and Politburo "conservatives" engineered Juquin's expulsion from the party at almost the same time that the Twenty-sixth Congress—called earlier than expected to allow preparations for the election campaign—met to ratify Marchais's handpicked stand-in candidate, Central Committee secretary and PCF National Assembly leader Lajoinie. Dissidents continued throughout the year to flail party leaders with accusations of self-serving blindness to recent failures of policy and their consequences for the communist vote. The leadership and Politburo hard-liners persistently deflected demands for open debate from self-styled *renovateurs* by emphasizing party unity as the primary exigency of the election campaign and by accelerating attacks on former Socialist allies and the center-right government as the twin agents of austerity, military spending, and public suffering. The leadership also fended off pointed reformist claims that PCF renewal should begin with leadership resignations as the only way to take full responsibility for past mistakes and for the party's precipitous slide toward political oblivion. Party international activity, meanwhile, quickened somewhat as PCF leaders embraced more fully General Secretary Mikhail Gorbachev's "openness" and "restructuring" initiatives.

Leadership and Party Organization. Strikes by subway drivers, electric workers, and railway men—joined by thousands of students—crippled France for a short period during the winter of 1987, damaging the government's image of effectiveness. Strikers also forced Prime Minister Jacques Chirac to withdraw or withhold key elements of his center-right government's legislative program, most notably bills on French nationality and privatization of French prisons—measures that excited considerable hostility across much of the French left. Although the communist-dominated trade union—the CGT—led the charge against controversial government policies, the communist party itself made only a lackluster attempt to mobilize its militants for demonstrations, and communist-affiliated groups, such as the communist youth movement, played only a minor role among the contingents of student protesters. Most important, according to knowledgeable observers, the PCF failed to gain either internal strength or public support from the difficulties of the conservative government. Instead, the party was self-absorbed in its growing factionalism, as "reformers" stepped up their campaign of the past two years to challenge Marchais and party hard-liners to permit a genuine debate within the PCF about the failure of the leftist coalition government with Socialists between 1981 and 1984 and about the PCF's relationship with other communist parties—an oblique reference to well-known charges of PCF subservience to Moscow's line and to the concept of the Stalinist state as a "model" of modern social evolution toward communism. (*Insight*, 23 March; *WSJ*, 3 February; Paris, AFP, 27 January.)

Rifts widened substantially in late January when two of the PCF's old guard—both former close allies of Marchais—resigned from the Central Committee in open defiance of "conservative" efforts to bludgeon critics into silence (*L'Express*, 30 January–5 February; *Libération*, 27 January). Marcel Rigout, former minister of vocational training in the defunct Unity of the Left government that Marchais had engineered with the Socialists between 1981 and 1984, challenged Marchais's use of the term *liquidator*—a term reminiscent of the worst images of the Stalinist purges and, in the PCF, a harbinger of imminent expulsion from the party—to brand Juquin and all those demanding internal reforms. Rigout exchanged several letters with Marchais and the Central Committee—all widely reprinted in the French press—in which he rejected Marchais's accusations as "a public blow to the party's unity" (*L'Humanité*, 27 January). In a move that took observers by surprise, Rigout next resigned from the Central Committee and placed his National Assembly seat at the party's disposal (party leaders did not accept the latter). Rigout also accused the leadership of stonewalling legitimate questions from well-meaning comrades (Paris, AFP, 27 January).

The Central Committee's riposte was swift and bitter, backing Marchais completely and condemning Rigout's defection. Most important, *L'Humanité* director and Politburo member Leroy attacked Rigout for failing to distinguish between dissent within the rules of democratic centralism and criticisms that clearly ran counter to the Twenty-fifth Congress line, aiming "to turn the PCF into a substitute for the PS [Socialist Party] (*L'Humanité*, 28 January). Leroy argued in a television interview that the Central Committee had first used the term *liquidator* in a resolution of the previous May to describe the activities of renovateurs in the strife-ridden Meurthe-et-Moselle federation and that Rigout had voted for the resolution (*L'Humanité*, 29 January 1987). Indeed, only Juquin abstained. Not surprisingly, prominent renovateurs—Juquin, Claude Poperen, Félix Damette, and Claude Llabres—abstained in voting the Central Committee's rejoinder to Rigout, but Poperen quickly followed Rigout into exile, resigning both his Central Committee and Politburo posts.

Rigout was a communist hero of the Resistance, and Poperen, a syndicalist hero of the long struggle to unionize Renault; their boisterous defections jolted the leadership and cast into bold relief the failure of Marchais's efforts to gag dissent. Press leaks painted an emotional scene in the Central Committee meeting, with old friends reportedly accusing one another of betraying the party (*WSJ*, 3 February; Michel Samson, "Le PC Liquide Ses Liquidateurs," *Libération*, 27 January). The Politburo and the Central Committee nonetheless pronounced Rigout guilty of stepped-up and concentrated attacks on both the Central Committee and the general secretary and both fell back on democratic centralism as the only valid channel for discussion of party policy. The Central Committee's resolution concluded with a stern "warning to those party members who engage in such unacceptable attempts at liquidation" (*L'Humanité*, 27 January, 16 February).

Hard-line reaction to the Poperen-Rigout resignations was reportedly sharpened by escalating rumors that renovateurs intended to run Juquin as a "divisionist" candidate for president, in direct rejection of Central Committee secretary Lajoinie—widely considered a shoo-in as Marchais's hand-picked stand-in on the PCF hustings (*WSJ*, 3 February). Each candidate elicited vigorous and cynical reactions—Lajoinie as the potential fall guy who would salvage Marchais's continued leadership by sparing the general secretary the shame and added embarrassment of leading the party to yet another historic humiliation at the polls and Juquin as the convenient dupe of Socialist strategy to split off disaffected PCF voters and drive the party still farther toward the margins of French political life. As the expulsions and Juquin's continued talk of launching a "new revolutionary organization" excited fears of "the Spanish syndrome," Marchais and majority conservatives in the leadership tried to divert rank-and-file attention toward preparations for the Twenty-sixth Congress and the coming presidential elections (*L'Express*, 30 January–5 February).

Meanwhile, notable support for renovateur leaders continued to trickle up from dissident federations like the Hérault, where protests over the Poperen-Rigout resignations welled up in the national media and where one powerful communist mayor bucked the leadership's election strategy of attacking Socialists by announcing in favor of "union with the PS" in the forthcoming election campaign (*L'Humanité*, 29 January). Over the next weeks, dissident communists and leftist intellectuals organized to focus even greater media pressure on the leadership to sponsor debate and enact reforms. Most important, 35 PCF members met "at a secret location" in Paris in direct response to the Poperen-Rigout resignations, styling themselves a "coordinating collective" of communist "reformers." Although the membership of the "collective" remained largely secret, various media with good access to renovateurs reported that it comprised militants from departmental federal committees, former Central Committee staffers, elected city officials, and other activists representing fifteen departmental federations and including "isolated members" from the Paris "red belt." Disavowing factionalist intentions and loyalty to any particular PCF leader, the collective promised a "Manifesto" that would challenge the leadership's record in strong Marxist and revolutionary terms and that would reportedly give no quarter to "the PS's dream of hegemony over the left" (*Le Monde*, 3 February). At the January Central Committee meeting—which defended the Marchais initiative against liquidators—Juquin reportedly delivered a frequently interrupted speech that pounded away at similar themes, notably that "the PCF is in danger of disappearing as a political force that counts" because it had lost the strength and optimism to challenge ascendant "neoliberalism" (*Libération*, 28 January).

Despite mounting evidence to the contrary, Marchais and PCF leaders continued to maintain that so-called rifts in the party were "pure misinformation"—a fabrication and exaggeration of rightist and Socialist media (*L'Humanité*, 12 February). Declaring in one television interview that "the PCF is not going through a crisis," party bosses launched a campaign that at once minimized the extent of internal discontent and defended party "democracy" achieved through the mechanisms of democratic centralism ("91 percent of delegates to federal conferences and 96 percent of delegates to the congress" approved the Twenty-fifth Congress line). Although dissidents had previously demanded an extraordinary congress to deal with issues of internal reform, none applauded the advent of the Twenty-sixth Congress in preparation for the 1988 presidentials (*L'Humanité*, 12 February; Paris Television Service, "Hour of Truth," 25 February).

In the run to the national conference—set for June and intended to ratify a PCF candidate and a resolution for the Twenty-sixth Congress—party leaders were dogged by media questions not only about the prospect of Juquin's rival presidential candidacy but also about persistent reports of shrinking voter support and membership. Stung by intense questioning about the party's diminished strength and influence, Leroy hired a poll—conducted by the PCF weekly *L'Humanité-Dimanche*—that consoled party leaders by showing that Frenchmen believed that communists were willing to "change society," but that also revealed that large numbers of voters believed the PCF was involved in financial shenanigans ("secret funds" and suitcases of money "from Moscow") and that a solid majority held an unfavorable overall image of the party (*WMR*, February). Pressed by interviewers and notwithstanding party efforts to put a positive spin on recent electoral disasters, Marchais acknowledged that voter support had fallen to less than half its historic high (Paris Television Service, 25 February). But on the basis of unsubstantiated claims that the PCF could boast "45,000 new members," Marchais maintained late in the year that recently declining party membership had recovered to the 600,000 level claimed since 1984. (Informed French observers have disputed this figure, however, maintaining that real PCF strength stands around 150,000 [*L'Humanité*, 14 September; *WMR*, February; *Pravda*, 14 January].) Significantly for the approaching election, barometers throughout the year showed that communist voter support remained stubbornly at or below the recent disappointing performance of about 9 percent. When the leftist weekly *Le Nouvel Observateur* polled voters early in January on the eighteen top potential presidential candidates, Lajoinie finished dead last behind extreme-right National Front leader Jean-Marie Le Pen and actor-turned political gadfly Yves Montand. Still other surveys throughout the year predicted Juquin and Lajoinie candidacies would split the communist vote almost in half, with each in various soundings showing strength of 4 or 5 percent (*WSJ*, 3 February; *Le Nouvel Observateur*, January).

Leadership efforts to mobilize the party's diminished strength for the coming presidential contest and for legislative elections that could follow focused on preparations for the Twenty-sixth Congress. The Politburo scheduled its national conference in mid-June, with regular Central Committee meetings in the months before and after—all orchestrated to manage the PCF's internal electoral process for the Twenty-sixth Congress but also geared to periodically boosting the PCF's assiduously dull campaign. Lajoinie's soft-spoken manner of the quintessential party functionary appealed to few in the noncommunist media, which noted how often Marchais seemed to do all the talking when they appeared together (*Le Monde*, 16 June). The campaign failed in its one brief opportunity to catch fire, when in mid-September Lajoinie rose to debate National Front leader Le Pen on television in the wake of Le Pen's claims that the Nazi gas chambers were a mere detail in the history of World War II. Billed as a "battle of the extremists," the confrontation became a meaningless exchange of insults and invective, which viewer polls nonetheless gave to Le Pen (Reuters, 22 September).

If Lajoinie's campaign lagged, Juquin's fared little better. As an unofficial candidate most of the year, the more articulate Juquin was constrained from throwing his full energies into forging a campaign organization. Yet, as an active noncandidate, he came under increasing derision from party leaders—Marchais, in particular—who chided him to produce his PCF membership card (suggesting that he had thrown it away) and even suggested that his Central Committee membership was in question. Juquin, meanwhile, stressed themes intended to keep the leadership on the defensive, notably the uselessness of "models," the party's continued acceptance of the *force de frappe*, and the PCF's lack of an effective policy on ecology issues (*Libération*, 28 January; *Paris Match*, 28 June; Paris Domestic Service, 15 October). On Marchais's recommendation, the Central Committee meeting of mid-May officially nominated Lajoinie as the party's candidate "unanimously" because the two abstaining votes—well-known renovateurs Llabres and Damette—did not propose an alternative candidate (*L'Humanité*, 21 May). Juquin angered party leaders by failing to attend the May Central Committee meeting—ostensibly because of a prior commitment to visit New Caledonia—but he sent a letter that struck several critical chords (*L'Humanité*, 19 May).

Juquin's reception at the national conference in June was a study in the ability of democratic centralism both to filter out dissent and to punish and isolate miscreants. The 1,200 delegates jeered and whistled when Juquin appealed to them to reject Lajoinie and denounced the party's "bureaucratic, sectarian, and closeted behavior." When he addressed the conference, the sound was mysteriously cut (technical problems, organizers said later) but came back on for the next speaker. Juquin's seat at the conference was isolated from other delegates by rows of benches deliberately left empty. Finally, the assembly unanimously confirmed Lajoinie's candidacy but only after Marchais had asked for a show of hands on Juquin's candidacy that failed to get a single vote (Reuters, 14 June). After the conference, Marchais declared Juquin undemocratic because he had refused to accept the expressed will of the party and stated flatly that if Juquin ran for president, he would "be primarily a Socialist candidate"—taking no votes from the PCF. Finally, Juquin resigned from the Central Committee, setting the stage for his long-expected showdown with party leaders (*L'Humanité*, 19 June; Paris Domestic Service, 24 June).

Apart from the histrionics of demonstrating Juquin's isolation in the party, the conference and the leadership focused on two questions about the elections that had beset the party since the 1986 legislative contests and that gained strength through reformist machinations: in Marchais's phrasing, "what will you do if there is a second communist candidate?" and "what will you do in the second round of the election, when the two-stage process will have reduced the field to two candidates?" Marchais pointed to the events of the conference to dismiss the first question, suggesting that any so-called communist candidate but Lajoinie would be a fraud, or worse, a Trotskyist. The second and more difficult issue harkened back to overtures and warnings—from renovateurs and from PS officials like First Secretary Lionel Jospin—that the PCF's best hope of regaining lost political terrain would be renewed unity with the Socialists. Marchais, however, made it clear that hard-liners would have nothing to do with anything that smacked of the old "unity of the left" tactics nor would they compromise their antirightist/anti-Socialist platform. While holding out the prospect that communists might support the PS candidate in the second round, Marchais promised anew (also a favorite Lajoinie theme) that this could only be a result of Socialist acceptance of the authentically Marxist program of the PCF (*L'Humanité*, 6 April, 13 June; *Le Monde*, 18 February, 16 June).

The national conference left Juquin with almost no maneuvering room within the party, guaranteed up to then by the convenient fiction that he was still a bona fide member of the Central Committee. Juquin's declaration of candidacy (on 12 October), however, came only after the September Central Committee confirmed his total alienation from the levers of PCF power and the near-complete success of party hard-liners in once again stacking the deck in delegate selection for the party congress (*Le Monde*, 13 October). Breaking the recent party custom of excluding troublemakers by declaring that they had excluded themselves, a quickly convened session of the Central Committee expelled Juquin outright because he had "played an active part, with others, in organizing factional activity within the party aimed at combating its policy, its leadership, and its principles" (Paris, AFP, 14 October; *L'Humanité*, 15 October).

Meanwhile, preparations for the Twenty-sixth Congress intensified after the party's annual September "Fête de *l'Humanité*," as did the din of protest and defections of well-placed renovateurs. Damette—PCF European Parliament deputy—led the charge at the September Central Committee meeting, along with Llabres, another Juquin supporter and well-known reformer. Llabres won dismissal from the Central Committee by refusing to support the Central Committee's approval of the draft resolution of the Twenty-sixth Congress. Damette, in fact, attacked the resolution even more forcefully, declaring it a "diversion" that proved the leadership was evading its responsibility for strategic mistakes of the recent past (*L'Humanité*, 10 September).

"Lack of renewal" became Damette's favored rhetorical theme for much of the year (even after losing his Central Committee seat at the Twenty-sixth Congress) as he ridiculed with special gusto the leadership's argument that issues of internal reform need not be considered by the forthcoming congress because the previous congress had "already settled everything" (*L'Humanité*, 10 October). Growing perceptions that the leadership intended to invoke the full power of democratic centralism to stifle dissent at the Twenty-sixth Congress and Juquin's declaration of candidacy provoked a wave of new defections from the party, none more dramatic than the mass resignation of 30 leaders of the Haute-Vienne departmental federation, including the beleaguered Rigout. Most of the defectors reportedly flocked to Juquin's campaign (*Le Point*, 4–9 November), which came to full steam in November. The organizational leadership featured a diverse assortment of disaffected leftists such as renovateur notable Alain Amicabile, former head of the faction-ridden Meurthe-et-Moselle federation, and student leader David Assouline, a coordinator of the previous winter's massive strikes. The campaign also attracted left-wing Socialists, Trotskyists of the Communist Revolutionary League (LCR), and activists from the fiercely anti–National Front SOS-Racisme. Juquin argued, with apparent justification, that his supporters averaged half the age of the PCF Central Committee and said publicly that his campaign aimed to mobilize immigrant voters as well as all those fed up with the PCF (Paris Domestic Service, 15 October; *Le Point*, 19 October). By year's end, however, various polls suggested that Juquin's 4 or 5 percent of the vote was mostly looted from traditional PCF constituencies.

The PCF congress convened on 2 December, as in the past, at the sports arena of the Paris communist stronghold of Saint-Ouen. Only Damette—the last and soon-to-be-marginalized renovateur on the Central Committee—caused something of a reformist ruckus. Otherwise, the 1700 delegates—many of them newly risen in the ranks of federation leaders as a result of renovateur defections—re-elected Marchais as general secretary for his seventh term and returned all members of the Politburo. They also dutifully ratified all the work of the party leadership since the last congress, especially the mobilization for the presidentials. Organizers reportedly worked overtime to ensure that the few sour notes coming from the PCF bandwagon were drowned out by a chorus of unity themes, lest the bourgeois media succeed in its planned "Juquinisation" of the congress (*Le Monde*, 2, 4, 5, 6–7 December).

The congress held few surprises in the sphere of personnel changes. There were virtually no changes in the Politburo, where former Transportation Minister Fiterman retained his post despite past suspicions of reform sentiments by hard-liners and press reports that he was still under attack. Especially noted among the new arrivals were François Duteil, head of the powerful energy federation of the CGT, Jackie Hoffmann, deputy for the Yvelines department, and Antoine Casanova, director of the PCF magazine *La Pensée*. Rumored departures from leadership posts, such as *La Révolution* editor Hermier, did not materialize, but the noncommunist press reported that many—including Hermier, Fiterman, and former ministers Jack Ralite and Anicet Le Pors—were barely elected (Paris Domestic Service, 6 December; *Le Monde*, 8 December).

Domestic Affairs. Hewing closely to the slogan "Justice, Freedom, and Peace" party leaders spent much of the year serving up almost equal portions of contempt for the policies of the Chirac government and loathing for Socialists who were "cohabiting" with it. Continuing the pattern of relentless derision of former Socialist allies established in the previous year's legislative elections, Marchais's domestic policy speeches, in particular, played variations on two themes: that rightists were only furthering the antiworking class policies of "austerity and the arms race" begun under the Socialists and that differences between Socialists of the Elysée and conservatives of the Matignon were differences of degree rather than of kind (*L'Humanité*, 19 June; Speech to National Association of Elected Communists, Paris Domestic Service, 24 May).

Blaming Socialist president François Mitterrand's betrayal of the joint leftist program of 1981 for both the ensuing "economic crisis"—replete with layoffs, declining purchasing power, and attacks on Social Security—and the return of the right after March 1986, Marchais asserted in his national conference address that

> on all the essential issues, the class decisions are now shared by the leaders of the PS, RPR [neo-Gaullists], and UDF [Centrists]. The existing separation between the policy of capital and the new policy no longer passes between Right and Left, but within the Left, between the PS and the Communist Party (*L'Humanité*, 13 June).

Similar charges were echoed in speeches by other hard-liners, notably Leroy's blistering anti-Socialist report to the January Central Committee meeting (*L'Humanité*, 28 January).

More specifically, Marchais and other hard-liners lambasted Socialist initiatives on which, in their view, the right was able to build, particularly Socialist economic policies designed to encourage greater competition in French capital markets and national enterprises (the harbinger of Chirac's privatization drive) and introduction of employment reforms aimed at instilling greater flexibility in hiring and firing. In the human rights sphere, Marchais and others assailed the similarity in Chirac's and Laurent Fabius's immigration policies—their equal gusto for "expelling Basque refugees" and their "joint refusal to impose sanctions on South Africa" (*L'Humanité*, 18 May).

Communists also intensified attacks on the perceived joint Socialist-conservative enthusiasm for the European Community (EC) and especially the moves envisioned in the Single European Act (approved at the Luxembourg summit, December 1985) toward more complete European integration by 1992 (*L'Humanité*, 18 May). Lajoinie in particular criticized the "supranational" European policy of the Chirac government in his voluminous report to the PCF national council in March (7,000 words, excerpted in *L'Humanité*, 16 March) and together with Marchais assailed the EC as a "yoke" by which the goal of "real cooperation" among Europeans was persistently thwarted by "U.S domination." In fact, Lajoinie argued in one attack on NATO, Europe would not escape U.S. vassalage until "general disarmament" had been achieved (*Le Monde*, 16 June).

With regard to other domestic issues, the PCF fired this year's "human rights" bombshell, embodied in the long-predicted declaration of fundamental freedoms finally produced by the party's Freedoms and Human Rights Defense Committee, at the industrial and employment policies of the RPR-UDF coalition. Identifying the unemployment "crisis" as a by-product of the Chirac government's privatization schemes, party leaders accused the conservatives of attempting to shatter the Labor Code by permitting "the unlimited multiplication of temporary and part-time jobs" and by employer attacks on the social insurance system. Marchais reserved special venom for the so-called Dalle report (authored under government auspices by the pharmaceuticals magnate François Dalle) that among other things recommended raising the official work schedule to 45 or 48 hours per week, pay at the 40-hour rate, and a decrease in the base wage (*L'Humanité*, 20 February, 13 June).

Against long-standing and thoroughly convincing evidence of the PCF's virtual desertion by significant French intellectuals—precipitated by the party's role in the events of 1968—the Politburo ordered a study of relations between the party and intellectuals. Gerard Streiff—the former *L'Humanité* correspondent in Moscow and present deputy editor of the Central Committee's theoretical organ *La Révolution*—produced an analysis that equated intellectuals with white-collar workers (in terms reminiscent of Stalinist efforts to identify party functionaries as true proletarians) that rang throughout with such shopworn aphorisms as "we have to convince the intellectuals that although the present struggle is a hard one the future is not dead" ("Intellectuals in Present-Day French Society," *WMR*, July).

Spokesmen for the PCF fought Chirac's privatization program at virtually every legislative juncture, but hard-line leaders lashed out most vigorously at two cases—television and Renault. Early in the year, Lajoinie and Fiterman attacked plans to denationalize France's flagship television network (TF1) as the machinations of "vultures of finance capital" calculated to gain complete control of the levers of public opinion and as a rightist assault on pluralism. ("Keeping Television a Public Service," *WMR*, May; *L'Humanité*, 6 April). Most important, the PCF decided late in the year to join the CGT—its affiliated trade union— in declaring a showdown with Chirac over a government bill to change the Renault auto company's status from that of a privileged state group (*régie*) to an ordinary state-controlled company, thus diminishing its financial support and exemption from bankruptcy. Apparently convinced that the act would be the first step toward privatization of one of its traditional bastions, the PCF leadership decided to disrupt the National Assembly debate by tabling more than 3,000 amendments. The CGT, meanwhile, which had seen its influence at Renault diminished by three years of labor cuts, staged a "day of action" to protest the firing, arrest, conviction, and sentencing of ten union militants (including Marchais's son-in-law) who had sacked some Renault offices in a protest last year (*Financial Times*, 9 December; *Le Monde*, 1 December).

French communists either organized or participated in a number of demonstrations aimed at changing other government policies, notably the large November mobilization by SOS-Racisme "against racism and xenophobia." The protest was directed partly at anti-immigrant police brutality and partly at the discriminatory deportation policies associated by leftists with Interior Minister Pasqua and French security minister Pandraud (*Le Monde*, 1 December).

Foreign Affairs and Security Issues. Communists shifted their stance significantly in 1987 on the issue of nuclear deterrence and disarmament, reversing a decade-old policy that supported the necessity of an independent nuclear deterrent as the linchpin of French nuclear policy. Although the party's new position stopped short of advocating unilateral nuclear disarmament, it nonetheless demanded elimination of all French nuclear weapons by the year 2000, the scrapping of all but land- and sea-based strategic systems, abandonment of steps toward the Strategic Defense Initiative (SDI) and European strategic defense, retreat from plans to professionalize the military, an end to the arms race, and—as a first step toward denuclearization—an end to nuclear testing on the French Pacific island of Mururoa ("National Defense at France's Service," *L'Humanité*, 22 January). Marchais emphasized various facets of the new defense policy periodically throughout the year, notably at a Dijon rally where he seconded Gorbachev's goal of a nuclear-free world by 2000 and later on Moscow television when he reportedly charged that France's nuclear deterrent, "previously intended for the defense of national territory," was "now changing as a result of plans to create a so-called European defense" (Moscow, TASS, 18 May; *Pravda*, 23 June). PCF leaders celebrated their revolt against their 1977 decision to support nuclear deterrence by attempting to stage a revival of the defunct communist-led French peace movement. The June peace march—ballyhooed by a lavish *L'Humanité* publicity campaign and predicted by party brass to turn out hundreds of thousands of protesters—attracted only modest support (*Financial Times*, 14 June).

Communists emphatically protested the perceived commonality of Socialist and conservative views on defense policy—ranging from continued support for nuclear deterrence ("the arms race") to passage of Defense Minister Giraud's ambitious new military program's law and budget. Lajoinie amplified such concerns at every turn, often arguing that the Socialist/conservative penchant for boosting military spending sent the wrong signal in an environment of superpower efforts to achieve arms reductions and flew in the face of the "fundamental changes" occurring in the Soviet Union (*L'Humanité*, 6 April). Lajoinie called in the National Assembly for significant channeling of defense expenditures into education and housing (Moscow, TASS, 15 October).

Communist leaders found little to criticize in Socialist support for the proposed U.S.-USSR treaty for the global elimination of intermediate-range nuclear forces (INF), but they attacked conservative reservations—often voiced by Giraud and the conservative defense lobby (Defense 2000)—as the feeble machinations of negative militarism ("For an Independent France in a World of Peace," *PCF Information Bulletin*, August; *L'Humanité*, 4 March, 10 April). The Politburo's first endorsement of INF negotiations in March and all subsequent leadership declarations completely backed the Soviet line that serious negotiations were a result of Gorbachev's initiative rather than a U.S. initiative that Moscow had rejected for some months because of the Strategic Defense Initiative (*L'Humanité*, 4 March).

Other party foreign policy initiatives maintained pressure for sanctions against South Africa, rejected government efforts to stage an all-parties referendum in New Caledonia, lambasted multinational naval escort operations in the Persian Gulf, and continued verbal support for Soviet military operations in Afghanistan. The leaking of a secret government report that charged the former Fabius government and the Socialist Party with profiting from kickbacks on the illegal sale of arms to Iran (the Luchaire affair) touched off a scandal that threatened Mitterrand's second presidential candidacy and compounded significant PS embarrassment from similar revelations in the Carrefour du Développement scandal a year earlier. Communists made every effort to portray Socialists as venal and PS counterterrorism policy as a farce and even hinted at advancing a bill to require public disclosure of political party finances (an idea later expropriated by Mitterrand in his own counterattack against the Chirac government) (*WMR*, February).

International Activities. The initiative on nuclear disarmament and preparations for the Twenty-sixth Congress excited somewhat more intense international activity than in the previous year. In general, party spokesmen vigorously touted the PCF's wholehearted admiration for the "openness" and "restructuring" reforms of Soviet leader Gorbachev. Several PCF leaders made official visits to Moscow throughout the year, none better publicized or more effective than Marchais's lengthy visit of April–May—his first visit since September 1985, when PCF-CPSU officials attempted to patch up differences stemming from the era of the PCF-PS coalition government. Marchais used the visit to court Gorbachev's support for leadership initiatives within the PCF and, more important, to express French communist support for Gorbachev's internal reforms and disarmament themes. Marchais gave interviews and made speeches on Moscow television, most of them elaborating on already well-established PCF habits of extolling Gorbachev's reforms and bemoaning the state of French-Soviet relations. Marchais also traveled to Soviet Armenia, where he reportedly discussed the same topics with local officials (*L'Humanité*, 7, 13 May;

Reuters, 24 April; Kevin Devlin, "Western Communist Reactions to Soviet Changes," *RAD Background Report* 28, 27 February; Moscow, TASS, 4, 6 May; *Pravda*, 8 May).

Marchais and others attended the celebrations for the 70th anniversary of the October Revolution, but on this occasion symbol overshadowed substance. Marchais, however, addressed a forum of delegates from international communist parties during which he repeated most of the disarmament and *glasnost'* themes of his previous visit. Leroy traveled to Moscow as part of a delegation of French citizens organized by Initiative-87—a French-Soviet group devoted to promoting bilateral understanding. Leroy and Anatolii Dobrynin reportedly discussed launching a PCF media campaign in support of Gorbachev's reforms (*L'Humanité*, 5 November; Moscow, TASS, 30 September; *Le Point*, 26 October). PCF delegations and leaders also made significant interparty visits to Warsaw, Madrid, Budapest, and Beijing; the latter was led by Lajoinie (*FBIS*, 21 August; *JPRS*, 26 January, 2 March; Madrid, *Mundo Obrero*, 5–11 February). The Twenty-sixth Congress brought a number of delegations from fraternal parties, but most were led by lower-level party leaders. The Soviet delegation, however, was headed by CPSU central committee secretary Egor Ligachev, who took the occasion to meet with numerous French—as well as PCF—officials and to stress Moscow's favorite arms control theses (Paris, AFP, 3 December; Moscow Television Service, 5 December).

International initiatives by the PCF's foreign affairs bureau included meetings and conferences devoted to the problems of development in Africa and, in particular, an international conference on Third World debt aimed at discovering new ways of financing and freeing developing states from dependence on Western states for military aid (*Le Point*, 26 October). Gremetz, who traveled widely in 1987 (especially in the Third World), enunciated the PCF's four-point plan for attacking Third World debt, which centered largely on "debt annullment" and a "new financing" from developed countries that would amount to a Marshall Plan for the underdeveloped world ("Propositions du PCF sur les Problèms de la dette et du développement," *Cahiers du Communisme*, no. 7–8, July–August).

Edward A. Allen
Washington, D.C.

Germany:
Federal Republic of Germany

Population. 59,131,000, excl. West Berlin (1987)
Party. German Communist Party (Deutsche Kommunistische Partei; DKP)
Founded. 1968
Membership. 50,800 (claimed, 1986); 40,000 DKP alone or 64,000 including youth and student movements (Federal Office for the Protection of the Constitution)
Chairman. Herbert Mies (since 1973)
Presidium. 19 members: Herbert Mies, Ellen Weber (vice-chair), Jupp Angenfort, Kurt Bachmann, Irmgard Bobrzik, Martha Buschmann, Werner Cieslak, Heinz Czymek, Gerd Deumlich, Kurt Fritsch, Hermann Gautier, Wolfgang Gehrcke, Willi Gerns, Dieter Keller, Georg Polikeit, Rolf Priemer, Birgit Radow (youth organization chair), Karl-Heinz Schröder, Wilhelm Spengler, Werner Sturmann
Secretariat. 14 members: Herbert Mies, Ellen Weber, Vera Aschenbach, Werner Cieslak, Gerd Deumlich, Kurt Fritsch, Willi Gerns, Marianne Konze, Jofel Mayer, Fritz Noll, Rolf Priemer, Karl-Heinz Schröder, Wilhelm Spengler, Werner Sturmann
Executive. 94 members
Status. Legal
Last Congress. Eighth, 2–4 May 1986, in Hamburg
Last Election. 1987, about 0.5 percent for "Peace List," in which DKP participated; no representation in federal parliament or any land (state) parliament.
Auxiliary Organizations. Socialist German Workers' Youth (Sozialistische Deutsche Arbeiter Jugend; SDAJ), about 15,000 members, Birgit Radow, chair; Marxist Student Union-Spartakus (Marxistischer Studentenbund-Spartakus; MSB-Spartakus), about 6,000 members; Young Pioneers (Junge Pioniere; JP), about 4,000 members, Gerhard Hertel, chair

Publications. *Unsere Zeit* (Our Time), Düsseldorf, DKP organ (editor: Georg Polikeit), daily circulation 30,000, weekend edition, 55,000, Monday edition discontinued. Many issues are distributed to socialist states through East Berlin. *Elan-Das Jugendmagazin*, SDAJ monthly organ, circulation about 25,000; *Rote Blätter* (Red Pages), MSB-Spartakus monthly organ, circulation about 15,000; *Pionier* (Pioneer), JP monthly organ.

The DKP, which is unswervingly loyal to Moscow and East Berlin, grew out of the Communist Party of Germany (Kommunistische Partei Deutschlands; KPD). The KPD had been officially founded 31 December 1918, by left-wing Spartakists, who had broken away from the Social Democratic Party of Germany (SPD) following the Bolshevik Revolution in Russia a year earlier.

After World War II, the KPD was the first party to be legalized on 11 June 1945. It merged with the SPD as a unified German workers' party in the Soviet zone of occupation on 22 April 1946, when the Socialist Unity Party of Germany (Sozialistische Einheitspartei Deutschlands; SED) was formed. Because of bitter opposition to such merger by leading Social Democrats in the Western zones, no unification took place in the West. The KPD had two representatives (out of a total of 65) on the Parliamentary Council, which existed from September 1948 to May 1949 to produce a Basic Law (constitution) for the Federal Republic of Germany (FRG); in the end, the KPD decided to oppose the Basic Law, which came into effect in 1949.

In the first federal elections in 1949, the KPD won 5.7 percent of the votes and gained fifteen members in the Bundestag (lower house of the parliament). In the 1953 election its vote plummeted to 2.2 percent, far short of the minimum 5 percent required. Communists never again won seats, and their percentage of votes declined steadily. The weakening popular support for the KPD merely increased its dependence upon a foreign patron, notably the SED in the German Democratic Republic (GDR). Such dependence contributed to the Constitutional Court's outlawing of the KPD in August 1956.

By the time the party was renamed the DKP and, as a concession by Chancellor Willy Brandt to the Kremlin, again legalized in 1968 (with new statutes and statements of purpose carefully crafted to be compatible with the Basic Law), two important developments had occurred: the party's membership had shrunk to about 7,000, and the tumultuous 1960s had produced in the FRG scores of radical and independent communist or radical leftist groups, which compete with the traditional orthodox party. The DKP does not regard itself as having supplanted the KPD, which in theory continues to exist underground. Indeed, the DKP continues to demand that the decision to ban the KPD be rescinded. Most of the DKP's present leaders and about half its members once belonged to the KPD.

Leadership and Organization. The DKP's Eighth Party Congress took place in Hamburg in May 1986 under the banner "For a new policy: A world without nuclear weapons and work for all." The congress was attended by 718 DKP delegates and 165 guests from affiliated and communist-influenced organizations and by representatives of 42 fraternal communist and workers' parties, seven "anti-imperialist liberation movements," and thirteen socialist embassies. It confirmed Mies as party chairman, elevated Weber to vice-chair, and elected the 94-member party executive, the nineteen-member Presidium, and the fourteen-member Secretariat. According to the DKP's own information, 99.3 percent of the delegates were trade union members (624 of whom were union officers or in workers' councils in factories) (*Handelsblatt*, 22–23 May 1986). About 43 percent of the delegates were women.

Mies gave a broad policy statement that reiterated the DKP's opposition to "Star Wars" and "U.S. imperialism." Supporting Soviet peace initiatives, such as a nuclear test ban treaty and the formation of a "worldwide alliance of reason," he declared that West German communists are on the side of peace and progress. He demanded the removal of U.S. medium-range missiles from Germany and nuclear and chemical weapons–free zones in Europe. He called for a "security partnership" with the East. He asserted that the DKP's most important task is to support the peace movement and therefore that the DKP had joined forces with other peace groups. He emphasized that the DKP is still an integral part of the world communist movement and is guided by class solidarity.

This congress supplemented the 1978 party program by adopting certain "theses," which, along with the executive's report, serve as the political-ideological orientation for every communist. They prescribe Marxist-Leninist principles as the guide for the party's actions, which are aimed at the establishment of a socialist state in the FRG. They authorize communists to support movements and citizens' initiatives with the aim of attempting to lead them toward basic changes of the social system.

Reliance on the SED. A variety of financial sources—membership dues, income from the sale of party publications, the keeping of DKP functionaries on the payrolls of communist firms and travel agencies directed by the SED, and direct subsidies of more than 65 million marks from the SED—are essential to financing the high costs of maintaining party headquarters in Düsseldorf, an office in Bonn, and more than 200 local offices; producing and distributing propaganda materials; providing for mass rallies and election campaigns; and subsidizing DKP-affiliated or -influenced organizations. In fact, no other Western communist party is as reliant on a foreign party as is the DKP on the SED. The DKP is controlled by the Department of International Politics and Economics (which until 1984 was known as "West Department") of the SED's Central Committee. Leaders of both the SED and the DKP must agree on an annual plan for West German communists, and the DKP leadership regularly reports to the SED. Even the DKP personnel files are kept in East Berlin.

In the past, the DKP's total loyalty to both East Berlin and Moscow created few problems for the party, except to reduce the DKP's electoral strength in the FRG to practically zero. Like the SED, the DKP has consistently pointed to the Soviet Union as the exalted model of "real socialism" and as the country to be emulated. The Communist Party of the Soviet Union (CPSU) was seen as almost unerring, and the DKP's motto was "To learn from the Soviet Union means to learn to be victorious." Both the DKP and the SED have always lined up behind the Soviet Union's foreign and defense policy objectives and have lent their full weight to their accomplishment. Both SED chief Erich Honecker and Mies (in 1987) were awarded the Lenin Peace Prize. However, the emergence in the Soviet Union of a new generation party leader Mikhail Gorbachev, who attacks corruption and self-serving privilege within the party and advocates intraparty democracy, openness (*glasnost'*), and general restructuring (*perestroika*), has created a dilemma for the DKP.

On the one hand, Gorbachev's calls for democracy have been avidly embraced by the DKP's rank and file, who have long been restless over the "lack of possibilities for intraparty influence and participation," to use the words of party author Erasmus Schöfer. The possibility of embarking on a new path has its risks, Schöfer admits, but "communists in the FRG have nothing to lose but their lack of success!" (*Spiegel*, 7 September). Thomas Riecke, a top functionary of the MSB-Spartakus, declared in regard to *glasnost'* that "we must know everything and be able to decide about everything" (*Die Zeit*, 16 October). There are calls for free election of cadres, who are now appointed by the party leadership.

Mies had to admit in a May 1987 interview in *Unsere Zeit* (*UZ*) that "there is hardly another topic on which so many party functions and with such a large number of participants have been held over the past several years . . . The sympathy for the changes in the Soviet Union is unanimous." He recognizes that "the attractive power of existing socialism has been growing" under Gorbachev, who, polls indicate, enjoys greater popularity in the FRG in 1987 than does President Ronald Reagan. Mies goes on to say that Gorbachev's welcome disarmament proposals present the DKP with

> fresh opportunities in, among other things, our united action and alliance policy [and has] made it easier for communists to act as respected and equal partners in the peace movement and other democratic movements. Not least important among the fresh opportunities is the possibility of using the growing sympathy for Soviet policy to spread the influence of the DKP as the party of socialism. (*UZ*, 20 May.)

On the other hand, the SED remains cool toward the Gorbachev reforms. In August 1987 Max Schmidt, director of the International Institute for Economics and Politics in East Berlin, told a DKP delegation that "much has yet to reach fruition" and "much will perhaps be undone." The SED prevented *UZ* from publishing a January 1987 speech in which Gorbachev asserted that "we need democracy as air to breathe." It threatened not to distribute any copies via East Berlin to other socialist countries (*Spiegel*, 7 September). The SED's message is "Go slowly, and wait and see!" It apparently does not want to be exposed to the bacillus of *glasnost'* from both West and East.

The DKP cannot ignore these warnings from East Berlin. Confronted with what the relatively liberal Hamburg DKP organization calls "a crisis in the party," the DKP leadership must try to dampen the enthusiasm caused by the "strong impulses" coming from Moscow. In *UZ* a cautious Mies warned that in a capitalist country like the FRG "there can be no imitation of the Soviet approach" and that the party must be careful "not to throw the baby out with the bathwater." One must not "reduce the splendid history of the Soviet Union . . . to economic and moral problems." DKP members should inform themselves through reports by "fraternal parties," not by "reading the tea leaves or using the slanders cooked up by the bourgeois mass media." While there is much need for

> invigoration of inner-party life, encouragement of inner-party discussions, and broader involvement of the party membership in the decision-making process, it is not a matter of weakening the principles of democratic centralism in the CPSU . . . Inner-party democracy for us is not a game, not an end in itself. It is designed to mobilize the party's collective knowledge and strength, and to unite it for the purposeful and centralized actions in the fight against the highly organized class enemy facing us. We need to have a further development of inner-party democracy, while keeping our communist principles intact. (*UZ*, 20 May.)

Thus, the party has resorted to censorship to try to silence the enthusiasm for the reform impulses from Moscow. When Peter Schütt, the party poet and member of the 94-member party executive, wrote a poem in early 1987 with the lines "After decades of radio silence, the red star is again sending signals," and "there are comrades who have held their hands in front of their faces for so long that they have unlearned how to understand the new radio code," he was encouraged by the chief party ideologue, Willi Gerns, not to publish the poem. To Schütt's surprise, the poem was published by the moderately conservative *Frankfurter Allgemeine Zeitung* (FAZ). The DKP leadership was reportedly embarrassed by this and especially by the fact that the editors of the Moscow publication *New Time* thanked Schütt for supporting *perestroika*, which was unfolding in the Soviet Union (*Spiegel*, 7 September).

Ideological training and propaganda. The GDR and the Soviet Union provide vital educational support for the DKP. More than a third of its members have attended courses in the GDR and the USSR. The DKP also maintains long-established institutions for this purpose. Founded in 1968, the Institute for Marxist Studies and Research (IMSF) in Frankfurt am Main cooperates closely with the Institutes for Marxism-Leninism of the Central Committees of both the SED and CPSU. Its director, Heinz Jung, is in the party's Presidium, and most of the sixteen members of the "scholarly advisory council," including Presidium members Josef Schleifstein and Robert Steigerwald, are DKP members. Party official Richard Kumpf directs the Marx-Engels Foundation in Wuppertal, which serves as a venue for seminars and conferences. DKP presidium member Hans Schneider directs the Marxist Workers' Education (MAB), founded in Frankfurt in 1969 to organize all the FRG courses and lectures, which features intructors from both Germanies for politically active Germans who are not members of the DKP. The DKP annually organizes approximately 8,000 educational lectures, seminars, and courses on such subjects as security in the atomic age; communists' roles in economic policies, global affairs, and culture; and electoral alliances and strategy.

Party publications. The DKP is so insignificant in the FRG that it receives very little attention in the noncommunist press. East German publications, such as the SED party organ *Neues Deutschland* (ND), give it much broader coverage, but they do not report on disagreements or problems within the DKP or with the SED or on how little electoral support the DKP receives within the FRG.

The DKP produces many publications of its own. They include the daily party organ (*UZ*), founded in April 1969 as a weekly, but appearing five times a week since October 1973; the eight-page daily now has a circulation of 30,000. Its sixteen-page weekend edition, published Fridays, has a circulation of 55,000. It sometimes publishes special editions, called *Extra Blätter*, of up to 300,000 copies. The editor claims that the FRG's "ban on occupations" (legal restrictions on members of anti-democratic parties serving in the public service) discourages some potential subscribers; in some cases, this is probably true. *UZ* is guided by party decisions and operates in close contact with the party leadership, who appoint the editor in chief and editorial board. It strives to uphold the German communist press tradition begun by *Rote Fahne* (Red Banner), founded by Rosa Luxemburg and Karl Liebknecht, and continued by *Freies Volk* (A Free People). In the words of *UZ*'s editor in chief, Georg Polikeit, it wages "an uphill struggle against the anticommunist inventions spewed by the mass media the big bourgeoisie controls" (*WMR*, September). An internal survey revealed that 94 percent of DKP members do not regularly read *UZ* (*Spiegel*, 7 September). Other party publications are the *Deutsche Volkszeitung/Die Tat* (German

People's Newspaper/The Deed), which has a circulation of about 30,000, and the quarterly *Illustrierte Volkszeitung* (Illustrated People's Newspaper). There are other party publications: the *DKP Pressedienst* (DKP Press Service), *Infodienst* (Info Service; *IS*), which provides print for the party's factory, residential area and student newspapers, and the *DKP-Landreview* (DKP Rural Review), which appear at irregular intervals. On a bimonthly basis, the DKP Presidium produces *Praxis—Erfahrungen aus dem Leben und der Arbeit der Partei* (Practice—Experiences from the Life and Work of the Party). The monthly *Marxistische Blätter* is the party's theoretical organ. The party also publishes approximately 340 factory and 450 local newspapers, some of which annually have a dozen editions with as many as 120,000 copies.

Providing these publications with news are two principal news agencies. The Progressive Press Agency (PPA), with headquarters in Düsseldorf and offices in Bonn, Mannheim, Munich, and Kiel, has approximately fifteen editors and correspondents and publishes the *PPA Daily Service*, which features party activities and selected articles from the noncommunist press five times a week. About one-third of the material in DKP publications comes from the Allgemeiner Deutscher Nachrichtendienst (ADN), the news agency of the GDR.

Youth Organizations. The largest group is the SDAJ, which has approximately 15,000 members in more than 900 local groups. Its self-image is the "revolutionary young workers' organization" devoted to "the teaching of Marx, Engels, and Lenin" and fighting for a "socialist Federal Republic," with a planned, socialist economy and power being exercised by the workers. Birgit Radow is not only SDAJ chairperson but a member of the DKP Presidium and Executive as well. Hans-Georg Eberhard, deputy chairman, belongs to the DKP, and most of the land chairmen are members of the DKP's land presidia.

The last SDAJ federal congress, 2–3 May in Frankfurt am Main, was attended by 750 delegates with an average age of twenty-one; 14 percent represented school groups, and 34 percent had functions in labor unions or youth councils in factories. DKP chairman Mies spoke of "a common struggle" with the DKP, and the first secretary of the central council of East German Free German Youth (FDJ), Eberhard Aurich, spoke of an "indestructible alliance" between the two youth organizations and asserted that "We have the same ideals and goals. We have the same friends and we hate the same enemies." Radow assured the Soviet Komsomol representative, Nikolai Palzew, that the SDAJ was "enthused" about the "revolutionary restructuring" in the Soviet Union and that the effect on the FRG was to strengthen "the appeal of socialism." To both the Russian and the East German visitors, Radow said:

> We are proud of our friendship with the GDR and with the young revolutionaries in the FDJ, who make socialism strong in our neighboring country . . . We are spreading far and wide in the FRG the example of the Soviet Union, the GDR and the other socialist countries. There the new social order is being built for which we want to fight in our own country. (*IS*, 24 July.)

The group's activities support those of the parent party and aim particularly at students, apprentices, and soldiers. It seeks contacts with Young Socialists (Jusos), Greens, and various groups within the peace movement. To be appealing to those groups, the SDAJ calls for peace and disarmament and for shutting down all nuclear energy plants in capitalist countries (but not in socialist countries for the time being because nuclear power is "indispensable" there) (*IS*, 24 July). It maintains ties with Communist youth groups in the GDR and other countries. SDAJ members participate in such organizations as the Solidarity Brigade in Nicaragua and the Soviet-controlled World Federation of Democratic Youth. It sponsors evening courses, group leader schools on the land level, and courses lasting a week at the Youth Education Center at Burg Wahrburg. It also publishes a variety of materials: *Elan—Das Jugendmagazin* is a monthly with a circulation of about 25,000, which every month puts out an *Artikeldienst für Betriebs–, Lehrlings, Stadtteil– und Schülerzeitungen* (Article Service for Plant–, Apprentice, Neighborhood– and Pupils' Newspapers). The SDAJ also publishes *Jugendpolitische Blätter* (Youth Political Pages), which appears in approximately 2,500 copies.

The Young Pioneers (JP) is for children and has 4,000 members. Its functionaries are trained at the Youth Education Center at Burg Wahrburg, and many, including its chairman, Gerd Hertel, belong to the SDAJ and/or the DKP. Its executive publishes a monthly *Pionierleiter Info* (Pioneer Leader Info), a child's newspaper, *Pionier*, and *Diskussionsmaterial für Pionierleiter* (Discussion Material for Pioneer Leaders). JP has ties with children's groups in the GDR and other socialist countries and with the International Commission of Children's and Adolescents' Movements (CIMEA), an auxiliary of the World Federation of Democratic Youth.

Represented at more than 100 postsecondary institutions is the MSB-Spartakus, which has about 6,000 members. It is the largest and most powerful left extremist organization at the university level, and it cooperates with all left-wing groups, including the Liberal Students' League (affiliated with but to the left of the Free Democratic Party; FDP) and Jusos. MSB-Spartakus and its permanent alliance partner, the Socialist University League (SHB), occupy about 18 percent of the seats in student parliaments and are represented in about half of such assemblies. All leftist extremist groups and groups influenced by them occupied 26.5 percent of such seats in 1987 (*IS*, 24 July). The MSB-Spartakus represents the United German Students' Association (Vereinigte Deutsche Studentenschaft; VDS) in diverse coordinating committees for protest and peace movements. Most top MSB-Spartakus leaders are DKP members. MSB-Spartakus regards "the struggle for peace" as one aspect of the class struggle and as a revolutionary objective and works feverishly to undercut NATO and the Strategic Defense Initiative (SDI) and to gain support for nuclear-free zones and other objectives that have a high priority for Kremlin leaders. The DKP considers its well-organized students to be the essential contact point between the intelligentsia and the working class.

The DKP regards the intelligentsia in the FRG as a lucrative reservoir for influence. Presidium and Secretariat member Gerd Deumlich wrote that

> past and present experience shows that the intelligentsia in the FRG is largely in opposition to the ruling circles [because of the] ignominy of fascism and the guilt of German capital in starting World War II, [even though] the views of many intellectuals can hardly be regarded as consistently progressive, and while their thinking is under the influence of bourgeois illusions and anticommunism . . . The FRG is a visual example of the crisis of capitalism permeating and interweaving every aspect of life in the society: economics, politics, ideology, morality and culture. (*WMR*, September.)

Cover groups and citizens' initiatives. For decades the DKP and other communist groups have faced mistrust and rejection on the part of the FRG's general population. For this reason, it has operated through a wide variety of cover groups and has sought to cooperate with protest groups that enjoy greater respectability. The DKP is supported by approximately 50 organizations and action groups, which it heavily influences but that appear to be independent; the majority of their members and leaders do not belong to the DKP. Party members are indeed appointed to certain high positions, but the key to these groups' effectiveness is that the DKP's role be underplayed. Many of the larger of these cover groups are also affiliated with Moscow-directed front groups, such as the World Peace Council (WPC).

Among the more important DKP front groups is the Association of Victims of the Nazi Regime/League of Antifascists (VVN/BdA), with about 13,500 members. The German Peace Union (DFU), with about 1,000 members was able to mobilize 100,000 protesters in April 1987 (300,000 according to DFU claims) for its annual Easter Marches. The central manifestos and accounts for contributions were almost exclusively traceable to functionaries of the DKP and the DFU (*IS*, 15 May). The goal of the 1987 marches was to appeal to Western governments to be receptive to Gorbachev's disarmament proposals (*This Week in Bonn*, 27 April).

The German Peace Society/United War Resisters (DFG/VK), with about 13,000 members, is the largest DKP front group with the greatest number of noncommunists, but it is plagued by declining membership and revenues and has had to reduce spending for its publication *Civil Courage*. Other groups are the Committee for Peace, Disarmament and Cooperation (KFAZ); the Democratic Women's Initiative (DFI); the Association of Democratic Jurists (VDJ), with about 1,000 members; and the Union of Democratic Doctors. The Anti-imperialistic Solidarity Committee for Africa, Asia, and Latin America (ASK) serves as the framework for joint efforts on behalf of "liberation movements" and in opposition to such U.S. objectives as SDI. The ASK publishes about 3,000 copies of a monthly, the *Anti-imperialist Information Bulletin*. The Patron Circle of the *Darmstädter Signal* was founded by DKP, SPD, and Greens and Protestant and Catholic clergymen in 1983 to dissuade federal army (Bundeswehr) soldiers from taking part in nuclear warfare.

Domestic Attitudes and Activities. Mies openly acknowledges that a party that has never received more than 0.3 percent of the votes in federal elections has a problem. As he explained in an interview in the Polish newspaper *Trybuna Ludu* on 20 July,

> the DKP has not been able to win a suitable place among representative bodies; its influence on the working class as a whole does not suit today's needs. The party realizes this . . . and right now it is at a stage of productive unrest, involving the seeking of ways generally to increase our influence on the working class.

The DKP tries to break out of its isolation by forming electoral alliances, trying thereby to contribute in some way to parliamentary life, and by jumping on the bandwagon of extraparliamentary movements, whose momentum stems from dealing with issues of broad concern in the FRG. Looking back over land (state) elections in 1986, the party saw nothing but dismal failures: 0.1 percent in Lower Saxony in June and 0.2 percent in Hamburg in November; it did not even enter the Bavarian election in October. Thus, facing the January 1987 Bundestag elections, it decided to form an electoral alliance in order that its demands "be represented in an alliance more effectively" and "in that way to establish contact with more people, with people whom we Communists do not yet reach" (*UZ*, September 1986). Its Peace List invited the Greens to join in a common front, an invitation which the ambitious Greens rejected (*FAZ*, 12 March 1986). Nevertheless, the DKP decided to ask its supporters to cast their first vote to the direct candidates of the Peace List and their second vote to either the Greens or the SPD, in an attempt to create a "majority left of the CDU" (*IS*, 3 April). (Every voter has two votes: the first is for a candidate in an electoral constituency elected by plurality; the second is for a specific party and determines the percentage and number of seats the party will receive in the lower house. To win any seats at all, though, the party must win at least 5 percent of second votes in the entire FRG; this is a hurdle that the communists have not come close to clearing since 1949, which is why it was no genuine sacrifice to recommend the communists cast their second ballots to other parties.)

More than 40 percent of the Peace List candidates in 1987 were DKP members or functionaries, and a further 30 percent were in the DFU. The DKP and its affiliated organizations—the MSB-Spartakus, the SDAJ and the DFU—bore the brunt of the work and expense for the campaign. However, knowing the average voter's antipathy toward the DKP, there were great pains to blur the role of the DKP and DFU in the Peace List. The three top candidates were not communists, and in party publications, only selections of candidates pictures were published in which communists were a small minority (*IS*, 3 April).

Peace List candidates received 188,602 (0.5 percent) of the first votes. Their best land results were in the city-states of Bremen (1.3 percent) and Hamburg (0.8 percent). In various university towns the Peace List topped its countrywide average: Tübingen, 3.8 percent; Freiburg, 1.8 percent; Marburg, 1.7 percent; and Münster, 1.6 percent. The DKP found these meager results to be "relatively satisfactory." In the party leadership's view, the DKP had helped to "debilitate the right-wing parties," particularly the "Steel Helmet faction of arch-conservatives," and to reverse the slide to the right that the FRG had experienced since 1985. The DKP claimed to have "made the issue of peace and détente the focus and touchstone of its electoral effort," to have "forced each party to speak up on it too," and to "reject the policy of subjecting West Germany to the interests of the Washington administration" (*WAR*, vol. 17, no. 2). In the words of Presidium member Rolf Priemer, the DKP's electoral strategy had given

> an uplift to the forces to the left of the CDU/CSU, stimulated positive changes in the SPD, reinforced the position of the Greens in the Bundestag, and raised our party's own prestige in the nation at large and particularly among the Social Democrats, the Greens, and activists of the peace movement and of the working class movement. All this provided an immense incentive for future joint or parallel actions in the common front and in the democratic alliances. (*WMR*, May.)

In actual fact, there is very little evidence that the DKP made significant contributions to or progress toward any of these goals. Both the SPD and the Greens are aware that their electoral performance would be harmed, not helped, by collaboration with the communists and that the DKP's minuscule vote-getting potential would be irrelevant to any electoral outcome. There are discussions within the SPD and the Green parties concerning possible alliances, but these discussions revolve around alliances with each other, not with the DKP. Although the SPD is conducting party-to-party talks with the SED to discuss such goals as nuclear-free zones and more visibly defensive military postures, it is not conducting such talks with the DKP. Nor are the SPD or the Greens dealing with defense issues because they have been prodded by the DKP. Defense and arms control questions are very much on the political agenda in the FRG, an exposed country in the middle of Europe located along the border with the Warsaw Pact nations and in which there are a million troops from six different countries and thousands of nuclear warheads; all parties therefore pay close attention to defense issues.

The DKP will continue, as its Presidium announced after the 1987 Bundestag elections, to follow "its line, adopted by its eighth congress, to broaden extraparliamentary action, its policy of alliances and unity of action, and to enhance on this basis its own political role as a mobilizing and motive force, and increase its membership." (*IB*, May). Its membership has not grown in recent years, a matter of some concern for the leadership. In a paper published by the party's executive, the party sets a 7–10 percent target in annual recruitment of members. But the paper also warns about the potential risks of bringing in new members from extraparliamentary alliances. The danger is that

> the allies' ideological and organizational attitudes also have an influence on the communists. When working in the alliances, they [communists] use the tactics of compromise, but often also carry it over to relations within their own party, so ignoring the fundamental distinction between a patchwork association and the Marxist-Leninist vanguard of the working class.

The report notes that "there is a change in the social make-up of the DKP." The DKP is recruiting among a broader social strata than the working class. Indeed, only 20 percent of communists now work in "material large production." For instance, the biggest DKP plant group in North Rhine–Westphalia, the FRG's largest land, is not to be found in the coal and steel industry, but in the city hospitals (*Spiegel*, 7 September). Thus, concludes the DKP report, "it is not right to forget that most of the new members lack what the workers acquire in fighting for their rights at enterprises and in the trade unions, namely, the conscious need for organized and collective action" (*WMR*, January).

The DKP tries to appeal to workers, a steadily declining class in the FRG's modern economy, by demanding such measures as a 35-hour work week without pay cuts, job creation programs, job security, higher real wages, the saving of the declining steel and shipbuilding industries, the protecting of the right of participation in the management of mining and steel-producing facilities, and an end to mass layoffs and social welfare cuts (*WMR*, May). But the DKP has trouble recruiting workers at a time of high unemployment in the FRG. In a well-publicized case, a postal worker was fired when the Federal Administrative Court in West Berlin ruled that his activities with the DKP were not compatible with his "obligation to loyalty" to the state. This is not the first instance of such firings, and a dismissed DKP member has great difficulty getting another job. As one such person remarked bitterly, "the alleged black mark of DKP membership is an insurmountable hurdle" (*Spiegel*, 19 October). Thus, a new recruit must be prepared to possibly sacrifice his livelihood. It is no wonder that the DKP calls for an end to the "bar to occupations" (*Berufsverbot:* used by those who oppose this law; the official title is *Radikalenerlass*—Radicals' Decree) against those deemed to be risks to the state (*ND*, 29 January).

The party orders its members to take an active role in trade unions to persuade trade unionists that workers' interests are only served by class struggle. It places great value on its "educational work," particularly for the union youth organizations; many union instructors are products of the student movement and advocate orthodox Marxism. Although few DKP members have risen to leading positions in the unions, they exercise influence in some, particularly those of printers, journalists, and mass media. In 1985 a Mass Media Trade Union was set up to include the Union of Print Workers, the Union of Journalists, the Union of Writers, the Union of Radio and Television Workers, and the main unions in music, drama, and the figurative arts. According to Gerd Deumlich, DKP Presidium and Secretariat member, this new union "wants to put an end to the power of the monopolies" in the media and is "a strong response to those who have been conducting a reactionary policy in the mass media and who want to limit the sphere of union political activity" (*WMR*, September). According to a 1987 BfV report, the number of communist workers groups has risen to about 400, about one-third of which are active in the metal industry and about a fourth, in the public service sector, principally in communal and land administrations. Some have only a few members and engage in action only irregularly. The number of DKP factory newspapers has declined to 340, each with a circulation of several hundred to several thousand and most appearing irregularly (*Handelsblatt*, 22–23 May).

Despite possible dangers, the party works to form broad alliances. These can be the "working class unity of actions," namely DKP cooperation with trade unionists, workers not affiliated with any party, Christian workers, and Social Democrats. They can also be with intellectuals and the bourgeoisie. Such "coalitions of reason" can seek broader objectives, such as foiling SDI. DKP members need not occupy leading offices, and they can use "political flexibility" while maintaining "ideological conviction." That is, cooperation should be based on common interests and should not be brought about through compromises with reformist positions (*IS*, 12 May 1986).

The DKP leadership believes it sees the wall breaking down between Social Democrats and communists, a wall which has existed since the foundation of the KPD in 1918 and which was strengthened by the effort of the KPD to absorb the SPD after World War II. Indeed, it has long sought to eliminate or lessen the "fears of contact" (*Berührungsängste*) that have made most groups in the FRG disinclined to deal with the DKP. Although there are no party-to-party contacts and no talk within the national SPD of any alliance or formal cooperation with the DKP, some Social Democrats serve on governing boards of DKP-influenced organizations, as well as on "citizens' initiatives" and friendship societies with certain socialist countries. Speakers from both parties sometimes appear at the same discussions or meetings. Also, some interviews with Social Democrats are printed in *UZ*, although such speeches and interviews seldom involve prominent Social Democrats. At the university level, the predominantly leftist Social Democratic SHB has for years joined in "unity of actions" with the MSB-Spartakus and, unlike the larger SPD, favors an SPD-DKP alliance. (*IS*, 12 May).

The DKP also joins broad-based protest efforts that bring it into contact with a wide spectrum of noncommunist groups and, it hopes, widens its appeal. It opposes nuclear power and reprocessing plants and participates in the often-bloody protests against such installations as the Wackersdorf nuclear reprocessing plant. The DKP claims to have helped expose Wackersdorf's true purpose: "to be a center for the manufacture of West Germany's own nuclear weapons" (*WMR*, September). (In fact, no responsible West German leader advocates the FRG's acquisition of such weapons.) The DKP advocates protection of the environment and cleaning up the polluted Rhine River. It joined in the movement against the taking of a census, reasoning that the information would strengthen the FRG's character as an "authoritarian surveillance state," as well as support the FRG's "antidemocratic security laws," and thereby serve ultimately "the preparation for war" (*IS*, 15 May).

Perhaps most important in the party's efforts to reach out to other groups has been its participation in the peace movement. Kurt Schacht, a member of the DKP executive, maintained that

> the participation of DKP members in the peace forums has unquestionably given the party valuable experience and . . . has had a positive effect on the peace movement itself. Cooperation between the Communists, Social Democrats, and Greens has been fostered by the considerable concurrence of their views on questions of war and peace. (*WMR*, March.)

Operating within the peace movement is particularly comfortable for the DKP because it is thereby able to devote its energies to supporting Soviet and GDR security objectives. As the SED organ ND wrote on 26 May,

> the GDR places extraordinary value on the contribution which the Communists in the FRG make in the struggle for peace and disarmament . . . That is why it [the DKP] energetically set about, with no ands-ifs-or-buts-about-it, having the proposal of the Soviet Union for a zero-option for medium-range missiles realized.

Neither the DKP nor the many communist splinter parties (called K-Groups) are the initiators or string-pullers of the peace movement, within which they remain a small minority. The noncommunist elements within the peace movement do not reject all forms of logistical support, which is probably the communists' greatest contribution to the movement; the DKP and its affiliated organizations are disproportionately represented in many of the movement's operational coordinating committees. For example, DKP delegates regularly attended meetings of the Coordinating Committee of the Peace Movement (KA) despite the fact that the party did not formally belong. Nevertheless, the Greens and other noncommunist activists in the peace movement intensified efforts to distance themselves from communists.

Communists have no reason to be happy about their attempts to work together with the badly divided Greens, although they recommended that

DKP members give their second vote in the 1987 elections to the Greens (or the Social Democrats) on the grounds that the Greens are a consistent radical-democratic force that supports the extraparliamentary struggle. Although there are former communists within the Greens, including Thomas Ebermann, who in 1987 won the speakership of the Green party caucus in the Bundestag, these former communists are from the militant communist splinter parties, which tend to be hostile or uncooperative toward the DKP.

The fundamentalists (*Fundis*), the majority within the Greens, are fiercely independent, rejecting arguments made by the realists (*Realos*) that coalitions with the SPD be formed. Coalitions with the communists are not even discussed, although when cases of East German spies have surfaced in recent years, the Greens have ridiculed the need for classified information and refused to sign a security pledge (*CSM*, 9 February). The DKP also agrees with the Fundis' position on violence in demonstrations, which is that there should be an end to the state's "monopoly on the use of force" (*CSM*, 24 November). Responding to a government statement by Chancellor Kohl, the DKP Presidium declared that "Kohl's stinging attack on those who allegedly resort to 'violence' during demonstrations disguises the intention to curtail still more the right to meetings and demonstrations" (*IB*, June). However, few if any of the several hundred militant demonstrators who travel throughout the FRG to turn every demonstration into a violent conflict with the police are following orders from the DKP. Such "chaotics" (*Chaoten*) are not suited for the discipline of the DKP.

The DKP's hope to gain advantages by riding the extraparliamentary protest wave and by participating in the peace movement are bound to be disappointed because the momentum and drive of the movement had largely vanished by 1987. This was largely due to the INF agreement signed in December 1987 between Soviet and U.S. leaders calling for the removal from Europe of all U.S. and Soviet medium- and short-range missiles and the prospect of further steps to reduce strategic arsenals by half. This agreement was made possible by Gorbachev's implicit admission that Soviet missiles are not purely defensive in nature and are part of the problem. This admission undercuts the DKP's persistent efforts to show that the United States and its president were the sole obstacles to disarmament. Also, in contrast with the early 1980s, the peace movement's demands are now incorporated in the SPD and Green manifestos. Thus, the former extraparliamentary opposition against the arms race has been brought directly into parliament, which has eliminated much of the raison d'être of the extraparliamentary peace movement. (*FAZ*, 27 May).

International Views and Party Contacts. The DKP's statements on foreign policy are in perfect harmony with those made by the GDR and USSR and follow Moscow's and East Berlin's lead in supporting whatever groups they define as liberation movements, including the Sandinista government in Nicaragua. The DKP invariably supports all aspects of the Soviet Union's peace propaganda, including demands for ending SDI and for removal of U.S. atomic weapons from Europe. It applauds the SPD's party contacts with ruling parties in Eastern Europe and the SPD-SED security policy talks, which call for a "security partnership" between both Germanies and the Soviet Union and for the creation in Europe of corridors or zones free of nuclear and chemical weapons, and demands a cut of 10 percent in the FRG's defense budget and an ultimate end to arms exports. The DKP roundly criticizes the Bonn government's making "a big issue of the mythical 'military threat' from the East" and its position "that there is no alternative to the deterrence doctrine in the foreseeable future and that a continued peace will still require armed forces with well-balanced conventional and nuclear weapons." Finally, the DKP unflaggingly supports the SED's interpretations of the GDR's legal status. It criticizes Bonn's "resurgent fiction of a 'single German nation' and hackneyed contentions that the German question 'remains open in the legal, political and historical sense' and that it is still necessary to maintain the concept of single citizenship." It calls for "a definitive renunciation of great Germany dreams." (*IB*, June.)

The DKP maintains close contacts with all ruling parties in Eastern Europe, especially with the Soviet Union and the GDR. It sends high-level delegations to their party congresses and receives such delegations to its own. West German communists were not the most important discussion partners for SED leader Honecker during his historic visit to the FRG in September; most probably Honecker's most important visit with a DKP member during his stay was with his sister, Gertrud Hoppstädter, in his hometown in the Saarland. DKP leaders of course attended the 70th anniversary of the Bolshevik Revolution in Moscow in November 1987.

Other Leftist Groups. In addition to the DKP, there are many active leftist-extremist small groups and parties, initiatives, and New Left revolutionary organizations. All renounce the pro-Soviet/SED policies and are deeply divided ideologically, although most of them cooperate in action alliances. Total membership in these organizations, after reducing for multiple affiliations, climbed slightly to approximately 63,000, with an additional 49,000 in organizations influenced by leftist-extremists. They produce about 250 publications with a total circulation of more than 4.9 million. By far the favored cause for cooperation is protesting against atomic power. About one-third of all terrorist acts were attributed to the struggle against the peaceful use of nuclear energy. SDI and NATO were also important targets. (*IS*, 24 July.)

The new left, composed of Marxist-Leninists, Trotskyists, anarchists, autonomists, and antidogmatic revolutionaries, preaches class struggle. It identifies the proletariat as the essential revolutionary force leading the fight to tarnish the image of the FRG's political order in the eyes of its citizens and to overthrow the bourgeois state and capitalist system. Most advocate establishing a dictatorship of the proletariat culminating in a socialist and ultimately communist order. They are confident that the bureacratic failures in communist-ruled regimes can be prevented. The autonomous anarchist groups advocate the eradication of the state, to be superseded by a "free" society. Most new leftists unabashedly advocate using violence to achieve their aims.

Dogmatic new left. There are a variety of Marxist-Leninist groups, loosely called K-groups. The strongest of these groups is the Marxist-Leninist Party of Germany (Marxistisch-Leninistische Partei Deutschlands; MLPD), which has from 1,100 to 1,300 members organized in twelve districts and approximately 100 local units. Its chairman is Stefan Engel, and its official organ is *Rote Fahne* (Red Banner), whose weekly circulation is about 10,000. It participated in the 1987 Bundestag election, winning 13,821 second votes. This 0.0 percent of the total vote indicates how little electoral hope there is for the K-groups. Nevertheless, party spokesman Klaus Vowe called this result "satisfactory," in that the party had expected to receive only 10,000 votes. Vowe noted that the party would have gotten more votes were it not for the "falsification" of the party's arguments by the bourgeois media (*IS*, 3 April).

The MLPD has three ineffective affiliated organizations with about 300 members. They are the Marxist-Leninist Workers' Youth Association (AJV/ML) with a press organ, *Rebell*, and a children's group, *Rotfüchse* (Red Foxes); the Marxist-Leninist Pupils' and Students' Association, whose organ is *Roter Pfeil* (Red Arrow); and an active Marxist-Leninist League of Intellectuals.

The United Socialist Party (Vereinigte Sozialistische Partei; VSP) was born from the 1986 merger of the Communist Party of Germany-Marxist Leninist (KPD, earlier known as KPD-ML) and the Trotskyist Group International Marxists (GIM). The VSP is led by Horst-Dieter Koch and has its headquarters in Cologne. Its biweekly publication, *Sozialistische Zeitung* (Socialist Newspaper), replaced the KPD's earlier *Roter Morgen* (Red Morning) and the GIM's *Was Tun* (What To Do). Its youth group is the Autonomous Socialist Youth Group (ASJG).

Members of the KPD who opposed the merger that resulted in the VSP reconfirmed their adherence to the old party statutes and program. Calling themselves the "correct KPD," they maintain headquarters in West Berlin. A separate Workers' League for the Reconstruction of the KPD claims about 300 members, maintains a Communist University League in Bavaria, and publishes two editions of the *Kommunistische Arbeiterzeitung* (Communist Worker Newspaper; KAZ).

The League of West German Communists (Bund Westdeutscher Kommunisten; BWK), which emerged from a split in the now-defunct Communist League of West Germany (KBW), counts approximately 400 members organized in groups in seven lands. It publishes the biweekly *Politische Berichte* (Political Reports), with a circulation of about 1,300 copies, and the *Nachrichtenhefte* (News Booklets), with a circulation of about 1,000. The BWK is the dominant member of the People's Front, whose business office is in the BWK's main office in Cologne. The People's Front is an instrument for an alliance of leftist-extremists, and the BWK is willing to cooperate with the DKP and its affiliated or influenced organizations.

The Communist League (Kommunistischer Bund; KB) has its headquarters in Hamburg, where about half of its 400 followers live. It has considerable influence within the Green-Alternative List (GAL), which won more than 10 percent in the November 1986 Hamburg elections running with an all-female slate. The KB publishes a monthly, *Arbeiterkampf* (Worker Struggle), which has a circulation of about 4,500. Group Z split from the KB in 1979 and joined the Greens, with many of its members rising to top positions in the Greens' federal and land organizations.

About a dozen Trotskyist groups, some only in certain regions, have a total of about 450 members. Advocating "permanent revolution" and the "dictatorship of the proletariat," they decry "real existing socialism" in communist-ruled countries as "bureaucratic" or "revisionist decadence." The League of Socialist Workers is the German section of the International Committee of the Fourth International in London. Together with its Socialist Youth League, it counts fewer than 100 members, and its weekly organ, *Neue Arbeiterpresse* (New Workers' Press), has advocated a general strike for overthrow of the government. The smaller Trotskyist groups, such as the Trotskyist Liga of Germany, the International Socialist Workers' Organization, the International Communist Movement, the Socialist Workers' Group, and the Posadistic Communist Party, protest against animosity directed toward foreign workers in the FRG and for revolutionary struggles in the Third World.

The Marxist Group (MG) is a Marxist-Leninist cadre party with a rigidly hierarchical structure, severe discipline, intensive indoctrination, and secrecy. Its 1,700 members and several thousand sympathizers are mainly students and academics, and the focus of its efforts is Bavaria. It is convinced that trained agitators must spark a class-conscious proletariat to engage in class struggle. It communicates through the monthly *MSZ-Marxistische Streit und Zeitschrift-Gegen die Kosten der Freiheit* (Marxist Controversy and Magazine-Against the Costs of Freedom, 10,000 copies), the *Marxistische Arbeiterzeitung* (Marxist Workers' Newspaper; MAZ, which appears irregularly), and the *Marxistische Schulzeitung* (Marxist School Newspaper).

Autonomous anarchist groups of the undogmatic left. These groups renounce strict organizational structures and are extremely divided over aims and whether to utilize violent or nonviolent action in order to change society.

The Free Workers' Union (FAU), which has 200 members in 22 local groups, is a member of the anarcho-syndicalist International Workers' Association (IAA) and publishes *Direkt Aktion* in Dieburg. It founded Schwarze Hilfe (Black Help) to assist imprisoned anarcho-syndicalists, anarchists, and autonomists. It also maintains contact with the international coordinating office of the anarchist Black Cross in London. The principles espoused by anarcho-syndicalists can be summarized as antistate, antiparliamentary, and antimilitary. FAU adherents oppose Western capitalism and the "state capitalism" practiced in communist countries. They see as their supreme task the revolutionary work in factories to create collective resistance against capitalism. They dream of a society characterized by decentralization and self-administration. There are some independent opposition FAU organizations that wish to work outside the factory arena.

The Violence-Free Action Groups—Grass-Roots count about 800 followers in 70 groups and collectives. The contact and coordinating body is the Grass-Roots Revolution–Federation of Violence-Free Action Groups (FoGA), which advocates a nonviolent revolution and creation of a decentralized society based on anarchy and self-administration to replace present state power. Its aims, as indicated by its actions and its monthly publication, *Grasswürzelrevolution* (Grass Roots Revolution), which has a circulation of about 4,000, are primarily antimilitarism, peace, and "social defense." Environmental protection, especially against nuclear power and reprocessing plants, is also important.

The diverse autonomous anarchist groupings within the undogmatic new left tend to be tiny, loosely organized, short-lived, and prone to violence. They attract several thousand predominantly young people, who engage in "solidarity actions" to support Third World liberation movements. But their contacts with like-minded leftist-extremist groups outside the FRG are sporadic and generally limited to specific actions.

The FRG has many foreign extremist organizations that operate within the country. Their numbers grow as the FRG becomes a haven for refugees from the Third World. This alien presence creates domestic political tensions and provides a convenient scapegoat and target for right-wing West German extremist circles. The BfV estimates that about 81,600 foreigners belong to leftist-extremist organizations (more than twice as many as belong to corresponding right-wing extremist groups). The most active and violence-oriented group is the orthodox-communist Workers' Party of Kurdistan (PKK). The Liberation Tigers of Tamil Ealam (LTTE) make their presence felt, as do violent Palestinian, Iranian, Turkish, and Yugoslavian groups. (*IS*, 24 July.)

Hard-core terrorist groups. Deadly and destructive terrorist actions continue. The hard-core, command-level (Kommandobereich) Red Army Faction (Rote Armee Faction; RAF) is still composed of about twenty underground killers, approximately the same number as in the mid-1970s. They engage in political assassinations and dramatic bombings. Closely supporting the RAF terrorists is a second echelon of RAF Militants, numbering approximately 200 persons. Recruited from the anti-imperialist resistance circles, they handle logistics for the command level such as documents, vehicles, weapons, explosives, and secret housing. These militants reportedly engage in violent actions against material targets but not against human beings. A further echelon is composed of RAF Sympathizers, who number around 2,000. They engage in propaganda and public relations for the terrorists and assist those who are in prison. (*IS*, 24 July).

As was proven in February when French police captured four leaders of Action Directe in a farm near Orléans, the RAF maintains close political collaboration with like-minded foreign terrorist groups. French police found weapons stolen in a raid on a weapons business in Maxdorf/Ludwigshafen, most likely committed by the RAF. They found the same kind of explosives stemming from a raid on a quarry in Belgium, which had been used by the RAF during a failed bombing attack in 1984 on the NATO school in Oberammergau. They also found an identity card with similar characteristics to one found on an RAF suspect arrested in Rüsselsheim. It is hoped that the raid was a setback for the RAF's efforts to intensify its contacts with Action Directe, the Fighting Communist Cells in Belgium, and the Red Brigades in Italy, in order to build a unified Western European guerrilla movement. (*IS*, 24 July.)

The Red Cells (Rote Zellen; RZ), their female affiliate, Rote Zora, and various "autonomist groups" also launch terrorist attacks. The RZ are in basic ideological agreement with the RAF's "socialist revolutionary and anti-imperialist" aims. The various other groupings and individuals lumped together as "autonomists" also choose their victims in the same basic way as the RAF and RZ and apply the same rationales for their attacks as are expressed in the "letters taking responsibility" sent by the RAF and RZ. The common characteristics of all these groups are hatred of the political, social, and economic systems of the FRG and a rigorous readiness to use violence, no matter what it may cost in life and limb (*IS*, 24 July).

The Greens and the SPD's youth, student, and women's organizations are not leftist-radical groups. Some of their members do share some of the views of the extreme left in an abstract way, and some have been willing to take part in "unity of actions" with leftists and communists. Common ground can often be found in support of the Soviet Union's disarmament campaigns, nuclear- or chemical-free zones in Central Europe, or efforts to reduce the power of the U.S. military, the Bundeswehr, or NATO.

A storm of emotional controversy among the Greens was unleashed by statements made in the fall by Green spokesman (and Fundi leader) Jutta Ditfurth. She said that "this state needed and again needs almost nothing so longingly as terror, in order to divert attention from its own daily violence." A majority of Green members of the Bundestag were incensed not only because they do not agree with this assertion but because it delivers a welcome pretext to the other traditional parties to portray the Greens as accomplices and allies to terrorists in the FRG. This intraparty debate heated up in late 1987 when two policemen were killed during a demonstration in Frankfurt and when violence broke out over squatters' occupation of houses in Hamburg. Realo leader Otto Schily emphasizes that nonviolence should be "clearly and jointly supported by all." Another Realo criticized the Fundis' approach: "They don't say we support an alliance with militants, but say that we should not split the opposition" (*Westdeutsche Allgemeine*, 21 November).

The debate also applies to the question of what the state should do to lure those who wish to drop out of their terrorist circles and re-enter society. Ditfurth's position is that since the "deformed society" drove people to terrorism in the first place, the society has a responsibility to take the first step in leading them back out. Until this matter is sorted out, most Greens agree that the strict conditions under which terrorists are handled in prison must be done away with. (*Spiegel*, 19, 26 October.)

WEST BERLIN

Population. 1,869,000 (1987)
Party. Socialist Unity Party of West Berlin (Sozialistische Einheitspartei Westberlins; SEW)
Founded. 1949
Membership. 7,000 (SEW's figures; the Federal

Office for the Protection of the Constitution, BfV, estimates 4,500); 70 percent joined after 1966.

Chairman. Horst Schmitt

Politburo. 19 members: Horst Schmitt, Dietmar Ahrens (deputy chairman), Inge Kopp (deputy chair), Ralf Derwenskus, Uwe Doering, Helga Dolinski, Detlef Fendt, Klaus Feske, Harry Flichtbeil, Margo Granowski, Heinz Grünberg, Klaus-Dieter Heiser, Volker June, Jörg Kuhle, Hans Mahle, Margot Mrozinski, Monika Sieveking, Eberhard Speckmann, Erich Ziegler

Secretariat. 7 members: Horst Schmitt, Dietmar Ahrens, Klaus Feske, Harry Flichtbeil, Margot Granowski, Inge Kopp, Jörg Kuhle

Executive. 65 members

Status. Legal

Last Congress. Eighth, 15–17 May 1987

Last Election. 1985, 0.6 percent, no representation

Auxiliary Organizations. Socialist Youth League Karl Liebknecht (Sozialistischer Jugendverband Karl Liebknecht; SJ Karl Liebknecht), 550 members; Young Pioneers (Junge Pioniere; JP), 250 members; SEW–University Groups, 400 members

Publications. *Die Wahrheit* (The Truth), SEW daily organ, circulation 13,000. The party also publishes a magazine, *Konsequent* (Consistent), for its propaganda work, and its university groups publish *Rote Wochen* (Red Weeks) for their agitation activities.

West Berlin remains under Allied occupation by the armed forces of the United States, the United Kingdom, and France, which maintain about 10,000 troops there. West Berlin is under the NATO defense umbrella. The 1971 Quadripartite Agreement, signed by the three powers above and the Soviet Union, confirms Berlin's special status. It states that West Berlin is not part of the FRG but that it has links with the FRG. Despite the fact that this agreement was intended to cover the entire area of greater Berlin, the Soviet-occupied eastern sector of the city has been declared as the capital of the GDR, which refers to the eastern part simply as "Berlin."

West Berlin is, for all practical purposes, ruled by its own elected Senate (parliament), but the three allied powers can and sometimes do veto a law or action of the Senate. Both West Berlin and the FRG seek to maintain close ties with each other; these ties are a diplomatic and economic necessity for West Berlin and a political imperative for Bonn. West Berlin is represented in the federal parliament in Bonn by nonvoting deputies. Residents of West Berlin are not required to serve in the Bundeswehr, a fact that prompts many young German dissidents to resettle there and thereby greatly enlivens the alternative scene in the city. Indeed, many new left, leftist-extremist, and terrorist groups are active in West Berlin.

The SEW has, according to its own sources, about 7,000 members, which is about how many votes it received in the last Senate elections in March 1985 (7,713). Its 0.6 percent of the total vote was far short of the minimum required for seats in the city parliament. Such poor electoral performances are likely to continue as long as the SEW retains its character as an unswervingly pro-SED and Moscow party, tightly organized along standard Marxist-Leninist lines, and financially dependent upon East Berlin. West Berlin voters are keenly aware of the truth expressed by SED Politburo member Alfred Neumann when he brought greetings from the SED to the SEW's party congress in May 1987: "The SED and the SEW are linked not only by common roots, traditions, and the same goals and class interests but also by the socialist world view and the Communists' confidence in victory" (ADN, 16 May).

The SEW is broken down into twelve suborganizations (Kreisparteiorganisationen) and a number of affiliated organizations; communist youth are organized in the SJ Karl Liebknecht, which has 550 members, and the JP, with about 250. Its university organizations garner around 400 students. The SEW-influenced Action Group of Democrats and Socialists embraces approximately 500 persons. Its Democratic Women's League—Berlin has about 600 members, the Society for German-Soviet Friendship, about 500, and the West Berlin organization of the Victims of the Nazi Regime/League of Antifascists (VVN/BdA) also about 500.

The Eighth Party Congress took place 15–17 May 1987 under the slogan "With the SEW for Peace, Work, Democracy, and Social Progress." There were 587 delegates and guests from 37 foreign parties and organizations, including delegations from the DKP, the CPSU, led by Central Committee Secretary Vadim Medvedev, and the SED, led by Neumann. SED chairman Honecker sent a telegram to re-elected SEW leader Schmitt wishing him "success, creativity, and health in implementing the decisions of the Eighth SEW Congress" (ADN, 15 May). The only major newspaper that provided extensive coverage of this congress was the SED's official organ, *Neues Deutschland* (*ND*) (New Germany).

The demands and resolutions produced by the congress provide an accurate picture of the SEW's overall policies and positions. In defense, it totally backs Soviet and GDR demands, with party Chairman Schmitt saying, "We—the Communists of West Berlin—support with all our strength the peace policy of the Soviet Union, the GDR, and the other socialist states." The SEW favors all disarmament proposals made by the Soviet Union, asserting that "this is evermore necessary because the most aggressive quarters in the United States and Western Europe bound up with the military-industrial complex are concocting evermore pretexts to frustrate disarmament moves." It calls for a replacement of deterrence by "a security partnership with the socialist states." Nuclear- and chemical-free zones in Central Europe should be created, nuclear tests stopped, SDI terminated, and no SDI research permitted in West Berlin, and the city should not be "illegally" involved in NATO strategy or "as a NATO policy tool" (*ND*, 17 May; *IB*, September).

In foreign affairs the SEW is an unfailing spokesman for the SED's policies, especially with regard to the status of West Berlin. It states that it is time to end the backward-looking "myth of a metropolis"—of one Berlin. "West Berlin is not 'part' of a whole city; it is a large city developed in nearly 40 years under the special conditions of an occupied territory." Schmitt asked rhetorically "if it is not time for the governing mayor [of West Berlin] to state publicly that his competence is confined to West Berlin and nothing else." West Berlin's need for broad contacts with the GDR requires that its government recognize the GDR and "stop interfering in the internal affairs of the GDR. Indeed, it corresponds to the spirit of the present for the Senate to recognize the GDR borders as state borders. It is time for all West Berlin authorities at least to respect the GDR citizenship."

Schmittt specifically criticized speeches made on 30 April by Chancellor Kohl and Mayor Diepgen on the occasion of the 750th anniversary of Berlin, which, in Schmitt's words, were "slanderous attacks against the GDR." It should be noted that Honecker, after some deliberation, decided not to accept the Senate's invitation to attend these ceremonies on the grounds that his taking part in a ceremony with representatives of the Bonn government would imply his approval of the ties between Bonn and West Berlin. Honecker would have been embarrassed to hear Kohl and Diepgen criticize the Berlin Wall and state again publicly that the "German question" (reunification) remains open. The GDR officially denies that reunification is a future possiblity or that Berlin is "in a waiting mode to become the German capital." The SEW agrees entirely with the SED's rationale for the Berlin Wall, which it calls "the secured state border of the GDR vis-à-vis West Berlin: it has led to stability in the area and will remain in place until the reasons [Western meddling] for which it was erected in the first place disappear" (*ND*, 16–17 May; *IB*, September; ADN, 25 May).

Like the DKP in West Germany, the SEW is open to "unity of action" with Social Democrats, the Alternative List (in which the West Berlin Greens participate), and trade unions, especially in the "fight for peace." It joined in the opposition to the census, invoking the "right of resistance" on the grounds that it violates "basic constitutional rights." It also struggles against unemployment; "poverty caused by social dismantling"; "hopelessness"; denial of renters' rights; capitalist application of education and technology that harms workers; destruction of the environment, especially the "continuing liquidation of small gardens, fields, and forests for the profit-oriented housing development policy"; relegation of thousands of artists to a minimal standard of living; and discrimination against women and foreigners. "Our party takes the view that the foreign workers are part of the working class and that we have a common enemy: monopoly capital" (*ND*, 16–17 May; *IS*, 15 May).

The objective of the joint struggle is to develop alternatives to the policies of the ruling Christian Democratic Union (CDU), without the SEW having to "renounce our basic principles." It joined many other groups in a demonstration protesting against "police terror and for democratic rights" on the occasion of President Ronald Reagan's visit to West Berlin 12 June, when he demanded that the wall be torn down (*ND*, 29, 30 June).

The SEW shares in the "spirit of proletarian internationalism" and sends delegations to fraternal party congresses, especially in the GDR and Soviet Union. For the first time, it sent a representative to a congress of the U.S. Communist Party. Schmitt concluded his address at the SEW's Eighth Party Congress with these words: "Our future lies in our Marxist-Leninist firmness in principle, in our undeviating orientation to the interests of the working people, and in our indestructible alliance with the

CPSU, with the SED, and with the entire world communist movement" (*ND*, 16–17 May).

Wayne C. Thompson
Virginia Military Institute

Great Britain

Population. 56,845,195
Party. Communist Party of Great Britain (CPGB)
Founded. 1920
Membership. 9,700 (*Morning Star*, 6 January)
General Secretary. Gordon McLennan
Political Committee. 9 members: Ron Halvarson (chairman), Gordon McLennan (general secretary), Ian McKay, Gary Pocock, Martin Jacques, Jack Ashton, Kerin Halpin, Vishnu Sharma, Nina Temple (*Morning Star*, 21 May 1985)
Executive Committee. 45 members
Status. Legal
Last Congress. Fortieth, 14–15 November 1987
Last Election. June 1987, 0.1 percent, no representation
Auxiliary Organizations. Young Communist League (YCL); Liaison Committee for the Defense of Trade Unions (LCDTU)
Publications. *Morning Star*, *Marxism Today*, *Communist Focus*, *Challenge Spark*, *Our History Journal*, *Economic Bulletin*, *Medicine in Society*, *Education Today and Tomorrow*, *New Worker*, *Seven Days*

The CPGB is a recognized political party and contests both local and national elections. It does not, however, operate in Northern Ireland, which it does not recognize as British territory. The party has had no members in the House of Commons since 1950 but has one member, Lord Milford, in the nonelected House of Lords.

Leadership and Organization. The CPGB is divided into four divisions: the National Congress, the Executive Committee and its departments, districts, and local and factory branches. Constitutionally, the biennial National Congress is the party's supreme authority, and except in unusual periods, such as the present, it rubber-stamps the decisions of the Political Committee. Responsibility for overseeing the party's activities rests with the 45-member Executive Committee, which is elected by the National Congress and meets every two months. The Executive Committee is comprised of members of special committees, full-time departmental heads, and the sixteen members of the Political Committee, the party's innermost controlling conclave.

Party leaders remain deeply preoccupied with the continuing decline in support for the party. Electorally, the party is so battered that it no longer contests as many seats as it once did. Membership, at fewer than 10,000 (only some 50 percent of whom have actually paid their fees), is at its lowest point since World War II. The YCL, with fewer than 500 members, is close to collapse. The decline in electoral support was most graphically illustrated in Britain's last general elections (1987) when the party's nineteen candidates polled a mere 6,078 votes.

However, the poor showing of the CPGB at the polls belies the party's strength in the trade union movement and in influencing opinion. Although it does not control any individual trade union, the party is represented on most union executive committees and has played a major role in most government-union confrontations of the recent years. The CPGB's success is partly attributable to low turnouts in most union elections, to the fact that it is the only party seeking to control the outcome of these elections, and to its close interest in industrial affairs, which ensures support from workers who might not support other aspects of the party's program.

Domestic Affairs. The long-standing conflict between the Eurocommunist leadership and the Stalinist hard left minority continued in 1987. The party remained in an obvious crisis that has been building for some years. It centers on the dispute between the party's Executive Committee and the *Morning Star*. The *Morning Star*, once recognized as the party's daily newspaper, is technically owned by the communist, but separate, People's Press Printing Society (PPPS). Throughout 1987 the PPPS continued to be in the hands of Stalinist opponents of the Executive Committee's Eurocommunist policies. The *Morning Star* group is bitterly opposed to the leadership's criticisms (muted though they were) of the Soviet Union and to the transformation of the party's theoretical journal, *Marxism Today*, into a popular, broad-based magazine.

The course of intraparty conflict in 1987 occurred in the context of, and in reaction to, several consecutive years of stinging defeats for the political left in Britain. Most important of these have been the miner's strike of 1984–1985, the left's debacle in controlling the Liverpool city government during 1985–1986, and the years of unsuccessful struggle with the Thatcher government on a whole range of issues. As a result, the already fractured communist movement drifted into an even sharper debate within itself. Who was to blame for these defeats? How should the movement proceed to bolster the party's position, along with the position of the left? Should the party adopt a more cooperative relationship with the Labour Party and even parties to the right? How should it deal with the British union movement?

The Eurocommunist majority in control of the CPGB has tended to answer these questions by advocating broad alliances with less ideological left parties and groups. This has infuriated the harder left, which has reacted angrily through the *Morning Star* and its political group, the Communist Campaign Group, as well as the breakaway New Communist Party. To be sure, there have been fractious problems within this opposition, but there is vocal agreement in charging that the Eurocommunist leadership is guilty of soft-headed thinking that has caused the movement to lose its leadership of the working class.

A pattern of vicious attacks from each side against the other together with Eurocommunist actions to expel rebels from the CPGB have almost completely dominated the time of all the participants, which has further hurt the appeal of the party. The 1987 election results graphically showed how extensive the damage has become. Whereas the party fielded 35 candidates and won more than 11,000 votes in 1983, it only offered 19 candidates and won less than 7,000 votes in 1987. Moreover, its membership has fallen to less than 10,000 and its full-time staff now numbers fewer than twenty.

The election results did nothing to soften the intraparty struggle. The executive was quick to restate the Eurocommunist views by noting that there is widespread acceptance in Britain "of Thatcherite concepts and arguments, even among those who vote Labour." The way forward, they argued, was just the opposite of what the hard left was advocating—that the party must "develop a strategy that can challenge the hold of Thatcherite thinking and lead to a level of mass movement higher than ever before, uniting broad sections of the population."

In the wake of postelection recriminations and continued purges, the CPGB held its Fortieth Party Congress in mid-November. The long intraparty conflict seemed to come to a head, as the congress, by a vote of four to one, broke the party's ties with the *Morning Star* and upheld the Executive Committee's numerous expulsions of prominent rebels.

The CPGB continued to support demonstrations against most aspects of government policy. The party led militant demands and protests over the issue of unemployment in Great Britain, continued to be an active supporter of the Committee for Nuclear Disarmament, and vigorously opposed the implanting of cruise missiles in Britain. The CPGB also supports unilateral nuclear disarmament by the United Kingdom, an issue it presses on the Labour Party and Neil Kinnock at every opportunity. In 1987, this issue was coupled with strong opposition to U.S. eagerness to encourage Star Wars, which was just as vigorously opposed by the Soviet Union.

Auxiliary Organizations. In industry, CPGB activity centers on its approximately 200 workplace branches. Its umbrella organization is the LCDTU. Although the CPGB is riven by internal disputes, its trade union structure can still command considerable support from prominent trade union leaders.

The YCL, the youth wing of the party, has fewer than 500 members.

The party retains a number of financial interests including Central Books, Lawrence and Wishart Publisher, Farleigh Press, London Caledonian Printers, Rodell Properties, the Labour Research Department, and the Marx Memorial Library.

International Views and Activities. Although the CPGB leadership is regarded as revisionist by its own dissident hard-line faction, there are in fact few areas in which the CPGB stints in its support of the Soviet Union. The party is still critical of the Soviet invasion of Afghanistan and Czechoslovakia. Otherwise, the CPGB favors arms reduction talks with the USSR and opposes the deployment of missiles in Europe and the development of U.S. space weapons. It is critical of Israel and seeks to promote recognition of the Palestine Liberation Organization.

Other Marxist Groups. Besides the CPGB, several small, mainly Trotskyist groups are also active. Although some of these groups were growing swiftly in the 1970s, their memberships are now waning.

The most important of the Trotskyist groups is Militant Tendency, which derives its name from its paper of the same name. Militant Tendency claims to be merely a loose tendency of opinion within the Labour Party, but there is no doubt that it possesses its own distinctive organization and for some years has been pursuing a policy of "entryism" (the tactic of penetrating the larger, more moderate Labour Party). Militant Tendency controls about 50 Labour Party constituencies.

The other significant Trotskyist organizations are the Socialist Workers' Party (SWP) and the Workers' Revolutionary Party (WRP). The SWP has been particularly active in single-issue campaigns, notably the antiunemployment campaign. It gave active support to striking miners' families but, in fact, enjoys little support in the coal mining industry. The WRP's activities are more secretive but are known to center in the engineering, mining, theater, and auto industries. It focuses its attention on the young and has set up six Youth Training Centres, which are primarily concerned with recruitment.

Gerald Dorfman
Hoover Institution

Greece

Population. 9,987,785
Party. Communist Party of Greece (Kommunistikon Komma Ellados; KKE)
Founded. 1921
Membership. 42,000 (estimated)
General Secretary. Kharilaos Florakis
Politburo. 9 full members: Kharilaos Florakis, Grigoris Farakos, Dimitris Gondikas, Nikos Kaloudhis, Orestis Kolozof, Loula Logara, Dimitris Mamatsis, Alexandra Papariga, Kostas Tsolakis; 4 candidate members: Dimitris Androulakis, Spyros Khalvatzis, Dimitris Karangoules, Dimitris Kostopoulos
Status. Legal
Last Congress. Twelfth, 12–16 May 1987, in Athens
Last Election. 2 June 1985, 9.9 percent, 13 of 300 seats
Auxiliary Organization. Communist Youth of Greece (KNE)
Publications. *Rizospastis*, daily: *Kommunistiki Epitheorisi* (KOMEP), monthly theoretical review

The major event for the KKE was its Twelfth Congress, held in Athens between 12 and 16 May. Another significant event in the area of the left was the spring congress held in Athens between 24 and 26 April by the KKE-Interior with the purpose of revamping the image of the party, changing its title, and clarifying its ideological principles. The congress resulted in a split between the two major factions, one led by Leonidas Kirkos and the other by Giannis Banias. The Banias group retained the title KKE-Interior adding the subtitle Renovating Left. The Kirkos group, which seems to have the relatively larger support, adopted the title Greek Left (E.AR), its acronym subtly suggesting the ancient Greek word for springtime.

The wider left, in addition to these three parties, now includes two factions of the United Democratic Left (EDA), the party that between 1950 and 1967 acted as a substitute for the-then outlawed KKE; the Socialist Party of Gerasimos Arsenis, the Panhellenic Socialist Movement (PASOK) minister of national economy till 1985; the Revolutionary Communist Party of Greece (EKKE); the Communist Marxist-Leninists; the Revolutionary People's Struggle; the Communist Internationalists of Greece; and several other smaller groups. The governing party, PASOK, also has in its ranks, as well as in its leading echelons, many individuals of a strong leftist orientation. Recent polls seem to indicate that KKE has increased its following, from approximately 10 percent to 15 percent, mostly thanks to the shift of voters dissatisfied with PASOK's more conservative economic policies.

Leadership and Organization. KKE is now legal, yet its organizational structure has not changed from the days when it was illegal. The party members are organized along the traditional patterns of cells in factories, work places, and universities and in party factions (*fraxies*) within the trade unions, professional organizations, and other associations and cooperatives. Neighborhoods are organized in *aktivs*, and smaller towns and villages have local party organizations. Major cities, such as Athens, Piraeus, and Salonika, have city organizations and city committees headed by powerful secretaries. Major sections of the country have regional party organizations with their own regional committees and secretaries.

The most powerful organ of the party is the Politburo, which is appointed by the Central Committee that, in turn, is elected by the party congress. By statute, the congress convenes every four years, but this rule has not been observed consistently. Recently, however, the party has held its congresses at regular intervals. The most recent congress (the twelfth) convened in May 1987. The Central Committee normally meets in plenary session once every six months. The actual decisionmaking power is in the hands of the Politburo, whose current membership is listed above. Although General Secretary Florakis is influential, decisions are reached by consensus. The individuals most likely to succeed Florakis are either Gondikas or Androulakis, with Gondikas seeming to have the edge. Both belong to the younger generation that rose in the KNE during the military dictatorship (1967–1974). KNE today is very active and has considerable influence in the universities and among young workers.

KKE-Interior came into being during the military dictatorship when KKE split into two factions. Through the years it adopted a less militant and less dogmatic line and indentified itself with Eurocommunism. Eventually it decided to drop the traditional marks of communist identity such as the hammer and sickle, democratic centralism, and the appellation "communist." In a congress held in April 1987, the KKE-Interior split into two factions, the smaller of which retained the name KKE-Interior and added the subtitle Renovating Left (KKE-Int./RL). The major faction, which is now called Greek Left (E.AR), elected Kirkos as the secretary of its 101-member Central Committee. In addition to Kirkos, the party's Executive Office includes Gr. Giannaros, D. Giatzoglou, Petros Kounalakis, K. Kourkoutis, Sp. Likoudhis, Ar. Manolakos, Mikh. Papagiannakis, Stergios Pitsiorlas, Giannis Toundas, M. Trandalidis, D. Khatzisocratis, and D. Psikhoyios. Recent polls indicate and that E.AR has approximately 2.5 percent of the electorate and that KKE-Int./RL has 1.5 percent. The mainstay of E.AR is leftist intellectuals and professionals.

Views and Positions. During the year KKE broadened its opposition to the government's austerity measures and instigated many strikes. Nevertheless, the militancy of its opposition was kept within bounds. KKE continues to be uncertain as to how to deal with the PASOK government, for it fears that a severe weakening of the government will benefit the conservative New Democracy Party. A return of New Democracy to power will deprive KKE of the many advantages it has enjoyed under the PASOK government, especially in the government-controlled mass media (radio and TV), which frequently present programs with themes favorable to KKE and the left in general. KKE has been advocating a coalition of the "forces of the left," including those leftist elements within PASOK. At the same time, the party supports a change in the electoral system, favoring a "pure proportional" system that would allow the various parties of the left to gain a corresponding number of seats in the legislature. With a "pure proportion," KKE would expect to gain more than 30 seats instead of its current 13. KKE rejects the current situation, which is dominated by the two major parties–PASOK and New Democracy—and hopes that if the "pure proportional" electoral system were applied KKE would hold the key to any government either in coalition with PASOK or as a parliamentary ally to a PASOK governement in exchange for major concessions. The party, of course, remains vehemently anti-American and opposes any agreement that would allow the U.S. bases in Greece to remain. Currently, the PASOK government is engaged in bilateral negotiations on the future of the bases. Under the existing agreement signed in 1983, the presence of the bases will be terminated in 1988 unless a new agreement provides for an extension.

The work of the Twelfth Congress—in which 582 regular and 190 alternate delegates together with foreign observers from 75 workers' and communist parties and "liberation movements" took part—showed that the party is uncertain as to how to deal with Mikhail Gorbachev's *perestroika* and *glasnost'*. For the most part, the leadership, as well as the rank and file, continues to think in traditional Stalinist terms. The names of the new Central Committee (CC) elected by the congress again were not made public. In spite of the presence at the congress of Mikhail S. Solomentsev, a CPSU/CC Politburo member, the party gave only half-hearted and rather cryptic endorsement to the *perestroika* aims of the Soviet leadership. After decades of denouncing "profit" as a cardinal sin, the KKE finds it rather difficult to accept the Gorbachev innovations. The Soviet leadership gives no sign that it finds the

KKE's reluctance to embrace *perestroika* annoying because KKE remains true to its Marxist-Leninist ideals and to its support of CPSU initiates in the international arena.

Relations between Premier Andreas Papandreou and Florakis remain fairly good in spite of disagreements over the government's economic policies and Papandreou's refusal to accept the "pure proportional" electoral system. As the electoral support for the governing PASOK declines, KKE calculates that in the next election—unless the New Democracy Party wins a clear majority and forms a government—PASOK will be unable to muster a majority in the legislature and will have to turn to the KKE parliamentary deputies for support. Although KKE may not take part in a coalition PASOK-KKE government, its bargaining power will be extensive.

Domestic Activities. During the year the party focused on the preparation of the Twelfth Party Congress. The generational gap between the older leaders that control the party, who rose in the ranks during the 1946–1949 "civil war," and the younger generation, who gained prominence during the military dictatorship, prevented the congress from charting new policies. The resolutions of the congress reflect the major compromises reached between the two groups.

Although in 1986 KKE rejected PASOK's overtures for a dialogue among the forces of the left, this year a key KKE campaign focused on the promotion of cooperation among the "democratic and progressive forces" (KKE labels for the left). Calls for such a coalition were rejected by Kirkos and other leftist leaders. To expand its influence among the workers, KKE encouraged several strikes throughout the year, although it kept the intensity low key to avert serious political damage to the governing PASOK. The party supported PASOK's clash with the Greek Orthodox Church over the church's independence and the disposition of church property. In November, KKE was the major participant in the annual march from the Polytechnic School to the American Embassy, in commemoration of the student takeover of the school in November 1973 in a massive protest against the military dictatorship. This year the New Democracy Party refused to paticipate in this strident display of anti-American and anti-Western slogans. PASOK's participation was less extensive than in previous years. Although KKE cannot be directly connected with terrorist activities, leftist terrorist organizations such as the 17th November Revolutionary Organization, the Revolutionary People's Struggle (ELA), and the 1st of May Revolutionary Organization were active during the year setting bombs off in public buildings. ELA claimed responsibility for a major explosion on 12 February and again on 14 May. The 17th November claimed responsibility for the explosion that on August 10 damaged a bus carrying U.S. military. Several soldiers were wounded. Another explosion severely damaged the Commerce and Industry Chamber building in late December. On Christmas Day a major explosion occurred in the Malakasa Depot of the Greek Army.

International Contacts. Florakis traveled extensively during the year. From 9 January to 17 January, he visited Cuba and Nicaragua. During a stopover in Prague, Florakis met with Vasil Bil'ák, secretary of the Czechoslovak Communist Party. In Cuba he met with Fidel Castro, and in Nicaragua, with Daniel Ortega. On 28 January Florakis went to East Germany, where he met Erich Honecker, secretary of the Socialist Unity Party of Germany's Central Committee. On 15 February, a delegation of the Turkish Communist Party led by General Secretary Haydar Kutlu visited Greece at the invitation of the KKE CC and held talks with Florakis. On 17 March, at the invitation of the Communist Party of China, a KKE delegation headed by Orestis Kolozov visited Beijing. Kolozov later disclosed that his delegation disagreed with the Chinese over the responsibility of the Soviet Union in fomenting international tension. The KKE view is that tension is caused only by U.S. "imperialism." On 26 April, Nicolae Ceauşescu of Romania sent Ian Stoian, a candidate member of the Romanian Communist Party Political Executive Committee, to Athens to invite Florakis to Bucharest. Relations between the two parties have been cool. In May, during the party's Twelfth Congress, more than 70 communist and workers' parties sent delegations. Many delegation leaders held talks with Florakis and other members of the KKE Politburo. The Soviet delegation was led by Solomentsev, who was accorded the distinction of being the only foreign delegate to appear on the platform with Florakis during the closing ceremonies at the Sports Stadium of Peace and Friendship. On 14 October Florakis visited Romania and held talks with Ceauşescu. On 22 October in Athens, Florakis addressed a two-day conference of communist and workers' parties from Eastern Mediterranean, Near and Middle Eastern, and Red Sea countries.

Other Marxist-Leninist Organizations. Most other Marxist-Leninist organizations in Greece are small, peripheral groups with insignificant followings. Because the new E.AR does not consider itself a Marxist-Leninist party, only the splinter group under Giannis Banias still operates under the KKE-Interior label. Other organizations include the Greek Internationalist Union-Trotkyists, the Revolutionary Communist Party of Greece, and the Communist Party of Marxists-Leninists. Also included are the ELA, the 17th November Revolutionary Organization, and the 1st of May Revolutionary Organization, which primarily engage in terrorist activities, justifying their acts with profound ideological diatribes against capitalism, the oligarchy, and the Americans.

D. G. Kousoulas, Professor Emeritus
Howard University

Iceland

Population. 244,676
Party. People's Alliance (Althydubandalagid; PA)
Founded. 1968
Membership. 3,000 (estimated)
Chairman. Olafur Ragnar Grimsson
Executive Committee. 10 members: Olafur Ragnar Grimsson, Svavar Gestsson, and 8 others
Central Committee. 70 members, 20 deputies
Status. Legal
Last Congress. Biennial, 1–10 November 1987
Last Election. 1987, 13.2 percent, 8 of 63 seats
Auxiliary Organization. Organization of Base Opponents (OPO; organizer of peace demonstrations against U.S.-NATO bases)
Publications. *Thjodviljinn* (daily), Reykjavik; *Verkamadhurinn* (weekly), Akureyri; *Mjolnir* (weekly), Siglufjördhur

Although Iceland figured less prominently in world politics in 1987, its domestic politics were lively. The year's political events included a sudden split within the center-right Independence Party only five weeks before the 25 April parliamentary elections, significant changes in party strengths following the April general elections, and a new governing coalition after two months of political negotiation. While the superpowers did not hold a summit conference in Reykjavik in 1987, Prime Minister (now Foreign Minister) Steingrimur Hermannsson traveled to Moscow in March for personal talks with Soviet leader Mikhail Gorbachev. Late in 1986 Hermannsson also visited Beijing, which has not previously seen a top Icelandic politician. In June the NATO council held its meeting in the Icelandic capital. All the above made quite a full plate for a nation of fewer than a quarter of a million inhabitants.

The PA occupies the left flank of Icelandic politics. It is the successor to a line of leftist parties dating back to 1930, when the Icelandic Communist Party (Kommunistaflokkur Islands) was established by a left-wing splinter from the Labor Party. In 1938, the Social Democratic Party (SDP) splintered from the Labor Party and joined with the communists to create a new party, the United People's Party—Socialist Party (Sameiningar flokkur althydu—Sosialista flokkurinn; UPP-SP). Although its ideology was based on "scientific socialism—Marxism," the UPP-SP had no organizational ties to Moscow. Its first goal was support for complete Icelandic independence from Denmark. By the time this was achieved in 1944, the UPP-SP was accepted as a responsible democratic leftist party and had participated in governing coalitions. In 1956, the UPP-SP formed an electoral alliance with other small leftist and neutralist groups, and the coalition became known as the People's Alliance (PA). In 1968, the UPP-SP dissolved itself into the PA, which then became the current pragmatic Marxist party. It has participated regularly in coalition governments, most recently joining the Progressive Party (PP; agrarian liberal) in a coalition headed by the late maverick Gunnar Thoroddsen, formerly of the Independence Party (IP). That coalition lasted until the April 1983 parliamentary elections, which were a setback for all the constituent parties. The PA held three cabinet posts: social and health affairs (Gestsson), finance (Ragnar Arnalds), and industry (Hjorleifur Guttormsson).

The PA's electoral setback in April was the second in a row and occurred despite the strong showing in 1986 local elections. The PA received 20,382 votes (13.4 percent) and eight seats, down more than 4 percentage points since 1983. For the first time since 1942, the reformist SDP, which received 15.2 percent of the vote and ten seats (a gain of two), has more parliamentary seats than the PA. Clearly the PA has been outflanked by the pragmatic SDP, under Jon Baldvin Hannibalsson's effective if somewhat idiosyncratic leadership, and by the unconventional radicalism of the Women's Alliance (Samtok um kvinnalista; WA). The WA was declared the "winner" of the election because it proved that it was not a short-term protest movement by doubling its parliamentary bloc to six and attracting 10.1 percent of the vote.

The PA was not the only traditional party whose fortunes suffered. The IP lost five seats (to eighteen) as a result of the split; it remains the country's largest party, but its share of the vote fell from 38.7 to 27.2 percent. The other governing party, the agrarian PP, did better than expected, with 18.9 percent of the vote (a gain of 0.4 percent) and a loss of one seat (to thirteen). The 1987 elections were the first held under a new electoral law that reduced the overrepresentation of rural areas (which had benefited the PP), increased the size of the Althing (parliament) to 63, and reduced the voting age to eighteen. With so much partisan turmoil, voters had more than enough choices, and nearly 90 percent of the electorate voted. The new Citizens' Party (Albert Gudmundsson's loyalists from the IP) did surprisingly well for a party of five weeks and won seven seats and nearly 11 percent of the vote. Another new party to enter parliament was the Regional Equality Platform, which wants further electoral law changes. With one member (and 1.2 percent of the vote), it is likely to be ignored. A small number of remaining Social Democratic Alliance diehards (most having returned to the SDP from whence they came) closed that brief chapter of Icelandic party life by receiving 0.2 percent of the vote. Two other parties (the Humanists and the National Party) each received about 1.5 percent of the vote. Thus the new parliament has seven parties (*News from Iceland*, May).

Icelandic politics do not fall easily into Western European categories. A recent survey indicated that about 40 percent of the blue-collar vote goes to the centrist IP. The PA's vote comes increasingly from male blue-collar workers, public employees, and various other radicals. It is not enough to build a winning coalition when faced with so much competition. Personal loyalties are strong across the political spectrum, as witnessed by scandal-ridden Gudmundsson's political following.

Leadership and Organization. The PA's dismal electoral performance rekindled intraparty strife, which has plagued the party since 1983. In August Gestsson announced that he would not be a candidate for re-election as PA chair. Gestsson and his allies represent the party's left wing, and this "old guard's" dogmatic attachment to Marxism allows their opponents to refer to them as "commies" despite their independence of any foreign movement. Competition arose over his successor. Sigridur Stefansdottir, a member of the Akureyri City Council, was reportedly urged to run by former PA ministers including Gestsson, Arnalds, and Guttormsson, who are seen as the party's parliamentary leaders. Grimsson, who represents the PA's academic wing as opposed to those more closely associated with the party's labor wing, also announced his candidacy. A sophisticated political scientist at the University of Iceland, Grimsson is well-traveled and known outside Iceland. Grimsson had been chair of the PA's Executive Board, but he resigned, along with several others, from the editorial board of the party paper *Thjodviljinn* in August (*Morgunbladid*, 23 June). Despite an active and personal campaign, Grimsson failed to win a parliamentary seat in April.

PA affairs were also illuminated in a lengthy report on the party edited by Gudrun Helgadottir and published in June. It reported that the party was perceived as "stagnant, boring, and undemocratic." It went on to lay most of the blame on the three former ministers, who had lost touch with the party's rank and file as well as with its voters. This attitude extended throughout the party, particularly to its parliamentary group. The parliamentary leadership runs the group as a closed clique without making its goals well-known. Kristin A. Olafsdottir, another PA critic, claimed in the report that the leader sought to run the party along "Eastern European" lines, "against all innovations, even technology in general; they fight against marketing, service, and businesses, as long as they are in the hands of people other than municipalities and state." They are "preachers of pessimism" and envy against those who are more affluent. In his essay, Grimsson attacked the party's sentimental ties to the state socialist model, which had proven bankrupt in the Soviet Union and Eastern Europe (*Morgunbladid*, 25 June).

The PA has never followed a strict Leninist organizational model, and the leadership is divided among several independent and assertive personalities. Hence, public bickering is a sign of a relatively open, pluralistic, and lively party. At the November party congress attended by 370 delegates, Grimsson was elected party chair over Steffansdottir by a vote of 221 to 144 (with 5 abstentions). Svanfridur Jonasdottir was elected deputy chair and Bjoern G. Sveinsson, party secretary. Both are supporters of Grimsson. While the winners celebrated, the defeated wing retaliated by selecting a majority of the Executive Committee. The Grimsson faction then responded by winning a majority of the party's Central Committee (*News from Iceland*, November). Several supporters of the ousted leadership resigned from the party. This turmoil suggests that it may be some time before the PA regains internal cohesion.

Domestic Affairs. Economic affairs dominate Icelandic politics. The PA generally speaks for the urban wage earner, but by no means does it dominate the labor union movement, including the Icelandic Federation of Labor (ASI). Although PA groups are often the largest, some unions (particularly in the private sector) have strong factions loyal to the moderately conservative IP, and there are signs that the revived SDP is making inroads in some unions. Periodic collective bargaining negotiations are decisive for the nation's economy and affect most employees. The government was forced to legislate an end to a strike of fishermen and merchant seamen in January that threatened the country's vital communications links. The seamen had demanded a 40 percent wage increase (ibid., February).

On the whole 1987 was another banner year for the Icelandic economy. Real economic growth is expected to be 8.7 percent, and unemployment is only 0.5 percent of the labor force. Inflation had, however, doubled, to more than 20 percent by the autumn (Central Bank of Iceland, *Economic Statistics Quarterly*, November). The Organization for Economic Cooperation and Development called for economic restraint, which the new government adopted by raising domestic taxation and restricting credit (*Financial Times*, 18 June). Improved terms of trade and record fishing catches were the main causes of the economic boom. The new government's austerity policy is expected to produce little if any growth in 1988, which makes domestic political and labor strife likely in the new year.

The financial scandal involving the government bailout of the bankrupted state Fisheries Bank (which finances the fishing fleet) became personal when it was disclosed that former Finance Minister Gudmundsson had personally profited from the bank. The sums involved were small, but, as they were hidden from the tax authorities, many saw the finance minister's behavior as inexcusable. When the scandal broke Gudmundsson was industry minister, and the ensuing turmoil led to his resignation from the government and the IP and his organization of the new Citizens' Party (*News from Iceland*, February). The PA joined other parliamentary groups in denouncing the affair but also opposed the new government's solution to the Fisheries Bank problem because it allowed for direct foreign investment in an Icelandic financial institution. The PA has been a consistent opponent of foreign investment (*Nordisk Kontakt*, nos. 11–12).

Foreign Affairs. Three traditional issues dominate Icelandic foreign policy debates: the NATO bases at Keflavik and elsewhere on the island, trade relations with its main export markets, and national economic control of resources on shore and in adjacent waters. Although Icelanders are sophisticated, well-informed, and widely traveled, their view of the world reflects their small size, geographic isolation, and limited foreign policy experience. At times, foreign policy discussions become surrealistic as in early 1987 when Tom Clancy's latest international thriller, *Red Star Rising*, hit the Icelandic book market. Clancy's hypothetical account of a sudden Soviet invasion of Iceland dominated the country's security policy debates (encouraged, of course, by press sensationalists and perhaps clever book marketers).

There were few new issues in 1987, but Iceland's increasingly active foreign policy broadened the domestic debate. Prime Minister Hermannsson's visit to Moscow in March was in part a reciprocation by the Soviet leadership, but substantive discussions on European and North Atlantic affairs, as well as on Soviet-Icelandic trade, did take place.

The year's first foreign policy debate occurred in January over whether Iceland was obstructing a joint initiative by the Nordic countries to create a regional nuclear weapons–free zone. Both the PA and the WA strongly favor such a zone, but the SDP's Hannibalsson was skeptical. He felt that such a Nordic zone should include parts of the USSR and be thoroughly discussed in the NATO context. PA leader Gestsson noted that the SDP position was unique among Nordic and European social democratic parties and closer to the "hawks" in Washington (ibid., no. 3).

In March, just before parliament was dissolved for the elections, foreign Minister Mathiesen presented his formal report on the international situation. He noted that despite improved East-West relations, the Icelandic Defense Force (IDF) still intercepts Soviet aircraft every other day (on average). The IDF continues to be "internationalized," with Danish and Norwegian staff officers added in 1986. Nearly all of the military personnel remain American, however. The IDF employs some 2,400 Icelanders and spends about $125 million in Iceland. In February agreement was reached for Iceland to supply meat and other foods to the IDF, worth about $20 million annually (*News from Iceland*, March). The PA has been suspicious of the substantial economic stake that Iceland has gained from the NATO bases.

Despite PA opposition, construction is progressing on several long-range radar stations being built with U.S. assistance. These installations will be manned by Icelanders and will have both military and civilian applications. Likewise, the United States paid for a portion of the new air terminal in Keflavik. PA foreign affairs spokesman Hjorleifur Guttormsson noted that improvements in world affairs have been mainly a result of changes in Soviet policy. U.S. policies have made less progress, and Guttormsson regretted that Iceland had not protested U.S. attacks in Libya in 1986 or voted with the other Nordic countries in various U.N. arms control resolutions. He found the government's foreign policy "unprincipled and servile" toward the Americans (*Nordisk Kontakt*, no. 6).

In June NATO defense and foreign ministers met in Iceland, symbolizing the country's higher profile in the alliance and in Atlantic affairs generally. The movement of Steingrimur Hermannsson to the foreign ministry in the new three-party coalition suggest that there will be substantial continuity in the country's foreign and security policies. In his announcement of the new government's program at the opening of parliament in October, Prime Minister Palsson stressed continuity and an independent Icelandic foreign policy. He also warned against using the country's well-established defense arrangements as a negotiating tool in other areas of relations with the United States, a tactic advocated by several Icelandic parties. With the SDP now included in the goverment, it is likely to be the most pro-NATO government in 25 years (ibid., no. 15).

As mentioned, Grimsson, the new PA chair, is a specialist in international and comparative politics who has been critical of the party's xenophobic, nationalistic, and dogmatic foreign policy program. Although critical of NATO bases, he would use the issue as part of the multilateral effort to reduce the ongoing militarization of the North Atlantic. It is likely that the PA will develop some new approaches to its foreign policy goals under Grimsson's leadership.

U.S.-Icelandic relations continued to improve with the resolution of the shipping issue, which had previously deprived Icelandic ships of lucrative IDF cargoes. In competitive bidding, the Icelandic freight line won 65 percent of the traffic. Another dispute involving whaling also relaxed as Iceland agreed to reduce its catch for scientific purposes by 50 percent. The United States remains Iceland's largest export market, mainly for fish products, which account for nearly half of Icelandic exports. The British market is rapidly growing. Although the Soviet Union has signed large trade agreements with Iceland, it is a much smaller market. The PA raised the new Soviet-Norwegian herring contracts as a possible threat to Icelandic interests (*Nordisk Kontakt*, no. 4).

International Party Contacts. The PA and its predecessors have always remained aloof from international communist movements. In recent decades the PA has been the least international of the country's political parties. It relates, to a limited degree, with social democratic and radical socialist parties in the other Nordic countries, and interacts at annual meetings of the interparliamentary Nordic council. Under Grimsson's leadership the PA is likely to identify closely with the Norwegian Socialist Left Party and the Danish Socialist People's Party. Over the years, there have also been sporadic contacts with the Italian and the Yugoslav communist parties, but there are no regular ties.

Other Marxist and Leftist Groups. The PA's internal pluralism has discouraged the formation of independent leftist groups even though the PA itself has often resembled an organized argument rather than a political party. After brief flurries in the 1970s, Maoism and Trotskyism have no organizational structure. It will be interesting to see how those defeated at the PA Congress in November react to their fate. They still hold power in the party's Executive Committee and parliamentary bloc as well as in local government, which may reduce their temptation to bolt from the PA. The SDA was a short-lived faction of the SDP, but most of its elements have rejoined the mother party. A few determined SDA activists participated in the April election but attracted almost no support.

The WA is an interesting Icelandic phenomenon. There has been a rapid rise of women to positions of prominence in all areas of public life, symbolized, of course, by the republic's president, Vigdis Finnbogadottir (whose powers are largely ceremonial but not irrelevant during cabinet crises, as in 1987). The alliance is a loosely organized radical feminist group with a pragmatic domestic program that attracts wide support in this highly egalitarian society. As noted, its large electoral gains made it a logical candidate for participation in the new government. All other parties accord the WA's parliamentary leaders considerable respect. Nevertheless, given the requirements for economic austerity that faced the new government, the WA's demands for massive wage increases for low-paid employees (overwhelmingly women) would have made it a problematic coalition partner. The WA's general line tends to be less interested in economic growth and investment and more interested in redistributional questions involving wages, public services, and social policy. On foreign affairs issues its position is strongly pacifist and opposed to Icelandic NATO commitments. The WA has clearly attracted many voters who might otherwise have supported the PA.

Eric S. Einhorn
University of Massachusetts at Amherst

Ireland

Population. 3,534,553
Party. Communist Party of Ireland (CPI)
Founded. 1933 (date of record)
Membership. 500 (estimated)
General Secretary. James Stewart
National Political Committee. Includes Michael O'Riordan (chairman), Andrew Barr, Sean Nolan, Tom Redmond, Edwina Stewart, Eddie Glackin
Status. Legal
Last Congress. Nineteenth, 31 January–2 February 1986, in Dublin
Last Election. February 1987, no representation
Auxiliary Organization. Connelly Youth Movement
Publications. *Irish Socialist*, *Irish Workers' Voice*, *Unity*, *Irish Bulletin*

The CPI was founded in 1921, when the Socialist Party of Ireland expelled moderates and decided to join the Comintern. During the Civil War, the party became largely irrelevant and virtually disappeared, although very small communist cells remained intact. The CPI was refounded in June 1933, the date the communists now adopt as the founding date of their party.

The party organization was badly disrupted during World War II because of the neutrality of the South and the belligerent status of the North. In 1948, the communists in the South founded the Irish Workers' Party and those in the North, the Communist Party of Northern Ireland. At a specially convened "unity congress" held in Belfast on 15 March 1970, the two groups reunited.

The CPI is a recognized political party on both sides of the border and contests both local and national elections. It has, however, no significant support and no elected representatives.

Leadership and Organization. The CPI is divided into two geographical branches, north and south, corresponding to the political division of the country. In theory, the congress is the supreme constitutional authority of the party, but in practice it tends to serve as a rubber stamp for the national executive. The innermost controlling conclave is the National Political Committee. Such little support as the CPI enjoys tends to be based in Dublin and Belfast.

Domestic Affairs. The continuing political division of the country and Ireland's economic problems remained the main issues in 1987. The CPI views the United Kingdom as an imperialist power that gains economically from holding Ireland in a subordinate position. Although continuing to advocate the creation of a single, united socialist Ireland, the party remains opposed to the use of violence and denounces the use of force by armed gangs on either side of the communal divide. For example, it was particularly vehement in its denunciation of the Provisional Irish Republican Army's bombing of the Grand Hotel in Brighton in 1984, which nearly killed several members of the British Cabinet including Prime Minister Margaret Thatcher.

The party believes Irish unification can be achieved only by promoting working-class solidarity and thus overcoming the communal divide between Protestants and Catholics. Executive Committee member Morrissey put the CPI view succinctly: "As long as the working class is divided along religions or other lines, the exploiting classes will dominate the political stage and Ireland will remain subordinate to imperialism."

The Nineteenth Congress of the CPI met during late January and early February 1986. The delegates devoted the majority of their time to the problem of the North. They strongly denounced the Anglo-Irish agreement, demanding that Britain immediately declare a fixed date by which it would withdraw its political, administrative, and military presence. Additionally, they declared their support for the establishment of a devolved Assembly for the North during the transition to a united socialist Ireland. This assembly should have broad political and social powers, sufficient to radically restructure the state, and these powers should be accompanied by a strong Bill of Rights. Interestingly, the delegates also urged that, as a united socialist Ireland is established, it adopt the more liberal North Irish laws on divorce and abortion to replace what it described as the backward prohibitions existing in the South.

International Views and Activities. The CPI is quite untouched by the phenomenon of Eurocommunism and remains staunchly pro-Soviet. Indeed, in a country where there are several larger Marxist groups in operation, the distinctive feature of CPI attitudes is perhaps, simple pro-Sovietism. The party is strongly anti-American and denounces U.S. policy in Central America, the Middle East, and elsewhere. It favors arms reduction talks in Europe and opposes the deployment of missiles and President Ronald Reagan's Strategic Defense Initiative.

The party also remains hostile to the European Economic Community, which it regards as a device for drawing Ireland into NATO planning.

Gerald Dorfman
Hoover Institution

Italy

Population. 57,350,850
Party. Italian Communist Party (Partito Communista Italiano; PCI)
Founded. 1921
Membership. 1,505,000
General Secretary. Alessandro Natta (69)
Deputy Secretary General. Achille Occhetto (51)
Secretariat. Alessandro Natta, Achille Occhetto, Massima D'Alema (37; organization), Livia Turco (31; women's commission), Piero Fassino (37), Gianni Pellicani (55), Claudio Petruccioli (46)
Directorate. 39 members
Program Office. 10 members (established 29 July)
Central Control Commission. 60 members; Gian Carlo Pajetta (76) replaced Paolo Bufalini (72) as president 29 July.
Central Committee. 216 members
Status. Legal
Last Congress. Seventeenth, 9–13 April 1986, in Florence
Last Election. 1987, 26.6 percent, 177 of 630 seats, in the Chamber of Deputies and 28.3 percent, 100 of 315 seats, in the Senate (1983, 29.9 percent, 198 seats, in the Chamber of Deputies, and 30.8 percent, 107 seats, in the Senate)
Auxiliary Organizations. Italian Communist Youth Federation (FGCI), Italian General Confederation of Labor (CGIL), National League of Cooperatives
Publications. *L'Unità*, official daily, Gerardo Chiaromonte (63), editor, Fabio Mussi (39), coeditor; *Rinascita*, weekly, Franco Ottolenghi, editor; *Critica Marxista*, bimonthly theoretical journal; Aldo Zanardo, editor; *Politica ed Economia*; *Riforma della Scuola*; *Democrazia e Diritto*; *Donna e Politica*; *Studi Storici*; *Nuova Rivista Internazionale*. The party also runs a publishing house, Editori Riuniti.

The PCI was founded in 1921 when a radical faction of the Italian Socialist Party (PSI) led by Amadeo Bordiga, Antonio Gramsci, and Palmiro Togliatti seceded from the PSI and joined the Comintern. Declared illegal in 1926 by Mussolini's regime, the PCI went underground, its party headquarters were moved to France, and its membership dropped to a few thousand during the 1930s. The PCI leaders regrouped in Italy in 1943–1944, and the party participated in broad coalition governments from the spring of 1944 until the spring of 1947. Meanwhile, membership grew from some five thousand in mid-1943 to about one and a half million by late 1945. The party won 18.9 percent of the votes in the first postwar election in 1946. (The PSI won 20.7 percent and the Christian Democrats, 35.2 percent.)

After the Comintern's purge of Bordiga and the Fascists' imprisonment of Gramsci in 1926, the PCI was led by Togliatti until his death in 1964 and then by Luigi Longo (who had headed the Communist Youth Federation in the mid-1920s) until his 1972 retirement in favor of Enrico Berlinguer. The Comintern matrix of Togliatti and Longo is important because both men were Marxist-Leninists in the early Bolshevik tradition, yet both had also experienced firsthand Stalin's use of divide-and-conquer machinations to control foreign communist parties, their own above all. They were therefore determined to preserve the cohesion of the PCI's leadership even if that meant forbearance toward internal party dissent. They viewed such cohesion as essential to the pursuit of their fundamental policy choice of a democratic path to socialism in Italy.

This ambiguous Comintern matrix of the Togliatti-Longo leadership contrasted sharply with the wartime matrix of the party's rank and file. The one and a half million Italians who joined the PCI between late 1943 and early 1946 were sentimentally pro-Soviet and pro-Stalin even though, in practice, they were called on to build an electoral machine geared to a constitutional, democratic system. As the Cold War escalated, moreover, the dual creed of pro-Sovietism and anti-Americanism couched in Marxist-Leninist rhetoric became the party's public philosophy.

The character of the postwar PCI base helps explain the party's development over the next four decades. Because of its reflexive pro-Sovietism, Togliatti's tentative departures from CPSU orthodoxy under the rubric of "polycentrism" in 1956 were premature. Only in the 1960s could the Togliatti-Longo leadership begin to take autonomous positions within the Moscow-centered international communist movement. By then the emergence of a younger generation of Italian militants who were not imbued with the wartime image of Soviet heroism, coupled with the Sino-Soviet split and the challenge posed by successive center-left coalition governments in Italy, favored such an initiative. The Soviet-led invasion of Czechoslovakia along with the repressiveness and foreign adventurism of the Brezhnev regime fueled the process, as did the transfer of authority from Longo to Berlinguer in 1972. The Solidarity crisis of 1980–81 and the ultimate declaration of martial law in Poland finally prompted Berlinguer to declare that the October Revolution had "exhausted its propulsive force" and to reject the very idea of an international communist movement separate and distinct from other left-wing forces. The result was the brief but intense polemical *strappo* (breach) in Soviet-PCI relations in 1982.

All the while, the postwar mass communist party observed the democratic rules of the game within Italy, and its share of the votes in national elections gradually grew from 18.9 percent in 1946 to 27.2 percent in 1972 and then jumped to 34.4 percent in 1976. This seven-point electoral leap forward was not, however, followed by a political breakthrough into the national government, the PCI's goal of a "historic compromise" notwithstanding. Although the communists participated widely in municipal, provincial, and regional councils and took part briefly in a parliamentary majority in the late 1970s, they were not offered cabinet posts in a coalition government at the national level.

Thereafter the PCI's strength declined to about 30 percent in the parliamentary elections of 1979 and 1983. Communist losses were also registered in regional and local contests. Only in the 1984 elections to the European Parliament was this trend reversed. Winning 33.3 percent of the vote, the PCI slightly surpassed the Christian Democrats for the first time. But this turned out to be a sympathy vote for Berlinguer, who had died of a stroke just days earlier.

Leadership and Organization. In the June 1987 parliamentary elections the PCI suffered what Natta, Berlinguer's successor, called a "serious defeat" (*L'Unità*, 26 June). In the vote for the Chamber of Deputies, the communists won only 26.6 percent, down from 29.9 percent in 1983 (*L'Unità*, 17 June). It was the party's worse showing since the 1960s. The impact of this electoral decline was felt in all areas of PCI activity.

First off, the defeat at the polls prompted Natta to propose Occhetto as deputy general secretary of the PCI, a position that had been vacant since 1972 when Berlinguer was promoted to general secretary after serving for three years as Longo's deputy.

Natta nominated Occhetto as his presumptive successor with almost no advance warning or consultation at a meeting of the 39-member Directorate the morning of 25 June (*La Repubblica*, 28–29 June). After a "lengthy" debate, "27 Directorate members voted for the proposal and 11 against, while Occhetto himself naturally abstained" (*L'Unità*, 26 June). Thereafter the nomination of Occhetto was debated at a three-day session of the Central Committee (CC), and the Central Control Commission (CCC) convened 25–27 June to discuss the parliamentary election results. When it came time to vote, 257 of 276 members were present, of whom 194 voted in favor of Occhetto, 41 voted against him, and 22 abstained (*L'Unità*, 28 June). (The arguments for and against the motion will be treated in the next section.)

Since the Sixteenth PCI Congress in 1983, party procedures had called for public disclosure of CC-CCC debates and votes. What was striking about the June plenum was, therefore, not the openness of the proceedings but the divisiveness of the vote. Even during the heyday of the Soviet-PCI *strappo*, less than 5 percent of the CC-CCC opposed or abstained from the Berlinguer position (*La Repubblica*, 27 November 1982). Natta was elected to succeed the late Berlinguer by a vote of 227 yeas and eleven abstentions (*L'Unità* 27 June 1984). At the Seventeenth PCI Congress in April 1986, the only divisive issue had to do with civilian nuclear energy usage (a reflection of the growing intensity of environmental concerns among PCI members and supporters). An amendment to defeat the party leadership's qualified support for new nuclear plant construction lost by a narrow margin of only seventeen votes, 457 to 440. (*L'Unità*, 14 April 1986.)

At the June 1987 plenum, Directorate member Emanuele Macaluso justified his vote against Occhetto with reference to the many important issues on which the Directorate or Secretariat had been divided in the past ((*L'Unità*, 28 June). However valid his point, it was nonetheless unprecedented for a personnel choice of such magnitude to be debated and sharply contested in the public eye.

Some participants favored voting on the nomination of Occhetto by secret ballot. This was proposed by Salvatore Cacciapuoti, secretary of the CCC, the first day of the plenum and reiterated by Paolo Spriano the final evening, 27 June. Spriano argued that use of the secret ballot might stimulate "freer discussion at all levels of the party." But others felt no need to vote in secret since so many persons (104) had already expressed their opinions during the plenum debate. Natta objected, moreover, that the secret ballot had not hitherto been used in similar circumstances and that this was a question on which the CC-CCC should adopt appropriate procedures. An open vote was thus taken. (*L'Unità*, 29 June.)

At the end of July a second plenum was held to assess the party's postelection debate (which will be discussed below) and to make adjustments in the PCI's organizational structure. The Secretariat was reduced from nine members to seven to make it a more effective administrative and coordinating body. In addition, a new ten-member Program Office (composed entirely of Directorate members) was established with the specific task of preparing for a National Program Conference to clarify the party's policy options. Of the five persons removed from the Secretariat as constituted after the 1986 congress, four were elected to the new Program Office: Alfredo Reichlin (62), who was named coordinator of the body, Giorgio Napolitano (61), Aldo Tortorella (61), and Giuseppe Chiarante (58). The six others elected to the Program Office were Natta, Occhetto, Antonio Bassolino (40), Renato Zangheri (62), Ugo Pecchioli (62), and Gianni Cervetti (54). Finally, Gian Carlo Pajetta replaced Paolo Bufalini as president of the CCC, and Bufalini was reconfirmed as a member of the Directorate with primary responsibility in the International Affairs Commission headed by Napolitano. (*L'Unità*, 30 July.)

The increasing openness of the PCI's decision-making process was accompanied by the leadership's quest for more information about the views of the party's middle-echelon cadres. To this end, the findings from a poll of delegates to the Seventeenth PCI Congress were published in January. (About 60 percent of the 1,091 delegates responded to the questionnaire distributed on the floor of the congress.) The gist of the answers suggested that the party was becoming ideologically "laicized," a term used by Directorate member Gavio Angius when he presented the data at a press conference 14 January. For example, only 7 percent said they joined the party because it represented the working class. More than 82 percent did not consider it realistic to pursue the classic communist objective of the "abolition of private ownership of the means of production" in Italy. Almost 54 percent said that no country had achieved a just society, whereas only 13.1 percent felt the Soviet Union had done so. And 54 percent also considered the capitalist and socialist countries to be "both, equally" in a systemic crisis, whereas only 24.6 percent thought that capitalism faced a greater crisis than socialism. (*L'Unità*, 15 January; *JPRS*, 14 May.)

This tone of ideological laicization had pervaded Natta's 1986 congress report, in which he did not once refer to Marx or Lenin and rarely spoke of the "working-class" character of the PCI. Instead he emphasized the party's alignment with "reformist forces" at home and with "the European left" in general. (*L'Unità*, 10 April 1986.)

In response to such ideological secularization, pro-Soviet CC member, Armando Cossutta (who had lost his position on the Directorate at the 1986 congress), founded an Association for the Study of Marxism in February (*NYT*, 15 February). In November the first issue of a bimonthly journal, *Marxism Today*, appeared under Cossutta's sponsorship with the goal of reviving the "Marxist scientific and cultural patrimony" in Italy (*L'Unità*, 15 November).

Meanwhile, the PCI's membership declined from 1,551,000 in late 1986 to 1,505,000 at the end of the annual recruitment drive on 26 November (supplement to *L'Unità*, 13 December). This represented a continuation of the downward slide that had begun after 1977, when membership reached a high of 1,814,000. In early December organizational secretary Massimo D'Alema proposed to reverse this trend by enacting several party reforms, including a reinvigoration of the 13,000 local sections by "simplifying and reducing" their number and by the introduction of a three-year membership term. He also proposed changes in the method of leadership selection at the federation and national levels, including the use of the secret ballot and the creation of autonomous nominating committees. These suggestions were slated for deliberation at the next CC-CCC plenum. (*L'Unità*, 4 December.)

Domestic Affairs and Party Debates. If the PCI was the big loser in the June parliamentary elections, the small lay parties of PSI leader Bettino Craxi's outgoing five-party coalition also suffered losses. Although the PCI's share of the vote for the lower house declined by 3.3 percentage points, with a loss of 21 seats, the combined showing of the Republican, Social Democratic, and Liberal parties was also 3.3 percent lower than it had been in the 1983 elections, resulting in a loss of 19 seats among them. On the other hand, notable gains were registered by all three of the PCI's main rivals: the Christian Democrats (DC), the PSI, and the new radical environmentalist group, the Greens. The DC, with 34.3 percent of the vote for the Chamber of Deputies, improved its showing over 1983 by only 1.4 percent, but this at least reversed its 1979-1983 downward slide of 5.4 percent. The PCI, in contrast, won just 14.3 percent of the votes cast, but this translated into a rise of 2.9 percentage points and 21 seats with respect to 1983. And the Greens won 2.5 percent of the Chamber vote and thirteen seats, proving themselves an equal competitor with the small centrist lay parties in their first parliamentary race. (*Corriere dell sera*, 17 June.) Preliminary analysis suggests that the PSI gained at the expense of the Republicans and Social Democrats, while the Greens gained at the expense of the communists, among whom sensitivity to environmental issues had already shown up dramatically at the 1986 PCI congress in the confrontation over civilian nuclear energy usage.

For the rest of the year the PCI was preoccupied with getting its own political house in order. The opposition to Natta's nomination of Occhetto as his deputy at the June plenum was triggered mainly by doubts about the correctness of the party's program and activity as elaborated since the 1986 congress in Florence. This uncertainty dominated the debates both in June and at the second CC-CCC session 28–29 July.

The discussion at the June plenum was punctuated with assertions that what was at stake was not the designation of Occhetto as deputy general secretary but the assessment of the party line. As the widely respected Bufalini put it, he voted no to the election of Occhetto not because of any lack of esteem or even political differences but because "the measure proposed today is entirely inadequate and out of place: it ought to be examined in the context of the conclusions of the political debate under way" (*L'Unità*, 29 June).

As for the substance of that political debate, three general tendencies surfaced that may be roughly labeled leftist, centrist, and liberal. The left blamed the election results on the reformist moderation of the 1986 congress. Lucio Magri, for example, deplored the weakening of the party's identity as a "communist force" with its own "particular theoretical and organizational tradition," and he urged a "higher and richer phase of social struggle." The center, in contrast, defended the party line adopted at the congress and ascribed the electoral drop to errors in its practical implementation. Its spokesmen often alluded to the need to win more support among Catholic democratic forces.

As for the liberal group, it also backed the Florence congress but tended to be skeptical about the extent to which the party base fully understood or accepted it. According to Directorate member Roberto Speciale, "It has often been a question of passive resistance in the body of the party rather than true and proper dissent." This group was likewise concerned with procedural matters. Gerardo Chiaromonte, editor of *L'Unità*, not only called for more open debates but also explicitly endorsed decisionmaking by majority vote, enjoining the party not to fear majority-minority divisions on specific questions. The procedural concerns of the liberal wing were often cited as the reason why many of its members voted against Occhetto. (*L'Unità*, 28 June.) These divisions were somewhat muted at the late July plenum when the centrist and liberal wings of the party coalesced into a new majority.

Natta stressed in his introductory report that the PCI's political profile, or "image," had become "blurred" in the public mind as a result of the changes in its ideological and international posture over the past decade. Because of this, he called on the party to work out an explicit "program and plaform for the renewal of society" that would clearly convey to Italian voters what the PCI meant by a "democratic alternative." (*L'Unità*, 29 July.)

The most notable response to Natta's speech came from the left. Bitter protests were voiced by ex-*Manifesto* leader Luciana Castellina, Directorate member Pietro Ingrao, and Cossutta. All three opposed the moderate reformism of Natta's current recommendations as well as of the 1986 congress, calling instead for the radical transformation of Italian society. Castellina blamed the party's electoral defeat on its failure to resolve "the great contradiction between minimalist reformism and reformism of the great transformations." Ingrao, evoking the long-discarded slogan of a *terza via*, insisted on "the necessity of constructing paths to structural transformations" and lamented the failure at the Florence congress to confront openly the "differences in analysis and line existing among us." (*L'Unità*, 29 July.) Cossutta declared that one question above all dominated the party's work: whether or not the PCI could or should devise a policy "that impinges on the very structures of this society and works for its change." And he deplored that this was no longer simply a rhetorical question. (*L'Unità*, 30 July.)

For the most part, the more prominent figures of the centrist and liberal wings of the party declined to speak at the July plenum, in contrast to the previous month. An exception was Giorgio Napolitano, chief spokesman of the liberal current and earlier opponent of Natta on the Occhetto issue. After commenting on the time, care, and reflection still needed to work out a concrete program capable of mobilizing broad support for a "reformist alternative," he suggested withdrawing a draft resolution on that theme that the Directorate had presented at the start of the plenum. (Ibid.)

In his brief closing speech, Natta rebutted the views of Castellina, Ingrao, and Cossutta, explaining that he considered "correct the results that we laboriously achieved in Florence" regarding the strategy of building "an alternative signifying a change in government policies and in the country's leadership groups" through "unity on the left." He then withdrew the draft resolution to which Napolitano had objected and asked that the plenum simply approve the guidelines set forth in his opening report, including the reorganization of the central party leadership. The plenum readily approved his report, with only nine votes against it and six abstentions. The negative votes came largely from the left, the abstentions from the most extreme liberals. The changes in the leadership organs described in the preceding section were then proposed by Natta and endorsed by unanimous or near-unanimous votes. (Ibid.)

While the PCI underwent its postelection self-analysis, the members of the five-party coalition that had governed Italy since 1983 searched for common ground on which to form a new cabinet. The June elections had been called a year ahead of schedule because of bickering between the two main coalition partners, the PSI and the DC. Late in the winter Craxi had refused to abide by an agreement he made in August 1986 to turn over the post of premier to a Christian Democrat for the last year of the regular parliamentary term. Instead he resigned, complaining of an "ultimatum" from the DC and asserting that "the political atmosphere" within the coalition had become "unbreathable and noxious for all." (*LAT*, 4 March.) At one point during the eight-week crisis that followed, Nilde Iotti, the communist leader of the Chamber of Deputies and Togliatti's long-time companion, was asked to mediate among the feuding coalition partners, to no avail (*WP*, 28 March). Finally, on 28 April President Francesco Cossiga dissolved Parliament and ordered general elections for 14 June, amid ongoing recriminations among the former alliance partners (*NYT*, 29 April). During the summer, with a total gain of only eleven seats in the lower house and none of its earlier differences resolved, the five-party coalition was reconstituted under the premiership of Giovanni Goria, a 44-year-old Christian Democrat (*WP*, 6 August). The instability of the new government became evident when it nearly collapsed after fifteen weeks because of budgetary disagreements between Goria and the small conservative Liberal Party (*NYT*, 15 November; *LAT*, 19 November).

Against this backdrop of ongoing intracabinet skirmishes, Occhetto delivered his first report as Natta's deputy before a CC-CCC plenum that met 26–28 November. His main topic was "the crisis of the Italian political system," which he defined as a situation of permanent jockeying for power within successive coalition cabinets at the expense of governing in the national interest. And he enjoined the the PCI to concentrate not on "polemics between the communists and socialists" but on the resolution of this crisis. (*L'Unità*, 27 November.)

Occhetto spoke of the "exhaustion" of a long historical phase during which political renewal had been expected to result from the "gradual and progressive broadening of the bases of the democratic State, to be pursued through successive governing formulas (centrism, opening to the left, centerleft, national solidarity)." This expectation, which was shared by Togliatti and Berlinguer, turned out to be unfounded by the late 1970s. At that time it became clear that political programs must take precedence over party alignments. It was to the credit of the PSI, said Occhetto, to have been the first to perceive this institutional crisis even though the socialists now seemed more interested in using it to further their party interests than in resolving it. (Ibid.)

Henceforth, declared Occhetto, the PCI must take a programmatic stand in favor of "reform of the State and of the political system." Such institutional reforms might include a constructive vote of no confidence as well as a revision of the electoral law (all the while safeguarding proportional principles). But whatever the specific content, a programmatic agreement must form the basis of party alliances, of an "alternative" to the governing five-party coalition, and not the other way around. (*L'Unità*, 27 November.)

Toward the end of his report, Occhetto made several conciliatory gestures toward the PCI's left wing, speaking of the need for "structural transformations" of Italian society that would go beyond "the old Keynesian compromise" and rejecting "acritical ruptures" with communist tradition even though certain discontinuities were necessary. He also reassured both leftist and liberal dissenters that they were free to express their opinions "even after different choices have been made." Indeed, the PCI should be "not the party of the majority but of all its components" despite the fact that votes should be taken on specific issues when there are sharp divergences. (Ibid.)

Occhetto's report was well received by the plenum participants. On a declaration approving its basic guidelines, there were only five negative votes and nine abstentions. Like the July plenum, the opposition came from the left—from Ingrao, Magri, Castellina, Cossutta, and Francesco Mandarini (*L'Unità*, 29 November), and the abstentions included a mixture of leftists and extreme liberals (*La Repubblica*, 29–30 November). At the same time, prominent members of the liberal wing who had opposed Occhetto's election as Natta's deputy now expressed warm support for him and the policies he set forth. Bufalini described the plenum's atmosphere as "calming and unifying," while former trade union leader Luciano Lama said he voted in favor of the declaration because he agreed with "the fundamental lines of the report" and thus wanted "to encourage Occhetto" (*L'Unità*, 29 November). In a concluding step, unanimous consent was given to a motion by one of the abstaining liberals, Napoleone Colajanni, to set up a committee to look into ways of giving publicity to the deliberations of the party Directorate (ibid.).

Occhetto's initiatives at the November plenum had a certain resonance on the wider Italian political scene. The PCI's strong stand in favor of institutional reform prompted Craxi, long a standard-bearer of this idea, to initiate a series of top-level interparty consultations on the subject. After a rare personal meeting with DC head Ciriaco De Mita, the PSI invited Natta for similar talks (*La Repubblica*, 16 December). Natta, accompanied by Occhetto, met with Craxi for several hours on 16 December at PSI headquarters, the first time in years (just how many neither Natta nor Craxi could quite recall) that the secretaries of the two parties had held talks of such a formal and wide-ranging nature. Although no agreement on specific institutional reforms was reached, both Occhetto and Craxi appraised the meeting in positive terms, conveying the impression that a period of "closer collaboration between the PCI and the PSI" had begun. (*La Repubblica*, 17 December.) The next day, during the course of a two-page interview with *La Repubblica*, Craxi remarked that "the Italian communists are not made of the same stuff as the French or Portuguese, they don't have hardening of the arteries . . . If their evolution continues, at a certain moment we will find them on our road, there will be a meeting sooner or later" (*La Repubblica*, 18 December).

Natta's meeting with Craxi was preceded by a collapse during the first week of December of the five-party centrist junta that had governed the city of Milan since 1985. The PSI mayor, Paolo Pillitteri, immediately put together a new majority comprising the PSI, PCI, Greens, and Social Democratic Party. (*La Repubblica*, 11 December.) Throughout the rest of the month, however, he was thwarted in winning the communal council's approval for his proposed "red-green" junta by procedural obstructionism on the party of the DC and covert opposition from within the ranks of the new majority itself (*La Repubblica*, 23, 24, 29 December).

All the same, as the year drew to a close there were signs that the PCI's political isolation was lessening somewhat, notwithstanding (or perhaps because of) the party's electoral decline in June and subsequent organizational and programmatic reassessment.

International Views and Contacts. The PCI devoted less attention to foreign affairs in 1987 than had usually been the case in recent years. The preelection campaign was oriented primarily to domestic matters, and during the three postelection plenums little reference was made to international issues.

Party spokesmen nevertheless frequently reaffirmed that the PCI was "an integral part of the European left." (The adoption of this position represented the party's major foreign policy initiative at the 1986 congress.) To underscore the PCI's identity as part of the broader West European left, Natta made a trip to East Germany, Finland, and Sweden (11–17 February), meeting with both socialist and communist leaders in the two Scandinavian countries. At a news conference in Stockholm, Natta described his talks with Swedish prime minister Ingvar Carlsson as so harmonious that Italian journalists accompanying him tried to find out with whom Natta was in greater agreement, the Social Democratic prime minister or the Swedish communists (*Svenska Dagbladet*, 17 February; *FBIS*, 19 February).

During the first half of October, Natta undertook a similar visit to Portugal and Spain. In Portugal, where he met with Socialist president Mario Soares and communist leader Alvaro Cunhal, he spoke publicly of his differences with Cunhal over European integration and the reform program of Mikhail Gorbachev (*La Repubblica*, 9 October). In Spain, where he met with Socialist prime minister Felipe Gonzalez and communist leader Gerardo Iglesias, Natta commented that the Spanish communists' position on the European Community was much closer to the PCI's view than that of the Portuguese communists (ANSA, 13 October; *FBIS*, 15 October).

The only concrete change in the nature of PCI contacts with the noncommunist leftist parties in Europe, however, involved the Italian Communist Youth Federation (FGCI). In early autumn the FGCI joined the Socialist Youth International in a consultative capacity, all the while remaining a member of the Soviet-sponsored World Federation of Democratic Youth (WFDY). Objections to this step by Cossutta as well as by the PSI youth group were rebutted by FGCI leader Pietro Folena on the grounds that the Italian communist youth could work within the WFDY "in order to change it," while "the young European socialists have moved very much to the left recently. Antonio Gramsci is one of the most cited authors at their meetings." The PCI leadership endorsed the FGCI's action but insisted that the party itself reject affiliation with any international organization. (*La Repubblica*, 9 October.) Natta reiterated this position during an interview concerning his trip to Portugal and Spain (*L'Unità*, 18 October).

Meanwhile, there was no notable change from 1986 in relations with the CPSU. The PCI's praise for Gorbachev's reform program was combined with critical detachment in assessing its prospects for implementation and unabashed pride in the fact that Gorbachev's criticisms of the Soviet system vindicated those made earlier by the Italian communists. In January Occhetto touched on these points in press interviews after his return from a private vacation in Moscow during which he met informally with Gorbachev and Egor Ligachev. Occhetto maintained that Berlinguer's "analysis of the exhaustion of the propulsive thrust [of the October Revolution] was so accurate that the new leadership group itself spoke recently of a profound stagnation of the Soviet system." He also noted the existence of an internal political struggle in the Soviet Union on the part of "sectors which, on the basis of privileges secured in the past, are now resisting the internal reform for fear of losing these privileges." The presence of such a struggle "is now being discussed openly," he added. But above all, he praised Gorbachev's new course, declaring that he was "among those who hope that the plan will succeed and that it will embrace not only the economy but also the more general field of political freedoms, involving the East European countries too." (*L'Unità*, 8 January; *FBIS*, 13 January.) With specific regard to the Soviet leader's late January report to the CPSU Central Committee, Occhetto commented, "It seems important to me that Gorbachev has said (for the first time, unless I am mistaken) that liberal acts from the top are no longer enough and that it is necessary to address the issue of 'objective guarantees'" (*L'Unità*, 28 January; *JPRS*, 3 March).

These themes were elaborated on in a series of 21 articles on the Soviet reform movement and its impact on Eastern Europe that appeared in the PCI weekly, *Rinascita*, from November 1986 through the end of April. The discussion opened with five introductory pieces by the Czechoslovak exile and 1968 activist Zdenek Mlynar and included contributions from Western experts, other East European dissidents, and the PCI's East European specialist, Adriano Guerra. Assessments of the prospects for democratization in the USSR ranged from guarded optimism to outspoken skepticism. In late May the entire series was published in a 176-page paperback, *Il Progetto Gorbaciov*, which was distributed free to *Rinascita* readers. Napolitano, in a speech celebrating the volume's publication, reaffirmed the PCI's support for the 1968 Prague Spring and pledged his party's commitment to ending the practice of branding the 1968 Czechoslovak reformers as criminals and ideological deviationists. (Kevin Devlin, *RFE Research*, 30 April, 21 May, 16 June.)

The pattern of praise for Gorbachev's planned reforms combined with skepticism and/or criticism regarding their implementation continued throughout the year. A key PCI spokesman in this respect was *L'Unità*'s Moscow correspondent, Giulietto Chiesa, whose ties with dissident Soviet intellectuals were underscored by his publication in April of a book of conversations with Roy Medvedev entitled *L'URSS che cambia*. Chiesa welcomed the June plenum of the CPSU, at which a detailed package of economic reforms was approved, as "a victory for the reformist line of Gorbachev" (*L'Unità*, 28 June). Yet he then proceeded to write extensive accounts of attacks against Gorbachev's program by his conservative enemies (*L'Unità*, 24, 26 July). In a similar vein, despite his reservations on certain points, Chiesa called Gorbachev's 2 November speech celebrating the 70th anniversary of the Bolshevik Revolution a "long step forward on a new road" (*L'Unità*, 3 November). Yet for the next several weeks his stories from Moscow focused almost exclusively on the fate of deposed Politburo member Boris Yeltsin, whose life Chiesa reported to be in danger in one dispatch (*L'Unità*, 16 November).

As in previous years, the idea of an international communist conference once again became a bone of contention in direct Soviet-PCI interactions. The PCI's positive appraisals of Gorbachev's January reform initiatives notwithstanding, Napolitano asserted that his party would "not return to any kind of special relationship with the CPSU and the other ruling communist parties" (*Corriere della Sera*, 1 February). When Romanian president Nicolae Ceauşescu proposed an international gathering of communist parties, Antonio Rubbi, Napolitano's deputy in the party's International Affairs Commission, ruled out such a meeting as "not only untimely but clearly inadequate" (ANSA, 16 May; *FBIS*, 18 May). Yet Gorbachev persisted in championing the idea in a lengthy interview with the editors of *L'Unità* in late May. In a written reply to one question, he said, "Frankly speaking, I do not understand the circumspection that exists in some parts of our movement toward proposals for multilateral meetings of the world's communists . . . It is necessary to deal with this question without prejudices, to dispense with fears and old stereotypes." *L'Unità* editor Chiaromonte, in a story covering the interview, retorted that there was no dearth of disagreements, "as on the idea of an informal meeting among communist parties." (*L'Unità*, 20 May.)

In a more informal question-and-answer conversation with the *L'Unità* editors, however, Gorbachev suggested a gathering of "not only communists but also representatives of other parties" during the forthcoming 70th anniversary festivities of the October Revolution. In reply, Chiaromonte specified that such a meeting should include socialists and social democrats, and Gorbachev agreed. (Ibid.) This was the kind of international meeting that the PCI had urged for at least a decade.

On November 3, during the formal celebrations in Moscow of the 70th anniversary of the October Revolution, Natta's speech recalled Togliatti's conviction that nuclear weapons posed a threat to all humanity, reaffirmed Berlinguer's assertion made ten years earlier in Moscow regarding the "universal value" of democracy, and declared that efforts to recreate "a closed international communist movement" would be anachronistic. Natta hailed the October Revolution as "one of the decisive events of our century" but went on to say that, "as you have recognized, a new transformation has become indispensable today" in order "to revive the ideals of the October Revolution." (*L'Unità*, 4 November.) Afterward the Italian delegation had a brief but "friendly and very cordial" meeting with Gorbachev (*L'Unità*, 5 November). Natta's speech was carried in full over Moscow TV (Moscow Television Service in Russian, 3 November; *FBIS*, 4 November).

An informal international forum of foreign delegations was then held 4–5 November in which 180 parties and movements participated. According to Napolitano (who represented the PCI at these proceedings), of the 65 speeches, 20 were given by delegates from the "noncommunist Western left." (*L'Unità*, 7 November.) The PSI took part in the festivities for the first time in more than twenty years (Rome International Service, 1 November; *FBIS*, 2 November).

The cordial tone of Soviet-PCI contacts in early November soon gave way to public recriminations over *L'Unità*'s coverage of the dismissal of Yeltsin as head of the Moscow party organization. Chiesa sent a series of dispatches detailing the reactions, both negative and positive, of the Soviet public as well as the rumored ill health of Yeltsin (*L'Unità*, 13, 14, 16, 17 November). Finally, on 19 November Soviet foreign ministry spokesman Gennadi Gerasimov announced that Yeltsin was fine and attacked *L'Unità* for reporting that he was dying, deploring the fact that "such information was transmitted back to the Soviet Union by the Voice of America." The editorial board of *L'Unità* retorted that it didn't know, or care, what the Voice of America reported, but that the Soviet government had let eight days elapse before giving any official information on the state of Yeltsin's health and that during that time *L'Unità* was obliged to report whatever information was available. (*L'Unità*, 20 November.) Two days later CCC president Pajetta wrote a stinging rebuttal as well, saying inter alia, "Dear Comrade Gerasimov, if we haven't seen clearly, it is because you haven't turned on the light for us, it is because on this occasion there wasn't enough *glasnost*'" (*L'Unità*, 22 November).

This was apparently a passing episode, for at the end of December Rubbi announced that Natta and Gorbachev would hold a formal bilateral meeting in early 1988 (their first since January 1986) (*La Repubblica*, 27–28 December).

During the year the PCI's contacts with other communist parties included "a lengthy and cordial conversation" between Natta and Polish leader Wojciech Jaruzelski while the latter was on a state visit to Italy (*L'Unità*, 15 January). A regularly scheduled annual meeting between Natta and top-ranking Yugoslav leaders took place in Rome in May, after which Natta reported that the PCI and the League of Yugoslav Communists were developing "exceptionally close and cordial relations" (Tanjug, 14 May; *FBIS*, 20 May). Nilde Iotti met with Deng Xiaoping on August 29 while on vacation in the People's Republic of China (Xinhua, 29 August; *FBIS*, 31 August). Piero Fassino of the Secretariat and Cristina Cecchini of the Central Committee represented the party at the French communists' Twenty-sixth Congress (*L'Unità*, 2 December).

Before the government crisis and national elections, there was also some talk in the Italian press of plans for Natta to visit the United States. Rubbi, who was in Washington early in the year with a delegation of the Interparliamentary Union, said that he had tried to "lay a new brick in the structure of the delicate relations between the American political world and the PCI." (Kevin Devlin, *RFE Research*, 6 March.) The elections and their aftermath put an end to such speculation.

On a broader foreign policy note, PCI leaders were unstinting in their praise of the Reagan-Gorbachev summit and the signing of the INF treaty. Before the summit, *L'Unità* ran a full-page photograph of the two leaders shaking hands, accompanied by the pithy caption, "true power is peace" (*L'Unità*, 7 December). Editorial reactions were effusive (*L'Unità*, 9–10 December). To be sure, primary credit for the event was accorded to Gorbachev. As Chiaromonte put it, "In truth, what is happening in the capital of the USA is the first, concrete, most important sign of that 'new way of thinking' about international problems and the future of humanity on which the general secretary of the CPSU has been insisting for some time" (*L'Unità*, 10 December). On the other hand, Napolitano no longer viewed the U.S. Strategic Defense Initiative as an insurmountable obstacle to an agreement on strategic arms. As for conventional forces in Europe, he reiterated the PCI's support for reaching "an equilibrium at the lowest level" between NATO and the Warsaw Pact. (*La Repubblica*, 10 December.)

Biography. *Achille Occhetto.* Occhetto was born in Turin on 3 March 1936, the son of an "editorial director." He attended university in Milan, where he joined the FGCI in 1953 and was also active in the Italian Goliardic Union, an organization of lay, leftist university students. Immersed in politics, he gave up his philosophy studies and entered the National Secretariat of the FGCI in October 1960.

In October 1962 Occhetto was elected head of the FGCI, defeating by a narrow margin Luciano Guerzoni (currently a Directorate member and president of the Emilia-Romagna region). By virtue of his new position, he also entered the party Central Committee and Directorate. As FGCI leader, he was militant and eclectic, referring in an oration at Togliatti's funeral to "the people who salute you with clenched fist, who salute you also with the sign of the cross."

He left the FGCI in 1966 to become head of the PCI's central section for press and propaganda. After drawing criticism from Giorgio Amendola, he became a party functionary in Sicily for eight years. He returned to work in the PCI's headquarters only in 1977. At the 1983 party congress he reentered the Secretariat and once again became responsible for press and propaganda.

Occhetto figured prominently in the organization of the 1986 PCI congress in Florence. He headed the "committee of 77" that drafted the congress theses and also presided over the political commission at the congress. He was named coordinator of the Secretariat as constituted after the congress. (*L'Unità*, 28 June.) Occhetto was elected deputy general secretary of the PCI on June 27.

Joan Barth Urban
Catholic University of America

Luxembourg

Population. 366,127
Party. Communist Party of Luxembourg (Parti communiste Luxembourgeois; CPL)
Founded. 1921
Membership. More than 600
Chairman. René Urbany
Executive Committee. 10 members: Aloyse Bisdorff, François Hoffmann, Fernand Hübsch, Marianne Passeri, Marcel Putz, René Urbany, Jean Wesquet, Serge Urbany, André Moes, Babette Ruckert
Secretariat. 1 member: René Urbany
Central Committee. 31 full and 7 candidates members
Status. Legal
Last Congress. Twenty-fourth, 4–5 February 1984
Last Election. 1984, 4.9 percent, 2 of 64 seats
Auxiliary Organizations. Jeunesse communiste Luxembourgeoise; Union des femmes Luxembourgeoises
Publication. *Zeitung vum Lëtzeburger Vollek* (Newspaper of the Luxembourgian People), daily, 1,000–2,000 copies (CPL claims up to 20,000)

Because of the country's size, which barely equals the area of Rhode Island, and because the government is a constitutional monarchy, the pro-Soviet CPL plays no significant role in the European communist movement and only a minor domestic political role. In federal and municipal elections alike, the communist vote has continued to decline since 1968.

Leadership and Organization. The CPL seems to be a family operation, with the political as well as the theoretical leadership of this still-active party dominated by the Urbany family. The secretary's father, Dominique Urbany, was one of the party's founders and led it until 1977. He remained in the CPL as honorary chairman until his death in October 1986 (*Neues Deutschland*, 27 October). Most key positions within the party and its auxiliaries are occupied by members of the same family. René Urbany also serves as director of the party press, which is heavily subsidized by the Society for the Development of the Press and Printing Industry, an organization founded by the Socialist Unity Party of Germany (SED; the East German communist party). The CPL's publishing company, COPE, not only prints and distributes the French edition of the *World Marxist Review* but also serves other communist parties abroad. Since 1976 René Urbany has held a communist seat in the Luxembourg parliament.

Domestic Affairs. The major event of 1987 for the CPL was winning a court victory when the lawsuit against its party newspaper was dismissed (*WMR*, April). The charges against *Zeitung vum Lëtzeburger Vollek* were brought by two Belgians, former Minister of Defense Jose Desmartes and retired General Robert Close, due to the paper's reporting on the 1986 Luxembourg conference of the World Anti-Communist League (WACL). According to the *World Marxist Review* (March), the newspaper published strictly documented evidence "exposing the fascist and racist character of this international organization active in the crusade against communism." Even the newspaper's charge that the WACL was behind the assassinations of Olof Palme and Indira Gandhi was rejected by the court, and it was cleared on all counts.

In late 1986 the CPL released a brief statement denying reports that it intended to form a coalition with Jean Huss's Greens alternative party at forthcoming communal elections. The party successfully organized its annual press fest in September in Luxembourg and invited several entertainers from East Germany (ADN, 12 September). The principal speaker was René Urbany.

International Affairs. Internationally the party's activities in 1987 were dominated by René Urbany's 60th birthday. On 7 February *Pravda* published a birthday message to Comrade René Urbany and reported his being awarded the Order of the October Revolution on behalf of the Supreme Soviet Presidium. The State Council of Bulgaria awarded him the Order of the People's Republic of Bulgaria, First Class (BTA, 7 February), and the Central Committee of the SED honored him with the Great Star of Friendship Among Peoples (ADN, 7–8 February). In addition several birthday messages were published on the front pages of party newspapers.

In February and March René Urbany represented his party at the congress of the Swiss Labor Party. In April he traveled to Moscow and was warmly received by Mikhail Gorbachev in the Kremlin, where Andrei A. Gromyko presented him with the order.

To maintain international contacts, René Urbany visited the *World Marxist Review* offices in Prague in June to discuss further ways of enhancing the cooperation between the two institutions. On 29 July he had a friendly meeting with Hermann Axen, secretary of the SED Central Committee in East Berlin (ADN, 29 July).

Besides these CPL activities there were several indications of intense contacts between Luxembourgian union members and SED officials in East Berlin and Magdeburg (ADN, 19–20 September).

Kurt R. Leube
California State University at Hayward

Malta

Population. 344,479 (Malta Central Office of Statistics, September)
Party. Communist Party of Malta (Partit Komunista Malti; CPM)
Founded. 1969
Membership. 300 (estimated)
General Secretary. Anthony Vassallo (63)
Central Committee. 12 members: Anthony Baldacchino (president; 49), Lino Vella (vice president), Anthony Vassallo, Victor Degiovanni (second secretary; 35), Karmenu Gerada (international secretary; 47), Mario Mifsud (propaganda secretary; 35), Lawrence Attard Bezzina (financial secretary; 40), Michael Schembri (33), Paul Caruana (63), Joseph Borda (42), David Mallia (34).
Status. Legal
Last Congress. Extraordinary Congress, 18–25 May 1984
Last Election. 9 May 1987, 0.08 (1987); no rep.
Auxiliary Organizations. Peace and Solidarity Council of Malta, Malta-USSR Friendship and Cultural Society, Malta-Czechoslovakia Friendship Society, Malta-Cuba Friendship and Cultural Society, Malta-Poland Friendship Society, Malta-Korean Friendship and Cultural Society, Communist Youth League (Ghaqda Zghazagh Komunisti; CYL), Women for Peace, Association of Progressive Journalists
Publications. *Zminijietna* (Our Times), monthly tabloid, part in English and part in Maltese, Anthony Vassallo, editor; *International Political Revue*, monthly, Malta edition of *World Marxist Review*; *Bandiera Hamra* (Red Flag) issued by CYL; *Bridge of Friendship and Culture Malta-USSR*, quarterly journal of Malta-USSR Friendship and Cultural Society

The CPM contested its first general election on 9 May. The result was disastrous and is worth detailed analysis. Maltese elections are held under the system of proportional representation. There are thirteen electoral constituencies, and each party could field any number of candidates to contest one or two constituencies. The CPM fielded six candidates, each of whom contested two constituencies in Malta. The party showed no interest in the sister island of Gozo. Out of 246,292 eligible voters, 236,169 cast their votes (96.11 percent). The total number of votes cast for the CPM candidates was 119. Vassallo, the general secretary, won just 3 votes in one constituency and 10 in another. Propaganda Secretary Mifsud polled 1 vote in one constituency and 6 in another. (*Malta Government Gazette*, 15 May; *Report of Electoral Commission*, November.) The election result reduced the CPM to less than its real size because the elections were weighted against the small parties as a result of last-minute changes to the island's constitution.

Ever since the 1981 elections, the Malta political scene has been in turmoil because the Malta Labor Party had won a majority of seats in the island Parliament despite the fact that the Nationalist Party in Opposition had polled an absolute majority of votes. This result followed a gerrymandering exercise involving constituency borders. To avoid a similar situation, the constitution was amended so that if a party secured more than 50 percent of the votes cast in the 1987 elections, it would be entitled to an allocation of additional seats in Parliament if it does not win a majority of seats. As it happened, the Nationalist Party polled 51.91 percent of the total vote but won 31 seats against 34 won by the Malta Labor Party. This entitled the Nationalist Party to a bonus of four additional seats to form a majority in the House.

In the postelectoral inquest that followed, comrade Vassallo came in for tough criticism from anonymous writers in the noncommunist press, most of which consisted of allegations that the party was in the grip of one man who administered the funds and dictated the run of policy by himself. In July, the CPM monthly, *Zminijietna*, published a terse analysis of the election results. It claimed that government regulations did not permit public employees to contest the elections and alleged that this restricted the number of eligible CPM candidates. The article denounced the monopoly of the broadcasting media by the major parties and the undemocratic implications of the amendments to the constitution before the elections.

Although the election experience may have chastened the CPM general secretary, he continues to enjoy the support of Moscow and the Soviet embassy authorities in Malta. He was an honored guest on the occasion of the 70th anniversary of the October Revolution in Moscow during November (*Sunday Times*, Malta, 1 November) and is a distinguished guest at all the Soviet embassy functions in Malta. Earlier, Vassallo led a CPM delegation to the Soviet Union, which was a familiarization visit with special reference to *perestroika*. The delegation held discussions with Vadim Zagladin, deputy head of the International Department of the Central Comittee of the Communist Party of the USSR (*Zminijietna*, September).

The Soviet embassy came to the forefront with an intensive performance that has gained momentum since the change of government.

The first senior visitor to arrive from Moscow was Nikolai Atanasievsky, the head of the first European department at the Soviet Foreign Ministry, who had "a long and frank discussion" with Dr. Vincent Tabone, the new Maltese minister of Foreign Affairs. They "touched on a wide range of subjects concerning international European and Mediterranean affairs as well as problems of security and cooperation." Both sides surveyed the bilateral relations existing between them as well as future developments. (*Times*, Malta, 2 July.) News of the retirement of Soviet ambassador Victor Smirnov was broken on 24 July (*In-Nazzjon Taghna*). His successor, Nikolai Va Plechko, is a new generation, urbane, low-profile diplomat. Born in 1934, Plechko has been in the diplomatic service since 1958. He held a number of posts in the Soviet Foreign Ministry, rising to senior counselor of the department for planning foreign policy, a post he held between 1971 and 1978. During 1979 and 1980, Plechko was USSR consul general in New York. From 1980 to 1985, he was deputy permanent representative of the USSR at the U.N. (*Weekend Chronicle*, Malta, 19 September.)

When he presented his credentials, Plechko indicated his targets: namely, to "raise the level of cooperation" between the two countries, to develop friendly ties on the basis of mutual respect, and to accommodate "each other's interests" (*Times*, Malta, 2 October). Indeed, progress was registered across a wide spectrum. Gennadi Bakthin, a representative of the Soviet Ministry of Mercantile Marine, visited Malta "to discuss problems" relating to the oil bunkering agreement between Malta and the Soviet Union (*In-Nazzjon Taghna*, 3 June). Agreement was reached to renew the cultural agreement between the two countries, which was due to expire at the end of the year. (*In-Nazzjon Taghna*, 13 June.) Enemalta Corporation signed a five-year storage, transportation, and fuel supply agreement with Aeroflot as a result of which five to six Aeroflot aircraft traveling to or from Latin American and

African countries will transit in Malta each week (*Times*, Malta, 21 November).

On the trade side, results have been disappointing partly because of Soviet foreign exchange difficulties and partly because of the upheavals and uncertainties arising from the *perestroika* reforms in the USSR. Unofficial estimates suggest that the level of Maltese exports to the USSR is substantially lower than the targets fixed in terms of the 1987-1990 trade agreement. That agreement provided for the purchase by the USSR of Maltese visible exports to the value of $40 million (U.S.) each year and another $140 million for the purchase of eight timber carriers to be constructed in Maltese dry docks (*Times*, Malta, 11 December 1986).

The Malta Labor government, which signed the trade agreement with the USSR, was worried before the May elections because it wanted to step up the process of implementation. A high-level delegation led by Mikhail Filipov of the Moscow Ministry of Foreign Trade visited the island for talks (*Orizzont*, 3 April). The delegation visited 25 factories and concluded some new contracts (*Weekend Chronicle*, Malta, 11 April). A Soviet textile exhibition was held in a local hotel to coincide with the visit (*Times*, Malta, 15 April). In July, the Soviet Union participated in the Malta International Fair. A trade seminar was organized by the Soviet commercial counselor and addressed by Filipov. (*Times*, Malta, 14 July.) A second seminar for Maltese businessmen was held on 16 December and attended by the Soviet ambassador. The event concentrated more on hopes about the future than on past results. The Soviets are trying to redress in part the balance of their commitment by sending more tourists to visit the island. Hundreds of them come to Malta by Aeroflot to board Soviet liners, which discharge their passengers after a Mediterranean cruise to be sent home by the same Aeroflot planes. (*Weekend Chronicle*, Malta, 7 November.)

On the political side, the Kremlin has been making entreaties to the Malta Labor Party, which is social democratic and a member of the Socialist International. The secretary general of the MLP, Marie Louise Coleiro, and the party international secretary, Leo Brincat, were invited to Moscow for talks about international affairs with particular reference to the Mediterranean region. They held discussions with Vadim Zagladin among others. (*Orizzont*, 15 October.) Brincat returned to Moscow in November to represent his party at the 70th anniversary of the October Revolution. At a meeting presided over by Mikhail Gorbachev, Brincat emphasized the MLP's policy "in support of all initiatives that ensure stability and security in the Mediterranean region" (*Orizzont*, 9 November).

It is in the propaganda and public relations field that the Soviet Union is most active in Malta. It has sent medical specialists, journalists, youth delegations, a sextet from the Bolshoi, musical groups, a water polo coach, and peace delegations to the island. Elaborate programs and extensive press coverage were designed to make an impact. The USSR has offered and awarded scholarships, shown prestigious cultural films in the island's cinemas, offered the Malta television service a constant supply of programs, made book presentations to schools and to the university, and sent a merchant marine officer cadet training ship to visit the island. The repertoire was practically in constant motion.

Soviet interest in Malta has been so steady and on such a scale that steps have now been taken to open a Soviet cultural center in Valletta. This will be Soviet-run and will eventually house the Malta-USSR Friendship and Cultural Society, which now has its own headquarters. Viktor Barinov, the secretary of the Union of Soviet Friendship Societies, came from Moscow with his legal adviser on 15 August to sign a deed for the acquisition of the new premises (*Orizzont*, 15 August).

Auxiliary Organizations. This cascade of Soviet activity has been supported by local auxiliary organizations. There is a strong presence of CPM members in most of these organizations. The most active is the Malta-USSR Friendship and Cultural Society. The society offered a number of scholarships in more than 80 different subjects for Maltese students interested in studying in Soviet universities and institutions (*Orizzont*, 17 February). Successful Maltese students studying in the USSR are given publicity wherever possible. Among those mentioned in the press during the year was one who is studying at the Lunacharskii Drama Institute of Moscow, another who had graduated as music conductor and composer at a Kiev conservatory, and a girl chosen for a six-year course in drama direction.

The society hosted several official and other visitors from the USSR and provided facilities for some of them to deliver public lectures and to meet interested members from the public. Anton Cassar, the president of the society, was one of 194 overseas delegates from USSR friendship societies from 98 countries who took part in a special Leningrad meeting organized by Friendship House in that city (*Orizzont*, 2 November). A Malta-Poland Cultural

Association was formed during the year with CPM members predominating in the committee (*Zminijietna*, July). The other friendship societies were conspicuous by their inactivity, except the Peace and Solidarity Council and the newly formed Women for Peace organization. These have participated in foreign manifestations and held various local activities at different intervals.

Malta Government Policies. The incoming Fenech Adami administration had to review and adjust Malta's foreign policy and repair Malta's image in the West. One early decision of the new prime minister was to address a special meeting of ambassadors accredited to Malta. Within the constraints of the constitution, namely, neutrality and nonalignment, the new government is anxious to project the image of "a stable country that can be trusted both as regards its internal policies as well as its foreign policy." Malta will not host "any foreign military base" or "seek to form part of any military alliance." This notwithstanding, Malta will seek "its rightful place" in the European Economic Community. It regrets that "Maltese government policies have at times been made to appear cool or antagonistic to a close relationship with the USA, a country which shares and practices our belief in parliamentary democracy." Adami declared that his government "will do its best to change this image because it strongly believes that closer links with the USA will bring mutual benefits" to the two countries. Malta will also seek to further cooperation with neighboring Arab countries, as well as with socialist countries and Commonwealth countries. (*Times*, Malta 10 June.)

Within these parameters, Malta's relationship with the Soviet Union and its satellites would be one of political disengagement, but there will be no attempt to scale down the level of economic and trade cooperation. This was made clear by Adami at a public meeting before the election when he said that a nationalist government would uphold Malta's commitments in the field of economic cooperation and international trade as well as through joint ventures such as those existing with Czechoslovakia. (*In-Nazzjon Taghna*, 9 March.)

In terms of the existing four-year trade agreement, Malta is building eight timber carriers for the Soviet Union, of which two have been launched and are soon to be delivered. According to the general manager of the Marsa Shipbuilding Yard, where these ships are being built, the Soviet Union may order 35 more ships if the present contract is concluded satisfactorily and on time (*Orizzont*, 1 May). The USSR provides an additional volume of ship repair work to Malta dry docks and buys quantities of clothes, textiles, and other consumer goods each year.

The Soviet Council of Ministers quickly opened a channel of communication with Adami as soon as he was elected prime minister. In a message of congratulations, Adami was told that "We are confident that the positive development of our relation corresponds to the interests of our peoples and is a constructive element of peace in Europe and the Mediterranean" (*Times*, Malta, 19 May).

J. G. E. Hugh
Valletta, Malta

The Netherlands

Population. 14,641,554
Party. Communist Party of the Netherlands (Communistische Partij van Nederland; CPN)
Date Founded. 1909
Membership. 12,000 (estimated); 27,000 (claimed)
Chairman. Elli Izeboud
Executive Committee. (Partijbestuur). 55 members, including Elli Izeboud, Ina Brouwer, Marius Ernsting, Nico Scouten, Jan Berghuis, Leo Molenaar, Boe Thio, Ton van Hoek, Geert Lameris
Central Committee. 46 members, including Henk Hoekstra, secretary; Ton van Hoek, international secretary; Joop Morriën, John Geelen
Status. Legal
Last Congress. Thirtieth, 29 November–2 December 1986, in Amsterdam
Last Election. 1986, 0.6 percent, no seats in the Second Chamber (lower house); 1987, 1 of 75 seats in First Chamber (Senate)
Auxiliary Organizations. General Netherlands Youth Organization (ANJV), CPN Women, Stop the Bomb/Stop the Nuclear Arms Race, CPN Youth Platform, Scholing en Onderwijs, Women Against Nuclear Weapons
Publications. *De Waarheid* (Truth), official daily, circulation 9,000–14,000; *CPN-Leden krant*,

membership journal published ten times annually; *Politiek en cultuur*, theoretical journal published ten times yearly; *Komma*, quarterly published by the CPN's Institute for Political and Social Research; CPN owns Pegasus Publishers.

In 1909, radical Marxists from the revolutionary left wing of the labor movement and the Labor Party (PvdA) founded the Social Democratic Party (Sociaal-Democratische Partij). In 1919, as the Communist Party of Holland, it affiliated with the Comintern, and in 1935 it took its present name. In 1940, Nazi Germany occupied the Netherlands, but the party remained legal as long as Germany was allied with the Soviet Union. It was suppressed from 1941 to 1945.

In its ideological and social composition, the CNP resembles the other northern European communist parties. Like them, it is a small party that has never captured more than a few percent of the vote. Its leadership has always been loyal to the CPSU and has had little contact or concern with the practical issues and problems facing the working class and the labor movement, such as pay, living conditions, profit sharing, or influence on national economic policy. When Nikita Khrushchev gave his Secret Speech in 1956 denouncing Stalin, the CPN did not undertake any process of de-Stalinization in its own ranks or methods. Even so, the CPN managed to score some gains on municipal councils and even in the national parliament during the social and ideological turmoil that began in the late 1960s. In 1971, the CPN gained 3.9 percent of the vote and six seats in the Second Chamber, a score that rose to 4.5 percent and seven seats in 1972.

In the early 1970s, a few intellectuals sympathetic to the CPN began arguing that if the party would renew itself by developing a broad left strategy using new themes, like pacifism, feminism, and environmentalism, it would be even better placed to attract elements of the progressive middle class and thus turn itself into a genuine rival of the PvdA on the left. It was important to do so because if the CPN missed this chance it would be seized by other radical parties that were springing up at the time—the Pacific Socialist Party (PSP) and the Radical Political Party (PPR). These arguments had no effect on the CPN until 1977. In the heavily polarized election of that year the PvdA recaptured most of the votes lost to the extreme left, including the CPN, in earlier years. The CPN won only 1.7 percent of the vote and two seats. As a result, the CPN leadership accepted the arguments for a broad left strategy, dropped its rigid adherence to Marxism-Leninism and CPSU leadership, and adopted a Eurocommunist line including the prospect of alliances with the PSP, the PPR, or even sympathetic elements on the left of the PvdA. The old guard within the CPN, however, argued that this attempt to abandon proletarian orthodoxy and become the basis of a broad alliance of forces to the left of the PvdA was not only doomed to fail but was ideologically wrong and that the CPN must remain a completely Marxist-Leninist party no matter what the effects on its popularity.

In the early 1980s the supporters of the broad left strategy, led by radical feminists, narrowly gained control of the party, and starting in 1982 the CPN declared itself officially committed to cooperation with the other extreme left parties. The CPN took an active role of leadership within the peace movement, which grew explosively in 1980–1983. These moves led to further internal division. In 1984, part of the Marxist-Leninist old guard departed and formed a rival party, the Association of Communists in the Netherlands (VCN). On the other side, a number of pacifists and feminists, who had joined in the hope that the CPN was about to become the party of their movements, left again in 1985 because change was not coming quickly enough.

These developments on both flanks weakened the CPN going into the 1986 elections. Despite attempts to build electoral alliances with the PSP and the PPR, the CPN competed on its own in these elections, which were a disaster for the party. In the municipal elections in March, it lost a third of its seats on municipal councils. In the parliamentary elections in May, it won only a third of the vote of 1982, namely, 0.6 percent. This was too few to win any seats, so as a result there were no communists in the Second Chamber for the first time since 1918. As in 1977, the PvdA took votes and seats from all three of the small radical parties. It nevertheless failed to oust the center right coalition of Prime Minister Ruud Lubbers, which continued in office with 81 out of 150 seats.

Apart from internal divisions, another reason for the electoral failure of the CPN was that its agenda was indistinguishable not only from that of the PSP or the PPR but even from that of the dominant left wing of the PvdA. A Dutch voter sympathetic to feminism or the peace movement might well ask why he should vote for the CPN or another small party if the PvdA, one of the three major parties in the country, was open to his views. In short, the turn to Eurocommunism of the 1980s had seemingly served only to make the CPN irrelevant.

Internal Party Affairs. There was no party congress in 1987 because the leadership advanced the one originally scheduled for that year to November 1986 to elect a new executive and to plan strategy for the spring 1987 elections to the provincial legislatures, known as the Provincial Estates. Apart from administering the individual provinces, these bodies also chose the members of the First Chamber, or Senate. Since the CPN had lost its representation in the Second Chamber, it was vital that it retain a foothold in the Senate to have any voice at all on the national parliamentary level.

At the congress, the orthodox Marxist-Leninist faction led by Geert Lameris tried to impose a party executive that would reject the broad left strategy of the previous years and take the CPN back to its past. The tactic failed, and the congress re-elected the previous leadership, all of whom were committed to the broad left strategy, including the chairman, Elli Izeboud (*YICA*, 1987). Some months earlier a special study group convened by the CPN's research bureau, the Institute for Social and Political Research, had debated the future of the party. The general tenor of the discussion was that the broad left strategy of renewal and cooperation with feminists and pacifists had not failed; it had simply not gone far enough yet.

Although Izeboud and Ina Brouwer, one of the three members of parliament defeated in 1986, had some doubts about the continuing validity of the broad left strategy, they agreed to negotiate with the PSP and the PPR to present joint lists for the elections to the Estates (and indirectly to the Senate). Brouwer also stated that communists might return to parliament by working through the PvdA. This reminded some observers of PvdA leader and former Prime Minister Joop den Uyl's statement of 1985 that ever since the CPN adopted the broad left strategy, most of its members could belong to his own party. Like most other northern European social democratic parties, the PvdA had abandoned, in the 1970s, its long-standing policies of preventing "entryism" by communists and enforcing loyalty to democratic socialism among its members.

The orthodox faction under Lameris that had tried to unseat the Izeboud leadership at the Thirtieth Congress was largely based in the two provinces of Groningen and North Holland. In these two provinces, the party submitted its own lists for the spring elections. It made little difference. The combined broad left lists won 2.5 percent of the vote as against 4.5 percent in the previous election to the Estates in 1982. This yielded fifteen seats in the Estates and three in the Senate, or one for each of the parties, CPN, PSP, and PPR.

For the communists, this was a slight improvement over the Second Chamber elections of 1986, but it offered little hope of dramatic progress. Morriën, a member of the Central Committee, argued that "the CPN recovered strongly and . . . will be amply represented in the Provincial [E]states." He further argued that the elections "have created the basis for further recovery" but that "much will depend on the force of the extraparliamentary struggle" (*WMR*, August).

The supporters of the broad left strategy were heartened by Mikhail Gorbachev's promises of *glasnost'* and *perestroika* (openness and restructuring) in the Soviet Union. The Soviet reforms appeared to prove that the Soviet Union was capable of dynamic change and of moving in a democratic direction. Hoekstra, an executive member and spokesman for the broad left strategy, argued in *De Waarheid* (7 January) that Gorbachev's reforms "give hope to peace fighters everywhere" and provide a good argument for the alliance of the CPN with other progressive forces. Morriën stated that "the spectacular developments in the Soviet Union evoke a growing interest in our country" (*WMR*, August). He was right insofar as Gorbachev's book *Perestroika* was by far the best-selling nonfiction book in the Netherlands for several weeks in late 1987.

The broad leftists interpreted the arms control negotiations between the United States and the Soviet Union in 1976–1987 in a similar vein. According to them, the talks were due to the pressure put on the United States and NATO governments by the Western European left, especially the peace movement, and to the goodwill of the Soviet Union. When the U.S. and Soviet leaders signed the treaty banning intermediate-range land-based ballistic missiles in December 1987, all the forces of the Dutch left regarded this accord as a vindication of their opposition to nuclear weapons since the late 1970s. "The Communist Party of the Netherlands views this agreement as the result of the activity of all peace-minded forces given all their diversity and differences," as Izeboud said in Moscow at the celebrations of the 70th anniversary of the October Revolution (*FBIS*, 6 November). She continued, "Creating a nonclass alliance of forces committed to peace is of exceptional importance" and went on to insist that the agreement should mean that no cruise missiles should come to the Netherlands at all.

As in other matters the CPN was barely ahead of the PvdA or even the Dutch government; no sooner had President Ronald Reagan and General Secretary Gorbachev signed the intermediate-range nuclear forces agreement than Dutch foreign minister Hans Van Den Broek announced that it was no longer necessary for the Netherlands to accept cruise missiles—as his government had promised in 1985—since they were to be scrapped anyway under the new treaty.

International Contacts. The most important event in 1987 was the visit of Chairman Izeboud and a delegation to the 70th anniversary of the October Revolution. In addition, Erich Honecker, the East German communist leader and chairman of the State Council, paid an official visit to the Netherlands in June 1987 with a delegation of 120 people including East German foreign minister Oskar Fischer. Although his visit was aimed at the Dutch government, he also spoke to members of the CPN, while members of his delegation met with working groups of the party.

The CPSU had not officially approved of the broad left strategy, and relations with the CPN appeared cool on the surface, at least, through 1985. This despite the fact that the CPSU itself since the mid-1970s had pursued a sort of broad left strategy of finding allies outside the communist parties in the struggle to oppose Western defense policies. Under Gorbachev, the CPSU appeared more willing to recognize this similarity. The Soviet papers covered the Thirtieth CPN Congress at some length and attributed an important role to the CPN in upholding antimissile sentiment among Dutch voters.

Conclusion. Despite the optimistic assessments of Morriën and Izeboud, the CPN failed in 1987 to significantly turn the tide of electoral loss. The modest recovery in the spring elections helped to heal the splits between broad leftists impatient with perceived immobility of the party apparat and orthodox Marxist-Leninists worried that the broad left strategy was compromising the party's ideological integrity. This seemed a temporary respite, however. The real problem was that the CPN, as a party appealing to the broad left of the new middle classes, offered no distinctive platform. Political sociologists might point out that the PvdA was always seeking power by moving to the center, and that there was therefore always room for an ideologically more committed party to its left. This rule of thumb no longer applied in the Netherlands, where the center itself was increasingly open to the egalitarian, pacifist, feminist, and environmentalist ethos offered by the new look CPN. On the other hand, orthodox retrenchment was no option either. Traditionally, the CPN had found what few members it had in the old textile and shipbuilding industries. Both of these were virtually gone by the late 1980s. Whether these two challenges will lead to a permanent alliance of the far left in Dutch politics or to complete disintegration remains to be seen.

David R. Gress
Hoover Institution

Norway

Population. 4,178,545

Parties. Norwegian Communist Party (Norges Kommunistiske Parti; NKP); Socialist Left Party (Sosialistisk Venstreparti; SV); Workers' Communist Party (Arbeidernes Kommunistiske Parti; AKP runs as Red Electoral Alliance (Rod Valgallians; RV) in elections.

Founded. NKP: 1923, SV: 1976, AKP: 1973

Membership. NKP: 5,500, SV: 2,000, AKP: 10,000 (all estimated)

Chairs. NKP: Kaare Andre Nilsen, SV: Theo Koritzinsky, AKP: Kjersti Ericsson

Central Committee. NKP: 8 full members: Kaare Andre Nilsen, Ingrid Negard (deputy chair), Trygve Horgen (deputy chair), Paul Midtlyng (organizational secretary), Grete Trondsen, Asmund Langsether, Gunnar Wahl, Ornulf Godager; 2 alternate members: Knut Vidar Paulsen, Knut Jarle Berg

Status. Legal

Last Congress. NKP: Nineteenth, 23–26 April 1987, in Oslo; SV; 2–5 April 1987, in Trondheim; AKP: December 1984, "somewhere in Norway" (*Arbeiderbladet*, 18 December 1984)

Last Election. 1985; NKP: 0.2 percent, no representation; SV: 5.5 percent, 6 of 157 representatives; Red Electoral Alliance, 0.6 percent; AKP: 0 percent, no representation

Auxiliary Organization. NKP: Norwegian Communist Youth League (NKU)

Publications. NKP: *Friheten* (Freedom), semiweekly, Arne Jorgensen, editor; *Vart Arbeid*, internal organ; AKP: *Klassekampen* (Class Struggle), daily

Until 1979 the Norwegian Labor Party (Det Norske Arbeiderparti; DNA)—a moderate social-democratic reform movement—dominated postwar Norwegian politics. During this era, the DNA was the main governing party and all but monopolized the left in the country's politics. Three Marxist parties have stood to the left of the DNA: the NKP and the SV, both pro-Soviet, and the Maoist AKP, which has campaigned in parliamentary elections as the RV. In the 1981 elections the DNA was ousted from power by a center-right coalition led by Conservative Party leader Kaare Willoch.

Willoch's coalition was re-elected in the general election of 9 September 1985, and he became the first conservative prime minister ever to win a second term in Norway. His coalition held only a one-seat majority in the Storting (parliament), however, and was forced to depend for support on the two representatives of the right-wing Progressive Party (which advocated the dismantling of the Norwegian welfare state). In May 1986 Willoch resigned after losing a vote of confidence in the Storting over the austerity policies introduced by his government to cope with delining oil revenues. Gro Harlem Brundtland, head of the DNA, became the new prime minister. Her socialist alliance held only 77 parliamentary seats—two short of a majority and one less than the conservative coalition.

The Norwegian Communist Party. The NKP began as a small splinter group of radical trade unionists and politicians who left the DNA in 1923. It experienced many lean years until after World War II, when its support for the war effort against Nazi Germany and the Soviet liberation of northern Norway boosted the NKP's popularity at the polls (eleven seats in the first postwar Parliament). However, the party's fortunes fell with the onset of the Cold War.

The weakness of the NKP was due, in large part, to its decision in 1975 to remain a staunchly pro-Soviet, Stalinist party. Its membership and popularity dwindled when Reidar Larsen, then its chairman, and several other leaders abandoned the NKP and established the SV.

Although differences still exist between the NKP and the SV, former NKP chair Hans I. Kleven looked favorably on SV chair Theo Koritzinsky's call for a broad united front of left-wing parties in Norway. Kleven believed that it is especially important to establish unity of action in the labor movement, both in the unions themselves and in the political parties close to labor—the DNA, the SV, and the NKP.

In addition, Kleven supported Koritzinsky's proposals for electoral cooperation between the NKP and the SV. Kleven suggested running SV and NKP candidates on joint election lists. He also backed Koritzinsky's idea for the NKP and SV to cooperate on specific issues in order to reshape Norwegian society in a socialist direction.

The NKP continues to be one of the weakest communist parties in Western Europe. It received a mere 7,025 votes (0.3 percent) in the last parliamentary elections in 1981, far short of the number needed to win a seat in the Storting. In the local elections of 1983, the NKP captured only 0.4 percent of the vote, and in the general elections of September 1985, the party polled just 0.2 percent.

The Nineteenth Congress. At its Nineteenth Congress, held in April 1987, the NKP unanimously adopted the draft of a new party program. The program's statement of principles reaffirmed the NKP's adherence to Marxism-Leninism and "proletarian internationalism." Outgoing Chairman Kleven remarked that "Marxism needs neither renewal nor modernization but can always be developed further, adding new analyses and conclusions based on life's experiences." (*Friheten*, 23 April.) The congress proclaimed peace and housing to be the two most important issues of the current period. Securing peace and contributing to the peace movement have been recurrent emphases of congresses: the NKP finds peace movements effective carriers of NKP foreign policy positions (major foci of the 1981 and 1984 congresses, as well as party infighting and reporting thereof in *Friheten*, are discussed in detail in *YICA*, 1987, pp. 569–71). According to an article in *Friheten* on 30 April, shortly after the conclusion of the congress,

> Securing world peace has always been part of the historic task of the working class. Today it is the most important part . . . No one can win either an arms race or a new war. This realization is not only deeply

> ingrained in the working class, it also extends into the petit bourgeoisie and the middle class. It is starting to penetrate . . . into sections of the upper middle class and its political spokesmen. These are a basis for creating a worldwide peace front.

The NKP's avowed objective, to be pursued through the Norwegian peace movement, was to isolate U.S. "imperialism" by obliging the United States to institute a nuclear test ban, by preventing the implementation of the Strategic Defense Initiative, and by creating a Nordic nuclear-free zone. The NKP credited the Soviet Union with the "zero option" on removal of intermediate- and short-range nuclear missiles from Europe and urged support for Soviet advocacy of a 150-km nuclear-free corridor along the East-West divide on the continent. The party congress called for halting all nuclear test and expediting plans for a Nordic nuclear-free zone. On other international issues, it criticized Norway's "mini-Europe" policy, which was closely tied to (although not a member of) the European Economic Community. The NKP advocated a pan-European approach, with broad East-West economic, commerical, and scientific cooperation.

On the domestic front, the NKP congress lamented that even though the Labor Party was in power, it was succumbing to pressures from capitalist elements that were steering it away from a Socialist program. Moreover, declared the NKP, the country's unemployment, environmental, and ecological problems could not be resolved outside a Socialist framework. According to *Friheten* (30 April),

> Our strategy for Socialism is based on an alliance of the working-class parties that is able to unite all those who are objective opponents of monopoly capital and imperialism in the struggle to limit the power of monopoly capital and expand democracy. This struggle must take place both inside and outside parliamentary organs . . . The Social Democrats are our most important alliance partners on all the major political issues today. We must accomplish the task of developing a constructive and comradely cooperation with the Social Democrats while at the same time maintaining our fundamental criticism of their policies.

The NKP emphasized the importance of defending and broadening the scope of human rights and of further developing democracy in Norway. It also called for strong national ownership and control of the Norwegian oil industry. The party proposed the end of speculation in both state-owned and privately owned housing and the abolition of the value-added tax on housing and food.

The Soviet delegation to the NKP Congress was headed by Georgiy V. Aleshin, candidate member of the CPSU Central Committee and second secretary of the Central Committee of the Latvian Communist Party. The congress discussed *perestroika* (restructuring) in the Soviet Union and proclaimed that the "new thinking" inspired by General Secretary Gorbachev offers for the entire world "a worthy example for emulation" (*Pravda*, 24 April). The congress also condemned the moves by the Norwegian government to restrict Kongsberg Vapenfabrikk's trade with the Soviet Union after the enterprise allowed the export of technology for making quieter submarine propellers.

The NKP congress elected a national executive committee by secret written ballot. The newly elected representatives were unable to appoint the party's new leadership before the close of the congress. On 9 May the new national committee met and elected Kare Andre Nilsen as party chairman. Kleven, 60, announced his resignation on grounds of poor health and a desire to bring in younger blood. Nilsen, 42, has a long record of service with the party's youth wing and has been a member of the Norwegian Peace Council since 1976.

International Activities. The NKP's international links revolve largely around meetings of the Nordic communist parties and consultations with the Soviet and East European parties. During 1985, however, delegates from the NKP visited China and Korea. The wide-ranging issues discussed at Nordic communist gatherings were typified in a communiqué published after the parley of northern European communist parties in Finland in November 1982. The document covered, inter alia, the inability of capitalism to solve unemployment problems in Scandinavia, the campaign for peace and disarmament, and a Nordic nuclear-free zone, as well as the right of the Palestinians to establish a national homeland (*IB*, February 1983).

In October 1984, Kleven led a party delegation to Bulgaria, where he and General Secretary Todor Zhivkov talked mostly about peace and security in the Balkans (Sofia, BTA, 26 October 1984). In December of that year, the NKP participated in a meeting in Czechoslovakia of world communist parties under the auspices of *World Marxist Review*. In February 1985 Kleven led a delegation to Prague for talks with General Secretary Gustáv Husák.

They condemned "U.S. imperialism," demanded an end to the arms race, and called for celebrating the 40th anniversary of the defeat of Nazi Germany by stepping up the struggle for international peace and détente (*FBIS*-Eastern Europe, 22 February 1985). In May, the Norwegians organized a series of events commemorating their World War II victory. The Soviets sent a delegation headed by D.B. Golovko, secretary of the Kiev section of the Ukrainian Communist Party (*Pravda*, 8 May 1985). Representing the NKP at a *World Marxist Review*–sponsored meeting of communist party delegates in Prague, Gunnar Wahl spoke in favor of more frequent international gatherings and more vigorous discussion of major issues facing the movement. He cited the concept of unity in diversity put forward at the Twenty-seventh Congress of the CPSU to make the point that international communist parleys need not result in the adoption of collective documents that would bind member parties (*WMR*, October 1986).

The Socialist Left Party. The SV is the strongest Marxist party to the left of the DNA. In the 1981 parliamentary elections, it received 4.9 percent of the vote and four seats in the Storting. The SV campaigned as a parliamentary ally of the DNA in the local elections of 1983 (in which it received 5.2 percent of the vote) and in the general election of 1985 (in which it won 5.4 percent and six parliamentary seats). For details on activities and developments in the SV leadership since 1983, and on the 1985 congress and elections, see *1987 Yearbook on International Communist Affairs*, pp. 573–75.

During 2–5 April 1987 the SV held a national congress to deal with leadership and other issues. Theo Koritzinsky expressed a desire to resign the party chairmanship to devote more time to his work on defense and foreign policy questions in the Storting. He apparently was persuaded to keep his post, however, so as to preclude a conflict over party leadership.

The cries of the 1985 congress for solutions to the problems of unemployment, of a nuclear-free life for Norway, of fairer distribution of goods, and of reduction of the work-week, have been muted by the emphasis placed during the 1987 congress on a call for nuclear and conventional arms reduction by both superpowers. The congress passed a resolution exhorting the Norwegian government to take the initiative for a broad international conference on the Nordic region. Declaring that the Soviet naval buildup in the north and the new U.S. maritime strategy were threatening Nordic security, the resolution called for negotiations to reverse the arms buildup and reduce tensions. The SV congress also urged Norway to make an immediate contribution to demilitarizing the seas in the region by banning the entry into Norwegian ports of any ship that was not certifiably free of nuclear weapons (*Aftenposten*, 3 April).

The Workers' Communist Party. The AKP was born in the late 1960s as an amalgam of various Maoist organizations that were disenchanted with the Soviet economic model and with Soviet foreign policy. The AKP was founded as a formal organization in 1973. Its electoral front, the RV, has not fared well, and the party has never garnered enough votes for even a single seat in the Storting. Far from being a genuine working-class party, the AKP is composed largely of well-educated and relatively affluent Norwegians. For details of AKP activities and developments in the 1980s, see *1987 Yearbook on International Communist Affairs*, pp. 575–76.

The Red Electoral Alliance. The RV is no longer simply an offshoot of the AKP. It is a combination of the AKP and independent Socialists. The development and evolution of the RV is discussed in the *1987 Yearbook on International Communist Affairs*, p. 576.

Marian Leighton
Defense Intelligence Agency

Portugal

Population. 10,314,727
Party. Portuguese Communist Party (Partido Comunista Português; PCP)
Founded. 1921
Membership. More than 200,000 (claimed) (Lisbon Domestic Service, 4 March; *FBIS*, 6 May)
General Secretary. Álvaro Cunhal (since 1961)
Secretariat. 8 full members: Álvaro Cunhal (73), Carlos Costa, Domingos Abrantes, Fernando Blanqui Teixeira, Joaquim Gomes, Jorge Araújo, Octávio Pato, Sérgio Vilarigues; 2 alternate members: Jaime Félix, Luísa Araújo

Political Secretariat. 5 members: Álvaro Cunhal, Carlos Brito, Carlos Costa, Domingos Abrantes, Octávio Pato

Political Commission. 18 full members: Álvaro Cunhal, Angelo Veloso, Dias Lourenço, António Gervásio, Carlos Brito, Carlos Costa, Diniz Miranda, Domingos Abrantes, Fernando Blanqui Teixeira, Jaime Serra, Joaquim Gomes, Jorge Araújo, José Soeiro, José Casanova, José Vitoriano, Octávio Pato, Raimundo Cabral, Sérgio Vilarigues; 7 alternate members: António Lopes, António Orcinha, Artur Vidal Pinto, Bernardina Sebastião, Carlos Ramildes, Edgar Correia, Zita Seabra

Central Committee. 91 full and 74 alternate members; 92 under 40 years of age, 122 under 45 (*Avante!*, 20 August; *FBIS*, 24 August)

Status. Legal

Last Congress. Eleventh (Extraordinary), 2–6 February 1986, in Lisbon

Last Election. 1987, United Democratic Coalition (CDU, communist coalition), 11 percent, 30 of 250 seats (*NYT*, 20 July)

Auxiliary Organization. General Confederation of Portuguese Workers (Confederação Geral de Trabalhadores Portugueses—Intersindical Nacional; CGTP), which, with 1.6 million members (*World Affairs Report*, vol. 16, no. 3), represents more than half of Portugal's 2.5 million unionized labor force out of a work force of 4.59 million (*World Fact Book*, 1987)

Publications. *Avante!*, weekly newspaper, António Dias Lorenço, editor; *O Militante*, theoretical journal; and *O Diário*, semiofficial daily newspaper (all published in Lisbon)

The Stalinist PCP controls the Portuguese communist movement, along with most labor unions and southern farm collectives, and has organized cells within the armed forces. Its attempts to infiltrate military intelligence units have reportedly been frustrated. (Lisbon, *Tempo*, 26 February; *JPRS*, 2 June.) The party's political influence continues to weaken from the 19 percent share of national votes it won in 1979. It has not participated in the government since a frustrated 1976 coup attempt.

Organization and Leadership. There was much speculation during 1987 about a possible renewal of the PCP leadership at the party congress scheduled for March 1988. Cunhal, the 73-year-old general secretary, countered that the devotion and experience of the older comrades made them valuable and difficult to replace but that in any case many younger men had been chosen for top posts at recent congresses. He denied that the issue of his own replacement needed to be broached but acknowledged that it may be debated. (*Diário de Notícias*, 3 August; *Avante!*, 20 August; *FBIS*, 18, 24 August; *JPRS*, 14 September.) The general expectation was that Cunhal's orthodox political line would not be altered and that any leadership changes could only be triggered by him (*O Jornal*, 21 July; *JPRS*, 4 September).

Veloso, a party member mentioned as a possible "dauphin" of the secretary general, was advanced from Porto to an influential position in Lisbon, where he was placed in charge of the political-ideological orientation of *O Diário*, the daily newspaper that normally reflects the views of the PCP. The appointment was seen as a reaffirmation of orthodoxy and was a blow to many staff members who had allegedly pled for a "cheerier" and less sectarian newspaper and less authoritarianism on the part of their superiors. Veloso, a member of the political commission of the Central Committee, was briefly the PCP candidate for president in early 1986. (Lisbon, *Expresso*, 1 November 1986; *JPRS*, 31 December 1986.)

Domestic Affairs. A censure vote, supported by the left of center opposition including the communists, overturned the minority government of Prime Minister Aníbal Cavaco Silva in April. The expectation that President Mário Soares, a socialist, would appoint a left-wing coalition to replace it was frustrated by his call for the July election of a new Assembly. (*WP*, 4 April, 20 July.) This was to coincide with elections for the European Parliament.

The PCP's Cunhal insisted that an election was unnecessary because the parties disposed to support a "democratic" government held a comfortable majority in the existing Assembly. He even said communists would support but were willing to forgo participation in such a government. The president's decision, he concluded, actually constituted support for the right just when it had been defeated. (*Avante!*, 2 April, 7 May; *FBIS*, 16 April, 18 May.)

To face an unwanted election, the PCP maneuvered to attract the Greens Party and "many independent democrats" into a new electoral alliance called the United Democratic Coalition (CDU). This replaced the defunct United People's Alliance (APU) that in previous elections had allied the communists with the Portuguese Democratic Movement/Democratic Electoral Commission (Movimento Democrático Popular/Comissão Electoral Democrática; MDP/CED). (Lisbon Domestic Service, 4 March; *FBIS*, 6 May.) However, the communists through the CDU were only able to attract some 11 percent of the July vote, compared with 15 percent through the APU in 1985. This gave the CDU 30 seats in the Assembly, 8 less than the APU in 1985, and 31 seats in the European Parliament. Of the 30 CDU Assembly seats, 25 were PCP members. (Lisbon Domestic Service, 20 July; *Avante!*, 24 July; *FBIS*, 21, 31 July.)

A worse blow for the communists was the impressive accomplishment of the Social Democrats (Partido Social Democrático; PSD) in winning 50 percent of the popular vote and a majority of seats in the new Assembly. The PCP saw this as a grave threat for the "democratic gains" of the April 1974 revolution since the prime minister had pledged constitutional revision to permit extensive denationalization. (*Avante!*, 24 July; *FBIS*, 31 July; *WP*, 18 August.)

Communists attributed the PSD victory to an externally caused improvement in the country's financial situation that permitted the government to acquire an image of "competence" and "efficiency" and to government deception of the electorate through manipulation of the news media it controlled. CDU losses were explained as partly resulting from the proliferation of minor parties that refused to join with communists in electoral agreements and from some voter shifts to the socialists—who won two more seats than in the previous election—and even to the PSD. Equally to blame, according to the PCP, were abstentions by many workers because of vacations, seasonal migrations abroad, and lack of confidence in the formation of a democratic government. (*Avante!*, 24 July; *FBIS*, 31 July.)

Asked to explain the PCP's relative isolation from "other" major parties, which do cooperate with each other from time to time, Cunhal responded that it was because the communists, unlike others, "resolutely defend the interests of workers. . . against capitalist exploitation" and have defended the gains of the April revolution against every government offensive of the last eleven years (*Avante!*, 20 August; *FBIS*, 24 August).

Reportedly actively recruiting youth in Portugal is the Reconquest Cultural Center, a branch of a Brazilian-led network of anticommunist organizations (Lisbon, *Tal & Qual*, 24 April; *JPRS*, 16 June).

Auxiliary Organizations. The MDP-CDE, heretofore considered a communst front "satellite" party, decided in March to sever its ties with the PCP in the United People's Alliance (APU). More than 80 percent of the delegates reportedly resolved not to give in to the PCP's conditions for a local election agreement; the organization had previously decided to abandon the "incompatible" alliance at the national level (see *YICA*, 1987). Calling the breakup of the APU "a great setback for the forces of democracy," the PCP enticed a number of individuals to move out of the MDP and into the CDU coalition as "independents." (*Diário de Notícias*, 15 March; *FBIS*, 24 March; Lisbon, *O Jornal*, 16 May; *JPRS*, 29 June.)

International Views and Activities. Effusive praise by Cunhal for Soviet domestic reforms was ridiculed by Portuguese jounalists. They wondered whether the PCP intended to assimilate Mikhail Gorbachev's internal democratization policy or merely continue "passively to watch this revolution." Communists responded that the party's drive for democracy in Portugal, including inner-party democracy, was always a crucial part of its policies (*Diário de Notícias*, 13 February; *Avante!*, 26 February; *IB*, June.) Cunhal further contended that Soviet restructuring (*perestroika*) to accelerate social and economic development was an advance by socialism, not, as charged by some, a retreat (*FBIS*, 6 November).

Delegations of the PCP and the Comnmunist Party of Spain (PCE) exchanged visits in March and April, ending a long period of mutual snubbing. Cunhal attributed the reconciliation to "favorable changes" in Spain; at the same time, he acknowledged some continuing differences. The PCP, he said, disagreed with the PCE's emphasis on Eurocommunism, on its promotion of unity of the European left as opposed to strengthening the communist movement, and on entry into the Common Market. (*Avante!*, 2 April; *FBIS*, 20 April.)

Cunhal made a lengthy tour of China, Vietnam, Cambodia, Laos, and the Soviet Union. He cited differences with the Chinese over their support for NATO (which they saw as necessary to contain Soviet expansion), their belief that Portuguese entry in the Common Market was advantageous for the Portuguese people, and their refusal to establish ties with the Soviet Union, Vietnam, Cambodia, Laos, and Afghanistan (*Avante!*, 8 January; *JPRS*, 3 March.)

There were also consultations between the PCP

and officials of East Germany, Poland, Czechoslovakia, Hungary, and Bulgaria. Cunhal's failure to attend the funeral of Samora Machel in Mozambique was interpreted by some as an indication that PCP relations with the government party, FRELIMO (Front for the Liberation of Mozambique), are strained (Lisbon, *Expresso*, 1 November 1986; *JPRS*, 31 December 1986).

Communists criticized the Cavaco Silva government for allowing a ship carrying arms to Iran to dock at Setúbal (Lisbon Domestic Service, 8 February; *FBIS*, 9 February). PCP deputies called for an investigation of alleged secret Portuguese involvement in Washington's Iran-*contra* scandal (*Pravda*, 8 February; *World Affairs Report*, vol. 17, no. 2).

H. Leslie Robinson, Professor Emeritus
University of the Pacific

San Marino

Population. 22,791
Party. Communist Party of San Marino (PCS)
Founded. 1921
Membership. 1,200 (claimed, *WMR*, July)
General Secretary. Gilberto Ghiotti
Honorary Chairman. Gildo Gasperoni
Status. Legal
Last Congress. Eleventh, 27 January 1986
Last Election. 29 May 1983, 24.3 percent, 15 of 60 seats

The PCS is an extension of the Italian Communist Party, just as the other political parties of San Marino, the Christian Democrats (DCS), Socialists (PSS), Social Democrats (PSUS), and Republicans (PRS), are extensions of their Italian counterparts.

The PCS, the PSS, and the PSUS worked in a coalition until the summer of 1986, when a falling out about governmental methods and financial scandals caused the PCS to pull out of the coalition and align itself with the DCS, a rather unusual move. It was prompted by the mellowing of the DCS conservative stance and the fact that there was no other way to form a government (*WMR*, July).

In a government (Congress of State) that consists of three secretaries of state and seven ministers of state, the CPS has the secretaryship for internal affairs (Alvaro Selva) and the ministries for education and culture (Fausta Morganti), industry and handicrafts (Amici Giuseppe), transport and communications (Gastone Pasolini), and tourism and commerce (Ariosto Maiani) (ibid.). It remains to be seen whether the coalition will hold after the next election (probably in 1988, since elections are held every five years): the CPS values its independence, but—according to Alberto Mino, member of the CPS Directorate and Secretariat—it also knows the value of slow and steady transformation within established institutions and trade unions (*WMR*, July).

Three major contacts with the communist superpowers took place. Wu Xuegian, foreign minister of China, stopped off to compliment the Sanmarinese on their neutrality and achievements and to assure them of the Chinese Communist Party's (CCP) equal regard for large and small nations (Xinhua, 20 March; *FBIS-China*, 23 March); during 8–13 April, Zhao Ziyang (then acting CCP general secretary) returned the hospitality to the CPS delegation, headed by General Secretary Ghiotti, when it visited Beijing and Shanghai to discuss China's economic development and San Marino's role as an agent of peace and cooperation (Shanghai City Service, 11 April; *FBIS-China*, 15 April; Xinhua, 13 April; *FBIS-China*, 17 April). In the fall, Morganti, the secretary for education and culture and a CPS member, visited Beijing. This was the first San Marinese ministerial-level visit to China since the two countries had established diplomatic relations in 1971 (Xinhua, 14 October; *FBIS-China*, 15 October).

During 8–13 October, a parliamentary delegation headed by Deputy A. Carattoni toured Moldavia and then was greeted in Moscow by the chairman of the Supreme Soviet, Lev N. Tolkunov. Again, this was the first parliamentary-level visit at the invitation of the Supreme Soviet since the two countries had established diplomatic relations in 1956 (*Izvestiia*, 6 October; *FBIS-Soviet Union*, 9 October). Carattoni praised the Soviet political system, which is "moving forward," and welcomed the progress in arms talks (TASS, 9 October; *FBIS-Soviet Union*, 14 October). Soviet parliamentarians praised San Marino's "active neutrality" and potential as an "organizer of cooperation among smaller states" (*Izvestiia*, 14 October; *FBIS-Soviet Union*, 20 October).

Margit N. Grigory
Hoover Institution

Spain

Population. 39,000,804
Parties. Spanish Communist Party (Partido Comunista de España; PCE); Communist Party of the Peoples of Spain (Partido Comunista de los Pueblos de España; PCPE); Spanish Workers' Party–Communist Unity (Partido de los Trabajadores de España–Unidad Comunista; PTE-UC)
Founded. PCE: 1920, PCPE: 1984, PTE-UC: 1987
Membership. PCE: 60,000 (estimated), PCPE: 25,000–26,000 (Prague, *Rudé Právo*, 3 October; *FBIS*, 7 October), PTE-UC: 14,000 (*RFE Research*, 17 March)
General Secretaries. PCE: Gerardo Iglesias (42), PCPE: Juan Ramos, PTE-UC: Adolfo Pinedo
President. PCE: Dolores Ibárruri (91, legendary La Pasionaria of Civil War days)
Chairmen. PCPE: Ignacio Gallego, PTE-UC. Santiago Carrillo (72)
Secretariat. PCE. 11 members: Andreu Claret Serra, José María Coronas, Enrique Curiel Alonso, Francisco Frutos, Gerardo Iglesias, Francisco Palero, Juan Francisco Pla, Pedro Antonio Ríos, Francisco Romero Marín, Simón Sánchez Montero, Nicolás Sartorius
Executive Committee. PCE. 28 members
Central Committee. PCE. 102 members
Status. Legal
Last Congresses. PCE: Eleventh, 14–18 December 1983, in Madrid; PCPE: Second, April 1987; PTE-UC: First, 8 February 1987
Last Election. 1986, United Left (coalition of 7 parties, dominated by the PCE and including the PCPE), 4.6 percent, 7 of 350 seats; PTE-UC (campaigned as Board for Communist Unity), 1.12 percent, no seats
Auxiliary Organization. Workers' Commissions (Comisiones Obreras; CC OO), claimed membership of about 1 million, almost a third of Spain's some 3.4 million unionized workers, Marcelino Camacho, chairman. The CC OO is considered an auxiliary organization of the PCE, but all three parties have direct influence in it.
Publications. PCE: *Mundo Obrero* (Labor World), weekly; *Nuestra Bandera* (Our Flag), bimonthly ideological journal (both published in Madrid); PCPE: *Nuevo Rumbo* (New Direction), biweekly, Armando López Salinas, editor

Two main rival communist groups and some minor ones compete with the mainstream PCE. However, differences dividing them have been narrowed by a new climate of unanimous goodwill toward the Soviet Union and by continuing conciliatory overtures by the PCE to dissidents.

Gallego led pro-Soviet loyalists out of the Eurocommunist PCE in 1983. His PCPE claims to have trebled its membership since 1984 (Prague, *Rudé Právo*, 3 October; *FBIS*, 7 October). Carrillo, former general secretary of the Spanish Communist Party, left the PCE in 1986. His newly formed PTE-UC, successor to a grouping called "Board for Communist Unity," reportedly has limited influence in some cities and in CC OO trade unions. It refuses to join the United Left (Izquierda Unida; IU) and calls for communist unity under its own banner. (*RFE Research*, 17 March.)

Terrorist acts have declined but are still carried out by Marxist guerrillas of Basque Homeland and Liberty (Euzkadi ta Askatasuna; ETA) and by Catalan separatist groups called Free Land (Terra Lliure) and the Catalan Red Army of Liberation.

Organization and Leadership. Iglesias boasted in September that the PCE was being rehabilitated and that its crisis was over. This was because "monolithism" had given way to an open atmosphere that permitted questioning any policy or person—"starting with the general secretary." (*WMR*, September.) Iglesias was optimistic that the PCPE would heed the PCE's appeals for reconciliation, and he went so far as to insist in October that even Carrillo was not excluded from the invitation (Milan, *L'Unità*, 13 October; *FBIS*, 19 October). The latter claimed he was being snubbed by the PCE leadership (Madrid, *Epoca*, 11 May; *JPRS*, 29 June). Discussion at the PCE's Twelfth Congress planned for February 1988 was to focus on steps to achieve reunification of all communist groups in Spain (TASS, 18 July; *FBIS*, 28 July).

Domestic Affairs. Communists made some gains in June municipal and regional elections, but they were unable to capitalize significantly on a decline in the socialist vote. The IU won 7 percent of the municipal vote count compared with 4.6 percent of the national vote for Parliament in 1986; the socialist count was 38 percent compared with 44 percent in 1986. (*NYT*, 12 June; *WMR*, August.) Iglesias indicated that this represented a loss of more than a million votes for the Spanish Socialist Workers' Party (Partido Socialista Obrero Español; PSOE) but that the IU gained only 10 percent of these. Some 50 percent resulted, he said, from abstentions by disgruntled socialists, and the rest went to regional or nationalist groups. He attributed the IU's modest showing to its weakness in rallying together the Spanish left, its shortage of campaign resources, the television service's bias against the IU, and the "confusing presence" of Carrillo's lists on the ballot. Iglesias pointed out that the IU won more votes in the simultaneous elections for the European Parliament, which gave it three seats, than in the local races. (*Mundo Obrero*, 25 June–1 July; *FBIS*, 11 June; 29 July.)

The PCE general secretary was gratified withal that PSOE losses would strengthen calls among socialists for a swing to the left and for self-criticism of the "arrogance and power cult" within the party (ibid.). Further, a weakened PSOE in need of the votes of IU deputies in many municipalities would be obliged to shift to a more leftist policy (*WMR*, September). Iglesias declared that wherever the IU did not hold a majority it should avoid taking part in coalition governments so that it could exercise effective opposition (*Mundo Obrero*, 25 June–1 July; *FBIS*, 29 July). Even so, he insisted that the PCE was not seeking to overthrow the socialist government because it was impossible at this time to advance toward socialism without the PSOE (Sofia, *Rabotnichesko Delo*, 13 September; *FBIS*, 16 September).

As the PCE celebrated its 10th year as a legal party, one Spanish publication cited that legalization as "one of the great successes" of the transition period following the death of dictator Francisco Franco. The communist movement in Spain had become greatly diminished with the consolidation of democracy, whereas a clandestine party might well be powerful and influential today. (*Diario 16*, 9 April; *FBIS*, 14 May.) Some PCE officials attribute the party's decline to the leadership's "mistake" of having abandoned mass movements in favor of overinvolvement in elections and institutions. Also, Carrillo is blamed for the "patrimonial" attitude he had toward the party. (*Diario 16*, 9 April; *JPRS*, 14 May.)

Auxiliary Organizations. During the first half of 1987, much of Spain was paralyzed by a series of sometimes violent demonstrations and strikes against the government's austerity policies. Trade union leaders of the CC OO and of the larger socialist-backed General Workers' Union (Unión General de Trabajadores; UGT) balked at continuing their previous agreement to soften demands for wage increases until the economy could be stabilized; they said it was now time for their years of cooperation to be rewarded. (*WP*, 7 May.)

With the approach of elections in which workers choose their union affiliation, a UGT rift with the government was seen as necessary to avoid losses to the aggressive communist unions (*NYT*, 28 October). The IU and the CC OO were said to have spearheaded the protest movements (Madrid, ABC, 23 March; *FBIS*, 3 April). Wage settlements concluded in May and June averaged closer to the 7 percent demanded by the unions than to the 5 percent government guideline (*NYT*, 11 June).

International Views and Activities. The first half of 1987 found the PCE mending fences with a number of communist parties abroad from which it had been estranged. With "cordial" fanfare, relations were "normalized" with parties in the Soviet Union, Czechoslovakia, Poland, Portugal, France, and Cuba. Iglesias attributed the prior alienation to his party's independent stance and to the "arrogance of a nucleus" within the PCE. (*RFE Research*, 17 March; Lisbon, *Avante!*, 16 April; FBIS, 1 May; Prague, *Rudé Právo*, 1 July; *JPRS*, 2 August.) More pointedly, he noted the great contrast between Soviet policies of recent years which were unacceptable to Spanish communists, and the current "inspirational" policies of *perestroika* (restructuring) and *glasnost'* (openness). These would eliminate the "many shackles" on the Soviet economy and introduce "pluralism" into the Soviet system. (Madrid Domestic Service, 15 November; *FBIS*, 6, 16 November.) PCE officials stressed that while they opposed the re-establishment of the Communist International, they accepted the need for mechanisms to facilitate international coordination (*Pravda*, 10 October; *FBIS*, 14 October).

Communists accused the government of "seriously jeopardizing national security" with alleged plans to reinforce instead of closing the Torrejón air base near Madrid. Fearing that U.S. personnel might end up being replaced by Spaniards, they charged that reinforcing the base would further integrate the Spanish armed forces into the NATO military structure. (*Ya*, 14 January; *JPRS*, 3 March.) A PCE campaign against the U.S. bases in Spain and for a nuclear-free Europe included an

October peace march and rally in Madrid led by Iglesias, Gallego, and Marcelino Camacho (*Neues Deutschland*, 26 October).

Iglesias expressed the PCE's solidarity with the Chilean people's struggle against Augusto Pinochet's dictatorship and with the demands of Clodomiro Almeyda, exiled general secretary of the Chilean Socialist Party (ibid., 11, 12 April).

PCE consultations with communists abroad took place during visits to the Soviet Union, Czechoslovakia, East Germany, Hungary, France, Italy, Portugal, Nicaragua, Cuba, Syria, and China. Communist delegations visiting Madrid came from the Soviet Union, Czechoslovakia, East Germany, Romania, France, and Portugal.

Rival Communist Parties. At its Second Congress in April, the PCPE proposed a joint PCPE-PCE commission to try to resolve contentious issues. The congress called for the creation of a united communist party but refused to merge with the PCE if the latter tolerated various ideological trends alongside Marxism-Leninism. It concluded that Eurocommunism, which had caused the "gravest crisis" in the history of the Spanish communist movement, had demonstrated its "complete bankruptcy." The congress was attended by 30 delegations of communist and workers' parties and "national liberation movements." (*Pravda*, 28 April; Prague, *Rudé Právo*, 3 October; *FBIS*, 8 May, 7 October.)

A member of the PCE Secretariat assured the gathering that his party reaffirmed its "ideological class substance" rather than nurturing dreams of a "new left" (*Mundo Obrero*, 7–13 May; *FBIS*, 26 May). Later in the year, the PCPE expressed the hope that the "streams of unification" would be strengthened at the PCE's next congress because little progress had been made in the formation of the proposed exploratory commission (*Rudé Právo*, 3 October; *FBIS*, 7 October).

The call for communist unity was also a recurring theme at the February founding Congress of the PTE-UC (*RFE Research* 17 March). Chairman Carrillo said he was willing to negotiate but later claimed that Iglesias would not tolerate any contacts with him and had reprimanded one PCE official for having approached him. Carrillo alleged there were reports of an internal crisis in the PCE, with two deputy general secretaries rarely attending meetings, and attributed his own unpopularity in the PCE to an "inferiority" and "guilt" complex of those around Iglesias that compelled them to think they could lead only by hating the former general secretary. (Madrid, *Epoca*, 11 May; *JPRS*, 29 June.)

At the party congress, Carrillo disavowed the Eurocommunism that he had launched in the PCE and enthusiastically lauded current Soviet reforms. It was clear, however, that the Kremlin had not forgiven him for his previous anti-Soviet attacks. The only foreign delegation attending his congress was the North Korean Workers' Party. Also, the Soviet ambassador in Madrid pointedly stated in an interview published in the PCE's *Mundo Obrero* that the Kremlin was on good terms only with the PCE and the PCPE. (*Mundo Obrero*, 12–18 February; *RFE Research*, 27 February, 17 March.)

Left-Wing Terrorist Groups. The ETA was thought to be severely crippled by a series of police raids in the Spanish and French Basque region in October and November. Large supplies of arms and supplies were captured, and key terrorist leaders were arrested. Those detained in France were either handed over to Spanish authorities or deported to other countries, especially Algeria. The latter country had agreed to accept 30 ETA members under house arrest in return for Spanish vigilance over Algerian exiles in Spain. Prime Minister Felipe González was encouraged to announce that the government was "winning the war against terrorism." He predicted that the organization would be dismantled because it had lost its capacity for organized offensives and was not renewing its membership with the ease and speed of a few years ago. (*Insight*, 9 November; *NYT*, 29 November.)

Shattering the government's optimism was a car bomb explosion in December that wrecked a barracks for Civil Guard families in Zaragoza. Eleven were killed and 34 wounded, bringing to 49 the number killed by Basque terrorists in 1987. This was ETA's first major attack since a car bomb killed 24 shoppers in a Barcelona supermarket in June. (*NYT*, 12 December.)

In an October meeting with González, the PCE general secretary repeated his party's demands that the antiterrorist law be repealed, that Basque autonomy be strengthened, and that local police and judges be given more authority. He insisted that his party would sign a pact that did not include the Basque political parties, especially Herri Batasuna (People's Unity), ETA's political voice. (Madrid Domestic Service, 15 October; *FBIS*, 19 October.) Incidentally, the latter party won one seat in the European Parliament in June elections (*FBIS*, 11 June).

Police sources cited possible ETA links with an

Italian terrorist group, the Union of Fighting Communists, said to be based in Spain. Arrested in April in Barcelona were eight suspected members of that organization, including one Spaniard. (Ibid., 30 April.) Also in Barcelona two Catalan separatist organizations, Terra Lliure and the Catalan Red Liberation Army, claimed responsibility for a number of bomb attacks on U.S. targets during the year. Terra Lliure justified its violence as a means of directing media attention to the rise in proindependence feeling in Catalonia and to opposition to holding the 1992 summer Olympic Games in Barcelona. The second terrorist group first surfaced in May but issued no political statement. (*FBIS*, 15 September; *NYT*, 28 December; *WP*, 28 December.)

H. Leslie Robinson, Professor Emeritus
University of the Pacific

Sweden

Population. 8,383,026
Party. Left Party Communists (Vänsterpartiet Kommunisterna; VPK)
Founded. 1921 (VPK, 1967)
Membership. 17,800, principally in the far north, Stockholm and Göteborg
Chairman. Lars Werner
Executive Committee. 9 members: Lars Werner, Viola Claesson (vice-chairwoman), Bertil Mabrink (vice-chairman), Kenneth Kvist (secretary), Gudrun Schyman, Jörn Svensson, Bitte Engzell, Birgit Hansson, Bo Leinerdahl
Party Board. 35 members
Status. Legal
Last Congress. Twenty-eighth, 23–25 May 1987
Last Election. September 1985, 5.4 percent, 19 out of 349 seats
Auxiliary Organization. Communist Youth (KU)
Publications. *Ny Dag* (New Day), semiweekly; *Socialistisk Debatt* (Socialist Debate), monthly; both published in Stockholm

The ancestor of the VPK, Sweden's Communist Party (Sveriges Kommunistiska Partiet), was established in 1921. Its greatest moment came right after World War II, when it obtained 11.2 percent of the vote in local elections, largely due to the popularity of the Soviet Union at the end of the war. Since that time the communist party (later the VPK) has usually garnered about 4 or 5 percent of the vote. The party, which has never made a truly major contribution to communist history, has had marginal influence in Swedish politics. Perhaps its most important role has been to allow the Social Democrats to govern during much of Sweden's recent history. During the last half-century, the Swedish Social Democrats have been Europe's most dominant social democratic party, and during many of their years in power, they have relied on a combined majority with the communists in the Riksdag (parliament). The communists, however, have never been part of the government.

In Sweden, a party has to clear 4 percent to be represented in the Riksdag, and after the bitter reaction to the Soviet invasion of Czechoslovakia in 1968, the VPK went under 4 percent and was not represented. In the 1970 and 1976 elections it received 4.8 percent, and in 1979 and 1982, 5.6 percent of the vote. The VPK dropped to 5.4 percent in 1985.

The communists changed both the name and the direction of the party congress in 1967. Blue-collar workers constituted the majority of the communist electorate in previous years, but during the 1970s the VPK increasingly attracted white-collar and younger voters. In the 1979 elections, 56 percent of the voters were under the age of 30, and 36 percent of the voters were in the white-collar class. In the 1982 elections, those under 30 slipped to 45 percent, but those in the white-collar class rose from 36 to 41 percent. Over the years, the VPK has projected a Marxist image, even though it is generally regarded as one of the more moderate West European communist parties.

Party Internal Affairs. The history of the VPK has been characterized by stormy internal fighting, and the internecine battling in 1987 was worse than usual. Throughout the first half of the year, the arguments focused on policy and personnel decisions that were to be made by the Twenty-eighth Party Congress in late May. Much of the dispute centered around Werner, who has served twelve years as party leader, longer than any other leader in the history of the VPK. (His predecessor, C. H. Hermansson, served eleven years.) Werner has considerable support among the party rank and file but is under increasing criticism from party inner circles because of his low profile and "diffuse ideology" (*Svenska Dagbladet*, 17 May). Also, many of his colleagues think he should take a tougher line against the Social Democrats in Parliament. One reason there is more infighting than usual is that national elections will be held in September 1988, and the VPK is trying to position itself.

Those in the party who are trying to oust Werner come from two main groups: the "environmental communists," who stress nuclear and energy issues as well as women's issues and cultural policy, and the more orthodox and hard-line group, which has close connections to union activity. Both groups perceive Werner as too tepid on the issues that concern them. (*Dagens Nyheter*, 25 April.) An editorial from Sweden's most influential paper stated,

> There scarcely seems to be any real party strategy any more. The VPK failed to attract antinuclear power supporters after the 1980 referendum, and later on it was unable to appeal to dissatisfied Social Democrats. The party has been weakened organizationally, and it has had dwindling support among younger voters. (*Dagens Nyheter*, 25 April.)

In late April, approximately one month before the party congress, Claesson, one of the two vice-chairpersons of the VPK, notified the VPK's election committee that she would be stepping down after the Twenty-eighth Congress because of difficulties with Werner and her unhappiness with the lack of women on the party's board. After expressions of dissatisfaction with Werner's leadership at the 1984 party congress, Claesson and Mabrink, the VPK group leader in Parliament, were made vice-chairpersons to divide the party's leadership functions (and thereby take some power away from Werner) (*Dagens Nyheter*, 25 April).

Svensson, a member of the Riksdag and one of the nine members of the party's executive committee, offered himself as an alternative to Werner at the Twenty-eighth Congress. Svensson, an academician and a county planning director on leave, had served in the Riksdag since 1971. Svensson, a leading critic of Werner's for several years, has been described as more dogmatic than Werner and also as "the visionary and analyst of the party, one of the few who has tried to sketch, in detail, a model of how a socialist Sweden would function" (*Svenska Dagbladet*, 17 May).

Several days before the party congress, the elections committee unanimously recommended a new leadership structure for the VPK that, in effect, would have significantly reduced Werner's power. Lennart Beijer, chairman of the elections committee, announced the recommendation that Werner stay on as chairman but that the party's leadership become collective. Werner would share the leadership with three vice-chairpersons and one executive committee chairman. All four were highly critical of Werner's job performance. The effect of the elections committee recommendation was to instill those divisions that existed in the VPK into the party leadership.

The Twenty-eighth Party Congress voted to retain Werner as party leader and rebuked Beijer and the recommendations of the election committee by turning down their proposal. The congress also removed Beijer and two other critics of Werner, Brit Rundberg and Lars-Ove Hagberg, from the Executive Committee and replaced them with Werner supporters. The overall outcome, however, was far from a ringing victory for Werner. The two vice-chairpersons, Mabrink and Claesson (who changed her mind and agreed to stay on), are both opponents of Werner as is, of course, Svensson, who remains on the Executive Committee. In the press conference that followed the party congress, Werner said little about the internal debate, that the leadership team would continue to work hard together (*Dagens Nyheter*, 14 June). The consensus of observers was that serious internal struggles within the VPK would continue into the foreseeable future. An editorial in *Dagens Nyheter* (27 May) said,

> It was clearly demonstrated during the VPK congress that Werner does not have a grip on the party machine. The conflicts within the VPK will continue even after the congress . . . A divided and paralyzed VPK has little chance of reversing a falling membership trend, of winning support among today's young, or even of running an effective election campaign.

There is some speculation that Werner retained the party leadership because polls show that his popularity ranges beyond the VPK. According to Statistics Sweden, "Werner was his party's major asset in the last election" (*Ny Dag*, 15–21 April).

The VPK and the Social Democrats. The party congress was not only a defeat for Svensson and a hollow victory for Werner, but it also has given the Social Democrats some pause for concern. The Social Democrats have been able to govern for most of the last three decades because they could count on the VPK voting with them (or not against them) in the Riksdag. If the VPK had given undivided support to Werner, the Social Democrats need not have worried about continued support. However, because a number of leading members of the VPK are negative about cooperating with the Social Democrats on some pet economic issues, the Social Democrats might have to look to their political right for support. (*Svenska Dagbladet*, 26 May; *Dagens Nyheter*, 1, 14 June.)

Foreign Affairs. The assassination of Prime Minister Olof Palme on 28 February 1986 continued to be an important topic in Swedish domestic and foreign politics. As of this writing, no one had been arrested, although there were rumors that various groups with roots in the Middle East were responsible. The Palme Commission was set up as a fact-finding commission to sort out evidence and look into possible shortcomings of the police's investigative work. The most controversial appointment to the commission was Svensson, who pointed to the United States as responsible for the murder, although he didn't present any evidence. (*Svenska Dagbladet*, 22 February.)

The VPK, which disassociated itself from Moscow for many years, has warmed up to the Soviet Union since Mikhail Gorbachev assumed power. Mabrink, who is Moscow-trained and considered the Soviet expert of the VPK, referred to the changes in the Soviet Union as "the Moscow Spring" and said that it reminded him of the Prague Spring of 1968. Mabrink said that in the past, the VPK lost election support because of Soviet transgressions against democracy. He felt that because of a more favorable political climate in the USSR, the VPK's public image would be enhanced.

Soviet-Swedish relations have suffered during the past several years because of sightings—real or imaged—of Soviet submarines in Swedish territorial waters. Related to this, *Svenska Dagbladet* (10 August) ran a story about large numbers of Soviet fishing vessels anchoring in Swedish territorial waters. According to the paper, 542 foreign ships anchored in Swedish waters during the previous year. Of that number, 530 were Soviet. *Svenska Dagbladet* intimated that the ships had more than fishing as their intended missions.

Nevertheless, according to the leading Swedish public opinion poll SIFO, a decreasing number of Swedes perceive the Soviets as unfriendly. The percent of those who thought that the Soviet Union was unfriendly or a threat to Sweden dropped from 80 to 72 percent in a two-year period (*Dagens Nyheter*, 19 December).

International Party Contacts. Alessandro Natta, the Italian communist leader, visited Sweden in February and had talks with both Werner and Prime Minister Ingvar Carlsson. Natta said that Gorbachev's policies showed that the Italian criticism of previous regimes had been correct. (*Svenska Dagbladet*, 17 February.) During the VPK congress, messages of greetings and friendship were sent to Werner by Nicolae Ceauşescu, general secretary of the Romanian party, and also by Erich Honecker, general secretary of the Socialist Unity Party of the German Democratic Republic (*Scinteia*, 23 May; *Neues Deutschland*, 26 May). Kenneth Kvist, secretary of the VPK, made a working visit to Bulgaria at the invitation of the Bulgarian Communist Party (*Rabotnichesko delo*, 3 October).

Rival Communist Groups. The pro-Soviet Communist Workers' Party (APK), founded in 1977, received only 5,877 votes (less than 0.1 percent) in the last election and therefore plays a minimal role in Swedish politics. During 1987, there was virtually no reportage of activities of the APK.

Peter Grothe
Monterey Institute of International Studies

Switzerland

Population. 6,573,000
Party. Swiss Labor Party (Partei der Arbeit der Schweiz/Parti suisse du travail/Partito Swizzero del Lavoro; PdAS)
Founded. 1921; outlawed 1940; re-established 1944
Membership. 4,500 (estimated)
General Secretary. Jean Spielmann
Honorary President. Jean Vincent
Politburo. 14 members
Secretariat. 5 members
Central Committee. 50 members
Status. Legal

Last Congress. Thirteenth, 27 February–1 March 1987
Last Election. 1987 (no accurate data)
Auxiliary Organizations. Communist Youth League of Switzerland (KVJS), Marxist Student League, Swiss Women's Organization for Peace and Progress, Swiss Peace Movement, Swiss-Soviet Union Society, Swiss-Cuban Society, Central Sanitaire Swiss
Publications. *VO Réalités* (Geneva), weekly, circulation 8,000 copies; *Vorwärts* (Basel), weekly, circulation 6,000 copies; *Il Lavatore*, Italian-language edition; *Zunder*, KVJS organ

Although Switzerland has three organizations of some significance that can be labeled "communist parties," the last election on a federal level showed a further decline of the political influence of the Moscow-line communist movement. The largest and oldest of these three groups is the PdAS, which is officially recognized by communist fraternal parties. The other two are the Progressive Organizations of Switzerland (POCH) and the Sozialistische Arbeiterpartei (Socialist Workers' Party; SAP).

The Social Democratic Party of Switzerland (SPS), which has some radical wings, suffered its worst defeat since proportional representation was introduced in 1919 (*NYT*, 20 October). Some left extremist SPS members, however, gained greater influence within the party's leadership.

POCH was founded in 1972 in Basel by students disappointed with the sterile politics of the PdAS. Under Georges Degen, its secretary, the now-Zurich-based organization recently replaced old-fashioned, doctrinaire Marxism with the more modern, ideological concepts of the Greens movement. There are two Greens parties in Switzerland: the first group, the Swiss Ecologist Party, is known as a "cucumber" because it is (supposedly) all Green; the second organization, the Green Socialist Alternative, is called a "watermelon" because its green peel covers a red, or Marxist, core (*NYT*, 18 October). POCH's new policies along the latter's party lines proved quite successful in the November election, where the "watermelons" gained nine seats, though the result was well below their expectations. A POCH subsidiary, the Organization for Women's Affairs, is the most important women's group in Switzerland and is quite active among students. POCH publishes the weekly *POCH-Zeitung*, with an estimated circulation of 6,000 copies. The membership is reported to be somewhat lower, with 65 percent women. This organization was more active than the other.

The SAP was founded in 1969 by a group of young Trotskyists who left the PdAS; it was renamed in 1980 and operates mainly in the larger cities. Because it is a cadre party, its membership seems to remain constant at about 2,000, but is supported by at least 3,000 sympathizers. Its leading theoretician is Fritz Osterwalder. In recent years SAP members have attained some important positions, especially in the educational system and the trade unions. It exercises, therefore, a far greater influence than its small membership would indicate. The SAP still advocates the revolutionary class struggle in centers of production and believes in central planning and the nationalization of industry. It is active among students under the name Revolutionary Socialist Youth (RSJ) and from time to time in the anti–nuclear power movement. Its main weekly publication appears in four languages: *Bresche*, *La Brèche*, *Rosso*, and *Roia*.

In addition there are several other radical socialist splinter organizations, such as the Autonomous Socialist Party (PSA), which, under the leadership of Werner Carrobbio, operates exclusively in the Italian part of Switzerland and has a membership of about 1,000. There were some indications that this party, the result of a split within the SPS in 1960, was considering merging with the SPS again. Two other small groups must be mentioned: the Communist Party of Switzerland/Marxist-Leninist (KPS/ML) and the SAP-connected Gruppe Schweiz ohne Armee/Group for a Switzerland Without Military (GSoA). The two major Swiss peace groups—the Schweizerische Friedensbewegung/Swiss Section of the World Peace Council (SFB) and the International Women's League for Peace and Freedom (IFFF)—are controlled by the PdAS. They all seem to be somewhat dormant, though they cooperate on special occasions. The majority of sympathizers of the older socialist ideas are mainly recruited in the country's western part and Basel, whereas the more modern, environmental-oriented approaches have more followers in the German-speaking areas.

Leadership and Organization. The central event of 1987 for the PdAS was its Thirteenth Party Congress, held in Geneva under the motto For Politics, Economy and Culture Advancing Peace on 27 February–1 March. Because each of the 23 cantons has a PdAS organization, there were some 110 delegates. The congress was also attended by several foreign communist party delegations, including representatives from the Soviet Union, Nicaragua's Sandinista front, Cuba, and the African National Congress of South Africa. The senior guest was Ivan V. Kapitonov, chairman of the Soviet Central Revisionist Commission. The delegation from East Germany was headed by Waldemar Liemen, a member of its party's Central Committee. The party congress opened with a solidarity meeting in which Herman Estrada of the Sandinista front and Tomy Wassen of the African National Congress reaffirmed the internationalism of the Swiss communist movement (ADN, 28 February). The two rather ambitious documents of the congress, a domestic action program and an international political resolution, were unanimously approved after two days of "open and enthusiastical" discussion (*IB*, June).

The main organizational change and one of the most notable aspects of the congress was the strong effort to rejuvenate the party's leading bodies, reflected in the election of Spielmann as the new PdAS general secretary. He replaced Armand Magnin, who has led the party since 1978. Spielman, born in 1944 in Geneva, joined the PdAS as early as 1967. As a postal worker, he has been active in the trade union movement since 1964 and served as the party's deputy general secretary since 1983 (*WMR*, July). Eleven members of the Central Committee were replaced with younger delegates. By now 39 percent of the delegates are under 40, and 26 percent are between 40 and 50 (*IB*, June). In addition the Politburo has three newcomers and a somewhat stronger representation of the German-speaking part of Switzerland. Although well over 42 percent of the Swiss labor force is employed in the service industries and thus aspires to be part of the middle class (*Neue Züricher Zeitung*, 2 October 1984), the PdAS seems to be stuck with old class struggle ideology, vocabulary, and slogans, and the exodus of about a hundred young intellectuals in 1969 deprived the party of its future intellectual leadership. The recent defeat in the federal election reflects the party's failure to adjust to sociological changes.

Domestic Affairs. The Thirteenth Congress passed one major domestic action program based on the struggle for a "peace economy" and winning the allies needed to pass it. In his report tracing domestic developments, outgoing General Secretary Magnin publicly admitted the party's painful electoral losses in the past, its lack of appeal to the younger generation, and its failure to grasp the full significance of the new demands pertaining to the protection of the environment, quality of life, and consequences of the scientific and sociological revolutions. In order to gain new appeal, the action program emphasized radical options such as completely banning arms exports (which would hurt the Swiss economy), reducing military spending, lifting the banking secrecy, or even calling for a working week of 35 hours with full pay. According to *WMR* (July), the document also underlines the party's continued efforts to fight "resolutely in the traditional spheres of class battles—for improving the position of the working people and for defending their gains against the offensive from the Right." In local elections in the Geneva canton in 1987 the PdAS had 29 candidates elected, with ten members now sitting on Geneva's municipal council.

International Affairs. The main international resolution of this congress upgraded the party policies as outlined in the 1971 theses, the 1979 Regensdorf program, and the 1982 decisions and promoted the idea of a "peace-advancing economy." This approach aims at five areas: the repudiation of the arms race; gearing and controlling the economy to solve important problems; balancing scientific and technological progress against protection of the environment; massive support of the Third World and radical changes in the political ties with less-developed countries; and peaceful coexistence.

Early in February General Secretary Magnin visited East Berlin, where he was received by Hermann Axen, a member of the Politburo and secretary of the Central Committee of the East German Communist Party. This meeting served as a booster for the then-forthcoming Swiss Party of Labor Congress. The PdAS used its congress for several international contacts, though the most intense relationship seemed to be with the delegation from East Germany. Shortly after the congress, Spielmann, the newly elected general secretary, met with the East German delegation in Geneva to discuss the U.S.-Soviet arms treaty and other issues of mutual interest (ADN, 3 March). In May Spielman met in Geneva with the editor in chief of *World Marxist Review* to discuss the development of cooperation between PdAS and the journal (*WMR*, May).

General Activities. During 1987 there was occasional cooperation between several more or less autonomous leftist student groups. Several anti-apartheid actions and organized divestment demonstrations took place in the major urban centers and universities, the most active of which seems to be the University of Zurich. Other than some minor actions organized by the SFB and IFFF among the Swiss student body, there were no signs of significant political activity.

Kurt R. Leube
California State University at Hayward

Turkey

Population. 52,987,778
Party. Communist Party of Turkey (TCP)
Founded. 1920
Membership. Negligible
General Secretary. Haydar Kutlu
Leading Bodies. No data
Status. Illegal
Last Congress. Fifth, October or November 1983
Last Election. N/a
Auxiliary Organizations. Progressive Youth Societies of Turkey (PYS)
Publications. *Atilim* (according to Voice of the Turkish Communist Party, this was a monthly publication slated to become weekly; no other information is available); *Ileri* (Forward), reportedly published by PYS; *Proleter Istanbul*, reportedly published by the Istanbul chapter of the TCP.

Although the TCP remained illegal during 1987, its legal status became the subject of public discussion for the first time in many years. The issue came to a head at about the time of the general election, which was held on 29 November.

The election was preceded by a referendum on the repeal of the ban on those political leaders who had been stripped of power by the military junta that came into office in the coup of 12 September 1980. The ban, preserved in the Constitution adopted in November 1982, was due to expire in 1987 for secondary figures and in 1992 for the major leaders of the old regime. Prime Minister Turgut Ozal had indicated his readiness to support repeal as early as the fall of 1986. He apparently won President Kenan Evren over by spring 1987. The referendum removed the president from the procedure and also enabled Ozal to avoid full responsibility for the decision. In fact, the prime minister favored a vote *against* repeal. In any event, a razor-thin majority (50.2 percent) of a heavy vote (94 percent of registered voters participated) supported the restoration of political rights to the old politicians; fewer than 90,000 votes out of almost 24.5 million separated the ayes from the nays. This sobering result reaffirmed the Turkish commitment to democracy but also served notice that the former political leaders seemed to have lost much of their popular appeal. In both respects, the referendum boosted Ozal's political fortunes.

The referendum set the stage for the general election. On 6 September, as the referendum was coming to an end but before the results were known, Ozal announced that the general election would take place in November, which was a year before the legal expiration of the parliamentary term. The prime minister, anticipating a favorable vote for repeal in the referendum, hoped to get through the election before his older competitors could get their political feet on the ground. He also drafted a new election law that included two formidable barriers: to attain parliamentary seats, a party would have to gain (1) at least 10 percent of the national vote and (2) at least 20 percent of the vote of the province in which the seat was at stake. Not surprisingly, there were numerous charges of unfairness.

The election results were as follows; Ozal's Motherland Party (MP) garnered just over 36 percent of the vote and won control of 292 of the 450 seats at stake for a 65 percent parliamentary majority; the moderate left Social Democratic Populist Party (SDPP), led by Professor Erdal Inonu, won almost 25 percent of the vote and gained 99 seats; and the True Path Party (TPP), led by former Prime Minister Suleyman Demirel (a previously banned politician) won 19 percent of the vote and gained 59 seats. No other party passed the 10 percent threshold. The Democratic Left party (DLP), led by another banned politician (Bulent Ecevit), won about 8.5 percent of the vote, and the religiously oriented Prosperity Party won 7 percent. Significantly, this distribution of votes was not very different from that of the 1977 election, the last before the military coup. The moderate right (MP and TPP) had the support of roughly 55 percent of the electorate, whereas the moderate left (SDPP and DLP) had the support of about 33 percent, with the remaining 12 percent scattered among more extreme parties, mostly on the right. The contrast between the popular vote and the distribution of seats was sharp enough to cause considerable comment. The combined vote for the two left parties, for example, was only slightly less than the MP vote, but the MP gained a 65 percent majority in the new Parliament while the left won only 22 percent of the seats, somewhat less than the SDPP's share of the popular vote, not counting the DLP vote. However, the overwhelming presence of the MP in the new Assembly was a favorable omen for continuing political stability, at least in the short run. Demirel, reported in 1986 to feel that he was unstoppable, appeared to have been effectively stymied, and his counterpart on the left, Ecevit, announced his retirement from politics.

The TCP experienced rather important developments during 1987 as well. Early in the year, the Central Committee released a report of a national conference, allegedly held in one of Turkey's industrial cities during November 1986. The conference was chaired by Kutlu (reportedly an alias for Nabi Yagci), general secretary of the Central Committee of the TCP. The theme set in his opening address dominated party propaganda all through 1987: preservation of peace at home and abroad and restoration of democracy in Turkey. The Evren-Ozal regime was denounced as a stooge of U.S. imperialism and as a dictatorship guilty of torture and repression. A new theme, which emerged as the year progressed, was that religious piety could be accepted as a genuine expression of nationalist sentiment and one with which communists could coexist. President Evren reciprocated by denouncing religious fanaticism as a threat as serious as communism. He also publicly excoriated the communists for their tactic of cooperation with fundamentalists, although he claimed this was consistent with communist strategy over a 30-year period. He accused both groups of trying to infiltrate the army to drive a wedge between the army and the people. Thus both extremist groups recognized that the army stood in their way; Evren promised that, as in the past, Turkey would overcome the forces of fundamentalism and communism (*FBIS*, 9 January).

This theme was developed by General Secretary Kutlu at a plenum of the TCP Central Committee in February. He compared the current situation with the Independence War of the early 1920s when the nationalist leader Kemal Atatürk made common cause with religious militants in the struggle to establish Turkish sovereignty. Kutlu accused Evren of surrendering Turkish independence to the imperialists and declared that secularism without democracy was meaningless (*FBIS*, 18 February). This newfound warmth toward Islamic fundamentalism was also reflected in formal cooperation between communist and fundamentalist organizations in Europe (*FBIS*, 25 February). It had its counterpart in the revelation of the Evren regime's arrangement with a Saudi-backed Islamic League to pay Muslim clergy to minister to Turkish *gastarbeiter* in Europe.

Perhaps the most notable development affecting the TCP was the return to Turkey of General Secretary Kutlu along with Nihat Sargin, General Secretary of the Turkish Labor Party, which was set to merge with the TCP. The merger of the two parties was announced in the wake of the September constitutional referendum and was apparently part of a TCP campaign to urge unification of all left parties and cooperation among all opposition forces in the upcoming general election. The new entity was to be known as the United Communist Party of Turkey (*FBIS*, 1 October; *Morning Star*, 8 October). The merger was announced jointly by Kutlu for the TCP and by Behice Boran, leader of the TLP, early in October, but Professor Boran apparently passed away shortly thereafter; it is not clear whether the original plan called for her to accompany Kutlu on his return to Turkey in November (*FBIS*, 12 November).

Plans for the return to Turkey of Kutlu and Sargin were announced in late October. The purpose of the return was ostensibly to establish the "legal activities" of the new United Communist Party; the two party officials also called for the legalization of the new party, for permission of political refugees to return to Turkey, and for the release of political prisoners (*Cumhuriyet*, 27 October; in *FBIS*, 12 November). The announcement of these plans triggered a debate involving the communist party officials, newspaper columnists and editors, and both the prime minister and the president. In a newspaper interview, Prime Minister Ozal was asked if he would join the leaders of the TPP, DLP, and SDPP in supporting legalization of the communist party. He responded by declaring that he had no fear of the communists because their front organizations had never polled more than 3 to 5 percent of the vote. However, he noted that it was not just a question of legalizing communist organizations but also of legalizing Islamic fundamentalism (outlawed since the beginning of the Republic). As for Kutlu and Sargin's plans to return to Turkey, Ozal warned that if they were subject to a pending investigation by state prosecutors, that investigation would continue, nor could they set up a communist party because it was still illegal. They would be better advised to wait for the law to change. Change in the law was, however, at the bottom of Ozal's agenda. He argued that others might freely advocate legalization but that he had to be more careful because he was still head of the government (*Hurriyet*, 29 October; in *FBIS*, 5 November). The communist response was to argue that democracy does not allow for a double standard and that the impending return of Kutlu and Sargin was not a challenge to Turgut Ozal but part of the general democratization of Turkey (Our Radio, 4 November, in *FBIS*, 5 November). Some newspapers supported this contention. *Milliyet*, for example, commented that if Turkey's application for full membership in the European Economic Community was to be taken seriously, it must allow the TCP to operate legally, as do Spain and Portugal. Ugur Mumcu noted in *Cumhuriyet* that if Kutlu and Sargin were arrested, the MP could no longer claim the label of liberalism, and he reminded his readers that the constitutional ban on links between political parties and labor unions remained in effect (*Milliyet*, 28 October; *Cumhuriyet*, 1 November; both in *FBIS*, 5, 6 November). A columnist in *Tercuman* (3 November), however, suggested that communism in Turkey was dangerous because the Soviet Union is an immediate neighbor and because it is "equated with treachery against the homeland and the nation. Once it gains legal status, it will upset all the values in the country, confuse the minds of the people, and create chaos in all establishments, organizations, and institutions." (*FBIS*, 10 November.) Ankara Radio, meanwhile, announced on 6 November that the two travelers risked arrest on "charges of crimes against the state," with possible penalties of eight to fifteen years imprisonment (*FBIS*, 9 November).

Kutlu and Sargin continued to argue for legalization and made appeals for cooperation to other party leaders, including Necmettin Erbakan of the religiously oriented Prosperity Party. They proclaimed their commitment to democracy and multiparty politics, even after the establishment of socialism; accepted the continued membership of Turkey in NATO; and called for the legalization of religious fundamentalism. They noted that the legal ban on fundamentalism had not prevented the spread of Islamic piety and declared that different beliefs can coexist: "we can find points of agreement with the religious movements on solutions to Turkey's many problems." (Voice of the TCP, 7 November; in *FBIS*, 9 November; news conference in West Berlin, 11 November; broadcast on Our Radio, 12 November; in *FBIS*, 12 November.)

Prime Minister Ozal was quoted by Ankara Radio on 14 November as announcing that Kutlu and Sargin would be detained because their organizations were charged with

> carrying arms, shipping arms to regions where action was being taken, using arms against members of a political party, extorting money, issuing illegal documents, establishing cells, engaging in activities to topple the government through revolutionary means and to divide the nation, resorting to violence among their own factions, disrupting education, and engaging in militant and ideological activities in universities, high schools, and secondary schools.

The trip was a plot "to distance Turkey from Europe," but it would not spoil the impending general election (*FBIS*, 16 November).

On 16 November, Ankara Radio reported that Kutlu and Sargin had arrived (apparently in the company of a retinue of parliamentary deputies from such countries as France, Italy, the Netherlands, West Germany, and the European Parliament, as well as a number of European journalists) and that they were immediately detained (*FBIS*, 17 November). On the same day, President Evren declared that the prohibitions on communism and fundamentalism could not be abolished because that would re-create the conditions that prevailed before the 1980 coup, although he allowed that the day for their abolition might come in the distant future. Why, he asked, did Kutlu and Sargin come with so many journalists and why now? (*FBIS*, 17 November). TASS, meanwhile, reported that "dozens of European parliamentarians and journalists" were shocked by the arrests (*FBIS*, 18 November). The speaker of the Grand National Assembly of Turkey formally received the parliamentarians who had accompanied Kutlu and Sargin and politely listened to their appeals for legalization of the communist party. A few days later, Prime Minister Ozal spoke to the foreign press at his official residence and told them that neither communists nor fundamentalists were as dangerous as in the past but that a general amnesty was not on his agenda (*FBIS*, 27 November).

Finally, on 25 November, Our Radio reported that both the TCP and the TLP had renounced terror, that the TCP is not controlled by foreign powers, that those who fear legalization reflect scorn for the Turkish people, and that a democratic move could not be portrayed as provocative (*FBIS*, 27 November). Tercuman denounced the TCP as a Soviet fifth column intended to destroy democracy in Turkey and warned that if these efforts succeeded, only the Armenians and others of their ilk would win (*FBIS*, 18 November). On 13 November, the journal *Bulvar* in Istanbul reported that the secretary general of the Turkish Communist Party-B (TCP-B) severely criticized Kutlu and Sargin's trip to Turkey on grounds that "they have reached an agreement with the Turkish state. The TCP has been led astray by the devil." The TCP-B threatened to launch armed struggle in Turkey against police torturers and possibly even against Evren and and Ozal but would not engage in terrorist actions outside Turkey (*FBIS*, 17 November).

Frank Tachau
University of Illinois at Chicago

Select Bibliography, 1986–1987

GENERAL

Amnesty International. *Amnesty International Report 1987*. London: Amnesty International Publications, 1987. 391 pp.

Baylis, Thomas A., ed. *East Germany, West Germany and the Soviet Union: Perspectives on Changing Relationships*. Ithaca, N.Y.: Cornell University Press, 1986. 64 pp.

Brock, Lothar. *Die beiden deutschen Staaten in der Dritten Welt*. Berlin: Westdeutscher Verlag, 1986. 426 pp.

Brohm, Jean-Marie, et al. *Marx...ou pas?* Paris: Etudes et Documentation Internationales, 1986. 340 pp.

Djilas, Milovan. *Of Prisons and Ideas*. San Diego, Calif.: Harcourt Brace Jovanovich, 1986. 166 pp.

Fritsch-Bournazel, Renate. *Das Land in der Mitte: die Deutschen im europäischen Kräftefeld*. Munich: Iudicium Verlag, 1986. 169 pp.

Gordon, Lincoln. *Eroding Empire: Western Relations with Eastern Europe*. Washington, D.C.: Brookings Institution, 1987. 359 pp.

Hammer, Manfred, et al., eds. *Das Mauerbuch: Texte und Bilder aus Deutschland von 1945 bis heute*. 3d rev. ed. Berlin: Oberbaumverlag, 1986. 308 pp.

Haraszte, Miklós. *The Velvet Prison: Artists under State Socialism*, A New Republic Book, New York: Basic Books, 1987. 160 pp.

Holmes, Leslie. *Politics in the Communist World*. Oxford: Oxford University Press, 1987. 420 pp.

Hyland, William. *Mortal Rivals: Superpower Relations from Nixon to Reagan*. New York: Random House, 1987. 320 pp.

Luchinova, S. M. *Osvobodivshiesia strany: Klassovaia sushchnost' i dvizhushchie sily revoliutsionno-demokraticheskikh preobrazovanii*. Moscow: Izdatelstvo Moskovskogo universiteta, 1987. 122 pp.

Mayer, Nonna. *La Boutique contra la gauche*. Paris: Presses de la Fondation Nationale des Sciences Politiques, 1986. 346 pp.

Nawrocki, Joachim. *Die Beziehungen zwischen den beiden Staaten in Deutschland*. Berlin: Verlag Holzapfel, 1986. 128 pp.

Pravda, Alex, and Blair A. Ruble. *Trade Unions in Communist States*. Boston: Allen and Unwin, 1986. 281 pp.

Sesay, Amadu, ed. *Africa and Europe: From Partition to Interdependence or Dependence?* Dover, N.H.: Croom Helm, 1986. 272 pp.

Shumikin, N. F., chief ed. *Sotsializm i sovremennyi mir*. Kiev: Vyshcha shkola, 1987.

Smith, Tony. *Thinking like a Communist*. New York: W.W. Norton, 1987. 244 pp.

Soley, Lawrence C., and John S. Nichol. *Clandestine Radio Broadcasting*. New York: Praeger, 1986. 288 pp.

Staar, Richard F., ed. *1987 Yearbook on International Communist Affairs*. Stanford: Hoover Institution Press, 1987. 640 pp.

Strashun, B. A., et al., eds. *Konstitutsii sotsialisticheskikh gosudarstv*. 2 vols. Moscow: Iurizdat, 1987.

Timmermann, Heinz. *The Decline in the World Communist Movement*. Boulder, Colo.: Westview Press, 1987. 275 pp.

Turner, Henry Ashby, Jr. *The Two Germanies since 1945*. New Haven, Conn.: Yale University Press, 1987. 228 pp.

Wagenlehner, Günther. *Abschied vom Kommunismus*. Herford: Verlag Busse und Seewald, GmbH, 1987. 491 pp.

Weeks, Albert L., comp. *Brassey's Soviet and Communist Quotations*. Washington, D.C.: Pergamon-Brassey, 1987. 368 pp.

World Federation of Democratic Youth. *12th Assembly of the Member Organizations of the World Federation of Democratic Youth. Budapest, Hungary, 23–29 November 1988*. Budapest: WFDY, 1987. 230 pp.

AFRICA

Abdel-Rahim, Muddathir. *Imperialism and Nationalism in the Sudan*. Khartoum, Sudan: Khartoum University Press, 1986. 275 pp.

Akinyemi, A. E., ed. *Economic Cooperation between Nigeria and the Socialist Countries*. Lagos, Nigeria: Nigerian Institute of International Affairs, 1986. 210 pp.

Ayida, A. A. *Reflections on Nigerian Development*. Lagos, Nigeria: Malthouse Press, 1987. 278 pp.

Babatiope, Ebenezer. *Nigeria, the Socialist Alternative*. Benin City, Nigeria: Jodah House, 1986. 127 pp.

Bach, Daniel C., ed. *Le Nigeria contemporain*. Paris: Editions du Centre national de la recherche scientifique, 1986. 336 pp.

Bridgland, Fred. *Jonas Savimbi: A Key to Africa*. New York: Paragon House, 1987. 512 pp.

Butler, Jeffrey; Richard Elphick; and David Welsh, eds. *Democratic Liberalism in South Africa: Its History and Prospect*. Middletown, Conn.: Wesleyan University Press, 1987. 426 pp.

Campbell, Kurt M. *Soviet Policy Towards South Africa*. New York: St. Martin's Press, 1987. 272 pp.

Chabal, Patrick, ed. *Political Domination in Africa: Reflections on the Limits of Power*. New York: Cambridge University Press, 1986. 240 pp.

Dejene, Alemneh. *Peasants, Agrarian Socialism, and Rural Development in Ethiopia*. Boulder, Colo.: Westview Press, 1986. 162 pp.

Duignan, Peter, and Robert H. Jackson, eds. *Politics and Government in African States, 1960–1985*. Stanford: Hoover Institution Press, 1986. 190 pp.

Egero, Bertil. *Mozambique, A Dream Undone: the Political Economy of Democracy, 1975–84*. Uppsala, Sweden: Nordiska afrikainstitutet, 1987. 230 pp.

Frankel, M. Iu., et al., eds. *Afrika: problemy istorii: sbornik statei*. Moscow: Nauka, 1986. 266 pp.

Gavrilov, N. I., et al. *Desat let efiopskoi revoliutsii*. Moscow: Progress, 1986. 194 pp.

Groupe d'Etudes et de Recherches du Parti Socialist du Sénégal. *Le Parti Socialiste du Sénégal: de Senghor á Abdou Diouf*. Dakar, Senegal: Nouvelles Editions Africaines, 1986. 176 pp.

Harbeson, John W. *The Ethiopian Transformation: Revolution in a Traditional Polity*. Boulder, Colo.: Westview Press, 1987. 200 pp.

Harbeson, John W., ed. *The Military in African Politics*. New York: Praeger, 1987. 200 pp.

Harris, Myles F. *Breakfast in Hell: A Doctor's Eyewitness Account of the Politics of Hunger in Ethiopia*. New York: Poseidon Press, 1987. 271 pp.

Ikejiani, Okechukwu. *Nigeria, Political Imperative: Desiderata for Nationhood and Stability*. Enugu, Nigeria: Fourth Dimension Publishers, 1986. 276 pp.

Jansson, Kurt; Michael Harris; and Angela Penrose. *The Ethiopian Famine*. Atlantic Highlands, N.J.: Zed Books, 1987. 196 pp.

Kamil, Leo. *Fueling the Fire: U.S. Policy and the Western Sahara Conflict*. Trenton, N.J.: Red Sea Press, 1987. 104 pp.

Keller, Edmond J., and Donald Rothchild, eds. *Afro-Marxist Regimes*. Boulder, Colo.: Lynne Rienner Publishers, 1987. 333 pp.

Lamb, David. *The Africans*. New York: Vintage Books, 1987. 371 pp.

Libby, Ronald T. *The Politics of Economic Power in Southern Africa*. Princeton, N.J.: Princeton University Press, 1987. 361 pp.

Liebenow, Gus. *African Politics: Crises and Challenges*. Bloomington: Indiana University Press, 1986. 305 pp.

Lopes, Carlos. *Guinea-Bissau: From Liberation's Struggle to Independent Statehood*. London: Zed Books, 1987. 194 pp.

Makinda, Sam. *Superpower Diplomacy in the Horn of Africa*. London: Croom Helm, 1987. 241 pp.

Mandaza, Ibbo, ed. *Zimbabwe: The Political Economy of Transition*. Dakar, Senegal: CODESIRA, 1986. 430 pp.

Mandela, Nelson. *The Struggle Is My Life*. London: International Defense and Aid Fund for Southern Africa, 1986. 249 pp.

Markakis, John, and Michael Waller, eds. *Military Marxist Regimes in Africa*. London: Frank Cass, 1986. 166 pp.

Markowitz, Irving Leonard, ed. *Studies in Power and Class in Africa*. New York: Oxford University Press, 1987. 400 pp.

Mazrui, Ali. *The African: Triple Heritage*. Boston: Little, Brown and Co., 1986. 336 pp.

McCaul, Colleen. *Satellite in Revolt: KwaNdebele, an Economic and Political Profile*. Johannesburg: South African Institute of Race Relations, 1987. 125 pp.

Mozambique News Agency. *Samora, Why He Died*. Maputo, Mozambique: AIM, 1986. 95 pp.

Munslow, Barry, ed. *Africa: Problems in the Transition to Socialism*. London: Zed Books, 1986. 220 pp.

National Union of South African Students. *Action for Democracy; 1986 NUSAS Theme Publication*. South Africa: NUSAS, 1986. 73 pp.

———. *NUSAS Talks to ANC: Report Back on Meeting*

between NUSAS and the African National Congress, Held from Sunday, 31 March to Tuesday, 2 April in Harare, Zimbabwe. South Africa: NUSAS, 1986. 32 pp.

Oculi, Okello. *Food and Revolution in Africa*. Zaria, Nigeria: Vanguard, 1986. 215 pp.

Parti de la révolucion populaire du Bénin, Comité Central. *Rapport d'activités et d'orientation du Comité Central: deuxième congrès national ordinaire, Cotonou du 18–24 novembre 1985*. Cotonou, Benin: O.N.E.P.I., Maison de la Presse, 1986. 91 pp.

The Role of the Southern Sudanese in the Building of Modern Sudan: Selected Papers. Khartoum, Sudan: University of Juba, 1986. 146 pp.

Ronin, Dov, ed. *Democracy and Pluralism in Africa*. Boulder, Colo.: Lynne Rienner Publishers, 1986. 220 pp.

Rosenblum, Mort, and Doug Williamson. *Squandering Eden: Africa at the Edge*. San Diego, Calif.: Harcourt Brace Jovanovich, 1987. 326 pp.

Ravenhill, John. *Africa in Economic Crisis*. Basingstoke, Hampshire, England: Macmillan, 1986. 359 pp.

Santos, Eduardo dos. *A Questão do Barotze*. Lisbon: Instituto de Investigação Cientifica Tropical, 1986. 174 pp.

Saul, John S., and Stephen Gelb. *The Crisis in South Africa*. Rev. ed. New York: Monthly Review Press, 1986. 245 pp.

Schärer, Therese. *Das Nigerian Youth Movement*. Frankfurt am Main, West Germany: P. Lang, 1986. 376 pp.

South African Communist Party. *SACP Directive-Discussion Document*. South Africa: The Party, 1986. 16 leaves.

United States Committee for Refugees. *Refugees from Mozambique: Shattered Land, Fragile System*. Washington, D.C.: U.S. Committee for Refugees, 1986. 31 pp.

Usman, Yusufu Bala. *The Manipulation of Religion in Nigeria, 1977–1987*. Kaduna, Nigeria: Vanguard, 1987. 153 pp.

Van der Ross, R. E. *The Rise and Decline of Apartheid: A Study of Political Movement Among the Coloured People of South Africa, 1880–1985*. Cape Town: Tafelberg, 1986. 416 pp.

Verschuur, Christine. *Mozambique: dix ans de solitude*. Paris: L'Harmattan, 1986. 182 pp.

Wallerstein, Immanuel Maurice. *Africa and the Modern World*. Trenton, N.J.: Africa World Press, 1986. 209 pp.

Williams, Robert. *Political Corruption in Africa*. Aldershot, Hampshire, England: Gower, 1987. 145 pp.

Wilmot, Patrick F. *The Right to Rebel*. Oguta, Nigeria: ZIM Pan African Publishers, 1986. 151 pp.

Wright, Stephen, and Janice N. Brownfoot. *Africa in World Politics: Changing Perspectives*. Basingstoke, Hampshire, England: Macmillan, 1987. 214 pp.

THE AMERICAS

Alinin, S. F., et al. *Gibel' Dzhonstauna—prestuplenie TsRU*. Moscow: Iurizdat, 1987. 224 pp.

Bark, Dennis L., ed. *The Red Orchestra: Instruments of Soviet Policy in Latin America and the Caribbean*. Stanford: Hoover Institution Press, 1986. 139 pp.

Davidson, Scott. *Grenada: A Study in Politics and the Limits of International Law*. Aldershot, Hampshire, England: Gower, 1986. 196 pp.

di Palma, Giuseppe, and Laurence Whitehead, eds. *The Central American Impasse*. New York: St. Martin's Press, 1986. 252 pp.

Dix, Robert H. *The Politics of Colombia*. Westport, Conn.: Greenwood Press, copublished with Hoover Institution Press, Stanford, 1986. 272 pp.

Falk, Pamela S., ed. *The Political Status of Puerto Rico*. Lexington, Mass.: Lexington Books, 1986. 125 pp.

Green, Jim. *Against the Tide: The Story of the Canadian Seamen's Union*. Toronto: Progress Books, 1986. 324 pp.

Hahn, Walter F., ed. *Central America and the Reagan Doctrine*. Lanham, Md.: University Press of America, 1987. 336 pp.

Hodges, Donald C. *Intellectual Foundations of the Nicaraguan Revolution*. Austin: University of Texas Press, 1987. 378 pp.

Keeran, Roger. *The Communist Party and the Auto Workers' Union*. New York: International Publishers, 1986. 340 pp.

Leiken, Robert S., and Barry Rubin, eds. *The Central American Crisis Reader*. New York: Summit Books, 1987. 717 pp.

MacKinnon, Janice R., and Stephen R. MacKinnon. *Agnes Smedley; the Life and Times of an American*

Radical. Berkeley: University of California Press, 1987. 425 pp.

Moore, John Norton. *The Secret War in Central America: Sandinista Assault on World Order*. Frederick, Md.: University Publications of America, 1987. 195 pp.

Newsom, David D. *The Soviet Brigade in Cuba*. Bloomington: Indiana University Press, 1987. 122 pp.

Osinskii, Igor. *Mirazhi Ameriki*. Minsk: Vysheishaia shkola, 1987. 157 pp.

Pashchuk, V. V. *Latinskaia Amerika: Srazhaiushchiisia kontinent*. Kiev: Radians'ka shkola, 1987. 231 pp.

Pryor, Frederic L. *Revolutionary Grenada: A Study in Political Economy*. Westport, Conn.: Greenwood Press, 1986. 395 pp.

Radu, Michael, and Vladimir Tismaneau. *Revolutionary Organizations in Latin America*. Boulder, Colo.: Westview Press, 1987. 420 pp.

Ratliff, William E., ed. *The Selling of Fidel Castro*. New Brunswick, N.J.: Transaction Books, 1987. 197 pp.

Smith, Wayne S. *The Closest of Enemies: A Personal and Diplomatic History of the Castro Years*. New York: Norton, 1987. 308 pp.

Taliia, Fung R. *Sotsialisticheskaia revoliutsiia na Kube*. Moscow: Mysl', 1987. 152 pp.

Turner, Robert F. *Nicaragua vs. United States; A Look at the Facts*. Washington, D.C.: Pergamon-Brassey, 1987. 165 pp.

United States Central Intelligence Agency, Directorate of Intelligence. *Directory of the Republic of Nicaragua*. Washington, D.C.: National Technical Information Service, 1987. (LDA 87-12849). 73 pp.

Valenta, Jiri, and Esperanza Duran, eds. *Conflict in Nicaragua*. Winchester, Mass.: Allen and Unwin, 1987. 440 pp.

Varas, Augusto, ed. *Soviet-Latin American Relations in the 1980s*. Boulder, Colo.: Westview Press, 1987. 290 pp.

Wiarda, Howard J., and Mark Falcoff, eds. *The Communist Challenge in the Caribbean and Central America*. Washington, D.C.: American Enterprise Institute, 1987. 249 pp.

ASIA AND THE PACIFIC

Alagappa, Muthiah. *The National Security of Developing States: Lessons from Thailand*. Dover, Mass.: Auburn House, 1987. 224 pp.

Babrin, E. P., and A. I. Taksubaev. *Mogol'skaia Respublika: spravochnik*. Moscow: Politizdat, 1987. 111 pp.

Bresnan, John, ed. *Crisis in the Phillipines: The Marcos Era and Beyond*. Princeton, N.J.: Princeton University Press, 1986. 284 pp.

Bridges, Brian. *Korea and the West*. London: Routledge & Kegan Paul, 1987. 112 pp.

Bui Diem, and David Chanoff. *In the Jaws of History*. Boston: Houghton Mifflin, 1987. 367 pp.

Buszynski, Leszek. *Soviet Foreign Policy in Southeast Asia*. New York: St. Martin's Press, 1986. 303 pp.

Chao Tzang Yawnghwe. *The Shan of Burma: Memoirs of a Shan Exile*. Singapore: Institute of Southeast Asian Studies, 1987. 276 pp.

Chapman, William. *Inside the Philippine Revolution*. New York: W. W. Norton, 1987. 288 pp.

Cheng, Peter P. *Chronology of the People's Republic of China, 1970–79*. Metuchen, N.J.: Scarecrow Press, 1986. 621 pp.

Dawa Norbu. *Red Star Over Tibet*. New York: Envoy Press, 1987. 303 pp.

Gao Yuan. *Born Red: A Chronicle of the Cultural Revolution*. Stanford, Calif.: Stanford University Press, 1987. 380 pp.

Gregor, A. James. *The China Connection: U.S. Policy and the People's Republic of China*. Stanford: Hoover Institution Press, 1986. 263 pp.

Johnson, Bryan. *The Four Days of Courage*. New York: Free Press, 1987. 290 pp.

Jussawala, Meheroo; Dan J. Wedemeyer; and Vijay Menon, eds. *The Passing of Remoteness: Information Revolution in the Asia-Pacific*. Singapore: Institute of Southeast Asian Studies, 1986. 172 pp.

Kobelev, Yevgeny, comp. *Kampuchea: From Tragedy to Rebirth*. Moscow: Progress Publishers, 1987. 187 pp.

Komisar, Lucy. *Corazon Aquino*. New York: George Braziller, 1987. 290 pp.

Korneev, Viktor L. *Indiia, 80-e gody*. Moscow: Mysl', 1986. 204 pp.

Kovalenko, I. I. *Kommunisticheskaia partiia Iaponii*. Moscow: Nauka, 1987. 528 pp.

Kuo, Tai-chun, and Ramon H. Myers. *Understanding Communist China: Communist China Studies in the United States and the Republic of China*. Stanford: Hoover Institution Press, 1986. 172 pp.

Levine, Steven I. *Anvil of Victory: the Communist Revolution in Manchuria*. New York: Columbia University Press, 1987. 314 pp.

Matveeva, G. S., et al., eds. *Mongol'skaia Narodnaia*

Respublika: spravochnik. Moscow: Nauka, 1986. 438 pp.

Michael, Franz. *China Through the Ages: History of a Civilization*. Boulder, Colo.: Westview Press, 1986. 278 pp.

Ngor, Haing, with Roger Warner. *A Cambodian Odyssey*. New York: Macmillan, 1987. 478 pp.

Olsen, Edward A. *U.S. Policy and the Two Koreas*. Boulder, Colo.: Westview Press, 1987. 96 pp.

Park, Jae Kyu; Byung Chul Koh; and Tae-Hwan Kwak. *The Foreign Relations of North Korea*. Boulder, Colo.: Westview Press, 1987. 491 pp.

Perkins, Dwight H. *China: Asia's Next Economic Giant*. Seattle: University of Washington Press, 1986. 108 pp.

Pike, Douglas. *Vietnam and the Soviet Union*. Boulder, Colo.: Westview Press, 1987. 271 pp.

Pin, Yathay, and John Man. *Stay Alive, My Son*. New York: Free Press/Macmillan, 1987. 256 pp.

Rajaretnam, M., ed. *The Aquino Alternative*. Singapore: Institute of Southeast Asian Studies, 1986. 158 pp.

Sanders, Alan J. *Mongolia: Politics, Economics and Society*. London: Francis Pinter, 1987. 179 pp.

Scalapino, Robert A. *Major Power Relations in Northeast Asia*. Washington, D.C.: University Press of America/New York: Asia Society, 1987. 92 pp.

Shaw, Yu-ming, ed. *Mainland China: Politics, Economics and Reforms*. Boulder, Colo.: Westview Press, 1986. 664 pp.

Somsakdi Xuto, ed. *Government and Politics of Thailand*. Singapore: Singapore University Press, 1987. 243 pp.

Stuart-Fox, Martin. *Laos: Politics, Economics and Society*. London: Frances Pinter, 1986. 664 pp.

Sukhumbhand, Paribatra, and J. Soedjati Djiwandono. *Asia in Regional and Global Context*. Berkeley, Calif.: Institute of East Asian Studies, 1987. 357 pp.

Thurston, Anne F. *Enemies of the People*. New York: Alfred A. Knopf, 1987. 323 pp.

Vickery, Michael. *Kampuchea: Politics, Economics and Society*. London: Frances Pinter/Boulder, Colo.: Lynne Rienner Publishers, 1987. 211 pp.

Wei, Betty Peh-ti. *Shanghai: Crucible of Modern China*. Hong Kong: Oxford University Press, 1987. 241 pp.

Wortzel, Larry M. *Class in China: Stratification in a Classless Society*. Westport, Conn.: Greenwood Press, 1987. 171 pp.

Zakaria bin Haji Ahmed. *Government and Politics of Malaysia*. Singapore: Institute of Southeast Asian Studies, 1987. 178 pp.

Zhang Xinxin, and Sang Ye. *Chinese Lives*. New York: Pantheon Books, 1987. 367 pp.

EASTERN EUROPE

Alia, Ramiz. *Report to the 9th Congress of the Party of Labor of Albania*. Tirana: 8 Nëntori Publishing House, 1986. 214 pp.

Andorka, Rudolf, and Laszlo Bertalan, eds. *Economy and Society in Hungary*. Budapest: Karl Marx University, 1986. 331 pp.

Baerns, Barbara, ed. *Die DDR in Deutschland*. Cologne: Verlag Wissenschaft und Politik, 1986. 119 pp.

Boyes, Roger, and John Moody. *The Priest Who Had to Die*. London: Victor Gollancz, 1986. 204 pp.

Budkin, V. S. *Internatsionalizatsiia sotsial'no-ekonomicheskogo razvitiia evropeiskikh stran-chlenov SEV*. Kiev: Naukova dumka, 1987. 248 pp.

Bugajski, Janusz. *Czechoslovakia: Charter 77's Decade of Dissent*. New York: Praeger/Washington, D.C.: Center for Strategic and International Studies, 1987. 118 pp.

Coutouvidis, John, and Jaime Reynolds. *Poland: 1939–1947*. Leicester, England: Leicester University Press, 1986. 393 pp.

Danilenko, V. M. *Sotrudnichestvo SFRIu so stranami-chlenami SEV*. Kiev: Naukova dumka, 1987. 111 pp.

Ernst Thälmann: Unsere Partei erfüllt sein Vermächtnis. Wissenschaftliche Konferenz zum 100, Geburtstag, Berlin 12 und 13 März. East Berlin: Dietz Verlag, 1986. 207 pp.

Fejtö, François. *Mémoires de Budapest á Paris*. Paris: Calmann-Lévy, 1986. 323 pp.

Fricke, Karl Wilhelm. *Zur Menschen- und Grundrechtssituation politischer Gefangener in der DDR*. Cologne: Verlag Wissenschaft und Politik, 1986. 255 pp.

Gadney, Reg. *Cry Hungary! Uprising 1956*. London: Weidenfeld and Nicholson, 1986. 180 pp.

Garrett, Stephen A. *From Potsdam to Poland: American Policy toward Eastern Europe*. New York: Praeger, 1986. 108 pp.

Germany, East. *Dokumente und Materialien der Zusammenarbeit zwischen der Sozialistischen Einheitspartei Deutschlands und der Kommunisti-*

schen Partei der Sowjetunion, 1980 bis 1985. East Berlin: Dietz Verlag, 1986. 640 pp.

Gibianskii, L. Ia. *Sovetskii Soiuz i novaia Iugoslaviia, 1941–1947*. Moscow: Nauka, 1987. 204 pp.

Graham, Lawrence S., and Maria K. Ciechocińska, eds. *The Polish Dilemma: Views from Within*. Boulder, Colo.: Westview Press, 1987. 258 pp.

Grothusen, Klaus-Detlev, ed. *Ungarn*. Göttingen: Vanderhoeck & Ruprecht, 1987. 781 pp.

Hackel, Renate. *Katholische Publizistik in der DDR, 1945–1984*. Mainz, West Germany: Matthias Grünewald Verlag, 1987. 163 pp.

Halliday, Jon, ed. *Memoirs of Enver Hoxha*. London: Chatto and Windus, 1986. 394 pp.

Honecker, Erich. *Reden und Aufsätze*. Band 11. East Berlin: Dietz Verlag, 1987. 467 pp.

———. *Report of the Central Committee of the Socialist Unity Party of Germany to the 11th Congress of the SED*. East Berlin: SED, 1986. 109 pp.

Hoxha, Enver. *The Superpowers*. Tirana: 8 Nëntori Publishing House, 1986. 678 pp.

Institut für Marxismus-Leninismus beim ZK der SED. *Dokumente und Materialien zur Zusammenarbeit der Sozialistischen Einheitspartei Deutschlands und der Kommunstischen Partei der Sowjetunion 1980 bis 1985*. East Berlin: Dietz Verlag, 1986. 462 pp.

Joseph, Philip, ed. *The Economies of Eastern Europe and their Foreign Economic Relations*. Brussels: NATO, 1987. 363 pp.

Kalvoda, Josef. *The Genesis of Czechoslovakia*. New York: East European Quarterly/Columbia University Press, 1986. 673 pp.

Kanturkova, Eva. *My Companions in the Bleak House*. Woodstock, N.Y.: Overlook Press, 1987. 314 pp.

Kaplan, Karel. *The Communist Party in Power*. Boulder, Colo.: Westview Press, 1987. 231 pp.

———. *The Short March*. London: Christopher Hurst, 1987. 207 pp.

Klein, Fritz. *Friedliche Koexistenz: Erfahrungen-Chancen-Gefahren*. East Berlin: Akademia Verlag, 1987. 300 pp.

Kopácsi, Sándor. *In the Name of the Working Class: The Inside Story of the Hungarian Revolution*. New York: Grove Press, 1986. 304 pp.

Linden, Ronald H. *Communist States and International Change: Yugoslavia and Romania in Comparative Perspectives*. Winchester, Mass.: Allen and Unwin, 1987. 340 pp.

Litavrin, G. G., ed. *Kratkaia istoriia Bolgarii*. Moscow: Nauka, 1987. 568 pp.

Lydall, Harold. *Yugoslav Socialism: Theory and Practice*. New York: Clarendon Press, 1986. 302 pp.

McConville, Michael. *A Small War in the Balkans*. London: Macmillan, 1986. 336 pp.

Meiners, Jochen. *Die doppelte Deutschlandpolitik: zur nationalen Politik der SED im Spiegel ihres Zentralorganes "Neues Deutschland," 1946–1952*. New York: Peter Lang, 1987. 654 pp.

Molnár, Miklós. *De Béla Kun á János Kádár: Soixante-dix ans de communisme hongrois*. Paris: Presses de la Fondation Nationale des Sciences Politiques, 1987. 335pp.

Monticone, Ronald C. *The Catholic Church in Communist Poland*. Boulder, Colo.: East European Monographs, 1986 (New York: Columbia University Press, distributors). 227 pp.

Moody, John. *The Priest and the Policeman: The Courageous Life and Cruel Murder of Father Jerzy Popieluszko*. New York: Summit Books, 1987. 251 pp.

Omari, Luan. *The People's Revolution and the Question of State Power in Albania*. Tirana: 8 Nëntori Publishing House, 1986. 230 pp.

Pacepa, Ion Mihai. *Red Horizons: Chronicles of a Communist Spy Chief*. Chicago: Regnery Gateway, 1987. 446 pp.

Sanford, George. *Military Rule in Poland*. New York: St. Martin's Press, 1986. 288 pp.

Sozialistische Einheitspartei Deutschlands. *Direktive des XI. Parteitages des SED zum Fünfjahrplan für die Entwicklung der Volkswitschaft der DDR in den Jahren 1986 bis 1990*. East Berlin: Dietz Verlag, 1986. 125 pp.

———. *Vom X. zum XI. Parteitag der SED: Eine aussenpolitische Bilanz in Daten und Fakten (1981–1985)*. Potsdam: Akademie für Staats-und Rechtswissenschaft der DDR, 1986. 132 pp.

Steussloff, Hans. *Worauf vertrauen wir? Humanistische Werte in der DDR*. East Berlin, Dietz, 1986. 167 pp.

Toch, Marta [pseud.]. *Reinventing Civil Society: Poland's Quiet Revolution, 1981–1986*. New York: U.S. Helsinki Watch Committee, 1986. 101 pp.

United States Central Intelligence Agency. *Directory of Yugoslav Officials*. Washington, D.C.: National Technical Information Service, December 1986. 207 pp.

Vasary, Ildikó. *Beyond the Plan: Social Change in a Hungarian Village*. Boulder, Colo.: Westview Press, 1987. 308 pp.

Vine, Richard D., ed. *Soviet-East European Relations as a Problem for the West*. London: Croom Helm, 1987. 262 pp.

Vladislav, Jan, ed. *Vaclav Havel or Living in Truth*. London: Faber and Faber, 1987. 315 pp.

Wałesa, Lech. *A Way of Hope*. New York: Henry Holt and Company, 1987. 325 pp.

Weber, Wolfgang. *Solidarność, 1980–1981, und Perspektive der politischen Revolution*. Essen, West Germany: Arbeiterpresse Verlag, 1987. 124 pp.

Weichelt, W., et al. *Der Staat im politischen System der DDR*. East Berlin: Staatsverlag der DDR, 1986. 400 pp.

Wozniuk, Vladimir. *From Crisis to Crisis: Soviet-Polish Relations in the 1970s*. Ames: Iowa State University Press, 1987. 176 pp.

Zitzlaff, Dietrich. *DDR-Jugend heute*. Stuttgart, West Germany: Metzler, 1986. 153 pp.

USSR

Adomeit, Hans; Hans-Hermann Höhmann; and Günther Wagenlehner, eds. *Die Sowjetunion als Militärmacht*. Stuttgart, West Germany: Verlag W. Kohlhammer, 1987. 288 pp.

Agursky, Mikhail. *The Third Rome: National Bolshevism in the USSR*. Boulder, Colo.: Westview Press, 1987. 425 pp.

Alexiev, Alexander R., and S. Enders Wimbush, eds. *Ethnic Minorities in the Red Army: Asset or Liability?* Boulder, Colo.: Westview Press, 1987. 180 pp.

Andreyev, Catherine. *Vlasov and the Russian Liberation Movement*. Cambridge, England: Cambridge University Press, 1987. 251 pp.

Antiukhina-Moskovchenko, V. I., et al., eds. *Istoriia mezhdunarodnykh otnoshenii i vneshnei politiki SSSR v trekh tomakh, 1917–1987*. 3 vols. Moscow: Mezhdunarodnye otnosheniia, 1986.

Bilocerkowycz, Jaroslaw. *Soviet Ukrainian Dissent: A Study of Political Alienation*. Boulder, Colo.: Westview Press, 1987. 240 pp.

Black, Cyril E. *Understanding Soviet Politics: The Perspective of Russian History*. Boulder, Colo.: Westview Press, 1986. 308 pp.

Borcke, Astrid von. *KGB: Die Macht im Untergrund*. Neuhausen and Stuttgart: Hänssler, 1987. 205 pp.

Broido, Vera. *Lenin and the Mensheviks: the Persecution of Socialists under Bolshevism*. Boulder, Colo.: Westview Press, 1987. 216 pp.

Buck, Trevor, and John Cole. *Modern Soviet Economic Performance*. New York: Basil Blackwell, 1987. 192 pp.

Campbell, Kurt M. *Soviet Policy Toward South Africa*. New York: St. Martin's Press, 1986. 223 pp.

Chernev, Anatolii Dement'evich. *Partiinaia informatsiia: voprosy istorii i teorii*. Moscow: Izd-vo Moskovskogo universiteta, 1987. 157 pp.

Cline, Ray S.; James Arnold Miller; and Roger E. Kanet, eds. *Asia in Soviet Global Strategy*. Boulder, Colo.: Westview Press, 1987. 176 pp.

———. *Western Europe in Soviet Global Strategy*. Boulder, Colo.: Westview Press, 1987. 176 pp.

D'Agostino, Anthony. *Soviet Succession Struggles*. Winchester, Mass.: Allen and Unwin, 1987. 320 pp.

Dizard, Wilson P., and S. Blake Swensrud. *Gorbachev's Information Revolution*. Boulder, Colo.: Westview Press, 1987. 128 pp.

Dyker, David A. *The Soviet Union under Gorbachev: Prospects for Reform*. London: Croom Helm/New York: Methuen, 1987. 227 pp.

Dzhirkvelov, Ilya. *Secret Servant: My Life with the KGB and the Soviet Elite*. London: Collins, 1987. 398 pp.

Ebon, Martin. *The Soviet Propaganda Machine*. New York: McGraw Hill, 1987. 439 pp.

Egorov, G. M. *Delo vsego naroda*. Moscow: DOSAAF, 1987. 255 pp.

Feofanov, O. A. *Agressia lzhi*. Moscow: Politizdat, 1987. 319 pp.

Gassman, Leonard R., moderator. *Glasnost: How Open? Two Seminars*. New York: Freedom House, 1987. 130 pp.

Gladyshev, Anatolii N. *Rossiia v dvenadtsatoi piatiletke*. Moscow: Sovetskaia Rossiia, 1986. 285 pp.

Goldman, Marshall I. *Gorbachev's Challenge*. New York: W. W. Norton, 1987. 296 pp.

Gorbachev, Mikhail. *Izbrannye rechi i stat'i*. 4 vols. Moscow: Politizdat, 1987.

———. *Perestroika: New Thinking of our Country and the World*. New York: Harper and Row, 1987. 255 pp.

Granick, David. *Job Rights in the Soviet Union: Their Consequences*. New York: Cambridge University Press, 1987. 344 pp.

Hammer, Darrell P. *Russian Nationalism and Soviet Politics*. Boulder, Colo.: Westview Press, 1987. 200 pp.

Hansen, James H. *Correlation of Forces: Four De-*

cades of Military Development. New York: Praeger, 1987. 236 pp.

Hazan, Baruch A. *From Brezhnev to Gorbachev: Infighting in the Kremlin*. Boulder, Colo.: Westview Press, 1987. 260 pp.

Helf, Gavin. *A Biographic Directory of Soviet Regional Party Leaders*. Part I, *RSFSR Oblasts, Krais, and ASSRs*. Munich: Radio Liberty Research, 1987. 90 pp.

Heller, Mikhail, and Aleksandr Nekrich. *Utopia in Power: The History of the Soviet Union from 1917–Present*. New York: Summit Books, 1986. 878 pp.

Herlemann, Horst, ed. *Quality of Life in the Soviet Union*. Boulder, Colo.: Westview Press, 1987. 192 pp.

Heyns, Terry L. *American and Soviet Relations since Detente: the Framework*. Washington, D.C.: National Defense University Press, 1987. 244 pp.

Iatskov, V. S. *Kadrovaia politika KPSS: opyt i problemy*. Moscow: Mysl', 1986. 315 pp.

Ioffe, Olimpiad S., and Mark S. Janis, eds. *Soviet Law and Economy*. Boston: Martinus Nijhoff Publishers, 1987. 335 pp.

Kahan, Stuart. *The Wolf of the Kremlin*. New York: William Morrow, 1987. 331 pp.

Keizerov, N. M., and E. A. Nozhin. *Ideologicheskaia bor'ba: Voprosy i otvety*. Moscow: Politizdat, 1987. 256 pp.

Kelley, Donald R. *The Politics of Developed Socialism: The Soviet Union as a Post-Industrial State*. Westport, Conn.: Greenwood Press, 1986. 226 pp.

Korbonski, Andrzej, and Francis Fukuyama, eds. *The Soviet Union and the Third World*. Ithaca, N.Y.: Cornell University Press, 1987. 318 pp.

Krivoruchenko, V. K., and N. V. Trushchenko, comps. *Dokumenty KPSS o Leninskom komsomole i pionerii*. Moscow: Molodaiai gvardiia, 1987. 383 pp.

Kuhne, Winrich. *Sowjetische Afrikapolitik in der "Ära Gorbachev*." Ebenhausen: Haus Eggenberg, 1986. 146 pp.

Litvin, Valentin. *The Soviet Agro-Industrial Complex: Structure and Performance*. Boulder, Colo.: Westview Press, 1987. 161 pp.

Lopatov, V. V. *The Soviet Union and Africa*. Moscow: Progress, 1987. 191 pp.

Matthews, Mervyn. *Poverty in the Soviet Union: The Life-Styles of the Underprivileged in Recent Years*. New York: Cambridge University Press, 1986. 227 pp.

McCauley, Martin, ed. *Khrushchev and Khrushchevism*. Basingstoke, Hampshire, England: Macmillan, 1987. 243 pp.

———. *The Soviet Union under Gorbachev*. New York: St. Martin's Press, 1987. 259 pp.

Manjuelo, A. N., chief ed. *The USSR and International Economic Relations*. Moscow: Progress, 1987. 493 pp.

Motyl, Alexander J. *Will the Non-Russians Rebel?: State, Ethnicity, and Stability in the USSR*. Ithaca, N.Y.: Cornell University Press, 1987. 188 pp.

Narkiewicz, Olga A. *Soviet Leaders: From the Cult of Personality to Collective Rule*. Sussex, England: Wheatsheaf Books, 1986. 256 pp.

Nissman, David B. *The Soviet Union and Iranian Azerbaijan: The Use of Nationalism for Political Penetration*. Boulder, Colo.: Westview Press, 1987. 116 pp.

Novik, F. I. *SSSR-FRG: problemy sosushchestvovaniia i sotrudnichestva, 1975–1986*. Moscow: Nauka, 1987. 137 pp.

Phillips, Ann L. *Soviet Policy Toward East Germany Reconsidered: The Postwar Decade*. Westport, Conn.: Greenwood Press, 1986. 274 pp.

Reid, Carl V. *Soviet Social Reform in the 1980's: the Anti-Alcohol Campaign as Antidote for the Flagging Economy*. Ottawa, Canada: Department of National Defence, 1986. 110 pp.

Richmond, Yale. *U.S.-Soviet Cultural Exchanges, 1958–1986; Who Wins?* Boulder, Colo.: Westview Press, 1986. 170 pp.

Roxburgh, Angus. *Pravda: Inside the Soviet News Machine*. New York: George Braziller, 1987. 285 pp.

Schneider, Eberhard. *Moskaus Leitlinie für das Jahr 2000*. Munich: Olzog Verlag, 124 pp.

Shapiro, L. B., ed. *Organizatsiia KPSS Evreiskoi avtonomnoi oblasti, 1934–1985: khronika*. Khabarovsk, USSR: Khabarovskoe knizhnoe izdatelstvo, 1986. 223 pp.

Shapiro, Leonard. *Russian Studies*. New York: Viking Press, 1987. 400 pp.

Shapiro, Leonard, and Peter Reddaway, eds. *Lenin: The Man, the Theorist, the Leader—A Reappraisal*. Boulder, Colo.: Westview Press, 1987. 320 pp.

Shlapentokh, Vladimir. *Soviet Public Opinion and Ideology: Mythology and Pragmatism in Interaction*. New York: Praeger, 1986. 256 pp.

Sleeper, Raymond S., ed. *Mesmerized by the Bear: the*

Soviet Strategy of Deception. New York: Dodd, Mead and Company, 1987. 384 pp.

Slusser, Robert M. *Stalin in October*. Baltimore, Md.: Johns Hopkins University Press, 1987. 281 pp.

Solov'ev, A. A. *S'ezdy i konferentsii KPSS: spravochnik*. 2d rev. ed. Moscow: Politizdat, 1986. 335 pp.

Staar, Richard F. *USSR Foreign Policies After Détente*. Rev. ed. Stanford: Hoover Institution Press, 1987. 308 pp.

Thompson, Terry L. *Ideology and Policy in the USSR*. Boulder, Colo.: Westview Press, 1987. 224 pp.

Tritten, James J. *Soviet Naval Forces and Nuclear Warfare*. Boulder, Colo.: Westview Press, 1986. 282 pp.

Umanskii, L. A., and S. S. Shaboldin. *Gody truda i pobed, 1917–1987*. Moscow, Politizdat, 1987. 368 pp.

USSR. Sovet Ekonomicheskoi Vzaimopomoshchi. *Statisticheskii ezhegodnik stran-chlenov soveta ekonomicheskoi vzaimopomoshchi, 1986*. Moscow: Finansy i statistika, 1986. 462 pp.

Veen, Hans-Joachim, ed. *From Brezhnev to Gorbachev: Domestic Affairs and Soviet Foreign Policy*. New York: Berg, 1987. 378 pp.

Vishnevskii, S. S., chief ed. *Sotsialisticheskii obraz zhizni*. Moscow: Politizdat, 1986. 335 pp.

Walker, Martin. *The Waking Giant: Gorbachev's Russia*. New York: Pantheon, 1987. 298 pp.

Williams, Robert C. *The Other Bolsheviks: Lenin and His Critics, 1904–1914*. Bloomington: Indiana University Press, 1986. 233 pp.

Zagladin, V. V., and G. A. Kiselev, eds. *Politicheskie partii: spravochnik*. Moscow: Politizdat, 1986. 382 pp.

Ziegler, Charles E. *Environmental Policy in the USSR*. Amherst: University of Massachusetts Press, 1987. 195 pp.

Zubarev, V. I., chief ed. *XXVII S'ezd KPSS i zadachi kafedr obshchestvennykh nauk*. Moscow: Politizdat, 1987. 269 pp.

Zuev, V. V., comp. *Rytsari dolga: vospominaniia chekistov*. 2d ed. Donetsk, USSR: Donbas, 1986. 251 pp.

THE MIDDLE EAST

Agaev, S. L. *Iran mezhdu proshlym i budushchim: sobytiia, liudi, idei*. Moscow: Politizdat, 1987. 319 pp.

Amstutz, J. Bruce. *Afghanistan: The First Five Years of Soviet Occupation*. Washington, D.C.: National Defense University Press, 1986. 545 pp.

Dawisha, Adeed. *The Arab Radicals*. New York: Council on Foreign Relations, 1986. 144 pp.

Farr, Grant M., and John M. Merriam. *The Afghan Resistance: The Politics of Survival*. Boulder, Colo.: Westview Press, 1987. 235 pp.

Hodson, Peregrine. *Under a Sickle Moon: A Journey through Afghanistan*. London: Century Hutchinson, 1986. 226 pp.

El-Hussini, Mohrez Mahmoud. *Soviet-Egyptian Relations, 1945–1985*. New York: St. Martin's Press, 1987. 276 pp.

Ismael, Tareq Y. *International Relations of the Contemporary Middle East*. Syracuse, N.Y.: Syracuse University Press, 1986. 344 pp.

Ismael, Tareq Y., and Jacquelin S. Ismael. *The People's Democratic Republic of Yemen: Politics, Economics and Society*. Boulder, Colo.: Lynne Rienner Publishers, 1986. 183 pp.

Kramer, Martin, ed. *Shi'ism, Resistance, and Revolution*. Boulder, Colo.: Westview Press, 1987. 324 pp.

Lessing, Doris. *The Wind Blows Away our Words, and Other Documents Relating to the Afghan Resistance*. New York: Vantage Books, 1987. 171 pp.

Norton, Augustus Richard. *Amal and the Shia: Struggle for the Soul of Lebanon*. Austin: University of Texas Press, 1987. 238 pp.

Roy, Olivier. *Islam and the Resistance in Afghanistan*. Cambridge, England: Cambridge University Press, 1987. 253 pp.

Seale, Patrick. *The Struggle for Syria: A Study of Post-War Arab Politics, 1945–1959*. New Haven, Conn.: Yale University Press, 1987. 384 pp.

Taheri, Amir. *Holy Terror: Inside the World of Islamic Terrorism*. Washington, D.C.: Adler and Adler, 1987. 313 pp.

United States Central Intelligence Agency, Directorate of Intelligence. *Directory of Iranian Officials*. Washington, D.C.: National Technical information Service, December 1987. 94 pp.

Weinberger, Naomi Joy. *Syrian Intervention in Lebanon*. New York: Oxford University Press, 1986. 337 pp.

WESTERN EUROPE

Andersen, Arne. *"Lieber im Feuer der Revolution sterben, als auf dem Misthaufen der Demokratie verrecken;" die KPD in Bremen von 1928–1933*. Munich: Minerva, 1987. 526 pp.

Ardagh, John. *Germany and the Germans*. London: Hamish Hamilton, 1987. 478 pp.

Bakker, Schut. *Stammheim: Der Prozess gegen die Rote Armee Fraktion: die notwendige Korrektur der herrschenden Meinung*. Kiel, West Germany: Neuer Malik Verlag, 1986. 685 pp.

Balsen, Werner. *Hoch die internationale Solidarität: Zur Geschichte der Dritten-Welt-Bewegung in der Bundesrepublik*. Cologne, West Germany: Kölner Volksblatt Verlag, 1986. 616 pp.

Bambery, Chris. *Ireland's Permanent Revolution*. London: Bookmarks, 1986. 87 pp.

Bell, J. Bowyer. *The Gun in Politics: An Analysis of Irish Political Conflict, 1916–1986*. New Brunswick, N.J.: Transaction Books, 1987. 371 pp.

Bergdorfer Gesprächkreis zu Fragen Freien Industriellen Gesellschaft. *Die Beziehungen zwischen der Sowjetunion und der Bundesrepublik Deutschlands*. Hamburg: R. Van Decker's Verlag, 1987. 119 pp.

Bruneau, Thomas, and Alex MacLeod. *Politics in Contemporary Portugal*. Boulder, Colo.: Lynne Rienner Publishers, 1986. 236 pp.

Calice, Nino. *Il PCI nella storia di Basilicata*. Venosa, Italy: Osanna Venosa, 1986. 211 pp.

Cardoze, Michel. *Nouveau voyage à l'interieur du parti communiste français*. Paris: Fayard, 1986. 346 pp.

Cornelsen, Dirk. *Ankläger im hohen Haus: die Grünen im Bundestag*. Essen, West Germany: Klartext Verlag, 1986. 176 pp.

Dankert, J. *Westeuropa in den Ost-West Beziehungen*. East Berlin: Staatsverlag der DDR, 1987. 103 pp.

Deutsche Kommunistische Partei. *Thesen der 8. Parteitages der DKP: Neue Fragen des Kampfes der Frieden und Arbeit—für eine demokratische Wende*. Neuss, West Germany: Plumbeck, 1986. 111 pp.

Dräger, Klaus. *Aus für Grün: die Grüne Orientierungskrise zwischen Anpassung und Systemopposition*. Frankfurt an der Oder, East Germany: ISP-Verlag, 1986. 318 pp.

Dubla, Ferdinando. *Gramsci e la fabrica: Produzione, tecnica e organizzazione de lavoro nel pensiero gramsciano 1913/1945*. Manduria, Italy: Lacaita, 1986. 192 pp.

Federal Republic of Germany. *Materialien zum Bericht zur Lage der Nation im geteilten Deutschland*. Bonn: Bundesministerium für innerdeutsche Beziehungen, 1987. 819 pp.

Flores, D., ed. *La questione communista: interviste a E. Berlinguer, N. Bobbio, E. Collotti, C. Donolo, et al*. Milan: Angeli, 1986. 225 pp.

Frey, Eric G. *Division and Détente: The Germanies and their Alliances*. New York: Praeger, 1987. 194 pp.

Gelb, Norman. *The Berlin Wall*. London: Michael Joseph, 1986. 298 pp.

Hanley, David. *Keeping Left? CERES and the French Socialist Party*. Manchester, England: Manchester University Press, 1986. 278 pp.

Heffer, Eric S. *Labour's Future: Socialist or SPD Mark 2?* London: Verso, 1986. 159 pp.

Herlemann, Beatrix. *Auf verlorenem Posten: kommunistischer Widerstand im zweiten Weltkrieg*. Bonn: Verlag Neue Gesellschaft, 1986. 311 pp.

Huber, Peter. *Kommunisten und Sozialdemokraten in der Schweiz, 1918–1935*. Zürich: Limmat Verlag, 1986. 239 pp.

Kayman, Martin. *Revolution and Counter Revolution in Portugal*. London: Merlin Press, 1987. 275 pp.

Kolinsky, Eva, ed. *Opposition in Western Europe*. Benckenham, Kent, England: Croom Helm, 1987. 416 pp.

McDonald, Michael. *Children of Wrath: Political Violence in Northern Ireland*. Cambridge, England: Polity Press, 1986. 159 pp.

Mies, Herbert, ed. *Deutsche Kommunistische Partei: Bericht des Parteivorstands der DKP den 8. Parteitags Hamburg, 2–4 Mai 1986*. Neuss, West Germany: Plumbeck, 1986. 76 pp.

Minrath, Axel. *Friedenskampf: die DKP and ihre Bündnispolitik in der Antinachrüstingsbewegung*. Cologne, West Germany: Verlag Wissenschaft und Politik, 1986. 176 pp.

Natta, Alessandro, et al. *Il diritto alla giustizia*. Rome: L'Editrice Unitá, 1987. 158 pp.

Paggi, Leonardo. *I comunisti italiani e il reformismo: un confronto con le socialdemocrazie europee*. Turin, Italy: Einaudi, 1986. 219 pp.

Pala, Gianfranco, et al. *Attualità di Marx: Atti del convegno, Urbino, 22–25 novembre 1983*. Milan, Italy: Unicopli, 1986. 486 pp.

Panitch, Leo. *Working-class Politics in Crisis: Essays on Labour and the State*. London: Verso, 1986. 250 pp.

Partito Comunista Italiano. *Tesi, programma, statuto: I documenti approvati dal 17. Congresso del PCI*. Rome: Editrice L'Unitá, 1987. 174 pp.

Pascual, Pedro. *Partidos politicos y constituciones de España*. Madrid: Fraga, 1986. 521 pp.

Penniman, Howard R. *Italy at the Polls: A Study of the National Elections*. Durham, N.C.: Duke University Press, 1987. 216 pp.

Raphael, Samuel, et al., eds. *The Enemy Within: Pit Villages and the Miners' Strike of 1984–85*. London: Routledge and Kegan Paul, 1986. 260 pp.

Reader, Keith A. *Intellectuals and the Left in France since 1968*. London: Macmillan, 1986. 208 pp.

Riddell, John, ed. *The German Revolution and Debate on Soviet Power: Documents, 1918–1919*. New York: Pathfinder Books, 1986. 540 pp.

Sbarberi, Franco. *Gramsci: un socialismo armonico*. Milan, Italy: Angeli, 1986. 88 pp.

Shinn, Rinn S., ed. *Italy: A Country Study*. 2d. ed. Washington, D.C.: U.S. Government Printing Office (for American University Foreign Area Studies), 1987. 412 pp.

Sundelius, Bengt, ed. *Neutral Democracies in the New Cold War*. Boulder, Colo.: Westview Press, 1987. 245 pp.

Togliatti, Palmiro, et al. *Essere communisti: il ruolo del PCI nella società italiana*. Rome: Editori Reuniti, 1986. 248 pp.

Verdes-Leroux, Jeannine. *Le réveil des somnanbules: le parti comuniste, les intellectuels et la culture (1956–1985)*. Paris: Fayard/Ed. de Minuit, 1987. 491 pp.

Wahlen '87—vor einem neuen Aufbruch? Gesellschaftsprogramme und Strategien der SPD, der Grünen und der KPD: Analyse und Kommentare. Frankfurt an der Oder, East Germany: IMSF, 1986. 96 pp.

Yannopoulos, George N. *Greece and the EEC: Integration and Convergence*. Basingstoke, Hampshire, England: Macmillan, 1986. 178 pp.

Cumulative Index of Biographies

Index of Names

Index of Subjects